Yearbook on
International
Communist Affairs
1990

Yearbook on International Communist Affairs 1990

Parties and Revolutionary Movements

EDITOR:	Richard F. Staar
ASSISTANT EDITOR:	Margit N. Grigory

AREA EDITORS

Africa	•	Thomas H. Henriksen
The Americas	•	William Ratliff
Asia and the Pacific	•	Ramon H. Myers
Eastern Europe and the	•	Richard F. Staar
Soviet Union		Robert Conquest
The Middle East and	•	James H. Noyes
North Africa		
Western Europe	•	Dennis L. Bark

HOOVER INSTITUTION PRESS
Stanford University, Stanford, California

The text of this work is set in Times Roman;
display headings are in Melior. Typeset by
Harrison Typesetting, Inc., Portland, Oregon.
Printed and bound by Braun-Brumfield, Inc.,
Ann Arbor, Michigan.

Hoover Press Publication 394

International Standard Book Number 0-8179-8941-2
International Standard Serial Number 0084-4101
Library of Congress Catalog Number 67-31024

Contents

ASIA AND THE PACIFIC

EASTERN EUROPE AND THE SOVIET UNION

THE MIDDLE EAST AND NORTH AFRICA

WESTERN EUROPE

viii   CONTENTS

Preface

This edition of the *Yearbook*, the 24th consecutive one, includes profiles by 85 contributors, covering 132 parties and revolutionary movements as well as 18 international communist fronts and 2 regional organizations (the Council for Mutual Economic Assistance and the Warsaw Pact). In addition, biographic sketches of prominent communist leaders follow individual profiles. This year we also have an essay on Soviet foreign propaganda. The names and affiliations of contributors are given at the end of each essay.

This *Yearbook* offers data on the organization, policies, activities, and international contacts of communist parties and Marxist-Leninist movements throughout the world during all of 1989. Information has been derived primarily from published sources, including official newspapers and journals, as well as from radio transmissions monitored by the U.S. Foreign Broadcast Information Service. Dates cited in the text without a year refer to 1989.

Whether to include in the *Yearbook* a party or a group that espouses a quasi–Marxist-Leninist ideology, yet may not be recognized by Moscow as "communist," always poses a problem. It applies specifically to certain of the so-called national liberation movements and, more significantly, to some ruling parties. In making our decisions, the following criteria have been considered: rhetoric, the organizational model, participation in international communist meetings and fronts, and adherence to the USSR's foreign-policy line. It seems realistic to consider the Sandinista regime of Nicaragua, until it lost the February 1990 national election, in the same category as that of Cuba. The ruling parties in the so-called "vanguard revolutionary democracies" appear to be clearly affiliated with the world communist movement. They also are discussed in the introduction.

Our thanks go to the librarians and staff of the Hoover Institution for checking information and contributing to the bibliography. The latter was compiled by the *Yearbook*'s assistant editor, Mrs. Margit N. Grigory, who also provided liaison with contributors.

Richard F. Staar
Hoover Institution

The following abbreviations are used for frequently cited publications and news agencies:

CSM	*Christian Science Monitor*
FBIS-AFR	*Foreign Broadcast Information Service-Africa*
FBIS-CHI	*Foreign Broadcast Information Service-China*
FBIS-EAS	*Foreign Broadcast Information Service-East Asia*
FBIS-EEU	*Foreign Broadcast Information Service-Eastern Europe*
FBIS-LAT	*Foreign Broadcast Information Service-Latin America*
FBIS-NES	*Foreign Broadcast Information Service-Near East and Southern Asia*
FBIS-SOV	*Foreign Broadcast Information Service-Soviet Union*
FBIS-WEU	*Foreign Broadcast Information Service-Western Europe*
HUM	*L'Humanité*
FEER	*Far Eastern Economic Review*
IB	*Information Bulletin* (of the *WMR*)
JPRS-EEU	*Joint Publications Research Service-Eastern Europe*
JPRS-LAT	*Joint Publications Research Service-Latin America*
JPRS-WEU	*Joint Publications Research Service-Western Europe*
LAT	*Los Angeles Times*
ND	*Neues Deutschland*
NYT	*New York Times*
PR	*Pravda* (Moscow)
UN	*L'Unità*
VS	*Volksstimme*
WMR	*World Marxist Review*
WP	*Washington Post*
WSJ	*Wall Street Journal*
YICA	*Yearbook on International Communist Affairs*
ACAN	Agencia Central Americano Noticias
ADN	Allgemeiner Deutscher Nachrichtendienst
AFP	Agence France-Presse
ANSA	Agenzia Nazionale Stampa Associata
AP	Associated Press

BBC	British Broadcasting Corporation	MTI	Magyar Távirati Iroda
BTA	Bulgarska Telegrafna Agentsiia	NCNA	New China News Agency
CANA	Caribbean News Agency	PAP	Polska Agencja Prasowa
ČTK	Československá Tisková Kancelář	RFE	Radio Free Europe
DPA	Deutsche Presse Agentur	RL	Radio Liberty
EFE	Agencia EFE, Spanish News Agency	TASS	Telegrafnoe Agentstvo Sovetskogo Soiuza
KPL	Khaosan Pathet Lao	UPI	United Press International
MENA	Middle East News Agency	VNA	Vietnam News Agency

Party Congresses

Country	Congress or National Conference	Date (1989)
Federal Republic of Germany	9th	6–9 January and 8 February
Nicaragua	FSLN Assembly	18 February and 24 September
India (CPI)	14th	6–12 March
Spain (PCPE)	3rd extraordinary	10 March
Dominican Republic	4th	16–19 March
Italy	18th extraordinary	17–22 March
Belgium	26th	18–19 March
Cambodia	National conference	5–12 April
Netherlands	31st	8–11 April
Norway (NKP)	National Conference	23 April
Sweden (APK)	29th	4–6 May
Chile	15th	5–12 May
Mexico (PRD)	2nd	14 May
Pakistan	3rd (2nd was convened in 1985, but was postponed)	25–27 May
India (UCPI)	National conference	29 May
South Africa	4th	? June
Tunisia	10th	? June
Finland (KTP)	1st	17 June
United States	National conference	14–16 July
Mozambique	5th	24–30 July
Congo	4th	26–31 July
Saudi Arabia	3rd	? August
Hungary (HSWP/HSP)	14th	6–10 October
Ireland	20th	28–29 October
Romania	14th	20–24 November
Australia	30th special	2–3 December
(CPA voted to dissolve and form New Left Party in coalition with other leftist parties)		
German Democratic Republic	Special	8–17 December
Sri Lanka	Extraordinary	9–11 December
Hungary (re-established HSWP)	14th (first session)	14–17 December
Zimbabwe	4th	19–22 December
Czechoslovakia	Extraordinary	20–21 December

Register of Communist Parties

Status: * ruling   # unrecognized
            + legal   0 proscribed

Country: Party(ies)/Date Founded	Mid-1989 Population (est.) (World Factbook)	Communist Party Membership (claimed or est.)	Party Leader (general sec.)	Status	Last Congress	Last Election (percentage of vote; seats in legislature)
AFRICA (11)						
Angola Popular Movement for the Liberation of Angola (MPLA), 1956 (MPLA-PT, 1977)	8,533,989	45,000 cl.	José Eduardo dos Santos	*	Second 9–11 Dec. 1985	(1980); all 203 MPLA approved
Benin People's Revolutionary Party of Benin (PRPB), 1975	4,663,832	2,600 est. (WMR; First-Hand Information, p. 119)	Mathieu Kérékou (chairman, CC)	*	Second 18–24 Nov. 1985	89.6 (1989); all 206 PRPB approved
Congo Congolese Party of Labor (PCT), 1969	2,227,744	9,912 cl. (Nguesso, at 4th congress)	Denis Sassou-Nguesso (chairman)	*	Fourth 26–31 July 1989	95.0 (1984); all 153 PCT approved
Ethiopia Workers' Party of Ethiopia (WPE), 1984	49,762,492	70,000 cl.	Mengistu Haile Mariam	*	First (Const.) 6–10 Sept. 1984	85.0 (1987); 835 all WPE members
Lesotho Communist Party of Lesotho (CPL), 1962	1,711,072	no data	Jacob M. Kena	0 (tolerated)	Seventh "early 1987"	(1985); n/a

Country / Party, year founded	Population	Membership	Leader	Symbol	Congress	Election results
Mozambique Front for the Liberation of Mozambique (FRELIMO), 1962	14,275,301	130,000 cl. (*WMR, First-Hand Information*, 1988, p. 133)	Joaquim Albert Chissano	*	Fifth 24–30 July 1989	(1986); incomplete
Réunion Réunion Communist Party (PCR), 1959	565,548	2,000 est.	Paul Vergès	+	Fifth 12–14 July 1980	35.0 (1988); 13 of 44 left coal., 9 for PCR (local assembly); 2 in Paris
Senegal Independence and Labor Party (PIT), 1957	7,506,197	no data	Amath Dansoko	+	Second 28 Sept.–2 Oct. 1984	0.84 (1988); none
South Africa South African Communist Party (SACP), 1921	38,509,312	no data (increase of 90% in five years since last congress)	Joe Slovo (in exile); Dan Tloome (chairman)	0	Seventh June 1989, in Havana (*Africa Confidential*, 12 Jan. 1990)	n/a
Sudan Sudanese Communist Party (SCP), 1946	24,476,290	9,000 est.	Muhammad Ibrahim Nugud Mansur	+/0 (illegal after 30 June 1989)	Fourth (legal) 31 Oct. 1967	1.67 (1986); 5 of 301; 2 in territ., 3 in grad. constituencies
Zimbabwe Zimbabwe African National Union–Patriotic Front (ZANU-PF), 1963	10,022,000 [3,000,000] (Interestingly, only 2,026,976 votes were cast for Mugabe [*NYT*, 1 Apr. 1990]). (*Pravda*, 20 Dec. 1989)	Robert G. Mugabe (president and first secretary)	*	Fourth 12–19 Dec. 1989	76.0 (1987); 77 of 100 (in by-election for 30 parl. seats formerly reserved for whites)
TOTAL	162,253,777	268,512 (not counting Zimbabwe)				

Country: Party(ies)/Date Founded	Mid-1989 Population (est.) (World Factbook)	Communist Party Membership (claimed or est.)	Party Leader (general sec.)	Status	Last Congress	Last Election (percentage of vote; seats in legislature)

THE AMERICAS (28)

Country: Party(ies)/Date Founded	Mid-1989 Population (est.) (World Factbook)	Communist Party Membership (claimed or est.)	Party Leader (general sec.)	Status	Last Congress	Last Election (percentage of vote; seats in legislature)
Argentina	31,914,473					
Communist Party of Argentina (PCA), 1918		80,000 cl.	Athos Fava to April; Patricio Echegaray (Fava chairman since Apr.)	+	Sixteenth 4–7 Nov. 1986	5.3 (1987); none in Broad Front coal. parliamentary and provincial by-elections 6 Sept. 1987; none
Bolivia	6,558,601					
Communist Party of Bolivia (PCB), 1950 (split, 1985)		500 cl.	Humberto Ramírez (majority faction) Carlos Soria Galvarro (minority faction)	+	Fifth 9–13 Feb. 1985 Extraordinary 26–29 April 1986	7.2 (1989); 12 of 130 are in United Left (IU) coalition; PCB's share of 12 seats not listed
Brazil	150,750,232					
Brazilian Communist Party (PCB), 1922		130,000 cl. (Pravda, 9 Apr.)	Salomão Malina (chairman)	+	Eighth (called National Meeting of Communists) 17–20 July 1987	(1986); 3 of 559
Canada	26,310,836					
Communist Party of Canada (CPC), 1921		3,000 est.	George Hewison (general secretary) William Kashtan (chairman)	+	Twenty-seventh 20–24 May 1988	.09 (1988); none

Country / Party (founded)	Population		Party leader	Membership	Last congress	Last election
Chile Communist Party of Chile (CPC), 1922	12,827,411	0	Luís Corvalán Lepe (in exile) to May; Volodia Teitelboim	20,000 est.	Fifteenth 5–12 May 1989	ca. 6.00 (1989); none; candidates via coalition of Broad Party of Socialist Left (PAIS)
Colombia Communist Party of Colombia (PCC), 1930	31,945,165	+	Gilberto Vieira White	18,000 est. (incl. youth org.)	Fifteenth 12–15 Dec. 1988	1.4 (1986); 9 of 199; Patriotic Union
Costa Rica Popular Vanguard Party (PVP), 1931	2,953,908	+	Humberto Vargas Carbonell	7,500 est. (for all left parties)	Sixteenth 15–18 Sept. 1988	0.8 (1986); 1 of 57; Popular Alliance
Costa Rican People's Party (PPC), split from PVP, 1984		+	Lenin Chacón Vargas	no data	Fifteenth 23–24 Aug. 1987	(1986); 1 of 57; United People's Coalition
Cuba Cuban Communist Party (PCC), 1965	10,450,360	*	Fidel Castro Ruz	600,000 est. (WMR, Oct. 1989)	Third 4–7 Feb. and 30 Nov.–2 Dec. 1986	(1986); all 499 PCC approved
Dominican Republic Dominican Communist Party (PCD), 1944	7,106,114	+	Narciso Isa Conde	750 est.	Fourth 16–19 Mar. 1989	0.28 (1986); none
Ecuador Communist Party of Ecuador (PCE), 1928	10,262,271	+	René Mauge Mosquera (member of parliament)	600 est.	Eleventh 21–23 July 1988	3.6 (1988); 2 of 71; Broad Leftist Front, FADI
Marxist-Leninist Communist Party of Ecuador (PCE-ML), 1972		+	Jaime Hurtado González (national director, MPD)	600 est.		no % data (1988); 2 of 71; participates as Movimiento Popular Democratico (MPD)
El Salvador Communist Party of El Salvador (PCES), 1930 (one of five in FMLN)	5,124,931	0	Jorge Shafik Handal	1,000 est.	Seventh Apr. 1979	(1988); n/a

Country: Party(ies)/Date Founded	Mid-1989 Population (est.) (World Factbook)	Communist Party Membership (claimed or est.)	Party Leader (general sec.)	Status	Last Congress	Last Election (percentage of vote; seats in legislature)
Grenada Maurice Bishop Patriotic Movement (MBPM), 1984	84,480	no data	Terrence Marryshow	+	Second May 1988	5.0 (1984); none
Guadeloupe Communist Party of Guadeloupe (PCG), 1958	341,430	3,000 est.	Christian Céleste	+	Ninth 12–13 Mar. 1988	no % data (1988); 22 of 42 (local assembly); left coal. (PCG: 10 of 22); also 1 of 3 in Paris
Guatemala Guatemalan Party of Labor (PGT), 1952	9,116,877	250 est.	Carlos González Orellana ("Camarilla" faction) Juan Manuel Díaz/ Mario Sánchez (National Leadership Nucleus faction has taken the new name of "PGT 6 de Enero")	0	Fourth Dec. 1969; First 1988	(1985); n/a
Guyana People's Progressive Party (PPP), 1950	765,461	300 est. (100 leadership)	Cheddi Jagan	+	Twenty-third 30 July–1 Aug. 1988	16.8 (1985); 8 of 53 elected members
Haiti Unified Party of Haitian Communists (PUCH), 1968	6,322,198	350 est.	René Théodore	+	First 1979	(1988) (PUCH boycotted)

Country / Party	Population	Membership	Leader		Last Congress	Election data
Honduras						
Communist Party of Honduras (PCH), 1954 (one of six in the Honduran Revolutionary Movement, MHR, 1982)	5,103,772	100 est. (less than 100)	Rigoberto Padilla Rush (in exile) Mario Sosa Navarro (leader in Honduras)	0	Fourth Jan. 1986 (clandestine)	(1985); n/a
Jamaica						
Workers' Party of Jamaica (WPJ), 1978	2,484,957	100 est.	Trevor Munroe	+	Fourth 11–13 Sept. 1988	(1989) (WPJ did not contest)
Jamaican Communist Party (JCP), 1975		no data	Christopher Lawrence	+	no data	
Martinique						
Martinique Communist Party (PCM), 1957	331,511	1,000 est.	Armand Nicolas	+	Ninth 12–13 Dec. 1988	no % data (1988); 2 of 45 (local assembly); none in Paris
Mexico						
Mexican Socialist Party (PMS), 1987	86,336,019	90,000 cl.	Gilberto Rincón Gallardo	+	First 14 May 1989	(1988) (presid.)
Democratic Revolution Party (PRD), May 1989		no data	Cuauhtémoc Cardenas (noncommunist coordinator general)			
Nicaragua						
Nicaraguan Socialist Party (PSN), 1937	3,519,620	1,400 est.	Gustavo Tablada	+	Tenth Oct. 1973	1.3 (1984); 2 of 96
Communist Party of Nicaragua (PCN, splinter of PSN), 1970		1,600 est.	Eli Altamirano Pérez	+	Second June 1986	ca. 2.0 (1984); 2 of 96
Sandinista Front of National Liberation (FSLN), 1961		5,500 est. (La Prensa, 27 Oct. 1989)	Daniel Ortega (coord. of Executive Commission)	*	FSLN Assembly 18 Feb. & 24 Sept. 1989	63.0 (1984); 61 of 96

Country: Party(ies)/Date Founded	Mid-1989 Population (est.) (World Factbook)	Communist Party Membership (claimed or est.)	Party Leader (general sec.)	Status	Last Congress	Last Election (percentage of vote; seats in legislature)
Panama People's Party (PDP), 1943	2,373,053	25,600 cl. (based on signatures) (750 militants, est.)	Rubén Darío Sousa	+	Eighth 24–26 Jan. 1986	02.0 (1984); none
Paraguay Paraguayan Communist Party (PCP), 1928	4,522,172	4,000 est.	Julio Rojas (acting) Antonio Maidana (arrested in 1980)	0 (but tolerated)	Third 10 Apr. 1971	(1989); n/a
Peru Peruvian Communist Party (PCP), 1928	21,448,501	4,000 est.	Jorge del Prado Chavez	+	Ninth 27–30 May 1987	26.0 (1985); 48 of 180 United Left Coalition; 6 PCP repr. of 48
Puerto Rico Puerto Rican Communist Party (PCP), 1934	3,300,707	100 est.	Frank Irrizarry	+	Fourth 1954	(1988); none (did not contest)
United States of America Communist Party USA (CPUSA), 1919	248,231,030	20,000 cl. (4,000–6,000 est.)	Gus Hall	+	Twenty-fourth 13–16 Aug. 1987 (nat'l conference, 14–16 July)	(1988); none (did not contest)
Uruguay Communist Party of Uruguay (PCU), 1920	2,988,813	11,000 cl. (*Pravda*, 14, 22 Dec. 1987)	Jaime Perez Gerschuni Rodney Arismendi (chairman) (died, 27 Dec.)	+	Twenty-first 7–11 Dec. 1988	34.0 (1989); 22 of 99; Frente Amplio coal. (10% and 11 seats for PCU)

Country / Party	Population	Membership	Leader		Last Congress	Electoral/Parliamentary
Venezuela Communist Party of Venezuela (PCV), 1931	19,263,376	4,000 est.	Alonso Ojeda Olaechea	+	Seventh 24–27 Oct. 1985	2.0 (1988); 1 of 201
TOTAL	712,738,279	1,034,250				

ASIA AND THE PACIFIC (20)

Country / Party	Population	Membership	Leader		Last Congress	Electoral/Parliamentary
Australia Communist Party of Australia (CPA), 1920	16,451,955	1,000 est.	Brian Aarons, et al. (nat'l executive)	+	Thirtieth/special 2–3 Dec. 1989 (voted to dissolve, create New Left Party)	0.3 (1987); none
Socialist Party of Australia (SPA), 1971		500 est.	Peter Dudley Symon Jack McPhillips (pres.)	+	Sixth 3 Oct. 1988	negl. (1987); none
Bangladesh Communist Party of Bangladesh (CPB), 1948	114,718,395	5,000 est. (9,911 cl.)	Saifuddin Ahmed Manik Nurul Islam, sec. of CPB (FBIS-NES, 12 May 1989)	+	Fourth 7–11 Apr. 1987	(1988) boycotted
Burma Burmese Communist Party (BCP), 1939	40,451,732	3,000 cl. (several hundred, est.)	[Thakin] Ba Thein Tin (chairman)	0	Third 9 Sept.–2 Oct. 1985	(1985); n/a
Cambodia Khmer People's Revolutionary Party (KPRP), 1951	6,838,033	10,000 cl. (*JPRS-SAS*, 29 June)	Heng Samrin	*	Fifth 13–16 Oct. 1985 (national conference of cadres, 5–12 April)	99.0 (1981); all 117

Country: Party(ies)/Date Founded	Mid-1989 Population (est.) (World Factbook)	Communist Party Membership (claimed or est.)	Party Leader (general sec.)	Status	Last Congress	Last Election (percentage of vote; seats in legislature)
Party of Democratic Kampuchea (PDK), or Kampuchean Communist Party (KCP), 1951		no data	Pol Pot (officially until 1981)	0	Third 14 Dec. 1975	n/a
China	1,112,298,677					
Chinese Communist Party (CCP), 1921		48,000,000 cl. (N.D., 21 Sept.)	Zhao Ziyang (to 24 June) Jiang Zemin	*	Thirteenth 25 Oct.–1 Nov. 1987	(1987); all 3,202 CCP approved
India	833,421,982					
Communist Party of India (CPI), 1928		467,539 cl.	C. Rajeswara Rao	+	Fourteenth 6–12 Mar. 1989	no % data; (1989); 12 of 545
Communist Party of India-Marxist (CPM), 1964		450,000 cl.	E. M. S. Namboodiripad	+	Thirteenth 26–31 Dec. 1988	(1989); 32 of 545
United Communist Party of India (UCPI), 1989		negligible	Mohit Sen (gen. sec.) S. A. Dange (chmn.)	+	nat'l conf. in Salem, negl. (1989) 29 May 1989	(1989)
Indonesia	187,651,163					
Indonesian Communist Party (PKI), 1920 (split)		1,500 est. ca. 200 exiles	Jusuf Adjitorop (pro-Beijing faction) Thomas Sinuraya (pro-Moscow faction)	0	Seventh Extraord. Apr. 1962	(1987); n/a
Japan	123,220,129					
Japan Communist Party (JCP), 1922		470,000 est.	Hiromu Murakami to June; Tetsuzo Fuwa (Presidium chairman) Kenji Miyamoto (CC chairman)	+	Eighteenth 26–28 Nov. 1987	8.8 (1989); 27 of 512

Country / Party (founded)	Population	Party membership	Party leader		Last congress	Last election
Korea (North) Korean Workers' Party (KWP), 1946 (as united party, 1949)	22,521,223	3,000,000 cl.	Kim Il-song	*	Sixth 10–15 Oct. 1980	100 (1986); all 706 KWP approved
Laos Lao People's Revolutionary Party (LPRP), 1955	3,935,786	40,000 cl.	Kaysone Phomvihane	*	Fourth 13–15 Nov. 1986	(1989); Supreme People's Assembly (65 of 79 are LPRP members)
Malaysia Communist Party of Malaya (CPM), 1930 (may be active under new party name per agreement of 2 Dec.)	16,726,766	1,300 est.	Chin Peng (pseud.)	0	1965 (last known)	(1984)
Communist Party of Malaysia (MCP), 1983		800 est.	Ah Leng	0	unknown	(1984)
Mongolia Mongolian People's Revolutionary Party (MPRP), 1921	2,145,463	89,312 cl. (WMR; First-Hand Information, p. 96)	Jambyn Batmonh (Dzambiin Batmunkh)	*	Nineteenth 28–31 May 1986	93.5 (1986); 346 of 370 MPRP approved
Nepal Nepal Communist Party (NCP), 1949 (factions)	18,699,884	10,000 est. (75% pro-Beijing and neutral)	Man Mohan Adhikary	0	Third 1961 (before split; right wing held its own third in 1968)	(1986); n/a
New Zealand Communist Party of New Zealand (CPNZ), 1921	3,372,763 (N.Z. Dept. of Stat.)	100 est.	Harold Crook (chairman)	+	Twenty-third 22 Apr. 1984	(1987); none
Socialist Unity Party (SUP), 1966		300 est.	George H. Jackson (pres.) Marilyn Tucker (gen. sec.)	+	Eighth 22–24 Oct. 1988	(1987); none

Country: Party(ies)/Date Founded	Mid-1989 Population (est.) (World Factbook)	Communist Party Membership (claimed or est.)	Party Leader (general sec.)	Status	Last Congress	Last Election (percentage of vote; seats in legislature)
Pakistan Communist Party of Pakistan (CPP), 1948	110,407,376	under 200 est.	Ali Nazish	+	Third 25–27 May 1989	(1988)
Philippines Philippine Communist Party (PKP), 1930	64,906,990	5,000 est. (range 5–8000)	Merlin Magallona (gen. sec.) Felicismo Mac-apagal (chmn)	+	Ninth Dec. 1986	(1987)
Communist Party of the Philippines (CPP), 1968		30,000 est. (range 30,000–40,000)	Benito Tiamzon (acting chmn.) Jose Maria Sison (chmn. in absentia)	0	Founding/Reest. 26 Dec. 1968–7 Jan. 1969	(1987)
Singapore Communist Party of Malaya, Branch (CPM), 1930	2,674,362	300 est.	Chin Peng (pseud.)	0	unknown	(1984)
Sri Lanka Communist Party of Sri Lanka (CPSL), 1943	16,883,130	5,000 est.	Kattorge P. Silva	+	Thirteenth 22–26 March 1987 Extraordinary 9–11 Dec. 1989	2.9 (1989); 3 of 225, as part of United Socialist Alliance
Janatha Vimukthi Peramuna (JVP), 1968		no data	Rohana Wijewwera (leader) Upatissa Gamanayake (dep.) (both killed Nov. 1989)	+	no data	did not contest

Country / Party (founded)	Population	Membership	Leader(s)		Party Congress	Last Election
Thailand Communist Party of Thailand (CPT), 1942	55,524,352	375 est. (range 250–500)	Thong Jaensri (unconfirmed; pseudonym?)	0	Fourth Mar.–Apr. 1984 (clandestine)	(1988); n/a
Vietnam Vietnamese Communist Party (VCP), 1930	66,820,544	2,195,824 cl. (*Nhan Dan*, 3 Feb. 1989)	Nguyen Van Linh	*	Sixth 15–18 Dec. 1986	98.8 (1987); 496, all VCP endorsed
TOTAL	2,819,668,705	54,787,250				

EASTERN EUROPE AND USSR (9)

Country / Party (founded)	Population	Membership	Leader(s)		Party Congress	Last Election
Albania Albanian Party of Labor (APL), 1941	3,208,033	147,000 cl.	Ramiz Alia	*	Ninth 3–8 Nov. 1986	100 (1987); all 250 Democratic Front
Bulgaria Bulgarian Communist Party (BCP), 1903	8,985,800	984,000 cl. (*Pravda*, 31 Jan 1990)	Todor Zhivkov, to 10 Nov. 1989; Petŭr Toshev Mladenov	*	Thirteenth 2–5 Apr. 1986	99.9 (1986); all 400 Fatherland Front
Czechoslovakia Communist Party of Czechoslovakia (KSC), 1921	15,658,079	1,574,690 cl. (Adamec claims 400,000 at KSC plenum 17 Feb. 1990, as per *RFE/RL Daily Report* no. 35, 17 Feb. 1990; ca. one-fourth of 1,574,690, reported by ČTK, 8 Jan. 1990; *FBIS-EEU*, 9 Jan 1990)	Miloš Jakeš Karel Urbanek Ladislav Adamec (chmn.) Vasil Mohorita	*/+	Seventeenth 24–28 Mar. 1986 Extraordinary 20–21 Dec. 1989	99.94 (1986); all 350 National Front
Germany: German Democratic Republic Socialist Unity Party (SED), 1946; Socialist Unity Party–Party of Democratic Socialists (SED-PDS), 1989	16,586,490	ca. 1,000,000 cl. (*Pravda*, 28 Jan. 1990) (*FBIS-EEU*, 2 Feb. 1990)	Erich Honecker to Nov. Egon Krenz to Dec. Gregor Gysi	*/+	Eleventh 17–21 Apr. 1986 Extraordinary 8–10, 16–17 Dec. 1989	99.94 (1986); all 500 National Front

Country: Party(ies)/Date Founded	Mid-1989 Population (est.) (World Factbook)	Communist Party Membership (claimed or est.)	Party Leader (general sec.)	Status	Last Congress	Last Election (percentage of vote; seats in legislature)
Hungary						
Hungarian Socialist Workers' Party (HSWP), 1956; reconstituted	10,566,944	82,000 cl. (*Pravda*, 28 Jan. 1990; *FBIS-SOV*, 7 Feb. 1990)	Károly Grósz to 7 Oct. 1989 Gyula Thurmer	*/+	Reconst./ Fourteenth 14 Dec. 1989	98.9 (1985); all 352 Patriotic People's Front
Hungarian Socialist Party (HSP), split from HSWP, 1989		50,000 cl.	Rezsö Nyers	+	Founding/ Fourteenth 6–10 October 1989	(1990)
Poland						
Polish United Workers' Party (PZPR), 1948–27 Jan. 1990, when the party dissolved itself	38,169,800	1,000,000 est. (2,000,000 cl. *Sovetskaya Rossia*, 25 Jan. 1990; *FBIS-SOV*, 6 Feb. 1990)	Wojciech Jaruzelski to July 1989 Mieczyslaw F. Rakowski to 27 Jan. 1990	*	Eleventh 27 Jan. 1990	78.8 (1985); all 460 Fatherland Front
Social Democracy of the Polish Republic (SDRP), Jan. 1990		5,000 est. (*San Francisco Examiner & Chronicle*, 18 Feb. 1990, quoting Kwaśniewski)	Aleksander Kwaśniewski	+	Founding 29 Jan. 1990	(1990)
New Party of Polish Leftist Forces (USDRP; split from SDRP, 29 Jan. 1990)		ca. 100 est. (*Pravda*, 30 Jan. 1990)	Tadeusz Fiszbach (pres.)	+		(1990)
Romania						
Romanian Communist Party (PCR), 1921	23,153,475	none (ceased 22 Dec.; 3,813,000 cl. at Nov. PCR congress)	Nicolae Ceauşescu to 25 Dec.	*/+	Fourteenth 20–24 Nov. 1989	97.8 (1985); all 369 Socialist Democracy and Unity Front
National Salvation Front		no data	Ion Iliescu (chairman)			

	Population	Members	Leader		Last Congress	Last Election
USSR Communist Party of the Soviet Union (CPSU), 1898	288,742,342 (TASS, 25 Apr. 1988)	19,487,822 cl. (*Izvestiia, Tsk KPSS* no. 2, Feb. 1989)	Mikhail S. Gorbachev	*	Twenty-seventh 25 Feb.–6 Mar. 1986	(1989); 2,250 (87.6% are CPSU members)
Yugoslavia League of Communists of Yugoslavia (LCY), 1920	23,724,919	ca. 1,868,000 cl. (before Emergency Congress, *Pravda*, 21 Jan. 1990; *FBIS-SOV*, 25 Jan. 1990)	Štipe Šuvar (pres. of Presidium until May) Milan Pančevski	*	Thirteenth 25–28 June 1986	(1986); all 308 LCY-approved Socialist Alliance
TOTAL	428,795,882	26,198,612				

MIDDLE EAST (15)

	Population	Members	Leader		Last Congress	Last Election
Afghanistan People's Democratic Party of Afghanistan (PDPA), 1965	14,825,013	30,000 est. (200,000 cl., Radio Kabul, 21 July; *FBIS-NES*, 1 July)	Mohammed Najibullah	*	Second nat'l. conference 18–19 Oct. 1987	38.0 (1988); 69 of 184 elected of 234 total (National Front) (22.6% and 42 for PDPA)
Algeria Socialist Vanguard Party (PAGS), 1920	24,946,073	no data	Sadiq Hadjeres (first secretary)	0/+	Sixth Feb. 1952	(1982)
Bahrain Bahrain National Liberation Front (NLF/B), 1955	496,759	negligible	Saif ben Ali (gen. sec.) Yusuf al-Hassan al-Ajajai (chairman; not noted since 1983)	0	unknown	n/a
Egypt Egyptian Communist Party (ECP), 1921	54,777,615	500 est.	Farid Mujahid (apparently)	0	Second Sept. 1984	(1987); n/a

Country: Party(ies)/Date Founded	Mid-1989 Population (est.) (World Factbook)	Communist Party Membership (claimed or est.)	Party Leader (general sec.)	Status	Last Congress	Last Election (percentage of vote; seats in legislature)
Iran						
Communist Party of Iran (Tudeh Party), 1941 (dissolved May 1983)	53,866,523	1,500 est.	Ali Khavari (first sec. of CC, party leader in exile)	0	National Conference 1986	(1988); n/a
Iraq						
Iraqi Communist Party (ICP), 1934	18,073,969	no data	Aziz Muhammad (first secretary)	0	Fourth 10–15 Nov. 1985	(1989); n/a
Israel						
Communist Party of Israel (CPI, "RAKAH"), 1948 (Palestine Communist Party, 1922)	4,371,478 (excl. E. Jerusalem and the West Bank)	2,000 est.	Meir Vilner	+	Twentieth 4–7 Dec. 1985	3.7 (1988); 4 of 120 (with Dem. Front of Peace and Equality)
Jordan						
Communist Party of Jordan (CPJ), 1951	2,955,660	no data	Dr. Ya'qub Zayadin	0	Second Dec. 1983	(1989); 1 of 80 (but not as CPJ member)
Lebanon						
Lebanese Communist Party (LCP), 1924	3,300,802	2,500 est. (14,000–16,000 cl.)	George Hawi	+	Fifth 3–5 Feb. 1987	(1972); none
Organization of Communist Action in Lebanon (OCAL), 1970		1,500 est.	Muhsin Ibrahim	+	First 1971	
Morocco						
Party of Progress and Socialism (PPS), 1974 (Moroccan Communist Party, 1943)	25,605,579	ca. 4,500 est. (50,000 cl.)	'Ali Yata	+	Fourth 17–19 July 1987	2.3 (1984); 2 of 306
Palestine Communist Party (PCP), 1982	4,500,000 est. Palestinians (incl. E. Jerusalem, Gaza, Jordan and the West Bank)	no data	Bashir al-Barghuti (presumably)	0	First 1984 (or late 1983)	n/a

Country / Party	Population	Membership	Leader		Last Congress	Last Election
Saudi Arabia Communist Party of Saudi Arabia (CPSA), 1975	16,108,539	negligible	Mahdi Habib	0	Third Aug. 1989	n/a (absolute monarchy)
Syria Syrian Communist Party (SCP), 1924 (as separate party, 1944)	12,010,564	5,000 est.	Khalid Bakhdash to May Yusuf Faysal (succeeded Bakhdash)	+	Sixth July 1986	(1986); 8 of 195
Tunisia Tunisian Communist Party (PCT), 1934	7,916,104	2,000 est. (4,000 cl.)	Muhammad Harmel (first secretary)	+	Tenth June 1989	(1989); none
Yemen (PDRY) Yemen Socialist Party (YSP), 1978	2,503,641	31,000 cl. (incl. cand. members)	'Ali Salim al-Bayd	*	Fourth 20–21 June 1987	(1986); all 111 YSP approved
TOTAL	246,258,319	80,500				

WESTERN EUROPE (23)

Country / Party	Population	Membership	Leader		Last Congress	Last Election
Austria Communist Party of Austria (KPÖ), 1918	7,584,766	15,000 est.	Franz Muhri (chairman)	+	Twenty-sixth 25–28 Mar. 1987	0.72 (1986); none
Belgium Belgian Communist Party (PCB/KPB), 1921	9,887,998	5,000 est.	Louis van Geyt (president)	+	Twenty-sixth 18–19 Mar. 1989	0.8 (1987); none
Cyprus Progressive Party of the Working People (AKEL), 1941 (Communist Party of Cyprus, 1922)	700,009	15,000 cl. (official AKEL cl.)	Dimitris Christofias	+	Sixteenth 26–30 Nov. 1986 Extraordinary Congress 20 Dec. 1987 (*Pravda*, 21 Dec. 1987)	27.4 (1985); 15 of 56

Country: Party(ies)/Date Founded	Mid-1989 Population (est.) (World Factbook)	Communist Party Membership (claimed or est.)	Party Leader (general sec.)	Status	Last Congress	Last Election (percentage of vote; seats in legislature)
Denmark	5,129,659					
Communist Party of Denmark (DKP), 1919		7,400 est. (Jyllands-Posten, 26 Nov. 1989)	Poul Emanuel (party sec.) Ole Sohn (chairman)	+	Twenty-eighth 16–19 Apr. 1987	0.8 (1988); none
Finland	4,963,359					
Finnish Communist Party (SKP), 1918		21,000 est.	Heljä Tammisola (gen. sec.) Jorma Wahlström (chairman)	+	Twenty-first 12–15 June 1987	9.4 (1987); 16 of 200 SKDL Front (11 of 16 for SKP)
Finnish Communist Party-Unity (SKP-Y), 1986		13,500 est.	Yrjö Häkanan (gen. sec.) Jouko Kajanoja (chmn. to Oct., replaced by Esko-Juhani Tennilä)	+	First 5–7 June, 1987	4.3 (1987); 4 of 200 DEVA Front
Communist Workers' Party (KTP), 1988		200 est.	Heikki Mannikko (gen. sec.) Timo Lahdenmaeki (chairman)	+	First 17–18 June 1989 (Founding, 23–24 May 1988)	registered; part of DEVA Front
France	55,994,085					
French Communist Party (PCF), 1920		200,000 cl. (FBIS-WEU, 30 Jan. 1989)	Georges Marchais	+	Twenty-sixth 2–6 Dec. 1987	11.3 (1988); 25 of 577 (and two from overseas depts.)
Germany: Federal Republic of Germany	60,977,195 (excl. W. Berlin)					
German Communist Party (DKP), 1968		27,500 (BfV est.) (400,000 cl.)	Herbert Mies (chairman)	+	Ninth 6–9 Jan. 1989	0.5 (1987); none for Peace List in which DKP participated

Country / Party	Population	Membership	Leadership		Party congress	Last election
Great Britain						
Communist Party of Great Britain (CPGB), 1920	57,028,169	7,500 est. (*NYT*, 2 Feb. 1990)	Gordon McLennan (resigned at congress)	+	Forty-first 25–28 Nov. 1989	0.01 (1987); none
Greece						
Communist Party of Greece (KKE), 1921	10,041,414	50,000 est.	Grigoris Farakos (gen. sec.) Kharilaos Florakis (chairman)	+	Twelfth 12–16 May 1987	10.97 (1989); 21 of 300 (Coalition of the Left and Progress)
Communist Party of Greece–Interior (KKE-I), 1968; (KKE-I Renovating Left), 1987; and	(split into two factions) no data		Giannis Banias	+	Fourth May 1986	(1989)
Greek Left (E.AR), 1987	no data		Leonidas Kyrkos	+	24–26 April 1987	
Iceland						
People's Alliance (PA), 1968	248,501	3,000 est.	Olafur Ragnar Grimsson (chairman)	+	Biennial Congr. 16–20 Nov. 1989	13.2 (1987); 8 of 63
Ireland						
Communist Party of Ireland (CPI), 1933	3,550,352	500 est.	James Stewart	+	Twentieth 28–29 Oct. 1989	(1989); none
Italy						
Italian Communist Party (PCI), 1921	57,557,767	800,000 cl. (*FBIS-WEU*, 11 Jan. 1990)	Achille Ochetto	+	Eighteenth 17–22 March 1989	26.6 (1987); 177 of 630
Luxembourg						
Communist Party of Luxembourg (CPL), 1921	366,329	600 est.	René Urbany (chairman)	+	Twenty-fifth 23–24 Apr. 1988	3.6 (1989); 1 of 64
Malta						
Communist Party of Malta (CPM), 1969	351,307 (Malta Office of Statistics, Sept. 1989)	300 est.	Anthony Vassallo	+	Fourth 15–17 July 1988	0.08 (1987); none

Country: Party(ies)/Date Founded	Mid-1989 Population (est.) (World Factbook)	Communist Party Membership (claimed or est.)	Party Leader (general sec.)	Status	Last Congress	Last Election (percentage of vote; seats in legislature)
Netherlands Communist Party of the Netherlands (CPN), 1909	14,790,125	4,000 est. (range of 3,000–5,000)	Elli Izeboud (chairman)	+	Thirty-first 8–11 April 1989	4.1 (1989); 6 of 150 (with Green Left)
Norway Norwegian Communist Party (NKP), 1923	4,202,502	ca. 1,750 est.	Kåre André Nilsen (chairman)	+	Nineteenth 23–26 Apr. 1987	0.84 (1989); none (Joint with AKP)
Workers' Communist Party (AKP), 1973		ca. 6,000 est.	Siri Jensen (chairman)	+	Fifth Dec. 1988 (secret)	(1989); none (see NKP above)
Portugal Portuguese Communist Party (PCP), 1921	10,459,701	over 199,275 cl. (*Avante!*, 3 Nov. 1988)	Álvaro Cunhal	+	Twelfth 1–4 Dec. 1988	11.0 (1987); 30 of 250 United People's Alliance Coalition (25 of 30 for PCP)
San Marino Communist Party of San Marino (PCS), 1921	22,980	1,200 cl. (300 est.)	Gilberto Ghiotti	+	Eleventh 27 Jan. 1986	28.71 (1988); 18 of 60
Spain Spanish Communist Party (PCE), 1920	39,417,220	83,000 cl. (*FBIS-EEU*, 17 Aug. 1989)	Julio Anguita González	+	Twelfth 19–21 Feb. 1988	9.05 (1989); 18 of 350 United Left Coalition
Communist Party of the Peoples of Spain (PCPE), 1984		16,500 est.	Juan Ramos Camarero	+	Third extraord. March 1989	as above
Spanish Workers' Party–Communist Unity (PTE-UC), 1987		14,000 est.	Adolfo Pinedo (gen. sec.) Santiago Carrillo (chairman)	+	First 8 Feb. 1987	(1989); none

Country / Party	Population	Voting	Leader	Membership	Congress	Election result
Sweden						
Left Party Communists (VPK), 1921	8,401,098	+	Lars Werner (chairman)	17,800 cl.	Twenty-eighth 23–25 May 1987	5.8 (1988); 21 of 349
Communist Workers' Party (APK), 1977		+	Rolf Hagel (chairman)	5,000 cl.	Twenty-ninth 4–6 May 1989 (*Pravda*, 4 May 1989)	(1988); no data
Switzerland						
Swiss Labor Party (PdAS), 1921 (re-established, 1944)	6,611,019	+	Jean Spielman	4,500 est.	Thirteenth 27 Feb.–1 Mar. 1987	0.8 (1987); 1 of 200
Turkey						
United Communist Party of Turkey (UCPT), 1988	55,355,831	0	Haydar Kutlu (gen. sec.) Nihat Sargin (chairman)	negligible	First 12–13 Oct. 1988	(1987); n/a
West Berlin						
Socialist Unity Party of West Berlin (SEW), 1949	1,869,000	+	Horst Schmitt, died Apr. 1989; Dietmar Ahrens	7,000 cl.	Eighth 15–27 May 1987	0.6 (1989); none
TOTAL	415,546,386			1,526,525		
GRAND TOTAL	4,785,261,348			83,895,649		

MAJOR INTERNATIONAL FRONT ORGANIZATIONS*

Organization (12)	Year Founded	Headquarters	Claimed Membership	Affiliates	Countries
Afro-Asian Peoples' Solidarity Organization (AAPSO) (Murad Ghalib*; Nuri Abd-al Razzaq Husayn*)	1957	Cairo	unknown	87	unknown
Asian Buddhist Conference for Peace (ABCP) (Kharkuu Gaadan*; G. Lubsan Tseren*)	1970	Ulan Bator	unknown	15	12
Berlin Conference of European Catholics (BCEC) (Franco Leonori*; Hubertus Guske*)	1964	East Berlin	unknown	unknown	45
Christian Peace Conference (CPC) (Károly Tóth*; Lubomir Mirejovsky)	1958	Prague	unknown	unknown	ca. 80
Continental Organization of Latin American Students (OCLAE) (Jorge Arias Diaz[2], Angel Arzuaga Reyes*[3])	1966	Havana	unknown	34[1]	26[1]
International Association of Democratic Lawyers (IADL) (Joe Nordmann; Amar Bentoumi)	1946	Brussels	25,000	unknown	ca. 80
International Federation of Resistance Movements (FIR) (Arialdo Banfi; Alix Lhote)	1951	Vienna	5,000,000	78[4]	27[4]
International Institute for Peace (IIP) (Erwin Lanc[5]; Max Schmidt[5])	1957	Vienna	unknown	unknown	unknown
International Organization of Journalists (IOJ) (Kaare Nordenstrang; Dušan Ulcak*)	1946	Prague	ca. 250,000	unknown	120 plus
International Radio and Television Organization (OIRT) (Karel Kvapil[6]; Gennadij Codr)	1946	Prague	unknown	29[7]	23[7]
International Union of Students (IUS) (Josef Scala*; Georgios Michaelides*)	1946	Prague	ca. 40,000,000[8]	117	110
Organization of Solidarity of the Peoples of Africa, Asia and Latin America (OSPAAAL) (Susumu Osaki?; René Anillo Capote*)	1966	Havana	unknown	unknown	unknown
Women's International Democratic Federation (WIDF) (Freda Brown*; vacant?[13])	1945	East Berlin	200,000,000	142	124

Organization	Founded	Location	Membership		
World Federation of Democratic Youth (WFDY) (Walid Masri*, György Szabó*)	1945	Budapest	150,000,000	ca. 270	123
World Federation of Scientific Workers (WFSW) (Jean-Marie Legay; Stan Davison)	1946	London	1,000,000[9]	ca. 46	70 plus
World Federation of Teachers' Unions (FISE) (Lesturuge Ariyawansa; Gérard Montant)	1946	East Berlin	26,000,000	150[12]	79
World Federation of Trade Unions (WFTU) (vacant[10]; Ibrahim Zakariya*)	1945	Prague	ca. 214,000,000	92	81
World Peace Council (WPC) (Romesh Chandra*; vacant[11])	1950	Helsinki	unknown	unknown	145[14]

New information is footnoted.

*World Peace Council Presidential Committee member (Helsinki). *New Perspectives*, June 1989, p. 2.

1. *World Student News* (Prague), no. 8, p. 11.

2. Ibid.

3. *New Perspectives* (Helsinki), June 1989.

4. *Neues Deutschland* (East Berlin), 26–27 August.

5. Ibid., 10 January; Schmidt is director of Scientific Council.

6. *IOJ Newsletter* (Prague), no. 11.

7. *Yearbook of International Organizations, 1989/90* (Munich: K. G. Saur, 1989), entry CC2391.

8. Prague TV, 15 Nov.; *FBIS-EEU*, 16 Nov.

9. Sofia, BTA, 7 Oct.; *FBIS-EEU*, 13 Oct.

10. Budapest, MTI, 24 March; *FBIS-EEU*, 3 April.

11. *Peace Courier* (Helsinki), no. 7/8.

12. *Teachers of the Whole World* (East Berlin), special edition, Sept., p. 4.

13. *Kansan Uutiset* (Helsinki), 20 Sept.; *Helsinggin Sanomat* (Helsinki), 21 Sept.

14. Prague, ČTK, 18 March 1988; *FBIS*, 21 March 1988.

Introduction
The Communist World in 1989

After *YICA* had appeared for almost a quarter century, Peace and Socialism International Publishers in Prague issued a concise 140-page paperback on the "85 million communists in almost 100 countries of all continents."[1] This handbook provides entries on 107 countries, most of the data derived from information supplied by those movements which have contacts with *World Marxist Review* (*WMR*). The latter's Commission on Exchanges of Experience in Party Work had initiated the requests.

Ten years earlier, a much more detailed volume appeared in Warsaw under the auspices of the Polish United Workers' (communist) Party. It had been prepared by twenty coauthors, who spent seven years on research and writing.[2] This compendium covered only 94 countries. It has never been updated. Nor is there any plan to do so, according to Tadeusz Iwinski, who headed the revolutionary-movements section of the central apparatus for the Polish United Workers' (communist) Party until the latter dissolved itself toward the end of January 1990, changing its name to Social Democracy of the Republic of Poland.[3]

This last development had first occurred in Hungary and has since been replicated by most of the East European bloc movements. Notable exceptions are Romania, where the ruling communist party just disappeared after Christmas Day of 1989, and Bulgaria, whose BCP still maintains itself in power.[4] In addition, where a change of name occurred, two or more splinter groups have appeared. Each of them claims to be the true heir of the dissolved movement.

The CPSU daily newspaper summarized conditions in Eastern Europe at the beginning of 1990 as follows:

> In a number of countries, communists have been left in the minority in the government. Many people are leaving communist ranks. Primary party organizations are disbanding and ceasing activity in the army, law enforcement, state organizations and, in a number of cases, also at enterprise levels. The explosive way in which events are developing has thrown some communists into confusion and disarray.[5]

It appears that the CPSU Politburo has decided that nature should run its course, at least in Eastern Europe. More comments on Soviet relations with the so-called bloc parties appear below under the section on that region of the world.

There have been no recent claims from Moscow that the world Marxist-Leninist movement has been growing. This volume of *YICA* treats 106 countries or territories: Nigeria and Suriname, where no activity could be registered, have been dropped. A year ago, the communist parties themselves claimed, or it was estimated that *ca.* 90,500,000 individuals were carried on their rolls. That number today is 83,896,149, more than six and a half million fewer members than one year ago. Not included in this total are three million claimed members of ZANU-PF in Zimbabwe.[6] The Communist Party of the Soviet Union (CPSU) recognizes more than one movement in Australia, Costa Rica, Finland, Greece, Hungary, India, New Zealand, Spain, and Sweden. It also maintains contacts with communist movements in nonsovereign geographic entities such as Guadeloupe, Martinique, Palestine, Puerto Rico, Réunion, and West Berlin.

The CPSU and, therefore, the government of the USSR classifies the following countries as being governed by "vanguard revolutionary democratic" parties: Angola, Afghanistan, Congo-Brazzaville, Ethiopia, Madagascar, Mozambique, and South Yemen.[7] Moscow also maintains relations with such "revolutionary democratic" movements as the ones in Bahrain, Burundi, Cambodia, Cape Verde, Grenada, Nicaragua (the Sandinistas), Sao Tomé and Principe, the Seychelles, and the State of Palestine (PLO). [8]

Several of the 106 geographic entities include significant Marxist-Leninist movements, not recognized by the CPSU. All population figures are from July 1989 and the same source, with the exception of those for Malta and New Zealand, for whom the essays' authors provided local statistics.[9] The most important party leader has the title of general secretary or first secretary, whereas the chairmanship is frequently an honorific position held by a retired former leader. The tables also provide the date(s) of the party's most recent congress or conference, its legal status, percentage of the vote and number of seats won in the latest election. If the party did not participate, the year of the last nation-wide vote is given in parentheses. The first table lists 27 congresses and four national conferences held during calendar year 1989.

Among the sixteen ruling communist parties, the Chinese again claimed the largest gain in numbers (one million) over the past year.[10] The North Koreans announced an increase of 500,000; Cuba about 100,000; and Vietnam 76,000. Apart from Bulgaria, with a listed growth of more than 15,000 and the Soviet Union's additional 19,000, the remaining East European movements had either no reported gain (Albania) or substantial losses.

The communists in Czechoslovakia admitted a loss of over 1.1 million; the ruling party in East Germany approximately 1.3 million; in Hungary, almost 690,000, when one adds up the membership for both splinter groups; in Poland, the former ruling party of only one million, which had about 2.2 million a year ago, dissolved itself at the end of January 1990 (5,100 remained in both splinter groups); in Romania, from 3.8 million party membership dropped to zero within a few days in December; and in Yugoslavia, the party lost almost 212,000 members.

A few of the nonruling parties showed gains: Brazil (10,000); the PCE faction in Spain (17,000 claimed). These gains were, however, outweighed by losses in India (12,000), the Philippines (2,000), France (405,000 cl.), West Germany (10,500 est.), and Italy (582,000 cl.). Never in the past have the admitted or estimated losses been higher, especially throughout Eastern and Western Europe.

The status of several communist parties changed during the past year. In Algeria, PAGS became legal, as of September 1989. The movement in Malaysia (CPM) dissolved itself at the start of December 1989, but regrouped as the Malayan People's Party under former CMP general secretary Chin Peng. The communists of Australia also merged with other leftist groups into the New Left Party. The movement in Pakistan is now legal. A United Communist Party of India has been formed with groups in the south from Salem and Tamil Nadu, as well as the Alliance of All-India CP and some former CPI members. In Mexico, a new Democratic Revolutionary Party, led by noncommunist Cuauhtémoc Cárdenas, held its first congress during May 1989.

A record number of fourteen leadership changes occurred during the past year. The long-time general secretary in Argentina became chairman in April, having been succeeded in his former post by a younger man. The same thing took place in Chile at the party congress in May. In Uruguay, Chairman Rodney Arismendi died toward the end of December 1989. The riots during June led to replacement of the Chinese general secretary. A game of musical chairs in Japan resulted in the general secretary's retirement for health reasons and his predecessor's assuming the top position; this also occurred in June. An acting chairman was named in place of the captured chairman kept in detention in the Philippines. In Syria, the long-time leader was replaced, although neither time nor place of the event has become known. The CP of Finland (SKP) and the Finnish CP-Unity (SKP-Y) replaced both their chairmen and general secretaries. The long-time British general secretary resigned in November, succeeded only in January 1990 by 31-year-old Nina Temple. Finally, in Greece the general secretary became chairman, making place for a younger leader. Before the end of 1989, five East European leaders had been replaced: in Hungary, Bulgaria, East Germany, Czechoslovakia, and Romania. In the last named country both the leader and his wife were executed by firing squad.

During the year under review, some eighteen parliamentary or presidential elections took place. In Sri Lanka, communists picked up a full percentage point and two additional deputies. Laos allowed its ruling party (LPRP) to have only 65 of 79 seats, rather than all of them as before. In Argentina and Norway, the parties did not win even one seat; in the Netherlands, as part of the Green Left, the party won 6 of 450 seats. As expected, both Benin and Zimbabwe's ruling movements took all seats in their legislatures. The communists of Spain joined a leftist coalition which elected 18 deputies; in Greece, the KKE's seats went up from 13 to 21. The two communist parties in India improved their standing from 6 to 12 legislators, in the one instance, and from 22 to 32 in the other. Even though banned, in Jordan the communist party ran under a popular-front umbrella, which won a single seat.

Major regional developments, and a more detailed discussion follow below.

Africa. The most sweeping development among the Marxist-Leninist regimes in Africa came on 7 December, when the People's Republic of Benin renounced Marxism-Leninism as the official ideology of the country.[11] President Mathieu Kérékou and the Revolutionary Party of the People of Benin faced mounting economic problems and pressure to liberalize the nation's economy from domestic opponents as well as from Western creditors and supporters, mainly France. Benin's ideological commitment never had been as deep as that of Angola or Mozambique, where Marxist-Leninist regimes came to power after protracted guerrilla struggle.

The People's Republic of Mozambique also announced changes, at least in its official jargon. In that southeast African country, the ruling party, FRELIMO (Front for the Liberation of Mozambique) held its fifth congress, which sanctioned discarding its previous Marxist-Leninist vocabulary.[12] Although FRELIMO reaffirmed its commitment to socialist principles, the party congress eliminated the old terminology from all pronouncements. The Central Committee, chosen by the congress, re-elected President Joaquim Chissano, who ran unopposed for the position of party leader.

In the People's Republic of Angola, the political focus of the year centered more on agreements leading to independence for Namibia than on internal restructuring. In late 1988, the Brazzaville agreement had paved the way for a cessation of foreign participation in the Angolan civil war. The agreement was carried out in part during 1989 by South Africa's terminating its support for the Angolan rebel movement, UNITA (National Union for Total Independence of Angola), while Angola ceased its support of the South West Africa People's Organization (SWAPO) and the African National Congress (ANC), both of which challenge white rule in the Republic of South Africa (RSA). The Brazzaville protocol also required the RSA to permit United Nations–sponsored elections in Namibia, which were held in November 1989. In them SWAPO gained 57 percent of the vote and 41 of the 72 seats in the constituent assembly. The latter set 21 March 1990 as the date on which Namibia would attain independence.

Cuba agreed to a phased withdrawal from Angola, to be completed by July 1991, as part of the protocol.[13] Cuban military forces had buttressed the ruling MPLA-PT (popular Movement for the Liberation of Angola–Labor Party) since the start of the Angolan civil war in 1975. While the Brazzaville protocol facilitated Namibian independence and opened the way for a de-internationalization of the Angola insurgency, it did not end the fighting in the southern region of the country between the Cuban-supported MPLA-PT, which launched a determined offensive at year's end, and Jonas Savimbi's UNITA forces.

Internally, Angola continued to move away from its centralized Marxist economy in modest steps, without abandoning the regime's control over society. These reform efforts were recognized and rewarded with membership in both the IMF and World Bank. The MPLA remained badly divided on the future of economic change and on which approach to follow with UNITA.[14]

In the People's Republic of the Congo, divisions within the ruling Congolese Party of Labor (CPL) were pronounced. Two spokesmen for the ideological hard line were dropped from the CPL's Central Committee, while a number of less ideological younger bureaucrats were promoted to that body. Other realignments took place within the Politburo, where, for the first time since the CPL's establishment, civilian members outnumbered the military.

At the fourth CPL congress in July, moderate and pragmatic elements emerged strengthened. President Denis Sassou-Nguesso also moved to maintain his grip over the armed forces by having his military supporters promoted to the Central Committee. For its part, the latter appeared to go along with the change toward less strong adherence to ideology by demanding the purge of "ultraconservatives" and bringing new blood into the leadership.[15]

Across the continent, the Zimbabwe African National Union-Patriotic Front (ZANU-PF) continued its pragmatic course, despite preindependence promises to create a Marxist-Leninist state. However, President Robert Mugabe held firm to his determination to build a one-party political system.[16] This course resulted in dissent among formerly loyal supporters. An opposition party, the Zimbabwe Unity Movement, was formed to counter the government's moves toward a one-party system and to criticize the corruption which had become a major national issue.

At its congress of December 1989, ZANU-PF also made arrangements for an enlargement of both the Politburo and the Central Committee. The ruling party reaffirmed its adherence to the principles of Marxism-Leninism, although the leadership supports policies favoring a mixed economy. ZANU-PF claims to have 3,000,000 members,[17] the first time that figure has been announced.

In Ethiopia, the hard-line Marxist-Leninist regime of Mengistu Haile Mariam faced near collapse owing to military defeats. After the regime lost control of the Tigre region, senior officers staged an unsuccessful coup in May 1989. Mengistu executed eleven generals for their role in the attempt to depose him, a measure which further weakened the central government's campaign against the secessionists.[18]

The African continent's oldest Marxist-Leninist movement, the South African Communist Party (SACP), reportedly held its seventh congress in Havana. Brief reports disclosed that Chairman Dan Tloome and General Secretary Joe Slovo were re-elected to their posts. Delegates approved a new program, entitled *The Path to Power*. It concentrates on "a seizure of power," while not ruling out a negotiated transfer of power by white rulers of the RSA.[19]

The SACP has been closely aligned with the Communist Party of the Soviet Union for decades. While they have been critical of Stalinism, without mentioning Stalin's name, the South African communists struck an ambivalent note with regard to Mikhail Gorbachev's policies of *perestroika* and *glasnost'*. They gave cautious endorsement, however, to his reforms, expressed in the new party program.[20]

To the north, the Sudanese Communist Party (SCP) fell on hard times during 1989, after the military coup which ended parliamentary government in June. The new regime arrested the SCP leadership and suppressed party activities. Management of the SCP, therefore, came into the hands of those who were either outside the country or had gone into hiding after the arrests.[21] Prior to the coup, the party leadership had been reformist rather than revolutionary. Since the coup, the nature of the underground SCP leadership is unclear.

Off the coast of Africa, on the island of Réunion, the communist party (PCR) continued to be concerned with social equality, economic development, and metropolitan France. The PCR hailed as a victory the signing of an agreement at year's end which brought the compensation of unemployed Réunionese into line with that of their counterparts in France. General Secretary Paul Vergès, who had left his post as mayor of Le Port in order to run at Saint-Paul, was not elected.[22] While the PCR lost seats in some areas, it won in others and thus maintained a political position on the island.

The Americas. Marxist-Leninist governments, political parties and organizations throughout the Americas sought during 1989 to cope with domestic challenges, while simultaneously struggling to adjust to the unprecedented upheavals in the communist-ruled world. Ten South American communist parties met at Quito, Ecuador, in early February 1990 to express their support for multiparty systems and the unity of the region's revolutionary, social-democratic, and Christian democratic forces. The meeting—attended by observers from Cuba, Nicaragua, and El Salvador—called for new elections in Panama. Participants reaffirmed their support for the "immortal ideas" of scientific socialism and attacked the "ideological offensive of imperialism," which dishonestly tries "to sell the idea of the death of socialism."[23]

The pressures of coping were most consequential in Cuba and Nicaragua, where the communists are in power. However, parties in other countries were tested, and sometimes battered, by the need either to compete in a political system—democracy—which is antithetical to their nature or to try simply to seize power through violence in the traditional Marxist-Leninist fashion. As in other parts of the world, communists throughout the Americas attempted to prove that the abysmal failure of Soviet-bloc governments did not demonstrate flaws fundamental to communism. This meant arguing that virtually every communist-ruled government in the world had somehow fallen into the hands of leaders who betrayed, or simply failed to achieve, communist ideals.

In Cuba, Fidel Castro has had a particularly difficult time reconciling the facts of communist failures and the fiction of continuing a communist "truth" which he claims to uphold. The Cuban economy is a disaster, and foreign currency reserves are virtually nonexistent there; early in 1990, new rationing was announced.[24] Castro still defiantly rejects the lessons provided by most of the remaining communist world, and promoted by USSR leader Mikhail S. Gorbachev. Instead of freer markets, he continues to tighten controls; instead of offering Cubans rewards for higher production, he provides only "moral" incentives. Meanwhile, by the end of 1989, economic reforms in Eastern Europe and the U.S. invasion of Panama were accelerating Cuba's economic decline by cutting or diminishing the aid it received and its possibilities of trade.

As 1990 began, Castro was proclaiming that, even if all other communists betrayed and defamed Marx—that is, those in the Soviet-bloc countries—he would preserve the eternal verities. This stubborn determination to persist in proven failure, along with corruption, repression of human rights and other problems, led to internal dissent and repression.[25] The most spectacular example of this was the "Ochoa affair," a Stalinist show trial and execution, at midyear of Cuba's best and most famous military leader (in Ethiopia, Angola, and Nicaragua), General Arnaldo Ochoa, on trumped-up corruption and drug charges. As President Oscar Arias of Costa Rica said at the end of the year, "I believe Fidel is a sort of Caribbean Kim Il-song. He [Castro] is a man whose watch stopped in 1959." At the beginning of the new year, Castro also halted Cuba's withdrawal of troops from Angola.[26]

The Nicaraguan government was burdened with an even more deteriorating economy—sometimes described as the worst in Latin America—characterized by hyperinflation, scarcity, and resultant social disaffection and unrest. Added to this were domestic and international pressures that have never been applied to Castro, for free elections and the need to adapt to the major reforms undertaken by all of its allied countries except for Cuba. Amidst uncertainty as to long-term support from Soviet-bloc allies, the Sandinistas found themselves under intense pressure to permit free elections also from domestic groups as well as the Central American presidents and the United States. Elections were scheduled for 25 February 1990, although Sandinista leaders said they had no intention of turning over full power to anyone else, even if the opposition were to win at the ballot box. The election deck was stacked against the opposition (led by *La Prensa* publisher Violeta Barrios de Chamorro); harassment was common; and torture and psychological pressure continued.[27] Sandinista leaders regularly equated the opposition with the armed resistance (the Contras), and "U.S. imperialism." President Daniel Ortega dramatically ended the cease-fire with the Contras on 1 November 1989, claiming repeated attacks by the Contras against the Nicaraguan people, which the resistance denied. The Sandinistas received about $500 million in military aid from the Soviet bloc during 1989, most of it through Cuba, while the Contras obtained no military aid from the outside. The Sandinistas continued to send arms—a shipment toward the end of the year included Soviet ground-to-air missiles—to the Salvadoran guerrillas in open defiance of the Esquipulas II peace accords signed by all five Central American presidents. In January 1990, Ortega asserted that he had discovered a Contra plan backed by the United States to assassinate him.[28] Not even this ploy could stave off the Sandinistas' electoral defeat.

Marxist-Leninists in other Latin countries split—with few exceptions—between those who attempted to overthrow democratic governments and those who tried to compete within the democratic process.

Among the former were guerrilla groups in El Salvador, Guatemala, Honduras, Colombia, and Peru, and, to a lesser extent, in Brazil and Argentina. The Salvadoran FMLN insurgents waged war at home, while they generally talked peace abroad, during a year that brought a significant increase in right-wing and military violence as well. Just weeks before the March 1989 presidential election, the FMLN offered to lay down its arms if the government would postpone the voting and make other concessions. The government, citing constitutional limitations, refused to do so. Nonetheless, the guerrillas were to some extent represented in the election, since their long-time political spokesman, Guillermo Ungo, ran on the Democratic Convergence ticket. He received less than 4 percent of the vote in what international observers proclaimed a free and fair election. In the most important FMLN statement of the year, which has been largely ignored, guerrilla leader Joaquín Villalobos admitted that because of "ideological rigidity" the guerrillas had not given peace a chance during 1979 and, thus, they themselves were in large part responsible for the ten years of heavy bloodshed in El Salvador which have taken about 60,000 lives.[29]

Shortly after Villalobos's statement was published, the guerrillas, supposedly in response to right-wing terrorism and the government's refusal to combat it, launched an offensive during which their forces occupied some sections of San Salvador, deliberately drawing military fire into heavily populated areas. They suffered heavy losses, in personnel and to some extent in reputation, but the government also had losses. Criticism of the latter resulted from firing by its army into populated areas and the murder of several Jesuit priests. Salvadoran President Alfredo Cristiani later announced that the killings had been committed by members of the armed forces. The assassination of the priests, in particular, was used by some in the United States to argue that American aid to the Cristiani government should be cut off. Late in 1989, the Salvadoran war escalated substantially when the guerrillas received ground-to-air missiles that they had for years sought to obtain from the Nicaraguan government. In early 1990, the insurgents were again proposing peace talks.[30]

Throughout Guatemala and Honduras there occurred escalations in armed violence. In the former country, one faction of the Guatemalan Party of Labor (the official communist party) joined the guerrilla National Revolutionary Unity of Guatemala (URNG) and thus subscribed to armed struggle. The URNG seemed better coordinated during 1989 than ever before, although as yet it is a faint shadow of the FMLN in El Salvador. Several new terrorist groups appeared in Honduras, where violence remains as yet a small factor in national life.

Guerrilla groups have been fighting in Colombia longer than in any other country of the Western hemisphere. Several of these organizations were active off and on during 1989, some cooperating with, and others fighting against the narco-traffickers. Even as the National Liberation Army increased its attacks toward the end of the year, the M-19 guerrillas agreed to participate in the March 1990 legislative elections.[31] Throughout 1989, many members of the Leftist Patriotic Union were assassinated by the right. In Brazil, several radical groups promoted violent land seizures and strikes.

More sporadic or even isolated violence took place in other countries. Argentina witnessed a bloody attack on the La Tablada military garrison outside of Buenos Aires in January 1989. This event involved the Popular Resistance Front which includes former members of the People's Revolutionary Army, one of the Marxist-Leninist groups that precipitated the "dirty war" in the mid-1970s. Two small groups engaged in armed attacks throughout Chile, while several of the larger movements, including the communist party[32] and parts of the socialist party, supported violent demonstrations in Santiago and other parts of the country. At the end of January, some 24 members of the Manuel Rodriguez Patriotic Front (half of those making the attempt) broke out of jail and escaped.[33]

The most successful guerrilla group in South America continues to be the Shining Path in Peru, which was responsible for the great majority of the more than 2,600 lives lost in political violence in that country during the year 1989. Much of Peru is in a perpetual state of siege because of these Maoist guerrillas, though the latter largely failed in their effort to disrupt the November municipal elections. The Shining Path has close links to some of the drug dealers in the Upper Huallaga Valley. Taken together, the guerrillas[34] and the narcoterrorists offer an almost insurmountable barrier to successful government by whoever becomes president after the April 1990 elections.

Elsewhere Marxist-Leninists played an active role in nonviolent, often electoral, politics. The People's Progressive Party under Cheddi Jagan remains the second-largest in Guyana. Yet it never wins many legislative seats, owing in part to fraudulent elections. In Uruguay, the communist party is the leading force in the Broad Front, which ran a strong third during the 1989 presidential election and won control of the government in the capital city of Montevideo. Communist movements have long been important in the governments of Martinique and Guadeloupe. The communists in Mexico are split into a minority that maintains a semi-independent identity and the majority, which has marched from one alliance to another and, in 1989, joined the Democratic Revolution Party headed by Cuauhtémoc Cárdenas, who is not a communist.

In Colombia, the communists have some representatives in local and national government, as they do in Peru where they are a pivotal member of the important United Left (IU) front. There and elsewhere, communist movements were involved in labor and student groups, as well as in electoral politics. These parties were active, although relatively insignificant, in Costa Rica, Ecuador, Brazil, Argentina, and Chile. Communists would have won several seats in the December 1989 election in Chile,[35] except for voting laws that favored center and rightist candidates. While the communist party in Venezuela continues to stagnate, the Movement to Socialism (MAS), a democratic-socialist group that broke away from the communists in 1971, has become a major actor in national politics.

Among the virtual nonentities of the communist world during 1989 were the parties in Grenada, Paraguay, Haiti, the Dominican Republic, Canada,[36] and the United States. The CPUSA reluctantly moved toward endorsing reforms in the Soviet bloc, though some of Chairman Gus Hall's remarks on the subject raised the question of replacing this aging leader.

Asia and the Pacific. Ruling party leaders in the People's Republic of China, the Democratic People's Republic of Korea, and the Socialist Republic of Vietnam responded to the collapse of communist regimes in Eastern Europe and to Gorbachev's reforms in the Soviet Union by consolidating their authority and boldly asserting that they would forever adhere to the "socialist road."

In China, a fierce power struggle erupted during late spring 1989, at a time when massive demonstrations were being held in major cities across the country. Hu Yaobang's death on 15 April sparked those peaceful activities, which continued until 4 June, when units of the People's Liberation Army entered Beijing and ruthlessly removed the demonstrators—mostly students—who had occupied Tiananmen Square, killing and injuring perhaps several thousand young people in the process.

The power struggle ended when the party faction led by Deng Xiaoping, the old cadre, and Li Peng ousted General Secretary Zhao Ziyang on 24 June and replaced him with the mayor of Shanghai, Jiang Zemin. The party and government cracked down by arresting tens of thousands, executing many, and imprisoning untold numbers. Martial law was imposed and continued into January of the new year. [37]

China's economy continued to deteriorate during the last quarter of 1989, with industrial output growing only 6.8 percent for the year, slightly more than one-third of the 17.7 percent growth claimed in 1980. Rising debt and a severe shortage of energy and raw materials forced numerous factories to close down. Living standards dropped; unemployment grew; and in the cities the mood was angry and tense. [38]

The party controls information and public discussion as rigidly as during the Maoist years. The regime's press repeatedly publishes articles extolling the virtues of socialism under the leadership of the Chinese Communist Party (CCP), justifying the mid-1989 suppression of urban demonstrations as necessary to save the Revolution, as well as to defend CCP rule and policies. Meanwhile, all sources of information controlled by the party and state continue to attack "bourgeois thinking" and Western-style democracy. China's state-run news agencies provided only minimal information about events in Romania, and the Chinese leadership placed its security forces on the highest degree of alert in late December. [39]

The new regime, led by Jiang Zemin, Li Peng, Yang Shangkun, and the old cadres, promised the people hard work and plain living. In the speech delivered by Deng Xiaoping five days after the Tiananmen massacre, a speech that became required reading for all CCP members, he emphasized the need to cultivate the "enterprising spirit in hard struggle and plain (frugal) living." Most important for Deng was that "promoting plain living must be a main objective in education, and this should be grasped in the next 60 to 70 years."[40]

After the Tiananmen tragedy, Sino-American relations suffered their most serious setback since exchange of ambassadors between the two states had taken place in December 1978. President Bush ordered mild sanctions and suspended high-level contacts with the Beijing regime on 20 June. Despite more executions and arrests in China and widespread purges in the government and party, the U.S. president vetoed an act of Congress guaranteeing that Chinese students in the United States would not be forced to return home as long as they were in danger. On 9 December, a top-level U.S. mission was sent to Beijing. Between 10 and 24 December, President Bush repeatedly stated that some sanctions would be lifted. On 11 January 1990, he said that China had taken a "very sound step" by lifting martial law. [41]

Shortly before 4 June, the astrophysicist and dissident Fang Lizhi and his wife Li Shuxian received sanctuary in the U.S. embassy in Beijing, where they still remain. Chinese authorities protested the U.S. action as a violation of international law. [42]

In North Korea, the regime of Kim Il-song hosted the World Youth Festival in July 1989 and continued to extol the virtues of Kim's son, Kim Chong-il. Both father and son began to prepare for the Seventh Congress of the Korean Workers' Party, which will take place at a time yet to be announced. During the sixteenth Central Committee plenum in June, Yi Yong-mu was elected a Committee member and Hong Song-nan added to the Politburo. The party and government lashed out at bourgeois influence and called for ideological vigilance. [43]

Throughout the year, the regime continued its campaign to meet the ambitious goals set forth in the third Seven-Year Plan. Pyongyang admitted that the country had suffered food shortages, blaming "chronically bad weather" for the poor harvests. [44] The leadership still has not introduced market incentives or economic reforms and continues to rely on orthodox central planning through state and collective organizations.

In Vietnam, a complex power struggle, begun following the death of Le Duan in July 1986, rages on. The old cadres still dominate the ruling party's Politburo, and they remain committed to the "socialist road." At the seventh Central Committee plenum in August, General Secretary Nguyen Van Linh reported that "ideological deviation had emerged among a large number of party cadres and rank-and-file members," who represented "deviant ideological viewpoints." Linh admitted that such deviation was due to poor party leadership. [45]

Certain groups, such as the older, southern party members and elements from the military, have challenged the central leadership. The Club of Former Resistance Fighters, located in Ho Chi Minh City, sent an open letter to the Central Committee in June, calling for "true elections" rather than those hitherto orchestrated by the party. Reports appeared in the press—an instance is an article published in *Quan doi nhan dan*—that the party had pursued a "no-win" policy in the war it had waged in Cambodia. While appealing for ideological unity, Linh and other leaders outlined the economic scarcities that had become serious and the measures required to solve these difficulties. Several important personalities died during the year: Le Thanh Nghi, a retired Politburo member; Huynh Tan Phat, chief theoretician of the National Liberation Front; and Nguyen Huu Chinh and Hoang Truong Minh, both Central Committee members.

New information became available about the People's Revolutionary Party of Kampuchea, the communist party in Cambodia, founded on 30 September 1951, and which now has a membership of some 10,000; a 13-member Politburo (plus three alternates), and a Secretariat of 8 members. The party's Central Committee includes 49 full members and 16 alternates. Throughout the year, the party held numerous regional conferences, and its second national cadres conference in April, at which time 21 new Central Committee members were elected (11 full and 10 alternates). Regional party conferences defined the duties of cadres and set forth the rules for local party meetings, as well as for linking lower cells with superior bodies.[46] The party also took the initiative in recruiting new members and supporting economic reforms that permitted the expansion of private enterprise and free markets.

In communist-ruled Laos, elections were held on 26 March 1989, for the 79 seats in the Supreme People's Assembly, the highest-ranking legislative body of the Lao People's Democratic Republic. These elections provided a small channel for ordinary people to express their demands at the national level, rather than through the apparatus of the communist party. A new constitution was also being drawn up, and preparations made for the Fifth Party Congress.[47] Laos resumed diplomatic relations with China, and Premier Phomvihane Kaysone visited Beijing in October. This significant move gave Laos the opportunity to deal with both Beijing and Hanoi, much in the manner in which Ho Chi Minh had balanced off Moscow and Beijing during the 1960s.

Early in 1989, some 1,000 members of the Communist Party of Malaya living along the Thai-Malaysian border surrendered to the 4th Army Command in Thailand. These insurgents were to be resettled on Thai territory in Songkhla and Yala provinces. They agreed with government officials to give up their armed struggle in return for being allowed to live permanently in Thailand without harassment.

Between mid-January and mid-February 1990, several thousand Mongolians staged rallies in Ulan Bator, the capital of the People's Republic of Mongolia, demanding an end to their country's communist system. The rallies were organized by the Mongolian Democratic Union. A spokesman for the group declared, "We must increase our efforts to overthrow the present system, which is haunted through and through by the ghost of Stalinism."[48] Landlocked between the Soviet Union and China, Mongolia has the second oldest communist system in the world (established in 1921), after that of the Soviet Union.

Documents of the Philippine Communist Party (CPP), seized by government troops during 1989, provided new information about the background of Central Committee cadres and also revealed details of Politburo meetings on Luzon. Of particular interest is documentation showing influential CCP ties to labor unions which include some 400,000 workers, as well as many urban and rural "front" organizations.

The CPP began a campaign of selective attacks against U.S. personnel, military installations, and foreign-aid projects. Such attacks began on 9 April, with a bombing attempt against a United States Navy communications relay station atop Mount Santo Tomas in Benguet Province.[49] Twelve days later the New People's Army (NPA) assassinated a U.S. army colonel, James N. Rowe, outside the Quezon City compound of the Joint U.S. Military Assistance Group. On 26 September, NPA guerrillas killed three American civilian military-contract employees. The day before Christmas, the United States Information Service office in Davao City on Mindanao was strafed. The CPP also attacked other foreigners, such as Japanese and Canadians.

The tactics of assaulting foreigners showed the dominance of the "militarist" faction in the CPP leadership. Founder and reputed chairman in absentia José Maria Sison recently published a book[50] outlining the strategy of "protracted people's war" for the CPP with stages of defense and offense that will serve to incite a revolution and mobilize the masses to overthrow the present government of the Philippines and its supporters. Sison now resides in the Netherlands.

The Middle East. The governments of both the Republic of Afghanistan and the People's Democratic Republic of [South] Yemen (PDRY), the only two Middle East states ruled by Marxist-Leninist parties, attempted to broaden their political bases, which have consisted chiefly of these countries' communist parties. The end of the Iran-Iraq war, withdrawal of Soviet forces from Afghanistan, the death of the Ayatollah Khomeini in Iran, and dramatic changes in the USSR and Eastern Europe all contributed to a new regional political climate that demanded at least a cosmetic response. Afghan media followed the official trend of virtually omitting any reference to activities of the ruling People's Democratic Party of Afghanistan (PDPA) or to the party titles of its leaders, preferring instead to use official state designations of their offices. A notable exception was the State Security Ministry's (WAD) "Independence Day" message to President Najibullah, in which the latter's title of PDPA general secretary title was repeatedly used, that concluded as follows: "we have learned patriotism from our beloved party. We are proud of our patriotic party and proud of our membership of [sic] this party."[51]

As Najibullah's core support comes from WAD, the message ironically exemplified the contrast between the regime's broad public relations efforts to present itself as popular, politically diverse, and Islamic, in contrast to the reality of Marxist-Leninist cadre control of the regime. Similarly, when Najibullah declared a state of emergency, following the departure of the last Soviet troops in mid-February 1989, he appointed a twenty-man Supreme Defense Council "with the aim of implementing central leadership under conditions of a state of emergency"; all the members, with the possible exception of the civilian vice-president were ranking party or military/security cadres.[52] The same gap between pretense and reality was revealed when Najmuddin Kawiani, head of the PDPA Central Committee's international relations department, told a Soviet interviewer that "our party . . . is Marxist in terms of its ideology," directly contradicting the Afghan leadership's basic position over the past two years.[53]

The continuing survival of the Najibullah regime depends both on the bitter divisions among the mujahideen groups and on continuing massive Soviet support. From early March to the end of August 1989, Moscow airlifted an estimated 550 SCUD missiles, 160 T-55 and T-62 tanks, 615 armored personnel carriers, and 1,600 five-ton trucks into Kabul.[54] Although the Afghan foreign ministry denied the following month that any Soviet advisers remained in the country, a USSR diplomat refuted this claim the next day by stating that 300 advisers were still at work in Afghanistan. [55]

The dramatically quickened pace of development in the long discussed plans for merger of the PDRY and the Yemen Arab Republic (YAR) also appeared part of the [Marxist-Leninist] Yemen Socialist Party's (YSP) urgent need to broaden its ideological base in the PDRY and end its isolation from the mainstream Arab world. At the end of November 1989, the presidents of the two states signed a formal agreement ultimately to merge their countries following ratification of a draft constitution and a national plebiscite six months thereafter.[56]

This projected unification of basically tribal states, each with its own bitter divisions, would involve, first, resolution of long standing and serious disputes between the two countries and, second, the development of a working ideological relationship between the PDRY's hard-core Marxists and the highly conservative tribal leaders, mullahs, and merchants of the YAR. Rumors that the PDRY initially had rejected the merger of foreign and defense ministries were denied by Rashid Thavit, the PDRY minister for union affairs who, in a triumph of understatement, acknowledged that "the views inside any society might include some differences [and] some groups and parties might also have their own trends."[57]

The YSP relationship, if any, to the recently surfaced YAR Yemeni Popular Unity Party (YPUP) is unknown, but the Marxist YPUP appears to represent a small group of merged revolutionary groups and organizations which split in 1979 from the opposition National Democratic Front.[58] The underground YPUP would seem to have dim prospects for serious competition with increasingly powerful YAR forces, like the Wahabi fundamentalists and Moslem Brotherhood.

Iran's decimated Tudeh Party remained a sore point in the USSR's dealings with Iran, inhibiting the hectic push by both Teheran and Moscow dramatically to improve relations following the Ayatollah Khomeini's death and President Hashemi Rafsanjani's visit to Moscow in June 1989. Reacting to a Moscow Radio commentary praising the Tudeh, a leading Teheran newspaper editorial asked whether the act "does not defeat the Soviet purpose [of] attempting to polish their image before the world and trying to put the past behind them in their relations with Iran."[59]

In its 48th anniversary statement, the Tudeh repeated its plaintive call for a united front against "the despotic regime which is the cause of increasing poverty, hunger, and public corruption," in which all progressive, democratic, and nationalist organizations "must unite, because one party or one organization cannot replace the present regime."[60] Teheran media also rebuked the USSR for an expected multibillion-dollar economic agreement with Iraq that would include a gas pipeline to Eastern Europe, plans which "reveal [Soviet] lack of concern about peace and calm in this part of the world."[61]

The Iraqi Communist Party (ICP) continued to be under the siege which began as the Gulf war ended and Baghdad stepped up its retribution against the Kurds and their ICP allies for wartime help to Iran. The resulting transfer of Kurds to areas distant from their original homes, bordering on Iran and Turkey, has been coupled with stringent government security measures sharply limiting the activities of the already beleaguered ICP. Apart from occasional appearances of exiled ICP leaders in Damascus or Eastern Europe, there was no evidence of ICP activities. Official promises to permit the organization of previously banned political groups have excluded the ICP. The speaker of the assembly, for instance, said that the ICP and its Kurdish allies have "no place among honorable Iraqis, because they denied their homeland during [its] ordeal."[62]

In contrast, both the Palestine Communist Party (PCP) and the Lebanese Communist Party (LCP) appeared to be playing substantive roles in the struggles surrounding them. The PCP general secretary (whose name is unknown) claims that because the party has gone with the tide of the *Intifada* movement throughout the occupied territories, there was a rapid increase in party membership, principally from among "18- to 22-year-olds participating in the uprising," and that two-thirds of the Palestinians, "who have died in Israeli prisons were communists."[63] Given the rivalry among groups within the *Intifada* movement, these and similar claims may be exaggerated. In a likely case of the pot calling the kettle black, PCP Politburo member Naim al-Ashhab asserted that the Islamists' role in the uprising "is being exaggerated," suggesting that they were colluding with King Hussein of Jordan.[64] The majority of observers, however, credit the Islamic groups with a growing role, which has become of some concern to the PLO leadership. It is interesting to note the visit of a high-level delegation from the Israeli Communist Party in Moscow.[65]

Lebanon's continuing turmoil and multitude of shifting alliances between militias has enabled the LCP to function militarily as a small faction, while as yet not achieving a secure base within any of the country's major religious groupings. In mid-August 1989, the Politburo issued a statement praising the battles in Souk-el-Gharb between the Popular Liberation Army—in which the LCP participated—and the soldiers of General Michel 'Aun's Christian militia.[66] Expectedly, the LCP was allied with the effort to oust 'Aun in favor of the plan for a reconstituted Lebanon, to allow better political representation for all major groups, which is supported by President René Muawad', the Arab League, the Soviet Union, and the United States.

Western Europe. Not only did the power and position of most ruling parties in Eastern Europe collapse, but the structures of Western Europe's communist movements underwent dramatic changes as well. The opening of the Berlin Wall on 9 November 1989, gave visible and emotional meaning to the idea of freedom. The communist parties in Western Europe were "shaken and squabbling" at year's end.[67]

One of the most interesting of the changing and conflicting tides engulfing the continent were the elections to the European parliament in Strasbourg, held in mid-1989. In the third direct election throughout the twelve European Community (EC) countries for 518 seats, the socialists and social democrats won 182, whereas communist parties gained only 42. The remainder is held by "Greens" (48 seats), Christian democrats (107), liberals (45), conservatives (50), the far right (16), and several other parties (38). The "left" won a two-seat majority.[68] This outcome assumes increasing significance as the 1992 program to establish the EC internal market moves forward.

By the end of 1989, on the other hand, strong leadership in the West European communist movement had almost disappeared. It had been decisively affected by the crumbling of every single communist regime in Eastern Europe, except for those in Albania and Yugoslavia, within a matter of months between August and the end of December.

The French Communist Party (PCF) continued to suffer from factionalism and electoral failure. Frustrated communists outside the party and determined critics within it developed a stronger organization with which to pressure the leadership for open debate and systemic reforms. One result was the formation of the "New Left for Socialism, Self-Management, and Ecology" (NG), under the leadership of Pierre Juquin.[69] Out of the NG emerged another group of dissidents that called itself the "Movement of Communist Renewalists." Finally, a third group remained within the PCF and throughout the year pressed Georges Marchais (leader since 1972) for internal reforms; these party members called themselves the Communist Reconstructionist Initiative.

The Communist Party of Italy (PCI) made a showing in elections to the European Parliament in June 1989 that exceeded all expectations. It received 27.7 percent to the Socialists' (PS) 14.8 percent of the vote. The election's real importance to the PCI was that it represented a moral victory after ten years of consistent electoral decline. However, it did not thrust the party to the forefront of Italian political life, since the party's membership dropped from almost 1.5 million in March to about 800,000 at year's end.[70]

Throughout the year, the PCI struggled to establish its own identity. The efforts to do so ranged from General Secretary Achille Occhetto's remark that he felt himself to be more a child of the French than of the Russian Revolution to his open pursuit of a closer alliance with the Italian socialists and affiliation with socialists of Western Europe in general via the Socialist International. At the end of December, the PCI set the date for its nineteenth congress, to be held from 7–10 March 1990, at Bologna. The previous month Occhetto had introduced a proposal that the congress consider establishing "a new democratic political formation, reformist, open to progressive lay and Catholic components," and therewith, after months of debate, endorsed the proposal to drop the word *communist* from the party's name, as well as to eliminate the hammer and sickle as its symbol.[71]

The Spanish Communist Party (PCE), under the leadership of Julio Anguita, claims a total of only 83,000 members. A pro-Soviet faction has its own Communist Party of the Peoples of Spain (PCPE), headed by Juan Ramos. The third and smallest group, led by Santiago Carrillo, is called the Spanish Workers' Party-Communist Unity (PTE-UC). At the beginning of 1989, the PCE pursued a policy of "ideological renewal," in an effort to bring together all communist groups under a coalition of the United Left. In June, the United Left received 6.1 percent of the vote and 4 of Spain's 60 seats in the European parliament. At national elections during

October, this same umbrella organization garnered 9 percent of the vote and 18 out of 350 parliamentary seats (compared with 4.4 percent and 7 seats in 1986). This result marked a notable improvement in the political fortunes of Spain's communist parties, despite the government's assertion that the United Left was merely "a front for the PCE, though they do not dare say so, because communism has failed throughout the world."[72]

The Portuguese Communist Party (PCP) had claimed almost 200,000 members in November 1988. The party has been led by Alvaro Cunhal over the past three decades and holds 30 of the 250 seats in parliament. Its political influence, however, has declined significantly under a pro-Moscow leadership. The PCP controls much of unionized labor and remains one of the most Stalinist parties in Western Europe. Although it formally supports Soviet domestic and foreign policy, the PCP stopped receiving funds from the USSR since the start of *perestroika*. The East Germans provided financial assistance until the fall of Erich Honecker.[73]

The primary focus of attention within the PCP during 1989 was the division of opinion over Cunhal's successor. In ill health, Cunhal encouraged a debate on the merits of Dominos Abrantes versus those of José Luís Judas, a Stalinist and a moderate, respectively. The latter is considered head of "a new political organization."[74] Argument within the party intensified after Cunhal's criticism of changes taking place in Eastern Europe, and his insistence that communist ideology held the solution to all problems of the modern world. The thirteenth PCP congress has been announced for the first half of May 1990, and it is not inconceivable that a new leader will be chosen at that time.

In Cyprus, Greece, Malta, San Marino, and Turkey, the communist parties do not play significant roles in the formation of domestic or foreign policy. The Communist Party of San Marino (PCS) is an extension of the Italian Communist Party. Holding 18 of the 60 parliamentary seats, the PCS has continued its coalition with the Christian Democratic Party (PDCS).

The Communist Party of Malta (CPM) is led by General Secretary Anthony Vassallo (age 70). In the most recent election, the CPM received .08 percent of the vote and, since that time, has been in decline. It ceased publishing a national edition of *World Marxist Review*, and the monthly publication *Zminijietna* (Our times) came out in only three issues during 1989. The United Communist Party of Turkey (UCPT) is proscribed, the only one in

Western Europe to operate illegally. Its direct influence on domestic politics is negligible, although it supports a wide range of leftist activities throughout the country. On Cyprus, the Progressive Party of the Working People (AKEL) draws its support primarily from the Greek majority. Discontent within the party focused on the rigidity of its ideological views and positions that had prevented much real change in policy, and by early 1990 the twelfth Central Committee member had resigned.[75]

The affairs of the Communist Party of Greece (KKE) had been decisively affected by the political fortunes of the Socialist prime minister, Andreas Papandreou. The movement is split between the larger pro-Soviet KKE and smaller Eurocommunist KKE-I (Interior) factions. The latter divided itself into the Greek Left (E.AR) and a weaker rump group (KKE-I), which added "Renovating Left" to its title.

Talks between KKE and the Greek Left resulted in the February 1989 formation of a "Coalition of the Left and of Progress." It adopted a position highly critical of the economic scandals surrounding the then-governing Panhellenic Socialist Movement (PASOK) of Papandreou. The Coalition of the Left won 28 seats in the June 1989 parliamentary elections. The conservative New Democracy Party obtained 144 mandates, 7 fewer than needed to govern. A majority was attained when the Coalition of the Left decided to join the conservatives. This development legitimized the communists as full-fledged participants in the Greek political process. However, following special national elections held in November 1989, the left lost 7 of the 28 seats it had won in June (its share of the vote dropping from 13.1 to 10.8 percent). This outcome produced an "all-party" coalition government at year's end.

The Communist Party of Great Britain (CPGB) has only 7,500 members, as compared with a postwar high of 56,000. General Secretary Gordon McLennan resigned at the 41st congress, held toward the end of November, and was succeeded only in January 1990 by 33-year-old Nina Templeton.[76] The communist movement includes the New Communist Party, the Revolutionary Communist Party, and the Communist Party of Britain. This last group claims 1,500 members and publishes *Morning Star*.

Communist groups in Belgium, Denmark, Luxembourg, and the Netherlands continue to exercise only marginal influence on the politics of their respective countries. In Luxembourg, communists won a single seat in parliament during elections held in June 1989, receiving less than 4 percent of

the vote and sustaining a loss of one seat. They traditionally maintained close ties with the formerly ruling SED of East Germany. The party leader in Luxembourg acknowledged that "the building of a socialist society in Western Europe is not an immediate prospect."[77]

In the Nordic countries of Iceland, Norway, Sweden, and Finland, communist movements were active, although without much influence. The Norwegian Communist Party (NKP) has no representation in parliament and competes with several small groups on the left, especially the Socialist Left Party (SV) and the Workers' Communist Party (AKP), both of which are larger than the NKP. The general election in September 1989 resulted in an increase of the SV's seats in parliament from six to seventeen. The NKP, in an electoral alliance with the AKP, received only 0.84 percent of the vote and no seats.

The Left Party Communists (VPK) in Sweden continue to hold 21 out of 349 seats in parliament. They have been, nonetheless, affected by political events in Eastern Europe. During late November 1989, after the dramatic opening of the Berlin Wall, the party chairman gave an interview in which he acknowledged that the VPK was considering a change of name by removing the word "communist."[78] He seemed to be advocating a broadly based left-wing party that could present a new "socialist" alternative.

Internal affairs of the Finnish Communist Party (SKP) have been dominated by factional strife, which has led to a four-way split and debate over the merits of a new party program entitled *Socialism with a Finnish Face*. Much of this is described in an article by the SKP general secretary.[79]

The Communist Party of Austria (KPÖ) and the Swiss Labor Party (PdAS) also play minimal roles in their respective countries. The former polled less than one percent of the vote during regional elections held in March 1989 throughout Carinthia, Salzburg, and the Tyrol. The KPÖ's 27th congress was held at the beginning of 1990. Political scientist Susanne Sohn and attorney Walter Silbermayr succeeded Franz Muhri as party co-chairpersons.[80] The party has maintained its pro-Soviet position and, while endorsing *perestroika*, also emphasized the necessity to continue the class struggle. Primary activities included opposition to Austria's application for membership in the Common Market, criticism of Hungarian political reforms, and condemnation of the decision to allow East German refugees to travel unimpeded via Hungary to Austria.

The Socialist Unity Party of West Berlin (SEW) has a new chairman in Dietmar Ahrens, who succeeded Horst Schmitt following the latter's death in April 1989. The group holds no seats in West Berlin's legislature, having received only 0.6 percent of the vote during last year's elections. In a city that had been divided by the Berlin Wall and surrounded with mine fields, the SEW never appealed to the population. During 1989, however, it concluded that *glasnost'* and *perestroika* must be recognized as principles of socialism. As the communist regime in East Germany showed signs of disintegration, the SEW made adjustments accordingly. The party newspaper, *Die Wahrheit* (The truth) changed its name to *Neue Zeitung* (New newspaper) in the hope that it would appeal to "the growing need of the leftist, democratic, trade union spectrum."[81] Following the opening of the Berlin Wall, the entire SEW Politburo resigned. An extraordinary congress was scheduled for February 1990.

In the Federal Republic of Germany, the German Communist Party (DKP) is not represented in the *Bundestag*, having received only 0.5 percent of the vote in the last national elections. Characterized by dogmatism and opposition to change, the DKP has been plagued by internal dissension that deepened internal divisions. The disintegration of the SED in East Germany brought financial ruin to the DKP (as well as to the SEW in West Berlin). The seriousness of its predicament was acknowledged at a meeting of the Central Committee in mid-December 1989. The DKP announced a continuing decline in membership, dismissed more than 80 percent of its employees, terminated many leases on buildings and offices, and changed *Unsere Zeit* (Our times) from a daily into a weekly.[82]

At its ninth congress in January 1989, the DKP chairman acknowledged that the party is beset with hitherto unparalleled inner contradictions. In a move that posed a direct threat to the credibility of the DKP, the East German party changed its name to "SED–Party of Democratic Socialism." The DKP chairman and his deputy announced that they would resign their posts at an extraordinary party congress scheduled for February 1990; their prospective resignations suggest the demise of the East German client movement.[83]

Eastern Europe and the USSR. Representing until recently the core of the "socialist commonwealth of nations," the Soviet Union and the seven countries of Eastern Europe are in the throes of fundamental change that is altering relations of the latter with the center: the USSR. The majority of the national legislatures, which includes that of the Soviet Union, are in the process of eliminating from their constitutions the article guaranteeing a "leading role" to their respective communist parties. Indeed, the very names of these movements and countries are being changed by deleting "communist" and "people's" from their previous designations.

The lack of popular support is suggested also by the self-dissolution of previously ruling parties (Polish United Workers' Party) or their disappearances (Romanian Communist Party). The 1990 national elections, beginning with those of East Germany and Hungary in March and ending with those of Czechoslovakia and Yugoslavia in June, could result in the defection of previously subordinate political parties to the opposition (as happened during August 1989 in Warsaw) or in coalition governments such as are already evolving in Budapest, Prague, and East Berlin.

The leader of the Soviet communist party and the Soviet government, Mikhail Gorbachev, has not attempted to block this process. If anything, by sending personal emissaries to the former satellite capitals and receiving new communist or noncommunist leaders in the Kremlin, he has encouraged the inevitable. With the official condemnation of the invasion of Czechoslovakia at the meeting of the Warsaw Treaty Organization (WTO) in Moscow on 4 December 1989, the notorious Brezhnev Doctrine was buried.[84]

Neither Albania nor Yugoslavia is a WTO member. The former has restored diplomatic relations with most of the East European countries, except for Yugoslavia and the USSR. The Albanian Party of Labor (APL) leader, Ramiz Alia, in his speech on the 45th anniversary of communist rule of Albania, stated that the APL, "since the first symptoms of the emergence of revisionism, [had] set in a clear-cut way a demarcation line with it and detached itself from the Soviet Union and its camp."[85]

Dramatic change, however, did occur in Bulgaria less than three weeks before the above-quoted address by Alia, when Todor Zhivkov was removed from his post of general secretary after 35 years in power. Subsequent purges removed all of his cronies from both the Politburo and Central Committee. The previously subordinate Bulgarian Agrarian Union (BANU) was permitted to reconstitute itself as a political party, and the ruling BCP underwent reorganization at a congress in early February 1990. Both BANU and the opposition Union of Democratic Forces refused to join a new cabinet a few days after that congress.[86] A new Alternative Socialist Party, with about 600 members, split off from the BCP. National elections were announced for May.

Only nine days after Zhivkov's fall, the police in Czechoslovakia brutally suppressed a demonstration by students in Prague. This event, reminiscent of the Tiananmen Square massacre, triggered strikes and massive protests that drew crowds numbering hundreds of thousands. Within less than a week, the entire Presidium (politburo) and Secretariat resigned. A month later, an extraordinary party congress removed Soviet collaborators. Before the end of the year, the leader of the oppositional Civic Forum, Vaclav Havel, had been installed as president,[87] and after 30 January 1990, when they lost their majority in parliament, the communists appeared to be in disarray. New elections are to take place on 8 June.

Developments in Budapest where the ruling Hungarian Socialist Workers' Party (HSWP) dissolved itself in early October 1989, proceeded at a more rapid pace. The Hungarian Socialist Party, one of the HSWP's successors, could attract a fraction of the communists, and the group retaining the old name only half of that fraction. All political organizations were banned from the workplace.[88] The largest opposition group is the Democratic Forum, which will run in the elections of 25 March 1990.

The SED or Socialist Unity Party of Germany in the [East] German Democratic Republic was the only ruling movement throughout Eastern Europe to support the Chinese suppression of the pro-democracy demonstrations in Beijing in mid-1989. It was soon to face similar mass protests that led to Erich Honecker's forced retirement and the opening of the Berlin Wall on 9 November. The following month, at an extraordinary congress, the SED added "Party of Democratic Socialism" (PDS) to its name.[89] By the end of January 1990, a new cabinet of 27 members included 11 noncommunists. Elections were moved up to 18 March, with West German political parties openly supporting their counterparts.

Within a month of its fourteenth congress, the Romanian Communist Party had disappeared. A few days after that meeting, an otherwise perceptive analyst wrote: "There is no opposition in Romania and even dissent is weak and encompasses only a handful of individuals."[90] Nobody, of course, could or did predict the uprising in Timisoara and later in Bucharest which resulted in decapitation of the RCP leadership on Christmas Day. A proliferation of peasant, democratic, liberal, and other prewar or newly formed political movements will contest the elections on 20 May 1990. The great majority of those in the ruling National Salvation Front are former communist officials who had served willingly until their removal by the Ceauşescus. The military,[91] which turned against the RCP leadership, may play a decisive role again.

In Poland, too, the ruling Polish United Workers' Party (PUWP) voted to dissolve itself after losing all credibility with the voters and even its own membership. Both of the groups that succeeded the PUWP are small. The elections during April 1990 should sweep from provincial and local government the vast majority of the approximately 111,000 former PUWP bureaucrats who still hold their posts. If national elections are held in the near future (the last were in June 1989),[92] they would allow a new government to replace the four communists who head the ministries of defense, interior (police), foreign trade, and transportation.

Finally, on 20 January 1990, the League of Communists in Yugoslavia (LCY) opened its fourteenth extraordinary congress, which was suspended two days later after delegates from Slovenia had walked out because of disagreement over political and economic changes. Elections to the Federal Assembly, scheduled for April, and to be contested by a number of parties, could dislodge the LCY from power. Several of Yugoslavia's six constituent republics have permitted other political parties to establish themselves. At the end of the fourteenth congress, the LCY "renounced its constitutionally guaranteed leading role in society" and called upon parliament to enact "political pluralism including a multiparty system."[93]

Faced with these developments, the Communist Party of the Soviet Union (CPSU) has been discussing elimination of Article 6 from the USSR's constitution, a step which would open the way for other political movements to compete in elections and, perhaps, even share power with the CPSU. The CPSU, torn by conservative and progressive factions, has suffered a loss in both authority and prestige. In the case of the USSR, however, it is not pressure from below that has brought about these conditions. Rather, it appears to be Gorbachev himself who wants to remove the CPSU from policymaking in the government. If he survives the

28th party congress, scheduled for early July 1990, he may decide to lobby for close associate and confidant Aleksandr N. Iakovlev as the new CPSU leader and for himself, the much more powerful position of president of the USSR.

It is not inconceivable that the CPSU will follow the footsteps of its East European fraternal parties straight into the dustbin of history.

Richard F. Staar

Hoover Institution

NOTES

1. Alexander Subbotin, gen. ed., *First-Hand Information: Communist and Revolutionary Democrats of the World Presenting Their Parties* (Prague: Peace and Socialism, 1988), p. 9.

2. Henryk Sobieski et al., eds., *Partie komunistyczne i robotnicze swiata* (Warsaw: Ksiazka i Wiedza, 1978), 879 pp.

3. A. Starukhin and M. Tretiakov, "Rozhdenie partii," *Pravda*, 29 January 1990, p. 5.

4. For details on what took place in each of these countries, see "1989: A Year of Upheaval," in RFE/RL, *Report on Eastern Europe*, vol. 1, no. 1 (5 January 1989), 42 pp.

5. V. Shavrov, "Emergency Congresses, Extraordinary Congresses," *Pravda*, 4 January 1990, p. 6.

6. *Pravda*, 20 December 1989, p. 5.

7. Receptions were held at USSR embassies on the 72nd anniversary of the October Revolution in the capital cities of these countries. See *Pravda*, 10 November 1989, p. 5.

8. Telegrams, with greetings on the same Soviet national holiday, were received from these groups and listed in *Pravda*, 9 November 1989, p. 4; 10 November 1989, p. 7.

9. U.S. Central Intelligence Agency, *The World Factbook 1989*, CPAS WF 89-001 (Washington, D.C.: U.S. Government Printing Office, May 1989), 367 pp.

10. Sheryl WuDunn, "Millions in China are Submitting to Analysis (the Political Kind)," NYT, 18 February 1990, p. 13.

11. Cotonou Domestic Service, 7 December 1989; trans. in *FBIS-AFR*, 8 December 1989, pp. 11–12.

12. William Clayborne, "Mozambique Shifts from Marxism," *WP*, 29 July 1989.

13. Moscow Radio, on 10 January 1990 (*FBIS-SOV-90-008*, 11 January 1990, p. 36), announced meetings in Moscow of Angolan, Cuban, and Soviet armed forces' chiefs of staff. On cooperation of the USSR with Angola, note Moscow Radio on 19 January 1990 (trans. in *FBIS-SOV-90-015*, 23 January 1990, pp. 24–25).

14. Radio Luanda, 22 Jan. 1989; trans. in *FBIS-AFR*, 25 January 1989, p. 18. Clyde Farnsworth, "Angola Is Admitted to the World Bank and IMF," *NYT*, 20 September 1989, p. C-16. "Angola: War and Peace in the MPLA," *Africa Confidential*, 11 August 1989, pp. 1–2.

15. AFP, 31 July 1989; trans. in *FBIS-AFR*, 2 August 1989, p. 1.

16. "Update: Zimbabwe," *Africa Report*, vol. 34, no. 4, July/August 1989, p. 7. See also George B. N. Ayittey, "Zimbabwe: Another Ghana?," *Defense & Diplomacy*, vol. 8, no. 1–2, January–February 1990, pp. 43–61.

17. I. Tarutin and Iu. Pichugin, "The ZANU-PF Congress," *Pravda*, 20 December 1989, p. 5.

18. Daniel Wattenberg, "Revolt Signals A Crumbling Regime," *Insight*, 12 June 1989, pp. 38–39. Jane Perlez, "Insurgents Begin...Offensive," *NYT*, 10 February 1990, p. 5.

19. "Don't Trust South Africa! Set Up the Fight for Namibian Independence," Editorial Notes, *African Communist* (London), second quarter, 1989, no. 117, pp. 11–12; Christopher S. Wren, "In Pretoria, Last Throes of Marxism?," *NYT*, 19 February 1990, pp. A-1 and 12.

20. "The Path to Power: Program of SACP adopted at the 7th Congress," *Africa Confidential*, third quarter, no. 118, 1989, p. 79. See "The Main Task," *Pravda*, 13 January 1990, p. 5, for an interview with Joe Slovo.

21. *Al-Maydan*, no. 1895, July–August 1989.

22. "Réunion," *Europa World Yearbook, 1989*, vol. 1, p. 1062.

23. AFP (Paris) in Spanish, 5 February 1990; trans. in *FBIS-LAT-90-026*, 7 February 1990, p. 1.

24. Havana Radio Rebelde, 22 January 1990; *FBIS-LAT*, 23 January 1990, pp. 11–12. See also A. Kamorin, "Who Is to Blame?," *Izvestiia*, 24 January 1990, p. 4.

25. Joseph B. Treaster, "Other Walls May Fall...," *NYT*, 28 January 1990, section 4, p. 2. See also A. Moiseev and S. Sereda, "Extraordinary Plenum," *Pravda*, 18 February 1990, p. 5; report from Havana.

26. *La Nación* (San José), no date given, cited in DPA, 29 December 1989; *FBIS-LAT*, 2 January 1990, p. 7. "Cuba suspende el retiro de las tropas de Angola," *La Prensa* (Panama), 26 January 1990, p. A-3; see also foreign ministry statement, Havana Tele Rebelde Network, 25 January 1990; *FBIS-LAT*, 25 January 1990, p. 1.

27. Mark A. Uhlig, "Opposing Ortega," *NYT Magazine*, 11 February 1990, pp. 35 ff.

28. "Nicaragua interceptó planes para asesinar a D. Ortega," *La Estrella de Panamá* (Panama), 26 January 1990, p. B-5; Contra leader Enrique Bermúdez's denial of such plans was reported by DPA, 25 January 1990; *FBIS-LAT*, 25 January 1990, p. 10.

29. *La Vanguardia* (Barcelona), 21 September 1989; *FBIS-LAT*, 10 October 1989, pp. 28–29.

30. TASS, from Havana, "Ready for Negotiations," *Pravda*, 21 January 1990, p. 6.

31. "El M-19 se incorporá a elecciones colombianas," *La Prensa* (Panama), 27 January 1990, p. A-3.

32. See the interview with Oscar Asocar, member of the Chile CP political commission, in *Pravda*, 19 February 1990, p. 5.

33. Shirley Christian, "A Jailbreak by Leftist Guerrillas...," *NYT*, 2 February 1990, p. A-10.

34. Shining Path violence was condemned by Radio Peace and Progress (Moscow), 20 January 1990; trans. in *FBIS-SOV-90-015*, 23 January 1990, p. 37.

35. See the PCCh statement on that election, broadcast over Moscow radio, 16 December 1989; trans. in *FBIS-SOV-89-248*, 28 December 1990, pp. 33–34.

36. V. Shelkov reported from Ottawa on how to join the CP Canada in *Pravda*, 28 January 1990, p. 5.

37. "Martial Law in Beijing Is Lifted by the Chinese," *NYT*, 11 January 1990, pp. 1 and 4.

38. Nicholas D. Kristof, "China's Leaders Seek a Painless Way to Respectability," *NYT*, 14 January 1990, pp. E-1 and E-3.

39. Claudia Rosett, "The Powderkeg That Is China," *WSJ*, 28 December 1989, p. A-6.

40. "The Storm Was Bound to Happen," *South China Morning Post*, (Hong Kong), 20 June 1989, p. 8. See also Sheryl

WuDunn, "Millions in China Are Submitting to Analysis (the Political Kind)," *NYT*, 18 February 1990, p. 13.

41. A. M. Rosenthal, "Chronology of Betrayal," *NYT*, 14 January 1990, p. E-23.

42. *Renmin ribao* (Beijing), 12 July 1989, p. 2.

43. *Nodong sinmun* (Pyongyang), 22 August 1989, p. 1; trans. in *FBIS-EAS*, 28 August 1989, pp. 23–27.

44. Pyongyang Domestic Service, 16 February 1989; trans. in *FBIS-EAS*, 7 March 1989, p. 14. Note, however, the claim of North Korean economic success in the TASS report, "Development Issues Discussed," *Pravda*, 11 January 1990, p. 7.

45. Hanoi Domestic Service, 28 August 1989; trans. in *FBIS-EAS*, 29 August 1989, pp. 66–67. Steven Erlanger, "Hanoi Remains True to Communism . . .," *NYT*, 11 February 1990, p. 16.

46. Phnom Penh Domestic Service, 11 April 1989; trans. in *FBIS-EAS*, 11 April 1989, p. 31. *JPRS-SEA*, 29 June 1989, pp. 7–9. Jacques Bekaert, "The Party—Still a Dominant Force," *Bangkok Post*, 19 May 1989, p. 6.

47. P. Tsvetov, "Toward a People's Democracy," *Pravda*, 7 February 1990, p. 7.

48. "Anti-Communist Rally Reported in Mongolia," *San Francisco Chronicle*, 15 January 1990, p. A-15. See also A. Nabatchikov, "Mongolia: Accelerating Renewal Process," *Izvestiia*, 19 January 1990, p. 4; AP from Beijing, "Mongols Protest Party's Monopoly," *NYT*, 12 February 1990, p. A-6.

49. AFP (Hong Kong), 10 April 1989; trans. in *FBIS-EAS*, 11 April 1989, p. 39.

50. José Maria Sison, *The Philippine Revolution: The Leader's View* (New York: Crane Russak, 1989), 241 pp.

51. *Kabul Times*, 23 August 1989, p. 1.

52. TASS, 20 February 1989; trans. in *FBIS-SOV*, 22 February 1989, p. 20.

53. *Argumenty i fakty* (Moscow), 28 April–5 May 1989; trans. in *FBIS-SOV*, 9 May 1989, p. 34.

54. *WP*, 2 September 1989, p. A-20.

55. *AFP* (Paris), 3 and 4 September 1989; trans. in *FBIS-WEU*, 5 September 1989, p. 14.

56. "Fourteen Days in Brief," *Middle East International* (London), no. 365, 15 December 1989, p. 14.

57. *Al-Musawwar* (Cairo), 22 December 1989; trans. in *FBIS-NES*, 28 December 1989, p. 16.

58. Garalla Omar [First Secretary, YPUP], "Northern Yemen: Working With Undiminished Vigour," *World Marxist Review* (Toronto), vol. 32, no. 6 (June 1989), pp. 67–70.

59. *Keyhan Havai* (Teheran), 18 October 1989, p. 8; trans. in *FBIS-NES*, 31 October 1989, p. 60.

60. Radio of the Iranian Toilers (clandestine from Baku), 2 October 1989; trans. in *FBIS-NES*, 6 October 1989, p. 54.

61. Iran National News Agency (Teheran) in English, 23 November 1989, citing *Teheran Times* of same date; *FBIS-NES*, 24 November 1989, p. 68.

62. *Al-Siyasah* (Kuwait), 1 October 1989; trans. in *FBIS-NES*, 4 October 1989, p. 23.

63. Interview by editors, "Intifada Continues," *World Marxist Review*, vol. 32, no. 8 (August 1989), p. 48.

64. Ibid., p. 49.

65. TASS, "An Exchange of Views," *Pravda*, 18 February 1990, p. 5. All four Israelis are identified by name and title, yet none of the Soviets is even mentioned.

66. LCP daily newspaper *Al-Nida* (Beirut), 18 August 1989, p. 1.

67. Alan Riding, "Communist Parties in West . . .," *NYT*, 9 January 1990, pp. A-1 and 5.

68. Serge Schmeman, "Environmentalists and Socialists Gain . . .," *NYT*, 19 June 1989, pp. A-1 and 5; Julian Baum, "European Parliament Shifts to Left," *CSM*, 29 June 1989, p. 4.

69. V. Bol'shakov, "In Paris," *Pravda*, 28 January 1990, p. 5.

70. Rome Radio, 9 January 1990; *FBIS-WEU-90-008*, 11 January 1990, p. 24.

71. Giorgio F. Polara, "Let's Not Stop Here . . .," *L'Unita*, 16 November 1989, p. 3; trans. in *FBIS-WEU-90-009*, 12 January 1990, pp. 1–7.

72. *Diario 16* (Madrid), 13 December 1989. See also the articles by V. Volkov in *Pravda*, 11 and 28 January 1990, pp. 7 and 5, respectively.

73. Helena Sanches Osorio in *O Independente* (Lisbon), 20 October 1989, p. 6; trans. *FBIS-WEU-89-235*, 8 December 1989, pp. 44–45.

74. *Expresso* (Lisbon), 15 December 1989, pp. 1 and 20; trans. in *FBIS-WEU-90-001*, 2 January 1990, p. 18.

75. *Cyprus Mail* (Nicosia), 24 November 1989; ibid., 31 January 1990, p. 1, in *FBIS-WEU-90-022*, 1 February 1990, p. 11.

76. Sheila Rule, "New Name and New Age . . .," *NYT*, 2 February 1990, p. A-4.

77. René Urbany, "An Optimistic View of the Prospects," *World Marxist Review*, vol. 32, no. 7 (July 1989), p. 8.

78. *Svenska Dagbladet* (Stockholm), 23 November 1989.

79. Heljä Marjä Tammisola, "To Be the Conscience of Society," *Problemy mira i sotsializma* (Moscow), no. 11 (November 1989), pp. 9–12.

80. For coverage, see articles by I. Mel'nikov and V. Smelov in *Pravda*, 20 and 21 January 1990, both on p. 7. *Die Presse* (Vienna), 22 January 1990, p. 1.

81. *Frankfurter Allgemeine Zeitung*, 16 October 1989.

82. Kevin Devlin, "Orphans of the Revolution: West Germany's Bankrupt Communists," *RAD Background Report/222* (19 December 1989), p. 2.

83. Ibid., p. 4.

84. "Meeting of Leaders from Governments-members of the Warsaw Treaty, Moscow, 4 December," *Vestnik Ministerstva Inostrannykh Del SSSR*, no. 24 (31 December 1989), pp. 42–43.

85. Speech on 29 November, quoted in "Albania: 'Pure' Communism," *RFE/RL Soviet East European Report*, vol. 7, no. 10 (10 December 1989), p. 4.

86. Reuters from Sofia, "Communist Cabinet for Bulgaria," *NYT*, 9 February 1990, P. A-8.

87. A. Krushinskii, "New President of Czechoslovakia Elected," *Pravda*, 30 December 1989, p. 5.

88. Alfred Reisch, *Hungary in 1989: A Country in Transition* (Munich: RFE/RL, 4 December 1989), p. 5. (Pamphlet)

89. S. Baigarov et al., "Extraordinary Congress Closed," *Pravda*, 18 December 1989, p. 8.

90. Michael Shafir, *Romania in 1989* (Munich: RFE/RL, 30 November 1989), p. 4. (Pamphlet)

91. John Kifner, "Romanian Leaders Courting Military," *NYT*, 18 February 1990, p. 10.

92. Richard F. Staar, "Poland: Renewal or Stagnation," *Current History*, vol. 88, no. 541 (November 1989), pp. 373–376, 405–409.

93. Cited in "The Story of Yugoslavia," *NYT*, 23 January 1990, p. A-7. See also Marlise Simons, "Yugoslav Communists Vote . . .," ibid.

AFRICA

Introduction

The dramatic events convulsing the communist regimes in Eastern Europe were echoed in weaker form by some African Marxist countries. For example, in Angola and Mozambique, people have become disenchanted with programs for collectivized agricultural and fixed wages and prices. Reformers thus sought to allow a modest amount of private enterprise to take place within the context of a command economy. Additionally, the Marxist regimes have also begun to alter their strictures against foreign investment and international aid.

Possibly the most spectacular development among the Marxist regimes, however, came on 7 December when the People's Republic of Benin renounced Marxism-Leninism as the official ideology of the country (Cotonou Domestic Service, 7 December; *FBIS-AFR*, 8 December). President Mathieu Kérékou and the Revolutionary Party of the People of Benin faced mounting economic problems and pressure from domestic opponents and Western creditors and supporters, mainly France, to liberalize the nation's economy. But Benin's commitment to Marxism was never as deep as that of Angola and Mozambique, where the Marxist regimes came to power after protracted guerrilla struggles.

The People's Republic of Mozambique also announced changes in its official language. In that southeast African country, the ruling Marxist party, Front for the Liberation of Mozambique (FRELIMO), held its Fifth Congress, which sanctioned the discarding of its previous Marxist-Leninist vocabulary. (William Claybourne, "Mozambique Shifts from Marxism," *WP*, 29 July.) Although FRELIMO reaffirmed its commitment to socialist principles, its party congress eliminated Marxism in its pronouncements. The Central Committee appointed by the congress re-elected President Joaquim Chissano, who was unopposed.

During the year, FRELIMO also abandoned its no-negotiations stance with the Mozambique National Resistance (RENAMO), which has been engaged in a countrywide insurgency with the central government for fourteen years. At RENAMO's First Congress, President Afonso Dhlakama was re-elected. The liberalization of the economy that began with FRELIMO's 1987 economic rehabilitation program began to show some modest results. But the ongoing guerrilla war with RENAMO continued to disrupt large sections of the country.

In the People's Republic of Angola, the political focus of the year was more on Namibian independence than on internal restructuring. In late 1988 the Brazzaville agreement paved the way for a withdrawal of international involvement in the Angolan civil war. The agreement was carried out in part during 1989, with South Africa terminating its support for the Angolan rebel movement, the National Union for Total Independence of Angola (UNITA), while Angola stopped its support of the South West Africa People's Organization (SWAPO) and the African National Congress (ANC), which challenges white rule in South Africa. The Brazzaville protocol also required South Africa to permit U.N.-sponsored elections in Namibia, which were held in November with SWAPO gaining 57 percent of the vote.

As part of the protocol, Cuba agreed to a phased withdrawal from Angola to be completed by July 1991. Cuban military forces had buttressed the ruling Popular Movement for the Liberation of Angola–Labor Party (MPLA-PT) since the 1975 Angolan civil war. Although the Brazzaville protocol facilitated Namibian independence and opened the way for a deinternationalization of the Angolan insurgency, it did not end the fighting in the southern region of the country between UNITA and the Cuban-supported MPLA-PT, which launched a determined drive against Jonas Savimbi's forces at year's end. ("Angola: War and Peace in the MPLA," *Africa Confidential*, 11 August.)

The MPLA's efforts to reduce the size of the government in the private sector were rewarded when Angola was admitted to the International Monetary Fund (IMF) and the World Bank in September, allowing Luanda to seek loans from the two international financial institutions (Clyde Farnsworth, "Angola Is Admitted to the World Bank and I.M.F.," *NYT*, 20 September). Despite the growing economy, the MPLA began to experience divisions in its ranks over the degree of reform from the Marxist blueprint (Radio Luanda, 22 January; *FBIS-AFR*, 25 January). Reports of tensions between reformers and hard-liners surfaced in news stories.

In the People's Republic of the Congo the divisions within the ruling Congolese Party of Labor (CPL) were even more pronounced than in Angola's ruling movement. Two spokesmen for the ideological hard-line were dropped from Central Committee membership whereas a number of less ideological, younger bureaucrats were promoted to it (AFP, 31 July; *FBIS-AFR*, 2 August). Other realignments took place within the Politburo, where for the first time since the party's establishment the civilian members outnumbered the military.

At the Fourth Party Congress in July, the moderate and pragmatic elements emerged strengthened. President Denis Sassou-Nguesso moved to maintain his grip over the military by promoting his military supporters to the Central Committee. For its part, the military appeared to go along with the ideological change in direction by demanding the purge of "ultraconservatives" and the bringing of "new blood" to the leadership.

Across the continent in Zimbabwe, President Robert Mugabe's Zimbabwe African National Union–Patriotic Front (ZANU-PF) continued its pragmatic course despite preindependence promises to create a Marxist state. But Mugabe held firm to his determination to build a one-party political system. ("Update: Zimbabwe," *Africa Report* 34, no. 4 [July August].) This course resulted in opposition from formerly loyal supporters. An opposition party, the Zimbabwe Unity Movement, was formed to oppose the government's moves to a one-party system and to criticize corruption, which became a major national issue. Criticism also came from university students and trade unions for Mugabe's handling of a major corruption crisis involving six cabinet ministers and a provincial governor.

Despite criticism, ZANU reaffirmed its plans for a one-party state and formally merged with the former opposition party, Zimbabwe African People's Union, at the December congress. The congress also made arrangements to enlarge both the Politburo and the Central Committee. The new party reaffirmed its adherence to the principles of Marxism-Leninism, although the leadership supports policies favoring a mixed economy.

In Ethiopia, the hard-line Marxist-Leninist government of Mengistu Haile Mariam faced a near toppling due to military defeats. When the Ethiopian government lost control of the Tigre region in May, senior officers staged an unsuccessful coup. Mengistu executed eleven generals for their role in the attempted coup, which further weakened the central government's campaign against secessionists. (Daniel Wattenberg, "Revolt Signals a Crumbling Regime," *Insight*, 12 June.) Moscow reportedly pressured Mengistu to negotiate a settlement with the rebels and to change Ethiopian agricultural policies because of crop failures and mismanagement.

The African continent's oldest Marxist-Leninist party, the South African Communist Party (SACP), reportedly held its Seventh Congress in Cuba. Brief reports disclosed that Chairman Dan Tloome and General Secretary Joe Slovo were re-elected to their posts. The congress delegates approved a new program, The Path to Power, to replace the previous party program. Although the new program concentrated on "a seizure of power," it did not rule out a negotiated transfer of power with the white rulers of South Africa.

The SACP had been closely connected with the Communist Party of the Soviet Union (CPSU) for decades. Like the CPSU, the SACP was critical of Stalinism but without mentioning Stalin's name. South African Communists, ambivalent in regard to Mikhail Gorbachev's reforms of *perestroika* and *glasnost'*, gave cautious endorsements of Gorbachev's policies. ("The Path to Power: Program of SACP Adopted at the 7th Congress," *African Communist*, no. 18.)

To the north, the Sudanese Communist Party (SCP) fell on hard times during 1989 with the military coup that ended parliamentary government in June. The new government of military officers arrested the SCP leadership and suppressed the party's activities. The SCP's management, therefore, was in the hands of those who were outside the country or who remained at large after the arrests. (*al-Maydan*, no. 1895 [July/August].) Before the coup the party leadership was reformist rather than revolutionary, but since the coup the nature of the SCP leadership in the underground party has been unclear.

In Senegal the communist parties continued to confront their crushing defeat in the February 1988 national elections. Throughout the past year the two major Marxist parties—the Independence and Labor Party (PIT) and the Democratic League/Movement for the Party of Labor (LD/MPT)—denounced the conduct of the 1988 elections and demanded new elections with sweeping political reforms. The Marxist parties joined with other opposition movements to criticize the government of President Abdou Diouf and his ruling Socialist Party (PS). The Marxists also joined with other government opponents in staging violent demonstrations during the Independence Day celebrations.

But during most of the year, the two major Marxist parties split on their response to the government's policies. Whereas PIT voiced its willingness to work with the PS to find solutions to the West African nation's economic and political problems, the LD/MPT criticized the ruling party's corruption, "anti-democratic nature," and neocolonial character—evidenced by its implementation of economic policies dictated by the IMF and the World Bank. (*Fagaru*, January; *FBIS-AFR*, 15 March.)

Off the coast of Africa on Réunion island, the Réunion Communist Party (PCR) continued to be concerned about social equality with metropolitan France and about economic development. The PCR hailed as a victory the signing of an agreement at year's end that brings into line the compensation of Réunionese unemployed with their French counterparts. General Secretary Paul Vergès, who left his post as major of Le Port in order to run in Saint-Paul, lost the election. (Réunion, *Europe World Yearbook*, vol. 1, p. 1062.) Although the PCR lost seats in some areas, it won in others, thus maintaining a political position on the island.

With communist and Marxist political forces continuing to be such a scant presence on the Nigerian political scene, the editors decided to drop Nigeria from the *1990 Yearbook on International Communist Affairs*. Although some Marxist leanings were apparent among the roughly 88 associations that sprouted up following military President Babangida's lifting of the ban on political parties on 3 May, there emerged no Marxist or communist political party with enough popular support to win official recognition as one of the two political parties that will be allowed to compete in the emerging Third Republic. The Nigerian Labour party, based in the trade unions and incorporating social democratic, socialist, and some Marxist perspectives, was ranked fifth by the National Electoral Commission among the thirteen parties that ultimately filed for registration. In a surprise announcement on

7 October, however, President Babangida rejected the bids of all these aspiring parties and said that his military government would move to establish two new parties—the Social Democratic party and the National Republican Convention. Explicitly intended to "lean a little to the left and a little to the right," the new party system seems certain to entrench the marginal standing of Marxist and radical-left forces in the Nigerian political system.

Thomas H. Henriksen
Hoover Institution

Angola

Population. 8,533,989 (July 1989)
Party. Popular Movement for the Liberation of Angola–Labor Party (Movimento Popular de Libertação de Angola–Partido do Trabalho, MPLA-PT)
Founded. December 1956 (renamed December 1977)
Membership. 45,000 (Radio Luanda, 8 December; *FBIS-AFR*, 9 December 1987)
General Secretary. José Eduardo dos Santos
Politburo. 11 members
Central Committee. 90 members
Status. Ruling party
Last Congress. Second, 9–11 December 1985
Last Election. 1980; all 203 candidates MPLA-PT approved
Auxiliary Organizations. National Union of Angolan Workers (UNTA), Organization of Angolan Women (OMA), MPLA Youth (JMPLA), People's Defense Organization (ODP), Agostinho Neto Young Pioneer Organization
Publications. *O Jornal de Angolan* (official newspaper, daily); ANGOP is the Angolan news agency.

During the first few months of the year, the People's Republic of Angola (PRA) basked in the glow of the Brazzaville Protocol signed 22 December 1988. The agreement paved the way for the deinternationalization of the Angolan civil war. Cuba agreed to withdraw all its combat forces by July 1991. South Africa terminated its relationship with the National Union for the Total Independence of Angola (UNITA), the Angolan insurgent movement, whereas Angola ceased to support the South-West Africa People's Organization (SWAPO) and the African National Congress (ANC), which had to move its bases from Angola to Uganda, Ethiopia, and Tanzania. The Brazzaville Protocol also obliged South Africa to allow U.N.-sponsored elections in Namibia. Those elections were held 7–11 November, with SWAPO winning 57 percent of the vote.

Although the Brazzaville Protocol ended foreign power involvement in the Angolan civil war, the internal components remained. Despite a dozen official four-party talks (United States, Cuba, Angola, South Africa), UNITA did not participate in the negotiation process. Thus as 1989 began, an end to the civil war was not in sight, although both UNITA and the MPLA realized a military solution was unlikely.

For economic reasons many southern African leaders desired that the civil war be peacefully resolved. Joseph Mobutu of Zaire and Kenneth Kaunda of Zambia sought to find a common ground between UNITA and the MPLA. Both Angolan president dos Santos and UNITA's Jonas Savimbi were under intense pressure to compromise. Dos Santos presented his seven-point peace plan; on 13 March Savimbi stated that he would "exclude himself from the negotiations and from a subsequent transitional government as it prepared for elections." (*WP*, 28 March.)

In May the government of Angola invited representatives from Zambia, Zaire, Congo, Gabon, Mozambique, Zimbabwe, and São Tomé e Príncipe to Luanda for a presentation of President dos Santos's peace plan. The meeting adjourned with an agreement to meet in June at Gbadolite, Zaire.

On 22 June the heads of eighteen African nations met at Gbadolite. That evening, President dos Santos and Jonas Savimbi shook hands, agreeing to a cease-fire and the beginning of peace talks on a government of national reconciliation. Confusion reigned, however, as to what had been agreed on during the six-hour meeting. President Kaunda claimed Savimbi would go into self-exile as part of a cease-fire accord. President Mobutu said that "there was nothing about exile." Savimbi's view was that "if you don't defeat a man, you can't send him into exile." Angola stated that the Gbadolite participants had accepted MPLA's proposal of a Savimbi exile, a cease-fire, a reintegration of UNITA members into

existing institutions, and an end of U.S. support for UNITA.

With the different interpretations of the Gbadolite Declaration, the entire peace process quickly degenerated into a series of acrimonious exchanges between the major participants. The official text on the Gbadolite Declaration stated that both sides agreed "to end the war and to proclaim national reconciliation." A cease-fire was to begin 24 June. Finally, MPLA and UNITA agreed to establish a commission to prepare for national reconciliation. (Radio Luanda, 23 June; *FBIS-AFR*, 26 June.)

The cease-fire was immediately broken by both sides, and the National Reconciliation Commission made little progress. The rest of the year focused on the multitudinous interpretations of the Gbadolite Declaration, although by December, UNITA announced its readiness to sign another cease-fire agreement. Meanwhile, MPLA presented another peace plan.

Party Leadership. Although his control of the party and state remained firm, President dos Santos continued to shuffle the cabinet. In late December 1988, dos Santos relieved Interior Minister Alexandre Rodrigues ("Kito") of his portfolio. President dos Santos had voiced concern about "reports of the existence of special forces of a commando nature, two battalions or a brigade, established without my knowledge and without the decision of the party leadership." The president also made reference to "preparations for a coup d'état." (Radio Luanda, 14 December 1988; *FBIS-AFR*, 15 December 1988.) "Kito" was a proponent of national reconciliation and may have been positioning himself to challenge dos Santos's supremacy within the MPLA. "Kito" maintained his cabinet status and position on the political bureau until 28 March, when he was dismissed. General Francisco Magalhaes Paiva ("Nvunda") was appointed as interior minister. (Radio Luanda, 28 March; *FBIS-AFR*, 29 March.)

On 24 January, Foreign Minister Afonso Van-Dunem ("Mbinda") was replaced by Pedro de Castro Van-Dunem ("Loy"). "Loy" had been minister of state for petroleum and energy. (Radio Luanda, 23 January; *FBIS-AFR*, 24 January.) The appointment of "Loy" to the foreign ministry was further evidence of Luanda's attempts to woo the West, especially the United States. Zeferino Cassa Yombo, a cabinet newcomer, replaced "Loy" as the oil minister. (*Africa News*, 6 February.) In addition, dos Santos replaced Angola's ambassadors to Britain, France, the Soviet Union, Yugoslavia, and Algeria.

Thrice more during the year, dos Santos relieved various commissioners, ministers, and ambassadors from their posts. (Radio Luanda, 13 February; *FBIS-AFR*, 15 February; Radio Luanda, 28 March; *FBIS-AFR*, 29 March; Radio Luanda, 21 October; *FBIS-AFR*, 23 October.)

In September various events were held throughout Angola to celebrate President dos Santos's ten years in office (ANGOP, 21 September; *FBIS-AFR*, 28 September). Despite a decade in power, dos Santos was jockeying to maintain his position and the pre-eminence of his policies. In less than a year, dos Santos moved to eliminate sources of potential friction to his leadership from the interior ministry and police service. (Radio Luanda, 19 January; *FBIS-AFR*, 23 January; Radio Luanda, 5 June; *FBIS-AFR*, 9 June.)

Party Affairs. President dos Santos used his New Year's message to urge Angolans abroad "to join the Angolan family and to contribute toward national reconstruction." This hand of friendship also included "compatriots who may have served interests alien to the Angolan nation." Dos Santos reminded listeners that the amnesty law had been promulgated 24 December 1988. The law stipulated that those who turned themselves over to government authorities and renounced violence would be granted amnesty. The law took effect 4 February and was to last one year. On 2 February, the Standing Commission of the People's Assembly approved a law to ensure that amnesty recipients would be quickly reintegrated into Angolan society. The amnesty law guaranteed all Angolans the right to medical care, education, and cultural activities. (Radio Luanda, 4 February; *FBIS-AFR*, 8 February.) UNITA rejected the amnesty offer, launching instead a "general offensive" across Angola (*NYT*, 3 February).

The First Special Session of the Defense and Security Council's Economic Commission convened 14 January. The economic commission recommended approval of a package of measures within the framework of the economic and financial restructuring program Saneamento Economico e Financiero (SEF). (Radio Luanda, 14 January; *FBIS-AFR*, 17 January.)

The Council of Ministers approved the economic commission's recommendations on 20 January, including establishing currency exchange rates, launching a fight against black marketeering, and decentralizing the price fixing system (Radio Luanda, 22 January; *FBIS-AFR*, 25 January).

On 24 January the first ordinary session of the Defense and Security Council met. The council agreed to modernize Angolan Airlines (TAAG) by purchasing new aircraft. More important, the group amended bills concerning the front's defense councils, which coordinated all political, military, economic, and social activities "in the fight against counterrevolutionary subversion." (Radio Luanda, 25 January; *FBIS-AFR*, 27 January.)

The fifth ordinary session of the People's Assembly met in Luanda on 1 March. President dos Santos, in his opening speech, focused on the two major issues confronting Angola: the UNITA issue and implementation of SEF.

The UNITA issue would be resolved in seven phases: (1) an end to interference in Angolan domestic affairs by South Africa, the United States, and their allies, (2) respect for Angola's constitutional laws, including the maintenance of a one-party political system, (3) application of active political and military measures to end the subversive war, (4) amnesty within the framework of the policy of clemency and national harmony, (5) voluntary reintegration of all Angolans in an effort of national reconstruction, (6) special treatment in the case of Jonas Savimbi, and (7) support from the international community to national reconstruction programs.

On SEF, dos Santos urged the delegates to approve measures on "the treasury bond law, readjusting prices, interest rates, the value of the kwanza in relation to the dollar, and actions conducive to increased production and salaries."

Dos Santos warned the delegates that there was no other option than full implementation of SEF (Radio Luanda, 1 March; *FBIS-AFR*, 2 March).

Before ending on 4 March the fifth ordinary session of the People's Assembly voted to devalue the kwanza by 200 percent. The devaluation was a necessary condition for admission to the International Monetary Fund (IMF) and the World Bank. By year's end, however, the devaluation process had not begun. Other measures passed included the Economic Recovery Program for 1989–1990, the 1989 state budget ($3.75 billion), clemency and national harmony legislation, and the remaining SEF package.

The sixth national meeting of MPLA's Control and Audit Commission was held from 19 to 23 April. The participants dealt with party discipline and established guidelines for the party's Third Congress. (Radio Luanda, 23 April; *FBIS-AFR*, 26 April.) The MPLA also held a national unity debate

23–29 April to formulate plans for the party congress (Radio Luanda, 28 April; *FBIS-AFR*, 1 May).

The 23rd ordinary session of the MPLA labor party Central Committee began 23 May. Topics of discussion included the political and military situation, education, health, and Angola's "internal problem." MPLA internal activities were reviewed in preparation for the Third Party Congress. (Radio Luanda, 23 May; *FBIS-AFR*, 24 May.)

The sixth ordinary session of the People's Assembly met from 16 to 18 August. The delegates heard reports from the president on implementation of SEF guidelines and on the results of the Gbadolite summit.

President dos Santos expressed his belief that positive results of the SEF program "will begin to surface next year and that we will perhaps achieve the main planned goals by 1991." (Radio Luanda, 17 August; *FBIS-AFR*, 17 August.) The Angolan president, however, cautioned the delegates that the devaluation of the national currency would have a negative effect "on the workers' living standards, on supplies to the population, on public and commercial transportation, and on small business."

The economy and the SEF program received a major stimulus on 19 September when Angola was admitted to the IMF and the World Bank. Finance Minister Augusto Teixeira de Matos indicated that the government would immediately seek loans to rebuild the economic infrastructure destroyed by the civil war. (*NYT*, 20 September.) Despite Angola's being a favorable investment opportunity, the unsettled status of the civil war made large Western investments there unlikely in the near future.

Angola's petroleum industry continued to prosper, as the government acted to open bidding on offshore blocks located between Lobito and the Namibian border, effectively opening all of Angola's petroleum reserves to exploration and production. Oil revenues totaled more than $2 billion. Ninety-five percent of Angola's foreign earnings come from oil revenues. (*NYT*, 24 April.)

The diamond industry also posted some impressive gains under the rehabilitation program begun in late 1986. Production for the year was expected to exceed one million carats, with diamond sales to earn approximately $100 million.

The Angolan government received pledges for hundreds of millions of dollars to rehabilitate the Benguela Railroad. In January, $94 million was pledged by the Southern African Development Coordination Conference (SADCC) and a group of Arab, Western, and African donors. However, reconstruction would not begin until the donors received assurances that UNITA forces would not disrupt or harass the project. (*Africa News*, 29 May; *NYT*, 13 November.)

The true problem for the MPLA in 1989 was not the socioeconomic costs of implementing SEF, but the UNITA question. The Brazzaville Protocol successfully resolved Cuban and South African involvement in the civil war, but other internal and external factors remained. The United States announced it would continue to support UNITA after both President George Bush's inauguration and the Gbadolite Declaration. (*WP*, 12 January; *NYT*, 25 June.) The MPLA desperately needed U.S. diplomatic recognition as a precursor to economic growth. The United States, however, insisted that UNITA be included in a government of national reconciliation. The MPLA split over how to achieve those goals.

In January, General Antonio dos Santos Franca, deputy defense minister, publicly admitted for the first time that the MPLA had talked with UNITA (*NYT*, 28 January). Later the deputy defense minister said he had been "misinterpreted" (Radio Lisbon, 27 January; *FBIS-AFR*, 30 January). President dos Santos offered his own clarification, saying that the Angolan government would hold talks with individuals under the amnesty program, not negotiate with UNITA (Radio Luanda, 29 January; *FBIS-AFR*, 30 January). In February, dos Santos was quoted as saying that the MPLA would never share power with UNITA (Radio Johannesburg; *FBIS-AFR*, 10 February). In his speech to the People's Assembly, dos Santos emphasized the importance of maintaining a one-party state in Angola.

The president and other government ministers continued to urge the United States to abandon UNITA and grant Angola diplomatic recognition (Radio Luanda, 12 January; *FBIS-AFR*, 13 January; Radio Luanda, 30 May; *FBIS-AFR*, 31 May). Various MPLA commentators argued that UNITA was an internal Angolan matter in which the United States should not interfere. After the Gbadolite Declaration, Angola blamed the United States for UNITA's rejection of the MPLA version of events. (ANGOP, 19 August; *FBIS-AFR*, 21 August; *Dakar Pana*, 23 September; *FBIS-AFR*, 26 September.)

Jonas Savimbi again visited Washington, D.C., in October and met with President Bush. The United States reconfirmed its support for UNITA demands of "face-to-face negotiations" and "ultimately free and fair elections." (*WP*, 6 October.) Yet in September, President dos Santos, at the invitation of 101 congressmen, accepted an invitation to visit the United States (*WP*, 29 September). The visit was scheduled for February 1990.

The MPLA, in a quandary over UNITA, split into several factions. One group advocated reintegrating UNITA members into the MPLA on an individual basis. In this way, UNITA militants would not outnumber MPLA members, thus preserving the MPLA's privileged position. Another group—dos Santos and his immediate supporters—maintained a delicate position of attempting to attract U.S. recognition and investment while focusing diplomatic efforts on splitting UNITA from Savimbi. The military men were alarmed at the Cuban withdrawal from Angola; the disengagement of Cuban forces would hamper Angola's army should the smoldering civil war reignite. Finally, the ideological purists feared an MPLA betrayal of the socialist principles of Agostinho Neto. (*Africa Confidential*, 11 August.) One point that all the MPLA factions agreed on was their fear of the charismatic Jonas Savimbi.

President dos Santos had to maintain a delicate balance among the various MPLA factions while seeking a favorable negotiated solution to the civil war. MPLA was under intense pressure from the United States, the USSR, South Africa, Zambia, and Zaire to negotiate with UNITA. Cuban forces were withdrawing, leaving Angola less and less of a military solution. The UNITA insurgency, although unable to defeat MPLA militarily, could prevent Angola's economic recovery. The Angolan government spent 40–50 percent of its state budget on defense; a resolution to the civil war would free resources for economic development.

Also, both the MPLA and UNITA were castigated by the human rights organization Africa Watch for violations of international law resulting "in serious and systematic abuses of human rights" (*NYT*, 9 April).

Additionally, UNITA was shaken by reports that dissidents had been tortured and killed. Some unconfirmed allegations stated that dissidents had been branded as witches and burned at the stake. Although nothing was proven, UNITA had to allocate valuable resources to prevent support from eroding. (*NYT*, 11 March.)

Further, in November the Angolan Catholic bishops issued a pastoral letter calling for "free elections," "personal, direct, and frank dialogue between one Angolan and another Angolan," and a political system based on "peace, progress, liberty, and democracy" (Voice of the Resistance of the Black Cockerel; *FBIS-AFR*, 19 December). This placed added pressure on both groups to negotiate an end to the war.

Mass Organizations. The National Agostinho Neto Party School was reconstituted as Angola's first higher party institute of learning. The school was administered by the Central Committee. Important functions included "raising the political and ideological level of the cadres of the party, state apparatus and mass public organizations." (*WMR*, December 1988.)

In February, the National Union of Workers of Angola (UNTA) signed agreements with its counterparts in Zaire (National Union of Workers of Zaire [UNTZA]) and the Congo (Congolese Trade Union Confederation [CSC]). The agreements formed a social security technical commission that would strengthen ties between the unions (Radio Luanda, 23 February; *FBIS-AFR*, 28 February).

The OMA, UNTA, and JMPLA participated in varying degrees to the implementation of SEF and preparation for the Third MPLA Party Congress.

International Affairs. Angola's relationship with the Soviet Union and Cuba remained uncertain. Under the terms of the Brazzaville Protocol, Cuba withdrew 25,000 combat troops during 1988. The first of these soldiers left 10 January. By June, 10,000 Cubans had departed; by October, 21,400 had left. Phase I of the Brazzaville Protocol was completed in November. (Radio Luanda, 11 January; *FBIS-AFR*, 12 January; Johannesburg Domestic Service, 13 June; *FBIS-AFR*, 14 June; Radio Luanda, 3 October; *FBIS-AFR*, 4 October.) The remaining Cuban forces were north of the thirteenth parallel, that is, north of the Benguela Railroad that splits Angola in half. This meant that Angolan forces could not employ Cuban military forces in the annual dry season offensive against UNITA's main base—Jamba. There were reports that the Cubans were replaced by Vietnamese and black Cubans, but there was no independent confirmation. (Johannesburg Domestic Service; *FBIS-AFR*, 8 March; Voice of Resistance of the Black Cockerel, 19 April; *FBIS-AFR*, 21 April.)

On 13 February, Angolan deputy trade minister Ambrosio Silvestre traveled to Havana to attend a meeting of Council of Mutual Economic Assistance interior trade ministers. The meeting focused on trade specialization issues and ways to increase technical mechanization. The Angolan delegation attended as guests. (ANGOP, 13 February; *FBIS-AFR*, 15 February.)

President dos Santos traveled to Cuba on 4 December to attend a ceremony to honor Cubans killed in Angola and to discuss with Fidel Castro the implementation of the Brazzaville Protocol (Radio Luanda, 4 December; *FBIS-AFR*, 5 December).

Angolan-Soviet relations fluctuated throughout the year. In March, President dos Santos met with the Soviet deputy foreign minister, Anatoly Adamishin, to strengthen existing cooperation between the Soviet Union and Angola (Radio Luanda, 28 March; *FBIS-AFR*, 29 March). The two men met again in July; Adamishin expressed full Soviet support for "the Angolan government's efforts to reach national reconciliation" (TASS; *FBIS-SOV*, 11 July).

The sixth regular meeting of the Soviet-Angolan Intergovernmental Commission on Economic, Scientific and Technical Cooperation and Trade met in July. The two sides agreed to allow Angola to supply coffee on a compensation basis. Joint enterprises were created in the field of oil, quartz, and diamond extraction. The Soviet side vowed cooperation in "running energy projects, restoring bridges and tunnels, carrying out geological exploration . . . and training national specialists." (TASS, 7 July; *FBIS-SOV*, 11 July.)

Manuel Bernardo de Sousa became Angola's ambassador to the USSR in April. He replaced Jose Cesar Augusto, who had occupied the post since 1983. (TASS, 21 April; *FBIS-SOV*, 25 April.)

There were some problems between the two allies. The Joint Soviet-Angolan Fishing Cooperation Commission met in Luanda on 30 April. After evaluating overall cooperation, the two sides failed to agree on current operations. According to Angolan fisheries minister Ramos da Cruz, "We failed to reach agreement on ways to share this quota . . . the Soviet side wants fish to be distributed within certain parameters, but the Angolan side feels these parameters are not in its best interests. . . . The differences that emerged were not overcome." (Radio Luanda, 30 April; *FBIS-AFR*, 3 May.) Vladimir Burmistrov, Soviet deputy minister of foreign economic relations, was asked to comment about Angola's debt to the Soviet Union. In the spirit of *glasnost'*, Burmistrov's answer was revealing:

I think the time has come for Angola to adopt a more responsible attitude regarding its undertakings vis-à-vis the USSR. I think that the Angolan side has re-

sources, for Angola pays its debts to the Western countries on a quite regular basis. We are prepared to consider any Angolan proposals for repayment not just in the form of goods but also services." (Radio Moscow, 26 August; *FBIS-SOV*, 28 August.)

Angolan-Eastern bloc ties remained solid although future relations were uncertain. A Polish parliamentarian group visited Luanda in January and met with Angolan government and party officials (Radio Luanda, 15 January; *FBIS-AFR*, 18 January). The German Democratic Republic (GDR) and Angola signed an accord on technical and professional training of Angolan students in GDR educational facilities (Radio Luanda, 18 April; *FBIS-AFR*, 26 April).

On 17 July, President dos Santos left for Czechoslovakia on "a friendly ten-day working visit." There dos Santos met with Yassir Arafat of the Palestine Liberation Organization and underwent "very thorough medical tests." (Bratislava Domestic Service, 25 July; *FBIS-EEU*, 26 July.) The Angolan leader also visited Hungary in September.

The political upheaval in the Eastern bloc may cause the new leaders there to re-examine commitments and pledges made by the now powerless communist parties of Eastern Europe.

The People's Republic of China (PRC) urged Angola not to allow events in Beijing "to affect relations." PRC embassy personnel in Luanda described occurrences in China as "isolated events." (Radio Luanda, 4 January; *FBIS-AFR*, 4 January.)

For the first time the South African-Angolan relationship was based on diplomacy rather than on military confrontation. In January, Angola accused South Africa of violating the tripartite agreement by refusing to allow the U.N. to inspect South African facilities at the Caprivi Strip in Namibia. (Radio Luanda, 24 January; *FBIS-AFR*, 24 January.) The Angolan defense minister, Pedro Maria Tonha Pedale, charged that South Africa was continuing to supply UNITA forces (Maputo Domestic Service; *FBIS-AFR*, 27 January). Later the defense minister accused South African forces of a border incursion in Cuando Cubango province in southern Angola (Radio Luanda, 9 February; *FBIS-AFR*, 10 February).

The joint commission established by the Brazzaville Protocol to monitor the peace treaty met for the first time in Luanda 23–25 February. The commission consisted of Angola, South Africa, and Cuba, with the United States and the USSR as observers. The agenda called for discussion on "SWAPO terrorists being south of the tenth parallel, the alleged South African attack on MPLA forces in the south of Angola...the prisoner of war question, and the matter of establishing direct communication between the South African, Cuban and Angolan delegations." (Johannesburg TV Service; *FBIS-AFR*, 24 February). The second session met 20–21 March in Havana; the third met in Cape Town from 28 to 29 April (ANGOP, 22 March; *FBIS-AFR*, 23 March; Radio Luanda, 28 April; *FBIS-AFR*, 27 April). The fourth session was held in Luanda 7–8 July. The delegates verified Cuban compliance with the withdrawal schedule. (Radio Luanda, 6 July; *FBIS-AFR*, 7 July.)

The fifth meeting took place in Havana from 13 to 15 September. The meeting focused on South African violations of the accord. (ANGOP, 15 September; *FBIS-AFR*, 18 September.)

The sixth and final session of the joint commission met 27 November at Hazyview in South Africa's eastern Transvaal. Representatives from Namibia's political parties, SWAPO, and the Democratic Turnhalle Alliance (DTA) were also present. All members of the commission expressed satisfaction with the first year of the commission. (ANGOP, 28 November; *FBIS-AFR*, 29 November.)

An emergency session of the joint commission, held 8–9 April, monitored and evaluated the 1 April SWAPO incursion into Namibia (ANGOP, 17 October; *FBIS-AFR*, 18 October).

President dos Santos was active throughout Africa searching for support of Angola's peace plan. On 28 February, Zambian president Kenneth Kaunda visited Angola to discuss "possible ways of ending the policy of destabilization of southern African countries by South Africa" (Radio Luanda, 28 February; *FBIS-AFR*, 1 March). After formally introducing his seven-point peace plan in March, dos Santos sent envoys to Chad, Zaire, Central African Republic, Gabon, and Congo. President dos Santos formally presented his proposal to the Organization of African Unity's ad hoc committee for southern African heads of state 21–22 March. (Radio Luanda, 21 March; *FBIS-AFR*, 22 March.) President Mobutu of Zaire traveled to Angola on 26 April. Zaire and Angola pledged "stronger bilateral friendship, solidarity and cooperation." (Radio Luanda, 26 April; *FBIS-AFR*, 27 April.) After the May summit, President dos Santos continued to cultivate relations with President Mobutu; on 5 June, dos Santos met again with the Zairean president. So successful was dos Santos that at one point Savimbi said Mobutu could no longer be an

impartial mediator. Savimbi insisted Angola's civil war would continue "if another mediator cannot be found." (Johannesburg Television, 17 September; *FBIS-AFR*, 18 September.) President Mobutu responded by cutting off UNITA's flow of U.S. military supplies. Only the direct intervention of President Bush was able to reopen the arms pipeline through Zaire. Savimbi and Mobutu met in France to resolve their differences. (*WP*, 16 October.) The 27 November crash of an American cargo plane in southern Angola was proof of the resumption of U.S. military aid through Zaire (*NYT*, 1 December).

After the 22 June Gbadolite handshake, dos Santos intensified his diplomatic efforts (Radio Luanda, 3 July; *FBIS-AFR*, 5 July; Radio Luanda, 8 August; *FBIS-AFR*, 9 August). Angola sent Foreign Affairs Minister Pedro de Castro Van Dunem throughout southern Africa explaining the MPLA's position and seeking support for the Angolan government's interpretation of the Gbadolite Declaration (Radio Luanda, 24 June; *FBIS-AFR*, 27 June; Radio Luanda, 18 July; *FBIS-AFR*, 19 July; Radio Luanda, 19 July; *FBIS-AFR*, 20 July; ANGOP, 21 October; *FBIS-AFR*, 23 October). Throughout the rest of the year, dos Santos worked to garner support for the MPLA's peace program, especially with the mediator, President Mobutu of Zaire. On 18 November, Mobutu went to Luanda to present UNITA's plan for a cease-fire. The final communiqué made no mention of substantive progress. (London, BBC, 20 November; *FBIS-AFR*, 21 November.)

The Angolan government continued to emphasize relations with Brazil. On 27–28 January, Brazil's president Jose Sarney visited Angola. Sarney condemned "UNITA terrorist acts" and praised dos Santos as "among the great men in the world." (ANGOP, 25 January; *FBIS-AFR*, 27 January.) Angolan defense minister Pedro Maria Tonha Pedale confirmed that Angola was purchasing Brazilian military equipment and would increase those contracts. Angola was offered a $1.1 billion line of credit.

In January the European Economic Community granted Angola $72 million to "rehabilitate infrastructures, rural development, and to generate employment" (Radio Maputo, 26 January; *FBIS-AFR*, 31 January).

Angola rescheduled its debt service payments to Japan over six years. The Paris Club approved Angola's rescheduling of debts to Western creditors in July, and Angola signed the Lome IV Accord on aid and trade in December. (ANGOP, 18 December; *FBIS-AFR*, 19 December.) The government's total external debt was $4 billion, with the USSR and Brazil the two largest creditors.

Diplomatically, Angola established ties with Panama and Swaziland during the year (ANGOP, 18 February; *FBIS-AFR*, 21 February; ANGOP, 10 November; *FBIS-AFR*, 15 November).

As the year concluded, the SEF program was advancing, albeit slowly. The UNITA problem posed the major obstacle to a climate of peace and economic development in Angola. To negotiate with UNITA, the MPLA would have to forsake the one-party state, and President dos Santos may not be able to convince the MPLA militants to support such a position. UNITA, in contrast, refused to negotiate without Jonas Savimbi or to integrate the party with the MPLA. Under those circumstances, peace was still a distant hope.

W. Martin James III
Henderson State University

Benin

Population. 4,663,832
Party. Revolutionary Party of the People of Benin (Parti Révolutionnaire du Peuple du Bénin, PRPB)
Founded. 30 November 1975
Membership. 2,600 (*First-Hand Information*)
General Secretary. General (ret.) Mathieu Kérékou
Politburo. Mathieu Kérékou, Martin Dohou Azonhiho, Joseph Deguela, Gado Giriguissou, Roger Imorou Garba, Justin Guidehou, Sanni Mama Gomina, Romain Vilon Guezo, Vincent Guezodje, Idi Abdoulaye Mallam, Simon Ifede Ogouma
Central Committee. 45 members
Status. Sole and ruling party
Last Congress. Second, 18–24 November 1985
Last Election. 18 June. Running unopposed, the PRPB list of 206 candidates for the National Revolutionary Assembly received 89.6 percent of the vote. On 2 August, the newly elected assembly re-elected Mathieu Kérékou president of Benin, with 198 votes in favor, 2 against, and 6 absentees.
Auxiliary Organizations. Organization of the Revolutionary Youth of Benin (PJRB), Organization of the Revolutionary Women of Benin (OFRB), National Federation of Workers' Unions of Benin (UNSTB), Committees for the Defense of the Revolution (CDR)
Publications. *Handoria* (PRPB publication), *Ehuzu* (government-controlled daily), *Bénin-Magazine* (monthly), published by the government-sponsored National Press, Publishing and Printing Office).

Party Affairs. By far the most spectacular development of the year was the 7 December joint decision of the Central Committee, the National Revolutionary Assembly, and the cabinet to renounce Marxism-Leninism as the official ideology of the country (*Le Monde*, 8 December; *WP*, 9 December).

This radical step was the immediate result of a speech Kérékou gave at a joint meeting of the National Executive Council (cabinet), the PRPB Central Committee, and the National Revolutionary Assembly on 6 December. After noting that "the current situation in our country is marked by a profound social upheaval which was caused by the effects of the acute national crisis" (*FBIS-AFR*, 7 December), the president and party chairman rhetorically asked whether "the choice of a socialist development process based on Marxism-Leninism" conforms with "national demands" for the liberalization of the economy and promotion of the private sector, whether the principle of party control over the state apparatus allows participation of all the people, and whether the present legal, constitutional and practical frameworks of the country are adequate to face the serious challenge of the present (ibid.). The following day the three assembled bodies declared that "from now on Marxism-Leninism is no longer the official ideology of the state of Benin," that the term *comrade* is no longer compulsory, and that a "healthy political climate" is to be introduced in 1990 (*NYT*, 9 December).

Kérékou's conversion from Marxism-Leninism was seen at least by the Soviets as a demonstration of the regime's superficial commitment to that ideology. As Radio Moscow put it,

The leaders of Benin have simply changed their course with amazing ease, abandoning Marxism overnight. Apparently that happened because there were only formal signs of socialism in the country—slogans, banners, and socialist rhetoric. It is common knowledge that President Kérékou at the beginning of this year said that he would abandon Marxism if attempts to improve the situation in the country by November had failed. (*FBIS-SOV*, 13 December.)

Although there is some truth in such observations, it seems that the 7 December statement was the logical conclusion not only of Kérékou's superficial knowledge of and belief in Marxism-Leninism and of his self-proclaimed adaptability, symbolized by his choice of the chameleon as personal symbol, but also of a calculated choice among various sectors of the opposition.

Benin's colonial history has meant that the country has a larger-than-usual intelligentsia, bureaucracy, student body, and ideological polarization. Thus in 1989, in the regime's opinion, the most politically dangerous enemy and the one offering nothing toward economic crisis was the far-left Parti Communiste du Dahomey, illegally but widely supported by the regime's most vocal enemies: the students. (*NYT*, 17 December.) Between the PCD and those elements of the bureaucracy, the students, and the public employees supporting liberalization, Kérékou chose the latter, encouraged by his Western creditors and supporters. His choice was based on the economic situation and the immediate political threat its impact has represented for the regime throughout the year.

The Economy and Unrest. The stringent economic measures adopted by the regime as a result of conditions imposed by the International Monetary Fund, the World Bank, France, and the United States continued to have a serious political impact. Spearheaded by relatively privileged social groups such as students and teachers, protests against austerity not only continued but, in light of the obvious weakening of the regime, intensified during 1989.

By the beginning of January most of the country's teachers, beginning with those in the high schools of Cotonou and Porto Novo, were on strike, some under the leadership of underground PCD cadres (*FBIS-AFR*, 10 January). In a matter of hours, the high school teachers' strike spread to their students and to university students and faculty at the campuses of Cotonou and Porto Novo (ibid.). After first denying the existence of student and teachers' strikes on 10 January (*FBIS-AFR*, 13 January), the regime was forced into an admission following massive demonstrations in Cotonou, particularly at the Technical High School and the University of Benin (ibid., 18 January).

The main grievances of both students and teachers were nonpayment of scholarships and salaries. Politburo member Vincent Guezodje tried to explain that the government cannot pay both scholarships and salaries at the same time and claimed that academic freedom is just a "neocolonial concept" inasmuch as it contradicts national security. (*FBIS-AFR*, 23 January.) On 23 January the president ordered Interior Minister Edouard Zodehougan to fire on protesters without warning if they engaged in vandalism (ibid., 24 January). Neither the education employees nor the students nor the civil servants joining their strike on 26 January seemed intimidated; thus they continued their activities, with greater and greater political content. Although Kérékou decreed that salaries of state employees, unpaid for four months by January, were to be paid for two months, he also made it clear that the military will have priority in collecting back pay. (Ibid., 27 January.) Attempts to fire striking civil servants were renounced, and accusations that the strikes were foreign plots were dropped after a few students were killed in March by security forces (*FBIS-AFR*, 3 March) and after the regime withdrew from attempts to suppress the opposition.

In August, following the elections (where even official figures indicated an 80 percent increase in opposition votes), the regime tried another approach to its opposition that involved amnesty for all opponents, with the PCD cadres the main beneficiary. More than 45 PCD cadres, perhaps a majority of those active at any time and including leaders like Souleymane Baparape, a "student leader" of 1985, were released. (*FBIS-AFR*, 1 September.) In an unusual interview with *Jeune Afrique*, Kérékou stated that the 29 August amnesty included all former "bourgeois" politicians and even recognized the role of some of the past leaders in the creation of postindependence Benin (*Jeune Afrique*, 4 December).

International Views, Positions, and Activities. Despite the spectacular changes in Benin's official ideology, there was a clear pattern of continuity in regard to the country's foreign affairs. France remained and became even more significant as the main financial, economic, and ultimately political factor in Benin. Paris not only conditioned further aid to Cotonou on economic reforms but also "suggested" that Kérékou resign (*FBIS-AFR*, 3 March). Most important, Paris encouraged President Houphouet-Boigny of Ivory Coast to press Kérékou toward reforms or, alternatively, exile (ibid.). It was French and Ivorian pressures that forced Kérékou to reshuffle his cabinet in August and to appoint Robert Dossou, a nonparty technocrat, as minister of planning and Rafiatou Karimou, the first woman minister in Benin's history, as health minister (*FBIS-AFR*, 7 August). As it turned out, Dossou openly challenged the president and his regime on political prisoners, asked for wide privatization and democratization (*FBIS-AFR*, 22 September), and generally positioned himself as both a future leader and France's favorite in Benin.

By February Cuba and Benin still had close relations, as demonstrated by the enthusiastic editorial of *Ehuzu* on 2 February claiming that there were historical and cultural ties between the two countries (*FBIS-AFR*, 13 March). At the beginning of the year the Soviets also donated a few vehicles, which was made a great deal of by the Porto Novo regime (*FBIS-AFR*, 4 January).

Michael Radu
Foreign Policy Research Institute, Philadelphia

Congo

Population. 2,227,744
Party. Congolese Party of Labor (Parti Congolais du Travail, PCT)
Founded. December 1969
Membership. 9,912 (591 women) (opening speech of Sassou-Nguesso at the Fourth Congress, 27 July). Official figures claim that workers constitute 17 percent of the membership; peasants, 11 percent; low-level employees, 17 percent; middle-level employees, 31 percent; and others, 26 percent. Of the total membership, 27 percent are semi–illiterate or illiterate (ibid.).
President of the Central Committee. General Denis Sassou-Nguesso
Politburo. 13 members (compared with 10 before the Fourth Congress): Denis Sassou-Nguesso, Justin Lekoundzou Ithi-Ossetoumba, Ange Edouard Poungui, Louis Sylvain-Goma, André Obami-Itou, Jean Michel Bokamba-Yangouma,

Charles Madzous, Bernard Combo-Matsiona, Alphonse Poaty-Souchlaty, Daniel Abibi, Raymond Damasse-Ngollo, Pierre Moussa, Gabriel Oba-Apounou
Secretariat. Justin Lekoundzou Ithi-Ossetoumba, organization; André Obami-Itou, foreign affairs; Daniel Abibi, education, ideology, and political/civic training; Luis Sylvain-Goma, constitutional council; Pierre Moussa, planning and economy commission
Central Committee. 75 members (4 women)
Status. Ruling and only party
Last Congress. Fourth, 26–31 July
Last Election. 1984; the party received 95 percent of the total vote for the 153 seats in the legislature.
Auxiliary Organizations. Congolese Trade Union Confederation (CSC), claiming 115,000 members; Revolutionary Union of Congolese Women (URFC); Union of Congolese Socialist Youth–Party Youth (UJSC–JP), claiming 30,000 members.
Publication. *Etumba* (daily, circulation 5,000)

Current Leadership and Party Organization. The year's developments were dominated by two related factors: the growing economic and social crisis and internecine party fighting. The intraparty struggle was dominated by the clash between the remnants of the ideological "purists," some left over from the late 1960s, and the more technocratically oriented, less-ideological young cadres supported by the CPL chairman. These conflicts came to a head during the CPL's congress in July.

As expected, the two spokesmen of the hard ideological line within the party, Camille Bongou and Pierre Nze, were dropped from the Central Committee (both had been Politburo members as well), while a number of bureaucrats like Prime Minister Poaty-Souchlaty and two protégés of Pierre Moussa (the regime's economist), Bernard Tchibambelela and Hilaire Babassana, were promoted to it (World Bank, office memorandum, 3 August).

More radical still was the reshuffling of the Politburo, despite that body's having lesser importance than in traditional communist regimes. Camille Bongou, National Assembly president Jean Ganga Zanzou, and Hilaire Monthault, formerly an important player and mediator between the bureaucracy and the regime, were dropped. Those newly elected included the ubiquitous Pierre Moussa; the new prime minister, Poaty-Souchlaty; Combo-Matsiona; Damasse-Ngollo (the oldest survivor of all CPL purges); and technocrats like Daniel Abibi, Gabriel Oba-Apounou, and Charles Madzous. For the first time since the party's creation, civilians hold a clear majority in the Politburo (nine of thirteen members). The general outcome of the purges at the congress seems to have been the strengthening of the moderate and pragmatic elements in the party (ibid.; *FBIS-AFR*, 2 August). President Sassou-Nguesso continued to maintain his grip over the army and promoted some of his military supporters to the Central Committee, the most prominent being Colonel Pierre Oba, director of public security. It is significant that, after the hardliners at the congress resisted the economic policies proposed by the president, the armed forces sent a message demanding the purge of "ultraconservatives" and the bringing of "new blood" to the leadership (*FBIS-AFR*, 31 July).

Domestic Affairs and Relations with the Government. As during the previous few years the main problems facing the regime are economic. The collapse of oil prices, the accumulation of budget deficits over the years—mostly as a result of subsidies, inefficient state companies, and a bloated public sector—and the loss of credit worthiness abroad have forced radical modifications in economic policies. The appointment of Poaty-Souchlaty as prime minister and the growing influence of Pierre Moussa are the most important symbols of those changes.

In substantive terms, Sassou-Nguesso's opening address at the CPL congress provided both the diagnosis of and the treatment for the economic ills of the country. Graft, corruption, the state sector's expenditures, and the losses of the parastatal enterprises were cited as the causes of the economic crisis, together with decreasing prices of Congo's exports. The measures proposed included a drastic reduction in investments and the virtual abandonment of all major projects, dismantling or reorganization of state enterprises, cuts in the number and salaries of state employees, liberalization policies (i.e., encouragement of private practice) in health services and urban transportation, reduction or elimination of subsidies for essential products and the freeing of agricultural prices, and privatization or the sale of parts (including majority shares) of state enterprises, including sugar, energy, and other monopolies.

Throughout the year the regime felt some pressure from more radical elements in the CPL and from the previously privileged urban strata, against

what was seen as a trend toward watering down Congo's commitment to socialism. Thus, in a March interview, then Prime Minister Ange-Edouard Poungui denied any ideological shift and rhetorically asked: "Is it because we took privatization measures to help government enterprises that could no longer survive without state subsidies that we are allegedly guilty of deviation and suspected of a shift toward liberalism?" (*Jeune Afrique Economie*, March).

Sassou-Nguesso not only pledged a continuing commitment to socialism, which he described as "the only option to the people of Congo, who have suffered from exploitation" (*FBIS-AFR*, 31 July), but also claimed that privatization of state enterprises "did not bring this policy into question" and that it "does not automatically mean the state's disorderly and undue disengagement" (ibid.). Such protestations notwithstanding, the regime did engage in a rapid process of economic liberalization. Furthermore, it not only shifted its economic development priorities from heavy industry and the state sector toward agriculture and the private sector, but, by replacing four previous taxes on investment and private income with a value-added tax in October (*FBIS-AFR*, 6 November), it shifted the economic burden of recovery from producers to consumers.

None of these changes went over well with some of the previously privileged groups, particularly the university students. The latter's reaction to austerity measures that included a four-month delay in government payment of scholarships was a strike at Marien Ngouabi University (the country's only university). Begun on 22 February in the humanities, law, and economics departments, the strike soon spread to the rest of the university; by the beginning of March it involved 8,000 of the 10,200 students and ten of twelve departments. (*FBIS-AFR*, 7 March.) In March the regime offered two months' back pay of scholarships, but the problem remained.

The students aside, the regime had no significant opposition. An irrelevant, exile-based opposition group led by Sylvain Bamba, a former junior official of the Youlou regime of 1960–1963, now 52 years old, announced in Abidjan the formation of a Union for Congolese Democracy (UDC) 17 November (*FBIS-AFR*, 21 November), but it has no recorded following in the country.

International Views, Positions, and Activities. The foreign policy of Congo provided signs of continuity, rather than any shift of importance. Relations with Cuba and the USSR were still important; Sassou-Nguesso, in his opening speech to the congress, praised Cuba as a "country of consistent internationalism" that "Africa could never say enough thanks to." However, never during his address to the CPL did he attack any Western country by name, despite expressing support for the Sandinistas and the Salvadoran Farabundo Martí People's Liberation Forces. Furthermore, at the congress and throughout the year the president refrained from any attacks on the West. On the contrary, he credited Moscow and Washington for the elimination of East-West tensions and French president Mitterrand for France's dominant role in helping African countries.

The regime was, however, among the first to recognize the Palestine Liberation Organization's proclamation of a Palestinian state (*FBIS-AFR*, 5 April), supported the Luanda regime in its negotiations with the National Union for the Total Independence of Angola, and increased ties with Pyongyang, Tripoli, and Belgrade. In September, Sassou-Nguesso visited Libya, Yugoslavia, and Italy. During the events in China, Brazzaville remained loyal to the Beijing regime and described the June massacre against China's students as "an internal affair" of Beijing, while expressing the hope that China would resist "difficulties caused by the sanctions imposed by certain Western countries" (*FBIS-CHI*, 22 September).

Biography. *Alphonse Poaty-Souchlaty, prime minister*. Born to a peasant family in Pointe Noire in 1940, Poaty-Souchlaty, now married and the father of fourteen children, is a French-trained lawyer by profession. Minister of finance in 1976–1977, he was dismissed as a result of his insistence on monetary and budgetary discipline. He was appointed minister of trade and small business in 1985. An ordinary party member before the Fourth Congress, at that time he was promoted to membership in the CPL Politburo and the Central Committee.

Michael Radu
Foreign Policy Research Institute, Philadelphia

Ethiopia

Population. 49,762,492
Party. Workers' Party of Ethiopia (WPE)
Founded. September 1984
Membership. 70,000
General Secretary. Mengistu Haile Mariam (48, career soldier)
Politburo. 11 full members: Mengistu Haile Mariam, Fisseha Desta, Tesfaye Gebre Kidan, Berhanu Bayih, Legesse Asfaw, Addis Tedlay, Hailu Yimenu, Alenu Abebe, Shimelis Mazengia (2 positions vacant); 6 alternate members
Secretariat. 8 members: Fisseha Desta, Legesse Asfaw, Shimelis Mazengia, Fasika Sidelil, Shewandagn Belete, Wubeset Desie, Ashagre Yigletu, Emibel Ayele
Central Committee. 136 full members, 64 alternate members
Status. Ruling party
Last Congress. First, 6–10 September 1984, in Addis Ababa; 10th regular session of WPE Central Committee, 28 August
Last Election. June 1987, to parliament (National Shengo): 85 percent (13.4 million) elected 835 deputies; all are WPE members.
Auxiliary Organizations. All-Ethiopian Peasants' Association, Kebelles, All-Ethiopia Trade Union, Revolutionary Ethiopia's Women's Association, Revolutionary Ethiopia's Youth Association
Publications. *Serto Ader* (Working Man), *Meskerem* (September), *Yekatit*, *Addis Zemen*, *Ethiopian Herald*, *Negarit Gazeta*. All are WPE organs, and all articles must be approved by the WPE Censorship Committee.

In 1989 the Ethiopian government lost control of the Tigre region to northern rebels. Because of the extraordinary military defeats suffered by the government, an abortive military coup took place. As a result of increasing military and political pressure, Ethiopia and the northern rebels agreed to begin negotiations aimed at resolving their disputes.

Civil War. The loss of the Tigre region in February began in December 1988 when twenty thousand soldiers were routed when they tried to reopen land communications to Asmara, Eritrea. Three thousand soldiers were killed as the local populace gave its support to the rebels. By early 1989, Ethiopia had withdrawn all its troops from Tigre. (Voice of the Tigray Revolution, 9 March; *Africa Confidential*, 17 March.) The retreat was followed up by sustained rebel attacks leading to the virtual occupation of Gondor and Wollo regions by the Tigre People's Liberation Front (TPLF) in its efforts to overthrow the Ethiopian government; at the same time the TPLF moved into and took towns in the northern Shoa region where Addis Ababa, the capital, is located. A major rebel offensive in Eritrea led by the Eritrean People's Liberation Front (EPLF), which seeks secession, took place in March. With tens of thousands of casualties, the loss of Tigre, continuous defeats in Eritrea, and the war moving south, the Ethiopian military was humiliated and the government powerless to halt the erosion of its authority.

Coup Attempt. Senior military officers, angered at President Mengistu's approach to the secessionist wars, led an attempted coup in May. While Mengistu was on a visit to East Germany, a number of generals tried to take over the government. Mengistu rushed back to Ethiopia. Eleven generals involved in the coup were executed, including army chief Demissie Bulto; another leader of the coup, Industry Minister Fanta Belai, was arrested as were more than four hundred officers of the Defense Ministry (*Izvestiia*, 20 May). The uprising, centered in the Defense Ministry in Addis Ababa and the army headquarters in Asmara, "was a direct result of the defeats in Eritrea and Tigre" (*Insight*, 6 November); all reports indicate that the plotters botched their attempt through poor planning and coordination (*Insight*, 12 June). The coup's aftermath was the destruction of the military high command, further weakening Ethiopia in its battles in the north. In addition the abortive coup's political ramifications affected some major figures in the Ethiopian political high command. Prime Minister Fikre-Selassie Wogderess was relieved of his position due to "health reasons" (*Pravda*, 8 November), but the Voice of the Tigray Revolution (10 November) reported that he was fired for differences he had with Mengistu. He was also removed from the Politburo. In addition Teka Tulu was removed as alternate Politburo member, and Debela Dinsa was removed from the Central Committee. Both were apparently considered suspect by Mengistu. In late November other political changes were also an-

nounced. Berhanu Bayih was promoted to vice-president of the State Council, leaving his post as foreign minister, and was replaced by Tesfaye Dinka. Ashagre Yigletu of the WPE Secretariat was given the additional rank of deputy prime minister, Tekola Dejene was appointed Minister of Finance, and Yilma Kasaye was chosen as commissioner for relief and rehabilitation (Addis Ababa Domestic Service, 21 November). During this period, Lema Gutema of the WPE Central Committee was also selected as a vice-president of the State Council; Amanuel Amde Michael, a member of the WPE Politburo, had earlier defected. Replacements for the positions held by Fikre-Selassie and Amanuel Amde Michael were not announced.

Peace Talks. As a direct result of the failed coup and the string of military and political victories by the TPLF and EPLF, in June the Ethiopian parliament endorsed unconditional peace talks with the Eritrean and Tigrean rebels. Within weeks both groups had agreed to peace talks without political conditions. Soviet President Mikhail S. Gorbachev informed Mengistu that "the Soviet party and government would unrelentingly support the success of this peaceful solution" (Addis Ababa radio, 19 June). The talks began in Atlanta, Georgia, 7 September with former President Jimmy Carter mediating the talks under the auspices of the International Negotiating Network, his Atlanta-based organization. There were broad discussions between the Ethiopian government and the EPLF regarding a cease-fire. The talks resumed in Nairobi 21 November. It was agreed that seven international observers should attend comprehensive peace talks and that Carter and former Tanzanian president Julius Nyerere should cochair the talks and choose a secretariat. In early November the TPLF and Ethiopia began their negotiations in Rome.

The Soviet Union generated extensive political pressure on Ethiopia to successfully conclude the talks. In late October, First Deputy Foreign Minister Yuli M. Vorontsov arrived in Addis Ababa, reportedly to inform Mengistu that the USSR looked unfavorably at the deteriorating war policy, which thus far had bred only failure (*Pravda*, 29 October). However, in June, Mengistu maintained that any negotiations regarding secession or his removal was "unthinkable" and that because the rebel groups' demands include these points, it was difficult to assume that these talks will lead to a nonmilitary solution.

International Relations. Given Soviet military retraction around the world and Gorbachev's policy of seeking peaceful settlements of violent disputes so as to limit Soviet expenditures, Mengistu has been forced to accept reduced Soviet aid and increased Soviet pressure for negotiations. In a 1989 analysis of Ethiopia, the Soviet Academy of Sciences criticized Mengistu for being a Stalinist, failing to understand the nature of his own society, exacerbating ethnic problems, and stubbornly persisting in attempts to deal with separatism by military means (*Report on the USSR*, 13 October). The Soviets informed Ethiopia that the military treaty between the two states will not be renewed when it expires in 1991, and on 15 December all Soviet advisers in Eritrea were withdrawn (*NYT*, 27 December). As a direct result of Soviet cutbacks, Mengistu announced in September that the remaining 2,094 Cuban troops would leave Ethiopia by the end of the year. In August, Mengistu expressed his desire for closer U.S.-Ethiopian relations (Addis Ababa Domestic Service, 5 August). Talks were held between Mengistu and U.S. assistant secretary of state Herman J. Cohen in August in an effort to begin a thaw in relations between the two states. In August, Mengistu aided the United States in its search for Congressman Mickey Leland and his official party, who were reported missing on a flight to visit a refugee camp in Ethiopia. All were found dead on 13 August, but President George Bush, in a letter to Mengistu, thanked him for Ethiopia's efforts during the search.

During the year, a trade agreement was signed with South Yemen and an agricultural barter agreement was coordinated with Cuba. Palestine Liberation Organization head Yassir Arafat and Jimmy Carter visited Ethiopia. Diplomatic relations were established with Iraq. The new government that took over after Erich Honecker in East Germany announced that it would no longer supply weapons to Ethiopia or continue to train the Ethiopian security services. Relations with Romania were expected to deteriorate after the execution of General Secretary Nicolae Ceauşescu, whose relations with Ethiopia had been firm. The rise of democratic movements in Eastern Europe in 1989 will have a negative effect on Ethiopia because East Germany, Bulgaria, and Romania supplied Ethiopia with agricultural and military aid, aid that will now come to an end.

Domestic Affairs. Ethiopian agricultural policy continued to deteriorate; Soviet president Gorbachev told Mengistu that if Soviet support were to continue the USSR wanted substantial changes in Ethiopian agricultural policies (*Africa Confidential*, 17 February). In addition, East Germany, once one of Ethiopia's strongest allies in terms of agricultural support, is in political turmoil and its role as an agricultural supplier, unclear. In 1989 the U.N. listed Ethiopia as one of fifteen countries that would require exceptional food assistance, partly due to the continuing low-level famine and the presence of 850,000 refugees from Somalia and the Sudan. Coffee prices plunged from $1.53 per pound to 68¢ per pound on the international commodities exchanges. The collapse caused economic dislocation, for coffee is Ethiopia's primary export crop, accounting for 60 percent of its exports.

In February, Mesfin Tassie, the Ethiopian chargé d'affaires in Sweden, defected. In September, Ethiopia released 87 political prisoners including former envoy Berhanu Dinka and three grandsons of the late emperor Haile Selassie. In August, Amnesty International accused Ethiopia of "a high level of human rights abuses" and maintained that Ethiopia had "one of the poorest records among African states."

Ethiopia re-established diplomatic relations with Israel and thus began allowing some of the twenty thousand Ethiopian Jews still in Ethiopia to leave for Israel. For its part, Israel began shipments of small arms to the Ethiopian military (*NYT*, 5 November). Early in the year a virulent strain of meningitis reached epidemic proportions; some ten thousand people died in the Sidamo region alone. The WPE through its auxiliary organizations has, with help from the World Health Organization (WHO), begun what one WHO epidemiologist called one of the most forthright AIDS prevention programs on the African continent.

Peter Schwab
State University of New York at Purchase

Lesotho

Population. 1,711,072
Party. Communist Party of Lesotho (CPL)
Founded. 1962
Membership. No data
Chairman. R. Mataji
Secretariat. Jacob M. Kena (general secretary), John Motloheloa, Khotso Molekane

Status. Illegal (but tolerated)
Last Congress. Seventh, early 1987
Last Election. September 1985
Auxiliary Organizations. Mine Workers' Union, Writers' Association of Lesotho, Union of Lesotho Journalists, Students' Representative Council, Lesotho Peace and Solidarity Committee

Although political party activity is presently suspended in the country, the CPL is tolerated because it is not looked on as a major opposition movement. The CPL in turn sees the Lesotho ruling establishment as a spectrum running from the relatively "progressive" (anti–South African) King Moshoeshoe II to the "reactionary" (pro–South African) right-wing faction of the Military Council. The CPL's illegal party activities, assuming that it is following through on its intention of organizing cells throughout the country (see *YICA*, 1988), are balanced by its legal trade union ones (e.g., CPL general secretary Jacob M. Kena holds the same position in the legal Mine Workers' Union) (ibid.).

The authoritative, Soviet-edited *First-Hand Information* (Prague: Peace and Socialism Publishers, 1988) noted that, aside from the labor field, CPL cadres were active in "youth and solidarity organizations" (p. 129). Presumably this refers to the Students' Representative Council and the Lesotho Peace and Solidarity Committee, which are affiliated with the Prague-based International Union of Students (IUS) and the Helsinki-based World Peace Council (WPC), respectively (*This is the IUS* [Prague: IUS, 1985], p. 57; WPC, *List of Members 1983–1986* [Helsinki: WPC Information Center, n.d.], p. 112). These two international organizations are major Soviet fronts.

A third such organization, the Prague-based International Organization of Journalists, has two Lesotho affiliates: the Union of Lesotho Journalists and the Writers' Association of Lesotho (see *YICA*, 1989). Sam Moeti, still noted as the CPL's representative on the staff of Prague's *World Marxist Review* (Toronto, *WMR*, July), is probably a key figure in the former and possibly in the latter.

First-Hand Information also noted that the CPL's Seventh Congress cited the party's main tasks as improving its work among the "rural working masses" and the migrant workers employed in South Africa (p. 129). Thus the former, said to be 80 percent of the country's population (ibid.), are regarded as the party's major untapped resource; the latter are the object of continued recruiting by the

Mine Workers' Union (whose main clientele are the Basotho working in South Africa).

Wallace H. Spaulding
McLean, Virginia

Mozambique

Population. 14,275,301
Party. Front for the Liberation of Mozambique (Frente de Libertação de Moçambique; FRELIMO)
Founded. 1962
Membership. 130,000 (*WMR*, 1988)
President. Joaquim Alberto Chissano
Politburo. 12 members: Joaquim Alberto Chissano, Marcelino dos Santos, Alberto Chipande, Armando Emilio Guebuza, Feliciano Gundana, Mariano de Aráujo Matsinhe, Jacinto Soares Veloso, Mário de Graça Machungo, Rafael Maguni, Pascoal Mocumbi, Eduardo da Silva Nihia, Jorge Rebelo
Secretariat. Joaquim Chissano, Mario Machungo, Julio Carrilho, Pascoal Mocumbi, Eduardo Aaro, José Oscar Monteiro, José Luís Cabaço, Jorge Rebelo
Status. Ruling party
Last Congress. Fifth, 24–30 July 1989, in Maputo (700 delegates)
Last Election. 1986
Auxiliary Organizations. Organization of Mozambican Women (Organização da Mulher Moçambicana); Mozambique Youth Organization; Mozambique Workers' Organization; War Veterans' Association
Publications. *Notícias* (daily); *O Tempo* (weekly); *Diário de Moçambique* (daily); *Domingo* (Sunday paper); *Voz de Revolução* (Central Committee organ); *Economia* (Chamber of Commerce magazine)

The year 1989 witnessed a shift in the ruling FRELIMO party's official rhetoric in its description of itself and its programs and marked FRELIMO's Fifth Party Congress, which sanctioned discarding its Marxist-Leninist language. Although

FRELIMO reaffirmed its commitment to socialist principles, it further softened its former hard-line policies and eliminated references to Marxism in its documents. The changes conform to the economic reform that FRELIMO began in preceding years and instituted in 1987 with the economic rehabilitation program. The year also saw efforts to reach some sort of accord with the rebel movement, the Mozambique National Resistance (*Resistência Nacional Moçambicana*; RENAMO, formerly MNR), which has fought against the central government for fourteen years. RENAMO responded to the government's initiatives, but no accord had been reached by the end of the year.

These changes, a Mozambican version of *perestroika*, also brought a respite to the deteriorating economy and the starvation-racked countryside, although guerrilla war and anarchy still ravaged the rural regions. Refugees continued to flood into urban areas and neighboring countries to avoid the conflict. Industry and agriculture remained hobbled by the lack of skilled laborers, by outdated machinery, and by the lingering party apparatus and doctrine. The People's Republic of Mozambique, therefore, stayed a prisoner of its Marxist past and recent history (for background, see *YICA*, 1982, 1989).

Organization and Leadership. FRELIMO held its Fifth Party Congress during 24–30 July. The Central Committee appointed by the congress re-elected President Joaquim Chissano, who was unopposed. The Central Committee also elected the Political Bureau and the Central Committee Secretariat. The Central Committee expanded its number from 131 to 160 members (Maputo Domestic Service, 31 July; *FBIS*, 1 August) and approved a set of sweeping economic and social directives for development in the next five years. Stripping away from its official platform most references to the Marxist-Leninist doctrine, the congress documents proposed "gradual socialism" of the rural areas by supporting voluntary cooperatives, not forced collectivizations as in past years. Although the revised policy retains FRELIMO's leading role in the state, the new program no longer calls for the state to be "a revolutionary democratic dictatorship of workers," as it did in the Fourth Congress in 1983. In fact, FRELIMO now refers to itself as the "vanguard of the worker-peasant alliance" instead of focusing exclusively on workers (William Claiborne, "Mozambique Shifts From Marxism," *WP*, 29 July).

The congress went on to redefine agriculture as the dynamic foundation of development and industry. Along with giving agriculture greater emphasis, the new direction put a priority on family farming and cooperatives to increase food production. These decisions continued the declining reliance on state farmers of the past few years.

FRELIMO maintained its primacy in the health and housing sector, but opened the way for participation of private schools in education, a departure from established practice (Maputo Domestic Service, 30 July; *FBIS*, 31 July).

Plans to increase membership and to lessen reliance on the Marxist-Leninist doctrine were part of the effort to end the guerrilla war and implement President Chissano's call for "a national consensus to normalize society." Chissano's concept called for "a party of all the people"; toward that end the Central Committee recommended that the property owners and businesspeople who had previously been excluded from party membership be permitted to join to broaden the base of FRELIMO (United Kingdom, *Guardian*, 25 July). One report noted that full and candidate members of the party increased from 110,323 at the time of the Fourth Congress in 1983 to 201,440. Party branches increased from 4,244 to 8,174, or 93 percent (South Africa, *New Nation*, 28 July).

The congress also endorsed Chissano's plans to end the war with RENAMO. Early in July he announced that a government delegation and church leaders were prepared to meet with RENAMO, which represented a turnaround in FRELIMO's policy. Instead of just offering amnesty to the rebels, FRELIMO reached out to seek a settlement of the war. Negotiations continued to the end of the year but no settlement was reached.

Mass Organizations. The People's Republic of Mozambique followed other communist states in creating and using a number of mass organizations to strengthen the party's hold on the population. One of the strongest of these organizations is the Organization of Mozambican Women. FRELIMO also established the Mozambique Youth Organization and the Mozambique Workers' Organization. In 1988 the party set up the War Veterans' Association. The war and political changes have undercut the smooth functioning of these organizations in the last several years.

The People's Forces for the Liberation of Mozambique. (FPLM). Mozambique's vicious guerrilla war has ravaged the country for a decade and a half. According to FRELIMO statistics this war has killed between 600,000 and 700,000 Mozambicans, displaced a further 1.6 million refugees in neighboring countries, and destroyed or closed 2,599 primary schools, 822 health clinics, and 44 factories (Christopher Wren, "Finally, Mozambique Sees a Way to Halt Its Own Devastation," *NYT*, 6 August). During the year RENAMO managed to cut the electricity supply to the capital on more than one occasion.

Although the central government continued to blame RENAMO for the countryside destruction, outside observers also held FRELIMO guilty, as well as renegade elements of the FPLM and roving bands. An anonymous Soviet expert stated that RENAMO was only part of the problem because many others took up arms against the government's policies. He argued that these actions led to a "general social mutiny" (E.W. Wayne, "US Seeks End of Mozambique War," *CSM*, 12 July).

Military officials announced that there are eleven thousand party members in the Mozambican army, navy, and air force (Maputo Domestic Service, 18 May; *FBIS*, 8 June). Estimates of the Mozambican army place its numbers at about 30,000.

RENAMO's first national congress, at Gorongosa in central Mozambique during 5–9 June, decided to respond positively to FRELIMO's peace initiatives. RENAMO, accepting the government's conditions for talks, stated a willingness to renounce violence and announced an agreement to work out differences within a constitutional framework. Afonso Dhlakama, RENAMO's head, renounced personal ambitions and the overthrow of the FRELIMO government. The congress also dropped demands for immediate free elections and the withdrawal of all foreign forces that support the central government, the main group of which came from Zimbabwe's ten thousand–man force. (*Africa Confidential* 30, no. 14 [7 July].) But at year's end the fighting still had not stopped.

At the RENAMO congress, Dhlakama was reelected president and confirmed the abolition of the general secretary's post. Many posts were given to members of the internal wing of the movement in what was interpreted as an effort to better control the activities of the external faction as a prelude to negotiations with FRELIMO and other governments. The Department of External Affairs went to Raul Manuel Domingos, who had been chief of staff. This position had been formerly occupied by Artur Janeiro da Fonseca, based in West Germany. Faustino Adriano replaced Domingos as commander of the rebel forces (*Indian Ocean Newsletter*, 24 June; *FBIS*, 4 August).

In an interview with the Portuguese press, Dhlakama reacted to charges that RENAMO lacked a political program and said that RENAMO opposed "communist villages, communist cooperatives." He added that the rebel movement rejected a "regime with only one party." RENAMO, according to Dhlakama, wanted "the judiciary to be independent from the political power, and we want respect for human rights" (*O Seculo*, 9 June; *FBIS*, 3 August). In the same interview, the RENAMO leader declared that its movement has 25,000 men fighting in the ten Mozambican provinces and accused FRELIMO of bombing villages to empty the countryside of inhabitants and isolate the rebels from the population (ibid.).

Domestic Affairs. The dramatic changes in politics were unmatched in the economy, although the economic improvement, which started in 1988, continued in 1989. The most striking example of this trend was in the Indian Ocean port city of Beira, where the rehabilitation of the facilities proceeded during the year, despite guerrilla attacks on the railway line linking the seacoast town with the interior. One source reported that Beira expected to handle 2.5 million tons of goods this year—a twofold increase over the tonnage shipped in the early 1980s. Beira reportedly transported about 20 percent of Zimbabwe's exports (Jane Perlez, "Road to Prosperity Has a Special Hazard: Rebels," *NYT*, 21 February).

The restructuring of the economy away from central planning toward one based on market forces achieved some of its goals. The capital city of Maputo, for example, witnessed a commercial revival, dampening the black market trade for cigarettes, alcohol, and the necessities of life. The government reduced the size of the public service sector by laying off a reported 14 percent of its employees. It also devalued the national currency, the metical, over the year in response to pressure from the World Bank and the International Monetary Fund.

But the changes have their downside. Without food subsidies urban dwellers paid much more for food, and there were reports of underfed children in the city ("Mozambique Finds That Market Forces Galvanize Its Capital," *WSJ*, 10 March). Begun in 1987, the Economic Rehabilitation Program (PRE, its Portuguese acronym) caused price hikes in basic commodities with the devaluation of the currency.

The increased crop prices have resulted in more foodstuffs, but the full impact of the market-oriented policy has been retarded due to the rural strife (Antonio Gumende, "Making Ends Meet in Maputo," *South African Economist*, April). In the first strike since independence, students at Eduardo Mondlane University blamed the decline in living standards for their protest in May. Concessions were made to the students in the form of better food.

Among other domestic activities was the approval by the People's Assembly, which considers itself a parliament, of a draft law repealing flogging. Under the chairmanship of Marcelino dos Santos, the People's Assembly also approved a social security system, the main provision of which allows pensioners to undertake paid work without fear of losing their pension rights (Maputo Domestic Service, 19 September; *FBIS*, 22 September).

Conditions within the countryside remained perilous. Central Mozambique, especially Zambezia province, faced famine brought on by the ongoing rural insurgency. Crops and transport systems were destroyed. In Niassa province the government shipped corn by air rather than use unsecured roads.

International Affairs. The dramatic events in Central Europe during the fall could hamper FRELIMO's foreign-assisted development plans, for the collapse of East European communist regimes means the loss of allies to Marxist Mozambique. For example, in May President Chissano received promises from Romania to develop bilateral trade and cooperation in the fields of agriculture, industry, transportation, and mining; Romania also agreed to establish joint ventures with Mozambique (Maputo Domestic Service, 24 May; *FBIS*, 25 May). The downfall of the Ceauşescu government in December and the turmoil in Romania, however, end the likelihood of any aid from that country in the immediate future. Chissano received similar promises in May from the Honecker government in East Germany, which also collapsed in late 1989 (ADN, 24 May; *FBIS*, 25 May). The unchallenged communist regime in Cuba made good its promise to accept Mozambican secondary students, bringing the total for the year to more than three thousand (Maputo Domestic Service, 25 March; *FBIS*, 28 March).

In midyear the Soviet Union announced that it planned on withdrawing nearly all of its military advisers by the end of 1990. If this plan is implemented, it would coincide with the expiration of the current five-year military cooperation agreement between the two countries. The Soviets gave no figures on the number of advisers in the southeast African country, but diplomatic and Mozambican Defense Ministry sources estimated that the Soviet Union has anywhere from seven hundred to fifteen hundred military experts in Mozambique. Despite the withdrawal pledge, Moscow plans on continuing to send military equipment to the Maputo government in the form of helicopters, trucks, and communications equipment rather than heavy weapons (Karl Maier, "Soviet Military Advisers to Leave Mozambique," *WP*, 3 June).

Mozambique continued to receive financial support from foreign countries and international organizations. The African Development Bank, for example, agreed to provide a loan of $80 million to finance three development projects—the Beira transport corridor, the Massambissa sugar refinery, and primary school teachers' training colleges (Maputo Domestic Service, 4 June; *FBIS*, 5 June).

West Germany canceled Mozambique's debt of $83 million. In April the United States announced that it would provide Mozambique with $100 million in food and economic assistance (*Indian Ocean News*, 22 April). This and past U.S. aid improved relations with Mozambique, but did not guarantee Washington a favorable vote from Maputo in U.N. decisions. One U.S. newspaper carried a story that Mozambique voted in agreement with the United States during U.N. votes in only 5 percent of the cases, despite $38 million from Washington in 1987, but voted 100 percent with the USSR ("How Top U.S. Aid Recipients Voted at UN," *WSJ*, 1 June).

Portugal and Mozambique signed fourteen protocols and agreements for aid programs to Maputo. One agreement reschedules for the second time Mozambique's debt to Portugal, another provides $9 million for the operation of Portuguese companies in Mozambique, and still others cover fisheries and television stations. In another agreement, Lisbon will provide additional military assistance and training to the FPLM (Maputo Domestic Service, 30 September; *FBIS*, 5 October).

The British have been training Mozambican troops in neighboring Zimbabwe, and Prime Minister Margaret Thatcher dispatched the Royal Engineers to clear mines from the track of the Nacala railway. That decision (to send the engineers into Mozambique) was made after Prime Minister Thatcher met with Mozambican refugees in Malawi (United Kingdom, *Guardian*, 1 April).

Relations with the Republic of South Africa remained problematic. On the one hand Maputo accused South Africa of continuing its policy of supporting RENAMO, and on the other FRELIMO received South African assistance. In June a FRELIMO periodical, *Boletim da Celula*, stated that the South African military intelligence directorate maintained support to RENAMO and argued that the Conservative party and military were behind this aid and working within the South African establishment (Dakar, *PANA*, 13 June; *FBIS*, 14 June).

Mozambique did, however, welcome South African investment and business activity within its borders. For example, during the year, South African businesses reopened a brewery and a match factory and increased tourism. Pretoria renewed a labor agreement with Mozambique to recruit migrant workers and spent millions of South African rand to upgrade Maputo's port, allowing for greater South African use and permitting Mozambique to earn much-needed foreign exchange (*FBIS*, 5 May). On 7 July the first phase of a preferential trade agreement between the two countries went into effect, thus eliminating surcharges on specific Mozambican goods crossing the border (South Africa, *News Review*, 13 July).

Publications. FRELIMO controls the media, using a number of print publications as well as broadcasts to put forth its message. It has the daily paper, *Notícias*; the *Diário de Moçambique* in Beira; the Sunday paper, *Domingo*; and a national magazine, *O Tempo* (for additional background, see *YICA*, 1982). *Voz da Revolução* deals with Marxist theory and FRELIMO policies. The party created *Economia* in 1987 under the direction of the Chamber of Commerce in its move toward economic liberalization.

Thomas H. Henriksen
Hoover Institution

Réunion

Population. 571,600
Party. Réunion Communist Party (Parti communiste réunionnais, PCR)
Founded. 1959
Membership. 7,000–10,000 claimed; 2,000 estimated.
General Secretary. Paul Vergès
Politburo. 12 members: Julien Ramin; remaining members unknown.
Secretariat. 6 members: Paul Vergès, Elie Hoarau, Jean-Baptiste Ponama, Lucet Langenier; remaining members unknown.
Central Committee: 32 members: Bruny Payet, Roger Hoarau, Daniel Lallemand, Hippolite Piot, Ary Yee Chong Tchi-Kan, Alexis Pota; remaining members unknown.
Status. Legal
Last Congress. Fifth, 12–14 July 1980 in Le Port
Last Election. 17 April, 24 April 1988, president of the French Republic; 5 May, 12 May 1988, French National Assembly, 2 of 5 seats, 35 percent of popular vote; 25 September, 2 October 1988, Réunion General Council, 9 seats of 44, 27.2 percent of popular vote; 11 March, 18 March, Réunion municipal elections
Auxiliary Organizations. Anticolonialist Front for Réunion Autonomy, Réunion Front of Autonomous Youth, Réunion Peace Committee, Réunion General Confederation of Workers (CGTR), Committee for the Rally of Réunionese Unemployed (CORC), Committee for the Rally of Réunionese Youth (CORJ), Réunion Union of Women (UFR), Réunion General Union of Workers in France (UGTRF), Réunion General Confederation of Planters and Cattlemen (CGPER)
Publications. *Témoignages* (daily), Elie Hoarau, chief editor; *Travailleur Réunionnais* (semimonthly), published by CGTR; *Combat Réunionnais*, published by UGTRF.

In 1989 social equality with metropolitan France and economic development continued to be the main concerns of the PCR. PCR general secretary Vergès marked the new year with a policy speech emphasizing the need for Réunion to assert its cultural identity whereas at the same time achieving a level of equality between the Réunionese and the French. In this connection, 1989 found the PCR dedicating its energies to redressing the lag between the guaranteed minimum incomes (*revenu minimum d'insertion*) of France and Réunion. Further challenges resulting especially from a united European market also await Réunion, which, according to Vergès, by the year 2000 risks facing a housing shortage and a doubling of the number of unemployed (*Témoignages*, 2 January). To the extent that the island as a French overseas department is considered European, the PCR claims that it should benefit from the rights and privileges guaranteed countries of the continent. The success of Programme d'Options Spécifiques à l'Eloignement et à l'Insularité des D.O.M. (Program of Options Specific to the Remoteness and Insularity of Overseas Departments), which would in effect create a doubling of European funds for overseas departments, is therefore essential to the PCR project; it would grant Réunion an integral partnership in the European Economic Community and promote the recognition of its regional realities by the continental powers. The European attempt to reform the *octroi de mer*, a kind of tax that guarantees local prices, also concerned a PCR opposed to the idea of substituting a European tutelage for a French one (ibid., 25–26 March). A 77 percent abstention rate in Réunion from the June European elections was claimed by the PCR as approval of their position toward Europe and of their policies for development and equality (ibid., 24–25 June). At year's end the signing of an agreement to bring into line the compensation of Réunionese and French unemployed was hailed as a PCR advance (ibid., 27 December).

In the wake of Hurricane Firinga, the PCR found grounds for further claims of abandonment by France. With three dead, six thousand evacuated, hundreds of homes destroyed, crops and roads devastated in what amounted to more than one billion francs worth of damages and the declaration of Réunion as a disaster area, the PCR, in a maneuver tied to the upcoming municipal elections, boasted of its role in hastening emergency aid from metropolitan France and publicized in *Témoignages* messages in the wake of the 1987 Hurricane Clotilda addressed to Jacques Chirac by Paul Vergès and Elie Hoarau, then deputies to Parliament, that promoted the establishment of an institute to study, predict, and prepare for hurricanes in Réunion.

The death in late 1988 of Laurent Vergès, son of the general secretary and PCR deputy to the Euro-pean Parliament, sent shock waves through the party that intensified in 1989. A disagreement between Laurent's replacement in Europe, Alexis Pota, director of the communist division in Saint-Paul, and his father, Paul, who had asked Pota to resign the European post (*Europa World Yearbook*, vol. 1, p. 1062), escalated into a full-scale opposition between the two in the March municipal elections. Amid allegations of electoral fraud and politically motivated violence, second-round balloting presented a strange admixture of running mates and opponents, with Vergès allied with the Rassemblement pour la République's Christophe Kichenin and Pota allied with the incumbent anticommunist mayor, Cassam Moussa. These odd combinations resulted in a loss for Vergès, who had left his post as mayor of Le Port in order to run in Saint-Paul, and the dismissal of Kichenin and Pota from their respective parties. Elsewhere, PCR incumbent mayor Mario Hoarau lost his seat in Saint-Leu and a close race in Sainte-Rose also ended with a PCR loss. Although not victorious, the PCR claimed it had made advances in Saint-Paul and maintained its level of support in Saint-André. There were some PCR victories: Lucet Langenier in Saint-Suzanne, Pierre Vergès (another of Paul's sons) in Le Port, Claude Hoarau in Saint-Louis, Elie Hoarau in Sainte-Pierre, and Christophe Payet in Petite-Ile.

In a year that saw the PCR turn 30; its major mouthpiece, *Témoignages*, 45; and the French revolution, two hundred, Réunion was visited by such noteworthies as French prime minister Michel Rocard and Pope John Paul II (both in May). March, a month of municipal elections, also inaugurated a period of union activity that brought strikes among construction workers, dockers, and store clerks that would last into the summer (*FBIS-AFR*, 14 July). The PCR did not greet the French bicentennial with enthusiasm. The Saint-André section of the party boycotted all bicentennial activities, and the 13 July edition of *Témoignages* claimed that the anniversary of the storming of the Bastille was, in Réunion, a "normal day of slavery" because the Réunionese, in their view, still await *liberté, égalité, et fraternité*.

Biography. *Emilien Apalama*, one of the pioneers of syndicalism in Réunion and general councilor from Grands-Bois in 1945, died 9 February at the age of 83. In 1936 he helped to create the Syndicat d'Ouvriers d'Usine (Factory Workers' Union) and was elected to the position of general councillor in 1945 under the rubric of the Comité

Réunionnais d'Action Démocrate et Sociale (Réunion Committee for Democratic and Social Action). (*Témoignages*, 10 February.)

Gerald Seaman
Stanford, California

Senegal

Population. 7,506,197
Party. Independence and Labor Party (Parti de l'indépendance du travail, PIT)
Founded. 1957
Membership. No data
General Secretary. Amath Dansoko
Politburo. 14 members: Amath Dansoko, Samba Dioulde Thiam, Maguette Thiam, Mady Danfaka, Sadio Camara, Seydou Ndongo, Semou Pathe Gueye, Makhtar Mbaye, Bouma Gaye, Mohamed Laye (names of other 4 not known)
Secretariat. 7 members: Amath Dansoko, Semou Pathe Gueye, Maguette Thiam, Samba Dioulde Thiam, Mady Danfaka, Makhtar Mbaye (replacement of Seydou Cissoko not yet named)
Central Committee. 55 members (Semou Pathe Gueye, secretary)
Status. Legal
Last Congress. Second, 28 September–2 October 1984, in Dakar
Last Election. 1988, 0.84 percent, no seats
Auxiliary Organization. Women's Democratic Union
Publications. *Daan Doole*, *Gestu*

Senegal's communist parties continued to struggle throughout 1989 with the legacy of their crushing defeat in the February 1988 national elections (they failed to obtain a single seat in the 120-member National Assembly) and with their own multiple and increasing divisions. During the year, the two major Marxist parties—the PIT and the Democratic League/Movement for the Party of Labor (LD/MPT)—repeatedly denounced the conduct of the 1988 elections and demanded new elections and sweeping political reforms (including greater opposition access to the media, protections for secret

balloting and against electoral fraud, and a lowering of the voting age to eighteen). In this stance they were joined by the liberal Senegalese Democratic Party (PDS), their dominant partner in the opposition Sopi ("change") alliance. The return in March (after seven months abroad) of the PDS leader Abdoulaye Wade, whose 1988 presidential candidacy was supported by both the PIT and the LD/MPT, led to an acceleration of opposition activity and ultimately a split in the opposition alliance when, in a sharp turnabout, the PIT embarked upon a path of cooperation with the ruling Socialist Party (PS).

Seeking to establish a national consensus to deal with the country's deep economic and social crisis, during which thousands of workers were laid off and bloated state structures were forced to retrench, President Abdou Diouf proposed a reform of the electoral code in his 3 April speech on the eve of Independence Day. These reforms were widely rejected by the various opposition party leaders, however, as inadequate and insincere. Independence Day celebrations were accompanied by demonstrations in which vehicles were set afire and 150 people were arrested. The demonstrators were praised by the three party leaders in the liberal-communist alliance—Wade and Dansoko of the PIT and Abdoulaye Bathily, general secretary of the LD/MPT, who declared that "violence has become the only resort" (AFP, 5 April; *FBIS-AFR*, 12 April).

In fact, the situation between government and opposition remained generally free of violence, but the opposition parties criticized President Diouf and his PS in strident tones. Appearing jointly on Independence Day, Wade, Dansoko, and Bathily denounced the government as authoritarian and vowed to "continue their joint battle to win back the victory snatched from them." They also warned of a second "wasted school year" because of the government's inability to settle the schoolteachers' strike (*FBIS-AFR*, 23 June). Bathily, through his frequent public comments and his writings and interviews in *Fagaru*, the LD/MPT monthly, throughout the year assertively criticized the ruling party for its corruption, its "anti-democratic nature," and its neo-colonial character, as evidenced by its willingness to implement economic liberalization policies dictated by the International Monetary Fund (IMF) and the World Bank and by its domination by the French-born minister of state for the presidency, Jean Collin (*Fagaru*, January; *FBIS-AFR*, 15 March). (Collin is regarded by many as the most powerful figure in the ruling party and, partly because of his background as a French colonial official in preindependence Senegal, has become a particular target of the left opposition.)

Although Bathily called for a broad-based national unity government excluding the ruling PS, Dansoko, the PIT's leader, from the very beginning of the year signaled his willingness to work with the PS government to find solutions to the country's economic and political crisis. In a news conference with Dansoko on 31 January, PIT Central Committee secretary Semou Pathe Gueye called for a "national union government" and hinted at the PIT's willingness to join if the government changed its policies (*Sud Hebo*, 2 February; *FBIS-AFR*, 14 April). The pretext for a rapprochement emerged in April when violence erupted along Senegal's border with Mauritania in a dispute between Mauritanian pastoralists and Senegalese farmers over rights to land along the Senegal River. The dispute degenerated into ethnic rioting that claimed the lives of more than two hundred Senegalese nationals in Mauritania and Moors in Senegal, followed by massive repatriations and a rupture in diplomatic relations.

In early May a dialogue began between the PS and the PIT that continued through June and July. Dansoko, the PIT leader, had several meetings with PS leaders, including President Diouf, and declared his party in full support of the government's stance on the Mauritanian crisis. At the PS national convention in July, President Diouf pointedly praised the PIT for its "nationalistic stance" while implicitly condemning the PDS for its futile thirst for power. Following the meetings of the PIT and PS leaders, youth wings of the two parties held several rounds of talks that were widely commented on by state radio and television (Amadou M. Sireye, "Herculean Task," *West Africa*, 18–24 September).

The PIT dialogue with and backing for the PS brought a bitter reaction from its two partners, the PDS and the LD/MPT, that effectively ruptured their "alliance of three." On 13 June, the latter two parties met and adopted a joint communiqué that in effect accused the PIT of betraying the alliance and going over to the PS. In late June, LD/MPT leader Bathily denounced the PIT for its unilateral initiative, declaring, "because the PIT has sovereignly decided to cooperate with the PS from top to bottom, and since the alliance is based on struggle against the PS and its government, . . . our party sees no reason to continue the alliance of three." In a sign of the personal bitterness underlying the break, Bathily accused the PIT of tarnishing the opposition's image and, responding to PIT secretary Se-

mou Pathe Gueye's suggestion that the LD/MPT had no specific proposals, stated that Gueye was out of touch "since he lives abroad most of the time." Conceding that the split constituted a hard blow for opposition forces, Bathily vowed that his party and the PDS would stick with their struggle against the PS government and would continue their call for "new, free, and democratic elections based on a new [electoral] code." (*Sud Hebdo*, 29 June; *FBIS-AFR*, 20 September.) At the same time, Dansoko denied rumors that he had received 25 million francs, a house, and a car for talking to Abdou Diouf and the PS (*Sub Hebdo*, 29 June; *FBIS-AFR*, 27 September).

The PIT vigorously defended its accommodation with the ruling party. In an interview in early June, Dansoko said pointedly, "We need a political solution to the crisis, and in all languages that spells negotiations" (*Wal Fadjri*, 2 June; *FBIS-AFR*, 8 August). In a public meeting in Dakar, Dansoko cited the conflict with Mauritania, structural adjustments, strikes in the educational system, and the ongoing political dispute as problems that could lead the country to civil war. "An exceptional situation" that requires a government of national union including the PS, "history has proven that solutions involving exclusions are harmful," he said, and added that the PS had realized its mistake in thinking it could solve all the country's problems by itself. PIT leaders toured the country explaining their new positions and defending themselves against what they called the "denunciation campaign" of their former partners (*Wal Fadjri*, 14 July; *FBIS-AFR*, 27 September). This campaign continued throughout the year, however, with the LD/MPT's September issue of *Fagaru* accusing the PIT of forgetting all its past convictions and accepting "the PS and its power as our country's inescapable fate" (*Fagaru*, September; *FBIS-AFR*, 21 November).

The PS did little to encourage opposition accommodation, however, pushing an electoral law that opposition leaders condemned as regressive and then delaying until 1990 local government elections that were supposed to have been held by 25 November. The new electoral law failed to respond to opposition demands that electoral oversight be transferred from the public service and Supreme Court to a new, independent national electoral commission, that the secret ballot be made obligatory, and that opposition parties be given wider access to the media. In fact, Bathily argued, the new proposed law was worse in that it shortened the electoral campaign from three weeks to two and eliminated the national system of proportional representation, which benefits small parties and has to date been used to fill half the seats in the National Assembly. Along with other opposition leaders, Bathily also denounced the postponement of elections for municipal and rural executives and councils, alleging that the PS acted out of its increasing weakness (Kaye Whiteman, "An Opposition Voice," *West Africa*, 13–19 November).

Although remaining on the fringes of political debate, the minor parties, grouped in a "cadre of eight," took every opportunity to denounce the PS and demand political reform. Some, however, also criticized the strategy of the Sopi alliance. Mamadou Dia, head of the Movement for Socialism and Democracy (MSD)—created by the merger of the People's Democratic Movement (MDP) and the Communist Workers League (LCT)—inveighed at a 25 March rally against "the treason" of the PDC, PIT, and LD/MPT for proposing a national union government. Like other speakers at the rally sponsored by the "cadre of eight" parties, he attacked the PS government for massive layoffs and plant closings and for the continuing crisis in the school system. Landing Savane, general secretary of the And-Jef/Revolutionary Movement for the New Democracy (AJ/MRDN), denounced the useless "hole plugging" of economic policies proposed by the IMF and the World Bank, tracing the cause of economic imbalance to "the corruption of the ruling class, which is actively supported by imperialistic structures." Savane proposed that economic stabilization be achieved instead "through substantial economies in luxury item consumption, adequate taxation, and the development of national production" and warned that if the crisis were not solved sooner or later there would be a military coup. The rally revealed that the "cadre of eight" had shrunk to a grouping of six parties—including the African Independence Party (PAI), the People's Liberation Party (PLP), the (Trotskyist) Socialist Workers' Organization (OST), and the People's National Front (FNP) (*Sud Hebdo*, 30 March; *FBIS-AFR*, 26 May).

As one Senegalese newspaper observed, however, "only a few of the sixteen parties contribute any specific content to the political battle" in Senegal. "It is quite obvious that some parties have dried up. Except for the leader it is sometimes impossible to find anyone or anything behind the party's name."

The article implied that the PAI and OST fall into this category and quoted the OST general secretary, Amadou Guiro, as conceding that the party had little money, was unable to stage public demonstrations on its own, and had chosen to keep some of its members underground because it "has no illusions about bourgeois democracy" (*Wal Fadjri*, 30 June; *FBIS-AFR*, 20 September).

Foreign Affairs. Signaling both its own increasing international pragmatism and the marginal standing of Senegal's communist parties, the Communist Party of the Soviet Union (CPSU) moved during the year to establish contacts with the ruling SP of Senegal. Two CPSU representatives, Aleksey Vassiliev, assistant director of the African Institute of the USSR Academy of Sciences, and Sergei Nenashev, adviser to the International Department of the CPSU Central Committee, visited Senegal in February to discuss possibilities for future bilateral collaboration with a delegation of PS leaders headed by Djibo Ka, PS secretary of international relations. "New political thought" dictated an international emphasis on moderation and the political resolution of conflicts, said the two representatives of the CPSU, which had to date concentrated on building "relations of brotherly cooperation" with the PIT and LD/MPT (*Wal Fadjri*, 13 January; *Le Soleil*, 8 February; *FBIS-AFR*, 29, 31 March). In March officials of the Soviet textile and light industry union were hosted by Senegalese trade union leaders in a tour of the country's light industries.

Also in March, President Diouf made a three-day state visit to Libya at the invitation of Colonel Moammar Khadafy aimed at intensifying bilateral cooperation. On 14 March the two leaders signed an agreement establishing a joint high commission to foster cooperation "in all fields, particularly the political, social, economic, scientific, and cultural areas." Their joint statement reaffirmed the two countries' support for the liberation movement in South Africa, for the struggle of the Palestinian people for an independent state, and for the Islamic Conference Organization, whose 1990 summit meeting will be held in Senegal (*FBIS*, 27 June). More tangible assistance came from Japan, which extended a 2.5-billion-yen grant to Senegal to help relieve its economic difficulties (KYODO, 14 March; *FBIS-AFR*, 16 March).

Larry Diamond
Hoover Institution

South Africa

Population. 38,509,312
Party. South African Communist Party (SACP)
Founded. 1921
Membership. No data
Chairman. Dan Tloome (70, teacher)
General Secretary. Joe Slovo (63, barrister)
Politburo. Chris Hani, chief of staff of the military wing; Ray Simons (pen name, R. S. Nyameko), labor theoretician; Mac Maharaj, political strategist, directs recruitment inside South Africa; Thabo Mbeki, information chief; John Nkadimeng, general secretary of SACTU, the banned labor union; all elected in 1984 at Moscow congress (*Africa Confidential*, 26 August, vol. 29, no. 17).
Leading Organs. Composition unknown
Status. Proscribed
Last Congress. Seventh, June
Last Election. N/a
Auxiliary Organizations. None
Publications. *African Communist* (quarterly, published abroad); *Umsebenzi* (published clandestinely in South Africa).

The SACP, the continent's oldest Marxist-Leninist party, operates underground in South Africa and in exile in Africa and Europe, continuing its longtime intimate alliance with the also banned and exiled African National Congress (ANC), the continent's oldest African nationalist organization and South Africa's major black opposition body.

Established in Cape Town in 1921 as the Communist Party of South Africa—the country's first political party open to all races—the party maintained a legal, but frequently harassed, existence. Ill-prepared for clandestine activity, it dissolved itself in June 1950 in the face of the threat of banning under the impending Suppression of Communists Act. Its multiracial membership of several thousand established a record of activism within the ANC, emerging black trade unions, and black and white electoral politics that continued after the dissolution of the party. In 1953 prominent members of the disbanded party reversed the 1950 decision, establishing the SACP as the underground successor that

revealed its existence only during the post-Sharpeville state of emergency in 1960 when the ANC was also proscribed and forced underground.

Like the Communist Party of South Africa, the ANC was ill-prepared for illegality and ruthless government persecution, having engaged in only open, legal, and nonviolent protest since its establishment in 1912. Drawn together by their shared experiences of antiapartheid campaigns of the 1950s and the necessity of survival, leaders of the ANC and the SACP (including Nelson Mandela and Joe Slovo, the present general secretary of the SACP) joined in 1961 to create Umkhonto we Sizwe, the military wing of the ANC, organized to conduct sabotage and to prepare guerrillas for eventual armed struggle. The shift from the militant nonviolence of the 1950s to the use of violence was a radical departure for both organizations. Similarly, the SACP and the ANC were forced to shift primary activity out of the country by the success of the South African government in destroying their nascent underground structures in the early 1960s, symbolized by the capture and subsequent conviction of key leaders at Rivonia.

Lengthy association in exile tightened the alliance between the ANC and the SACP; in the wake of the resurgence of black opposition in the 1970s and the infusion of younger recruits in the wake of the Soweto uprising of 1976, both bodies and Umkhonto were able to reconstruct their underground structures within the country. Starting in the late 1970s the government under President Pieter W. Botha introduced cautious reforms—giving blacks limited new opportunities for economic advancement and worker organization and desegregating some public facilities—but continued to exclude Africans from participation in national politics. Black trade unions grew explosively in the 1980s as did unprecedented mass opposition activity anchored in locally based grass roots organizations and expressed in school boycotts, rent strikes, stay-at-homes, and well-supported demonstrations against government authority even in the face of bans on political meetings. The new surge of aboveground black politicization and militancy was given focus by the United Democratic Front (UDF), formed in 1983, and the Congress of South African Trade Unions (COSATU), established in 1985 with a membership of some half million black workers. The underground presence of the ANC and the SACP was reflected in an upsurge of Umkhonto sabotage and armed attacks. Since mid-1985 the government has sought to contain the challenge to its authority with a draconian state of emergency under which thousands of activists were arrested and hundreds more were wounded and killed. Only since President Botha's stroke on 18 January and the subsequent struggle for power within the ruling National party, concluded by the election of President F. W. de Klerk on 14 September, has government repression relaxed. As the Botha era came to an end, the *African Communist* commented that

> for 95 per cent of the South African population there has been no "reform" under President Botha. On the contrary, their life-style has deteriorated. The economy is in tatters, unemployment is at record levels and inflation soars, leading to a sizable reduction in income per head of population. Strike and conflict continue—in the mines and factories, in the schools and universities, on the borders. The increased activity by Umkhonto we Sizwe is a direct consequence of the deep freeze into which normal political activity has been placed by the regime...with the regime ever more shaky in its grasp of power, paralyzed by uncertainties over all its policies, on the defensive, ideologically bankrupt—this is the time for mounting a new offensive against the apartheid edifice. Given the right combination of circumstances, it can be brought to the ground. (*African Communist*, no. 117.)

Organization and Leadership. In June at a location not disclosed in the party press, but reported to be Havana by a nonparty source (*Africa Confidential*, 12 January 1990), the SACP held its Seventh Congress just over four years after the Sixth Congress of late 1984, also held at a location not identified by the party, but reported to have been Moscow (ibid.). Brief published reports did not disclose the number or names of the delegates with the exception of Chairman Dan Tloome and General Secretary Joe Slovo, who were re-elected to their posts. Delegates elected by party units and regional committees including "leading activists from the ANC, SACTU [South African Congress of Trade Unions], and our people's army, Umkhonto we Sizwe," both "veterans and younger members" (*African Communist*, no. 117). In discussions characterized as "extensive," "substantial," "intensive, highly theoretical, and eminently practical," the delegates approved a new party program, The Path to Power, replacing the previous party program, The Road to South African Freedom, which was adopted at a clandestine conference of the SACP held in South Africa in 1962. "The depth of political and theoretical maturity demonstrated by delegates

who had been recruited into the SACP since 1976" was cited as "testimony to the political calibre of the revolutionary alliance headed by the ANC" (ibid.).

The re-election of Tloome and Slovo continued the party practice of reserving public leadership positions for members of the older generation who joined the then legal party in the 1940s, but remained active in re-establishing the underground SACP in the 1950s before following party orders in 1963 to leave South Africa to continue work in Africa and Europe in association with the external leadership of the ANC. Dan Tloome, re-elected to the ceremonial and diplomatic post of chairman, is a 70-year-old African teacher by training who has been active in the trade union movement and the ANC for almost five decades, serving in exile on the executive committees of the ANC and SACTU, the trade union organization associated with the ANC since the early 1950s. Joe Slovo, re-elected to the political and administrative post of general secretary, is a 63-year-old Lithuanian barrister who was a prominent defense lawyer for members of the ANC and allied organizations in South Africa in the 1950s and early 1960s. In exile he has been intimately associated with organizing armed struggle for the ANC and with articulating military-political strategies and tactics. In 1964 he became a member of the Revolutionary Council of the ANC and subsequently served as chief of staff of Umkhonto (until 1987), receiving recognition in 1985 as the first white elected to the National Executive Council of the ANC when non-Africans were made eligible for membership on the ANC's directing body.

Slovo, Tloome, and the bulk of other party leaders shuttle between major centers of activity in Africa and Europe, including Tanzania, Zambia, England (London), and Eastern Europe, where party members are concentrated within the ANC and party structures. Within South Africa membership in the banned party is concentrated in the major urban centers where antiapartheid activism and the trade union movement are centered. Their presence is highlighted by the display of SACP banners and hammer and sickle flags at trade union rallies and political demonstrations. At the 29 October rally in Soweto of 70,000 ANC supporters welcoming Walter Sisulu and the other Rivonia prisoners freed by President F. W. de Klerk on 15 October, a message of greeting from General Secretary Slovo was read to the crowd (*Sechaba*, December, pp. 10–11). The Seventh Congress "reaffirmed that at this juncture of our struggle, the SACP should remain a working class party composed primarily of professional revolutionaries" (ibid., p. 11). The party has not published precise membership figures, but it did announce that membership had increased 90 percent in the five-year period since the Sixth Congress (*Weekly Mail*, 23–29 June).

Domestic Activities and Attitudes. Observing that "after 27 years there have been major changes in the world, in our region, and within South Africa itself," the new party program, The Path to Power, reaffirmed that the

> immediate aim [of the SACP] is to win the objectives of the national democratic revolution, whose main content is the national liberation of the African people in particular, and the black people in general, the destruction of the economic and political power of the racist ruling class, and the establishment of one united, non-racial, democratic South Africa in which the working class will be the dominant force.

Realization of this goal "is the essential condition and the key for future advance to the supreme aim of the Communist Party: the establishment of a socialist South Africa, laying the foundations of a classless, communist society" (*Sechaba*, December, p. 74).

The Path to Power reiterates the argument of the earlier 1962 program—that capitalist relations in South Africa developed within the context of colonialism, resulting in "colonialism of a special type" in which "the essential features of colonial domination in the imperialist epoch are maintained and even intensified....In South Africa the colonial ruling class with its white support base on the one hand, and the oppressed colonial majority on the other are located within a single country." (Ibid.) Analyzing the alliance of white classes and strata that constitute the colonial bloc, the program contends that monopoly capital (concentrated in four large companies that control 80 percent of the shares on the Johannesburg stock exchange) is dominant. Nevertheless, with its interests in "a more stable, better qualified and higher consuming work force," domestic monopoly capitalism is seeking "a political and economic restructuring of colonialism of a special type" (ibid., p. 94).

Among the white middle strata, a large number of Afrikaners are state employees and "highly dependent for their positions on having in power a political organization committed to a strong, racially privileged state bureaucracy," but other sectors, "professionals and particularly the intelligentsia, often feel least threatened among the white community by the prospect of a non-racial future." In contrast, white wage earners (most of whom hold clerical, supervisory, administrative, and technical positions) in many ways constitute a "classical 'labor aristocracy'" as a result of "decades of racial privilege [that] have brought them real material gains" and "have instilled an extremely reactionary outlook within a significant proportion" of this group. "Non-monopoly white farms . . . the most backward sector of the capitalist economy" also have little interest in change, being highly dependent on government loans and subsidies and "the most barbaric oppression and exploitation of their black laborers." (Ibid., p. 93.)

Although all-white classes and strata previously united around white minority rule, the program asserts that "the growing revolutionary challenge, and increased international isolation are now dramatically weakening the cement uniting the white bloc. Today the white community is more confused, more divided and more demoralized than in many decades," permitting "many possibilities for detaching significant sectors of whites from at least an unquestioned faith in white minority rule." (Ibid., p. 94.) Noting that an increasing number have actually espoused "an antiapartheid position, joining the broad front of forces aligned against the Pretoria regime," the program also suggests that a small, but growing number of whites are willing to make the "fuller, revolutionary commitment" to the "struggle for a united, non-racial and democratic South Africa" of the sort that white communists pioneered in the early years of the party in the 1920s. (Ibid., pp. 94–95.)

"The largest and most significant class force," however, is the six million strong black working class, an "industrial proletariat, concentrated in the large urban complexes [that] has emerged as the most organized and powerful mass revolutionary contingent in our country," with a "proletarian class consciousness . . . developed and deepened by decades of militant trade unionism" (ibid., p. 95). Closely allied to the black proletariat are the African "oppressed rural masses," both the 1.3 million on white farms and the 13.5 million crammed into the bantustans. All of the first group and the overwhelming majority of the second group are landless and linked with the working class "in their outlook and in their objective interests" through migratory work patterns and other ways. The majority of the small African middle strata are also closely linked "in terms of their living conditions, their social origin and their political aspirations" and have actively participated in the revolutionary struggle, as have the majority of the colored and Indian population who have rejected collaboration with the government. (Ibid., p. 97.)

The achievement of the national democratic revolution, which is in "the immediate interests of the overwhelming majority of the South African people," will come through the revolutionary alliance headed by the ANC.

> The ANC—as head of the revolutionary alliance— occupies a virtually unchallenged place as the popular vanguard force in the liberation struggle.... The ANC does not represent any single class or any one ideology. As head of the liberation alliance and prime representative of all oppressed, the ANC welcomes within its ranks all—from whatever class they come— who support and are ready to fight for the aims of the Freedom Charter [adopted by the ANC-led Congress of the People in 1955]. South African Communists consider that the achievement of the aims of the Charter will answer the pressing and immediate needs of the people and lay the indispensable basis for the advance to socialism. (Ibid., p. 103.)

According to the party program,

> The foundation of the national democratic state will be popularly elected representative institutions based on one-person, one-vote: universal and direct adult franchise without regard to race, sex, property and other discriminatory qualifications...The state will guarantee the basic freedoms and rights of all citizens, such as the freedom of speech and thought, of the press and of organization, of movement, of conscience and religion and full trade union rights for all workers including the right to strike. To fully eliminate the system of colonial domination it will be necessary to ensure democratic ownership and control over decisive aspects of the economy. At the same time, the state will protect the interests of private business where these are not incompatible with the public interest. (Ibid., p. 104.)

In the view of the party program, the trade union movement is "another important organized contingent of the democratic forces" (ibid., p. 110). The party states that militant trade unionism is "today embodied in the South African Congress of Trade Unions (SACTU) and in the giant federation, the Congress of South African Trade Unions (COS-

ATU)" (ibid., p. 95). By this formulation it gives equal recognition to the shell of the 1950s SACTU organization with which it and the exiled ANC have long been associated and to COSATU, the largest black trade union organization with its membership of hundreds of thousands, formed in 1985 by both ANC supporters and nonaffiliated labor activists leading the burgeoning trade unions established in the last two decades. "It is of crucial importance that the working class builds and strengthens its own independent class organizations while cooperating with, and indeed leading, the broad democratic forces" (ibid., p. 107). In the estimation of the program "the role of black workers as the dominant force in our struggle is absolutely crucial to ensure that the national democratic revolution lays the basis for a transition for socialism" (ibid., p. 106); at the same time "by placing the attainment of socialism on the immediate agenda would, in fact, be to postpone the very attainment of socialist transformation" (ibid., p. 105).

A proper workers' vanguard party is necessary for the achievement of socialism. The ANC considers that "the overwhelming majority and most strategically placed of our people are workers. The ANC therefore, recognizes the leading role of the working class." Yet the program explicitly states that "the ANC is not a workers' vanguard political party" (ibid., p. 110) and that "the basic character of a trade union means that . . . a trade union movement cannot play this role" of a workers' vanguard party either (ibid., p. 111). It is the SACP, working "consistently to forge the South African working class into a powerful force, capable of playing the leading role in the struggle for national democracy and in carrying out its historic mission of abolishing exploitation and creating a classless society" that is the workers' vanguard party.

> The SACP plays its role both as an independent organization and as part of the revolutionary alliance headed by the ANC. There is no contradiction between the multi-class leadership role of the ANC, and the working class vanguard role of the Party... Communists have never sought to transform the national democratic movement into a front for the Party. Participation by communists in the ANC, Umkhonto we Sizwe and other revolutionary organizations is based on our class appreciation of their distinct but complementary tasks. (Ibid., pp. 111–12.)

Looking into the immediate future the party program is cautiously optimistic: "the situation has within it the potential for a relatively rapid emergence of conditions which make possible seizure of power" (ibid., p. 122). In the program's analysis the likely path is an "insurrection," which, in contrast to a coup, is "a mass revolutionary upsurge of the people in conditions which hold out the possibility of a seizure of power." Such a possibility will present itself when the following elements converge

> in a sufficient measure: mass upsurge, in which working class action at the point of production will play a key role, mass defiance, escalating revolutionary combat activity, intensified international pressure, a situation of ungovernability, a deteriorating economy and growing demoralisation, division, vacillation and confusion within the power bloc. Above all, a political vanguard is needed to plan for, and lead, the insurrectionary assault at the crucial stage. (Ibid., p. 124.)

Although The Path to Power is through insurrection—"an act of *revolutionary force*, [which] is not always an *armed* uprising (ibid., p. 123)—the program is also explicit that "there is no conflict between this insurrectionary perspective and the possibility of a negotiated transfer of power." It warns that "we should be on our guard against the clear objective of our ruling class and their imperialist allies" who aim to pre-empt revolutionary transformation *"by pushing the liberation movement into negotiation before it is strong enough to back its basic demands with sufficient power on the ground."* In careful terms the program spells out that

> we are not engaged in a struggle whose objective is merely to generate sufficient pressure to bring the other side to the negotiating table. If, as a result of a generalized crisis and a heightened revolutionary upsurge, the point should ever be reached when the enemy is prepared to talk, the liberation forces will, *at that point*, have to exercise their judgment, guided by the demands of revolutionary advance. But until then its sights must be clearly set on the perspectives of a seizure of power. (Ibid., pp. 124–25.)

International Views and Activities. The new party program blandly states that "the South African Communist Party is part of the world communist forces. True to the principles of working class internationalism, the Party works for the unity of the workers of the whole world, and especially of the Marxist-Leninist parties." (Ibid., p. 82.) The world socialist system is characterized as contribut-

ing to the "world revolutionary process" in three main ways:

> First, the existence of socialist countries, their growing might, and their foreign policies, based on working class internationalism, have brought about gradual changes in the world-wide balance of forces between imperialism and all the forces opposing it . . . Secondly, the advances of the socialist countries inspire the working people throughout the world to struggle for social and national emancipation, raising the level of their demands and programmes of action. Thirdly, socialist countries provide significant and many-sided support to revolutionary movements throughout the world. (Ibid., p. 78.)

Spelling out how "proletarian internationalism" has manifested itself in southern Africa, the program notes that

> progressive and revolutionary forces have a long and warm experience of the consistent, selfless assistance of the socialist countries. In particular, the contribution of the Cuban internationalist forces, the Soviet Union and other socialist countries to the defeat of apartheid and imperialist plans in Angola has been of decisive importance for our whole region. (Ibid., p. 79.)

Historically closely oriented toward the Communist Party of the Soviet Union (CPSU), the SACP in its program reiterated its assessment of the deleterious consequences of Stalinism without mentioning Stalin:

> For a number of decades democratic procedures were neglected in the Soviet Union, and the cult of the personality dominated the leadership, the Party and the whole country. Given the pre-eminent position of the Soviet Union within the world communist movement, some of these negative tendencies also affected Communist Parties around the world, including our own.

Continuing to the Brezhnev period the program noted that

> within the Soviet Union elements of stagnation and other phenomena alien to socialism began to appear. Since the 27th Congress of the CPSU an important process has been initiated for democratization, restructuring [*perestroika*] and openness [*glasnost'*], with the aim of ensuring the fuller realization of the

economic, moral and cultural possibilities opened up by socialism. (Ibid., p. 79.)

The cautious endorsement of President Gorbachev's policies in the party program reflected ambivalence about aspects of trends in the Soviet Union that have been expressed by party spokespersons elsewhere. In the wake of Gorbachev's path-breaking December 1988 speech to the United Nations in which inter alia he declared that the new era required "de-ideologizing relations among states," *African Communist* commented that "some of his formulations in the UN speech strike one as tentative and experimental" and noted that imperialist countries were not responding to Soviet initiatives. *African Communist* concluded:

We do not have to abandon our ideological perspectives in order to fight for peace. We do not ask Gorbachev to turn back, but on the contrary applaud his achievement to date and urge him forward. At the same time we will continue to play our part in mobilizing the people of our country and the world to ensure that his advances meet with an adequate response and that victories continue to be notched up on the road to peace and social progress. (*African Communist*, no. 117.)

Earlier Brian Bunting, editor of the *African Communist* who was invited to the Nineteenth Conference of the CPSU as a representative of the press of a fraternal party, confessed that "it was a fascinating and, in some respects, disturbing experience, but one which in the end reinforced confidence in the Soviet Party and people" (*African Communist*, no. 115). In a subsequent issue he printed without comment extracts from an interview with Fidel Castro in which Castro acknowledged differences with President Gorbachev and extracts from an article by Gus Hall, chairman of the Communist Party of the United States, in which Hall criticized unrestrained debate within the Soviet Union and critical assessments of Stalinism in which there was "no discussion about the nature of the class enemy, or what the problems were in building socialism in a backward country" (*African Communist*, no. 116).

Several recent Soviet popular and scholarly assessments of South Africa also have come under fire, in particular the work of Boris Asoyan, longtime African correspondent of *New Times*. In a critical assessment of his book, *South Africa: What Lies Ahead?* the reviewer in *African Communist* concluded that

this book gives some insight into the "new thinking" that is going on amongst certain Soviet "experts" on South Africa and the liberation struggle. This calls for a more vigorous approach by our revolutionary alliance to explain to these people our position, perspective, analysis and strategy and tactics. We should engage these comrades in comradely discussion and debate (*African Communist*, no. 118, p. 68).

In response to an article by Asoyan in *Pravda* of 20 August, General Secretary Slovo wrote a critical letter in which he took Asoyan to task on a number of points of interpretation, including the statement that the "ANC represented simply one among many forces opposing apartheid," which Slovo suggested approached the formulations of Pretoria and Margaret Thatcher (*Pravda*, 1 October).

South African Communists have continued to be active diplomatically both for the SACP and as part of ANC delegations. In December 1988 a SACP delegation of Brian Bunting and Essop Pahad made the first official visit by the SACP to the Norwegian Communist party (*FBIS-AFR*, 7 March). In March, General Secretary Slovo was a member of an ANC delegation headed by President Oliver Tambo that was received in the Kremlin (*Pravda*, 12 March). Three years after the last visit by an SACP delegation, General Secretary Slovo headed a delegation that spent at least nine days in May in the People's Republic of China, concluding with a meeting with the head of the Chinese Communist party, Zhao Ziyang (*FBIS-AFR*, 8, 12 May). No visits to Eastern European parties were reported nor did the party press comment on the rapid changes that took place late in the year in Eastern Europe. There were also no visits reported to African parties, but the party program reaffirmed its longtime commitment to cooperation, stating that "the Party works for the deepening of the comradely unity and cooperation among Marxist-Leninist Parties of Africa" (*African Communist*, no. 118).

Publications. Observing the 30th anniversary of its publication, the party quarterly, *African Communist*, continued to characterize itself, as it did in its initial 1959 issue, as a journal published "in the interest of African solidarity, and as a forum for Marxist-Leninist thought throughout our Continent." Its contents continued to focus on South Africa, but it regularly contained a section, "African Notes and Comment," in which developments elsewhere on the continent were analyzed. Electronically typeset in London and printed in Leipzig

(German Democratic Republic), the *African Communist* is distributed from London. Within South Africa the SACP clandestinely publishes *Umsebenzi*, the Zulu/Xhosa word for worker and the name of the legal party newspaper from 1930 to 1936. It also disseminates party flyers and leaflets, along with smuggled Marxist-Leninist classics.

SACP publications are complemented by those of the ANC, also published in exile and illegally within South Africa; the major journal, the monthly *Sechaba*, is published with support from the German Democratic Republic. The ANC also beams "Radio Freedom" to South Africa using the shortwave services of the state radios of Angola, Ethiopia, Madagascar, Tanzania, and Zambia.

Sheridan Johns
Duke University

Sudan

Population. 24,476,290 (July)
Party. Sudanese Communist Party (al-Hizb al-Shuyu'i al-Sudani, SCP)
Founded. 1946
Membership. 9,000 (estimated)
General Secretary. Muhammad Ibrahim Nugud Mansur
Secretariat. Before 30 June: Muhammad Ibrahim Nugud Mansur, Ali al-Tijani al-Tayyib Babikr, Izz al-Din Ali Amir, Abu al-Qasim (Gassim) Muhammad, Sulayman Hamid, al-Gazuli Said Uthman, Muhammad Ahmad Sulayman (Suleiman)
Central Committee. Before 30 June: Sudi Darag, Khidr Nasr, Abd al-Majid Shakak, Hasan Gassim al-Sid, Fatima Ahmad Ibrahim, Ibrahim Zakariya, and members of the Secretariat
Status. Illegal (after 30 June)
Last Congress. Fourth, 31 October 1967, in Khartoum
Last Election. 1986: 1.67 percent of the total vote in territorial constituencies; 5 seats out of the contested 264 (2 in territorial constituencies and 3 in special ones for "graduates") (Sudan News Agency [SUNA], 25 May 1986)
Auxiliary Organizations. Before 30 June: Demo-

cratic Federation of Sudanese Students, Sudanese Youth Union, Sudanese Workers' Trade Union Federation, Sudanese Defenders of Peace and Democracy, Union of Sudanese Women
Publications. *Al-Maydan* (official party newspaper; suspended operations in July), *al-Shuyi*.

Organized communist activity began in the Sudan in the 1920s, but it was not until 1946 that Sudanese intellectuals and students created a formal party organization. The group adopted the name of the SCP in 1956 and has been active both publicly and clandestinely in Sudanese politics since that early era. Initially part of the Anti-Imperialist Front in the first period of parliamentary politics (1953–1958), it was then part of the opposition to the first military regime (1958–1964). SCP members played a leading role in the 1964 revolution, which overthrew military rule, and participated in the transitional government. Despite winning eleven seats in the 1965 parliamentary elections, however, opposition to the SCP by the new prime minister, Sadiq al-Mahdi, led to the party's exclusion from parliament (see *YICA*, 1968). When the second era of civilian politics was brought to an end by a military coup in 1969, the SCP strongly supported the coup's leader, Ja'far Numayri.

Communists were influential in the first two years of the Numayri regime, but tensions led to an abortive leftist coup in the summer of 1971 and the subsequent vigorous suppression of the SCP and the execution of many of its leaders. The SCP joined other civilian parties in opposition to Numayri and again in 1985 played a leading role in popular demonstrations that led to the overthrow of military rule for a second time. The SCP became an active participant in the restored partisan civilian political arena and won 5 of the 264 contested seats in the 1986 elections. Because of its experienced leadership and ties with other social and political groupings, the SCP was able to emerge as an important part of the new parliamentary groupings. The military coup of 30 June led by Umar al-Bashir brought an end to the third parliamentary period, and the SCP again became part of the underground opposition.

Leadership. The leadership of the party was arrested by the new military government in the summer of 1989, and management of SCP affairs was in the hands of those leaders who remained at large or out of the country. General Secretary Nugud and others in the party leadership have long been active in civilian politics in the Sudan and are respected by the supporters of civilian rule there. Nugud was on the SCP executive committee in the 1960s, and he and others participated in important political events like the favorably viewed revolutions of 1964 and 1985. The party leadership was reformist rather than revolutionary in its programs, and more radically oriented Marxists did not have a major role in party leadership. In the conditions of the suppression by the new military regime, however, the nature of the leadership of the underground party is unclear.

Domestic Issues. The third era of civilian politics since Sudanese independence was brought to an end on 30 June, when military officers led by Umar Hasan Ahmad al-Bashir took control of the government. Civilian political leadership had been unable to resolve the Sudan's major problems. Civil war continued in the southern regions of the country with the major opposition group, the Sudan People's Liberation Movement (SPLM), gaining strength. In addition, natural catastrophes and financial mismanagement made efforts to resolve the major problems of foreign debt and internal economic disorder ineffective. The SCP had been active in the political manipulations of the first half of 1989 and was part of the coalition government that was overthrown by the military.

At the beginning of the year, the SCP was part of the parliamentary opposition to the coalition government of Prime Minister Sadiq al-Mahdi. In February, however, the Sudanese military leadership demanded that the government take major steps toward resolving the problems of national disunity and the economy. During March, al-Mahdi created a new coalition government that included all of the political parties except the National Islamic Front. The SCP representative in the cabinet, Abu Zayd Muhammad Salih, was the minister of public service. The cabinet also included two representatives from the trade unions who were sympathetic to the SCP.

The general program of the new coalition, which received the full support of the SCP, included a freezing of the implementation of Islamic law, undertaking a major new initiative in negotiations with the SPLM, and convening a national constitutional convention in the fall of 1989. Although there was some success in opening talks with the SPLM, economic conditions continued to deteriorate, and the political situation remained highly unstable. It

was in that context that the group of officers led by al-Bashir took control of the government.

Immediately after the coup, the Central Committee (CC) of the SCP issued a privately circulated statement that reaffirmed the party's commitment to "democracy based on political pluralism, national sovereignty, judicial independence, the rule of law, and respect for human rights" as "the only principles accepted as basis for rule." The CC also rejected "any attempt or stance which aims at establishing a military or civilian dictatorship." In a special issue of *al-Maydan* published after the coup and the suppression of the SCP, the party leadership identified the new military regime as a creation of the Islamic fundamentalists: "All decisions and decrees passed by the putschists are in conformity with the programme of the National Islamic Front. This shows that the coup has been staged to block the way to peace and the planned constitutional conference." (*al-Maydan*, no. 1895, July–August.) This set the tone for the secularist line of opposition that was followed by the SCP in the subsequent months.

The SCP worked with trade unions and other civilian parties to rouse opposition to the new regime, but the government was able to suppress these attempts and remain in power through the end of the year. The strength of the communist efforts is reflected by the fact that al-Bashir specifically cited the danger of the communist threat to the regime on a number of occasions (*FBIS-AFR*, 18 July, 20 December). However, he also reminded an interviewer that the government did not reject the work of someone simply because he was a communist, citing the work of Abu Zayd Muhammad Salih, the former communist cabinet member, as the chair of the board of the Sudanese Maritime Lines in the new government (*FBIS-AFR*, 17 October).

At the end of 1989, the SCP joined with other civilian parties in opposition to a military regime for the third time in its history. Although it can play a role in organizing popular demonstrations, as it did in 1964 and 1985, the party remains small, urban based, and on the periphery of power politics in the Sudan. Its weakness in appealing to intellectuals was reflected in its inability to win any seats in the University of Khartoum student council elections in December, all of which were won by Islamic activists (*FBIS-AFR*, 21 December). Its orthodox Marxist and socialist ideas have less appeal than the special radicalism of the SPLM or the revivalism of emerging Islamic groups.

International Positions. The SCP is a relatively orthodox, Soviet-oriented communist party whose leaders have had regular ties with Soviet bloc party officials. The internal domestic changes in the Sudan have occupied the attention of the SCP leaders, and their response to changes in Eastern Europe and the Soviet Union was muted.

The Soviet Union, maintaining friendly if formal contacts with the governments of the Sudan, has not provided special support for the SCP. Despite the fact that al-Bashir is actively anticommunist in his ideology, stating, for example, that "communism has fallen...communism has collapsed with the Berlin Wall" (*FBIS-AFR*, 5 December), the military regime maintained relatively good relations with the Soviet Union. Discussions regarding Soviet aid for Sudanese agriculture were held late in the year (*FBIS-AFR*, 3 October). The Soviet Union has not made any significant moves in support of the SCP in this context.

In terms of positions on international issues, 1989 was not a year of dramatic initiatives by the SCP. It continued to support the idea of a negotiated settlement of the Arab-Israeli conflict in the framework of support for the Palestine Liberation Organization, and it maintained its strong opposition to apartheid in South Africa.

In general, the SCP continues to be a party of intellectuals, students, and organized working groups. It maintains good ties with the union movement in the Sudan and, in opposition, can organize actions like the doctors' strike in December, which caused great concern to the military regime (*FBIS-AFR*, 8 December). However, the SCP continues to face the competition of nontraditional Islamist groups like the Muslim Brotherhood. There is little indication that the SCP made significant progress during 1989 in expanding the base of its support. The new conditions created by the rule of an apparently Islamist military regime provide opportunities for the SCP to speak for the secularist opposition. Its international connections may aid it in this. However, the party continues to be a small one on the margins of the political scene.

John O. Voll
University of New Hampshire

Zimbabwe

Population. 10,022,000
Party. Zimbabwe African National Union–Patriotic Front (ZANU-PF)
Founded. 1963
Membership. 3,000,000 claimed (*Pravda*, 20 December)
First Secretary and President. Robert G. Mugabe
Politburo. 22 seats
Central Committee. 160 members (full list, *FBIS-AFR*, 26 December)
Status. Ruling party
Last Congress. Fourth, 19–22 December
Last Election. October: by-elections for parliamentary seats
Auxiliary Organizations. People's Militia, Youth Wing
Publications. *Zimbabwe News*. Nearly all news organs are government owned in whole or in part. The major exception is the privately owned weekly the *Financial Gazette*, which operates independently of party and government.

Party Organization and Domestic Political Conditions. The true power in Zimbabwe is in the recently enlarged ZANU Politburo, although ultimate authority rests with Robert Mugabe, who serves as party head. Mugabe's position in both government and party continues to grow as a result of the new party structure established at the Second Congress in 1984, the constitutional amendment of 1987 creating a more powerful presidency, and the stunningly successful absorption of the Zimbabwe African People's Union (ZAPU), the opposition party, by ZANU, the ruling party.

As executive president, Mugabe is simultaneously the head of the party, the government, and the state. Before independence, Mugabe committed himself to the ultimate establishment of a Marxist state, but his increasingly pragmatic economic policies and purges of radical ideologues from party leadership have won the collaboration of key white leaders in the capitalist sectors and contributed to the viability of those areas of private enterprise that are considered essential to economic growth.

Nevertheless, President Mugabe's movement

away from the economic models of Marxism-Leninism coupled with his determination to build a one-party political system triggered a brushfire of opposition from cadres that had hitherto been among his strongest supporters. In 1989 an opposition party, the Zimbabwe Unity Movement (ZUM), was formed by Edgar Tekere, former general secretary of ZANU. ZUM, drawing its electoral strength almost solely from the insecure eastern regions along the Mozambique border, lashed out against government moves toward a one-party system and criticized the regime for tolerating corruption. (*Africa Report*, July/August.) In October, Mugabe overreacted by arbitrarily arresting two key ZUM leaders on the eve of by-elections. ZUM, failing to attract a national following, secured few votes (*Economist Intelligence Unit*, no. 4). ZANU won handily, but a low voter turnout indicated growing public disillusionment with a government leadership that is seen as veering from its revolutionary principles (*Financial Times*, 23 October).

In 1989 corruption became a major national issue; six cabinet ministers and a provincial governor were dismissed after allegations of black market racketeering of motor vehicles. Maurice Nyagumbo, a powerful cabinet member and a key ZANU leader, committed suicide in the wake of this so-called Willowgate scandal (*Washington Times*, 11 May). Nyagumbo had helped author the leadership code that discouraged government officials from pursuing private business interests (*FBIS-AFR*, 18 April). Weeks later, Mugabe shocked the nation by pardoning the Willowgate group and restoring some of them to high posts. Some observers questioned his ability to deal objectively with the issue of corruption in his regime.

Antigovernment demonstrations at the University of Zimbabwe in October led to the closure of the campus, the arrest of student leaders, and the detention of a prominent officer in the Zimbabwe Congress of Trade Unions (ZCTU). This action drew strong criticism from the press and the judiciary, which threw out most of the charges. Africa Watch, an international human rights group, joined Zimbabwe's Catholic bishops in calling for an end to detentions without trial and government intimidation of its critics. Trade unionists and intellectuals accused Mugabe of falling under the sway of corrupt capitalists and of seeking to move the economy off its socialist course (African Consulting Associates). Students demanded that Mugabe live up to his promise of land reform. In defense of the regime, Dr. Herbert Ushwokunze, chairman of ZANU-PF,

warned that "capitalists are trying to devour the children of the revolution" and accused ZUM of trying to subvert the nation's socialist goals (*New African*, October).

Mugabe and the ruling ZANU-PF party leadership, seemingly undeterred by the rising criticism, renewed the state of emergency that, since the days of white rule in 1965, allowed the government to suspend normal civil rights protection (*FBIS-AFR*, 14 November). At the party congress in December, ZANU-PF reaffirmed its call for a one-party state and formally merged with ZAPU, its old opposition. The congress also made arrangements for an enlargement of both the Politburo (15 to 22) and the Central Committee (90 to 160). Months earlier, the House of Assembly voted to abolish the Senate, thus paving the way for a unicameral parliament in 1990 (*FBIS-AFR*, 23 November).

Mugabe, president of the reconstituted ZANU-PF, serves with Joshua Nkomo, his long-standing adversary and the former leader of ZAPU, as one of its two vice-presidents. The new party affirmed its adherence to the principles of Marxism-Leninism, even though its key leaders support policies favoring a mixed economy. Indeed, some members of the party's Central Committee have prospered in their own private enterprises (Political Risk Services, October).

Domestic Economic Conditions. In the first half of 1989, Zimbabwe's economy continued to display robust growth. By September, however, it had begun to slow, partly in response to dry conditions and lower agricultural production (*FBIS-AFR*, 15 September). Unemployment exceeded 25 percent, taxation had begun to absorb nearly 45 percent of national product, and little fresh capital had flowed into the country since independence.

Zimbabwe's ambitious public sector development plans could not succeed without fresh infusions of capital. With the economies of the Soviet Union and communist bloc countries in disarray, Zimbabwe would have to seek greater support from the West. That reality greatly strengthened the role of the party's non-Marxist moderates.

In April the government, in a dramatic shift in economic policy, announced moves toward market-oriented approaches and decentralization (*Africa Economic Digest*, 24 April). The sweeping liberalization program was designed to attract new foreign investment. Finance Minister Bernard Chidzero, the chief architect of the capitalist-oriented program, set up a National Consultative Council comprised of representatives of all sectors of the economy to advise the government's National Planning Agency (*African Business*, May). In May a new investment code was unveiled to encourage local investment and foreign capital. The code will allow 100 percent foreign ownership by foreign corporations of firms involved in so-called high priority projects and will sanction full profit remittability (*African Business*, July). A one-stop Foreign Investment Centre was then set up to speed the process. In addition, Zimbabwe agreed to join the World Bank's Multilateral Investment Guarantee Agency. The government also promised to give new vigor to the Small Enterprises Development Corporation, a parastatal. Coupled with these bold initiatives was a new export promotion program aimed at seeking new markets overseas and regionally. Key leaders in the private sector and moderates in government would like to improve trade ties with Pacific Rim countries, including Malaysia. Others are fearful that the lure of the European Economic Community after 1992 will divert attention from Africa.

The liberalization trend was met with resistance from old-line party ideologues as well as from more-youthful intellectuals. To quell their concerns, Mugabe has maintained his Marxist rhetoric and continues to court the more hard-line communist countries, particularly China and North Korea. He has also resisted lifting price controls and passed new rules making disinvestment more difficult.

In 1989 there were growing concerns among socialists that Mugabe was veering from his original Marxist course. That concern was best expressed over the smoldering issue of land reform. At independence, Mugabe had pledged to resettle 162,000 families on farmland by 1985, but by the end of 1989, less than 51,000 of them had actually received land (African Consulting Associates). The Lancaster House Agreement with the British, which will expire in April 1990, forbids expropriations or large-scale land redistribution; however, Zimbabwe has been unsuccessful in acquiring much land on a willing-seller basis. Indeed, 4,400 white Zimbabweans, less than 1 percent of the nation's population, own more than a third of the country's land area. In August, Mugabe promised "uninhibited land redistribution in the near future" (*Africa Economic Digest*, 28 August). Nevertheless, a month later, in the face of pressure from white farmers who earn much of Zimbabwe's desperately needed foreign exchange, Mugabe said he would not seize private property (*FBIS-AFR*, 21 September). Zimbabwe's population growth rate, nearly 4 percent, is one of the highest in the world, and the pressure for land is bound to increase dramatically. Moreover, many veterans of the liberation struggle of the 1960s and 1970s are threatening to turn against one-time guerrilla leader and now president Mugabe if he does not deal with the problem of landlessness soon. Many observers forecast that land reform will be the paramount issue of the 1990s.

Although the government tolerates, and in some cases supports, the private sector, it continued to pursue its policy of acquiring equity in key private enterprises and thus ran against the continentwide trend toward privatization of the public sector.

International Relations. Relations with the United States greatly improved in 1989, partly in response to Zimbabwe's decision to liberalize its investment procedures. President Mugabe toned down his criticism of U.S. foreign policies, and Zimbabwe welcomed the U.S. decision to renew its aid (*Africa Analysis*, 3 March). Relations with Great Britain have also warmed, despite Mugabe's continuing criticism of Prime Minister Margaret Thatcher's stance toward South Africa on the issue of economic sanctions. The British have contributed generously to the Southern African Development Coordination Conference (SADCC), especially toward the rehabilitation of Beira's railway and port facilities. Such projects will benefit both Mozambique and Zimbabwe.

Mugabe's policies toward Pretoria have not changed, even in the face of Zambia's active encouragement of dialogue with white South African public and private leaders (African Consulting Associates). Nevertheless, economic contacts with its southern neighbor quietly continue, and bilateral trade remains brisk.

Zimbabwe plays a major role in the SADCC, and its trade with SADCC members continues to grow. Zimbabwe also remains a staunch supporter of Mozambique, contributing funds to its anti-insurgency campaign against the Mozambique National Resistance and providing military cover for vital transport routes from Zimbabwe to Mozambican seaports (ZIANA, 9 December).

Zimbabwe's relationships with the African National Congress and the Pan-Africanist Congress have become warmer. Bowing to pressure from South Africa, however, Mugabe has steadfastly refused to permit either organization to establish headquarters or any kind of guerrilla operations within Zimbabwe.

Relations with communist bloc countries are extremely confused as a result of recent political events in Central and Eastern Europe. Mugabe was shocked by the overthrow of the communist leadership in Romania and East Germany; he admired their tough ideological stances, and Zimbabwe was conducting a brisk barter trade with the former.

Despite their condemnation in the world press, Mugabe continued to support such hard-line communist countries as North Korea, Cuba, and the People's Republic of China. These countries have been enthusiastic supporters of Zimbabwe since the days of the liberation struggle. Mugabe sided with the Chinese ruling clique in their suppression of the student rebellions in 1989. Weeks earlier, China had offered to supply Zimbabwe with $105 million in air defense equipment, including combat aircraft and missiles (*Africa Economic Digest*, 6 March). Relations with Cuba also remain cordial, and in 1989 Fidel Castro agreed to accept more Zimbabwean students, who already number more than a thou-sand (*FBIS-AFR*, 7 January). Relations with the Soviet Union are correct, but not always cordial (*Pravda*, 12 November). Many key leaders in ZANU-PF are fearful that Gorbachev's *perestroika* will fatally weaken Marxism-Leninism everywhere. They are also frustrated by low levels of economic aid from the Soviet Union and other bloc countries (African Consulting Associates).

In conclusion, Mugabe has reached a turning point. In 1990, Zimbabwe, freed from its obligations under the British-imposed Lancaster House agreement, will put Mugabe under increasing pressure from the political right and left to make long-range decisions about the country's future direction. Should Zimbabwe become a de jure one-party state? Can the regime afford to pursue a Marxist-Leninist economic course at a time when the rest of the world, including its immediate neighbors, are moving toward a more capitalist approach? Can Mugabe, an avowed Marxist, swim against these swiftly changing currents? Clearly, the country has reached a critical crossroads.

Richard W. Hull
New York University

THE AMERICAS

Introduction

During 1989 the Marxist-Leninist governments, parties and organizations in the Americas faced the same kinds of challenges encountered by their counterparts in other regions of the world: coping with domestic affairs, which should have been their primary concerns, while simultaneously trying to adjust to both the collapse of communism throughout the world and the resulting shifts in Soviet-bloc economic and foreign policies.

The pressures of coping were most intense and consequential in Cuba and Nicaragua, where the communists were in power. But parties were tested, sometimes battered, in other countries as well, under pressures to show why anyone should take communism seriously, as an ideology or system of government, except as an oppressor, in the face of its utter failure everywhere—not least in Cuba and Nicaragua. Most nonruling communist parties and movements in Latin America professed their belief in democracy and, through often Byzantine rationalizations, sought to distinguish their local versions of communism from many decades of history in Europe and elsewhere which have demonstrated the incompatibility of communism in power and any kind of serious free choice. This meant arguing for their difference from every communist-ruled government in the world, virtually all of which somehow had fallen into the hands of leaders who failed to achieve, usually even betrayed, communism's professed ideals of freedom and equality.

Soviet policy toward Latin America did not always coincide with what Soviet leaders said was their broad international objective of defusing tensions. While Moscow's relations with major countries in the region were national rather than communist, that is to say focused on trade and other traditional contacts rather than ideology and revolution, ties to Cuba and Nicaragua, and through them to groups in several other smaller nations, were more murky. Despite talk of *perestroika*, Soviet

economic aid to Cuba continued at about $4–5 billion, but far more important, military aid also continued at the level of about $1 billion and included the newest MiG-29 aircraft. Soviet bloc economic and military aid continued to Nicaragua as well, at about $500 million for the year, and Soviet-made ground-to-air missiles were for the first time delivered, by the Sandinistas, to the Salvadoran guerrillas. Soviet arms deliveries continued into early 1990—MiGs in January, for instance—even though the Soviet Union reportedly lectured Castro on the evils of the latter's aggressive Central American policy.

In Cuba, Fidel Castro has had a particularly difficult time reconciling the facts of Soviet-bloc upheaval, communism's repeated economic failures in Cuba, and the fiction of an immutable socialist/communist truth, of which Cuba, under Castro's very self-conscious guardianship, is almost the last impregnable fortress in the world. "The last Stalinist" is the phrase most often applied to Castro, even by some of the world's communists.

Much of Castro's attention during 1989 was directed toward the so-called socialist world. With ever-increasing concern and defiance, Castro rejected the lessons to be learned from the changes sweeping the rest of the Soviet bloc, despite visits to Cuba by Soviet leader Mikhail S. Gorbachev and Soviet foreign minister Shevardnadze. During 1989 Castro even prohibited the circulation in Cuba of two Soviet magazines he found particularly offensive because of what he considered their criticism of Soviet history and socialism: *Moscow News* and *Sputnik*.

But the eternal communist verities Castro defended have made the Cuban economy a perpetual wreck, with little in the way of foreign-currency reserves. Instead of moving toward freer markets, however, as other Soviet-bloc countries are doing, Castro continues to tighten controls; instead of offering Cubans rewards for higher production, Castro promises only "moral" incentives. Predictably, the desperate Cuban economy deteriorated further, a fact of great concern to Gorbachev, since massive Soviet aid and trade benefits have bailed Castro out for more than two decades.

Meanwhile, by the end of 1989, economic reforms in Eastern Europe had accelerated Cuba's economic woes by cutting off or diminishing its access to aid and trade with former allies. On 28 January 1990, Castro told delegates to a Cuban Trade Union Congress: "We didn't foresee any of the catastrophic problems that hit the socialist camp recently," and he concluded by warning darkly that Cuba cannot predict what new problems there may be in 1990 and beyond. He even speculated that at some point the provision of Soviet oil to Cuba might be cut off entirely, putting the latter on what would amount to a war footing even in peacetime. Indeed, burgeoning difficulties in receiving supplies from former Soviet-bloc allies led to new rationing in late January 1990. The Cuban economic situation was worsened also by the U.S. invasion of Panama, which closed down a source of goods that bypassed the U.S. trade embargo of Cuba.

Castro's stubborn determination to persist in proven domestic and international failures, along with corruption, the repression of human rights, and other problems, has led to internal dissent and repression. The most spectacular example of this was the "Ochoa affair," a Stalinist show trial and execution in mid-1989 of General Arnaldo Ochoa, Cuba's best and most famous military leader, who had led Cuban military missions in Ethiopia, Angola, and Nicaragua, on trumped-up corruption and drug charges. In a vitriolic and often incoherent attack on Ochoa, Cuban defense minister and heir apparent Raúl Castro said that remaining dissidents in the military should go to Hungary or Poland; he would even get them visas from his "friend General Jaruzelski," a comment that was omitted from the official published version of the speech. In December, Fidel blasted internal critics he called "charlatans associated with a subtle form of counterrevolution," and warned, "we cannot allow trust in the party to be subverted." As Costa Rican president Oscar Arias said at the end of the year, "Fidel is a sort of Caribbean Kim Il-song, a man whose watch stopped in 1959." (The Communist Party of Cuba announced in mid-February 1990 that it would hold its Fourth Congress in 1991.)

Castro continued his 31-year campaign against capitalism, which he said was rejoicing at the problems in the socialist world, and against the United States. He condemned Washington's "fascist imperialist invasion and massacre" of Panama in December, which the Cuban Communist Party's organ *Granma* called "a warning for Latin America," and praised the heroic Panamanian people's resistance, evidently having missed the news that the vast majority of Panamanians consider the U.S. intervention a liberation.

Under Castro's guidance, Cuban foreign policy remained more assertive than that of the Soviet Union. Cuba's ties to the Salvadoran FMLN, for example, remained strong and Castro loudly praised the guerrillas' November offensive, while the Soviet Union urged a negotiated settlement. At the end of January 1990, Castro decided to "temporarily halt the withdrawal of Cuban military personnel" from Angola, just as the Soviet government supported a new offensive against UNITA. The Cuban Foreign Ministry announced that as of 24 January Cuba had withdrawn 31,000 troops from Angola, more than half its forces in that African country.

In Nicaragua the government was burdened with an even weaker economy—sometimes described as the worst in Latin America—characterized by hyperinflation, massive unemployment, scarcity, and resultant social disaffection and unrest. Purchasing power at the end of 1989 was about 10 percent of what it had been when the Sandinistas took over a decade earlier. Added to this was the need to adapt to the major reforms undertaken by all of its Soviet-bloc allies, except for Cuba.

President Daniel Ortega dramatically ended the cease-fire with the contras on 1 November 1989, claiming repeated contra attacks against the Nicaraguan people, which the Nicaraguan Resistance—the contras—denied. Meanwhile, the Sandinistas received about $500 million in military aid from the Soviet bloc during 1989, most of it from Cuba, though the contras received no military aid from the United States. The Sandinistas put about 50 percent of their budget into the military.

Beginning especially with the Central American summit in August 1987, international pressures were put on the Sandinistas to allow free elections. The international pressures from the Central American presidents and the United States were matched by pressures from nonviolent domestic groups and the remains of the armed resistance forces based in Honduras and portions of Nicaragua. As the domestic economy became increasingly depressed, and uncertainty grew regarding long-term support from Soviet-bloc countries, the Sandinistas themselves began to see some advantage to gaining the international legitimacy elections would bestow, so as to open doors to financial aid and trade.

The elections scheduled for 25 February 1990 pitted ruling Sandinista President Daniel Ortega against an opposition alliance, UNO, made up of more than a dozen anti-Sandinista parties ranging from conservatives to communists, under the leadership of *La Prensa* publisher Violeta Barrios de Chamorro. The election deck was stacked against Chamorro: harassment was common, and torture and psychological pressures continued, as noted by such human-rights groups as Americas Watch. Sandinista leaders regularly equated the opposition with the armed resistance (the contras) and "U.S. imperialism." The Organization of American States and some other observers noted the unequal access to major media. Still, the election was judged fair by several thousand international observers, among whom were very few known critics of the Sandinistas, either individuals or groups, as most such critics had been denied visas. Chamorro won by about 55 to 41 percent; if the 400,000 or more Nicaraguans who have voted with their feet and gone into exile had cast ballots—relatively few could return to Nicaragua to do so—she would have won by 75 to 80 percent.

During 1989 the Sandinistas continued to send arms to the Salvadoran guerrillas in open defiance of the letter and spirit of the Esquipulas II and subsequent peace accords signed by all five Central American presidents since August 1987. This included the shipping of Soviet-made ground-to-air missiles to the guerrillas at the end of the year, a major escalation of the conflict and an action which reportedly drew a severe reprimand from the Soviet Union. According to some sources, the Sandinistas were pushed into the shipment by Fidel Castro and resented the Cuban pressure because it led to international criticism and isolation of the Sandinista government. (*Le Monde*, 30 November; *FBIS-LAT*, 1 December.)

Elsewhere in the hemisphere, nonruling Marxist-Leninist parties and movements sought either to compete for power within democratic systems or to seize power through violence in the true Leninist fashion, though these latter groups were often under pressure to lay down their arms.

In February 1990, ten South American communist parties met in Quito, Ecuador, to express their support for multiparty systems and unity with the region's revolutionary, social democratic, and Christian democratic forces. The meeting, which was attended by observers from Cuba, the Sandinistas of Nicaragua, and the FMLN of El Salvador, called for the ousting of new Panamanian president Guillermo Endara and the holding of new elections. (Like the People's Party of Panama, communist parties around the hemisphere proclaimed the Panama Electoral Tribunal's ruling of December 1989 that Endara had won the May 1989 elections to be illegal.) The ten parties reaffirmed their support for the "immortal ideas" of scientific socialism and attacked the "ideological offensive of imperialism," which dishonestly tries "to sell the idea of the death of socialism." Just before the Quito meeting, the communist Workers Party of Jamaica went so far as to formally open WPJ membership to noncommunists. At the same time, some communist party leaders from Canada to Colombia admitted that they had not always been "objective" in analyzing conditions in the Soviet Union and Eastern Europe, or honest in reporting to their party members and the public.

In Peru, the Communist Party, operating for several decades under the leadership of Jorge del Prado, was the pivotal member of what was the second strongest political group in the country, the United Left (IU), which holds seats in local and national government bodies. Del Prado, a member of the national senate, was chosen president of the IU at its First National Congress in January, though only for six months, during which time, despite PCP efforts, the IU split into competing radical and moderate sections. The PCP eventually stayed with the "radical" faction, though its presidential candidate for the April 1990 election is no more extreme than the candidate of the "moderates."

The Brazilian Communist Party's (PCB) vice-president, Roberto Freire, ran in the first round of Brazil's November–December presidential elections. He garnered only 1.07 percent of the vote in November, but was an articulate spokesman who made a good public impression. In the run-off, the PCB supported the popular, though not victorious, leftist candidate of the Workers' Party, Inácio Lula da Silva. In Guyana, the People's Progressive Party under Cheddi Jagan remained the second-largest in the country. Yet it wins relatively few legislative seats, in large part due to perpetually fraudulent elections. In Uruguay, the communist party was the leading force in the Broad Front (FA), which ran a strong third in the 1989 presidential elections and won control of the government in the capital city of Montevideo. In Mexico, the communists are split into a minority that maintains a semi-independent identity and the majority, which has marched from one alliance to another; in 1989, the latter joined the Democratic Revolution Party headed by noncommunist Cuauhtémoc Cárdenas. Communist parties have long been significant in the governments of Martinique and Guadeloupe.

In Colombia, the communists are the leading member of the moderately effective Patriotic Unity front and have significant representation in local and national government. There and elsewhere, communist parties were involved in labor and student groups, as well as in electoral politics. Communist parties were sometimes active, although relatively insignificant, in Costa Rica, Ecuador, Argentina, and Chile. Communists would have won several seats in the election of December 1989 in Chile, had it not been for voting laws that favored center-left and center-right candidates. While the Communist Party of Venezuela continues to stagnate, the Movement to Socialism (MAS), a democratic-socialist organization that broke away from the communists in 1971, has become a major actor in that country's national politics.

The virtual nonentities of the Latin American communist world during 1989 were the parties in Grenada, Paraguay, Haiti, Panama, the Dominican Republic, Canada, and the United States. The CPUSA reluctantly moved toward endorsing Soviet-bloc reforms, though some of Chairman Gus Hall's remarks on the subject raised questions about his awareness of reality.

Among the groups relying mainly on armed struggle to take power were guerrillas and others in El Salvador, Guatemala, Honduras, Colombia, Peru, and, to a lesser extent, in Brazil and Argentina.

In El Salvador, the FMLN guerrillas pursued a double-track policy of alternating and overlapping war and peace. They waged armed struggle and infiltrated unions and other organizations at home, while they talked peace at home and abroad, during a year that also brought a significant increase in right-wing and military violence. Just weeks before the presidential election in March, the FMLN offered to lay down its arms if the government would postpone the voting and make other major concessions to the guerrillas. The government refused to do so, citing constitutional limitations and arguing that if the FMLN had really been interested in opening up to democracy, it could have done so a couple of months earlier within the well-known schedule of planned democratic elections. Nonetheless, the guerrillas were to some extent represented in the election, which they nevertheless tried to disrupt through intimidation and violence, since their long-time political spokesman, Guillermo Ungo, ran on the Democratic Convergence ticket. Ungo received less than 4 percent of the vote in what

international observers proclaimed was a free and fair election.

The question of government-guerrilla negotiations came up again after the election. In the most important FMLN statement of recent years, which has been largely ignored everywhere, top guerrilla leader Joaquín Villalobos admitted that because of ideological rigidity a decade ago, the guerrillas had not given peace a chance, and thus they themselves were in large part responsible for the ten years of heavy bloodshed in El Salvador, during which tens of thousands have lost their lives (Barcelona, *La Vanguardia*, 21 September; *FBIS-LAT*, 10 October).

Then in another reversal, on 11 November, supposedly in response to right-wing terrorism, the government's refusal to combat that terrorism, and alleged government indifference to sincere negotiations, the guerrillas launched the largest offensive of the ten-year-long war. Their forces occupied some sections of San Salvador, deliberately drawing military fire into heavily populated areas. The guerrillas suffered heavy losses in personnel—at least 400 guerrillas were killed—and to some extent in reputation and infrastructure. For example, prominent members of some well-known Salvadoran organizations, including the Committee of Mothers of the Disappeared (Comadres), a much-cited human-rights group, joined the guerrillas and announced they were no longer pretending to be nonpartisan. (*CSM*, 21 November.)

But the government also had losses. Its military forces were criticized for firing into populated areas where the guerrillas had taken a foothold and for the murder of several Jesuits. After an investigation, Salvadoran president Alfredo Cristiani announced that the killings had been done by members of the military who would be tried. But the assassination of the priests, in particular, was used by some in the United States to argue that U.S. aid to the Cristiani government should be terminated. Guerrilla leader Villalobos put the murder of the Jesuits in perspective when he said their murder "is going to come back and provoke the isolation of the government." (Ibid.) Late in 1989, the Salvadoran war was escalated substantially when the guerrillas received from the Nicaraguan government Soviet ground-to-air missiles they had been seeking for years.

There were increases in armed violence throughout Guatemala and Honduras, though some in the latter country may have been instigated more by the Salvadoran FMLN and the Sandinistas than by Honduran revolutionaries. In the former, one faction of the Guatemalan Party of Labor, the country's official communist party, joined the guerrilla National Revolutionary Unity of Guatemala (URNG) and thus subscribed to armed struggle. The URNG was better coordinated during 1989 than ever before, although as yet it is a faint shadow of the FMLN.

The most successful guerrilla group in South America continued to be the Sendero Luminoso, or Shining Path, in Peru, if success is measured by deaths and destruction over a broad area. More than 2,600 people died from political violence between January and November, the considerable majority in actions involving Sendero, but some also involving the Revolutionary Movement of Túpac Amaru (MRTA), raising the total for the past decade to about 16,000. Sendero chooses its victims carefully, aiming in particular at poor peasants who do not cooperate with guerrilla dictates, law-enforcement officials, and political leaders. Half of Peru's citizens now live under states of emergency, though the guerrillas failed in their major immediate objective of the year: the sabotaging of the November municipal elections. The Shining Path has close links to some of the drug dealers in the Upper Huallaga Valley. Taken together, the guerrillas and the drug dealers offer an almost insurmountable barrier to successful government by whoever becomes president in the April 1990 elections.

Guerrilla groups have been fighting in Colombia longer than in any other country of the Western hemisphere. Several of these forces were active off and on during 1989, some cooperating with and others fighting against the narcotraffickers. Even as the National Liberation Army increased its attacks toward the end of the year, the M-19 guerrillas agreed to participate in the March 1990 legislative elections. Throughout 1989, many members of the Colombian Leftist Patriotic Union were assassinated by the right. In Brazil, several radical groups promoted land seizures and violent strikes.

More sporadic or isolated violence occurred in several other countries. Argentina experienced a bloody attack on the La Tablada military garrison outside of Buenos Aires in January 1989. This event involved the Popular Resistance Front, which includes former members of the People's Revolutionary Army, one of the Marxist-Leninist groups that precipitated the "dirty war" in the mid-1970s. Its appearance strengthened the presidential bid of Carlos Menem, the Peronist who was elected and took power at midyear. Argentine authorities were particularly concerned that Peru's Sendero Luminoso held at least one meeting in the northern Argentinian city of Tucumán. Two small groups engaged in armed attacks throughout Chile, while several of the larger movements, including the Communist Party and parts of the Socialist Party, supported violent demonstrations in Santiago and other parts of the country after the December elections and on other occasions. Early in 1990, the Chilean communists announced that with the advent of an elected government in March they would no longer support armed struggle by the masses.

Increasingly, Latin Americans are questioning the relevance of communist parties, though not always to the degree found in most other parts of the world. As to some outspoken U.S. academics, the causes of the Sandinistas, the FMLN, and some other groups still seem so appealing to some Latin Americans that their failures—and the failures of all other groups professing anything like the same objectives—are ignored or discounted. With Soviet-bloc support declining, many Marxist-Leninist groups will find funding more difficult to obtain in the future. A few have already turned to drugs as a means of obtaining dollars, and others may persist underfunded until the full political, social, and economic failures of communist systems around the world are finally grasped.

William Ratliff
Hoover Institution

Argentina

Population. 31,914,473 (1989)
Party. Communist Party of Argentina (Partido Comunista de la Argentina; PCA)
Founded. 1918
Membership. 80,000 (claimed; 25,000 militants)
General Secretary. Patricio Echegaray
Politburo. 12 members: Patricio Echegaray, Athos Fava, Jorge Pereyra, Luis Heller, Ernesto Salgado, Fanny Edelman, Guillermo Varone, Miguel Balleto, Eduardo Sigal, Rodolfo Casals, Enrique Dratman, Francisco Alvarez
Central Committee. 100 members, 15 alternates

Status. Legal
Last Congress. Sixteenth, 4–7 November 1986
Last Election. 14 May 1989 (presidential, parliamentary), no representation
Auxiliary Organizations. Communist Youth Federation, Union of Argentine Women, Committee in Solidarity with Nicaragua, local branch of the World Peace Council
Publications. *Nuestra Propuesta* (weekly); *Ideología y política* (theoretical bimonthly); *Juventud* (biweekly youth magazine)

During 1989 Argentina experienced a serious economic and political crisis, with ramifications for civil-military relations, public order, and armed insurgency. The so-called Spring Plan, intended to bolster the faltering economy, collapsed in February, sending the country into an inflationary tailspin and causing the dollar to rise from 17 australes (the local unit of currency) to 850 in six months. The cost of living increased 70 percent in the month of May, and 114 percent in June. In elections—the first since 1928 in which one civilian government was chosen to immediately follow another—Peronist Carlos Saúl Menem predictably defeated the candidate of President Raúl Alfonsín's ruling Radical Party. Shortly thereafter, food riots broke out in Rosario and Córdoba, Argentina's second and third largest cities. President Alfonsín declared a 30-day state of siege, permitting the arrest of nearly a thousand people. Among them were the presidential candidate of the tiny Partido Obrero—a leftfringe group—and several militants of the PCA and the Revolutionary Workers' Party (POR), all of whom stood accused of inciting crowds to violence and looting. The militants were subsequently released on judicial orders for lack of evidence. PCA general secretary Patricio Echegaray heatedly denied party involvement in the unrest, claiming that "the government discovered eight million agitators disguised as hungry people." (*NYT*, 31 May.)

Deteriorating public order and financial panic continued to sap confidence in the government's authority throughout the month of June, causing President Alfonsín to step down in favor of his elected successor on 9 July, some seven months early. President Menem immediately restored a measure of calm and sought to rebuild national consensus, partly by reaching out to members of the Argentine business and military establishments, both of whom had feared that his election would lead to a new round of reckless populism, demagoguery, and class conflict.

In early October, as part of a grand gesture of national reconciliation, Menem pardoned officers active in military uprisings against President Alfonsín (see *YICA*, 1987, 1988), as well as most of the military chiefs linked to the fight against subversion during the period from 1976 to 1983. In addition, however, he also amnestied nearly sixty leftist terrorists, most of whom had long since fled to foreign exile. Public reaction was unexpectedly negative, causing the president to cancel plans to pardon former junta leaders Gen. Jorge Videla, Gen. Roberto Viola, and Adm. Emilio Massera, all condemned to life imprisonment, as well as Mario Firmenich, former chief of the Montoneros, a group of urban guerrillas, serving a 30-year sentence for kidnapping and murder.

Though Menem received considerable public support for his new economic plan, which included a drastic reduction of the deficit, privatization of money-losing state enterprises, and wage and price controls, he immediately ran into difficulty with his own trade-union movement. Though he managed to purge an uncooperative secretary general of the Peronist General Confederation of Labor, Argentina was plagued by strikes in November, including a nationwide transport stoppage that snarled traffic in Buenos Aires and many provincial capitals for nearly a week. For his part, the new president pledged his willingness to "face a thousand strikes" as he piloted Argentina into wholly uncharted waters. (*NYT*, 13 November.)

In December, the alliance between Menem and the business sector broke down over disagreements on exchange rates, tariffs, and macroeconomic policy generally. Meanwhile, the Peronist labor federation had split in two, and, in spite of the pardon given to the officers, the military continued to be restive. One of the leading rebels of 1988, Col. Mohammed Seineldín, "seemed to challenge authority by openly leading a hundred or so of his followers in workouts in a public park" in November. (*NYT*, 26 December.) The year ended with Menem appearing to lose control of the situation, as left and right each struck out in its own direction.

The La Tablada Affair. The most sensational event of the political year was a mysterious attack on a garrison at La Tablada, a distant suburb of the capital of Buenos Aires, on 23 January. The operation was carried out by the Popular Resistance Front (FRP), made up of members of the All for the Fatherland Movement (MTP) and former militants of the People's Revolutionary Army (ERP), an urban guerrilla group which had been active in Argentina during the early 1970s and hitherto thought extinct. After a 30-hour pitched battle, much of it in full view of television and news cameras, 28 guerrillas and 11 soldiers and police officers lay dead, including the deputy commander of the post, whose tongue had been cut out before he was murdered. Some 70 persons were injured; 18 of the assailants were captured. The rest escaped, including, apparently, Enrique Haraldo Gorriarán Merlo, the intellectual author of the plot.

The La Tablada affair illuminated several dark corners of Argentine politics. For one thing, it discredited frequent claims by the Alfonsín administration that the only political violence which constituted a threat to authority came from the right (and, very specifically, from insubordinate military officers). For another, it pointed to a possible connection between Argentine leftist terrorists and the government of Nicaragua, since Gorriarán Merlo had been a frequent visitor to Managua since the Sandinistas' assumption of power and had apparently received military training there. (He was thought as well to be involved in the 1980 murder in Paraguay of exiled Nicaraguan dictator Anastasio Somoza.) Further, it held up to public suspicion both the human-rights community and the small radical wing of the Argentine church, since among the attackers were human-rights lawyer Jorge Baños and Rev. Antonio Puigjané, a Franciscan priest from the "progressive" diocese of Quilmes. Many critics of the Radical administration—including then–presidential candidate Carlos Menem—even suggested that the attack was deliberately provoked by the Radicals in a last-ditch attempt to save their faltering presidential campaign, a theory rendered somewhat less probable by the complex political architecture of the event itself.

According to documents purportedly captured from the guerrillas and subsequently released to the press by the Argentine government, the plan was to create the impression that the officers within the garrison were launching a new uprising against the Alfonsín government. Having captured the barracks, the revolutionaries would use the army's radio network to broadcast a call to rebellion, sowing confusion within the ranks of the armed forces.

Then they would announce that they, as representatives of the "popular resistance," had managed to abort the uprising. They would lead a convoy, headed by captured armor, to the main square in Buenos Aires, where they would call on President Alfonsín to place himself at the head of an armed popular movement. The ultimate objective was a "peoples' government" that would replace the army with a People's Resistance Front; expropriate the financial market; suspend interest payments on the foreign debt; and expropriate properties in excess of one house and one car belonging to military officers and trade-union leaders.

The first phase of the plan worked so well that it took the government almost a day and a half to realize it was not facing a military uprising. And their high degree of military preparedness suggests that the attackers had received serious training, presumably abroad; their intention to use captured armor reinforced the hypothesis. (*Noticias Argentinas*, 26 January; *FBIS*, 27 January; *Latin American Weekly Report*, 9 February.) For his part, President Alfonsín later told an interviewer from Italian television that the plan to execute the officers "might have led us to civil war. Had this happened, I would not have had the confidence of the military, who in turn would have believed that I had set a trap for them. All of this would have meant chaos." When asked what the terrorists expected to gain, he replied, nothing "from the viewpoint of reason. But, as you see, it has happened because there is another logic, the logic of terror."

The La Tablada affair also tilted the ideological balance of Argentine politics—which had been firmly left-of-center during the last five years—back toward the right. As President Alfonsín warned in the same television interview, "People who side with the left must be careful of the ultra left... the left cannot afford to simply say that an attack was a foolish thing because it only helps the right. This would suppose that had it helped the left, it would not be a foolish but an intelligent act... Violence is evil and the pursuit of power through violence is an aberration. This must be admitted by both the right and the left." (TELAM, 1 February; *FBIS*, 3 February.)

In the aftermath of the battle in La Tablada, President Alfonsín issued Decree 327, conceding to the military the right to carry out domestic intelligence operations against potential subversives. He would be advised in this by a newly created National Security Council, composed, in part, of the three service chiefs of staff. Critics claimed that this amounted to turning over to the army the function of "preventing the formation or activity of armed groups," a step backward from the civilian control achieved since 1983. (*CSM*, 17 April.) Many leftist groups regarded this as an overreaction, particularly since the La Tablada raid had been promptly denounced by the PCA, The Movement Toward Socialism (MAS), Firmenich, and Nestor Vicente, the presidential candidate of the United Left (see below).

For their part, from Montevideo, in neighboring Uruguay, where those insurgents who managed to escape were apparently in hiding, the FRP promised "to continue the struggle until a final victory is achieved" (*Diarios y Noticias*, 1 February; *FBIS*, 2 February).

Domestic Party Affairs. For the past several years Communist party leadership has gradually moved from critical support of the center-left government of President Raúl Alfonsín to open hostility. It has been particularly alienated by the administration's economic and foreign policies, as well as its efforts to conclude trials of military men accused of human rights abuses during the 1970s.

In both the congressional and gubernatorial races of 1986, and the presidential and congressional elections of May 1989, it opted to run a common opposition slate with other left-wing parties. In this year's elections, the party presented a joint list (the so-called United Left) in combination with the Trotskyist party MAS, as well as (in some provinces) left-wing schismatics from the Peronist, Radical, or Intransigent parties. The United Left's presidential candidate Nestor Vicente, though himself not a communist, was generally regarded as the party's choice over several other, more notably independent possibilities. Though the communists gained no representation in parliament, under a complicated system of joint lists MAS managed to send two deputies to the lower house for the first time.

In April, General Secretary Athos Fava was replaced by Politburo member (and deputy general secretary) Patricio Echegaray, who also succeeded him as chairman of the Central Committee plenum. In October the party weekly *¿Que Pasa?* was replaced by another publication, *Nuestra Propuesta*, with an announced initial press run of 25,000.

Auxiliary and Front Organizations. The party has territorial organizations in every province, including Tierra del Fuego, and a Communist Youth Federation active in promoting party policy at schools and elsewhere.

The party controls a local chapter of the World Peace Council and also the Argentine Permanent Commission on Human Rights. It has unusually close relations with—such as to suggest covert control of—the Argentine Military Center for Democracy (CEMIDA), a group of retired officers and soldiers who purport to favor human rights, democracy, and anti-imperialism—that is, opposition to U.S. military influence in Latin America.

It is the principal component of the Broad Front for Liberation (FRAL), an all-purpose political umbrella organization that brings together small leftist political groups and dissidents from the major parties.

International Views, Positions, Activities. As it is one of the most orthodox (that is, pro-Soviet) parties in Latin America, recent events in the USSR have posed something of an ideological challenge for the PCA. After the sixteenth party congress, much of the party's top leadership was purged to bring it closer into line with Gorbachev's "new thinking" (see *YICA*, 1988). Nonetheless, there is some evidence that Argentine communist leaders are still somewhat behind the Moscow curve.

For example, at a symposium of communist leaders from many countries held in Prague early in the year, PCA representative Jorge Bergsten took pointed exception to the notion advanced by a Soviet colleague that "the revolutionary forces should lead the struggles in their countries in a way that would prevent them from setting off a world nuclear conflict." Bergsten argued that "such a view results in an unjustifiable narrowing of the class struggle, with the revolutionaries yielding to the nuclear blackmail of imperialism and restricting their activities." His position was seconded by Tran Thanh of Vietnam and Antonio Díaz Ruiz of Cuba. ("Forum: Peace and Revolution in the Nuclear Age," *WMR*, February.)

Argentine communist leaders Patricio Echegaray and Athos Fava also held consultations with their Soviet and Czech counterparts in Moscow and Prague in October. The subjects were said to be the international situation and the evolving situation of the socialist countries.

Relations with the Soviet Bloc. Argentine-Soviet commercial and maritime relations continued at their normally intense level. Soviet trade representatives announced the opening of a local branch of the Bank for Foreign Economic Activities, and a high-level Argentine delegation visited Moscow from October 24 to 26 to discuss (and possibly revise) existing fishing agreements, as well as trade in cereals and cereals byproducts.

Anatoly Timoshenko, the new Soviet trade representative in Argentina, announced that his country would explore new areas of commercial involvement, including joint industrial and construction projects and joint enterprises and plants, with both public and private enterprises.

Timoshenko reminded the Argentine-Soviet Chamber of Commerce in April that "the volume of our commercial exports to Argentina is the highest of any Latin American country"—$950 million in 1988, mostly in agricultural products. He expressed some concern, however, over the continued one-sided nature of the exchange, which clearly favored the Argentines. (*La Prensa*, 2 April; *FBIS*, 19 May.) However, it was expected that the actual volume of Argentine-Soviet trade would be smaller in 1989, owing to a drought.

Other Leftist Groups. Even apart from the La Tablada affair, there were indications throughout 1989 that terrorist activity was reviving to a modest but troubling extent. In February, two individuals wearing military uniforms and carrying submachine guns robbed a hospital in a town in the province of Corrientes of large quantities of blood, serum, and medicine.

In April, Vice Admiral Barry M. Hussey, secretary of the National Security Council, confirmed that Sendero Luminoso, a terrorist group which normally operates in Peru, had held a meeting at a hotel in the northern Argentine city of Tucumán. He could not say, however, whether the recent activities of the MTP had anything to do with this event.

In late December, an unexplained bomb exploded in front of army headquarters, and the same week another explosive charge blew up a car in a military housing project in La Plata, some 30 miles from Buenos Aires.

Meanwhile, however, the leaders of the Montoneros—the largest and most active of several guerrilla groups during the 1970s—publicly repudiated their past tactics. In a document released in April ("Solemn Commitment for National Pacification and Reconciliation Based on Social Justice and Soul Searching"), the Montoneros renounced violence and clandestine struggle as legitimate tools, and promised to work within the democratic system under the banner of "Revolutionary Peronism." Among those subscribing to the document were Roberto Perdía, Fernando Vaca Narvaja, and former Buenos Aires governor Oscar Bidegain, all of whom were outside the country, as well as (from his prison cell) Mario Firmenich.

A few days after their pardon by President Menem, Vaca Narvaja and Perdía returned from Uruguay, offering to return some of the $60 million in ransom money that they had obtained by kidnapping the brothers Juan and Jorge Born, owners of Argentina's most important grain-trading consortium. Vaca Narvaja and Perdía not only paid a call on the president to thank him for their pardon, but also met for a conciliatory tea with the Born brothers in a hotel in downtown Buenos Aires.

Notable Figures or Newsmakers. Patricio Echegaray, new general secretary of the PCA, was born in 1946. Educated as a teacher, he worked for many years as a trade-union leader. He joined the Federation of Communist Youth in 1965, becoming a member of its Central Committee in 1970 and its general secretary in 1980. In 1981 he was elected a member of the party's Central Committee and the Political Commission, and appointed editor in chief of its weekly, *¿Que Pasa?* In May 1986, he was appointed a member of the secretariat of the Central Committee, and deputy general secretary.

Paulino Gonzalez Alberdi, a Communist party member since 1923, died in September at the age of 86. For many years he served on the editorial board of *World Marxist Review*.

Mark Falcoff
American Enterprise Institute

Bolivia

Population. 6,588,601 (July 1989)
Party. Communist Party of Bolivia (Partido Comunista de Bolivia; PCB)
Founded. 1950 (latest split 1985)
Membership. 500 (claimed)
General Secretary. Humberto Ramírez (majority faction); Carlos Soria (minority faction)
Status. Legal
Last Congress. Fifth, 9–13 February 1985; extraordinary, 26–29 April 1986
Last Election. 7 May 1989. The United Left (IU), the coalition in which the PCB participated, gained only 7 percent of the vote and 12 of the 130

seats in the elections and played no role in the
Congressional vote which saw Jaime Paz Zamora
of the Movement of the Revolutionary Left (MIR)
elected president.

Auxiliary Organizations. Communist Youth of
Bolivia

Publications. Both factions of the PCB publish a
paper called *Unidad*.

In a country where presidential elections can become the focal point of attention to the virtual exclusion of all other events, 1989 was a good year for
Bolivia. A remarkable election took place, in which
a former "radical leftist revolutionary" was elected
to the presidency by the Congress in August largely
because a former "right-wing dictator," who had
finished ahead of him in the general elections in
May, gracefully stood aside. Moreover, the incumbent party, which had undertaken to curb hyperinflation and save the economy, was surprisingly not
punished by the public, but instead finished in first
place in the general elections. Bolivia being
Bolivia, however, it was the third-place finisher who
finally ended up wearing the presidential sash. In
the midst of all this, the parties of the far left, which
included the Communist Party of Bolivia (PCB),
continued their downward slide, and are now
largely irrelevant in the Bolivian political process.

Jaime Paz Zamora, who bore the twin burdens of
being both a former "radical" and a former vice-
president in the administration of Hernán Siles
Zuazo (1982–1985), whose economic policies
brought the country to near ruin, was sworn in as
president on 6 August after the three-month confu-
sion-filled period between the elections and the inauguration. Representing the Movement of the Revolutionary Left (MIR), the one-time seminarian
had finished in third place with 19.6 percent of the
vote, behind former president and general Hugo
Banzer of the National Democratic Action Party/
Christian Democrat Party coalition (itself an interesting combination), which gained 22.7 percent of
the votes cast, placing just behind the top vote
getter, Gonzalo Sánchez de Losada of the incumbent National Revolutionary Party (MNR), who
obtained 23 percent (*LAT*, 3 August). In a distant
fourth place, but displaying a potential for the future, was a new party that appealed to Bolivia's
Indian majority with a theme of ethnic unity, the
Conscience of the Fatherland (CONDEPA), led by
former television personality Carlos Palenque. Although Palenque gained only 11 percent of the vote,
he played a critical role in delivering the presidency

to Paz Zamora in the vote in the Congress in the
early days of August. He could have just as easily
swung the vote to either Banzer or Sánchez de
Losada, and in fact his strong showing in La Paz
effectively denied Banzer the plurality that would
have given him the presidency.

The parties of the far left had joined together in
1988 to form the United Left (IU). Staking out the
position that Bolivia's economic recovery had been
carried out on the backs of the poor, the IU appeared
in 1988 to be poised to play the role of spoiler/
kingmaker in 1989. This latest coalition of the far
left attracted only about 7 percent of the votes cast,
however. It was in IU that the PCB made its latest
effort to align with like-minded groups as a means
to gain political power. Its previous effort to do so
had been successful: in 1980 it joined with Siles
Zuazo's party, and the PCB had been rewarded with
key positions in the cabinet. Because the memories
of the Siles Zuazo era remain so bitter for many
Bolivians, the PCB's access to power then is probably now considered a Pyrrhic victory.

If the results of the 1989 elections are any guide,
the party appears to have little future. Its younger
members are deserting it for other elements on the
left side of the political spectrum. There is, of
course, strong sympathy in a poor country like
Bolivia for the "egalitarian" and distributive notions
of the far left, but the PCB does not appear to have
the confidence of those on the left that it is the
vehicle with which to achieve these goals. And the
apparent demise of the Communist parties of Eastern Europe has reinforced the notion among Bolivians that the PCB is finished in that country as a
viable political force.

The Rise and Fall of the PCB. The PCB is
badly split; its most recent schism occurred in 1985,
when, after its Fifth Congress, it split into two
factions. The main element of the PCB does have
influence in the Bolivian labor movement, and its
leader, Simón Reyes, was elected general secretary
of the Bolivian Labor Federation (COB) in 1987.
He then turned over the leadership of the PCB to his
long-time ally Humberto Ramírez. In April the
PCB's latest off-shoot surfaced, calling itself the
"Revolutionary Left" (IR), sounding the familiar
refrain that U.S. "imperialism" had changed strategies in backing democracies instead of military
governments, but that the goal of Washington was
still capitalist exploitation but now through the
means of "controlled democracies." (La Paz, La

Red Panamericana [radio broadcast], 14 April; *FBIS-LAT*, 18 April.)

Ironically, the demise of the PCB in the 1980s is a reflection of the very conditions that propelled it into existence in 1950. Young radicals in that year became frustrated with the actions of Bolivia's communist standard bearer, the Revolutionary Party of the Left (PIR). These university students felt that the PIR leadership had compromised the revolutionary ideals of the party by collaborating with the conservative elements that dominated Bolivia in the late 1940s. They broke away and created the PCB.

The PIR, along with the MNR, had come into existence in the aftermath of the 1930s Chaco War, the seminal event of twentieth-century Bolivia. The two radical parties became the political magnets for young Bolivian intellectuals who felt the country had been betrayed by the conservative parties whose bumbling had caused Bolivia to suffer an ignominious defeat by Paraguay.

The PIR—unified in its populist Marxism—was initially the stronger of the two parties, as the MNR, with competing factions, struggled to find its place on the Bolivian political landscape.

The MNR enjoyed a brief period in power as a result of a coalition with the military in the mid-1940s. It was toppled in 1946. Many of its key leaders, such as Paz Estenssoro, were driven into exile. The PIR, in contrast, survived as a political party by collaborating with the conservative parties, and in 1950 was surpassed as the dominant voice on the left by the breakaway PCB. The MNR, meanwhile, stormed back from exile in 1952, defeated the Bolivian army in a populist uprising fueled by charges of electoral fraud, and set in motion the reforms of the Bolivian National Revolution, adopting many of the positions long espoused by the PIR, which soon vanished as a political actor.

Just as it supplanted the PIR, so too has the PCB now been moved from the center stage of radicalism in Bolivia. As is the case in so many countries of Latin America where the old-line communist parties are considered discredited remnants of the past, the PCB holds little attraction for the younger generation of Bolivians, who see the other parties of the left as more promising routes to power. As noted above, the near eclipse of the Communist parties in Eastern Europe in the remarkable year of 1989 will certainly do little to help the PCB recapture any political power, and in fact will serve to increase its hemorrhaging.

The PCB's Quest for Power Through Coalition. The PCB has attempted over the years to parlay what political strength it has by participating in the recurring coalitions of the far left. Despite its own internal problems, the PCB continues to preach that unity is the only way the left in Bolivia can achieve power. This theme was emphasized in an article written in 1988 by PCB general secretary Humberto Ramírez. Ramírez demonstrated that the PCB is cognizant of the problems it faces in Bolivia, and sees unification of anti–right-wing forces as essential. He wrote that "the Communist Party of Bolivia is aware of the need to overcome certain obstacles, such as sectarianism and anti-communist attitudes which play into the hands of right wing forces. It is also important to eliminate other factors of disunity among the left, democratic and progressive forces" (*WMR*, August 1988). The election results in 1989 show just how much short of the mark the PCB and its allies have fallen, and how they have been unable to reach the Bolivian people with their message.

The most recent effort of the PCB and other parties of Bolivia's far left to gain political power was the creation of the aforementioned United Left in September 1988. The IU's presidential candidate for the elections of 7 May 1989 was Antonio Aranibar, who formerly headed the far-left faction of the MIR, but then broke away and formed the Free Bolivian Movement (FBL), which gained a surprising 89,000 votes in the 1988 municipal elections (*El Diario*, 11 June 1988). In the 1985 general elections, Aranibar had given the support of his faction of the MIR to the PCB, and also supported Reyes in the COB election in 1987. The IU's intention to run a populist campaign, criticizing the MNR's "neo-liberal" economic policy which the left claims has placed the burden of Bolivia's economic recovery on the backs of the poor, was to a great extent coopted by Palenque's CONDEPA.

In commenting on the prospects of the IU shortly after it was formed in 1988, one of Bolivia's most astute political columnists, Father José "Pepe" Gramunt, a Spanish Jesuit who has lived in Bolivia for 35 years, wrote that "the IU would bring in even more votes if it were capable of offering the country a convincing alternative economic policy...The majority of the voters...no longer have any confidence in the various forms of Utopia which the radical left was in the habit of proposing until just a short time ago...These and other solutions...no longer appear convincing, even to leftist voters in the Western democracies. I fear these proposals will not win over any majorities here either" (*El Mundo*, 14 September 1988). The results of the election in 1989 proved just how accurate and prophetic were Father Gramunt's words.

If the IU had followed Father Gramunt's advice, it perhaps could have played a more important role in the elections, and in fact been able to garner enough votes to have gained some valuable IOUs from Paz Zamora, including positions in the cabinet, as it had during the Siles Zuazo presidency. Because the PCB's strength is concentrated in the labor movement, the party could be expected to exert influence in any government in which it participates far out of proportion to its vote-pulling strength. But it must be adroit enough to place itself into the pivotal kingmaking role, and the IU, with the PCB at its core, failed utterly to live up to its own expectations in the 1989 elections.

Background to the 1989 Election Campaign. To grasp the significance of the elections of 1989, it is necessary to examine the political context from which they evolved. Bolivia is a country where political instability has been the norm since independence was achieved in 1825. Military rule has predominated, and some estimates place the number of violent and near-violent changes of government at close to 190, more than any other country in Latin America. There has not, however, been a military coup in ten years, and democratization seems to be taking root.

Unlike many other countries in Latin America, Bolivia has not seen fit to change its electoral law so that a clear-cut winner can be selected in a run-off between the two top vote getters in a general election. The result in Bolivia's multiparty system is that the person eventually chosen as president by the newly-elected Congress comes into office with the burden of having had the majority of voters cast their ballots for someone else. Delicate coalition-building is a requirement, but continual crises in confidence are almost guaranteed, given the lack of a clear mandate for the president. In a country with a strong tradition of military rule, the temptation is ever present for political factions to "knock at the barracks' doors" in order to have the soldiers "save the country" once again.

Even with the apparent changes in the Bolivian political environment, this cannot be ruled out. The Bolivian military often refers to itself as the "tutelary institution," although its tendency to teach the country civic virtues has been stifled in recent years. The inherent fragility of the political system, however, could eventually see the return of the "man on horseback." Amending the electoral law to allow a president to come into office with a majority of the people having voted for him in a run-off election would at least place another obstacle in the path of those in the military, and their civilian supporters, who may be inclined to unseat the president during the recurrent crises that seem destined to be a part of the Bolivian political landscape.

In 1989, as in the previous election in 1985, the man who emerged victorious had neither an electoral plurality nor a legislative majority. But in 1989 Jaime Paz Zamora was able, as had been his uncle, the venerable Victor Paz Estenssoro in 1985, to put together a coalition to gain the presidency and a working majority to govern. Paz Estenssoro had the difficult task of attempting to recover from the disastrous, indecisive presidency of his one-time revolutionary colleague, Hernán Siles Zuazo, whose administration had seen inflation surpass 20,000 percent. Paz Zamora, while facing the overwhelming challenges of any president of Bolivia, has an easier road to follow as a result of the tough and politically unpopular decisions taken by his predecessor. Perhaps only Paz Estenssoro, the "grand old man" of Bolivian politics, could have taken the measures needed to save Bolivia. Now over 80, Paz Estenssoro will surely be remembered as one of the country's greatest leaders. But he owed much to the man who devised and implemented these harsh but necessary measures, Planning Minister Gonzalo Sánchez de Losada.

The 1989 Campaign for the Presidency. As the election campaign got under way in 1988, it appeared that the MNR would suffer a stinging defeat at the polls in 1989 because of its austerity-based "New Economic Policy." The December 1987 municipal elections certainly did not augur well for the MNR. In Bolivia's first such elections in 40 years, MNR candidates received less than a third of the votes the party gained in the 1985 presidential elections—138,906 to 456,754. Even more ominous was the decline in the percentage of MNR votes of the total votes cast—from 24 percent in the 1985 general elections to 8 percent in 1987. Left-of-center parties made the most significant gains at the MNR's expense, especially the MIR of Paz Zamora. The MIR pulled in 31 percent of the total votes cast—308,714, about twice as many as it received in the 1985 elections (*El Diario*, 11 June 1988). The MIR, which was considered by the military governments of the past a party of the far left—its name, inflammatory rhetoric, and many of its actions certainly suggested this orientation—had modified its position and is thought by the Marxist elements to have deserted the leftist cause.

The ADN, led by a former president, General Hugo Banzer, saw its vote total decrease from 493,375 in the 1985 general elections to 336,684 in 1987, but this still represented 35 percent of the total votes cast, more than any other party received (ibid.). After nudging out Paz Estenssoro in the 1985 general elections, Banzer gracefully accepted the vote of the new Congress, which gave the MNR the victory, and the MNR-ADN "Pact for Democracy" was formed. It was this agreement that enabled President Paz Estenssoro and Planning Minister Sánchez de Losada to implement the economic reforms so badly needed, which included the closing of many unproductive government tin mines and resulting unemployment in one of the pillars of MNR strength, the mine workers. The MNR success of 1985–1989 would have been impossible without the cooperation of Banzer and the ADN. Given his identification with the relatively harsh MNR economic program, Banzer perhaps sensed the need to move to the center to bolster his political strength. Consequently, he forged an alliance with the Christian Democrats, and asked their leader Luis Ossio to be his running mate in the 1989 elections.

The architect of the Paz Estenssoro administration's efforts to tame the economic monster, Sánchez de Losada, to the surprise of many, captured the MNR nomination for the presidency. He beat out candidates that carried less baggage than he in an aggressive campaign for the nomination that signaled the type of campaign he would wage in the general election.

Perhaps because he felt he had little to lose, given the unpopularity of the economic measures he had instituted as Paz Estenssoro's "hatchet man," Sánchez de Losada launched hard-hitting attacks against his main rivals, Banzer and Paz Zamora. As the campaign progressed, Sánchez de Losada took on the bellicose posture of a U.S. candidate of the 1980s: he engaged in so-called negative campaigning. He was, in fact, assisted by U.S. consultants. Adding to the "made in the U.S.A." image was his strong "gringo" accent, a product of having lived until he was 21 in the United States. A line that Banzer used for sure-fire applause was that, unlike another candidate for the presidency of Bolivia, he spoke Spanish fluently. There is some speculation that "Goni" actually capitalizes on his accent to set him apart from other Bolivian politicians.

He constantly referred to Banzer as a former "dictator," and reminded one and all that Paz Zamora had been the vice-president in the Siles Zuazo government, and therefore likely to return the country to the economic chaos of those years. Although he may have gained some votes by this tactic, the net result seems to have been to drive Banzer closer to Paz Zamora and the MIR, rather than to Sánchez de Losada and the MNR, whose political and economic philosophy more closely resembled that of the ADN. When the votes were cast in the congress, Paz Zamora received the support of Banzer, who reportedly had developed an intense dislike for Sánchez de Losada. In Bolivian politics, personal feelings and loyalties frequently transcend ideology in the formation of political alliances. Sánchez de Losada may have won the battle for popular votes with his negative tactics, but they were his undoing in the war for the presidency.

Banzer ran on the promise to return Bolivia to the period of relative prosperity it had enjoyed during his almost unprecedented length of time in office (1971–1978). Only the presidency of Marshal Andres Santa Cruz, who ruled from 1829 to 1839, was longer than that of Banzer. He and his party, although in alliance with the MNR through the "Pact of Democracy," were only partially blamed for the austerity measures of 1985–1989, and the ADN had going for it a reputation for efficiency, as much because of the nostalgia for the "good old days" of the first Banzer presidency as for the competency displayed by ADN mayors in cities and towns around the country.

When the ADN announced that it had formed an alliance with the Christian Democrats, and that Luis Ossio would be Banzer's running mate, it caught observers in Bolivia by surprise, given the distinct differences between the statist Christian Democrats and the free-market ADN. But stranger alliances have been formed in Bolivia's flexible politics, and both parties saw benefits deriving for them. For Ossio and the Christian Democrats, it was a chance for national office, something they could not achieve on their own. For Banzer and the ADN, what really counted was the chance to broaden their appeal and perhaps get the extra votes in the general election in May and vital seats in the Congress that would be needed for the election in August.

The Aftermath of the Election. Despite charges of fraud in the vote counting, and the posturing by the candidates and their "spin doctors," most observers considered any irregularities as inconsequential. But because the Bolivian electoral law and Constitution call for the newly-elected congress to elect a president from the three top vote getters—and congress is not sworn in until 4 August—political maneuvering for position continued for three months, and the media gave daily reports on the worsening political "crisis."

The area of most contention was the throwing out of ballots because of irregularities. Banzer made much of this for a very understandable reason: Having been confident that he would gain a plurality, he had campaigned on the basis that the candidate who garnered the most votes in the general elections should be viewed as the people's choice, and therefore given the presidency by the Congress. (*Latin American Weekly Report*, 27 April.)

Having finished second to Sánchez de Losada, Banzer made an effort to have enough of the MNR ballots declared null that he would in fact have the plurality when congress convened. Sánchez de Losada's narrow lead held up, however. But the daily intrigue allowed Bolivians to continue to enjoy the electoral game long past 7 May.

With the inauguration on 6 August, the backroom politicking to see which candidate would be selected continued almost until the eve of the inauguration, and most foreign delegations left for Bolivia unsure of whose inauguration they would be attending. Banzer finally broke the logjam by giving his votes to Paz Zamora. When Palenque did likewise, Sánchez de Losada lost any chance to be president, although he had gained a narrow plurality in the elections. Perhaps a "kinder, gentler" Sánchez de Losada might have been able to persuade Banzer to swing the needed votes to him, given their convergence of views on political and economic issues. But months of being branded a "dictator" by the MNR candidate caused Banzer to direct his delegates to vote for Paz Zamora, who had been imprisoned for subversive activities during Banzer's presidency. (*San Francisco Examiner and Chronicle*, 6 August.)

His decision to support Paz Zamora did not sit well with Banzer's supporters, who felt betrayed. Although there was a "mini-rush" on the banks, calm returned as soon as it became evident that Banzer and the ADN would exert considerable influence in the new government, particularly in economic matters. (*Latin America Weekly Report*, 31 August.) The ADN now has nine of the eighteen cabinet seats; Banzer occupies a key advisory position; and Luis Ossio, Banzer's running mate from the Christian Democrats, is the vice-president.

The CONDEPA Factor. The real surprise in the election was the strong performance of Carlos Palenque and his CONDEPA. Palenque had a wide following in La Paz due to his radio and television background, and he parlayed this grass-roots sympathy into a political machine concentrated in the capitol and its environs. His was a basic indigenous message: the Indians were the true owners of Bolivia, and their rightful place had been usurped by the Spanish. The indigenous-racist argument can have, and did have, a powerful appeal to the *Cholos* of the Altiplano. Starting with no political organization, Palenque used his media background and his communication skills—including fluency in the Indian dialects—to cut deeply into Banzer's strong political base in La Paz.

A favorite theme of the charismatic Palenque was the economic self-sufficiency of pre-Colombian times. This would bring the normally stoic Indians to their feet with the cry: "We want to feed ourselves with the wheat that is produced in this country, we want our bread made by Bolivians, we want the clothes we wear made by Bolivians." (*Latinamerica Press*, 25 May.)

Although Palenque drew votes from all three top vote-getters, there is little doubt that he hurt Banzer the most, probably denying him both the votes for a clear plurality and the seats in the Congress needed for the presidency. Two of the three seats in the Senate are now in the hands of CONDEPA, and few doubt that the party will become a central force in Bolivian politics. If Palenque is to have a chance at the presidency in 1993, however, he will have to broaden his geographic base. Given the extreme regionalism of Bolivia, it is unlikely that the *Cambas*, as the citizens of the eastern part of Bolivia describe themselves, would vote for a candidate with distinctly "altiplano" bias.

Drugs, Bolivia's Cash Crop. Bolivia and Peru produce virtually all of the world's coca, and it is then processed into cocaine in Colombia. According to some reliable estimates, illegal drug trafficking—principally of coca—accounts for close to half of Bolivia's export revenues, although these figures do not show up in balance-of-payments ledgers (*WSJ*, 11 September). It was probably the monies from drugs that slipped into the Bolivian economy that enable the country to survive the austerity measures of 1985–1989.

The Colombian government's crackdown on the drug cartel in 1989 has had some success, and Bolivian coca growers found that prices dropped sharply in the latter half of the year, as there was less demand for their erstwhile cash crop. Should that trend continue, it would facilitate the government's efforts to encourage growers to substitute other crops for coca. In December, over 1000 acres were converted, a record for any single month and almost triple the number of acres converted in November (*WP*, 15 February 1990). The government has also taken the politically risky decision to declare coca growing illegal and that therefore coca crops can be forcibly eradicated. Prospects for a continuation of this action are not likely, as coca has long been a part of the Bolivian diet, both for medicine and to deaden hunger pains.

If crop substitution is to be successful, U.S. economic aid is essential. But here U.S. antidrug policy and its own internal politics are in conflict. U.S. laws on the books to protect American agriculture may make it impossible for foreign-aid funds to be used to help Bolivians grow crops such as citrus fruit, that would compete with U.S. farmers. (Ibid.)

Preparations got under way at the end of the year for the antidrug summit meeting of the presidents of Peru, the United States, and Colombia at Cartagena, Colombia. Paz Zamora was expected, in unison with the other Latin American presidents, to press President Bush for additional economic and military assistance to aid in the fight against drugs. Additionally, the three Latin American leaders were expected to remind the American president that, as long as the United States was the "consuming country," providing a limitless market for cocaine, there would be only limited success at the supply/manufacturing end, where the proceeds from the drug industry provide great economic benefits for the people of Latin America, especially in Bolivia.

Bolivia's Prospects. Having now carried out its third consecutive transfer of power through democratic means, and with its economy showing signs of growth for the first time in a decade, Bolivia appears to have turned a corner. According to President Paz Zamora, bank deposits almost doubled between the date of his inauguration in August and 31 December 1989, and Bolivia's inflation was in

the range of 2–3 percent at year's end, the lowest in all of Latin America.

Unemployment, in excess of 20 percent, and underemployment, continue to plague the country, and this is a potentially volatile situation. The PCB and the other parties of the far left continue to blame the government for creating economic growth at the expense of the poor. Carlos Palenque, looking to broaden his political appeal for another try at the presidency in 1993, may move further to the left, perhaps even heading an alliance that would fuse leftist ideology with racial and ethnic resentments. With Paz Zamora not being able to run again in 1993, elements of his party could unite to form a CONDEPA-IU-MIR coalition.

As for the immediate future, how Paz Zamora, the former "radical," works with Hugo Banzer, the former general who had him jailed in the early 1970s, will tell the story of Bolivia. It is not a natural alliance, as was the "Pact for Democracy" that united Paz Estenssoro and Banzer. Banzer will surely attempt to maintain control over "his" members of Paz Zamora's cabinet, and may attempt to use his own position to form a type of "copresidency." Paz Zamora and his followers would not countenance such interference, and the ensuing internecine disputes could undo much of what cooperation among disparate elements has been achieved in recent years.

Bolivia has had a tumultuous history and remains desperately poor and subject to the vagaries of international markets. But in the last half of what has been called Latin America's "lost decade," Bolivia has proven to be a model of consensus-building that other countries with much more going for them would be well advised to emulate.

Col. Lawrence L. Tracy, U.S. Army (Ret.)
Americans for Democracy in Latin America

Brazil

Population. 150,750,232
Parties. Brazilian Communist Party (Partido Comunista Brasileiro; PCB), pro-Soviet; Communist Party of Brazil (Partido Comunista do Brasil; PCdoB), pro-Albanian; Workers Party (Partido dos Trabalhadores; PT), strong Marxist-Leninist-Trotskyist influence

Founded. PCB: 1922; PCdoB: 1961 split from PCB; PT: 1981

Membership. PCB: 130,000 (*Pravda*, 9 April); PCdoB: 50,000 claimed, 20,000 estimated (*Folha de São Paulo*, 28 June 1987); PT: 600,000 (*O Estado de São Paulo*, 11 June)

Top Official. PCB: Salomão Malina (67), president; PCdoB: João Amazonas (77), president; PT: Luiz Gushiken, president

Executive Committee. PCB: vice-president Roberto Freire, Amaro Valentin, Carlos Alberto Torres, Domingos Tódero, Flávio Araújo, Francisco Inácio Almeida, Geraldo Rodríguez dos Santos, Givaldo Siqueira, Jarbas de Hollanda, José Paulo Netto, Luiz Carlos Moura, Paulo Elisiário, Regis Fratti, Sergio Morães, Severino Teodoro Melo. Alternates: Luiz Carlos Azedo, Paulo Fábio Dantas, Byron Sarinho, Raimundo Jinkings; PCdoB: José Duarte, Dyneas Fernández Aguiar, José Renato Rabelo, Roberto D'Olne Lustosa, Ronaldo Cavalcanti Freitas, Elsa de Lima Monnerat, João Batista de Rocha Lemos, Pericles Santos de Souza, Alanir Cardoso, María do Socorro Morães Vieira; PT: 19 members, including General Secretary José Dirceu, Luis Inácio Lula da Silva, Olivio Dutra, José Genoino, Eduardo Jorge, Eduardo Suplicy, Helio Bicudo, Plinio de Arruda Sampaio

Central Committee. PCB: 63 active members, 23 alternates

Status. All legal

Last Congress. PCB: eighth, 17–20 July 1987

Last Election. 17 December, a run-off between the two front runners in the 15 November presidential election. PCB candidate Roberto Freire won 1.07% of the first round vote. PT candidate Luis Inácio Lula da Silva took second place on 15 November with 16% of the vote but lost the run-off to right-wing candidate Fernando Collor de Mello of National Reconstruction Party (Partido de Reconstrução Nacional; PRN).

Auxiliary Organizations. The PCB seems to have lost virtually all influence in the General Workers' Central (Central Geral dos Trabalhadores; CGT) as well as in the Agricultural Workers' Confederation (Confederação Nacional dos Trabalhadores na Agricultura; CONTAG). The PCdoB is taking its 200-member unions from the CGT to the PT-dominated Single Labor Central (Central Unica dos Trabalhadores; CUT), and CONTAG is expected to do the same. The PT also has strong influence in the National Student Union (União Nacional dos Estudantes; UNE), the Basic Chris-

tian Communities (Comunidades Eclesiais de Base; CEBs), and the Landless (or Roofless) Movement (Movimento dos Sem Terra, *or:* Sem Teto)

Publications. PCB: *Voz da Unidade*, Luiz Carlos Azedo, director; PCdoB: *Tribuna da Luta Operária*, Pedro de Oliveira, director

A general strike called by the two labor centrals on 14–15 March was moderately successful, and individual private and public sector strikes continued to proliferate through the first half of the year. The increasing violence of these movements adversely affected Lula's presidential campaign, and PT pressure may have been responsible for eventually curbing the worst excesses. That a left-wing radical came so very close to winning the election, however, shows that the grievances are real, and that Lula will constitute a formidable opposition to the new government. His loss to a young, unknown candidate with virtually no party organization points up the disarray of the traditional parties and the rejection suffered by their leaders. Voters seemed unwilling to give any more chances to the politicians who have failed to turn the economy around during the past five years.

PCB. For the most part, Roberto Freire, leader of the PCB's three-member parliamentary group, was allowed to run his campaign without much interference, and he made a good job of it. With very little money or infrastructure, he attracted good television ratings, frequent and consistently favorable press coverage, and respectable crowds at rallies. This did not translate into votes, nor was it expected to, but it did provide a forum for the projection of a modern and more democratic image of the party. The PCB platform promises that democracy will not be just a phase of the movement toward socialism, but "the very essence of a society in which social justice goes hand in hand with political pluralism" (*WMR*, October). Freire feels that Brazil's new constitution opens the way for the installation of a pluralistic socialism in the country, with the participation of private enterprise and some nationalized sectors (*Folha de São Paulo*, 8 February; *FBIS*, 22 March).

Unfortunately for the PCB, the new image is too little, too late for some members. Three party leaders in Rio de Janeiro defected to the governing Brazilian Democratic Movement party (Partido do Movimento Democrático Brasileiro; PMDB). National executive committee member Hércules Corrêa and regional directors José Alves de Brito and Carlos Alberto Muniz had helped elect PMDB governor Moreira Franco in 1986, and they all hold posts in his administration. According to Corrêa, the need for a mass party to fight for change in the economic system is imperative; the PMDB could become such a party of the center-left, but the PCB could not conceivably do so. Upon hearing the news, Salomão Malina lamented the party's loss of influence among intellectuals in recent years and recalled the earlier defections of Leandro Konder and Carlos Nelson Coutinho to the PT. (*Jornal do Brasil*, 10 January.) The newsweekly *Veja* reports that Freire himself is going to call for the creation of a new social-democratic party inspired by the drastic changes in Eastern Europe. He expects the new organization to attract progressives from the PMDB, the Brazilian Social Democratic Party (Partido Social Demócrata Brasileiro; PSDB), and disaffected leftists. (*Veja*, 13 December.)

The PCB has tried to take advantage of the good will Freire's campaign generated by entering as many union elections as possible. It hopes to reestablish, step by step, its former pre-eminence in the labor movement. PCB deputy Augusto Carvalho said the party is planning a big labor conference in 1990 and will probably announce its withdrawal from the CGT at that time; if anticommunist sentiment in the CUT cannot be overcome, the PCB may then form its own central (*O Estado de São Paulo*, 23 August). The CGT is currently split between its old, independent leader, Joaquín dos Santos Andrade, and newly elected "pragmatic" Rogerio Magri. Andrade apparently suffered for his too close association with the CUT during the general strike. Magri, on the other hand, has been tarnished by accusations of having accepted extraordinary funds from the AFL-CIO, a regular contributor to the CGT. (Ibid., 19 March, 23 May.) Some members of the PCB reportedly objected to Freire's criticism of the Chinese government's repression of the students' movement; this was a justifiable repression in the eyes of the old guard (Ibid., 2 July). In February, Salomão Malina led a PCB delegation to Beijing, where they met with Politburo Standing Committee member Qiao Shi (XINHUA, 20 February; *FBIS*, 3 March).

PT. PT founder and presidential candidate Luis Inácio Lula da Silva ran on a ticket of the Popular Brazil Front (Frente Brasil Popular), which included the PT, the Brazilian Socialist Party (Partido Socialista Brasileiro; PSB), the PCdoB, and the Green Party (Partido Verde; PV), headed by former guerrilla Fernando Gabeira. The platform called for suspension of foreign-debt payments, a break in relations with the IMF, stepped up expropriations and distributions of land under a new agrarian reform, a doubling of the minimum wage, a price freeze, and replacement of the military ministries with a civilian-led defense ministry.

Lula's 16 percent return in the first round put him less than 1 percent ahead of Leonel Brizola of the Democratic Labor Party (Partido Democrático dos Trabalhadores; PDT). Brizola is a vaguely left-wing populist. By the end of the highly suspenseful second round, Lula had increased this to about 48 percent, with support from the PCB, the PDT, and Mario Covas's mainstream PSDB. This outstanding performance should guarantee his continued control of the PT and makes him a strong contender for the governorship of São Paulo in the 1990 election.

The campaign was by no means an unbroken progression. From a reasonably healthy beginning, Lula's standing in the polls dropped in July to 5 percent. Reasons for the decline included nepotism and corruption scandals in the administration of PT mayor Luiza Erundina in São Paulo, as well as a long-running dispute among Popular Brazil Front members on the choice of a vice-presidential candidate. This was resolved only in July with the compromise nomination of Senator José Paulo Bisol (PSB). More important than either of these, however, were the radical labor policies of the PT-dominated CUT and the same tendencies in some of the PT's 39 municipal administrations. Lula's moderate faction, Articulation (Articulação), won more than 50 percent in internal party elections and even kept the word socialism out of the party platform. Some of the Trotskyist factions, Convergência in particular, do not feel bound by the policies of the majority (although they are in fact so bound by the bylaws). For example, the PT generally supports the hundreds of ongoing Catholic Church– and CEB-backed land invasions as a necessary adjunct to sluggish agrarian reform. It nonetheless expelled the vice-mayor of Diadema (state of São Paulo) and two councilmen for leading a land invasion of 1500 families onto territory specifically reserved by the mayor for construction of low-cost housing. (The mayor belongs to Articulation; the others to Convergência and another small faction.) In the same way, the PT began to move against other municipal directorates that are distributing pamphlets or otherwise calling for armed struggle in the name of the PT. (*O Estado de São Paulo*, 17, 25 August.)

Similar radical tendencies within the CUT were perhaps more damaging and still harder to control. With annual inflation topping 1,000 percent, justifiable strikes for restoration of eroded wages proliferated and became more violent. During the general strike of 14–15 March, mayors Erundina in São Paulo and Olivio Dutra in Rio Grande do Sul were criticized for promoting the strike rather than insuring basic services. This did not bother the PT, but it was concerned by bomb throwing during a bank strike in Pernambuco; the Convergência bank worker responsible was expelled. Metal workers in São Bernardo trashed a Volkswagen factory while carrying out their new policy of forcibly removing nonstrikers from workplaces. Clashes with police were commonplace, and police reaction to attacks from strikers also became more violent; rifles and, in some cases, machine guns replaced sticks. (In May, an Oscar Niemayer monument honoring three workers killed by the army during the repression of a strike at the Volta Redonda steel mill in 1988 was blown up. A soldier on guard at the time, who might have identified the perpetrators, was shot to death two days later.)

The Articulation faction of CUT agreed that this situation had become too frightening for voters and was threatening the presidential campaign. Convergência saw no need for a truce. Its leaders not only favored a continuation of "saturation bombing" (*O Estado de São Paulo*, 10 May), but urged another general strike to begin in September for an indefinite period. Cyro García, president of the Rio de Janeiro bank-workers union, and the only member of Convergência on the CUT executive board, said, "In our view, the heart of the situation today is the class struggle, the battle against the wage squeeze, [while] Articulation believes the presidential election is the focus." CUT general secretary Gilmar dos Santos Carneiro argued that "Articulation, when it is in power, faces crises just as all groups in power do . . . Members of Convergência take advantage of these crises to assert their role as revolutionaries, calling other people reformists." (*Gazeta Mercantil*, 17 August; *FBIS*, 20 September.) Articulation prevailed this time, and the strikes diminished, with a corresponding recovery in the polls for Lula. The dispute can be expected to continue, however, as both the PT and the CUT move into the mainstream.

Lula traveled to Cuba and Nicaragua in January and also visited the president of the Italian Communist Party, Achille Occhetto, whom he greatly admires. The elections in Poland pleased him, as he had previously been compared unfavorably to Lech Walesa, for having left the union to enter politics: "Walesa discovered, as I did, that the labor question is also political . . . The victory of Solidarity in the election is not a victory of capitalism over socialism but the cry of revolt of a people tired of bureaucracy." Of the repression in China, he said, "What happened there should not happen in either a capitalistic or socialistic regime . . . the Left must be the first to vehemently repudiate such things." (*O Estado de São Paulo*, 11 June.)

Guerrillas. On 17 December Brazilian police arrested ten members of an international kidnapping ring that was funneling millions of dollars in ransom money to the Chilean guerrilla group, the Revolutionary Left Movement (Movimiento de la Izquierda Revolucionaria; MIR). Those captured in the foiled kidnapping of São Paulo supermarket executive Abilio dos Santos Diniz included five Chileans, two Canadians, two Argentines, and one Brazilian. According to Chilean police, three of the Chileans are MIR members. One of them, María Emilia Badilla, said "the Left in Chile had no way of growing and the money from the kidnappings would help agitation and propaganda work" in her country. Brazilian police established that members of the group had trained in Cuba, Nicaragua, and Argentina. Two previous kidnappings of a banker and an advertising executive in São Paulo had netted the group $6.5 million in ransoms. (*NYT*, 30 December.)

Carole Merten
San Francisco, California

Canada

Population. 26,310,836
Parties. Communist Party of Canada (CPC); Communist Party of Canada (Marxist-Leninist) (CPC-ML); Revolutionary Workers' League (RWL); Trotskyist League (TL); International Socialists (IS)
Founded. CPC: 1921; CPC-ML: 1970; RWL: 1977; TL: 1975

Membership. CPC: 3,000; CPC-ML: 500; RWL: 200 (all estimated)

General Secretary. CPC: George Hewison; CPC-ML: Hardial Bains; RWL: John Riddell

Central Committee. CPC: 65 members

Status. All legal

Last Congress. CPC: Twenty-seventh, 20–24 May 1988, in Toronto; CPC-ML: Fifth, 28–30 December 1987, in Montreal; RWL: Sixth, 28 July–3 August 1986, in Montreal

Last Federal Election. 21 November 1988; CPC: 52 candidates, average vote 126; no representatives; CPC-ML: no official candidates; RWL: no official candidates

Auxiliary Organizations. CPC: Parti communiste du Québec, Canadian Peace Congress, Conseil québecois de la paix, Association of United Ukrainian Canadians, Congress of Canadian Women, Young Communist League, Workers' Benevolent Association of Canada; CPC-ML: Peoples' Front Against Racist and Fascist Violence, Revolutionary Trade Union Opposition, Democratic Women's Union of Canada, Communist Youth Union of Canada (Marxist-Leninist), Canada-Albania Friendship Association; RWL: Young Socialist Organizing Committee, Comité de la jeunesse révolutionnaire (CJR)

Publications. CPC: *Canadian Tribune* (Tom Morris, editor), *Pacific Tribune*, *Combat*, *Communist Viewpoint*, *Le Communiste*, *Rebel Youth*, *Jeunesse militante*; CPC-ML: *Marxist-Leninist*, *Le Marxiste-Leniniste*, *Voice of the Youth*, *Voice of the People*, *Democratic Women*, *Peoples' Front Bulletin*, *Canadian Student*, *BC Worker*; RWL: *Socialist Voice* (Michael Prairie, editor), *Lutte ouvrière*; TL: *Sparticist Canada*; IS: *Socialist Worker*

A number of tiny Marxist-Leninist organizations exist legally in Canada. The oldest, largest, and best organized is the always-pro-Soviet CPC. The CPC-ML, founded in 1970, was Maoist until changes in Chinese domestic and international policies led it to shift its ties to Albania. The most active of several Trotskyist groups is the RWL.

The Marxist left in Canada considers the Conservative government of Prime Minister Brian Mulroney little more than a Canadian appendage of U.S. business and whatever American president is in office. Consequently many CPC and other leftist critiques of Canadian domestic and international policies are at least in part attacks on Ottawa's real and alleged ties to Washington. Increasingly during

1989, however, the CPC also had to wrestle with the profound changes taking place in the Soviet Union and Eastern Europe, trying to argue that these changes do not signal the death of socialism, but its revitalization after decades of control by Stalinist elites.

CPC Internal Affairs. The CPC has recently been declining from its original insignificance in Canadian life. It got less than one-tenth of one percent of the votes in the 1988 federal election. Party membership has been stuck for years at about 3,000, and the party presses evidently print about 9,000 copies of the CPC's weekly organ *Canadian Tribune*. This stagnation was reflected in the reduction in 1988 of the CPC Central Committee from 77 to 65 members. At a meeting of the CPC's Central Committee on 6–8 January 1989, party leader George Hewison said "this is an historical turning point in our party" and declared his personal relief that "things are out in the open now." Among the things now in the open are the fact that the party has been operating with "unacceptable" deficits, and that even by the January meeting steps had been taken to cut party staff and reduce operating costs. (*Canadian Tribune*, 16 January.) A nationwide campaign was launched to recruit new party members and to improve circulation of the party weekly by getting 1,000 renewals and 450 new subscribers during the year (ibid., 13 November). Nonetheless, Gerry van Houten, in particular, continued to travel in Europe on behalf of the party, attending conferences on municipal government, change, and peace. The editors of CPC publications visited with the editors of the Soviet paper *Pravda* in Moscow in November.

Coping with Change. CPC leaders spent much of their time trying to explain to party members and others how things had gone so obviously wrong in the communist world and yet it is only "imperialist" propagandists or fools who assert that socialism is dead. The *Canadian Tribune* (4 September) editorialized that the USSR, "which built a modern, industrial society in just 70 years, today is 'retooling' for the future. . . Perestroika is the struggle for socialism, for renewal, restructuring, democratization and progress."

Canadian Tribune editor Tom Morris argued that recent events "require 'new thinking' about an array of formulas and dogmas heretofore considered sacred." He continued that in Europe "the people" are carrying out a "second socialist revolution," this time deposing "those who, in the name of socialism, violated and abused socialist democracy and norms." He concluded that the CPC had contributed to this abuse of power by refusing to take principled stands—for example, on the invasion of Czechoslovakia in 1968—when such stands were called for. (Ibid., 20 November.)

In December, CPC general secretary Hewison acknowledged that "we are living through gale force winds of change," but warned that "the big business media and capitalist politicians" are responding with "an immense ideological assault," alleging the "failure or collapse of socialism and invincibility of capitalism." On the contrary, he asserted, the future is bursting with promise for socialism if communists—most pointedly including Canadian communists—learn some basic lessons from what happened in recent decades. These lessons are:

- CPC members must sharpen their "critical eyes" in evaluating world events and in commenting on the performance of allied parties;
- Party members must "distinguish more accurately between those questions which are of universal significance in building socialism and those which are peculiar to this or that country";
- Canadian communists should recognize the "enormous theoretical defect" that has emerged "around the nature of the class struggle in the aftermath of achieving working class power." "What is clear in all of the cases in Eastern Europe is the alienation of the Communist Parties from the people" and that "the link between democracy and socialism must be seen to be indivisible." This means the examination of the effect of Stalinism— "the substitution of bureaucratic centralism for democratic centralism." Hewison continued: "The basic principles of communist parties need not be threatened, but the application of those principles must be cleansed of anti-socialist, anti-popular, corrupt, dogmatic, unscientific, non-Marxist content."
- The final lesson is of "ideological stagnation linked to organizational entropy...Why did nearly 100 million communists worldwide engage in the same self-hypnosis, for so long?...This is related to the stagnation of theory and the severing of the vital link between theory and practice and to inner-party democracy." (*Canadian Tribune*, 11 December.)

The CPC itself, Hewison noted on an earlier occasion, has "initiated a party-wide debate on the 'legacy of Stalinism,'" the "subjective baggage of the past that artificially separates us from the Canadian people." These include: the "denial or lessening of inner-party democracy"; the "substitution of conceited, manipulative, devious and paranoid behavior for open, frank, and modest relations"; "the substitution of the living science of Marxism-Leninism by dogmatic formulations"; and "an uncritical attitude to every practice of the Soviet Union and other socialist countries." (*WMR*, September 1989.)

The CPC on the Mulroney Government. The CPC had nothing but criticism for Mulroney's "cowardly and sleazy gang of politicians," the "trained seals of the Conservative caucus" or what it called the "pro-U.S., anti-people Mulroney gang" (*Canadian Tribune*, 14 August, 2 and 9 October). The Canadian government, it says, is racist, defiantly against aboriginal rights, and sexist (ibid., 23 January, 6 March, 4 December). By "peddling free trade and neo-conservatism" (ibid., 3 April) and turning Canada into an appendage of U.S. and Canadian big business (ibid., 14 August), the Tory government had declared "open season on average Canadians"; this attitude was manifested in "plant shutdowns, new massive tax grabs, privatization drives, abandonment of public program commitments, new cuts in social services, government by Cabinet, targeting of organized labour, and more" (ibid., 4 December). More specifically, *Canadian Tribune* editorials hit the government for its "regressive, punitive" Goods and Services Tax and for policies which "cannibalized, victimized and privatized" the rail system (2 October); for "sweeping reactionary changes" to the Unemployment Insurance Act and "brutally slashed funding" for public broadcasting, foreign aid programs and research (9 October); and for abortion legislation that is "wrong—ideologically, legally and medically" (13 November).

The CPC response to this daunting challenge was outlined in a *Canadian Tribune* editorial of 4 December:

It will take a concerted effort to turn this around. It will require clearly-posed alternatives to corporate Canada's agenda. It will take the maximum united effort by every Canadian who shares our belief in our country's sovereignty, in Canada's economic and political independent role in an increasingly inter-depen-dent global community.

Canadian politics on the Left is not what it was just a few years ago. The addition of many new, young and militant forces—a powerful women's movement, Native peoples, environmentalists, a Canada-wide peace coalition, organized seniors and others mobi-lized on local, regional, national and international issues, all with a developing understanding of the key role of the organized trade union movement—bring a bold and dynamic new ingredient to political reality.

New Democrats, headed by a new leader and armed with policies designed to take on the transna-tional corporations, can help inject [the] new vision which is so needed at this juncture of our history.

The CPC on Canada's International Pol-icies. It is clear to the CPC that in most of these and other policies, Canada is subservient to the United States. According to one *Tribune* editorial (13 Feb-ruary), "Whether in military matters, trade, bank-ing, natural resources, the environment, fishing rights, foreign policy, the 'level playing field' of regional development and social programs, or cor-porate takeovers—Washington's shopping list will be endless." Canada should not have become asso-ciated with the Organization of American States, which is nothing but "a vehicle for direct U.S. hemispheric control" (*Canadian Tribune*, 16 Oc-tober); it has never imposed total sanctions on South Africa (ibid., 18 September); it has refused to cut all financial support to the government of El Sal-vador (ibid., 27 November); and it has denied that the Soviet Union has launched a peace offensive which is nothing less than "an all-out war on war" (ibid., 1 May). Consequently, Mulroney leads a "military-minded Tory government" (ibid., 29 May) that backs continuing U.S. oppression of Third World governments (ibid., 20 November), shame-lessly allows Washington to test Cruise missiles over Canada, and plays "high profile war games designed for a first strike attack against the Soviet Union," the latter including allowing overflights of Canada by B-1, B-52 and F-111 bombers (ibid., 13 February, 19 June).

Maoists, Trotskyists, et al. Other Marxist-Leninist organizations were smaller and had less effect than the CPC. Most were beset by mem-bership, organizational, and ideological problems,

and focused much of their commentary on Soviet bloc affairs, South Africa, and Latin America.

Lynn Ratliff
Stanford, California

Chile

Population. 12,827,411
Party. Communist Party of Chile (Partido Com-unista de Chile; PCCh)
Founded. 1922
Membership. 20,000 (estimated)
General Secretary. Volodia Teitelboim
Politburo. (Political Committee) 20 members
Secretariat. 5 members
Central Committee. 55 members
Status. Illegal, but functions freely
Last Congress. Fifteenth, 5–12 May, 1989; pre-ceded by discussion of draft program by cells and local organizations
Last Election. 14 December 1989. Party presented candidates through front group. None elected to Senate (has 38 elected and 9 appointed members) or Chamber of Deputies (120 members)
Publications. *El Siglo*, began nonclandestine pub-lication in September 1989; *Principios* (the-oretical journal)

In 1989, the party held its first public congress since it had been forced underground by the coup of September 1973. It elected new leadership and re-affirmed the policy of "mass popular rebellion" adopted in 1980. In the elections of 14 December 1989, for a congress which is to take office in March 1990, it presented several candidates, but although two or three did well, none was elected.

The communists did not join the opposition Coalition (*Concertación*) of Parties for Democracy when it was formed in January 1989, nor were they asked to do so by the seventeen parties which were members. The party had recommended that its members participate in the plebiscite of October 1988 on the continuation of General Augusto Pi-nochet's rule only shortly before it took place. It had not registered as a legal party (it would have been rejected for being in violation of article 8 of the 1980 constitution that forbids "totalitarian" parties, but in late 1988, when a leftist "instrumental" coalition, the Broad Party of the Socialist Left (PAIS), was formed, the communists became active members.

The period between March and May 1989 was devoted to discussion by the cells and regional party organizations of a lengthy draft program which was voted on at the Fifteenth Party Congress in early May. The congress reaffirmed the policy of "mass popular rebellion" which had been followed since 1980, and admitted that the communists were responsible for the importation of a cache of large quantities of arms which was discovered in 1986. However, the congress recommended against participation in the extremist Manuel Rodriguez Popular Front (FPMR), which itself had earlier split over the issue of relations with the communists. The party congress reinterpreted its current policy so as to permit support for the presidential candidate of the united opposition in the December elections.

The congress also replaced Luis Corvalán as the party's general secretary with another old-time communist ex-senator, Volodia Teitelboim. The meeting was widely reported in the Chilean press, and its internal dynamics were analyzed by a Socialist journal (*Apsi*, 22 May; *FBIS*, 21 June). It was made up of 130 voting delegates from the outgoing Central Committee and the regional assemblies as well as 30 "invited guests," mostly leaders of related social organizations and youth groups. In June the party officially abjured armed struggle during the election period, and in July it formally endorsed Patricio Aylwin, the Christian Democratic presidential candidate of the Coalition of Parties for Democracy.

Also in July the Pinochet government called a constitutional referendum on 54 amendments that had been agreed upon by the government and the opposition. The communists recommended abstention, and when the amendments were overwhelmingly adopted and only 4 percent abstained, the Pinochet government argued that the results demonstrated a striking decline in communist strength. One of the amendments repealed article 8, which outlawed totalitarian parties, leaders, and ideas, but the constitution retained a provision punishing subversive activity, including advocacy of revolution.

Teitelboim repeatedly stated that electoral participation was an example of mass popular rebellion, but there was continuing tension within the party between the advocates of electoral action and those who favored violence. However, the bombings and occasional murders of policemen in 1989 were carried out by the Manuel Rodriguez Patriotic Front (FPMR), now no longer related to the party, and by the Lautaro Youth Movement (MJL), which became increasingly active in 1989. The Movement of the Revolutionary Left (MIR), which had formerly occupied the far left end of the Chilean political spectrum, was now divided over the use of violence. In early September the leader of its moderate faction, Jacar Nighme, was assassinated by a right-wing extremist group, the September 11th Movement (named after the date of the 1973 coup). In late August, Teitelboim repudiated the attacks by the FPMR as well as those of the MJL (*Cosas*, 31 August; *FBIS*, 19 September) and argued that popular rebellion of the masses included struggling for democracy by supporting Aylwin's candidacy. When Luis Corvalán returned to Chile in October, he also pledged his support for Aylwin.

Three well-known communist leaders ran for the Senate in the elections of December 14. None was elected, although two of them received more votes than those who were elected; but they were not seated because of an election law designed to benefit the center-left and center-right coalitions. The communists' lack of electoral success, and the movement of the Almeida Socialists, who had been their close allies, to join other, more moderate socialist movements in a single federation, were indications of the declining influence of the communists in Chilean politics.

They still could organize demonstrations and create effective front groups, but their claim to be the leading party of the Chilean left was rapidly being undercut by the Socialists. After Aylwin's strong victory (55 percent to 43 percent), the party announced that it would pursue an independent course. The question for the future was whether it would become increasingly marginal to the Chilean political scene, as has become the case with the Spanish Communist Party, or whether it can forge new alliances with other left parties—particularly the reformed Socialist Party—so as to re-establish itself as a major force in Chilean politics. The answer will depend on the conduct of the Aylwin administration over the next four years, on the political skill of the communists in the newly democratized Chilean political scene, and on the firmness of the armed forces' determination to prevent them from regaining their former power and influence.

Paul E. Sigmund
Princeton University

Colombia

Population. 31,945,165 (July)
Party. Communist Party of Colombia (Partido Comunista de Colombia; PCC)
Founded. 1930
Membership. 18,000 (estimate, including Communist Youth Organization)
General Secretary. Gilberto Vieira
Executive Committee. 14 members
Central Committee. 80 members
Status. Legal
Last Congress. Fifteenth, 12–15 December 1988
Last Elections. 1988: 18 mayors, 364 municipal council members, 13 deputies and 5 alternates to state assemblies; 1986: presidential, 4.5 percent; congressional, 1.4 percent, 5 of 114 senators, 9 of 199 representatives
Auxiliary Organizations. United Workers Confederation (CUT); Federation of Agrarian Syndicates; Communist Youth of Colombia (JUCO), claims 2,000 members
Publications. *Voz* (weekly), 40,000 circulation; *Margen Izquierda*, political journal, 6,000 circulation; Colombian edition of *World Marxist Review*, 2000 circulation.

Efforts by President Virgilio Barco's government to resolve Colombia's long-standing guerrilla conflict were overshadowed in 1989 by a dramatic increase in violence attributed to rightist paramilitary groups, death squads, self-defense groups, and bands of assassins organized by drug interests.

The threat to peace in Colombia is exacerbated by persistent charges that middle-level army officers are involved in the activities of paramilitary groups and right-wing death squads. The continued assassinations of political and trade-union leaders and the massacres of peasants are disturbingly reminiscent of the lawlessness associated with *La Violencia* of the 1940s and 1950s. In addition, bands of assassins sponsored by drug traffickers have proliferated in recent years and are responsible for an alarming number of murders and attacks on leftist leaders and high-level military and government officials.

The assassination of presidential hopeful Senator Luís Carlos Galán on 18 August and the resulting crackdown on drug interests focused international attention on the war of attrition between the government and Colombia's drug cartels. The cartels were believed responsible for the crash of a Colombian jet on 27 November, in which 107 were killed, and the bombing on 6 December of the headquarters of the Department of Administrative Security in Bogotá, in which 62 persons died. The government responded with the death of drug baron Gonzalo Rodríguez Gacha on 15 December and a resolve to press forward its antidrug campaign, including the extradition of suspected drug criminals to the United States.

Although the Barco government's peace initiatives dramatically reduced guerrilla violence in 1989, the persistence of paramilitary, criminal, and drug-related violence continues to undermine Colombia's democratic institutions. Still Colombia is in no immediate danger of being taken over by leftist extremists or a security-conscious military.

PCC. The communist movement in Colombia has undergone various transformations in both name and organization since the party was formed in December 1926. The PCC was publicly proclaimed on 17 July 1930. In July 1965, a schism within the PCC between pro-Soviet and pro-Chinese factions resulted in the latter's becoming the Communist Party of Colombia, Marxist-Leninist (PCC-ML). Only the PCC has legal status. It has been allowed to participate in elections under its own banner since 1972. In 1988, the PCC participated in mayoral, municipal-council, and state-assembly elections as the leading member of a leftist coalition called the Patriotic Union (Unión Patriótica; UP). The UP was formed in 1985 on the initiative of the Revolutionary Armed Forces of Colombia (FARC) as a broad front to achieve political and social reforms. From the day the movement was founded, the PCC has been active in its leadership and work.

According to U.S. intelligence sources, the PCC has 18,000 members, including those of JUCO. The party claims more than 50,000 members, "23 percent of them women," operating through 320 regional and 2,000 grassroots organizations (*WMR*, May). Although the PCC's growth has been less rapid than its leaders had hoped, especially outside the Federal District of Bogotá, in recent years the party has expanded its influence in rural areas of Arauca, Urabá, César, Caquetá, Meta, Bolívar, and Santander. The PCC maintains several national theoretical and education centers, including the National School for Party Cadres and the Center of Study and Social Research, as well as various regional party schools (ibid.). The PCC exercises only marginal influence in national affairs.

The highest party authority is the congress, convened at four-year intervals. At the Fifteenth Party Congress in December 1988 the Central Committee was enlarged to comprise 80 full and 10 alternate members. The composition of the Central Committee and of the Executive Committee was renewed by 50 percent. Gilberto Vieira was re-elected general secretary, and Alvaro Vásquez was elected to the newly created post of vice-general secretary (ibid.).

A major source of the party's influence is its control of the United Workers Confederation, reportedly Colombia's largest trade-union confederation with 800,000 members. Although the party officially disclaims any control over the CUT, it insists on the right to "occupy and exercise any leadership positions that may be assigned to it" (*YICA*, 1988). The CUT's vice-president, Gustavo Osorio, and its secretary general, Angelino Garzón, are members of the PCC's Central Committee. In February, the CUT's Executive Committee peacefully occupied the Labor Ministry's offices to protest the murders of two trade-union leaders. They demanded talks with government officials and called for greater guarantees of safety. They charged that some 250 CUT members have been murdered, and another thousand have received death threats since 1986 (AFP, 24 February). The CUT held its Second Congress from 4 to 8 December in Bogotá.

The PCC's youth organization, the JUCO, plays an active role in promoting party policy among university and secondary-school students. The JUCO's Central Committee held a plenary meeting in Bogotá from 10–12 February. It called for youth organizations to undertake actions in support of a new dialogue for peace and proposed that the government replace compulsory military service with a form of social service. The plenum also discussed the JUCO's participation in the Thirteenth World Youth Festival in North Korea and organizational plans for its own Seventh Congress, held from 2–6 August in Bogotá (*Voz*, 16 February).

According to documents prepared for the PCC's Fifteenth Congress, the party must pay greater attention to the JUCO's political and organizational development. The JUCO continues to be "weak, vulnerable to cyclical leadership, and with little impact on the principal youth concentrations." The party also criticized JUCO leaders for their "lack of initiative, irresponsibility, and formalism" (*YICA*, 1988). Although the JUCO plays an active role in student politics at the national level, its middle-level leadership is weak and only marginally involved at the regional and grassroots levels. The JUCO's political role in support of the PCC's electoral and organizational objectives is carried out through the Union of Patriotic Youth. The JUCO's national secretary is Omar Calderón.

Guerrilla Warfare. Although not a serious threat to the government, guerrilla warfare has been a feature of Colombian life since the late 1940s; the current wave began in 1964. The four main guerrilla organizations are the Revolutionary Armed Forces of Colombia (FARC), long controlled by the PCC; the M-19, which began as the armed hand of the National Popular Alliance (ANAPO); the pro-Chinese People's Liberation Army (EPL), which is the guerrilla arm of the PCC-ML; and the Castroite National Liberation Army (ELN). Other, smaller guerrilla movements that have emerged in recent years include the Trotskyist-oriented Workers Self-Defense Movement (ADO); the Revolutionary Workers Party (PRT); the Free Fatherland (Patria Libre), which some observers believe to be a spin off of the EPL; and the Quintín Lamé, a pro-Indian group that operates primarily in the Valle del Cauca and Cauca Departments. In September 1987, leaders from the six principal subversive movements in the country created the Simón Bolívar National Guerrilla Coordinating Board (CNG). The principal leadership within the CNG is provided by the FARC. Estimates of guerrilla strength range from 10,000 to 15,000 men and women spread over some 80 different fronts (*NYT*, 15 December 1988).

FARC. According to Colombian military sources, the FARC has a total of 4,500 people (other estimates range as high as 12,000) operating on more than 40 fronts (*YICA*, 1988). According to the movement's principal leader, Manuel Marulanda Vélez, the FARC has expanded its areas of influence in recent years to include portions of the departments of Huila, Caquetá, Tolima, Cauca, Boyacá, Santander, Antioquia, Valle, Meta, Cundinamarca, and the intendancy of Arauca. The FARC's general headquarters is located at La Uribe. Jacobo Arenas is Marulanda's second in command; other members of the FARC's central staff are Alfonso Cano, Raúl Reyes, and Timoleón Jiménez. Although Marulanda has never confirmed officially that the FARC is the armed wing of the PCC, it is widely believed that the leadership mechanisms and general policy of the FARC are determined by the PCC's bylaws, and political resolutions made at party congresses and plenums are presumably transmitted to the fronts through Marulanda's directives.

Although the FARC's high command declared a unilateral cease-fire through Christmas 1988, the government considered the M-19 the only guerrilla group seriously interested in peace talks. In January, the Defense Ministry accused the FARC of illegally attempting to import a weapons shipment valued at $8 million from Portugal. Army commander General Nelson Mejía Henao rejected Arenas' denial and declared a major offensive against the FARC (*AFP*, 12 January). In February, newspaper sources announced the emergence of a new FARC front in northern César Department and reported numerous clashes between the army and guerrilla forces (*El Tiempo*, 11 February).

The FARC declared in early February that it was prepared to join the peace process if the government's dialogue included all the guerrilla groups within the CNG. On 28 February, Arenas announced a unilateral cease-fire of indefinite duration after the government accepted the appointment of a five-member "Commission of Notables," including several former Colombian presidents, proposed by the FARC to promote "understanding" with the government (*El Tiempo*, 1 March; *Voz*, 2 March). FARC leaders accused the M-19 of breaking guerrilla unity by signing a separate peace accord with the government on 17 March (*Voz*, 31 March).

The military accused the FARC of breaking its unilateral truce in late March by conducting operations in Antioquia, Meta, and Huila in which four soldiers and three civilians were killed (*El Tiempo*, 27 March). Government authorities subsequently announced that a major FARC intelligence network and arms supply in Bogotá had been dismantled (*El Espectador*, 20 April).

At the conclusion of the fourth guerrilla summit held in the Sumapaz mountains in July, the FARC, the EPL, and Quintín Lamé proposed a "direct dialogue" with the government. In a communiqué delivered to the Commission of Notables, the CNG called for "a negotiated solution to the armed conflict, political solutions to the 'dirty war,' lifting of the state of siege, a realistic solution to the foreign-debt problem, constitutional reforms to regain democracy, and genuine guarantees for individual rights" (*Voz*, 6 July; *El Tiempo*, 14 July).

In August, the CNG renewed its demand that the government's dialogue with guerrillas include all armed groups. Speaking for the CNG, Arenas requested an "open agenda" for all talks and reaffirmed the guerrillas' belief that "only a national constituent assembly with broad popular participation will ensure that the changes demanded by the majorities will be made" (EFE, 8 August; *FBIS*, 9 August). Government representatives and leaders of the FARC and EPL met in October and agreed to discuss means to achieve greater progress toward the demobilization and reintegration of guerrilla groups into civilian life (AFP, 21 October). Despite such overtures, many officials, particularly in the military, continue to question the trustworthiness of the FARC's declared intentions.

Domestic Attitudes and Activities. The PCC recognizes the experience of the Communist Party of the Soviet Union (CPSU) as an ideological source, but it also takes "maximum account of the national characteristics and revolutionary and democratic traditions of the Colombian people." The practice of combining legitimate, peaceful action and clandestine, armed struggle has been an integral part of the party's strategy for several decades. The documents and declarations approved by the PCC's Fifteenth Congress indicate that the strategy and tactics of the PCC will continue to be a combination of all forms of struggle. According to PCC member José Arizala, the congress reaffirmed that "the communists do not aim at total war: they seek to preserve and consolidate the political ground necessary for launching constitutional action." The PCC proposes the creation of a democratic-convergence government as "a step towards a popular, anti-imperialist and democratic revolution which will open the way to socialism" (*WMR*, May).

Much of the PCC's political activity in 1989 directly concerned its participation in the leadership and activities of the Patriotic Union. The UP was established by the PCC, trade-union, and other independent leftist forces in November 1985 to facilitate the transition of FARC guerrillas to legal political life. Since its inception, the UP has counted on the decisive and open participation of the PCC, which assigns members of its political directorate at all levels to participate in the UP's activities. The official communist view is that the UP has emerged as an alternative to the traditional parties with a well-defined program of social, economic, and political reforms. According to a plenary report by the Central Committee in July, the

PCC does not expect the UP to be a mechanical reflection of the PCC's criteria and objectives in its pronouncements and daily activity: "It is clear to us that the UP does not run the PCC, nor does the PCC run the UP" (*Voz*, 13 July). In discussing its strategy for the UP's Second Congress, the PCC's leadership proposed to seek agreements that "will guarantee that the UP remains in essence a broad-based movement capable of bringing together popular sectors and attracting the independent forces of the traditional parties." The PCC is critical of the UP's failure to combine its high-level contacts and meetings with more direct work among the masses. To accomplish the latter and further the PCC's goal of forming alliances with different political sectors, it will be necessary for the UP to clarify its organizational line, without simply attempting mechanically to transform the PCC's organizational entities into UP organizations. (Ibid.)

The PCC supports the UP's position that it is a legal movement, unlike the FARC, and can therefore demand guarantees for its followers' lives and its political activities. The year 1989 was marked by increased violence against PCC and UP leaders. The systematic assassination of UP partisans continued in various regions of the country, with sixteen murders reported during the first six weeks of the year. UP president Bernardo Jaramillo Ossa went into self-exile on 28 February after four UP leaders had been killed in downtown Bogotá, including the PCC's organizational secretary and prominent labor leader Teófilo Forero (*El Tiempo*, 1 March). Only days later, José Antequera, former JUCO president and a member of the PCC's central committee was assassinated at the El Dorado Airport in Bogotá (ibid., 4 March). A delegation from the PCC met with President Virgilio Barco following Forero's murder and renewed its appeal to the government to dismantle right-wing paramilitary groups and death squads (*Voz*, 2 March). According to Vieira, the most reactionary Colombian sectors, including the military, have "unleashed a plan to exterminate the PCC, the UP, other leftist organizations, the labor movement, and human rights activists" (ibid., 30 March). The UP claimed in August that 854 of its members had been killed since their alliance with the PCC was formed (Reuter, 4 August; *FBIS*, 7 August).

The PCC's Executive Committee issued a statement on 27 March calling for the government to suspend its talks with the M-19 and to engage instead in a broad-based dialogue that would include all insurgent groups. The committee also an-nounced its support for the UP's determination not to attend any roundtable discussions between the government, the M-19, and the traditional political parties "until the government makes a stronger commitment to end the dirty war and to combat hired assassins" (*Voz*, 30 March). UP leaders seized a government minister's office in early August to protest the murder of eleven UP members in various parts of the country during the last week in July. They ended their one-day occupation after the government promised to "intensify its efforts" against the illegal activities of rightist paramilitary groups and reinforce its protection of leftist and union leaders (Reuter, 4 August; *FBIS*, 7 August). Ironically, Gustavo Guerra, coordinator of the UP in Córdoba, was assassinated while UP leaders still occupied the minister's office (EFE, 3 August; *FBIS*, 7 August).

According to Alvaro Vásquez, an essential element in raising the people's consciousness is the struggle against militarism. This means the party's continued opposition to the state of siege, paramilitary actions, disappearance of popular leaders, persecution of the UP, discrimination against the labor movement, and militarization of the universities and popular barrios. The party also demands that the army be purged of "fascist elements," and that a civilian be put in charge of the Ministry of Defense. The PCC has repeatedly denounced the military's Condor Plan and charges that military intelligence carries out some of its actions under cover of dissident guerrilla groups, which it claims are acting in the name of the FARC. According to Vieira, militarism in Colombia is "above all at the service of North American imperialist interests." The only way to defeat it, in the party's view, is through the broadest patriotic coalition possible, and "that is what we [the PCC] are promoting in Colombia through the work of the UP" (*YICA*, 1988).

At its plenary meeting on 8 and 9 July, the PCC's Central Committee discussed the problems of communist trade-union efforts and proposed to develop a major national campaign for the defense of trade-unionism and for unity. Specifically, an effort will be made to "strengthen the CUT at the national level in terms of its unity, democracy, and pluralism, and to establish large unions and federations in the service and production sectors" (*Voz*, 13 July). The PCC contributed to the preparation of the second CUT congress during 4–8 December by encouraging trade-union assemblies to elect delegates to the congress and by promoting the congress among workers.

The PCC played a prominent role at the UP's Second National Convention in Bogotá from 8–10 September. At its plenary session preceding the convention, the PCC's Central Committee proposed that the UP launch a government program seeking "convergence with the broadest possible sectors" (*Voz*, 7 September).

The convention elected Bernardo Jaramillo Ossa as the UP's presidential candidate for the 1990 elections, with Diego Montaña Cuellar assuming the position of UP president. Although the party did not rule out the possibility of forming strategic coalitions with the majority Liberal and Conservative parties in selected departments, its official strategy is to campaign alone until the March general elections, at which time it will support a convergence candidate who "represents the nation's interests." The UP's political platform calls for mandatory voting; state financing of political campaigns; popular election of governors, municipal authorities, the attorney general, and the comptroller; state compensation to victims of the dirty war; and a government with the participation of all political sectors. The convention also drafted guidelines for a constitutional reform intended to break up the traditional parties' political monopoly and to facilitate the creation of a democratic-convergence government. (Ibid., 14 September.)

International Views and Positions. The PCC faithfully follows the Soviet line in its international positions. According to Vieira, the party is engaged primarily in the struggle for the emancipation of the Colombian people. However, the PCC insists that it is impossible to remain neutral in the "great international struggle" between socialism and capitalism. The party therefore "enthusiastically" supports the socialist countries and particularly the Soviet Union "because it defends genuine socialism, despite its imperfections" (*YICA*, 1988). At the same time, the party claims that it is not dependent on Moscow, Havana, or "any foreign place," nor does it serve as the agent for the international policy of any foreign country. The PCC wants a Colombian international policy that is "independent and autonomous." It therefore seeks to maintain relations with all international organizations, participating in as many events as possible. The PCC believes that its experience in employing all forms of popular action is proving useful in other Latin American countries.

The PCC is consistently internationalist and invariably displays solidarity with the struggles of fraternal parties and peoples. Some party members were critical of the documents prepared for the party's Fifteenth Congress for failing to "reflect properly the transformations underway in the Soviet Union and other socialist countries." The congress described *perestroika* in the Soviet Union as a "revolutionary renewal of socialism." The PCC leadership admitted that in the past it had not always been objective in assessing international developments or "the mistakes, deficiencies and violations of socialist principles in socialist countries." The delegates concluded that the party should extend its contacts with organizations and movements operating under different conditions, and "with those parties from which we used to distance ourselves because of ideological differences" (*WMR*, June).

The UP's Second National Convention adopted resolutions harshly critical of the U.S. government for its antidrug policy and for having promoted the breakup of the world coffee pact. Bernardo Jaramillo called for an end to extraditions of suspected drug traffickers to the United States and stated the convention's opposition to any U.S. military intervention in Colombia (*Voz*, 7 September). According to the PCC, "under cover of measures and actions against drug trafficking, U.S. imperialism has increased its interference in the country to a dangerous extent." The $65 million U.S. aid program announced in August "is clearly directed against the revolutionary movement and mass sectors" (ibid., 14 September). Delegates from foreign countries issued statements expressing support for Panama, the FMLN, and "the democratic electoral process urged by the Sandinista government" (ibid.).

Soviet leader Mikhail Gorbachev congratulated Gilberto Vieira in connection with his re-election as general secretary and wished him and all Colombian communists "great success in the struggle for the interests of the working people of Colombia, and for the development of the country in the direction of peace, democracy, and social progress" (*El Siglo*, 3 January).

José Arizala represented the PCC at international symposiums in Prague and Vienna organized by the *World Marxist Review* to discuss the dialectics of the struggle for peace and social progress in the late twentieth century and the role of communists in local government.

The Maoists. The PCC-ML is firmly pro-Chinese, although in recent years the party has looked more toward Albania for political guidance. Its present leadership hierarchy is not clearly known, although Francisco Caraballo is recognized as the movement's first secretary. The PCC-ML has an estimated membership of one thousand. Unlike the PCC, it has not attempted to obtain legal status, and its impact on Colombia's national life is insignificant. Its official news organ is *Revolución*. The Marxist-Leninist League of Colombia publishes the monthly *Nueva Democracia*. PCC-ML statements are sometimes found in Chinese publications and those of pro-Chinese parties in Europe and Latin America.

The PCC-ML's guerrilla arm, the EPL, was the first to attempt a "people's war" in Latin America. The EPL has conducted only limited operations since 1975, although according to Colombian intelligence it still has an estimated 750 guerrillas organized over fifteen fronts (*YICA*, 1988). The EPL operates mainly in the departments of Antioquia, César, Córdoba, and Risaralda, with urban support networks in several of the country's larger cities. Francisco Caraballo is the EPL's principal commander. Other members of the central staff are Javier Robles, Antonio Cáceres, and Beto Martínes.

In February, an EPL front operating in Córdoba accused the FARC of massacring EPL partisans and declared an "all-out war" against the FARC's "anti-revolutionary and fascist practices" (*El Tiempo*, 15 February). In a joint communiqué with the ELN, the EPL announced a new offensive against the government and condemned the M-19 for holding talks with government officials in violation of previous agreements adopted by the CNG (*AFP*, 20 February).

In early May, the EPL general command stated its willingness to accept the Barco administration's peace proposal and announced its decision to begin preparations for a unilateral cease-fire (*El Espectador*, 3 May). In June, military authorities announced the capture of two EPL leaders and the dismantlement of an urban network in Bucaramanga, Santander (Inravision Television Cadena, 3 June; *FBIS*, 5 June). Troops of the 2nd Army Division killed five EPL guerrillas in a clash in southern César (ibid., 25 June; *FBIS*, 27 June). The EPL ambushed a truck convoy in Bolívar Department on 29 June, killing five marines (ibid., 30 June; *FBIS*, 3 July).

In late July, Caraballo praised the work of the Commission of Notables and insisted that a direct dialogue with the government could improve the possibility for achieving peace (*El Espectador*, 1 August). EPL leaders met with President Barco's peace adviser on 29 September at an EPL camp in

Córdoba as part of the government's policy to prepare a dialogue agenda and search for points of agreement with guerrilla groups belonging to the CNG (*El Tiempo*, 30 September). In November the Defense Ministry reported that one soldier and five guerrillas had been killed in raids carried out by EPL forces in Northern Santander and Chocó (Radio Cadena Nacional, 10 November; *FBIS*, 13 November). The army reported that 21 guerrillas had been killed during intense fighting with EPL units operating in the area of Puerto Libertador, Córdoba (ibid., 15 November; *FBIS*, 16 November).

The Independent Revolutionary Workers' Movement (MOIR) has aspired since 1971 to become the first mass-based Maoist party in Latin America. Its leadership and organization are independent of those of the PCC-ML. The MOIR has no military branch and has been unable to strengthen its political position in recent years. The MOIR's general secretary is Francisco Mosquera.

The M-19. The M-19, which first appeared in January 1974 as the self-proclaimed armed branch of ANAPO, takes its name from the contested presidential election of 19 April 1970. Since 1976, the M-19 has been actively involved in Colombia's guerrilla movement, pursuing "a popular revolution of national liberation toward socialism." Over the years the M-19 has suffered heavy battle losses. The Colombian Defense Ministry's official estimate of the M-19's strength is 450 men operating on two fronts (*YICA*, 1988). Other estimates on the movement's size range up to several thousand. The M-19's principal commander is Carlos Pizarro Leongómez. Other surviving members of the M-19's central staff, some of whom operate from self-exile in Mexico, are Antonio Navarro Wolff, Otto Patiño, Germán Rojas Niño, Ramiro Lucio Escobar, and René Ramos Suárez.

The M-19 was the only guerrilla group that welcomed President Barco's peace plan in September 1988. In January the government agreed to hold direct talks with the M-19 as a first step toward the M-19's demobilization and its incorporation into the country's democratic life (*El Tiempo*, 14 January). At a follow-up meeting in Mexico City, government representatives and M-19 leaders agreed to hold a working meeting to draw up an agenda for a direct dialogue with other groups in the country (AFP, 5 March). As part of the peace process, the M-19 agreed on 17 March to relocate its forces and general headquarters to a demilitarized zone near Santo Domingo, Cauca, which the M-19 promptly renamed "Peace Village." In announcing the agreement, President Barco acknowledged that this "transitional stage" in the peace initiative did not require the M-19 to surrender its weapons (*Voz*, 21 March). For his part, Carlos Pizarro dismissed speculation that the M-19's internal weakness was a key factor in its decision to pursue a separate peace agreement. He called on the Catholic Church and the UP to participate in the roundtable discussions between the government, the M-19, and political parties represented in the Colombian Congress to prepare a proposal for political, social, and economic reforms (*El Siglo*, 22 March). Following an M-19 attack on the police station in Bruselas, Huila, on 28 March, the army declared it would mount operations against any M-19 members who failed to relocate to the neutral zone (AFP, 1 April).

President Barco officially opened the first round-table talks on 4 April. The M-19's negotiating platform included demands for modifications to the antiterrorist statute; disbanding of the self-defense paramilitary organizations; a new state economic plan, including distribution of food and housing to the poor; and constitutional changes intended to emphasize popular plebiscites and break the electoral dominance of the country's two traditional parties (*NYT*, 27 June). On 8 April, three M-19 leaders were murdered, including Alfranio Parra, the commander of the M-19's urban militias, resulting in a two-week suspension of the talks (*Voz*, 13 April).

In a joint declaration issued on 13 April, the M-19 and the UP affirmed their determination to work together and agreed on the need to consolidate the various peace processes (*El Siglo*, 14 April). In a subsequent interview, Pizarro stated that the M-19 would not repeat the history of the UP, but he confirmed that the movement's ultimate goal is to become a political party. As the only non-Marxist guerrilla group, M-19 leaders consider their movement atypical. Although Pizarro did not rule out any type of alliance, he expressed the view that "communism has no chance in Colombia" (*El Tiempo*, 17 April). According to Pizarro, the difference between the M-19 and the UP is that the latter is "a part of a section of the Communist Party and is deeply attached to the theory that all kinds of struggle can be waged at the same time... This stance seems to be in crisis in Colombia... and the UP has paid a high price for its mistaken views" (Lisbon, *Expreso*, 11 November; *FBIS*, 7 December).

On 17 July, the M-19 and the government agreed to form a commission to establish the judicial and political guarantees for guerrillas who return to civilian life (ibid., 17 July). An additional accord in September included agreement on a pardon for the guerrilla forces, contingent on congressional approval, and the M-19's pledge to surrender its weapons. The two sides agreed that a bilateral commission be created to discuss the manner in which the guerrilla group will be demobilized and the security mechanisms that would protect the lives of M-19 members (ibid., 27 September). On 2 November, the government and the M-19 signed a "Political Pact for Peace and Democracy" during a ceremony at the Colombian Congress. The peace accord formalized arrangements for the demobilization and the incorporation of the guerrillas into civilian life and also included constitutional reforms, electoral modifications to permit the M-19 to participate in the 1990 elections as a legal political party, and establishment of compulsory voting (*El Espectador*, 6 November).

In late December, the government announced that the peace process had been "suspended" by mutual agreement. To prevent the Congress from voting for a referendum on the issue of extradition for those involved in drug trafficking, the executive branch elected to sacrifice, at least temporarily, its political agreements with the M-19, which had included the M-19's demand for approval of a constitutional reform package as a condition for demobilization. Although the Congress approved a law that authorizes the president to "pardon" over the next six months the armed groups that have demonstrated their desire for peace, the M-19 announced that for the time being it will not surrender its weapons. At year's end, the government and the M-19 were calling for an extraordinary meeting early in 1990 in an attempt to redirect the peace process and prevent its permanent collapse (AFP, 23 December).

ELN. The ELN was formed in Santander in 1964 under the inspiration of the Cuban revolution. It undertook its first military action in January 1965. Once recognized as the largest and most militant of the guerrilla forces operating in Colombia, the ELN has never recovered from the toll exacted on its leadership and urban networks in the 1970s. The ELN was the only major guerrilla movement which did not sign a cease-fire agreement with the government in 1984.

According to Colombian intelligence, the ELN has approximately 950 men distributed over fifteen fronts. Its principal leader is Manuel Pérez Martínez. Other members of the central staff are Nicolás Rodríguez, Milton Hernández, and Gabriel Borja. The ELN operates in a vast region of northeastern Colombia, in North and South Santander, Bolívar, Cauca, and Antioquia, and in the intendance of Arauca. Because of its revenue from kidnappings, extortion, and bank robberies, the movement is believed to be financially self-supporting.

The ELN was the most active guerrilla movement in 1989. ELN units intensified their operations early in the year, actively engaging the military in various parts of the country. In a communiqué to the governor of Antioquia in February, the ELN rejected the peace plan proposed by the government and reaffirmed its intention to continue the armed struggle (*El Espectador*, 2 February).

In March authorities reported that fifteen guerrillas had been killed following an ELN attack on Tenjo in northern Cundinamarca (Inravision Television Cadena, 9 March; *FBIS*, 10 March). Later in that month military sources reported twelve guerrillas killed over a four-day period and large quantities of war material seized during clashes with ELN forces in Cauca, Boyacá, Nariño, Antioquia, and Bolívar (*El Tiempo*, 22 March). On 31 March, an ELN commando unit kidnapped Liberal Senator Félix Salcedo Baldión and two journalists in Cucutá in a propaganda move to announce the beginning of its campaign "against militarism and the dirty war" (EFE, 1 April; *FBIS*, 4 April).

The ELN continued its attacks against Colombia's petroleum infrastructure in 1989 in an effort to force the government to nationalize the oil industry and "prevent the exploitation of the country's natural resources." During the first six months of the year, the ELN carried out over twenty attacks on Colombia's main petroleum pipeline between Caño Limón and Covenas, which links the eastern plains and the Caribbean coast.

Following several dynamite attacks on oil installations in April, the defense minister declared that "no guerrilla group in Colombia is invulnerable," and proclaimed a new offensive against the ELN "to protect the country's oil resources" (AFP, 23 April). On 16 June, the ELN destroyed the main oil terminal in Covenas, halting the export of crude oil for three weeks. The ELN's clandestine radio simultaneously announced an oil-policy proposal calling for the nationalization of the Caño Limón oil field, suspension of Ecopetrol's partnership contracts with multinational corporations, and the creation of a national petroleum council (Radio Patria Libre, 16 June; *FBIS*, 19 June). According to Colombia's Interior Minister, the ELN's multiple acts of sabotage have caused "catastrophic economic and ecological consequences" and reduced hydrocarbon production by as much as 20 percent (AFP, 25 June).

The military deployed some two thousand troops of the 2nd Army Division in an effort to counteract ELN attacks on the pipeline in the Arauca and central Magdalena regions. Thirteen ELN guerrillas and four soldiers were reported killed during clashes in late July (Emisoras Caracol Network, 27 July; *FBIS*, 28 July). The ELN launched its own offensive in August, killing at least eight soldiers during skirmishes in rural areas of César, Santander, and Antioquia. On 16 August, a Defense Ministry spokesman reported that the army had killed five guerrillas in a raid on an ELN camp near the Venezuelan border. The camp reportedly served as a base to train new recruits and to plan attacks on petroleum installations (Reuter, 16 August; *FBIS*, 21 August).

ELN attacks continued throughout the year, despite appeals from the CNG and the UP asking ELN leaders to consider negotiating a cease-fire with the government. Authorities reported in October that four ELN guerrillas had been killed when they had attempted to ambush a military patrol near Urabá, Antioquia (Radio Cadena Nacional, 13 October; *FBIS*, 17 October). The ELN's Domingo Laín front claimed responsibility for the assassination on 14 October of Bishop Msgr. Emilio Jaramillo Monsalve of Arauca for his "obstinate meddling in the front's domestic matters" (*El Tiempo*, 20 October). In November, ELN guerrillas ambushed an army convoy in El Playón area of Santander, killing four soldiers and wounding seven. Army sources reported the death of seven guerrillas in clashes following the ambush (Radio Cadena Nacional, 17 November; *FBIS*, 20 November). On 22 November, some fifty guerrillas occupied the town of California, Santander, where they harangued the citizens, demanded the elimination of paramilitary groups, and painted pro-ELN slogans on the walls (ibid., 22 November; *FBIS*, 24 November).

At year's end, the ELN remained the only major guerrilla group that had not entered into negotiations with either the government or a private peace commission.

Daniel L. Premo
Washington College

Costa Rica

Population. 2,953,908
Party. Popular Vanguard Party (Partido Vanguardia Popular; PVP). A splinter faction is the Costa Rican People's Party (Partido del Pueblo Costarricense; PPC), up to 1988 led by PVP founder and former general secretary Manuel Mora Valverde and his brother Eduardo. Other secondary leftist parties are the Broad Democratic Front (Frente Amplio Democrático; FAD) associated with the PVP and led by Rodrigo Gutiérrez; associated with the PPC are the New Republic Movement (Movimiento de la Nueva República; MNR) led by Sergio Erick Ardón; the Socialist Party of Costa Rica (Partido Socialista Costarricense; PSC) led by Alvaro Montero Mejía.
Founded. PVP: 1931; PPC: 1984; MNR: 1970 (as the Revolutionary People's Movement, MRP); PSC: 1972
Membership. 5,000 to 10,000 for all of the abovementioned parties and groups (est.)
General Secretary. PVP: Humberto Vargas Carbonell; PPC: Lenin Chacón Vargas (replaced Manuel Mora Valverde, 6 February 1988)
General Undersecretary. PVP: Oscar Madrigal; PPC: Eduardo Mora Valverde
Central Committee. PVP and PCC each has 35 members, 15 alternates
Status. Legal in all cases
Last Congress. PVP: Sixteenth, 15–18 September 1988; PPC: Fifteenth, 23–24 August 1987.
Last Election. 1986: Popular Alliance (Alianza Popular; AP), including PVP, less than 1 percent of the presidential vote, 1 legislator elected; United People (Pueblo Unido; PU), including PPC, less than 1 percent of the presidential vote, 1 legislator elected.
Auxiliary Organizations. Unitary Workers' Central (Central Unitaria de Trabajadores; CUT); General Workers' Confederation (Confederación General de Trabajadores; CGT); National Peasants' Federation (Federación Campesina Nacional; FCN); Costa Rican Peace and Solidarity Council (umbrella group of approximately 50 unions and solidarity committees)
Publications. PVP: *Libertad Revolucionaria* became *Adelante* (weekly), Manuel Delgado, director; PPC: *Libertad* (weekly), Rodolfo Ulloa B., director.

1989 was the year Costa Ricans prepared for the general elections of February 1990. Like everyone else in the country, Costa Rican Marxists were caught up in that process. Faced with a historically strong two-party system, as well as their consistently poor record at the polls, they began the year with a serious attempt to create a leftist coalition behind a single candidate. Three leftist parties (the PVP, the FAD, and the PPC) had agreed on 11 December 1988 to form a new coalition called Frente Patriótico. The date of the national convention at which a single candidate would be selected was set as 22 April 1989. By February, however, dissension within the ranks of the coalition was quite evident. In a scathing critique of "partisan vanities," "antidemocratic procedures," and "bureaucratism," the weekly *Libertad* (16 February) noted that only a small part of the left in Costa Rica was supporting the Frente Patriótico. No candidate was ever selected, and the search for a new coalition began around mid-year. Again, the task was to come up with one presidential candidate and a minimal program and platform. This was finally done at a National Convention on 1 October. The coalition was called Pueblo Unido, and Dr. Daniel Camacho Monge, a politically unaffiliated sociologist, was chosen as the coalition's single candidate. Pueblo Unido's platform contained the usual anti-imperialist and anti-IMF rhetoric but placed special emphasis on two other threats: the trend toward privatization of state agencies, and the perceived deterioration of the "moral climate" of the country. Narcotrafficking and generalized corruption were cited as prime examples of the latter and were portrayed as endemic in both major parties. The campaign took on airs of a crusade, with candidate Camacho stating at one point that Pueblo Unido would have to fight "like the early Christians" to clean out the national stables. (*Adelante*, 17–23 November.)

Presidential candidate Camacho spoke of the creation of a "third force," of a "left of center coalition" (*La Nación*, 3 November).

The resulting coalition appeared to have been the result of a decision made at the Sixteenth Congress (September 1988) of the PVP to "remove the obstacles to consolidation of left unity and the unification of the broad masses" (Resolución del XVI Congreso del Partido Vanguardia Popular, San José, 1988, p.

2 [multilith]). The broader context was—judging from the numerous stories in the PVP press—*perestroika* and *glasnost'*.

The new openness was evident in the revelation (*Libertad*, 23 February) that part of the generalized Stalinism which governed the left parties was systematic suppression of any information which would "demoralize" party members. The long-suppressed results of a 1983 poll of the working class were revealed: the percentage of those polled who were members of a socialist party, or who identified with a revolutionary regime (i.e., Cuba or Nicaragua) was "1 to 3%." Those who identified with worker or trade-union demands: 20 percent; who identified with "patriotic and nationalist demands": 60 percent. The revelation of the poll's results was obviously intended to support the PPC leadership's decision to join a broad coalition for the 1990 elections.

There appeared good social and political reasons for the left to attempt to establish a coalition which would encompass the considerable discontent evident in the society. The peasant sector seemed especially restless. Some of the IMF-imposed policies of economic adjustment, that is, deregulation of supports on prices for fertilizers, were especially opposed by farming groups. The general secretary of the PVP, Humberto Vargas Carbonell, pointedly noted that it was the peasantry which was "most active" in the fight against deregulation (*WMR*, April). It must not have been lost on Carbonell that that same peasantry has also been the one most prone to oppose the governing, and largely urban-based, National Liberation Party (PLN) by voting for its major opponent. This explains the Pueblo Unido's constant emphasis on the absence of differences between the PLN and the oppositional Partido Union Social Cristiano. Whatever their hopes of electoral success might have been, the member parties of Pueblo Unido hoped, at a minimum, to retain the two seats (out of 57) in the Chamber of Deputies which coalition partners had won in 1986. The Partido Vanguardia Popular (PVP) held one, and the Partido del Pueblo de Costa Rica (PPC) also one.

Despite the serious efforts at coalition forming in 1989, however, it was clear that the divisions which have historically bedeviled the left and, most recently, destroyed the Frente Patriótico, were also affecting Pueblo Unido. In November, Javier Solís, a deputy originally elected by Pueblo Unido and general secretary of the Partido del Progreso, resigned from the coalition (as well as from the Par-

tido del Progreso), stating that the crisis in the left was so great that "the left can die" in Costa Rica (*La Nación*, 9 November). As Costa Rica entered the final stretch of the political race, the traditional two-party system did not appear to be seriously menaced by a "third force."

But internal dissension was not the only habit lingering from the Stalinist days. Secrecy and censorship still reared their ugly heads. One example will illustrate how, despite the rhetorical support in both *Adelante* and *Libertad* for *perestroika* and anti-Stalinism, changing Soviet attitudes toward Central America were not always revealed to the readers of these newspapers. On invitation of the Costa Rican Legislative Assembly, several members of the Soviet parliament spent six days studying the Costa Rican assembly. Questioned on the USSR's stance on Central America, Aleksandr Mokanu, deputy chairman of the Supreme Soviet Presidium, responded that the USSR had stopped supplying military equipment to Nicaragua because it supported the peace initiative of Esquipulas II. Soviet attitudes toward the armed struggle? It was, he noted, "an internal affair." Alfredo Cristiani's government—was it legitimate? "All governments elected by the people," he responded, "are legitimate." (*FBIS*, 11 August; AFP, 10 August.)

None of the left newspapers reported these answers. The fear of "demoralizing" their followers that leftist leaders had had in the early 1980s was clearly still very much alive.

Anthony P. Maingot
Florida International University

Cuba

Population. 10,450,360 (July 1989)
Party. Communist Party of Cuba (Partido Comunista de Cuba; PCC)
Founded. 1965
Membership. About 600,000 full and probationary members. Industrial workers account for one third of that total, managerial and office workers for 20 percent, professionals and technicians for 13 percent and peasants for 2 percent. Persons

aged 36 to 45 make up 38 percent of the total; those aged 46 to 55, 23 percent; those over 55 account for 25 percent; and those aged 27 and younger for 3 percent. (*WMR*, September 1989.)

General Secretary. Fidel Castro Ruz, 63; title: first secretary

Politburo. 14 members: Fidel Castro Ruz, Raúl Castro Ruz (second secretary), Juan Almeida Bosque, Julio Camacho Aguilera, Osmany Cienfuegos Gorrián, Abelardo Colomé Ibarra, Vilma Espín Guillois, Armando Hart Dávalos, Esteban Lazo Hernández, José R. Machado Ventura, Pedro Miret Prieto, Jorge Risquet Valdés-Saldana, Carlos Rafael Rodríguez, Roberto Veiga Menéndez; 10 alternate members

Secretariat. 9 members: Fidel Castro Ruz, Raúl Castro Ruz, José R. Machado Ventura, Jorge Risquet Valdés-Saldana, Julián Rizo Alvarez, José Ramón Balaguer Cabrera, Sixto Batista Santana, Jaime Crombet Hernández-Baquero, Lionel Soto Prieto

Central Committee. 162 members, about 70 alternates. In 1989, one member, General Arnaldo Ochoa, was tried and executed by a firing squad; several others, among them Generals José Abrantes, interior minister, and Diocles Torralba González, transportation minister, were arrested and received long jail sentences.

Status. Ruling party; no dissident group allowed to operate

Last Congress. Third, two sessions: 4–7 February, 30 November–2 December 1986

Last Election. In 1986, all members of the National Assembly of People's Power were approved, and they re-elected Fidel Castro Ruz and Raúl Castro Ruz as president and first vice-president of the Council of State for the 1987–1992 period. The council has a secretary and 23 members (ministers).

Auxiliary Organizations. Union of Young Communists (Unión de Jovenes Comunistas; UJC), Union of Cuban Pioneers (Unión de Pioneros de Cuba; UPC), Federation of Cuban Women (Federación de Mujeres Cubanas; FMC), Committees for the Defense of the Revolution (Comités de Defensa de la Revolución; CDR), Confederation of Cuban Workers (Confederación de Trabajadores Cubanos; CTC), National Association of Small Farmers (Asociación Nacional de Agricultores Pequeños; ANAP)

Publications. *Granma* (six days a week), official organ of the Central Committee, Enrique Román, editor; *Juventud Rebelde* (daily), organ of the UJC

In 1989, Cuba, under the leadership of Fidel Castro acquired the dubious distinction of being the only Soviet bloc country untouched by the winds of revolutionary change sweeping Eastern Europe. Very strongly and explicitly, Castro proclaimed his unwavering devotion to communist orthodoxy and his opposition to internal liberalization and political and economic restructuring. At the year's end, for Castro the most dangerous counterrevolutionaries were not external enemies, the Miami-based exiles, but those in Cuba who favored *glasnost'* and *perestroika*. But whatever pressure there was on the Cuban regime to fall into line with other communist countries and open up to new ideas, if not to substantially change the one-party-and-total-control principle, it did not manifest itself on the streets. A purge of high military and state-security officers, although officially linked to their alleged drug-trafficking activities, had more to do with the desire by many Cuban officials to at least explore the possibilities of change. By executing four of his former close collaborators and jailing many others, Castro clearly warned the top party, military and government echelons that even to talk about change was treason, and that his unipersonal rule and his views could not be challenged. A minor change in voting in the grass-roots party organizations announced 5 January 1990, appeared to be a cosmetic measure which did nothing to alter the PPC's central control.

Leadership and Party Organization. More than ever before, in 1989 the leadership of the country was in the hands of Fidel Castro, who relied on his brother, Defense Minister Raúl Castro, to support his ideas and execute all his orders. Although some of the policy decisions were supposedly made at meetings of the Politburo, for practical purposes that group, the PCC Secretariat, the Central Committee and the party apparatus were merely rubber-stamp bodies. Castro, in his many speeches, laid down a policy line which then would be approved by the agency that has jurisdiction over the particular issue. In a process that apparently began a year earlier, by mid-1989 over 400,000 party members were interviewed in a course of a "grass-roots-level" campaign to "confirm" membership cards. The "basic aim" of the campaign was to give party members an opportunity for self-criticism, to enhance their political activity and production performance, and to check whether the members' behavior was in line with party policy. According to the party's announcement, over 6,000 people were disciplined, and close to 2,000 were expelled from the organization, with 40 percent of the reprimands issued arising from noncompliance with party rules and 31 percent from irresponsibility and indiscipline at work. (*WMR*, September.)

Those sanctioned for poor discipline included high party officials. In August, several departmental directors and other top officials of the Ministry of Transportation were dismissed following an investigation that was conducted after two serious railway accidents which left 51 people dead and some 300 injured. The investigation concluded that "the lack of discipline, supervision, and good work methods in the Cuban rail system was the fundamental cause" of the two derailments. (*Granma*, 17 September.) The arrest on 11 June of Transportation Minister General Diocles Torralba, a Central Committee member and a vice-president of Cuba, Havana said, was not related to the problems of his agency, but was motivated by his "personal conduct," as was the jailing of Luís Leonardo Domínguez, a high party official and a former head of the Cuban civil-aviation agency and once Castro's protégé. Domínguez' successor, Vicente Gómez Lopez, was arrested after only a few months in office, and was replaced by General Rogelio Acevedo. Torralba was tried and sentenced to twenty years in jail for "stealing public funds... falsifying public documents... gross immoral actions... corruption and dissipated and licentious conduct." He was replaced by General Senen Casas Regueiro, an alternate member of the Politburo.

The visit of Mikhail S. Gorbachev to Cuba from 2 to 5 April, the first such trip of the top Kremlin leader since 1973, appeared to have been an unsuccessful effort by the Soviet president to convince Castro of the necessity to initiate a process of political and economic rectifications in the party and government. The Soviets, whose annual subsidy of Cuba is calculated at between $4 billion and $6 billion, for years have been known to be frustrated by the Castro regime's economic mismanagement. Despite that huge Russian largesse (whose openhandedness has been criticized publicly in the Soviet parliament), according to foreign observers in Havana Gorbachev was not awarded the courtesies any top Soviet leader would be expected to receive during a Cuban trip. Castro was often visibly annoyed because newsmen covering the visit appeared to ignore him and addressed most of their questions to Gorbachev. On one occasion, Castro brushed aside a Latin American correspondent who addressed a question to his Soviet host by stating that it was out of order, just as Gorbachev was about to respond. Castro's introduction of the Soviet president to the Cuban National Assembly, the country's parliament, was longer than Gorbachev's speech that followed, in what appears to have been a breach of diplomatic custom. "Those who march along with time and draw the necessary conclusions from change can count on success," Gorbachev told the Assembly.

But the advice apparently fell on deaf ears. Shortly after the Soviet leader left Cuba, the country's press began to emphasize the principle of "diversity of socialism" and the right of every communist party to choose its own solutions to its peculiar socioeconomic problems, but solutions always based on "resolute loyalty to the principles of Marxism-Leninism" which Havana said was the only correct line for a communist leader to follow.

In August, Havana banned the circulation in Cuba of the weekly *Moscow News* and the monthly *Sputnik*, the first such action in nearly three decades of close relations between Cuba and the Soviet Union. Cuba accused the two Soviet publications of promoting "bourgeois democracy" and the American way of life. In addition, Havana said, explaining the ban, that the magazines were misinforming Cuban youth about history and Marxist ideology. At the same time, the Havana press attacked two Hungarian journalists for asserting that there were violations of human rights in Cuba, whose economy, they wrote, was stagnated. On 5 October, Soviet foreign minister Edward Shevardnadze visited Cuba for a talk with Castro, presumably on the situation in Central America. Havana did not give any details of their conversations. *Granma*, the party newspaper, printed a headline saying: "Very Good Climate At Fidel-Shevardnadze Talks," over the photograph of the two grim-looking leaders taken in Castro's office.

Castro was leading his regime's antichange drive. In his 26 July speech, he spoke of the possibility of a "great civil war in the USSR" and the possibility that the Soviet Union could "disintegrate." Apparently shaken by the news from Eastern Europe, he commented that this could never happen in Cuba because the country would continue to struggle along the correct path of socialism, which included a centrally controlled economy. But in the same address, the Cuban leader began to prepare the country for an economic decline, saying that, as a result of changes in the Soviet bloc, socialist supplies would not be arriving in Cuba in the same quantities and with the same regularity as before. In the speech of 7 November on the same subject the Cuban leader reiterated that the events in Eastern Europe could cause "serious difficulties" for the country and *Granma* assailed Hungary for raising the prices of goods bought by Cuba. "We are amazed by some of the things we are witnessing" in the Soviet bloc, Castro said. "Where will it all lead? Of course we respect everyone's right to solve problems as they see fit. We have no right to rule over others, nor do others have the right to rule over us... When there are reports of strikes over there, you can be sure we run the risk that certain equipment will not reach our country... certain materials and equipment we were counting on for our plans have been delayed or have not come at all... We will continue defending socialism, and we will continue building socialism, come what may. We never have any thought, not even the remotest thought, of returning to the filth and repugnance of capitalism." (*Granma*, 19 November.)

On 7 December, Castro, in his fiercest attack of the year on the East European reformist governments, pledged to resist changes even if it meant parting ways with his allies. "It is disgusting to see how many people, even in the USSR itself, are engaged in denying and destroying the history-making feats and extraordinary merits of that heroic people... Thus we didn't hesitate to stop the circulation of certain Soviet publications that are full of poison against the USSR itself and socialism. Some of those publications have already started calling for an end to the fair and equitable trade relations that were established between the USSR and Cuba during the Cuban revolutionary process. They want the USSR to begin practicing unequal trade with Cuba by selling its products to us at even higher prices, just as the United States does with other Third World countries—in short, they want the USSR to join the U.S. blockade against Cuba." Castro indicated that he and Gorbachev did not see eye to eye during their April encounter in Havana. He said that the two had had a "frank, in-depth exchange of views." Perhaps referring to a reported meeting in late November of the Soviet ambassador in Managua with Cuban and Nicaraguan officials, during which the Russian diplomat is said to have strongly criticized Castrista and Sandinista aid to the Salvadoran rebels, Castro said: "The imperialist government of the United States demands that no one help the Salvadoran revolutionaries and tries to blackmail the USSR into ending its economic and military assistance to Nicaragua and Cuba because

we express solidarity with the Salvadoran revolutionaries, even though we abide strictly by our commitment concerning the weapons supplied by the USSR, in accord with the agreements signed between our sovereign nations. Meanwhile, that same imperialist government... is helping the genocidal Salvadoran government and sending special combat units to El Salvador... organizing coups d'état in Panama; sending military aid to UNITA in Angola... and continuing to supply the rebel forces in Afghanistan with large amounts of weapons." In a stinging criticism of East European communists, but without mentioning any country in particular, Castro commented: "Cuba is not a country in which socialism came in the wake of the victorious divisions of the Red Army... Those of us in our country's leadership aren't a bunch of bumbling parvenus, new to our positions of responsibility... The banners of revolution and socialism won't be given up without a fight... giving up is for cowards... Socialism or Death." (*Granma*, 17 December.)

During the last days of December and in early January 1990, Castro continued what appeared to be a propaganda marathon, making public speeches practically every day. At a three-day-long December meeting in Havana of top government and PCC leaders, recognizing dissent within his regime, he castigated internal critics, calling them "charlatans associated with a subtle form of counterrevolution," and saying that they "allow themselves to doubt the ability and experience of the cadres that lead the party and the country." He warned that "we cannot allow trust in the party to be subverted." (*The Miami Herald*, 15 December.) In his New Year's message to the country, broadcast on radio and television, Castro called on the Cubans to defend the "ideological and military trenches of the revolution." He also urged them to fight against the "doubters and the divisionists" to preserve unity in government and party ranks.

While Castro was mentioning the changes in the Soviet bloc in general terms, the Cuban media were reporting daily on these developments, as well as on the Bush-Gorbachev summit meeting at Malta. Pictures of demonstrations in Poland, Hungary, East Germany, and Romania were shown on Cuban television. The Cuban press frequently printed articles about the adverse consequences for Cuba of the Soviet bloc's economic and political changes, reportedly the prime topic of conversation among people from all walks of life. Although judging by Castro speeches, the impact of the East European developments must have been considerable in

Cuba, where many officials travel to the Eastern bloc nations, and many more people study or work, there were no reports of public expressions of dissatisfaction, or demands for change by the populace. By preparing the people for more austerity, and pledging to continue the still-undefined campaign of "rectification of errors and negative tendencies" begun in 1986, Castro was trying to prevent an anti-government explosion caused by a spark of discontent.

The Cuban security police were also active in silencing any type of protest. In August, it arrested three of the country's leading civil-rights workers who theretofore had been allowed to operate on a modest, strictly supervised, scale. Arrested and later sentenced to two years in jail were Elizardo Sánchez Santa Cruz, the head of the Cuban Commission for Human Rights and National Reconciliation; Hiram Abi Cobas, the acting head of the Human Rights Party of Cuba; and Humberto Jerez Marino, the president of the José Martí Commission on Human Rights. The three were charged with "disseminating false information dangerous to the state." Sanchez, who had met with foreign journalists a few days before his arrest, told reporters that the Cuban government was going to become more authoritarian than before. A government official told the journalists who interviewed Sanchez and other human rights activists that they might be expelled or barred from future visits to Cuba if they met with the dissidents. (*NYT*, 7 August.) A total of 27 human-rights monitors were in Cuban jails at the year's end, making the country, according to the international human-rights groups, one of the world's worst violators. The New York–based West Watch said that Cuba had more political prisoners per capita for longer periods than any other country. (*Insight*, 30 October.) Castro also appeared unmoved by widespread criticism abroad. "While the breezes of freedom surge through much of the Communist world, Fidel Castro is resolutely turning Cuba into a fortress of reaction," wrote *The New York Times* in an editorial on 9 August commenting on Sanchez' arrest. On 12 December, the paper called Castro a "Marxist fossil with teeth," suggesting that President Bush talk to Mikhail Gorbachev about finally cutting the USSR's arms aid to Cuba, in a quid pro quo for disbanding the contras. On 1 January 1990, in an open letter to Fidel Castro published in the principal U.S. newspapers, some 200 political figures, intellectuals, and artists known worldwide, asked the Cuban leader to release all political prisoners, to give Cubans the right

to travel freely in and out of the country, to allow free association, free expression, and a plebiscite on the governing of the country. Among the signatories were Lech Wałęsa, Milovan Djilas, Yves Montand, Jacek Kuroń, Federico Fellini, Leslie Caron, Susan Sontag, Elie Wiesel, Mario Vargas Llosa, and Paloma Picasso. A few days after the letter, entitled "Fidel Open Your Wall," was published, *Granma* strongly criticized its signatories and reiterated that Cuba would not deviate from its correct Marxist-Leninist course.

But evidently the events in Eastern Europe were having their effect on Castro. For the first time since he came to power there was no multitudinous celebration of the anniversary of 1 January 1959, a celebration which had been usually accompanied by a military parade. It was as though Castro were afraid that a huge rally in Havana could result in a massive repudiation of his rule, as had happened days earlier in Bucharest to Nicolae Ceaușescu. On 6 January, Havana announced that communist party organizations at grass-roots levels would be allowed to elect their leaders by direct secret vote, with more than one candidate on the ballot. The announcement, published by *Granma*, appeared an effort to allay discontent within the party's rank and file, discontent which reportedly has existed in Cuba for years. The new voting rules affect party cells with more than fifteen members, and candidates for party leaders are to be proposed at open meetings. Heretofore, base-level party leaders were actually appointed by higher-ranking communist officials, who prepared a list containing their names, which was then approved openly by communist cell members.

On 6 January *Granma*, in a front page article, said the voting changes were part of the Cuban process of "rectification" that had been launched by Castro in 1986. But rather than liberalizing the governance of Cuba, the "rectification" process has been aimed at tightening state control over the economy and most other activities in Cuba. Since 1986, small private enterprises and the sale of agricultural products on a free market in the cities has been outlawed.

The aim of the new party election rules, *Granma* said, is to "perfect the system of electing party leaders at grass-roots levels." Party organizations at these levels are to hold their elections and present their annual reports by April, the newspaper said. The new measure does not appear to alter the party structure in any significant way, nor does it signify an effort to invigorate the PCC. Delegates for the higher-level party bodies, the municipal and provincial assemblies, have already been elected from a slate of several candidates.

New Cuban Purge. Even before the political upheaval in Eastern Europe had shaken the Cuban leadership and populace, the arrest, trials, and executions of several of Fidel Castro's closest collaborators became the most intensely watched political event in Cuba since the 1959 revolution. On 13 June, the country was stunned by the announcement that General Arnaldo Ochoa Sánchez, one of Cuba's most decorated officers and commander of Cuba's expeditionary forces in Ethiopia and Angola, was arrested on charges described only as "serious acts of corruption and mismanagement of economic funds." Also arrested in what became known as the Case No. 1 were General Patricio de la Guardia Font, top-ranking official of the Interior Ministry; his twin brother Colonel Antonio de la Guardia Font, head of the ministry's "MC" department (an abbreviation of *Moneda Convertible*, convertible currency), who had been entrusted with the task of obtaining abroad American products Cuba has difficulty in purchasing because of the U.S. trade embargo; five other officers; and five civilian officials of the Interior Ministry, all later charged with drug trafficking and corruption.

The 57-year-old General Ochoa had been credited with having devised the tactics which resulted in a brilliant victory of Cuban troops over strong South African military units that had entered Angola, in a campaign culminating in the battle of Cuito Cuanavale. He was a member of the PCC Central Committee and of the Cuban legislature, and was one of a handful of officers awarded the title of "Hero of the Revolution." His 30-year-long military career included fighting as a guerrilla commander in Venezuela in the early 1960s, acting as head of the Cuban military mission to Nicaragua, and serving as commander of the Cuban forces in Ethiopia, where he led his troops to a victory over the Somali army in the Ogaden desert. Shortly before his arrest, General Ochoa, known to be very popular with his troops, had been appointed head of Cuba's Western Army, its largest military grouping, whose territory includes the province and city of Havana.

The two de la Guardia brothers were known to be close and trusted aides of Fidel Castro, at one time supervising his personal security. Antonio de la Guardia had been sent by Castro on many sensitive, commercial-intelligence missions abroad. He had visited the United States on a number of occasions, these visits indicating that he was acting with full authority of the "Maximum" leader. Castro, never accused of being a hands-off leader, was also said to be closely following the operations of the secret "MC" department, which was earning badly needed dollars through a series of trading companies set up abroad, among other places in Panama, the Caribbean, and Western Europe.

Adding to the bewilderment of the populace, was a rambling, incoherent speech delivered one day after General Ochoa's arrest to some 1,000 army officers by defense minister General Raúl Castro. He accused Ochoa of "unbridled populism," of engaging in illegal sugar sales in Angola, of always "yakking and joking." "Ochoa's behavior (his penchant for commercialism) was concealed by his apparent concern for the troops' living conditions. We knew of the unrestrained populism he resorted to in recent months when he had not yet been named chief of the Western Army, and when he was already presenting his 'credentials' to his troops by offering gifts and other objects of value, chiefly to officers, over and above the established norms in an exercise of self-indulgence, and with a total lack of principles and ethic, to create his image and establish ties of gratitude toward him." After stating that "it is preferable that Cuba sink to the bottom of the ocean like Atlantis before having the capitalist system prevail here," General Castro said that those who disagreed with the policies of the Cuban government could leave the country for Hungary or Poland, and that he would even get them visas by calling his "friend General Jaruzelski." Significantly, the reference to possible political dissidence within the Cuban armed forces was omitted from the official text of the nationally televised speech that later appeared in *Granma*.

Two days after Raúl Castro's speech, *Granma*, in an editorial, accused General Ochoa and other persons arrested in the Case No. 1 of "making contact with international drug traffickers," and possibly of providing them means of moving drugs through or near Cuban territory. This was the first mention by the Castro regime of a high-level Cuban involvement in the international drug traffic. On June 25, with reports from Cuba that hundreds of officers and officials were being detained (whose number later was said to have passed 1,000), a special tribunal of 47 senior generals and admirals was convened to review the drug-trafficking charges against the 14 persons accused. By that time, the Cuban public was being conditioned to expect severe punishment for the 14 arrested officials. *Granma* was repeating accusations against Ochoa and the others hinting that details of their involvement in the drug trade would be revealed at the military tribunal.

Work practically stopped in Cuba during the sessions, lasting two days, of the tribunal, major parts of which were televised, and which was seen as an effort of the Castro regime to involve the entire top military leadership in the Ochoa process and its bloody end. No foreign observers or journalists were allowed to witness the proceedings. General Castro, addressing his principal subordinates in the army and navy, urged them to give "exemplary punishment" to General Ochoa, who was seen watching impassively his former colleagues. "Ochoa's behavior was covered up by an apparent concern for the living conditions of his troops, [which] in reality served as a pretext for acquiring money," Raúl Castro said. Not a single officer spoke up for Ochoa and recalled his faithful 30-year-long military service, most of it abroad. The 47 unanimously ruled that General Ochoa be courtmartialed for "high treason against the fatherland," stripped of his rank and decorations, and dishonorably discharged from the armed forces. They also recommended that he be expelled from the Communist Party and the National Assembly.

Two days after the ruling of the tribunal, the country received another jolt when Havana announced the dismissal, because of "great failings" in leadership, of General José Abrantes Fernández, interior minister and chief of the Cuban government's powerful security apparatus. Abrantes, for many years a close aide to Fidel Castro, was replaced by General Abelardo Colomé Ibarra, a full member of the Politburo and the third-ranking military leader after Fidel and Raúl Castro. Simultaneously, five other generals, heads of the Interior Ministry's principal departments, including General Arsenio Franco Villanueva, national police chief, were dismissed. (When the dust settled two months later, 23 top military and civilian officials of the Interior Ministry had been shot, sentenced to prison terms, or dismissed. One, Colonel Rafael Alvarez Cueto, the ministry's finance director, committed suicide.)

The court-martial of General Ochoa and thirteen others in the Case No. 1 began 30 June, and it was also nationally televised. Specific charges were brought by the prosecution. Ochoa was accused of contacting through an aide, Captain Jorge Martínez Valdéz, Colombian drug boss Pedro Escobar, one of the heads of the Medellín cartel, for the purpose of devising ways and means to facilitate for a price the transport of drugs through Cuban territory, and to sell valuables, among them ivory obtained in Angola. Colonel Antonio de la Guardia was described by the prosecutors as the leader of a group within the MC department which between 1987 and early 1989 had helped Colombian drug traffickers smuggle through Cuba six tons of cocaine bound for the United States, accepting $3.4 million in bribes for this assistance in nineteen smuggling operations. Ochoa and Martínez were not charged with carrying out any drug smuggling, but with "damaging the image of the Cuban Revolution abroad." General Ochoa admitted having sent his aide to explore the possibility of collaborating with Escobar, but said his purpose was not personal enrichment, but to earn for Cuba badly needed foreign exchange. All his commercial operations in Angola were permitted by military regulations, duly recorded and accounted for, he testified, conceding he had erred in contacting the drug dealers. De la Guardia also admitted helping Colombian traffickers, but insisted that he had turned over the major part of the proceeds from the smuggling operations to the Cuban treasury and had been in the process of depositing the rest when he was arrested and several hundred thousand dollars were found in his and his MC subordinates' homes. During the trial, Captain Miguel Ruiz Poo, accused of being de la Guardia's contact man with Cuban-American drug traffickers in the United States, said that smuggling activities had been approved "at the highest level," testimony which was denied by the prosecution. On 7 July, the military tribunal, composed of three generals, sentenced Ochoa, Martínez, Antonio de la Guardia, and his aide Major Amado Bruno Padrón Trujillo to death by firing squad. The ten other defendants were given prison sentences ranging from 10 to 30 years.

From all over the world, appeals for mercy began to arrive in Havana, from Pope John Paul II, U.N. secretary general Javier Pérez de Cuéllar, Spanish prime minister Felipe González, other West European and Latin American heads of state and government, and even Julio Anguita, secretary general of the Italian Communist Party. But to no avail. On 11 July, the Cuban Council of State, presided over by Fidel Castro and the highest governing body in Cuba with power to overrule judicial verdicts, voted 29–0 to uphold the death sentences. After the Council's action, and explaining his affirmative vote, Castro revealed in a public speech that previously the issue had been discussed in other Cuban party and government organizations, and that all 14 members of the Politburo had endorsed the death sentence, that 10 of the 162 members of the Central Committee had voted against it, as had 2 of the 45 members of the Council of Ministers and 1 of the 404 deputies of the National Assembly of People's Power. Admitting that the death sentences were causing a deep trauma in the country, he said: "We know what the people think. But it is my duty to say that for us, in these circumstances, this does not constitute a determining factor. The leader must think in long-run terms and recognize what is best for the Revolution and the nation." He added that even if he wanted to, he could not grant a stay of execution because he had only one vote in the Council. In his speech he also tried to minimize the role General Ochoa had played in the Cuban victories in Angola and Ethiopia. (*Granma*, 12 July.) At dawn on 13 July, Ochoa, de la Guardia, Martínez, and Padrón were executed by firing squad in Havana.

In July and August, the purge continued. There was a complete shake-up in the Interior Ministry, with army generals appointed as vice-ministers and heads of all of the ministry's departments. On 31 July, former interior minister Abrantes, dismissed in June (when *Granma* declared that he still enjoyed the "confidence of the party's leadership"), and several of his collaborators were arrested. He was accused, among other charges, of "introducing cronyism, moral decay, and corruption into the Ministry," and of improperly using foreign-currency funds belonging to the Immigration Department to purchase abroad during the preceding 14 months, 1,200 cars for the ministry's personnel and for other officials. After a secret trial, explained by the sensitivity of the ministry's work, Abrantes was sentenced on 31 August to 20 years in prison, and six of his aides were given lesser jail sentences.

The sentencing of General Abrantes and his subordinates in the Case No. 2, did not end the purge. There were frequent reports of the jailing and firing of lesser officials throughout the country. A campaign to denigrate Ochoa continued, and pro-Ochoa officers were cashiered or reassigned to non-sensitive positions in the provinces. But the impact of the purge did not diminish. This was conceded and elaborated on by an unusual, one-page-long editorial published by *Granma* on 10 September and undoubtedly approved by Fidel Castro. Although it stated that "there has been no crisis," the editorial presented a grim picture of the profoundly disturbed Cuban populace: "The entire nation real-

izes that the problems faced by the country this summer go far beyond the fate of a handful of corrupt and disloyal individuals. The working people . . . realize that these have been decisive and historic months . . . Thus the most important aspect of this [affair] does not end with the Court's decision. It may be just beginning." The editorial said that the country was "shaken" by the trials and added that in the Case No. 1 "public opinion favored benevolence toward the main defendant" [Ochoa]. Reflecting on the country as a whole, *Granma* said that "the Tony de la Guardia mafia of drug traffickers reflects a cancer that was starting to eat away at the state institutions [Ministry of Interior] and whose metastasis was reflected in crimes such as petit bourgeois lifestyles, slackening of morals, cronyism, and arbitrary conduct . . . There are more profound problems in our society at the root of what has happened. We cannot limit ourselves to the implication that attributes all these problems to the lack of control." The editorial ended by saying: "This is not the time for useless lament or pessimism, much less for falling prey to groundless speculations."

Nevertheless, there were many speculations outside Cuba and, according to many journalistic reports, in Cuba about the true origins of the purge and its timing. Almost all observers agree that most of the accusations against Ochoa, de la Guardia, and Abrantes were factual. The question of who knew about the Cuban drug involvement and for how long, has not been answered by Havana. The most plausible theory is that Fidel Castro knew for years what the so-called Tony de la Guardia gang was doing. In fact, in 1982 the United States had indicted one of the 47 senior officers who recommended that Ochoa be tried, Admiral Aldo Santamaria, as a member of a group engaged in smuggling Colombian drugs to Cuba. Throughout the 1980s, there were many reports, documented in scores of Florida indictments, that Cuban ports and territory had been used for transshipment of cocaine, or that Cuban authorities, also for a high price, repaired and sold fuel to drug-transporting ships bound for the United States, choosing to ignore the nature of their cargo. Castro only acted, according to this theory, which was widely believed in Cuba, when he realized that General Ochoa had begun talking about *perestroika*-like changes in Cuba. It became known that Ochoa's modest house in Havana had become a gathering point for Africa veterans who came to visit their former commander, who was expected to take over soon the Occidental Army, to vent their frustration at finding the situation in the country much worse than when they had left it years before. Many veterans were also complaining to Ochoa of an entrenched military bureaucracy, headed by Defense Minister Raúl Castro, which had reneged on promises of special treatment they were to receive in return for their "internationalist service." It is widely believed that it would have been impossible for Ochoa and the de la Guardia twins to engage in "immoral behavior" without Fidel Castro learning about it, since their actions were said to have spanned several years. Equally, it is considered unthinkable that the purchase by Abrantes of some 1,200 new automobiles and their distribution to hundreds of high officials over a period of eighteen months would not have been reported to Castro, or even noticed by him on the streets, where a new car is a rarity. Fidel Castro turned a blind eye to the involvement of his subordinates in the drug trade as long as they were doing only that. He must have been told of millions of dollars being deposited by Ochoa and de la Guardia in the National bank, and their statement to that effect at the trial was not contradicted by the prosecution. But the Cuban president, who already had had some differences with Ochoa over the tactics used in the Angolan campaign, was aware that the advocacy by the popular general of political and economic liberalization was directly threatening his unipersonal rule. By executing Ochoa and Antonio de la Guardia, Castro warned his subordinates that mere talk about reforms would be regarded as treason, no matter what position advocates of changes would occupy in the armed forces, the government, or the party.

There were indications, however, that demands for reforms continued to be voiced, especially by the younger Cubans, among them, significantly, members of the UJC, the Cuban Communist youth organization. A dispatch of 12 January 1990 sent from Havana by the Spanish news agency EFE, reported that four University of Havana students had been arrested in connection with criticism of the Castro rule at a meeting of the UJC, of which they were members. The dispatch said that shortly before his arrest, one of the students, Jorge Quintana, in a letter to the national leadership of the UJC, had said that the Cuban Revolution "has been transformed into Stalinism" by Castro. The letter, which criticized the cult of personality of Castro, indicated that a group of dissident UJC members, who call themselves "Followers of Mella" (communist youth leader Julio Antonio Mella, assassinated in 1929), has embraced Gorbachev's *perestroika* and *glasnost'*. The Spanish agency also reported that a public meeting at the University of Havana, scheduled for 6 January, had been canceled at the last moment without explanation.

The Cuban Economy. The 1989 production of sugar, Cuba's main export, amounted to 8,124,000 metric tons, 800,000 more tons than for the previous year. But, also according to Havana, the economy grew by 1.5 percent, whereas the 1988 growth was 2.3 percent. Low world sugar prices reduced the Cuban foreign-exchange reserves, further depleted by Moscow's cut in petroleum deliveries (prior to this, Cuba had been able to re-export surplus Soviet oil for foreign currency). Cuba increased exports to socialist countries by 29.7 percent, but imports remained at the 1988 level. According to an economic analysis by *Granma*, "the effects of financial restrictions on hard currency, together with other problems such as delays in the arrival of important products [from the Soviet bloc], and unsuccessful efforts to find local substitutes, had a negative effect on the economy. There was a decline in the availability of fuel, corrugated steel bars, nickel products, gray cement, fabrics and clothes, cheese, beef, leaf tobacco, canned vegetables, and fish, among other things." *Granma* said that Cuba owed Western creditors $6.77 billion, and that the country's hard-currency reserve had dropped to $87.9 million by the middle of the year. Cuba was forced to delay payments to foreign creditors, and "short term loans are virtually the only sources of finances open." Housing in Cuban cities was "the most serious problem," the newspaper said, with 284,000 of Havana's two million people living "in slums and that's not counting those in overcrowded acceptable homes. Other serious problems are the water and sewer systems, both obsolete...There is a critical state of public transportation...In terms of communication, Havana is one of the most backward cities in Latin America." (*Granma*, 5 November.)

Bad as the situation was in Cuba in 1989, that of 1990 promised to be bleaker. The decision of the 10 socialist countries of the Council of Mutual Economic Assistance (COMECON) to move toward a free-market trading system was expected to strongly affect Cuba with its extremely small hard-currency reserve. Also, as a result of the changes in the COMECON trading practices, Cuba faced a steady decrease of aid from the Soviet bloc, which accounts for 90 percent of its trade. While a special trade treatment Cuba receives from the Soviet

Union was likely to continue in 1990, after that it was expected to be scaled down. Already Hungary was reported to have told Havana to pay 20 percent more than in 1989 for the chassis and other parts Cuba needed to assemble Ikarus buses, and 40 percent more during the next five years. Given the already decrepit state of its transportation system, Havana agreed to the demand.

To compensate for the dwindling East European aid, Cuba began to look toward China and Latin America in a search for new trading partners. Following a visit to Havana in December by Zheng Toubin, the Chinese minister of foreign economic relations, Cuba and China signed a trade agreement that will increase goods exchanges to $500 million in 1990, an 11 percent increase over 1989. But Cuba's trade with China has been on a barter basis only, which will not make Havana able to increase imports of badly needed Western products. In Latin America, Cuba has been courting Brazil, Venezuela, the Dominican Republic, and Chile, whose new government was expected to resume relations with Cuba. On the other hand, the downfall of the Noriega regime in Panama could adversely affect Cuba if the new Panamanian government decides to crack down on Cuban front companies based in Panama City, which for years have been circumventing the U.S. trade embargo.

Late in December, President Castro told the country that domestic food production must be the country's no. 1 priority, even above sugar output, in view of economic problems expected to result from political changes in Eastern Europe. "Sugar is sacred, but above all we must guarantee food and vegetables for the people," he said. He added that the country was facing a "tense" economic situation, which the Cubans must confront with "a spirit of combat, intransigency and firmness." (*Granma*, 14 January 1990.) Many basic foodstuffs produced in the country, such as rice, beans, meat, coffee, butter, and even sugar, have been rationed for years in Cuba, which receives other staples, principally wheat, from the Soviet Union.

Foreign Relations. In 1989, all Cuban troops sent more than a decade ago to Ethiopia to help its Marxist government in the war with Somalia, came home, and those in Angola continued their steady withdrawal. In 1978, at the height of the fighting in Ethiopia, Cuba had about 20,000 troops in that country. Also the remains of Cuban soldiers who had fought in Africa were brought home for burial. Bodies of 2,289 soldiers were buried on 7 December in a mourning ceremony attended by President José Eduardo dos Santos of Angola, where most of the dead had been killed. Since 1975, more than 400,000 Cuban "internationalists," both men and women, had been sent by the Castro regime to fight alongside leftist governments and revolutionary movements in the Third World. The mass burial in Havana appeared to signal an end to Cuba's military intervention abroad and a turn inward to face critical problems at home.

Castro reacted strongly to the U.S. invasion of Panama, saying it was being carried out in "the style of Nazis and Fascists." At the same time, he said that although the U.S. action had brought upon the United States the "revulsion of the world," Soviet bloc countries had not been outspoken about the "aggression" against Panama. (*Granma*, 21 December.) Havana reported factually on the American arrest of General Manuel Antonio Noriega, and Radio Havana reported that thousands of Panamanians had staged spontaneous street celebrations when they had learned of his capture.

The Castro government repeated throughout the year its determination to prevent the transmissions of a U.S.-funded television program, called TV Martí, from reaching Cuban viewers. In December, the Cubans demonstrated to a U.S. congressional delegation and a group of American broadcasters in Havana their ability to jam a television channel. TV Martí, designed as a sister program of Radio Martí, is to beam signals to Havana from a balloon floating 10,000 feet above the Florida Keys. A 90-day test of TV Martí has been delayed several times because of technical difficulties. Cuba regards the TV Martí project as a violation of international broadcasting treaties, which, it says, give each country the right to use any channel it wishes without interference. Havana's retaliation could include, in addition to jamming the TV signal in Cuba, counterbroadcasting Cuban radio transmissions to the United States, interfering with many American commercial stations and jamming Radio Martí whose broadcasts have been interfered with only intermittently.

In January 1990, Cuba assumed for two years a seat on the United Nations Security Council, and earlier several major Latin American countries called for Havana's return to the Organization of American States from which it was expelled a quarter of a century ago.

George Volsky
University of Miami

Dominican Republic

Population. 7,106,114 (July 1989)
Party. Dominican Communist Party (Partido Comunista Dominicano; PCD)
Founded. 1944
Membership. 750 (estimated)
General Secretary. Narciso Isa Conde, 47
Central Committee. 21 members
Status. Legal
Last Congress. Fourth, 16–19 March 1989
Last Election. 1986, 0.28 percent, no representation in Congress
Auxiliary Organizations. No data
Publications. *Hablan los Comunistas* (weekly), Arsenio Hernández F., editor; *Impacto Socialista* (theoretical journal, appears every two months)

The Dominican Communist Party held its Fourth Congress in March, electing a new 21-member Central Committee, which then re-elected Narciso Isa Conde as the PCD's general secretary. Elected as members of the Central Committee were: Pedro Juan Persia, Odalis Martínez, Alfredo Pierre, Lourdes Contreras, Tancredo Vargas, Octavio García, Rafael Tavárez, Santiago Guillermo, Nelson Pérez Duarte, Silvano Lora, Carlos Ascuasiati, Arnulfo Mateo, Rolando Bretón, Ramón Rodríguez, Mario Robles, Fausto López, Tomás Reyes, Jorge Santana, Ramón Vargas, and Domingo Rosario.

Given the continuing division and the consequent weakness of the country's extreme left, the principal theme of the congress was unity, a new effort to band together the Dominican Marxists in order to present a joint bloc in the next presidential and congressional elections, scheduled for 16 May 1990.

But the PCD had trouble keeping peace in its own house, let alone persuading other leftist organizations, all with minuscule membership, to join forces under its umbrella. The congress witnessed "long and stormy debates," and some former members of the Central Committee preferred not to stand for re-election, saying that "they did not accept the adopted decisions, as they believed them wrong," wrote Rafael Tavárez, later a member of the Central Committee. He added: "Unfortunately, those comrades did not argue their cases either before or after the Congress. Instead, most of them preferred gradually to abandon their party responsibilities." (*WMR*, November.)

The congress approved a strategy of "popular mass power" to be reached by political means through "the revolutionary unity," which is to be attained by a "national coordination of popular organizations." It deferred the decision as to whether the PCP, and in what form, would participate in the 1990 elections; it added ecology to its stated concerns and approved the principle of removing leaders who "fail to fulfill the democratic mandate or lose support of the masses." (*Hablan los Comunistas*, 6–13 April.)

Other Marxist organizations continued to operate independently of the PCD. They were the Dominican Popular Movement (Movimiento Popular Dominicano, MPD); the Anti-Imperialist Patriotic Union (Unión Patriótica Anti-Imperialista, UPA); the Movement of the United Left (Movimiento de Izquierda Unida, MIU); the Party of the Dominican Working League–Iván Faction (Partido de Trabajadores Dominicanos–Iván, PTD-I); the Socialist Bloc (Bloque Socialista, BS); and the Party of the Dominican Working People–Maria Faction (Partido de Trabajadores Dominicanos–Maria, PTD-M). The last two, BS and PTD-M, did not participate in PCD-sponsored unitary movement. Rather, they sought alliance with the two traditional non-Marxist leftist parties, the Dominican Liberation Party (Partido de Liberación Dominicana; PLD) and the Dominican Revolutionary Party (Partido Revolucionario Dominicano; PRD) to win a seat in parliament in the May 1990 election.

There was also a division in the Dominican labor movement, which in July showed its force by paralyzing the country during a two-day general strike over economic issues. There were several worker groupings of unions, each following its own policy and frequently changing alliances. The intellectual community, many of whose members support the Marxist left, was also fractioned. With constant internal squabbles, the left was more interested in internal Dominican affairs than in the changes taking place in the Eastern bloc. Isa Conde, in a long article on the history of revolutions, dedicated only a few lines to *perestroika*. He said that *perestroika* was "an example of onward movement . . . an effort to eliminate red tape and promote political democracy and self-government on the basis of public ownership not necessarily identified with the State, centralization or the like. But can transformations within a single system be regarded as a revolution? I believe they can." (*WMR*, October).

With economic problems that appear intractable, the Dominican Republic was preparing for the election. A measure of the fragmentation of the country's political life was the fact that by the year's end 47 parties qualified to present presidential and congressional candidates were engaged in unending quarrels, making and breaking deals and alliances. But two men, both octogenarian, dominated the scene. One was President Joaquín Balaguer, leader of the ruling Social Christian Reformist Party (Partido Reformista Social Cristiano; PRSC), and the other was Juan Bosch, leader of the PLD, who had been elected president in 1962 and overthrown after only seven months by a military coup. The other traditional political party, the left-of-center Dominican Revolutionary Party was divided into two factions and appeared unlikely to be a contestant in the election. Fighting for the supremacy of the PRD were José Francisco Peña Gómez and Jacobo Majluta, who lost the 1986 election by a small margin to Balaguer. Majluta, who represented the conservative faction of the PRD, was being courted by Balaguer to strengthen his position in relation to Bosch. Should the two join forces, Peña Gómez might support Bosch, who has moderated his leftist positions, stopped criticizing the United States and the armed forces, and begun seeking the support of the middle and upper classes.

The election could well be decided by the state of the economy in the spring. By the end of 1989, the country faced a 300 percent rise in inflation in the next three years, a 125 percent devaluation of its currency, declining production, and continual power shortages.

George Volsky
University of Miami

Ecuador

Population. 10,262,271 (July 1989)
Party. Communist Party of Ecuador (Partido Comunista Ecuatoriano; PCE), pro-Moscow, participates in elections as part of the Frente Amplio de Izquierda coalition (FADI); Marxist-Leninist Communist Party of Ecuador (PCE-ML), participates in elections as the Movimiento Popular Democrático (MPD); Ecuadorean Socialist Party (Partido Socialista Ecuatoriano; PSE); Popular Socialist Party (Partido Socialista Popular; PSP)
Founded. PCE: 1928; PCE-ML: 1972; PSE: 1926
Membership. PCE: 600; PCE-ML: 600—both estimated
General Secretary. PCE: René Maugé Mosquera; chairman, Central Party Control Commission, Milton Jijón; MPD: Jaime Hurtado González (national director); PSE: Víctor Granda; FADI: Xavier Garaicoa (president); PSP: Napoleón Saltos (president)
Status. Legal
Last Congress. PCE: Eleventh, 21–23 July 1988, in Quito; PSE: Forty-second, 26–27 May 1989, in Quito; FADI: 30 September 1989, in Guayaquil
Last Election. 31 January 1988 (for president): Frank Vargas Pazzos, coalition including PSE, 10.5 percent; Jaime Hurtado González, coalition including FADI and MPD, 4.2 percent. 31 January 1988 (for congress): PSE: 4 of 71 seats; FADI, 2 of 71 seats; MPD: 2 of 71 seats
Auxiliary Organizations. PCE: Ecuadorean Workers' Confederation (Confederación de Trabajadores del Ecuador; CTE), comprises some 20 percent of organized workers; Ecuadorean University Students' Federation (Federación de Estudiantes Universitarios del Ecuador; FEUE); Ecuadorean Indian Federation (Federación Ecuatoriana de Indios; FEI)
Publications. PCE: *El Pueblo*, weekly, editor, René Maugé Mosquera; *La Bandera Roja*, occasional; MPD: *Patria Nueva*

The recently inaugurated social democratic government of Rodrigo Borja Cevallos dominated political affairs in 1989. Coming in the wake of the conservative, free-market government of León Febres

Cordero (1984–1988), it confronted a host of economic difficulties which allowed little leeway for new programs or expenditures. It was necessary to impose austerity measures similar to those of Febres when he first came to power. Febres's free-spending efforts to court popular support during his last year in office had aggravated the conditions which Borja inherited. Although the latter had defeated Abdalá Bucaram by 53 to 47 percent in the 8 May 1988 runoff, he proceeded to build a coalition in which the Communist Party and FADI participated.

Domestic Affairs. The FADI had been the one Marxist group to back Borja in the runoff, and subsequently agreed to join the alliance between Borja's Democratic Left (Izquierda Democrática; ID) and the Popular Democracy (Democracia Popular; DP) of former president Osvaldo Hurtado, a Christian Democrat. Constituting a bloc of 39 votes in the 71-member congress, the resultant majority generally provided a practical working margin for the government during the three-month session. During the remainder of the year, congressional business was handled by the customary plenum of four permanent committees: Civil and Penal, Labor and Social, Agricultural and Commercial, and Budget. Of the twenty-eight members, there were 16 from the ID, 5 from the DP, and one member of the FADI.

Since the 1988 presidential runoff, the FADI had viewed the Borja-led forces as the best and most progressive vehicle with which to attack the local oligarchy. The FADI's major member, the Communist Party of Ecuador, had confirmed this judgment at its eleventh congress in Quito in July 1988. General Secretary René Maugé Mosquera explained that, while no illusions were harbored about social democracy, the PCE could support many of the reforms promised by the new government. Reflecting the pragmatism of the PCE, he declared that "no one can deny the communist involvement in Ecuador's current political life: *in spite of the strategy of imperialism and the Right, we have succeeded in avoiding isolation.*" (*WMR*, December 1988.)

When the new Congress was convened, the Ecuadorian communists were invited to share in guiding the permanent committees, while receiving a handful of positions in such institutions as the Tribunal of Constitutional Guarantees (Tribunal de Garantías Constitucionales; TGC), in which they held the vice-chairmanship. Two of Borja's cabinet members, although not party members, had enjoyed earlier links to the FADI: Labor Minister César Verduga and Alfredo Vera of the Education Ministry.

On 28 January 1989, the FADI National Council reconfirmed the coalition's electoral stance as collaborative, although insisting that its fundamental position was "independent." With the re-election as FADI president of José Xavier Garaicoa, a member of the Communist party, three points of "constructive criticism" of the government were outlined. They called for: a new program to meet mass needs; political action dedicated to strengthening progressive forces; and an effort to broaden the alliance. Garaicoa and FADI vice-president Napoleón Saltos of the PSP emphasized that the government did not consult with the Marxists in formulating its policies. Thus the possibility for "independence" was underlined as a valid description of the FADI position (*Punto de Vista*, 6 February).

Internal stresses gradually mounted as the PSP increasingly questioned the collaborationist position of the PCE, which dominated FADI. The issue came to a head when the FADI held its congress in Guayaquil on 30 September. Xavier Garaicoa told the 600 delegates that FADI's so-called independent line remained valid, meanwhile attacking the PSP's Saltos for opposing it. The PCE position was reaffirmed by over three-fourths of the delegates, but Saltos and the PSP reiterated their opposition, attacking the collaborationist image of the FADI and demanding the withdrawal of all members from bureaucratic posts, especially Dr. Hugo del Pozo, director of the Labor Ministry. Independents, the PSP, and the PCE advocated internal democratization, along with a more even distribution of leadership posts. The PSP ultimately withdrew from FADI's central directorate, although two of its members defied their party's directive and accepted vice-presidencies alongside the FADI's René Maugé Mosquera (*El Universo*, 2 October).

Other Marxist organizations were in opposition to the government. Thus the four PSE congressmen and the pair from the MPD were generally critical of Borja and his program. At their forty-second congress held in Quito on 26 and 27 May, the PSE ratified its view of the government as "continuist liberalism" serving internal and external banking and financial sectors (*Punta de Vista*, 5 June). A frontal attack on the government was pledged, with the party's General Secretary Víctor Granda promising to give top priority to a reunification of the left.

On 10 November, the ID-DP accord was terminated under the pretext of disagreement over a price increase for vegetable oil. Both parties preferred going it alone at this juncture, with off-year congressional elections coming in early 1990 (*Vistazo*, 23 November). FADI's position was not immediately clear, but the communist-dominated Front—with the PSP still sitting on its hands—remained the only Marxist organization offering a modicum of support to the government.

Auxiliary Organizations. Ecuador's three major trade-union confederations continued to work together through an umbrella organization known as the Workers' United Front (Frente Unitaria de Trabajadores; FUT). Rodrigo Borja's austerity measures had initially been accepted, but workers' attitudes soon hardened. A series of strikes and threatened work stoppages reverberated throughout the year. The first, which came on 4 January, made little impact on the nation. In May, however, the FUT called for a general strike to protest the government's labor policy. At the core of the dispute was the magnitude of a rise in the monthly minimum wage. The government's 22.7 percent increase (roughly 60 at the official exchange rate) was termed inadequate by the FUT, which demanded 172.7 percent more (the equivalent of $133). The latter was termed "absurd" by the government, while Labor Minister César Verduga called the strike "an antidemocratic political stance" (*FBIS*, 1 June).

Labor problems were aggravated when Ecuadorean transportation workers threatened their own work stoppage, while rejecting government fare increases ranging from 35 to 46 percent. It went into effect on 30 May despite government opposition and the criticism of the FUT itself. Despite minor occurrences of conflict, these and similar disputes later in the year failed to provoke the extensive violence that had occurred during the time of the Febres government. Middle ground was usually found between government and labor positions. It was also true that the majority of Ecuadorean workers were still unorganized or, in such cases as that of the Federation of Professional Drivers, were independent of the FUT. The FUT itself also experienced rifts like those of the FADI, suffering from the divisions endemic in Ecuador's Marxist movement.

Guerrilla Activity. Despite the heightened guerrilla activity in both neighboring Colombia and Peru, Ecuador was free of serious armed insurgency. Alfaro Vive, Carajo! (Alfaro Lives, Dammit!) had been subjected to harsh reprisals from the Febres government. Rodrigo Borja had extended a call for national reconciliation shortly after taking office, and this undertaking culminated in negotiations revealed by the president on 25 January. The following day, Interior Minister Andrés Vallejo announced on Radio Quito that the AVC was laying down its arms "immediately and completely," thus accepting political life "within a framework of legality and under the protection of constitutional guarantees" (*FBIS*, 27 January). A few hours earlier, an AVC representative identified merely as "Comandante Joaquín" had made a similar announcement on Quito television.

While there were discrepancies in details between the announcements—especially regarding the matter of the AVC's laying down its arms—it was evident that an understanding had indeed been reached (*Latin American Weekly Report*, 9 February). On 7 March, a joint statement was released at a press conference attended by Vallejo and César Verduga for the government and by Pedro Moncada and Marco Troya for the guerrillas. By the four-point accord, the AVC renounced all forms of violence and returned to political life. In exchange, the government guaranteed the constitutional rights of AVC members, while promising further efforts to meet the national social crisis (*FBIS*, 8 March).

Alfaro Vive, Carajo! itself underwent internal dissent as a consequence, and recalcitrant members claimed in early May that the government had reneged on the agreement. Rosendo Santamaría therefore denied that the AVC had laid down its arms (*FBIS*, 15 May). However, in the main the truce held throughout the rest of the year, and on 16 December the AVC underscored its position by mounting a public rally at the Plaza de la Independencia. This so-called *Encuentro Unitario* called for participation in forthcoming elections in conjunction with all democratic and progressive forces (*Punto de Vista*, 11 December).

Meanwhile the smaller Free Homeland Montoneros (Montoneros Patria Libre; MPL) refused to follow the path of the AVC. Shortly after the initial AVC accord, the MPL rejected this course, calling for actions consistent with "the rebelliousness and courage of the Ecuadorean people" (*FBIS*, 22 March). However, since its founding in 1986, the MPL has rarely taken direct action. A bomb thrown outside the National Congress in mid-June was commonly attributed to the MPL, although responsibility for the deed was uncertain. No damage occurred, and for the rest of the year the MPL was rarely heard from.

International Affairs. The PCE maintained the usual fraternal ties with Communist parties elsewhere. In January it sent Central Committee member José Regato to attend an international symposium: "Communists in Municipal Councils," organized by the Austrian Communist Party in conjunction with the *World Marxist Review* (*WMR*, June). The PCE was joined informally by other Marxist groups for the official visits of Nicaraguan Interior Minister Tomás Borge and Cuban Education Minister Fernando Vecino Alegret (*FBIS*, 22 May). There was little else of note in terms of international dealings, although the impact of Gorbachev's reforms in the Soviet Union were subjected to frequent analysis in conferences and in occasional newspaper commentaries.

John D. Martz
Pennsylvania State University

El Salvador

Population. 5,124,931
Major Marxist Leninist Groups

• The Communist Party of El Salvador (Partido Comunista de El Salvador; PCES)
Founded. March 1930; destroyed 2 years later; reorganized during the late 1940s
Membership. Fewer than 1,000
Leadership. Jorge Schafik Handal (general secretary since 1970)
Governing Body. Central Committee
Last Congress. Seventh, April 1979
Status. Illegal
Fronts and Auxiliary Organizations. The Armed Forces of Liberation (Fuerzas Armadas de Liberación; FAL) are the party's military branch. Together with elements of FARN and FPL (for definitions of acronyms, see below), the PCES controls the National Union of Salvadoran Workers (Unión Nacional de Traba-

jadores Salvadoreños; UNTS), established on 8 February 1986, and led by Humberto Centeno and Marco Tulio Lima. The Nationalist Democratic Union (UDN) has been the PCES political front since 1965; after participating at cabinet level in the 1979 junta, it was declared illegal in 1980. In July–August 1988, its leaders, including General Secretary Mario Aguinada Carranza, Tirso Canales, and Aronette Díaz de Zamora returned to El Salvador and became openly active once again.
Publications. *Voz Popular* (irregular); *Fundamentos y Perspectivas* (theoretical, irregular)

• Farabundo Martí Popular Liberation Forces (Fuerzas Populares de Liberación Farabundo Martí; FPL)
Founded. 1 April 1970, by dissidents from the PCES, led by former general secretary Salvador Cayetano Carpio and Central Committee member Mélida Anaya Montes ("Ana María")
Membership. Ca. 1,200 cadres and fighters
Leadership. Leonel González, first secretary of the Central Committee since August 1983, commander of the Popular Liberation Army (EPL; see below); second in command of the EPL and of the FPL, Dimas Rodriguez; chief of staff of the EPL, Ricardo Guttiérez; Salvador Guerra
Governing Body. Central Committee (membership unknown, except for above)
Status. Illegal since inception
Last Congress. Seventh Revolutionary Council, August 1983
Front and Auxiliary Organizations. The People's Revolutionary Bloc (BPR) was established on 20 July 1975 as an FPL-controlled umbrella, including unions and professional groups. The "subregional governments of people's power" in the department of Chalatenango were sporadically operative in certain areas until 1985, when the group lost permanent control over them; their leader was Evaristo López.
Publications. *El Rebelde* (irregular); *Farabundo Martí Weekly Informative* (external propaganda); the BPR (see below) publishes irregularly the *Weekly Popular Combat* (abroad) and the *Juan Angel Chacón Bulletin*, since 1981; the FPL also controls the second most active radio station of the FMLN, the Radio Farabundo Martí.

• People's Revolutionary Army (Ejército Revolucionario del Pueblo; ERP)

Founded. 1971, as an urban terrorist group known as The Group (El Grupo); acquired the present name following bloody internal purges in May 1975

Membership. Ca. 2,000 cadres and fighters, and as many as 20,000 civilian supporters and dependents

Leadership. Seven main leaders, doubling as the Political Commission of the PRS (see below): Joaquín Villalobos (alias of René Cruz), chief leader, Ana Guadalupe Martínez, Ana Sonia Medina Arriola ("Mariana"), Mercedes del Carmen Letona ("Luisa"), Claudio Rabindranath Armijo ("Francisco"), Juan Ramón Medrano ("Balta"), and Jorge Meléndez ("Jonas"); in addition, former army captain Francisco Mena Sandoval ("Manolo"), who defected in 1981, is an increasingly prominent military leader on the northwestern front.

Governing Body. Political Commission of the ERP-PRS

Status. Illegal since inception

Last Congress. July 1981 (last of the 3 PRS plenums ever to take place)

Front and Auxiliary Organizations. Party of the Salvadoran Revolution (PRS) and the popular front organization of Popular Leagues–28 of February (LP-28) were both established in 1977 as largely fictitious expansions of the militaristic ERP. Both are now largely defunct or inoperative.

Publications. The ERP is in total control (ensured by "Luisa") of the FMLN Radio Venceremos.

• Armed Forces of National Resistance (Fuerzas Armadas de la Resistencia Nacional; FARN)

Founded. May 1975, as a result of the ERP purges (see above) by a group of dissident youth from the PCES, FPL, and the Christian Democratic Party. The Party of National Resistance (PRN) established in 1975, and supposed to control the military branch, remains ineffectual.

Membership. Fewer than 1,000 cadres and guerrillas and some 10,000 civilian supporters and dependents

Leadership. Fermán Cienfuegos (alias of Eduardo Sancho Castañeda); "Luis Cabral" is second in command

Governing Body. A seven-member National Leadership (equivalent of a politburo) which selects an "extended leadership" (i.e., a central committee)

Status. Illegal since inception

Fronts and Auxiliary Organizations. The United People's Action Front (FAPU) was established by Marxist Jesuit priests in the early 1970s and transferred to FARN; since 1981 it has become largely nonexistent. FARN is by far the most successful FMLN group in infiltrating legal organizations, particularly student groups at both the National and Central American (Catholic) universities, as well as various human rights organizations, such as COMADRES (Committee of the Mothers of the Disappeared).

Publications. *Pueblo Internacional* (irregular); *Parte de Guerra* (war bulletin).

• The Revolutionary Party of Central American Workers (Partido Revolucionario de los Trabajadores Centro Americanos; PRTC)

Founded. 26 January 1976 in San Jose, Costa Rica, as a regional, Trotskyist party with branches planned in Costa Rica and Guatemala, which were never formed; and in El Salvador and Honduras, which were established and became officially independent on 29 October 1980

Membership. Fewer than 200 members, mostly urban, with some 1,000 sympathizers and dependents

Leadership. Francisco Jovel (a.k.a. Roberto Roca) is the supreme leader; Jaime Miranda is the representative to Mexico; important Central Committee members include Mario González ("Mario"), urban terrorist leader Ismael Dimas Aguilar ("Ulysses"), and María Concepción de Valladares ("Nidia Díaz")

Governing Body. Central Committee (complete membership unknown)

Front and Auxiliary Organizations. The Popular Liberation Movement (MLP), established in 1979, had largely disappeared by 1981. No other is known of today.

• The Revolutionary Democratic Front (Frente Democrático Revolucionario; FDR)

Founded. 1980, as an umbrella alliance between the Marxist-Leninist guerrillas of the newly established Farabundo Martí National Liberation Front (FMLN), including all of the above and their fronts, and a few minor civilian parties, including the allegedly social-democratic National Revolutionary Movement (MNR), led by Guillermo Ungo, a vice-president of the Socialist International, and the even smaller splinter from the Christian Democratic Party, the Social Christian Popular Movement (MPSC), led by Rubén Zamora

Membership. A few hundred intellectuals and internationally connected professionals

Leadership. The Politico-Diplomatic Commission, led by Ungo and having Zamora as vice-president, includes representatives from the MNR, MPSC, UDN, FAPU, LP-28, BPR, and MLP, represented, respectively, by Ungo, Zamora, Mario Aguinada Carranza, José Rodríguez Ruiz, Ana Guadalupe Martínez, and Salvador Samayoa.

Status. Technically illegal under its original name; however, in 1988 prominent members, including Guillermo Ungo, Rubén Zamora, Hector Oqueli, and Mario Aguinada returned to El Salvador and formed a legal organization, the Democratic Convergence, while publicly retaining their links with and sympathies for the FMLN

Last Election. The Democratic Convergence participated in the March 1989 presidential elections, receiving 3.8 percent of the votes.

Developments on the Left. The most surprising development on the Marxist-Leninist left was the unity of the FMLN elements during the year, particularly in light of the double-track strategy of the organization. The double-track strategy embraced a massive public-relations campaign proclaiming the FMLN's desire for a negotiated solution to the Salvadoran civil war and a simultaneous secret campaign of assassinations, military attacks, and economic sabotage.

The second track, that of assassination of prominent anti-communist figures, became apparent in January, and continued until November. On 12 January, Miguel Castellanos, a.k.a. Napoleon Romero, the highest ranking FMLN defector (he was third in command of the FPL at the time of his defection), was murdered by his former comrades, who took credit for the assassination (*FBIS-LAM*, 12 January). On 9 June, José Antonio Rodríguez Porth, the main adviser to newly elected president Alfredo Cristiani, was murdered. The FMLN denied its involvement (*FBIS-LAM*, 13 June), but ballistic tests, mentioned by President Alfredo Cristiani, demonstrated that both Rodríguez and Castellanos were killed by the same weapon, i.e., by the FMLN (*FBIS-LAM*, 26 October).

Through threats and killings, the FMLN forced some 35 locally elected mayors out of their jobs (*NYT*, 9 January). The FMLN campaign also in-

cluded the murder of Ernesto Flores Serpaz, governor of Usulutan department (*NYT*, 5 March); the attempted murder of vice-president-elect Francisco Merino's family on 14 April (*FBIS-LAM*, 17 April), when he was widely known to be out of the country, and the killing of Attorney General Roberto García Alvarado, on 19 April (*NYT*, 20 April). Merino accused the FPL urban commandos of the attack against his family (*FBIS-LAM*, 18 April), while the president of the Legislative Assembly, Ricardo Valdivieso, blamed the FMLN for García's murder (ibid., 30 April).

On 27 September, the FMLN attacked the home of Col. Mauricio Ernesto Vargas, then the commander of the San Miguel garrison (San Salvador, *Diario Latino*, 28 September); on 17 October, the daughter of retired Col. Edgardo Casanova Vejar was murdered by an FMLN urban commando (*FBIS-LAM*, 18 October). On 28 November, former chief justice, presidential candidate (in 1984), and main leader of the National Reconciliation Party (he received over 4 percent of the votes in the March 1989 elections), Francisco José "Chichi" Guerrero was killed by FMLN squads (*NYT*, 29 November).

Finally, on 11 November, at the beginning of the FMLN offensive, the guerrillas first targeted the political leadership of the country: attempts were made to murder President Alfredo Cristiani, Legislative Assembly president Ricardo Valdivieso Alvarenga (*WP*, 12 November), Army Chief of Staff Emilio René Ponce, and other members of the political and military leadership (*San Francisco Examiner*, 12 November).

The series of FMLN assassinations was part of a longstanding plan, elements of which were captured by the Salvador military on 2 April in the area of the Guazapa Volcano near San Salvador; the plan bore the title "Synthesis sobre la Conyuntura actual . . ." (text available at the Hoover Institution). The document explicitly mentioned attacks against the families of senior officers and politicians, in order to "bring the war to the rulers."

The FMLN Offensive. On 11 November, following unsuccessful assassination attempts against most top political and military officials, including an attempt to kill or kidnap President Cristiani (*FBIS-LAM*, 15 November), the FMLN engaged in the largest, most spectacular and, as it turned out, the most costly military offensive in its history.

The offensive started simultaneously in the major cities of San Salvador, San Miguel, and Santa Ana, as well as in Zacatecoluca, Usulután, and La

Union departments, in addition to the FMLN's traditional strongholds in the Chalatenango and Morazan departments. The FMLN took over marginal suburbs of San Salvador, including Mejicanos, Soyapango, and Zacamil, and tried to stir up a popular insurrection.

No popular insurrection occurred, however, and the FMLN suffered the largest losses in its history. By December, the FMLN was said to have lost 2,132 killed and 638 captured, in contrast with 476 military men killed and some 500 civilians. (*FBIS-LAM*, 18 December.) Equally important, top cadres of the FMLN were killed in action or captured. In other words, some 25 percent of the estimated total of FMLN cadres were killed, and 10 percent captured; it is impossible to estimate the number of those wounded in action. More important perhaps, those killed were hardline fighters with long experience in guerrilla warfare, as well as in the organization of fronts; their presence on the front line of the offensive destroyed their usefulness as legal operators.

Those captured included Carlos Ernesto Morales Carbonell (a.k.a. Esteban), the son of the former Christian Democratic mayor of San Salvador, and Antonio Morales Erlich, captured on 15 December, a self-admitted FPL cadre (*FBIS-LAM*, 18 December). Morales admitted his role as an important propagandist for the FPL and the FMLN in Costa Rica, Mexico, and Ecuador, and his role as a fundraiser for the guerrillas, in which he dealt with Salvadoran Catholic and Mexican university groups (ibid.). More important, however, were the deaths of important FMLN military leaders. The most important of those was Nicolás Hernán Solorzano Sánchez, a.k.a. commander Dimas Rodríguez, second in command of the FPL, probably the highest-ranking FMLN leader ever killed in combat. On 19 December the FMLN, for the first time ever, provided a list of its own casualties: 401 killed since the beginning of the offensive on 11 November (*FBIS-LAM*, 19 December). The list included 9 commanders, in addition to Dimas Rodríguez, one of whom was Misael Gallardo, a prominent PCES leader (ibid.). In fact, it appears that the PCES and its armed branch, the FAL, took a major part of the FMLN casualties in San Salvador, proportionate to its dominant role in the fighting there. Indeed, ex-FDR "political" communist leader Facundo Guardado was the commander of the area around the Sheraton Hotel and barely escaped after an unsuccessful attempt to capture a number of U.S. military advisers.

The Peace Process. During the year the FMLN began to lose most of its foreign support and sympathy, largely as a result of its opposition to negotiations with the government within the framework of the Esquipula peace process. In fact, the FMLN's duplicitous attitude toward the peace negotiations required by the Central American Peace Plan (the "Arias Plan") was so obvious throughout the year that even Nicaragua's president, Daniel Ortéga Saavedra, had to subscribe to its condemnation at the summit in Costa Rica on 12 December.

On the one hand, the FMLN encouraged its front, the FDR, to participate in the presidential elections in March under the name of the Democratic Convergence, while on the other hand it proposed its own plan for participation in elections, totally contradicting the FDR position. Indeed, on 23 January, the FMLN demanded a postponement of elections until September, in opposition to the letter of the Salvadoran Constitution, but did not accept that its members should lay down their weapons (*NYT*, 25 January). At the same time, as noticed by the *New York Times* (12 February), as well as by the Salvadoran army, the FMLN was preparing for a major offensive against whatever government was to be formed after the March elections.

The dismal failure of the Democratic Convergence in the presidential elections on 19 March, blamed by some ex-FDR politicians on the FMLN's militarism (*CSM*, 27 March; *NYT*, 25 March), did not influence the FMLN leadership. On the contrary, the guerrillas continued, throughout the year, to accumulate military supplies from Nicaragua in preparation for the November offensive. To every proposal of negotiations, including those issuing from the Central American presidents' meetings in El Salvador, Honduras, and Costa Rica, the FMLN responded by proclaiming its peaceful intentions, while demanding the dismissal of all the top army officers and the reduction of military strength in exchange for vague promises of participation in the political process.

On 12 December, the latest Central American summit in Costa Rica resulted in explicit condemnation of the FMLN's offensive, support for negotiations, and a demand that both the contras and the FMLN lay down their weapons. (The text of the statement can be found in *FBIS-LAM*, 13 December.) The FMLN immediately rejected the resolution, claiming that "the Costa Rica declaration is neither realistic nor viable," and that the meeting itself was nothing but an attempt "to pull Cristiani out of international isolation" (*FBIS-LAM*, 14 December). By summarily rejecting the declaration made at the Costa Rican summit meeting, the FMLN became completely isolated in Central America.

Foreign Affairs. On 26 November the government of El Salvador suspended diplomatic relations with Nicaragua, because of a long pattern of official Nicaraguan aid to the FMLN (*NYT*, 27 November). The most immediate reason was the crash in El Salvador of a Cessna airplane from Nicaragua that was transporting weapons, including SAM-7 anti-aircraft missiles (*FBIS-LAM*, 27 November; *NYT*, 26 November; *Newsweek*, 2 December). The Managua government did not deny that the plane originated in Nicaragua. In December, Managua's deputy foreign minister, Victor Tinoco, inadvertently admitted the role played by Nicaragua in supplying the FMLN (*FBIS-LAM*, 14 December).

The year 1989 was a crucial point in the history of the Salvadoran Marxist-Leninist movement. On the one hand, the FMLN lost credibility with the Central American presidents for its duplicity in peace negotiations; it also suffered major, probably disastrous, and possibly terminal losses after its failed attempt to provoke an insurrection on 11 November. On the other hand, the murder of six Jesuit priests, including the rector and vice-rector of the University of Central America on 16 November, which President Cristiani blames on members of the military, provided the FMLN with very vocal, massive, and effective support in the United States, which could result in the denial of U.S. military and economic aid to the government of El Salvador.

Michael Radu
Foreign Policy Research Institute, Philadelphia

Grenada

Population. 84,480
Party. Maurice Bishop Patriotic Movement (MBPM)
Founded. 27 May 1984
Membership. Unknown
General Secretary. Dr. Terrence Marryshow (age 37, medical doctor)

Status. Legal
Last Congress. Second, May 1988
Last Election. 1984, 5.0%, no representatives
Publication. *Indies Times* (weekly)

The sudden death of Prime Minister Herbert Blaize on 19 December lent further uncertainty to Grenada's political direction during the 1990s. While the 71-year-old Grenadian leader had been gravely ill for several years, he had tenaciously held onto power despite the splintering of his electoral coalition. Blaize's passing from the Grenadian political scene means that the island's upcoming elections will be contested by a variety of parties, ranging from former prime minister Sir Eric Gairy's Grenada United Labour Party (GULP) to the Maurice Bishop Patriotic Movement (MBPM).

During the course of the year, the MBPM continued its strategy of relatively low-key political organizing. Attention was devoted to revamping the party's radical-leftist image. At the beginning of the year, the MBPM announced that it had set itself the goal of doubling or tripling party membership by the end of 1989, as well as increasing sales of its newspaper, *Indies Times*. Party leader Dr. Terrence Marryshow promised that under an MBPM government, opposition groups would be allowed free media time on state-owned radio and television. (Bridgeton, CANA, 10 April.) The party manifesto also calls for free medical and dental care for needy families, and the party has established a small scholarship program for underprivileged children. Marryshow also worked to distance the party from Bernard Coard and sixteen other former revolutionary leaders sentenced to death or long jail terms for the murder of Maurice Bishop, stating that it would be "political suicide" for the MBPM to be openly associated with that cause (*Morning Star*, 22 September).

Although the MBPM plans to field candidates in all fifteen of Grenada's constituencies during the 1990 general elections, it is unlikely that the party will capture even a single seat. MBPM leaders hope that a return to the autocratic rule of Sir Eric Gairy, or a weak centrist government, will generate strong public dissatisfaction and greater support for the left.

Timothy Ashby
Washington, D.C.

Guadeloupe

Population. 341,430
Party. Communist Party of Guadeloupe (Parti Communiste Guadeloupéen; PCG)
Founded. 1944 as section of the French Communist Party (PCF), 1958 as independent party
Membership. 3,000 (estimated)
General Secretary. Christian Céleste
Politburo. 14 members: Henri Bangou, other members unknown
Central Committee. Christian Céleste (secretary)
Status. Legal
Last Congress. Ninth, 11–13 March 1988
Last Election. 24 April, 8 May 1988, president of France; 5 and 12 June 1988, French National Assembly; 25 September, 2 October 1988, Guadeloupan General Council, 10 (members and allies) of 42 seats
Auxiliary Organizations. Union of Guadeloupan Communist Youth (Union de la Jeunesse Communiste Guadeloupéenne; UJCG; Fred Sablon, general secretary), Union of Guadeloupan Women (Union des Femmes Guadeloupéennes; UFG), General Confederation of Guadeloupan Labor (CGTG)
Publications. *L'Etincelle* (PCG weekly), *Madras* (UFG monthly)

In 1989 Christian Céleste further consolidated his leadership of the Communist Party of Guadeloupe, while an earlier generation of leaders was honored and not kept at arms' length. Guy Daninthe, Céleste's predecessor as general secretary, participated in some events and wrote an important commentary on reform in Eastern Europe. The party honored Hégésippe Ibene, one of the founders, on his 75th birthday and then mourned his passing in May.

The theme of the last party congress, the ninth, held in March 1988, was reiterated: National independence with a socialist orientation, but it took second place to concerns about European integration after 1992 and events in the USSR.

Party leaders met with the PCM—Communist Party of Martinique—in October, and the general secretary of the French Communist Party, Georges Marchais, visited Pointe-à-Pitre from 20 to 24 No-

vember. The purpose of the exchanges was the sharing of information and a discussion of the confusing and unsettling changes elsewhere.

The terrible destruction wrought by Hurricane Hugo during the night from 16 to 17 September, which left 16,000 people homeless and laid waste over $80 million worth of property, bananas, and sugar crops, made a mockery of demands for independence, as the PCG, along with everyone else, made urgent appeals to Paris for assistance. On 9 October, President François Mitterrand made a brief but welcome visit to the island, and the PCG greeted him. At a press conference on 26 October, Christian Céleste asserted that Hurricane Hugo proved as never before that Guadeloupe depends on France.

The party held on to its constituency during the municipal elections held earlier in the year on 12 and 19 March. Even though communist candidates, like the socialists and others, usually run under purely local names such as the Democratic and Progressive Union of Basse Terre, everyone knows who is who. Elections took place in 34 towns, of which the PCG already controlled six city halls. With the victory of Ernest Moutoussamy's list in St. François, the election results brought to seven the number of towns governed by the party. Moutoussamy is a deputy to the French National Assembly. The socialists won eight, and various right groupings won eleven. In the partial canton elections of 28 May for the General Council, two PCG candidates, including Deputy Moutoussamy, won.

In the course of these elections the party issued a new rallying cry: "Status Politique Spécifique," or Special Political Status, meaning that Guadeloupe should not be fully integrated into the European Economic Community after 31 December 1992, when the twelve European countries and their dependencies will become economically integrated as never before. In anticipation of what PCG members perceive to be a disaster for the island, measures were proposed to protect its fragile economy.

The Common Market authorities put forward POSEIDOM in an attempt to ease the transition of Guadeloupe, Martinique, Guyane, and Réunion, the four French overseas departments or DOM. The acronym stands for "Program of options relating to the distance and specificity of the overseas departments" for 1989 to 1992. The PCG denounced the proposed suppression of Guadeloupe's "octroi de mer," a type of sales tax on all goods coming into the department from anywhere outside, including from metropolitan France. The revenues thus generated went in large part to the town budgets, but they are in violation of the provisions of EEC agreements.

The PCG led the effort to reject POSEIDOM, and it spoke ceaselessly against the full integration of Guadeloupe.

In reaction to the Common Market proposal, the PCG called on Guadeloupans to boycott the elections to the European Parliament of 18 June. The rate of boycott, usually quite high anyway, reached 83.9 percent. The Union for French Democracy, or UDF, of Valéry Giscard d'Estaing won 43.45 percent of the votes cast, and the Socialists won 35.6 percent. The communists denounced the EEC as an "enterprise of collective colonialism."

General Secretary C. Céleste traveled to the Soviet Union for two weeks in March and April, and a delegation flew to North Korea for the Thirteenth World Festival of Youth and Students.

The weekly newspaper *L'Etincelle* published muted reports of events in Eastern Europe and the USSR. Reforms were quietly noted, but former party leader Guy Daninthe proposed that the PCG study changes in Poland; he said it was healthy for communist parties to engage in auto-criticism, for some of them had been too authoritarian in the past.

Closer to home, the PCG had less than usual to say about Cuba, but it denounced the arrest of the number-two person in Haiti's communist party, PUCH.

Because of the death of party stalwart H. Ibene, there was no festival of *L'Etincelle*, the 45-year-old newspaper. *Madras*, published by the Union of Guadeloupan Women, celebrated its 31st anniversary.

Dr. Henri Bangou, PCG leader, senator of Guadeloupe and mayor of Pointe-à-Pitre, published his latest book, *La Révolution et l'Esclavage en Guadeloupe 1789–1802*, which provided an agenda for party discussion of the bicentennial of the French Revolution.

Brian Weinstein
Howard University

Guatemala

Population. 9,116,877
Major Marxist-Leninist Organizations

• The Guatemalan Party of Labor (Partido Guatemalteco de Trabajo; PGT)
  Founded. September 1949. The first Guatemalan Communist Party was created by the Comintern in 1922, and was destroyed in 1932. In September 1949 an illegal, new party was formed, which became legal three years later under the present name, then became illegal again following the 1954 coup. The other PGT factions were established as follows: National Leadership Nucleus in 1978; PGT–6th of January in February 1988; Revolutionary October (Octubre Revolucionario; OR) in June 1987;
  Membership. Unconfirmed estimates of 200–300 for all party factions
  Factions and Leadership. PGT–Central Committee ("*Camarilla*") faction: Carlos Gonzáles (also general secretary of the Central Committee and head of the Political Commission); Elfidio Cano, Central Committee member; National Leadership Nucleus faction: Daniel Ríos (Ríos seems to have been supplanted in 1988 by José Manuel Díaz; the faction took the new name of PGT–6th of January (PGT–6 de Enero): main leader is José Manuel Díaz; also Mario Sánchez, who is "in charge of general political questions"; membership unknown; OR faction: the main leader, a former Ejécito Guerrillero de los Pobres cadre, is known only as "Benedicto"; membership unknown. Only the PGT-Central Committee faction is recognized by the Soviet Union and its allied communist parties.
  Leading Body. PGT-Central Committee faction: the Political Commission. The membership and size of the Political Commission are unknown. The nature of the top structures of the other factions is also unknown.
  Legal Status. All factions illegal
  Last Congress. PGT ("Camarilla"): Fourth, 1969; PGT–6 de Enero: first, 1988
  Last Election. N/A
  Auxiliary Organizations. Autonomous Federa-

tion of the Guatemalan Trade Unions (FASGUA); Patriotic Youth of Labor (JPT)
Publications. PGT-CC: *Verdad* (appears irregularly, published abroad); OR: *Opinión Pública*

• Rebel Armed Forces (Fuerzas Armadas Rebeldes; FAR)
Founded. 1962; broke with the PGT in 1968; largely inactive 1968–1978
Membership. Probably less than 800
Leadership. Jorge Ismael Soto García (alias Pablo Monsanto)
Status. Illegal
Auxiliary Organizations. National Committee of Trade Union Unity (CNUS), founded in 1976, now practically defunct
Publication. *Guerrillero* (appears irregularly, published abroad)

• Armed People's Revolutionary Organization (Organización Revolucionaria del Pueblo en Armas; ORPA)
Founded. 1971; militarily active after 18 September 1979
Membership. Ca. 600
Leadership. Rodrigo Asturias Amado (alias Gaspar Ilom)
Status. Illegal
Auxiliary Organizations. Infiltrated FAR's CNUS and EGP's CUC (see below)
Publication. *Erupción* (appears irregularly)

• Guerrilla Army of the Poor (Ejército Guerrillero de los Pobres; EGP)
Founded. January 1972, in Mexico; militarily active since 1979
Membership. Ca. 700
Leader. Rolando Morán (alias Ricardo Ramírez de León)
Auxiliary and Fronts Organizations. Peasant Unity Committee (CUC); January 31st Popular Front (FP-31); Vicente Menchú Revolutionary Christians; Robin García Revolutionary Student Front (FERG). Most are now inactive or defunct.
Publications. *Compañero* (appears irregularly, published abroad; sometimes translated into English); *Informador Guerrillero* (irregular)

• National Revolutionary Unity of Guatemala (Unidad Nacional Revolucionaria de Guatemala; URNG), an umbrella organization which includes FAR, ORPA, EGP, and the National Leadership

Nucleus faction of the PGT. The URNG has never succeeded in actually unifying the insurgent organizations, all of which continue to operate autonomously. The guerrillas' respective fronts, allied minor civilian groups of exiles and other sympathetic groups, such as the Guatemalan Church in Exile, are more or less united under the political umbrella of the Representación Unitaria de la Oposición Guatemalteca (RUOG). RUOG's most prominent figures are Francisco Villagrán Kramer, a former vice-president, Rigoberta Menchú, and Rolando Castillo. It operates largely out of Mexico, Nicaragua, and Cuba.
Founded. 7 February 1982
Publications. URNG distributes its propaganda through *Noticias de Guatemala* (in Mexico); the press agency CESGUA; the clandestine radio station La Voz Popular de Guatemala.

In 1989, for the first time in almost five years, the violent Guatemalan left took the offensive, albeit in a minor way, both in the field and in legal front activities.

The military activities of the URNG groups expanded in a number of departments where they had been absent for a number of years. On the political front, the developments within the left suggest better cooperation among the URNG groups and a dramatic shift in the attitudes of various PGT factions.

Developments Within the Communist Movement. The most interesting developments of the year took place among the multiplying factions of the PGT. The Central Committee faction, under Carlos Gonzáles, formally joined URNG on 4 March and thus became formally associated with armed struggle. The URNG communiqué of 4 March, signed by Morán, Ilom, and Monsanto, stated that "with a broader interpretation of the present and vision for the future" the PGT had decided to join the URNG—implying that the PGT had accepted the other three URNG groups' approach to the revolutionary struggle. (*Central American Review*, 17 March.) Despite claims to the contrary, both the old URNG groups and the PGT made concessions, the former by stressing negotiations as the only solution to the conflict in Guatemala, a position long advocated by the PGT and repeated as late as March. Indeed, Elfidio Cano wrote that "Progressive circles in the country favor negotiations" and "are not advocating the creation of a revolutionary army to defeat the reactionary, counter-insurgent armed forces" (*WMR*, March). On the other hand, by joining the URNG the PGT has implicitly accepted the other member groups' refusal to lay down their arms as a precondition for negotiations with the government. Thus Pablo Monsanto stated that "we are prepared and are willing to seek a way out of the critical political situation in the country, but that does not imply that we shall lay down our arms" (*WMR*, January). Not by coincidence, almost the same terms were used in one of the first URNG statements in which Carlos Gonzáles joined his signature to those of Morán, Ilom, and Monsanto (text in *FBIS-LAM*, 15 June).

While the PGT-Central Committee's decision to join the URNG was a significant development, it apparently had little impact on the main problem plaguing the party: factionalism.

The PGT-Central Committee faction deplored the splits in the party that occurred in 1978 and 1984, but refrained from blaming anyone and claimed that "Comrades have been working to overcome the ideological, political and organizational consequences [of the splits] by joining...the URNG" (*WMR*, July). In fact, the PGT-Central Committee's joining the URNG only resulted in a rapprochement, perhaps even some sort of re-unification with the Military Commission faction (see *YICA*, 1987), a faction that had previously been part of the URNG in any case (*Central America Review*, 24 February; that article confuses the Military Commission faction with the National Leadership Nucleus). At the same time, however, the PGT-Central Committee's new bellicosity did nothing to improve ties with the apparently more reform-minded factions, particularly the PGT–6th of January and the OR. On the contrary, almost at the same time the PGT joined the URNG, the leader of PGT–6th of January, José Manuel Díaz, announced that his group will probably seek legal recognition from the Cerezo government (*Central America Review*, 17 March). Furthermore, at the end of the year it seemed that Díaz's group had joined the OR to create a "Marxist-Leninist party of a new type."

The OR, whose name recalls the Bolshevik revolution and the insurrection in Guatemala in 1944, is, despite the associations of its name, a rather mild and reformist faction of the Guatemalan Marxist-Leninist left. Founded in 1987 by disgruntled EGP members, including one of that group's fifteen founders, "Benedicto," it made public its existence in February 1988 through the fifteenth issue of the journal *Opinion Publica*. The initial OR manifesto included demands for agrarian reform, a broad coalition government, renegotiation of the foreign debt, regional autonomy for Indian groups, and a policy of anti-imperialism, antimilitarism and self-determination. (*Central America Review*, 24 February.)

By September the PR–6th of January and OR claimed that they had a joint political project, that they were seeking a "unity convergence" based on the "best aspirations and traditions of the PGT," while pursuing "energetically" the struggle to renew the party by "converting it into a party modern in [both] its thought and its revolutionary action," modernizing the party's "organic structures," and by "the reforming of its leadership and methods" (Mexico City, *6 de Julio*, 30 September).

While the communist party factions reshuffle themselves, the old URNG group seemed to have reached a level of unity unattained before. Previous hints of disagreement between the "militarist" ORPA and the FAR or EGP appeared to have been buried for the time being. The former's tenth anniversary on 18 September was celebrated by a joint URNG statement that mentioned ORPA as "one of the powerful detachments that make up the URNG" and expressed "special honorable greetings to Commander Gaspar Ilom, ORPA's creator and founder and undoubtedly one of the leaders of the Guatemalan people's united vanguard." (*FBIS-LAM*, 28 September.) Such statements, as well as the almost perfect unanimity among the top FAR, EGP, and ORPA leaders in their public statements, suggest a degree of unity and commonality of interests among the Guatemalan insurgent groups previously unheard of, and perhaps a trend toward the formation of a unified politico-military front along the lines of the Salvadoran FMLN.

Auxiliary Organizations. While it was clear that the post-1985 democratic opening in Guatemala has offered the left, including its violent sectors, new opportunities for legal action, 1989 was dominated by the renewed discussion of the legitimacy of some of the URNG's legal fronts. The spark for the furious debate over the role of the URNG's front organizations was provided by the statements made in January by one of ORPA's former leaders, Angel Reyes Melgar, who defected and accepted amnesty in Guatemala.

Reyes's revelations included data long suspected of being true by the government and the military, particularly about the most vocal, foreign-supported, and self-proclaimed "human rights" organization in the country, the GAM (Grupo de Apoyo

Mutuo; Mutual Support Group). Responsible for URNG propaganda, Reyes was in charge of disinformation in Western Europe and Mexico. He claimed that GAM leader, Nineth Garcia, was an ORPA cadre who had proved incompetent and had been replaced by ERP cadre Amilcar Méndez. (*FBIS-LAM*, 24 January.) The latter was already the self-appointed "president" of the Rujunel Junam ("Everyone is Equal") Ethnic Council (CERJ) (*Central America Review*, 27 January; *Latinamerica Press*, 21 September). Furthermore, Reyes stated that European, particularly French humanitarian groups, indiscriminately used his propaganda as facts, and channeled funds to URNG fronts, mostly GAM (*FBIS-LAM*, 24 January).

Whatever Reyes's allegations would prove in courts, and whether or not GAM would ever be tried for subversion, the group's diminished credibility in Guatemala was hard hit by the Reyes testimony. President Cerezo, the National Assembly, and the military all gave Reyes credit for spelling out facts long suspected. (*Central America Review*, 27 January.)

As a former important ORPA member, Reyes's claim that GAM is simply an ORPA front that also has armed units totally discredited that organization. As he put it, "I was the founder of GAM, as part of ORPA, when the latter group was planning to create an urban front" (*FBIS-LAM*, 10 March). Whether the Reyes revelations will have any impact on GAM's image abroad remains to be seen. Writing in the *New York Times Magazine* (26 March), Stephen Kinzer described Amilcar Méndez simply as a teacher and human rights activist, without mentioning the Reyes revelations.

Guerrilla Activities. The most important impact of the renewed URNG (and specifically EGP) military activities was demonstrated by the decision of Amoco to pull out of Guatemala in April, as a result of the insecurity in its exploration areas in El Quiche and Huehuetenango (*Central America Review*, 21 April).

However, it was clear already in January that the URNG was prepared for a massive increase in guerrilla activities, although those still followed the previous territorial patterns: EGP was active in El Quiche and Huehuetenango; FAR in Peten and, indicating growing logistical cooperation among URNG groups, in Escuintla as well, ORPA in Solola and Chimaltenango (*Central America Review*, 13 January). Fights also took place in San Marcos (*FBIS-LAM*, 17 January), as well as in the more

traditional URNG areas of Solola, El Quiche, and Huehuetenango.

In March, President Cerezo stated that "The military is concerned...There are between 700 and 1,000 guerrillas in the country" (*FBIS-LAM*, 8 March). In April, URNG elements shot Colonel Lizandro Garcia Arandi, the deputy commander in Huehuetenango (*FBIS-LAM*, 26 April). In June, the military high command admitted that the guerrillas had more modern radio communications equipment than the army (*FBIS-LAM*, 16 June)—an old story, mostly explainable by ORPA's electronic talents. In August, the military admitted the loss of a lieutenant in Chimaltenango (*FBIS-LAM*, 17 August), and further losses were conceded by the end of the year.

All these indications suggest that the URNG, while far from being a serious threat to the government of Guatemala, has become, once again, a considerable military problem in most of the country.

Peace Negotiations. In light of its renewed military capabilities, the URNG has increasingly become more demanding in its attitudes toward negotiations. In January, the URNG only asked for preliminary talks with the Cerezo government (*FBIS-LAM*, 30 January). By the end of that month, the main propaganda strategy of the guerrillas had become obvious: separate talks with the military, described as the actual rulers of Guatemala. "Perhaps," the guerrillas said, "the officers will be more realistic than Cerezo." (*FBIS-LAM*, 30 January.)

On the other hand, URNG cooperation with the Salvadoran FMLN, long known, became more concrete. In November, following the massive FMLN offensive against the Salvadoran regime, the URNG slavishly repeated the FMLN's propaganda claims: that the Cristiani government was "fascist"; that Guatemalan military moves to the Salvadoran border were "proofs" of Cerezo's support for "fascism" in San Salvador; and that the URNG expressed "profound solidarity [with] and admiration" for the FMLN. (*FBIS-LAM*, 21 November.)

The PGT's position is a very peculiar one. On the one hand, it received a greeting from the North Korean Communist Party (*FBIS-Northeast Asia*, 29 September), and was applauded by the Cuban communists; on the other hand, the Prague-based *World Marxist Review* still accepted the newly violent PGT-Central Committee as a legitimate member of the international communist community.

Ideologically, militarily, and politically, 1989 was, for the Guatemalan left, a crucial year, whose full import will become clear only with the passage of time.

Michael Radu
Foreign Policy Research Institute, Philadelphia

Guyana

Population. 765,461
Party. People's Progressive Party (PPP); Working People's Alliance (WPA)
Founded. PPP: 1950; WPA: organized 1973, became formal party in 1979
Membership. PPP: 100 leaders and several hundred militants above non-Marxist rank and file (estimated); WPA: 17 leaders, with membership estimated in the hundreds
General Secretary. PPP: Cheddi Jagan
Leadership. PPP, 9-member party secretariat elected August 1988: Cheddi Jagan, general secretary; Janet Jagan, executive secretary; Harry Persaud Nitka, organization secretary; Shree Chand, finance secretary; Clinton Collymore, information and publicity secretary; Feroze Mohamed, education secretary; Donald Ramotar, membership secretary; Clement Rohee, international secretary; Pariag Sukhai, mass organization secretary. WPA, 17-member collective leadership body announced May 1988: Eusi Kwayana, Rupert Roopnarine, Moses Bhagwan, Andaiye, Clive Thomas, Karen De Souza, Wazir Mohamed, Tacuma Ogunseye, Josh Ramsammy, Nigel Westmass, Ameer Mohamed, Stanley Humphrey, Bissoon Rajkumar, Danuta Radzik, Eric La Rose, Kassim Kamaludin, Vanda Radzik
Status. Legal but often harassed
Last Congress. PPP: Twenty-third, 30 July–1 August 1988
Last Election. 9 December 1985. PPP: 45,926 votes, 16.84 percent, 8 of 53 seats in National Assembly. WPA: 4,176 votes, 1 seat in National Assembly
Auxiliary Organizations. PPP: Progressive Youth Organization (PYO), Women's Progressive Organization (WPO), Guyana Agricultural Workers' Union (GAWU)

Publications. PPP: *Mirror* (weekly), *Newsletter* (monthly), *Interior Special* (monthly), *Thunder* (quarterly); WPA: *Dayclean* and *Open Word* (weeklies)

Under the direction of President Hugh Desmond Hoyte, the ruling People's National Congress (PNC) maintained in 1989 the two-track policy course initiated in 1986 in both domestic and foreign affairs. Economic restructuring was aimed at improving relations with the private sector, Western nations, and the International Monetary Fund (IMF). At the same time, ties with the Eastern bloc and Third World radical states established during the rule of the late Forbes Burnham (1964–1985) were actively maintained.

Economic reform, however, was not matched by domestic political opening. Although the private sector continued to enjoy a measured relaxation of governmental control of the media, the PNC retained its authoritarian grip on the government and all repressive sectors of the state. But because Moscow, Washington, and their respective allies remained generally sanguine about Hoyte's effort to revive a destitute economy through increased Western engagement, and because the West did not appear eager to press the government for domestic democratization, the Moscow-line PPP and the democratic-socialist WPA were left to their own devices as the reign of the minority-backed PNC entered its 26th year.

In April, following prolonged negotiations, the Hoyte government finally agreed with the IMF on an austerity program and monitoring agreement that resulted in a drastic devaluation of the Guyanese dollar and a steep increase in the cost of living. By the end of the year, however, relations with the IMF had reached an impasse as economic targets set for the first phase of the IMF-tied Economic Recovery Program were not met.

Production levels fell when workers, backed by the PPP and WPA, struck the key sugar and bauxite industries for nearly two months in the spring. There were also delays in the provision of a U.S. $20 million Western aid package from a seven-member support group headed by Canada and including Great Britain and the United States. In November, a Caribbean Community (CARICOM) economic team determined that Guyana had replaced Haiti as the poorest nation in the Western hemisphere (*Miami Herald*, 2 December). When IMF monitors arrived in Guyana in December, worried Guyanese officials admitted that prospects for a long-sought agreement on a standby loan remained uncertain.

As he had the year before, Hoyte toured the United States seeking support for his economic program, but again with mixed results. In June, he visited five Midwestern states promoting private U.S. investment in Guyana; his calling card was Guyana's designation in late 1988 as a beneficiary of the United States' Caribbean Basin Initiative. After meeting with U.S. secretary of state James Baker in Washington, he reported that the United States was willing to assist in Guyana's economic recovery (CANA, 22 June; *FBIS-LAT*, 26 June). However, with Guyana near the bottom of the U.S. foreign policy agenda, any significant aid from Washington, as well as from other Western governments, seemed unlikely until Guyana had reached a new agreement with the IMF.

In the United States, Hoyte also was forced to answer criticism about continued authoritarian rule by the PNC, particularly from a few key Democrats on Capitol Hill, who pressed the Bush administration to link U.S. aid to Guyana to democratic reform and free and fair elections.

On the other side of the international relations agenda, Guyana maintained its ties with the Eastern bloc and with revolutionary states and movements in the Third World. At the end of January, Hoyte led a high-level delegation to Cuba for a four-day official visit, making him the second Guyanese head of state to be received in Havana since diplomatic relations were established in 1972. Fidel Castro presented Hoyte with the medal of the Order of José Marti, the highest decoration awarded by the Cuban government (Havana Tele-Rebelde Network, 27 January; *FBIS-LAT*, 31 January). The reception held by Castro for Hoyte was attended by Nicaraguan interior minister Tomas Borge, who was also visiting Havana (EFE, 28 January; *Diario Las Americas*, 29 January).

Although officials from both countries hailed the strength of Cuban-Guyanese relations, the main purpose of Hoyte's visit was to address problems in economic cooperation. In the area of trade, neither country had been able to meet its commitments, and a number of projects dating back two and three years had failed to get off the ground (CANA, 27 January; *FBIS-LAT*, 30 January). On 22 February, a new trade protocol and agreements on bilateral cooperation in the fields of science, technology, education, and culture were signed at the fourteenth session of the Guyana-Cuba joint commission held in Georgetown (CANA, 23 February; *Carib News*,

7 March). The trade protocol envisaged a doubling of bilateral trade from the 1988 figure of U.S. \$3 million (*Caribbean Insight*, March).

In September, Prime Minister Hamilton Green, the second man in the PNC government, paid a two-week visit to Cuba where he was received by Fidel Castro and other high-level Cuban officials. The length of Green's stay and the Guyanese government's description of the visit as "semi-official" caused speculation that Green was also receiving medical treatment (CANA, 22 September; *FBIS-LAT*, 25 September).

In July, a delegation from the Guyanese National Assembly led by Speaker Sase Narain of the PNC was received in Beijing by Wan Li, chairman of the Standing Committee of the Chinese National People's Congress. Wan Li remarked favorably on the strength of diplomatic relations established between the two countries in 1972, and stated that "relations between China and Guyana are solid and the friendly, cooperative relations between the two assemblies, two peoples and two countries will be further developed in various areas" (*Renmin Ribao*, 2 July; *FBIS-CHI*, 5 July).

According to official Chinese news reports, "Narain said his delegation happily witnessed that the situation in China has returned to normal" (XINHUA, 1 July; *FBIS-CHI*, 3 and 5 July). Narain was quoted as saying, "I believe the Chinese government can make correct judgements of its internal affairs and do things in line with the interest of the people" (ibid.).

In August, the PNC's eighth biennial congress was attended by more than 2,000 delegates and observers, principally from the Eastern bloc and nonaligned countries (*Caribbean Insight*, September). According to the PNC, official delegations were sent by North Korea, Romania, Zimbabwe, Mozambique, India, Barbados, Cuba, Jamaica, East Germany, the USSR, Yugoslavia, and the People's Republic of China, among others (CANA, 14 August; *FBIS-LAT*, 15 August). Also attending were delegations from the African National Congress of South Africa, the South West Africa People's Organization, and the Palestine Liberation Organization (ibid.).

The CPSU delegation was led by V. V. Ryabov, deputy chief of the CPSU Central Committee's Ideological Department, who met privately with President Hoyte. According to *Pravda*, Hoyte "emphasized that the two parties and countries have traditionally good and sound relations, and the Guyanese side intends to continue to develop them and raise them to a higher level" (*Pravda*, 19 August).

In October, Guyana and the USSR signed an agreement extending for the third time and for another three years a barter protocol dating back to a series of bilateral agreements signed in 1978. Both sides acknowledged that Guyana had been unable to meet its commitments in supplying the USSR with bauxite, but expressed hope that a joint mining project being worked out between the two countries would end the shortfall (CANA, 25 October; *FBIS-LAT*, 31 October).

At the PNC congress in August, Hoyte appeared to solidify his control of the party by restructuring the PNC leadership. Hamilton Green was named PNC deputy leader, replacing Ranji Chandisingh, a Marxist and former member of the PPP suspected of disagreeing with Hoyte's economic policies. Chandisingh, who earlier had been named ambassador to Moscow, also lost his post as secretary general of the PNC.

At the beginning of 1990, Hoyte also moved to consolidate his control of the government. He abolished the Ministry of National Mobilization, an instrument for directing public funds to the PNC that had been headed by Chandisingh since the Burnham years. The removal of Chandisingh from the cabinet, coupled with the demotions of Yvonne Harewood-Benn and Viola Burnham, the widow of Forbes Burnham, seemed to deal a blow to the hardline Burnham faction within the PNC. Three Hoyte supporters were promoted to full minister, giving Hoyte a majority in the cabinet for the first time.

PPP's Domestic Views and Activities. In 1989, the Marxist-Leninist PPP again failed to resolve the contradictions in its strategy for confronting the PNC. After the fraudulent elections of December 1985, the PPP entered into the Patriotic Coalition for Democracy (PCD) with the WPA and three small centrist parties—the Democratic Labor Movement (DLM), the National Democratic Front (NDF), and the People's Democratic Movement (PDM). The unlikely coalition was formed to pressure the PNC to effect electoral reform and to give its opponents a fair chance to defeat the PNC at the ballot box.

At the same time, the PPP, still headed by party founder Cheddi Jagan, continued to call for the creation of a "national front government" incorporating the PNC, the WPA, and itself (CANA, 4 May; *FBIS-LAT*, 10 May). However, by threatening the PNC with the stick of representative democ-

racy in order to achieve a share of power in a nondemocratic government, Jagan remained vulnerable to Hoyte's political manipulation.

Regarding the PCD's long-standing demand for negotiations on electoral reform, Hoyte reiterated that it was nonsensical to discuss reforms with a coalition that "pursues a one-party state through the backdoor" (ibid.). Hoyte's response served to exacerbate the ideological tension within the PCD and, in the manner of the late Forbes Burnham, raise the specter of a Marxist Guyana to quiet Western criticism of PNC rule.

Stonewalled by Hoyte, the PCD attempted to hammer out a common platform with the other members of the coalition for the general elections constitutionally due by March 1991. However, negotiations bogged down over the PPP's insistence that the program be overtly socialist. The PPP was opposed by the other four coalition parties, with the WPA stating that "under the slogans of socialism, Burnham was systematically destroying the country" (*Financial Times*, 26 May). Asked in the spring about the PCD's effort to deepen its alliance, Hoyte remarked, "Frankly, I don't take them seriously" (*Caribbean Insight*, August).

Squabbling between the PPP and the WPA grew worse during the strike of sugar and bauxite workers against the government's austerity program. When the PPP-affiliated Guyana Agricultural Workers' Union (GAWU) agreed to Hoyte's offer of a separate deal with the government, it broke the unity of the Federation of Independent Trade Unions of Guyana (FITUG). FITUG's seven members, including the GAWU, had apparently agreed to stay out at least until the government granted formal recognition to the independent labor federation formed in late 1988. Two of the unions, as well as the rank and file of other FITUG affiliates, joined the WPA in criticizing Jagan for breaking ranks and letting the government off the hook.

Following the setback to Jagan's authority, the PPP began a concerted effort to re-establish his image as the country's chief opposition leader, which only added to the disputes within the PCD. In April, Hoyte had hinted that he would consider opening talks with the PCD if the coalition could agree on a single spokesman. The WPA proposed the designation of an independent lawyer trained in electoral procedures, then backed DLM leader Paul Tennassee for the position. But the PPP refused to consider anyone other than Jagan. After months of wrangling, the WPA appeared willing to let Jagan have his way for the sake of unity, but the DLM and the other centrists balked.

In the spring, the PCD appeared to present a serious political challenge, as it rallied to the support of independent labor and drew more than 5,000 people to an April protest march in Georgetown. But Hoyte, pressing the right buttons, had once again exposed the inherent instability of the PCD; by the end of the summer, the coalition was in considerable disarray and unable to take advantage of deepening popular discontent with the government. Not until the end of September, when Hoyte announced that municipal elections would take place in November, did the PCD begin to get back in gear.

Shelving their differences for the moment, the five parties announced they would boycott the vote unless Hoyte agreed to discuss electoral reform. The PCD's principal demands were: an independent electoral commission; the public counting of votes at polling stations; the confining to barracks of all military personnel on the day of the vote; and authorization of international monitors. These demands were also supported by the Anglican and Catholic churches, the prestigious Guyana Human Rights Association, and a growing number of prominent professional groups and private sector leaders.

Hoyte repeated that there would be no discussion until the PCD had agreed on a leader "authorized to speak on its behalf and give binding assurances" (*Caribbean Insight*, November). The PCD carried out its threat to boycott the balloting, and on 15 November the PNC-dominated electoral commission declared the PNC slate of municipal candidates to be victorious in all five districts, just as it had in 1986.

By the end of the year, Hoyte's intransigence appeared to bring about a closing of the ranks within the PCD. Amid speculation that Hoyte was preparing to hold early general elections, Jagan declared that he would not stand in the way of a consensus PCD platform, and that the PPP would not seek to dominate a PCD government if one were elected (CANA, 10 December; *FBIS-LAT*, 12 December).

Perceiving renewed concord within the PCD as a threat, Hoyte moved quickly to undermine it. Less than a week after Jagan's declaration, he invited Jagan for a personal discussion, not about electoral reform but about developments in the sugar and bauxite industries. Moreover, Jagan was invited not as a representative of the PCD, but as the leader of the PPP opposition in the National Assembly. Hoyte's maneuver was reminiscent of the tactics

utilized by the late Forbes Burnham against the PPP. Burnham discovered in the 1960s that whenever the PPP appeared to threaten the PNC's grip on the government, Jagan could be neutralized by holding out the prospect of sharing power in exchange for Jagan's cooperation.

During the fall, Jagan had assailed Hoyte, accusing him of "making a unilateral declaration of war on legitimate opposition demands" (CANA, 8 October; *Carib News*, 10 October). But after noting that Hoyte had never invited him for talks on major developments before, Jagan met with the president for two hours in mid-December. In the days following the meeting, however, Jagan appeared reluctant to issue a statement about the issues discussed, saying only that the talks were "cordial and wide-ranging" (CANA; *Carib News*, 2 January 1990). The question was whether Jagan had pressed Hoyte on the issue of electoral reform on behalf of the PCD or succumbed yet again, as the Cliff Barnes of Guyana, to the promise of a deal.

PPP's International Views and Activities. In January, the PPP issued a statement calling on Hoyte to strengthen relations between Cuba and Guyana during his visit to Havana. The PPP hoped that Hoyte's stay in Cuba "would suffice to educate him at first hand about the economic success of that socialist state under the dynamic leadership of Fidel Castro" (CANA, 24 January; *FBIS-LAT*, 26 January).

At the end of September, Jagan traveled to Prague at the invitation of Miloš Jakeš, general secretary of the Central Committee of the Communist Party of Czechoslovakia. It was reported that Jakeš and Jagan "expressed their support for increasing collaboration and for expanding the mutual flow of information among Communist, workers', and leftist parties and progressive movements" (*Rudé právo*, 30 September; *FBIS-EEU*, 5 October).

At the end of the year, the PPP issued a statement welcoming the changes taking place in the socialist world, particularly in Eastern Europe. "The PPP has always stood for the rule of law based on constitutional, fundamental human rights, a pluralist political/ideological system, separation of the party from the state and government, and periodic free and fair elections," the statement said. Singling out changes in the USSR, the PPP said these reforms "are clearly intended to build a democratic and humane socialism." (CANA, 8 December; *FBIS-LAT*, 12 December.)

The PPP's international activities also involved, as a member of the PCD, seeking Western pressure on the Hoyte government for electoral reform. Jagan lobbied for support among the CARICOM countries, traveling to Trinidad in May and Jamaica in October. In July, the PPP issued a formal statement in Georgetown calling on CARICOM leaders to express the same concern over electoral fraud in Guyana as they had regarding fraud in Haiti and Panama. A similar statement was issued to the other nations of the British Commonwealth.

The PPP also lobbied figures of the political opposition in Canada and the United States to press the Mulroney and Bush administrations for support of democratic reform in Guyana. In August, Jagan announced that the PCD would invite the Organization of American States, CARICOM, the Caribbean Conference of Churches, and former U.S. president Jimmy Carter to monitor the next general election (CANA, 19 August; *FBIS-LAT*, 22 August).

WPA's Domestic Views and Activities. Despite the WPA's commitment to collective leadership, Eusi Kwayana emerged as one of the most effective WPA leaders and played an increasingly prominent role in the PCD. "Our main drive," he stated, "is for free and fair elections, to mobilize public opinion, and especially to direct our views to aid donors who are running a terrible risk sinking millions into this country without knowing what is going to happen under the control of a regime that has no mandate" (CANA; *Carib News*, 29 August).

In the spring, following the implementation of the PNC's economic program, the WPA organized demonstrations outside the office of Frank Jackman, the Canadian High Commissioner to Guyana. The WPA charged that Canada, the head of the seven-member international economic-support group for Guyana, was shoring up a "discredited and decadent" government, while ignoring the need for political reform and social justice (CANA, 16 April; *FBIS-LAT*, 20 April).

The WPA played a low-key but effective role during the spring bauxite and sugar strikes. While Jagan was criticized for allowing the PPP-affiliated GAWU to negotiate its own deal with the government, the WPA strengthened its mass appeal by supporting the Sugar and Bauxite Workers' Unity Committee, a rank-and-file body that began to attract disaffected members of the GAWU. In recent years the WPA has aimed to broaden its base to increase its leverage against the considerably larger PPP, as well as the PNC.

The WPA appeared to take a softer line than the PPP on dealing with the IMF. According to Jagan, "We are going down, like the rest of Latin America, with policies imposed by North America" (AP; *LAT*, 28 May). For his part, Kwayana stated, "We oppose the nature of the program negotiated with the IMF, not the IMF itself" (*Financial Times*, 26 May).

The ideological differences between the WPA and the PPP became more pronounced in 1989, particularly during the negotiations for a common PCD electoral platform. Having formally adopted social-democratic principles in 1986, the WPA became increasingly frustrated by the PPP's ideological rigidity.

WPA's International Views and Activities. The WPA became a "consultive member" of the Socialist International (SI) in 1986. However, because of its scarce resources, the party was unable to play an active role in SI activities in 1989. Nonetheless, the WPA continued to seek SI support for its domestic objectives.

Douglas W. Payne
Freedom House, New York

Haiti

Population. 6,322,198
Party. Unified Party of Haitian Communists (Parti Unifié des Communistes Haïtiens; PUCH)
Founded. 1934 (PUCH, 1968)
Membership. 350 (estimated)
General Secretary. René Théodore
Politburo. René Théodore, Max Bourjolly, Gérard Joseph (?)
Status. Legal since 1985; in the open in Haiti with the return of Théodore in March 1986
Last Congress. 1979 (first)
Last Election. 29 November 1987, canceled; 17 January 1988, boycotted
Auxiliary Organizations. No data
Publications. Publications in French and Creole: account of first congress in 1978; explanations about PUCH

PUCH, the Unified Party of Haitian Communists, celebrated the twentieth anniversary of its creation from 18 through 21 January. Its two leaders, René Théodore and Max Bourjolly, hosted a news conference, cultural events, and various social activities. Delegates arrived from Cuba, Venezuela, Uruguay, the Dominican Republic, Martinique, and Guadeloupe. Observers marveled that Haitian communists could stage public events in a country where until 1986 being a communist was a capital offense.

The resignation of party intellectuals marred the party's effort to present itself as a reasonable, progressive force. Dr. Gérard Pierre-Charles, a famous economist, made a reserved but public announcement of his resignation, which was followed by the resignation of his wife, the social historian Dr. Suzy Castor, and those of Michel Hector, and Guy Pierre. The four refused to go into details about their separation from a party they had supported over the years—some even believed that Pierre-Charles had once headed the party from Mexico. Speculation about the four's reasons centered on the party's effort to downplay revolution and on the personalities of Théodore and Bourjolly, who, it was said, want to dominate the party.

Another challenge from the left came from possibly ephemeral groups, which distributed tracts calling for immediate revolution and seizure of food stocks by the poor of Port-au-Prince. A heretofore-unknown organization called the FCPLN, the Charlemagne Front for National Liberation, along with the FDP, or Democratic Population Front, challenged the communist party with their own version of communist programs.

Frustrating to some party members but intriguing to other political movements has been the explicit effort of PUCH leaders to join in the non-revolutionary political process in Haiti. René Théodore, general secretary, never tired of calling for a government of national coalition. He participated in the National Forum in February to discuss the electoral process, and he joined with others in pledging loyalty to the constitution and its article 291, in particular. This article eliminates Duvalierists from the political process in the coming years. He agreed with other parties that the military government must dissolve itself, but he said the PUCH would accept the military as part of a future government. He expressed skepticism about the efficacy of elections in the short term. He called for agrarian reform, however, which other parties do not generally mention. In a widely publicized event,

René Théodore met with General Prosper Avril, who is the current head of state.

In spite of these actions, the military arrested the party's number-two man, Max Bourjolly, on what were alleged to be trumped-up charges of holding illegal weapons. In December another party member, Philippe Delva, was arrested for joining with other parties in trying to organize a protest against continuing military rule.

Other parties and movements were subject to similar harassment and arrest, as the military tried to consolidate its position and neutralize efforts to lead Haiti to an elected civilian government. The military began to use methods of the former Duvalier regime, a turn of events which was not surprising since General Avril was very much part of the Duvalier apparatus.

PUCH and others began to blame the United States for many of the current problems, even though the U.S. government has ceased to aid the Haitian government. When Washington demanded the extradition of reputed drug lord Colonel Jean-Claude Paul, General Secretary Théodore denounced the American action as an affront to Haitian sovereignty. Fellow communists in other lands were not mentioned in Théodore's speeches, particularly as changes occurred in Eastern Europe, but considerable publicity was given by the party to the trip of eleven Haitians to North Korea for the World Youth and Student Festival in June.

René Théodore had free access to government and private media. He spoke over the government-owned Radio Nationale and Radio Soleil, which belongs to the Roman Catholic Church. In its edition of 10–17 March 1989, the New York–based *Haiti Observateur* interviewed René Théodore (p. 11). Haitians and others who knew the history of suppression of political opinions in Haiti over the past decades marveled at the wide range of free expression. At the same time, unmistakable signs of military crackdown were appearing.

Brian Weinstein
Howard University

Honduras

Population. 5,103,772
Major Marxist-Leninist Organizations

• Communist Party of Honduras (Partido Comunista de Honduras; PCH)
  Founded. 1927, dismantled by 1932, re-established 10 April 1954
  Membership. Probably less than 100 permanent cadres in the country
  General Secretary. Rigoberto Padilla Rush
  Status. Illegal
  Last Congress. Fourth, January 1986
  Publications. *Trabajo* (theoretical); *Voz Popular*; both irregular, published abroad

• Revolutionary Party of Central American Workers (Partido Revolucionario de los Trabajadores de Centro America; PRTC)
  Founded. 1976 in Costa Rica, as Honduran branch of regional party, became independent in 1979
  Membership. Probably less than 100 cadres
  Leadership. Wilfredo Gallardo Museli
  Status. Illegal
  Last Congress. No data
  Publications. No data

• Morazanist Front for the Liberation of Honduras (Frente Morazanista para la Liberación de Honduras; FMLH)
  Founded. 1969 claimed, but was inactive until 1980
  Membership. Probably less than 100
  Leadership. Octavio Pérez, Fernando López (both aliases)
  Status. Illegal
  Last Congress. No data
  Publications. No data

• Lorenzo Zelaya Popular Revolutionary Forces (Fuerzas Populares Revolucionarias Lorenzo Zelaya; FPR-LZ)
  Founded. 1980
  Membership. 100 (estimated)
  Leadership. No data
  Status. Illegal
  Last Congress. No data
  Publications. *Lorenzo Zelaya* (irregular, published in Mexico)

• "Cinchoneros" Popular Liberation Movement (Movimiento Popular de Liberación Cinchoneros; MPL-Cinchoneros)
  Founded. 1981, as successor to the People's Revolutionary Union, established in 1980 as Honduran front for the Salvadoran Popular Liberation Forces
  Membership. Some 300
  Leadership. No data
  Status. Illegal
  Last Congress. No data
  Publications. No data

Umbrella Organization

• Unified Directorate of the Honduran Revolutionary Movement (Dirección Nacional Unificada del Movimiento Revolucionario Hondureño; DNU-MRH)
  Founded. 1982, though largely ineffective
  Membership. All the above parties, as well as the Socialist Action Party (Partido de Acción Socialista de Honduras; PASOH), led by Virgilio Carias, headquartered in Nicaragua

Party Affairs. The PCH, as the only Honduran group on the far left with a public presence abroad, had a rather mixed attitude toward the developments in the rest of the communist world. That Rigoberto Padilla was the undisputed spokesman of the party suggests that his position as party leader is now unchallenged. On 18 February, Padilla gave an interview to Havana's International Service, describing his country as "a dependency" of the United States, subject to "dictates" from the World Bank and the International Monetary Fund, and defined the impact of IMF and AID policies as "a catastrophe." He also condemned U.S.-Honduran joint military maneuvers, describing them as directed against the people and "alleged guerrilla activities." (*FBIS-LAM*, 23 February.)

On 15 May, Padilla visited Prague and was received by Michal Stefanek, then secretary for international affairs of the Central Committee of the Communist Party of Czechoslovakia. In June, in an interview with the soon-to-be-dismantled Hungarian Communist Party newspaper *Népszabadság*, Padilla, described as a 59-year-old man who joined the communist movement in 1948, made a call for "realism." Since Central America is under U.S. control, he stated, peace rather than revolution is the immediate aim. He mentioned the successes of the PCH in organizing front groups, particularly among union and youth organizations. He also mentioned his party's main aims: the withdrawal of U.S. troops, the removal of the contras and friendship with Nicaragua. (*FBIS-EE*, 19 May.)

The year 1989 witnessed a strong revival of the Honduran Marxist-Leninist left, as well as the appearance of new violent organizations on both the left and the right. Furthermore, it became apparent that for the first time in many years the violent left is beginning to succeed in establishing effective legal fronts.

Salvadoran, Nicaraguan, and, to some extent, Guatemalan revolutionary interests all contributed to the revival of the Honduran left. It is still unclear to what extent local, as opposed to regional and external factors, are responsible for this year's wave of violence.

The three interconnected factors explaining the resurgence of the violent left in Honduras are the growing activities of the Salvadoran FMLN on Honduran territory, the continuing presence of the Nicaraguan contras and the spillover of their confrontation with Managua into Honduras, and the U.S. military presence in the country.

The most active of the groups belonging to DNU-MRH throughout the year have been the Cinchoneros and the Morazanist Front. The Cinchoneros, closely allied with FMLN elements ever since their beginnings in 1981, started the year with the spectacular murder of General Gustavo Alvarez Martínez, former chief of the Honduran armed forces, on 25 January. A recent born-again Christian, Alvarez was not politically active at the time of his murder. The Cinchonero communiqué taking credit for the assassination accused Alvarez of having "filled many homes of worthy patriots with mourning, grief and fear" and having supported "the dirty war, the low intensity war," but also of direct participation in executions and of religious hypocrisy. (*FBIS-LAM*, 26 January.) Interestingly, and indicative of the Cinchoneros' regional contacts and ties with the FMLN, the statement started with a mention of the "revolutionary duty to avenge the Honduran and Central American martyrs" (ibid.). Alvarez's murder was the third spectacular political assassination in the same month, following the killing of top Nicaraguan resistance leader Manuel Rugama ("Aureliano") on 7 January

and of Carlos Díaz del Valle Lorenzana, a prominent lawyer, whose clients included convicted drug trafficker Juan Ramon Matta (*Latin America Weekly Review*, 9 February). While Rugama's death was clearly attributable to the left (personal communication from Honduran military sources), no one took credit for it, and Díaz del Valle's murder could have been related to the drug traffic underworld, with no political significance.

Cinchonero attempts to attack U.S. servicemen in Honduras, such as the assault on 3 February in the Yoro Department, were largely ineffective (*FBIS-LAM*, 6 February). Equally ineffective were repeated Cinchonero attempts to establish a guerrilla *foco* on Honduras's Atlantic coast, specifically in the Yoro and Atlantida departments. Such a *foco* was dismantled by the military at the beginning of March in the region around San Pedro Sula (*FBIS-LAM*, 21 March).

The Morazanistas (FMLH) became active again by bombing an electric tower in San Pedro (*FBIS-LAM*, 27 February), with a statement protesting the U.S. presence in Honduras, an attack on a U.S. military convoy in Olancho on 11 April, in which they claimed they had killed one and wounded four persons (*FBIS-LAM*, 20 April), and yet another anti-U.S. bombing on 15 July, for which they claimed seven wounded (*NYT*, 16 July).

Three new violent leftist revolutionary groups made their appearance during the year. The first was the Revolutionary United Front Movement (Movimiento Frente Unido Revolucionario; MFUR), which took credit for three anti-American attacks in February: a large bomb that killed eight persons at Tegucigalpa's city hall on 21 February; another bomb attack three days before in Comayagua that injured eight people, including three U.S. soldiers; and a victimless bombing at a government office in Tegucigalpa on 20 February (*FBIS-LAM*, 23 February).

The second new revolutionary group to appear on the Honduran scene was the May 9th People's Revolutionary Forces (Fuerzas Populares de Liberacion 9 de Mayo; FPL-9), which claimed credit for a series of bombings in July. These included pamphlet bombs in La Ceiba and San Pedro Sula, as well as in Tegucigalpa's Central Plaza on 23 July (*FBIS-LAM*, 25 July). The initial statement of the new group claimed it had emerged "as a result of a serious division in the Honduran People's Movement" (a reference to the DNU-MRH) (ibid.).

On 11 November, the explosion of two propaganda bombs in Tegucigalpa announced the appearance of yet another revolutionary organization, the Patriotic Resistance Army 1827 (Ejercito de Resistencia Patriótica 1827; ERP-1827), taking its name from both the highly successful Salvadoran ERP (see *YICA*, 1990) and the date of the victory on 11 November 1827 of Honduras's national hero, Francisco Morazán, over Guatemalan and Salvadoran forces (*FBIS-LAM*, 13 November). The new group's initial statement also demanded the dismantling of the Nicaraguan contra forces, the departure of U.S. forces from Honduras, and total support for Nicaragua's objectives in Central America (ibid.).

The claims of these groups should be regarded with much skepticism, since none of the three has demonstrated any ability to persist beyond its initial actions. They may well be nothing but new names for specific operations conducted by older Honduran groups or, equally likely, by FMLN elements or Nicaraguan intelligence. Their common denominator—support for Managua's aims in Central America, including the elimination of the U.S. military presence there and of the contras, and the halting of the limited Honduran cooperation with the Salvadorans against the FMLN—suggest that they may well be ephemeral creations of Sandinista intelligence and FMLN groups in Honduras. Such suspicions, still unconfirmed, are only strengthened by the timing of the appearance of these groups, consistently related to approaching Central American summits where Nicaragua would be isolated and in need of allies.

Throughout the year the Honduran military had to cope with repeated FMLN attacks against, and operations in Honduran territory. The pattern of FMLN activities in Honduras was the same throughout the year: taking advantage of the unmarked border areas, the FMLN used them as refuges and accused the Hondurans of invading Salvadoran territory; when under Salvadoran attack in those same areas, the FMLN used its radio stations to claim Salvadoran attacks against Honduras.

On 29 May Honduran sources, as well as the FMLN, claimed that a Salvadoran attack had occurred in the Carolina area of the border, but it turned out that the entire invasion, as the event was described by the FMLN, was a single strafing by the Salvadorans of pseudo-refugees, who were actually fleeing FMLN cadres (*FBIS-LAM*, 30 May). A Honduran spokesman made it clear that the whole incident was to be seen as part of the FMLN's "political campaign" and the Salvadoran guerrillas' fight against their government (*FBIS-LAM*, 1 June). On 30 July, the Honduran military captured a mas-

sive shipment of arms from Nicaragua to the FMLN, which included 60 AK-47 rifles (*FBIS-LAM*, 30 July). A similar occurrence took place on 19 October, when Uzi and AK-47 submachineguns, RPG grenade launchers, mortars, radio equipment, and ammunition were captured in Honduras on their way to El Salvador (*FBIS-LAM*, 20 October).

There are strong indications that the pattern of violence apparent in 1989 will continue in 1990, originating in the same basic factors present in the previous year: Honduras's geographic position, which makes it a natural focus for revolutionary groups from neighboring states, including the FMLN, the URNG, and the Managua regime; the relative openness of the political system of the country, allowing the left more legal possibilities to operate than in most Central American countries; and the long-standing ties between the Honduran revolutionaries and those of Nicaragua, El Salvador, and Guatemala.

Michael Radu
Foreign Policy Research Institute, Philadelphia

Jamaica

Population. 2,484,957
Party. Workers Party of Jamaica (WPJ)
Founded. 1978
Membership. 100 (est.)
General Secretary. Dr. Trevor Munroe
Status. Legal
Last Congress. Fourth, 11–13 September 1988
Central Committee. 31 members (one-third women; one-third from rural parishes; one-third workers and small farmers)
Last Election. 1989 national election; did not contest.
Auxiliary Organizations. University and Allied Workers' Union (UAWU)
Publications. *Struggle*

The general elections of 9 February brought Michael Manley and his Peoples' National Party (PNP) back to power. This was a dramatically changed Manley and PNP. "I think we have all grown a little older, a little wiser, a little more mellow with years," was how Manley explained the change after his victory. (*Latin American Regional Report, Caribbean Report*, 23 February.) From his statements, cabinet appointments, and initial program initiatives, it appears that the PNP's left-leaning policies of the 1970s are things of the past.

This shift of the PNP to the ideological center has left Jamaica's communist party, the Workers' Party of Jamaica (WPJ), quite isolated on the hard left. During 1989, this political isolation was evident from the WPJ's absence from significant political activities.

The general secretary of the WPJ, Dr. Trevor Munroe, explained that the party was engaged in a "process of fairly *profound rethinking*" of tactics and concepts. This was necessary, he admitted, "because there is no popular upsurge on the agenda." (*WMR*, March.) He called for a new "humanism" in the party's agenda. It is unclear what that means exactly. What is clear is that his traditional emphasis on race has not changed: He concludes that the interests of the Caribbean people and the interest—in fact the core—of Marxism-Leninism as a revolutionary doctrine require that "we caribbeanize—indeed, we 'blacken'—Marxism-Leninism to link with our people and for our people to link with it more." (Ibid.)

But, if the WPJ was insignificant in the open political arena, it was hardly dead. Its years-long battle to gain acceptance by workers in the sugar-producing areas bore fruit in 1989. Labor in those areas had long been controlled by the two trade-union branches of the dominant parties: the PNP-linked National Workers' Union (NWU) and the JLP-linked Bustamante Industrial Trade Union (BITU). The WPJ utilized every stratagem in the book to break that monopoly. Interestingly enough, the trade-union branch of the Worker's Party of Jamaica, the University and Allied Worker's Union (UAWU), had recourse to one of the few remaining "colonial" ties between Jamaica and Britain: it made a legal appeal to the Privy Council. After a four-year-long legal struggle, the Privy Council mandated that workers be allowed to vote on whether UAWU should represent them. Workers on one estate (Hampden Estate, in Trelawny) voted 534 to 17 to have the UAWU represent them. In November 1989 it was agreed that the UAWU would join in industrial negotiations together with the NWU and the BITU as a joint partner.

The conservative *Daily Gleaner* (4 November) complimented the UAWU by saying in an editorial

that ever since its inception in the early 1970s it "has shown very bold characteristics: it has fought on where other unions of similar size have backed off." Perhaps this compliment from the very established *Gleaner* was an accurate reflection of the WPJ's effectiveness in trade-union activity despite its political decline in 1989.

Anthony P. Maingot
Florida International University

Martinique

Population. 331,511
Party. Martinique Communist Party (Parti Communiste Martiniquais; PCM)
Founded. 1921 (PCM, 1957)
Membership. Less than 1,000
General Secretary. Armand Nicolas (62; French citizen)
Politburo. 3 members
Secretariat. 4 members
Central Committee. 33 members
Status. Legal
Last Congress. Ninth, 12–13 December 1988
Last Elections. 24 April, 8 May 1988, president of France; 5 and 12 June 1988, French National Assembly, no seats; 25 September, 2 October 1988, Martinique General Council, 2 of 45
Auxiliary Organizations. General Confederation of Martiniquan Labor (CGTM); Martiniquan Union of Education Personnel (SMPE-CGTM); Union of Women of Martinique (Union des Femmes de la Martinique); Martiniquan Committee of Solidarity with the Peoples of the Caribbean and of Central America
Publications. *Justice* (weekly newspaper)

The very small Martinique Communist Party seemed weak and on the defensive. Members followed Guadeloupe's lead in denouncing measures taken by the European Economic Community, but followed the French Communist Party (PCF) in voting in the elections for the European Parliament. The party's general secretary Armand Nicolas, met with leaders of the Communist Party of Guadeloupe, and from 24 to 28 November Georges Marchais, leader of the French Communist Party, visited the island.

During municipal elections in 34 towns on 12 and 19 March, the PCM won in Lamentin, Martinique's second largest city, and in Macouba. In both towns there had been a communist administration, but in June the Macouba elections were annulled because of alleged irregularities. Aimé Césaire's Progressive Martinique Party (PPM) retained control of Fort-de-France, the city which dominates the island and is its capital.

In July, the communist-allied trade union, the CGTM, or General Confederation of Martinique Workers, refused to join in celebrations of the bicentennial of the French Revolution, partly because of the anticipated negative consequences for Martinique of European economic integration, to be effected in 1992. On 29 October, the PCM led a demonstration for a special status for Martinique, which is what the Guadeloupan communists had earlier proposed.

The party was particularly upset about the Common Market transition proposal, called POSEIDOM, which stands for "Program of options relating to the distance and specificity of the overseas departments." The proposal would abolish the "octroi de mer," which is a tax on all incoming products for the benefit of town budgets. Such a tax would be illegal after 1992. The PCM also feared the loss of a guaranteed banana and rum market in France.

Unlike the Communist Party of Guadeloupe, the PCM decided to participate in elections to the European Parliament, supporting the French communist list. Because the latter opposes complete integration of Martinique, the PCM could support it. Only 5.38 percent of the vote went to the PCF list.

The PCM followed events in Eastern Europe and the Soviet Union, defending socialist reform in its reports and giving an unusual twist to events. According to one author, "The new leaders of the Unified Socialist Party of Germany are accelerating the rhythm of reform and are opening the frontier with the West thereby putting the Occident in a state of shock" (*Justice*, 16 November). Changes were seen by the PCM's leaders as part of a communist peace initiative to which the West should respond.

The PCM also reported interethnic conflicts in the Soviet Union as well as the coal miners' strike. They admitted there were problems of corruption and a low quality of life in the USSR, but denied that communism was dead. There is considerable disin-

formation in the French press about changes in Eastern Europe, party leaders asserted.

On 2 and 9 July the PCM celebrated the "Fête de *Justice.*"

Brian Weinstein
Howard University

Mexico

Population. 86,336,019
Party. Partido Comunista Mexicano (PCM); during the 1980s, most Mexican communists joined with other leftists to form a series of parties, most recently the Mexican Socialist Party (PMS), founded in 1987, which further broadened its base in 1989, when it became part of the Democratic Revolution Party (PRD); some Mexican communists continue to operate as the PCM
Founded. PCM, 1919; PMS, November 1987; PRD, May 1989
Membership. PCM, unknown; PMS, 90,000; PRD, unknown
General Secretary. Juan Pablo Sainz Aguilar, of continuing PCM faction; Gilberto Rincón Gallardo, of communists joined together in PMS and then PRD; general coordinator of PRD, noncommunist Cuauhtémoc Cárdenas
Status. All legal
Last Congress. 14 May 1989, PMS
Last Election. 6 July 1989, gubernatorial, Baja California Norte; state representatives, Michoacán
Publications. *La Unidad* (PMS), ended May 1989; *6 de Julio, periódico de la revolución democrática* (PRD), a biweekly, commenced publication on 6 July 1989; editor, Antonio Bulmaro Castellanos

Since 1981 Mexican communists have been in an almost constant flux. Most members and leaders of the Mexican Communist Party have on several occasions joined with other groups to form everbroader unified parties of the left. Some communists disapproved of the mergers, arguing that they dissipated their power, and either withdrew from active politics or maintained a rump PCM. In 1989, the merging communists dissolved their Mexican Socialist Party (PMS) to become part of the far broader Democratic Revolution Party.

The rump PCM, meanwhile, signed an agreement to unite in action with one of Mexico's oldest parties, the Popular Socialist Party (PPS), both asserting their goal of advancing organic unity among Mexican Marxist-Leninists, while maintaining their political autonomy. According to Sainz Aguilar, there are cells of the original PCM in at least ten organizations throughout Mexico. When the PCM and PPS signed their agreement in late August, Sainz stated that organic unity—a merger—would not be possible until a consensus was reached within the PCM's rank and file, but in the meantime the two parties would cooperate in those areas where agreement already exists. Should the PCM be interested in an electoral front, the PPS would help draft the political platforms and support the sole candidate representing both parties. (*FBIS-LAT*, 14 September.)

The entrance of most Mexican communists into the PRD, however, indicates the left's desire to reposition itself in order to broaden its membership, as well as to ride the wave of social and economic discontent that has weakened the legitimacy of the ruling PRI. It clearly is a move away from an ideological base towards popularism and Mexican nationalism. This strategy is being played out against the backdrop of the country's most serious crisis since the Mexican Revolution of 1910.

For the Mexican left, these truly are the best of times and the worst of times. It generally is believed that poor and worsening economic conditions favor the political opposition, and the left in particular. As a rule of thumb this notion has proven to be too simplistic. From a socioeconomic standpoint, the situation could not be more propitious for the left. Years of austerity have cut the purchasing power of wage earners by 50 percent and forced drastic changes in diets and family economics. In 1982, a worker receiving the minimum wage worked 45 minutes a day to buy a pound of chicken; by 1987 that same worker had to labor three and one-half hours. Per capita consumption of milk has fallen, to be replaced by use of cheaper soft drinks. Soft-drink consumption is now three times that of milk. Meat has all but disappeared from the diet. Poor Mexicans eat almost the same amount of meat as the poor in Ethiopia and other Third World countries where consumption is below 30 grams a day. Malnutrition has already stunted a new generation, both physically and mentally. Only one in five rural children under four years of age is of normal weight and stature. (*NYT*, 25 July.)

Widespread desperation, reaching from the poor far up into the middle class, has forced entire families to look for work of any kind. Enrollment in elementary schools has dropped since 1985, in spite of annual population growth of 1.5 million. Efforts to deal with the crisis are compounded by capital flight and debt. Approximately 30 percent of Mexico's gross national product is swallowed up by the servicing of the country's debt. The amount of capital that has fled is estimated at close to 50 billion dollars. Reducing government budgets, a 50 percent reduction in health and education, closing or selling state enterprises, ending subsidies of food and gasoline help the financial picture and hold down inflation, but in the short term require heroic sacrifices from people with little left to give. Hope for better times can sustain these people only up to a certain point. Meanwhile the gap between the rich and the poor has widened. The richest 10 percent have more income than the bottom 67 percent of the population combined. Whether Mexico can pull through is still in doubt. Who is responsible for the socioeconomic disaster appears self-evident. One-party rule, corruption, economic mismanagement, and social disaster are associated inevitably with the PRI. It would seem a fatal burden.

Nevertheless, the nature of Mexican politics makes the socioeconomic reality more of a theoretical advantage for the left rather than a concrete opportunity. The Cuauhtémoc Cárdenas phenomenon of 1987–1988, while tremendously exhilarating for the left, has not resulted in further electoral breakthroughs. Cárdenas, seriously challenging the PRI candidate for president, Carlos Salinas de Gortari, captured at least 31 percent of the vote, and opened up the possibility of ending PRI domination of the government. Cuauhtémoc Cárdenas, personally not a magnetic individual, drew upon the historical charisma of his populist father, Lázaro Cárdenas, whose presidency appeared to be the most radical of those that followed the Mexican Revolution of 1910. Huge crowds responded to the exciting combination of the man and his father's myth, a myth fostered, ironically, by PRI propaganda. Without a political party of his own, Cárdenas ran for president at the head of an impossible coalition, the National Democratic Front (FND). The Mexican Socialist Party (PMS) joined the coalition in the last two weeks of the campaign.

The PMS moved slowly because of concern that it would be lost in the ideological morasses of the

Cárdenas movement. As a result, the PMS did not profit much from the coalition. As the PMS entered the new year, the most effective strategy for it was far from clear. Maintaining an independent party risked missing the Cárdenas wave. Moreover, the future of a Marxist-Leninist party was complicated by *perestroika*, *glasnost'*, and the crumbling of communism in Eastern Europe, as well as by reforms in the USSR. The future of the left appeared to lie with the democratic socialism of Felipe González in Spain, or an even more watered down Euro-Communism. A reformed and cleansed PRI might be closer to that vision than the PMS.

In January of 1989, the Movement Towards Socialism (MAS) constituted itself a task force to form the Party of the Democratic Revolution (PRD) to unite the left behind the leadership of Cuauhtémoc Cárdenas (*Uno Mas Uno*, 22 January). The PMS role in the new party was outlined in a discussion document approved by the Eighth Plenum of the National Council. In short, historical difference and conflicts had to be laid aside in the interest of democracy and Mexican nationalism. A willingness to talk to all opposition parties, including the National Action Party (PAN), and to form alliances when they would be useful became a guiding principle. Such toleration stemmed in part from a well-founded belief that an alliance between the PRI and the PAN could spell disaster for the left. Within the new party, former PMS members would continue to be an organized "current" but not a sectarian interest group. Top leadership would not be based on proportional representation. (*FBIS-LAT*, 16 March.)

The submergence of the PMS into the PRD called for in January became a reality on 14 May when the majority of PMS members voted to change the name of the party to the PRD by a vote of 1,079, with 18 against and 10 abstentions (*FBIS-LAT*, 17 May). That act ended the separate organization of most of the left that had begun in 1919 with the founding of the Mexican Communist Party. Cuauhtémoc Cárdenas, who had planned the formation of the PRD in late 1988, assumed the leadership.

The major disappointment for the left opposition in 1989 was the ability of the PRI to hold itself together under the leadership of President Carlos Salinas de Gortari. Lacking personal charisma, the Mexican president strengthened his popularity with a publicly tough anticorruption campaign aimed at all levels of the bureaucracy, as well as labor unions. The dramatic seizure of Joaquín Hernández Galicia ("La Quina"), union boss of the oil workers, impressed the entire country. While some called it political revenge against a powerful enemy of Salinas de Gortari, it nevertheless demonstrated that the president remained in control and would use his power. Other labor leaders denounced the act as illegal, yet hesitated to do more.

In March, a highly publicized meeting between Salinas de Gortari and the former PAN presidential candidate, Manuel Clouthier, took place. Newspapers throughout the republic splashed photos across their front pages of the two political arch-enemies shaking hands. It should be noted that Clouthier had called Salinas de Gortari a "bald-headed vote thief." To balance off the political sideshow, a delegation of CPSU workers headed by A. Yu Urnov, deputy chief of the Central Committee's International Department, visited Mexico from 19 to 27 April at the invitation of the PRI, meeting with PRI organizations in the federal district and throughout the country. Salinas de Gortari clearly had the political initiative.

The political events of the year were the gubernatorial election in the increasingly important state of Baja California Norte and state representative elections in the state of Michoacán, the home state of Cuauhtémoc Cárdenas. Cárdenas had served as a PRI governor of that state from 1980 to 1986. The elections would either confirm or damage the legitimacy of the regime of Salinas de Gortari. All the rhetoric about honest elections and the end of the unbelievable, but victorious voter tallies compiled by the "alquimistas," would be tested. International publicity and pressure had to be managed to avoid any negative effect on the issue of debt relief and general confidence in the regime.

In the Baja California campaign, the left proved totally ineffectual and unable to work together. A large part of the problem arose from their inability to define the PRD. As Tijuana newspaperman José Luis Pérez Canchola observed, the PRD appeared to be an odd mixture of ex-PRI and communist party members in a desperate but vain search for a program. Consequently, the right opposition took the election with their candidate Ernesto Ruffo. The PAN now has had an effective and significant electoral victory. It should be noted that during the race the PAN broke its long standing refusal to accept federal election funds (*CSM*, 14 July).

In Michoacán, the situation differed, and the message could not be clearer. The PRI demonstrated that it would not tolerate a PRD victory and would use all its old devices, as well as force, to deny the left a victory. Cárdenas claimed that the

PRD had won fourteen of the eighteen seats at stake in the state legislature. The PRI's "selective democracy" did not extend to Cárdenas. (*6 de Julio*, 8 August.) A PRD attempt to enlist the PAN in an effort to contest the Michoacán result fell upon deaf ears. An enraged PRD merely appeared impotent.

In the aftermath of the Michoacán elections, the PRD was left reeling and beset by intraorganizational ideological struggles, as well as by important defections. The scent of victory for the left has all but disappeared. The only hope remaining is that the PRI will not be able to get the economy working at an acceptable level nor be able to mitigate the effect of external and internal debts. This hope is made slimmer by the international impression that Salinas de Gortari is an effective pragmatic reformer and able to control the political situation in an acceptable manner. Cárdenas unintentionally bolsters support for the government with strong statements in favor of debt suspension that holders of both the external and internal debt find unacceptable. President Salinas de Gortari is playing international and domestic politics with an unexpected brilliance, while Cárdenas appears as a slightly updated 1930s popularist.

Financial constraints on the PRD are severe and likely to worsen unless some tangible victory is achieved very soon. *La Unidad*, the PMS weekly, has been replaced by a biweekly, *6 de Julio*. As an official organ of the PRD it is distributed throughout the republic, adding to the financial strain. So far *6 de Julio* has been devoted to strengthening support for the PRD as an organization rather than presenting an action program. Running a national party on a limited amount of money requires the personal involvement of many unpaid followers, whose morale must be kept sufficiently high to assure their continued efforts—not an easy task.

The left entered the year excited by the impressive turnout for Cárdenas in the 1988 presidential elections, and ended the year confronting a more sobering reality. The tendency to splinter has always characterized the Mexican left. Now the weight of disappointment and frustration can be expected to place an added strain on the PRD.

Everything depends on making the PRD effective. While no one expected the PMS to become a governing party—it depended on long range education of the workers—the expectations for the PRD are much more immediate. The inability to mobilize mass support at a time when socioeconomic conditions are so favorable to the opposition is another factor. It appears to be a golden opportunity

that remains out of reach because of the political incapacity of the left. The government's decision to declare the state-owned copper producer, the Compañia Minera de Cananea, bankrupt and put it up for sale stunned both labor and the left. Willingness to use troops to break the mining union once again demonstrated Salinas de Gortari's toughness. The events in Cananea, the cradle of the Mexican Revolution of 1910, symbolize in a vivid fashion the PRI's pragmatic flexibility and readiness to drop old political loyalties and historical groups. By refusing to be a captive of its history, the PRI has become politically unpredictable and able to keep the opposition off balance. The response of the left has been yet another umbrella group, the Patriotic Front (FP), formed by the PRD, PPS, PSD, and other minor groups (*6 de Julio*, 1 September).

The most serious problem for the PRD in 1989 has been its inability to put forth a program that goes beyond old-fashioned rhetoric, honest elections, Mexican nationalism, and other well-worn emotional issues. Almost as serious is the growing alliance between the PRI and the PAN, which is designed to deny the left more than a token victory. The PRI's new economic policy, its crackdown on labor, and its willingness to end agrarian reforms and stimulate modern agriculture, have narrowed the gap between them. A two-party governing system may be in Mexico's future, but it is unlikely that the PRD will be one of them.

Colin M. MacLachlan
Tulane University

Nicaragua

Population. 3,519,620
Major Marxist-Leninist Organizations.

• Sandinista Front of National Liberation (Frente Sandinista de Liberación Nacional; FSLN)
  Founded. 1961
  Membership. 5,500 (*La Prensa*, 27 October)
  National Directorate. 9 members: Daniel Ortega Saavedra, Humberto Ortega Saavedra, Victor Tirado López, Tomás Borge Martínez, Bayardo

Arce Castaño, Henry Ruíz Hernández, Jaime Wheelock Román, Luís Carrión Cruz, Carlos Nuñez Téllez.

Executive Commission. 5 members: Daniel Ortega Saavedra (coordinator), Bayardo Arce Castaño (deputy coordinator), Humberto Ortega Saavedra, Tomás Borge Martínez, Jaime Wheelock Román

Main Party Organs. The Sandinista Assembly (105 members), supposed to convene yearly. Routine party operations are under the control of eight auxiliary departments: general affairs (René Nuñez); organization (Lea Guido); agitation and propaganda (Dionisio Marenco); communication (Carlos Fernando Chamorro Barrios); political education (Vanessa Castro Cardenal); international affairs (Julio López Campos); finance (Plutarco Cornejo); studies of Sandinismo (Flor de Maria Monterrey)

Party-State Relationship. The following top leaders of the FSLN are also in charge of the most important state institutions: Daniel Ortega Saavedra, president of the republic; Humberto Ortega Saavedra, minister of defense; Tomás Borge Martínez, minister of the interior; Victor Tirado López, responsible for the labor movement and labor-relations policies; Luís Carrión Cruz, minister of the economy; Henry Ruíz Hernández, minister of external cooperation; Jaime Wheelock Román, minister of agriculture and the agrarian reform; Carlos Nuñez Téllez, president of the National Assembly

Status. Ruling party

Last Congress. FSLN Assembly, 18 February and 24 September 1989

Last Election. 4 November 1984; presidential election, 47.43 percent of the official list of registered voters, 63 percent of ballots cast; National Assembly, 61 out of 96 seats; according to Jaime Chamorro Cardenal of the newspaper *La Prensa*, in "Farsa Electoral en Numeros, Datos Estadisticos y Porcentages," (1985), the FSLN obtained only 29.17 percent of the true votes cast in the 1984 elections; 400,000 false votes were added after the election.

Auxiliary Organizations. FSLN activist membership estimated between 12,000 and 16,000 (*La Prensa*, 27 October); Sandinista Defense Committees (Comités de Defensa Sandinista; CDS), estimated membership 80,000, led by Omar Cabezas Lacayo; Sandinista Youth–19 of July (Juventud Sandinista–19 de Julio; JS-19), estimated membership 11,000, led by Ajax Del-

gado; Luisa Amanda Espinosa Association of Nicaraguan Women (Asociación de Mujeres Nicaraguenses Luisa Amanda Espinosa; AMNLAE), led by Glenda Monterrey; Sandinista Workers Central (Central Sandinista de Trabajadores; CST), led by Lucio Mendez; Farmworkers Association (Asociación de Trabajadores del Campo; ATC), led by Edgardo García

Front Organizations of FSLN. Federation of Health Workers (Federación de Trabajadores de la Salud; FETSALUD), led by Gustavo Porras; National Union of Agricultural and Cattle Producers (Unión Nacional de Agricultores y Ganaderos; UNAG), led by Daniel Nuñez; National Association of Teachers (Asociación Nacional de Educadores; ANDEN), led by Guillermo Martínez; National Union of Journalists (Unión Nacional de Periodistas; UPN), led by Lily Soto; National Council of Professional Associations "Martyrs and Heroes" (Consejo Nacional de Asociaciónes Profesionales "Heroes y Martires"; CONAPRO); Union of Nicaraguan Writers (Unión Nicaraguense de Escritores; UNE), led by Michelle Najlis; National Union of Artists (Unión Nacional de Artistas Plasticos; UAP), led by Roger Perez De La Rocha; Evangelical Commission for the Promotion of Social Responsibility (Comisión Evangelica de Promocion de la Responsabilidad Social; CEPRES), led by Miquel Angel Casco (*Barricada*, 8 November)

Status Change. The auxiliary organization, Sandinista Association of Cultural Workers (Asociación Sandinista de Trabajadores de la Cultura; ASTC) was renamed and became front organization Institute for the Promotion of Culture (Instituto de Promoción Cultural; IPC), led by Rosario Murillo (*Barricada*, 24 February).

Publications. *Barricada* (party daily, circulation 120,000); *El Nuevo Diario* (government daily, 45,000); *Nicarahuac* (ideological journal); *Segovia* (army journal); *Bocay* (Interior Ministry monthly); all television stations and the two major radio stations, Radio Sandino and La Voz de Nicaragua, are party-controlled and owned.

• Socialist Party of Nicaragua (Partido Socialista de Nicaragua; PSN), oldest pro-Soviet communist party in the country

Founded. 1937; first official congress, 3 July 1944

Membership. 1,400 (estimated)

General Secretary. Gustavo Tablada

Political Commission. Luís Sánchez Sancho, Gustavo Tablada, Alejandro Solorzano, Roberto Guzman, Adolfo Evertz, Juan Gaitan, and José Luis Medina (elected by the plenums, which also elect the general secretary)

Status. Legal

Last Congress. 45th Anniversary Plenum, July 1989

Last Election. November 1984; 14,494 votes, less than 2 percent, two seats in National Assembly (Sánchez Salgado and Sánchez Sancho)

Auxiliary Organizations. General Confederation of Workers-Independent (Confederación General de Trabajadores-Independiente; CGT-I), led by Alejandro Solorzano, 31,000 members (estimated), joined in November 1987 with the other three major independent labor union confederations (CUS, CTN-A, and CAUS) to form the coalition front: Permanent Congress of Workers (Congreso Permanente de los Trabajadores; CPT); Union of Construction Workers of Managua (Sindicato de Carpinteros, Albaniles, Armadores y Similares de Managua; SCAAS), led by Domingo Sánchez Salgado

Publications. *El Popular* (weekly, circulation ca. 7,000)

• Communist Party of Nicaragua (Partido Comunista de Nicaragua; PCN)

Founded. 1970, as splinter of PSN

Membership. 1,600 (estimated)

General Secretary. Eli Altamirano Pérez

Politburo. 7 members: Eli Altamirano Pérez, Ariel Bravo Lorio, Alan Zambrana Salmerón, Angel Hernández Cerda, René Blandón Noguera, Manuel Pérez Estrada, Alejandro Gutiérrez Mayorga

Status. Legal

Last Congress. Second, June 1986; National Conference, December 1986

Last Election. November 1984; 16,034 votes, less than 2 percent, two seats in National Assembly (Zambrana and Hernandez)

Auxiliary Organizations. Central for Trade Union Action and Unity (Central de Acción y Unidad Sindical; CAUS), led by Roberto Moreno, 19,000 members (estimated); joined together with the other three major independent labor confederations to form the coalition front: Permanent Congress of Workers (Congreso Permanente de los Trabajadores; CPT) founded in November 1987

Publication. *Avance* (weekly, circulation ca. 20,000)

• Popular Action Movement–Marxist-Leninist (Movimiento de Acción Popular-Marxista-Leninista; MAP-ML); before 1989 called Nicaraguan Marxist-Leninist Party (Partido Marxista-Leninista de Nicaragua; PMLN)

Founded. 1970, as a splinter of FSLN; expelled from FSLN in August 1972; struggled for an independent political line after the 1979 revolution until it adopted an ultraleft tactical support position toward the FSLN with which it has a tacit alliance (*Barricada*, 8 September).

Membership. Unknown

General Secretary. Isidro Téllez (chilo)

Other Party Leaders. Fernando Malespín, Carlos Cuadra, Carlos Lucas

Governing Body. Central Committee, last meeting in August 1985

Status. Legal

Last Election. November 1984, 11,352 votes, less than 2 percent, two seats in National Assembly (Cuadra and Lucas)

Auxiliary Organization. Workers Front (Frente Obrero; FO), a very small membership

Publication. *Prensa Proletaria* (bimonthly)

Others: The far-left Workers Revolutionary Party (Partido Revolucionario de los Trabajadores; PRT) and the Central American Unionist Party (Partido Unionista CentroAmericano; PUCA) were founded in late 1984; neither was allowed to participate in the 1984 elections; both have presidential and vice-presidential candidates running in the February 1990 elections; Bonifacio Miranda Bengochea and Juan Carlos Leyton for the PRT, elected in their Fourth Congress (*Barricada*, 29 August); Blanca Rojas Echaverry and Daniel Urcuyo Castrillo for PUCA. Other PRT leaders are René Tamariz and Leslie Pérez; other PUCA leaders include its founder Alejandro Pérez Arevalo and Giovanni D'Ciofalo. The PRT publishes a biweekly newspaper *El Socialista*. The PRT had its origin in the small circle of radical students organized in the early 1970s in the Marxist Revolutionary League (Liga Marxista revolucionaria; LMR), the Nicaraguan section of the Fourth International. The PRT had for a long time criticized the FSLN for its alleged authoritarian-bureaucratic political line and for moving too slowly toward the consolidation of the dictatorship of the proletariat. In the electoral campaign, the PRT became a tactical ally of the FSLN, granting it legitimacy from the far-left; the FSLN reciprocated by boosting this minuscule party of less than two dozen members to the proclaimed legitimacy and rank of the largest organization of the left with supposedly 2,585 members (*Barricada*, 29 August). The PUCA, on the other hand, according to its leader Alejandro Baca Muñoz (*Barricada*, 10 February), has made public its support for the FSLN, which has never challenged its obscure status as a minuscule organization.

The major challenges that the FSLN faced in 1989 were to meet the demands of the Central American presidents' peace plans that required creating the conditions for free elections and the adaptation to the new international climate created by the changes in the Soviet Union and its Eastern bloc allies. Both major adjustments were to be performed under the extreme difficulties of a disastrous economical situation, characterized by hyperinflation, social dissatisfaction, and unrest; together with the growing dependency on the financial subsidies provided by the Soviet Union, Czechoslovakia, East Germany, and the other Eastern bloc trading partners. The dominant trend of the Nicaraguan scene in 1989 was the contradiction between the accelerating insertion of the nation into a collapsing communist political and economic international system and the institutional changes to democratize the country's internal political structures and allow greater freedoms in the workings of civil society. The tensions created by this contradiction brought forth internal dissension within the ranks of the FSLN and forced the leadership to choose between two conflicting long-term strategic options: either to sincerely embrace democratic reform, abandoning its self-proclaimed vanguard predominance over Nicaraguan society; or to continue its policy of deception, of appearing democratic while embracing Marxist-Leninist orthodoxy, which legitimates their monopoly of state power, a policy that has already failed. The latter can only assure further economic disasters and continuation of the nation's civil war. The campaign for the February 1990 election and their record of international relations in 1989 were indicators of the alternative the FSLN leadership chose.

Party Affairs. The ideological direction of the FSLN during 1989 was defined in Havana by the speech of Fidel Castro on 1 January that pledged total allegiance to the principles of Marxism-Leninism and their defense until death (*Barricada*, 3 January). President Daniel Ortega Saavedra who participated in the thirtieth anniversary celebrations of the Cuban Revolution, was the only head of state, besides Fidel Castro, to sign the Declaration of Havana, which called for the formation of a united Latin American front against the United States, against imperialism, for the victory of the Salvadoran FMLN guerrillas, in support of the regime of Manuel Antonio Noriega in Panama, and in opposition to payment of the foreign debt. (*Barricada*, 6 January.)

The joint Cuban-Nicaraguan response to the process of *perestroika* led by the Soviet Union was explained by the leading FSLN ideologue, Victor Tirado López, the day before in Managua at a public party meeting in the César Augusto Silva Convention Center. He stated: "Since the appearance of *perestroika*, Marxism-Leninism and all the revolutionary doctrines have been submitted to new tests and trials"; in order to face this situation, and uphold Marxism-Leninism, Commander Tirado recommended that the Sandinistas needed to "be capable of proving by the facts that this doctrine is of actuality, alive and fertile . . ." (*Barricada*, 5 January.)

The task of ascertaining the validity of Marxism-Leninism in the Nicaraguan experiment did not take long to be completed; the public debate that was reviewing the obligatory inclusion of Marxism-Leninism in the curriculum at all levels of public education soon came to an end; and on 13 January the decision not to remove the teaching of Marxism-Leninism from the required curriculum of public schools and private schools was made (*Barricada*, 13 January). The same day the FSLN was successful in provoking the split of the leadership of the PSN, inducing the leader of the old-guard orthodox Marxist-Leninist line, Domingo Sánchez Salgado, to break from his party's strategy of opposition and endorse the FSLN's hard line. Domingo Sánchez, cofounder of the first pro-Moscow communist party of Nicaragua, criticized his party for establishing alliances with the "class enemies" of the democratic opposition (*Barricada*, 13 January). The FSLN invited Sánchez and Clemente Guido, the third and second vice-presidents of the National Assembly, to be members of the official delegation led by Carlos Nuñez Téllez to visit East Germany and express President Ortega's personal thanks to Erich Honecker for the solidarity he had demonstrated toward his regime during the "years of war" (*Barricada*, 8 March).

However, the highpoint of President Ortega's success was the official party-to-party visit that the general secretary of the Communist Party of Czechoslovakia, Miloš Jakeš, made to Nicaragua, giving Ortega the opportunity to host Jakeš in one of the latter's last foreign trips. Ortega bestowed on Jakeš the order of Augusto César Sandino in its highest grade, that of the "Battle of San Jacinto." The formal introduction of the FSLN into the world of official Marxism-Leninism was sealed with Miloš Jakeš's recognition and fraternal endorsement of it. (*Barricada*, 8 January.) *Pravda* also recognized the leadership role of Daniel Ortega Saavedra, and P. Bogolomov portrayed the Nicaraguan president as a man who does not differentiate himself from the common people of Nicaragua (*Barricada*, 11 January).

The FSLN extended its ideological indoctrination and political training to all levels of the Sandinista Popular Army (Ejército Popular Sandinista; EPS) by developing sections of the Sandinista Youth–19 of July organization throughout that institution. Colonel Hugo Torrez, at the celebration of the first conference of the Sandinista Youth for pilots, antiaircraft gunners, and radar operators of the Sandinista Air Force (FAS-DAA), stated: "With this event, we conclude a whole process of valuable work developed by the Sandinista Youth Organization inside the army during the last year and the first few months of 1989." (*Barricada*, 26 February.) Oscar Balladares was designated as the coordinator of the Sandinista Youth–19 of July Organization within the Sandinista Popular Army.

After the meeting of Central American presidents at Tesoro Beach, El Salvador, in early February, at which President Ortega promised to hold free elections in Nicaragua, the FSLN initiated significant changes in the party structure. The Sandinista Assembly held a general meeting on 18 February in which it supported the decision to hold elections in 1990 (*Barricada*, 18 February). The next day Miguel D'Escoto, minister of foreign relations, explained in *Barricada* that the elections would mean a third war for the FSLN; the first war ended with the overthrow of Somoza; the second war was the struggle against the contras; and the third and final war would be for the ultimate consolidation and legitimation of the FSLN's regime and would consist of the electoral campaign. D'Escoto identified the stakes that the FSLN was playing for in the elections: the credibility they were seeking to gain

from their compliance with the political accords, and the international recognition that it could produce.

However, the endorsement of the elections did not mean that the FSLN was willing to renounce the policy of class war that had justified its monopoly of power; Henry Ruíz Hernández, of the National Directorate of the FSLN, stated: "Nobody that feels or calls himself a revolutionary can fall into the illusion that the changes that have been announced imply that class struggle has disappeared" (*Barricada*, 24 February). According to TASS, in the March meeting in Moscow, when commenting on the new political line of the FSLN, Shevardnadze told Henry Ruíz Hernández that "The line followed by the Nicaraguan government is an example and a considerable contribution to the just political settlement of the Central American problem" (cited by *Barricada*, 27 March).

Following its new political line and putting its electoral policy to the test, the FSLN was able to win the university student government elections in which the candidates of the Sandinista Youth Organization ran unopposed at the university in Léon, gaining the presidency and vice-presidency of the National Student Union of Nicaragua (Unión Nacional de Estudiantes de Nicaragua; UNEN) for Mauricio Alvarez Arguello and Gerardo Gallo (*Barricada*, 19 March).

The electoral process forced the FSLN to reassign some of its cadres and to create new party structures. The departments and secretariats of agitation and propaganda, organization, political education, and communications, among others, were suspended. The new electoral party structures were: the Commission of Investigation and Training, led by Vanessa Castro Cardenal; the Commission on Publicity, led by Ivan García; the Commission on Informational Policy, led by Dionisio Marenco; the Commission on Foreign Image Management, led by Alejandro Bendana; and the Institutional Commission, under the direct supervision of Bayardo Arce Castaño, which was responsible for monitoring the Supreme Electoral Council and the regional, district, and local electoral-action committees of the FSLN (*La Prensa*, 1 November).

The final selection of Sandinista candidates and local party electoral structures was decided by the Commission of Electoral Organization of the FSLN, led by Bayardo Arce Castaño, in September. The process was scheduled to include the meeting of the regional FSLN secretariats on 23

September, the final approval of candidates, which took place on 24 September during the special session of the Sandinista Assembly and concluded with the public presentation of candidates on 25 September in the meeting of the Great Convention of the People (La Gran Convención del Pueblo) that was held in Managua. (*Barricada*, 6 September.) The supporters of Tomás Borge Martínez at the newspaper *El Nuevo Diario* launched a campaign promoting Borge as candidate for the vice-presidency, in opposition to the chosen candidate, Sergio Ramírez Mercado, but were not able to alter the decision of the FSLN leadership (*El Nuevo Diario*, 21 September).

The FSLN devoted the National School for Cadres, which took place on 26 August, to discussion of the problems that the electoral process had brought on the party. In the opinion of Bayardo Arce Castaño, the inflation could lead to the defeat of the FSLN in the coming elections (*La Prensa*, 31 October). In fact, the labor strikes and the political mobilization that developed in the country seemed to confirm the FSLN's worst fears and induced its government to restrict and control the political activity of the opposition through intimidation and the abuse of power. In his document on the plan for the election campaign, Carlos Carrión Cruz, FSLN coordinator for Region Three and the mayor of the city of Managua, identified the main source of concern for his party as the competition that could come from leftist parties with credibility among the members of their support base, and which are not integrated into the United Nicaraguan Opposition (UNO) coalition, as in the case of the candidacy of Moises Hassan.

According to Carlos Carrión Cruz, the FSLN feared losing votes to Hassan, the presidential candidate of the Movement of Revolutionary Unity (Movimiento de Unidad Revolucionaria; MUR). Hassan's candidacy is not judged to pose any threat to UNO, but is capable of competing for votes with the FSLN (*La Prensa*, 26 October). Moises Hassan, a member of the junta that governed after the 1979 revolution and later the mayor of Managua, is a Sandinista who withdrew from the FSLN government because of its widespread corruption and antidemocratic policies (*La Prensa*, 20 July, 7 September). The MUR was established in August 1988 by a great number of former members of the FSLN, with support from the PSN and the PCN. Today the party is not part of any coalition and is led by Francisco Samper Blanco.

More interesting changes took place in the party structures and ideological outlook of the country's largest labor-based leftist organizations: the Socialist Party of Nicaragua (PSN) and the Communist Party of Nicaragua (PCN).

Luís Sánchez Sancho, leader of the PSN, which was the first party to proclaim Marxist ideals in the country, stated: "Marx was obviously mistaken in some of his predictions." Explaining his misgivings about Soviet Marxism, he added, "In practice, it makes the human person into an impotent subject confronting a powerful state machine while services and economic production are in the hands of an incompetent state bureaucracy" (*NYT*, 24 January).

Mutual cooperation between the PSN and the PCN began in 1987 with the foundation of the Permanent Congress of Workers (CPT). The congress brought together the two parties' labor-union auxiliary organizations and the other two largest democratic labor confederations: the Autonomous Nicaraguan Workers Central (CTN-A), with 25,000 members and closely associated with the Social Christian Party (PSC) of Erick Ramírez and the Popular Social Christian Party (PPSC); and the Confederation of Labor Unification (CUS), with 25,000–35,000 members and closely linked to the Social Democratic Party (PSD). This cooperation extended to the political coalitions formed in 1989.

In March, the National Democratic Alliance (Alianza Democrática Nacional; ADN) was founded. The alliance included the Nicaraguan Socialist Party (PSN), the Communist Party of Nicaragua (PCN), the Social Christian Party (PSC) of Erick Ramírez, the Popular Social Christian Party (PPSC), and the Independent Liberal Party (PLI) of Virgilio Godoy. (*Barricada*, 30 March.)

The spirit of unity among the major opposition parties, which had been demonstrated since the joint march organized by the Democratic Coordinating Board (CDN) at Nandaime in 1988, with the participation of the PSN and the PCN, continued in 1989. On 16 January, the "Ramiro Sacasa" Democratic Coordinating Board (CDN), made up of fourteen parties and civic organizations, started off the political year with a march in Managua led by Violeta Barrios de Chamorro that counted on the support of the PSN and the PCN. More than 8,000 participated in the march, which showed that the population was not intimidated by the crackdown and jail sentences with which the Sandinista authorities had responded to the Nandaime demonstration six months before (*Barricada*, 16 January). In March, the CDN, putting to the test the government's commitment to respect public liberties made in the agreement signed at Tesoro Beach, El Salvador, organized a march in the city of Léon demanding the "democratization" of Nicaragua. Under the direct leadership of Duilio Baltodano, and with the participation of all the opposition parties in Léon, the demonstration was able to draw more than 3,000 marchers (*Barricada*, 13 March). Despite the blockade of the city by the Sandinista police in order to prevent supporters from nearby communities from joining the march, the PSN, the PCN, and the rest of the opposition demonstrated their skills and political will to work in a broad democratic front.

Under the auspices of the Permanent Congress of Workers, the opposition rallied at the city of Masaya, again gathering over 8,000 marchers. The leadership of the demonstration was in the hands of the PSN, the PCN, and the other labor confederations (*Barricada*, 3 April). In August, 3,000 more marched under the banners of the CPT in Chinandega, demanding reforms of the labor laws and increase of the minimum wage (*La Prensa*, 15 August). During the electoral campaign, the CPT promoted marches in working-class neighborhoods in Managua and other cities in support of UNO and against the candidacy of Daniel Ortega Saavedra, "the candidate of hunger" (*La Prensa*, 6 October). On every occasion, the CPT had to face the harassment of Sandinista mobs that tried to provoke the marchers.

The traditional opposition, made up of the Democratic Coordinating Board (CDN) and the Superior Council of Private Enterprise (COSEP), was dominated by centrist and right-wing organizations, which were led by liberal professionals and business people. The political following of the CDN, with the exceptions of a few labor and grassroots groups, was made up of the middle-class and rural populations. The participation and leadership provided by the PSN and the PCN greatly contributed to the enlargement of the active popular support of the democratic opposition and to the mobilization of segments of the urban working class and their integration into its political structures. The recognition of their role by the rest of the parties of the opposition was reflected by the dominant positions granted to the PSN, the PCN, and the other parties affiliated with the Permanent Congress of Workers in the governing body of UNO, a coalition of thirteen political parties, founded in June (*La Prensa*, 7 June).

Of the six governing commissions of UNO, four were designated to be chaired by these parties: the International Relations Commission, by Gustavo Tablada of the PSN; the Electoral Commission, the most strategic and largest of UNO commissions, by Eli Altamirano Pérez of the PCN; the Communications Commission, by Luís Humberto Guzman of the PPSC; and the Finance Commission, by Guillermo Potoy of the PSD.

Of the five parties that formed the National Democratic Alliance, only the Social Christian Party (PSC) led by Erick Ramírez did not join in the founding of the UNO coalition. Ramírez had previously been expelled from the Democratic Coordinating Board because, according to Edmundo Castillo Ramírez of the Nicaraguan Conservative Party (PCN), Erick Ramírez was "collaborating" with the FSLN government (Managua, Radio Corporacion, 15 June; *FBIS*, 19 June). The Independent Liberal Party was chosen to chair the Negotiations Commission of UNO, led by Jaime Bonilla; and Virgilio Godoy was elected UNO's vice-presidential candidate for the 1990 elections and to preside over UNO's leadership structure as chair of its Political Commission. UNO's Political Commission (Consejo Político Nacional) was established in July and formed of the heads of each political party in the alliance (*La Prensa*, 28 July).

It is indisputable that political hegemony within UNO is in the hands of the coalition's center-left component: the National Democratic Alliance (ADN), and not in those of the center-right component: the Democratic Coordinating Board (CDN). Mauricio Diaz abandoned UNO in September and joined the PSC of Erick Ramírez in order to run on a separate list in the coming elections (*La Prensa*, 30 September). Erick Ramírez, Mauricio Diaz, and Edén Pastora (Commander Zero) joined together in the FSLN-inspired electoral alliance called the "Centrist Block," the purpose of which was to develop a "constructive opposition," according to FSLN sources (*La Prensa*, 15 August). The hold of the PSN and the PCN on the Permanent Congress of Workers and their influence within UNO increased significantly after the split of the PPSC and the reduction of the coalition's political center. Both the union branches and the major political leadership of the PPSC remained with UNO; however, the party was weakened by the division. Luís Humberto Guzmán and José Gabriel Moya continued as UNO's National Assembly candidates for Managua in fifth position, and Luisa del Carmen Larios and Antonio Jarquin (general secretary of the CTN-A) in the second position for Boaco and Chontales. The

PPSC presented candidates for UNO in the electoral districts of Ocotal, Masaya, Chinandega, and Estelí (*La Prensa*, 29 September).

The first political party of Nicaragua to present Violeta Barrios de Chamorro as its presidential candidate for the 1990 elections was the PSN, publishing its resolution in *La Prensa* on 1 July. Two days later, during the 45th Anniversary Party Congress, the plenum confirmed the decision of the political commission. During the process of candidate selection within UNO, both the PSN and the PCN did not waver in their support for Chamorro, nor did the other parties linked to the Permanent Congress of Workers. The Congress announced its public endorsement of Chamorro, and of all UNO candidates as soon as they were selected (*La Prensa*, 5 September). Most of the right-wing and centrist political parties that were members of the Democratic Coordinating Board sponsored the presidential candidacy of Enrique Bolaños Gueyer of the Superior Council of Private Enterprise (COSEP), who lost the nomination.

The list of UNO's candidates for the National Assembly included thirteen labor leaders of the PSN, the PCN, and the other parties related to the union confederations which are members of the Permanent Congress of Workers. These candidates were: Antonio Jarquin, Roberto Moreno, Emilio Marquez, Alejandro Solorzano, Nilo Zalazar, Francisco Caceres, Leopoldo Guevara, Dagoberto Caceres, Alvin Guthrie, Santos Tijerino, David Williams, Daniel Tate, and Nicolas Morales (*La Prensa*, 6 November). In order to balance the political representation of the other parties in the UNO alliance, the Electoral Campaign Committee was enlarged so that it had a majority of representatives of the mainstream centrist organizations. This alteration of the committee became a source of friction between the two wings of the coalition all through the campaign (*La Prensa*, 17 October).

The 1990 Election Campaign. The convening of a national dialogue with "all domestic political opposition groups" was the very first commitment the Nicaraguan government made in signing the Esquipulas Accords. The FSLN government allowed one-to-one consultations between certain leaders of the opposition and FSLN officials. The consultations were held before the National Assembly issued its final reforms of the electoral law on 20 April (*Barricada*, 20 April). The opposition, which must be recognized now to mean principally the 13 parties participating in UNO, continued to demand the revision of the electoral provisions enacted by the government. President Ortega agreed on 4 August to meet and discuss all grievances with all the parties at the Olof Palme Convention Center in Managua. Of the nineteen amendments that UNO presented, the government refused to accept the three most vital ones needed to ensure a fair and free election and campaign. First, it did not accept the creation of a voter's identification card that could prevent multiple voting and fraud. Second, it did not accept the creation of an independent private television station that would operate free of FSLN control during the electoral campaign. Third, it did not accept that the Nicaraguan citizens forced into exile could vote in the February 1990 elections (*La Prensa*, 4 August).

The demand that the Supreme Electoral Council be made up of a balanced number of FSLN supporters and opponents and presided over by a mutually acceptable and distinguished Nicaraguan, was not presented again by the opposition, which was discouraged from continuing to press for acceptance of this point. On 22 April, President Ortega announced at a press conference that he wanted "all the parties that are going to participate in the elections" (that is, not just the parties represented in the National Assembly) to offer him proposals for "a 'notable' person to be named as the fifth member and president of the CSE [Supreme Electoral Council], as long as he is of recognized impartiality . . ." (*Barricada*, 23 April). However, Daniel Ortega selected Dr. Mariano Fiallos Oyanguren, a former president of the National University, who had presided over the CSE since the 1984 elections, and who is a member of the FSLN. Dr. Fiallos's "impartiality" became most noticeable on 31 September, when he cosponsored a nationwide radio broadcast imposed by the Ministry of Interior on all radio stations, together with Dionisio Marenco, head of the Secretariat of Agitation and Propaganda of the FSLN, as part of the electoral campaign promoting FSLN candidates in the 1990 elections (the broadcast was announced in *La Prensa*, 30 September).

Of the other four members of the Supreme Electoral Council, the FSLN could count on the support of Dr. Leonel Arguello, president of a governmental insurance company, who was also a member of the CSE in 1984, and is a member of the FSLN. Dr. Aman Sandino, a cardiologist, is a member of the Democratic Conservative Party of Clemente Guido, second vice-president of the National Assembly and supporter of the FSLN government. Dr. Rodolfo Sandino Arguello, dean of the Law School at the government-run Central American University, is not currently active in any political party, and does not represent the opposition in the SEC. Dr. Guillermo Selva is a member of the Independent Liberal Party and was elected to the council with 45 votes from the Sandinista majority in the National Assembly; he is the only member of the CSE whom the opposition recognizes as representing its view.

However, the government assured only a selective compliance even on the demands that the government agreed to accept, as for example, point one, which stated: The President of the Republic will make effective a reprogramming of the Patriotic Military Service (the draft), so that there will be no recruitment between September 1989 and February 1990. In towns like Somoto, for example, the military authorities continued to draft into the army those opposition youths who were active in the campaign against the FSLN. On 6 October, Juan Martínez, Francisco Rodriquez Ochoa, and Mariano Gonzalez, all activists of the Christian Democratic Party (Partido Democrático de la Concordia Nacional), were notified by Lieutenant Antenor Pérez Andara that they were to present themselves to the 63-15 Battalion or be arrested by the police of the city of Condega (*La Prensa*, 6 October).

The second amendment, which was accepted by the FSLN government, transferred to the CSE jurisdiction over the application of the media law in electoral matters. To comply with the Tesoro Beach Accords of February, the Nicaraguan government enacted on 24 April a new statute to replace the patchwork of decrees that had been in force since the 1979 revolution. The new law (number 57), which is administered by a Media Directorate set up by the Ministry of Interior, is to be overseen by a National Communications Council, to be chaired by Tomás Borge Martínez, the minister of the interior, or by his designee, who in this case would be Lenin Cerna, head of the State Secret Police. According to this new law, "any broadcast that is contrary to the state, the national integrity, peace, law and order is a violation of the law." The directorate's finding of a violation and its imposition of a penalty are not appealable to a court of law; the only appeal is to the minister of the interior (*Barricada*, 25 April).

The opposition was able to obtain from the government the concession that it would be allowed to use a half hour a day of television time from Monday to Saturday. President Ortega granted the opposition access to channel 2 of the Sandinista Television System, the time to be distributed evenly

among all the parties by the CSE. However, the president of the CSE, Dr. Mariano Fiallos Oyanguren, was forced to admit on 3 November in a public letter addressed to Ivan Garcia, the director of the Sandinista Television System, that the broadcast signal of the channel 2 station is so weak that it can be received only near Managua, and that he was able to confirm that it is hardly perceptible in the rest of the country. In contrast, the other Sandinista television station, channel 8, which does not allow access to the opposition, has strong reception throughout the country (*La Prensa*, 6 November). The final decision permitted the opposition parties to have twenty minutes of news time between 6:30 p.m. and 7:00 p.m. on channel 2 until 2 December (*Barricada*, 26 August). The Soviet Union contributed significantly to enhancement of the Sandinista campaign efforts for the 1990 elections by contributing to the enlargement of the capability of the FSLN party's radio network to reach all of Nicaragua. Soviet ambassador Valery Nikolayenko appeared beside President Daniel Ortega and Oscar Benavides, director of la Voz de Nicaragua, a radio station under direct FSLN control, during the inauguration of the new broadcasting plants donated by the Soviets, which are situated in the city of Estelí (*Barricada*, 23 August).

The fourth amendment agreed upon by the FSLN government was the reform of the law granting jurisdictional functions to the Sandinista Police. In October, when the reform was completed, the results were not what the opposition had expected. The new law was judged to be unconstitutional by the opposition because it violated the right of habeas corpus. The Nicaraguan Constitution establishes that the police can hold a citizen for only 72 hours before surrendering him or her to the jurisdiction of the courts; the new law gave the police the authority to detain and interrogate a citizen for up to fifteen days without making a charge. (*La Prensa*, 11 October.) The common practice of the Sandinista Police, especially in smaller cities during the electoral campaign, was to arrest political activists of the opposition in order to intimidate them. Cases like that of the four UNO youth leaders of Masaya, Manuel Carrión, Carlos Lacayo Enriquez, Felipe Barrios Lopez, and Alberto Valverde Ruíz, who were arrested on 1 August, were repeated all over the country (*La Prensa*, 1 August).

The most important concession that Daniel Ortega Saavedra granted was the approval of a full amnesty for all political prisoners. However, the number of political prisoners and their whereabouts remained a mystery all through the year. On 15 August 1987, according to Lino Hernández Triguero, president of the independent Nicaraguan Human Rights Commission (Comisión Permanente de Derechos Humanos de Nicaragua; CPDHN), Daniel Ortega reported to Tom Harkin, U.S. senator from Iowa, that an amnesty would benefit all of the 10,000 political prisoners held in Nicaragua (*La Prensa*, 19 August). The FSLN refused to present the list of all political prisoners, in violation of the accords it had signed with the opposition (*La Prensa*, 22 August). The official list the government submitted included only 1,440 political prisoners. Ninoska Robles de Jarquin of the Nicaraguan Human Rights Commission had a list of nearly 7,000 political prisoners, supplemented by information from families that had reported relatives who had been captured by the Sandinista authorities (*La Prensa*, 23 August). The Sandinista authorities have not yet agreed among themselves on the number of political prisoners they acknowledge to have in jail. Tomás Borge Martínez, head of the Ministry of the Interior, which is responsible for administering all the prisons in the country, stated that they had in custody over 1,832 former National Guardsmen and 1,532 prisoners connected with the contras, the Nicaraguan Resistance (*Barricada*, 23 August). However, President Daniel Ortega after the Tesoro Beach summit meeting of Central American presidents, declared that his regime had less than 2,000 political prisoners. Again, when he met with Jürgen Warnke, the minister of foreign cooperation of the Federal Republic of Germany, he acknowledged that his government was holding 3,000 political prisoners (*La Prensa*, 16 August). After 15 August, after the accords with the opposition had been signed, the Independent Nicaraguan Commission for Human Rights claimed that the FSLN government had at least 6,000 political prisoners, and that the numbers continued to grow (*La Prensa*, 15 August).

The officially stated policy of the FSLN government was to assure a political climate that would encourage the members of the Nicaraguan Resistance to abandon their armed struggle and peacefully reintegrate themselves into Nicaragua's civil life. The offers of a general amnesty and political freedoms, together with respect of their human rights, were seen to be part of the commitments that President Ortega made to the other Central American presidents, so there could be free elections in Nicaragua in 1990 and a free electoral campaign in 1989. Not only was the offer of a general amnesty

compromised by the lack of an independent verification of the true number of political prisoners in the country, but the gross violation of human rights—torture and executions of prisoners and other atrocities committed by the Sandinista security forces—revealed the continuation of the terrorist policy followed since 1979.

According to the human-rights organization Americas Watch, a number of summary executions by the Sandinista security forces of people suspected of collaboration with the Nicaraguan Resistance were confirmed. The fact that these executions continued in 1989 led Americas Watch to conclude in their April report that these violations were not isolated cases, but confirmed the impression of Americas Watch that the security forces of the government of Nicaragua were engaged in the practice of violent abuses in the Jinotega and Matagalpa regions of the country. In the opinion of Americas Watch, the fact that the government had not put an end to these practices deserved to be condemned in the most severe terms (*La Prensa*, 27 July). Americas Watch added that it had presented to the Nicaraguan government since March the following list of confirmed cases of Nicaraguan citizens executed by the government's security forces (the army [EPS], the State Security of the Ministry of Interior [DGSE], and the Sandinista Police of the city of Bluefields): Felix Pedro Herrera Carballo, Celso Socorro Herrera Carballo, Miguel Angel Ramírez Davila, Francisco Ramon Castro Gonzalez, Rodolfo Cordero Lopez, Jacinto Sevilla Duarte, Felicito Peralta, Albio Toledo, José Esteban Hernández Gutierrez, José Francisco Martínez Murillo, Carlo Oliver Huls Downs, and David Michell Mcklin (*La Prensa*, 27 July).

In October, Americas Watch concluded that torture had been practiced in the detention centers under the control of the Ministry of the Interior. It stated: "Our findings in this respect are the same as in the past: isolation and other forms of psychological pressure, such as short term food, water and sleep deprivation, have been practiced in Nicaragua as a matter of policy. These practices must be condemned. In addition, psychological torture such as verbal threats and display of weapons, including mock executions, have been frequent in the past, and higher authorities have not done enough to curb them. There have also been sporadic instances of physical torture, generally in the form of beatings." (*News From Americas Watch*, no. 12, October 1989.)

Amnesty International (*Nicaragua: The Human*

Rights Record 1986–1989) recently concluded that the executions of alleged civilian collaborators with the contras after the cease-fire agreements had been signed continued during 1989. That organization reported:

> Testimonies by family members and other information received during Amnesty International's February 1989 visit indicate that there have been dozens of new cases of apparent extrajudicial executions since the cease-fire took effect in April 1988, particularly in the central and northern provinces of Matagalpa and Jinotega. Many of the victims were allegedly detained by government soldiers at their homes and then taken away under armed guard, only for their abandoned bodies, sometimes mutilated, to be discovered by relatives or neighbors a short distance away. The victims were often relatives of people who had joined the *Contras* or had been imprisoned as alleged civilian collaborators.

Violence, abuse of power, and intimidation were not restricted to Nicaraguans allegedly affiliated with the contras. The FSLN authorities did not spare any segment of the population in 1989. Robert Beckel, who managed the presidential campaign of Walter F. Mondale in 1984, was a witness to the attack by Sandinista mobs against a rally of UNO in the city of Masatepe; one person was killed in the attack and eleven others were wounded. According to Mark A. Uhlig of the *New York Times* (12 December), the Sandinista attack of 10 December "followed more than six weeks of increased election violence that opposition leaders and witnesses have blamed on Sandinista mobs." Sandinista mobs attacked the marchers of UNO in the city of Jalapa (*La Prensa*, 30 October), and at a rally in the city of Matagalpa threw stones at the peaceful demonstrators (*La Prensa*, 4 November).

Private citizens have also suffered from Sandinista violence. The following events occurred in a period of 24 hours: Juan Mairena Salgado and his brother Porfirio were reported to have been killed by Sandinista military when they refused to be drafted (*La Prensa*, 14 August); the Sandinista army (EPS) killed the whole family of Mrs. Santos Matus Morales, as its members were celebrating the fifteenth birthday of her daughter Arracely (*La Prensa*, 15 August); six passengers were killed in a bus at Pueblo Nuevo by a member of the Sandinista army (EPS); and the army patrol sent out to find the killer stole 3,000,000 cordobas and raped Genara Castro as her eleven-year-old son, Donald Antonio

Castro, watched (*La Prensa*, 15 August). Even the chauffeur of General Humberto Ortega Saavedra, minister of defense, sought asylum in Costa Rica after having been tortured and imprisoned because he had received a letter from his mother who lives in the United States. Carlos Felipe Carrión Cano, 30 years of age, was placed in the "La Granga" prison on 6 April and kept isolated for over eight days. He escaped on 28 April and stayed in hiding until he was able to reach Costa Rica on 14 July, according to Carlos Jimenez Guíllen, the spokesperson of the public-security office of the Costa Rican government (*La Prensa*, 14 July). According to the same source, Carrión Cano was the fourth Nicaraguan military officer to desert in fifteen days. The others were Major Douglas Zuniga Zalazar, his brother Lieutenant Walter Zuniga Zalazar, both on 23 June, and Dorian Otoniel Alvarado Pérez, on 26 June (*La Prensa*, 14 July).

Leaders of the Oppositionist Youth Organization were threatened with assassination, according to Manuel Carrión Garcia, secretary of the organization. Other young UNO members in the city of Masaya alleged that death squads were emerging in Nicaragua: the Commandos for Popular Executions (Comandos de Ajusticiamiento Popular; CAP); and have declared Alejandro Cruz Téllez, a local Sandinista activist, responsible for the death threats received (*La Prensa*, 17 August). On 26 July, during the celebration of the tenth anniversary of the foundation of the Sandinista Workers' Central (CST), Victor Tirado Lopez of the FSLN National Directorate threatened that the labor leaders of the Permanent Congress of Workers (CPT) would all end up committing suicide; Lucio Mendez, general secretary of the CST, declared that the FSLN did not lack the energy to eliminate all the CPT's leadership from the map (*Barricada*, 27 July). The FSLN had publicly threatened the lives of Alvin Guthrie of the CUS; Antonio Jarquin of the CTN-A; Roberto Moreno of the CAUS; and Alejandro Solorzano of the CGT-I (*La Prensa*, 27 July).

According to Jaime Wheelock Román of the FSLN directorate, even diplomats in Nicaragua are under close surveillance by the Sandinista secret police. Minister Wheelock confirmed to President Oscar Arias of Costa Rica that his government had listened to the telephone lines of Costa Rica's embassy in Managua and carried out a 24-hour surveillance of the contacts and movements of Costa Rican ambassador Farid Ayales (*La Prensa*, 17 October).

Threats in Nicaragua are taken seriously. When

President Ortega threatened that he could do away with the mixed economy, and that he could confiscate the lands of all the private producers, if necessary, his words had the weight of previous deeds (*La Prensa*, 24 July). Three days before, Jaime Wheelock Román, the Sandinista minister of agriculture, had confiscated the farms of three leaders of the national business and professional association on the grounds that they had expressed their opposition to a government policy. The official FSLN newspaper reported that the three had "assumed an attitude of open confrontation toward the process of economic reorganization the government has put into effect" (*Barricada*, 21 July). Concerns over the sanctions the government might take against those who exercised their freedom of expression moved the opposition to demand from President Ortega assurances that politically motivated expropriations would end. In the accords of 4 August, the FSLN acceded to that demand and reaffirmed in article 9 of the agreement with the opposition that the different forms of property guaranteed by the Constitution of Nicaragua would be respected (*La Prensa*, 4 August).

Another of the major concessions the opposition achieved was the agreement with President Ortega that whoever won the February 1990 elections would be able to take over the executive office of the government after three months. Until the accords of 4 August, the date set by the National Assembly for the effective transmission of power to the winners of the 1990 elections was for a year later, in 1991 (*La Prensa*, 2 August). However, the real issue, according to President Ortega was not the date of the transferral of power, but rather what degree of power would be transferred to the opposition, if it won the coming election. President Ortega declared that if the Sandinistas lost the election they would only turn over to the opposition a "quota of power," but never all the power. (*La Prensa*, 25 July.) According to Daniel Ortega, in case of victory by the opposition, the FSLN would not release all power, but only just enough so that the new government could run the executive branch of the government (*La Prensa*, 26 July). As the electoral campaign unfolded, the FSLN began to reconsider even sharing "quotas of power" with the opposition and threatened to call off the elections altogether. When President Ortega reincited war with the contras in November, he also warned that the entire electoral process could be canceled. (*La Prensa*, 1 November.)

According to Luís Sánchez Sancho of the PSN,

and a member of the National Assembly, Daniel Ortega's notion that if the opposition won the election, he would surrender to them only a share of power is a feudal understanding of power and reflected the belief "that political power won is a conqueror's patrimony"; in addition, it was "an attempt to make a Stalinist doctrinal interpretation of the nature of political power." For Sánchez, the ruling FSLN party's position was reactionary and Stalinist; he stated:

> According to Stalinism, political power is an expression of the resolve of the ruling class, not the entire population...Stalinism does not make provisions for the distribution, independence, and democratic balance of state powers. Stalinists think power is indivisible and must be controlled by the vanguard of the ruling class. According to Stalinism, state power does not exist, only state organs that act according to the instructions of the ruling class vanguard. According to this anachronistic Sandinist and Stalinist scheme, the opposition could rule the executive and legislative branches, but would never achieve power, even if the majority of the people vote for the opposition... Yet the Sandinistas are trying to impose totalitarianism on us, presenting it as a revolutionary novelty... (Managua, Radio Católica, 27 July; *FBIS*, 28 July.)

The Military Situation. President Ortega renewed the war with the contras (the Nicaraguan Resistance) officially on 1 November by not extending the cease-fire agreement in effect since March 1988 (*La Prensa*, 1 November). The decision to continue the war publicly was interpreted as a sign that the FSLN had serious fears that the coming elections were not going to show the population's support of its candidates. The official FSLN newspaper *Barricada*, four days before Ortega's announcement, published a poll showing that only 36.5 percent of the voters supported the FSLN, and that 41.8 percent were undecided (27 October). However, *La Prensa*, the day before President Ortega's declaration of war, published the results of the CID-Gallup poll, in which the FSLN obtained the preference of only 32 percent of the voters, the opposition alliance UNO garnered 36 percent, and only 32 percent of the voters were undecided (31 October). The pro-FSLN poll found only 2 percent support for other political parties outside of the UNO alliance, a recognition that the true confrontation was between the FSLN and UNO. When the candidates were directly identified, Violeta Barrios de Chamorro, the UNO candidate, obtained 42.8 percent of the preference and Daniel Ortega Saavedra, of the FSLN, scored only 21.3 percent (*La Prensa*, 7 November). The two-to-one lead of the opposition candidate Chamorro over Ortega was steady throughout the entire electoral campaign. In July, the poll by *La Prensa* and *New Herald* of Miami also gave her a lead: 45.7 percent to 26.1 percent for Ortega (*La Prensa*, 25 July).

To be understood, Sandinista military strategy has to be closely correlated with the FSLN's domestic and international political strategy in 1989. The FSLN's regional objectives were defined as "their militant engagement with the victory of the FMLN guerrillas in El Salvador" and their "endorsement of the cause of Manuel Antonio Noriega of Panama" (*La Prensa*, 1 November). The widely reported secret shipments of arms to Noriega in October and November (*NYT*, 27 December), and the military support of the Ortega government for the insurrection launched by the FMLN, which was denounced by President Cristiani (UPI, 31 October), was followed by the FSLN's own war initiative against the contras. The diplomatic and political pressures to demobilize the contras were directly linked by the FSLN to public efforts to trade an end to support for the contras for free elections. Both objectives were in accord with official Soviet policy, as stated by President Gorbachev in Havana in April: "The Contras should demobilize before the 1990 February election, and the FMLN troops should not be demobilized, nor their case linked to the Contra issue, because that would contradict the spirit of the Central American presidents' accords" (*Barricada*, 5 April).

However, the contras rejected the Sandinista invitations to surrender and did not turn in their weapons in 1989. On the contrary, they assured that "they will hold out until after the elections, and don't want to give Ortega any reason to crack down" (*West Watch*, December). In August, Israel Galeano Cornejo (nom de guerre: Commander Franklin), rejected General Humberto Ortega Saavedra's proposal that he accept the amnesty offered by the government and challenged Ortega to meet him on the battlefields of Chontales (a department of south central Nicaragua) if the elections were fraudulent (*La Prensa*, 12 August). Franklin was elected to command the resistance by his fellow commanders in September, after Enrique Bermudez relinquished actual power (*West Watch*, December). Commander Quiche (a nom de guerre) declined to head the general staff of the Resistance's army in March

(*Barricada*, 1 April). José Lara (nom de guerre: Commander Ganso) is the general commander of the southern front of the Resistance's army (*La Prensa*, 7 November).

The Sandinista military and secret police were accused of being responsible for a series of assassinations of contra officials in 1989. José de Jesus Peña, head of security of the Nicaraguan Embassy in Honduras, was accused by Luís Fernando Ordonez Reyes of organizing and planning the killing of Dr. Manuel Adan Rugama (Aureliano), the Nicaraguan Resistance's medical commander, on 7 January in Tegucigalpa, Honduras. The other participants: José Bautista Nuñez Amador, Rigoberto Matute, and Cano Ortega, all in the custody of the Honduran authorities, confirmed the allegations (*Barricada*, 9 February). The Sandinistas were also charged with the killing of a bodyguard of contra leader Fabio Gadea Mantilla during an attack on his home in San José, Costa Rica; the assassination of Gustavo Sánchez Herdocia (El Licenciado), cousin of Aristidez Sánchez, a member of the directorate of the Nicaraguan Resistance; and also the alleged murder attempt against his brother Enrique (Cuco) Sánchez in Miami (*Barricada*, 25 August).

The Sandinistas' public military policy was to give the impression that they had reduced their military budget and weapons imports. General Humberto Ortega declared that in 1989 the military budgets of the Ministry of Defense and the Ministry of Interior would decrease by 29 and 40 percent; however, sources in the National Assembly estimated that military spending would represent 52 percent of the total government budget for 1989 (*La Prensa*, 3 January). The Sandinista government, together with the Soviet government, stated that weapons imports had been suspended in early 1989; at the end of the year, this claim was still widely accepted by the media: "Since the beginning of 1989, Soviet leaders have declared a suspension of all direct arms shipments to Nicaragua, and American intelligence officials estimated that total military aid received by the Sandinista Government has fallen by perhaps 20 percent" (*NYT*, 27 December).

In late summer, the news media in Nicaragua published a commentary on a broadcast by Radio Moscow which stated that President Gorbachev had sent a letter to President Bush in May indicating that all military aid to Nicaragua had been suspended since December 1988 (*La Prensa*, 11 August). The White House said in May that Gorbachev had promised to halt Soviet weapons shipments to Nicaragua, but that there was evidence that arms were still going to the Sandinistas (*NYT*, 17 May). At the August summit of Central American presidents in Tela, Honduras, Alexander Lezkin, vice-president of Novosti, a Soviet press agency, confirmed in an interview that all Soviet military aid to Nicaragua had ceased (*La Prensa*, 8 August). President Arias of Costa Rica demanded in a letter of 7 March to President Gorbachev that military shipments to Nicaragua be suspended. President Arias received his response through the visit to Costa Rica of Aleksandr Mokanu, deputy chairman of the Soviet parliament, who assured him of Gorbachev's suspension of arms shipments to Nicaragua, as part of the Soviet contribution to the peaceful solution of the problems of Central America (*La Prensa*, 11 August).

However, the suspension of Soviet weapons exports to Nicaragua was not yet a reality. In fact, on 10 August, Radio Moscow was quoted as announcing that Bernard Aronson, assistant secretary of state for inter-American affairs, was meeting in London with his Soviet counterpart, Yuri Pavlov, who was responsible for Latin America, to address precisely the "burning issue of Soviet military aid to Nicaragua" (*La Prensa*, 11 August). In September, Secretary of State James Baker was still insisting to Soviet foreign minister Eduard Shevardnadze at their meeting in Wyoming that Soviet military assistance to Nicaragua be curbed (*La Prensa*, 20 September). It was not until 4 October, during Shevardnadze's trip to Managua, that an official accord was signed with the Sandinista government by which military aid was "temporarily suspended," and only light weapons and ammunition would continue to be delivered (*La Prensa*, 5 October). The day before the Baker-Shevardnadze meeting, President Daniel Ortega, together with the Soviet ambassador to Nicaragua, Valery Nikolayenko, admitted at a public news conference the reception of new Soviet heavy weapons consisting of four M-24 gunship helicopters and three torpedo-armed speed boats for the Sandinista air force and the Sandinista navy (*La Prensa*, 21 September).

According to the United States Defense Department's third quarter report, in the first nine months of 1989, 55 shipments carrying an estimated 14,000 metric tons of arms, with a value of 410 million dollars, had been received in Nicaragua. In all of 1988, there had been only 68 shipments, with a total cargo of 19,000 estimated metric tons of weapons at a value of $515 million; at the rate reported by the Defense Department, the total arms

shipments for 1989 would exceed those of 1988. The Pentagon report concluded that Nicaragua had received a total of 152,500 metric tons of weapons valued at $3,160 million; that Cuba had doubled its shipments of small arms and ammunition to Nicaragua; that North Korea had sent patrol boats; and that Nicaragua's other suppliers were Bulgaria, Czechoslovakia, Vietnam, East Germany, Poland, Romania, the People's Republic of China, Libya, and the PLO. (UPI, 17 October; *La Prensa*, 17 October.)

After the Central American presidents' summit meeting at Tela, White House spokesman Marlin Fitzwater said that the United States would support demobilization of the contras (*WP*, 9 August). On 12 September, a U.S. delegation including senior State Department officials and members of Congress met with President Daniel Ortega Saavedra. According to State Department official Janet G. Mullins, the purpose of the meeting was to indicate that relations between the United States and Nicaragua could improve if Managua held free and fair elections (*NYT*, 13 September). The new policy toward the Nicaraguan Resistance was signaled by James Baker's interview with Robert Pear of *The New York Times* in March, in which the secretary of state declared that the contras were abusing their prisoners (*NYT*, 23 March); that the contra headquarters in Miami should be dismantled, their leadership pressured to return to Nicaragua, and the political and diplomatic support for the Resistance canceled. The Sandinista army remained 70,000 strong, and, according to *Time Magazine*, it "exists to defend the ruling party, not the country" (*Time*, 24 July). The new U.S. policy in effect reduced by two-thirds the cost to the USSR of subsidizing Nicaragua. Eduard Shevardnadze stated in October at a news conference in Managua that the Soviet Union had delivered $1,690 million to Nicaragua in "civil aid" during the preceding ten years (*La Prensa*, 5 October). The Pentagon's October report estimated that the value of arms delivered to Nicaragua in the past ten years represented $3,160 million, of which the greatest part had come from the Soviet Union; both "civil" and military aid would reach close to $5 billion. In the future, without a military threat from the contras, the military component of Soviet aid could be saved; that reduction presented a formidable incentive for continued Soviet presence, because of the lower cost incurred. After the invasion of Panama by the United States, the Sandinistas were not very likely to reduce their army or halt the import of weapons from the Soviet Union. According to Danilo Aguirre, an editor of the pro-government daily newspaper *El Nuevo Diario* and a Sandinista member of the National Assembly, "Nicaragua has justified to the world the reasons for its defense," adding, "With what moral standing can the United States now ask the Soviet Union to stop sending arms to Nicaragua" (*NYT*, 27 December). However, the overgrown military continued to have devastating effects on the Nicaraguan economy long before the new-found justifications were available.

The Economic Situation. In the year of the tenth anniversary of the revolution, the Sandinista government witnessed the drop of the nation's per capita income to the level of 1920, around $300 a year, placing Nicaragua below Haiti as the poorest country in the hemisphere (*Latinamerica Press*, 20 July; *Time*, 24 July). The government's economic policy was a repeat of the preceding year's and consisted of a continual reduction of imports, further eliminations of subsidies to consumption, added devaluations of the national currency, and increase of domestic prices, but without a significant reduction in public spending. The result was an extension of the state of hyperinflation, with the additional hardship suffered by the population because of the lack of price controls and the overpricing of fuel, which has been thought to finance the continued military expenses. The worsening of the economy in 1989 was affected by the lack of reduction in military spending; the loss, because of the drought, of the first harvest of food crops; the reduction of external credits; and increased government spending due to the electoral campaign (*La Prensa*, 22 July). The exchange rate of the córdoba fell from 4000 to one U.S. dollar at the start of the year to 26,400 to one U.S. dollar by the end of 1989. In April, the price of gasoline was 12,300 córdobas a gallon (*Barricada*, 24 April); by November it had risen to 48,100 córdobas a gallon (*La Prensa*, 4 November).

According to Alejandro Martínez Cuenca, minister of planning and budget, by November the accumulated inflation rate for the year was 959 percent (*La Prensa*, 6 November). According to Francisco Mayorga Balladares, a graduate of Yale University and professor of economics at INCAE in Managua, the "devaluation was a tactic to reduce private purchasing power, notably the purchasing power of coffee growers, who had just been paid in local currency for their last year's crop" (*NYT*, 6 July). The government pleaded this year with

business leaders to resume production, especially of agro-export crops. The devaluation of 11 June, and the expropriation on 21 June of three large coffee growers by Minister of Agrarian Reform Jaime Wheelock Román, ended what headway the government had made with the private sector.

Exports were hard hit. Coffee, cotton, meat, and bananas decreased by 40 percent; manufactured goods for Central American markets were down 84 percent. Imports were four times greater than exports. Last year's $579 million foreign-trade deficit, largely financed by loans from the Soviet bloc, represented one-third of the total national income (*NYT*, 6 July). According to Alejandro Martínez Cuenca, planning and budget minister, the salaries paid by the government only permitted the purchasing of 70 percent of the basic foods needed by the state workers and only 40 percent of their total basic needs (*Barricada*, 30 August). The cost-of-living increases affected large numbers of wage earners in both the public and private sectors. The government had to face growing unrest among public employees, scattered walkouts by teachers, many of whom earn less than $20 a month, and a mass protest by taxi drivers, who were upset over the doubling of gas prices in June. The Sandinista Police used tear gas on the crowd of protesting cab drivers (*Latinamerica Press*, 20 July).

The greatest effect of the economic disaster has been the massive exodus of Nicaraguans from their country. According to Alejandro Martínez Cuenca, 155,000 citizens emigrated since 1979 (*Barricada*, 27 March). However, the real number of Nicaraguans in exile was not acknowledged by the government. The FSLN's daily newspaper, *Barricada*, was willing to admit at the beginning of 1989 that 100,000 Nicaraguans were residing in Miami alone (*Barricada*, 17 January). Larger concentrations of Nicaraguans could be found within the United States in Los Angeles and San Francisco. Other sources estimated the number of Nicaraguans in exile to be 250,000 (*Time*, 24 July). The Honduran government's National Refugee Commission (CONARE) placed the number of Nicaraguans in Honduras at 23,498 refugees in four camps, with 220,000 more Nicaraguans spread about the country (Panama City, ACAN, 16 August; *FBIS*, 17 August). Approximately the same number of Nicaraguans was also in exile in Costa Rica. Large numbers of Nicaraguan refugees were also living in Guatemala, Mexico, and Panama. Two out of every ten Nicaraguans had been forced into exile, and three out of every ten into unemployment, according to other estimates (*LAT*, 25 March).

The Nicaraguan population, which has had a steady population growth rate of 3.3 percent per year, reached an estimated 3,384,000 people in 1989, according to an immigration official of the Sandinista government, First Lieutenant Efrain Delgado (*Barricada*, 27 March). A country that, according to Ajax Delgado, general coordinator of the Sandinista Youth Organization–19 of July, has a population 50 percent of which is under fifteen years of age (*Barricada*, 27 March), and in which students number 1,000,000 (*Barricada*, 3 January) could not have a total voting-age population of more than 1,692,000 people (Nicaraguans can begin voting at age 16). However, the official number of registered voters certified by the Supreme Electoral Council of the Sandinista government was 1,691,974 as of 22 October, and it was projected that the total would reach 1,730,000 eligible voters by the end of the election campaign (*La Prensa*, 23 October). The only way Nicaragua could have the official Sandinista figure of 1,691,974 registered voters as a true number of eligible voters for the 1990 elections would be that 100 percent of all eligible voters had registered, and that not one single Nicaraguan had been forced to leave the country since 1979.

In 1989, the Soviet Union added to its list of "civil aid" items food for the Nicaraguan government. After the loss of $800 million caused by the preceding year's Hurricane Joan, the drought caused additional shortfalls of 31 percent of corn production, 50 percent of beans, 53 percent of rice, and 71 percent of sorghum produced for human consumption (*NYT*, 15 August). Valery Nikolayenko, ambassador of the Soviet Union to Nicaragua, declared in an interview to the FSLN's daily newspaper that the 35,000 tons of rice and 35,000 tons of wheat donated by the USSR to Nicaragua in 1988 would be replicated in 1989. Also, the Soviet aid package would include, as in the previous year, close to $400 million in long-term credits, $50 million in donations, and $90 million for the construction of economic infrastructure and investment. He added that the Soviet Union was the principal supplier of petroleum, raw materials, machinery, and food to Nicaragua (*Barricada*, 1 April).

Alexander Chujorv, Soviet commercial representative in Nicaragua, later confirmed that in 1989 the Soviet Union continued to supply Nicaragua with oil, rice, and wheat, and had expanded its cooperation into new fields, such as joint ventures. Chujorv stated that the Soviet Union was interested in developing the analysis of Nicaragua's mining resources and programs for the fishing industry, joint investment in the textile industry. . .and the making of a detailed topographic map of Nicaragua, and in continuing the training programs for technicians in all fields. As an example of the joint ventures he had in mind, Chujorv mentioned the formation of BANANIC, the banana export and production company, which is an enterprise jointly owned by the Soviet and Nicaraguan governments that emerged from the merger of the Soviet AGROLIT and the Nicaraguan MIDINRA banana company. Chujorv indicated that similar joint ventures would be explored in the mining, fishing, and textile industries (*Barricada*, 28 August).

Nicaragua's reliance on other Soviet bloc countries continued to increase in 1989. As a result of a visit by Miloš Jakeš, general secretary of the Communist Party of Czechoslovakia, to Nicaragua, Henry Ruíz, minister of external cooperation, stated that the relations between the two parties and countries "had reached a new height" (*Barricada*, 20 March). The total amount of Czechoslovakian aid grew to $159 million; the aid included machinery, raw material for the small-industry sector, energy production, and the textile industry. Emilio Rappaccioli, minister of energy, confirmed that in 1989 Czechoslovakia had delivered 240,000 tons of oil, 60,000 tons on very favorable terms—an equivalent of 8 percent of the nation's needs—and would receive the same amount in 1990 (*Barricada*, 20 March). Joint investments were also studied with the first vice-minister of foreign trade of Czechoslovakia, Ladislav Vodrazka, who presides over the Nicaraguan-Czechoslovakian Mixed Commission on Trade, during his visit to Nicaragua. According to Vodrazka, joint investments in the textiles and footwear industries producing for export were discussed (*Barricada*, 21 March).

James Zablah, vice-minister of foreign trade, signed the renewal of the Nicaraguan-Cuban Trade Agreement in August with his Cuban counterpart Alberto Betancourt for $26 million. According to Zablah, the trade agreement was very favorable to Nicaragua because "it permits us to sell in Cuba two dollars for every one dollar we import" (*Barricada*, 25 August). However, Zablah was forced to admit that the gain was not equivalent to the loss of trade Nicaragua had incurred because of the embargo that the Bush administration was continuing to impose on that country. According to Zablah, speaking in November, the total loss to Nicaragua due to the trade embargo in force since May 1985, had reached a total of $1,092 million (*Barricada*, 6 November).

According to *Latinamerica Press*, President Ortega came back from his tour of eleven European nations in May with $50 million in hard cash— enough to prevent a sharp decline in Nicaragua's GNP, but far short of what was needed to jump-start the country's moribund economy (*Latinamerica Press*, 20 July). During 1989, the Nicaraguan government's credit from traditional European sources dried up, and the country grew increasingly dependent on Soviet bloc governments that were not likely to continue in power. The only hope the Sandinistas had of reviving their crippled economy was to meet the democratic demands of their opposition, fulfill their regional agreements on democratization, obtain the suspension of the U.S. embargo, and obtain renewal of the credit that the Western democracies had withdrawn.

International Affairs. When Vice-President Quayle stated that there existed a "Havana-Managua-Panama axis," and that it was a threat to democracy and peace in Central America (remarks made on 19 July, on the tenth anniversary of the Sandinista Revolution), he asserted: "This axis is held together by more than just hatred and fear of democracy. Both Noriega and senior officials of the Castro regime have been deeply involved in narcotics trafficking." However, the Sandinistas were not directly implicated in the narcotics side of the axis by the vice-president, even though the armed forces of Colombia had discovered that since 19 July 1988 one and a half tons of cocaine processed in a plant operated by the Colombian Armed Revolutionary Forces (FARC), a Marxist guerrilla group, have been transported daily to Cuba and Nicaragua (Cuban American Foundation, *Cuba Today*, August 1989). On 19 April 1985, former drug runner James A. Herring, Jr., testified before a Senate subcommittee that he had "worked with Cuban government officials and American fugitive Vesco to help the Nicaraguan government build a cocaine-processing laboratory near Managua." Herring said that the purpose of "our project" was to earn foreign exchange for Nicaragua's troubled economy. (*NYT*, 19 April 1985.)

In fact, the connection that Cuban Intelligence had set up in Colombia to run the narcotics operation since 1982 had been discovered by U.S. federal judiciary authorities, who indicted in Miami on 5 November 1982 Fernando Ravelo Renedo, former Cuban ambassador to Colombia and high-ranking official in the Foreign Ministry, on charges of smuggling narcotics into the United States. On 1 April, Cuban ambassador to Nicaragua Norberto Hernández Curbelo was retired, after sixteen months of duty, and was replaced by the indicted drug trafficker Fernando Ravelo Renedo (*Barricada*, 1 April). After the arrest this year of Cuban division general Arnoldo Ochoa, Ambassador Fernando Ravelo Renedo was called back to Havana from Managua on 12 June to testify in the trial, but was not indicted by the Castro regime and continued as Cuba's ambassador to the Sandinistas. The first duty of Fernando Ravelo Renedo in Nicaragua was to assist in the selection and training of the new Nicaraguan ambassador to Panama, Antenor Ferrey, a close friend of General Humberto Ortega Saavedra and a former military intelligence operative of the FSLN. Ferrey was confirmed publicly as ambassador to Panama two days after the departure of the former Cuban ambassador Norberto Hernández Cubelo (*Barricada*, 3 April). As reported by *West Watch* in March, a U.S. federal grand jury indicted a close associate of Bahamian prime minister Lynden O. Pindling and leaders of the Medellín cocaine cartel, charging them with a wide-ranging conspiracy to smuggle more than $1 billion of cocaine into the United States, and charging that Pindling and several Bahamian cabinet ministers received cash payoffs in return for their assistance. The indictment charged the defendants with using a Nicaraguan military air base, Cuban airspace, and a Bahamian island as part of a "continuing criminal enterprise." The Nicaraguan air base in question, Los Brasiles Air Force Base, just west of Managua, was the same one that figured widely in the press five years ago in photographs of drug lord Pablo Escobar and Sandinista soldiers led by a close aide of Interior Minister Tomás Borge Martínez loading cocaine onto a plane destined for the United States (*West Watch*, June). During the trial of General Ochoa in Havana in June, Interior Minister Borge was absent from Managua for over three weeks, allegedly testifying in Ochoa's case. Vice-Minister René Vivas publicly acted as interior minister, in accordance with Nicaraguan law.

The Ochoa case also had internal political effects on the relations between Cuba and Nicaragua. Two days after Ochoa's arrest, Minister of Defense Raúl Castro delivered a speech accusing Ochoa of "unbridled populism," saying "there is no place [in the Cuban military] for those who are tempted to follow

Gorbachev's vision of glasnost'" (*The Cuban Monitor*, vol. 2, no. 3, August). General Ochoa was very close to the Ortega brothers; he had directed the organization of the Sandinista army and received the highest medal of the Nicaraguan government, being declared a hero of the Nicaraguan Sandinista Revolution. Also the two brothers Patricio and Tony (Antonio) De la Guardia had been friends of all the Sandinista leadership since the 1960s, because they were the contacts of the Cuban Ministry of the Interior with the FSLN; both were tried and condemned at the show trials set up by the Castro brothers. The Sandinistas did not withdraw the military honors and decorations they had bestowed upon Ochoa and the De la Guardia brothers.

The Sandinistas did not amuse Castro when they praised *perestroika* in the accord signed with Shevardnadze on 4 October in Managua, including it as article 15 of the agreement with their principal patron. The year started with a visit to Cuba, during which President Ortega began his political year with interviews, including Georges Marchais, general secretary of the French Communist Party, and Sam Nujoma, president of SWAPO (*Barricada*, 8 January). For the Sandinistas, the year ended with a relative need to choose between the advice of the Soviets, who supply them with everything, and their loyalty to Castro, who did not show much loyalty to his friend Ochoa and could not save their common friend Noriega.

President Ortega's entry into the gala reception of the meeting of nonaligned states in Belgrade beside his mentor Colonel Moammar Khadafy was celebrated as his major international success (*Barricada*, 6 September). After the meeting, he had planned to spend a day with Nicolae Ceauşescu in Romania (*Barricada*, 7 September). Before the planned visit, Ceauşescu was sent a message that had been twice published as an open telegram in *Barricada* (23 and 27 August); it expressed the "sincere joy of the Nicaraguan people at the time of the 45th anniversary of the Romanian people's new victories on the road to Socialism and to wish him to continue harvesting new and better successes," signed with fraternal greetings by Daniel Ortega Saavedra, president of Nicaragua.

Among the new friends that the Sandinistas made in Europe, the Green Party of the Federal Republic of Germany distinguished itself by contributing $250,000 to the election-campaign fund of the FSLN (*La Prensa*, 25 October). In Eastern Europe, the FSLN was able to sign a party-to-party convention with the Communist Party of Hungary

(SWPH), before the party was officially dissolved later in the year. Carlos Nuñez Téllez signed the agreement for the FSLN, and Mátyás Szürös, president of the National Assembly, signed for the Hungarians (*Barricada*, 18 March). In Asia, the Sandinistas strengthened their ties with North Korea, receiving the visit of Lualg Doc Chan, vice-president of the youth organization and member of the organizing committee of the Thirteenth World Youth Festival held in that country from 1 to 8 July (*Barricada*, 23 April). Bayardo Arce Castaño, together with Rosario Murrillo, assured North Korean ambassador Pak Miong-Jak that the FSLN would send the best of Nicaragua's youth to the festival (*Barricada*, 22 February). Closer ties were also established with the People's Republic of China after the suppression of the student pro-democracy movement. The joint communiqué signed by the president of the People's Republic of China, Yang Shangkun, and the new Nicaraguan ambassador to that country, Roger Baldizon Ibarra, pointed out that both China and Nicaragua were "victims of North American meddling" and called for the victory of the FSLN in the 1990 Nicaraguan elections (*Barricada*, 27 August).

Finance minister William Huper was to preside over a twelve-member commission charged with promoting the idea of building a canal through Nicaragua. According to Huper, the government was in contact with a group of Japanese scientists, engineers, and businessmen interested in studying the feasibility of a second canal (*WP*, 11 February). The Japanese ambassador to Nicaragua, Yoshizo Konishi, evidently embarrassed by the published statements attributed to Professor Yasunobu Somura, a member of the technical team that visited Nicaragua in March, and who declared that the canal project had the backing of the Japanese government, denied that his government had any intentions to collaborate in a canal study (*Barricada*, 21 March).

After the invasion of Panama, partly justified by the threats to the security of the canal, new talk of a canal through Nicaragua would have introduced a new concern for the Sandinista government. The location of the country in the only segment of the Central American isthmus where a canal could be built without extensive excavation has long aroused justified concerns about foreign domination. Because Lake Nicaragua and the San Juan River would make up a large part of the waterway, the site has attracted, throughout the nation's history, the interest of foreign powers, first of Europeans, later of the

United States, and in the twentieth century that of Japan and recently the Soviet Union. The fears of domination and military interventions that aroused nationalist sentiments in the past could have turned against the Sandinistas if the population feared that the nation's future would be placed under foreign control through sale of the rights to a canal.

Antonio Ybarra-Rojas
University of Wisconsin at Platteville

Panama

Population. 2,373,053
Party. People's Party (Partido del Pueblo; PdP or PDP) or People's Party of Panama (Partido del Pueblo de Panamá; PPP).
Founded. 1930 (PdP; 1943).
Membership. 25,600 members claimed on basis of signatures presented to government electoral commission in October 1988; 500–1,000 militants (estimated)
General Secretary. Rubén Darío Souza Batista (more commonly known as Sousa)
Politburo. Includes César Agusto de Léon Espinosa, Miguel Antonio Porcella Peña, Anastacio E. Rodríguez, Cleto Manuel Souza Batista, Luther Thomas (international secretary), Felix Dixon, Darío González Pittí, Carlos Francisco Changmarín
Central Committee. 26 members
Status. Legal; regained registered status in November 1989 after submission of approximately 25,600 signatures to government electoral commission (Tribunal Electoral de Panamá; TEP) (19,252 signatures required)
Last Congress. Eighth, 24–26 January 1986
Last Election. 1984, obtained less than 3 percent of the vote, no representatives in the National Assembly 1984–89; also participated as one of eight parties of progovernment Coalition of National Liberation (COLINA) ticket in elections of 7 May 1989, which were annulled on 10 May
Auxiliary Organizations. Panama Peace Committee; Committee for the Defense of Sovereignty and Peace; People's Party Youth; National Center of Workers of Panama (Centro Nacional de Trabajadores de Panamá; CNTP); Union of Journalists of Panama; Federation of Panamanian Students (Federación Estudiantil de Panamá; FEP); National Union of Democratic Women
Publication. *Unidad* (weekly), Carlos Francisco Changmarín, director (also member of Central Committee)

As Panama entered the final month of 1989, it appeared that the year would end uneventfully—with the Noriega regime still in power, the economy continuing in its downward spiral, and the U.S. government's efforts to dislodge General Manuel Antonio Noriega at a near stand-still. But on the morning of 20 December it was evident that the approaching new year would be very different for Panama because of the U.S. invasion of Panama, "Operation Just Cause," a military action of a magnitude greater than any undertaken by U.S. forces in nearly two decades.

What brought U.S.-Panamanian relations to this critical juncture? While a full recounting of the events is beyond the scope of this essay, the following summary may serve. In June 1987, the then–chief of staff of the Panamanian Defense Forces (PDF), Colonel Roberto Diaz Herrera, broke ranks with the PDF and aired their dirty laundry in public, accusing that institution, which was led by General Noriega, of widespread corruption. In response to these allegations, the National Civic Crusade for Democracy took to the streets, demanding Noriega's resignation and the return to civilian, democratic rule. Utilizing all means at its disposal, the Noriega-dominated government of President Eric Arturo del Valle successfully repressed the riots.

In 1988, the Panamanian crisis—which at its roots was a domestic affair—exploded into a full-scale U.S.-Panamanian confrontation. In February, two South Florida grand juries handed down sealed indictments of General Noriega on narcotics-trafficking charges. In response, President del Valle attempted to remove Noriega from his position, but was himself unseated by a rump session of the National Assembly. In less than 24 hours, Minister of Education Manuel Solis Palma was appointed minister in charge of the presidency. In mid-March a coup attempt within the PDF was successfully repressed, but more important was the event's aftermath: the creation of the Strategic Military Council (CEM). Designed to curry favor with junior-level officers, the twenty-member CEM was created; it acted as an advisory body to the general. In order to further increase the pressure on Noriega and the PDF, Washington invoked the International Emergency Economic Powers Act (IEEPA) and put Panama under severe economic sanctions.

At this juncture, the regime's leftward drift as it conducted an anti-American campaign became more than evident. In April, Solis Palma, at Noriega's behest, named a new cabinet which increased from six to nine the ruling party's (Partido Revolutionario Democrático; PRD) share of a total of twelve positions. Of key importance in this leftward drift was the appointment of Orville Goodin as treasury minister, one of the leaders of the left-leaning segment of the PRD, the *tendencia*. In essence, the *tendencia* is composed of leftist and Marxist groups that dissolved themselves in 1978 in order to assist in the creation of the PRD, which was intended to act as the PDF's political party.

The year 1989 began as a hopeful one. In an effort to fend off both international and domestic criticism, as well as to relegitimize itself, the regime decided to maintain the nation's electoral calendar and moved toward presidential, legislative, and municipal elections on 7 May.

Two principal coalitions formed for these elections. Representing the domestic opposition, ADO-Civilista (Democratic Alliance of Civic Opposition; ADOC) was formed from three political parties: the National Republican Liberal Movement (MOLIRENA); the Christian Democratic party (PDC); and the Authentic Liberal Party (PLA). Its presidential ticket consisted of Guillermo Endara (presidential candidate, from the PLA), Ricardo Arias Calderón (first vice-presidential candidate, from the PDC), and Guillermo "Billy" Ford (second vice-presidential candidate, from MOLIRENA).

Representing the Noriega regime was the Coalition of National Liberation (COLINA) ticket, composed of eight political parties: the Labor Party (PALA); National Action Party (PAN); the Chiari faction of the Liberal Party (PL); the People's Party (PdP); the Revolutionary Panamenista Party (PPR); the José Young faction of the Republican Party (PR); the Democratic Revolutionary Party (PRD); and the Revolutionary Workers Party (PRT). Its presidential ticket was led by Juan Carlos Duque (presidential candidate, from the PRD and a businessman crony of Noriega), Ramón Sieiro (first vice-presidential candidate, from PALA and brother-in-law to Noriega), and Aquilino Boyd (second vice-presidential candidate and former ambassador to the United Nations and Organization of American States, as well as former foreign minis-

ter). By far, the two largest parties in COLINA were the PRD and PALA; the PdP brought an almost negligible amount of support to the ticket.

In a classic Noriega tactic, the general attempted to divide and confuse his opposition. The regime-controlled Electoral Tribunal recognized a rump faction of the Panamenista Party as the legitimate heir to Arnulfo Arias, patriarch of civilian opposition to the PDF, under the banner of the authentic Panamenista Party (PPA) led by presidential candidate Hildebrando Nicosia.

The tenor of the campaign was, to say the least, vitriolic. COLINA's slogan epitomized its platform: "COLINA Si, Colonia, No" (COLINA Yes, colony No), in an overt attempt to paint the crisis as an attempt to deny Panama her nationalism and sovereignty. The heart of ADOC's message was its opposition to the continuation of the corrupt PDF-dominated regime. With charges of electoral fraud by the government completing the setting, the stage was set for a tense election.

On the basis of the results of "quick-counts" carried out shortly after voting had been completed, ADOC was estimated to have secured a three-to-one victory over COLINA. After charges of fraud were made against the regime by election observer and former president Jimmy Carter, election-related violence by government forces ensued. On 10 May, Electoral Tribunal president Yolanda Pulice de Rodriguez, under pressure from Noriega, annulled the elections, charging that international interference had irrevocably marred the process.

In response to the violent turn of events within Panama (including the public beating of leading opposition candidates), the Bush administration requested that the OAS attempt to negotiate a transition of power in Panama—given that a change in administration was to occur on 1 September. From June to late August, a three-member OAS negotiating team met with the principal Panamanian actors, but was unable to broker a compromise. As had been the case in the previous two years, Noriega was unwilling to relinquish power, and the opposition was unwilling to enter into any power-sharing arrangements with the regime's civilian loyalists.

On 1 September, Solis Palma relinquished his ministry, and Francisco Rodriguez, who had studied with and befriended Noriega in Peru, was appointed provisional president. The National Assembly was dissolved and replaced with the *corrigimiento* system of local representation—all members of which were hand picked by Noriega.

While at this point it appeared that the rest of

1989 would be a fairly low-keyed period for Panama, a series of events altered this expected course. On 3 October, a PDF-led coup attempt, with minor American logistical support, was repulsed by Noriega. Another purging of the PDF then occurred, with attendant promotion of Noriega loyalists. Then, on 15 December, Noriega was named "Maximum Leader"—merely a de jure recognition of a long-time de facto situation—but the conferring of the title was accompanied by harsh "anti-Yanqui" rhetoric. Furthermore, Panama was declared to be in a state of war with the United States.

On the following weekend, a U.S. marine was killed, and two American witnesses (a Navy officer and his wife) were interrogated and beaten by a combination of PDF forces and the dreaded Dignity Battalions. The manner in which these events occurred seemed to suggest that an "open season" on Americans in Panama had begun.

On 20 December, Operation Just Cause was launched by the United States. The PDF, as an institution, was dismembered, and after taking refuge in the Nunciature (the Vatican's embassy) in Panama City, Noriega surrendered to U.S. forces and is presently awaiting trial in Miami. In Panama, the triumvirate of Endara, Arias Calderón, and Ford have provided the new leadership for the civilian government, and the PDF has been reborn as the Public Forces, under the leadership of Colonel Eduardo Herrera-Hassan.

During 1989, the PdP played an almost negligible role in Panamanian developments. As its weekly publication, *Unidad*, suggests, it was highly supportive of the efforts of the now-defunct Noriega regime. Furthermore, it viewed its internal opposition as nothing more than lackeys of the United States' government and considered the beleaguered regime a victim of U.S. aggression and neo-colonialism, which was simply seeking sovereignty.

But aside from participating in the COLINA ticket for the annulled elections of May 1989, the PdP was virtually invisible during 1989. With its militant supporters numbering no more than 1000, even in a nation of 2.3 million, it evidently lacked any base of popular support. Instead, the PdP was in obvious collusion with the PRD—the PDF's political party. Furthermore, Panama's links to the international communist community have been managed either directly through the Noriega regime or through the PRD and its left-wing *tendencia* faction.

Before examining the particulars of Panamanian contact with the communist bloc, a note of explanation is warranted. Although the Noriega regime clearly drifted leftward in both policy and rhetoric, attempting to cloak itself in nationalistic issues, there is no evidence to suggest that the senior levels of the PDF ever embraced this philosophy. Instead, it was an opportunistic effort to gain international support in its confrontation with Washington. Thus, although friendship was extended by the communist bloc, the relationship was certainly handled in an opportunistic manner by both sides.

The Soviet Union began the year 1989 highly supportive of the Noriega regime. On 2 January, a high-profile agreement on trade and economic cooperation was signed with Moscow. But given the dismal state of the Panamanian economy, and despite the bestowal on it of the status of most-favored nation, this agreement offered few benefits to Panama in the economic realm. Thus, despite public statements to the contrary, the agreement represented more a political gesture of support to the beleaguered Noriega regime than it gave economic benefits. Furthermore, as the year wore on, public support by the Soviet Union appeared to wane: fewer public pronouncements of support were made by governmental officials of the USSR. Finally, in a confirmation of the opportunism which guided Soviet strategy, the U.S. invasion of Panama was publicly condemned by the Soviet leadership. However, understanding that the invasion represented a death knell for the type of regime Noriega represented, the USSR offered no overt support to either Noriega or his allies in its aftermath.

Having had a long-term and more than cordial relationship first with the Torrijos regime, and later with Noriega, Cuba remained a fairly stalwart—if opportunistic—defender of the general. Beginning during the Torrijos years, Cuba has used Panama as a site for front companies, through which to circumvent controls of foreign exchange with the United States.

Under Noriega, the politico-diplomatic relationship with Cuba was visibly strengthened. In 1988, rumors surfaced that military cooperation had also begun. According to Major Villalaz, participant in the coup attempt of March 1988, the Panamanian Air Force had flown large arms caches into Panama throughout the year. (Much of this inventory was uncovered and captured during the 1989 U.S. invasion.) In addition, Cuban advisers were reportedly sent to Panama to assist in the training of PDF troops.

Finally, it is apparent that the Dignity Battalions were modeled, at least in part, on the Cuban Territorial Troop Militia (MTT). In Cuba, the MTT was created in the early 1980s principally for political reasons: the training of civilians for militia service not only increased support for the Castro government, but sent a powerful message to any enemy contemplating invasion of the island, namely, that high levels of civilian casualties would be incurred.

In Panama, during 1988–89, the Dignity Battalions were created by Noriega, with Cuban assistance and training, to shore up civilian support for his regime. Headed by Benjamin Colomarco, whose title was elevated from that of *comandante* to that of colonel, the Dignity Battalions were in essence gangs of armed thugs designed to roam the capital and intimidate the citizenry. Their actions were described by the regime as spontaneous expressions of public support for Noriega, and their presence on the streets of Panama served principally as provocation, with PDF forces backing them up.

Following the December invasion, Cuba's opportunism with regard to Panama once again became clear. In the numerous public speeches denouncing U.S. actions in Panama, much more time has been devoted to this theme than to expressions of support for Noriega. While Noriega's future inside the Nunciature was yet to be decided, a few fleeting comments were made regarding Cuban willingness to offer asylum to Noriega. However, since it was evident that U.S. forces would not permit Noriega's safe exit to Cuba, these gestures of support can only be seen as halfhearted. Instead, Cuba attempted to utilize the invasion as a means to foster additional anti-American sentiment in the international community. Finally, a few of Noriega's cronies took refuge in the Cuban embassy in Panama.

Nicaragua also had cordial relations with the Noriega regime. But the Nicaraguan presence in Panama was far behind that of Cuba, and Nicaraguan support does not seem to have gone much beyond public declarations. However, one incident underlined Nicaragua's potential involvement: acting on reports of an arms cache there, U.S. forces illegally raided the residence of the Nicaraguan ambassador to Panama. The reports from different sources vary greatly with regard to the quantity and kinds of weapons found there. (*NYT*, 31 December; *San Francisco Chronicle*, 30 December.) In keeping with Cuba's line toward Panama, the Nicaraguan government roundly condemned the American invasion and voiced halfhearted support for Noriega's asylum in Panama. It was also reported

that a few of Noriega's loyalists had sought refuge in the Nicaraguan embassy.

As 1990 begins, Panama's long-term future has yet to be determined. Neither the Soviet Union, Cuba, or Nicaragua has been willing to recognize the new Endara government, although their embassies have not been closed down. As for Panama's internal political landscape, a few leading members of the PRD (including former minister of commerce and industry, Mario Rognoni) have indicated their desire to rebuild the PRD as the leading party of loyal opposition. In fact, the PRD has already levelled charges of corruption against the new government. Finally, the future of the PdP is even more open to question than the PRD's. While at this juncture it may be presumed that the PdP will also seek to play the role of loyal opposition, that party's lack of popular support suggests a grim future for it.

Eva Loser
Center for Strategic and International Studies,
Washington, D.C.

Paraguay

Population. 4,522,172
Party. Paraguayan Communist Party (Partido Comunista del Paraguay; PCP)
Founded. 1928
Membership. 4,000
General Secretary. Júlio Rojas
Status. Illegal, but tolerated
Last Congress. Third, 10 April 1971
Last Election. N/a
Auxiliary Organizations. No data
Publications. *Adelante* (underground weekly); *Perspectivas* (underground magazine)

General Alfredo Stroessner, Paraguay's ruler for more than 34 years, was overthrown in the early morning hours of 3 February by tank and infantry units led by General Andrés Rodríguez. On the day after his surrender Stroessner and his family were sent to Brazil, to remain there in exile, but many of his political cronies were kept under arrest. General Rodríguez was immediately sworn in as provisional president. Speculation soon arose concerning his intentions, since he was known to be a Stroessner protégé; indeed, he had been so close to the fallen dictator that his daughter had married Stroessner's younger son. Meanwhile, the Paraguayan Communist Party addressed itself to the new situation. On 4 February its Central Committee issued a statement calling for the release of all political prisoners and information about all of those who had "disappeared" into Stroessner's prisons—particularly the PCP's former secretaries, Miguel Angel Soler and Antonio Maidana. The PCP also demanded the establishment of a "real democracy," with improved living standards for the workers and peasants. (*FBIS*, 6 February.)

On 7 February Rodríguez announced that general elections would be held on May Day, and that all political parties, except the Communists, would be allowed to participate. The PCP's exclusion was based on Article 118 of the Constitution, which outlaws political parties whose aim is to subvert the constitutional order, or who receive instructions from abroad. Other dissidents who previously were considered "subversive" by the state were permitted to return from exile, however. Among them were the leaders of the left-wing Movimiento Popular Colorado (MOPOCO). The MOPOCOs, who had been members of the National Accord, a coalition of anti-Stroessner parties, were even invited to rejoin the ruling Colorado Party, which was supporting General Rodríguez's presidential candidacy. They accepted the invitation, deserting their former allies and dampening the opposition's electoral hopes.

The PCP naturally protested its exclusion from the elections and began a campaign to obtain its legalization. The Colorados pretended sympathy. Their leading spokesman, former interior minister Edgar L. Ynsfrán, claimed he favored the legalization "since the Communist Party does not scare anyone anymore." When he worked for Stroessner, however, Ynsfrán had labeled all political opposition as "communist" and persecuted it with considerable ferocity. In any case, the elections took place without the PCP. Rodríguez easily won a four-year term and the Colorados retained control of Congress with 74 percent of the vote. Seven other parties split the remainder, the Authentic Radical Liberals establishing themselves as the chief opposition with 20 percent of the vote. Rodríguez promised that he would not seek a second term.

After the elections there were signs that the new government might not differ greatly from the old *stronato*. Rodríguez quickly let it be known that he

had no intention of establishing diplomatic relations with the Soviet Union or any other communist country (*FBIS*, 1 May). And, despite the repeal by Congress of two sweeping antisubversive laws in August, there was little sign that the government intended to legalize the PCP. Nevertheless, the Communists were able to take advantage of a much more liberal political atmosphere. On 19 June a Communist-led student delegation left for North Korea, via Buenos Aires and the Soviet Union, to attend the International Youth and Students' Festival. Included in the group were representatives of the Authentic Radical Liberals, the democratic-socialist Febrerista Party, the Paraguayan Students' Federation, the Humanist Party, and the Workers' Party. Only the personal intervention of the parent organization prevented a Christian-Democrat youth from joining the delegation (*FBIS*, 27 June).

Other indications of a rightward tendency in the new government were furnished by its heavy-handed treatment of protestors. On 23 June police dispersed a Catholic Church–sponsored march on Congress by landless peasants, using police dogs to attack the demonstrators. On 11 October they used clubs and water cannon to break up a protest by some 1,000 trade unionists demanding the release of three of their leaders. The three men had been arrested after delivering a petition to the Presidential Palace demanding the reinstatement of several union organizers recently dismissed by factory owners. Two days later the police used water cannon and electric prods to disperse some peasants demonstrating for land reform. (*Latin American Monitor*, *Southern Cone*, November.) Naturally, the PCP made common cause with these victims and demanded the dismantling of the government's "repressive apparatus." In a manifesto issued late in June it suggested that the Rodríguez administration was little more than "Stroessnerism without Stroessner" (*FBIS*, 28 June). In early December, the PCP held its first public rally in 42 years and called for its legalization (Asunción, *Hoy*, 5 December; *FBIS*, 6 December).

Although the PCP was forced to admit that Paraguay's press was freer than it had been in years, and was unearthing horrifying stories about corruption and human-rights abuses under Stroessner, it insisted that there were few "concrete actions toward socioeconomic change" (*FBIS*, 29 June). Moreover, the charge that Rodríguez was scheming to keep the Stroessner apparatus intact gained force on 26 September when twenty top army generals issued a statement calling for more unity and discipline in the Colorado Party. This was universally interpreted as an endorsement of the conservative "traditionalist" wing of the party, as opposed to the reformist *contestatario* wing that had been formed by the MOPOCOs and other former Colorado mavericks. On the other hand, it was rumored that the *contestatarios* had the support of the younger officers (*Latin American Weekly Report*, 30 November). As this eventful year came to an end, there was much speculation as to which way Rodríguez would turn in the months ahead.

Paul H. Lewis
Tulane University

Peru

Population. 21,448,501 (*World Factbook*, 1989)
Party. Peruvian Communist Party (Partido Comunista Peruana; PCP)
Founded. 1928
Membership. 4,000 est.
General Secretary. Jorge del Prado Chavez (b. 1910, member of Senate; member of the National Executive Committee of the United Left, coalition)
Central Committee. 47 members
Status. Legal
Last Congress. Ninth, 27–30 May 1987; Sixteenth Plenary, 29–30 November 1986
Last Election. November 1989 municipal elections. The PCP participated as part of the United Left coalition, which won 22 percent nationwide, 52 provincial mayor's offices, and 8 districts in Lima.
Auxiliary Organizations. General Confederation of Peruvian Workers (Confederacíon General de Trabajadores Peruanos; CGTP), the Peruvian Peasant Confederation (Confederacíon Campesino Peruana; CCP)
Publications. *Unidad* (newspaper of the PCP, Carlos Esteves, editor); *El Diario* (pro–Sendero Luminoso newspaper); *Cambio* (magazine that is pro–Revolutionary Movement of Túpac Amaru)

The Peruvian Communist Party (PCP) is a pivotal member of the Izquierda Unida (United Left; IU), which since 1985 has been the second strongest political force in Peru. At the beginning of 1989, it appeared that the IU was poised for electoral victory in the 1990 presidential elections, but the year ended with the movement split in two. This division occurred despite considerable effort by the PCP and its general secretary, Jorge del Prado, to reconcile the disputing factions. The beneficiary of the collapse of the IU was the Democratic Front (FREDEMO), a right-wing coalition under the leadership of novelist Mario Vargas Llosa. The results of municipal elections, held on 12 November, indicate strong public support for FREDEMO with its promises of economic reactivation, Peru's reintegration into the international financial community, and a "law and order" counteroffensive against terrorism. Not only did the IU division weaken party loyalty, FREDEMO's campaign to identify the failures of President Garcia's administration with leftist policies also drew independent support toward the resurgent right. While the IU captured only 22 percent of the national vote in the municipal elections, its leaders still expect to make a strong showing in the elections of April 1990.

As defined by the Central Committee of the PCP, the party's major goals are to end the guerrilla insurgency which has cost 16,000 lives in nine years, to avoid the further militarization of Peruvian society, and to prevent the right from eroding the democratic gains of the working class. To do so, the party plans to strengthen the unions, bolster the United Left, support the formation of self-defense groups, and demand the observation of human rights (*World Marxist Review*, April).

Leadership and Party Organization. Izquierda Unida had retained a semblance of unity in its nine years of existence because it remained an opposition bloc. The original members of the alliance—the PCP; the Revolutionary Communist Party (PCR); the Revolutionary Socialist party (PSR); the Trotskyist Worker, Peasant, Student, and Popular Front (FOCEP); the Union of the Revolutionary Left (UNIR); and the Unified Mariateguista Party (PUM)—have acted jointly or separately, as their interests dictated, forming coalitions around different issues within the broader bloc. The tenuous nature of the alliance became more apparent as grass-roots pressure, and the prospect of electoral victory, moved the IU toward becoming a full-fledged political party requiring a unified program and a single slate of candidates.

The First National Party Congress, held on 19 January in Huampaní, was the culmination of 400 district congresses and 60 provincial assemblies. Jorge del Prado hailed it as the "most important and transcendental step in the history of the Peruvian left..." marking the moment when "IU passed from being an electoral alliance to a revolutionary front of the masses" (*Resumen Semanal*, 20–26 January). There were 3,153 delegates in attendance; 75 percent of them had been elected from local committees and 25 percent were representatives of the component parties of the IU (*Resumen Semanal*, 13–19 January).

At the congress, tension between the moderate and the radical factions was pronounced. The PCP provided the critical balance, as the communists voted with the moderates (the PSR, PCR, the non-party socialists, independents, and other small social-democratic groups) in defining the party's policy line, and then backed the radical wing on the selection of the National Executive Committee (CDN). The Accords of Huampaní defined the IU's opposition to the García administration as a "political struggle," explicitly rejecting the use of armed confrontation to achieve power and supporting democratic processes. The goal of the moderate program was to consolidate the different elements of the IU into an organization capable of launching a winning electoral campaign and establishing a popular, democratic, anti-imperialist government in 1990. (*Resumen Semanal*, 20–26 January.)

The party program had been discussed in pre-congress sessions and was the product of intense debate at Huampaní. The selection of the leadership, however, was done by acclamation at the last session of the congress, and the result was a radical majority. The leadership was composed of Jorge del Prado (PCP), who became the first president for a six-month term, Manuel Dammert (PCR), Alfredo Filomeno (PSR), Eduardo Cacerces Valdivia (PUM), Jorge Hurtado (UNIR), Gustavo Mohme (Socialist Popular Action, APS), Genero Ledesma (FOCEP), and Henry Pease (Independent) as representatives of various IU entities. From the plenary were selected Rolando Ames (Movement of Socialist Affirmation; MAS), Santiago Pedraglio (Revolutionary Mariateguista Party; PMR), César Barreda Bazan (UNIR), Javier Diez Canseco (PUM), and Guillermo Herrera (PCP). The composition of the CDN became the major target of moderate dissension.

The rules of the Peruvian National Election Jury allow group inscription as well as party alliance registration. Therefore, on 15 February, the dissident faction formed the Socialist Accord (Acuerdo Socialista; AS). This group included the PCR, the Regional Mariateguista Committees, and the Socialist Convergence (CS)—formed by the PSR, non-Marxist socialists, and independents. Its goal was to restructure the IU from within by holding internal elections to simultaneously select candidates for the municipal and presidential elections and elect a new CDN. The moderates argued that the present leadership was unrepresentative, and said they were not convinced that a "radical" CDN would carry out the "moderate" accords. (*Resumen Semanal*, 3–9 March.)

As president of the IU, Jorge del Prado attempted to reconcile the most popular IU candidate, Dr. Alfonso Barrantes, with the organization. But the CDN refused to accept that its constitution was in any way illegitimate, and the moderate Barrantes refused to participate in elections internal to the IU which did not offer to restructure the leadership. Finally, in May, the Socialist Accord held a plenary which called for internal elections of all IU members. Del Prado and the IU declared the act "organic and political parallelism," and the PCP leader expressed disappointment that Barrantes would take this step which would divide the grass-roots organizations. (*Resumen Semanal*, 12–18 May.)

Internal elections held by the IU on 11 June for municipal candidates and on 1 October for the presidential nomination, brought a turnout of 15,000 and 35,000 voters, respectively. The AS faction held its combined elections on 9 July, and 70,000 members went to the district and provincial polls, thus reinforcing its claim that it represents the majority of IU militants (*Resumen Semanal*, 9–15 June; 14–20 July).

Del Prado had wanted a consensus slate for the IU presidential nomination, but no compromise could be reached and two tickets went forward; one from the radical line, composed of Agustín Haya de la Torre (PMR), César Barreda Bazan (UNIR), and Alfonso Benavides Correa (Independent), and the other with moderates Gustavo Mohme (APS), Rolando Ames (MAS), and César Guzman ("non-party" members). Haya took 61 percent in Lima and 71 percent nationally to win, but afterwards the CDN tried to form a consensus slate to win over the PCP and FOCEP, which had abstained from the elections. Del Prado and the PCP central committee still wanted reconciliation with Barrantes, arguing that low turnout was an indication the people wanted a unified movement, which was the only way to seriously contest the election. But on 7 October, in Piura, Barrantes announced that he was the presidential candidate of the alliance Socialist Left (Izquierda Socialista; IS). This cemented the break and forced a consensus formula within the IU. On 11 October, the PCP accepted a slate with Henry Pease as candidate for president, Agustín Haya de la Torre for first vice-president, and Gustavo Mohme for second vice-president (*Resumen Semanal*, 6–12 October). It was a ticket that was *barrantista* without Barrantes, acceptable to the leaders, but not based on internal democracy.

While the differences in ideology and organizational goals between the moderates and radicals were substantial, the radicals' ultimate support of Henry Pease, an independent who was Barrantes's vice-mayor, indicated that their major objective was to get rid of Barrantes, rather than present a radical electoral platform. Barrantes is, without doubt, the most popular leftist politician. He is well-known, and his service as mayor of Lima (1983–86) is widely respected. He repeatedly called for the left to set aside its sectarian squabbles and unify against the dangers posed by FREDEMO, yet he refused to compromise with the IU radicals. By creating a separate organization to run for president, he attempted to eliminate the far left—UNIR and PUM—believing that the majority of the IU supporters would rally to his position.

The platforms of both Pease and Barrantes are moderate and progressive, having been pulled toward the center by FREDEMO's definition of the issues and the results of the municipal elections. Both reject nationalization of finances. Barrantes, for example, said he would not nationalize any industry that was not already state-owned. What distinguishes them from Mario Vargas Llosa is their antipathy to privatization and support for all labor-stability laws. In terms of foreign investment, neither candidate stuck to the IU's previous nationalist stance, calling instead for it to be "complementary" to national investment, rather than "interdependent," as they claimed FREDEMO would have it. Barrantes's principal concerns—a national accord to fight drug traffic and terrorism, reactivation of agricultural production to reduce hunger and extreme poverty, and the defense and development of natural resources—are calculated to appeal to a broad spectrum of Peruvian society. Pease's call for the government to meet the basic needs of the people is very similar. Both candidates warn that a

FREDEMO victory would mean the loss of national sovereignty, economic austerity, and increased social tension. (*Resumen Semanal*, 22–28 September; 1–7 December.) Because the differences between the two leftist slates are more rooted in personality than in substance, the danger for the PCP in the 1990 presidential campaign is that the IU and the IS will attack each other more than FREDEMO.

Domestic Affairs. In 1989 dissatisfaction with the government of President Alan García was widespread. The energetic president, who had started his term in 1985 with unprecedented popular support, now faced repudiation within his own ranks and demands of resignation from the opposition. His economic policies—*paquetazos* (packages of price hikes, elimination of subsidies, and devaluations) and *maquinazos* (printing money to pay state employees)—were drastic measures to break the nation's financial tailspin. At the end of the year, recession had contracted the GDP by 10–14.5 percent. Peru's foreign-debt burden was $17 billion, and inflation for the year was 3,000 percent. Real wages had dropped 52 percent below 1970 levels, and observers looked increasingly to the "informal economy" to find out how people were surviving. (*Latin America Weekly Report* [*LAWR*], 11 January 1990; David Scott Palmer, "Peru's Persistent Problems," *Current History*, January 1990.) The result of such economic stress was, predictably, greater social tension and debilitating strikes. This atmosphere merely fed the political violence of two revolutionary guerrilla movements, Sendero Luminoso and the Revolutionary Movement of Túpac Amaru (MRTA), and a much smaller rightist paramilitary group, the Comando Rodrigo Franco (CRF).

In 1989 the PCP-oriented General Confederation of Peruvian Workers (CGTP) confronted numerous difficult problems. Its leaders had to decide whether to press for raises above the government's ability to pay, or merely to demand job security. Complicating the situation, they found themselves under increased attack from guerrillas, paramilitary, and security forces, while at the same time they struggled to maintain the cohesiveness of the leftist movement.

Strike actions were different from previous years in terms of the duration of "indefinite" walk-outs. The transport workers struck for three weeks, the fishing sector was off two months, judiciary employees took 65 days to settle, the most active group, the Intersectoral Confederation of State Employees (CITE), went out 77 days, and the doctors of the national health service struck for a record 97 days.

Activity mounted with each new *paquetazo* and its devaluation of the inti and increases in controlled prices and wages. But wage hikes never caught up with prices; for instance, the daily minimum wage in February would not purchase one kilo of chicken. The IU's complaint about the Aprista reactivation plan was that "gradualist" reductions were essentially the same as the IMF's demands and would only lead to capital flight, recession, and unemployment. (*LAWR*, 16 February.)

Within hours of the February adjustment, riots and looting broke out in some poorer Lima markets. State employees from various sectors took to the streets to demand salary increases and a 77 percent bonus for specialized categories. On 7 February, the demonstrations turned violent, and police used tear gas and water cannons to disperse the crowds. IU congressmen intervened, and one, CDN member César Barreda, was beaten by police. (*Resumen Semanal*, 27 January–17 February.)

By June, the gradual adjustments were eliminated, and talks with the IMF accelerated. Monthly inflation had declined, but the nation was into a full recession, with the automobile industry at a standstill, manufacturing output down by 35.5 percent, construction off by 36.6 percent, and, more ominously, food consumption down by 20 percent. IU union leaders worried that along with low wages, the contraction of the economy was going to mean 500,000 wage earners on forced vacations or working part-time would soon be unemployed. The CGTP called an assembly to analyze the recession and find ways to save jobs. (*LAWR*, 6 July.)

Taking advantage of the economic distress, the revolutionary organizations sought to infiltrate the unions and incite unrest. In April, the IU unions defeated an offensive by Sendero in the industrial zone of the Carretera Central in Lima. The militant revolutionaries sought to gain influence in the neighborhood and labor organizations controlled by the IU, but they were unable to carry out a successful armed strike such as they had done in the sierra. (*Resumen Semanal*, 14–20 April.) The MRTA was accused of being involved in the police strike on 16 October. A clandestine group, called "Progressive Police of Peru," initiated actions which resulted in other striking workers clashing with on-duty police. Some local police posts were "closed," and transit police were hard to find, but the minister of the interior maintained that only a

very small number of junior officers were involved. (*Resumen Semanal*, 13–19 October.)

The 70,000-member Federation of Miners and Metallurgic Workers suffered a major loss when its general secretary, Saúl Cantoral, was assassinated on 13 February. It was unclear who was responsible. The note on his body bore Sendero's motto "Thus die traitors," but he had received death threats from the Comando Rodrigo Franco. The CGTP maintained that the right-wing organization did not want the miners' strike settled with gains for the workers. The government claimed that the assassination was Sendero's doing, and also that it was intended to prevent any accommodation in the miners' strike. (*Resumen Semanal*, 27 January–17 February.) The *senderistas* did intimidate the union into shutting down the mines for the armed strike called by the guerrillas for 10–12 May. The federation's second walk-out of the year was halted after two weeks of violence instigated by the MRTA and harassment from security forces (*Resumen Semanal*, 1–7 September).

Given the confederation's desire to avoid bloodshed, CGTP leader, Valentín Pacho, was willing to participate in the government's efforts to reactivate the economy. In February, he met with representatives of the Ministry of Economics and the Confederation of Private Enterprise Institutions (CONFIEP), and with other labor, university, and religious leaders to discuss an "economic pact of national solidarity." The goal was to formulate a coherent strategy to combat inflation and recession and to reactivate the economy. Pacho participated in these discussions, but refused to make a formal commitment until labor problems had been dealt with "sincerely." (*Resumen Semanal*, 25 February–3 March.)

The CGTP was also concerned about the prospects of a FREDEMO government and was willing to work with García to ensure workers' benefits. Valentín Pacho warned that Mario Vargas Llosa's "antipatriotic program" represented "a danger to all the social, economic, and political conquests that have been achieved with struggle, demonstrations, and blood in this century" (*Resumen Semanal*, 10–16 November). One means of protecting these gains was to strengthen the union movement, which the García government did by officially recognizing the CITE, thereby ending the 77-day state employees' strike. On 29 November, the CITE became the primary bargaining unit for the 500,000-member union. General Secretary Luis Iparraquirre called it an historic step, and at the same time announced that CITE's first move would be to denounce candidate Mario Vargas Llosa before the judiciary for threatening the right of job stability for public servants. (*Resumen Semanal*, 25 November–1 December.)

The only positive news on the economic scene was that sluggish domestic activity had reduced imports, and that high prices for mineral exports had thus resulted in Peru's first trade surplus in three years. García also worked out a deal with the IMF. While he maintained that the organization had bent its rules to help Peru pay $800 million in arrears with easier than normal conditions, many on the left saw the IMF's cooperativeness as the international financial community getting ready for Vargas Llosa's assumption of power. (*LAWR*, 7 December; 11 January 1990.)

One of the greatest problems for García was a perceived "lack of control," which increased the level of resignation and fear with regard to the guerrilla insurgency. Polls showed that 56 percent of the population believed the country was on the brink of a civil war, and 55 percent said they would obey a call for an armed strike by Sendero (EFE, 25 July; *FBIS*, 27 July).

In 1989, criticism of the administration's ineffective counterinsurgency policy mounted. The security forces' inability to defend their own troops, rural communities, or candidates for public office, generated demands for better protection of the citizenry. Much attention focused on the military failure at Uchiza. The police post, in the heart of Peru's coca cradle, was attacked by Sendero Luminoso and Colombian *narcotrafficantes*. The six-hour siege left 10 policemen, 3 civilians, and 50 *senderistas* dead. After the police had run out of ammunition, the guerrillas ransacked the town, destroying the bank, the public records office, and several stores. The question was why the military had been unable to reinforce the besieged post once they learned of the attack. The military said they hesitated in order to avoid a massacre. More to the point, perhaps, was the government's response that there was no way to land reinforcements at night, and, worse yet, transport equipment is in such poor repair that 70 percent of the planes are not functioning at any one time. By mid-year, however, with U.S. equipment for the war on drugs and the delivery of 23 new helicopters from the Soviet Union and West Germany, the Peruvian army was better equipped to pursue columns of guerrillas and take the offensive (*LAWR*, 11 May).

The government's increased support for military activity meant more military engagements and deaths, as well as a rise of human-rights violations. There were 348 deaths among the security forces (military and national police) in 1989. This compares to a 1987 total of 198 and a 1988 count of 266. Also significant is the fact that the percentage of all victims made up by the security forces' casualties is rising. In 1985, the losses suffered by the military and the police forces accounted for only 5 percent of the deaths, but in 1989 they exceeded 11 percent. (*Resumen Semanal*, 1985–1989; *Andean Newsletter*, 15 January 1990.) In fact, this percentage may be higher, as some sources argue that the unverified counts of 50–70 *senderistas* killed in jungle battles may be exaggerated by the military merely to show it is effective. In Lima there is evidence that efforts to project a "winning" image has led to severe human-rights abuses. For example, it appears that MRTA was correct when it charged that three of its members and two innocent bystanders were killed *after* they had been detained, not during a terrorist attack as claimed by the police. (*Andean Newsletter*, 13 August.)

In August, Amnesty International (AI) issued its second report on Peruvian human-rights violations. For three years in a row, Peru has had more forced disappearances than any other nation in the world. In 1987 there were 78; in 1988 that number rose to 170; and as of August 1989, 288 cases had been reported (*Andean Newsletter*, 4 December). AI denounced the security forces for the disappearances, for torturing prisoners, and for extrajudicial civilian deaths. The Peruvian government was also castigated for not prosecuting soldiers charged with human-rights violations. At the same time, AI condemned Sendero Luminoso for its campaign of assassination, sabotage, and armed attacks, charging that the group has "spread a veil of terror over the country." (*Resumen Semanal*, 18–24 August.)

Counterinsurgency failures have also spawned paramilitary groups willing to take matters into their own hands. The Andean Commission of Jurists claims that unidentified paramilitary groups were responsible for 153 assassinations in 1989. The two-year-old Comando Rodrigo Franco, named for an Aprista leader killed by Sendero, is blamed for 11 assassinations and hundreds of threats to union leaders, journalists, and leftist politicians. (*Andean Newsletter*, 15 January 1990.)

Worried that violence in Peru is becoming endemic, IU congressmen have pressed for government investigations and accountability for misconduct, and they made some progress in 1989. A commission to investigate paramilitary groups, specifically the CRF, was created on 31 May (*Resumen Semanal*, 26 May–1 June). In June, Interior Minister Agustín Mantilla gave detailed accounts of the activities of the MRTA and Sendero Luminoso, but he claimed that the CRF was just several local groups with no national cohesion (*Expreso*, 7 June; *FBIS*, 15 June). Information gathered by the congressional commission, however, provided some evidence that sophisticated Israeli weapons and security systems were being smuggled into the country, ostensibly for the Central Bank. Ties with the Aprista party and Minister Mantilla were revealed, and charges made that Italian and Israeli combat trainers had connections to the CRF. At this point several Apristas resigned from the commission in protest. (*Resumen Semanal*, 1–7 September; *Andean Newsletter*, October–November; EFE, 21 August; *FBIS*, 23 August.)

There have been some minor gains in accountability for authorities' misconduct. The prefect of Pucallpa was removed in February after nine persons had been killed when police attempted to stop peasants who were demonstrating to be paid for commodities given in sale to state companies (*Andean Newsletter*, 6 March). And in December, two officers were sentenced to prison for the 1986 massacre in Lurigancho prison (*LAWR*, 21 December).

Military intelligence gains were also made against the second largest guerrilla force, the MRTA. (For background see *YICA*, 1984–1988.) The majority of the MRTA's operations have been in Lima, where attacks on buildings, the hijacking of deliveries, and the kidnapping of wealthy businessmen have produced few fatalities. The group's attempt to expand into the interior, especially into the coca-production areas where they confront both Sendero and the military, has not been as successful. By November 1989, there had been 93 actions claimed by the group, and the number of deaths resulting from them totaled 195. The MRTA itself lost 125 members in confrontations with the police, with Sendero, or through terrorist accidents. (*Resumen Semanal*, 1987–1989.) In February, the commandant of the MRTA's northeast front, Victor Polay Campos, was captured in Huancayo. He was charged with 102 kidnappings and 200 terrorist attacks in Lima. His capture was rumored to have been the result of internal bickering. The fall of twelve more leaders in the northern sierra in October led some analysts to say the group had been "decapitated." (EFE, 15 October; *FBIS*, 17 October.)

International Affairs. The major international issues for Peru in 1989 were the nation's position on the repayment of its foreign debt, the conduct of an internationalized drug war, and increased emphasis on Latin American integration. President García, supported by the left wing of his party and the IU, had rejected any discussions of reconciliation with the IMF until the organization had recognized the special needs of debtor nations. But when García was pushed more toward the center by Vargas Llosa's campaign, his Aprista economic advisors devised a plan whereby Peru avoided threatened expulsion from the IMF and actually received a bridge loan at reasonable interest rates. On 11 December, Peru paid $43 million to the IMF as part of the $800 million owed to the fund. Both leftist candidates supported this move as a way to salvage the economy. (*Resumen Semanal*, 8–14 December.)

The role of the United States in Peruvian affairs increased as a result of the war on drugs. But the García administration and the left resented the implication that the drug war could be "lost" in Peru, or that the solution is eradication of the source; rather, they view the problem as one of consumption in the United States. They argued that attacking the problem in Peru is best done by means of economic incentives, such as greater access to U.S. markets for legal crops. In addition, they believed that the European nations have to be included in any international effort to stem demand for drugs. Finally, with only $261 million of the $7.9 billion to be spent in the drug war, allocated to the three producer countries, the amount Peru will receive from the Bush administration is seen as a token commitment (*Lima Peruana Television*, 11 September; *FBIS*, 12 September).

The government's resolve to destroy the coca trade has been mixed at best. First, García has been responsive to the concern of IU politicians and ecological groups in Peru and elsewhere about the environmental consequences of spraying broad-spectrum pesticides on the coca plants. Second, local officials and soldiers have operated within a network of protection and corruption, and the overall economy is, according to some analysts, dependent upon the injection of foreign exchange in the form of coca dollars. Third, destroying the peasants' livelihood will only increase the appeal of the *senderista* message. Finally, the antidrug police lack the skills, training, and equipment to be effective.

U.S. investment is changing this situation, however. In Santa Lucia, the United States has constructed a $3 million base from which to conduct the drug war. There are approximately 130 Americans and 450 Peruvians conducting antinarcotics patrols in the Upper Huallaga Valley (*NYT*, 31 October).

U.S.-Peruvian cooperation in combatting drugs was threatened, however, when the United States invaded Panama. Earlier, García had condemned the dictatorial regime of General Manuel Noriega and supported the democratic opposition. But he immediately denounced the invasion of 20 December, recalling the Peruvian ambassador. He characterized the event as an insult to Latin America that violated the principles of the U.N. and the OAS. On 22 December, the Peruvian congress voted to withdraw from the Interamerican Mutual Assistance Treaty if the principles of the treaty were not put into practice within two years. García asserted that the United States "has no right to impose new authorities by armed invasion," and he announced that the would not attend the scheduled drug summit. Criticism of the United States did not mean support for Noriega, however. In fact, García "deauthorized" the Order of the Sol that had been awarded to the general three years before. (*Resumen Semanal*, 15–22 December; 22–28 December; *LAWR*, 11 January.)

The CDN of Izquierda Unida held a demonstration in Lima and sent a letter to the U.S. embassy condemning the invasion. Militants burned a U.S. flag with a pirate insignia on it. The CGTP and other unions wrote a letter to George Bush noting that "the brutal aggression. . .demonstrated potential imperialist abuse in Latin America." IS candidate Barrantes called for the immediate withdrawal of the U.S. troops. (*Resumen Semanal*, 22–28 December.)

Good relations with the communist-bloc nations were sustained by the president and the leftist political parties. But as popular opinion swung to the right in 1989, criticism of some earlier trade arrangements became more prominent in the business community. For instance, fishing contracts with the Soviet Union and Cuba were denounced because of perceived tax benefits. García defended the agreements, saying that it was wise to let others develop the resources since Peruvian investors had not done so. Moreover, Peru receives 17.5 percent of the catch, which is limited so that it is ecologically safe. While the Soviets' 27-ship fleet waited for the bureaucratic haggling to be worked out, the Cubans withdrew theirs, which resulted in a loss to Peru of 30,000 tons of fish. (*Lima Television Peruana*,

6 January; *FBIS*, 9 January; *Lima Television Peruana*, 26 April; *FBIS*, 26 April.)

The processing of fish is a very important component of the Peruvian economy, one that actually grew during 1989, and one upon which the nation bases its trade. The purchase of 500 buses by Lima Transport from the People's Republic of China will be effected by giving in exchange processed fish from PESCA-PERU. (*Lima Television Peruana*, 26 March; *FBIS*, 27 March.)

Perhaps the most important shift by Peru in international matters has been a new emphasis upon mutual cooperation with other Latin American nations. Discussions on integration were given renewed priority. The Andean Pact presidents met for the twentieth anniversary of the Cartegena agreement and decided to reactivate the group, which is to meet once every six months. The Group of Eight met in Peru in October to discuss integration by 1992 and cooperation on dealing with drug trafficking. (*Resumen Semanal*, 6–12 October.)

Two moves taken by García, which were supported by the IU, but denounced by the opposition party FREDEMO, were the recognition of North Korea on 3 November, and a departure from the traditional Peruvian stance on Bolivian access to the sea. García met with Bolivia's chief executive, Jaime Paz Zamora, three times during the year. At the summit at Lake Titicaca on 18 October, they established free-trade zones in the ports of Matarani and Ilo and created a binational maritime-transport company. Most important, García agreed that if Chile gave Bolivia passage to the sea through former Peruvian territory, Peru would not object. The Chileans, and many Peruvians, quickly said that this was only a "personal" opinion of the president. (*Resumen Semanal*, 20–26 October.)

Terrorist Activities. The Peruvian Communist Party-Sendero Luminoso has maintained a nine-year-old insurgency that has proved more resilient than analysts expected. (For background see *YICA*, 1982–1988.) That portion of the public that believes that Sendero will eventually be victorious has increased from 4 percent in 1988 to 15 percent in 1989 (*Christian Science Monitor* [*CSM*], 16 March). Political violence from January to November 1989 claimed 2,642 lives, raising the ten-year death toll to approximately 16,000. One half of the population now lives with restricted civil and political liberties under states of emergency established in ten departments. Sendero is not the only group responsible, but as of July, a congressional investigation attributed 757 attacks to them, 148 to the MRTA, and 27 to the CRF. (*Resumen Semanal*, 7–13 July.)

Sendero has been successful in demonstrating the government's lack of control and ineffectiveness. It has provoked a repressive military response and injected fear and apprehension into the daily lives of the citizenry. It did not thwart the municipal elections in 1989, and although the group's activities brought forth demands for "law and order," the response has not been a military coup, but a turn to the right by Peruvian voters.

The extension of Sendero Luminoso's influence and control has been greatest in those areas where popular organizations have been weakest, or where antigovernment sentiment is strongest and can be easily manipulated. Thus, the three geographic areas where Sendero's activities have been most successful are: their own Andean base in Ayacucho, the coca cradle of the Upper Huallaga Valley, and the Mantaro Valley in the strategic central highlands. Although some estimates claim that one-third of the national territory is "controlled" by guerrilla groups, most of the Sendero's liberated zones are in Ayacucho, Huancavalica, and Húanuco, inside the military emergency zone, and constitute a no-man's land for civilians that has become virtually depopulated as thousands have fled to avoid the confrontations between the guerrillas and the military.

The second major area is the coca region of the Upper Huallaga. The benefits of this region to Sendero are that antigovernment sentiment is high, and there is substantial opportunity for tapping vast financial resources. But, this area requires a different mode of operations than Sendero has traditionally employed. Autarchic peasant communities could survive in isolation in the Andean highlands, but the *cocales* of the Upper Huallaga are intricately tied to the Colombian drug cartel's network of distribution and are the main target of the international war on drugs.

The Upper Huallaga Valley is the source of 60 percent of all the coca reaching the United States. In the 300-mile-long area, 60,000 families, each with from three to four hectares, produce coca leaves worth as much as $3 billion on the international market, of which $800 million–$1.2 billion a year stays in the country. It is estimated that 30 percent of the nation's foreign exchange is generated by drug trafficking (EFE, 9 September; *FBIS*, 11 September; *CSM*, 18 August). As protector and middleman, the guerrillas earn 10 percent for every kilo

of paste sent out of the valley (*Wall Street Journal*, 17 January). The easy-to-grow crop brings peasant families ten times the revenue they could earn from any substitute. Thus crop substitution and eradication programs are easy rallying points for the *senderista* movement.

When it infiltrated the Upper Huallaga region, Sendero portrayed its mission as one of protecting the indigenous culture and the region's livelihood, pointing to the Peruvian police and U.S. DEA officials who were waging a "war on drugs," as the enemy. But it has not been easy for Sendero to gain control of the region. Its members are susceptible to corruption; the military offensive is increasingly effective; and the population is still not supportive. Despite efforts to identify with local economic interests, Sendero Luminoso must resort to terror to control the population. Raids on cities, armed strikes, and the mass indoctrination of students and workers in the fields and factories are commonplace.

Although less extensive geographically than the sierra, and less lucrative financially than the coca region, the Mantaro Valley is more crucial strategically. Here terrorism is most effective because it can halt normal activity in the country's most populous region. Sendero threatens to encircle Lima, disrupting the distribution of food, cutting the transmission of electricity, and halting the transportation of export minerals. Using intimidation and extortion, Sendero has induced merchants and service providers to close down, thus paralyzing highland towns and even entire regions with "paros armados" (armed strikes).

In May, President García sent the military to patrol the streets in the department capitals of Junín, Pasco, and Húanuco, and he visited Huancayo himself to demonstrate that the government could and would protect citizens' day-to-day business in the face of these strikes. Sabotage continued, however. Between 26 and 31 July, the worst attacks in nine years toppled 33 electric towers, causing $570,000 in damage and affecting most of the central coast. Over 40 percent of Lima suffered as industry was shut down, stores and banks could not function, and even traffic lights did not work. Half of Lima could not hear or see García's last Independence Day address. (*Resumen Semanal*, 4–10 August.)

In areas with strong popular organizations, such as Puno, Cuzco, the sierra mining areas, and industrial Lima and Callao, Sendero has made few inroads, causing them to turn to particularly brutal methods, including the assassination of well-known leaders. The targets of Sendero's violence are not random, but are chosen as part of the group's revolutionary strategy. A prime target has been the peasant community itself. Between January and August 1989, 76 percent of Sendero's victims (588) were campesinos or *pobladores* (poor urban dwellers), who would not conform to the group's life style. (DESCO, *Buletin Informativo*, September 1989; David Scott Palmer, "Terrorism as a Revolutionary Strategy: Peru's *Sendero Luminoso*," in Barry Rubin, *The Politics of Terrorism: Terror as a State and Revolutionary Strategy*, SAIS: Washington, D.C. 1989; *CSM*, May 2, 1989).

Another target group was outsiders who threatened peasant isolation with technology, education, or ideology. This included domestic and foreign research and development efforts. In Puno, the 25-year-old Institute for Rural Studies in Ayaviri and an experimental farm in Chuquibambilla were destroyed. In Ancash, $8 million worth of equipment at a livestock station was demolished (*Andean Newsletter*, 12 June; *EFE*, 17 October; *FBIS*, 18 October). Environmental journalist Barbara D'Achille and a coworker on a project to protect alpacas and vicuña were stoned to death May 31 in Huancavelica (*Andean Newsletter*, 12 June). In fact, it was reported that 70 percent of the public-works projects in the central sierra have been abandoned as a result of terrorist attacks (*LAWR*, 22 June).

Sendero's major goal for 1989 was to sabotage the November municipal elections in an attempt to undermine the legitimacy of the democratic system. Their strategy involved a cumulative attack that was psychologically as well as physically damaging. According to DESCO figures, 92 public officials had been assassinated as of August 1989, leaving 80 districts and four provinces with no municipal authorities. Of the six district mayors of the province of Leoncio Prado in Húanuco, three were murdered and three resigned after receiving death threats (*Resumen Semanal*, 30 June–6 July; 9–15 June; *Andean Newsletter*, 12 June). IU politicians were prominent targets. An IU mayor in Puno was killed on 19 May, the PCP regional secretary in Huacho was killed on 14 September, and IU mayor Fermín Azparrent of Huamanga, who had survived nine previous attacks, was assassinated on 19 September. The lack of adequate protection immediately led to the withdrawal of 16 APRA, 6 IU, 4 FREDEMO, and 3 independent candidates. (*Resumen Semanal*, 15–21 September.) Provincial politicians in remote localities were not the only vic-

tims; Lima was shaken when two congressmen were killed there. IU deputy from Piura, Eriberto Arroyo Mío, was assassinated on 28 April, and on 6 May, Aprista deputy Pablo Nolberto Li Ormeño was shot in Villa El Salvador (*Resumen Semanal*, 21–27 April; 5–11 May). Sendero's boldness was underscored by its ambush on 3 June of the Palace Guard in downtown Lima, in which six soldiers were killed. (*LAWR*, 15 June.)

The month before the election was called "Red October," as Sendero launched an even more brutal campaign. More than 420 persons were killed, and 263 of the 50,000 candidates seeking office withdrew (*LAWR*, 16 November). On 1 November, they infiltrated a religious procession and then fought a pitched battle on Lima streets in which three persons died. Such actions inspired the political parties and the government to exert a greater effort in support of the elections. In response to a call by IU candidate Henry Pease, all the political parties and church leaders rallied on 3 November for a "March for Peace" in central Lima to support the democratic process. This was the largest demonstration for peace the capital had seen, and it was in direct confrontation of a senderista "armed strike." (*Resumen Semanal*, 3–9 November.)

The government support of the elections brought unprecedented security measures. As Sendero sought to disrupt the process by stealing electoral cards, halting transportation, and cutting off electricity on election day, there were massive preemptive detentions of known "trouble-makers," military personnel patrolled neighborhoods, transportation was protected, and the police guarded vulnerable places such as banks, gas stations, and buses. The administration increased protection for voting tables, extended voting hours, and eliminated the use of indelible ink to signify those who voted because Sendero had made a practice of cutting off fingers so marked.

The elections of 12 November demonstrated that Sendero's ability to undermine Peruvian politics is geographically limited to Ayacucho, where 66 percent of the votes were blank, and a few other highland areas where contests were annulled because of low turnout or a high number of blank or spoiled ballots. Nationwide, however, most citizens disregarded threats and went to vote, producing a 70 percent turnout and a relatively normal distribution of invalid votes. (*LAWR*, 23 November.)

The election results, did, however, indicate rising voter frustration with the major parties and a rightward shift in popular sentiment. Television personality Ricardo Belmont, running as an independent, was elected mayor of Lima with 45 percent of the vote, and nationwide independents attracted almost 30 percent of the votes. Belmont won in traditionally leftist strongholds, which the right wing interpreted as a repudiation of García's economic and social policies. Indeed, the big loser was the governing party, APRA. With only 18 percent of the national vote, it hung on to a departmental majority only in traditionally Aprista La Libertad.

The divided left did poorly. Henry Pease drew less than 10 percent, which cast doubt on his appeal as head of the IU slate, and Enrique Bernales of AS drew only 2 percent of the votes in Lima. Izquierda Unida polled a disappointing 22 percent of the vote nationally, but did win at least 52 of the provincial mayoral posts. In Lima, AS fielded candidates in 13 of the 41 districts. They won one, IU won eight, and two were lost to FREDEMO because of the split. FREDEMO captured 30 of the 41 districts in Lima and had the highest total nationally with 37 percent. (*Resumen Semanal*, 25 November–1 December.)

If Sendero's strength is inversely related to the level of organized leftist opposition, the 1989 split of Izquierda Unida (IU) must be viewed as a positive development for the guerrillas as well as for FREDEMO. The amorphous nature of the IU, however, may mean that the split will not be as detrimental as would be expected. The *personalismo* and/or sectarianism that undermines organization building may still provide a measure of success for IU and IS in the general elections. The alliances, the fronts and the names listed on the ballots are so confusing that the population votes for individuals anyway, and the leftist politicians who are community-based should do as well as previously. If Barrantes, on the strength of his own personality, forces a presidential run-off, the PCP and a majority of the leftist movement would quickly coalesce behind him. In a polarized run-off, the Aprista party would provide the balance, most likely in the direction of FREDEMO. The familiar position of opposition bloc should provide enough impetus to support a reconstitution of the IU under the direction of the IU congressional representatives. But to keep the majority of the IU in congress as an ally against revolutionary terrorism, FREDEMO will have to maintain respect for a plural democratic system which includes the participation of revolutionary communists.

Sandra Woy-Hazleton
Miami University

Puerto Rico

Population. 3,300,707
Parties. Puerto Rican Socialist Party (Partido Socialista Puertorriqueño, PSP); Puerto Rican Communist Party (Partido Comunista Puertorriqueño, PCP)
Founded. PSP, 1971; PCP, 1934
Membership. PSP: 150; PCP: 100 (both estimated)
General Secretary. PSP: Carlos Gallisa; PCP: Franklin Irrizarry
Leading Bodies. No data
Status. Legal
Last Congress. PSP: Second, 1979; PCP: Fourth, 1954
Auxiliary Organizations. No data
Publications. PSP: *Claridad* (weekly); PCP: *El Pueblo* (monthly).

Because of relative prosperity in Puerto Rico in 1989, the island's Marxist left was less active than during recent years. Puerto Rico had the most prosperous economy in the Caribbean, with industry surpassing agriculture as its leading economic sector. Mainland American corporations continued to invest heavily in the island, a trend that developed in the 1960s after they had obtained tax incentives and duty-free access for their products to the continental United States. Among the new industries were pharmaceuticals, electronics, textiles, petrochemicals, and processed foods. Tourism boomed in 1989, and even agriculture staged a comeback after years of declining production caused by the flight of farm workers to the cities. The island's 1988 GNP was $18.4 billion, or $5,574 per capita, and the real growth rate of its economy was 4.9 percent.

The only political issue that for a while was hotly debated in Puerto Rico (although interest in it abated noticeably at the end of 1989) was a plebiscite on the future status of the island proposed for 1991. Backed by the Bush administration, a bill was introduced in the Senate earlier in the year that would give Puerto Rico the right to become the 51st state, an independent country, or remain a commonwealth but with greater control over its own affairs. The bill was expected to reach the floor in the spring of 1990, and its final form, or indeed its future was uncertain.

The issue of the island's status has divided Puerto Ricans for a generation. In the latest plebiscite, which took place in 1967, 60.4 percent voted for the commonwealth status, with additional powers, but the vote did not oblige Congress to discuss the question with Puerto Rican authorities. The Puerto Rican Independence Party (PIP), a non-Marxist leftist group which boycotted the 1967 plebiscite, announced it would welcome the proposed 1991 referendum. In June, tens of thousands of demonstrators marched in San Juan for Puerto Rican independence; the march was organized by the PIP.

But the *independentistas* have not increased appreciably in strength, which is estimated at five percent of the electorate. For, while many people might support independence emotionally, the majority of Puerto Ricans are afraid of the huge economic and social problems with which such a change would saddle the new country. The rest of the voters were sharply split over the issue, with the commonwealth supporters believed to have a 5 to 10 percent edge over those of statehood. The current governor, Rafael Hernández Colón, leader of the Popular Democratic Party (PPD), wants to preserve the commonwealth status. The New Progressive Party (PNP), led by Baltasar Corrado del Río, advocates joining the Union.

During the summer, the population was split along socioeconomic lines. Poorer people supported commonwealth status, and wealthier Puerto Ricans statehood. But when more details of the referendum bill became known, many of the poorer partisans of the status quo switched sides, and so did many of the wealthier ones, with their own economic advantages or losses dictating their new preference. Puerto Ricans realized that statehood offered them the prospect of immediately benefitting from social-welfare programs that do not now apply to them. This would favor the poor, who are not concerned about having to pay federal income tax as full-fledged U.S. citizens. On the other hand, the U.S. income tax would be a new burden to the middle and upper classes, who would also lose a number of business tax breaks they enjoy today. They were also afraid that large U.S. companies might not remain in Puerto Rico if it became a state because they, too, would lose the tax break given for investment in Puerto Rico.

Another problem would be the use of the Spanish language in Puerto Rico. As the 51st state, the island would be obliged to use English as its official language, although 90 percent of Puerto Ricans speak Spanish, and only 20 percent of them are fluent in English. Statehood would also mean that three million new citizens would vote for the president, elect two senators and three to four representatives. Judging by the political trends of the past, the vote would favor the Democratic party, which could pick up two senators and possibly all the House seats.

The illegal terrorist, extreme left-wing groupings Armed Forces for National Liberation (FALN); Volunteers of the Puerto Rican Revolution; Boricua Popular Army, or Los Macheteros; and the Armed Forces of Popular Resistance remained very small and inactive in 1989. The only known terrorist actions for which Los Macheteros claimed responsibility were the explosions in June of several pipe bombs in downtown San Juan and Bayamón, fifteen miles outside San Juan, which caused small damage and no injuries.

In a letter delivered to the Associated Press, the group said it had planted the bombs to protest, among other things, the "farcical plebiscite" planned for 1991 and the imprisonment of a Machetero member for the robbery of a Wells Fargo depot in Hartford, Connecticut, in 1983, in which $7 million was taken.

George Volsky
University of Miami

United States of America

Population. 248,231,030 (July 1989)
Party. Communist Party U.S.A. (CPUSA)
Founded. 1919
Membership. 20,000 (claimed); 4–6,000 (probable)
National Chairman. Gus Hall
National Board. Gus Hall, Evelina Alarcon, Kendra Alexander, John Bachtell, Arnold Becchetti, Barry Cohen, Elsie Dickerson, Louis Diskin, Lee Dlugin, Joelle Fishman, Clyde Grubbs, James

Jackson, Maurice Jackson, Judith leBlanc, Robert Lindsay, Carole Marks, Scott Marshall, George Meyers, Charlene Mitchell, Rick Nagin, Daniel Rubin, Betty Smith, James Steele, Sidney Taylor, Jarvis Tyner, Sam Webb, Jim West, Michael Zagarell
Status. Legal
Last Congress. 24th National Convention, Chicago, 13–16 August 1987
Electoral Activity. The party did not run a presidential candidate in 1988, but fielded or supported several local candidates. Its share of the presidential vote in 1984, the last year it had a national candidate, was under 0.1 percent
Publications. *People's Daily World* (New York), Barry Cohen, editor; *Political Affairs* (theoretical monthly), Michael Zagarell, editor

The CPUSA is the largest Marxist-Leninist organization in the United States. Emerging from the fusion of two groupings founded in 1919, the CPUSA attained considerable influence during the 1930s and 1940s, playing a significant, if controversial role in the labor movement and finding allies and support among liberal, labor, and farm-oriented politicians in a number of states. Beginning in the 1920s, the party also exercised an important influence in the Black community.

The party reached its greatest size, claiming some 80,000 members, during World War II, thanks to the general national warmth toward America's then-ally, the Soviet Union.

Leadership and Party Organization. From 1956 to the present, the CPUSA has remained a marginal element of American political life. With the departure of the "Gatesites," the party, put under the guidance of the internally popular but intellectually limited Gus Hall in 1959, was effectively re-Stalinized. The elderly Gus Hall continued as party leader through 1989 with no immediate succession in view. Hall (born Arvo G. Halberg) has led the CPUSA longer than any other individual and is among the longest-tenured communist-party leaders in the world. Other major figures include Jim West, head of the National Review Commission (the control commission of the CPUSA); John Bachtell, head of the YCL; Maurice Jackson, leader of the party in Washington, D.C.; Michael Zagarell, a New York activist; Carl Bloice, Moscow correspondent for the party newspaper *People's Daily World* (published four days per week); and Herbert Aptheker, a semiacademic historian of uneven reputa-

tion who is known within the party as an ideological watchdog.

The *People's Daily World* (*PDW*) is the party periodical directed to "the masses." It emerged in 1986 from a fusion of the former *Daily World*, begun in 1967 to replace *The Worker*, then a semiweekly publication, and the then-weekly *People's World*, published first in San Francisco, then in Berkeley, beginning in 1938. The *PDW*, a multicolor daily tabloid of twelve pages with a weekend edition of 24 pages (including a Spanish-language supplement), reports a daily circulation hovering around 70,000, but its circulation documents do not specify whether this alleged figure represents daily or weekly sales (*PDW*, 27 October). In addition, communist dailies have never submitted their circulation to audit.

The CPUSA's 24th national convention, held in 1987, was attended by 400 delegates and some 600 guests. Statistics show that 60 percent of the delegates were under the age of 45; 40 percent had been members of the party for fewer than 10 years; 43 percent were women; 21 percent were Black; 4 percent were Mexican-American; and 2 percent were Puerto Rican. Union members comprised 33 percent and represented 43 labor organizations.

Domestic Party Affairs. CPUSA activities were slowed this year by the impact on the organization of foreign events (see section on International Views, Positions, and Activities). However, one notable incident was the election of Illinois state CP organizer Scott Marshall to a school council in the Chicago area (*PDW*, 20 October).

Allied Organizations. The party has an affiliated youth section, the Young Communist League, and several foreign-language groupings. In addition, the party maintains a number of active front groups, the most prominent of which is, currently, the National Council of American-Soviet Friendship, headed by the actor John Randolph, who is, aside from Angela Davis, the only well-known public figure aligned with the party. The U.S. Peace Council, affiliated with the World Peace Council, had been very active in protest activities against U.S. involvement in Central America, but has not played a dominant role. Other such groups include the National Alliance Against Racist and Political Repression and Trade Unionists for Action and Democracy. However, most of these fronts are not very active at the present time. Perhaps the most successful among them in recent years has been the long-established Labor Research Association, regarding which some debate took place during the early part of the year (see Arnold Beichman, "Wooing labor with guile?" *Washington Times*, 22 March).

Activities directed to speakers of foreign languages constitute a feature of the left-wing tradition in the United States that today is little known, but in which the party has maintained an interest (see *1989 YICA*).

One area of American life in which the CPUSA enjoys a certain attractiveness is the community of academic historians. Of several biographies and related works on party figures and activities that appeared during the year, the most controversial was undoubtedly *Paul Robeson* by Martin Bauml Duberman, published by Alfred Knopf, which revealed the deep ambivalence about Stalinism suffered by this outstanding Black figure and prominent CPUSA partisan, which led to profound depression and mental problems.

By contrast, the continuing romanticization of party history was well illustrated by an article, titled "Outlasting the FBI. A Determined Widow Restores Her Husband's Reputation as a Loyal Communist," by the 1960s writer James Simon Kunen, published in the mass-circulation photo magazine *People* (20 November). This article told of the "martyrdom" of Lillie Albertson, whose husband William, a long-time stalwart, was expelled from the party in 1964 following an FBI provocation labeling him a government agent inside the party. More comical, but similar in its naive presentation of the party's heritage, was a profile in the *San Francisco Examiner*'s Sunday magazine *Image* ("Marathon Man," by Maria Brooks, 18 June) of Walter Stack, an octogenarian graduate of the Lenin School known as one of the most Stalinist of communist labor bosses in the 1940s, who has become well-known in the San Francisco Bay region as a booster of exercise by the elderly. The article included the bizarre claim that Stack's success in sport had been helped by the "self-discipline" of party membership.

International Views, Positions, and Activities. In this, the 70th year of the CPUSA's history, the party found itself profoundly confused by bloody events in China and Romania, the overall collapse of communism in Eastern Europe, and sweeping reforms in the USSR.

This consequence was predictable, since the CPUSA is one of the last communist parties in the

world to carry on with a "1956 restorationist" leadership, i.e., a group imposed on the membership in the wake of the turmoil of the Twentieth Congress and the Hungarian insurrection.

After the crisis that exploded in the party that year, with many party leaders defending the uprising, the CPUSA never undertook a major ideological examination of Stalinism. One seemingly trivial but illustrative example of this is that the United States was the only major country not represented at the Eighteenth Congress of the Italian Communist Party in March (*The Italian Communists*, foreign bulletin of the ICP, January–March 1989). There have always been hints that party chief Hall, who had been put in place partially because of his popularity with the rank and file and his reputation as a closet reformer, has felt strong but necessarily suppressed desires for the renovation of the party. But Belgian Trotskyist Ernest Mandel characterized the CPUSA attitude toward *glasnost*'as "hesitant. It has not declared itself one way or another" (*International Viewpoint*, 30 October).

Hall and his colleagues put forward contradictory positions as the critical year 1989 wore on, and as the rigid posture of the party made it a subject for comment in the mainstream press. In an interview in the *Wall Street Journal* quite late in the year ("Communist Party in U.S. Is being Left Right on a Limb," by Jane Mayer, 7 November), Hall still described the Soviet invasion of Afghanistan as "legitimate" and said he "thought Stalin was a good leader." He added, "I didn't join the party because of Stalin, and I won't leave it because of him."

A similar article ("The Party's Shaky Line," by Bill Turque, 13 November) appeared in *Newsweek*. In it Hall repeated criticisms he had elsewhere voiced about the new freedom of the Soviet press. "Under glasnost, the editors have gone wild with untruths, especially about history and capitalism," he warned. He had similarly accused Soviet journalists of "whitewashing" fascism, concealing the nature of the kulaks (who, according to Hall, "killed, terrorized, and burned crops,"), and, in *Moscow News*, spreading anti-Semitic slanders— all this appeared in a speech by Hall reprinted in the issue for the first quarter of 1989 of the South African exile communist journal *The African Communist*.

Perhaps the point of lowest comedy in the CPUSA's struggle to deal with the winds of change from the East came in September, when Hall spoke to a New York audience and compared the flight of East Germans to the West to an American-style student beer bust: "You know in Florida you have Fort Lauderdale and you have Easter exodus to Fort Lauderdale of young people, for a good reason, excitement and so on. I have a feeling that many of these young [East Germans] have got the same idea about excitement and West Germany" (*Workers Vanguard*, 29 December).

But the party's spokespersons gave the overwhelming impression of a movement at sea, unable to find its bearings. Jarvis Tyner, one of the best-known activists, plaintively insisted "we are not pro-Stalin, we are pro-Socialist" (*PDW*, 28 November). The party's dilemma had already been summarized by Alexander Amerisov, editor of *Soviet-American Review*, when he excoriated party-supporter Michael Parenti for such remarks as "If this is glasnost, who needs anti-Communism?" and "Socialism is too important to be left in the hands of the revisionists." Amerisov also blasted a well-known polemicist, Alexander Cockburn, for praising the Brezhnev era as "a golden age for the Soviet working class" (Amerisov's text appeared in *NYT*, 27 May).

However, a slow change in perspective was visible through the second half of the year, and parallel to the march of events. In June, the party was clearly shocked by the massacre of the Chinese students at Tiananmen Square. Hall commented, "No one—students, government or Communist Party leaders—had any inkling that the protests would lead to bloodshed," but he further argued that the main problem was the ideology of the students, and intimated that the United States, where 250,000 Chinese had studied, was somehow to blame (*PDW*, 8 June).

The party ranks were not so sanguine. Margy (Lima) Wilkinson, a tested second-generation party leader, wrote, "I am appalled that [a letter writer] would 'applaud the Chinese victory over counter-revolution.' What evidence does he have that there is 'counter-revolution'? Does he expect us to believe that there weren't serious problems in China [or] that the CIA would be able to 'promote' demonstrations of two million?" Veteran supporter Morris Sharnoff, wrote, "The bloodshed [in Beijing] should be denounced and the students' lack of prudence should be censured." At the same time, in an exchange on Stalinism, party ideologist Harry Martel insisted that "Stalin's achievements cannot be expunged from the history of the Soviet Union, however much we may be overtaken by our moral outrage over unjustified execution of so many outstanding Marxists as 'enemies of the people' [during

the purges of the 1930s]". But Marxist student David Englestein wrote, "There is no scale that can balance the sentencing to prison and the killing of millions of innocent people by Stalin and his clique with any individual acts that Stalin may have performed in the interest of socialism and peace." (It is perhaps significant that Wilkinson, Sharnoff, and Englestein are all from California, traditionally known for heterodoxy within the CPUSA; all the above citations appeared in *PDW*, 11 October.)

In July the party held its first-ever national ideological conference, attended by some 600 delegates. Debate was tame, and it was reported that one participant felt the event was controlled by "brain police." (*Workers Vanguard*, 29 December.)

Another convulsion struck the party in September with the visit of Boris Yeltsin, a prominent Soviet reformist, to the United States. *PDW* chimed in with a chorus of attacks on Yeltsin, calling him "a political charlatan" and remarking on his "easy seduction" (*PDW*, 21 September, 5 October).

In line with this general hard-line stance, the party rallied to the Honecker regime in the German Democratic Republic (GDR), as the first major cracks in Eastern Europe's status quo appeared. Articles in *PDW* (17, 18 October) praised Honecker for encouraging "input" on the advance of "GDR socialism" and dwelt on problems GDR emigrés might have in finding housing and employment in the West. Within a month, however, following the (brief) replacement of Honecker by Egon Krenz, *PDW* shifted its position to argue that the growing crisis of East German society demonstrated the superiority rather than the weakness of the system (10, 14 November).

Soon William Pomeroy, a party elder statesman resident in London and active in international work (which included a stint as a communist guerrilla in the Philippines) was cautioning the faithful in terms hitherto unimagined in the CPUSA press: "Capitalist politics have a built-in safety valve: the alternation between parties...Perestroika and its program of socialist renewal are opening doors and windows to vent all pent-up grievances and protests" (*PDW*, 29 November).

The next step came in Czechoslovakia, where, for the first time since 1956, American communists indicated support for a democratization process in the Eastern bloc. Simultaneously, a remarkable mea culpa was delivered by Margrit Pittman, an authoritative party leader with long service in her native Germany, in the United States, and in the GDR. Pittman admitted "the slowness of [East Germany's] leadership in implementing the extension of democracy . . . During the eighties I heard increasing complaints about the lack of real popular participation in decision-making . . . about conspicuous consumption among the leadership and about evidence of corruption . . . The leadership had failed to broaden democratic expression, kept the lid on . . . Another source of dismay was the lifestyle of the leadership. Too many privileges, friends told me, special shops . . . huge vacation homes, fancy imported cars, large exclusive vacation recreational facilities. 'They no longer know how the average person lives,' people would say . . . [T]here were incidents of corruption . . . Some of the events taking place are painful to us . . . The mistakes . . . can only be overcome by opening the opportunities of democratic development." (*PDW*, 30 November.)

By December a formal change, at least, had taken place. *PDW* began publishing a number of useful documents, such as a statement by Hans Modrow, the new head of the East German government, and CPSU theses on elections and other democratic issues. *PDW* remained silent on the crisis of the Ceaușescu regime until 22 December, when it came out in support of the popular uprising there. (See also *PDW*, 27, 28 December.)

It should be noted that throughout the period of transformation in the Eastern bloc, the party maintained a rigid line in support of Castro and the Sandinistas, and in strong opposition to U.S. intervention against Noriega in Panama.

Other Marxist-Leninist Organizations. The American left is replete with small, sectarian groups of Marxist-Leninist as well as other casts. Remnants of the Socialist Labor Party and the Industrial Workers of the World survive, although the death of their veterans and the devolution of responsibility for these organizations on children of the 1960s have transformed them from once distinctive, if not unique political formations into leftist groupings indistinguishable from the CPUSA in their general approach to issues. The same can be said of the Catholic Worker Movement, led for so long by Dorothy Day.

There is a fairly serious agglomeration of groups under the banners of the many varieties of Trotskyism. During the 1930s the American Trotskyists, mainly organized in the Socialist Workers Party (SWP; founded 1938), were something of an inspiration for their fellow Trotskyists around the world.

The SWP itself fell apart in the 1980s, with most of its veterans leaving to form a group called Socialist Action. Smaller groups of former SWP militants constituted themselves as the North Star Network, the Fourth International Tendency, etc. The remnant of the SWP has become a kind of public relations firm for Castro and the Sandinistas. It controls a publishing house, Pathfinder Press, and a chain of 35 bookstores that also function as SWP headquarters. On its way, the Trotskyist movement spawned many sectlets.

The third main grouping of Marxist-Leninists in the United States, alongside the CPUSA and the Trotskyists, consists of groups originating in the Maoist movement of the 1960s. Some of these groups, such as the bizarre mixture of Trotskyism and Maoism known as the Workers World Party, or the quasicult known as the League of Revolutionary Struggle (publishing the newspaper *Unity*) have attained some limited success in electoral coalitions with Black politicians in Chicago, the San Francisco Bay Area, and elsewhere. For example, the League of Revolutionary Struggle saw election of one of "its" candidates, Oscar Ríos, to a vice-mayorship in the rural town of Watsonville, California. The largest such group, formerly known as the Line of March, changed its name to Frontline Political Organization.

A case apart seems to be that of the Revolutionary Communist Party (RCP), a group faithful to the memory of Mao and the "gang of four," with a high profile of public propaganda and provocation, and which runs a chain of twelve bookstore/headquarters around the country. RCP claims to serve as an American solidarity network for the Peruvian terrorist movement Sendero Luminoso (Shining Path), but such claims seem clearly exaggerated.

So great is the proliferation of such groups in the broad reaches of the American political landscape, in which, nonetheless, they remain only microscopically evident, that it would require a separate yearbook to describe them all. For each example mentioned above, there seem to be dozens of similar entities, Trotskyist, Maoist, feminist, and Black nationalist. Finally, there are strains influenced by anarchism and the extremist leftism of European communism during the 1920s. Altogether, Marxism-Leninism in the United States provides a complicated, if fundamentally irrelevant inventory of groups and types.

Stephen Schwartz
San Francisco, California

Uruguay

Population. 2,988,813 (*World Fact Book*, 1989)
Party. Communist Party of Uruguay (PCU)
Founded. 1920
Membership. 30,000 (estimate based on claims; 11,000, *Pravda*, 22 December 1987; and 27,000 increase in last three years according to Report to 1988 Congress)
General Secretary. Jaime Pérez
Executive Committee. Pérez, general secretary; Rodney Arismendi, president (until his death on 27 December); Daniel Baldassari, Leopoldo Bruera, Thelman Borges, Félix Díaz, Edgar Lanza, León Lev, José Luis Massera, Jorge Mazzarovich, Rafael Sanseviero, Juan Angel Toledo, Pedro Toledo, Andrés Toriani, Esteban Valenti, Eduardo Viera
Status. Legal
Last Congress. Twenty-first, 7–11 December 1988
Last Election. November 1989; PCU ran with Frente Amplio coalition, with ca. 34 percent of votes and 22 of 99 seats (PCU's share, 10 percent and 11 seats)
Auxiliary Organization. Union of Communist Youth
Publications. *La Hora*; *El Popular*

If democracy has something to do with free, contested elections and public suffrage on important issues, then 1989 found Uruguay in the full flush of democratic expression. The year saw Uruguayans voting on whether to uphold an amnesty law regarding the military abuses committed during over eleven years of dictatorship (1973–1984), a first-time primary election to determine the presidential candidate of the Batallista wing of the ruling Colorado Party, and university elections. Finally, on 26 November, the first totally unrestricted national and local elections since 1971 took place.

The election of November 1984 that brought Julio Maria Sanguinetti to the presidency proved to be one of the more successful examples of transition politics in Latin America. The Colorado government that emerged from the negotiations with the military which ended in the so-called Pacto de Club Naval can pride itself on the full restoration of civil

and political rights and a marked improvement in the Uruguayan economy from the near depression levels experienced from 1982 to 1984, when the GDP fell by over 16 percent. The government managed to increase the GDP by more than 7 percent in 1986 and some 5 percent in 1987, while raising real wages almost 20 percent from 1985 to 1988. In 1988 the country's economic performance was much poorer, with growth of the GDP a meager .5 percent (the GDP has still not reached its 1980 level). (An invaluable source of economic data is *Búsqueda*, Uruguay's most professional and influential newsweekly.) This slowdown has important political consequences that will be discussed below. Nevertheless, Uruguay's steady and conservative monetary and fiscal policy has pleased the U.S. and international financial institutions. Its foreign policy and trade policy, brilliantly guided by former foreign minister Enrique Inglesias for the first three and a half years of the Sanguinetti government, has paid dividends in terms of international respect and increased trade opportunities.

Human Rights and the Plebiscite. The one issue that the government did not resolve during its first three years was the question of human-rights violations. When he campaigned for the presidency during the dictatorship, Sanguinetti promised justice, but also made clear that the government itself (probably as a result of negotiations with the military about the latter's relinquishing of power) would not seek prosecutions. He made it equally clear, however, that individual citizens who had grievances could use the judicial system to seek redress. By mid-1986, after the Supreme Court had ruled in favor of civilian court jurisdiction, some 38 cases were making their way through the courts. Several active and retired officers were subpoenaed to testify in cases involving disappearances, death, and torture. When Army Commander Hugo Medina refused to serve the subpoenas on his men, a potential constitutional crisis began to brew. Two amnesty proposals (one of which would have involved two or three trials) were defeated in Parliament. The issue festered until late 1986 when, just 24 hours before three officers were due in court, Wilson Ferreira Aldunate, head of the principal opposition party in Parliament, decided to support the government's call for a blanket amnesty and thus avoid a crisis.

But the story does not end there. Uruguay's constitution permits a referendum on laws passed by Parliament, provided that 25 percent of the electorate sign a petition requesting it. In late 1988, after many hurdles and obstacles had been overcome by the pro-referendum forces, the court announced that the requisite number of signatures had been obtained.

The plebiscite took place on 16 April and was preceded by intensive campaigning on both sides of the issue. The governing Colorado Party counselled support of the amnesty law (yellow ballot) as did most of the Blanco leadership, the exceptions being Senator Carlos Julio Pereyra and his Movimiento Nacional de Rocha. Those in favor of an abrogation of the law (green ballot) waged an energetic and effective media campaign based on the idea that no one should be above the law.

In the end the plebiscite was defeated by a margin of 57 to 43 percent. The green vote won in Montevideo by a clear-cut 55 to 45 percent, but a massive 60+ percent support of the law in the interior doomed the initiative.

The defeat of the plebiscite was a victory for the government, but an even bigger victory for Defense Minister Hugo Medina. The retired commander in chief of the army had staked his reputation with his colleagues on his ability to negotiate their surrendering of the government without danger of reprisals for, or repercussions from their actions while they were in power.

The armed forces remained backstage and let electoral politics play itself out. They do, however, have a clear agenda after the installation of the new government in March 1990. Domestically, they want a coalition government that will assure a parliamentary majority for the implementation of economic liberalization and the passage of legislation regulating the unions and reforming the university. Internationally, they want a creditable administration that can persuade Washington to provide them with the modern equipment they desire. The military's goals are quite compatible with the programs presented by president-elect Lacalle.

Elections and the Rules of the Game in Uruguay. In order to understand the elections of November 1989 and their implications for the future stability and development of Uruguay, we need to be familiar with the country's peculiar electoral and party system. (This discussion is adapted from my study, *Uruguay: Democracy at the Crossroads*, Boulder, Colo.: Westview Press, 1988, pp. 86–89.)

Uruguay's electoral laws, which were ultimately unaltered by the military, provide for a Senate and a Chamber of Deputies elected by strict proportional representation. The president is elected by means of

the "double simultaneous vote," which results in a concurrent primary and election. Basically, the election is conducted by means of a list system that allows several presidential candidates to run under the banner of the same party, with the ballot counting for both the candidate and his party. The candidate who receives the most votes from the party that receives the most votes gains the presidency, as seen in the following example:

Colorado Party		*Blanco Party*	
Candidate A:	40	Candidate D:	45
Candidate B:	30	Candidate E:	30
Candidate C:	30	Candidate F:	20
Total	100	Total	95

Given this distribution, the Colorado Party wins the presidency by 100 votes to 95, and candidate A—the Colorado candidate with the most votes—becomes president, even though candidate D of the Blanco party received more votes (45) than did candidate A (40). This electoral system has been conducive to party factionalism and citizen identification with these factions rather than with the party or the nation as a whole.

The University and Politics in Uruguay. The university continued to struggle in a highly politicized atmosphere with considerable antipathy from the Colorado government. Since the university is the principal focus of Montevideo's 18–30-year-olds, one would hope to find some expression of new energy and the potential for change. The reality is disappointing.

Uruguay's sole public university, in the tradition of the Córdoba reforms of 1918 and in accord with a law passed in 1958, is autonomous and governed by school (*facultad*) councils and a university assembly, all elected by students, alumni, and faculty. This past June, some 100,000 Uruguayans were eligible to vote in the university elections, with some 60 percent of these doing so. The slates of candidates reflected party structures and allegiances, the one anomaly being the weakness of Colorado representation. The results were no surprise. The left, which has controlled teaching and governance of the university since the early 1960s (with the exception of the period of military rule), continues its dominant, but not monopolistic position.

The leftist student coalition (ASCEEP-FEUU) received some 52 percent of the vote, winning a majority in eight of eleven *facultades*. The Blanco Student Group (CGU) won a majority of seats in three schools: Agronomy, Veterinary Medicine, and Law, obtaining about 30 percent of the vote. A student faction supporting social-democratic Senator Hugo Batalla and his PGP after its split from the Frente Amplio managed to get a little over 10 percent of the vote.

The Elections and the Left. The left, which united in 1971 under the aegis of the Frente Amplio (Broad Front), underwent a split in 1989. Senator Hugo Batalla, head of the PGP (Partido por el Gobierno del Pueblo), took his social-democratic party out of the Frente, which had already seen the defection of the small Christian Democratic Party. Batalla polled more than 40 percent of the left's vote in 1984. Batalla ran for president in 1989 with the support of the Christian Democratic Party and another small social-christian party, the Unión Cívica, under a new party label, Nuevo Espacio.

The Frente Amplio, consisting mainly of the Communist and Socialist parties with the participation of smaller groups including dissident Christian Democrats and members of the ex-guerrilla movements—the Tupamaros and the Partido por la Victoria del Pueblo—ran their 1971 candidate, General Líber Seregni, for president once again, and shrewdly put up a popular doctor and soccer-club president as their candidate for mayor (*intendente*) of Montevideo. As the campaign began, the Frente was given little chance of capturing Montevideo, which they had lost by only 18,000 votes in 1984, because of the departure from the front of the social democrats. But the November 1989 elections proved a watershed event.

The first truly unfettered contest since the military coup in 1973 brought historic changes. The election gave the Blancos the presidency and the Frente Amplio control of the government of Montevideo, thus proving historic on several levels. Luis Alberto Lacalle will be only the third Blanco president in this century, although the Blancos did gain majority control of the collegial executive system during the 1920s. The Frente's clear victory in Montevideo, where half the country's people live, will bring a socialist doctor, Tabaré Vásquez, to the Intendencia. This will give the left its first experience with executive power at any level in Uruguay, and they are starting with the second–most import elective office in the country. The Frente's presidential candidate actually received almost as many votes as Lacalle, but he was the only candidate in his

party, whereas Lacalle benefitted from the significant number of votes Carlos Julio Pereyra received for his presidential candidacy within the Blanco Party. The Blancos received 38 percent of the presidential vote to 30 percent for the Colorado's and 22 percent for the Frente. The electoral collapse of the Colorado Party, which had received 41 percent of the vote in 1984, made the above breakthroughs possible.

Uruguay now has a three-party political system (some would say four, if Nuevo Espacio remains independent). The historic electoral dominance of the Colorado and Blanco parties has been shattered. The Frente Amplio and Nuevo Espacio polled more votes than the Colorado Party. As indicated, the Frente, with 35 percent of the vote in Montevideo, won the mayoralty of the capital. With half the country's people, its only institutions of higher education, the only national TV and radio stations and press, Montevideo is truly Uruguay's heart. The new *intendente*, Tabaré Vásquez, proved to be a tireless and charismatic campaigner. He has pledged to improve sanitation, build thousands of units of low-cost housing, reduce busfares, and improve the collection of municipal taxes. His program will not be welcomed by President Lacalle, and friction with the central government is to be anticipated.

Given the left's frustration over the loss in the human-rights plebiscite, its victory in Montevideo gives progressive forces a stake in the system as well as executive responsibility and accountability. They must demonstrate that the left can act as far more than merely a vocal opposition coalition. They must act wisely and temper their victory with the knowledge that they won the capital with only 2 percent more votes than they received in 1984. Again, it is important to stress that the left's victory in Montevideo, like Lacalle's at the national level (the Blanco received only 3 percent more of the votes than they did in 1984), was partially the result of the electoral collapse of the Colorado Party, whose share of the total vote fell from 41 to 31 percent.

The Frente's victory in Montevideo is nevertheless remarkable, given the fact that some nine months earlier the social-democratic factions which had received over 40 percent of the coalition's vote in 1984, had left the coalition to form a new party. How then, did the Frente manage to keep and slightly expand the total number of votes it obtained? The youth vote is a major part of the explanation. It appears that first-time voters and those that were young adults during the dictatorship are tired of traditional party politics. Another major factor was Senator Batalla's supporters. Many of those who voted for him in 1984 stayed with the Frente. His showing reflected disenchanted Colorado voters, not ex-Frentistas.

Within the left, the Communist Party of Uruguay (PCU) was the big winner. Running under the title of Democracia Avanzada (List 1001), the PCU received some 10 percent of the total vote and almost 50 percent of the Frente's vote. The PCU will have four senators, including the current party leader, Jaime Pérez. The party will also have eleven deputies. Former general secretary, Rodney Arismendi, gained one of the seats, but died unexpectedly on 27 December. The PCU's success is partly the result of effective television commercials broadcast during the campaign, in which the rhetoric was clearly toned down.

Within the Frente Amplio, the PCU, with its 46 percent, was followed by the Socialist Party, which obtained some 22 percent of the coalition's total number of votes. A group that included dissident elements of the Christian Democrats was third, with 16 percent. A more radical group, which includes two former guerrilla groups, the Tupamaros and the Partido por la Victoria del Pueblo, were next, with 11 percent, which represents only 2 percent of the total number of votes cast in the election.

In an interview granted to Uruguay's leading newsweekly, *Búsqueda*, General Secretary Jaime Pérez of the PCU conceded that the party has to come to grips with its historic ties to Stalinism and some aspects of Leninism. He strongly implied that significant party reforms would take place at the next party congress, scheduled for September 1990, at which time it would become clear whether there is a split between renovationist and more conservative sectors of the party. (*Búsqueda*, 14 December.)

Senator Hugo Batalla's social-democratic party, Nuevo Espacio, was disappointed with its showing of less than 9 percent. Nevertheless, its members could point to the fact that they pulled many votes away from the Colorado Party. Nuevo Espacio will remain a separate party for the time being, but a merger with the Frente Amplio by the time of the 1994 elections should not be ruled out.

Looking back at this extraordinary year in Uruguay, one can safely conclude that its citizens voted for change and against the inertia that overtook the Sanguinetti government after its gracious and effective first three years in office. The voters, and especially the young, decided to shake things up. They did it democratically and completely non-violently. Uruguayan politics should prove to be a lot more interesting in the next few years. The transition from military to civilian rule has ended, although military power has not. The building of an effective and vital economic system is the immediate challenge. The political system has now been opened up enough to make that possible.

Lacalle, individually, received some 22 percent of the total vote. His party received 38 percent. Thus he can only be guaranteed a parliamentary majority for his program if he receives a significant amount of support from other parties. However, the Frente and Nuevo Espacio will not support Lacalle's privatization efforts, nor his call for union and university reforms; hence Lacalle will have to make a deal with the Colorados. Such a deal could prove easy to conclude, once the bitterness between Senator Batalla and ex-president Sanguinetti is overcome or at least neutralized. Lacalle will offer several ministries to the Colorados and hopefully get the "coalition" government he has spoken about since the start of his campaign for president.

Lacalle has pledged to reduce the fiscal deficit (now running at some 6 percent of the GDP), streamline government bureaucracy, privatize or get at least some private capital participation in the ailing state enterprises, and resolve the country's foreign-debt problems. He also wants to encourage foreign investment and believes that the unions must be regulated in order to attract foreign investment. He intends to submit legislation which would call for a secret ballot before a strike could be called.

Many of the above goals will put Lacalle's government in conflict with the leftist government in Montevideo, that city's municipal unions, and other unions, almost all of which are controlled by the left, especially by the communists. Yet it is the communists who will probably argue for the most cautious and statesmanlike positions within the Frente. Running Montevideo is a huge challenge for the left. If they can do it with some success, they would certainly be re-elected in 1994 (for elections to all offices in Uruguay take place simultaneously once every five years) and also have a realistic chance to gain the presidency if the Blancos falter.

Martin Weinstein
The William Paterson College of New Jersey

Venezuela

Population. 19,263,376 (July 1989)
Parties. Communist Party of Venezuela (Partido Comunista de Venezuela; PCV), pro-Soviet; Movement to Socialism (Movimiento al Socialismo; MAS), democratic socialist
Founded. PCV: 1931; MAS: 1971, PCV splinter
Membership. PCV: 4,000 estimated
Chief Officials. PCV: General Secretary Alonso Ojeda Olaechea (71); MAS: President Pompeyo Márquez
Politburo. PCV: Seven members, Alonso Ojeda, President Jesús Faría, Pedro Ortega Díaz, Trino Melean, Silvio Varela, Alí Morales, (Eduardo Gallegos Mancera died on 3 July); three alternates, including Luis Ciano and José Manuel Carrasquel
Executive Committee. MAS: 15 members, including Pompeyo Márquez, General Secretary Freddy Muñoz, Teodoro Petkoff, Victor Hugo de Paola, Mayita Acosta, Rafael Thielen, Leopoldo Puchi, Manuel Molina Peñaloza, and Luis Manuel Esculpi
Central Committee. PCV: 65 members; MAS: National Directorate, 45 members
Status. Both legal
Last Congress. PCV: seventh, October, 1985; MAS: sixth national convention, June–July, 1985
Last Election. 3 December, for governors, mayors, city councils. PCV: did not elect any governors or mayors; city council results not yet available. The PCV has one of 201 federal deputies. MAS: elected one governor; claims to have elected 25 mayors and more than 300 councilmen. The MAS has 18 federal deputies and three of 46 senators.
Auxiliary Organizations. PCV: Unitary Central of Venezuelan Workers (Central Unitária de Trabajadores Venezolanos; CUTV), Communist Youth (Juventud Comunista; JC)
Publications. PCV: *Tribuna Popular*, weekly, previously edited by the late Eduardo Gallegos Mancera; *Canta Claro*, monthly ideological supplement of Central Committee

On 3 December Venezuelans chose governors and mayors for the first time by direct vote and also elected city councils. State governors had previously been appointed by the president, and the office of mayor did not exist. Despite these important reforms, abstention was high everywhere, and reached 70 percent in Caracas. The apathy was attributed in large part to the disillusion generated by ongoing disclosures of outrageous financial scandals from the administration that had left office in February. The blatant corruption of former leaders of President Carlos Andrés Pérez's own party, Democratic Action (Acción Democrática; AD), did not sit well with lower- and middle-class voters who have been seriously affected by the current economic austerity program. The measures were suggested by the International Monetary Fund to promote a free-market, anti-statist economy in Venezuela. Introduced by Pérez shortly after his inauguration, they produced steep price increases. Annual inflation of about 78 percent has annulled the February wage hikes. Increases for January 1990, projected at 24 percent, may have to be higher.

Public sector wages had been raised, but the private sector was expected to conduct its own bargaining and had no immediate cushion at all. Protests degenerated into two days of the worst rioting and looting in 30 years. At least 300 people were killed on 27 and 28 February before state-of-emergency and curfew decrees stemmed the worst of the violence. Calm slowly returned with the decree of compensatory wage increases for the private sector and restored price controls for a basket of basic goods. The calm is not an easy one, however, and fears return with each new student protest. So far, they have not escaped control, nor did the successful general strike called on 18 May.

PCV. The PCV participated in two opposition coalitions that backed winning gubernatorial candidates, and this should give them an administrative post or two. Data is not yet available on the city-council elections, but a strong showing is considered unlikely. The party was more active on the labor front. The Politburo published a document which called the riots an "explosion of national discontent"; urged the workers to unite in the struggle to defend their rights to a better life; and said congress must take steps to protect the people from the effects of inflation (*Neues Deutschland*, 2 March).

The AD-dominated Confederation of Venezuelan Workers (Confederación de Trabajadores Venezolanos; CTV) held one May Day parade; President Pérez attended and was booed by the 80,000 workers present. Another parade, attended by three or four thousand, was held by the National Council of Workers and People, representing the CUTV, some CTV dissidents, the Social Christian Confederation (CODESA), the Federation of University Professors, and others. CUTV president José Manuel Carrasquel called the parade a warm-up for the general strike on 18 May: "It is not a protest against the CTV . . . Although we do not share the ideas of some CTV directors, we believe that the struggle for labor unity is more necessary than ever to confront those who would deny the rights and conquests of the workers" (*El Universal*, 29 April).

Ricardo León represented the PCV on the general-strike committee headed by CTV president Juan José del Pino (now retired and replaced by Antonio Ríos until the CTV convention in 1990). Del Pino said the twelve-hour strike on 18 May was "98 percent effective" (ibid., 19 May). It was declared illegal by the government but not contested; workers agreed to maintain basic services and not to stop essential industries. President Pérez established a government-labor-management commission to seek "concertación" (agreements) on issues such as renegotiation of the foreign debt, wage policy, privatizations, and petroleum. The CUTV submitted a paper but was not invited to commission meetings. Public-sector strikes continued throughout the year, affecting, among others, police, teachers, health and justice workers and social-security doctors.

The leader of the East German delegation to Pérez's inauguration, Manfred Gerlach, chief of the State Council of Ministers, met with several political leaders, including Jesús Faría and Alonso Ojeda. A PCV delegation led by Perfecto Abreu was received in East Berlin in April by Politburo member and Central Committee secretary Horst Dohlus. (*Neues Deutschland*, 6 February, 26 April.) In an article warning of anti-communist "cultural imperialism" by the United States, Hector Mujica admits that Latin American communist parties have been guilty of "dogmatism and sectarianism, but this is now history." According to Mujica, these parties must reach out to broader sectors of the intelligentsia, especially the "greens" and the liberation theologists. (*WMR*, August.) A release from the PCV Politburo "condemns and protests the U.S. invasion of Panama . . . an imperialistic act which threatens the atmosphere of peace and détente that was being created in the world." It asks the Venezuelan government to assume a "Latin American, Bolivarian" attitude toward this crime against the Panamanian people. (*El Nacional*, 21 December.)

MAS. The Revolutionary Left Movement (Movimiento de la Izquierda Revolucionária; MIR) has merged with the MAS. Former MIR secretary general Moisés Moleiro is now under general secretary of MAS. With eighteen deputies, three senators, and now one governor, the MAS can no longer be ignored by the two major parties, AD and the Social Christian COPEI. MAS president Pompeyo Márquez is vice-president of the senate, and Carlos Tablante was first vice-president of the Chamber of Deputies until he resigned to run for governor of the state of Aragua. His winning coalition included the Peoples' Electoral Movement (Movimiento Electoral del Pueblo; MEP), the PCV, and three regional groups. MAS delegates sat on the National Committee for Political Reform, where their preference for maintaining proportional representation on city councils prevailed. Victor Hugo de Paola, Freddy Muñoz, and Luis Alvaray are permanent delegates to the "Concertación" Commission.

Former presidential candidate Teodoro Petkoff held Central Bank president Pedro Tinoco and his shock program directly responsible for the February riots (*Latin America Weekly Review*, 30 March). Later, he also criticized Pérez, who, during ten years out of office, had "talked like a social democrat" and has now "bought all the postmodernist neoliberalism of his technocrats . . . He has unleashed inflation with no protection for workers, forgetting that time is necessary to convert a controlled market—with all its fat cats and their privileges—to a free market with relatively balanced competition" (*El Universal*, 2 May). By August, Petkoff saw the first six months of Pérez's presidency as "an economic disaster. What we have in front of us is a prolonged recession" (*NYT*, 23 August).

Pompeyo Márquez visited Moscow in May as a member of the Permanent Conference of Political Parties of Latin America (Conferencia de Partidos Políticos de América Latina; COPPAL). In discussions with *WMR*, he named the U.S. policy of intervention as the chief external obstacle to the democratic process in Latin America: "Washington does not seem to understand that Latin Americans are going to continue on the road to independence and sovereignty" (*WMR*, May). Petkoff had hard words for the U.S. intervention in Panama: "an act of absolutely inadmissible imperial insolence." He also deplored the Venezuelan reaction, which was to condemn the invasion but agree to recognize the new government as soon as U.S. troops are withdrawn: "It cancels all Pérez's ambitions to exercise a leadership beyond our frontiers . . . By recognizing the Endara government, he sanctions the invasion. Noriega was no hero of democracy but the crisis really began with the U.S. decision to disown the Torrijos-Carter Treaty. The invasion is therefore the continuation of a chain of interventions." (*El Nacional*, 21 December.)

Other Leftist Parties. The MEP gubernatorial candidate Ovidio Gonzáles won on a coalition ticket of the Opposition Front in the state of Anzoátegui. The MEP is a CTV-based socialist party that broke away from AD in 1968. It has three deputies in congress.

Bolívar was the only state where the opposition won without a coalition. Andrés Velásquez of the union-based Causa R (Radical Cause) polled 52 percent of the vote there. Until his election, he was one of three Causa R deputies in congress and the party's presidential candidate in 1988. Velásquez said he was taking over a governorship that had been "the mecca of inefficient bureaucracy and parasitism . . . at the service of party patronage and a corrupt political class that never thought of the people's interests but governed for its personal benefit" (report from Joseph Mann, Caracas). He pledges to eliminate corruption, improve health and education, and promote economic development in the region. He would support domestic and foreign investment in downstream transformation industries and services such as tourism but strongly opposes privatization of the basic industries. Velásquez will have to work with a state assembly where his party holds only two of nineteen seats; AD has twelve and COPEI five. (Ibid.)

Causa R was founded by Alfredo Maneiro in the late 1970s along the lines of other radical Marxist-Leninist groups that proliferated at that time. (The Popular Struggle Committees [Comités de Lucha Popular; CLP] and the Revolutionary Armed Group [Grupo Armado Revolucionário; GAR] have disappeared; the Trotskyist Socialist League [Liga Socialista; LS] resurfaced this year in election coalitions but is insignificant.) Causa R had four national bases: workers in Guayana, the poor in Catia, students in Carabobo, and intellectuals in Agua Mansa. The Agua Mansa group has some influence, but the party's growth after Maneiro's death in the early 1980s is a result of Velásquez's tenacious union work. Revolutionary rhetoric has been largely discarded in favor of working within the system.

Guerrillas. In August a low intensity bomb exploded in front of Congress, scattering flyers signed by an unknown group, the Bolivarian Military Unit (Unidad Militar Bolivariana). The flyers protested government corruption. (*Diario Las Américas*, 25 August.) Sometimes-violent student protests continued throughout the year, but data on organized political involvement is scant and unclear. The Colombian National Liberation Army (Ejército de Liberación Nacional; ELN) kidnapped and released after payment of ransom at least one Venezuelan rancher and is believed to be implicated in other cases. The ELN or drug trafficking gangs killed five members of the Venezuelan National Guard in a border ambush in October. The Venezuelan Defense Ministry apologized for a raid into Colombian territory in late April in pursuit of guerrillas who had attacked a National Guard outpost. The guerrillas were identified as members of the Popular Liberation Army (Ejército de Liberación Popular; ELP). The Supreme Court is reopening the investigation of the massacre of fourteen fishermen by security forces at El Amparo in 1988 (see *YICA*, 1989).

Carole Merten
San Francisco, California

ASIA AND THE PACIFIC

Introduction

As the Marxist-Leninist regimes of Eastern Europe crumbled and collapsed in late 1989, the states with ruling communist parties in Asia tightened their control and appealed to communist orthodoxy as justification for adhering to the road of central planning, monopoly control by the communist party, and socialism. In other states the influence of communist parties seemed weak and faded; in Malaysia communist guerrilla forces surrendered to authorities in Thailand and then were taken away to be settled in distant rural areas of that country.

Except in the Philippines, where the New People's Army increased its attacks on U.S. armed forces personnel and installations and other foreigners, not since World War II had the future seemed so bleak for the communist movement in Asia. These developments can be briefly reviewed by classifying communist activity as follows: states with ruling communist parties, states with banned communist parties in opposition, and states with legal communist parties.

States with Ruling Communist Parties. In the People's Republic of China (PRC) a fierce power struggle erupted in late spring 1989 at the same time that massive, peaceful demonstrations were being held in major cities across the country. Hu Yaobang's death on 15 April sparked those demonstrations, which continued primarily in Beijing; on 4 June units of the People's Liberation Army entered Beijing and ruthlessly removed demonstrators from Tiananmen Square and patrolled streets, killing and injuring perhaps as many as several thousand people.

The communist party's power struggle ended when the faction led by Deng Xiaoping, some old cadres, and Li Peng ousted General Secretary Zhao Ziyang on 24 June and replaced him with the Shanghai mayor, Jiang Zemin. In the months after 4 June, the party and the government cracked down, arresting tens of thousands, executing many, and imprisoning untold numbers. Martial law was imposed and continued until 10 January 1990, when it was lifted in Beijing.

The economy continued to deteriorate in the last quarter of 1989: industrial output grew only 6.8 percent for the year, down from 17.7 percent in 1980. Rising domestic and foreign debt and a severe shortage of energy and raw materials forced numerous factories to shut their doors. Living standards dropped, unemployment grew, and in the cities the mood was angry and tense. Even though the country boasted the best harvest ever—in excess of 400 million metric tons of grain—the government had been forced to depreciate the currency against the dollar some 21 percent to boost sagging exports and slow imports.

The communist party continued to control information and public discussion as rigidly as it had in the Maoist years. The press repeatedly published articles extolling the virtues of socialism under the leadership of the communist party, justifying the suppression of the spring demonstrations by referring to them as counterrevolutionary, and defending the communist party and its rule since 1949 as the only salvation for China and socialism. At the same time, the government pushed an all-out attack on "bourgeois thinking" and Western-style democracy. The state provided only minimal information about the events in Romania in December, and the leadership put its security forces on a first-degree alert late that month.

The new leadership of Jiang Zemin, Li Peng, and Yang Shangkun promised the people hard work and frugal living, adhering to Deng Xiaoping's message some five days before the Tiananmen slaughter that the communist party must cultivate the "enterprising spirit in hard struggle and plain living." Deng particularly emphasized that "promoting plain living must be a main objective in education, and this should be grasped in the next sixty to seventy years."

Sino-American relations suffered their most serious setback since diplomatic relations were resumed between the two states in December 1978. On 20 June, President George Bush ordered mild sanctions against and suspended high-level contacts with the Beijing regime. On 9 December a second top-level U.S. mission went to Beijing. In the following days President Bush repeatedly stated that some U.S. sanctions would be lifted against the PRC. On 11 January 1990 Beijing finally lifted martial law, but despotic control over the country continues.

Active bilateral exchanges continued between the PRC and the Soviet Union despite the June crackdown. In September discussions began in Beijing on setting up a demilitarized zone along the entire length of the Sino-Soviet border. These talks ended with a statement that troops would begin withdrawing in six months. In early November, Deng Xiaoping criticized Mikhail Gorbachev and several socialist bloc countries for following a political course that was "not in conformity with true Marxism-Leninism."

In North Korea, Kim Il-song's regime hosted the World Youth Festival in July and continued to extol the virtues of Kim's son Kim Chong-il. Father and son began preparing for the Seventh Congress of the Korean Workers' party (time to be announced). Meanwhile the party and the government lashed out at bourgeois influences and called for ideological vigilance.

Throughout 1989 the DPRK government continued its campaign to meet the ambitious goals set in the Third Seven-Year Plan. The regime admitted that the country had suffered food shortages, but blamed bad weather for poor harvests. The leadership still has not introduced market incentives or other reforms, relying on orthodox central planning through state and collective organizations.

In the Socialist Republic of Vietnam a complex power struggle still rages. The old cadres dominate in the party's Politburo and remain committed to the "socialist road." At the Seventh Plenum in August, however, Party Secretary Nguyen Van Linh reported that "ideological deviationism had emerged among a large number of Party cadres and rank-and-file members" that represented "deviant ideological viewpoints." Linh admitted that this deviationism was due to poor party leadership.

Certain groups like the southern party members and elements of the military also challenged the party's leadership. The Club of Former Resistance Fighters, located in Ho Chi Minh City, sent an open letter to the Central Committee in June calling for true elections rather than the standard party-controlled elections. Reports surfaced in military newspapers that the party had a "no-win" policy for waging war in Cambodia.

Cambodia's communist party, founded on 30 September 1951, now has ten thousand members, a thirteen-person Politburo, and a Central Committee of 49 full members and 16 alternate members. In 1989 the party held numerous regional congresses as well as a second Party Cadres' Conference in April. The regional party congresses defined the duties of cadres and set forth rules for conducting local party meetings and linking lower cells with superior party units.

In communist-ruled Laos, elections took place on 26 March for 79 seats in the Supreme People's Assembly, the highest-ranking body of the Lao People's Democratic Republic. The party drew up a new constitution, and the country resumed diplomatic relations with China.

On 12 January 1990 several thousand Mongolians staged a rally in Ulan Bator, the capital of the People's Republic of Mongolia, demanding an end to their country's Stalinist communist system. Landlocked between the Soviet Union and the PRC, Mongolia has the oldest communist system in the world after Moscow's.

States with Banned Communist Party Opposition. In early 1989, some one thousand members of the Communist Party of Malaya who lived along the Thai-Malaysian border surrendered to the Fourth Army Command in Thailand. In an agreement with Thai government officials, these communists said they would give up armed struggle in return for being allowed to permanently live in Thailand without harassment. The former insurgents were to be resettled on Thai territory in Songkhla and Yala provinces.

In Indonesia the governor of the National Defense Institute, Major General Subiyakto, issued repeated warnings of government infiltration by underground activists of the Indonesian Communist party. Outside of various student demonstrations during the year, the communist party members seemed unable to organize labor or other groups in their efforts to destabilize Indonesian society.

In Burma the communist party began fragmenting in 1989 into new organizations. Three of these now claim an ethnic rather than ideological rationale for their activities. Another intends to join the broad opposition front forming to fight the military dictatorship in Rangoon. This breakup might mark the party's end as a significant communist insurgent force within the country.

Philippine Communist Party (CPP) documents captured by the armed forces of the Philippines in

1989 provide new information about the background of Central Committee cadres and reveal that the party's Politburo held various conferences throughout the year in Luzon. These documents also showed that the party has influential ties to labor unions that represent some 400,000 workers, as well as to many urban and rural front organizations.

In 1989 the communist party began a campaign of selective attacks against U.S. personnel, U.S. military facilities, and foreign aid projects. Such attacks began on 9 April with a bombing attempt against a U.S. Navy communications relay station atop Mount Santo Thomas in Benquet province. On 21 April, the New People's Army killed Colonel James N. Rowe (U.S. Army) outside the Quezon City compound of the Joint U.S. Military Assistance Group. On 26 September, NPA guerrillas killed three U.S. civilian military contract employees. On 24 December, more guerrillas strafed the U.S. Information Office in Davao City on Mindanao. The party's armed forces also attacked Japanese and Canadian nationals working on economic projects.

These attacks on foreigners represented the dominance of the militarist faction of the CPP leadership. The party's founder and reputed chairman in absentia, Jose Maria Sison, recently wrote in his new book, *The Philippine Revolution: The Leader's View*, about a strategy of "protracted people's war"—stages of defense and attack whereby the party can mount a revolution while mobilizing the masses to overturn the present government and its supporters. Sison now resides in the Netherlands.

States with Legal Communist Parties. In Pakistan the communist party openly held its Third Congress on 25–27 May, which was attended by 127 delegates from across the country. The congress re-elected Imam Ali Nazish as general secretary, considered a Central Committee report on past errors of the party, and approved a plan for future action.

In India the Bharatiya Janata party scored a big election win, acquiring more seats than all the leftist parties combined. The Indian communist party also failed to recruit new, young members, and the party continued to remain out of step with the voters. At the Fourteenth Party Congress there were no major changes in personnel or policies.

In Japan the Japanese Communist party made no progress with the voters, scoring as poorly as it had in previous elections. Kenji Miyamoto, the 81-year-old chairman of the Central Committee, remained in charge.

These examples of legal communist parties in a few Asian states indicate that the veteran leadership still dominates those parties, that those parties are increasingly out of touch with voters, and that they are unable to recruit young blood to expand party membership.

Ramon H. Myers
Hoover Institution

Australia

Population. 16,451,955

Parties. Communist Party of Australia (CPA); Socialist Party of Australia (SPA); Communist Party of Australia–Marxist-Leninist (CPA-ML); Democratic Socialist Party (formerly Socialist Workers' Party, DSP); Association for Communist Unity (ACU); New Left Party (NLP)

Founded. CPA: 1920; SPA: 1971; CPA-ML: 1964; DSP: 1972; ACU: 1985; NLP: 1989 (founding congress to be held in spring 1990)

Membership. CPA: 800–1,000 (1989); SPA: 500; CPA-ML: 50 (1989); DSP: 250–500 (1989); ACU: 50; NLP: 850–1,050 (estimated)

Leadership. CPA: Brian Aarons, Dennis Freney (spokesmen for National Committee); SPA: Jack McPhillips (president); CPA-ML: Bruce Cornwall (chairman); DSP: Jim Percy (national secretary)

Status. Legal

Last Congress. CPA: Thirtieth, 2–3 December; SPA: Sixth, 3 October 1988; DSP: Eleventh, 2–6 January 1986; CPA-ML: Seventh, October 1988

Last Election. 11 July 1987; official government report says communist party polled 0.3 percent of national vote.

Publications. CPA: *Tribune* (weekly; editorial collective; Peter Murphy, coordinator); *Australian Left Review* (monthly); SPA: *Guardian*; CPA-ML: *Australian Communist* (bimonthly); *Vanguard* (weekly)

Rapid changes in the communist world prompted a realignment of Australia's five principal leftist parties, whose total membership numbers perhaps two thousand (*Sydney Morning Herald*, 2 December). Foremost among these adjustments were plans by the Communist Party of Australia (CPA) to become dormant and commit its membership to the newly formed New Left party, a movement it hoped would unite Australia's various communist parties in framing a socialist program better adapted to current world conditions.

Meanwhile, Australian government contacts with the Eastern bloc continued throughout the year. The first official contact in nearly fourteen years with the Democratic People's Republic of Korea (DPRK) took place in January when two Australian diplomats traveled to Pyongyang for DPRK-initiated trade talks and an examination of Pyongyang's attitudes toward foreign relations, including the peaceful reunification of the Korean Peninsula. Government sources denied that the mission was intended to reciprocate North Korean interest in restoring the diplomatic ties broken off unilaterally and without explanation by the DPRK in late 1975 (Hong Kong, AFP; *FBIS*, 17 January). That stance was clarified by a November statement that full diplomatic relations would not be restored until various issues had been resolved, including the DPRK's relations with South Korea, its general international behavior, and its troubling interest in acquiring nuclear weapons (Melbourne Overseas Service, 21 November; *FBIS*, 22 November).

During a two-week visit to Indochina and North Asia in January, Foreign Minister Gareth Evans met with leaders in Vietnam and Laos for discussions on resolving the Cambodia conflict, a process in which Australia remained involved throughout the year (Hong Kong, AFP; *FBIS*, 17 January). On 29 January Evans went to Beijing, where he talked with People's Republic of China (PRC) leaders about the 1997 retrocession of Hong Kong, Chinese economic reforms, the prospects for Sino-Australian trade, and human rights, particularly in Tibet; while in Beijing, he also discussed proposals for settling the Cambodian war with Prince Norodom Sihanouk (Melbourne Overseas Service; *FBIS*, 18 January), a contact renewed by another Foreign Affairs Department official's December meeting with Sihanouk and Chinese officials in Beijing in December (Melbourne Overseas Service; *FBIS*, 20 December).

On 2 February, Australia established full diplomatic relations with Cuba for the first time since communist rule began there 31 years earlier. An agreement signed in Mexico City upgraded the relationship from the consular ties established in 1973 and provided for the exchange of nonresident ambassadors. (Melbourne Overseas Service; *FBIS*, 2 February.)

The government agreed to formalize a fisheries and trade agreement with the Soviet Union during the scheduled visit of Soviet premier Ryzhkov in mid-February 1990. That agreement, in process for two years, will grant the USSR's antarctic fishing fleet of some 50 boats access to Australian ports for repairs and reprovisioning and will give landing rights to Aeroflot charters for fishing crew changeovers; in exchange, the Soviet Union has committed itself to long-term Soviet purchases of Australian agricultural and mineral products. (*FBIS*, 2, 3 March; Melbourne Overseas Service; *FBIS*, 18 December.) The Soviet Union was reported eager to develop long-term bilateral access arrangements with various other South Pacific island states as well (Hong Kong, AFP, 2 April; *FBIS*, 4 April).

A 31-member contingent of Soviet peace activists arrived in Sydney in April for contacts with local peace and environmental groups (Melbourne Overseas Service; *FBIS*, 19 April).

A four-member Vietnamese delegation visiting Australia in May to discuss Australian-Vietnamese banking and financial ties canceled a scheduled seminar at Monash University after they were shouted down and jostled when they tried to address another seminar at the Australian National University (Melbourne Overseas Service, 3 May; *FBIS*, 4 May).

Canberra reacted forcefully to the Beijing massacre of dissidents in Tiananmen Square and the ensuing nationwide crackdown on protest: On 4 June Prime Minister Robert Hawke condemned the "brutally excessive use of force" with which Beijing authorities repressed prodemocracy demonstrations, and on 5 June Foreign Minister Evans lodged a formal protest with the PRC's Australian ambassador. Hawke canceled a planned October trip to China, but ruled out severing diplomatic relations with Australia's second-largest trading partner. (Hong Kong, AFP, 4, 5 June; Melbourne Overseas Service, 5 June; *FBIS*, 6 June). All nondiplomatic Australian nationals were ordered out of China on 6 June, and temporary visas for an estimated 15,500 Chinese nationals in Australia were extended for up to one year (Melbourne Overseas Service, 5, 6 June; *FBIS*, 6, 16 June).

During a 15 June debate in which Parliament

unanimously condemned the Beijing massacre and nationwide repression, Prime Minister Hawke announced that Dong Qi, a vice-consul at the Chinese consulate in Canberra, had been granted permanent asylum. Australian authorities denied reports that their Beijing embassy was harboring Chinese dissidents (including possibly student leader Chai Ling) or that Ms. Chai had been spirited into Melbourne (Hong Kong, AFP; *FBIS*, 15, 16 June).

On 21 June the government officially protested to a senior Chinese official the death sentences handed down to prodemocracy dissidents (Melbourne Overseas Service; *FBIS*, 21 June). The protest's failure to avert those executions led Australia to suspend all exchange programs with the PRC and call for the major Western nations to join it in imposing sanctions on China (Tokyo, KYODO; *FBIS*, 22 June).

November saw the first visit to Australia since 1975 by a senior official of the unrecognized regime in Cambodia, but Deputy Prime Minister Kong Sam-ol failed to persuade Foreign Minister Evans to drop Australian support for the Khmer Rouge role in an interim Cambodian administration (Hong Kong, AFP, 2 November; *FBIS*, 3 November).

Ignoring repeated Chinese threats of possible damage to relations, Canberra issued visitor's visas to two representatives of the dissident Federation of Democratic China. A spokesman for Australia's Department of Foreign Affairs said that China had been informed that the federation would be allowed to form an Australian branch, provided its activities were legal. (Melbourne Overseas Service; *FBIS*, 13 December.)

On 20 December a formal protest was lodged with Romania over the shooting of protesters in Timişoara (Melbourne Overseas Service; *FBIS*, 20 December).

Communist Party of Australia. At a Special National Congress (the party's 30th congress) in Glebe, New South Wales, 2–3 December, the CPA accepted proposals first discussed six years ago and decided to wind down its independent activities as of the end of the year, fully committing its members to working with other left activists in forming the New Left Party (NLP). The NLP, whose founding conference is scheduled for Sydney around Easter 1990, will focus, like the CPA before it, on causes such as aboriginal land rights, environmental issues, women's rights, and gay and lesbian issues (*Sydney Morning Herald*, 2 December). The CPA's initiative in planning the NLP is expected to give it a dominant role in its activities, an interpretation the CPA denies (Melbourne, *News Weekly*, 3 February 1990).

The Special National Congress was attended by 115 delegates elected by state and district conferences, where the party rank and file had voted five to one in favor of "A New Party for New Times," the CPA National Committee's blueprint for the NLP.

The Special Congress decided that the CPA would become dormant immediately, meeting again only after the NLP is fully established. If the new party is a success, the CPA plans to vote itself out of existence by 1992.

The congress received greetings from communist parties in Japan, Belgium, Sweden, and Britain and from the Greek Left party and the West German Greens. A "solidarity night" was held to raise funds for the National Coalition of Aboriginal Organisations and for "progressive" movements in the Philippines. (*Tribune*, 6 December.)

Led by Brian Aarons, a delegation of three CPA National Executive members made a 14–22 December visit—the first official visit in sixteen years—to Moscow and Leningrad at the invitation of the Communist Party of the Soviet Union (CPSU) Central Committee (*Tribune*, 6 December; *Pravda*, 24 December) to discuss "the world-wide renewal of socialism" and reportedly to secure the Kremlin's blessing for the slated New Left party.

The party retains significant political influence in the thinning ranks of labor unions as well as in education, the pacifist movement, a few radical feminist groups, and Third World solidarity fronts. Through its collaboration with the ACU, the CPA also exerts influence among the leadership of the Building Workers' Industrial Union, the Waterside Workers' Federation, and the Seamen's Union (the latter two are expected to merge soon) (Melbourne, *News Weekly*, 3 February 1990).

The CPA, whose reworked constitution reflects acceptance of a multiparty system and perhaps a toleration of private enterprise in Australia's projected new order (*Sydney Morning Herald*, 2 December), welcomed developments in Eastern Europe, saying they denoted the "bankruptcy and dismantling" of Stalinist socialism, not the failure of socialism itself (*Tribune*, 15 November).

The party's weekly newspaper, the *Tribune*, marked its 50th year in September and continued its emphasis on environmental, trade union, aboriginal, women's, and gay and lesbian issues. In November and December it held events in various cities to raise funds for rising expenses, as its press fund of $44,566 was said insufficient to ensure the paper's survival (*Tribune*, 6 December) and as the fund's average weekly increment of around $1,350 had brought in only 51 percent of the $80,000 goal (*Tribune*, 22 November). Noting that the increased candor of the mainstream media in recent years has challenged the survival of the *Tribune* (*Tribune*, 6 September), the paper conducted a November survey to elicit readers' views of the publication and their preferences for its future style and coverage (*Tribune*, 1 November).

Communist Party of Australia–Marxist-Leninist.

The CPA-ML remained reticent in explanation, if strident in commentary. Endorsing front activities rather than overt activism, *Australian Communist* acknowledged that few CPA-ML members are known even to one another; party consensus is achieved through "democratic consultation" by "special" (and unspecified) means (*Australian Communist*, September/October).

Upholding the correctness of the USSR's past hegemonism, but asserting the need for greater decentralization in the future, the 27 September *Vanguard* seemingly endorsed events in Eastern Europe. Later in the year, however, a party spokesman refused public comment on either East European developments or the attempt to renovate Australian socialism through the New Left party (*Sydney Morning Herald*, 2 December).

The 4 October issue of *Vanguard* criticized Soviet support for the Addis Ababa regime against Eritrean resistance, terming Soviet conduct hypocritical, and *Australian Communist* published an Afghani statement critical of the Soviet invasion of 1979 (September/October). The 8 November *Vanguard* said that it had been a mistake to consider the Soviet model of socialist construction as *the* road to socialism.

In contrast, a 27 September *Vanguard* article lauded Chinese socialism's past achievements and made no mention of June's events in Tiananmen Square, though it did characterize the revolution's progress as "uneven"; a later, generally noncommittal interview described the Tiananmen events as "somewhere in between" a massacre and the suppression of a Western-inspired counterrevolution (*Sydney Morning Herald*, 2 December). The 22 November *Vanguard* praised PRC rectification programs undertaken in response to the spring's democracy movement and lamented that the "intense

struggle" of building socialism sometimes involves "unnecessary losses" to innocent people.

The party tried throughout the year to bolster its residual influence with labor (particularly in the building industry [Melbourne, *News Weekly*, 3 February 1990]) by expressing its consistent solidarity with pilots, teachers, truckers, dockworkers, and other labor groups. It was equally persistent in condemning various cost-cutting and restructuring measures, whether by government (welfare, public housing, and public health care restrictions) (*Vanguard*, 22 November) or by private business (layoffs and increased productivity standards).

The 23 August–1 November issues of *Vanguard* featured a series of articles commemorating *The Communist Manifesto* designed to refute allegations that Marxism had grown irrelevant. That series was followed by one on Mao Tse-tung's *On Contradiction* that began in the 8 November issue and ran through at least the end of the year.

Vanguard focused on labor (especially pilot and teacher collective bargaining), income distribution, environmental, and aboriginal issues; decried privatization; continued to oppose the U.S. base at Nurrungar, South Australia, and other elements of U.S.-Australian military cooperation; and continued to decry "monopoly capitalism," particularly the "foreign monopoly domination" it accused the ruling Labor party and big business of toadying to. Throughout the year, *Vanguard* condemned multinational corporations' presence in Australia, noting that Marxism's mission in Australia is "to fight foreign monopoly domination" (*Vanguard*, 13 December). The *Australian Communist* invoked many of the same shibboleths, including nationalist sentiment, foreign trade issues, and environmental concerns.

The 20 September *Vanguard* called for increased availability of public transport, but then denounced Japanese involvement in plans for a Very Fast Train line between Sydney and Melbourne, adducing nationalist sentiments, ostensible ties between Japanese construction firms and organized crime, and the danger that development along that rail line might lead to technocratic colonization at taxpayer expense (*Vanguard*, 6 December). The 4 October number taxed efforts by the Australian Council of Trade Unions (ACTU) to enlist more workers in the ever-declining union movement as a continuation of its campaign to redistribute national income from wages to profits; the ACTU leadership, too, was called a tool of foreign economic imperialism throughout the year.

The 25 October *Vanguard* condemned Japanese economic and American cultural imperialism and inveighed against "imperialist" interference in the internal affairs of other countries under the guise of concern for human rights (Eastern Europe, China, Cuba, and Nicaragua were named). The *Australian Communist*, however, condemned Prime Minister Hawke's visit to a number of Asian nations for its emphasis on trade at the expense of human rights (September/October).

Socialist Party of Australia. Party president Jack McPhillips saw no reason to revise the SPA's earlier endorsement of the Soviets' 1968 repression of the Prague Spring (the cause of the SPA's 1971 schism from the CPA) and remained undaunted by events in Eastern Europe (*Sydney Morning Herald*, 2 December). The SPA's Central Committee met 28–29 October to reaffirm the party's traditional line and pointedly ignored events in Eastern Europe.

The SPA lost its main industrial cadres to the ACU a few years ago, but it still retains influence in the union movement and is active in the Australia-Soviet Friendship Society (Melbourne, *News Weekly*, 3 February 1990).

The SPA continues its slow amalgamation with the Democratic Socialist party (formerly the Socialist Workers' party), hoping to attract more youth into its pro-Moscow ranks. The SPA's unswerving loyalty to Moscow was rewarded by an Australian visit from *Pravda*'s deputy editor to the SPA's *Guardian* Festival (Melbourne, *News Weekly*, 9 December).

Association for Communist Unity. The ACU maintains fronts in the Building Workers' Industrial Union (BWIU) and the Australian Council of Trade Unions (Tom McDonald, an ACU leader, holds top positions in both); in the Waterside Workers' Federation; and in the Seamen's Union. BWIU and Seamen's Union support, however, totals only three hundred to four hundred supporters.

McDonald has expressed regret that his advocacy of the 1968 Soviet invasion of Czechoslovakia helped divide the Australian communist movement, and the ACU hopes for a rapprochement with other leftist parties in the slated New Left Party (NLP). If the NLP is a success, the ACU plans to vote itself out of existence in 1990. (*Sydney Morning Herald*, 2 December.)

Democratic Socialist Party. On 23 October the Socialist Workers' party changed its name to Democratic Socialist party, a change "designed to reinforce the Party's identification with the Gorbachev reform movement" (Melbourne, *News Weekly*, 3 February 1990). Jim Percy, national secretary, hailed Gorbachev and condemned the Tiananmen Square massacre as "a crime against socialism."

Although recognizing the need for leftist unity, the DSP declined to join other leftist parties in forming the New Left party. The DSP and the Socialist party of Australia, however, are gradually merging in hopes of attracting more youth into the Australian left.

The environmental movement is at the top of the DSP's agenda for the 1990s; it has already succeeded in infiltrating the Green Alliance. (*Sydney Morning Herald*, 2 December.)

New Left Party. Spurred by the declining influence and growing irrelevance of the Australian left, the Communist Party of Australia (CPA) and the Association for Communist Unity (ACU) committed their memberships to the newly formed NLP late in the year. The Democratic Socialist Party (DSP) explicitly refused to join, and it is likely that the Socialist Party of Australia will refuse as well, given its ongoing unification with the DSP; the position of the Communist Party of Australia-Marxist-Leninist is unclear. The CPA is expected to dominate the NLP, if by virtue of numbers alone; naturally, the CPA denies this (Melbourne, *News Weekly*, 3 February 1990). The CPA and the ACU plan to disband if the NLP is a success.

Plans for the NLP were first announced on 14 March with the release of a fourteen-point statement signed by 130 leading figures in the trade union, women's, and environmental movements, including Jack Mundy, Frank Stilwell, Betty Hounslow, and ACTU assistant secretary Laurie Carmichael. The new party hopes to counteract privatization measures and other government actions, to adapt the Australian left to changing times (Melbourne Overseas Service, 14 March; *FBIS*, 16 March), and to draw attention to causes like aboriginal land rights, the environment, women's rights, and gay and lesbian issues.

Responding to claims that the Federated Liquor Trades Union (FLTU) is a front for the NLP and the left wing of the ruling Australian Labor Party (ALP), NLP activists denied that the party has any intention of infiltrating the ALP by means of upcoming elections for leadership of the FLTU (*Tribune*, 13 September).

At the Launching Conference in late July 1988, it was decided that regional committees, elected at that meeting and later in September, should select their own campaign strategies. The Sydney and Melbourne groups chose to focus on toxic waste dumping, while the Sydney group also decided to campaign around falling living standards.

Signatories of the NLP's "Time to Act for a New Left Party" statement met in Sydney and Melbourne in September to select a name for the new party, a decision ratified by the prospective rank and file in November (*Tribune*, 15 November), and to plan for the Founding Conference, which is scheduled for Easter 1990 (*Tribune*, 20 September).

Timothy J. McGuire
Hoover Institution

Bangladesh

Population. 114,718,395 (July 1989)
Parties. Bangladesh Communist Party; National Socialist Party
Founded. Bangladesh Communist Party in 1948 as East Pakistan Communist Party; banned in 1954; re-emerged in 1971 following Bangladesh independence. National Socialist Party, unknown.
Membership. 5,000 (1987 estimate)
General Secretary. Bangladesh Communist Party: Saifuddin Ahmed Manik; National Socialist Party: Mohammed A. Jalil
Status. Bangladesh Communist Party proscribed from November 1987 to March 1988; now legal.
Last Congress. Fourth Congress of the Bangladesh Communist Party was held in April 1987.
Auxiliary Organizations. Trade Union Centre; Cultural Front; Chatra Union; Jubo Union; Khetmozdur Samiti; Mahila Parishad
Publication. *Ekota* (in Bengali)

In Bangladesh, General Mohammad Ershad remained very much in control, with the opposition splintered and much violence throughout the country.

Elections for local governing bodies were held in January despite opposition party protests, rallies, and violence (*FBIS-NES*, 26 January). In April, Ershad's ruling Jatiya party split; a few disgruntled party members formed a new political party supported by both the Awami League (AL) and the Bangladesh National Party (BNP). These two major opposition organizations accepted former Jatiya party members and began to form a new liberal democratic party to compete with Ershad. (*FEER*, 6 April.)

The AL and BNP leaders accused one another of complicity in the assassination of political leaders. AL leader Sheikh Hasina Wajed accused former President Zia Rahman of murdering her father, Sheikh Mujib Rahman, Bangladesh's first president. Zia's widow, Khalida Zia, head of the BNP, retorted that Sheikh Hasina and her AL had had a hand in the assassination of her husband. The charges and countercharges ended all hope of opposition unity. (*FEER*, 20 April.)

Party Affairs. This was a difficult year for the communist party of Bangladesh and its associated National Awami party as they tried to participate in a multiparty effort to oppose Ershad. However, General Secretary Saifuddin Ahmed Manik began using Moscow's new policies of democratization and pluralism and relaxed control over unions and student groups. (Prague, *WMR*, June.)

Hard-liners in the party Central Committee evidently disagreed with Manik's desire for change, and an internal philosophical struggle began that detracted from the party's political efforts (*Asia Yearbook*, 1990).

On 2 September, Manzurul Ahsan Khan, a senior party leader and member of the Secretariat, suddenly resigned (*FBIS-NES*, 15 September). Khan, a hard-liner and critic of *glasnost'*, called for a left front made up of the United Communist League, components of the Five-Party Alliance, and the National Awami party.

Relations with the Communist World. Bangladesh's relations with communist China continued to be close during the year. Beijing filled most of Dhaka's requests for military assistance and continued to be Bangladesh's principal source of military hardware. Relations with the Soviet Union improved slightly when Ershad replaced the

Bangladesh ambassador to Moscow with an official less pro-American.

Michael R. Potaski
Catholic University of America

Burma (Myanmar)[1]

Population. 40,451,732 (July 1989)

Party. Burma Communist Party (BCP). After rebellions against the BCP leadership in March and April, at least four splinter organizations have been established. None appears based on communist ideology, although rhetoric of at least one resembles that of the BCP.

Founded. BCP: 15 August 1939

Membership. 3,000 claimed, 1978–1979; after March–April 1989 rebellions, not more than several hundred. Armed strength formerly 8,000–15,000; currently estimated at less than 400.

Chairman. [Thakin][2] Ba Thein Tin (75), Sino-Burman. Ba Thein Tin was expelled from the BCP's old headquarters at Pang Hsang in April along with other party leaders, although it is not known exactly which ones. They are reported to be in Panwa, Kachin state, near the Chinese border.

Vice-Chairman. [Thakin] Pe Tint (73), Burman

Politburo. [Thakin] Ba Thein Tin, [Thakin] Pe Tint, Khin Maung Gyi (62), Myo Myint (65), Tin Yee (67), Kyaw Mya (74), [Bo] Kyin Maung (67), Chinese

Secretariat. Khin Maung Gyi (62)

Central Committee. 29 members: Aye Hla, Aye Ngwe, [Thakin] Ba Thein Tin, Bran Ba Di, Khin Maung Gyi, Kyauk Mi Lai, Kyaw Mya, Kyaw Myint, [Bo] Kyaw Zaw, [Bo] Kyin Maung, Mya Thaung (possibly still detained by the faction that

seized Pang Hsang), Myint Min, Myo Myint, Ni Tu Wu, Pe Thaung, [Thakin] Pe Tint, Po Ngwe Sai, Po Tint, [Sai] Aung Win, San Tu, [Saw] Ba Moe, Saw Han, Soe Hein, Soe Lwin, Tin Yee, Tint Hlaing, Tun Lwin, Ye Tun, Zaw Mai

Status. Illegal

Last Congress. Third, 9 September–2 October 1985

Last Election. N/a

Auxiliary Organizations. Three organizations have been reported (*YICA*, 1989); possibly dormant even before the March–April mutinies, these have probably since been dissolved.

Publications. *Pyeithu Ah Nar* (People's Power). First issue reported 1987. No copies are known to have reached the West. The BCP formerly broadcast over the Voice of the People of Burma (VOPB), located inside Burma near the Sino-Burmese border. VOPB broadcasting facilities were seized by Wa rebels on 12 April and are subsequently broadcasting as the Burma Nationalities Broadcasting Service (BNBS).

Two problems latent in the BCP since its reconstitution in the late 1960s came to a head early in the year and nearly destroyed the twenty-year-old party structure. The two were ethnic divisions, inherent in the BCP's reconstitution in an ethnic minority–dominated area in 1968–1969, and conflicts of interest with drug traffickers who had been incorporated into the BCP army. Ethnic problems were acknowledged by the BCP as far back as 1978; conflicts with drug interests, never explicitly acknowledged, were probably exacerbated by recent Chinese efforts to stop drug production in BCP territory.

The consequent rebellions in March and April split almost all of the former BCP armed forces into new organizations. Three of these now claim an ethnic, rather than ideological, basis for existence, and one has indicated the intent to join an existing opposition front to continue the fight against Rangoon. At least one other important element may have reached an agreement with the Rangoon government, evidently a modus vivendi to facilitate narcotics trading.

1. The Rangoon government changed the country's name to Myanmar effective 18 June. The United Nations officially adopted the change on 22 June. The U.S. Board on Geographic Names has not adopted the new name.
2. Honorifics are in brackets. Thakin signifies participation in Burma's independence struggle. Bo connotes a military commander. Sai and Saw are standard male honorifics among the Shan, Karen, and other ethnic minorities. The most common Burman honorifics (U, Daw, and Maung) are omitted. This article makes the standard distinction between *Burmese*, referring to the entire country, and *Burman*, referring to Burma's largest ethnic group.

The BCP breakup, which appears to mark the party's end as a significant insurgent force, came even as popular dissatisfaction with Burma's military rulers became deeper and more widespread. The Rangoon regime has responded to this dissatisfaction by claiming BCP infiltration of various sectors of Burmese society, particularly education, and alleging BCP responsibility for the 1988 disorders that brought down the Ne Win government. The regime appears determined to use a continuing BCP threat, whose existence is now problematical, to rally support within the military and to crack down on its most effective political opponents.

Leadership and Organization. A late 1988 Rangoon commentary, "The Last Problems of the BCP," by Nay Balu, outlined four factions within the BCP; in retrospect the article accurately describes the major fault lines along which the organization subsequently broke up (Rangoon, *Working People's Daily*, 24 December 1988). Along with the tiny ethnic Burman faction, which reserved to itself the top BCP posts, were an ethnic Kachin faction, a Kokang area faction, and a nationalities faction dominated by ethnic Wa. The Kachin faction was made up of the Kachin who followed Naw Seng from China back into Burma in the 1968–1969 campaign to establish the new BCP base area. Two of this group were said to have moved into higher positions within the BCP: Frangumdee and Zaw Maing, alias Kyauk Myint. The Kokang faction is led by a former associate of opium warlord Lo Hsing Han, Peng Chia-sheng. (Transliteration of names in Burma is not standardized. Peng Chia-sheng is elsewhere rendered Phonkyashin—in the article cited here, Pheung Kya-shin, in *FEER*, Peng Chia-Shin, Fung Kya-Shin in *YICA*, 1984, and Peng Chia Chang in Catherine Lamour and Michael R. Lamberti, *The Second Opium War* [London: Allen Lane, 1974], p. 165. Although this particular name is ethnic Chinese, the unavailability of the Chinese written form used by Peng himself makes uncertain at best any attempt to impose a standard Chinese transliteration.) Peng began his association with the BCP as an independent rebel permitted to trade in opium in BCP-controlled territory and was subsequently identified as vice-commander of the BCP's Northeast Command (*YICA*, 1984). The article asserted personal problems between Peng and Politburo member Tin Yee and cited Peng's subsequent "retirement" from his military post. The last group, the nationalities faction, was primarily ethnic Wa "who are humiliated most" and who "constitute the largest number and the lowest in rank in the BCP."

The first concrete sign of a problem was news of a 12 March open challenge to the BCP leadership by ethnic Chinese in the Kokang area of Shan state, led by Peng Chia-sheng. On 14 March, Peng, joined by other ethnic units, took over the BCP's northern headquarters at Mong Ko, arrested a large number of party cadres, and announced the formation of a Burma National Democracy Front independent of the BCP. His group is estimated to include about 9 percent of the former BCP army, that is, one thousand to two thousand men. (BBC, in Burmese, 18 March; *FBIS-EAS*, 20 March.)

On 18 April a radio broadcast, evidently coming from the site of the BCP's VOPB facility, announced a 12 April revolt at BCP headquarters at Pang Hsang (Wan Long) (BNBS, in Burmese, 18 April; *FBIS-EAS*, 19 April). Although dominated by ethnic Wa, this revolt is reported to have also included Shan, Kachin, and Kokang Chinese (*Bangkok Post*, 9 May; *FBIS-EAS*, 10 May). Apparently among its leaders were the signatories of a 12 April protest note (for content, see below): Pao Jue Tang, Jaung Ji Lang, Kim Sam Naw, Aw Ta Pang, Ko Lai Tham, Jan Jue Chan, Sao Jue Ji, Sai Ni, Ah Zone, Ah Li, Sao Mi Nam, Ah Lu, and Sao Wai Thein (names as heard by *FBIS*) (BNBS, in Burmese, 19 April; *FBIS-EAS*, 20 April). (There is some variety in the names given for the organization[s?] that have emerged from this revolt. The broadcast here cited gives the Wa Region Nationalities Provisional Committee and the Burma Nationalities Provisional Committee. The first rebel broadcast noted the Burma Nationalities Uprising Army Directorate [BNBS, 18 April; *FBIS-EAS*, 19 April]. A later broadcast cites the Wa Region Alliance party and the Wa Region Army [BNBS, 16 May; *FBIS-EAS*, 25 May]. The *Bangkok Post* cites the Burma National Democratic Alliance [9 May; *FBIS-EAS*, 10 May]. *FEER* cites the Burma National United party [1 June].) Elsewhere identified as leaders were General Secretary Kyauk Ni Lai (also noted as Ta Ngi Lai [*Bangkok Post*, 9 May; *FBIS-EAS*, 10 May]) and Burma National United party head Pao Yo Chang (probably identical with Chief of Staff Pao Yu Chang [*Bangkok Post*, 9 May; *FBIS-EAS*, 10 May]), both former alternate members of the BCP Central Committee (*FEER*, 1 June). Also reported joining the rebels was the ethnic Kachin military commander Zau Mai. The Wa claim to lead more than ten thousand armed men (*Bangkok Post*, 9 May; *FBIS-EAS*, 10 May); because the largest part of the former BCP army was composed of ethnic Wa, this claim, even if exaggerated, may not be far from the truth.

Taken by surprise, BCP leaders are variously reported to have fled into China (*FEER*, 1 June) or to have been captured and later forced across the border (*Bangkok Post, FBIS-EAS*, 5 May). BCP military commander Kyaw Zaw reportedly fled to China with about two hundred men after the rebellion (*Bangkok Post*, 9 May; *FBIS-EAS*, 10 May).

Also reported in revolt are the 768th Brigade, between Mong Yang and the Chinese border, the 815th War Zone, further east along the Chinese and Laotian borders, and the 101st Military Region, to the north along the Chinese border of Burma's Kachin state. The 768th Brigade has declared itself as Noom Suk Harn, the name of an early ethnic Shan rebel organization, under Chairman Khun Myint, identified as ethnic Shan, and his deputy the Welsh-Shan Michael Davies. Its military leaders are Sai Noom Pan, an ethnic Shan, and Zhang Zhi Ming, a Chinese volunteer who joined the 1968–1969 move into Burma that established the BCP Northeast Command. The 815th War Zone, now the National Democratic Army, is under Military Commander Lin Ming Xian, also a Chinese volunteer and son-in-law of Kokang leader Peng Chia-sheng. (*FEER*, 30 March, 1 June.) The BCP units of the 101st War Zone, reported by Rangoon to be under the command of Sai Khom Tin Win (Rangoon Domestic Service, 7 August; *FBIS-EAS*, 9 August), reportedly joined the insurgent Kachin (*FEER*, 24 August).

Chinese authorities first held the BCP leaders who escaped from Pang Hsang in Meng Lien and a group of refugees from Mong Ko at Man Hai. Some of the former leadership may still be detained in Pang Hsang, including Soe Thein, the political commissar of the northeast base area, and Mya Thaung, political commissar of the northern Wa district. (*FEER*, 1 June.) In June those who had escaped from Pang Hsang were trucked by the Chinese army north to the Burmese border at the now Kachin Independence Army (KIA)-run 101st War Zone. The KIA, itself allied with the BCP since 1976 (*YICA*, 1989), permitted them to settle in the village of Panwa in former BCP territory, reportedly on the condition that they not engage in further political activity (*FEER*, 24 August). Leaders identified by Rangoon as now in Panwa are Ba Thein Tin, Kyaw Zaw, Khin Maung, Khin Maung Gyi, and Tin Yee, with a total of 150 people including

families (Rangoon Domestic Service, 7 August; *FBIS-EAS*, 9 August).

BCP units numbering at most several hundred in Tennasserim and Arakan (Rakhine) districts have not been noted in recent reporting. Along with the group at Panwa, they may be among the last remnants of the former BCP.

Thakin Soe, a founding member of the BCP, died 4 May at 83, after a long illness. Soe led the Red Flag faction in its split from the White Flag BCP in 1946. He was captured by the Burmese army in November 1970 and later released in a government amnesty. In October 1988, with government permission for the formation of political parties, he was registered as the official patron of the Unity and Development party.

Party Internal Affairs. The Political Report of 1 November 1978 contained the first notable BCP references to ethnic difficulties in the Northeast Command. It recognized the need to acknowledge and teach in minority languages (albeit ensuring that the Burmese language was also taught), urged the recruitment of party cadres from the minorities, and specified that cadres working with a particular ethnic minority must speak the language of that minority (for text, see Charles B. Smith Jr., *The Burmese Communist Party in the 1980s* [Singapore: Institute of Southeast Asian Studies, 1984], pp. 71, 74, 77–78). The Political Report of 9 September 1985 to the Third BCP Congress, although asserting a BCP policy in dealing with the minorities of "genuine equality and unity" (VOPB, 11 May 1986; *FBIS*, 19 May 1986), in sharp contrast to the 1978 report, gave minimal attention to conditions inside BCP-controlled territory. Later information indicates that the party effectively ignored the recommendations of the 1978 report, regarding the minorities only as a reserve of draftees for the BCP army (*YICA*, 1988).

Also, subsequent to the Third Congress, the BCP reportedly implemented severe penalties on private opium trading. Although observers at the time predicted the policy would lead to splits in the party (*YICA*, 1988), inattention by the party hierarchy to local conditions and intense Chinese pressure against the drug trade prevented its retraction. This policy further alienated traditional opium growers among ethnic minorities and directly threatened groups, particularly Peng Chia-sheng's, that refine, transport, and sell opium and heroin.

Both factors were probably critical elements in the Wa rebellion, although added irritations, including leaders' exploiting their positions for material advantage, certainly contributed. The first announcement of the revolt described as its purpose "to oppose the narrow racial policy of the Burma Communist Party" (BNBS, 18 April; *FBIS-EAS*, 19 April). A later broadcast criticized the use of ethnic Burman students who defected to the BCP—they were not allowed to fight, but were appointed "to all important positions, controlling the political, military, and economic sectors." An additional, specific impetus was probably a BCP leadership crackdown on minority cadres after the Kokang revolt. (BNBS, 10 May; *FBIS-EAS*, 16 May.)

Notable in the BNBS broadcasts was the continuing influence of BCP rhetoric, if not BCP ideology. A "declaration" to the BCP Central Committee by the Wa Region Provisional Military Commission dated 11 April said,

Looking back at the past, we see the BCP leading us— the people of all nationalities in the Wa region—in their determined and unyielding struggle against all enemies. Conditions were good before 1979. But what has the situation come to now? No progress whatsoever is being made. Why?...because some leaders are clinging to power and are obstinately pursuing an erroneous line. They are divorced from reality, practicing individualism and sectarianism, failing to study and analyze local and foreign conditions, and ignoring actual material conditions. Pursuing an erroneous line of [words indistinct] dogmatic thinking in particular, they have cheated the people of the Wa Region, and...dragged us into their sham revolution...they have sacrificed the interests of the party and the people of all nationalities to further the interests of individuals and a small minority...we shall continue to grasp the practical aspects of the revolution as a whole and shall unite with all the other forces that sympathize with us. (BNBS, 27 April; *FBIS-EAS*, 28 April.)

Subsequent statements indicate a further distancing of the Wa rebels from BCP ideology, although still drawing heavily on standard BCP vocabulary. A protest note to the BCP from the Directorate of the Burma Nationalities Provision Committee, dated 12 April, asserted that BCP leaders

are obstinately pursuing an erroneous line. They [words indistinct] fail to integrate theory with practice, pursue individualism and sectarianism, and ignore the concrete conditions at home and abroad....

In our view, they have destroyed the interests of the party and the people to further the interests of a small group of people in the highest organs...your [i.e., the BCP leadership's] ideology is divorced from reality, and the path you have chosen is divorced from the people. (BNBS, in Burmese, 19 April; *FBIS-EAS*, 20 April.)

The main task of our party and army today is to unflinchingly strive and struggle to achieve that objective [of insurgent unity]. To do that, the line that should be strictly adhered to is as follows: 1. To always stay away from the leadership of the BCP while marching along the line of the Wa Region National Alliance Party....2. To unite with all the forces that can be united with." (BNBS, 16 May; *FBIS-EAS*, 25 May.)

The Wa group appears ready to carry on against Rangoon in the character of an ethnic rather than ideology-based insurgency. During 19–21 April the Democratic Alliance, an association of ethnic insurgencies and Burman opponents of the Rangoon government, was reported considering a Wa approach to join, sponsored by another ethnic Wa insurgent group (*Bangkok Post*, 25 April; *FBIS-EAS*, 26 April). A 16 May statement declared the "fervent wish of the people of Burma is for the consolidation of national liberation efforts." The line of the Wa Region National Alliance party, besides specifying its divorce from the BCP and its desire for alliance "with all the forces that can be united with," also included the declaration that "traders...will be allowed to conduct commerce, trade, and travel inside our territory." (BNBS, 16 May; *FBIS-EAS*, 25 May.) This last should probably be read as an explicit repudiation of the BCP attempt to restrict opium trading.

Sai Noom Pan of the former 768th Brigade, recounting having been wounded in Rangoon in 1962 as a student demonstrator against the Ne Win takeover, has also asserted his group's sympathy with the ethnic insurgent alliance and with anti-regime student activity. He said that the September 1988 assault on Mong Yang by his unit was intended to show solidarity with student demonstrations in Rangoon. (*FEER*, 1 June.)

The motivation for the Kokang uprising was evidently connected to the BCP attempt to ban private opium trading, judging from the reported accommodation between the Kokang group and the Rangoon government. On 24 March the Rangoon government confirmed reports of the 12 March Kokang revolt (Rangoon Domestic Service, 24

March; *FBIS-EAS*, 27 March). According to *FEER*, even before this announcement and at the initiative of the Rangoon military authorities, former opium warlord and Peng associate Lo Hsing Han visited Kokang 20–21 March for talks with Peng Chia-sheng. A second meeting took place 20 April in Lashio between Kokang representative Lo Hsing Han and Rangoon politician and former general Aung Gyi. A third meeting in Kunlong two days later between Brigadier General Khin Nyunt, Rangoon military intelligence chief, and Peng's younger brother, Peng Chia-fu, produced an agreement for a temporary cease-fire. (*FEER*, 1 June.) By August, *FEER* reported an apparent understanding involving in part two thousand bags of rice plus some $750,000 in Rangoon "development aid" for Peng's group (24 August). In September, Kokang area residents were reported "going all out to cultivate poppies and produce opium" with the "permission and encouragement" of the Burmese military authorities; three heroin refineries were in operation (Hong Kong, AFP, in English, 13 September; *FBIS-EAS*, 13 September).

The financial incentives of the narcotics trade are probably bigger than ever. The 1989 Golden Triangle opium crop, a record, was estimated at more than two thousand tons, compared with twelve hundred tons in 1988 (*FEER*, 23 November). The increased crop is likely to be matched by a substantial growth in drug movement out of the area. An Australian seizure of 43 kilos of heroin in October 1988 was a record for that country (*CSM*, 6 January), as was a U.S. seizure in early 1989 of 380 kilos along with $3 million in cash in New York. The latter was traced back through Hong Kong to Bangkok, according to Thai customs (*Bangkok Post, FBIS-EAS*, 24 February). The February 1988 Thai seizure of 1,282 kilos stands as the largest ever recorded (*CSM*, 6 January). Golden Triangle narcotics now account for 42 percent of the heroin reaching the United States versus 15 percent in 1985, according to U.S. officials (*FEER*, 23 November).

Further negotiations in November and December between the Kokang group and the Burmese military are also reported to have involved Zhang Zhi Ming from the 815th Military Region (this may be the same Zhang earlier identified with the 768th Brigade) and a representative from the old 101st War Zone. Rangoon is said to have offered the former BCP commanders rice and other aid and the right to convert their forces into government-sponsored militia. (*FEER*, 28 December.)

In August the Rangoon military authorities, in an elaborate presentation, described the structure and activities of a BCP underground organization that they alleged had been in operation from the mid-1960s, just before the collapse of the old Pegu Yoma headquarters, into 1989. Wai Lin was identified as head of the upper Burma underground group; the lower Burma group had been headed by Thet Khaing, whom the military claimed to have in custody. (Rangoon Domestic Service, 5–7 August; *FBIS-EAS*, 9 August.)

The Rangoon military broadcast a videotape (probably obtained through contacts with the Kokang mutineers) of a 10 September 1988 Politburo meeting at Mong Ko. Ba Thein Tin and other BCP leaders were shown discussing how to exploit the confused political situation by promoting the unilateral setup of a rival government of which they would then seize control. (*FEER*, 30 November.) In a six-hour briefing on 5 August, the government claimed that the members of the BCP Central Committee dispersed after the March and April mutinies, but gathered at Mong Yai on 4 May to discuss strategy. The BCP was said to have laid down a new political line: that in the short run they could survive only by depending on others. For the longer run, they would form the Democratic Patriotic Army (DPA) to create an armed uprising. (Rangoon Domestic Service, 7 August; *FBIS-EAS*, 9 August.) In a later speech military leader Saw Maung asserted that the DPA was intended to coordinate BCP efforts in the event of further demonstrations against his government and to create domestic unrest (Rangoon Domestic Service, 10 November; *FBIS-EAS*, 15 November). The inconsistency of this account of a 4 May meeting with other reports of BCP leaders fleeing to China is unresolved.

Outside observers have noted apparent distortions of the influence of the BCP by Rangoon's military leaders. Rangoon officials "appear to believe that everything would be fine if only an antiregime coalition of 'communists, certain diplomats, rightist elements, and organizations with foreign contacts' could be crushed" (editorial, "Paranoia in High Places," *Bangkok Post*, 18 September; *FBIS-EAS*, 18 September). The long 5 August briefing appeared to be addressed more to the army than to the public at large, "probably playing up the issue of the 'communist specter' in order to make the rank and file apprehensive of the [political] opposition" (*FEER*, 7 September). Such distortion may well be in part deliberate and in part the result of misperception. On 23 May, at the beginning of the abortive effort to mediate a truce between Rangoon and the ethnic minorities, Thai deputy supreme commander Pat Akkanibutr gave his view of the Burmese leader's goal: "Saw Maung wants peace with the minorities so the country can focus on development and fight the real enemy, the Burmese Communist Party" (*FEER*, 15 June). The government-controlled Burmese press has put substantial stress on the BCP issue. A seven-part series, "The Blood-Stained History of the BCP," ran in the *Working People's Daily* from 11 to 22 November 1988, and another series, "The Main Enemy of the People: The BCP, Underground Destructive Elements," began 14 February. In a 22 June news conference a military spokesman was specific about the conclusions the public should draw:

> Any plan to defy authority is always followed by the building up of red power. . . . We know whose method it is to defy authority first, then set up red power. This is the method of the BCP. . . . If there are attempts to set up a power base—red power—then we shall have to use our power to prevent it. (Rangoon Domestic Service, 22 June; *FBIS-EAS*, 26 June.)

An evolution during the year in regime portrayal of the BCP role in the 1988 demonstrations attributes more of their inspiration and organization to BCP agitation. In a February interview with *Asia Week*, Saw Maung conceded that the movement for democracy began with the students. "But we found that the influence of the leftists has taken over the movement. And especially I speak now of the BCP." (*Working People's Daily*, 13 February.) In March, regime spokesman Brigadier General Khin Nyunt noted the peaceful start of the demonstrations, which then fell "under the influence of elements at home and abroad. The so-called BCP, using its overt hardcore cells, politically exploited the situation." (Rangoon Domestic Service, 28 March; *FBIS-EAS*, 30 March.) The same spokesman in the 5 August briefing asserted that "the BCP organized student protests at Rangoon University and planned a national strike." The "mass uprising" was "due to agitation by the lower Burma underground group [of the BCP]." Further, it was due to agitation by the upper Burma underground group that civil disturbances spread to Mandalay and upper Burma. (Rangoon Domestic Service, 6 August; *FBIS-EAS*, 9 August.) In a later meeting with Education Department personnel, Khin Nyunt warned of BCP underground members "who have been infiltrating education circles since the parliamentary democracy era" and were able to control the student

unions. He advocated "extreme caution" to counter this. (Rangoon Domestic Service, 16 November; *FBIS-EAS*, 17 November.)

Later added to the equation and detailed in a seven-hour briefing on 9 September was a conspiracy of "certain right-wing elements," including "certain diplomats, overseas broadcasting stations, some foreign journalists and overseas antigovernment elements" (Rangoon Domestic Service, 9–12 September; *FBIS-EAS*, 13 September). As basically an outside factor, however, these elements do not seem to have assumed anything close to the importance of the BCP in the regime's conspiracy theory.

The most significant use of the BCP issue was an effort to discredit opposition politician (and daughter of independence hero Aung San) Aung San Suu Kyi and her National League for Democracy (NLD). Former General Aung Gyi continued to attack the NLD as influenced by communists (Rangoon, *Loktha Pyeithu Nezin*, in Burmese, 16 March; *FBIS-EAS*, 17 March). Outside observers cited "the presence of a dozen former members of the BCP" on the NLD's executive committee as providing the military with "a ready excuse" to cancel the May 1990 election plans or reject their results. Trade Minister Colonel David Able was quoted as warning, "Once you are a communist, you are always a communist. We would not sit idly by if we see armed communists coming in." (*WP*, 15 March.) The warning is from a military establishment that made a place for many former communists after Ne Win's 1962 coup—one of the most prominent being U Chit Hlaing, the leading theoretician of Ne Win's Burmese Way to Socialism. Aung San Suu Kyi commented, with considerable accuracy, that "there are no more communists in our party than there are in any other political organization in Burma" (*WP*, 15 March). National Democratic Front (NDF) critic Aung Gyi has been noted as losing public credibility as he moves closer to the military regime (*Asia Week*, 8 September); his participation in March in government negotiations with the Kokang group and Khin Nyunt's 5 August citation of his comments on NDF communist connections have likely contributed.

The military appears determined to use the issue to remove Aung San Suu Kyi from politics. On 21 July the government announced Aung San Suu Kyi had been put under house arrest for up to one year under a law protecting the state from "destructive elements" (*NYT*, 22 July). A substantial portion of the 5 August briefing cited above was devoted to

BCP infiltration of the NDF and BCP plans to use first her mother, then Aung San Suu Kyi, to put a BCP-controlled government in power (Rangoon Domestic Service, 5–7 August; *FBIS-EAS*, 9 August). In a warning of measures to come, a government declaration 3 November listed unlawful organizations, including the BCP, and a news conference the same day noted that any other organizations that "join, contact, and affiliate" with unlawful organizations would themselves be banned (Rangoon Domestic Service, 3 November; *FBIS-EAS*, 6 November).

The Insurgency. In contrast to its public evaluation of the BCP political threat, the Rangoon government has assessed the military situation around the former BCP base area as much improved. According to a 9 June statement, "at present, due to the offensive from the Defense Forces and the disintegration among themselves, [the BCP] are disbanding and the areas formerly dominated by them are becoming peaceful." Specific note was made of roads being built and of areas of improved security on the east bank of the Salween River. (Rangoon Domestic Service, 9 June; *FBIS-EAS*, 12 June.) According to the government, the 202d Battalion in Shweli valley was the last significant element of the BCP military organization and even its loyalties were now uncertain (Rangoon Domestic Service, 7 August; *FBIS-EAS*, 9 August). In November several units formerly based near BCP territory were reported transferred north to Kachin state (*FEER*, 16 November).

In general, available battle reports bear out the picture of sharply decreased fighting. Reported surrendered to the government were BCP soldiers from the Mawpa unit (Rangoon Domestic Service, 8 February; *FBIS-EAS*, 9 February) and the Ho-Tawng village unit and an operations commander of the 768th Brigade (Rangoon Domestic Service, 15 June; *FBIS-EAS*, 22 June). Two attacks—on 11 May in Namhsam township and on 12 May in Hopong township, both in Shan state—were attributed to BCP soldiers (*Working People's Daily*, 18 May).

In January, the Thai press reported a joint Thai-Burmese operation against Burmese communist insurgents on the Burmese border at Mae Ai and Fang districts (*Bangkok Post*, 19 January; *FBIS-EAS*, 19 January). Two attacks were later noted in the same area by forces of drug trafficker/insurgent Chang Chi-fu against a camp held by some 250 "former BCP" (*Bangkok Post*, 30 November, 1 December; *FBIS-EAS*, 30 November, 5 December).

As late as May the Wa group continued to maintain its determination to at least hold its area. "If others do not touch us, we will not touch them. Conversely, if others touch us, we will touch them. Our army will fight to the last man." (BNBS, in Burmese, 28 April; *FBIS-EAS*, 3 May.) A later broadcast was in some contrast: "We have an enormous duty to liberate not only the entire northern and southern Wa region, but the whole country as well" (BNBS in Burmese, 13 May; *FBIS-EAS*, 25 May).

International Views and Positions. Even though Chinese concern over the narcotics trade probably contributed to the BCP's disintegration, Beijing was nonetheless reported by a senior Kachin insurgent as having turned down a request from the exiled BCP leaders to set up a headquarters on Chinese territory (*Bangkok Post*, 20 May; *FBIS-EAS*, 22 May). Contributing to such a decision would certainly have been Beijing concern for continued good relations with Rangoon, already a factor in the late 1970s cutoff of arms aid to the BCP. An additional factor may have been Beijing's recognition of the essential failure of the BCP leadership to maintain a base area originally set up with substantial Chinese help. Even the leaders' presence as refugees, reportedly approved at first, quickly became an embarrassment, resulting in their being returned to Burmese territory, albeit in an area where their safety was at least temporarily assured. Thus a Burmese spokesman on 20 October could deny reports of their presence in China, asserting bilateral cooperation along the border as proof of good Sino-Burmese relations (Rangoon Domestic Service, 20 October; *FBIS-EAS*, 23 October). Bilateral visits continued throughout the year, notably the twelve-day visit to China, beginning 18 October, by a senior Burmese military delegation, including the defense minister, army commander, and intelligence chief (Beijing, XINHUA, in English, 18 October; *FBIS-CHI*, 19 October).

Facilitating narcotics smuggling and thus reinforcing Chinese concerns over narcotics is the substantial expansion over the past several years in Sino-Burmese cross-border trade, the official volume of which reached 860 million yuan in 1988—21 times the level of 1985. Although most official trade is between Chinese state-run stores and Burmese government organizations and merchants, business among the ethnic minorities on both sides of the borders is also reported to be brisk. One Chinese county near the main official crossing point counts 28 ferries and 64 passes along the border handling an annual flow of some eight million merchants and frontier residents. (Beijing, CEI Database, in English, 10 May; *FBIS-EAS*, 10 May.) Although rice supplies to the Wa mutineers are reportedly cut off, border trade in the area, presumably including opium, was continuing (*FEER*, 1 June). Opium trading along the border is reported to be profitable, despite Chinese-publicized executions of drug traffickers in border areas (*FEER*, 8 June). Opium addiction has been noted re-emerging as a problem in parts of China (*FEER*, 23 November).

The BCP collapse may be one factor in Thai army commander General Chawalit Yongchaiyut's suggestion that a 37-year-old anticommunist act be abolished. *FEER* notes the suggestion as recognition that "currently there are few communists left" (7 September).

Charles B. Smith, Jr.
Department of State

Note: The views expressed here are the author's own and do not necessarily represent those of the Department of State or the U.S. government.

Cambodia

Population. 6,838,033 (July 1989). Average annual growth rate is 2.2 percent
Party. People's Revolutionary Party of Kampuchea (PRPK)
Founded. The PRPK traces its origin to the Khmer People's Revolutionary Party (KPRP), which was formed on 30 September 1951 with the establishment of a provisional Central Committee pending the party's first congress. Authoritative PRPK histories, however, cite the founding date as 28 June 1951.
Membership. Approximately 10,000 (*JPRS–Southeast Asia*, 89-024, 29 June)
General Secretary. Heng Samrin (b. 1934), former Democratic Kampuchea political officer, commander of the Fourth Division, assistant chief of the General Staff, and member of the party Executive Committee of the Eastern Zone from 1976 to May 1978, when he became one of the leaders of an ill-fated rebellion in the Eastern Zone against Pol Pot. Fled to Vietnam in June 1978 and returned to Cambodia with the invading Vietnamese army in December 1978 as president of the Central Committee of the Kampuchean National United Front for National Salvation. Concurrently chairman of the Council of State.

Politburo. 13 full and 3 alternate members. Full members: Heng Samrin (b. 1934), chairman of the Council of State; Hun Sen (b. 1951), chairman of the Council of Ministers, minister of Foreign Affairs; Bou Thang (b. 1938), vice-chairman of the Council of Ministers; Chea Sim (b. 1932), chairman of the National Assembly, chairman of the Kampuchean United Front for National Construction and Defense (KUFNCD); Chea Soth (b. 1928), vice-chairman of the Council of Ministers; Men Sam-an (b. 1953), chairwoman of the PRPK Central Organization Commission; Mat Ly (b. 1925), vice-chairman of the National Assembly, chairman of the Kampuchean Federation of Trade Unions; Ney Pena, minister of interior; Nguon Nhel (b. unknown), chairman of the Phnom Penh provisional party committee; Sar Kheng (b. 1951), chief of the cabinet of the party Central Committee; Say Chhum (b. 1945), vice-chairman of the Council of Ministers, minister of agriculture; Say Phuthang (b. 1925), chairman of the PRPK Central Control Commission, vice-chairman of the Council of State; Tie Banh (b. unknown), minister of national defense, elected to full Politburo membership in April 1989. Alternate members: Pol Saroeun (b. unknown), deputy minister of national defense, chief of General Staff, elected to alternate Politburo membership, April 1989; Sim Ka (b. unknown), vice-chairman of the Control Commission, elected to alternate Politburo membership, April 1989; Sin Song (b. unknown), minister of interior, elected to alternate Politburo membership, April 1989.

Secretariat. Heng Samrin, Hun Sen (rumored to have been relieved of position on Secretariat during July or August 1988), Bou Thang, Men Sam-an, Ney Pena, Sar Kheng, Say Phuthang, Say Chhum

Central Committee. 49 full members and 16 alternate members. Full members: Bou Thang (b. 1938), vice-chairman of the Council of Ministers, chairman of the Kampuchean People's Revolutionary Armed Forces General Political Department, vice-chairman of the National Council of the

Kampuchean United Front for National Construction and Defense; Chan Phin (b. 1930), chairman of the Central Committee's Economic Commission through at least July 1988, secretary of the party Committee for Central Ministries and Offices; Chan Seng (b. 1935), vice-chairman of the PRPK Central Committee Control Commission; Chay Sangyun (b. unknown), deputy chief of the General Staff, commander of the Third Military Region of the Kampuchean People's Revolutionary Armed Forces, promoted to brigadier general on 1 January; Chea Sim (b. 1932), chairman of the National Assembly; Chea Soth (b. 1928), vice-chairman of the Council of Ministers; Chhay Than (b. unknown), minister of finance; Chheng Phon (b. unknown), minister of information and culture; Dith Munti (b. unknown), deputy minister of foreign affairs; Do Sohan (b. unknown), secretary of Kompong Thom Province Party Committee; El Vansarat (b. unknown), chief of the General Political Department of the Kampuchean People's Revolutionary Armed Forces, deputy minister of defense, promoted to brigadier general on 1 January; Heng Sam Kai (b. 1930), brother of Heng Samrin, secretary of the Svay Rieng province provisional party committee; Heng Samrin (b. 1934), chairman of the Council of State; Ho Nan (b. unknown, female), appointed minister of industry in August 1988; Hul Savoan (b. unknown), commander of the Fourth Military Region of the Kampuchean People's Revolutionary Armed Forces, promoted to brigadier general on 1 January; Hun Neng (b. unknown), secretary of the Kompong Cham province party committee; Hun Sen (b. 1951), chairman of the Council of Ministers, minister of foreign affairs; Keo Kimyan (b. unknown), first deputy minister of defense, relieved of the post of chief of the General Staff of the Kampuchean People's Revolutionary Armed Forces in August 1988, promoted to major general on 1 January; Kham Len (b. unknown), member of the Council of State; Khoy Khunhuor (b. unknown), chairman of the PRPK Central Committee, Propaganda and Education Commission; Kim Yin (b. 1928), director general of the Kampuchean Radio and Television Commission; Kong Korm (b. 1941), appointed minister of the state affairs inspectorate in August 1988; Kong Sam-ol (b. unknown), vice-chairman of the Council of Ministers; Koy Buntha (b. 1952), relieved as minister of defense and appointed minister of social action and war invalids in August 1988; Lak On (b. unknown, female), secretary of the Ratanakiri province provisional party committee; May Ly (b. 1925), vice-chairman of the National Assembly, chairman of the National Federation of Trade Unions; Mean Sam-an (b. 1956, female), chairwoman of the Kampuchean Revolutionary Women's Association; Men Sam-an (b. 1953, female), chairwoman of the PRPK Central Committee Organization Commission; Neou Sam (b. unknown), secretary of the Siem Reap-Oddar Meanchey province party committee; Ney Pena (b. unknown), relieved as minister of interior and appointed chairman of the PRPK Central Committee, Propaganda and Education Commission, in August 1988; Nguon Nhel (b. unknown), secretary of the Phnom Penh municipal party committee; Nhim Vanda (b. unknown), vice-chairman of the Committee for the Construction of the Cambodian-Thai Border Defense System; Pol Saroeun (b. unknown), deputy minister of national defense, chief of General Staff, elected to alternate Politburo membership in April; Pen Navut (b. unknown), minister of education; Ros Chhun (b. unknown), general secretary of the National Council of the Kampuchean United Front for National Construction and Defense; Ros Sreng (b. unknown), secretary of the Pursat province provisional party committee; Sam Sundoeun (b. 1951), first secretary of the People's Revolutionary Youth Union of Kampuchea, chairman of the Kampuchean-Vietnamese Friendship Association; Sar Kheng (b. 1951), chief of the cabinet of the PRPK Central Committee; Say Chhum (b. 1945), vice-chairman of the Council of Ministers, minister of agriculture; Say Phuthang (b. 1925), chairman of the PRPK Central Committee Control Commission, vice-chairman of the Council of State; Sim Ka (b. unknown), vice-chairman of the PRPK Central Committee Control Commission, chairman of the Kampuchean-Soviet Friendship Association; Sin Song (b. unknown), minister of interior; Som Kimsuor (b. 1949, female), editor in chief of the PRPK weekly publication *Pracheachon*; Tang Saroeum (b. unknown), minister for economic and cultural cooperation with foreign countries; Um Sarit (b. unknown), secretary of the Banteay Meanchey province party committee; Ung Phan (b. unknown), vice-chairman of the Committee for Training Administrative and Legislative Cadre, member of the Central Committee Emulation Commission; Ung Sami (b. unknown), secretary of Battambang province party committee; Yos Son (b. unknown), chairman of the PRPK Central Committee, External Relations Commis-

sion, president of the Kampuchean Committee for
Afro-Asian Solidarity. Alternate members: Chea
Chanto (b. unknown), minister of planning; Em
Sam-an (b. unknown), director general of Sarpor-
damean Kampuchea (SPK); Hen Khan (b. unknown), secretary of Kompong Speu province
party committee; Kang Nem (b. unknown), deputy minister of agriculture; Khim Bo (b. unknown), deputy secretary of Takeo province provisional party committee; Lim Nai (b. unknown),
secretary of the Kompong Som provisional municipal party committee; Lim Thi (b. unknown),
secretary of the Kandal province provisional party
committee; Phang Saret (b. unknown), deputy
minister of home and foreign trade; Sam Sarit (b.
unknown), director of the General Department of
Rubber Plantations; Say Sipon (b. unknown),
vice-chairman of the Kampuchean Federation of
Trade Unions; Sin Sen (b. unknown), deputy minister of interior; Som Sopha (b. unknown), secretary of the Stung Treng province provisional party
committee; Thong Khon (b. unknown), chairman
of the Phnom Penh People's Revolutionary Committee, deputy secretary of the Phnom Penh municipal provincial party committee; Um Chhunlim
(b. unknown), chief of an unidentified department
of the Central Committee; Yim Chhaylim (b. unknown), deputy minister of health; Yut Phuthang
(b. unknown), secretary of the Prey Veng province
provisional party committee.

Status. The PRPK is the sole authorized political
party of the regime in Phnom Penh. PRPK leaders
serve concurrently as officials of the government
of the People's Republic of Kampuchea (PRK),
renamed the State of Cambodia (SOC) at an extraordinary session of the National Assembly, 29
April–1 May.

Last Congress. The Fifth National Congress of the
PRPK was held in Phnom Penh during 13–16
October 1985. The congress was attended by 250
delegates from 22 subordinate party committees
representing provincial, municipal, military, and
sectoral PRPK entities. The Fourth National
PRPK Congress was held in May 1981 and was
attended by 162 delegates.

Last Election. The last election for the PRPK National Assembly was held in May 1981. The election, a single-party contest unchallenged by any
political opposition, seated 117 of the 148 candidates for the National Assembly. The remainder of
the candidates were fielded by mass organizations
and by other formal, organized interests recognized and legitimated by the ruling party.

Auxiliary Organizations. Kampuchean Afro-
Asian People's Solidarity Organization Committee (chair: Khien Kanharit), Kampuchean Center
of the Asian Buddhist's Council of Peace (chair:
Tep Vong), Kampuchean Committee for the Defense of Peace (chair: Yit Kamseng), Kampuchean Federation of Trade Unions (chair: Mat
Ly), Kampuchean Journalists' Association (chair:
Chey Sophon), Association of Revolutionary
Youth in Kampuchea, Kampuchean Red Cross
(chair: Phlek Phirum), Kampuchean Revolutionary Women's Association (chair: Mean Sam-an),
Kampuchean United Front for National Construction and Defense (chair of Presidium: Heng
Samrin; chair of National Council: Chea Sim)

Publications and Media. *Pracheachon* (People),
weekly publication of the PRPK Central Committee founded in 1985; editor in chief: Som Kimsuor; *Kangthap Padevat* (Revolutionary Army),
weekly publication of the PRK Army; *Phnom
Penh*, weekly publication of the Phnom Penh Municipal PRPK Committee; *Kampuchea*, weekly
publication of the Kampuchean United Front for
National Construction and Defense; Sarporda-
mean Kampuchea (SPK), official news agency of
the PRK; director general: Em Sam-an. SPK publishes *Daily Bulletin* in English, Cambodian, and
French and a monthly magazine, *Angkor*, in Cambodian. Voice of the Kampuchean People (VOKP)
radio; director: General Kim Yin. Kampuchean
Radio and Television Commission; director: Kim
Yin.

Leadership and Party Organization. In 1989
the PRPK sustained its efforts to upgrade the quality
of its constituent parts, to increase its membership
rolls by adding more trained and capable secretaries
and members at provincial and commune levels,
and to develop an organizational base in the countryside. Party strength and political influence, however, continued to vary directly with the distance
from provincial capitals and large district seats, and
provincial party structures continued to be composed of severely understrength committees with
weak commune-level structures and inadequate
leadership.

The membership of the PRPK hovered between
five thousand and seven thousand in the mid-1980s
and increased to between eight thousand and ten
thousand during 1986–1988. In 1989 the party
claimed to have topped the ten thousand–member
mark and spoke in terms of "tens of thousands" of
members, a calculation that probably included can-

didates and members of the party core groups (*krom snoul*). (*JPRS–Southeast Asia*, 89-024, 29 June.) The party center claimed substantial growth in provincial organizations. During the regional congresses held throughout the first half of 1989, many provincial party standing committees were enlarged through the addition of new permanent members, reflecting claimed growth in overall membership. (Hanoi, VNA, in English, 0710 GMT, 16 January; *JPRS–Southeast Asia*, 89-004, 26 January.)

The Second Party Cadre Conference in April announced the long-awaited expansion of the Politburo and Central Committee and the strengthening of the statutory role of the Central Committee. The conference elected 21 new Central Committee members, 11 full and 10 alternate. The conference also promoted three alternate Politburo members to full membership and elected three new alternates. Two of the three new full members were quick risers: Sar Kheng and Say Chhum were added to the Politburo as alternate members at the seventh plenary session in July 1988. Say Chhum was also added to the ranks of the Secretariat at that plenary session, along with Say Phuthang. Tie Banh was elected to full membership at the extraordinary Central Committee session preceding the conference. An August 1988 cabinet shuffle brought Tie Banh, an alternate member of the Central Committee, to the position of defense minister and relieved Central Committee member and Deputy Defense Minister Ke Kimyan of his concurrent position as chief of the General Staff of the Kampuchean People's Revolutionary Armed Forces. He was replaced by Pol Saroeun, who was also appointed to a vice-ministerial slot in the Defense Ministry. Those changes, and several other shifts within the Ministry of National Defense, left the military underrepresented within the Politburo and the Central Committee and in the peculiar circumstances of having a defense minister with alternate Central Committee membership who was outranked by two vice-ministers of defense with full Central Committee membership (El Vansarat and Keo Kimyan). Two other vice-ministers of defense (Nhim Vandy and Soy Keo) did not hold Central Committee membership, whereas the Third and Fourth Military Region commanders were full members of the Central Committee. The Second National Cadre Conference elevated Pol Saroeun to alternate Politburo status. The Second National Cadre Conference also strengthened the hands of cabinet ministers within the Politburo and Central Committee and at the same time injected some new

blood into a top-heavy structure. In 1988 the Central Committee consisted of 31 full members and 14 alternate members. By April 1989 the Central Committee had been expanded to 49 full slots and 16 alternate positions. Of the nineteen new full members of the Central Committee, twelve held ministerial or subministerial posts and six were provincial party committee secretaries. Five of the twelve governmental officials were of ministerial rank. Of the nine new alternate Central Committee members, five were central government officials, four were provincial party committee officials, and one was a Central Committee department chief.

Despite the reforms, which were intended to expand the base of political participation and slightly enfranchise interests represented by mass organizations, the contours of a Politburo-dominated system remain unaltered. Decision-making power remained in the hands of a closed circle of power brokers. Experiments in the pluralization of society—the widening of political and economic participation, enfranchisement of selected constituencies, the legitimation of social groups and interests—continued to be managed by power brokers in the Politburo. Elite succession was partial and controlled. The party offered no effective testing ground for the younger alternate members; the Secretariat remained dominated by party elders. There seemed to be no systematic effort to replace the dominant holders of provincial party power or to interject anything more than a token representation of technocrats into the Central Committee.

The founding fathers of the PRPK continued to wield unrivaled authority. For example, Heng Samrin made several major speeches on the subject of militia force expansion and party work within the military, establishing himself as the authoritative spokesman for this policy, a role that does not coincide with the widely shared impression of him as a doltish, vacuous, ill-educated man. In 1989 he took an active and public role in party affairs, especially in district- and provincial-level party congresses. He paid a significant number of visits to key installations, enterprises, and provincial seats, functioning as the honored guest or keynote speaker at party functions. Whereas he once seemed as dispensable as Pen Sovan, he now seems more of a fixture, the quiet and underestimated senior leader. Heng Samrin, whose brother Heng Sam Kai holds significant power as a provincial party committee chairman, conceivably has more authority and leverage within the system than he is generally given credit for. In midyear a party functionary told a Western journalist that when Heng Samrin spoke, party officials were attentive to his words.

In that context the national cadre conference this year provided an indication of the survivability of regime elders, including Samrin, and a measure of the upward mobility limits of provincial second-stringers. The announced relatively even mix of party stalwarts and young newcomers composing the expanded Central Committee seems to have maximized the chances of Samrin's political generation to stay in power in the same way that the seeding of fast-rising economic, provincial, and public security leaders into the ranks of tried and true party stalwarts ensured the basic stability of the Vietnamese old guard at the Sixth Party Congress in December 1986.

Domestic Party Affairs. During 1989 the PRPK convened regular and extraordinary sessions of the Central Committee to transact the basic business of the party. The PRPK continued to emphasize the development of regional and provincial organizations, took a more active role in supporting the economic reforms, and supported the expansion of state and legislative agencies.

Regional congresses convened by the provincial party organizations during the first half of the year defined reformist agendas that focused on improving municipal administrative committee services and party committees. The congresses seated clusters of provincial representatives at formal sessions under the chairmanship of individual Politburo members and focused these meetings on concrete regional issues, activating these geographic fulcrums for regional party activity. The sessions defined the responsibilities of district-level core cadres, sought ways to strengthen party organization officers, and set minimum requirements for the organization of party committee meetings and visits to subordinate organizations by representatives of superior party chapters. (Phnom Penh Domestic Service, 0430 GMT, 25 March; *FBIS-EAS*, 89-059, 29 March; Phnom Penh Domestic Service, 0430 GMT, 9 February; *FBIS-EAS*, 89-026, 9 February; Phnom Penh Domestic Service, 1300 GMT, 16 February; *FBIS-EAS*, 89-031, 16 February; Phnom Penh Domestic Service, 0430 GMT, 27 February; *FBIS-EAS*, 89-038, 28 February; Jacques Bekaert, "The Party—Still a Dominant Force," *Bangkok Post*, May.) Special party conferences and meetings conducted during the course of the year underscored the center's commitment to systematic reform of provincial political organizations, to the expansion of party membership, and to the development of subprovincial structures.

In early February an enlarged eighth plenary meeting of the Central Committee that included ministers emphasized multisectoral efforts to strengthen core groups and improve core cadres. The plenum gave priority to village and communal development in addition to supporting the convening of regional party congresses. (Phnom Penh Domestic Service, 2300 GMT, 7 February; *FBIS-EAS*, 89-026, 9 February.) An extraordinary Central Committee session held from 29 March to 1 April, which preceded the Second National Cadre Conference and which was chaired by General Secretary Heng Samrin, reiterated the basic themes of institutional development and membership expansion.

The Second National Conference of Party Cadres in April proclaimed the success of the central organization's efforts to expand and improve subordinate provincial and municipal party committees. According to the report presented to the Central Committee, provincial and municipal party committees had increased the size of their staffs, established control commissions, and encouraged the parallel growth of mass organizations. (Phnom Penh Domestic Service, 1300 GMT, 20 April; *FBIS-EAS*, 89-080, 27 April.) The cadre conference hailed the expansion of the party's leadership and troubleshooting role and demonstrated the party's strong hand in formulating and managing the new economic reforms.

During the course of 1989 the regime took steps to empower the government to act in a more independent, uncensored manner without the overbearing Politburo veto hanging over its head. The regime placed a premium on separating church and state, distinguishing the party's role in defining policy from the administrative structure's responsibility as the primary implementing agent. Phnom Penh sought to strengthen the hand of the mass organizations as representatives of social and sectoral interests and as vehicles through which those interests could participate more directly and actively in the political process. Additionally, the National Assembly took a more active role in formulating reformist legislation and sponsoring constitutional reforms, ventured into the realm of public debate, and placed its parliamentarian imprimatur on efforts to reorganize ministerial authority and to empower broadened political participation.

The sixteenth session of the National Assembly

in February favored a more vigorous role for the parliament and adjustments in the government's mode of operation. In his 13 February closing speech on the final day of the six-day session, National Assembly chairman Chea Sim reiterated the broad support for rethinking habits of governance and the practices of rule that occupied the attentions of the assembly. The session, according to Chea Sim, urged a leaner, more effective leadership and a bureaucracy with more precisely defined purviews and "fewer cadre, fewer formalities, but greater effectiveness." The parliamentarians stressed the importance of new laws in guiding these reforms, supported constitutional amendments, and proposed legislation regarding the reform of land tenure, solidarity production groups, and taxation. (SPK, in French, 1200 GMT, 13 February; *FBIS-EAS*, 89-029, 13 February; see also Michael Vickery's two-part article in Bangkok, *Nation*, 5 February and 12 February.) Additionally, the National Assembly took a more active role on selected local issues such as urging the Council of Ministers to devise practical solutions to urban housing shortages. Finally, the assembly demonstrated its willingness to tinker with the government's structure through proposals for amending and improving the ministerial bureaucracy. (The National Assembly proposed the establishment of positions for assistant counselors for strategic and economic research. Those counselors were to be assigned to the Council of Ministers.) (SPK, in French, 1200 GMT, 13 February; *FBIS-EAS*, 89-028, 13 February.)

In late March the State Council issued a decree on the establishment of a Commission for Amending the Constitution of the PRK, which was formed under Chea Sim's chairmanship and included two overseas Cambodians as vice-chairs: In Tam, a former Lon Nol general, and Pung Peng Cheng, Sihanouk's former chief of cabinet. (SPK, in French, 1124 GMT, 24 March; *FBIS-EAS* 89-058, 28 March.) The National Assembly convened an extraordinary session from 29 April to 1 May that debated and adopted amendments to the constitution proposed by Chea Sim's committee. The session renamed the country the State of Cambodia, designated Buddhism the national religion, declared Cambodian foreign policy to be based on neutrality and nonalignment, abolished the death penalty, altered the national flag, and guaranteed citizens the right to a legal defense. Follow-up sessions clarified and expanded the meaning of these constitutional amendments. A mid-May meeting of the Council of State accorded the chairman of the Council of State the concurrent roles of head of state, supreme commander of the armed forces, and chairman of the national defense. An early May circular by the Kampuchean United Front for National Construction and Defense (KUFNCD) empowered the ordination of monks in accordance with a January party Central Committee pronouncement on the necessity of preserving Buddhism, subject to official permission and KUFNCD concurrence. In June the regime pardoned one hundred political and common law prisoners. (Phnom Penh Domestic Service, 0430 GMT, 29 April; *FBIS-EAS* 89-082, 1 May; SPK, in French, 0407 GMT, 18 May; *FBIS-EAS* 89-095, 18 May; Phnom Penh Domestic Service, 2300 GMT, 4 May; *FBIS-EAS* 89-086, 5 May; SPK, in French, 0407 GMT, 15 June; *FBIS-EAS* 89-114, 15 June.)

The seventeenth session of the First National Assembly, convened in mid-July, adopted a raft of draft bills and proposals concerning ministerial restructuring and import-export taxation reform and legislated changes in civil laws including the marriage and family laws, the rules governing foreign investment, and legal procedures for criminal courts. According to official accounts, the assembly members discussed granting expanded rights to provincial governments, endorsed the economic reforms, elected Mrs. Pung Peng Cheng, an overseas Cambodian, to membership in the Council of State, and appointed her assistant minister to the chairman of the Council of Ministers. In September and October the regime began preparations for convening an extraordinary National Assembly session to discuss the timing for a national election. (Hong Kong, AFP, in English, 1151 GMT, 24 October; *FBIS-EAS* 89-204, 24 October.) The party took a central role in defining the program of economic reforms in 1989. The Central Committee placed its imprimatur on the land use and labor exchange policies and endorsed the policy entitling households and private citizens to engage in business activities at the April cadre conference. The PRPK also took a position as superintendent of the shifts in fundamental agricultural development and land use policy and strongly sponsored the expansion of the political role accorded peasant associations in pressing the reforms of production. (SPK, in English, 0413 GMT, 1 April; *FBIS-EAS* 89-062, 3 April; Phnom Penh Domestic Service, 1300 GMT, 22 April; *FBIS-EAS* 89-077, 24 April.)

The party underwrote government efforts to influence local economic activity by devolving decision-making authority over basic production choices to local factory levels, experimenting with mixed state-owned and privately owned companies, and defining foreign trade and investment opportunities to attract outside investment interest and to energize internal production for export.

The sixteenth session of the First National Assembly in early February supported the reforms that accorded the rights of self-management to factories, endorsed the high-level decision to authorize state and private economic entities, and approved improvements in production organization and the rules governing land management and utilization. (SPK, in French, 0426 GMT, 9 February; *FBIS-EAS* 89-026, 9 February.) The Second National Conference of Party Cadres in early April adopted a resolution on small industries and handicrafts in the household, private, collective, and joint state-private sectors that was intended to accord legitimacy to the unorthodox forms of individual and family ownership and management of production in select sectors. The state would play a continued central role, especially in governing the production of strategic goods and items requiring special control. Individual managers and producers were to be encouraged by the government to make production decisions based on market criteria, to apply technical innovations to production, and to bring to bear the capital assets from overseas Cambodians to import equipment or expand production facilities based on local assessments of economic conditions and marketability of products. (SPK, in French, 0137 GMT, 24 April; *FBIS-EAS* 89-078, 25 April.) At the February session the National Assembly also adopted amendments to the Land Ownership and Exploitation Law that authorized full rights to occupation and exploitation of land and the right to inherit land distributed by the state. The assembly also mandated the taxation of property, payable through direct remittance or the sale of agricultural products to the state, thus legislating stability in individual land tenure for agricultural producers. In July the National Assembly underwrote ministerial reform proposals and new tax and foreign investment laws aimed at enhancing the independent decision-making rights of family, private, and joint economic forms. (Phnom Penh Domestic Service, 2300 GMT, 28 February; *FBIS-EAS* 89-041, 3 March; Phnom Penh Domestic Service, 1300 GMT, 20 July; *FBIS-EAS* 89-139, 21 July.)

The regime supported efforts to develop foreign investment and trade activities at the early February National Assembly session, building on earlier efforts of the assembly to establish a legislative basis for internal and external investments. By late February district-level trade bureaus and specialized trade offices responsible for the supervision of provincial trade were involved in monitoring transactions with foreign countries, guiding purchases of grain and agricultural products, and controlling the distribution of supplies. As a consequence of the authorization of independent and joint state-private economic activities, by late February six wholesale companies had opened in Phnom Penh, matched by the establishment of provincial counterparts and a slow proliferation of district collectivized trading stores. Although the Phnom Penh regime did not have regulations governing foreign investment, joint ventures, and shareholding, an infrastructure of ministerial subordinates responsible for import-export policy and provincial services and trade agencies managed direct deals with Thai companies. By early January provincial governors, most of whom were deputy chairmen of the provincial party committees, had been authorized to oversee provincial trade with foreign countries. Regularly reviewed trade protocols with Laos and Vietnam governed long-term bilateral programs of economic cooperation. (Bangkok, *Nation*, 11 January, 26 March.) By mid-April the regime had begun to contemplate defining a foreign investment code. Early speculation suggested that the law would be drawn up by May and would include guidelines for joint ventures and foreign-owned companies based entirely on foreign capital. (Hong Kong, AFP, in English, 0232 GMT, 14 April; *FBIS-EAS* 89-073, 18 April.) Although little progress toward that goal was apparent through late April, the Second National Cadre Conference did adopt a resolution guaranteeing that the state would not nationalize or dissolve production establishments as long as such activities conformed with already existing laws.

Auxiliary and Front Organizations. In 1989 the regime continued to place a primacy on the expansion of mass organizations and sustained its commitment to grass roots–level work toward the integration of party, government, and mass organizational systems at the village and commune level. Key leaders reiterated their endorsement of a comprehensive "national reconciliation policy" calling for the blending of workers, intellectuals, ethnic groups, and clergy into organized citizen groups that would participate in national politics and serve the parallel aim of assisting the expansion of commune and village units. The Fourth National Conference of the KUFNCD, held in late January, elected a National Council replicating in a slightly expanded form the leadership named in December 1981 under Chea Sim's chairmanship. Front Secretary Ros Chhun emphasized the broadening of the united front and endorsed the formation of a "rational structure at all levels," an integration of front structures into district, township, and grass roots–level administrative bodies. He also lamented lingering opposition to front development in terms similar to Chea Sim's 1988 refrain about the need to eliminate opposition to the role of mass organizations: "Unfortunately, party authorities and the administration at certain places have not given due attention to the Front and other mass organizations. Instead of seeking their advice they simply regard them as mere attachments. That is un-Marxist, un-Leninist." (SPK, in English, 1113 GMT, 25 January; *FBIS-EAS* 89-020, 1 February.)

The Second Session of the Kampuchean Federation of Trade Unions (KFTU), convened in early April under the chairmanship of May Ly, focused on broadening the federation's responsibilities in the context of widened economic participation and the gradual marketization of the economy. (Phnom Penh Domestic Service, 2300 GMT, 5 February; *FBIS-EAS* 89-024, 7 February; Phnom Penh Domestic Service, 0705 GMT, 26 January; *FBIS-EAS* 89-020, 1 February; Phnom Penh Domestic Service, 1300 GMT, 11 August; *FBIS-EAS* 89-158, 17 August.)

The Kampuchean Youth Association, the Kampuchean Youth Union, and the Women's Union worked to expand membership, continued involvement in national defense and restoration projects, and played their customary roles in emulation campaigns including the clemency policy intended to attract defectors from the ranks of the Non-Communist Resistance (NCR) and Democratic Kampuchea (DK). The association and the unions had a hand in government-organized efforts to attract overseas Cambodians to travel to the PRK for firsthand looks at the performance of the incumbent regime. The visits were calculated to enhance the image of the regime at critical points in the regional diplomatic process. (SPK, in English, 0705 GMT, 26 January; *FBIS-EAS* 89-020, 1 February; *FEER*, 19 January.)

The regime patted itself on the back for reviving Buddhism, repairing pagodas, publishing and broadcasting sermons, breathing life into the Buddhist Association, and establishing a research group under KUFNCD auspices to sustain such government-sponsored activities. The regime also took credit for reviving Cham religious practices. In January, Hun Sen apologized for government "mistakes" toward religion in a speech to monks at a Kampot City pagoda. Several weeks after the April National Assembly vote that restored Buddhism as the national religion, the government decreed that Buddhist followers could be ordained as monks. Pagoda schools, however, remained in the hands of the Ministry of Education. The pre-1975 responsibilities for running local self-help and education programs were not restored to the pagodas, and the seminary was not reopened or authorized to train new monks. The modest revival took place under close government scrutiny. (*FEER*, 3 August; *Bangkok Post*, 13 January.)

International and Regional Issues. The year 1989 began with a series of important departures from long-standing diplomatic approaches to the Cambodian problem. In early January, Sitthi Sawetsila visited Hanoi for discussions about Cambodia, becoming the first Thai foreign minister to make such a journey in more than a decade. Sitthi announced substantial agreement on key bilateral issues and on the basic questions about a Cambodian settlement, as well as Hanoi's consent to consider the establishment of a peacekeeping "mechanism," a slight reversal of the Vietnamese opposition to the principle of an international peacekeeping force under U.N. auspices. On 16 January, Vietnam vice–foreign minister Dinh Nho Liem met in Beijing with his Chinese counterpart, Liu Shuqing, for the first direct talks in a decade. Thereafter, Hanoi agreed to a September 1989 date for the withdrawal of its forces from Cambodia, a concession made in response to China's offer to consider tandem and progressive decreases in its assistance to the DK in return for an earlier date for the completion of the People's Army of Vietnam (PAVN) withdrawal. On 21 January, Hun Sen was received by Thai prime minister Chatichai in an unprecedented private visit to Bangkok. Chatichai offered his visitor a vision of what a postconflict Indochina could expect from the Association of Southeast Asian Nations (ASEAN) in terms of normal, proper, and fruitful bilateral economic and political relationships. These events contributed to sustaining the momentum of diplomacy and set the context in which the incremental advances in negotiations—including the narrow, perishable accommodations between Hun Sen and Sihanouk—were seized upon by the extraregional constituency for a negotiated settlement as the basis for compromise. (*FEER*, 12 January; Bangkok, *Nation*, 17 January; Bangkok Domestic Service, in Thai, 1200 GMT, 25 January; *FBIS-EAS* 89-016, 26 January; Bangkok, *Nation*, 25 January.)

In mid-February, Prince Norodom Sihanouk returned to the presidency of the Cambodian resistance in advance of the convening of the Jakarta [*sic*] Informal Meeting (JIM) working group. Sihanouk resigned in July 1988 to protest Khmer Rouge actions in the field against the NCR. The second JIM session, from 19 to 21 February, brought into sharp relief the basic conflicts that divided the competing Cambodian parties, the Vietnamese, and ASEAN. Vietnam restated its basic case: that the withdrawal of the PAVN from Cambodia depended on the achievement of a political solution. ASEAN and the Coalition Government of Democratic Kampuchea (CGDK) insisted that the withdrawal of Vietnamese forces be unconditional and take place according to a timetable, in a geographic rather than a numerical manner. ASEAN and the CGDK continued to agree on the need for an international peacekeeping force (IPKF) under U.N. auspices. Vietnam and the PRK were prepared to accept a control commission with a military component, drawing armed forces from a number of countries and possibly including representatives from the four Cambodian factions. The CGDK and ASEAN continued to demand a legitimate provisional coalition government under Sihanouk's leadership. The PRK and the Vietnamese were prepared to offer Sihanouk the chairmanship of a national reconciliation council that would organize and implement elections leading to the creation of a quadripartite government without dissolving the PRK government before holding free elections. The Vietnamese viewed the second JIM as tactical in nature, not a key point in the process of solution. They therefore hardened their position regarding the legitimacy of the PRK, the irrelevance of Sihanouk, and the need to keep the internal and external aspects of the problem separate. (*FEER*, 4 February.) The second JIM session yielded no significant progress toward agreement among the four Cambodian factions. The meeting endorsed continued negotiations by the Cambodians and called for a status report to the JIM by June. The conclusion of the JIM left the sense that bilateral meetings involving the major actors would catalyze further progress and that an international conference was necessary to guide the Cambodian factions toward agreement.

On 5 April the three Indochinese states issued a joint statement that provided for a total withdrawal of all Vietnamese troops by the end of September and proposed a cessation of all foreign military aid to the Cambodian parties. The statement had a tactical dimension to it as an effort to prod the diplomatic process along, but was also the result of efforts to prepare the way for a maximum impact of the 15 May Sino-Soviet summit.

The fourth meeting between Hun Sen and Sihanouk took place from 2 to 4 May and yielded no great strides forward on key issues—specifically, the question of the interim government and the role of the Khmer Rouge. However, the flurry of tabled proposals and the general predisposition toward flexibility evinced by the two negotiators yielded a potential for compromise. As a result of the exchange Sihanouk appeared closer to a decision to jettison the Khmer Rouge than he was in July 1988, when he resigned as head of the CGDK, or any time before. Sihanouk did in fact give a bit on the question of the auspices of an international peacekeeping mechanism, conceding that an international conference that would include security council members could name an international control commission that could fulfill the necessary cease-fire and troop withdrawal monitoring responsibilities. Sihanouk also backed away from his insistence on "dismantling" of the PRK and began to speak of the possibility of "transforming" the PRK into a quadripartite government. Hun Sen promised to report back to his government regarding Sihanouk's demand for further constitutional change that would permit the formation of additional political parties and break the monopoly of the People's Revolutionary party. Although Hun Sen remained steadfast in his insistence that the PRK not be dissolved before the holding of an election, Sihanouk's musings that he would reach a decision on returning to Cambodia in the immediate aftermath of the Vietnamese troop withdrawal were enough of an incentive to Hun Sen to work hard to get everything in line. That the two scheduled another meeting for July seemed to indicate that both Sihanouk and Hun Sen saw a deal emerging that would satisfy each of them. (The PRK National Assembly—which convened in an extraordinary session in late April and amended the constitution to declare a neutral, nonaligned foreign policy course for the country, alter the national flag, and rename the PRK the State of Cambodia—was a calculated effort to make some of the substantive and cosmetic changes necessary to accommodate Sihanouk.) (*WP*, 2 May; *NYT*, 3 May.)

On 6 May, Hun Sen visited Bangkok for the

second time. Discussions between Hun Sen and the Thai prime minister focused on cease-fire proposals formulated by Chatichai and his advisers. On 8 May the Chinese and Vietnamese vice–foreign ministers held a second set of talks. From 8 to 15 May, China and the Soviet Union held a summit in Beijing that resulted in a joint communiqué outlining central areas of agreement on the issues of Vietnamese military disengagement from Cambodia, international supervision of the peace process, reduction of external assistance to the Cambodian factions, and the basic successes of the JIM process. One major area of difference was China's endorsement of the creation of a quadripartite coalition government and the contrasting Soviet support for quadripartite participation in a Sihanouk-led national reconciliation council that would organize elections and play a role in the formation of a coalition government. (Statement by Robert Kimmitt, under secretary of state for political affairs, before the Senate Foreign Relations Committee, 12 June; Tommy Koh, "The Failure of the Paris Conference and its Implications for a Cambodian Settlement," Washington Center of the Asia Society, 11 September.)

Following the Sino-Soviet summit French foreign minister Roland Dumas announced that Paris would host an international conference on the conflict in Cambodia during August, an event that Dumas had worked toward encouraging from the middle of the year. Sihanouk proposed a new constitution embodying a French-style multiparty democracy for Cambodia, signaling his view that Hun Sen's concessions were not yet sufficient and challenging Phnom Penh's chief diplomat to wring further accommodations from the PRK National Assembly. The early July meeting of the ASEAN foreign ministers in Brunei sought to state strongly the organization's support for the CGDK by rejecting the quick compromises that would leave Phnom Penh in a commanding position in an interim coalition. In early July, Sihanouk reiterated the position that an international control mechanism under U.N. auspices remained an essential part of the formula for solution and restated his demand for the simultaneous dismantling of the Phnom Penh government, backing away from earlier compromises.

On 24 July, Sihanouk and Hun Sen met for the fifth time, followed by a meeting of the four Cambodian parties that opened the way for the international conference that convened in Paris on 30 July. During the month-long conference Vietnam and the PRK continued to object to a U.N. role in the peacekeeping mission for Cambodia. China and the Khmer Rouge argued that the use of the term *genocide* in the documents of a negotiated settlement would give Hanoi justification for its invasion of Cambodia. Hanoi opposed dwelling on the issue of the Vietnamese settlers, pushed strongly as an issue by the CGDK. The PRK proposed a cease-fire in place, while the CGDK stressed the need for regrouping armed forces and disarming to specific levels under appropriate U.N.-managed monitoring forces. The PRK adamantly opposed the inclusion of the Khmer Rouge in such an interim coalition. Sihanouk took the position that excluding the Khmer Rouge from a coalition would guarantee continued armed conflict, whereas including the Khmer Rouge would help ensure the stability of a quadripartite interim government, especially in view of the Khmer Rouge's agreement to accept regroupment and disarmament, a U.N. peacekeeping force, and internationally supervised elections, as well as Chinese support for the position that the coalition need not be based on an equal distribution of power among the four parties.

At the end of August the Paris conference suspended its proceedings without having achieved a comprehensive agreement for the settlement of the conflict in Cambodia. The conference, which did leave a body of important basic agreements on the external aspects of the settlement, made a point of not adjourning and agreed to begin consultations within six months with a view toward reconvening. (*NYT*, 31 August; Secretary of State James Baker, "International Efforts for a Peaceful Cambodia," statement at the International Conference on Cambodia, Paris, 30 July.)

In the wake of the Paris conference, regional players scurried to organize meetings of the Cambodian factions, to re-engage the JIM process, and to push for compromise solutions building on the basic agreements of the Paris conference. ASEAN, especially Singapore, urged continued support for the two noncommunist parties and firmly expressed the hope that the Bush administration's proposal for lethal assistance to the NCR would receive bipartisan support in Congress. Thai prime minister Chatichai peddled his proposals for turning the Indochina battlefield into a marketplace, and his "academic advisors" flogged their plans for "parallel track diplomacy"—regional discussions on the subject of power sharing and simultaneous international participation in the formation of a control mechanism to verify the Vietnamese claim to have withdrawn their military forces. Indonesian foreign minister Alatas sought to reserve the JIM vehicle, recognizing that a regional meeting that did not obtain a compromise on power sharing would further squander ASEAN resources and contribute to a hardening of positions. In November, Alatas offered to convene a regional meeting in the Paris framework, involving the four Cambodian parties, Laos, Vietnam, France, and the ASEAN countries. In mid-November the ASEAN resolution on Cambodia was adopted at the 44th session of the U.N. General Assembly with a record high vote of 124 supporters rejecting the Phnom Penh regime. Australia offered a proposal for turning Cambodia into a U.N. trusteeship, an alternative initially formulated by U.S. congressman Stephen Solarz.

The Cambodians, clearly not in a bargaining mood, were intent on pressing their perceived advantages on the battlefield, effectively eliminating the opportunity for another spurt of diplomacy. In early October the noncommunist forces launched operations in northwest Cambodia with the aim of seizing control of large chunks of real estate in the vicinity of Sisophon. In early November the Khmer Rouge seized control of Pailin, mainly through sustained shelling of PRK units, which fell back to their home garrisons, offering little resistance to their adversary's grab for this gem-rich area. In early December, after repeated efforts, the KPNLF seized Svay Chek, north of Sisophon on Route 69.

In the context of this yearlong diplomatic industry, Phnom Penh reaffirmed the strength of the Indochina triangle in symbolic if not practical terms. A continuous two-way flow of senior officials underscored the special tie that united Vietnam and Cambodia. In early January, Vietnamese communist party general secretary Nguyen Van Linh attended the tenth anniversary celebrations of National Day in Phnom Penh. Senior PRK ministerial officials kept the Vietnamese fully informed of Hun Sen's talks with Thai leaders in early 1989 through consultations with Deputy Foreign Minister Tran Quang Co in Hanoi. In late February, Phnom Penh hosted the Indochinese foreign ministers conference, which highlighted the stability and developmental achievements of the PRK and coordinated the strategy for the second JIM meeting. In September, Heng Samrin visited Vietnam at the invitation of the Council of State and the Central Committee and heard ringing endorsements from top Vietnamese leaders for the policy of neutrality articulated by the PRK National Assembly meeting in July. The press communiqué issued by the Politburo at the end of the visit underscored the continued strength of close Vietnamese-Cambodian friendship, solidarity, and cooperation. Both Hanoi and Phnom Penh sought to demonstrate that the professed commitment to permanent neutrality was compatible with the treaty relationship between the two countries and would not compromise the commitment to enhanced relations and cooperation between the parties, states, and peoples because that relationship would be rooted in commitments to mutual respect of independence, sovereignty, and territorial integrity.

Hanoi and Phnom Penh sustained their entangling alliance through renewed protocols on trade and other specialized cooperation. In mid-January the two trade ministries signed a protocol on scientific and technological cooperation in trade and specialized training for 1989. A broader bilateral trade exchange protocol was signed by Phnom Penh at the end of April during the visit of a Vietnamese delegation. A midyear protocol on cooperation between radio and television services was signed in mid-June.

Phnom Penh also scurried to win wider recognition for the legitimacy and accomplishments of the PRK. Hun Sen calculated his public diplomacy to communicate an image of a sophisticated, reasonable, and mature regional player and had a good deal of success in portraying the PRK as a legitimate entity deserving of recognition if only for its incumbency. Phnom Penh maintained a constant rhythm of high-level contacts with the Soviet Union and Eastern European countries during 1989 and echoed Hanoi's admonition to diversify economic relations with traditional partners and expand contracts and commerce with other countries predisposed to friendship. The regime seized on contacts with the Thai prime minister and his advisers, who urged a formula for peace in Cambodia that relied less on the long-standing ASEAN position and more on an amorphous commitment to expanded regional dialogues and hardened commercial interactions. Phnom Penh entertained parliamentarian delegations from Bangkok, announced a Council of Ministers decision to establish a committee for Cambodian-Thai economic cooperation, and encouraged Chatichai's interest in direct cross-border trade, in joint fishing operations in Cambodian territorial waters, and in upgrading communications and transportation links between traditional corridors of trade. (Hanoi Domestic Service, in Vietnamese, 1100 GMT, 5 January; *FBIS-EAS* 89-003, 5 January; VNA, in English, 1515 GMT, 1 February; *FBIS-EAS* 89-021, 2 February; SPK, in

English, 1108 GMT, 18 February; *FBIS-EAS* 89-035, 23 February; Phnom Penh Domestic Service, 1100 GMT, 10 September; *FBIS-EAS* 89-174, 11 September; SPK, in English, 0450 GMT, 17 June; *FBIS-EAS* 89-116, 19 June.)

Party. Party of Democratic Kampuchea (PDK). The PDK is the successor to the Kampuchean Communist Party (KCP), the instrument of rule under Pol Pot from April 1975 to December 1978, when the Vietnamese invaded Cambodia and displaced the brutal DK regime.

Founded. The PDK traces its origin to the Khmer People's Revolutionary Party (KPRP), which was founded on 30 September 1951 with the establishment of a provisional Central Committee, pending the party's first congress. According to a party history issued under the authority of the Eastern Zone Military-Political Service in 1973, the decision to form a Marxist-Leninist party was made at the second congress of the KPRP in September 1960. The organization was renamed the Workers' Party of Kampuchea at that time. A 1977 speech by Pol Pot suggests that September 1960 was the first congress of the KCP, though the party did not bear that name until a September 1966 Central Committee decision authorizing the change in nomenclature. The KCP designation endured until the nominal dissolution of the party in 1981.

Membership. Unknown

General Secretary. Ever since the KCP was dissolved in 1981 the position of general secretary has not been publicly mentioned. Pol Pot was general secretary up to 1981 and was retired in August 1985 from his leadership role in the DK faction in an orchestrated effort to improve the group's image in the context of the tripartite Coalition Government of Democratic Kampuchea, founded in 1982.

Politburo. Possibly no longer functioning

Secretariat. Possibly no longer functioning

Central Committee. Possibly no longer functioning

Status. The KCP was officially dissolved in December 1981 in a calculated effort to facilitate the formation of an anti-Vietnamese coalition between the remnants of the DK regime, the Khmer People's National Liberation Front (KPNLF) of Son Sann, and Sihanoukist forces that remained hesitant about joining a coalition with the brutal DK to oppose Hanoi's occupation of Cambodia. A tripartite partnership aimed at opposing the Vietnamese military presence in Cambodia was established in mid-1982. The DK, or Khmer Rouge in the appellation preferred by Prince Sihanouk, has remained the dominant partner in the coalition, with the most disciplined, best-organized, and most completely supplied army. The KCP was replaced by the PDK, an organization that replicated the functional-level leadership structure and high command relationships of the KCP while publicly professing to have discarded the iconoclastic commitment to radical communism. The August 1985 public retirement of Pol Pot from his leadership roles was undertaken to further underscore the flexible nature of the organization.

Last Congress. The third and last party congress was held in Phnom Penh on 14 December 1975.

Last Election. The last election for the People's Representative Assembly of Democratic Kampuchea was held on 20 March 1976. One hundred and fifty peasants, 50 workers, and 50 soldiers were elected to the assembly.

Auxiliary Organizations. Organizations such as the Communist Women's Organization and the Alliance of Democratic Kampuchean Youth have probably been defunct since the fall of Pol Pot's regime in December 1978.

Media. The PDK maintains a radio broadcasting station called the Voice of the National Army of Democratic Kampuchea (VONADK), which operates clandestinely.

Leadership and Party Organization. In 1989 the PDK remained the best-equipped, the most capably organized and led, and the most efficient fighting force of all the Cambodian contestants. The DK thwarted the Vietnamese army's ten-year-long effort to pacify Cambodia; by late year the DK had claimed the nationalist mantle as vanquisher of Hanoi's occupation forces. The DK outclassed the Non-Communist Resistance (NCR) in command, control, and execution of tactical and strategic actions.

The estimated strength of the Democratic Kampuchean forces in 1989 ranged from 25,000 to 30,000 troops and porters. The organization was able to replace its losses, but was not capable of overall force expansion. China continued to supply the DK with basic infantry weapons, rocket-propelled grenades, and mortars in excess of its needs. The DK sustained its emphasis on political action in the interior and avoided large-scale attacks on Vietnamese and PRK forces during the year.

The PDK's organizational chart and the composition of the political high command remained shrouded in secrecy in 1989. Pol Pot was widely viewed as still exercising considerable behind-the-scenes power, and the fundamental KCP structures were widely assumed to have remained intact and unaltered by the cosmetic changes. In a June 1989 letter to Khieu Samphan and Son Sen, Pol Pot requested permission to resign as head of the High Institute for National Defense. In September, Khieu Samphan told a Western reporter that though Pol Pot had recovered from severe malaria attacks and was "fairly well," he had decided to remove himself from decision making. The PDK controls a system of refugee and insurgent base camps along the Thai-Cambodian border and operates in southeastern Cambodia in the vicinity of the Great Lake (Tonle Sap) and near Phnom Penh. In 1989 Khieu Samphan, the vice-president of Democratic Kampuchea in charge of foreign affairs, continued to function as the party head, in close consultation with the party's shadowy political high command. Ieng Sary, one of Pol Pot's oldest and closest associates, retained significant authority for foreign policy and military strategy. His wife, Ieng Thirith, held substantial power in the realm of foreign affairs, according to some observers. Son Sen, deputy premier for national defense under Pol Pot, held the position of supreme commander of the National Army of Democratic Kampuchea (NADK). Khieu Samphan and Son Sen were rumored to have formed an alliance representing a more moderate, conciliatory faction of the DK. That moderate grouping was opposed by the followers and soldiers of the barbaric Ta Mok (alias Chhit Choen), vice-chairman of the NADK Military Committee. The Khmer Rouge retained close control over civilian camps and satellites.

In 1989 the DK suffered some slight slippage in its organizational coherence through the defections of some battalion-level commanders and regimental officers and through a weakened ability to contain civilians under the jurisdiction of the DK in camps on Thai soil. In June approximately seven hundred Cambodians fled DK encampments in the vicinity of Kaiche, an area in which several secret DK facilities had been constructed, to the KPNLF camp at Sok Sann. (Anuraj Manibhandu, "Opposition to Site K By Khmer Rouge," *Bangkok Post*, 25 June; Steven Erlanger, "700 Cambodians Given A Reprieve," *NYT*, 29 June; *NYT*, 27 June; *Quan Doi Nhan Dan*, 28 March; VNA, in English, 1448 GMT, 28 March; *FBIS-EAS*, 89-059, 29 March.) Nevertheless the DK maintained its overall field command structure with the two military sectors

that were defined in 1987, the border and the interior. An entity that combined the functions of a general staff and a commander in chief sat atop the command structure and controlled the field commands and their subordinate divisions. Pailin, Samlot, and Koh Kong were battlefield commands assigned to individual field commanders, who held sway over divisions that operated against those specific geographic targets. Ta Mok was in charge of Command 1003, and Son Sen commanded the 1001 Battlefield Command in addition to his concurrent responsibilities for overall direction of DK military operations in Cambodia. Divisions subordinate to commands were assigned responsibilities within provinces, down to specific districts. They were apparently of uneven strength, and individual field commanders had differing numbers of divisions under their authority.

Domestic Affairs. In 1989 the interior of the Khmer Rouge organization remained inaccessible to outsiders. The DK continued to resist the presence of international aid organizations in five camps supplied by the United Nations Border Relief Organization (UNBRO)—Huay Chan, Na Trao, Au Trao, Bo Rai, and Ta Luan—though some slightly increased access was granted to UNBRO for the purpose of monitoring the distribution of humanitarian aid in Bo Rai and in Site Eight, the largest DK camp inside Thailand. In early 1989 increased numbers of Site Eight inhabitants departed for the neighboring KPNLF-controlled camp at Sok San to escape the draconian discipline and the severe, controlled life of the DK-administered camp. Civilians in Bo Rai, a DK camp of 4,500 people located near the southernmost portion of the Thai-Cambodian border, continued to be forced to provide military support for DK operations, largely as porters. Ta Luan, with a population of about six thousand, had been partially reconstructed through the forced relocation of eight thousand residents to a location closer to the border in the summer of 1988. The Thai government compelled DK authorities to improve living conditions at the original site and to allow increased access by international organizations. Approximately four thousand of those forcibly moved in 1988 remained in closed satellite camps close to the border, which served as staging areas for DK operations aimed at securing the Cambodian side of the border. Au Trao camp was reopened in late January after Thai authorities closed it to UNBRO for a month following the burning of a Catholic-run outpatient hospital and DK refusal to unload United Nations Educational, Scientific, and Cultural Organization food trucks, presumably a result of DK camp authorities' dissatisfaction with the increasing presence of international organizations that took exception to DK efforts to move the population to the border. Ten thousand people of the seventeen thousand–person camp were moved to satellite camps in the month before the original site was reopened. By February the camp had a population of six thousand, which was increasing with the return of those relocated to border settlements. (Bangkok, *Nation*, 4 January, 27 February; *Khmer Rouge Abuses Along the Thai-Cambodian Border*, An Asia Watch Report, February; Steven Erlanger, "The Return of the Khmer Rouge," *NYT Magazine*, 5 March; Lawyers Committee for Human Rights, *Refuge Denied: Problems in the Protection of Vietnamese and Cambodians in Thailand and the Admission of Indochinese Refugees into the US*, 1989, pp. 64–79.)

Auxiliary and Front Organizations. There was no information concerning PDK auxiliary or front organizations in 1989.

International Views, Positions, and Activities. Throughout 1989 the DK held to the demand for a role in the quadripartite interim coalition government that would accept authority for organizing elections in Cambodia under the vigilance of an international control mechanism, in the vision of the JIM. The DK endorsed Sihanouk's five-point plan during the first JIM in mid-1988. The five-point plan called for withdrawal of the Vietnamese troops, the simultaneous dissolution of the PRK and the DK, general elections under an international control mechanism outside the framework of the PRK, the establishment of a provisional quadripartite government and army, and the dispatch of an IPKF under U.N. auspices. (VONADK, in Cambodian, 2315 GMT, 19 January; *FBIS-EAS* 89-013, 23 January.) During the course of the year the DK moved to preserve the advantages that resulted from sustaining the coalition government, including the legitimacy and respectability conferred by alliance with Prince Sihanouk. The DK made symbolic adjustments in its public persona, undertook periodic gestures of conciliation, and sought to convey a more accommodating posture in the context of international diplomacy, while remaining single-minded about securing a place in the interim government as part of the settlement package endorsed by the CGDK, China, the United States, and ASEAN.

On 20 January, in a coordinated effort to stake out a position in advance of the second JIM and to counteract press reports that Prince Sihanouk had dropped two conditions from his five-point plan, DK leader Khieu Samphan, vice-president of the CGDK in charge of foreign affairs, signed a CGDK press communiqué along with KPNLF president Son Sann and Prince Norodom Ranarith, Sihanouk's personal representative, that reaffirmed united support for the prince's five-point program. At about the same time the same triumvirate publicized a letter to Sihanouk expressing strong support. (VONADK, 2330 GMT, 20 January; *FBIS-EAS* 89-013, 23 January.) The prince was reported to have agreed in mid-January to withdraw his demand that an IPKF be stationed in Cambodia, accepting in its place an enlarged control commission. Sihanouk also reportedly abandoned his condition that the PRK be dismantled before a provisional government was established. (Bangkok, *Nation*, 12 January.) The support for the five-point plan was strongly reiterated up to the convening of the second JIM in mid-February. Just before the JIM, Prince Sihanouk resumed the post of president of the CGDK, a decision that ultimately contributed to the DK's ability to manipulate the image of Sihanoukist support and alliance to their advantage.

The Khmer Rouge effectively froze progress at the JIM by demanding that all JIM decisions be unanimous and by focusing attention on extreme estimates of Vietnamese troop strength and clandestine Vietnamese plans to perpetuate DK occupation of Cambodia by utilizing the Vietnamese settlers to do Hanoi's bidding from afar. In the end the Khmer Rouge avoided isolation and effectively prevented a compromise on the demand for dismantling the PRK. The Khmer Rouge elicited strong Chinese opposition to a compromise that would have created a national reconciliation committee drawing representatives from the competing Cambodian factions under Sihanouk's leadership, with the authority to organize elections without first dismantling the government in Phnom Penh.

In the aftermath of the JIM, Sihanouk reaffirmed his commitment to the coalition and indicated his willingness to be bound by any agreement negotiated or found acceptable by the leadership of the three parts of that coalition. (VONADK, 0430 GMT, 9 March; *FBIS-EAS* 89-046, 10 March.) In a joint statement issued in Beijing, DK leader Khieu Samphan, Son Sann, and Sihanouk announced the establishment of a High Council for National Defense led by Sihanouk, with Son Sann and Khieu assuming vice-chairmanships. The three ministers on the CGDK's Coordinating Committee for National Defense and the CGDK's high command and general staff were included as permanent members of the National Council. (Beijing, in Cambodian to Cambodia, 1030 GMT, 14 March; *FBIS-EAS* 89-050, 16 March 1989.) Although Sihanouk later claimed that the council was intended to provide "coordination and united aid" in the fight against the Vietnamese army and to serve as a means of preventing clashes between the resistance factions, the prince had effectively allowed himself to be cast as the supreme commander of a united high command that included the Khmer Rouge army. In an interview in late March, Khieu built the case for an enduring match between the DK and Sihanouk citing Sihanouk's five-point plan, the prince's modalities for implementing the plan, and the 14 March joint statement of the three CGDK leaders. Khieu enshrined the High Council for National Defense, emphasizing that it was Sihanouk's idea and that it suggested that the first step toward the establishment of a single national army after Vietnam's withdrawal had already been taken. Khieu worked overtime to paint a picture of the prince as being bound by unbreakable commitments to the tripartite coalition when Sihanouk had the least to gain from a closer strategic commitment to the Khmer Rouge. (VONADK, 2315 GMT, 24 March; *FBIS-EAS* 89-059, 24–27 March; VONADK, 2315 GMT, 29 March; *FBIS-EAS* 89-060, 30 March; *La Vanguardia*, 13 March.) The Khmer Rouge also pledged themselves to a variety of accommodations intended to make the comprehensive solution— according the DK a seat in a four-party coalition— more palatable and more credible as a means of fencing in the Khmer Rouge with international guarantees and a free and fair supervised election. The Khmer Rouge repeated their willingness to allow a U.N. force to carry out spot investigations to determine whether and where they maintained arms caches. (*Le Monde*, 4 April.) In June the DK reiterated their acceptance of a U.N. international peacekeeping force and proposed the disarmament of all four Cambodian parties as a means of assuring that no faction could dominate an interim coalition government. The Khmer Rouge endorsed the paring down of each of the four Cambodian armed forces to a level of ten thousand troops, which would be situated in the framework of a provisional quadripartite national army. (VONADK, 2330 GMT, 19 June; *FBIS-EAS* 89-118, 21 June.) In mid-

June, not to be outdone by Phnom Penh, the Khmer Rouge proposed a new flag for Cambodia. (Hong Kong, AFP, in English, 2322 GMT, 16 June; *FBIS-EAS* 89-115, 16 June.) Finally, in the context of the Paris conference, the DK made it clear that they were willing to accept less than 25 percent of the positions in an interim coalition government.

Thus, at the Paris conference in August the Khmer Rouge position revolved around five commitments. First, it supported the proposal that, following a cease-fire agreement, all armed Cambodians should be regrouped in bases and disarmed. Second, they supported a strong and effective international peacekeeping force under the auspices of the United Nations. Third, they supported an internationally supervised election that would be free, fair, and democratic. Fourth, they would abide by the outcome of the election. Fifth, in the context of a comprehensive settlement, the Khmer Rouge would not insist on equal power sharing in the interim coalition.

Khmer Rouge sincerity was never put to the test at the Paris meeting, which was scuttled by PRK intransigence on the question of according Sihanouk substantive executive powers in an interim coalition government, by Hun Sen's refusal to include the DK in an interim authority, and by stiff Vietnamese opposition to according the United Nations a role in forming a peacekeeping force and control mechanism.

Lewis M. Stern
Assistant for Indochina in the Office of the Assistant Secretary of Defense for International Security Affairs

Note: The views expressed in this paper are those of the author alone and do not reflect the official policy or position of the Department of Defense or any portion of the U.S. government.

China

Population. 1,112,298,677 (excluding Taiwan, July, *World Factbook* 1989)
Party. Chinese Communist Party (Zhongguo gongchan dang; CCP)
Founded. 1921
Membership. 48 million (Beijing, XINHUA, 22 September; *FBIS*, 22 September)

Central Committee. 175 full members and 110 alternate members

General Secretary. Jiang Zemin (replaced Zhao Ziyang on 24 June)

Standing Committee of the Politburo. 6 members, in rank order: Jiang Zemin (61) (since 24 June); Li Peng (60), premier; Qiao Shi (64), first secretary of Central Commission for Inspection Discipline, member of Secretariat, vice-premier; Yao Yilin (71), vice-premier, minister of State Planning Commission; Song Ping (since 24 June); Li Ruihuan (since 24 June); (Zhao Ziyang and Hu Qili removed on 24 June)

Politburo. 14 full members: Wan Li, Tian Jiyun, Qiao Shi, Jiang Zemin, Li Peng, Li Tieying, Li Ruihuan, Li Ximing, Yang Rudai, Yang Shangkun, Wu Xueqian, Song Ping, Yao Yilin, and Qin Jiwei (Hu Yaobang died 15 April; Zhao Ziyang and Hu Qili were removed on 24 June); alternate member: Ding Guangen

Secretariat. 4 full members: Qiao Shi, Li Ruihuan, Ding Guangen, and Yang Baibing (Li and Ding since 24 June; Yang since 9 November; Hu Qili, Rui Xingwen, and Yan Mingfu removed on 24 June); alternate member: Wen Jiaobao

Central Military Commission. Chairman: Jiang Zemin (Deng Xiaoping resigned 9 November); first vice-chairman: Yang Shangkun (Zhao Ziyang removed on 24 June); vice-chairman: Liu Huaqing; general secretary: Yang Baibing

Central Advisory Commission. Chairman: Chen Yun; vice-chairmen: Bo Yibo and Song Renqiong

Central Commission for Discipline Inspection. First secretary: Qiao Shi; deputy secretaries: Chen Zuolin, Li Zhengting, and Xiao Hongda

General Office. Director: Wen Jiabao; deputy directors: Xu Ruixin, Yang Dezhong, and Zhou Jie

Department of International Liaison. Director: Zhu Liang; deputy directors: Jiang Guanghua, Li Shuzheng, Li Chengren, and Zhu Shanqing

Department of Organization. Director: Song Ping; deputy directors: He Yong, Liu Zepeng, Lu Feng, Meng Liankun, and Zhao Zongnai

Department of Propaganda. Director: Wang Renzhi; deputy directors: Gong Yuzhi, Li Yan, and Wang Weicheng

Department of United Front Work. Director: Yan Mingfu; deputy directors: Li Ding, Song Kun, Wan Shaofen, Wu Lianyuan, and Zhang Shengzuo

Work Committee for Government Organs. Secretary: Chen Junsheng; deputy secretaries: Wang Chuguang, Zhang Jingyuan

Work Committee for Party Organs. Secretary: Wen Jiabao; deputy secretaries: Gu Yunfei, Li Yan

Central Party School. President Qiao Shi (replaced Gao Yang); vice-presidents: Chen Weiren, Gao Di, Han Shuying, Su Xing, Xing Bensi, and Xue Ju

Status. Ruling party

Last Congress. Thirteenth, 25 October–1 November 1987

Last Election. 1987

Auxiliary Organizations. Communist Youth League of China (50 million members), led by Song Defu; All-China Women's Federation, led by Chen Muhua; All-China Federation of Trade Unions, led by Ni Zhifu; Chinese People's Political Consultative Conference (CPPCC), the party's leading united front organization, led by Li Xiannian; eight democratic or satellite parties.

Publications. The official and most authoritative publication of the CCP is the newspaper *Renmin Ribao* (People's Daily), published in Beijing. The theoretical journal of the Central Committee, *Hongqi* (Red Flag), published its last issue in June 1988. It was superseded by the new biweekly theoretical journal *Qiushi* (Seeking Truth), under the Central Party School, which published its first issue in July 1988. Influential in recent years has been *Liaowang* (Outlook), the weekly publication of XINHUA (the New China News Agency; NCNA), the official news agency of the party and government. The daily paper of the People's Liberation Army (PLA) is *Jiefangjunbao* (Liberation Army Daily). The weekly *Beijing Review* (*BR*), published in English and in several other languages, carries translations of important articles, editorials, and documents from these three publications and from other sources. *China Daily*, the first English-language national newspaper in the People's Republic of China (PRC), began official publication in Beijing and Hong Kong on 1 June 1981. It began a New York edition in June 1983.

Domestic Affairs. Throughout the socialist bloc 1989 was an exceptional year, and China was no exception. The year began with the country experiencing economic retrenchment and a sharply divided leadership, the reformers having lost some of their momentum during the preceding year's setbacks occasioned by fears of inflation. The death of Hu Yaobang in April provided the opportunity for sizable numbers of demonstrators to amass whose momentum was sustained through further fortuitous events, including the May Fourth anniversary celebration along with the meeting of the Asian Development Bank and the visit of General Secretary Mikhail Gorbachev in mid-May. The whole world witnessed the euphoria of the prodemocracy demonstrations of April and May, and even the initial restraint of the Chinese authorities, whether by design or indecision, struck a welcome note. This generally positive experience, however, was turned around when the Chinese government suddenly and brutally enforced martial law with awesome military might before a world television audience that saw many hundreds of people killed and wounded.

The entire face of China and the standing of its ruling party have changed dramatically. A country that had been in the forefront of the reform movement among the socialist countries only a year or two earlier suddenly reversed gears and since June has consciously identified with the most ideologically conservative of such nations, which were themselves being transformed, abandoning China in the process. Of course, there remained in China considerable reformist sentiment. Many Chinese were aghast and outraged at the behavior of their government, and this has not been mollified by the months of repression that followed the June crackdown. The CCP, while still the only viable political organization in China, has perhaps never been so unpopular, despite its poor overall record in the years before the 1980s. With the dramatic fall of the Ceauşescu regime in Romania in late December, the Chinese regime found itself isolated from many of its erstwhile friends and in need of placing its security forces on alert and reinforcing police on campuses in Beijing.

Before the June debacle the Chinese economy, despite serious problems, had continued to register a mixed performance. According to the State Statistics Bureau, the annual gross national product reached 1,385.3 billion yuan for 1988, an increase of 11.2 percent over 1987; national income reached 1,153.3 billion yuan, an increase of 11.4 percent. Total industrial output value in 1988 was 1,810 billion yuan, an increase of 20.7 percent (this figure would be 1,518.1 billion yuan if village-run industries were excluded, 17.7 percent more than 1987). The output of steel in 1988 was 59.18 million tons; coal, 947 million tons; crude oil, 137 million tons; and electric power production was 543 billion kilowatt-hours. Economic development, however, experienced major problems of "overheated social demand, a sharpening of the contradiction between supply and demand and of the structural contradictions, a hasty price hike and an evident inflation." Meanwhile, the total agricultural output value in 1988 rose to 561.8 billion yuan, up by 3.2 percent over 1987. Grain production reached only 394 million tons, a decrease of 2.2 percent from 1987. ("Statistics for 1988 Socio-Economic Development," *BR*, 6–12 March.)

Although Chinese students would play a particularly prominent role in 1989, much of it heroic, the year did not begin that way; Chinese students at the beginning of the year focused on issues of racism and incompatibility between students from Hong Kong and Macao and mainland students. African students were threatening to leave China en masse because four African students were expelled after an incident over a Chinese woman 24 December 1988 at Hehai University in Nanjing. Following the incident 44 African students were held in a guest house outside Nanjing for nine days and were not released until they staged a hunger strike. Three Chinese were arrested, but the Africans were insulted by one of the conditions: that male African students could only have one Chinese girlfriend at a time and she would have to be introduced to the local foreign affairs office (Hong Kong, *South China Morning Post*, 6 January; *FBIS*, 6 January). This ugly incident led to demonstrations by Africans in Beijing and by Chinese students in Nanjing and other cities. There had been similar incidents in recent years in China.

Meanwhile, in early January at Jinan University in Guangzhou, more than a hundred postgraduate students demonstrated against alleged attacks by Hong Kong and Macao students. (Students from those two areas constitute almost half of the university's four thousand undergraduates.) The disturbances seemed to stem from the considerable differences in life-style and ages between the different student groups. (Fan Cheuk-wan, *Hongkong Standard*, 10 January; *FBIS*, 10 January.)

Beijing reimposed martial law in Lhasa on 7 March following three days of violent clashes between Tibetans and Chinese police during which, according to official sources, at least twelve people were killed and more than a hundred injured. Unofficial Tibetan sources, however, claimed that the number of deaths ranged between 20 and 75, with several hundred injured. After the Panchen Lama died on 28 January, several proindependence demonstrations took place without interference, but as the 30th anniversary (10 March) of the 1959 uprising approached, the government made a show of force with the People's Armed Police. On 5 March the demonstrators began attacking police stations, Chinese-owned businesses, and government and party offices. Witnesses said that the rioters seemed to be urban youth rather than the monks or nuns who were calling for independence in nonviolent demonstrations. (Robert Delfs, Beijing, *FEER*, 16 March.)

The Second Session of the Seventh National People's Congress (NPC) was held from 20 March to 4 April with 2,967 deputies attending. Premier Li Peng delivered the report on the work of the government. The resolution approving this report, which underwent more than 120 changes and modifications in content and wording, passed with but two votes opposed and four abstentions. (Beijing, XINHUA, 4 April; *FBIS*, 5 April.)

Li Peng noted that in China's socialist modernization, "we were challenged by a great many problems and difficulties, the most outstanding ones being the obvious inflation and excessive price hikes." He said that the problems were caused by a tendency to be too impatient for quick results in economic and social development. The orientation of reform was "correct and generally successful," but

in our guidance of the work we often lacked a full understanding of the arduousness and complexity of reform, did not pay sufficient attention to taking comprehensive and coordinated measures, and failed to tighten control and supervision at the right moment and establish in time a system of macroeconomic regulation and control when we persisted in decentralizing power and invigorating the economy.

In the past six months the government did help slow the economic growth rate, alleviated panic over prices, and more or less stabilized urban and rural markets. Li said that the State Council has decided to reduce total investments in fixed assets this year by 92 billion yuan, a reduction of 21 percent from 1988. Also, institutional purchases nationwide this year will be 20 percent lower than in 1988. (Li Rongxia, "NPC Session Stresses Rectification," *BR*, 27 March–2 April, 17–23 April.)

The NPC approved two important laws: the Administrative Litigation Law, which will become effective on 1 October 1990, codifies the procedure for common people to sue government departments and officials. The second law, the NPC Rules of Procedure, is designed to provide a legal and demo-

cratic procedure for the NPC to exercise power. It was to become effective on the day of promulgation.

The NPC also approved six other resolutions, decisions, and bills, including the State Council's 1989 plan for national economic and social development, the implementation of state budgets for 1988 and 1989, a work report of the NPC Standing Committee, work reports of the Supreme People's Court and the Supreme People's Procuratorate, and an authorization bill. The resolution on the NPC Standing Committee's work report was approved overwhelmingly (12 opposed and 109 abstentions), even though the committee had been sharply criticized by a number of deputies during the session for its failure to supervise the government.

The bill to authorize a legislative right for the People's Congress of Shenzen, China's first special economic zone, and for its standing committee and the city government encountered unprecedented opposition. Of the 2,688 deputies present, 1,609 voted for the bill; 274 opposed it, and 805 abstained. (Chang Hong, *CD*, 5 April; *FBIS*, 5 April.)

On 3 April, Li Peng held a press conference at the Great Hall of the People. With Li were Yao Guang, spokesman of the Second Session of the NPC, and Vice-Premiers Yao Yilin, Tian Jiyun, and Wu Xueqian (Beijing Television Service, 3 April; *FBIS*, 4 April).

On 6 April, Li Peng, in response to criticisms by NPC deputies, announced that the central leaders and State Council leaders would not hold their usual summer meetings in Beidaihe this year and that the import of luxury cars is now banned (Hong Kong, *Zhongguo Tongxun*, 11 April; *FBIS*, 12 April).

Former General Secretary Hu Yaobang died on 15 April following a heart attack during a meeting of the Politburo a few days earlier. The death of the prominent but disgraced party reformer served as a pretext for several thousand students gathering at Tiananmen Square on 17 April. The students called for political reforms and an end to official corruption. About half of the protesters marched on Zhongnanhai, the compound where China's leaders reside. On 20 April about fifteen thousand students demonstrated for reform in Tiananmen Square, and again many of these marched on the party's headquarters. On 22 April more than 150,000 students from at least 30 universities defied government warnings and marched to the square for an illegal sit-in. The students announced a boycott of their classes until their demands were met and were joined by students from elsewhere and by workers. The boycott began on 24 April, with many professors and lecturers in support. On 26 April, *Renmin Ribao* published an editorial accusing the students of seeking to overthrow the government and warning them to cease, but on the following day more than 150,000 students and their supporters staged a 25-mile march through Beijing. On 29 April several senior government leaders met with a handpicked group of students, but student leaders accused the government officials of being insincere.

On 3 May, the government rejected an eleven-point petition presented by the student leaders. On the following day, 4 May, the 70th anniversary of the May Fourth Incident, tens of thousands of students defied new warnings from authorities and began to occupy Tiananmen Square. The class boycott ended the next day, but the occupation of the square occurred while hundreds of foreign bankers and officials, including the first official delegation from Taiwan, participated in the annual meeting of the Asian Development Bank (ADB) in the Great Hall of the People.

On 13 May, anticipating the arrival of Mikhail Gorbachev, more than three thousand students began a hunger strike in Tiananmen Square. Gorbachev arrived on 15 May, and the demonstrations on the following day, with more than a quarter million participants, forced Chinese authorities to make repeated changes in Gorbachev's schedule. On 17 May more than a million demonstrators marched in Tiananmen Square. The demonstrations, now a vast popular movement, upstaged the important visit of the Soviet leader, although Gorbachev himself was regarded a popular personality by the demonstrators. By the third and fourth day of the hunger strike, as collapsing students were taken off to hospitals, the ranks of the demonstrators were augmented by people from all walks of life, including media representatives, workers, soldiers, and government workers. By the time Gorbachev left for Shanghai, the demonstrations had spread to more than twenty provincial capitals and other cities. It had become a powerful popular movement beyond the control of government and party leaders. A remarkable feature of the movement was the moderation on the part of the student and other demonstrators up to and through Gorbachev's visit and on the part of the police as well. The atmosphere of the demonstrations was more festive than angry, although the student leaders maintained their demands in the face of conciliatory gestures by authorities that fell short of satisfying the students. While Gorbachev was in Shanghai four principal

leaders, including Zhao and Li Peng, visited students in the hospitals.

As the demonstrations gained widespread popular support, the official media began to report the historic phenomenon much more openly and honestly. It did not appear, however, that the political leadership fully comprehended how far things had developed. By the time Gorbachev left China, protesters were calling for the resignation, first of Deng Xiaoping and then of Li Peng as well. It soon became clear that conservative leaders would use the protests to get rid of Zhao Ziyang, an objective they had long had in mind.

For his part, Zhao Ziyang visited the students in the square early in the morning of 19 May. He would not be seen again publicly for the rest of the year. Later that day the government declared martial law, a measure opposed by Zhao, in much of Beijing and sent army units into the city. On the following day, however, more than a million Chinese again took to the streets, this time defying martial law. A number of protesters were injured by riot police, but Beijing citizens succeeded in blocking the advance of the army units. The students now abandoned their hunger strike, anticipating the need to marshal their strength for the struggle ahead.

On 24 May, Yang Shangkun gave a secret speech to the Central Military Affairs Commission entitled "To Yield Would Mean Our End" in which he spoke of two headquarters within the party, of Zhao Ziyang's criticism of the *Renmin Ribao* editorial of 26 April upon his return from Korea on 29 April, and of Zhao's speech to the ADB on 4 May, which was "the turning point" because it revealed to the students "divergent views in the Standing Committee and intensified their agitation." Yang also criticized Zhao's talk to the students on the square in the early morning of 19 May and his absence from the important meeting of leaders that same evening. Yang also said that Zhao's revelation to Gorbachev that all important decisions were referred to Deng Xiaoping was an effort "to avoid responsibility and to put Comrade Xiaoping into the line of fire." Hence, Yang concluded that "the root of the problem originates in the party." (Düsseldorf, *Handelsblatt*, in German, 14 June; *FBIS*, 16 June.)

On 30 May demonstrators unveiled, amidst cheering throngs in Tiananmen Square, a sizable statue dubbed "Goddess of Democracy." This modified replica of the Statue of Liberty was placed facing the Mao portrait on Tiananmen and posed an intolerable symbolic challenge to the aged Chinese leaders.

Late on 2 June a speeding PLA jeep (actually on loan to China Central Television) accidentally ran into and killed three civilians and severely injured another. Early on the following day a column of unarmed PLA soldiers jogged toward Tiananmen Square, but were turned back by civilians. Anticipating further assault, civilians began erecting barricades to the entrance of Tiananmen Square. Crowds of resisters took guns and ammunition from two stopped military buses, but students reportedly tried to return such weapons to authorities. There were intermittent clashes throughout 3 June. In the afternoon five thousand soldiers came out from behind the Great Hall of the People, and resisters and soldiers pelted each other with bricks and stones. At 6:30 P.M. on 3 June the authorities began warning residents to stay at home, and the military began to advance inexorably toward the square. For the next few hours there was great violence in different parts of the city. Some soldiers were killed and wounded; a great many more civilians, perhaps thousands, were killed and wounded. Subsequently, the Chinese government would claim that not a single student was killed or injured in securing Tiananmen Square, but this does not appear to be true. Some student accounts perhaps exaggerated the accounts of the bloodshed that occurred in the square; however, although there are few Western eyewitness accounts of actual killing, one Japanese newsman who was in the square testifies to having seen "at least 30–40 people killed or injured by shots fired from the guns of soldiers" (Junichi Taniguchi, "An Eyewitness in China," *Japan Times*, 31 July; translated from the Japanese original printed in the Japan National Press Club *Bulletin*, no. 232).

In any case, the Chinese army, under orders from China's top political leaders, did use tanks and automatic weapons, sometimes indulging in indiscriminate shooting, to suppress what had been an obviously popular movement, killing many Chinese people in the process. Ironically, by the time of the brutal crackdown, the nonviolent students had become anxious to suspend the demonstrations, although many had agreed to continue until the meeting of the NPC Standing Committee later in the month. The government and the party, as a result of their actions and with the world watching, immediately lost further credibility and legitimacy within China and abroad. For the rest of the year a repressive atmosphere replaced the euphoria of spring, as many activists were pursued and ar-

rested. An undetermined number of executions followed, the news on the subject being sparse after a few weeks.

On 9 June, Deng Xiaoping gave a speech entitled "Better that This Storm Comes Earlier than Later" to army commanders and high-ranking officers of the Beijing martial law enforcement units at Huairen Hall, Zhongnanhai. An abridged version was subsequently conveyed to party, army, and government organs and to others throughout the country; a videotape of the talk was shown on television on 28 June. (Hong Kong, *Ming Pao*, 17 June; *FBIS*, 19 June.) The speech was also read by a news announcer on 27 June (Beijing Domestic Service, in Mandarin, 27 June; *FBIS*, 27 June). The 2,800-character speech was printed in the *People's Daily* on 28 June. (*FBIS*, 29 June, notes some differences between the radio and printed versions.)

In mid-June, Deng Xiaoping reportedly gave a speech to members of the new Politburo Standing Committee. He told Li Peng and Yao Yilin that "after the new leadership establishes its working order, I will refrain from bothering about, or interfering in their work." With regard to the work to be grasped, the first thing

is that we must prevent our economy from declining.... The second thing which we must do is something with which the people will be satisfied. Our efforts must be exerted toward the following two major aspects. First, we must carry out reform and opening up in a bolder way. Second, we must firmly grasp the work of handling cases of corruption and punishing those involved in them.... The third thing for us to do is that we must carry the work of suppressing rebellion through to the end. This is a good chance for us to ban illegal organizations at one go.... To concentrate on the three things, all disputes, or arguments are not allowed for at least two years. (Hong Kong, *Tung Fang Jih Pao*, 15 July; *FBIS-CHI*, 18 July.)

The Fourth Plenum of the Thirteenth Central Committee, originally expected to be held in March before the Second Session of the NPC, was finally convened during 23–24 June with 170 members and 106 alternate members of the Central Committee. Attending the meeting as observers were 184 members of the Central Advisory Commission, 68 members of the Central Commission for Discipline Inspection, and 29 leading comrades of the "departments concerned." The plenum was preceded by an enlarged preparatory meeting of the Politburo during 19–21 June. The communiqué of the plenum found that "a very small number of people" had taken "advantage of student unrest, stirred up, planned, organized and premeditated political turmoil," which subsequently "developed into a counterrevolutionary rebellion in Beijing. The aim of the turmoil and rebellion. . . was to overthrow the leadership of the Chinese Communist Party and to subvert the socialist People's Republic of China." The plenum also pledged to continue the policies of the 1978 Third Plenum and to focus on economic construction, the upholding of the four cardinal principles, and carrying out economic reforms and the opening to the outside world. The plenum also "highly evaluated" Deng Xiaoping's speech of 9 June, "unanimously believing that the speech is a programmatic document for us to review the past, look forward to the future and unify the thinking and understanding of the whole Party." (*BR*, 3–9 July.)

The plenum heard and approved Li Peng's report on Zhao Ziyang's mistakes, who "at a critical juncture involving the destiny of the Party and the state . . . made the mistake of supporting the turmoil and splitting the Party and he had unshirkable responsibilities for the development of the turmoil." Thus Zhao was dismissed as general secretary, as a member of the Politburo Standing Committee, as a member of the Politburo and the Central Committee, and as first vice-chairman of the Military Affairs Commission of the Central Committee; it was said that his case would be further looked into. Also removed from his previous positions on the Politburo's Standing Committee and from the Politburo and the Secretariat of the Central Committee was Zhao's ally, Hu Qili. Similarly, Rui Xingwen and Yan Mingfu were removed from the Secretariat. (Ibid.)

Jiang Zemin, former party chief of Shanghai, was elected general secretary and a member of the Standing Committee of the Politburo (he had been a member of the Politburo since 1987). Song Ping and Li Ruihuan were elected to the Standing Committee of the Politburo. (Ibid.)

Jiang Zemin spoke to a forum attended by non-CCP members in Beijing on 28 June:

We are determined to dig out all instigators, organizers and conspirators of the turmoil and rebellion, leading members of illegal organizations and other criminals who engaged in assaulting and killing of soldiers, burning, looting and other crime. . . . We must mete out severe and timely punishment. . . Otherwise, there will be no peace and security. . . .

For those cruel enemies of the people, we should not have an iota of forgiveness or we shall make a serious historical mistake.

But he went on to say that distinctions are to be made between two kinds of contradictions, those among the people and those between the people and the enemies of the people. (*BR*, 10–16 July.)

On 30 June, at a meeting sponsored by the Organization Department of the Central Committee attended by more than 50 party veterans, Jiang Zemin said that many problems in party organizations and among party members had been revealed, "and some of them were serious. Zhao Ziyang's neglect of Party building has brought about very grave results, weakening the Party." (*BR*, 10–16 July.)

The NPC Standing Committee held its eighth meeting in late June presided over by its chairman, Wan Li, and attended by 133 of its 152 members. On 30 June, on a motion submitted by Deng Xiaoping, the body decided to dismiss Zhao Ziyang from his one remaining post, vice-chairman of the state Central Military Commission. It was reported that 126 of the 132 members attending voted for the decision. (Beijing, XINHUA, 30 June; *FBIS*, 30 June.)

At the session on 30 June, Beijing mayor Chen Xitong gave an eight-part report of more than twenty thousand words entitled "Report On Conditions About Suppressing Turmoil and Quelling Counterrevolutionary Riots." Chen said that more than two hundred civilians, including 36 college students, had died and that more than three thousand had been injured during the recent upheaval. He also said that more than six thousand soldiers and policemen had been wounded, that dozens of them had died (these figures were later scaled down considerably), and that more than 1,280 vehicles had been damaged or burned, including more than one thousand military trucks, 60 armored cars, 30 police cars, and 120 buses. (XINHUA, 30 June; *FBIS*, 30 June; Beijing Domestic Service, *Zhongguo Xinwen She*, 30 June.)

A report that Defense Minister Qin Jiwei (who reportedly had been reluctant to use the army to suppress the spring demonstrations) had been detained by troops loyal to President Yang Shangkun on 16 August was subsequently denied by the Ministry of Defense (London, BBC World Service, 18 August; *FBIS*, 18 August).

On 20 August distribution began nationwide of the *Selected Works of Deng Xiaoping (1938–1965)*, which contains 39 articles and speeches, 30 of which had not previously been published (Beijing, XINHUA, 20 August; *FBIS*, 23 August). Deng Xiaoping also wrote for *The Dictionary of Party Affairs of the CPC*. This dictionary was compiled by more than two hundred people in the Heilongjiang Provincial CCP Committee and other relevant departments. It includes fifteen main items such as party organizations, propaganda, united front work, and so forth. It also provides accounts of important meetings, documents, events, and figures of the party. The dictionary, published by Hanwang Publishing House, contains 4,888 entries and 2.15 million words. Bo Yibo and Song Renqiong were advisers to the book and wrote prefaces and inscriptions for it. Sun Weiben, secretary of the Heilongjiang Provincial Party Committee, was the editor in chief. (Beijing, *Renmin Ribao*, 19 June; *FBIS*, 22 June.)

In early September the State Council decided to begin checking identity cards on a national basis within days. Issuing identity cards had begun nationwide after a trial run in Beijing two years earlier, and more than 500 million such cards had been issued by the end of June. (Beijing, XINHUA, 8 September; *FBIS*, 8 September.)

In mid-September 160 political exile delegates from Chinese communities around the world held an unprecedented three-day conference in Paris, France. The delegates launched the Federation for a Democratic China and issued a charter committing them to work for multiparty rule, free enterprise, and human rights in China. Nonviolent change was stressed. They elected Yan Jiaqi as chairman, Wu'er Kaixi as vice-chairman, and Wan Runnan as secretary general. Yan was formerly director of the Political Science Institute of the Chinese Academy of Social Sciences and an adviser to Zhao Ziyang. Wu'er was a student at Beijing Normal University and had been one of the principal leaders in Tiananmen Square; he is now a student at Harvard University. Wan had established China's important Stone Computer Company in Beijing. The three had barely escaped capture after the June crackdown in China. (Jim Hoagland, Paris, *Honolulu Advertiser*, 25 September.)

On 29 September, Jiang Zemin gave a major speech at a meeting to celebrate the 40th anniversary of the PRC. He said that the history of the 40 years lead, minimally, to four conclusions:

1. The establishment, consolidation and development of the socialist system constitutes the objective law of the movement of China's modern society, and the greatest and deepest change in China's history . . . .

2. Socialism is a system that requires constant development and improvement on its own basis . . . .

3. To give full play to the spirit of patriotism and uphold the principle of independence and self-reliance . . . .

4. The Communist Party of China, armed with Marxism-Leninism and Mao Zedong Thought, is the vanguard of the Chinese working class and the faithful representative of the interests of the people of all nationalities in China; it shoulders the supremely important responsibility for China's independence and development. The correct choice of the Communist Party of China as the leading core of the Chinese revolution and construction was made by the Chinese people in a protracted process of practice. (*BR*, 9–15 October.)

The Seventh NPC's Standing Committee held its tenth meeting between 25 September and 31 October. It adopted China's first Law on Mass Rallies and Demonstrations at the closing session on 31 October to take effect that day. Among its measures is the requirement to submit written applications to the local police bureau five days before a planned demonstration; written confirmation must be received two days before the demonstration date. (Beijing, XINHUA, 31 October; *FBIS*, 31 October.)

The hundredth birthday anniversary of Li Dazhao, one of the founders of the CCP, was commemorated with a rally of more than one thousand people on 28 October. Jiang Zemin addressed the rally, which was also attended by Li Peng and Yang Shangkun. (*BR*, 13–19 November.)

The Beijing municipal government finally decided to replace the PLA martial law enforcement troops stationed in Tiananmen Square with armed police on 1 November, almost five months after the military occupation was imposed. PLA soldiers had been withdrawn from Beijing's major road junctions two days earlier, on 30 October. (*BR*, 13–19 November.)

The Fifth Plenary Session of the Thirteenth Central Committee was held in Beijing 6–9 November, preceded by a central working conference held by the Politburo, 30 October–3 November. The plenum endorsed Deng Xiaoping's resignation (his letter of resignation was dated 4 November) on 9 November from the chairmanship of the Central Committee's Military Affairs Commission, noting that following the Eleventh Central Committee's Third Plenum he "became the nucleus of the second-generation leading collective of our Party." Jiang Zemin was appointed the new chairman of the commission; Yang Shangkun, first vice-chairman; Liu Huaqing, vice-chairman; and Yang Baibing, general secretary. (*BR*, 20–26 November.) There was an earlier unconfirmed report that Deng Xiaoping had been considering establishing a high-level military committee within the party, tentatively to be called the Leading Group on Military Affairs, that would advise the Central Military Affairs Commission and the Defense Ministry on matters of strategy and long-term planning. This report, which appeared in the Japanese newspaper *Mainichi Shimbun*, also said that the members of this new leading group would be Deng Xiaoping, Yang Shangkun, Wang Zhen, Qin Jiwei, Hong Xuezhi, and Li Desheng. The report acknowledged that Jiang Zemin was to be appointed chair of the Military Affairs Commission. (Willy Wo-lap Lam, Hong Kong, *South China Morning Post*, 18 October; *FBIS*, 18 October.)

The Fifth Plenum also approved a decision on further economic revamping and reforms in China and reaffirmed that the current economic retrenchment policy was correct. The plenum called for

the grasping of four important links to improve the economic environment and straighten out the economic order:

1. Continued efforts should be made to cut the total social demand, persistently carry out the policy of tightening control over finance, credits and loans, resolve the problem of earmarking an excessive proportion of the national income for consumption, and be determined to lead a thrifty life for several years.

2. Vigorous efforts should be made to readjust the industrial structure, increase the effective supply, and strengthen the staying power of economic development. In particular, it is essential to swiftly bring about a high tide throughout the Party and the nation of paying great attention to, supporting and developing agriculture in a concerted effort to promote the development of agriculture and ensure the stable increase of the main agricultural products such as grains and cotton.

3. Effective steps should be taken to straighten out the economic order and great efforts should be made to screen and rectify various kinds of companies,

particularly those engaged in circulation, so as to overcome the serious confusion in the realms of production, construction, circulation and distribution.

4. The campaign of increasing production and practicing economy, of increasing revenue and cutting expenditure should be deepened. It is necessary to make hard efforts to improve management of enterprises, tap internal potentiality, raise their scientific and technological standards, and adopt an economic development strategy with less input, more output, high quality and better economic results. (Ibid., 20–26 November.)

Also on 9 December, Jiang Zemin gave a speech to the plenum in which he "elaborated on four points related to the implementation" of the Central Committee's decision on

further improving the economic environment, straightening out the economic order and deepening the reform: First, firmly embrace the idea of a sustained, stable and harmonious development of the national economy as our guiding thought.... Second, hold to the mass line and improve leadership style.... Third, strengthen democratic centralism and enhance the Party's fighting power.... Fourth, strengthen theoretical study and make Party work more scientific.

He went on to say that the plenum "is one featuring seeking truth from facts and one to pluck up our spirits, inspire our confidence and make us united for the future tasks." (*BR*, 4–10 December.)

Deng Xiaoping, now fully retired from all official positions, met with an enlarged meeting of the party's Central Military Commission 10–12 November, during which he urged the PLA to "remain loyal to the party, the state, socialism and the people" (*BR*, 27 November–3 December). Also present at the enlarged meeting were Hong Xuezhi, Qin Jiwei, Chi Haotian, and Zhao Nanqi, along with commanders of the PLA's General Staff Headquarters, General Political Department, and General Logistics Department and major army units and the Chinese People's Armed Police Force (Beijing, XINHUA, 13 November; *FBIS*, 14 November.)

On 13 November, Deng Xiaoping met his last foreign guests on an official basis. The occasion was the visit of Eishiro Saito, president of the Japanese Federation of Economic Groups, and Ryoichi Kaiwai, president of the Japan-China Economy and

Trade Association, leading a 35-member delegation. (Ibid.)

Toward the end of the year Chinese students desiring to go abroad for further education were worried about measures being imposed or about to be imposed that would impede their efforts to do so, as authorities were presumably heeding Li Peng's recently stated stricture that only "politically mature" students be sent abroad. One measure already in effect requires students to obtain permission from their college departments, work units, or neighborhood committees to take English-language proficiency tests. Another measure, to take effect in February 1990, would require payment of a passport fee of as much as 20,000 yuan (about $5,400) for Chinese students seeking to use private funds, including American university scholarships, to finance their education abroad. Also some Chinese students reported that their campus registrars are refusing to honor requests for official copies of transcripts, which are needed for admission to foreign schools. Another pending requirement would require students to work in China for up to seven years after graduation before they could travel abroad. (Louise Branson, Beijing, *Chronicle of Higher Education*, 29 November.)

Meanwhile, Beijing University's freshman class of 748 students was undergoing unprecedented military and political training at Shijiazhuang Army Academy. At the opening ceremony for the training program on 12 October, State Education Commission vice-minister He Dongchang said that it was "an experiment in exploring ways of nurturing qualified college students." Wu Shuqing, the new president of Beijing University, told the students that the training "will give you a fine environment to grow up in." Elsewhere in China, an eight-week military and political training course was being carried out at 143 colleges and universities. (*BR*, 30 October–5 November.)

Despite such measures on 9 December (coincidentally during the surprise visit to Beijing of Brent Scowcroft and Lawrence Eagleburger, see below), seven Chinese students from the University of Aeronautics and Astronautics, knowing they were acting illegally, apparently deliberately sacrificed themselves in order to show that China's suppressed democracy movement was still alive. They gathered in front of the Ministry of Radio, Film and Television and openly expressed support for the political liberalization taking place in Eastern Europe. It was said that many onlookers wept as policemen beat the students and dragged them away. (*Honolulu Advertiser*, 14 December.)

In mid-November it was reported that the Chinese government would crack down on the "six evils": prostitution; pornography; trading in women and children; growing, taking, and trading narcotics; gambling; and profiting by the use of superstition (Chang Hong, Beijing, *China Daily*, 14 November; *FBIS*, 16 November).

In the meantime the campaign against corruption had, in the past two and a half months, resulted in the surrender to judicial departments (31 October was the surrender deadline) of more than 53,000 economic criminal suspects and government officials involved in embezzlement and bribery. Among these suspects more than 5,300 were members of the CCP, 40 were senior officials above the bureau level, and 1 was at the vice-ministerial level. Optimism over such results was cautioned against, however, because the most serious cases have yet to be uncovered, according to Liu Fuzhi, the chief procurator of the Supreme People's Procuratorate. (XINHUA, 10 November; *FBIS*, 16 November.)

Nevertheless, in the first nine months of 1989 the CCP expelled more than 12,500 members from its ranks as a result of the continuing drive to eradicate corruption and other irregularities. As many as 60,000 party members have been given disciplinary punishments; of those, 10 were officials above the deputy provincial chief or army commander level, 113 were above the district head or division commander level, and 1,400 cadres were above the county magistrate or regimental level. By the end of the year it was expected that 210,000 cases will have been investigated since the Thirteenth Party Congress in late 1987. (Li Hong, Beijing, *China Daily*, 23 November; *FBIS*, 24 November.)

It was reported that by late October more than 30 million copies of pornographic books and magazines and 400,000 obscene audio and video tapes had been confiscated throughout China in the ongoing campaign against pornography (*BR*, 30 October–5 November).

Speaking at a seminar for editors in chief of party newspapers at the provincial, municipal, and autonomous regional levels on 28 November, Jiang Zemin said that China's journalism must serve the people and socialism. He said that the party has always regarded the media as "mouthpieces" of the party. He said, however, that "when bourgeois liberalization ran rampant in the country over the past couple of years and the anti-government riot took place in Beijing in June, some mass media departments provided a forum for the plotters and organizers of the unrest and counter-revolutionary rebellion, and added fuel to the flames." (*BR*, 11–17 December.)

The startling news that Nicolae Ceauşescu and his regime had been violently overthrown was greeted with consternation by China's leaders, following as it did the spectacular changes in other Eastern European countries in the preceding two months. Security forces were alerted in Beijing, and additional police were stationed on campuses. Students quietly celebrated the popular revolt in Romania, and a wall poster, "Learn from Romania," appeared, only to be torn down. Yuan Mu, the State Council spokesman, met with three hundred students at Beijing University who asked pointed questions that went unanswered. For example, one student asked why Zhao Ziyang was purged when it was senior leader Deng Xiaoping who decided policy in the past ten years. Yuan did not reply. Regarding Romania, Yuan said, "No matter what the situation is in the rest of the world, China will always walk the path of socialism, uphold the socialist flag and adhere to the leadership of the Communist Party of China." Yuan reportedly spoke with vehemence, standing up and banging his hand on the table. But when he went on to repeat familiar socialist principles, it was reported that some students made hissing noises. (Jim Abrams, AP, Honolulu, *Star-Bulletin*, 27 December.)

Taiwan-mainland relations continued to evolve rather briskly on a broad front through early 1989. By the end of 1988 the volume of indirect trade had reached $8.2 billion, with mainland exports to Taiwan totaling $1.5 billion and imports from Taiwan, $6.7 billion. The annual average of the volume of trade has increased by 48.6 percent over the past ten years. The total trade volume between both sides reached $1.75 billion in the first half of 1989. (Beijing, *Renmin Ribao*, 20 September; *FBIS*, 26 September.) Moreover, between January and October 1989, more than 450,000 Taiwan visitors traveled through Hong Kong enroute to the mainland, a 35 percent increase over the same period in 1988 (Beijing, XINHUA, 22 October; *FBIS*, 26 October). Thus although more than 800,000 Taiwan people have visited the mainland since the end of 1987, only 2,100 people from the mainland have been permitted to visit their relatives in Taiwan since November 1988 (Beijing, XINHUA, 15 September; *FBIS*, 18 September).

Meanwhile Taiwan continued to make notable progress in various ways, including the passage of three major political reform bills: the Civil Organization Law, the Electoral Law, and the Voluntary Retirement Law (calling for the voluntary retirement of elderly KMT legislators) (Chen I-hsin and Wu Wen-cheng, *Free China Journal*, 6, 16, and 20 February).

Taiwan president Lee Teng-hui made a successful state visit to Singapore on 6 April. Beijing, however, responded cooly to Taiwan's "flexible diplomacy," particularly as this foreign policy initiative began to attract diplomatic recognition for the Republic of China on Taiwan (see "Relations Elsewhere" below).

Taiwan finance minister Shirley Kuo led a high-level delegation of officials to attend the 4–6 May annual meeting of the Asian Development Bank (ADB) in Beijing, the first such official governmental delegation to go from Taiwan to the PRC. Taiwan had boycotted meetings of the ADB for two years, protesting the designation "Taipei, China," but this was lifted in April 1988 at the ADB annual meeting in Manila. The visit to Beijing was approved, it was said, because the meeting was merely being held in Beijing and was not organized by the PRC government; the delegation was also able to use its Republic of China passports. (Taipei, *Free China Journal*, 10 April.)

Lee Huan, former secretary general of the Kuomintang (KMT), became premier of the Republic of China on 1 June, replacing Yu Kuo-hwa (age 75), who had retired. James Soong, who had been deputy secretary general of the KMT, replaced Lee Huan as the new KMT secretary general. (Taipei, *Free China Journal*, 5 June.)

The historic elections (the first since the lifting of the Emergency Decree in July 1987) in Taiwan on 2 December resulted in a surprising setback for the KMT, which won fewer races than expected, although it remained dominant. The KMT captured or retained 208 (70.98 percent) of the 293 seats being contested in the Legislative Yuan, the Taiwan Provincial Assembly, and the Taipei and Kaohsiung city councils and 21 mayoral and county magistrate posts, according to the Central Election Commission. The KMT won only 14 of the 21 county magistrate and mayoral posts, a most notable setback for the dominant party. The main opposition party, the Democratic Progressive Party (DPP), won or retained 65 local, regional, and national seats, an increase of 25 from its 1986 showing. But the DPP won 30 percent of the popular vote, about half of that won by the KMT. More than nine million (75.39 percent) of Taiwan's eligible twelve million

Chinese voters went to the polls to cast ballots for the 722 candidates and sixteen political parties participating in the elections. (Chen I-hsin and Wu Wen-cheng, *Free China Journal*, 7 December.)

Among the natural disasters visited upon China this year were several earthquakes that hit Shanxi Province on 18 October, killing eighteen people (*BR*, 6–12 November).

Auxiliary and Front Organizations. The Second Session of the Seventh CPPCC was held between 19 and 27 March. This was the shortest session since the Second Session of the Second National CPPCC in 1956, the shortening of the session being regarded as a reform in itself. In October the CPPCC's National Committee held a three-day meeting to discuss Jiang Zemin's speech on the occasion of the 40th anniversary of the PRC's establishment. At the meeting, National Committee chairman Li Xiannian reiterated the CCP position that "China can neither introduce a Western multiparty system nor allow the existence of an opposition party." He said that the CPPCC, as part of China's unique socialist political system, "has a solid foundation and is a creation of common efforts of the Communist Party and non-Communist parties." He added that "Western democracy cannot compare with it." (*BR*, 23–29 October.) The CPPCC's Standing Committee held its eighth meeting on 16 November to study the guidelines of the CCP Central Committee's Fifth Plenary Session (Beijing, XINHUA, 17 November; *FBIS*, 21 November).

According to Yan Mingfu, a member of the Central Committee's Secretariat at the time, the eight noncommunist parties in China, which had a combined membership of 10,000 in 1949 and 60,000 after the Cultural Revolution in 1976, in 1989 had nearly 300,000 members (Beijing, XINHUA, 7 April; *FBIS*, 12 April).

International Views and Positions. Despite the economic retrenchment under way at the beginning of the year, China's external economic relations continued to register gains in the first several months of 1989. However, the unexpected turn of events in June dramatically reversed this trend, and China was subjected to various international sanctions affecting loans and investment. There was a sharp reduction in tourism. In mid-December China devalued its currency by 21.2 percent against the dollar, the first such devaluation since 1986. Accordingly, one dollar will now bring 4.7103 yuan

instead of 3.7128; the black market price for the yuan is between 5 and 6 to the dollar. (Honolulu, *Star-Bulletin*, 16 December.)

The Ministry of Foreign Economic Relations and Trade reported that China's foreign trade in 1988 totaled $79.419 billion, an increase of 16.6 percent over 1987. Exports came to $40.102 billion, which fulfilled the target of $38 billion set by the Seventh Five-Year Plan for 1990 two years ahead of schedule and represented a 15.5 percent increase over the previous year. Imports reached $39.317 billion, an increase of 17.7 percent, but China still had a favorable balance of trade by $785 million, consolidating the surplus registered in 1987. (*BR*, 6–12 March.) It should be noted, however, that Chinese customs, as usual, reported different statistics: total trade for 1988 as $102.79 billion, a 24.4 percent increase over 1987, with exports of $47.54 billion, up 20.6 percent, and imports of $55.25 billion, up 27.9 percent. On this reckoning, after taking into account such items as aid, donations, and so forth, there was a trade deficit of $3.09 billion. In 1988, China's nontrade foreign exchange income was $6.61 billion, 22 percent higher than 1987, with income $3.91 billion more than expenditure. (Ibid.) By the beginning of 1989, China had established trade relations with more than 180 countries and regions. Its largest trading partners for the first eleven months of 1988 were Hong Kong, Japan, the European Community, the United States, and the Soviet Union and Eastern Europe (ibid.). China used more foreign capital in 1988: $9.84 billion, up 16.4 percent, including $2.62 billion directly invested by foreign businessmen, up 13.1 percent. Contracts for overseas projects and labor service signed by China in 1988 were worth $1.83 billion, a 10.6 percent increase; business volume, amounting to $1.2 billion, registered a slight decrease. The tourist industry continued to grow in 1988, with 31.69 million tourists and visitors from 168 countries and regions, 17.8 percent more than in 1987, earning $2.22 billion in foreign exchange, up 19.2 percent. (Ibid.) According to the General Agreement on Tariffs and Trade, China's share of total world trade compared with other countries in 1988 ranked her sixteenth in exports and fourteenth in imports (*MOR China Letter*, April).

For the first time China's State Administration of Exchange Control announced the country's outstanding foreign debt for the 1985–1988 period. Year-end foreign debts were $15.8 billion in 1985, $21.5 billion in 1986, $30.2 billion in 1987, and

$40.0 billion in 1988. (Yao Jianguo, *BR*, 30 October–5 November.)

However, according to Zheng Tuobin, minister of foreign economic relations and trade, China's foreign exchange reserves increased from $3.3 billion in 1988 to $5.8 billion in late 1989. He said that China enjoyed a favorable foreign trade balance of $4 billion in the first nine months of 1989. (Beijing CEI database, in English, 10 November; *FBIS*, 16 November.)

Most Chinese ambassadors were recalled to Beijing for a major consultative session in July to discuss the country's international situation in the wake of the 4 June massacre. By the time of the meeting twenty Chinese diplomats stationed in Western countries had sought asylum. (David Chen, Hong Kong, *South China Morning Post*, 8 July, p. 7; *FBIS*, 10 July.)

Sociologist Zhu Qingfang of the Chinese Academy of Social Sciences (the first Chinese scholar to compare China's status in the world through indexes that China itself has selected) reported that by means of her sixteen indexes China ranks 70th out of 128 countries with at least one million population in overall social development. China ranks 105th in per capita income, but between 6th and 7th in gross national product. Thus China is at the lower-middle level among the selected countries, between the 37 low-income countries and the 56 countries of medium income. At the top of Zhu's list are Belgium, the Netherlands, the United States, Canada, Sweden, Denmark, Norway, Switzerland, France, and Japan, in that order. (Beijing, XINHUA, 12 April; *FBIS*, 12 April.)

Relations with the Soviet Union. General Secretary Mikhail Gorbachev made a historic visit to China 15–18 May, the first Soviet leader to do so since 1959. The visit normalized the Sino-Soviet relationship once again and formally restored the CCP–Communist Party of the Soviet Union relationship. The visit, which would have received full media attention in its own right, was upstaged by and contributed to the momentous popular uprising in Tiananmen Square and the streets of Beijing and many other Chinese cities during the Soviet leader's stay, affecting his formal schedule no fewer than five times in Beijing alone. He was unable, for example, to visit the Forbidden City.

Nevertheless, the visit was a successful one for Gorbachev. He gave a conciliatory 50-minute speech in the Great Hall of the People (which he had to enter and exit via the back door) that was in keeping with the line he had initiated at Vladivostok in July 1986. In Beijing he spoke of demilitarizing the Sino-Soviet border and itemized specific military reductions currently under way and in the offing, including the removal of sixteen warships from the Soviet Pacific fleet. A Sino-Soviet joint communiqué was issued in Beijing on 18 May (Beijing, XINHUA, 18 May; *FBIS*, 18 May).

Columbia Broadcasting System reported that the Soviet media did not report the demonstrations in China until Gorbachev began his return flight to the Soviet Union, noting that the demonstrations had gone beyond the control of the Chinese authorities.

Subsequently, Gorbachev expressed concern over the situation in China during his press conference in Bonn on 15 June and said he regretted some aspects of what happened there. Diplomatic sources said he was shocked to hear that the reason given for Zhao Ziyang's ouster was that Zhao had leaked party information to Gorbachev during his China visit. Gorbachev is said to have shared the most friendly feelings with Zhao of all Chinese leaders. In Bonn, Gorbachev disclosed that he had received letters from Chinese students and that he did not think that they had any bad intentions in their demonstrations. During his visit to China, Gorbachev is said to have shown a strong interest in the student prodemocracy demonstrations, saying that he would have responded to their hopes of direct dialogue with the government leaders. (The Bonn report of XINHUA did not mention Gorbachev's comment on the situation in China.) (Tokyo, *Kyodo*, 15 June; *FBIS*, 16 June.)

Active bilateral exchanges continued between China and the Soviet Union despite the June crackdown. It was reported in September that Jiang Zemin will likely visit Moscow in the fall of 1990, a prospect agreed on during the visit to Moscow that month by Zhu Liang, head of the Central Committee's International Liaison Department. Jiang had escorted Gorbachev around Shanghai during the Soviet leader's visit to that city in May. (Tokyo, *Kyodo*, 28 September; *FBIS*, 28 September.) Among the many further developments in Sino-Soviet relations was the establishment of the third airlink between the two countries with the opening, on 26 September, of an 80-minute service between Harbin and Khabarovsk. (Harbin, Heilongjiang Provincial Service, 26 September; *FBIS*, 28 September.)

The first round of discussions on setting up a demilitarized zone along the entire length of the Sino-Soviet border began in Beijing in September.

It was reported that if the talks are successful the pullback of troops could begin within six months. It was also reported that China would be the first to withdraw troops and tanks from the border. (David Chen, Hong Kong, *South China Morning Post*, 16 September; *FBIS*, 18 September.)

Deng Xiaoping, at a small discussion group meeting during the four-day Fourth Plenum in early November, is reported to have criticized Gorbachev and several socialist bloc countries for the changes taking place in Eastern Europe. He is said to have accused the Soviet leader of pursuing a political path that was "not in conformity with true Marxism-Leninism." He also accused Poland, Hungary, East Germany, and Czechoslovakia of "deviating from the correct line." (David Chen, Hong Kong, *South China Morning Post*, 25 November; *FBIS*, 27 November.) In December an internal document was circulated in China that attacked Gorbachev for undermining socialism in Eastern Europe (Honolulu, *Star-Bulletin*, 27 December).

Relations with the United States. President George Bush took advantage of his attendance at the funeral of the late Japanese emperor Hirohito to visit China in early February. The opportunity to make such a gesture so early in the new presidential administration was marred, however, by an incident during a banquet the president gave for his Chinese hosts. Dissident astrophysicist Fang Lizhi, invited to the dinner by the Americans, was prevented from attending by Chinese security guards. Chinese officials protested that such an invitation should have been cleared with the Chinese government.

Responding to the gross violation of human rights in Tibet, the U.S. Senate adopted a resolution on the Tibetan question on 16 March. This gesture was protested by the Chinese NPC Foreign Affairs Committee on 19 March as "gross interference in China's internal affairs." (Beijing, XINHUA, 19 March; *FBIS*, 20 March.)

The Chinese naval training ship *Zheng He* visited Pearl Harbor, Hawaii, in April, the first visit of the Chinese PLA navy to the United States and only the second PLA naval visit abroad (the previous visit was to Pakistan, Bangladesh, and Sri Lanka in 1985). In return, the U.S. Navy made its second visit to China, this time to Shanghai, on 19 May after having postponed the visit from 18 May reportedly in compliance with a Soviet request because of General Secretary Gorbachev's visit on that day. The navy's visit to Shanghai was a successful

one, but was obscured, just as was Gorbachev's visit, by massive prodemocracy demonstrations.

Following the June crackdown, President Bush said on 8 June that the United States and China could not have normal relations until Beijing authorities recognized the validity of the prodemocracy student movement (Bernard E. Trainor, *NYT*, 9 June). Subsequently, following growing pressure from Congress, Bush condemned the Chinese government's "outrageous" treatment of the student demonstrators and imposed sanctions, including the halting of military sales to China, the suspension of all high-level visits between U.S. and Chinese officials, and an indication that the United States will do what it can to stall action on China's international loan applications. The president's response was a measured one, and although it did not satisfy many in Congress and elsewhere, it was a course designed, it was said, to preserve, if possible, the economic and strategic relationship that had been developed over the last fifteen years.

Astrophysicist Fang Lizhi and his wife Li Shuxian were given sanctuary in the American embassy in Beijing, where they were to remain through the end of 1989. Chinese authorities protested the American action as a violation of international law. (Beijing, *Renmin Ribao*, 12 July; FBIS, 12 July.) The Chinese government was critical of the measures taken by the United States with regard to China, as well as of the reporting of the Voice of America during the spring crisis.

Zhu Qizhen was appointed to be China's ambassador extraordinary and plenipotentiary to the United States on 6 July, replacing Han Xu, who became the first Chinese ambassador to be replaced following the 4 June massacre. (Because of this change, Han Xu was not among the Chinese ambassadors recalled to Beijing for the major mid-July consultative session.) University-educated Zhu, 61, was born in Jiangsu and is proficient in English. He had served previously in the Chinese embassy in the United Arab Emirates and as deputy director of the Asia-Africa Department of the Foreign Ministry, counselor in the Chinese embassy in Australia, director of the U.S.-Canada Department of the Foreign Ministry, assistant minister of foreign affairs, and finally deputy foreign minister. (Hong Kong, *Hsin Wan Pao*, 6 July; *FBIS*, 6 July.)

Former president Richard Nixon made his sixth visit in seventeen years to China 28 October–1 November. During his 95-minute meeting with Deng Xiaoping on 31 October, Deng said that the United States should take the initiative to solve the problems that have cropped up in Sino-U.S. relations in the past few months, thus reforging ties for the future. . . . Frankly speaking, the U.S. was involved too deeply in the turmoil and counter-revolutionary rebellion. . . . China was the real victim and it is unjust to reprove China for it.

Nixon also met with Jiang Zemin, Li Peng, and Yang Shangkun. (*BR*, 13–19 November.) Although the Nixon meeting was characterized as cordial overall, the former president had some harsh words for his hosts, saying, among other things, that "many Americans had lost respect for Chinese leaders after the events in June" (Seth Faison, Beijing, *South China Morning Post*, 1 November; *FBIS*, 1 November).

U.S. ambassador to China James Lilley, in a speech in Hong Kong on 7 November, criticized the reintroduction of politics and ideology into economic decisions in China, in particular the intrusion again of party cadres into enterprise management. He said, "I think we can call this politicizing a marked step backwards for reforms in China." However, Lilley advised against further economic sanctions and observed that a World Bank decision to go ahead with $780 million in seven loans that had been suspended would be a "therapeutic injection" for China. (Robert Delfs, Beijing, *FEER*, 16 November.)

The U.S. Congress passed an emergency Chinese immigration relief act in November that waived the two-year home country service requirement for all Chinese studying in the United States on J-1 visas. Earlier, Congress had adopted an amendment to the State Department's authorization bill on sanctions against China. These gestures were vigorously criticized by the Chinese government as interference in China's internal affairs and held to be damaging to U.S.-China relations. On 30 November, President Bush vetoed the immigration bill and another seeking to expand economic sanctions, but strengthened his own executive order extending the stay in the United States of Chinese students.

In the middle of the night, Saturday, 9 December, the White House made the surprise announcement that national security adviser Brent Scowcroft and Deputy Secretary of State Lawrence Eagleburger were making a two-day visit to top leaders in China, thus ending the sanction imposed by President Bush in June on high-level meetings with Chinese leaders. The two emissaries visited with Deng Xiaoping, Jiang Zemin, Li Peng, and Yang Shangkun.

Scowcroft told Chinese leaders that the Bush administration wanted to bring "new impetus and vigor" into U.S.-China relations. (Daniel Sutherland, Beijing, *WP* Service, Honolulu, *Sunday Star-Bulletin & Advertiser*, 9 December.) President Bush subsequently justified the trip as necessary to keep China from becoming isolated, holding that other sanctions were still in force. The ostensible reason for the visit was to inform the Chinese leadership of developments at the Malta summit between Bush and Gorbachev. Bush indicated that one purpose of the trip was achieved, that is, persuading the Chinese not to sell M-9 missiles to Syria. The State Department said, however, that the Chinese had already provided assurances that they would not do so two weeks earlier. On 12 December Beijing announced the approval of Stephanie Mann Nealer as a new Voice of America (VOA) correspondent to replace VOA correspondent Al Pessin, who was expelled in June along with AP newsman John Pomfret. VOA director Richard Carlson said that he did not know if this decision was related to the Scowcroft-Eagleburger visit, but said that the next move would be for Beijing to stop jamming VOA Mandarin and Cantonese broadcasts to China as they have been doing since June.

Prominent Democrats and others immediately criticized this Bush initiative as unwarranted kowtowing to China's political leaders and saw it as likely to be construed as justifying the hardline policies employed by them. It was expected at year's end that if the Chinese did not make significant concessions to the United States before Congress convened on 23 January 1990, there would be further pressure on the Bush administration over its China policy. Critics of that policy were particularly galled by Scowcroft's toast to Chinese leaders in which he was quoted as saying, "In both societies there are voices of those who seek to redirect or frustrate our cooperation. We both must take bold measures to overcome these negative forces." (James McCartney and Owen Ullmann, Washington, D.C., Knight-Ridder Service, Honolulu, *Sunday Star-Bulletin & Advertiser*, 17 December.)

This controversy was heightened when Cable News Network disclosed on 18 December that Scowcroft and Eagleburger had made a previous secret visit to Beijing as early as July, apparently in direct contradiction to the suspension of all high-level contacts between the two governments imposed by Bush two weeks earlier! The explanation for the earlier secret, sanction-defying visit, according to White House press secretary Marlin

Fitzwater, was "to personally underscore the United States' shock and concern about the violence in Tiananmen Square and to impress upon the Chinese government the seriousness with which this incident was viewed in the United States." (*Honolulu Advertiser*, 19 December.)

Subsequently, Bush announced his decision to authorize licenses for three communications satellites for China and indicated that he would not impose new sanctions recently approved by Congress on export-import bank financing for projects in China. He cited national interest on both counts. The White House statement said that Bush had been urged to approve the licenses by Australian prime minister Bob Hawke and that the approval was "in keeping with the president's policy not to disrupt normal commercial relations with China." Bush said that he was awaiting positive signals from Beijing, but did not mention any concessions from China. The U.S. concessions were in addition to the decisions to go ahead with the sale of Boeing jetliners to China and to allow Chinese workers to return to work on a project in the United States to upgrade China's fleet of F-8 fighter planes with U.S. electronics. (*Honolulu Advertiser*, 20 December.)

Relations Elsewhere. A high-level, 26-member Chinese trade delegation of officials from several key agencies in Beijing and elsewhere in China led by Shen Jueren of the Ministry of Foreign Economic Relations and Trade, made a week-long visit to Japan to find ways of reducing China's trade deficit and speeding the flow of Japanese investment and technology transfer to China (Yuan Zhou, Beijing, *China Daily*, 15 March; *FBIS*, 15 March).

Li Peng visited Japan between 12 and 16 April in return for the visit of Japanese premier Takeshita to China in August 1988.

The Beijing office of Japan Air Lines said that it received a letter on 17 July from a group identifying itself as the "Blood-Bright Dare to Die Squad" saying that two Japanese would be killed each month beginning around 15 August. The number would be increased to one a week if Japan did not "change its attitude." (Seth Faison, Beijing, *South China Morning Post*, 19 July; *FBIS*, 19 July.) However, there was no fulfillment of this threat in August or subsequently.

The newly appointed ambassador to China, Hiroshi Hashimoto, said in an interview in October that Japan should exercise independent judgment on the matter of resuming economic aid to China, including the third yen loan that was frozen following the events of June, and that the loan would "contribute to China's economic development as well as benefit Japan. Japan made a pledge, and therefore must carry it out." (Tokyo, *Nihon Keizai Shimbun*, 13 October; *FBIS*, 25 October.)

As noted above, Deng Xiaoping's last official meeting with foreign guests was on 13 November with a delegation of the Japan-China Association on Economy and Trade headed by its director, Ryoichi Kawai, and its senior adviser, Eishiro Saito, director of the Federation of Japanese Economic Groups. Deng used the occasion not only to say that this was his last meeting with foreigners on an official basis, but to request that the sanctions imposed by the Japanese government following the Tiananmen Square massacre in June, including the freeze on the third yen-based loan, be removed. (Tokyo, NHK General Television Network, 13 November; *FBIS*, 13 November.)

In Beijing the deputy foreign ministers of China and Vietnam, Liu Shuqing and Dinh Nho Liem, discussed, for four days in mid-January, normalization of relations and matters of mutual interest including Cambodia, constituting the first such senior-level official Sino-Vietnam talks in ten years (David Storey, Ho Chi Minh City, Reuters, 20 January; Honolulu, *Star-Bulletin*, 20 January). Later in the year it became clear that relations had not improved significantly. Beijing reacted to Vietnam's 26 September declaration that it had withdrawn all of its troops from Cambodia by calling the withdrawal a "hoax." (Chen Jiabao, *BR*, 16–22 October.) China also announced in September that its first sea observation station—the Yongshujiao Sea Observation Station—on the Nansha Islands in the South China Sea had been completed ahead of schedule. (Beijing, *Zhongguo Xinwen She*, 29 September; *FBIS*, 6 October.)

On 9 January, at a meeting in Paris between foreign ministers Qian Qichen and Moshe Arens, China and Israel agreed to keep in contact through their permanent representatives to the United Nations (*BR*, 23–29 January).

On 28 February, Indonesian President Suharto instructed Foreign Minister Ali Alatas to prepare to resume diplomatic relations with China. Technical talks to this end were left to the two countries' permanent representatives to the United Nations. Suharto had discussed normalization of relations with Chinese foreign minister Qian Qichen in Tokyo, where both attended the funeral of the Japanese emperor Hirohito. (Beijing, XINHUA, 28

February; *FBIS*, 1 March.) These ties were not consummated by year's end, however.

China and Mongolia restored long-severed party ties during a visit to Ulan Bator by a CCP delegation in July. Zhu Liang, head of the CCP's International Liaison Department, led the Chinese delegation. (Beijing, AP, *LAT*, 16 July.)

Relations with the Democratic People's Republic of Korea (DPRK) were marked by two high-level visits during the year. Zhao Ziyang's only visit abroad since he became party general secretary in 1987 was to the DPRK from 24 to 28 April, responding to an invitation by DPRK president Kim Il-Song during the latter's visit to China in May 1987. (Beijing Domestic Service, in Mandarin, 24 April; *FBIS*, 25 April.) The second trip was an unofficial three-day visit to China by Kim Il-Song, 5–7 November. Kim met with Deng Xiaoping, Jiang Zemin, Yang Shangkun, Li Peng, and Deng Yingchao. (*BR*, 27 November–3 December.)

Kaysone Phomvihane, chairman of the Council of Ministers of the Lao People's Democratic Republic and general secretary of the Central Committee of the Lao People's Revolutionary Party, visited China for the first time in ten years in early October. He met with Deng Xiaoping, Jiang Zemin, Li Peng, and Yang Shangkun. (*BR*, 16–22 October.)

Thailand's prime minister, Chatichai Choonhavan, visited Beijing twice during the year. The first visit was in mid-March, during which he met with principal leaders including Deng Xiaoping, with whom he had had three previous meetings. Cambodia was the principal topic of their hour-and-40-minute meeting. Deng said that Thailand was China's best friend in Southeast Asia. However, Deng rejected the new Thai plan for resolving the Cambodia conflict. (Li Wei, Beijing, *Zhongguo Xinwen She*, 17 March; *FBIS*, 17 March.) During the second visit, on 26 October, he again met with Deng Xiaoping who rejected the new Thai plan to resolve the Cambodia conflict (Tokyo, *Kyodo*, 26 October; *FBIS*, 27 October). Chatichai told Deng that Thailand and China serve as a model of countries with different social systems getting along in friendship, with current ties being at a peak in which political, economic, and trade relations were growing rapidly. He also met with Jiang Zemin, Li Peng, and Yang Shangkun. Li told Chatichai that Vietnam had failed to withdraw all of its troops from Cambodia and blamed the failure of the Paris conference on Cambodia on Vietnam's lack of cooperation. Li also expressed appreciation of Chati-

chai's understanding of China's suppression of the popular demonstrations in Beijing in June. (*BR*, 6–12 November.)

China suspended ties successively with Grenada, Liberia, and Belize following their establishment of diplomatic relations with the Republic of China on Taiwan.

Formal diplomatic relations were established between China and Micronesia on 11 September (Beijing, *Renmin Ribao*, 11 September; *FBIS*, 18 September). Prime Minister Tofilau Eti Alesana of Western Samoa also visited China for a week in late October (*FBIS*, 27 October).

A Foreign Ministry spokesman said that the Chinese government opposed any attempt to "internationalize" the question of Hong Kong, a position reiterated by Li Peng the following day in his meeting with the visiting prime minister of Western Samoa. The position was stated in response to recent remarks by British leaders. (*BR*, 6–12 November.) Meanwhile, China had been putting pressure on Hong Kong not to allow the colony to be used as a base for "subversives." This pressure has caused Hong Kong authorities and many Hong Kong residents to exercise more self-restraint and self-censorship. (Barbara Basler, *NYT*, Honolulu, *Star-Bulletin*, 26 December.) Thus the situation in Hong Kong had changed drastically from the spring, when the largest demonstrations in the history of Hong Kong had massed in support of the pro-democracy movement on the mainland.

The Chinese government was particularly displeased with France for providing refuge for political exiles during the year. A *People's Daily* commentary of 26 September criticized France for supporting the establishment in Paris of the Federation for Democracy in China by the exiles, led by Yan Jiaqi and Wu'er Kaixi, among others. (*BR*, 9–15 October.)

On 7 October, a Chinese Foreign Ministry spokesman criticized awarding the 1989 Nobel Peace Prize to the Dalai Lama, which had been announced in Oslo two days earlier (*BR*, 16–22 October).

Premier Li Peng visited Pakistan, Bangladesh, and Nepal from 14 to 21 November.

Politburo member Qiao Shi led a CCP delegation to attend the Fourteenth National Congress of the Romanian Communist Party from 20 to 25 November, following which Qiao Shi visited Bulgaria from 27 November to 2 December. It was reported that in recent days there had been a flurry of meetings between Chinese officials and those from Romania, Bulgaria, North Korea, and Cuba. (Willy Wo-lap Lam, Hong Kong, *South China Morning Post*, 18 November; *FBIS*, 20 November.)

Beijing was increasingly distressed by developments affecting erstwhile hardline allies in Eastern Europe. The overthrow and execution of Romania's Ceauşescu in late December was the last and most stunning of these historic occurrences. China, reduced to only one relatively secure hardline ally of uncertain proportions, North Korea, found itself near year's end seeking to prevent discussion of the Romanian crisis in the U.N. Security Council, presumably because of the comparisons that might have been made to the June crackdown in China. (*Honolulu Advertiser*, 27 December.)

Stephen Uhalley, Jr.
University of Hawaii

India

Population. 833,421,982
Party. Communist Party of India (CPI), Communist Party of India—Marxist (CPM), minor communist splinter parties
Founded. CPI: 1928, CPM: 1964
Membership. CPI: 467,539; CPM: 450,000
General Secretary. CPI: C. Rajeswara Rao, CPM: E. M. S. Namboodiripad
Politburo. CPI: 9 members: C. Rajeswara Rao, Indrajit Gupta, Indradeep Sinha, Jagannath Sarkar, N. Rajashekara Reddi, N. E. Balaram, M. Farooqi, A. B. Bardhan, Homi Daji; CPM: 12 members: E. M. S. Namboodiripad, B. T. Ranadive, M. Basavapunnaiah, Harkishan Singh Surjeet, Jyoti Basu, Samar Mukherjee, E. Balanandan, Nripen Chakravarty, Saroj Mukherjee, V. S. Achuthanandan, L. B. Gangadhara Rao, A. Nallasivian
Central Committee. CPI: National Council, 125 members; CPM: 70 members
Status. Legal
Last Congress. CPI: Fourteenth, 6–12 March in Calcutta; CPM: Thirteenth, 27–31 December 1988 in Trivandrum
Last Election. 1989. CPI: 12 seats, CPM: 32 seats;

two CPM-allied communist parties (Revolutionary Socialist and Forward Bloc) won 8 seats (out of 524 contested seats in the 545-seat Parliament); CPM also dominates Left Front governments in two Indian states (West Bengal and Kerala) where CPI is a junior coalition partner.

Auxiliary Organizations. CPI: All-India Trade Union Congress, All-India Kisan Sabha, All-India Student Federation, All-India Youth Federation, National Federation of Indian Women, All-India Agricultural Workers' Union; CPM: Centre for Indian Trade Unions, Kisan Sabha, Students' Federation of India, Democratic Youth Federation of India, All-India Democratic Women's Association, Indian Federation of Working Journalists
Publications. CPI: *New Age* (Pauly V. Parakal, editor), Indian-language dailies in Kerala, Andhra Pradesh, West Bengal, Punjab, and Manipur; CPM: *People's Democracy* (M. Basavapunnaiah, editor), Indian-language dailies in Andhra Pradesh, Kerala, and West Bengal

National Election Results. Some three hundred million Indian voters went to the polls to elect a national government during three days of balloting between 22 and 26 November. Opposition willingness to sink political differences and downplay ideology paid off. Congress-I lost over half its 415 parliamentary seats, though Rajiv Gandhi won reelection handily. Despite this dramatic decline, Congress-I and its electoral partners led all parties with 193 seats (36 percent). The middle-of-the-road Janata Dal finished second with 141 seats (26 percent). A profusion of political interests—communists, Hindu fundamentalists, regional parties, and freewheeling independents—won the remaining seats.

Because no single party could claim the 273 seats required to form a government, the major political parties conducted around-the-clock negotiations to put together a workable coalition. The main players in the tense political drama included Janata Dal, a right-wing Hindu fundamentalist combine led by the Bharatiya Janata Party (BJP), and a leftist group headed by CPI and CPM. All the campaign platforms of the three groups had in common was an overriding desire to drive Gandhi from office. Nevertheless, the opposition rose to the challenge of forming a government.

The communists and the BJP held the balance of power, and both yearned to play a kingmaker role. The left and the right, however, were not willing to share power—the price of admission to the new

Election Year	CPI Seats	CPI Percent of Popular Vote	CPM Seats	CPM Percent of Popular Vote
1967	23	5.0	19	4.4
1971	23	4.4	23	5.0
1977	7	2.8	22	4.0
1980	11	2.8	36	6.1
1984	6	2.7	22	5.7
1989	12	—	32	—

government—with their ideological adversary. Their alternative—joining forces with Gandhi's Congress-I—was equally unpalatable. In the end political pragmatism prevailed over ideological considerations. The communists and the BJP agreed to back a non-Congress coalition government from the outside. Under this arrangement, neither side shared the spoils of office.

With the exception of the CPM-dominated state of West Bengal, voters in every corner of the country rebelled against incumbents regardless of their ideological coloration. In north India, Janata Dal and the BJP were the main beneficiaries of the voters' wrath. In the opposition-ruled south, Congress-I avoided national humiliation by scoring impressive gains at the expense of regional parties and the communists.

The leftist contingent—CPI, CPM, and two minor communist parties—performed respectably in the 1989 election, picking up 24 new seats for a combined strength of 52. The election did not symbolize an historic turning point for the Indian left, however. Both CPI and CPM made an impact only in those states where they traditionally enjoyed support. Moreover, communist strength was generally in line with the results of India's previous five elections (*India Today*, 15 November).

To be sure, CPI and CPM achieved some of their objectives: a Congress-I defeat, the formation of a government committed in principle to secularism and a progressive foreign policy, and a semblance of communist electoral unity. Although the leftist group in parliament is neither a loyal opposition nor a full-fledged ruling partner, the communists did acquire a degree of influence over central government policy. Once again, however, the communists could only hope to use their parliamentary foothold to expand their political base and roll back BJP inroads. With a combined membership of almost

one million, front membership totaling some 33 million, and the international backing of fraternal communist parties, CPI and CPM wield considerable clout outside parliament.

Last year's election was a bittersweet victory for the Indian communist faithful. From their perspective, the BJP's emergence as a national political force outweighed the modest parliamentary gains registered by CPI and CPM. The hated BJP, which had only 2 seats in the previous parliament, gained 88 seats in last year's election. With the BJP winning more seats than all the left parties put together, "the little islands of [communist] red have been swamped by a flood of [Hindu] saffron," declared the respected biweekly *India Today* (15 December). The BJP's performance dealt a severe blow to the communists' strategy of isolating "communalists" and "antinational elements" (codewords for the BJP and its allies). The BJP was the primary beneficiary of the Congress-I rout in the critical Hindu heartland of northern India, where communist support remained thin. Even more galling was the fact that the communist-backed Singh government owed its survival to the BJP. Spokesmen for both CPI and CPM warned early on that the communists would withdraw their support if Singh veered to the right in deference to Hindu fundamentalism. BJP spokesmen issued similar warnings about communist leverage over the National Front.

Regional voting patterns provided little consolation to the Communists. In the "red fort" state of West Bengal, the CPM-led Left Front coalition prevailed over all challengers, as expected. But CPM's anemic electoral performance outside West Bengal confirmed that the Marxist party remains essentially a Bengali regional organization. In Kerala, a southern state ruled by another CPM coalition, communist candidates won only two of twenty seats. In the Bengali-majority state of Tripura, the third CPM red fort, Congress-I captured the two seats at stake with ease.

CPI, the weaker of the two parties, managed to double its parliamentary strength, from six to twelve seats. Unlike CPM, CPI tapped pockets of support in the Hindu heartland, though here again the BJP dashed CPI hopes for an electoral breakthrough. All CPI legislators owed their victory to electoral compacts with CPM or noncommunist parties. All told, India's communist parties fielded 126 candidates. A breakdown of communist members of parliament by state is shown below.

State	Number of Seats at Stake	CPM	CPI	Minor Communist Parties
Bihar	54	1	4	—
Kerala	20	2	—	—
Maharashtra	48	—	1	—
Orissa	21	1	1	—
Rajasthan	25	1	—	—
Uttar Pradesh	85	1	2	—
West Bengal	41	26	3	8
Total		32	12	8

The CPI. In March twelve hundred CPI delegates and 60 fraternal delegates from abroad gathered for the Fourteenth Party Congress. The site of the six-day pageant was Calcutta, the capital of West Bengal and home of the rival CPM. CPI leaders chose Calcutta to underscore the party's determination to promote communist unity in advance of the national elections. Although the CPI is a junior partner in the CPM-led Left Front coalitions in West Bengal and Kerala, both parties failed once again to heal the ideological wounds of the 1964 split in the Indian communist movement.

The Calcutta congress did not alter the CPI party line laid down in the late 1970s. CPI supports the basic outlines of Indian foreign policy, particularly India's warm ties with the Soviet Union. On the domestic front, CPI follows the CPM lead in vigorously opposing Congress-I. In his opening remarks to the delegates, General Secretary C. Rajeswara Rao recapitulated the party's main objectives in the upcoming electoral battle. These included (1) the removal of Congress-I, (2) the installation of a "left, democratic and secular alternative," (3) the isolation of "communal forces," and (4) the unification of the Indian communist movement (*Statesman*, 8 March).

On the delicate issue of forming electoral alliances with ideologically suspect bourgeois parties, party bosses tried to avoid a breach in party unity and keep CPI's tactical options open. The rank and file was united in its opposition to the BJP, a party vilified as "communal" and "reactionary." "The BJP's entry into the central government," Rao warned, "would be a severe blow against the secular-democratic set-up in the country and a threat to its unity" (*WMR*, July). Excluding the BJP from the opposition camp was easier said than done,

however. A number of CPI's prospective partners were prepared to cooperate selectively with the BJP in the larger interest of patching together a winning coalition. This, in the view of some CPI cadres, tainted CPI cooperation with those parties.

CPI attitudes toward V. P. Singh's four-party National Front coalition were ambivalent. Formed in 1988 as a centrist alternative to Congress-I, the alliance grouped Singh's Janata Dal with shallow-based regional parties in Tamil Nadu, Andhra Pradesh, and Assam. Rao complained that the "National Front's understanding of foreign policy is confused and even retrograde. Its economic policy hardly differs from the Rajiv [Gandhi] government." On a more positive note, Rao characterized Janata Dal, the leading front component, as "considerably better" and worthy of guarded cooperation. (Ibid.)

The Fourteenth Party Congress broke no new ground on the international front. Speakers invoked ritual condemnations of "U.S. imperialism" and "Pakistani interference" in communist-ruled Afghanistan. Criticism of China was muted, however, because Beijing dispatched a delegation to the CPI congress for the first time. Resolutions heaped praise on the Soviet Union's leading role in world affairs. Party spokesmen avoided being drawn into second-guessing where Gorbachev was taking his country, a heated subject in Indian communist circles. After endorsing the general thrust of Gorbachev's policies of *glasnost'* and *perestroika*, CPI reserved the right to take its own political path. K. M. Makhamov, the Soviet delegation head, applauded the stand as a concrete expression of *glasnost'*. CPI delegates, however, were acutely aware that the Kremlin frowned on the communists' opposition to the Gandhi government. From Moscow's perspective, Gandhi's re-election probably offered the best hope for keeping Indo-Soviet relations on a sound footing. Makhamov and his Chinese counterpart, Jiang Guanghua, endorsed CPI efforts to reunify the Indian communist movement.

The CPI congress made few organizational changes. Rajeswara Rao agreed to serve another term as general secretary, although the aging communist veteran had made no secret of his desire to step down. Observers speculated that Rao's retention as general secretary was part of a deal struck with supporters of the Andhra Line who felt that Indrajit Gupta, Rao's handpicked successor, was insufficiently sensitive to their ideological concerns. Rao, a native of Andhra Pradesh, apparently agreed to guide the party through the elections in an effort to keep CPI cadres in line. Three new members (Y. V. Krishna Rao, Jagdish Tripathi, and Vimla Farooqi) were added to the 31-member central executive committee, the inner sanctum of the CPI's 125-member Central Committee. The other 28 members were re-elected unanimously. Politburo membership remained intact.

CPI claimed 467,539 members, an increase of fifteen thousand since the 1986 party congress. According to party statistics, 60 percent of the membership was classed as "rural poor" and 10 percent as "workers." Party documents complained that "the support the party gets during mass movements is not being translated into membership" (*Statesman*, 9 March). A regional breakdown of CPI membership bears out this complaint. Although the party boasts local chapters in 22 of India's 25 states, fully 41 percent of its membership is concentrated in the populous states of Uttar Pradesh and Bihar. States such as Punjab, where CPI chapters had staged agitations and recruitment drives, showed virtually no growth. Other pockets of support were noted in Kerala, West Bengal, and Tripura—states where CPI competed for members with powerful CPM state units. CPI also acknowledged its failure to attract women (only fourteen thousand are members).

Most telling, however, was the party's failure to inject young blood into the aging CPI structure. With only 2 percent of its membership listed as "young" (no ages specified), CPI found itself at a severe disadvantage in competing for the youth vote. The 1989 election was the first time Indians between the ages of 18 and 21 were allowed to exercise the franchise (*Patriot*, 21 March). Preliminary data strongly suggest many of these new voters flocked to more dynamic parties such as CPM and BJP. According to CPI's own figures, the party is failing to keep pace with the times.

The party congress reported no significant changes in CPI front group membership and activities. The party sponsors at least six such organizations that carry the CPI message to targeted constituencies—students, workers, peasants, and intellectuals. The most significant CPI fronts are the All-India Trade Union Council (AITUC), with a claimed membership of almost three million, and the All-India Agricultural Workers' Union (more than 500,000 members). AITUC has union affiliates in a number of state-owned enterprises that depend on Soviet and East European purchases of their output. In addition, CPI participates in the full range of Soviet-sponsored international fronts. *New Age*, the CPI organ, continued to carry the party's message with the help of generous Soviet subsidies. Throughout the year, *New Age* published a blizzard of articles calling on wayward communist factions, particularly CPM, to set aside their ideological differences and rejoin the CPI fold.

Communist Unity was the watchword of the Fourteenth Party Congress. Just before the conclave, national executive committee member Avtar Singh Malhotra published an appeal for unity. Malhotra conceded that serious stumbling blocks remained, but urged the two parties to pursue a strategy of "unity in action." Under this formula, the two sides would not dwell on the past, but would build on common objectives of removing Congress-I from power and fighting "religious obscurantism" (*WMR*, February).

Deputy General Secretary Gupta picked up this theme when he informed the Calcutta delegates that "the unity of the two parties is now a life-and-death question for the masses of the country." Recognizing the formidable obstacles that lay ahead, Gupta insisted that a full-fledged merger was not in the cards. "We want joint programmes and unity of action in the communist movement," he maintained. "Something may come out of these dialogues, something may not, but we are determined to go ahead in that direction" (*Telegraph*, 7 March). Rajeswara Rao went even further when he extended the olive branch to Maoist radicals who had bolted CPI and CPM in the late 1960s. "Our party will do everything possible to bring these groups into the mainstream," he promised (*WMR*, July).

As the weaker of the two parties, CPI has historically taken the lead in promoting Indian communist unity. Differences between the two sides have narrowed considerably in recent years. Although CPI enjoys closer ties with the Soviets, both CPI and CPM have adjusted to improvements in Sino-Soviet and East-West relations by forging party links with both wings of the international communist movement. In domestic affairs, CPI and CPM attitudes toward the Gandhi government and the Indian right are virtually identical. On a bedrock issue—the class character of the state—the two parties have fundamental differences, however.

A CPI minority eschews all cooperation with "bourgeois" parties that compromise with "feudal elements." This so-called people's democracy line championed by CPM was put to the delegates by veteran CPI leader Satpal Singh, who urged the party to abandon the hope shared by some cadres of eventually cooperating with "progressive" elements within Congress-I. A reformulation of the party line in this direction would bring CPI into conformity with CPM and remove the main obstacle to unity. Party leaders recognized, however, that abandoning the national democratic line would be a tacit admission that CPM's 1964 breakaway was ideologically correct. The Fourteenth Party Congress, unable to swallow such bitter medicine, balked at assuming responsibility for the 1964 split and invited CPM to rejoin the parent body on CPI terms.

True to form, CPM rejected CPI's unity overtures even before the Calcutta congress adjourned. On 12 March, CPM general secretary E. M. S. Namboodiripad responded to the CPI appeal in a hard-hitting editorial in the party's Bengali-language organ. Namboodiripad insisted that the 1964 divorce had strengthened, not weakened, the Indian communist movement and that CPM alone carried the banner of the working class. Moreover, CPM remained in the forefront of the struggles against revisionism and communalism. "Talking of reunification without seeing these important facts," Namboodiripad opined, "would be similar to the unity efforts of the bourgeois parties which go through the exercise of split and unification" (*Patriot*, 12 March). An editorial tirade by CPM Central Committee member Anil Biswas was even more blunt. "There can be anything but a communist unity between a non-Marxist organization [read CPI] and a Marxist party," he fumed. "At its root, it is a case of Marxist-Leninist thought versus social democratic ideas" (*Telegraph*, 15 March). Other indignant CPM spokesmen accused CPI of "carrying the Menshevik flag of class appeasement" (*Patriot*, 20 March).

Stung by CPM's insolence, CPI leaders retaliated in kind. "The Marxist party," lamented a party spokesman, "is getting vicarious pleasure in making the CPI dance to its tune by making regular but vague statements about unity . . . with the intention of exposing what they feel is [CPI's] ideological cretinism." CPM, he noted, displayed a "big brotherly attitude" toward smaller communist parties, a complaint often echoed by CPM's Left Front partners in West Bengal and Kerala. "It seems the CPM is fighting for dictatorship within the Left movement," the spokesman observed (*India Today*, 30 April).

Political mudslinging has been a regular feature of Indian communist polemics since 1964. Behind the scenes, however, last year's intramural disputes occasionally gave way to "unity in action" on issues where the two sides shared common objectives. The primary vehicle for cooperation was the National Coordinating Committee, a joint body of Politburo insiders who took responsibility for charting campaign strategy and organizing mass movements. In July, CPI and CPM joined more than one hundred opposition members of parliament who resigned their offices, ostensibly to protest Gandhi's alleged cover-up of a defense kickback scandal involving a multibillion dollar purchase of Swedish howitzers. In reality, the mass resignation was intended to flex opposition muscles in advance of national elections (*NYT*, 25 July).

The following month, CPI, CPM, and the National Front observed a one-day general strike to rally national opinion against Congress-I. The public relations ploy was surprisingly effective. The Gandhi government, sensing that political momentum was shifting in the opposition's favor, threatened to fire state employees who failed to report for work. Fearing that a shutdown of public transportation would prevent their commuting to work, many bureaucrats camped out in their offices. Press reports noted that the festive mood of the general strike was sullied by physical clashes between CPI and CPM demonstrators in Calcutta (*NYT*, 1 September).

In strife-torn Punjab, CPI and CPM mounted a coordinated campaign against Sikh terrorism, a growing Hindu backlash, and security force excesses. With pockets of support in the state, both parties rejected any compromise with Hindu communalists or Sikh separatists. According to CPI statistics, terrorists have assassinated more than two hundred Punjab cadres since 1983.

The CPM. Boasting widespread support in its regional bastions of West Bengal, Kerala, and Tripura, the CPM was in a strong position to influence the direction of the opposition campaign. Indeed, CPM has for years been a leading voice in the elusive drive to forge opposition unity. The party's electoral agenda, which was ratified at the 1988 Thirteenth Congress in Trivandrum, mirrored the CPI program. CPM sought to defeat Congress-I, isolate the BJP, and strengthen like-minded "secular and democratic forces." As with CPI, however, CPM was divided over tactics. (*YICA*, 1989.)

CPI adherents of the Andhra Line found similar expression among a CPM minority headed by General Secretary Namboodiripad. This faction, composed almost entirely of non-Bengali cadres, was reluctant to cement alliances with noncommunist groupings that cooperated with the BJP. Namboodiripad and his supporters invoked the Bolshevik shibboleth When Communists Win with the Right, the Right Wins. Accordingly, they wanted the party to distance itself from elements of the National Front in the larger interest of defeating communalism.

The powerful Bengal wing of the party, led by West Bengal party boss Jyoti Basu, urged a more flexible line that would allow CPM candidates to join forces with a broad spectrum of opposition forces. Their only condition was that the BJP must not be a formal partner. Dubbed the Bengal Line, Basu and his followers were less concerned with the BJP threat than with protecting their hard-won electoral gains in CPM's three red forts.

In January, Congress-I suffered a humiliating defeat in Tamil Nadu at the hands of a local affiliate of the National Front. Basu, sensing that the Congress-I setback could bolster the opposition's chances of unseating Gandhi at the national level, rallied the party behind his call for "synchronized action" with the National Front. Basu then met with V. P. Singh in Calcutta to hammer out seat adjustments. As a token of good faith, Basu allowed Janata Dal to run unopposed against a Congress-I candidate in a local by-election in West Bengal. Singh reciprocated by accommodating a handful of CPM parliamentary candidates elsewhere in north India (FEER, 10 August).

CPM-CPI relations in West Bengal were strained throughout the year. In May, CPI staged demonstrations in Calcutta in support of laid-off jute workers belonging to a CPM union. Basu complained, probably with justification, that the demonstrations were designed to embarrass the Left Front government (Indian Express, 24 May). In July, CPM party bosses decreed that Left Front constituents could not issue press statements without CPM approval. CPI refused to comply with the gag order and accused CPM of indulging in "big brother" behavior (Indian Express, 15 July).

CPM's well-oiled electoral machinery was already in high gear in October when Gandhi announced elections for the following month. The CPM election manifesto reiterated long-standing party staples, including lusty condemnations of Congress-I, the restructuring of center-state relations in favor of the states, negotiated settlements of separatist revolts in the Punjab and Kashmir, and safeguards for minorities (Delhi Domestic Service; FBIS-NES, 25 October).

On the first day of balloting, Jyoti Basu put to rest widespread speculation that CPM might throw its support behind Congress-I in the event no party emerged with a majority. Basu indicated that CPM would support a "friendly government" if the National Front emerged victorious. "We were not opposing Mr. Gandhi and his party just to form a coalition government with them. We are not going to scale down our ideology," he vowed (Hong Kong, AFP; FBIS-NES, 22 November). True to its word, CPM backed the National Front. CPM cadres interpreted the election results as a clear victory for the Bengal Line.

In West Bengal, a state ruled for twelve years by a CPM-dominated communist coalition, Left Front candidates won 36 of 41 seats. CPM won 26 of those seats, an increase of 10. As in other north Indian states, the opposition had the advantage of confronting a badly divided Congress-I state apparatus. At the state and local level, Congress-I will continue to have difficulty dislodging the well-entrenched CPM. The Left Front shrugged off Congress-I charges that CPM stole the election by stuffing ballot boxes. To the relief of CPM officials, BJP candidates were not a significant factor in the state.

CPM electoral performance in Kerala was a disaster. In line with Namboodiripad's hard-line stance against sharing a platform with communal parties, CPM candidates ran solely under the banner of the state's Left Democratic Front coalition. Although the BJP does not enjoy broad support in the state, its undeclared backing of Congress-I was a decisive factor. The Christian and Muslim minorities flocked to Congress-I, which won seventeen of twenty seats on the strength of 50.9 percent of the popular vote. Most observers predicted that a resurgent Congress-I would eventually unravel the CPM state ministry of Chief Minister K. Karunakaran (India Today, 15 December).

In Tripura, where a CPM coalition government fell to Congress-I in 1988, CPM failed to win either of the two parliamentary seats. The BJP was elated by CPM's poor showing. "With its defeat in Kerala and Tripura," crowed a BJP official, "the CPM has been reduced to a negligible party. Communism is dying everywhere in the world." (Ibid., 31 December.) Clashes between CPM and Congress-I party workers occurred throughout the year. In May, Congress-I thugs attacked CPM headquarters in Agartala and burned shops and buses. The melee was triggered by false rumors that CPM operatives had kidnapped a cabinet minister's wife. CPM state officials claimed that 68 party members have been killed in more than two hundred such incidents since the Congress-I government arrived in power (*Indian Express*, 15 May). Congress-I levels similar charges when CPM is in power.

In international affairs, CPM was unsure how to react to the many challenges facing the international communist movement in 1989. Ever since the 1964 split, many CPM cadres (particularly in West Bengal) looked to China as the bulwark of international communism. When the People's Liberation Army massacred students in Beijing's Tiananmen Square in June, CPM expressed "concern and anxiety," but concluded that Chinese leaders had acted responsibly. CPM interpreted the prodemocracy campaigns as an "action spearheaded by a mischievous section misleading the mass of students" (ibid., 6 June). Later in the summer, the CPM organ *Ganashakti* lent credence to the theory that the U.S. Central Intelligence Agency had masterminded the upheaval (ibid., 18 August). CPI, for its part, had "no comment" on events in China. (For a full discussion of the international implications of the Tiananmen massacre, see the profile on China in this volume.)

Other Communist Parties. Small communist parties exist on both the left and the right of CPM and CPI. On the right is the All-India Communist Party (AICP), established by nonagenarian S. A. Dange, a Lenin Peace Prize recipient who left the CPI in a disagreement over its decision to abandon the "united front" policy with the Congress party. The AICP has been virtually ignored by the Soviets because of its anemic electoral performance. Moreover, its separate existence conflicts with the Kremlin's long-standing desire to unify Indian communists.

In May, Dange's AICP merged with another CPI splinter formed in 1987 by a CPI Central Committee member. The new United Communist Party of India (UCPI) convened its inaugural congress in Salem, Tamil Nadu. According to Dange, the National Front presented a "sorry picture of intrigues, infighting and disarray." He urged the new party to reject "political opportunism" practiced by the established communist parties and to work jointly with progressive sections of Congress-I. (*Statesman*, 15 May.) The UCPI, with extremely limited support in industrial areas of Bombay and Tamil Nadu, had no impact on the November election.

To the left of CPI and CPM are a profusion of radical Maoist parties and underground cells collectively known as Naxalites. India's ultraleftists have lost the appeal they once enjoyed during the heyday of China's Cultural Revolution. Press reports noted that many Naxalites, who had terrorized eastern India in the late 1960s, were mellowing with age and turning their energies to pursuits such as social work and writing revolutionary memoirs (*India Today*, 31 July). Some factions, in fact, have disavowed the Naxalite line of "annihilating class enemies" and joined the political mainstream. One such group, the Communist Organization of India (Marxist-Leninist), held a unity convention in rural Bengal in February. Formed in 1985 by old guard Maoists such as the legendary Kanu Sanyal, the gathering called for "bold and practical steps" to reunite the fractured Naxalite movement. The group made little headway and observed that the "future path remains tortuous. Resolution of disputes has indeed proved difficult." On a militant note, Sanyal's followers vowed to arm themselves and subvert the Indian army in anticipation of the coming struggle (*Times of India*, 14 February).

Indian police sources reported in June that two hundred hard-line Naxalites from five states convened a clandestine strategy session in a tribal backwater of Madhya Pradesh. The unity conclave embarrassed local authorities, who noted that Naxalite kidnappers and extortion rings operated with impunity in the region (*Indian Express*, 13 June). Another notorious Naxalite band is the People's War Group, operating in the Telengana region of Andhra Pradesh. An independent who won a parliamentary seat in the November election is reportedly connected with Andhra Naxalites. Other pockets of Naxalite support can be found in backward tribal districts of West Bengal, Bihar, Orissa, and Tamil Nadu. Without the backing of China or other foreign powers, it appears that Indian Maoists have been reduced to a local security menace.

Douglas C. Makeig
U.S. Department of Defense

Note: The opinions expressed in this article are the author's own and do not necessarily reflect those of the U.S. government or any U.S. government agency.

Indonesia

Population. 187,651,163 (*World Factbook*, 1989)
Party. Indonesian Communist Party (Partai Komunis Indonesia; PKI)
Founded. 23 May 1920 (*First-Hand Information*, p. 71)
Membership. 1,000–3,000, with less than 10 percent engaged in organized activity (*World Factbook*, 1989, p. 140)
General Secretary. Tomas Sinuraya, Moscow wing; Jusuf Adjitorop, Beijing wing
Leading Bodies. N/a
Status. Illegal
Last Congress. Seventh Extraordinary, April 1962
Last Election. N/a
Front Organizations. None identifiable in Indonesia
Publications. *Tekad Rakyat* (People's Will) published abroad (monthly, according to entry in *First-Hand Information*, p. 76). No data on editor.

Summary. The PKI, once the third-largest communist party in the world, was officially banned in March 1966 following an abortive coup on 30 September 1965. The Indonesian government continues to attribute some instances of unrest in the country to communist activity, but has gradually relaxed certain strictures against some of those found guilty of participating in the coup, many now in their 60s and 70s.

Leadership and Party Organization. The only known PKI leaders are those few living abroad who are referenced in official communist documents. Satiajaya Sudiman continues to be cited as a member of the party's leadership and the PKI's representative on the *World Marxist Review* (Prague, *WMR*, June). The *World Marxist Review*'s compilation of data on world communist parties, *First-Hand Information*, provides no names of past or present leaders, but claims that the party is conducting political work among the masses and implies that it is the force behind strikes, peasant unrest, and student demonstrations in Indonesia.

The *World Marxist Review*'s summary of the history of the PKI predictably encapsulates the major tenets of the revisionist versions that have achieved such popularity in some U.S. academic circles. Madiun, the PKI's 1948 abortive military coup against the Indonesian government, is presented as an attack by reactionary forces against the vanguard of the revolution, the PKI. The summary attributes the party's isolation both in Indonesia and in the international arena during the early 1960s to opportunism among the leaders, the erosion of the party's class base, and the influence of Maoism. The PKI's attempted coup of 30 September 1965 is described as a putsch by young army officers to forestall a coup attempt by right-wing generals. The PKI failed to mobilize the popular masses because its leadership was split over the officers' actions, and the party was forced underground. (*First-Hand Information*, pp. 74–75.)

The *World Marxist Review* history does not, of course, take note of any PKI leaders currently in Beijing, but Sudomo, Indonesia's coordinating minister for politics and security, in a statement about the talks with China on normalization of relations, referred to Jawoto, a PKI leader, as one of the many former party members living in China (*Djakarta Post*, 21 March; *FBIS*, 29 March).

Information on PKI members or sympathizers in Indonesia remains spotty. Several officials were reported to have lost their jobs because of their "leftist connections." In the most widely publicized instance, the chairwoman of the East Java Provincial House of Representatives (DPR), Mrs. Sunardi, resigned her post amid reports that she had concealed the fact that her father had been "involved" in the PKI. Mrs. Sunardi, the only woman to have led a regional DPR, had been active in the ruling party, Golkar, since 1964 and had been elected chairwoman of the Malang regency DPR and, in 1988, of the provincial DPR. The military commander of East Java said that her resignation was a wise step, although he had concluded after a seven-months' investigation that she had never been involved in communist activity and had done her job flawlessly. He said that, like other former left-wing activists still holding important posts in the province, she was not ideologically motivated, but merely wanted to survive. (*Djakarta Post*, 5 January; *FBIS*, 10 January.)

Although urging continued national vigilance, the army's chief spokesman expressed the hope that the people would "be able to receive" those involved in the 1965 coup who had served their time and been released from prison. He spoke in connection with the release of Mrs. Sundari Abdulrahman, the former chairwoman of Gerwani, the banned communist women's organization. Originally sentenced to life imprisonment, she had received a presidential commutation. (*Antara*, 23 August; *FBIS*, 24 August.)

The leader of the Free Papua Movement (OPM) surrendered in late July, virtually crippling his organization. The OPM apparently receives some assistance from abroad, but there are no apparent ties between this movement and the suppressed PKI. (Djakarta Domestic Service, 1 August; *FBIS*, 2 August; *FEER*, 30 November.)

Domestic Party Activities. The *World Marxist Review*'s description of the PKI states that the party clandestinely publishes a monthly journal, *Tekad Rakyat*, in Indonesian and in English, but does not indicate if it is distributed in Indonesia or why it has an English-language edition (*First-Hand Information*, p. 76).

Government officials suspected communists were behind several incidents. One of the more violent involved an Indonesian army attack on a village in southern Sumatra where an army officer had been killed the previous day while investigating local unrest. The village, in Lampung province, is in an area where over the years many Javanese have been resettled, including suspected communists detained after the 1965 coup. The army first ascribed the unrest to Muslim extremists, but Armed Forces commander general Try Sutrisno linked the incident to a "communist comeback," accusing the communists of using Islam as a facade and making Muslims their primary target in an effort to create social or religious unrest. (*FEER*, 9 March; Djakarta Domestic Service, *FBIS*, 29 March.)

The governor of the National Defense Institute, Major General Subiyakto, issued repeated warnings of infiltration of the administration and bureaucracy by underground activists of the PKI. He stressed the need for constantly monitoring developments in the communist movement abroad, particularly in the Soviet Union and the People's Republic of China, to anticipate its influence on the underground movement of former PKI members in Indonesia. (Djakarta Domestic Service, 29 July; *FBIS*, 2 August.) Noting that the authorities had been able to detain only 0.1 percent of the total number of former PKI members and sympathizers, he said that cadres and sympathizers "intentionally trained by [former PKI leader] Aidit" were still involved in various organizations, but did not say how many former PKI supporters he believes are still "roaming around freely" in Indonesia. (*Djakarta Post*, 7 August; *FBIS*, 14 August.) Some idea of the size of the perceived threat is suggested by the government's statement that it maintains a list of seventeen thousand people who are not permitted to leave the country (*FEER*, 30 November).

When a food poisoning scare swept the country after several deaths had been traced to a poisonous chemical mistakenly used in some locally manufactured biscuits, the minister for political and security affairs warned that the PKI and other subversive groups might take advantage of the situation to stir up trouble (*Antara*, 27 October; *FBIS*, 1 November).

There were a variety of student demonstrations during the year, despite a 1970 ban on such activities that was reaffirmed in April (*Djakarta Post*, 11 April; *FBIS*, 18 April). A wave of student protests in Java beginning in March brought out the police and the army on several occasions. In June two thousand students from several cities in Java joined in a march to the parliament building in Djakarta where they sought to present a petition protesting the government's increase in electricity prices. Initially the students took great pains to indicate their independence of any outside influence, and their demonstrations focused chiefly on local issues. The demonstrations became more violent and more explicitly political, however, after two students in Jogja were given eight-year sentences and several students in Bandung were summarily expelled. Although some officials tried to mollify the students, others demanded that some of the detained students be tried on charges of subversion. (*Djakarta Post*, 11 April; *FBIS*, 18 April, 2 October; *FEER*, 20 April, 22 June, 21 September; *Antara*, 29 September.) Both students and faculty protested the government's decision to continue talks with the People's Republic of China (PRC) on normalization after Tiananmen Square (*Kompas*, 21 June; *FBIS*, 27 June).

The question of whether Sukarno, the country's founding father and first president, was a communist was raised again when President Suharto in his autobiography said that, in his view, Sukarno was not a communist (*FEER*, 19 January). In a major statement on the issue of succession, Suharto spoke of Pancasila Democracy as a system that does not draw on "Western liberalism" or "communist authoritarianism" as a source (*FEER*, 22 June).

International Views, Positions, and Activities. Satiajaya Sudiman is listed as a participant in the international symposium in Prague on Peace and Revolution in the Nuclear Age, sponsored by the *World Marxist Review* Commission on General Theoretical and Global Problems (Toronto, *WMR*, February). Sudiman also contributed an article, "A Life of Debt or 'Pakdes 24'?" on the Indonesian economy to the June issue of *World Marxist Review*. The article blames Indonesia's reactionary circles for an economic policy "which benefits not only imperialism but also themselves." Pakdes 24 refers to the government's 24 December package intended to stimulate the export of oil and oil products, but, Sudiman claims, does not provide for boosting output as a whole or for needed changes in the banking system. He recommends seeking a solution in line with Mikhail Gorbachev's December 1988 proposals to the United Nations on ways to ease the debt burden on developing countries.

Indonesian suspicions that the PRC still supports the PKI were much in evidence during the yearlong discussions between Djakarta and Beijing on normalization of relations. In February, at a meeting in Tokyo, President Suharto and Chinese foreign minister Qian Qichen agreed that the next steps toward normalization could begin. The talks were to be based on the Bandung principles, which include mutual abstention from intervention or interference in the internal affairs of another country. Nevertheless, President Suharto noted that the negotiation process would not lessen Indonesia's alertness toward possible dangers from China. (Djakarta, TVRI, 23 February; *FBIS*, 24 February; *Bernama*; AFP; *FBIS*, 27 February.)

The Indonesian Chamber of Commerce announced plans to send a sizable delegation to the April trade fair in China, but not all Indonesian officials were enthusiastic about the prospect of normal diplomatic relations with the PRC. Some weeks after the Suharto-Qian announcement, Minister Sudomo said that Indonesia remained reserved about normalizing ties with China and that there were certain assurances required of China before Indonesia could consider normalization, among them China's willingness to promise not to give protection to former PKI members. He also recommended seeking Chinese assurances that neither its party nor its government would support a communist movement in Indonesia. (*Djakarta Post*, 21 March; *Kyodo*, 27 March; *FBIS*, 29 March.)

Reactions to the events of 3–4 June reflected the divisions among Indonesian officials on the resumption of diplomatic ties with China. Although Indonesia's foreign minister said that he would not con-

demn the PRC government on the grounds that this would constitute interference in the internal affairs of another country, other leaders expressed misgivings about the talks. Defense/Security Minister L. B. Murdani recommended that normalization efforts should be continued, but not immediately. General Subiyakto proposed that Indonesia reconsider the question of normalization. He said that underground activities of the communist remnants involved in the 1965 attempted coup were inseparable from current developments in the communist movement abroad. China, he said, unlike Japan, could not exercise economic power to sustain its interests in Southeast Asia and would resort to political and military power and even subversive means to maintain its position in the region. The PRC's pledge to meet the Indonesian government's terms for normalization of ties was now in doubt, he said, because the man who made the pledge was a government official, not a party man, and the less progressive nature of the present party leadership in China presaged greater party problems, especially with regard to the ties to parties in the developing countries. (*Antara*, 26 June; *FBIS*, 27 June; *Antara*, 1 July, 4 July; *FBIS*, 5 July.)

In early December, Indonesia and the PRC began discussions expected to resolve the final details for the resumption of full diplomatic relations. Xu Dunxin, assistant foreign minister and head of the Chinese delegation, said the PRC was willing to accept Chinese nationals residing in Indonesia who wished to return to their homeland and could provide proof of their valid citizenship. For those who preferred to continue residing in Indonesia, the PRC would issue special passports including their status as Chinese citizens. (AFP, 5 December; *FBIS*, 5 December.) Despite these suggestions, no final agreement was reached on how to treat the estimated 350,000 Chinese nationals living in Indonesia (*FEER*, 21 December).

A somewhat different atmosphere surrounded the strengthening of ties with the USSR and East European countries, highlighted by President Suharto's September trip to Moscow, the first by an Indonesian head of state in 25 years. Minister Murdani noted that "there is a difference between communist teachings in Indonesia and in communist countries." Pointing out that the USSR had not backed the PKI in the attempted coup of 1965, Murdani said that Indonesia's national resilience is strong enough to withstand such teachings introduced from abroad and that although Indonesia should remain alert on communism, it should not overreact. President Suharto reportedly told his Soviet hosts that Indonesia would continue to ban the PKI, but that this did not mean that Indonesia is hostile toward countries professing Marxism or Leninism. (*Merdeka*, 13 September; *FBIS*, 15 September; *Djakarta Post*, 19 September; *FBIS*, 22 September; *FEER*, 21 September.) However, Minister Sudomo said that Indonesia needs to remain vigilant about the latent danger of communism, despite efforts to boost trade and economic cooperation with the Soviets (*Indonesian Times*, 26 September; *FBIS*, 2 October).

Auxiliary and Front Organizations. There is no information available on such organizations for this banned party.

Jeanne S. Mintz
Washington, D.C.

Japan

Population. 123,220,129 (*World Factbook*, 1989)
Party. Japan Communist Party (Nihon Kyosanto, JCP)
Founded. 1922
Membership. 470,000 (*World Factbook*, 1989); industrial workers: 65.6 percent; women: 38.3 percent
Central Committee Chairman. Kenji Miyamoto
Presidium Chairman. Tetsuzo Fuwa
Central Committee. More than 200 members
Status. Legal
Last Congress. Eighteenth, 26–28 November 1987
Last Election. July 1989: 8.8 percent of the popular vote in the House of Councillors. The JCP has 14 seats of 252 in the House of Councillors and 27 of 512 in the more powerful House of Representatives.
Auxiliary Organizations. All-Japan Student Federation, New Japan Women's Association, All-Japan Merchants' Federation, Democratic Foundation of Doctors, Japan Council of Students, Japan Peace Committee, Gensuikyo (Japan Council Against Hydrogen and Atomic Bombs)

Publications. *Akahata* (Red banner), daily circulation 550,000, Sunday circulation 2,500,000, total readership more than 3,000,000 in addition to frequent special issues and 90,000 copies of a poster called *Akahata Photo News*, published twice a month; *Bulletin of Information from Abroad* (Central Committee of the JCP); *Gakusei shimbun* (Student newspaper), weekly; *Shōnen shōjo shimbun* (Boys' and girls' newspaper), weekly; *Zen'ei* (Vanguard), theoretical journal; *Gekkan gakushū* (Monthly studies); *Josei no hiroba* (Women's tribune); *Gurafu konnichiwa-Nihon kyōsanto desu* (Hello, we are the JCP); *Asu no noson* (The countryside tomorrow); *Bunka hyōron* (Cultural review); *Keizai* (Economics); and *Rōdō undō* (Workers' movement)—all monthlies; *Sekai seiji: Rompyō to shiryō* (International politics: Critical reviews and materials), fortnightly

The JCP remains a Eurocommunist party advocating the parliamentary road to power. Nevertheless the party performed poorly in the House of Councillors election in July. JCP leaders explained the setback as a result of the Tiananmen massacre in China that occurred just before the election and of other Japanese political parties' falsely, but successfully, associating the event with the JCP.

The JCP continues to maintain an internationalist perspective, although its relations with China have been and remain bad and its ties with the Communist Party of the Soviet Union, while improving in recent years, are still not too friendly. Changes in Soviet policy toward other communist parties during the year did not help because JCP leaders regarded Gorbachev's "new political thinking" as abandoning class struggle. The JCP also criticized Soviet leaders for viewing international problems so seriously that monopoly capitalism and imperialism began to seem less threatening and more rational.

The JCP's relations with the other political parties in Japan remained strained as the opposition parties continue to align against the JCP. This in part accounted for the JCP's poor election performance even while the ruling conservative Liberal Democratic party suffered at the polls.

Party Leadership and Meetings. Kenji Miyamoto at age 81 remained chairman of the Central Committee of the JCP and the party's top leader and spokesman. Miyamoto, who has been the JCP's boss since 1958, was criticized by the press during the year for remaining in power while other aging party leaders have retired. Miyamoto replied that he would not discuss party organizational matters with outsiders and said that decisions about such things are made through "collective democracy" (*Asahi shimbun*, 10 June). Tetsuzo Fuwa, vice-president of the Central Committee, was reappointed chairman of the Presidium after Hiromu Murakami stepped down because of an eye ailment (*Japan Times*, 4 June). Fuwa, 53, joined the JCP in 1947 and became party secretary in 1970. He served as chairman of the Presidium from 1982 to 1987. (See *YICA*, 1983, for biography.) Fuwa is considered Miyamoto's most likely successor. There had been some speculation that Mitsuhiro Kaneko, the party's general secretary and the fourth-ranking JCP leader, might succeed Murakami. Koichiro Ueda, vice-chairman of the Presidium and the fifth-ranking JCP leader, was also mentioned as a possible successor. (*Japan Times*, 4 June.)

During the year the Japanese media speculated both about Murakami's health and about his disagreements with Miyamoto. The JCP responded by filing a libel suit. (*Asahi shimbun*, 10 June.) It was also reported by the Japanese press that the JCP had to consolidate its leadership before the July diet election and that this explained Fuwa's appointment.

The JCP convened its Fourth Central Committee Plenum meeting 1–2 February at party headquarters in Tokyo. The meeting was called less than three months after the Third Plenum because, according to JCP leaders, there were a number of important events and issues to discuss: the Recruit scandal, the death of Emperor Hirohito, the "pro-Emperor campaign" that followed his death, and preparations for the House of Councillors elections in July. Party leaders also wanted to discuss the continuing problem of the opposition parties' hostility toward the JCP and the other parties' support of the U.S.-Japan military treaty.

Regarding the Recruit case—a serious insider trading and payoff scandal that hurt the ruling Liberal Democratic party (LDP) and the other opposition parties as it unfolded throughout the year—the JCP boasted that none of its members was involved. JCP leaders criticized the press for withholding names of top leaders who purchased Recruit stock before it was put on the market and assailed the LDP for its involvement in the corruption and its attempts at a coverup. The JCP charged that the Recruit Company had succeeded in putting its people "at the

center of government" and had influenced important political decisions.

Central Committee chairman Miyamoto, at the Fourth Plenum, reiterated the party's position on the emperor. He declared that sovereignty resides with the people under the postwar democratic constitution. He chided the LDP and the opposition parties for "trying to use the issue to win votes in the next election" and the media for "clouding this fact by praising the Emperor." Miyamoto asserted that a "political party that stands for the people's interests and for the cause of peace can never acquit the Emperor of his responsibility for the great tragedy" (*Akahata*, 4 February). He noted that Japan's other political parties did not blame the emperor for World War II.

Miyamoto discussed efforts to ensure the party's victory in the July election. He expressed concern about localism, which he equated with "bourgeois parliamentarianism and degeneration into individualism, having nothing to do with JCP policy." (Ibid.) He observed that this problem was discussed at the Second Plenum of the Central Committee of the Seventeenth Party Congress in 1986, but that information "had not been disseminated sufficiently." Miyamoto was especially disturbed by JCP prospects in the proportional representation, or at-large, part of the election. He underscored "four basic points": everyday activity, mass propaganda, party papers and journals, and associations and mass organizations.

The JCP held its Fifth Plenum, also at party headquarters, 7–8 June. Miyamoto gave the introductory speech; Mitsuhiro Kaneko, acting chairman of the Presidium and head of the Secretariat, reported on party work; and Tetsuzo Fuwa, vice-chairman of the Central Committee, gave the presidium report.

Miyamoto called for special efforts to improve the party's chances in the upcoming election. He particularly mentioned the issues of the Uno cabinet, "political reform," the consumption tax, the attitude of the Japan Socialist party and other anticommunist opposition parties, the Anti-Subversion Activity Law, errors by the Soviet Union and China (especially the latter), and defining socialism in the context of changing conditions in the world. (*Akahata*, 9 June.) Miyamoto made a special effort to denounce the Chinese government and the Chinese Communist party for the Tiananmen massacre.

Tetsuzo Fuwa's report focused on international questions and the need for JCP members running for local office to understand foreign policy issues. Fuwa asserted that the other political parties had taken a weak position vis-à-vis China following the June massacre of students in Beijing and had not taken any action against China, but rather used the occasion to criticize communism in general and to associate the JCP with the incident. (*Akahata*, 10 June.) Fuwa described the Beijing massacre as the "most serious outrage since the 'Great Proletarian Cultural Revolution.'" He pointed out that the JCP had had no contacts with China for 22 years because of the Chinese Communist party's "unwarranted interference and attacks." (Ibid.) In the context of describing the situation in China, Fuwa promised that the JCP would implement socialism in Japan only when the people wanted it.

On 15 June the JCP held an emergency Presidium meeting to discuss the situation in China. Tetsuzo Fuwa addressed the meeting. He noted that "many witnesses, including the Japanese press," have attested to the fact that "a number of students were crushed under tanks and children were shot down with their mothers." He blamed the military dictatorship of Deng Xiaoping, "who holds the reins of the Army and dominates both Party and State." Fuwa asserted that the JCP had immediately condemned the brutality while the Japanese government and other opposition parties "hesitated to face up to the situation." (*Akahata*, 20 June.) Fuwa noted that the Japanese Socialist party said it had to refrain from comment because of "inadequate information," whereas the Komei party said it should "watch the development of the situation." The ruling Liberal Democratic Party (LDP), he said, tried to deceive the people, saying if it failed in the election, "Tokyo would become a Tiananmen." He said all three were being servile to China while trying to use the situation for anti-JCP propaganda.

Fuwa delineated JCP relations with China over the last twenty plus years and noted that relations between the two had not been good. In this context he referred to Deng Xiaoping as the "string puller of genocide in Cambodia" and quoted Mao and Deng about how during several wars the loss of life had been large, yet things were better afterward. He went on to condemn the Chinese leadership and point out differences between it and the JCP. The JCP's response seemed to mirror the party's reaction to events in China, differences with the Chinese communist party over a period of more than two decades, and an effort to counteract the use of the incident against the JCP in the upcoming election.

The JCP called its Sixth Central Committee Plenum meeting at party headquarters in Tokyo, 11 and 12 August. Chairman Miyamoto gave the introductory speech; Presidium chairman Tetsuzo Fuwa presented a party report. The meeting came soon after the last plenum and was held primarily to discuss the defeat in the House of Councillors election and plans for the upcoming House of Representatives election.

In his introductory speech Miyamoto noted that the LDP had suffered a crushing defeat in the election and that the Japan Socialist party had made a "quantum leap," winning many more seats than expected. He observed that the event "turned a new page" in the history of Japanese politics. (*Akahata*, 14 August.) Miyamoto argued that although the JCP had also suffered a major setback, the party had played a major leadership role in bringing issues to the attention of the public. He also referred to an "upsurge of the Mass movement" on three key issues: the consumption tax, plutocratic politics, and LDP misgovernment on agriculture. (Ibid.) Miyamoto stated that even though the JCP opposes the "power program" of the four other opposition parties and their approval of the U.S.-Japan Security Treaty and the Japanese Self-Defense Forces, he did agree to support Japan Socialist party chairwoman Doi's bid to the House of Councillors to proclaim her prime minister (even though only the House of Representatives is empowered to do this).

Miyamoto attributed the JCP defeat to the "negative impact" of the Tiananmen affair and to voters supporting the Japan Socialist party in order to "deal the LDP a blow." (Ibid.) He also stated that the JCP is plagued with localism and had not made adequate preparations for the at-large part of the election. He pointed out that only 40 percent of JCP branches had an official in charge of the proportional representation election and that no meetings were held for them. (Ibid.) He said that campaigning in the future for this part of the election process would be done for the party rather than candidates and that the party would set up a new Secretariat post to take this responsibility (ibid.).

Domestic Affairs and Issues. The major issues for the JCP during 1989 in terms of party public statements and articles in party publications were the status of the emperor and the role or future of communism in view of changes in the communist world. The Recruit scandal, the consumption tax, the U.S.-Japan military relationship, the Japanese Self-Defense Forces, the antinuclear movement, welfare, and the party's relationship to a new national union in Japan and to the other political parties were also important.

On the death of Emperor Hirohito on 7 January, the JCP declared that mourning for the emperor by the LDP and the government was in essence an effort to support the emperor as head of state or at least "to make him superior to the people." The party repeated its position that Japanese militarism was the worst event in the history of Japan, was brought about by the absolutist emperor at the top, and resulted in an anticommunist alliance with Germany and Italy and a brutal war of aggression against China and other Asian countries. (*Akahata*, 8 January.)

The JCP stated its position that "in the light of reason, the Emperor system should be abolished." Party leaders recognize that the constitution made the emperor the symbol of state, but argue that the emperor had gone beyond this and had become involved in matters of state, such as when he sanctioned the continued U.S. control of Okinawa and when he stated that the dropping of the atomic bombs was necessary. These statements prove that the "emperor totally lacked patriotism." (Ibid.) The JCP also assailed what it said were efforts to make the emperor head of state. (*Akahata*, 4 February.)

Both chambers of the diet met in plenary session after the emperor's death and adopted a resolution of condolences. The JCP boycotted the session, saying that the message ran counter to the constitution, which stipulates that sovereign power rests with the people. (*Japan Times*, 10 January.) *Akahata* subsequently eliminated the Japanese year designation from the paper, using only the Western year in protest (*FBIS*, 10 January).

During 1989 party leaders spent considerable time and energy on ideological issues arising out of what Miyamoto called "new political thinking" in the Soviet Union and elsewhere. In a speech made in 1988 but reprinted in the JCP's *Bulletin* (in English for overseas distribution), Miyamoto argued that the "earth sharing co-destiny" view arising out of the nuclear war issue and global ecology problems had given rise to wrong ideas. This view, he declared, assumed an end to class struggle and did not accord with Lenin's view or his own. Miyamoto went on to explain that Khrushchev and Brezhnev had argued that peaceful coexistence still assumed class struggle and the aggressive nature of imperialism and monopoly capitalism. He stated that they had based their view on Soviet great power chauvinism and that was wrong. However, the new view, he said, assumes the end of class struggle and the

rational and good nature of imperialists, which is not right either. Miyamoto asserted that the imperialists have not changed and that class struggle and confrontation between capitalism and socialism are necessary for people to have a choice of systems. (*Akahata*, 26 September 1988.) In this connection Miyamoto pointed out that President Bush has taken the position that the United States must continue to build weapons for nuclear war, that more than 5 percent of mankind would survive a war using all nuclear weapons, and that the United States would emerge a winner (*Akahata*, 4 February).

On the issue of the Recruit scandal, the JCP attacked the LDP for not making a self-examination. Party leaders cited public opinion polls indicating low public support for the Takeshita cabinet, with twice the number opposing it as supporting it. (*Akahata*, 1 January.) JCP leaders criticized the Regulation of Money for Political Activities Law, which permitted the sale of stock to be unreported, and called for the elimination of political contributions by businesses. The party also rebutted the LDP's contention that switching to a single-member electoral district system would reduce "money politics," characterizing it as an effort to aggrandize power and weaken the smaller parties. Finally, the JCP called on Prime Minister Takeshita to resign over the issue.

When the Geisha scandal hit newly installed Prime Minister Uno, the JCP quickly called for his resignation also. Party leaders similarly demanded the dismissal of Minister of Agriculture, Forestry and Fisheries Hisao Horinouchi, characterizing both as "looking down on women." (*FBIS*, 10 July.)

The JCP took a similarly strong position on the unpopular consumption tax promoted by the LDP and passed by the diet in April. Miyamoto had said earlier that the JCP would engage in "all out opposition." (*Akahata*, 1 January.) In trying to fulfill that promise the party said that the consumption tax "hit the poor and aged the most." JCP leaders throughout the year criticized the LDP for lying to the people and abandoning its earlier pledge not to push this tax and other opposition parties for their willingness to make concessions on the issue. The JCP took the strongest position against the tax of any Japanese political party. When the LDP promised to revise or get rid of the tax later in the year, the JCP accused its leaders of insincerity and compromise and of not abiding by their pledges or responding to public demands.

Related to the consumption tax, the JCP continued to advocate increased welfare and sponsored legislation to this end. In his New Year's address Miyamoto declared that in the past three years families covered by livelihood assistance have been cut by 90,000 and that the consumption tax on top of this will hurt even more. (*Akahata*, 1 January.) He also advocated that the pension age be raised from 60 to 65 and that the aged be paid more for medical costs (ibid.).

The party continued to oppose the U.S.-Japan military alliance and increased spending on arms. The party likewise sustained its support for the antinuclear movement. Early in the year Miyamoto charged that a JSP–Komei party agreement made in January 1980 and still in effect supports the Japanese Self-Defense Forces, thus making the JCP the only political party opposing the agreement. He noted that both parties are using this issue to attract union support and are trying to isolate the JCP. He vowed that the JCP would not change its stance. (*Akahata*, 1 January.) Miyamoto also attacked increased defense spending, arguing that it was unconstitutional and that tax money should be saved, making more funds available for welfare and other needs.

On economic policy, the JCP also called for an end to economic assistance to China. Mitsuhiro Kaneko, head of the Secretariat at the time, said it is "paid for by the sweat of the Japanese people's brows." (*Japan Times*, 25 June.) He also called for sanctions against China and the unconditional extension of visas of Chinese students in Japan (ibid.).

On the labor front the JCP expressed opposition to the merging of Sohyo, the general council of trade unions of Japan, with Rengo, the Japanese private-sector trade union confederation, to form Shin Rengo, or Japanese trade union confederation. Rengo, 5.5 million strong, planned to absorb Sohyo, 2.5 million strong, to become an 8 million-member organization with 65 percent of the organized workers as members. (*Japan Times*, 21 November.) Miyamoto described Rengo as "right-wing" and stated that Shin Rengo would be a "class-oriented center of trade unions" (*Akahata*, 1 January). The JCP instead supported Zenroren, the Japan confederation of trade unions, which officially formed in November in opposition to Shin Rengo. Zenroren, composed of 1.2 million workers, opposes Shin Rengo's policy of supporting the U.S.-Japan security treaty and stresses the class struggle side of the labor movement. (*Japan Times*, 21 November.) Because of Shin Rengo's size and because it ran twelve candidates in the July House of Councillors election—eleven winning—it is of con-

siderable concern to JCP leaders. Politically Shin Rengo envisions a left-of-center bloc that excludes the JCP and includes the other opposition parties and liberal elements of the LDP. Its union policies are also anticommunist. (Ibid.)

Elections. The JCP performed well in several local elections and some fill-in elections during the year. However, the JCP lost seats in the House of Councillors election in July—a major setback for the party in election politics. Moreover, this followed a defeat in the Tokyo Metropolitan Assembly election in June.

In the Kagoshima gubernatorial election in February, JCP-recommended candidate Isamu Kumamoto won three times as many votes as in the previous election in 1985, though failing to win (*FBIS*, 22 February). In the Tikushima mayoral race, JCP candidate Yutaka Yamada, while also losing, won the largest vote ever for a communist candidate in such an election (ibid.). In March a JCP candidate lost a close race in Chiba prefecture. Some considered it a breakthrough for the party because the margin was close in a basically conservative district. (*Japan Times*, 21 March.) Kiyoshi Takahashi, supported by the Japan Socialist party, the Social Democratic Federation, and the JCP, won the Kawasaki mayoral race in November—an election some said would be a bellwether for the next House of Representatives election (*Japan Times*, 20 November).

In contrast, the JCP, accusing all of the other parties of colluding on the issue of the consumption tax and attacking the Tokyo government on its welfare record, won only fourteen seats, for a loss of five, in the Tokyo Metropolitan Assembly election 2 July. This occurred in the context of the ruling LDP suffering a crushing defeat and the Japan Socialist party winning big. The other opposition parties, however, failed to gain seats. (*Japan Times*, 4 July.) The reasons for the JCP setback were nearly identical to the causes of its defeat in the subsequent House of Councillors election and are explained below.

The most important election during the year was the triennial upper house or House of Councillors election in July. Up for election were 126 seats in the weaker house of the diet: 50 proportional representation seats and 76 for 47 electoral districts. It was the first national election since 1986 and the first since the Recruit scandal in June 1988 and the imposition of the consumption tax in April 1989.

Both were major political issues and points of contention between the JCP and the ruling LDP.

JCP candidates won five seats, four in the proportional election and one in the district election. The party won 5,012,423 votes, or 8.81 percent of the total votes cast. Compared with its previous strength in the House of Councillors, this was a loss of three seats. The JCP now has fourteen seats in this 252-member body, ranking fourth in strength among the parties though far behind the ruling LDP and the Japan Socialist party. (See *FBIS*, 24 July for further details.) In terms of popular vote the JCP dropped from 11.42 percent to 8.81; in the proportional representation race, which reflects national strength, the party got 7.04 percent of the popular vote compared with 9.47 percent in 1986 (*FBIS*, 25 July).

The reasons for the JCP loss are many. The most important factor seems to have been the massacre of students in China in June. Although the JCP has had no connection with the Chinese communist party for more than twenty years and castigated the Chinese communist party for its actions, the JCP suffered from guilt by association. Moreover, the other parties took advantage of the situation to condemn communism and equate a vote for JCP candidates as an approval of the killing of Chinese students. The party Central Committee stated that both were important factors in explaining the JCP's defeat. (*Akahata*, 24 July.) Another factor, of course, was the anticommunist position taken by the opposition parties and their unwillingness to cooperate with the JCP in the campaign. This has been a serious problem for JCP candidates for a number of years. Also hurting the JCP was its failure to make the Recruit scandal and the consumption tax winning campaign issues. The JCP was the only party not implicated in the Recruit scandal; party members tried to make this known and use it, but were not very successful. The same was true of the consumption tax, even though both issues hurt the LDP. Another factor was Rengo—the newly formed national union organization—which ran its own candidates and thus took strength from the minor opposition parties. Finally, the JCP's stance on the emperor had angered a sizable portion of the electorate and was still fresh in the public's mind.

In the realm of election strategy, the JCP—as has often been true in the past because of its concern to educate the public through elections—put up too many candidates. The JCP fielded 70 candidates, second only to the LDP's 78. This caused JCP candidates to compete with each other and forced the party to spread its resources too thinly. Nineteen of the JCP's candidates were women, which, given the strength of the female vote and the anger of women about sex scandals in the government, should have helped the JCP. However, the JCP competed for votes with the Japan Socialist party, which was headed by a woman. Thus, though the JCP fielded more female candidates than any other party, it failed to win a significant part of the female vote. (*Japan Times*, 26 September.)

Auxiliary Organizations. The JCP throughout 1989 continued to support a host of organizations that help the party or agree with its policies and goals. Some of these receive financial support from the party; others provide material help to the JCP.

The most important events related to auxiliary organizations during the year concern the party's antinuclear efforts. Early in the year Miyamoto called for one billion signatures to the Hiroshima-Nagasaki appeal. He said that Henry Kissinger had said that the Stockholm appeal had stopped the planned use of nuclear weapons by the United States; likewise the Hiroshima-Nagasaki appeal would bring an end to nuclear deterrence. Miyamoto announced that there were already 33 million signatures. (*Akahata*, 1 January.) He also noted that 41 percent of local governments have signed nonnuclear declarations in areas that cover 62 percent of the population of Japan. He said the party seeks more nonnuclear municipalities. (Ibid.)

In the spring, Miyamoto stated that he anticipated prefectural antinuclear organizations would be set up in every part of Japan. He also cited progress in getting signatures for the Hiroshima-Nagasaki appeal and declared that the ten-year-old National Progressive Unity Forum had reached a membership of nearly four and a half million. (*Akahata*, 4 February.) However, Miyamoto also stated that membership in party mass organizations was down by 250,000 since the last national election in 1986 and that *Akahata* readership had declined. He called this a "poor performance." (Ibid.)

At the Sixth Central Committee Plenum, Miyamoto called on members of JCP-related organizations to help the party overcome problems created by the Tiananmen massacre, the other parties' use of this against the JCP, and the party's poor performance in the July election (*Akahata*, 14 August).

International Views and Activities. The JCP was active on the international front during 1989. Changes in the communist world, relations with the Soviet Union, and the Tiananmen massacre in China were the primary causes. JCP leaders felt they had to give attention to international events and consider their impact on the party for ideological as well as practical reasons.

On 15 January, Mitsuhiro Kaneko, head of the Secretariat, together with several other party leaders, traveled to Romania for a week of meetings. There they issued a joint document entitled "In Advance of the 2nd Anniversary of the Joint Declaration between Kenji Miyamoto, Chairman of the Central Committee of the Japanese Communist Party, and Nicolae Ceauşescu, General Secretary of the Romanian Communist Party." (*Akahata*, 25 January.) The earlier document set out "the method and perspective for resolving basic problems in the present world in five areas: peace—the elimination of nuclear weapons and disarmament; cooperation between peace and democratic forces; the imbalance in economic development throughout the world; the independence and security of nations; and communist movements in the world." The two parties recognized that this declaration has "proved its vitality" for two years. (*Akahata*, 26 January.)

The most important foreign issue for the JCP during 1989 was the action taken by the government of China and the Chinese Communist party against student demonstrators. The JCP criticized the government when martial law was ordered. *Akahata* stated that "the Japanese Communist Party expresses deep concern about the declaration of martial law in the capital of a country which calls itself socialist, and about the danger of armed suppression of peaceful mass movements." (*Akahata*, 29 May.) It went on to say that "an armed crackdown on all peaceful mass movement of students and other citizens should never be conducted under socialism" (ibid.).

On 4 June the JCP Central Committee issued a statement of condemnation: "The Japanese Communist Party, which firmly maintains the principles of scientific socialism and regards the enhancement of democracy and respect for human rights as basic, resolutely condemns with anger the leadership of the Chinese party and government for this brutal outrage." It described the event as "an inexcusably savage act [that] can never be condoned internationally, in the light of the socialist cause." (*Akahata*, 5 June.) It went on to say that "Chinese authorities have arbitrarily defined the peaceful movement of students and citizens as a 'counterrevolutionary riot'" (ibid.).

Akahata subsequently carried a series of articles on the issue, all extremely condemnatory of the Chinese government and the Chinese communist party. In May when Deng Xiaoping appeared in public after talks with Gorbachev, the fact that Deng was in command, the JCP said, "brought to light the seriousness of the problem of the present political system in China." *Akahata* went on to describe the Chinese political system and Deng's authority as not based on formal or constitutional positions. It noted particularly that he exerted supreme power through the Central Military Commission after he had resigned from the party's Central Committee and the Standing Committee of the Politburo in 1987. (*Akahata*, 16 June.)

The next day in another statement the JCP argued that it was legitimate for the international community "to denounce the Chinese authorities for their barbarous actions, the impermissible infringement of human rights." Rejecting the Chinese claim that it was a domestic matter and that it had to suppress a counterrevolutionary riot, the JCP asserted that regarding outside comment as interference in internal affairs is "far behind the times." (*Akahata*, 17 June.)

When Chinese authorities met with foreign journalists on 16 June and declared that no students had been shot or run over by tanks, the JCP referred to the statement as "an absolute lie on the bloody event in Tiananmen Square." The party paper noted that the Chinese authorities "believe that shooting and slaughter of unarmed students and citizens is unjustifiable . . . so they claim there was no bloodshed." The paper went on to compare the Chinese Communist party's statement with an "Announcement by the Imperial Headquarters" in prewar Japan. Going on to describe the event as an "atrocity," the JCP stated that "to pretend that this event did not take place shows that the military rule system under Deng Xiaoping, dominating both party and state, cannot exist without lies." (*Akahata*, 18 June.)

Later the JCP made efforts to distinguish its views from those of the Chinese Communist party, noting that the Chinese Communist party has seen the dictum "political power grows out of the barrel of a gun" as universally applicable, supporting Pol Pot, who killed three million people in Cambodia and invaded Vietnam. JCP leaders in this context stated that the JCP seeks an "independent, peaceful and parliamentary way of changing the social system." (*Akahata*, 29 June.)

During the year the JCP made a number of pronouncements about global trends and the role of communist parties in a changing world. On the occasion of the Italian communist party's Eighteenth Congress in March, the JCP observed that the Italian communist party had rejected the role of the political party and the scientific socialism movement. It had approved, the JCP noted, the existence of military blocs and Italy's continued membership in NATO. The Italian party had entertained proposals at the meeting to change the name of the party or drop the word *communist*, thus reflecting a nullification of the split in the Second International between scientific socialism and social democracy and an effort to become a social democratic party. According to the JCP this "disregarded Marxist tradition and socialist political experience." The JCP saw this as another example of a worldview leading to the abandonment of class struggle and much worse. (*Akahata*, 22 May.)

The JCP viewed the Italian communist party's worldview as similar to the "new political thinking" in the Soviet Union and elsewhere. It noted in this context that General Secretary Gorbachev's idea— priority must be given to dialogue and collaboration between the United States and the Soviet Union over the struggles of the people and the class struggle on the pretext that if nuclear war should break out there would be no chance for humanity to survive—is incorrect thinking. (Ibid.) The JCP subsequently published Gorbachev's December 1988 speech to the United Nations along with criticisms of its major tenets. It noted, for example, that Gorbachev's "new political thinking" wrongly assumes that people's struggles for the progress of human society do not open the way for a better future world, but that "universal consensus through agreement with the imperialists makes the world turn toward progress." (*Akahata*, 27 December 1988; republished in *Bulletin*, June.) The JCP also described Gorbachev's ideas as a "deviation from historical materialism, new collaborationism reflected in eulogizing the U.S. government, a passive attitude toward the elimination of nuclear weapons" (ibid.).

John F. Copper
Rhodes College

Korea
Democratic People's Republic of Korea

Population. 22,521,223
Party. Korean Workers' Party (Choson Nodong-dang; KWP)
Founded. 1946 (a united party since 1949)
Membership. 3 million
General Secretary. Kim Il-song
Standing Committee of the Politburo. 3 members: Kim Il-song, Democratic People's Republic of Korea (DPRK) president; Kim Chong-il, Kim Il-song's son; O Chin-u, minister of People's Armed Forces
Politburo. Kim Il-song; Kim Chong-il; O Chin-u; Pak Song-chol, vice-president; Yi Chong-ok, vice-president; Yon Hyong-muk, DPRK premier; So Chol; Ho Tam; Kim Yong-nam; Kang Song-san; So Yun-sok; Kye Ung-tae; Chon Pyong-ho; Han Song-yong; candidate members: Hyon Mu-kwang; Kim Pok-sin; Choe Kwang, chief of staff; Kang Hui-won; Cho Se-ung; Hong Si-Hak; Chong Chun-ki; Yi Son-sil; Hong Song-nam
Secretariat. Kim Il-song, Kim Chong-il, Kang Song-san, Yon Hyong-muk, Ho Tam, Kye Ung-tae, Hwang Chang-yop, Ho Chong-suk, Chon Pyong-ho, Chae Hui-chong, So Kwan-hui, Choe Tae-pok, Chi Chang-ik, Kim Chong-nin
Central Committee. 145 full and 103 alternate members
Status. Ruling party
Last Congress. Sixth, 10–15 October 1980, in Pyongyang
Last Election. 2 November 1986. 100 percent participation reported for Eighth Supreme People's Assembly, all 706 candidates on the slate elected.
Auxiliary Organizations. General Federation of Trade Unions of Korea, Union of Agricultural Working People of Korea, Korean Democratic Women's Union, Socialist Working Youth of Korea, Friends' (Chongdogyo religion) Party, Korean Democratic Party, Committee for Peaceful Reunification of the Fatherland

Publications. *Nodong Sinmun* (Worker's Daily), KWP Organ; *Minju Chosun* (Democratic Korea); *Kulloja* (The Worker), party theoretical journal; *Chosun Inminkun Sinmun* (Korean People's Army News). English-language publications include the *Pyongyang Times* and *Korea Today*; in Japan the *People's Korea* generally follows the North Korean line. The official news agency is the Korean Central News Agency (KCNA).

Leadership and Organization. Rumors in fall 1989 of Kim Il-song's death (Seoul, *Korea Herald*, 7 September) proved untrue. The Great Leader celebrated his 77th birthday in 1989, and his televised appearances revealed his age. Kim seemed particularly weary at the close of the World Youth Festival in July, when he met with numerous dignitaries from the communist and Third Worlds. Kim Chong-il, his son and political heir, made only 15 appearances in 1989, compared with at least 126 for his father, but was celebrated in the North Korean media as the author of virtually all important economic and political decisions.

The publication of transcripts of recorded conversations between Kim Chong-il and the film star Choe Un-hui and her director husband Sin Sang-ok, who had escaped to the West after being kidnapped in Hong Kong and brought to North Korea in 1978, revealed Kim Chong-il implying that North Korea started the Korean War in 1950, a position at odds with the official North Korean line (Seoul, *Yonhap*, 14 June).

Two North Korean students studying at an East German university repeated allegations that Kim Chong-il is unpopular in North Korea and that he is opposed by his half brother (or half brothers) and half sister—the children of Kim Il-song and his second wife, Kim Song-ae (*Kyodo*, 9 December).

Hong Song-nam, who served in various administrative capacities, became a candidate Politburo member, judging from the elevated ranking in his order of appearance at public ceremonies (KCNA, 31 March; Pyongyang Domestic Service, 6 April). Kang Hui-won, an alternate Politburo member, relinquished his longtime position as Pyongyang party boss to become a vice-premier (KCNA, 19 April). He was replaced in Pyongyang by Choe Mun-son (KCNA, 16 May). Alternate Politburo member Cho Se-ung was released from his duties as a vice-premier in October (Pyongyang Domestic Service, 17 October). In October, Paek Pom-su replaced Kim Chang-chu as chairman of the cabinet's Agricultural Council (Pyongyang Domestic Service, 25 October).

Other changes came at the Sixteenth Central Committee Plenum in June. Yi Yong-mu moved up from candidate to full member of the Central Committee and was appointed head of the party Inspection Board (KCNA, 9 June). Chang Song-taek, Yi Yong-ik, Kim Chang-ho, Kim Myong-kuk, Cha Yong-chin, and Kim Hak-sop filled vacancies as new Central Committee alternate members (Pyongyang Domestic Service, 9 June).

Two Central Committee members died in 1989. Yi Myon-sang had been a composer and chairman of the Korea Musicians Union (KCNA, 27 June); Colonel-General Chon Mun-uk had served with Kim Il-song during his guerrilla war against the Japanese (KCNA, 24 April).

Domestic Affairs. Kim Chong-il, "the one who knows no limit to thought and contemplation and who embraces the entire universe in his bosom" (Pyongyang Domestic Service, 22 February), continued to be publicly venerated as the acclaimed leader of those North Koreans now old enough to inherit the burdens of their parents. The media warned that the new generation was as much in need of the younger Kim's leadership as the old one was of his father's. The February issue of *Korea Today* included a complaint from Kim Chong-il that educators were not adequately inculcating North Korean youth with the proper values. Kim charged that "some officials" simply compiled statistics on the number of required study sessions and forced their students to memorize phrases for the purposes of public recital. He warned teachers and party bureaucrats to expunge ideological remnants of the "old society," but also heaped praise on the Confucian tenet of filial piety, stressing the "basic obligation" to love and respect parents, brothers, sisters, spouses, and children. More broadly, the younger Kim charged that party cadres were treating their jobs as mere administrative responsibilities and could not thus inspire the correct attitudes in the masses.

Related media commentary on Kim Chong-il's thoughts stressed that too many North Koreans were being corrupted by bourgeois influences and that the imperialists were creating millions of "mental cripples" in North Korea and elsewhere (KCNA, 5 May). Impressionable youths were likely to be "dazzled" by the "splendid external phenomenon" of the capitalist system without seeing its rotten core (Pyongyang Domestic Service, 26 January). A

North Korean radio editorial attacked "the different ideological trend" as evidence of the existence of dissent in the North (Seoul, *Hanguk Ilbo*, 20 August). *Nodong Sinmun* renewed the call for ideological vigilance two days later and in August published a long commentary detailing the younger Kim's concern that ideological indoctrination needs to be intensified (*Nodong Sinmun*, 22 August).

Young North Koreans were among those most affected by a major measles epidemic that ravaged the country in 1989. Rumors that the North had failed to contain the measles outbreak were confirmed by Mun Tae-sok, director of the Health Ministry's Anti-Epidemic Treatment Bureau, who told Indonesian reporters that 50 children had died from the disease. Dr. Mun claimed that measles had been introduced into North Korea by foreign visitors (Djakarta, *Antara*, 27 May).

The Economy. North Korea entered 1989 in the midst of the second "200-day battle," a classic Stalinist campaign to increase industrial and agricultural production and kick off new efforts to meet the ambitious goals set for the Third Seven-Year Plan. In what may have been a response to complaints about North Korea's food shortages, Premier Yon Hyong-muk claimed that the entire world was suffering from poor harvests as a result of "chronically bad weather" and that South Korea was only able to produce 40 percent of the food needed to feed its people (Pyongyang Domestic Service, 7 March).

The April session of the Supreme People's Assembly, convened for its yearly ratification of the budget, focused deliberations on problems in the light industry and consumption areas and virtually ignored the "200-day battle." Overall, the government announced that state revenues in 1988 stood at 31,905,800,000 won, 102 percent of the 1987 figure. Expenditures totaled 31,660,900,000 won, 5.2 percent more than in 1987 and 99.4 percent of the 1988 plan. Revenue and expenditure targets for 1989 were put at 33,550,700,000 won. Spending for capital construction and industrial construction increased 6.1 percent and 9 percent, respectively, but the increase of investment in light industry was pegged at 13 percent. Not only was this double the increase projected for the budget as a whole, but was higher than the 7 percent growth in spending for light industry in 1987, the last time an increase in this sector was announced. The regime pegged the defense budget at 12.1 percent of total budgetary expenditures (KCNA, 7 April).

In June the concern for light industry and consumption turned into a full-scale economic campaign. At its sixteenth plenary session since the 1980 party congress, the KWP Central Committee concentrated on issues related to public welfare and satisfaction and ignored the "200-day battle." In the main address, Kim Il-song called on North Koreans to improve the quality of food and textile products to bring "mass consumption" up to world standards—an unusual admission that North Korea's performance in that area was falling behind (KCNA, 10 June). On 14 June, Pyongyang announced that Kim Il-song and Kim Chong-il had ordered a special bonus amounting to 100 percent of monthly wages and stipends be awarded to every North Korean to reward them for their efforts in the "200-day battle" and in preparing the country for the huge influx of visitors attending the International Festival of Youth and Students of the World Peace Council (KCNA, 14 June). A few days later an editorial in *Nodong Sinmun* complained that officials in charge of light industrial enterprises were not adequately using their existing resources, were lagging behind in efforts to modernize their facilities and production methods, and were failing to ensure an improvement in the standard of living (*Nodong Sinmun*, 19 June). Another editorial implied that raw material producers were not yet allocating adequate supplies to light industrial enterprises or to construction projects related to that sector (*Nodong Sinmun*, 16 July).

There was no evidence in 1989 that the leadership had opened its mind to the value of market incentives or economic reform. Orthodox planning methods remained dominant in the North Korean economy, and the media issued standard appeals to managers to improve productivity using existing equipment and people.

North Korea also tried to expand its foreign trade and attract investment from businesses and developed countries. According to South Korean figures, North Korean exports grew 11.1 percent in 1987 (the most recent available reporting year) and imports grew 14.5 percent over the previous year. Overall, North Korea reportedly exported $1,464,000,000 and imported $2,076,000,000 worth of goods in 1987 (Seoul, *Korea Herald*, 29 January).

North Korea is also trying to increase its trade with the capitalist world. In 1987 exports to the Soviet Union, valued at $683 million, still accounted for 46.7 percent of total exports, but exports to the communist bloc declined 2.5 percent over 1986, whereas exports to Japan and the European Community countries rose 49.6 percent (the sources did not provide a dollar figure). More than 60 percent of North Korea's imports came from the Soviet Union.

Pyongyang continued to claim that its joint venture law permitted foreigners to make profits in business dealings with North Koreans, but there was little evidence of foreign interest in new investments. In the above-cited article, Kim Tal-hyon stressed that North Korea would have to pay off old debts and establish a good credit rating if it was to attract foreign capital and technology, but there was no evidence that Pyongyang was prepared to do so. The government, for the first time in "many years," issued bonds designed to attract investment from Koreans living in Japan and elsewhere (KCNA, 17 July).

North-South Relations. Kim Il-song's New Year's address, which usually sets the tone for North Korean policy, was notable in 1989 for its attention to relations with South Korea. Although Kim's comments on domestic affairs revealed no new initiatives or policy directions, his views on North-South issues suggested that Pyongyang was ready to break the stalemate of previous years. Kim said that "in keeping with the new trend of relaxation we should abandon the idea of confrontation...and refrain from exciting the nerves of the other side and straining the situation" (KCNA, 1 January). Kim invited South Korean president No Tae-u, the heads of South Korea's opposition parties, Catholic cardinal (Stephen) Kim Su-hwan, and dissident leaders Reverend Mun Ik-hwan and Paek Ki-wan to a meeting in Pyongyang, thus reviving discussion in both Koreas of the reunification issue and sparking debate at least in the South as to the best means of achieving national reconciliation.

South Korea's opposition politicians did not take the bait. They joined with the government in dismissing Kim's offer as a trick and rejected the contention that each South Korean faction should send its own representative to a meeting with a united North Korean leadership (Seoul Domestic Service, 4 January).

The South, however, was more attentive than usual to standard North Korean demands that it cancel the joint U.S.–South Korean Team Spirit military exercise, which the North called the "touchstone" of South Korean intentions (KCNA, 4 January). Defense Minister Yi Sang-hun reportedly proposed postponement of the exercise

(*Yonhap*, 5 January). Although this idea was rejected, officials in Seoul and Washington did suggest that they would scale back the number of troops involved in Team Spirit (*Yonhap*, 5 January). Other South Korean spokesmen denied that Team Spirit would be reduced (Seoul Domestic Service, 6 January), but the debate provided a clear signal to the North of a willingness to improve the atmosphere on the peninsula.

The first tangible indication of a peninsular thaw—and the only practical improvement in North-South relations in 1989—came in the commercial rather than political arena. The South used its growing economic power as a weapon in the dialogue by permitting individual deals between South Korean businessmen and the North Koreans. Shortly after Kim Il-song's speech, the chairman of the Federation of Korean Industries expressed his interest in increasing trade with the North (Seoul, *Korea Times*, 5 January). Within a few days Seoul announced that it would permit domestic companies to import 60,000 tons of coal from the North (*Yonhap*, 18 January). The first shipment reportedly transited Nampo in late January (Tokyo, *Kyodo*, 31 January). Other contracts were publicized involving South Korean imports of commodities ranging from electrolytic copper (*Korea Times*, 24 January) and fish (*Yonhap*, 31 January) to books (*Yonhap*, 3 February), and works of art (*Yonhap*, 7 January). According to one report, the South Korean Construction Ministry had requested a plan for an extensive road system that would link the two Koreas (*Korea Times*, 6 January).

Whereas Samsung, Daewoo, and other large South Korean companies sought a piece of the North Korean pie, Hyundai and its chairman, Chong-Chu-yong, appeared to have the best entrée to North Korea. In mid-January Hyundai Heavy Industries announced it had received an order for barges and trawlers from the North (*Yonhap*, 17 January). Later in the month the company said it would barter South Korean sweaters for North Korean marine products (*Kyodo*, 31 January). The Pyongyang-Hyundai relationship was apparently sealed in spectacular fashion when Chong himself visited the North at the end of the month. Chong spoke to the media in both Koreas, expressing delight at the good his contacts could do regarding North-South relations and announcing Hyundai's intention to develop the Mount Kumgang area in North Korea as a major tourist resort that presumably would be visited by North and South Koreans alike (Pyongyang Domestic Service, 31 January).

While in North Korea, Chong visited his home village—an emotional issue for the millions of Koreans separated from family members since the Korean War—and met with Politburo member Ho Tam and other North Korean officials (KCNA, 25 January). Rumors that he also saw Kim Il-song were denied by both sides.

North-South economic relations appeared to be ready to take off when economic experts from the two governments met in Switzerland on 27 January on the margins of an international economic conference (*Yonhap*, 28 January). But hopes for rapid progress collapsed as suddenly as they had appeared, suggesting a possible dispute within the North Korean leadership over the wisdom of opening to the South. Chae failed to appear for a second meeting, leading to a public expression of regret from his South Korean counterpart (*Yonhap*, 30 January). At the same time, North Korean media vehemently denied rumors that Pyongyang was willing to permit direct North-South trade or trade through third countries (Pyongyang Domestic Service, 29 January). North Korean commentators issued denials concerning the specific coal, copper, and marine products deals that had been reported in the press (Voice of National Salvation, 28 January). The next month, South Korean firms complained that the North Koreans had sent pulverized instead of lump coal and charged Pyongyang with breach of contract (*Yonhap*, 14 February). South Korean firms got the message that the North had changed its mind about economic exchanges, and requests to import goods from the North—which totaled $22.5 million in January—fell off to 3.3 percent of that figure in February (*Yonhap*, 30 March). The North's negative line was reinforced in April when Chong Chu-yong reportedly was denied permission to make a second trip to Pyongyang (*Yonhap*, 6 April).

Political, military, and humanitarian contacts proved to be even more disappointing. The North's initial willingness to negotiate proved weaker than the obstacles both Koreas put in the way of progress. The Koreas began the year by agreeing to accede to the 1925 Geneva Protocol on the prevention of chemical weapons (*Yonhap*, 10 January), a gesture that raised hopes that the two sides would be able to come to terms on their treatment of international agreements and on membership in international organizations. In addition, on 17 January the two sides held their first closed-door military talks as part of a meeting of the Military Armistice Commission at Panmunjom (*Kyodo*, 17 January). At the

same time, they agreed in principle to form a joint team for the 1990 Asian Games in Beijing (*Yonhap*, 8 January)—an agreement that survived the ups and downs of the year and remains on the books as of this writing. Late in January, according to South Korean press sources, South Korean presidential adviser Pak Chol-on met with a senior North Korean official—presumably Ho Tam—in Singapore (*Korea Herald*, 12 February).

Despite initial rejection from all South Korean parties, Pyongyang pressed Kim Il-song's offer for a meeting with President No and the leaders of the political opposition. Ho Tam sent letters to each of the would-be South Korean participants (Pyongyang Domestic Service, 30 January), provoking reports in the South Korean press—almost certainly at the initiative of the government—that President No hoped to hold a one-on-one meeting with Kim Il-song sometime in 1989 (*Yonhap*, 3 February). The South firmly rejected any formula that would dilute the government's monopoly on an official dialogue with the North, but held open the option of permitting unofficial contacts on a case-by-case basis.

The most promising North-South forum was that dealing with the question of a joint team for the 1990 Asian Games, the only discussion that progressed from polemical exchanges to practical discussions of relevant issues. Kim Il-song told Yugoslav journalists that the prospect for a single team "best demonstrated" his country's desire for reunification (Sarajevo, *Oslobojenje*, 25 July). The sides met on 9 March, restated their agreement in principle to a joint team, and even chose a team song (*Yonhap*, March 9). The North proposed that the team use a white and yellow flag with the name *Koryo* in blue or red letters. (*Koryo* is Pyongyang's preferred name for the Korean confederation and is at the heart of Kim Il-song's long-standing reunification proposal.) The South insisted on the name *Korea*.

The team selection process proved to be a difficult obstacle. The North proposed that the team be balanced to the extent possible: that is, when two athletes could represent Korea in a sport, there should be one from each side. The South responded that the best athletes should make the team, using purely athletic standards of selection. North Korea, however, expressed the hope that some participants would be chosen for their "contributions to national reconciliation." At the second round of talks, North Korea agreed that the best athletes—wherever they are from—should make up the team, but the sides remained divided over the number and location of selection trials. (*Yonhap*, 28 March.) It proved impossible to select a joint team by 22 June, the deadline for Asian Games entries, to meet North Korea's goal of beginning the joint trial/selection process in August (KCNA, 28 March).

North-South dialogue took an emphatic turn for the worse as a result of the unauthorized trip of South Korean dissident Reverend Mun Ik-hwan to North Korea in March. The North, which had already tried to dilute President No's authority through Kim Il-song's New Year's proposal, raised questions about its sincerity by staging Mun's well-publicized visit. The resulting flap—by going to North Korea, Mun violated the South's national security laws—put a damper on all negotiating forums and, ironically, strengthened South Korean resolve not to permit unofficial channels of dialogue to proceed without Blue House authorization.

Mun, along with an entourage of advisers and associates, arrived in Pyongyang on 25 March. He was met by Chong Chun-ki, an alternate Politburo member (KCNA, 25 March), and was received by Kim Il-song two days later (KCNA, 27 March). The South Koreans did not permit Mun to return via Panmunjom and arrested him when he came home by an indirect route. South Korean opposition politicians, put in an awkward position by the unauthorized visit, reacted negatively to Mun's initiative, with the exception of Kim Tae-chung, who expressed appreciation for the positive role played by individual efforts in further reunification (*Yonhap*, 27 March).

Pyongyang created a direct tie between Seoul's treatment of Mun and the immediate prospects for North-South talks. Kim Il-song, in a visit to Mun's quarters in Pyongyang, presented Mun's visit as a step toward a summit with No Tae-u and hopes for economic exchanges (KCNA, 1 April). The North not only protested loudly when Mun was arrested on his return to Seoul (Seoul Domestic Service, 13 April), but postponed a scheduled 12 April contact between negotiators working for a high-level meeting on political-military issues at first for two weeks (Seoul Domestic Service, 12 April) and then for two months (KCNA, 17 April). The North Koreans also rescheduled the third round of the Asian Games talks from 18 April to 18 July because South Korean authorities had arrested Mun Ik-hwan (Pyongyang Domestic Service, 17 April). On 24 April, Kim Il-song restated his willingness to meet with No Tae-u, but again presented a summit as a

logical result from the Mun Ik-hwan visit (KCNA, 24 April).

The dialogue suffered another blow when So Kyong-won, a representative in the National Assembly from Kim Tae-chung's Party for Peace and Democracy, was publicly accused of not only having traveled illegally to North Korea, but of having accepted money from Pyongyang and—in effect—acting as an agent for their interests in the South (*Korea Times*, 30 June). He allegedly had met with Kim Il-song and Ho Tam, and the South Korean Agency for National Security Planning released transcripts supposedly documenting their praise for his work (*Korea Times*, 18 July). So was arrested on 28 June (*Yonhap*, 28 June). Another South Korean lawmaker, this time a member of Kim Yong-sam's Reunification Democratic Party, said that North Korean officials had tried unsuccessfully to talk him into a meeting with Ho Tam (*Korea Times*, 1 July). Kim Tae-chung himself came under suspicion of criminal activities in connection with this affair (Seoul Domestic Service, 27 July). The South, miffed by the So and Yim incidents, cut off parliamentary talks with the North, although it remained willing to conduct negotiations through the Red Cross forum (*Yonhap*, 4 July).

No, however, took the opportunity presented by the So affair—virtually all South Korean politicians and commentators expressed shock at So's activities—to strengthen his control of North-South policy and restated his willingness to authorize visits to North Korea and meetings with North Koreans. Although the traditional dialogue was faltering, individual North-South meetings continued; rumors spread that Pak Chol-on, one of No's closest advisers, secretly visited Pyongyang during the World Festival of Youth and Students in July (*Korea Times*, 2 August). Seoul denied that this visit had taken place, but did not challenge press reports that Pak had conducted secret talks with high-ranking North Korean officials in Singapore in January (*Seoul Sinmun*, 6 August). The South Korean government also did not refute allegations that those discussions were part of a series of quiet negotiations that had been going on since 1985.

More spectacularly, Kim Yong-sam, Kim Tae-chung's rival as leading opposition politician, visited Moscow—with Blue House approval—where he met not only with Soviet officials but with Ho Tam (Seoul Domestic Service, 13 June) and the North Korean ambassador to the Soviet Union (Seoul, *Chosun Ilbo*, 14 June). In contrast to Mun Ik-hwan and So Kyong-won, whose actions served mainly to enhance North Korean propaganda, Kim elevated his public image by rejecting Ho's invitation to visit Pyongyang and by supporting South Korea's stated positions regarding the dialogue and reunification (*Yonhap*, 14 June). The North Korean media also reported the meeting in a favorable light, saying it was held in a "warm consanguineous atmosphere" and quoting Kim as hoping eventually to meet Kim Il-song (Pyongyang Domestic Service, 15 June).

By midsummer each side was trying to appear more interested than the other in promoting North-South dialogue, but it was unclear whether any of the forums would revive. No called for an "early" summit with Kim Il-song (*Korea Times*, 8 July), and the South proposed that Red Cross talks resume on 2 August (*Yonhap*, 12 July). The Blue House, in addition, permitted a Japan-based Korean pastor holding a South Korean passport to visit North Korea (*Yonhap*, 24 July). The North, for its part, pressed for parliamentary talks—the forum that had been its favorite before 1986—(Pyongyang Domestic Service, 18 July), suggested that political-military discussions resume on 20 August (Pyongyang Domestic Service, 20 July), and called for further negotiations for a joint Asian Games team (Pyongyang Domestic Service, 24 July).

These proposals finally served as the basis for a limited resumption of the dialogue. Hopes were raised initially when Pyongyang accepted the 2 August date for resumption of Red Cross talks (Pyongyang Domestic Service, 24 July), but the South put these negotiations on hold in reaction to North Korea's use of Yim Su-kyong (*Yonhap*, 29 July). It was still unclear whether either side sincerely wanted to negotiate, although South Korean media suggested that Seoul and Pyongyang were talking secretly and operating under an agreement whereby they would publicly deny the existence of any contacts (*Yonhap*, 3 August). The North appeared to be willing to reschedule parliamentary talks (its 25 August proposal to do so did not include provocative references to Yim or Reverend Mun), but made only a general comment that its meetings with South Koreans from various walks of life served a constructive purpose (Pyongyang Domestic Service, 25 August). The next day, Pyongyang called for resumption of Red Cross talks on 6 September, again using a tone that suggested the North wanted to improve the bilateral atmosphere (Pyongyang Domestic Service, 26 August).

Seoul responded with a diplomatic offensive designed to seize the high road on North-South talks without conceding to any of the dates suggested by the North. No proposed that the presidents, ministers, and other representatives establish consultative councils to discuss reunification (*Yonhap*, 11 September). In addition, he proposed resuming Red Cross talks on 27 September at a higher level than the North had suggested (Seoul Domestic Service, 5 September). The South also offered to hold another round of discussions preparatory to a prime ministers' meeting on 10 October and the next Asian Games talks ten days later. Press reports that seemed to come from official sources suggested that the South also was preparing to propose exchanges of students and professors (*Yonhap*, 19 September).

Pyongyang decided it was time to revive some of the old forums, but had its own ideas on how to form new ones. North Korea immediately rejected the idea of consultative councils—claiming it would reinforce the South's effort to legitimize the existence of two Koreas—(*Nodong Sinmun*, 14 September), but agreed to resume preparations for a prime ministers' meeting on 12 September. Pyongyang also accepted 27 September as the date for the next working-level Red Cross talks (Pyongyang Domestic Service, 20 September). At these talks—and at further rounds in October and November—the sides agreed in principle to a second exchange of family visits on 8 December. Brief hope that these visits would actually take place were dashed when the South rejected North Korea's demand that its artists be permitted to perform two revolutionary operas (*Yonhap*, 27 November, 4 December).

Little progress was made in other forums as the year ended. The sides differed over suggested dates for higher-level Red Cross talks (Seoul Domestic Service, KCNA, 27 September, 6 October, 16 October, 18 October, 8 November, 13 November), and squabbled when Pyongyang's delegates raised the issues of Mun Ik-hwan and Yim Su-kyong. These same issues marred the resumption of negotiations for parliamentarians' meetings (Pyongyang Domestic Service, 25 October; Seoul Domestic Service, 29 November) and talks designed to prepare for high-level political-military consultations (*Yonhap*, KCNA, 12 October, 15 November, 21 December). The two sides also resumed sports talks and agreed that a joint team for the Asian Games should be chosen through direct competition—the South's position (*Yonhap*, 1 December). As the year ended, however, differences over technical details still stood in the way of an agreement (XINHUA, 22 December).

At the same time the North again noted Kim

Il-song's New Year's offer of a North-South meeting to discuss reunification, suggesting that about 30 people from various political and social groups on each side meet in Pyongyang in February 1990 after a series of preparatory discussions (KCNA, 28 September). The South repeated its opposition to this approach, rejecting the notion that South Korean opposition politicians and dissidents should be represented at the talks (*Korea Times*, 30 September). Seoul reiterated its support for cultural and family exchanges (Seoul Domestic Service, 29 September) and—for the first time—gave a South Korean student permission to contact North Korean diplomats about obtaining information useful to his doctoral dissertation (*Yonhap*, 2 October).

Nuclear Issues and the Military Balance. The pessimism surrounding the North-South dialogue was deepened by U.S. and South Korean concerns that North Korea had embarked on a program to develop nuclear weapons. The North had signed the nonproliferation treaty in late 1985, but had not yet reached a safeguards agreement with the International Atomic Energy Agency—a step required of all signatories. South Korean charges that Pyongyang was "perilously close" to achieving a weapons capability seemed exaggerated (*Yonhap*, 13 July), but fears that the North's Yongbyon reactor was capable of producing enough plutonium for one or two weapons a year were probably more realistic. Japanese sources claimed that the North was building a nuclear fuel reprocessing facility at the Yongbyon site (*Kyodo*, 11 May). North Korea denied having the intention—or technical capability—to build nuclear weapons and reminded South Korea of the presence of U.S. nuclear weapons on the peninsula (KCNA, 16 August). But the *New York Times* (20 August) quoted two Asians who said they saw the reprocessing facility when they visited the North during the World Festival of Youth and Students. The North—in a development related to the weapons issue only in the terms of generic nuclear discussion—did claim to have achieved nuclear fusion using the controversial cold process publicized by two U.S. scientists (KCNA, 7 May).

Discussion of the nuclear question coincided with U.S. re-evaluation of the size of North Korea's conventional forces. Estimates early in 1989 placed overall military strength at one million people—5 percent of the North Korean population—including 930,000 ground groups (*WP*, 26 January). This amounted to an increase of 160,000 over previous estimates, themselves sizable upward revisions of figures used in the 1970s. The North scoffed at Washington's "ridiculous" claims, noted that it had already reduced its forces by 150,000 troops and assigned others to civil construction duties, and restated its offer to reduce forces on both sides to 100,000 by 1992 (Pyongyang Domestic Service, 31 January). Nonetheless, the International Institute of Strategic Studies in London, which had placed North Korean troop strength at 742,000 in 1989, raised that estimate to 1,040,000 (*Korea Times*, 6 October).

At the same time, a South Korean defense white paper placed North Korean active strength at 980,000 and claimed the North had six million reservists (*Yonhap*, 26 October). The paper's authors suggested that South Korea could not catch up to North Korean military power until the year 2006.

Relations with the Soviet Union and Eastern Europe. North Korea was clearly uncomfortable with the galloping changes in the Soviet Union and Eastern Europe caused by *glasnost'* and *perestroika*. An article in the July issue of *Kulloja*, the party theoretical journal, lambasted "anti-socialist commotions," which the author blamed on imperialist "machinations," but implied were the fault of irresolute communist leaderships. In August, media commentators complained that the "erosion" of revolutionary consciousness in some socialist countries was permitting the "ideological and cultural infiltration of imperialism" (*Nodong Sinmun*, 30 August). The Soviets seemed just as unhappy with the North's hard line; Politburo member Yakovlev criticized Pyongyang's "closed door" policy (*Yonhap*, 15 November).

Closer to home, the North was unable to stop the growth of relations between Moscow, East European capitals, and Seoul or restrict those relations to economic exchanges. Edging toward support for some version of the South's proposal for cross-recognition, Soviet spokesman Alexander Bovin told Japanese reporters that, in his opinion, "the most reasonable option would be to normalize relations between the governments in the North and South and have them join the international community (Tokyo, *Mainichi Shimbun*, 3 January). Bovin noted that, "of course," this would presuppose recognition of North Korea by Japan and the United States and of South Korea by China and the Soviet Union. He acknowledged Pyongyang's opposition to such a plan and said that it would take time before there could be diplomatic relations between South Korea and the Soviet Union. A Soviet Korean affairs specialist criticized her country's adherence to the North Korean line, insisting that it was time for Moscow to recognize the Seoul regime (*Izvestiia*, 2 September).

Other officials were more cautious in approaching the Korean question. Georgii Arbatov, director of the USSR's USA and Canada Institute, refused to comment on Bovin's position except to note that differences of view between the Koreas adversely affected the prospects for reunification (Seoul, *Chugang Ilbo*, 1 February). Both Bovin and Arbatov, however, declared that unofficial ties would grow between the Soviets and South Koreans, and Arbatov said that the Soviet Union would not support any "armed aggression" by North Korea (*Chugang Ilbo*, 12 September). The director of the Soviet Institute of Oriental Studies stated that cross-recognition would be a "favorable" development, but stressed that North Korean opposition to it remained a formidable roadblock (Tokyo, *Asahi Shimbun*, 30 July). Finally, an unsigned TASS report answered the North Korean specialist's piece in *Izvestiia* by denying that Soviet recognition of South Korea was imminent (*Pravda*, 6 September).

The Soviets took a position on the North-South dialogue befitting their growing ties with Seoul. Although issuing standard denunciations of South Korean "insincerity" (*Izvestiia*, 21 February), they quoted President No's comments on dialogue policy, in particular his announcement in response to Kim Il-song's New Year's address that his government would set up a council to arrange for domestic exchanges with the North (*Izvestiia*, 18 January).

At the same time, the Soviets did not hide their differences with a regime that seemed as little interested in diplomatic progress as in internal reform. Moscow demonstrated some irritation with the North's rigid opposition to dealings with the South, noting that even a "neutral word" about South Korea is likely to draw denunciations from Pyongyang (*Izvestiia*, 31 March). Thus *Pravda* correspondent Sergei Tikhomirov wrote in his first report after taking his assignment in Pyongyang of "ups and downs" in Soviet–North Korean relations (*Pravda*, 25 March). Komsomol chief Vladimir Mironenko, interviewed by Tikhomirov at the World Festival of Youth and Students, criticized this event—the most important of the year to the North Koreans—as marred by "extremism" and "pseudorevolutionary attitudes" (*Pravda*, 10 July). Mironenko said that he found the event "pompous" and believed that its successors should rethink its anti-imperialist character in line with "new realities." Subsequent com-

mentary complained that North Korean authorities had blocked efforts by Soviets attending the festival to make contacts with North Korean citizens (Moscow International Service, 18 September).

In this atmosphere, bilateral relations were quiet in 1989. According to press reports, North Korea received a few more SU-25 ground attack aircraft (*Korea Herald*, 31 January), but there was little evidence of other major weapons deliveries. In August, North Korea celebrated the anniversary of Japan's defeat in World War II by, as usual, giving the Soviets only a supporting role in Kim Il-song's campaign to liberate his country. Moscow, in contrast, said that Korea owed its freedom to the defeat of Japanese forces by Soviet troops. In addition, there were relatively few exchanges of high-level visitors during the year. Supreme People's Assembly chairman Yang Hyong-sop visited Moscow in August, where he was hosted only by A. I. Lukyanov, first deputy chairman of the Supreme Soviet and a Central Committee candidate member (*Pravda*, 1 August). General I. M. Tretiyak, Soviet deputy defense minister and commander of the air defense forces, visited Pyongyang later that month and met with Kim Il-song and Defense Minister O Chin-u (KCNA, 17 August). In addition, according to South Korean media, North Korea and the Soviet Union conducted a "secret" joint exercise involving 50 aircraft and 40 ships (Seoul Domestic Service, 2 October).

The relative paucity of North Korean–Soviet contacts stood in marked contrast to the explosive growth in direct Soviet–South Korean trade and visits—albeit largely of low-level functionaries. Relations between Seoul and Moscow, which barely existed before 1988, became commonplace in 1989. The most visible development was the trip to Moscow of South Korean opposition leader Kim Yong-sam in June. Kim spent a week in Moscow, not only seeing Ho Tam, as noted above, but also having dialogues with Soviet academicians and politicians (*Korea Times*, 3 June). Although he did not see either President Gorbachev or Foreign Minister Shevardnadze, the joint communiqué issued at the end of Kim's visit promised Soviet cooperation in cultural relations and in permitting visits to South Korea by Koreans who had been moved to the island of Sakhalin—now in the Soviet Union—when it was under Japanese control (*Yonhap*, 10 June). In fact, the first Sakhalin Korean visited South Korea in April (*Kyodo*, 10 April). The atmosphere created by Kim's visit—in part because his trip was sanctioned by the government—gave rise to euphoric expectations that South Korea and the Soviet Union might establish diplomatic relations in 1990 (*Yonhap*, 23 June). The Chinese noted the optimism on this score of South Korean foreign minister Choe Ho-chung (XINHUA, 20 June).

The Soviets initially were more interested in economic exchanges than in diplomatic relations. They took public note of Hyundai honorary chairman Chong's visit to North Korea (TASS, 2 February), and leapfrogged ahead of Pyongyang in arranging for bilateral trade. Moscow openly acknowledged this development (*Izvestiia*, 5 January) and permitted a variety of South Korean firms, academicians, and cultural groups to open institutional ties. For example, the Soviets asked Samsung to build a "mammoth" trade center in Moscow as a joint venture with Soviet enterprises (*Korea Times*, 29 January). The two sides began negotiations to open direct sea transportation routes (*Korea Times*, 21 March) and to permit South Korean fishermen to ply waters near the Soviet Union (*Korea Times*, 31 January). The Soviet Union, which praised South Korean business success (Moscow, *Argument i Fakti*, 18–24 March), opened its trade office in Seoul in April (*Yonhap*, 3 April). Forty leading South Korean firms formed the Korea-USSR Economic Association in July (*Yonhap*, 18 July), and a large business delegation went to Moscow later that month (TASS, 31 July). Overall, bilateral trade reportedly increased 270 percent during the first two months of 1989 (*Korea Herald*, 25 March).

Moscow was reluctant to move to direct political relations and pressed for South Korean approval to have its trade office in Seoul perform consular functions. The South Koreans demurred, insisting that the Soviets set up a separate consular office. The Soviets gave in, and consular facilities opened in Seoul and Moscow on 8 December (*Yonhap*, 8 December).

South Korean economic and political relations with other communist countries also improved dramatically. Bilateral trade with Yugoslavia, which had been worth about $33,000,000 in 1988, was more than $17,000,000 in the first four months of 1989; both sides estimated the final figure for the year could reach $100,000,000 (*Tanjug*, 7, 8 June). The South Koreans valued overall trade with all communist countries at $632,000,000 in the first quarter of 1989. Exports in the January–March period rose 44.4 percent, to $163,000,000, whereas imports rose 47 percent, to $469,000,000.

The South exchanged trade offices with Bulgaria and Poland (Slovenia and Hungary had done so in 1988). Bulgaria, which had tried to benefit from imports of Japanese technology in the 1970s, seemed to harbor similar hopes regarding South Korea, whereas reformist Poland embarked on a program of cultural as well as economic exchanges (*Yonhap*, 4 May).

Hungary, along with Poland, the East European country farthest on the road to political and economic change, continued to have the best relations of any bloc country with South Korea and to draw the bulk of North Korean wrath. Daewoo, for example, embarked on a major joint venture in Hungary in 1989 for the production of automobiles and spare parts (*Korea Times*, 19 January). The next week, the Hungarian Presidential Council announced that Hungary would be the first communist country to establish diplomatic relations with South Korea (Budapest, MTI, 27 January). South Korean foreign minister Choe Ho-chung visited Budapest in March, where he met with General Secretary Károly Grósz (XINHUA, 31 March). TASS gave these developments favorable coverage, referring to "tempting (economic) proposals which are desirable to both sides" (TASS, 12 February), and a joint Hungarian–South Korean delegation visited Vladivostok to discuss exploitation of Siberian resources (Moscow Domestic Service, 9 February).

Pyongyang was not amused. It immediately downgraded diplomatic relations with Hungary to the chargé level and warned that Budapest faced "grave consequences" for its actions (Pyongyang Domestic Service, 2 February). *Nodong Sinmun* (18 February) criticized the "ridiculous excuse of those with a guilty conscience" and accused Hungary of "treacherous" behavior. The North did little besides complain, however, and Hungary went out of its way to demonstrate that it was not impressed. Further anti-Hungarian diatribes in the North Korean press (for example, KCNA, 27 June, 17 July) interfered with Hungary's ongoing re-evaluation of the Soviet invasion of 1956 by referring to the Imre Nagy period as "counterrevolutionary." Budapest reacted by reintroducing the requirement that North Koreans obtain visas before visiting Hungary (MTI, 21 July), leading North Korea to retaliate amid denunciation of Hungary's "monstrous strange step" (KCNA, 24 July).

Poland followed the Hungarian example and established diplomatic relations with South Korea (AFP, 1 November). North Korean officials in Beijing were quoted as "regretting" this move, and Pyongyang attacked the Poles for permitting their economic problems to lead them to this "unjust act"

(Pyongyang Domestic Service, 3 November). North Korea also expressed its displeasure with Yugoslavia when it became the third East European country to establish diplomatic relations with South Korea, but did not react as viscerally as it had with regard to Hungary. Foreign Minister Kim Yong-nam's visit to Belgrade in April apparently did not resolve bilateral differences, and the Yugoslavs stressed their right to formulate policy toward South Korea without consulting "anyone" (*Tanjug*, 13 April).

North Korea's relatively mild response to Polish and Yugoslav policies toward South Korea probably resulted from the change in the international communist environment. The establishment of Hungarian–South Korean ties took place when East European communism was still more or less intact; the North, therefore, could concentrate on pressing a socialist state not to break ranks with established bloc policy. By the time Poland and Yugoslavia established political ties with the South, however, East European communism was collapsing with dizzying speed. North Korea—rather than wasting its venom on dying parties—concentrated on shoring up relations with the few states where old-time communism seemed to still show signs of life.

North Korea clearly had better relations with more orthodox communist states and must have been deeply concerned when many of their leaders were overthrown in a breathtaking sequence of popular activity. Kim Il-song, for example, quoted approvingly a speech by Czechoslovak party boss Miloš Jakeš in which he criticized restructuring as an expression of the "exhaustion of socialism" (Pyongyang Domestic Service, 13 November). Jakeš, however, was deposed a few days later. It must have been dismaying to Pyongyang when such orthodox stalwarts as East Germany's Erich Honecker and Bulgaria's Todor Zhivkov were overthrown by the irresistible demand for change.

The execution of Romanian dictator Nicolae Ceauşescu and his wife—as of this writing, his son Nicu and other relatives remain alive, but seriously imperiled—carried a particularly chilling message to the Kim family. Like Kim Il-song, Ceauşescu had tried to create a dynasty and had held to a hard line in the midst of the reform movements sweeping the communist world. The North Korean media—which had published a long interview with Ceauşescu a few weeks before his fall (*Nodong Simnun*, 15 November)—issued a factual report of his execution (KCNA, 26 December) and spoke of the breakdown in public order caused by the civil war.

Pyongyang denied reports that North Korean troops had fought on Ceauşescu's side and issued a speedy, if terse, recognition of the new regime (KCNA, 26 December).

The North had been in enthusiastic agreement with Ceauşescu's staunch adherence to communist orthodoxy in the months before his ouster. In the early fall, Chief of Staff Choe Kwang visited both Zhivkov and Ceauşescu (Bucharest, Agerpres, 27 September; Sofia, BTA, 2 October). Romanian defense minister Milea, who later committed suicide or was executed, was received by Kim Il-song and O Chin-u in Pyongyang (KCNA, 3 October). At the end of October, North Korea and Romania announced that their citizens would no longer need visas when they visited each other's country (KCNA, 31 October). North Korean premier Yon Hyong-muk led a delegation to the Romanian Communist Party congress in November (KCNA, 20 November). Kim Yong-nam visited Romania for six days in December, resulting in the announcement that North Korea and Romania had agreed to create an antireform front (Seoul, *Tong-a Ilbo*, 7 December).

Kim visited East Berlin on the same trip, where he doubtless found little to be happy about. East Germany's tumultuous autumn almost certainly was greeted with alarm in Pyongyang. Not only had one more communist country strayed from the correct socialist path, but the specter of German reunification suggested a natural comparison with the Korean situation. Pyongyang media were low-keyed concerning Egon Krenz's replacement of longtime leader Erich Honecker and virtually silent about liberalized travel policies and other changes. The North did not echo suggestions in the South Korean press that the opening of the inner German border raised hopes for similar Korean developments (*Yonhap*, 11 November).

The many high-level exchanges between North Korean and East European hard-liners suggested the possibility that those communists opposed to Gorbachevian *glasnost'* felt the need to circle their wagons—even as the wagons began to disappear. Other than those mentioned above, the most notable North Korean contacts with orthodox East Europeans were as follows: Kim Il-song received a Czechoslovak military delegation, led by Defense Minister Milan Vaclavik, and a group of East German educators (KCNA, 19 September). So Kwan-hui, Central Committee secretary, led a delegation to Czechoslovakia in April (KCNA, 17 April), as did Politburo member So Yun-sok a few months later (Prague, CTK, 14 September). General Yi Pong-won, first deputy chief of the Korean People's Army Main Political Directorate, also visited Prague, where he met with President Gustáv Husák (Prague, *Rudé právo*, 27 May). North Korean defense minister O Chin-u, the third-ranking North Korean leader, traveled to Czechoslovakia (KCNA, 16 September) and East Germany, where he met with party chief Honecker (East Berlin, ADN International Service, 2 June). Vice-President Yi Chong-ok also visited East Berlin and held talks with then security chief Egon Krenz (ADN International Service, 12 July). KWP secretary Choe Tae-pok visited East Berlin in September (KCNA, 18 September). In the same month, Ho Tam visited Bulgaria (KCNA, 28 September).

Will the Kims also be swept away by an angry populace? Kim Il-song still appears to enjoy some personal legitimacy, but the country's deepening economic problems and its outmoded brand of Stalinist orthodoxy are increasingly anachronistic. Although the father may be secure, the events in Eastern Europe almost certainly hurt his son's chances for succession. Kim Chong-il has neither his father's charisma nor anti-Japanese credentials and may eventually be pushed aside by other leaders, the army, or even a popular movement.

In the short run, however, North Korea's diplomatic problems with some communist countries may have actually helped Pyongyang achieve limited contact with the United States. Washington seemed less unwilling to permit meetings with North Korean diplomats, perhaps because South Korea was having so much success establishing ties with the Soviet Union and its East European allies. According to Chinese media the State Department "confirmed" that U.S. diplomats had met with North Koreans twice in Beijing, once on 6 December 1988 and once on 24 January (XINHUA, 27 January). South Korean media reported State Department briefings on a similar meeting on 28 February (*Tong-a Ilbo*, 21 March). Chu Chang-chun, North Korea's ambassador to China, told reporters that the fourth meeting between U.S. and North Korean diplomats—held in Beijing on 15 May— had included discussions on terrorism, North-South dialogue, and Korean War missing in action issues (*Tong-a Ilbo*, 31 May). The two sides discussed the same issues in their fifth meeting in Beijing on 1 November (KCNA, 3 November).

Other, more informal U.S.–North Korean contacts also took place. In April, three North Korean academicians were permitted to attend a conference at the University of Hawaii, the first time an academic visit had been allowed since North Korean historians attended a meeting at George Washington University in Washington, D.C., in 1985 (XINHUA, 11 April). In October, Gaston Sigur, former assistant secretary of state for East Asian affairs, visited Pyongyang, where he met with Yi Chong-ok, Kim Yong-nam, and Ho Tam (Pyongyang Domestic Service, 25, 27, 29 October). Sigur reportedly invited Ho Tam to visit the United States in 1990 (*Tong-a Ilbo*, 1 November), but denied rumors that he met with Kim Il-song (*Yonhap*, 29 October). The North Korean press carried positive appraisals of his talks, signaling Pyongyang's interest in further meetings (Pyongyang Domestic Service, 27 October). At the same time, the North Koreans hosted Arthur Hummel, former U.S. ambassador to China (KCNA, 27 October).

Relations with China. Chinese–North Korean relations improved somewhat in 1989 after the events in Tiananmen Square, but significant differences remained, in part because of continuing differences over China's economic reforms and its openness toward the West and South Korea. There was no evidence by the end of 1989 that Deng Xiaoping's crackdown against the students and the purge of Zhao Ziyang would lead to a change in China's willingness to deal with the South. Beijing, like Moscow, encouraged the North to be receptive to North-South dialogue, positively noting elements of South Korea's position on the various negotiating forums (for example, Beijing International Service, 10 January).

Beijing showed its enthusiasm in public for trade with the South. Premier Li Peng noted that the two countries had economic relations (XINHUA, 20 March). A reporter from Shanghai urged his country to develop economic relations with South Korea (Shanghai, *Shijie Jingji Daobao*, 16 January), and it appeared the Chinese would do exactly that. The two sides agreed in May to open a direct line for container ships through a joint venture shipping company (*Yonhap*, 25 May). In August—after the crackdown against the students—they set up a group to coordinate responses to problems arising between South Korean traders and Chinese officials (*Yonhap*, 1 August). The total value of trade in 1988 reportedly topped $3 billion, including $2 billion in direct trade. The South Koreans reportedly expected trade to drop a little in 1989, primarily because of China's economic austerity program (*Korea Times*, 13 May). The only apparent problems in bilateral relations stemmed from South Korea's first trade surplus in 1988—$383,000,000 in direct trade—and from the South's acceptance of a defecting People's Liberation Army major and his wife in July (Seoul Domestic Service, 29 July). Beijing demanded their return, claiming that "external factors" had influenced their decision to cross the demilitarized zone at Panmunjom (Hong Kong, AFP, 3 August). As to trade, the overall decline in exchanges reported after the Tiananmen Square crackdown led to a Chinese surplus of $5 million in April and May (*Yonhap*, 24 August).

North Korea did not permit China's dealings with South Korea to ruin the overall bilateral relationship. Ho Tam visited Beijing in March and held substantive discussions with Zhao Ziyang. According to the Chinese media, Zhao told Ho that Chinese economic development would be slowed over the next two years (XINHUA, 14 March). Zhao himself traveled to Pyongyang in April shortly before the onset of China's internal crisis. The visit apparently went well, although North Korean media implied that the relationship was going through "trials" (KCNA, 29 April). Zhao was met at the airport by both Kim Il-song and Kim Chong-il (Pyongyang Domestic Service, 24 April). He met twice with both Kims—a virtually unprecedented development (KCNA, 24–26 April). This treatment did not seem to indicate a general increase in Kim Chong-il's involvement in foreign policy because he neither held any public meetings with other leaders nor sent greater numbers of official greetings to foreign dignitaries.

North Korea, nevertheless, almost certainly was miffed by China's trade relations with South Korea and nervous about its improving relationship with the Soviet Union. Since at least 1961, Pyongyang had been able to play its two giant neighbors off against each other, attracting aid from them both while preventing either from gaining an overbearing influence on North Korean policy. The North gave virtually no coverage to the Deng-Gorbachev summit in May (a point noted in *Kyodo* on 18 May).

That development, which should have marked a cardinal development in international communist relations, was immediately overshadowed by the chaos in Tiananmen Square. North Korea did not immediately react to Chinese internal developments, although a Japanese newspaper reported that the North had evacuated five hundred of its students from Beijing (Tokyo, *Sankai Simbun*, 15 June). Kim Il-song sent pro forma greetings to Jiang Zemin, who replaced the disgraced Zhao Ziyang as

party boss in June (XINHUA, 26 June). The next month, however, Kim reportedly expressed support for the crackdown against the students, saying that he supported "all measures" taken by the Chinese regime (XINHUA, 6 July). Ho Tam told a visiting Chinese delegation that North Korea supported their government's suppression of the "counterrevolutionary riot" (Beijing International Service, 30 August). In October, North Korea returned a dissident to China who had fled to the North shortly after the crackdown (Hong Kong, AFP, 12 October). A 22 October article in *Nodong Sinmun*—reprinted approvingly in *Renmin Ribao* in support of the prevailing Chinese line—urged people to combat imperialist efforts to sow discord in the communist world using the tactic of "peaceful evolution" (*Renmin Ribao*, 23 October).

The pace of Sino–North Korean relations quickened in the wake of the crackdown in Beijing. Kim Yong-sun, director of the KWP's International Department, visited China in August and held "cordial and friendly" conversations with Chinese officials (Shanghai City Service, 8 August). General Choe Kwang, KPA chief of staff, also visited Beijing in August, where he met with his counterpart, General Chi Haotian, and with Jiang Zemin (Beijing International Service, 30 August). Jiang Zemin also met with visiting North Korean Supreme People's Assembly vice-chairman Song Son-pil in September (XINHUA, 19 September). Kim Il-song offered further praise for Beijing's crackdown the next week (XINHUA, 24 September), as did Kye Ung-tae, who headed a delegation visiting China (XINHUA, 25 September). PLA Military Commission deputy general secretary Liu Huaqing met with O Chin-u in Pyongyang (XINHUA, 3 October). Vice-President Yi Chong-ok led North Korea's delegation to the 40th anniversary of the People's Republic in October and met with Deng Xiaoping (XINHUA, 1 October).

Kim Il-song's greetings to the Chinese leadership on that occasion implied less than complete satisfaction with their performance by congratulating them for quelling "in time" the "counterrevolutionary riot" (KCNA, 30 September). It is likely that he reacted to China's troubles much as he had to the dislocations caused by the Great Proletarian Cultural Revolution two decades earlier. Kim dislikes chaos and almost certainly disapproved of Beijing's initial inability to control its internal developments. This distaste for disorder might explain his comments to Chinese students that "only after you secure stability can we have it" (Beijing Television Service, 8 July).

His concerns over developments in China and other communist countries may have spurred the Great Leader's visit to Beijing in November (Seoul Television Service, AFP, *Kyodo*, 5 November). Kim met with Deng Xiaoping, Jiang Zemin, and Li Peng (Pyongyang Domestic Service, 12 November). This trip was not announced beforehand, but was confirmed afterwards by the North Korean and Chinese press (XINHUA, Pyongyang Domestic Service, 12 November). An official of the North Korean embassy in Beijing originally denied that Kim was in town (Seoul, *Chosun Ilbo*, 7 November). Kim, who hosted Zhao Ziyang shortly before his fall, may have wanted to size up Jiang, Zhao's successor as party boss. Press reports speculated that Kim and his hosts also discussed their mutual antipathy toward reform in the communist world (*Korea Times*, 7 November). Some commentators also suggested that Kim met with former U.S. secretary of state Henry Kissinger—who was in Beijing at the same time—to discuss developments in U.S.-North Korean relations (*Kyodo*, 6 November).

As noted above, China showed no sign that its internal crackdown would lead to any change in its openness toward trade with South Korea. But Beijing may have appreciated—or even anticipated— North Korea's support for its actions. Chinese media issued strong rhetorical support for the North's position on reunification (Beijing, *Renmin Ribao*, 28 July) and noted the North's "celebration" of anti-U.S. struggle day (*Renmin Ribao*, 25 June). Late in the year—in an unusual nod to Kim Il-song's son and heir—the Chinese press quoted Kim Chong-il's interview with Cuban reporters concerning Korea's resistance to imperialism (*Renmin Ribao*, 5 December).

Relations with Japan. Although none of the issues marring North Korean–Japanese relations was settled in 1989, the bilateral atmosphere improved considerably. Pyongyang did not end its standard criticism of Japanese policies in East Asia, but it expressed willingness to discuss outstanding problems.

Pyongyang signaled its willingness to talk to Tokyo in January, when media sources reported the North's positive reaction to Japanese feelers through "various channels" (KCNA, 12 January). The North Koreans still demanded satisfaction on issues ranging from an apology for World War II atrocities to disputes over captured fishermen, the Japanese position regarding recognition of South Korea, and allegations that North Korea sabotaged a South Korean airliner in 1987. North Korea's official Foreign Ministry spokesman stressed the "obstacles" to better relations, suggesting the possibility of some disagreement within the Pyongyang regime over whether to soften relations with Japan (KCNA, 11 January). Later in January, North Korea issued a demand—which Japan rejected—that the latter return to North Korea a man who had stowed away on a ship to Japan in 1983 before Pyongyang would agree to free the crew of the *Fujisan Maru*, a ship that had been captured in 1987 (*Kyodo*, 27 January).

North Korea's traditional anti-Japanese policy was put under some pressure by discussions between South Koreans and officials of the Japanese Socialist Party (JSP), heretofore sympathetic to the North. Former JSP chairman Ishibashi Masashi held talks with Kim Yong-sam, a development probably revealed in advance to a group of North Koreans who visited Japan at JSP invitation (*Kyodo*, 21, 23, 30 January). After the meeting with Kim the JSP issued a statement promising a more "balanced" approach to the Korean Peninsula (*Korea Herald*, 1 February). Rumors that Japanese government officials would talk to the North Koreans—perhaps an appropriate balance to the Ishibashi-Kim meeting—proved false (*Asahi Shimbun*, 27 January).

By March, however, the Takeshita government was ready for better relations with North Korea. The prime minister himself issued an expression of "regret" for Japan's conduct toward *all* Koreans during World War II and referred for the first time to the "Democratic People's Republic of Korea" (*Kyodo*, 30 March). North Korea's ambassador to China—who could have chosen to be dissatisfied that this did not constitute a formal apology—praised the statement; South Korean officials said they would not oppose improved relations between Tokyo and Pyongyang (*Kyodo*, 30 March). But Ho Tam, after a meeting with a JSP delegation, called the Japanese statement "too vague" and insisted that Tokyo follow its words with action (*Kyodo*, March 31; Pyongyang Domestic Service, 31 March). In July, Ho once more criticized Japan's "hostile policy" and called on Tokyo to make a tangible demonstration of its sincerity (*Asahi Shimbun*, 11 July).

If these reactions reflected a difference of opinion over policy, that issue was at least temporarily settled by Kim Il-song's praise for the Takeshita remarks on 4 April (*Kyodo*, 4 April). Kim expressed his hope for better bilateral relations to a JSP delegation, whose leader—Secretary General Tanabe Makoto—said he hoped the way would now be open for contacts between North Korea and Japan's ruling Liberal Democratic Party (LDP). Japanese foreign minister Uno, in turn, said that North Korea had shown a "positive stance" in its reaction to Takeshita's comments (*Kyodo*, 4 April). LDP officials subsequently offered the hope of early talks with North Korea (*Kyodo*, 22 June), and the government announced it would support sports and cultural exchanges (*Korea Herald*, 26 May). In August, Japan relaxed restrictions on tours to North Korea that had been in effect since the alleged North Korean sabotage of the Korean airliner (*Korea Herald*, 13 August).

The Chinese, meanwhile, reported that Takeshita had sent a letter to Kim Il-song expressing hope for "early dialogue" (*Renmin Ribao*, 1 April). Chinese foreign minister Qian Qichen denied rumors that Premier Li Peng had agreed to mediate an improvement in Japanese–North Korean relations, but said that Li had praise for recent developments (*Kyodo*, 18 April).

Nothing tangible came of these feelers as Japan became preoccupied with its internal political scandals. In October, Foreign Minister Nakayama gave a speech supporting South Korea's drive for U.N. membership, thus eliciting the predictable North Korean denunciation (*Kyodo*, 3 October). Still, the North remained interested in improving bilateral relations and in October welcomed the first Japanese tourists since March 1988 (*Kyodo*, 8 October).

Relations with the Third World. Cuba continued to be a favored partner for North Korea both because of Havana's support for the North's position on the 1988 Olympic Games and as a result of Fidel Castro's leading role in criticizing reform movements sweeping the communist world. One remarkable sign of good bilateral relations was a rare interview granted by Kim Chong-il to the Cuban party organ *Granma* in December (KCNA, 4 December). In addition, Politburo member Kye Ungtae went to Havana in June and met with Castro (Pyongyang Domestic Service, 10 June). Yang Hyong-sop, chairman of the Standing Committee of the Supreme People's Assembly, had already visited Cuba in January (KCNA, 12 January). On 27 December, in the wake of the momentous changes that 1989 brought to the communist world, a *Nodong Sinmun* editorial singled out Cuba, China, and

North Korea as the special targets of an imperialist offensive that threatened to destabilize world socialism. The North criticized the U.S. invasion of Panama primarily in terms of its role in Washington's campaign against Cuba (KCNA, 28 December).

North Korea had its usual share of exchanges with other neutral and nonaligned states in 1989. Foreign Minister Kim Yong-nam attended a meeting of his colleagues from the Non-Aligned Movement in Cyprus in January (KCNA, 10 January). He paid a visit to Yugoslavia in April, where he held talks with President Raif Dizdarevic and Foreign Minister Budimir Loncar (Belgrade, TANJUG, 11 April). Premier Yon Hyong-muk attended the nonaligned summit in Belgrade in September (TANJUG, September 3). Vice-President Yi Chong-ok led a delegation to Nicaragua in July (KCNA, 10 July). Yang, in addition, was hosted by Togolese president Eyadema in March (KCNA, 18 March). Chong Chun-ki, a candidate member of the Politburo and a vice-premier, went to Pakistan in May and held talks with Prime Minister Bhutto (Islamabad Domestic Service, 23 May). Bangladeshi foreign minister Mahmud visited Pyongyang in August (Dhaka Domestic Service, August 25). External Economic Affairs Minister Chong Songnam was especially busy in 1989, visiting Iran in January (Teheran Domestic Service, 5 January), perhaps in preparation for Iranian president Ali Khamenei's visit to Pyongyang in May (KCNA, 14 May). Chong also visited Angola and Ethiopia in August (KCNA, 21 August).

After a flurry of diplomatic activity in 1987 and 1988, North Korea finally did host a meeting between the warring factions in the Cambodian conflict. Prince Norodom Sihanouk made his usual visits to Pyongyang, this year in April, June, and October, and saw Kim Il-song at least three times (*Renmin Ribao*, 10 June; KCNA, 8 April, 8 June, 31 October). As in previous years, there is no evidence Sihanouk saw Kim Chong-il. Khieu Samphan, Democratic Kampuchean vice-president, arrived in Pyongyang on 19 June and took part in a "working meeting" with Sihanouk (Beijing Radio, in Cambodian, 20 June).

North and South Korea took different tacks in their overall diplomatic competition in 1989. In the wake of its Olympic triumph in 1988, the South felt secure enough to close embassies in Burkina Faso, Niger, the Central African Republic, and Barbados (*Yonhap*, 19 May). This went against the grain of Seoul's traditional preoccupation with maximizing the number of its missions abroad in order to underscore its wide international presence compared to Pyongyang.

North Korea, in contrast, attempted to expand its international representation. In particular, it sent feelers to Australia (Hong Kong, AFP, 18 January) and the Philippines (Manila, *Manila Chronicle*, 18 January), countries traditionally suspicious of the Kim regime. Taiwan also indicated some interest in better relations with the North (Taipei, *Chung-kuo Shih Pao*, 15 August). In addition, North Korea established diplomatic relations with Peru (KCNA, 21 November).

The Thirteenth World Festival of Youth and Students. On 1 July, 30,000 participants from 170 countries took part in the opening ceremonies of the flagship celebration of the World Federation of Democratic Youth, a major Soviet front organization. This event was the largest ever held in North Korea. Pyongyang explicitly used it as a counter to the 1988 Seoul Olympic Games, quoting international press reaction that allegedly showed that the festival surpassed the Olympics "in all respects" (KCNA, 8 July). The main stadium could seat 150,000 spectators, 50 percent more than the Seoul main Olympic stadium. The North mobilized vast numbers of troops and construction workers to build facilities and transportation for the event, costing—according to various press sources—several billion dollars. Kim Il-song spoke at the opening and closing events and made visits to several international delegations—most notably the Cubans—during the week (KCNA, Pyongyang Domestic Service, 1–9 July). Kim Chong-il also made one of his rare public appearances at the festival (Pyongyang Television Service, 1 July).

Despite some problems posed by students unfurling banners protesting China's crackdown against its students (Pyongyang Television Service, 1 July) and by the negative Soviet commentary noted above, the North could be generally satisfied with the publicity it attracted. Although the festival could not compare with the Olympics in terms of its international television audience, North Korea did gather an impressive array of international leaders under one roof. The Soviet Union and its Warsaw Pact allies were represented at the Politburo level (TASS, 29 June; KCNA, 1–8 July).

David B. Kanin
Washington, D.C.

Laos

Population. 3,935,786. Growth rate is 2.2 percent.
Party. Lao People's Revolutionary Party (Phak Pasason Pativat Lao; LPRP)
Founded. 22 March 1955
Membership. 40,000
General Secretary. Kaysone Phomvihane (69), Lao-Vietnamese, premier
Politburo. 13 members: Kaysone Phomvihane; Nouhak Phoumsavan; Souphanouvong, president; Phoumi Vongvichit, acting president; Khamtai Siphandon; Phoun Sipaseut; Sisomphon Lovansai; Sisavat Keobounphan; Sali Vongkhamsao; Maichantan Sengmani; Saman Vi-gnaket, Oudom Khatthi-gna, alternate; Choummali Saignakon, alternate
Secretariat. 9 members: Kaysone Phomvihane, Khamtai Siphandon, Sisavat Keobounphan, Sali Vongkhamsao, Maichantan Sengmani, Saman Vi-gnaket, Oudom Khatthi-gna, Choummali Saignason, Somlat Chanthamat
Central Committee. 49 full members, 9 alternate members
Status. Ruling and sole legal party
Last Congress. Fourth, 13–15 November 1986, in Vientiane
Last Election. 26 March
Auxiliary Organizations. Lao Front for National Construction, Lao People's Revolutionary Youth Union, Federation of Lao Trade Unions, Federation of Lao Women's Unions, Lao Buddhist Fellowship Organization
Publications. *Pasason* (The People), LPRP central organ, published in Vientiane (daily); *Alun Mai* (New Dawn), LPRP theoretical journal, published in Vientiane (quarterly); the official news agency is Khaosan Pathet Lao (Pathet Lao News Agency; KPL)

Elections were held on 26 March for the 79 seats in the Supreme People's Assembly (SPA), which is officially described as the supreme power body of the Lao People's Democratic Republic (LPDR), with the duty of implementing the line, plans, and policies of the LPRP through the laws of the state (Radio Vientiane, 24 February; *FBIS*, 1 March).

The SPA replaces the Supreme People's Council, which was hastily organized by the LPRP on the eve of its consolidation of power in 1975.

The election of the SPA endows the LPDR for the first time with a channel for the national-level expression of popular will other than the "democratic centralism" of the LPRP. Its inaugural session during May and June dealt mainly with organizational matters and heard reports on the elections, the economy, and foreign affairs. A large part of the second session in November was taken up with deliberations of four draft laws on legal procedures. Work was reported going ahead on the "difficult task" of drafting the country's constitution, which most observers agree is the SPA's most important agenda item.

In international relations, the most noteworthy events were the normalization of relations with China at the party and state levels and Premier Kaysone's visit to China in October. Also important were Kaysone's visits to Japan in November and to France in December, which marked a further extension of the LPDR's opening to foreign countries. The normalization of relations with China allows the LPDR to gain freedom to maneuver by balancing its two powerful allies, Beijing and Hanoi, much in the manner Ho Chi Minh balanced Moscow and Beijing in the 1960s. This was not possible so long as the LPDR was constrained by Vietnam to treat China as an enemy.

Party Leadership and Organization. The LPRP observed its 34th anniversary by strongly affirming its role as the organizer and leader of all the victories of the Lao revolution and the genuine Marxist-Leninist party of the Lao workers, continuing the cause of the Indochinese Communist Party and showing the way to "the new glorious era of our Lao nation—an era of independence, democracy, and social progress" (Radio Vientiane, 22 March; *FBIS*, 24 March). Although General Secretary Kaysone is addressed on ceremonial occasions as "respected" by his Politburo colleagues, there is little evidence of the development of a personality cult within the LPRP, whose top leadership underwent no changes during 1989.

President Souphanouvong's 80th birthday on 13 July was the occasion for all-around praise, congratulatory messages from abroad, and awarding of medals. Souphanouvong, still recovering from an unspecified incapacitation in 1986, took it all calmly, vowing to continue contributing to the great cause of national liberation and social transforma-

tion under the LPRP's leadership (Radio Vientiane, 14 July; *FBIS*, 17 July).

Domestic Party Affairs. The date for elections to the SPA having been set in a decree from Premier Kaysone's office broadcast on 11 January (Radio Vientiane, *FBIS*, 11 January), eligible voters eighteen and over went to the polling places on 26 March. Party committees had received instructions to scrutinize carefully the goals of all candidates "to ensure that their standards are suitable" (Radio Vientiane, 17 February; *FBIS*, 24 February). Delaying and repeatedly revising the approved lists of candidates reportedly caused "a negative line of thinking; affecting confidence in the laws; and bringing about waste in energy, intelligence, money, and other assets" (Radio Vientiane, 20 May; *FBIS*, 31 May), but in spite of this 121 candidates passed the test. Voting appears to have proceeded uneventfully.

Sixty-five of the 79 members of the SPA are reported to be LPRP members. Two LPRP Politburo members were candidates: Nouhak Phoumsavan was elected from Savannakhet province and Sali Vongkhamsao was elected from Champassak province. Another notable member is Mrs. Thongvin Phomvihane, an LPRP Central Committee (CC) member and Kaysone's wife, elected from Vientiane municipality. LPRP CC member Thongsing Thammavong was elected from Houa Phan province, and LPRP CC alternate member Chaleun Yiapaoheu was elected from Luang Prabang province. Souban Salitthilat, a deputy foreign minister, was elected from Luang Prabang province. (Radio Vientiane, *FBIS*, 12 April.)

Ethnically, 66 SPA members belong to the Lao Loum, nine to the Lao Theuang, and four to the Lao Soung groups. Most have received secondary education or more, with 30 having university or graduate education. The majority are between 30 and 50 years old, the youngest being 32 and the eldest, 75.

Casting his ballot at Wat Pakthong in Vientiane, Premier Kaysone told reporters that the election marked a major turning point for Laos. He would not retire because the people would not let him. A draft constitution would be completed "in about one year or more" and then would be distributed to the people to be debated. After that, a new government would be formed. He did not know whether more than one party would be allowed "because that will be up to those who make the constitution." (Bangkok, *Nation*, 27 March; *FBIS*, 27 March.)

The SPA held its inaugural session from 30 May

to 1 June, with 71 of its members in attendance, and heard a report of the National Electoral Committee and a report on domestic and foreign affairs from Premier Kaysone. It elected Nouhak chairman and Thongsing vice-chairman. Standing Committee members were Somphavan Inthavong, Phai Oula, Phou Latsaphon, and Bounmi Pakthavong. The session also established the following commissions: Secretariat; Legal; Economy, Planning, and Finance; Foreign Relations; and Cultural and Social Affairs. The session approved the 1989 budget plan of the Council of Ministers. It heard a lecture by Nouhak on the duties and responsibilities of the SPA and its members. (Radio Vientiane, 1 June; *FBIS*, 2 June.)

Kaysone's speech represented a major statement of position and goals in foreign relations and domestic policy (Radio Vientiane, 3 June; *FBIS*, 20 June). In his lecture, Nouhak explained the SPA's organizational structure and role. (Radio Vientiane, 1–2 June; *FBIS*, 22 June.)

At the second session of the SPA, 20–24 November, Nouhak announced that the appointment of Det, director of the intermediate-level law school, to be chief of the Supreme People's Court had been unanimously endorsed; that the appointment of Phai Oula, member of the SPA Standing Committee and head of the Legal Commission, to be the director of the People's Judiciary Institute had been similarly endorsed; and that the SPA Standing Committee had been enlarged by the addition of Chaleun Yiapaoheu (Radio Vientiane, 24 November; *FBIS*, 27 November).

Kaysone gave the members a lecture in which, quoting Ho Chi Minh, he defined the three characteristics of laws: their class features, their use as a tool to regulate social relations with definite limits, and their use by the state to strengthen and increase the efficiency of its management (Radio Vientiane, 24 November; *FBIS*, 27 November). The session endorsed draft laws on criminal law, on procedures of criminal cases, on people's courts, and on people's judiciary institutes. Nouhak in his closing speech called the four draft laws "a direct contribution to the establishment of the draft constitution which we are now studying." (Radio Vientiane, 25 November; *FBIS*, 27 November.) He warned against acting in haste, quoting the Lao proverb "Firm steps, not running, lead to quick success," which apparently also applies to work on the draft constitution, for the only concrete step reported with respect to this task in the course of 1989 was the convening of a Constitution Drafting Commit-

tee under Nouhak's chairmanship on 16 August and the establishment of a standing committee and three subcommittees (Radio Vientiane, 16 August; *FBIS*, 17 August).

Aside from adding to the institutional structure of the LPDR, the year also saw passage of a number of important regulations. Regulations on the responsibilities, roles, rights, and duties of local people's councils were enacted on 25 January (Radio Vientiane, 4 February; *FBIS*, 6 February). A provisional regulation governing all types of agricultural land was issued on 21 March (Radio Vientiane, 5 April; *FBIS*, 14 April). A resolution on management of rates of exchange between the kip and foreign currencies was issued on 19 July (Radio Vientiane, 25 July; *FBIS*, 26 July). A decree on bank interest rates was issued on 1 July (Radio Vientiane, 27 July; *FBIS*, 28 July). A decree on bank credit policy was issued on 1 July (Radio Vientiane, 28 July; *FBIS*, 2 August). Regulations governing the registration of state and collective enterprises, state–private sector partnerships, and private firms were issued on 1 July (Radio Vientiane, 4 August; *FBIS*, 15 August). New income tax rates for state and collective business organizations, state–private sector partnerships, private companies, and individuals were promulgated in decree No. 47 (Radio Vientiane, 16 August; *FBIS*, 21 August). Kaysone gave a lengthy speech at the first nationwide banking conference in Vientiane on 20 July (Radio Vientiane, 7, 9–14 August; *FBIS*, 22 August).

In an important series of articles published in *Pravda* in December 1988, Kaysone described Lao as state capitalist (Radio Vientiane, 9–11 December 1988; *FBIS*, 19, 29 December 1988) and went on to describe at some length his thinking about the reforms that have been introduced to the LPDR economy since 1985 under the name New System of Economic Management. Initially, the reform program focused on extending autonomy to state enterprises, but emphasis increasingly was given to removal of government restrictions on trade, elimination of the system of multiple exchange rates, and placing greater reliance on markets and market-determined prices. In the agricultural sector, procurement prices were raised to market levels and preferential treatment of cooperatives and state farms was officially abolished. These policy shifts resulted in a substantial improvement in the domestic terms of trade in favor of agriculture and provided incentives for farmers to raise output. Market inflation also slowed considerably from its pre-1985 levels, although recently it has accelerated somewhat, mainly due to drought in 1987–1988. Several joint ventures have been formed, mostly with Thai firms, opening the possibility of export expansion. The regulations and decrees outlined above are part of the continuing effort to reduce consumer subsidies, reduce the size of the civil service, and place the country's finances on a stronger footing.

Although the LPDR's exports of hydroelectric power to Thailand have fallen off sharply in value terms in recent years—partly due to lower production because of drought and partly because of a new negotiated price less favorable to the LPDR— timber exports have increased at a rapid rate. In 1989 for the first time the LPDR had a trade surplus with Thailand. Timber exports have been particularly heavy since Thailand imposed a nationwide ban on logging and have led some to express alarm at the rate of deforestation in Laos. There are signs that the LPDR government is aware of the problem. An unusually sharp attack on Thai commercial interests broadcast on Radio Vientiane on 4 July, which implied that they represented an imperialistic policy, may not have been unconnected with this timber trade. The LPDR was quick to disavow the broadcast (which coincided with a visit to Vientiane by Vietnam Communist Party general secretary Nguyen Van Linh and Socialist Republic of Vietnam premier Do Muoi), and it had no lasting effect on LPDR-Thai relations. (*FEER*, 27 July.)

The Seventh Plenum of the LPRP Fourth Congress was convened from 25 January to 7 February in Vientiane (Radio Vientiane, 7 February; *FBIS*, 8 February).

The first official confirmation of the death of former King Savang Vatthana came in a press conference on 14 December by Premier Kaysone on his visit to France. Kaysone did not give the date of the king's death, but said he was aged 69. (AFP, 14 December; *FBIS*, 18 December.) Unconfirmed reports several years ago said the king had died in a reeducation camp in 1978.

Auxiliary Organizations. The Third Congress of the Lao Buddhist Fellowship Organization convened in Vientiane on 24 February. Acting President Phoumi Vongvichit told 150 monks in attendance that the government planned to enhance the role of Buddhism in Laos. (Radio Vientiane, 24 February; *FBIS*, 3 March.)

The Lao Front for National Construction, which had come in for considerable criticism for its man-

ifold failures in organizing the three rounds of elections to people's councils in 1988–1989, held a meeting in Vientiane on 21 April under the chairmanship of Phoumi Vongvichit. The meeting heard reports of achievements and shortcomings and "held penetrating discussions and consultations aimed at finalizing the report to be addressed at the enlarged meetings scheduled to be held in Vientiane Municipality, Xieng Khouang, Luang Prabang, and Champassak Provinces." (Radio Vientiane, 21 April; *FBIS*, 26 April.) The enlarged regional meetings were reported held during May and June.

The Federation of Lao Trade Unions (FLTU) held its second national congress in Vientiane on 26–28 April with 371 delegates (Radio Vientiane, 28 April; *FBIS*, 28 April). A new executive board of the FLTU CC was elected consisting of 27 members and a five-person standing committee. Elected president and vice-president, respectively, were Bounthan Souvannasouk and Amphonnali Keola. (Radio Vientiane, 29 April; *FBIS*, 1 May.)

International Views, Positions, and Activities. In line with the unannounced withdrawal from Laos of Vietnamese troops and economic advisers, relations between the LPDR and the Socialist Republic of Vietnam (SRV) took on the more normal aspects of relations between sovereign states. In LPRP statements, however, there continued to be evocation of "the special relations, great solidarity, and all-around cooperation between our two parties, two states, and two peoples" (message of greeting on the Communist Party of Vietnam (CPV) founding anniversary, Radio Vientiane, 6 February; *FBIS*, 7 February).

Exchanges of high-level visits between Laos and Vietnam were as frequent as ever in 1989. SRV defense minister Le Duc Anh visited Vientiane for the 40th anniversary of the Lao People's Army on 20 January (Radio Vientiane, 21 January; *FBIS*, 26 January). A delegation of the LPRP CC Organization and Inspection Board led by its chairman, Maichantan Sengmani, paid a five-day visit to the SRV in March (Radio Vientiane, 14 March; *FBIS*, 15 March). SRV interior minister Mai Chi Tho paid a working visit to the LPDR in April (Radio Vientiane, 8 April; *FBIS*, 10 April). Another SRV visitor in April was Information Minister Tran Hoan (Radio Vientiane, 14 April; *FBIS*, 17 April). Ho Chi Minh's birthday on 19 May was marked by a meeting in Vientiane attended by one thousand persons (Radio Vientiane, 22 May; *FBIS*, 23 May).

CPV general secretary Nguyen Van Linh and

SRV premier Do Muoi paid an official friendship visit to the LPDR 2–4 July; the concluding joint communiqué said the following of the two sides:

They expressed the firm confidence of the CPV and the LPRP in the final victory of socialism. The road to that goal for agriculturally backward and war-torn countries like Vietnam and Laos is long and strewn with obstacles and trials, but victory is certain. That glorious cause can and will certainly be brought to victory if the leading revolutionary party firmly grasps Marxism-Leninism and creatively applies it to the concrete historic conditions of the time, bases itself on the people, knows how to unite them, relies on the worker-peasant-intellectual alliance and international solidarity, and steadfastly marches forward on the road to socialism. (Radio Vientiane, 4 July; FBIS, 7 July.)

One of the results of the Linh–Do Muoi visit was the signing of a new agreement on cooperation in the economic, cultural, scientific, and technical fields (Radio Vientiane, 26 September; FBIS, 27 September).

Fresh reports of the diminishing Vietnamese presence in the LPDR circulated in 1989. One such report, based on Western sources in Vientiane, affirmed that there were fewer than twenty thousand Vietnamese troops left in Laos (AFP, 23 March; FBIS, 24 March). A Japanese report, quoting a Vietnamese high command source in Hanoi, stated that Vietnam no longer maintained battle-ready troops in Laos (Kyodo, FBIS, 12 April). Diplomatic sources in Phnom Penh were quoted in another Japanese report as saying that Vietnamese economic advisers, as well as two army divisions, had been withdrawn from Laos (Kyodo, 25 June; FBIS, 26 June).

LPRP CC secretary Oudom Khatthi-gna conferred medals on three Vietnamese experts in recognition of their contributions to Laos under a cooperation agreement between the two party organization boards (Radio Vientiane, 6 November; FBIS, 9 November). At another medal-awarding ceremony in Hanoi, eighteen Vietnamese experts received Laotian orders and medals for their contributions to national construction and defense in the LPDR (Radio Hanoi, FBIS, 29 November).

Relations between Laos and China were fully normalized in 1989. As one step in this process, an eight-member economic reform study group from the LPDR, led by Somsavat Lengsavat of the Council of Ministers Office, paid a two-week visit to China in May (Radio Beijing, 12, 18, 26 May). A trade agreement between the two countries was signed in Vientiane on 31 May (XINHUA, 2 June). A first round of talks on a draft provisional agreement on border affairs was reported to have concluded successfully in Vientiane (Radio Vientiane, 8 June; FBIS, 9 June). Radio Vientiane noted that when Kaysone received Chinese ambassador Liang Feng on 1 July he stated "that the Lao people have followed developments of the recent unrest in China with concern and stressed that all acts of imposing pressure or interfering in China's internal affairs run counter to international tradition." The meeting proceeded in a warm atmosphere of understanding, and Kaysone asked the ambassador to convey his best wishes to General Secretary Jiang Zemin. (Radio Vientiane, 2 July; FBIS, 3 July.)

Next, a delegation led by Thongsavat Khaikhamphithoun, deputy head of the Commission for Foreign Relations of the LPRP CC and first deputy foreign minister, paid a week-long official visit to China in August (KPL, 12 August; FBIS, 14 August). In Beijing, CC Politburo member Wu Xueqian was reported to have "expressed happiness over the agreement reached by the CPC and the LPRP on the restoration of their relations." He added, "Though bilateral relations [between China and Laos] once suffered some difficulties, that is now over." (Beijing, XINHUA, 15 August; FBIS, 16 August.)

The way having been carefully prepared, Kaysone himself visited China 5–12 October, meeting all the senior Chinese party and government leaders, including Deng Xiaoping (Radio Vientiane, 12 October; FBIS, 16 October). It is clear from a press release on the visit issued in Vientiane that the Chinese gave strong endorsement to Kaysone's economic reforms (Radio Vientiane, 13 October; FBIS, 16 October). Pasason hailed the visit as marking "a significant milestone in Lao-Chinese relations" (Radio Vientiane, FBIS, 16 October).

With respect to the Soviet Union, the relations of the LPRP and LPDR continued without significant change. These relations are characterized by frequent exchanges of official delegations and fraternal messages at all levels. Soviet aid to Laos, according to the Soviet embassy in Vientiane, is organized in 55 aid projects, including construction and repair of highway bridges, an agricultural experiment station, a tin mine, a satellite communications station, a radio station, a hospital, and a polytechnic school. In the period 1975–1986, 3,500 Lao cadres and students were trained in the USSR, and six thousand

Lao technicians were given on-the-job training. The USSR furnished the LPDR with 4,500 transport vehicles, 150 passenger buses, one thousand vehicles for agricultural production, fourteen aircraft, and seventeen helicopters. (Radio Vientiane, *FBIS*, 12 May.) Kaysone spent his usual annual three-week vacation in the USSR during August (TASS, 1 September).

The LPDR's relations with Thailand continued on an even keel, with the exception of the incident of the radio broadcast already mentioned. Following up in the spirit of goodwill initiated by the Thai prime minister's visit to Vientiane the previous November, Kaysone and the prime minister, Chatichai Choonhavan, jointly cut ceremonial ribbons opening the Phra That Phanom Homage Fair in Nakhon Phanom province in Thailand on 17 February. Kaysone in a speech on the occasion remarked that the Phra That Phanom pagoda is on an ancient site that was built up more than one thousand years ago. "The outer part of the pagoda was beautifully carved in artistic artwork by our people in ancient times," he said, referring to the ethnic Lao population of the district. He added, "We regard our participation in paying homage to this pagoda as an auspicious sign of the strengthening of true fraternity, affection, and unity between the Lao and Thai peoples." The formation of a Thailand-Laos Friendship Association was announced at the ceremony. (Radio Vientiane, 17 February; *FBIS*, 21 February.)

In other concrete steps by the two countries, joint border committees were inaugurated early in 1989 to deal with outstanding border disputes and ferry services across the Mekong River were reopened at a number of points. Thailand also lifted its ban on the export of the last of a list of so-called strategic goods (the list originally consisted of 363 items, having been shortened on two previous occasions). (Bangkok, *Bangkok Post*, 22 November; *FBIS*, 28 November.)

The LPDR also took part in tripartite talks with Thailand and the U.N. Office of the High Commissioner for Refugees on procedures for repatriating Laotian refugees from Thailand. It was stated that 495 such refugees have returned to Laos since the beginning of 1989 and that more than one thousand have decided to register in a voluntary repatriation program. (Radio Vientiane, *FBIS*, 14 August.)

An agreement on bilateral cooperation in economic, trade, cultural, scientific, and technical fields was signed in Vientiane on 6 October (Radio Vientiane, 6 October; *FBIS*, 10 October).

Nevertheless, a resolution of the border dispute in the mountains between Boten district of Laos's Sayaboury province and Chat Trakan district in Thailand's Phitsanulok province, where serious fighting occurred between December 1987 and February 1988, still appears to evade both countries. Kaysone said as much when interviewed by a French correspondent toward the end of the year. "I must say frankly that the border dispute has not been wisely settled," he said (Paris, *Le Monde*, 12 December; *FBIS*, 15 December).

The activities of anti-LPDR guerrillas—who made further claims, carried in the Bangkok press and largely unverifiable, of liberating territory and disrupting the LPDR during 1989—are another issue that threatens to raise complications in relations between Laos and Thailand. A press release, made available to the AFP in Bangkok signed by the United Lao National Liberation Front, spoke of "the proclamation of our liberated zones and the formation of the revolutionary provisional government of Laos after 15 arduous years of struggle against the socialist Vietnamese occupation armed forces with great success" (Bangkok, *Nation*, 6 December; *FBIS*, 6 December). According to a by-lined story in the *Bangkok Post* datelined Sayaboury, General Vang Pao, the Hmong leader now resident in the United States, and his supporters announced the formation of a revolutionary government of Laos and said they would invite the eldest son of former King Savang Vatthana, Prince Solignavong Vongsavang who is reported to be living in France, to be their king (Bangkok, *Bangkok Post*, 10 December; *FBIS*, 11 December). These claims were largely dismissed by other resistance groups and flatly denied by LPDR ambassador to Thailand Khamphan Simmalavong (Bangkok, *Bangkok Post*, 14 December; *FBIS*, 14 December).

The Bangkok press also reported in midyear that members of the clandestine Laos-based Phak Mai, once seen as a vehicle for LPDR irredentism toward the northeast of Thailand, had begun returning to Thailand in view of the improved relations between the two countries. Returnees said in interviews that LPDR officials told them their movement was no longer supported and that they could remain in Laos or sell their belongings and return to Thailand (Bangkok, *Nation*, 26 April; *FBIS*, 26 April).

The LPDR's slowly evolving relations with the United States also saw some rough passages during 1989. The year opened with the visit to Laos of a delegation headed by the U.S. National Security Council's Richard Childress. LPDR media noted that the delegation included representatives of the departments of State, Defense, and Commerce, as well as the National League of POW/MIA Families (Radio Vientiane, *FBIS*, 5 January). With respect to the matters under negotiation 2–3 January, LPDR media reported that the U.S. delegation reaffirmed the 1987 statement on bilateral relations respecting the independence, sovereignty, and territorial integrity of Laos and refraining from interfering in Laos's internal affairs. Concerning narcotics, the two sides agreed to form an expert group. The U.S. delegation agreed to review the drought situation in Laos, and the two sides agreed to hold further meetings to take measures to search for remains of those missing in action (MIA). (Radio Vientiane, 6 January; *FBIS*, 6 January.)

In March, however, U.S. National Security adviser Brent Scowcroft recommended censuring Laos for its alleged continued involvement in drug trafficking, reporting that opium production continues to expand and could reach three hundred tons. The LPDR in turn postponed a joint excavation to search for the bodies of MIAs. (*NYT*, 6 March.) A radio commentary on the State Department's expression of regret at the Lao decision noted that the LPDR had "consistently rendered humanitarian cooperation to the United States in the search for the remains of U.S. MIAs in Laos." It also noted that the LPDR had enacted laws to suppress production and trafficking in narcotic drugs and had meted out punishment to convicted drug traffickers. It called upon the U.S. administration "to match its words with deeds" and abide by the principles of respect for Lao independence and sovereignty. It said the Lao people "seek sympathy and justice from the American Government and people" in view of the damage wrought by the United States in Laos during the war. (Radio Vientiane, 10 March; *FBIS*, 13 March.)

This exchange was followed on 29 March by the visit to Vientiane of a congressional delegation headed by Congressman Lawrence Smith, chairman of the international narcotics task force of the House Foreign Affairs Committee. The visit allowed LPDR spokesmen to put forward their point of view on the problem. (AFP, 29 March.) The search for U.S. MIAs was resumed in May with an excavation in Savannakhet province (Radio Vientiane, 29 May; *FBIS*, 30 May).

In his lengthy report to the SPA, Kaysone touched on relations with the United States, saying,

Our government has been trying to respond to every issue in which the United States is interested. During the past years, relations between the two countries have expanded, but still at slow paces. We believe that Lao-U.S. relations will again be expanded if the United States will also respond to every issue of interest to us.

In one of her last official acts as chargé d'affaires of the American embassy in Vientiane, Harriet Isom dedicated a new clinic in Savannakhet province built with the assistance of an American foundation (KPL, 25 August; *FBIS*, 25 August). The choice of Savannakhet is significant, for it is in this Lao province that most of the joint excavations to search for remains of MIAs have taken place. Meanwhile, following a visit to Laos on 31 March by Charles Twining of the State Department, the provision of five thousand tons of rice through the World Food Program was finally approved as a U.S. gesture in response to the drought situation in southern Laos. The United States also signed an agreement with Laos for rural development projects in Houa Phan province over six years (KPL, 2 October; *FBIS*, 4 October).

A U.S. delegation led by Senator David Durenberger visited the LPDR 26–27 August and was received by Acting Foreign Minister Thongsavat Khaikhamphithoun and Bounmi Pakthavong, head of the SPA Foreign Relations Commission (Radio Vientiane, *FBIS*, 30 August). A U.S. delegation led by Deputy Assistant Secretary of State David F. Lambertson visited Vientiane for an exchange of views on issues of mutual interest 1–3 November (Radio Vientiane, 3 November; *FBIS*, 9 November).

LPDR deputy foreign minister Souban Salitthilat paid a four-day visit to Washington 12–15 September to discuss the narcotics issue, the search for U.S. MIAs, and the normalization of relations (Radio Vientiane, *FBIS*, 29 September). However, as one of his first duties after arriving in Vientiane, the new U.S. chargé d'affaires, Charles B. Salmon, received a "strong protest" against an anti-LPDR demonstration on 11 November in front of the LPDR embassy in Washington, D. C. in which Radio Vientiane reported a Lao flag was trampled. The radio said, "The Lao side is waiting for an appropriate reply from the United States within a reasonable period of time so that further action can be considered in this matter." (Radio Vientiane, *FBIS*, 15 November.)

Kaysone, apparently intent on broadening the

LPDR's foreign relations, visited Japan 7–11 November and France 11–16 December. During these visits, Kaysone had meetings with Emperor Akihito, President François Mitterrand, and government leaders. *Pasason* hailed the visit to Japan as "intended to promote and expand, even more efficiently in the years to come, the relations of friendship and cooperation between the two states and two peoples" (Radio Vientiane, 13 November; *FBIS*, 15 November). The tone of the corresponding editorial on the visit to France was more subdued, with the accent on restoration of relations based on an equal footing thanks to "the good will and efforts of both sides" (KPL, 18 December; *FBIS*, 20 December).

In line with the policy of the LPDR's opening to noncommunist countries, Deputy Foreign Minister Souban paid an official visit to Australia in October (Radio Vientiane, 24 October; *FBIS*, 25 October).

It was reported during the year that the LPDR had applied for membership in the General Agreement on Tariffs and Trade in 1988 (KPL, 19 September; *FBIS*, 22 September).

LPDR media carried no news of the dramatic events in Eastern Europe and the various republics of the USSR in 1989.

Arthur J. Dommen
Bethesda, Maryland

Malaysia and Singapore

Population. Malaysia: 16,726,766; Singapore: 2,674,362 (*World Factbook*)
Party. Communist Party of Malaya (CPM)
Founded. 30 April 1930
Membership. CPM: about 1,000 armed insurgents on Thai side of border, about 200 inside Malaysia; Sarawak (North Kalimantan Communist Party, NKCP): fewer than 100; Sabah: insignificant (*World Factbook*, 1989). Composition: 694 Thai; 494 Malay, 402 of whom are ethnic Chinese; 77 Malays. Singapore: 200–500; Barisan Sosialis infiltrated by communists (*World Factbook*, 1989).
General Secretary. Chin Peng (born name, Ong Boo Hwa, 67, also reported as 69).
Politburo. No data
Secretariat. No data
Central Committee. C. D. Abdullah, chairman (66); Rashid Maidin, member (72)
Status. Illegal
Last Congress. Singapore, 1965 (last known)
Last Election. No data
Auxiliary Organizations. Malayan People's Army (MPA); Malay Nationalist Revolutionary Party of Malaya (MNRPM)
Publications. MNRPM: *Suluh Rakyat*; clandestine radio station, Voice of Malayan Democracy (VOMD)

The CPM, which had once commanded an effective guerrilla force of close to five thousand, has dwindled to relatively weak units operating along the Thai-Malaysian border areas. In November 1987 two breakaway factions numbering more than one thousand put down their arms, leaving an estimated twelve hundred guerrillas on the Thai border at the beginning of 1989. In December, after more than a year of intensive negotiations, the general secretary of the CPM signed a peace accord with the military chiefs of Malaysia and Thailand, officially ending more than four decades of warfare.

Leadership and Party Organization. Some details about the party leadership that had been the subject of speculation for years were clarified when the CPM laid down its arms in December. Chin Peng, the shadowy figure long known as the party chairman but frequently reported as dead in recent years, emerged from Beijing, where he had been living since 1961, to ratify the accords. Earlier in the year, he sent his wife to Thailand to participate in the protracted discussions that preceded the final agreement.

Chin Peng, born Ong Boon Hwa, is 67. As general secretary of the CPM he led the principal guerrilla force cooperating with the Allies during the Japanese occupation, for which he was awarded the Order of the British Empire. He remained general secretary of the CPM when it was a legal political party in the early postwar years, but went into hiding in July 1948 when the CPM was outlawed. Chin Peng was last seen outside the communist world in late 1955 when he participated in truce negotiations with the Malaysian government. After those talks broke down, he returned to the jungle at the border of Malaysia and Thailand and later went to Beijing. His name continued to be invoked in party statements, but he did not reappear until the final stages of the negotiations leading to the 2 December accord. At the press conference after the signing ceremony, it was Chin Peng, speaking in Malay, Mandarin, English, and a little Thai, who fielded most of the questions. (Tokyo, KYODO, 6 May; *FBIS*, 10 May; *FEER*, 23 November; *Bangkok Post*, 27 November; *FBIS-EAS*, 28 November; Bangkok, *The Nation*, 1 December; *FBIS-EAS*; *Bangkok Post*, 1 December.)

Other CPM leaders who participated in the signing of the peace accords were party chairman C. D. Abdullah (66) and Central Committee member Rashid Maidin (72), both of whom had taken part along with Chen Ping in the abortive 1955 peace talks (*Bernama*, 2 December; *FBIS-EAS*, 4 December). Pohji Kasim (65), a senior party member identified as a deputy commander of one of the four guerrilla regiments operating along the Thai border, was also present as was former CPM chairman Musa Ahmad, who had defected in 1980 and returned to Malaysia from China (*FEER*, 23 November). The leader of the NKCP, Wen Min Chuan, is reportedly living in China (*FEER*, 21 December).

In the course of the peace negotiations, more information emerged about the composition of the guerrilla forces. Of the 1,188 remaining CPM members, 694 were born in Thailand and 494 claim Malaysian origin. Of those claiming Malaysian roots, 402 are ethnic Chinese and 77 are Malay, half of them aged 35 to 50. There were also 30 Singaporeans (all Chinese), thirteen *Orang Asli* (indigenous people), two Indians, and an Indonesian. One bizarre revelation was that the CPM guerrillas included two Japanese, the survivors of fifteen former members of the Japanese Imperial Army who had remained behind at the end of World War II and joined the guerrillas in 1948. (*Bernama*, 2 December; *Straits Times*, 3 December; *FBIS-EAS*, 4 December; *FEER*, 14 December.)

Domestic Party Activities. On 2 December, Chin Peng on behalf of the CPM signed two separate agreements with representatives of the governments of Malaysia and Thailand. The 35-minute ceremony at a hotel in Hat Yai, southern Thailand, was the culmination of more than a year of negotiations during which Thai and Malaysian officials met with CPM representatives in sixteen rounds of offi-

cial talks and held more than one hundred unofficial meetings with CPM forces in the jungle.

Early in the year Thai authorities promised resettlement in Thailand for those CPM guerrillas who so desired, an offer that the Malaysian Army Corps commander later said largely contributed to the communists' willingness to lay down their arms. The talks broke down when the Thai negotiators initially rejected the communists' demand for a written Thai government guarantee of their safety and the right to Thai citizenship for those who sought it. After an impasse of several months, a major breakthrough came in early November when Thailand's supreme commander, General Chawalit Yongchaiyut, agreed to the CPM's request. (*Bangkok Post*, 1 January; *FBIS-EAS*, 12 January; Kuala Lumpur International Service, 19 March; *FBIS-EAS*, 22 March; *Bangkok Post*, 1 November; *FBIS-EAS*, 2 November.)

A final round of talks focused on money and the issue of domicile, but the sticking point, one that almost brought the negotiations to a halt again, was whether former CPM members who returned to Malaysia would be allowed to take part in politics. The Thai government maintained its offer of land, housing, and some initial funding for those who chose to settle on the Thai side of the border. The official Malaysian position was less forthcoming. Five days before the signing of the peace accords, Prime Minister Datuk Sri Dr. Mahathir said that the government had not yet considered the matter of amnesty for former members of the CPM and that conditions relating to the return of those who wished to settle in Malaysia would be worked out later (Kuala Lumpur International Service; *FBIS-EAS*, 27 November). This led the CPM's Malayan People's Army (MPA) to issue a statement reiterating and defending its decision to dissolve the party, saying that for the sake of the country and the people, "we are willing to reach an agreement acceptable to both parties on fair and reasonable terms in order to realize peace in our country" (Bangkok, *The Nation*, 23 November; *FBIS-EAS*, 27 November). The final agreement, approved by the Malaysian parliament on 29 November, included a pledge by the Malaysian government to allow former CPM members to "freely participate in political activities within the framework of the Federal Constitution and the laws of Malaysia." The CPM in turn pledged to respect the laws of Thailand and Malaysia and to participate in socioeconomic developments for the benefit of the people. The joint communiqué issued by the two governments and the

CPM to mark the signing of the peace agreements referred to "this honorable settlement" as bringing "prosperity, stability and security to the Thai-Malaysian border region and Malaysians." (*Bernama*, 2 December; *FBIS-EAS*, 5 December.)

The CPM pledged to dissolve its army, but it was agreed that there would be no ceremony to mark the dissolution of the last armed group, for the guerrillas felt that such a ceremony would signify defeat. Instead, they would destroy their weapons in the presence of Malaysian and Thai officials during the month after the signing of the accords.

Throughout the period of negotiations, CPM spokesmen sought to present the coming peace agreement as a communist initiative. In a press interview in June, Pohji Kasim referred to the CPM statement of June 1988 that agreed to find a political solution to the armed struggle. The statement was in accordance with the world trend of resolving conflicts, he said, noting that "everything is gradually changing, even the situation in Malaysia. Is it worth keeping up the fighting? . . . The CPM has turned the situation from war to negotiations and from negotiations to peace." He asked the press not to use the term "surrender," saying that the CPM wants to end the war with justice and dignity and citing the CPM's pride at having fought alongside British troops in World War II. (*Bangkok Post*, 22 June; *FBIS-EAS*, 26 June.)

In the same vein of claiming the initiative, the CPM's resolution on ending the armed struggle began

Based on the situation at home and abroad and the subjective and objective conditions as well as the spirit of the statement of the Central Committee dated 18 June 1988, the 13th enlarged plenary session of the Central Committee has decided to immediately end the armed struggle and subsequently conduct a long-term peaceful and democratic struggle within the framework of the Constitution of the Federation of Malaysia.

The resolution, broadcast by the party's clandestine radio station some days after the peace accord but reportedly adopted on 25 November, cited the party's and the army's contributions to "our country's independence" and urged all comrades to "continue to develop under the new terms the spirit of whole-heartedly serving the people and fight hard for the democratic rights and justice of the society." (VOMD, 6 December; *FBIS-EAS*, 7 December.)

A VOMD editorial hailing the peace accords noted that former MPA members "will freely take part in political activities within the framework of the nation's constitution and law" and urged them to "unite and cooperate" with other political parties and organizations as well as "leaders of various circles to fight hard together to promote the people's democratic rights and achieve social justice" (VOMD, 6 December; *FBIS-EAS*, 7 December).

On the day of the signing, in a press statement later reported by VOMD, party chairman C. D. Abdullah emphasized the CPM's role in achieving Malaysian independence. He said that independence had been a joint effort of all parties and patriotic organizations, linking the CPM "in the field of armed struggle" with such mainstream parties as the United Malays National Organization and the Pan-Malaysian Islamic Party "in the struggle for independence." Welcoming the spirit of mutual understanding and compromise by all parties that made the signing of the agreements possible, the CPM chairman called on the people of all races, Malays and non-Malays, "to forge closer solidarity and cooperate to uphold democracy and social justice." (VOMD, 19 December; *FBIS-EAS*, 20 December.)

The ink was scarcely dry on the agreements when there were differences in interpretation of some key points. On the day of the signing, Prime Minister Mahathir said that the party was still banned. Chin Peng, however, told the press that the CPM army had been dissolved but not the party. (*Bernama*, 2 December; *FBIS-EAS*, 4 December.) There were conflicting reports through the end of the year on the CPM's plans for political activity in Malaysia. Although Malaysian radio reported that top leaders like Chin Peng would "of course" continue to live in China and that a few hundred of the rank and file would begin a new life on the border area inside Thailand, the Thai press reported that Chin Peng would return to Malaysia with a new "Malayan People Party." About three hundred former CPM members were expected to return with Chin Peng about the middle of the new year. Other leaders reportedly planning to join Chin Peng are C. D. Abdullah, Rashid Maidin, and Pohji Kasim. (Kuala Lumpur International Service, 19 December; *Bangkok Post*, 17 December; *FBIS-EAS*, 19, 22 December.)

In Malaysia, reactions to the accords reflected the prevailing skepticism about the CPM's true agenda. In July, while negotiations were actively under way, Malaysia's deputy minister for home affairs warned the public to be vigilant against "delicate tricks" by the communists, who still hoped to exploit ethnic and religious conflicts in the country (Kuala Lumpur Domestic Service, 23 July; *FBIS-EAS*, 24 July). On the day of the signing of the peace accords, the general secretary for home affairs said that Malaysia would not make new regulations to enable former CPM members to return easily; returnees would have to go through the existing legal process including security screening and assessment (Kuala Lumpur Domestic Service, 2 December; *FBIS-EAS*, 4 December). Former Prime Minister Tunku Abdul Rahman was one of those who questioned whether the CPM was giving up the struggle, recalling that Chin Peng had told him during the 1955 talks, "once a communist, always a communist." Chin Peng commented to reporters that those were not his words, but said that he had not given up his belief in Marxism. (Bangkok, *The Nation*, 1 December; *FBIS-EAS*, 1 December.)

Although there had been numerous leaks throughout the year to the Thai press about the progress of the negotiations, there were no similar leaks from Malaysian sources even though senior Malaysian officials fully participated in the talks. This appeared to be because of the persistent hostility to the CPM among Malaysians who recalled the period of the emergency from 1948 to the mid-fifties.

Reactions in Singapore were similarly guarded, although Chin Peng, reversing the CPM's long-held position, said that he recognized Singapore's independence (*Straits Times*, 3 December; *FBIS-EAS*, 5 December). Prime Minister Lee Kuan Yew urged caution, warning that "the signing of the peace treaty acknowledges that the communist attempts to seize power by force have collapsed, but is it the end of the communist movement?" He asked if those members of the CPM who had spent decades in the jungle would write off that time as a bad investment or see it as having lost one phase of the fight to seize power by force and wait for another time and place. All Singaporeans among the CPM returnees should be accepted back, he said, but the country's constitution requires that the government must be satisfied of their rehabilitation. (*FBIS-EAS*, 13 December.) A branch of the People's Action Party (PAP) issued a statement saying that the CPM continued to pose a threat with its Marxist-Leninist ideology. The statement congratulated the Malaysian government for successfully negotiating the end of the communist insurgency, but warned that the CPM still harbored hopes of a communist Ma-

laysia and Singapore. The laying down of arms only meant that the CPM would now turn to other ways to "undermine, subvert, infiltrate and control" the two countries (*Straits Times*, 22 December).

In Singapore only two of the alleged Marxist conspirators detained in May and June 1987 remained in custody: Vincent Cheng, accused of being the local mastermind, and Teo Soh Long, a lawyer who has refused to drop her legal challenges to detention. In June their detentions were extended for a year. (*NYT*, 3 June; *FEER*, 13 July.) In May the Singapore government released Chia Thye Poh, a political detainee held without trial for 23 years. He was permitted to live on an island off Singapore although he never admitted that he had any links with the CPM, an admission the government had demanded through the years as the price of his release. A Home Affairs Ministry official claimed that Chia, who had been a member of parliament from the now defunct Barisan Sosialis, was no harmless dissident, but had openly advocated violent overthrow of the government. Given the weakened state of the CPM, however, Chia's release was not a problem, he said. (*FEER*, 1 June, 28 September.)

During the last stages of the negotiations, Malaysia's defense minister said that the army had been directed to remain on alert. His concerns appeared to be justified when Thai forces clashed with a group of about fifteen guerrillas little more than a week before the signing of the peace accords. (*Siam Rath*, 25 November; *FBIS-EAS*, 28 November.)

At the time that the CPM was agreeing to lay down its arms, Prime Minister Mahathir and the Sarawak state secretary were urging the remaining guerrillas of the North Kalimantan Communist Party (NKCP) to follow suit. Reportedly, Wen Min Chuan sent a representative to Thailand to convey his party's desire to end its armed activities in Sarawak. Although Malaysian police officials described the 42 remaining guerrillas as more of a nuisance than a security threat, talks were still under way in mid-December between the NKCP representative and Malaysian officials. (*Bernama*, 8 December; Kuala Lumpur International Service, 9, 16 December; *FBIS-EAS*, 11, 14, 20 December.)

Auxiliary and Front Organizations. As the year and the negotiations progressed, statements by CPM affiliates reflected the shift from revolutionary opposition to political participation. The February broadcast celebrating the 40th anniversary of the founding of the MPA gave the traditional review of the history of that organization, including some statistics not likely to allay Malaysian fears about the CPM. Extolling the MPA's achievements, the broadcast stated that the MPA's predecessor, the Malayan National Liberation Army (MNLA), had fought against 400,000 British troops, initiated more than nineteen thousand battles and skirmishes, and shot dead or injured more than 26,000 British troops and police. "The CPM is a peace-loving political party" whose decision to establish an armed force was aimed at leading the people to "oppose the bloody oppression of British colonial rule." The broadcast gave credit for achieving independence to "all patriotic and democratic parties," but asserted that "every honest person admits that independence achieved in 1957 would not have been possible without the difficult armed struggle led by the CPM and the bloody battles fought by the MNLA." Although citing the June 1988 CPM proposal to seek a peaceful solution, the broadcast repeated the standard attacks on the government. (VOMD, 1 February; *FBIS-EAS*, 3 February.)

By autumn, the editorial celebrating the 40th anniversary of the MNRPM's publication *Suluh Rakyat* spoke of the new era of national development and national solidarity and paid tribute to the positive influence of the spirit of nationalism. Continuing the CPM's attempt to appeal to the Malay majority, the editorial endorsed the role of the national language, applauded Malay economic advances, and urged political, economic, and administrative reforms to strengthen Malaysia's multi-ethnic society. The national culture should be enhanced by fusing Malay culture with those of the other races. In the same way, political parties that advocate the interests of only one group should gradually be replaced by multiracial-based political parties. This is especially important, the editorial concludes, because of the widespread pressure throughout the country for a general election. (VOMD, 27 November; *FBIS-EAS*, 13 December.)

At the end of the year, after the signing of the peace accords, the CPM's clandestine radio station continued to broadcast. It is believed to be located in southern China.

International Activities. The predominantly pro-Beijing CPM has not played much of a role in the international communist meetings sponsored by Moscow. *WMR*'s compilation of data on world communist parties states that the CPM sent representatives to the international meetings of communist and workers' parties of 1957 and 1960.

Malaysia and China established diplomatic relations in 1974, soon after the People's Republic of China stated that it had renounced any material aid to the CPM. However, the Malaysian government continues to control trade and people-to-people ties because of China's insistence on maintaining fraternal ties with the CPM. A recent trade pact that includes weekly air service between Malaysia and South China has opened the door for greater economic cooperation between the two countries. In November, Malaysian authorities relaxed some of the restrictions on visits to China, lowering the age limits for those allowed to visit China alone or as members of tour groups. (*Bernama*, 6 May; *FBIS-EAS*, 11 May; Beijing, XINHUA, 16 November; *FBIS-CHI*, 22 November.)

The Chinese ambassador to Thailand was reported to be at the peace accord ceremony in Hat Yai.

The establishment of diplomatic relations between Singapore and China proceeded at a slower pace. In March, Prime Minister Lee reiterated Singapore's position that there is only one China and said that Singapore would establish diplomatic relations with China as soon as Sino-Indonesian relations were normalized (Beijing, XINHUA, 17 June; *FBIS-CHI*, 20 June). Nevertheless, as the first deputy prime minister pointed out, because Singapore already has cordial trading relations with China, it does not feel it has to move in haste to establish full diplomatic relations. Meanwhile, the Singapore government gave a low-key but cordial welcome to the president of Taiwan during his 6–9 March visit. (*FEER*, 16 March.)

Jeanne S. Mintz
Washington, D.C.

Mongolia

Population. 2,145,463
Party. Mongolian People's Revolutionary Party (MPRP)
Date Founded. 1 March 1921
Membership. 89,312 (*WMR Yearbook*, 1988); 30.9 percent women; 32.9 workers; 17.3 percent

Agricultural Association members; 49.8 percent intelligentsia

General Secretary. Jambyn Batmonh (63)

Politburo. 5 members: Jambyn Batmonh, chairman, Presidium of People's Great Hural; Dumaagiyn Sodnom, premier; Bujyn Dejid; Tserendashiyn Namsray; Paavangiyn Damdin. 3 candidate members: Sonomyn Lubsangombo, Lamsurendin Lantuu, Puntsagiyn Jasray

Secretariat. 5 members: Jambyn Batmonh, Tserenpilyn Balhaajab, Paavangiyn Damdin, Bujyn Dejid, Tserendashiyn Namsray

Central Committee. 85 full members; 65 candidate members

Status. Ruling party

Last Congress. Nineteenth, 28–31 May 1986, in Ulan Bator

Last Election. 22 June 1986; of 370 seats in People's Great Hural, 346 (93.5 percent) went to members or candidate members of the MPRP.

Auxiliary Organizations. Mongolian Revolutionary Youth League (269,000 members), Ts. Narangerel, first secretary; Central Council of Mongolian Trade Unions, B. Lubsantseren, chairman; Committee of Mongolian Women, L. Pagmadulam, chairwoman

Publications. *Unen* (Truth), MPRP daily organ, published Tuesday–Sunday; MONTSAME is the official news agency.

Leadership and Party Organization. The influence of *perestroika* and *glasnost'* became increasingly apparent in Mongolia in 1989. At the end of the year, in a plenum of the MPRP, three members of the Politburo retired, B. Altangerel—possibly against his will—D. Molomjamts, and B. Lhamjab, for reasons of age (Radio Ulan Bator, *FBIS*, 12 December). Candidate member P. Damdin was promoted to the Politburo, and L. Lantuu, first secretary of the Ulan Bator MPRP committee, and P. Jasray, first deputy chairman of the Council of Ministers, were made candidate members (MONTSAME, 12 December; *FBIS*, 13 December). Biam Suren was appointed deputy prime minister. Earlier in the year, Defense Minister Yondon retired and was replaced by Lieutenant General Lubsangombyn Molomjamts (Radio Ulan Bator, 15 September; *FBIS*, 19 September).

Perhaps even more significant than the leadership changes was the manner in which political affairs were conducted. For the first time an unauthorized demonstration demanding greater political reform received attention in the Mongolian press.

According to various accounts about one thousand demonstrators gathered in Ulan Bator and other cities to demand pluralistic elections by 1990, a more market-oriented economy, preservation of the environment, banking reform, and revocation of past statements by the MPRP supporting the 1956 invasion of Hungary and the 1968 invasion of Czechoslovakia. The demonstrators called for the end of special privileges for high officials, noted that colleagues of discredited leaders Choybalsan and Tsedenbal were still in power, criticized Mongols who send their children to Russian schools, and demanded that Genghis Khan be restored to his proper role in history (Radio Ulan Bator, 18 December; *FBIS*, 19 December; Beijing, U.S. embassy, unclassified cable). Clearly influenced by developments in Eastern Europe, Mongolia's dissident movement may be gaining steam.

The MPRP's response to developments in Eastern Europe was to shore up its own version of socialism. At the Seventh MPRP Plenum in December, Batmonh announced that the next congress of the MPRP would be moved up to November 1990 to consider new tasks for "social construction" and revision of party rules, elections, and guidelines for socioeconomic development. Batmonh pointed out that the MPRP would continue to "provide ideological and political unity to all the strata of society in the common task of building socialism." He also noted that the prestige of the party depended on how well the party fulfilled this duty. (Radio Ulan Bator, 11 December; *FBIS*, 12 December.) Batmonh, like Gorbachev, plans to save socialism by reforming it.

Domestic Affairs. In the spirit of *glasnost'* strong criticism of former leaders was amplified. In January the government announced it was restoring the original names of places named after Stalin (Radio Ulan Bator, 3 January; *FBIS*, 4 January). Throughout the year articles published in Mongolian journals carried accounts of the persecutions of prominent Mongol political and cultural leaders. *Novosti Mongolii* (6 December 1988) carried the account of A. Amar, a former prime minister who was falsely accused of counterrevolution, arrested, and removed by Choybalsan to die in obscurity (*FBIS*, 9 February). *Unen* carried an article, "Tragedy in the History of the Comintern," which claimed that Stalin and his henchmen were responsible for "dozens of thousands" of "particularly brutal repressions" of Mongols including party and state leaders, military personnel, ordinary people, and clergymen (MONTSAME, 22 May; *FBIS*, 30

May). In September a Politburo commission formally rehabilitated some of those so persecuted (Radio Ulan Bator, 21 September; *FBIS*, 25 September). Additionally, many street and place names changed to honor now discredited Mongolian leaders were changed back to the original.

During much of the year attention was focused on restructuring. In February, Batmonh appeared before a commission responsible for drafting a new constitution for the MPR and observed that a new constitution was required to facilitate restructuring and renewal (MONTSAME, 14 February; *FBIS*, 17 February). In an interview with the Japanese newspaper *Yomiuri Shimbun* (31 October), Batmonh stressed that restructuring would improve group and individual initiative and give greater independence to enterprises and management bodies. Batmonh also stated that Mongolia would not simply copy the reforms of other socialist nations, but would restructure in accordance with its own unique characteristics.

Several government organs held meetings to facilitate restructuring. In April, for example, the Foreign Ministry met to consider how to restructure foreign relations so as to meet Mongolia's specific interests, particularly foreign economic relations (MONTSAME, 24 April; *FBIS*, 12 May). Progress in restructuring was apparently satisfactory to the party leaders; Batmonh informed the December MPRP plenum that harvests had been stabilized and the losses of livestock reduced. He also insisted that the restructuring process should continue. (Radio Ulan Bator, 11 December; *FBIS*, 12 December.)

One result of restructuring was substantial reductions in Mongolia's armed forces. In February it was announced that the military would be cut by thirteen thousand personnel and defense expenditures reduced. These cuts were made in conjunction with reductions of Soviet forces in Mongolia. (Radio Ulan Bator, 13 February; *FBIS*, 14 February; MONTSAME, 4 March; *FBIS*, 6 March.) These cuts caused some dislocations. Many workers in defense-related industries lost their jobs or had their wages reduced; however, the government claimed that steps were being taken to shift these industries to civilian production (Radio Ulan Bator, 26 December; *FBIS*, 28 December).

Although restructuring may have made some progress, the economy showed substantial difficulties. The government acknowledged growing inflation, consumer shortages, and shoddy goods. Politburo member Molomjamts, in an interview with *Unen*, observed that economic reform was originally adopted eighteen months earlier in an MPRP plenum, but that shortcomings remained, such as unfulfilled government orders and contractual obligations, manufacture of poor-quality goods, and failure to maintain the pace of production (MONTSAME, 6 March; *FBIS*, 9 March). Other articles during the year continued to decry the destruction of the environment (MONTSAME, 16 May; *FBIS*, 25 May), inadequate food supply (MONTSAME, 27 May; *FBIS*, 2 June), and Mongolia's lower quality of life compared with other Council for Mutual Economic Assistance countries (*Novosti Mongolii*, 5 February; *FBIS*, 29 August).

One of the most serious problems was that of unemployment, especially among young people. The Council of Ministers released figures in April showing that 27,500 young people were unemployed (which by year's end grew to 31,000) of whom 15,300 were able-bodied. According to these figures the total population was growing by about 50,000 annually, with 30,000 entering the job market. The Council of Ministers stated that more steps must be taken to improve education and training and to assist people in being qualified for jobs (MONTSAME, 5 April; *FBIS*, 7 April). Many available jobs in stockbreeding and agriculture went begging as youths moved to Ulan Bator and other population centers in hopes of finding better jobs.

Livestock production achieved 9.5 million new head, a modest increase partly achieved by limiting quantities of meat shipped outside the country (Radio Ulan Bator, 18 July; *FBIS*, 24 July). Reforms to make livestock breeders and crop growers more independent encouraged leasing, contracting, and renting rather than direct state management. The government promised to improve the lives of livestock breeders to encourage greater production (Radio Ulan Bator, 6 July; *FBIS*, 7 July).

In social affairs, Mongolia continued to wrestle with problems of health and education. The attack against alcoholism launched last year was continued, and some favorable results were reported. About seventeen thousand students graduated from middle school, but only about 9 percent planned to continue higher education (MONTSAME, 30 May; *FBIS*, 31 May). The government also was more forthcoming in reporting problems of crime and corruption. In a wide-ranging interview in late 1989, the minister of public security, Lieutenant General Jamsranjab, stated that serious problems of black marketeering and other criminal activity existed. He decried the violation of human rights under previous regimes and called for greater discipline. He noted that crime had decreased since 1985; however, murder, rape, robberies, and other serious crimes were still common. He also observed that hundreds of people were killed in auto accidents each year. He further complained about a high rate of recidivism among convicts (*Novosti Mongolii*, 6 December 1988; *FBIS*, 27 March).

Mongolia also witnessed the gradual resurgence of some traditional elements of nationalism. Tsedenbal was criticized for dogmatic attitudes on the country's past heritage. Mongol writers began to treat Genghis Khan favorably and to call for a revaluation of his role in history. A new hotel in Ulan Bator will be named after him (XINHUA, 16 November; *FBIS-CHI*, 17 November). According to Alan Sanders, demand is strong for the publishing of new books in the Mongolian classical script and there is growing encouragement to wear traditional native dress (*FEER*, 23 February).

International Views and Affairs. Mongolia's relations with its two important neighbors, the Soviet Union and China, underwent substantial changes. Gorbachev's desire to normalize relations with the PRC had profound influence on Ulan Bator. Early in the year the Soviets said that they would withdraw 75 percent of their forces from Mongolia—some 50,000—by 1990. The first detachment was withdrawn on 15 May, the same day Mikhail Gorbachev arrived in Beijing for talks with Deng Xiaoping (Radio Ulan Bator, 15 May; *FBIS*, 16 May). The Soviets also reportedly will withdraw 850 tanks, about 1,100 infantry combat vehicles and armored personnel carriers, more than 820 artillery pieces, 190 fixed-wing aircraft, and 130 helicopters.

There was a gradual distancing in the Soviet-Mongolian relationship. Articles in the Mongolian press and journals increasingly questioned aspects of the relationship, leading some to speculate that the revival of nationalism was taking an anti-Soviet direction, according to Alan Sanders (*FEER*, 6 July). Similarly, James Pringle observed that the criticism of Mongolia's former leaders also cast suspicion on Soviet influence in Mongolia's history, noting the irreparable damage done to the historical and cultural heritage of the Mongols by Soviet-appointed dictators (*FEER*, 21 September). During a meeting with Batmonh in July, Gorbachev stated that "perestroika has entered probably the hardest phase of its development," implying that, facing its own difficulties, Moscow would probably be some-

what less lavish in its assistance to Ulan Bator (Radio Ulan Bator, 27 July; *FBIS*, 28 July).

Further evidence of the divergence may be seen in the Soviet decision to withdraw half of its 10,442 technical advisers working in Mongolia (Radio Ulan Bator, 26 October; *FBIS*, 31 October) and in Mongolia's efforts to join the nonaligned movement (Radio Ulan Bator, 17 June; *FBIS*, 20 June) and the group of 77 developing countries (Radio Ulan Bator, 24 June; *FBIS*, 28 June). In petitioning to join the nonaligned movement, the Mongolian Foreign Ministry observed that it was reconsidering its position in the United Nations, which had been previously characterized by ideological positions rather than the vital interests of the nation. In December, Foreign Minister Gombosuren visited Moscow and subsequently in an interview in *Unen* noted that the two sides were taking up the issues of remaining Soviet troops in Mongolia and historical questions in the bilateral relationship. He also stated that the two countries would begin to conduct bilateral trade in hard currency. The foreign minister further stated that Mongolia would strive to improve its ties with the West and would seek admission to the Asian Development Bank (Radio Ulan Bator, 30 December; *FBIS*, 4 January 1990).

Changes in Eastern Europe also began to affect Mongolia's international position. As communist parties began to lose power and disintegrate, the Mongolian reaction was first to denounce and then to accept. In October the MPRP quickly recognized the new Hungarian Socialist party. Batmonh visited East Germany in October and endorsed the hardline policies of the regime, but by December the Mongolian Foreign Ministry stated that the changes in Eastern Europe were "positive" and that each nation had the right to develop its own policies free of foreign intervention (Radio Ulan Bator, 23 December; *FBIS*, 27 December). Mongolia endorsed the revolution in Romania, sent medical aid to the people, and revoked a decree of 25 January 1988 conferring Mongolia's highest honor, the Order of Sukhe Bator, on Nicolae Ceaușescu (Radio Ulan Bator, 30 December; *FBIS*, 3 January 1990). Mongolia was the first satellite country of the Soviet Union and a model for the subsequent system of relations between the USSR and Eastern Europe in the post–World War II era. Mongolia now may become the recipient of the unraveling satellite system and see its own ties with Eastern Europe decline as attention is redirected toward Asia.

Relations with China improved dramatically. Mongolia reported, but made little comment on the

Chinese crackdown at Tiananmen. In January the People's Great Hural ratified the border treaty concluded with the People's Republic of China (PRC) in 1988, and in February a MONTSAME article stated that trade and "new thinking in international policy" had led to the normalization of Mongolia-PRC ties (Radio Ulan Bator, 10 February; *FBIS*, 15 February). Foreign Minister Gombosuren visited China in March, declaring that friendly and cooperative relations with China were a basic principle of Mongolia's foreign policy. Chinese foreign minister Qian Qichen stated that there were "no outstanding questions" between China and Mongolia (Radio Ulan Bator, XINHUA, 30 March; *FBIS*, 31 March). Mongolia praised the outcome of the Sino-Soviet summit in May. In September, Mongolia announced its first joint venture with China, the Terzlerki Hotel, and also concluded a tourism agreement with China. Direct border trade between Mongolia and China's Inner Mongolia Autonomous Region was opened, and the Inner Mongolian leader, Bu He, visited Mongolia (XINHUA, 13 November; *FBIS*, 15 November). Mongolia also proposed the establishment of a consulate in Huhehot to facilitate trade and tourism. At the end of the year, Gombosuren announced that a Sino-Mongolian summit would be held in 1990 (Radio Ulan Bator, 30 December; *FBIS*, 4 January 1990).

Mongolia also made strides in its newly declared emphasis on improving ties with noncommunist countries. Japanese foreign minister Uno visited in May, the first cabinet minister to visit Mongolia since relations were established in 1972. Uno agreed to expand trade with Mongolia, and his visit led to a new Japanese extension of credit, the first since 1981 (*Kyodo*, 5 May; *FBIS*, 8 May). In September the first British ministerial-level visitors to Mongolia arrived to discuss potential agricultural cooperation (Radio Ulan Bator, 21 September; *FBIS*, 25 September). Mongolia also sent a trade delegation to Britain and the United States to explore the possibility of improved trade.

Mongolia ended the year with a foreign policy flap. In an interview with *Playboy* magazine, chess champion Gary Kasparov said that the Soviet Union should sell Mongolia to China. The statement aroused strong indignation in Mongolia and resulted in a protest to the Soviet embassy in Ulan Bator. Soviet Foreign Ministry spokesman Gennadii Gerasimov voiced regret over the statement and declared that such an idea "has nothing in common with the official position of the USSR" (Radio Ulan Bator, 29, 30 December; *FBIS*, 3 January 1990).

William R. Heaton
Dumfries, Virginia

Nepal

Population. 18,699,884 (July 1989)
Parties. Nepal Communist Party–Marxist; Nepal Communist Party–Marxist-Leninist; Nepal Communist Party–Maoist; Nepal Workers' and Peasants' Organization; Democratic Front; numerous factions of the above
Founded. Nepal Communist Party Marxist: 1949; Nepal Communist Party–Marxist-Leninist: 1978; Democratic Front: 1980
Membership. 10,000 (1988 estimate)
Leadership. Nepal Communist Party–Marxist: Man Mohan Adhikary; Nepal Communist Party–Marxist-Leninist: Radha Krishna Mainali; Democratic Front: Ram Raja Prasad Singh; many of the factions and offshoots are personality centered.
Status. All illegal
Last Congress. The unified Nepal Congress party held its third and last presplit congress in 1961. The various factions have held congresses, most notably in 1975 and 1986.
Auxiliary Organizations. Nepal Progressive Students' Union; Nepal Progressive Democratic Youth Association; All-Nepal National Free Students' Union; People's Front; Nepal National Student Federation; Nepal National Youth Federation
Publications. *Naya Janabad* (New Democracy); *Nepal Patra*, *Barga Sangharsha* (Class Struggle); *Mukti-Morcha* (Liberation Front); *Mashal* (Torch); *Daily Diary Weekly*; *Samikshya Weekly*

In March, the Nepalese government began to build a popular consensus. The partyless Panchayat (parliament) legislators visited most of the major towns and districts in January and February to review the social, political, and economic conditions that prevailed in the kingdom. The members of parliament also sought to rally and unify the country and foster wider acceptance of the Panchayat. (*FBIS-NES*, 10 February.)

Students in Kathmandu's universities and colleges reacted to the sudden unavailability of goods in markets by mounting large-scale demonstrations against India and threatening Indian traders and businessmen. New Delhi began withdrawing assets from Nepalese banks, and rumors were widespread that India was considering an intervention, under the so-called Indira doctrine, to protect and evacuate its citizens. (*FEER*, 4 May.)

Many in Kathmandu saw striking parallels between the deteriorating situation they were experiencing and the activities that had led to the downfall of the monarchy in Sikkim in the middle 1970s. (Ibid.) The government reacted by closing all the institutions of higher education in Kathmandu Valley and sending the students to their hometowns and villages. This effort was both to reduce the potential for political unrest in a particularly trying time and to reduce demands in the marketplace by an unproductive segment of the population. (*FBIS-NES*, 11 May.)

India's blockade had a decided impact by mid-year. The growth rate of the gross domestic product plummeted to 1.5 percent, and the treasury was being bled to the tune of some $27 million per month. (*FBIS-NES*, 12 July.) To make matters worse, the pro-India Nepalese National Congress party had begun to agitate against government actions that had sparked the Indian effort (*FBIS-NES*, 23 June). The situation in the valley further heated up as those students still there began counter-demonstrations in support of the government. The students were joined by progovernment Panchayat members (*FBIS-NES*, 16 August). The turmoil in the capital caused the king to crack down and prorogue the Panchayat and finish dispersing the students to their homes (*FBIS-NES*, 25 August).

The Congress party and other banned opposition groups attempted to take advantage of the August turmoil by calling for a National Awakening Week to be held in early September. The program was aimed at criticizing the government's handling of relations with India, publicizing alleged corruption and inefficiency in the government, provoking a call for the dissolution of the Panchayat system and reinstitution of a multiparty system, and overthrowing the government of Prime Minister Shrestha. The government responded with the arrest of more than six hundred political party activists and workers. (*FBIS-NES*, 12 September.)

Nonetheless, the inflation and the attendant shortages that inevitably followed India's blockade made themselves felt by year's end. Discontent began growing alarmingly, and students and others began questioning the wisdom of the government's policies.

Foreign Affairs. The political and economic turmoil of 1989 is a direct result of Nepal's attempts to secure its national interests by following an independent path and balancing its relations with China and India.

Nepal had for some time been procuring small amounts of military matériel from the People's Republic of China. In June 1988 it took delivery of a small quantity of air defense artillery. The purchase in itself was fairly innocuous, but it raised concerns in New Delhi that Kathmandu intended to pursue an independent defense and foreign policy.

Although Beijing agreed to provide petroleum products, salt, and other consumer goods, its intentions were stymied by geography. The Chinese rail line in Tibet ends eight hundred kilometers short of the border with Nepal, and the road linking the two was closed during much of 1989 by avalanches and monsoon season landslides. A considerable effort was undertaken by the Nepal army to keep the road passable. (*FBIS-NES*, 25 April.)

Nonetheless, Kathmandu was not about to make concessions to India, but instead sought assistance to upgrade the overland route through Tibet. The World Bank, Swiss Development Corporation, and Asian Development Bank agreed to share nearly one million dollars of the cost of improving 114 kilometers of the most difficult section of the China-Nepal Friendship Highway. (*FBIS-CHI*, 21 July.)

Nepal also sought agreements to expand imports from and through other countries. Bangladesh agreed to send emergency supplies in the form of diesel fuel, kerosene, and sugar. Dhaka also allowed expanded use of direct air links between the two countries. (*FBIS-NES*, 10 April.) Pakistan also agreed to help out, and high-level delegations traveled between the two countries. Pakistan-Nepal economic cooperation talks were held 25 to 29 July to identify additional avenues of assistance. (*FBIS-NES*, 28 July.)

New Delhi blasted Kathmandu's efforts at expanding third-party trade and aid without attempting to deal through the Indians. New Delhi insisted that the Nepalese were endangering their own security in attempting to play a China card against India. New Delhi further threatened to halt what few supplies, mostly scarce petroleum products, were trickling through the two open border points and to cancel scheduled talks. (*FBIS-NES*, 28 July, 3, 4 August.) Although bilateral talks would subsequently be held, the year ended with a continuing impasse. Indian prime minister Rajiv Gandhi was facing national elections and could not afford to be seen as soft in his dealings with recalcitrant neighbors.

Party Affairs. The Nepal communist party continued to operate underground during the year. However, like other banned political parties, it had members seated in the Panchayat on a nonparty basis. The party's attitudes seemed to go through a metamorphosis as the year went on. Party activists, parliamentarians, and student groups were active in the anti-India activities that occurred in the spring. (*FBIS-NES*, 13 April.) However, by fall, communist party officials and workers were among those agitating against the government and for a resolution of the crisis with India (*FBIS-NES*, 12 September). The party is a cosponsor with the Nepal Congress party of a planned nationwide movement, which began in late 1989, against the Panchayat system and the Shrestha government (*Asia Yearbook*, 1990).

Michael R. Potaski
Catholic University of America

New Zealand

Population. 3,372,763
Parties. Communist Party of New Zealand (CPNZ); Socialist Unity Party (SUP); Communist League (CL), known before June 1989 as the Socialist Action League (SAL); Workers' Communist League (WCL)
Founded. CPNZ: 1921, SUP: 1966, CL: 1989 (from 1969 to 1989, SAL), WCL: 1980
Membership. CPNZ: 100, SUP: 300, CL: 50, WCL: 100 (all estimated)
Leadership. CPNZ: Harold Crook, chairman; SUP: George Jackson, president; Ken Douglas, chairman; CL (SAL): Russell Johnson, national secretary; WCL: Graeme Clark

Status. All legal
Last Congress. CPNZ: Twenty-third, 1984, special 50th anniversary of the *People's Voice* conference, 29–30 July 1989; SUP: Eighth, 22–24 October 1988; SAL: Eleventh, 26–31 December 1986, special conferences 28–31 December 1987 and 4–6 June 1988, Twelfth, 3–5 June 1989 when name changed to CL; WCL: Fourth, October 1988
Last Election. 15 August 1987 (parliamentary), no representatives elected; 14 October 1989 (local government), no official representatives elected, though a number of communists did stand on various broadbased community tickets.
Auxiliary Organizations. SUP: Youth in Unity, South Pacific United Youth Association, Workers' Institute for Scientific Education (WISE), Peace Council of New Zealand, New Zealand–USSR Society; CL (SAL): Young Socialists, Socialist Forum, Latin American Solidarity Committee, Cuba Friendship Society, Committee for a Workers' Front, Nicaragua Must Survive Committee; CPNZ: New Zealand–Albania Society
Publications. CPNZ: *People's Voice* (fortnightly); SUP: *Tribune* (fortnightly; editor, Jan Farr), *Socialist Politics* (every two months; editor, Marilyn Tucker); WCL: *Unity* (monthly)

During 1989 New Zealand continued to extend its relations with the Soviet Union and China, despite official New Zealand denunciation of the student massacre in Tiananmen Square. The SUP strengthened its influence in the trade union movement, supported the embattled Labour government, and welcomed the dramatic events in Eastern Europe as "positive developments of socialism, not victories for capitalism" (George Jackson, SUP president, *Auckland Sunday Star*, 26 November). The CPNZ opposed the SUP, its union leadership, and the Labour government. The SAL, which appeared to be fading into insignificance, changed its name to the CL. The WCL and a number of other small communist groups joined a New Labour party (NLP) formed after a Labour member of Parliament and former Labour party president, Jim Anderton, resigned from the Labour party and attacked its free market economic policies.

CPNZ. The CPNZ continued throughout 1989 to support Stalin as "the great revolutionary leader of the working class" and Albania as "the bastion of working class freedom in the world today" (*People's Voice*, 6 February). Rex Hollis of the *People's Voice* editorial board, who had visited Albania in late 1988, wrote a series of articles on Albania published throughout 1989. China, the Soviet Union, and Poland came under frequent attack as did the Labour, National, and Socialist Unity parties, which were described as "political stooges" of capitalism. The SUP was denounced for its "treachery" and "class collaboration" for advocating an industrial compact among government, employers, and unions (*People's Voice*, 6 February). The CPNZ was active in establishing and maintaining throughout New Zealand groups of Trade Unionists Against the Compact (TUAC) who protested incessantly against the "misleading rubbish" that a compact could "serve the workers and the bosses together" (*People's Voice*, 1 May).

In May the CPNZ Central Committee called for a "united front of labour" to contest the 1990 parliamentary elections with the slogan "Down with the Labour Government." A seventeen-point platform was proposed, and the CPNZ announced that it was prepared to work with the NLP, whose leaders, however, did not even reply to three letters sent by the CPNZ's National Executive requesting representation at the NLP's inaugural conference. When the SUP's Central Executive suggested a "formal party to party debate on policy . . . at national, regional and branch level," the CPNZ unanimously rejected the request (*People's Voice*, 10 July; *Tribune*, 24 July).

The *People's Voice*, which became a more substantial newspaper during 1989, celebrated its 50th anniversary (1939–1989) with a detailed history of the paper and its predecessors (*Communist*, 1924–1926, *Vanguard*, 1926–1929, *Red Worker*, 1929–1933, *Workers' Weekly*, 1933–1939, and the illegal Auckland *Forward* and Dunedin *Guardian* during World War II). The commemorative issue (*People's Voice*, 10 July) was followed by a conference on the party's propaganda work held in Auckland 29–30 July. Much of the *People's Voice* attention during the latter part of 1989 was devoted to the Labour government's cuts in public health services as well as to the continuing battle against the compact.

In October, Willie Wilson, a member of the Central Committee and leader of the CPNZ team during the 1988 March Against Unemployment, was expelled from the party for failing to carry out his Central Committee duties, going overseas in the course of his employment "without prior Party consultation or agreement," and doing "his own thing" in regard to "state sponsored Maori development schemes" (*People's Voice*, 16 October).

The National Executive of the CPNZ's Central Committee consists of three men: Grant Morgan, since 1987 a full-time party official after fourteen years on the railways; Barry Lee, who has "held responsible positions in the party" since 1972; and Harold Crook, the party's former secretary who became chairman in 1989, replacing Dick Wolf, who died in 1987.

SUP. Throughout 1989 the SUP's leaders supported the Labour government even after the formation of the more left-wing NLP. In April, Ken Douglas (chairman) and Marilyn Tucker (general secretary) of the SUP called publicly on trade unions to remain loyal to the Labour party (*NZ Herald*, 26 April).

There are four major reasons why the SUP, unlike New Zealand's other communist parties, is openly committed to the re-election of the Labour government in 1990. First, the SUP wants to entrench Labour's foreign and defense policies, notably its antinuclear ship ban. Second, it believes that a National party government would introduce voluntary unionism and deregulate the labor market. Third, the union movement is currently reorganizing itself into a smaller number of large industrial unions under the umbrella of the new Confederation of Trade Unions (CTU), which the SUP wishes to influence even more significantly than at present. Fourth, Douglas, as the CTU's president, already enjoys a powerful influence on the Labour government.

The SUP's attitude to and relations with the Labour party were analyzed for the international communist movement in two articles published during 1989 in the *World Marxist Review* (Prague). They were written by David Arthur, an SUP Central Committee member (*WMR*, March), and Douglas (*WMR*, July). In his article, Douglas noted that the suffering of many New Zealanders "also creates more favourable conditions for workers' struggle." That struggle would involve "political activists—both Communists and left Labour Party members—and trade union leaders (in New Zealand this refers primarily to the SUPNZ)." He revealed that unofficially "our activists and Labour Party activists have been working in a much more cooperative way" and that in future "progress will be impossible without joint action by SUP and Labour Party members." In November, 55 SUP, NLP, and WCL supporters and other unionists attended a WISE seminar in Auckland on the topic Building Left Unity (*Tribune*, 13 November).

Faced with some dissent from rank-and-file SUP members antagonistic to the Labour government and its continuing record of high unemployment and cuts in health and education, the SUP published a special four-page supplement to the *Tribune* in which Tucker argued that, as long as there was a two-party monopoly of government in New Zealand, Labour was better than the antiunion National party (*Tribune*, 4 September). The supplement followed a meeting 19–20 August of the SUP Central Committee on the theme Understanding the Nature of Change and Its Causes.

Twenty-three New Zealanders attended the Thirteenth World Festival of Youth and Students held at Pyongyang, North Korea, in July. Approximately half the New Zealand delegates were Maori, and one-third were women. Only three were *pakeha* (white males). Hannah Zwartz and James Nihoniho were elected to a newly formed South Pacific United Youth Association (SPUYA), which will address three major issues: a nuclear-free and independent Pacific, educating Pacific youth on environmental problems, and anticolonialism in New Zealand. SPUYA subsequently held an international peace forum in Wellington 6–8 October at which France was the major target. The forum was attended by a number of overseas delegates including Igor Abylgaziev, who heads the Committee of Youth Organizations in the USSR. A conference of SPUYA will be held at Waitangi 31 January–4 February 1990 to coincide with New Zealand's commemoration of the signing of the Treaty of Waitangi on 6 February 1840, when the Maori chiefs ceded sovereignty of the country to Britain. An SUP women's delegation also visited Moscow and Kharkhov for ten days in October.

George Jackson, the president of the SUP, is now 81, and a new generation of activist SUP leaders is starting to emerge, such as 40-year-old Marilyn Tucker, a pharmacist and the party's general secretary, Alan Ware, the SUP's vice-chairman, and Joe Tonner, a senior full-time official of the Public Service Association (the government employees' union) and assistant general secretary of the SUP. The most influential figures in the party, however, are two longtime SUP officeholders and major trade union officials, Ken Douglas and Bill Andersen.

WCL. Throughout 1989 the WCL campaigned in support of Maori self-determination, pay equity for women, and Marxist parties in Nicaragua, El Salvador, and the Philippines. The WCL criticized the Chinese "return to Stalinism" (*Unity*, 3 July), the

Labour government's decision to buy four frigates, and the industrial compact, which was described as a strategy to "keep the unions smiling while they are beaten to death" (*Unity*, 14 April).

During 5 and 6 August the WCL organized a Socialism Meets Feminism conference in Wellington. Two hundred women attended the fifteen workshops on such themes as Red Lesbians and A Vision of a Socialist-Feminist Aotearoa and listened to three speakers—Anne Else (feminist), Marilyn Tucker (SUP), and Dale Little (WCL)—on the topic of The Unhappy Marriage of Marxism and Feminism (*Unity*, 1 September).

On 2 September the WCL and the NLP explored the possibility of a Red-Green Alliance at a seminar on the environment addressed by Klaus Bosselman, a cofounder of the West German Green party. That environmental emphasis by the NLP was reinforced in its newspaper (*New Times* 1, no. 1, November–December) and at the NLP's regional conferences held during November.

The WCL, which at its 1984 national conference had decided to abandon "the monolithic approach to political leadership" by "rejecting the idea of party monopoly over socialist society and the mass movement" (*Unity*, 3 July), welcomed the formation of the NLP held in Wellington 3–5 June (*Unity*, 3 July). Delegates to the NLP's inaugural conference included two hundred former members of the Labour party and 250 other Marxists, feminists, environmentalists, peace activists, Maori radicals, and unemployed-worker organizers. A number of small existing Marxist parties and groups were represented: the WCL, some former members of the SAL, the Communist Left (Auckland Trotskyite), the Permanent Revolution (Wellington Trotskyite), the Revolutionary Communist League (Christchurch), and the People's Alliance, formed in 1988 by an amalgamation of the Auckland Left Alternative and the Wellington People First organizations (see *YICA*, 1989).

The two major positions in the NLP, which soon claimed three thousand financial members compared with the Labour party's nine thousand and the National party's 140,000, were won by Anderton (party leader) and Mat McCarten (president). Among the other key officeholders in the NLP are Sue Bradford (WCL and Left Alternative), the vice-president; Keith Locke (onetime SAL and current national coordinator of the Philippines Solidarity Network), the convenor of the NLP's international policy committee; and Jim Delahunty (People First spokesman), the chair of the NLP's social policy committee. Among the first candidates the NLP chose to contest key electorates in the 1990 parliamentary elections were Bradford and trade union lawyer Matt Robson, who in 1975 was an SAL candidate for Parliament and subsequently an officeholder in the Labour party.

The WCL decided, despite its involvement in the NLP, to try to retain its own separate identity "as a small organised centre of left activists committed to revolutionary change" (*Unity*, 5 May). The People's Alliance and its two affiliates, People First and Left Alternative, officially disbanded themselves and handed over their funds to the NLP. In July the NLP expelled the Auckland University–based Communist Left after Anderton and McCarten claimed that the tiny Trotskyite faction had only joined the NLP to provoke a split between moderate and militant wings of the new party (*Wellington Evening Post*, 3 July; *NZ Herald*, 4 July).

CL (SAL). The SAL largely withered away after twenty years of active existence. Its newspaper, *Socialist Action*, ceased publication during 1988, and the party now consists of a small and dwindling handful of rather dispirited members. Many of its idealistic student members, recruited at the height of the Vietnam War, chose to work in manual occupations, such as freezing work, where they became isolated into small, self-contained cells with limited influence over other workers. They became preoccupied with international affairs and took their lead from Castro's Cuba. Nicaragua, El Salvador, and the Philippines became more important to them than New Zealand, and today the SAL appears to be little more than a branch office of the Socialist Workers' Party of the United States and its publishing house, Pathfinder Press. The SAL held a conference 3–5 June at which the party decided to change its name to the Communist League (CL). Its activities and views are now printed from time to time in the New York–based weekly *Militant*, which the CL distributes in New Zealand. In October, Mel Elio, chairman of Lumad Mindanao, and Yul Caringas, deputy secretary general of the Philippines Organisation of Tribal People's Emancipation, toured New Zealand under the auspices of the Philippines Solidarity Network.

New Zealand and the Soviet Union. The biennial meeting of the Soviet–New Zealand Joint Trade Commission took place in Moscow in June. The New Zealand delegation, led by Richard Nottage, deputy secretary of the Ministry of External Relations and Trade, and the Soviets, led by Y. Chumakov, deputy minister of foreign economic relations, explored joint ventures such as the Sakhalin-SOVENZ peat moss extraction project and trade between the two countries (*NZ External Relations Review* 39, no. 3 [April–June]).

According to the New Zealand Department of Statistics, New Zealand exports to the USSR for the year ending 30 June totaled NZ$351.4 million. Imports from the Soviet Union were a mere NZ$13.3 million. Trade has continued to be in traditional products: wool, meat, and dairy products to the USSR and Lada cars from the USSR. Lada New Zealand, owned by the New Zealand Dairy Board subsidiary SOVENZ, has tried to increase its sale of Ladas in New Zealand to 250 a month (*NZ Herald*, 28 August).

The difficulties of extending trade and establishing joint ventures between the USSR and New Zealand were emphasized by the members of a six-man delegation from the New Zealand National Committee for Pacific Economic Cooperation when they returned from a visit to Moscow, Khabarovsk, Vladivostok, and Nakhodka from 17 to 24 July (*NZ Herald*, 12 July; *Auckland Star*, 17 August). The delegation, which included two of New Zealand's leading businessmen, Sir Ron Trotter and Alan Gibbs, did, however, express support for the Soviet Union becoming a full member of the Pacific Economic Cooperation Council (PECC) (for a full report of the visit see Roger Peren, "Internationalising the Soviet Economy," *NZ International Review* 14, no. 6 [November–December]). In November the Soviet National Committee for Asian-Pacific Economic Co-operation (SOVNAPEC) was represented at the seventh PECC meeting at Auckland 12–15 November by V. L. Malkevich (chairman, Soviet Chamber of Commerce and Industry), Y. V. Akhremenko (executive secretary of SOVNAPEC), V. P. Lukin (deputy head, Evaluation and Planning Directorate, Ministry of Foreign Affairs), and a Mr. Younousov (SOVNAPEC). The Soviets attended as guests, and although New Zealand favored future Soviet membership, the delegations from the United States and Japan appeared firmly opposed.

A number of joint ventures have been undertaken between New Zealand and the USSR. SOVENZ has signed contracts to build small meatworks and a dairy factory in the Soviet Union (*Auckland Star*, 1 September; *NZ Herald*, 24 November). A project estimated to be worth NZ$1.4 billion is proceeding despite the withdrawal of one of the New Zealand partners: the New Zealand Liquid Fuels Group decided not to be involved in the conversion to compressed natural gas or liquid petroleum gas of 50,000 Soviet cars, five thousand trucks, and two thousand buses every year or the building of four hundred to five hundred gas stations in the Soviet Union during the 1990s. The other two potential partners—the Maritime Pacific Group, led by Hugh Templeton, New Zealand's former minister of trade and industry, and Wellington lawyer Bruce Carran and the Soviet Ministries of Gas Industry and Automotive Transport—registered in July a joint venture company called Intertop, with the shareholding equally split between New Zealand and the Soviets (*NZ Herald*, 12 June; *Wellington Evening Post*, 3 July).

Among Soviet visitors to New Zealand who discussed trade with the New Zealand business community were Vladimir Arkhipov, general director of the Soviet Association for Business Cooperation, and Vadim Efremov, vice-president of the Soviet Chamber of Commerce and Industry (*Soviet News*, 15 June).

Other Soviet visitors during 1989 included Dr. Oleg Kolbasov, deputy director of the Academy of Sciences Institute of State and Law, Nikolai Kapralov, Institute of Far Eastern Studies, and Boris Makarenko, Soviet Peace Committee, who in April met New Zealand peace activists in Auckland, Christchurch, Wellington, and Napier and also had talks with Deputy Prime Minister Geoffrey Palmer and Disarmament Minister Fran Wilde. In the same month, Soviet economist Igor Guriev held discussions with union and SUP officials, and in September a Soviet trade unionist, Eugene Budarev, was an official observer at the first biennial conference of the CTU.

Also in September a delegation of three Soviet parliamentarians, Nikolai Dementei, Sergei Ambartsumiam, and Oleg Shenin, met a wide range of New Zealand politicians. Dementei, who is deputy chairman of the Supreme Soviet, advocated a permanent relationship with "systematic meetings" between the Supreme Soviet and the New Zealand Parliament. He also stressed the Soviets' wish to join PECC, the Asian Development Bank, and the General Agreement on Tariffs and Trade (GATT). Dementei proposed the creation of a new Asian-Pacific mechanism for handling disarmament negotiations in the region (*NZ Herald*, 5, 15 September).

Two major academic addresses were given by Soviet visitors. Rubin Azizian, from the Soviet Ministry of Foreign Affairs, gave a paper at a con-

ference on New Zealand, the Soviet Union, and Change, held at Otago University 12–14 May. The hundred participants in the conference were drawn from the universities, diplomatic corps, business community, and Ministry of External Relations and Trade. The papers, by speakers from New Zealand, Australia, the Soviet Union, and the United States, have been published (R. H. C. Hayburn, *New Zealand, the Soviet Union and Change*. Dunedin: University of Otago Press, 1990). The opening address by Fran Wilde, associate minister of external relations and trade, was also published in *NZ External Relations Review* 39, no. 3 (April–June). In October, Vladimir Kulagin, deputy director of research coordination with the Soviet Ministry of Foreign Affairs, addressed the Institute of Policy Studies at Victoria University of Wellington. Although his emphasis was on the dialogue and mutual understanding that would permit naval arms control to be implemented, Kulagin also argued that "the superiority of United States naval forces in the Pacific is becoming intolerable" (*NZ Herald*, 23 October). Kulagin, whose audience included the Soviet and Japanese ambassadors to New Zealand, pointed out that although

> the Northern Pacific looms largest in the Soviet consciousness . . . the South Pacific . . . is important to the Soviet navy in order to demonstrate that it has a capacity to disperse and cannot be confined to a limited area, and because in budget battles within the Soviet Union it helped if it can demonstrate a need for more ships and longer operations. (*IPS Newsletter* 20 [November], for summary of Kulagin's address and subsequent discussion.)

In January an influential radio talk host, Leighton Smith of Radio 1ZB Auckland, was a guest of the Soviet government, and later in the year a Novosti correspondent, Gennadi Belousov, took up residence in Wellington and was accredited to the parliamentary press gallery. In November a Soviet television crew filmed throughout New Zealand, accompanied by an Australian-based *Izvestiia* journalist, Vladimir Mikheyev.

The president of New Zealand's governing Labour party, Ruth Dyson, and a Labour member of Parliament, Richard Northey, were the guests of the CPSU during a visit to the USSR 8–19 July. They had a busy schedule of meetings with party, state, union, press, and academic representatives and were particularly impressed with the considerable amount of research on New Zealand, Australia, and the Southwest Pacific being undertaken by the Academy of Sciences Institute of Oriental Studies. At Dyson's invitation the CPSU sent a delegation consisting of N. B. Bikenin, editor in chief of the CPSU's theoretical journal *Kommunist*, and V. P. Kudinov, of the foreign department of the CPSU Central Committee, to attend the Labour party's annual conference in October.

On the cultural level, Dr. Michael Bassett, New Zealand's minister of internal affairs, visited the Soviet Union in August and subsequently announced three proposed Soviet contributions to New Zealand's 1990 celebrations of the nation's founding in 1840: an art exhibition from Leningrad's Hermitage collection, the Catherine collection of jewelry, and a troupe from the Kirov Ballet (*Wellington Evening Post*, 26 October).

The New Zealand government-sponsored Hillary Commission on Sport announced in July that the Football Association of the Soviet Union had established a "buddy programme" to help improve New Zealand's soccer and prepare New Zealand teams for the 1992 Olympics and the 1994 World Cup. Yuri Semin, a top Soviet coach, will spend six months in New Zealand in 1990, and the Soviets will help select and train the New Zealand team, which will spend some time training in the USSR during 1990 (*Wellington Evening Post*, 14 July; *Wellington Dominion*, 26 August).

The Soviets did not react in June to the New Zealand government's unexplained expulsion of the Soviet research ship *Akademik Oparin* from its two-hundred-mile economic zone. The ship, which went on to research Australia's northeast coast, had on board twelve Soviet and four American scientists who had intended, with four Auckland University biologists, to work in the Hauraki Gulf near Auckland. (*NZ Herald*, 21 June; *Christchurch Star*, 22 June; *Wellington Evening Post*, 23 June.)

After years of negotiations officials are ready to draft an agreement on landing rights for Aeroflot to fly in crews for Soviet fishing fleets off the coasts of New Zealand. New Zealand in return has sought access to Moscow for Air New Zealand (*Dominion Sunday Times*, 21 May). On 8 November a precedent was set when the giant *Antonov* An-124, the largest commercial cargo aircraft in the world, was the first Aeroflot plane to bring a cargo to New Zealand, landing in Auckland with a television broadcast van and flying out with a cargo of six large containers and 60 tons of aluminum (*NZ Herald*, 9 November).

Two polls indicated that New Zealanders were losing their distrust of the Soviet Union. An international Gallup survey revealed that 27 percent of New Zealanders had positive feelings toward the USSR, 11 percent negative, and the rest indifferent. This compared with positive and negative feelings toward the British of 69 and 4 percent; the Americans, 55 and 17 percent; the Japanese, 38 and 19 percent; and the French, 26 and 40 percent (*NZ Herald*, 26 August). A much smaller survey of first-year political studies students at Auckland University, taken shortly after enrollment, revealed that 80 percent saw New Zealand's relationship with the USSR as important, that only 18 percent believed the Soviets were a potential strategic threat, and that twice as many believed the USSR was more committed to peace and disarmament than the United States (36 to 18 percent). When ranking world leaders on a five-point scale (very favorable to very unfavorable), the students gave Mikhail Gorbachev a 75.6 percent favorable–very favorable rating and a 4.8 percent unfavorable–very unfavorable assessment. By comparison, Ronald Reagan received only 24.4 percent approval and 50.2 percent disapproval. That the students were not left-wing in their bias was shown by their highly favorable ranking of Britain's Conservative prime minister, Margaret Thatcher. (The poll is detailed in Hayburn, *New Zealand, the Soviet Union and Change*.)

New Zealand and the People's Republic of China. In April, New Zealand's foreign minister, Russell Marshall, visited China and had talks with Premier Li Peng and Foreign Minister Qian Qichen. They expressed general agreement on major international issues and satisfaction with the development of friendship, cooperation, and trade between the two countries.

Ever since New Zealand recognized the People's Republic of China in 1972, China has become New Zealand's fifth most important trading partner and its major market for wool, though during 1989 the Chinese were far less active in purchasing New Zealand wool. New Zealand exports to China for the year ending in June were NZ$539.5 million (NZ Department of Statistics). In recent years 20 percent of New Zealand's wool has gone to China, which also buys New Zealand timber, hides, aluminum, and dairy products. The New Zealand company Welgas Holdings Ltd. became in 1988 the first foreign company to introduce compressed natural gas technology to China, training engineers and technicians and supplying conversion equipment to convert oil tankers to gas and dual-fuel operations.

Five other New Zealand companies have joint venture investments in China, producing livestock feed, printed circuit boards, textile quilts, air compressors, and packaged fish.

New Zealanders were outraged by the massacre of students in Peking's Tiananmen Square in June, and Marshall summoned the Chinese ambassador and delivered a strong formal protest. The New Zealand minister of education, Phil Goff, cut short an eight-day visit to China, and a scheduled visit by the minister of police, Peter Tapsell, was canceled in protest. All social contacts between the two governments and their officials were suspended, and the New Zealand government expressed concern for the 450 Chinese students studying in New Zealand. A seminar on China, held on 4 October by the Institute of Policy Studies at Victoria University of Wellington and attended by government officials, businessmen, and academics, agreed that "condemnation of the Chinese Government's actions had to be combined with an acceptance of the importance of its participation in the international community" (*IPS Newsletter* 20, November).

Although the New Zealand government announced that there would be no trade embargo, the suppression of the students and subsequent international reaction made it difficult for the Chinese government to conclude negotiations for the foreign loans it required to complete the purchase of the New Zealand Steel Corporation by China's National Metals and Minerals Import and Export Company (Minmetals). The modern, high-technology, internationally competitive enterprise, with a steelmaking capacity of 630,000 tons of finished steel a year using New Zealand energy and ore, was to be sold to the Chinese at about a sixth of the initial cost of its establishment after the New Zealand government wrote off much of the NZ$3 billion it had invested in setting the industry up (*NZ Herald*, 25 March; *Auckland Star*, 17, 23 April). Although the steel sale fell through, by October another Chinese group had gained approval to submit a bid for New Zealand's 550,000 hectares of state forests, which the Labour government had put on the market hoping to obtain as much as NZ$5 billion to pay off government debt (*Wellington Domain*, 26 October; *NZ Herald*, 28 November). Most of the forests will probably be sold to New Zealand forestry groups rather than to the Chinese.

Biography. *George Harold Andersen.* George Harold ("Bill") Andersen was born in Auckland in 1924. Married, with three children, he was educated at Otahuhu College. A merchant seaman during 1942–1946, he was expelled from the seaman's union in 1948 for organizing an unofficial strike. He became a freezing worker, but was dismissed for union activities. As a waterside worker during the 1951 strike, Andersen was responsible for the distribution of illegal publications. Blacklisted by the employers after the strike, he worked as a cleaning contractor and then as a truck driver. In 1954, Andersen was elected organizer of the Northern Drivers' Union, centered in Auckland, and in 1958 became the union's secretary, a post he has held ever since. He was jailed briefly in 1974 for refusing to obey a court order during an industrial dispute. In 1976, Andersen was elected president of the Auckland Trades Council, holding the post until that body was replaced in 1988 by the Auckland District Council of the new CTU. Andersen has been chairman of the District Council and a National Executive member of the CTU since their formation. He had earlier served on the National Executive of the FOL. Andersen joined the British Communist Party in 1944 and the NZCP in 1946. In 1966 he was one of six leading CPNZ members who broke away from the pro-Chinese CPNZ to form a new Soviet-aligned SUP. In 1986, Andersen resigned the SUP's presidency to become the party's national secretary, but it was decided that he should devote his attention to his leadership role in the union movement. He has continued to be a member of the SUP's Central Executive and Central Committee. He stood unsuccessfully as an SUP candidate for Parliament in Tamaki against the National party leader, Sir Robert Muldoon, on four occasions: 1972, 1975, 1978, 1981. His highest proportion of the vote was in 1981 when he received 0.9 percent.

Biography. *Harold Crook.* Harold Crook was born in 1910, the son of a coal miner in Huntly. He joined the Labour party in 1924, but switched to the CPNZ in 1932. Sacked from the mines during the depression, Crook became active in the Unemployed Workers' Movement. During World War II he returned to the mines; by the time of the 1951 strike, which crippled the New Zealand economy for 151 days, Crook had become president of the Huntly Miners Union. He held that post until his retirement in 1971. When pro-Soviet members broke away from the CPNZ in 1966, Crook remained loyal to the CPNZ and China. In the 1970s he supported Wolf and helped oust the pro-Chinese faction when the CPNZ aligned itself with Albania.

He stood unsuccessfully as CPNZ candidate for Raglan in 1963 and 1966, but never polled more than 0.8 percent of the votes cast.

Biography. *Ken Douglas.* Ken Douglas was born in Wellington in 1935, the son of a truck driver. Married, with four children, Douglas was educated at Wellington College. After working as a trainee wool classer, laborer, and waterside worker, he became a truck driver. President of the Wellington Drivers' Union during 1958–1960, Douglas became the union's full-time organizer in 1960 and full-time secretary in 1963. He held that post until he was elected secretary of the New Zealand Federation of Labour (FOL) in 1980. When the FOL (private-sector unions) and Combined State Unions (CSU) joined to become the CTU in 1988, Douglas became the first national president of the CTU and the most powerful union leader in the country, presiding over 560,000 of the nation's 700,000 unionized workers. Douglas joined the CPNZ in 1961, switching his allegiance to the SUP after its formation in 1966. He stood as SUP candidate for Parliament in Porirua in 1972, 1975, and 1978, receiving his highest vote in 1972 when he recorded 0.5 percent of the vote. Since 1986 he has been the chairman of the SUP's National Executive.

Biography. *Bruce Skilton.* Bruce Skilton, who retired from the SUP's Central Committee at its October 1988 conference at the age of 80, arrived in New Zealand from England in 1925. After working on a sheep farm and hydroelectric power construction projects, he joined the New Zealand Railways and was elected chairman of the railway union's road services section. Skilton joined the CPNZ in August 1939 and was responsible throughout the war for the party's illegal publications in Christchurch. In 1945 he became chairman of the CPNZ's Christchurch committee and a member of the Central Committee. From 1949 to 1961, Skilton served as the CPNZ's organizing secretary, but left the party to help found the SUP in 1966. He remained on the SUP's Central Committee until his retirement 22 years later. In 1975, Skilton contested the Grey Lynn seat in Parliament, receiving 0.2 percent of the total votes cast.

Biography. *Victor George Wilcox.* Victor George Wilcox died on 29 April at the age of 77. The son of an immigrant London railway worker, Wilcox was a rural laborer during the depression. He joined the CPNZ in 1934, becoming its full-time secretary in Auckland in 1939. In 1956, Wilcox became the party's general secretary when its long-time leader Sid Scott resigned over the Soviet invasion of Hungary. Wilcox remained in that position until 1977. When the Sino-Soviet rift developed, Wilcox was influential in aligning the CPNZ with China. A friend of Rewi Alley, a New Zealander who spent much of his later life working in China, Wilcox visited that country almost every year during the 1960s and 1970s. In 1977, when the CPNZ rejected China, Wilcox was expelled from the party. He formed a small, short-lived organization known as the Preparatory Committee for the Formation of a CPNZ (Marxist-Leninist) and later another faction called the Organisation for Marxist Unity. Wilcox remained active in the New Zealand–China Friendship Society and loyal to the Chinese position in international communist affairs until his death. He stood for Parliament as a CPNZ candidate six times (Arch Hill, 1946, 1949, 1951; Auckland Central, 1954; Waitakere, 1960, 1963), but never received more than 4.6 percent of the votes cast (1946).

Barry Gustafson
University of Auckland

Pakistan

Population. 110,407,376 (July 1989)
Party. Communist Party of Pakistan
Founded. 1948; banned in 1954; re-emerged in 1989.
Membership. 200 with several thousand sympathizers (1989 estimate)
General Secretary. Imam Ali Nazish
Status. Legal
Last Congress. Third, 25–27 May
Leading Bodies. Unknown
Publications. Unknown

Summary. In November 1988 Benazir Bhutto led the Pakistan People's Party (PPP) to an electoral victory that gave the PPP 92 of the 205 seats in Pakistan's National Assembly (parliament). Bhutto pulled together a coalition that permitted her to take office as the country's first woman prime minister.

Party Affairs. The Communist Party of Pakistan benefited from Bhutto's political liberalization. After some 35 years of operating underground, the party openly held its Third Congress 25–27 May, attended by 127 delegates from across the country. The congress re-elected Imam Ali Nazish as party general secretary, received a Central Committee report on past errors, and approved a plan of action for the future.

Foreign Affairs. Afghanistan remained Pakistan's chief foreign affairs preoccupation during the year. The withdrawal of Soviet forces from Afghanistan in February fundamentally altered Pakistan's security environment. It also called for a reassessment of Islamabad's relations with Afghanistan and the Soviet Union as well as with Pakistan's allies and backers on its Afghan policy.

When Bhutto removed General Hamid Gul as czar of Afghan policy in May, she replaced him with retired General Shansur Rahman Khallu. Khallu was relieved by Zia for challenging Zia's assumption of the presidency while remaining chief of army staff. Khallu had been a Bhutto supporter, and his selection for the position was a way for her to get greater control over Afghan policy. Gul had been instrumental in directing foreign matériel and financial support toward fundamentalist Afghan resistance groups favoring a military solution to what had become a civil war. Bhutto favors a political solution to the Afghan war, perhaps one resulting from a negotiated settlement. (*NYT*, 26 May.)

Relations with the USSR. Pakistan's relations with the USSR continue to be influenced by events in Afghanistan. Moscow and Islamabad sought to improve relations and find common ground on Afghanistan. Moscow's first deputy foreign minister and the ambassador to Afghanistan, Yulii Vorontsov, went to Islamabad in early January, some six weeks before the completion of the Soviet troop withdrawal, to talk with Pakistani leaders and Foreign Ministry officials. Pakistan continued to press the Soviet Union to help establish a broad-based government in Afghanistan acceptable to all parties in the conflict. During the visit, Vorontsov continued talks, begun the previous month in Saudi Arabia, with members of the resistance Afghan interim government. Vorontsov's trip ended on a high note with the announcement that the Soviets

and the Afghan resistance would establish a consultative mechanism to bring about a settlement. (*FBIS-NES*, 9 January.) The year ended, however, with no progress.

The following month, Soviet foreign minister Eduard Shevardnadze went to Islamabad to follow up and expand upon the Vorontsov visit. Besides agreeing that a military solution would not work in Afghanistan, the visit examined areas where Soviet-Pakistan cooperation could be expanded in the economic, cultural, and technical fields. (*FBIS-NES*, 21 February.) Bhutto later emphasized her government's goal of promoting good relations with Moscow (*FBIS-NES*, 22 March).

In April the USSR and Pakistan signed agreements to implement greater cooperation between the two countries' chambers of commerce and industry. There was anticipation that a trade council would evolve that could promote stronger Soviet-Pakistani trade and economic relations. (*FBIS-NES*, 3 April.) These efforts were followed some months later with a visit to Moscow by the Pakistan minister of state for information and broadcasting. On his return he stressed that opportunities should be sought for greater Soviet cooperation and assistance in developing Pakistan's industrial sector. (*FBIS-NES*, 13 September.) The year ended with continued Pakistan-Soviet disagreement on the implementation of a political solution in Afghanistan. Islamabad supports the resistance consensus that the People's Democratic Party of the Afghanistan-led government must be removed. Moscow insists that the Kabul government participate in any transitional regime. (*FBIS-NES*, 27 October.) Islamabad did use its good offices with the resistance to secure the release of a number of Soviets who were prisoners of war.

Relations with the People's Republic of China. China continued to factor very heavily in Pakistan's foreign policy. Bhutto traveled to China in March to strengthen the existing relationship and seek further areas for cooperation. In Beijing she signed an agreement on reciprocal encouragement and protection of investments and a memorandum of understanding extending trade protocols. An agreement was also reached to hold the Fifth Session of the China-Pakistan Joint Economic Committee for Economy and Trade in late February in Islamabad. Bhutto went next to Shanghai, where she discussed Chinese assistance in textile production. (*FBIS-CHI*, 13 February.) In March a Chinese Communist party delegation visited Islamabad to promote closer ties with the PPP (*FBIS-NES*, 21 March).

The visit to China was reciprocated late in the year when Chinese premier Li Peng paid a four-day November visit to Islamabad and Karachi. Peng reviewed bilateral trade and economic cooperation and held talks on trade, finance, electrical generation, food and agriculture, industry, communications, and highway construction. Agreements were signed for expanded economic cooperation. (*FBIS-NES*, 15 November.)

Sino-Pakistan defense cooperation continued during the year both on a bilateral basis and as support for the Afghan resistance. China is an important source of low-technology, low-cost matériel assistance to the Pakistan armed forces. Moreover, as a solution to the Afghan imbroglio comes closer to fruition, Beijing becomes more important as a stalwart friend of Pakistan. Islamabad well remembers past U.S. embargoes of military goods. Many in Islamabad argue that Washington's periodic threats to cut both arms supplies and other aid because of Pakistan's nuclear program raise the value of Chinese support. (*FEER*, 23 February.)

Michael R. Potaski
Catholic University of America, Washington, D.C.

Philippines

Population. 64,906,990 (*World Factbook*, 1989)
Parties. Communist Party of the Philippines (CPP); Philippine Communist Party (Partido Komunista ng Pilipinas; PKP)
Founded. CPP: 1968; PKP: 1930
Membership. CPP: 30,000 (estimates range to more than 40,000); PKP: 5,000 (estimates as high as 8,000)
Leadership. CPP: Jose Maria Sison, chairman in absentia; Benito Tiamzon, acting chairman; PKP: Felicisimo C. Macapagal, chairman; Merlin Magallona, general secretary
Central Committee. CPP: regular members: Jose Maria Sison, Benito Tiamzon, Romolo Kintanar, Prudencio Calubid, Caridad Magpantay Pascual, Arturo Tabara, Leo Velasco, Ricardo Reyes, An-

tonio Tujan, Antonio Zumel, Sixto Carlos, Jose de Vera, Randall Echaniz, Antonio Cabanatan, Sotero Llamas, Allen Jasminez, Luis Jalandoni, Juliet Delima Sison, Jose Luneta, Salvador Bas, Julius Giron, Miel Laurenaria, Eugenia Magpantay Topacio, "Bart Paredes," Jesus Nacion, Geronimo Pasetes, Ruben Balistoy, Antonio Cabardo, Noel Itabag, Vicente Ladlad; alternate members: Edzel Sajor, Manuel Homina, Nilo Dela Cruz, Adelberto Silva, Vic Martinez, Alex de Vera, Angel Mendoza, Francisco Morales, Elizabeth Principe; captured in 1989: Manuel Warren Calizo, Satur Ocampo, Carolina Malay Ocampo, Federico Guanzon, Wilma Austria-Tiamzon (later escaped). PKP: Felicisimo C. Macapagal, Merlin Magallona, Alejandro Birones, Jesus Lava, Jose Lava, Aurora Evangelista
Status. CPP: illegal; PKP: legal
Last Congress. CPP: has never held a full congress; PKP: Ninth, December 1986
Auxiliary Organizations. CPP: New People's Army (NPA), National Democratic Front (NDF). Under its National United Front Commission, the CPP controls or influences many other organizations, listed here by sector. Religious: Christians for National Liberation (CNL); Ecumenical Movement for Justice and Peace; National Ecumenical Forum for Church Response; Ecumenical Partnership for International Concerns (EPIC); Mindanao Interfaith Pastoral Center (MIPC). Education, youth: Nationalist Youth (Kabatang Makabayan, KM); Youth for Democracy and Nationalism (KADENA); League of Filipino Students (LFS); National Union of Students of the Philippines (NUSP); Association of Nationalist Teachers (KAGUMA); Association of Concerned Teachers (ACT); Progressive Organization of Teachers for Enlightenment and Nationalist Transformation (POTENT). Labor: May First Movement (Kilusang Mayo Uno, KMU); Peasant Movement of the Philippines (Kilusang Magbubukid ng Pilipinas, KMP); National Federation of Sugar Workers (NFSW); Small Farmers' Association (SFAN); Federation of Small Fishermen. Women: Patriotic Movement of Women (Makabayang Kilusan ng Bagong Kababaihan, MAKIBAKA); Mothers and Relatives Against Tyranny (MARTYR); General Association Binding Women for Reforms, Integrity, Equality, Leadership, and Action (GABRIELA). Human rights: Task Force Detainees (TFD); Philippine Alliance for Human Rights Advocates (PAHRA); Families of Victims of Involuntary Disappearances

(FIND). Professional: Medical Action Group (MAG); Concerned Artists of the Philippines (CAP); Confederation for Unity, Recognition, and Advancement of Government Employees (COURAGE); Citizen's Alliance for Consumer Protection (CACP). General political: New Nationalist Alliance (Bagong Alyansang Makabayan, BAYAN); People's Party (Partido ng Bayan, PnB); Alliance for New Politics (ANP); Volunteers for Popular Democracy (VPD); Philippine Rural Reconstruction Movement (PRRM); Nuclear Free Philippines Coalition. CPP foreign auxiliaries and support groups: United States: Alliance for Philippine Concerns (APC); Philippine Workers Support Committee; Friends of the Filipino People in Honolulu; Church Coalition for Human Rights in the Philippines; Canada: Canada-Asia Working Group; Austria: Philippines-Austrian Committee; Belgium: Philippine Group-Gent; Britain: Philippine Resource Center; Philippine Support Group; Denmark: Danish-Philippine Group; Italy: Friends of the Filipino People in Italy (Solidarietà con il Popolo Filipino); Ireland: Filipino-Irish Support Group; Netherlands: Filipino People's Committee (Komite ng Sambayanang Pilipino, KSP); Dutch Philippines Group (FGN); Simbayan; Sweden: Swedish-Filipino Association; Switzerland: Samahang Pilipino; Gruppe Schweiz-Philippinen; West Germany: Aktionsgruppe Philippinen (AGPHI); Japan: Resource Center for Philippine Concerns; Australia: Philippine Action Support Group; New Zealand: Philippine Solidarity Network. PKP: Association of Agricultural Laborers; National Association of Workers (Katipunan); Philippine Committee for Development, Peace and Solidarity; Democratic Youth Council of the Philippines. CPP and PKP joint membership: Forward-Looking Organization of Women; Freedom From Debt Coalition; National Movement for Civil Liberties; Congress for People's Agrarian Reform.

Publications. CPP: *Ang Bayan* (The Nation), monthly; NDF: *Liberation*, monthly; *Balita ng Malayang Philipinas* (Free Philippines News Service) bimonthly; NPA: *Pulang Bandila* (Red Flag), bimonthly; Alex Bocayao Brigade: *Ang Partisano* (The Partisan); *Taliba ng Bayan*, biweekly; *Larab*, monthly, published in Samar; *NDF Update*, bimonthly, published in the Netherlands; *Filippijnenbulletin*, monthly, published by Dutch Philippine Group; *Pintig*, irregular, published by the Aktionsgruppe Philippinen

in West Germany; *Philippine Brief*, irregular, published by the Philippine Action Support Group in Australia; *Philippines Update*, monthly, published by the Philippine Solidarity Network in New Zealand; *Solidardad II*, quarterly, published by the Resource Center for Philippine Concerns in Japan. Books: Jose Maria Sison, with Rainer Werning, *The Philippine Revolution: The Leader's View* (Taylor and Francis, 1989); PKP: Merlin M. Magallona, *U.S. Marshall Plan for the Philippines: U.S. Military Bases and Foreign Monopoly Capital* (1989).

CPP. In 1989 the CPP escalated the largest communist insurgency in Asia by beginning to selectively target U.S. facilities and personnel in the Philippines. However, the CPP suffered further setbacks from a more aggressive government counterinsurgency program that led to the capture of key Central Committee members and a slight reduction in guerrilla numbers. The CPP's Robin Hood image was damaged by a widely publicized internal purge. Internationally, the CPP was embarrassed by its response to the violence in the People's Republic of China, expanded its contacts with North Korea, and continued to receive solidarity support from many Western leftist groups. There was a low-key CPP response to the nearly successful 1 December coup attempt by military factions.

Leadership and organization. Continuing to reside in the Netherlands, CPP founder and reputed chairman in absentia Jose Maria Sison maintained a high profile in 1989. His letters, which were captured by the military, revealed his continued influence on CPP decision making. Sison's new book, *The Philippine Revolution: The Leader's View*, is written in the form of a structured interview conducted between October 1987 and February 1988 by West German CPP solidarity activist Rainer Werning. It is a memoir of Sison's role in the CPP's formation and early growth and a commentary on current questions of CPP ideology, strategy, and international relations. In his preface, Sison says that his "experience and opinions are worth telling only as they are part of the people's revolutionary struggle for national liberation and democracy; and can somehow inspire others to understand and contribute their own share to this struggle." Sison says that following his release from jail by the Aquino government in 1986, he had no intention of working for the new government (Sison, p. 134). On the Aquino government he says, "let us then continue to assume that the Aquino regime follows its pro-imperialist and reactionary character and course to the bitter end. The revolutionary movement has no alternative but to wage fierce and bitter struggle against it" (Sison, p. 150).

There are indications that Sison now wants to return to the Philippines. In a letter from Sison to Benito Tiamzon, captured by the military with Wilma Austria-Tiamzon, Sison is alleged to have proposed returning to the Philippines in April 1988 (*FBIS*, 19 October). Yet in March, Sison said that he would not return to the Philippines, that to do so would "bare my chest to the bayonets of the reactionary state" (*Daily Globe*, 4 March). But in July he stated, "I hope to return home before the general offensive is carried out by the revolutionary movement" (*FBIS*, 31 July). There is some speculation that Sison may return to participate in a yet-to-be-held general CPP congress. Such a meeting would deal with the question of Sison's leadership.

In his new book on the CPP, journalist Gregg Jones notes that while in Europe, Sison and his wife "spent much of their time moving between the Netherlands and West Germany, where they were feted by European radicals as the first couple of the Philippine revolution" (*Red Revolution, Inside the Philippine Guerrilla Movement* [Westview, 1989], p. 252). Sison continues to deny that he has resumed chairmanship of the CPP or that he is raising funds for the party. But he faces more pressure. The Dutch government placed guards around his residence after the Manila government offered rewards for the capture of top CPP leaders (*FBIS*, 22 August). Sison has requested political asylum in the Netherlands, but Dutch news media reports indicate that Washington has urged the Netherlands not to grant Sison's request (*FBIS*, 15 August).

Regarding Acting Chairman Benito Tiamzon, Jones says that he was in his late 30s in 1988, that he studied engineering at the University of the Philippines where he became involved in radical politics, that he was captured by the military in 1973, and that he was released in 1974. He then played a key role in the CPP's rise on the island of Samar, was elevated in the mid-1970s to the Central Committee, where he was put in charge of the CPP's education department, and by the end of the 1970s rose to the Executive Committee of the Politburo. Jones notes that during his rise Tiamzon "made few enemies and impressed few people" and that his obscure background presents "an image problem" when compared with Sison (Jones, p. 254). Correspondence between Sison and Tiamzon captured by the Armed Forces of the Philippines (AFP) along with Wilma Austria-Tiamzon indicates that Tiamzon defers to the suggestions of Sison (*FBIS*, 18 December).

Romolo Kintanar, who was captured in 1988 and later escaped, is now presumed to be vice-chairman of the Central Committee's military commission. This commission is chaired by Benito Tiamzon and also includes Leo Velasco, Jose de Vera, Arturo Tabara, Caridad Magpantay Pascual, Antonio Cabanatan, Antonio Cabardo, and Prudencio Calubid. Kintanar is also chief of staff of the NPA General Command, with Antonio Cabardo as vice-chief of staff and Randall Echaniz as political director.

The AFP disclosed that the CPP held a Politburo conference in March and early April in southern Luzon and at least tried to hold another meeting in Manila during early November (*Manila Bulletin*, 15 August; *Daily Globe*, 6 November). Ideally, the Politburo meets every six months and is believed to contain at least nine Central Committee members: Jose Maria Sison, Benito Tiamzon, Caridad Magpantay-Pascual, Wilma Austria-Tiamzon, Arturo Tabara, Leo Velasco, Romolo Kintanar, Antonio Cabanatan, and Ricardo Reyes. Day-to-day decisions are made by a five-member executive committee that contains Benito Tiamzon, Jose Maria Sison, Wilma Austria-Tiamzon, Ricardo Reyes, and Romolo Kintanar. The AFP also made light of "conjugal dictatorships," an informal chain of command of powerful cadre couples. These were said to include Jose Maria Sison and Juliet Sison, Satur Ocampo and Carolina Malay Ocampo, Benito Tiamzon and Wilma Austria-Tiamzon, and Romolo Kintanar and Maria Gloria-Jopson. (Ibid.)

There was more turnover in the Central Committee. Alternate members elevated to full membership included Eugenia Magpantay Topacio, "Bart Paredes," Geronimo Pasetes, Miel Laurenaria, and Ruben Balistoy. Also added were at least six new alternate members.

The AFP also captured several more Central Committee (CC) members including Manuel Warren Calizo on 10 June (*Manila Bulletin*, 14 June), Satur and Carolina Malay Ocampo on 27 July (*WP*, 28 July), and Wilma Austria-Tiamzon on 4 October (*FBIS*, 5 October). Austria-Tiamzon later escaped from detention in Camp Crame, Manila, during a Christmas party (*FBIS*, 29 December). Alternate CC member and Negros regional party committee secretary Federico Guanzon was captured on 4 September (AFP, *Negros News and Features*, 12 September). Ignacio Capegsan, who was captured in

1988, was released on 19 April after charges against him were dropped for lack of evidence (*FBIS*, 20 April).

The AFP also identified the following regional CPP leaders: Leo Velasco, head of the Northern Luzon Commission; Julius Giron, deputy secretary of the Northern Luzon Commission; Caridad Magpantay Pascual, head of the Central Luzon Commission; Arturo Tabara, head of the Visayas Commission; Prudencio Calubid, deputy secretary of the Mindanao Commission; Sotero Llamas, secretary of the Bicol regional party committee; Miel Laurenaria, secretary of the Southern Tagalog party committee; and Ruben Balistoy, secretary of the Samar regional party committee (*FBIS*, 27 July).

In a sworn statement following his August 1988 capture, a bodyguard to National United Front Commission (NUFC) secretary Satur Ocampo identified the leadership of the NUFC: Carolina Malay Ocampo, deputy secretary; Allan Jasminez, chairman of NDF Secretariat; Domingo Anonuevo, vice-chairman, NDF Secretariat, in charge of Middle Forces Department; Fidel Agcaoile, in charge of the legal political party (Partido ng Bayan) and congress work; Lito Emong, in charge of Business/Bureaucracy Group of NUFC; Father Ted Anana, in charge of National Church Bureau of Middle Forces Department (sworn statement of Renato Constantino, 14 December 1988).

The AFP speculated that Allan Jasminez would succeed Satur Ocampo as head of the National United Front Commission (*FBIS*, 1 August). Former priest Frank Fernandez is believed to have succeeded Federico Guanzon as secretary of the Negros regional party committee (AFP, *Negros News and Features*, 28 November). Documents captured along with Satur and Carolina Malay Ocampo indicate that a Politburo investigation of the purge Operation Missing Link resulted in the disciplining of some Central Committee members. Jose Luneta and possibly Miel Laurenaria were demoted from the Central Committee. Luneta was stripped of all leadership positions and criticized for his alleged homosexuality. The Politburo also was said to have taken lesser disciplinary action against Satur Ocampo, Carolina Malay Ocampo, and Nilo Dela Cruz (*FBIS*, 10 August).

Captured documents revealed that another consequence of the Politburo deliberations on the purge was to dissolve the National Organization Commission headed by Antonio Tujan and the Manila-Rizal Party Commission headed by Edzel Sajor. The AFP revealed they have been succeeded by a National Urban Center Commission (*FBIS*, 21 August).

Domestic affairs. In 1989, for the first time, the CPP began a campaign of selective attacks against U.S. personnel, U.S. military facilities, and foreign aid projects that it judged were helping the government. There have been sporadic attacks against U.S. personnel, but despite years of debate the CPP had consistently avoided a deliberate policy of attacking foreigners. Warning of a policy change appeared in the December 1988 *Ang Bayan*, which stated, "The revolutionary movement must act against US military installations and business enterprises" (*FEER*, 16 February). Reasons for the change include a desire to change the conflict from a "civil war to a national war" by exploiting the increasing controversy over the U.S. military bases (ibid.; *CSM*, 3 May).

Attacks began on 9 April with an unsuccessful bombing attempt against a U.S. Navy communications relay station atop Mt. Santo Tomas in Benguet province for which the NPA claimed credit (*FBIS*, 12 April). The same day, an unsuccessful ambush on the Clark Base reservation tried to use homemade mines to blow up a bus carrying about 40 Americans to a practice shooting range. Then on 21 April the NPA killed U.S. Army colonel James N. Rowe outside the Quezon City compound of the Joint U.S. Military Assistance Group (JUSMAG). A statement signed by NPA commander Romolo Kintanar said Rowe was "a direct participant in the U.S. designed total war counter-insurgency program of the Aquino regime" and that the killing "signifies the firm commitment of the revolutionary forces to continue military actions against U.S. personnel and installations" (*FBIS*, 24 April). CPP chairman Sison called Rowe's killing "just punishment" (*FBIS*, 25 April). The assassination of Rowe, a Vietnam War hero, was widely reported in the United States and prompted Washington to reaffirm its support for the Aquino government. U.S. Pacific forces commander Admiral Huntington Hardisty said that U.S. troops would defend themselves if attacked by the NPA (*Daily Globe*, 6 May).

CPP attention then shifted to central Luzon as the NPA's Central Luzon Command stated it would "punish U.S. troops" and the AFP revealed an NPA list of U.S. personnel at Clark Base targeted for assassination (*FBIS*, 19 June). On 26 September, NPA guerrillas killed U.S. civilian military contract employees Donald Buchner and William Thompson outside Camp O'Donnell, about ten miles north of Clark. The killings occurred hours before the arrival of U.S. vice-president Dan Quayle (*FBIS*, 27 September). Finally, on 24 December NPA guerrillas strafed the U.S. Information Office in Davao City, on Mindanao, causing damage but no casualties. An NPA statement said the attack was "a reminder and a warning to the United States against continued intervention," referring to the U.S. support for Aquino during the 1 December coup attempt (*NYT*, 29 December).

On 25 February, the CPP on Negros Island burned a postharvest facility built with funds from the Canadian International Development Agency. The CPP called the complex part of the "Low Intensity Conflict program of the United States Central Intelligence Agency" (AFP, *Negros News and Features*, 6 March). The CPP also began to threaten Japan, Manila's largest economic aid donor. A captured letter from Sison instructed Satur Ocampo to warn Japan "against joining a U.S.-sponsored plan to buy off the U.S. bases"; if Japan joins the United States in exploiting Filipinos, then the CPP should "adopt a policy of resistance against Japanese interests" (*FBIS*, 15 August). Soon after this revelation a reported advance copy of an *Ang Bayan* article stated that Japanese aid was being used to suppress the CPP insurgency and that Japanese aid projects "will be properly dealt with by the people's democratic revolution" (*FBIS*, 7 September).

The decision to attack foreigners and the return of Romolo Kintanar highlighted the continued strength of the militarist tendency within the CPP leadership. In his book, Sison criticized the Nicaraguan-style insurrectionist strategy, with its political and urban emphasis, as reminiscent of the errors of the PKP in the 1950s (Sison, p. 129). He stated that his strategy of "protracted people's war," with its balanced rural-urban and military-political emphasis, provided more flexibility and has already laid the basis for later urban insurrection during the stages of "strategic stalemate" and "strategic offensive." A captured CPP assessment of its strategy noted that the protracted people's war "is already maturing" and that most errors have "had something to do directly with the failure to gain the participation and support of the masses" (*FEER*, 27 April).

But the December 1988 *Ang Bayan* noted that military strength "should not be made at the cost of neglecting . . . the mass organizations and the organs of political power. . . . The revolutionary struggle cannot be brought to total victory by armed struggle alone" (*FEER*, 16 February). However, the tendency favoring political struggle may have lost a

major proponent with the capture of Satur Ocampo (*Asiaweek*, 11 August). In a 15 September speech delivered for him at the University of the Philippines, Ocampo proposed greater "united front" building by the party. He said that current "united front efforts can be further developed, from tactical issue-based coalitions to the broad anti-fascist and anti-imperialist movement type formation of varied coalitions, towards a comprehensively programmatic national united front."

In the same speech, Ocampo said "some sections of the revolutionary movement committed serious political and military errors, starting in Mindanao in late 1985 to early 1986, up to more recent ones." He was referring to the CPP purge in Mindanao that is estimated to have killed eight hundred activists. Another purge, discovered in late 1988 called Operation Missing Link (OPML), created a media sensation. Estimates range from forty to two hundred victims in this purge, which sought to eliminate AFP "deep penetration agents" primarily in the National United Front Commission, National Finance Commission, and Southern Tagalog regional party committee. OPML survivors led the military to the mass graves of many victims, mainly in Quezon and Laguna provinces, and gave vivid accounts of torture, brutal executions, and the atmosphere of paranoia within the party (*Manila Chronicle*, 31 May, 1, 2 June). The purge originated in the accusation of captured CPP chairman Rudolfo Salas that he had been betrayed by a high-placed spy, a suspicion that was accentuated when more Central Committee members were captured in 1988 (*FEER*, 3 August). Witnesses said the purge was halted by Satur Ocampo, who also swore the survivors to secrecy.

A Politburo critique of OPML in the captured personal notes of Satur Ocampo for 25 March states there was "widespread use of torture . . . easy slide into suspicions of long standing party cadres/members on basis of circumstantial evidence, implications by others." The notes also list the mistakes of cadres who administered the purge and record the recommended expulsion from the Central Committee of Jose Luneta and Miel Laurenaria. Ocampo also says that past lessons have not been learned and that the "whole party leadership had not been able to systematically set guidelines and principles to guide anti-infiltration drives, despite Quezon-Bicol-Mindanao and other experiences." Another assessment of the purge captured along with Ocampo stated "there were no confirmed spies among those investigated . . . it devastated the cadre force, brought the organization to the brink of destruction and ruined the relationship of the movement without apprehending any definite enemy" (*FBIS*, 2 August).

The CPP received more adverse publicity from a widely reported 25 June NPA attack against a church in the village of Ranao, on Mindanao. Because the church members had been urged not to pay "revolutionary taxes" by their pastor, NPA guerrillas killed about 40 people, mainly women and children, during Sunday service. The pastor was beheaded. Reacting to the public outrage, the NPA in Mindanao apologized for the attack, but claimed they were defending themselves from anticommunist religious cult members (*Tempo*, 28 June). Following an NDF investigation of the massacre, spokesman Antonio Zumel called for the trial of the responsible NPA members (*FBIS*, 8 September).

Also damaging were the revelations of former CPP members that Jose Maria Sison had planned the infamous 1971 Plaza Miranda bombing (*WP*, 4 August). Although the late president, Ferdinand Marcos, had blamed the CPP, most blamed Marcos for this bombing, which he later used to justify his declaration of martial law. Sison correctly calculated that the bombing would increase the "contradictions" between the ruling classes, increase CPP membership, and lead to greater cooperation with legal political opposition parties (Jones, p. 62). Senate president Jovito Salonga, who was injured by the bombing, conducted a Senate hearing about the new revelations. Rudolfo Salas confirmed that CPP member Danny Cordero claimed to have carried out the bombing (*FBIS*, 25 August). Sison denied that he planned the bombing and denounced author Gregg Jones (*FBIS*, 8 August).

The AFP recorded a decline in NPA strength from 23,060 in January to 19,780 in December (*FBIS*, 29 December). An unofficial military estimate placed NPA strength closer to 34,000 (*FEER*, 27 April). From January to 30 June the AFP recorded 1,748 insurgency-related fatalities and 1,565 incidents, or 8.65 a day, down from 9.63 a day for 1988. "Sparrow" assassinations continued in Manila, including the 4 July killing of the police chief of the Makati financial district (*FBIS*, 17 July).

By midyear the AFP claimed that out of 41,864 *barangays* (barrios), there was a decline in the number of those affected by the CPP from 7,852 to 7,827. Other estimates place this number at 12,000 (*FEER*, 27 April). The CPP is said to maintain the initiative against the government in the Cagayan Valley in the Visayas and Bicol regions and to have

reduced but significant strength in Mindanao and Bataan provinces (*NYT*, 21 October). It is reported that half of the barangays in Pampanga province, which surrounds Clark Base, are influenced by the CPP (*Stars and Stripes*, 25 May). In Quezon province the governor negotiated with NPA commanders so that a sports festival would not be disrupted (*FBIS*, 8 May).

The government claimed that the CPP sought to capture the leadership of 60 percent of the barangays in nationwide barangay council elections held on 28 March; the CPP did win in some remote villages in Samar, Leyte, Negros, and Mindanao (*FBIS*, 4, 5 April). President Corazon Aquino said that communists who are elected to barangay posts can keep them as long as the elections were fair. The CPP is also reported to have formed provisional revolutionary governments, or "shadow" governments, in 17 towns plus 20 percent of the barangays in Isabela, 42 towns in central Luzon, 2 towns in Negros, 10 towns in Samar, 50 barangays in Bicol, and 25 towns in eight Mindanao provinces (*FBIS*, 7 April).

AFP chief of staff Renato de Villa estimated the CPP was able to collect $7.5 to $10 million from "revolutionary taxation" and another $6 to $9 million from abroad, mainly channeled through nongovernment organizations (*FBIS*, 6 October). The AFP also reported that the CPP has collected up to $60,000 from logging firms in the Cagayan Valley and up to $375,000 a year from businesses in Pampanga province (*FBIS*, 18, 26 July). Information captured along with several CPP leaders in Davao in early September indicated that the CPP collects up to $180,000 a year from businesses in the four provinces of Region Eleven in Mindanao (AFP, action report).

There were several proposals for peace talks, but none transpired. In response to President Aquino's 19 February offer to resume peace talks, Satur Ocampo said on 22 February that the NDF would begin such talks only if Aquino declared that the U.S. military bases would not be extended beyond 1991. Then on 23 February, NDF international representative Jalandoni said such talks could begin without the preconditions regarding the bases (*Manila Chronicle*, 25 February). In early April, Sison and Jalandoni said that if Aquino were willing to dismantle the U.S. military bases by 1991, then the CPP would consider a "unilateral ceasefire" (*FBIS*, 12 April). This offer was later rejected by AFP chief of staff de Villa (*FBIS*, 25 July). Jalandoni also proposed peace talks in a third country, but this was rejected by Aquino (*FBIS*, 17 August).

On several occasions government leaders claimed they could win the war by 1991 (*Manila Bulletin*, 16 May; *FBIS*, 23 August). In addition to more aggressive intelligence operations that led to the capture of more leadership cadres, the AFP applied greater military pressure. Nineteen specific CPP guerrilla fronts were targeted for military operations (*FBIS*, 23 August). The April to May Operation Thunderbolt on Negros was the largest offensive sweep of the year. It succeeded in chasing the CPP from strongholds in central Negros, but also created about 35,000 refugees who strained the government's ability to care for them (*NYT*, 13 June). The AFP also began offering one-million-peso ($50,000) rewards for the capture of top CPP leaders, identified on wanted posters (*FBIS*, 27 July).

The 1 December coup attempt by military factions seriously weakened the Aquino government. The CPP apparently had no direct role in the incident and only a limited reaction. The AFP reported a rise in small-scale NPA attacks in the countryside, and on 25 December the CPP called for a "broad anti-imperialist and democratic front" to combat "the approaching reimposition of fascist rule" (*FBIS*, 12, 26 December). The CPP's inability to take advantage of the coup attempt brought criticism of its structure and ideology from Professor Alex Magno of the University of the Philippines. He said the CPP's classification of Aquino as right-wing, which led to the decision not to support her against a "fascist" revolt, was a mistake that relegated the CPP to the same sideline role it played during the rapid fall of Marcos in 1986. Magno also noted that the CPP's structure made it unable to exploit opportunities offered by the coup attempt. Its decentralized leadership made it unprepared for "political initiative in an hour of great political crisis" and unable to "play fast-paced political games" (*FBIS*, 27 December).

Auxiliary and front organizations. After two years of consultations with its various component fronts, the National Democratic Front (NDF) issued a new fifteen-point program to succeed its twelve-point program of January 1985. The NDF international office described the new program as including "new points on trade unionism, freedom of religion and belief, women's emancipation and rights, science and technology development, and environmental protection." However, the program

remains committed to violent revolution: (point 2) "Wage a people's war to win total, nationwide victory"; (point 3) "Establish a democratic coalition government and a people's democratic republic." The new statement on religion says (point 12), "Guarantee the freedom of religion and belief and promote the conditions for both believers and non-believers to work together for a national-democratic society" (*BMP*, March–April).

A 33-page analysis entitled "The Role of the Broad Legal Alliance in the Open Mass Movement Under the US-Aquino Regime," captured with and apparently written by Satur Ocampo in late 1987 or early 1988, acknowledges setbacks for CPP fronts and recommends new tactics to counter the "US-Aquino regime." Following attacks the "PDC (BAYAN) is faced with the formidable task of preserving and consolidating its forces for political and organizational survival." It notes that fishermen's fronts in the Visayas region that numbered as many as fourteen thousand in 1986 have declined to eight thousand members and that organizations of the urban poor, trade unions, and teacher and student organizations have weakened. Regarding the CPP's political struggle it concludes, "it is, indeed, difficult to expect at this particular period the movement's resurgence in breadth and intensity to that manifested during the Marcos years...the ND [National Democrat] open mass movement, left on its own, is unable to effectively fend off these [the U.S.-Aquino regime's] attacks." To supplement BAYAN and begin to revive its political struggle, the paper says the BLA-CL (National Movement for Civil Liberties) was created as "an entry point...to broaden the campaign to include progressive forces and individuals outside the ND orbit." But the real goal of the new BLA-CL is to draw "into more militant forms of struggle the politically inexperienced...neutralizing, at a minimum, antagonism and fear of the revolutionary armed struggle from within their ranks."

Former National United Front Commission member Renato Constantino named several groups as "influenced by the CPP/NPA": National Alliance for Justice, Freedom, and Democracy, Citizens' Alliance for Consumer Protection (CACP), Ecumenical Studies and Development Center, Church-Based Consumer's Movement (CBCM), Task Force Detainees, Kapisanan para sa Pagpapalaya at Amnestiya ng mga Detenido sa Pilipinas (KAPATID), Families of Victims of Involuntary Disappearances (FIND), Mothers and Relatives Against Tyranny (MARTYR), Philippine Peasant Institute, Nuclear-

Free Philippines Coalition, Basic Christian Community-Community Organization (BCC-CO), Protestant Lawyers League, Commission on Trade Union and Human Rights (CTUHR), Ecumenical Partnership for International Concerns (EPIC), National Council of Churches of the Philippines–Human Rights (NCCP-HR), United Church of Christ of the Philippines–Human Rights (UCCP-HR), Ecumenical Center for Missions (ECM), Ecumenical Studies and Development Center (ESDEC), Ecumenical Center for Development–Protestant (ECD), Episcopal Commission on Tribal Filipinos (ECTF), IBON, Share and Care Apostolate for Urban Poor Settlers (SCAUPS), Philippine Assistance for Rural and Urban Development (PARUD), and Institute of Religion and Culture of the Philippines (IRCP) (sworn statement, 14 December 1988).

Constantino also identified as personal friends within the CPP three leftists whose deaths in late 1988 had been widely blamed on the AFP: Pearl Abaya, formerly of the finance staff of the NUFC, later deployed to the Human Rights Committee to oversee the Philippine Alliance of Human Rights Advocates (PAHRA); Lani S. Mercado, formerly of the Citizens' Alliance for Consumer Protection, later deployed to BAYAN; and Efren Banagua, with the finance staff of the NUFC and BAYAN (ibid.). CPP documents captured by the AFP listed them as having been victims of the OPML purge. Task Force Detainees (TFD) cited relatives of the three victims who rejected the AFP's accusations (*Philippines Human Rights Update*, 15 February). But in August the Ecumenical Movement for Justice and Peace (EMJP) criticized the CPP for its silence regarding the AFP charges (*FBIS*, 21 August). In July the EMJP said that peace talks were jeopardized by the capture of Satur Ocampo and the posting of rewards for the capture of CPP leaders by the government (*FBIS*, 31 July).

While in Japan in December 1988, TFD leader Sr. Mariani Dimaranan stated, "There is no substantial difference between the governments of Mrs. Aquino and Mr. Marcos" (*Solidardad II*, December 1988). TFD's credibility was challenged when, following the 25 June Ranao massacre, the TFD in Mindanao issued a statement saying, "Task Force Detainees does not consider the Ranao incident a violation of human rights" (*Daily San Pedro Express*, 7–8 July). TFD seeks to differentiate between CPP and government violations by saying that CPP violations "should not be seen on the same level and degree of violations by agents of the gov-

ernment. The former is an illegal organization while the latter is a duly constituted protector of the people" (*Human Rights Update*, international ed., 15 July).

Religious leaders had differing assessments of the strength of Christians for National Liberation (CNL). National Council of Churches of the Philippines secretary general Fely Carino estimated CNL members and supporters amounted to between two thousand and four thousand, or 10 to 15 percent of the Philippine clergy. Catholic bishop Francisco Claver, however, said, "the CNL has become marginalised" and noted that only 21 priests had taken up arms against the government since 1972 (*FEER*, 1 June). In February, CNL issued a 30-page report analyzing political currents in the religious sector. The report assesses the opinions of several church leaders and denominations toward cooperation with the AFP, land reform, and the U.S. bases. There is praise for liberals like Bishop Labayan, NCCP, and UCCP and much criticism for conservatives like Cardinal Sin and Archbishop Quevedo and Social Democrats seeking to displace the influence of "progressives" in church structures.

In the trade union sector, the CPP-controlled Kilusang Mayo Uno (KMU) tried to recoup the loss of the 50,000-strong United Lumber and General Workers Federation to the Philippine Democratic Socialist party by organizing a convention of the federation's pro-KMU locals (*Philippine Daily Inquirer*, 24 February). Captured documents were said to indicate that close to 400,000 workers were in CPP-led or -infiltrated unions (*Daily Globe*, 26 February). In February the Toledo City prosecutor filed charges of illegal association with the CPP against KMU chairman Crispin Beltran plus officials of the KMU-affiliated union of the Atlas Mining Co. (*Daily Globe*, 10 February). An assassin was reported to have confessed to having been hired by the KMU to kill Atlas Company executives (*Daily Globe*, 4 April). In May the KMU joined forces with the noncommunist Trade Union Congress of the Philippines and succeeded in pressing the Congress to agree to a 25-peso raise in the daily minimum wage (*FBIS*, 31 May). The KMU called off a *welgang bayan* (general strike) to protest oil price increases scheduled for 1 December because of the coup attempt by military factions.

On 10 December BAYAN issued a statement condemning Aquino's decision to invite U.S. support to put down the coup attempt and opposing Aquino's intent to declare a state of emergency (*FBIS*, 15 December). Several groups including the Philippine Democratic Socialist party and BAYAN—in a nonofficial capacity—formed the Kilusan Laban sa Kudeta (KILOS, Movement Against Coups) and proposed regular meetings with Aquino (*FBIS*, 18 December). University of the Philippines professor Alex Magno noted the "CPP-led forces, for reasons of political orthodoxy, did not participate in this rare opportunity [KILOS] for rebuilding the broad progressive united front that once enjoyed great mobilizing capability in the waning years of the Marcos dictatorship" (*FBIS*, 27 December). He also noted that the recent decline of the radical student movement inhibited CPP ability to conduct "street action on short notice." The League of Filipino Students claimed to have the support of 25,000 students organized in 245 chapters (*National Midweek*, 23 August).

International views. The CPP had little to say publicly about the dramatic changes in the communist systems in the Soviet Union and Eastern Europe. But Sison's book examined several questions regarding CPP–Soviet bloc relations. He said, "It is obvious that the CPP central committee is already taking steps to revive and improve relations with all Eastern European parties" (p. 186). He also seemed to express impatience with the lack of support received from the Soviet bloc. Sison responded to a question on CPP-CPSU relations by saying, "Communist or workers parties should be more ready to develop fraternal and friendly relations with a communist party that is waging a life-and-death struggle against U.S. imperialism and the reactionaries" (p. 189). Sison also appeared to criticize other communists "who have never had the experience of participating in armed revolution and who argue even against possible and necessary help to those who are waging armed revolution" (p. 190).

Sison indicated there was competition with the PKP for the favor of Eastern European parties, saying that when those parties examine the "misinformation" provided by the PKP, "they see the merit of the successful revolutionary practice of the CPP. . . . The CPP is confident that relations of some Eastern European parties with the Lava group are vestigial" (p. 188). He said the PKP "is not really a revolutionary party of the proletariat. It is only a small reformist group and it would be a big joke for any foreign party to consider it the only party worthy of fraternal relations" (p. 189). He then stated a general criticism of the PKP: "Although the Lava group is zero in terms of armed struggle and takes pride in being exclusively or mainly parlia-

mentarist and legal, it is puny and inconsequential in the legal or parliamentary struggle" (p. 190). Sison's statements contrast with evidence in 1988 that CPP and PKP fronts began cooperating in groups like the Freedom From Debt coalition and the National Movement for Civil Liberties.

On relations with Vietnam and Cambodia, Sison said that since the CPP's 1979 criticism of Hanoi's invasion of Cambodia, "relations have not been good, especially with the Vietnamese party. But efforts are being exerted to improve relations with these two parties" (p. 185). He also says that "the CPP has maintained excellent relations with the majority of the communist parties in Southeast Asia. I refer to the parties of Indonesia, Malaysia, Kalimantan Utara, Thailand and Burma" (p. 184).

North Korea has become an important supporter of the CPP. In his book Sison says, "The Democratic People's Republic of Korea is an example of a state that is independent and democratic and is building socialism in a sound and admirable way" (p. 191). Reportedly, a captured letter from Sison to Benito Tiamzon in 1987 described a foiled plan to send North Korean weapons to the Philippines with assistance from the People's Republic of China (*FBIS*, 24 October). In September 1988 a CPP delegation attended ceremonies celebrating the 40th anniversary of the Pyongyang regime (Jones, p. 305). A delegation from the CPP's League of Filipino Students joined a delegation from the PKP's Democratic Youth Council of the Philippines to attend North Korea's World Youth Festival in July.

Gregg Jones noted that "by the late 1980s, the CPP had dispatched cadres to Vietnam, Nicaragua, and the Soviet Union to study how revolutionary change had been carried out in these countries" (Jones, p. 278). Jones also says that Sison visited Nicaragua and Mexico in early 1988 (p. 252).

The CPP was embarrassed when it showed initial support for Beijing's crackdown on demonstrators. In an 11 June statement the KMU said it "expresses its full support to the Chinese people under the able leadership of the Chinese Communist Party . . . in spite of the consistent efforts by imperialist forces to sabotage and derail the correct path chosen by the Chinese people." This stand was widely criticized in the Philippine press (*Manila Bulletin*, 14 June). Reacting to the KMU's support for the massacre, the Dutch Christian Federation of Employees trade union cut its financial support to the KMU (*Philippine Journal*, 3 October). The AFP released a captured letter dated 19 July to Tiamzon from Sison requesting that the KMU be told to retract its statement and noting that KMU financial supporters in Europe were not pleased (*Malaya*, 26 November).

CPP support groups in Europe generated much criticism of Aquino during her July visit (*FBIS*, 3 July). They were aided by visiting KMP deputy secretary Felicisimo Patayan and eight other KMP members (*Pintig*, August). In April, Byron Bocar of the NDF's international office addressed the annual conference of West German Aktionsgruppe Philippinen (AGPHI) (*Pintig*, June). In May a West German Department of Foreign Affairs official reacted angrily to the disclosure of a report by a Philippine military attaché about West German groups aiding the CPP (*FBIS*, 9 May). However, on several occasions the Philippine ambassador to West Germany criticized those aiding the CPP (*FBIS*, 3 July, 27 December).

During the July meeting of the Association of Southeast Asian Nations (ASEAN), Philippine foreign minister Raul Manglapus was reported to say that foreign ministers of ASEAN, the United States, Japan, Australia, New Zealand, and the European Community pledged to take measures to stop aid to the CPP (*FBIS*, 12 July).

At the annual Congress of the Australian Council of Trade Unions (ACTU), the Executive Committee of the ACTU ended the ACTU's exclusive support for the KMU. However, pro-KMU unions within the ACTU continue their support. In January one hundred to two hundred activists, mainly from Australia and New Zealand, traveled to the Philippines to participate in marches, demonstrations, and a conference against the U.S. bases. Their activities were sponsored by several CPP fronts including BAYAN, KMU, KMP, ACT, GABRIELA, and EPIC. The conference led to the creation of a new organization, the Asia-Pacific People's Forum on Peace and Development (APPFPD), led by Fr. Arturo Balagat (letter from APPFPD, 22 February). The forum is intended to be a regional center for leftist activists and proposed an initial budget of $50,000 to be raised from Koreans in the United States, Australia, South Korea, Japan, and New Zealand (ibid.). In July, Balagat traveled to North Korea for an International Study Tour to Support Reunification (*FBIS*, 20 July).

There is a growing CPP interest in leftist movements in South Korea. Sison said, "There are objective conditions for the progressive and revolutionary forces in South Korea to gain strength" (p. 191). Dominador Mamangun, general secretary of the KMU's National Federation of Labor Unions, attended the International Conference for Korean

Workers Union Movement in October 1988 (KMU correspondence). On 27 July, the Asia-Pacific People's Forum for Peace and Development, KMU, and LFS picketed in front of the U.S. embassy in support of International Day of Solidarity with the Korean People (letter from APPFPD, 20 July).

When Aquino visited the United States in November, several groups, including the Alliance for Philippine Concerns (APC), sponsored protest activities when she visited New York, Washington, D.C., and California. The APC claims to be composed of twenty organizations in twelve U.S. cities, three in Canada, and one in Mexico (*Daily Globe*, 30 April). The APC also participated in the National Consultation of Philippine Support and Anti-Intervention Groups on 4 March in New York City (ibid.). An APC affiliate, the Washington Forum on the Philippines, issued a 2 December statement that condemned the military coup attempt and criticized Aquino's reliance on U.S. support.

It was revealed that in 1988 the Canadian Anglican church gave $6,024 (Canadian) to the KMP and provided funding for the pro-CPP Canada Asia Working Group (*Pacific Newsletter*, no. 289). In December 1988 the Toronto-based International Commission for the Coordination of Solidarity Among Sugar Workers sponsored a conference in Bocolod hosted by the KMU's National Federation of Sugar Workers (*Inquirer*, 14 December 1988).

Accusations of Western church funding for the CPP were made by Australia's National Civic Council. These centered on the Hong Kong–based Asia Partnership for Human Development (APHD), which was organized in 1973 to funnel money to charitable projects and has twenty member countries, but is not accountable to any Catholic bishops. Australian Catholic Relief gave over $7.6 million (Australian) to APHD between 1978 and 1988. From literature of the APHD, the Flemish Broederlijk, and the Walloon Entraide et Fraternite, they cited the following donations: 750,000 Belgian francs were given to Task Force Detainees in 1986; 700,000 francs in 1987 to the Fishermen's Alliance of Cavite, which is controlled by the NDF; and donations to GABRIELA and groups controlled by the KMU (*AD 2000*, April). The article also mentioned the September 1988 visit to Belgium of left-leaning Philippine bishop Julio X. Labayan, who is said to have told the Europeans that "different independent support groups" have been formed to replace the National Secretariat of Social Action (NASSA), which distributed foreign church project funds. The Philippine bishops had regained control of NASSA after accusations that it was funding CPP fronts. Labayan criticized the article's authors as "paranoid" and denied that he made such a statement in Belgium (*Manila Chronicle*, 18 July).

PKP. In 1989 the PKP did not appear to be as active as in 1988 and denied accusations of an impending merger with the CPP. It was also revealed to be competing with the CPP for Soviet bloc recognition.

Leadership. No changes reported.

Domestic affairs. In a series of articles columnist Tony Abaya described an impending "merger" between the PKP and the CPP based largely on the 1988 interview of "Reynaldo Dimal" in *Morning Star* (*Business World*, 12, 13 January). PKP chairman Felicisimo C. Macapagal responded in a letter saying,

The two columns mislead the public because they conjure visions of a "possible merger" of the Partido Komunista ng Pilipinas (PKP) and the Communist Party of the Philippines (CPP). Such visions have no basis in fact...It is true that the PKP has always called for the principled unity of all anti-imperialist forces. But talk of a PKP-CPP merger is pure imagination and smacks of the CIA. (*Business World*, 24 January.)

Macapagal expressed alarm over the assassination of U.S. colonel Rowe, saying, "it can only lead to greater and even more direct U.S. intervention, which in turn will strengthen U.S. machinations to hold on to the bases in the Philippines" (*Business World*, 4 May).

International views. General Secretary Magallona admitted that in 1988 the PKP tried to block the CPP's efforts to gain greater foreign communist recognition. He wrote letters requesting that those parties already aligned with the PKP monitor the CPP's attempts to gain recognition (*CSM*, 1 March).

Richard D. Fisher, Jr.
Asian Studies Center, The Heritage Foundation

South Pacific Islands

Populations. Federated States of Micronesia: 102,134; Fiji: 756,599; French Polynesia: 196,246; Kiribati: 68,826; Nauru: 9,053; New Caledonia: 152,386; Papua New Guinea (PNG): 3,736,386; Republic of the Marshall Islands: 42,018; Solomon Islands: 323,545; Tonga: 100,465; Trust Territory of the Pacific Islands (Republic of Palau): 14,208; Tuvalu: 8,624; Vanuatu: 159,830; Western Samoa: 181,984 (*World Factbook*, 1989); Commonwealth of the Northern Marianas: 20,350; Cook Islands: 17,754 (1981); Wallis and Futuna: 12,391 (1983) (*Pacific Islands Yearbook*, 1989)

Regional Overview. During the 1970s, when most of the island states became independent, the South Pacific region was regarded as something of a democratic success story. In all but one case— Vanuatu—the transition to independence had been peaceful and subsequent elections fair and orderly. For the most part the island leaders were politically conservative, with ideologies influenced by Christianity. The islands had a strongly pro-Western political orientation. The Soviet Union had almost no influence in the region, and no island state had a formal communist party. Two military coups d'état in Fiji during 1987 and political instability in the Melanesian states of Papua New Guinea (PNG), Vanuatu, and New Caledonia, however, challenge democratic forms of government in the region. Outside powers not traditionally associated with the South Pacific are becoming involved in the region, and there appears to be a growing disillusionment on the part of some groups with the current island leadership.

The present leadership is, in many cases, drawn from the people who brought their islands to independence in the 1970s. Some leaders have grown old in office, and over the next few years it is likely that power will pass to a younger generation that has somewhat less conservative views. One measure of the pressure for reform that the younger generation of leaders has been exerting has been the creation of a number of labor parties—especially in the Melanesian islands—which profess democratic socialist philosophies. Labor party members and supporters come from the urban areas and have weak ties to traditional authority.

During 1989 the Soviet Union continued a policy of active but quiet diplomacy in the region. Before leaving his post in February as second secretary in Canberra to take up a senior staff appointment with Foreign Minister Eduard Shevardnadze, Valeri Zemskov gave an interview stressing the Soviet desire to establish "good and efficient relationships with each and every country of the region" and also the need to treat Australia "with a great deal of attention and consideration" as the major regional power (*Pacific Report*, 16 February).

Fishing rights are still the major focus of Soviet activity. Discussions are going on between the Soviet Union and both Australia and New Zealand with regard to port access for the fishing fleet. The Soviets have also expressed an interest in signing an agreement that would cover the Melanesian states of PNG, the Solomons, and Vanuatu. The Soviet ambassador to Australia, Dr. Evgeni Samoteikin, visited the South Pacific Forum's regional body, the Forum Fisheries Agency, based in Honiara, in March to discuss a possible agreement with Vanuatu. A communiqué issued during the visit noted a desire to "explore areas of co-operation in the development of commercial fishing as well as scientific matters between Pacific island nations and the Soviet Union" (*Pacific Report*, 13 April; *News Weekly*, 29 April).

Soviet intelligence-gathering activity continues unabated in the region. One major Australian concern about the Soviet fishing fleet presence is that it will bring with it additional Soviet intelligence collection platforms. Soviet auxiliary general intelligence (AGI) vessels were sighted off the north coast of Australia during Exercise Kangaroo-89, a major Australian-U.S. military exercise. AGIs are routinely deployed around the Marshall Islands to gather signals intelligence (Sigint) from U.S. missile tests. In January, testifying before Congress, U.S. Navy admiral David Jeremiah said that the Soviet AGI presence around Hawaii has grown from 60 days a year in 1986 to more than 250 days a year in 1987 and 1988 (*Pacific Research*, February). In 1988 it was revealed that all Soviet space vehicles in the first half of their orbit after launching pass over, at low altitude, an area in the South Pacific northeast of New Zealand and south of

French Polynesia (Aadu Karemaa, "What Would Mahan Say About Space Power?" *Proceedings*, April 1988). This zone will therefore become an important strategic area once antisatellite devices become deployable at sea. Although this may be some years away, it suggests that there will be a growing Soviet naval interest in the region and hence an interest in gaining port access in the islands.

The last regionwide issue is the impact on island politics of regional trade union, antinuclear, and proindependence movements. Large numbers of Australian and New Zealand interest groups concerned with these issues are active in the South Pacific region. Gathered together under the generic title of the nuclear-free and independent Pacific movement—although there is no formal coordinating body between the various groups—it appears that there is reasonably close contact between organizations and a significant overlap of membership, with key individuals involved in several groups. Among the island-based organizations that have been involved in the nuclear-free movement are the Pacific Conference of Churches, which is affiliated with the Moscow-backed World Council of Churches, and the Pacific Trade Union Forum. (Stewart Firth, *Nuclear Playground* [Sydney: Allen and Unwin, 1987].)

Frequent international meetings bring together activists of the region. The Asia-Pacific Peace and Development Conference, held in Manila in January, was "sponsored by a coalition of Filipino trade unionists, social justice movements, church groups and the Partido ng Bayan [People's party]" (*Pacific Islands Monthly*, February). Bayan is said to be under the broad umbrella of the communist National Democratic Front (*News Weekly*, 1 February). The Australian delegation was the largest at the meeting and included members of the Communist Party of Australia (CPA) and antinuclear activists such as Australian independent senator Jo Vallentine. Among the islanders present was former Pastor Djoubelly Wea from New Caledonia. (*Pacific Islands Monthly*, February.) On 4 May, Wea assassinated two leading moderates in Kanak politics—the president and deputy of the Front de Liberation Nationale Kanak et Socialiste (Kanak Socialist National Liberation Front, FLNKS), Jean-Marie Tjibaou, and Yeiwene Yeiwene. Wea was opposed to their support for a plan that would give New Caledonia independence from France in 1998; he favored immediate independence, which was one of the platforms of the Peace and Development conference in Manila. The conference declaration also called for the removal of the French and U.S. presence in the region, total denuclearization, a return to democracy in Fiji, support for Vanuatu's antinuclear policies, and opposition to U.S. attempts to "subvert" Palau's antinuclear constitution. (Ibid.)

There continues to be a measure of contact between Soviet front organizations and island church, student, and union organizations. Attending such conferences is no clear indication of political commitment; indeed with the island elites such invitations to travel are attractive regardless of who pays the check. However, as antinuclear activist Stuart Firth points out, these meetings can be seen as "a major event in a small island state" that can have a significant impact on the development of attitudes to such things as the French or U.S. military presence in the region (Firth, *Nuclear Playground*, p. 135).

Papua New Guinea. PNG celebrated its fourteenth year of independence on 16 September. During the year a counterinsurgency conflict developed on Bougainville Island in the North Solomons province that in May closed down the Panguna gold and copper mine, which brings PNG 40 percent of its export income and 19 percent of government revenue (*Australian Defence 2000*, November). The central government in Port Moresby, led by Prime Minister Rabbie Namaliu, received no-confidence motions in Parliament and constant defections from the ruling coalition parties. The competence and loyalty of the Papua New Guinea Defence Forces (PNGDF) have come under question. Incidents of lawlessness and politically related violence have increased in number. Collectively, these developments have created what one analyst has called a "serious crisis of ungovernability" in PNG. (Yaw Saffu, "Military Roles and Relations in Papua New Guinea," November.)

There is little ideological motivation in PNG party politics. Like a number of Pacific island states, politics in PNG is characterized by strong individuals backed by friends and weak coalitions. In every election about half of the 108 members of the national Parliament lose their seats. Although Parliament is elected for a five-year term, no government since independence has been able to survive for a full term. In eleven years there have been sixteen no-confidence motions against governments. (*Pacific Islands Monthly*, March.) Two of these—in March and October—were against the Namaliu government. Namaliu's Pangu Pati, which

has 33 seats in Parliament, is in a coalition with five other minor parties, although over the course of the year there have been defections and additions as well as cabinet reshuffles to this coalition. On both occasions the no-confidence motions were withdrawn when it became apparent that the opposition parties did not have the numbers to unseat the government. Clearly this instability is not conducive to developing sound policy; too much time is spent simply holding the government together. Money and the perquisites of power are freely distributed in return for political support. Much of this can be attributed to a traditional Melanesian way of doing business, but there is a growing view that corruption on a very significant scale is undermining the central authority of the PNG government. (Saffu, "Military Roles.")

A major test of this authority has come from the North Solomons province, which has long entertained sympathies for secession from Port Moresby. From December 1988 on, militants on Bougainville Island led by Francis Ona have been carrying out a well-coordinated campaign of violence against the massive Panguna mine operations jointly owned by the PNG government and Australian mining companies. Among Ona's grievances are the extent of environmental damage caused by the mining operation and the lack of adequate financial compensation to both the North Solomons province and the traditional landowners. Ona has demanded many billions of dollars, and in June and July an additional demand of complete political independence for the North Solomons was made. Ona commands what is now being referred to as the Bougainville Liberation Army (BLA). With a provincial population of around 170,000, the BLA has been estimated to number about 150 individuals. (*Australian Defence 2000*, November.) With weapons and explosives (mainly shotguns and grenades) stolen from the mine at the beginning of the year, the BLA has blown up electricity pylons, staged attacks on mine workers and the PNGDF, and assassinated, on 11 September, the North Solomons provincial minister for commerce, John Bika. (*FBIS-EAS*, 12 September; *Pacific Islands Monthly*, November.) The central government has speculated that the BLA has received military training from foreign sources; but there is no firm evidence to show this, nor does the BLA appear to have access to military weaponry (*FBIS-EAS*, 10 April; *Pacific Islands Monthly*, October).

In responding to the crises, the central government deployed around four hundred PNGDF personnel to Bougainville on 21 March to support the local police. An additional two hundred troops were deployed in October. (*FBIS-EAS*, 21 March; *Islands Business*.) Australia has provided four helicopters for support operations, but in practice there is little three companies of troops can do to quell the BLA activities in the very rugged country around Panguna. In fact, the military have displayed a shocking lack of discipline in their handling of the crisis and may well have worsened the situation by alienating much of the population. In late June, PNGDF forces beat up civilians and razed a village to the ground because it was suspected of harboring BLA sympathizers. Riot squad police assaulted the North Solomons premier and one of his ministers as a payback after an attack on police by some militants. The minister lost an eye when he was jabbed in the face by rifle barrels. (*FBIS-EAS*, 27 June; *Pacific Islands Monthly*, November.)

By the end of the year more than 40 civilians were dead as well as eight members of the security forces (*FBIS-EAS*, 3 October). Ona rejected Namaliu's offer of US$338 million compensation; the actual security operation was estimated to have cost US$23 million (*FBIS-EAS*, 3 November). Having not been operational for most of the year, the Bougainville mine sacked two thousand of its workers on 28 December and will remain closed indefinitely with only a skeleton staff (*Australian*, 29 December). A resolution to the conflict does not appear likely in the short term; however, the Port Moresby government cannot afford to do without revenue from the mine without risking a collapse of its central functions.

The wider question of an upsurge in violence and disorder in PNG must be seen against this background. There are too many incidents to list, but since 1984 the PNGDF has been called out to respond to internal security problems on four occasions (Saffu, "Military Roles"). In particular major towns and cities have become subject to gang violence and lawlessness. Even the military contributes to this problem. In February around six hundred troops marched on Parliament House and created a lot of damage demanding pay raises (*FBIS-EAS*, 16 February).

Although it is in the nature of PNG politics to be undisciplined, developments in 1989 raise serious questions about the capacity of the existing political system to cope with these difficulties and about the potential for a complete breakdown of central authority. The possibility of a military takeover has been discussed, especially in the Australian press.

Certainly, the current political situation is one in which the advocacy of radical solutions to PNG's problems is encouraged.

In the area of foreign policy, PNG has openly expressed an intent to widen the range of its diplomatic contacts with the outside world. In late October, Foreign Minister Michael Somare said that PNG wanted to establish diplomatic relations with one hundred nations by 1990. Somare said that the government was considering establishing ties with countries from Eastern Europe, the Middle East, Africa, Latin America, and the Asia-Pacific region. (*FBIS-EAS*, 25 October.) The one hundred–nation goal was not reached in 1989; but diplomatic relations were established with Cuba in October, and a PNG Parliamentary delegation visited Beijing for the first time in March (*FBIS-EAS*, 17 October, 20 March).

Following the 1988 invitation of Prime Minister Namaliu, the Soviet Union has made a major diplomatic push in the region by conducting negotiations with PNG on establishing a resident embassy. When established, this will be the Soviets' first resident posting to a Pacific island state. Soviet ambassador to Australia Dr. Evgeni Samoteikin had discussions with Namaliu in Port Moresby in March, and a Soviet delegation visited in August to carry out more detailed work on establishing the embassy. It was stressed that the Soviets' main interest was in developing trade contacts. (*FBIS-EAS*, 31 March, 21 August.) Also in August, a five-man Soviet fisheries delegation visited Port Moresby with the intention of signing a fishing treaty that had already been drawn up. The PNG cabinet held up the signing at the last moment to give the treaty further consideration. (*Pacific Research*, November.) Earlier, in May, PNG lifted a 1979 ban on port access for Soviet cruise liners, which will now be able to dock and crew members allowed shore leave. This dispensation does not apply to the fishing fleet, a matter that was to be addressed in the fishing treaty.

The incident over the treaty demonstrates that there is still a good deal of suspicion about the Soviet Union in PNG. The defense minister, Ben Sabumei, has expressed concern that with the establishment of the Soviet embassy, "the KGB will follow as sure as night follows day" (*FBIS-EAS*, 25 October). Such concerns, of course, are not unfounded. Australian intelligence expert Desmond Ball estimated that in 1989 there were approximately 235 KGB personnel attached to Soviet diplomatic and trade establishments in Southeast Asia. Ball argued that Soviet signals intelligence (Sigint) gathering is a major priority in the Southeast Asia region. (Desmond Ball, "How Moscow Steals ASEAN's Secrets," *Pacific Defence Reporter*, June.) The Soviets may also have an interest in establishing a Sigint post in Port Moresby to monitor developments in the islands and the delicate relationships between Australia, PNG, and Indonesia. The island states, PNG among them, are beginning to make greater use of satellite communications technology, and facsimile machines are proliferating throughout the region. Few island communications systems would be encrypted, which suggests that from the Soviet viewpoint the possibility for Sigint collection from PNG may well be worth exploiting.

Fiji. Much of the political activity in Fiji during 1989 centered around various proposals for a new constitution to be implemented in time for an election in 1991. A constitutional advisory committee issued a draft constitution in September that was essentially a watered-down version of a September 1988 draft issued by the interim government of Ratu Sir Kamisese Mara—the administration installed by the Fiji Military Forces (FMF). Common to both constitutional proposals is the unambiguous establishment of ethnic Fijian political dominance. A permanent majority of seats in both Houses of Parliament will be reserved for the ethnic Fijians over the Indo-Fijians and people of Polynesian and so-called mixed-race origin. Not surprisingly, the coalition of the predominantly Indian National Federation Party (NFP) and the Fiji Labour Party (FLP), which was ousted in the 14 May 1987 coup, has rejected the new proposals. They are, however, an advance on the old inasmuch as they do not provide for the commander of the FMF to hold a permanent seat in the cabinet.

Shortly after the draft document was issued, Ratu Mara announced that he would continue on in government at least until the next election. Earlier, he had maintained that he would serve in the interim government only for two years, retiring on 5 December. Mara's decision to stay on was conditional on Major General Rabuka's agreeing to leave the cabinet to return to being the sole commander of the FMF. (*Pacific Report*, 28 September; *Pacific Islands Monthly*, October.) Although the December deadline has passed, neither Rabuka nor the three colonels in the cabinet have left for Queen Victoria Barracks. Neither, however, has Mara resigned, and this is probably the important point. Mara's eminence in Fijian politics makes his continued presence essential for a return to political stability and a necessary boost to business confidence. As for Rabuka, in or out of the cabinet, he and the FMF will continue to exert a dominating influence in Fijian politics that will ensure Fijian dominance in any constitutional structure. Thus the real issue is not *whether* the new constitution will enshrine ethnic Fijian political supremacy, but rather *to what degree* it will disenfranchise the Indian population.

If the military had its way it would opt for a much tougher political system. In late September an FMF secret briefing paper on options for Fiji's political future was leaked to the press. Presented to Ratu Mara and President Ratu Sir Penaia Ganilau in May, it argued for the adoption of what the FMF called *Fijian democratic socialism*. The proposals seemed neither democratic nor socialistic. Of the Indian population the document said, "their adamant refusal to accept reality and the objectives of the coup coupled with their selfish and unrealistic ideologies about the destiny of the nation has compelled us to believe that in the best interest of national peace, prosperity, and stability they should be neutralised." (*Islands Business*, November.) The FMF argued for a ten- to fifteen-year delay before returning to constitutional government, stronger executive powers for the army, replacing British common law with Fijian customary law, avoiding trade with Australia and New Zealand, and realigning foreign policies to bypass the Commonwealth. The document said that Fiji should "provide a supportive and contributory role in a treaty based alliance with the French, Asian countries and the United States of America." It argued that Fiji should be opened up to Chinese immigrants who would sharecrop Fijian land in place of the Indians. There would be a state religion and an army national youth scheme for all ethnic Fijian youths. The FMF advocated abolishing the trade union movement within Fiji and expressed concerns about the Fiji Trades Union Congress (FTUC), an affiliate of the Pacific Trade Union Congress (PTUC), which in turn is linked to the Moscow-backed World Federation of Trade Unions (WFTU). The document noted that the 1987 coup had curtailed the activities of the Soviet-backed Fiji Council of Churches, whose activists "must not be allowed to preach Marxist and anti-government doctrines from the pulpits." (Ibid.; *Pacific Report*, 28 September.)

Interim government leaders have distanced themselves from the report, but have nevertheless implemented policies that are similar in content if not in style to the FMF recommendations. Attempts have been made to diversify trade and to reduce dependence on Australia and New Zealand; in the absence of military cooperation with traditional allies, Fiji has looked to some Asian states and an accommodating France to provide training and equipment. (*FBIS-EAS*, 23 August, 7 November.) The Indian ambassador to Fiji was expelled on 3 November, allegedly for interfering in local political affairs (*FBIS-EAS*, 3 November). One consequence of the coups is that the coalition was denied the chance of implementing their ban on port access for nuclear-powered or -armed ships. The USS *Robert E. Peary* visited Suva harbor in late July—the first U.S. ship to do so since the coups. Its presence was protested by the Fiji Anti-Nuclear Group (FANG), but it was granted access under the U.S. policy of neither confirming nor denying that it was carrying nuclear weapons. (*FBIS-EAS*, 28 June.) U.S.-Fiji relations in general seem good. In November, Ratu Mara spent twenty minutes with President George Bush in Washington—a meeting that signaled to some commentators that the United States intends to take a more direct interest in the region (*Washington-Pacific Report*, 15 November).

Against this background the coalition has continued to press for the return to a full democracy. In early May the FLP and NFP agreed in principle to merge, although by year's end this had yet to happen. In November the Labour party leader Dr. Timoci Bavadra died. He was buried at his village on 8 November, with a crowd of between 20,000 to 30,000 attending. Shortly afterward, Bavadra's wife, Adi Kuini Vuikaba Bavadra, agreed to head a Labour-NFP coalition. Adi Kuini is a realist and acknowledges that there is little the Labour party can do to influence the constitutional deliberations; however, she is also of chiefly rank and a close cousin of Ratu Sir Penaia Ganilau and Ratu Mara. In the structured and hierarchical system of Fijian politics, this gives Adi Kuini a stature that her commoner husband could never enjoy. Combined with her acknowledged political ability, this may give the Labour party more influence in Fijian political circles than has been the case since 1987. (*Pacific Islands Monthly*, December.)

The Labour party was very much the party of the Fiji trade union movement (Brij Lal, *Power and Prejudice*, 1988). During 1989 the FTUC attempted to gain overseas support in opposition to the interim government. In April the FTUC announced its intention to mount a general strike. The government responded by threatening to implement a state of emergency that would have given it sweep-

ing powers to break the strike. The government has also complained that overseas union organizations like the Australian Council of Trade Unions (ACTU) have been interfering in Fijian domestic politics. (*Pacific Report*, 13 April; *Washington-Pacific Report*, 15 September.) To date, however, the general strike has not gone ahead, and although there continues to be significant contact between the FTUC and the overseas unions, neither the ACTU nor the New Zealand Federation of Labour has been able to implement significant sanctions against Fiji.

What seems remarkable about Fiji is that these developments have taken place with only a minimum of violence between racial communities. However, the apparent calm should not be taken for granted. Fiji is a deeply divided society of which the Indian–ethnic Fijian split is only the most apparent example. Within the Fijian community there is a significant divide between western Fijians and those from the east and outlying islands; the powerful Methodist church in 1989 split between radicals and moderates; and there is a growing divide between those subscribing to traditional tribal allocations of power and the urbanized Fijians for whom these old loyalties have lost some force. The Indian community, too, is divided between Muslims and Hindus and into various political factions. The interim government, and behind them the FMF, has been very inflexible in responding to the competing claims of these groups. In the 1990s pressure for political reform will grow and with it prospects for violence and political radicalization.

Vanuatu. The political battle that emerged during 1988 between the prime minister, Father Walter Lini, and Barak Sope for control of the ruling Vanua'aku Pati (Our Land party, VP) appeared to be decisively won by Lini in 1989. In late 1988, Sope, plus four VP supporters and eighteen members of the opposition Union of Moderate Parties (UMP), walked out of Parliament. The expectation was that Parliament would lapse for want of a quorum and that a general election would have to be called. However, a quorum vote was not taken by the sitting VP members, and under the terms of the constitution, the absent Parliamentarians were expelled from office after missing three consecutive sittings. By-elections to fill the vacant seats were held in December 1988 and December 1989. These too were boycotted by the UMP and Sope's new party, the Melanesian Progressive Party (MPP), with the net effect that the VP now holds 40 seats in the 46-seat Parliament. The UMP and the MPP have thus been politically sidelined by their own attempt to boycott Parliament. In the words of Canberra analyst Stephen Henningham, "Vanuatu has become, for the time being, in some respects a de facto one-party state." ("Pluralism and Party Politics in a South Pacific State: Vanuatu's Ruling Vanua'aku Pati and its Rivals," *Conflict* 9).

These developments appear to suit the temper of the VP leadership. Of all the political parties in the South Pacific, the VP is the one most characterized by a degree of ideological conviction and—Sope's defection aside—political unity. The VP carried the New Hebrides's struggle for independence from British and French joint colonial rule almost single-handedly. In power the party has exhibited some of the characteristics of one-party control, for example, in its dominance of the local media. Their sustaining ideology—termed *Melanesian socialism*—is a heady blend of support for local custom, adherence to Christianity, aggressive nationalism, and, externally, support for regional independence movements and antinuclear politics. (Ibid.)

The trial of Vanuatu president George Sokomanu, Barak Sope, UMP president Maxime Carlot, and three others for incitement to mutiny and seditious conspiracy took place during January and February. Sentence was passed in March. Sokomanu was sentenced to jail for six years, Sope and Carlot for five, Willy Jimme two years, and the two others were acquitted. It was a bizarre trial. During the proceedings, Sope told the court about a $21 million arms purchase he had concluded with the PRC on the orders of Lini in 1983. The final transaction apparently never took place, and with equal finality neither the court nor the international media saw fit to examine the issue further. (*Pacific Islands Monthly*, March.)

Following severe criticism of the conduct of the trial by the International Commission of Jurists, an appeals court comprised of three judges from Tonga, Papua New Guinea, and Vanuatu quashed the convictions of Sokomanu and the others and ruled that there should be no retrial (*Pacific Report*, 27 April). The four were released on 14 April. Sokomanu had earlier been relieved of his post as president by the Vanuatu Electoral College. He was replaced by Fred Timakata, a former VP health minister. (*FBIS-EAS*, 31 January.)

Vanuatu's next general election will be held in 1991. Sokomanu has said that he will run for office, and Sope on a number of occasions has announced that his MPP will merge with the UMP and some

minor opposition parties. To date, this does not appear to have happened. (*Canberra Times*, 31 August; *Pacific Islands Monthly*, September.) However, the underlying factors that gave rise to these political disputes will not go away. The personal animosities that color the relationship between Sokomanu, Sope, and the UMP's Carlot, on the one hand, and Lini and the VP, on the other hand, are underpinned by more fundamental rifts. There is a north-south split in Vanuatu: Sokomanu, Carlot, and Sope are from the southern islands, where there is a resentment of the predominantly northern and outer-island VP leadership. In addition the VP is a predominantly Anglophone and Protestant organization, whereas the UMP is Francophone and Catholic. (Henningham, "Pluralism and Party Politics.") Increasingly there is also a generational split between those who brought the country to independence and a younger group, educated overseas, that now aspires to power.

These cross-cutting issues and loyalties suggest that the potential for instability in Vanuatu politics remains strong. It is therefore important to note the extent to which outside powers have taken an interest in the affairs of the Port Villa government. In 1989 there were no reports about Libyan links to Sope or the national government. However, the Soviet Union has made a number of approaches about the possibility of re-establishing a fishing agreement. In mid-1989 the Soviet Union gave Vanuatu twelve tractors as an aid donation following the devastation caused in February 1987 by Cyclone Uma. However, the gift may not have done too much to enhance the Soviet's image in the region. Apart from the delay in presenting the equipment, this author understands that the tractors have never been uncrated, that the instruction manuals are in Russian, that there are no spare parts, and that Vanuatu does not have a tradition of using tractors.

In keeping with Vanuatu's nonaligned political stance ambassadorial-level relations were established with the Palestine Liberation Organization (PLO) on 17 October. The nonresident ambassador will be Ali Kazak, who is based in Australia. (*FBIS-EAS*, 19 October.) Vanuatu is the first South Pacific island state to establish formal relations with the PLO.

Lastly, on 14 November, France and Vanuatu agreed to re-establish normal diplomatic relations in 1990. In 1987, Vanuatu expelled the French ambassador, accusing him of interference in domestic political affairs. However, France's profile has improved in the region following the signing of the

Matignon Accords in June 1988. (*FBIS-WEU*, 20 November.)

Solomon Islands. The Solomon Islands held an election on 22 February, with the result that the ruling United party, led by Ezekiel Alebua, was put out of office by the People's Alliance Party (PAP) of Solomon Mamaloni. Politics is pursued with gusto in the Solomon Islands, but is lacking in party discipline. It was not until the end of March, after a number of victorious candidates announced their loyalty to the PAP, that Mamaloni was able to form a government. Of the 38 seats in Parliament, PAP now holds 21, although fewer than half that number were formal Alliance candidates during the election. Although coalition politics is the PAP's only unifying theme, the Alliance now has the rather tenuous distinction of being the only single-party government to rule the Solomon Islands since independence in 1978.

Of the remaining seats, the United party won six, the Liberal party of Bart Ulufa'alu, four, and independents and a minor party (the National Front for Progress), five (*FBIS-EAS*, 10, 31 March). The remaining two seats were won by the newly formed Solomon Islands Labour Party (SILP), led by Joses Tuhanuku, who was elected along with Jackson Piast. Tuhanuku is the secretary of the Solomon Islands National Union of Workers, the South Pacific's sole official affiliate of the Moscow-backed World Federation of Trade Unions (WFTU). The SILP fielded 21 candidates in the election on a platform based on what Tuhanuku called *socialist principles* (*FBIS-EAS*, 22 February). These included supporting the land rights claims of the New Zealand Maoris, Australian aborigines, black South Africans, and Palestinians (*Pacific Report*, 2 February). Domestically, Labour would nationalize key industries, and Tuhanuku has indicated that he would favor opening diplomatic relations with the Soviet Union. In 1987 the then Australian foreign minister, Bill Hayden, is reported to have expressed concerns that the SILP was offered financial support by Libya; however, this link is denied by Tuhanuku. (*FBIS-EAS*, 22 February; Parliament of Australia, Joint Committee on Foreign Affairs Defence and Trade, *Hearings on Australia and the South Pacific*, 21 March 1988.) Tuhanuku and other members of the National Union of Workers have maintained their association with the WFTU, which continues to provide travel opportunities to Eastern bloc countries for union members. On 9 September, for example, four mem-

bers of the National Union of Workers and the National Teachers Association, along with a number of others from Australia, New Zealand, Vanuatu, and Papua New Guinea, left for a study tour of the USSR. The stated purpose of the trip was to visit a number of industrial sites, collective farms, and cultural centers. Clement Waiwori, acting general secretary of the National Union of Workers, said the "study tour is part of a regular programme designed to help overseas trade unionists familiarise themselves with trade union functions in industries" (*PacNews*, 7 September).

Although the SILP has little influence in Parliament, the development of an ideologically based political party critical of the colonialist attitudes of other Solomon Island politicians is a significant development that may affect the conduct of politics in the 1990s.

In domestic politics the Alliance government announced a reorientation of foreign policy in mid-1989 that will see the closure of the Solomon Islands mission at the United Nations and the opening of a trade office in Brisbane, Australia (*Pacific Islands Monthly*, September). Mamaloni seems set on continuing the somewhat eccentric political style established by his predecessor. He refused to see Australian foreign minister Senator Gareth Evans or the British state minister for foreign and commonwealth affairs, Lord Glenarthur, when they visited in July. No reason for the refusal was given. (*FBIS-EAS*, 26 July.) In mid-November, tribally inspired rioting and looting in the capital, Honiara, necessitated the calling out of several hundred riot police to quell the disturbance (*Canberra Times*, 13 November).

New Caledonia. In mid-1988, New Caledonia looked to be heading for a protracted and bloody conflict. Opinion in the French territory was split between the native Melanesian Kanak population, which favored political independence, and the Caldoches, French settlers who wanted to keep the tie with Paris. Despite the granting by Paris of greater autonomy to New Caledonian authority, positions both for and against independence appeared to harden. Since 1984 radical Kanaks of the Front Uni de Liberation Kanak (United Kanak Liberation Front, FULK) had been cultivating relations with Libya and had sent representatives there to receive political training. (Helen Fraser, *New Caledonia: Anti-Colonialism in a Pacific Territory*, 1988.) In April 1988 a band of Kanaks on the FULK stronghold of Ouvea in the Loyalty Islands kidnapped 27 hostages, killing four gendarmes in the process. French security forces were used to free the hostages; however, during the operation two soldiers and nineteen of the Kanak kidnappers were killed. It is alleged that three of the Kanaks were summarily executed after the hostages had been freed. (Ibid.) As a result of this crisis, the numbers of French military and paramilitary forces based in New Caledonia were increased from around 6,000 to 9,500. The number has since declined to its former level.

A change of government in France probably helped to defuse the situation. Conservative prime minister Jacques Chirac was replaced by Michel Rocard of the Socialist party in June. Rocard brought with him a new set of proposals for New Caledonian autonomy and began a process of negotiations with the main political organizations of the territory. From July to August 1988 talks were conducted in France and New Caledonia between Rocard, Jean-Marie Tjibaou of the FLNKS, Jacques Lafleur, and Dick Ukeiwe of the anti-independence, predominantly Caldoche Rassemblement pour la Caledonie dans la Republique (Assembly for New Caledonia in the Republic, RPCR). On 22 August at Matignon in Paris an accord was signed by the FLNKS, RPCR, and the French government that offers the possibility for peace in New Caledonia. Under the terms of the accord a referendum on independence will be held in New Caledonia in 1998. As of 14 July the island was divided into three administratively autonomous provinces. Aid funds are to be channeled into the Kanak strongholds north of the main island and the outlying islands, and amnesty was granted to those imprisoned for politically related actions.

In November 1988 a referendum held throughout France and its overseas territories sanctioned the accord. In New Caledonia, 63 percent of the population, mainly Kanaks, did not vote. Of those who did, 57 percent countrywide voted in favor of the accord, but it was strongly rejected by the white population of the capital, Noumea. (*Pacific Islands Monthly*, June.) As expected, the 11 June provincial elections saw parties under the FLNKS umbrella win in the mainly Kanak Northern and Loyalty Islands provinces. The RPCR won resoundingly in the Southern province, where Noumea is located. Parties opposed to the accord, like FULK (which attempted to arrange a Kanak boycott of the elections) and the extreme right-wing National Front, were largely ignored by the electors. (*Pacific Report*, 22 June.) This latter point has

been taken as a hopeful sign that the accord will enable New Caledonia peacefully to determine its future. At best, that is an optimistic hope. There can be a truce between the two New Caledonian signatories to the accord only so long as both believe that their goals will be achieved in 1998. However, as the aims of the RPCR and FLNKS are diametrically opposed, one may suppose that support for the accord will end when either side believes the other is doing too well out of the arrangement. In any event, it is thought that the French elections of 1992 will be a crucial watershed in the implementation of the accord.

Tjibaou's assassination in May on Ouvea Island—a year to the day since the death of the eighteen Kanak militants—indicates disagreement within the Kanak community about the value of the accord. FLNKS is an umbrella organization made up of a number of smaller groups, each of which is free to develop its own position on the accord. Moving from the moderate to the radical end of the political spectrum, major FLNKS member organizations are as follows: The oldest and largest of the Kanak organizations is the Union Caledonienne (UC), led by Tjibaou and now by a former Catholic priest François Burck. The UC was originally skeptical of the value of the accord, but ultimately became a strong supporter of it. There are three other small parties that provide a political base for a number of Kanak activists: the Union Progressiste Melanésienne (Progressive Melanesian Union, UPM), the Parti de Libération Kanake (Kanak Liberation Party, Palika), and the Parti Socialiste de Kanaky (Kanak Socialist Party, PSK). These latter two are on the far left of the FLNKS. (Fraser, "New Caledonia," *Australian Left Review*, September/October.)

Further left still are two organizations that have rejected the Matignon Accord outright. These are the Union des Syndicats des Travailleurs Kanaks et Exploités (United Union of Kanak and Exploited Workers, USTKE), led by Louis Kotra Uregei, and FULK. In late July the USTKE announced that it will leave the FLNKS. (*FBIS-EAS*, 31 July.) Louis Kotra Uregei is related to Yann Celene Uregei of FULK—the organization that has the dubious distinction of being perhaps the most politically radical in the South Pacific during 1989.

FULK refused to sign the Matignon Accord or, indeed, to express regret at the assassination of Tjibaou. Because of his radical views, Yann Uregei was relieved of his role as FLNKS spokesman two years ago, and since May FULK has been excluded from FLNKS meetings. (*FBIS-EAS*, 18 May; *Pacific Report*, 25 May; *Pacific Islands Monthly*, June.) Yann Uregei has continued to cultivate contacts with Libya at a time when the rest of the FLNKS seems to have abandoned the relationship. He is known to travel extensively overseas. Uregei was present at the Non-Aligned Movement meeting in Zimbabwe in May, where he tried to pass himself off as the FLNKS spokesman until he was evicted from the meeting. (*Pacific Report*, 25 May.) In July it was reported that eight FULK militants had been sent to Pyongyang, North Korea. As well as attending the communist World Festival of Youth and Students, the eight were to undergo ten weeks of training in a course that was reported to include terrorist tactics. (*Pacific Report*, 6 July.) Uregei has not visited New Caledonia since April. He is apparently being hosted by the Libyan People's Bureau in Kuala Lumpur.

It remains to be seen whether the FLNKS will be able to preserve a measure of unity over the issue. In January 1990 the FLNKS will hold a congress to elect a president (*Pacific Report*, 23 November). The post has been vacant since Tjibaou's death. Burck of the UC has indicated that he will not run, and a front-running candidate has yet to emerge.

French Polynesia. French Polynesia is an overseas territory of France that retains great strategic significance for Paris because since 1965 it has been the site for the testing of nuclear weapons in the French strategic arsenal. In 1989 France carried out eight underground nuclear explosions at two test sites on the atolls of Fangataufa and Mururoa. Several thousand French troops and technicians occupy the islands under the aegis of the Centre d'Expérimentation du Pacifique (CEP), which carries out the tests.

The governments of Australia, New Zealand, and most of the Pacific island states have long opposed French nuclear testing in the region. On the islands of French Polynesia itself, nuclear testing as well as the question of achieving political independence from France have been taken up by a number of radical political groupings. In the middle 1980s there was some contact between these groups and Libyan representatives, but these links do not appear to have been developed to any significant extent.

A 41-member, popularly elected Territorial Assembly governs French Polynesia. The assembly elects a seven-member Council of Government, which since December 1987 has been led by the moderate Alexandre Leontieff. The territory also has one representative in the French Senate and two in the National Assembly. The French high commissioner, resident in the capital, Papeete, also has a considerable degree of administrative power.

There has always been a degree of antinuclear sentiment on French Polynesia; however, this has strengthened in the last few years to become an important factor in the conduct of island politics. Among the parties that have strong antinuclear platforms and also support political independence from France—the two issues are closely linked—are Ia Mana Te Nunaa, led by Jacqui Drollet, and Tavini Huiratira, or the Polynesian Liberation Front (PLF), led by Oscar Tumaru. Tumaru is a former seminarian and an advocate of a return to a more traditional Polynesian life-style. Both these parties gained ground in the March elections for 48 municipal councils. They are also expected to increase their representation in the Territorial Assembly at the 1991 elections. (*Pacific Islands Monthly*, April/May; *Sydney Morning Herald*, 28 October.) The PLF currently holds two seats (*FBIS-EAS*, 25 August).

Antinuclear feeling, however, is not only the province of the parties of the left. In June all French Polynesian parties called for a boycott of the metropolitan French election as an expression of concern about nuclear testing. A 90 percent abstention rate was achieved. (Ibid.)

On 7 July the president of the Territorial Assembly, Alexandre Leontieff, promised to hold a debate in the Territorial Assembly on three topics proposed by Oscar Tumaru. These were the future of French Polynesian relations with Paris, the role of the CEP, and the merits of conducting a referendum on the independence question. This move followed a hunger strike of proindependence activists. (*Pacific Islands Monthly*, August.) When French prime minister Michel Rocard visited French Polynesia in August, he was met at Papeete by 350 protesters led by Oscar Tumaru calling for an end to nuclear testing. Rocard agreed to grant more autonomy to the island group and also to hold round table discussions to hear island views on testing. (*Pacific Islands Monthly*, September.)

In October, Papeete was treated to the arrival of an antinuclear delegation from France—the first in fourteen years—led by Monsignor Jacques Galliot, bishop of Evreux. Organized by a French group, the Mouvement de la Paix, the bishop's party was hosted by Tumaru's PLF. (*Melbourne Age*, 13, 15 October.)

Nauru. Reports in October 1988 that the Soviet Union had expressed interest in providing aid to Nauru appear to have come to nothing. In early 1989 the Soviet ambassador to Australia presented his credentials to the Nauru government; however, it is not anticipated that the relationship will develop much beyond this essentially ceremonial level.

Domestically, it has been a turbulent political year. On 28 December 1988 a report on the costs of rehabilitating the island following exhaustive mining of phosphate resources was tabled in Parliament by Prime Minister Hammer DeRoburt. The report is highly critical of Australia, New Zealand, and the United Kingdom—the main mining states—for rendering 80 percent of the island useless for farming or habitation after some 70 years of mining. The report estimates that A\$215.9 million would be required to rehabilitate the island and that each of the three governments should pay about one-third of that cost. Australia maintains that it will not pay any part of this sum, and in May Nauru took Canberra to the International Court to seek a resolution of the dispute. (*FEER*, 29 June; New Zealand, *Evening Post*, 29 December.)

Relations between Australia and Nauru reached their nadir early in 1989. Nauru expelled the Australian high commissioner, and late the previous year a secret Australian report was leaked alleging massive corruption and incompetence on the part of the DeRoburt government. In August, DeRoburt—who has been prime minister for all but a few months since Nauru's independence in 1968—lost a no-confidence motion in Parliament and was replaced by his former Cabinet minister Kenas Aroi, who leads the Centre party. (*Pacific Defence Reporter*, December/January 1990.) In a series of cost-cutting measures, Aroi has closed down Nauru offices in London, Tokyo, Honolulu, Hong Kong, Western Samoa, American Samoa, and the Cook Islands. However, he is proceeding with the International Court action. (*Pacific Islands Monthly*, October.) National elections were held in mid-December. Aroi was re-elected but replaced as prime minister by Bernard Dowiyogo, who is also of the Centre party. Dowiyogo was prime minister in 1977 and the first half of 1978. DeRoburt was also re-elected, but lost a bid for the prime minister's position ten votes to six. A new Australian high commissioner will take up residence in January 1990.

Cook Islands. In 1965 the Cook Islands became self-governing in free association with New Zealand, which undertakes the responsibility of defense and foreign relations of the island group. Under previous administrations the Cook Islands have been critical of New Zealand's antinuclear policies.

A general election was held on 19 January. Some 88 candidates from a variety of political parties ran for 24 seats in the national legislature. The opposition Cook Islands party, led by Geoffrey Henry, won twelve seats in their own right and will govern for a five-year term with the support of the Demo Tumu party, led by Vincent Ingram. The former governing party, the coalition led by Dr. Pupuke Robati, won nine seats; the remaining seat was won by an independent. (*Pacific Islands Monthly*, February.) Two new parties ran in the election: the Labour party, which fielded fifteen candidates, and the People's party, which fielded eight. Neither was successful. With some nine thousand electors in total, the Cook Islands' largest single constituency is made up of voters living overseas—mainly in New Zealand—where more than eight hundred people voted. (*Parliamentarian*, July.) Despite the proliferation of political parties, Cook Islands politics is dominated by the influence of family and personal loyalties. Following the election, Henry made a series of allegations regarding political cronyism and misuse of public funds on the part of the previous government. Former ministers were accused of giving themselves exorbitantly large expense accounts on overseas travel. With some 39 percent of the island's residents on the government payroll, it is clear that the new administration will have a difficult task in reforming the country's aid-dependent economy. (*Pacific Islands Monthly*, June.)

Tonga. Tonga remains the last island state to be ruled by a hereditary monarchy. King Taufa'ahau Tupou IV retains executive power under the authority of a 114-year-old constitution that denies any legislative power to the island's 95,000 commoners. The Legislative Assembly is comprised of nine cabinet ministers who are appointed by the king and hold their positions until retirement, nine nobles elected by the 33 noble families of Tonga, and nine commoners elected by the general population. Despite the obvious inequalities of wealth and lifestyle enjoyed by the noble families and the increasing corruption stemming from official patronage, Tonga's deeply conservative population has, until this year, not challenged the political system.

On 12 September, however, eight of the nine elected commoners walked out of the Legislative

Assembly to express concern about the autocratic nature of government. Among them 'Akilisi Pohiva has emerged as a spokesman for the commoners, and his newspaper, *Kelea* (Conch Shell), as a vehicle for criticism of government ineptitude and cronyism. Although Pohiva has been called a socialist by the minister of police, the charge hardly seems accurate. After the Parliamentary walkout commoners and nobles alike called for a day of prayer and fasting to seek a resolution of the dispute. The commoners returned to Parliament a few days later, but maintained for some days thereafter a silent protest by refusing to participate in debates.

The commoners have not yet formed a political party or articulated a specific set of goals for government reform. Among the goals that most would like to see are greater representation of commoners in the assembly, some checks against executive corruption, and the right to initiate legislation, currently denied to the commoner representatives. These objectives are modest enough, but there is some skepticism that the noble families will allow the reforms to take place. In February 1990 the commoner seats will be contested in an election. If the radicals of the walkout are re-elected, then pressures for reform will surely grow. A number of statements have been made to the effect that violence will ensue if the king and nobles refuse to grant some measure of political reform. These developments may be some time away. But it is clear that pressures for political change in the first half of the 1990s will dominate Tongan politics and threaten to undermine the legitimacy of the constitution. Although some measure of reform would appear to be necessary, resistance to change on the part of the nobles may lead to the development of a genuinely radical political opposition in the next decade. (*Islands Business*, November.)

For the shorter term, however, even if the commoners manage to bring about a measure of political reform, it is doubtful that such changes would alter Tonga's profoundly conservative foreign policy. In February a Soviet oceanographic voyage to the South Pacific was reportedly canceled because Fiji and Tonga refused to allow the Soviet vessel into their waters. (*NZ Herald*, 4 February.)

Western Samoa. Like Tonga, Western Samoa has a political system that favors the chiefly class of land holders at the expense of the general population. However, in 1989 there were no developments of the sort that took place in Tonga. In September the prime minister and chairman of the ruling

Human Rights Protection party, Tofilau Eti, accepted a long-standing invitation from the People's Republic of China (PRC) to visit China. Eti announced his intention to visit Beijing following the October Commonwealth heads of government meeting at Kuala Lumpur, Malaysia. There has been no official confirmation that the visit took place, but Eti's visit would make him only the second foreign leader to visit China since the June crackdown on the freedom movement. (*Pacific Report*, 28 September.)

The PRC maintains a resident embassy in Western Samoa and has for a number of years provided foreign aid. Then Prime Minister Tupuola Efi visited China in 1980, and shortly thereafter Beijing provided Apia with a ten-million-yuan long-term loan with which a sports complex, two agricultural developments, and a water supply project were undertaken. (Thomas V. Biddick, "Diplomatic Rivalry in the South Pacific: The PRC and Taiwan," *Asian Survey*, August.)

Tuvalu. Following an election on 16 October, the new prime minister of Tuvalu is Bikenikbeu Paeniu. Twenty-six candidates ran for office in the twelve-seat Parliament. After several weeks of negotiations between the successful candidates, Paeniu formed a government with the support of seven members. He unseated the government of Dr. Tomasi Puapua, around whom an unofficial opposition will now form. Tuvaluan politics is based on informal party-style groupings and is heavily influenced by the politics of family and the personalities of prominent individuals. Paeniu says that he would like to see the development of a party system to facilitate the discussion of political issues. His main goal is to try to develop a capability for economic self-reliance through building up financial resources in a trust fund to which nations like Australia, New Zealand, Japan, and the United Kingdom have made substantial contributions. (*Islands Business*, November.) Interest from the investment funds a large part of Tuvaluan recurrent budget costs (*FBIS-EAS*, 10 October).

Paeniu has expressed an intention to diversify the sources of aid to include not only traditional donors like Australia and New Zealand but also the Asian states, Canada, and the European Community. It is doubtful, however, that this will include Eastern bloc countries. Paeniu, like most of his countrymen, is deeply religious and suspicious of the motives of countries like the Soviet Union. In 1985, Tuvalu turned down a Soviet offer of a fishing deal, a move which was rewarded by substantial increases in aid from Australia and New Zealand.

Kiribati. In 1985, Kiribati briefly became the subject of world attention when it signed a fishing deal with the Soviet Union. The deal lapsed after a year because the Soviets attempted to lower the price they were paying per ton of tuna to the Kirabati government. Prime Minister Ieremia Tabai indicated in May that the Soviets would be welcomed back if they could agree on a mutually acceptable price. (*CSM*, 21 May.) Tabai's comments come at a time when the Soviets do indeed appear interested in renegotiating regional fishing agreements. To date, however, Soviet efforts have been directed at the Melanesian islands southwest of Kiribati. Despite the 1985 Soviet fishing agreement, Kiribati politics is largely conservative, strongly influenced by Christianity, and characterized by a pro-Western outlook.

In July, Kiribati hosted the 1989 South Pacific Forum meeting at Tarawa. In keeping with Kiribati's stated intention to extend its diplomatic contacts, ambassadorial-level relations with Singapore were established 7 September. (*Pacnews*, 7 September.)

Trust Territory of the Pacific Islands (TTPI). Following the end of World War II in the Pacific, U.S. military forces retained control of the main Micronesian island groups north of the equator. In 1947 the United Nations granted the United States administrative control of these islands under a trusteeship arrangement. The 1970s and 1980s represented a transition period for the TTPI during which four main island groupings emerged to claim some degree of independent sovereign status while maintaining close political ties to the United States. The strategic location of these island groups has particular importance for the U.S. military posture in the Pacific region. Two of the four groups have recently joined the South Pacific Forum and are seeking to extend the range of their diplomatic ties. A third, Palau, will do the same some time in the 1990s. It is therefore worth considering each of these states separately because—with the exception of the Marianas—they are likely to become more politically active in the South Pacific region in the next decade.

Commonwealth of the Northern Marianas Islands (CNMI). The CNMI was the first of the TTPI island groups to adopt a different constitutional arrangement. In 1975 the islanders voted overwhelmingly in favor of becoming a commonwealth of the United States. The arrangement gives internal self-government responsibilities to a territorial legislature, but the United States retains control of foreign affairs and defense responsibilities. The U.S. Department of Defense leases more than two-thirds of the island of Tinian, on which military exercises have occasionally been held. Tinian is often named as an alternative site for U.S. forces in the Pacific should Subic Bay in the Philippines be closed.

In the November elections, Republican party candidates defeated their Democrat opponents for the positions of governor and lieutenant governor of the islands. In the Territorial Legislature, the Democrats continued to control the House of Representatives ten seats to five, but the Republicans retained control of the Senate, six seats to three. The CNMI has a nonvoting delegate in the U.S. House of Representatives. At the November election, Republican Juan N. Babauta defeated Democrat Herman T. Guerrero for the position. (*Pacific Islands Monthly*, December.)

Federated States of Micronesia (FSM). The FSM is comprised of four states—Kosrae, Pohnpei, Truk, and Yap—making up, with the Republic of Palau, the Caroline Islands chain. The FSM adopted a constitution on 10 May 1979 and has, in effect, been self-governing since that point. On 3 November 1986 a compact of free association with the United States came into force. This agreement gives the United States responsibility for the islands' defense and security, but leaves the conduct of internal and foreign affairs to the FSM. Although relations between the FSM and the United States are harmonious, there is potential for discord given this division of responsibilities. Since 1987 the FSM has been a full member of the South Pacific Forum and is seeking to extend its contact with the outside world. One example of potential discord with the United States is over the question of FSM support for the South Pacific Nuclear-Free Zone Treaty. John Haglelgam, FSM president since 1986, has indicated that he would like to sign the treaty despite a U.S. refusal to ratify the protocols. (*Pacific Islands Monthly*, November.) In September the FSM established full diplomatic relations with Beijing following a visit by the PRC ambassador to Australia, Zhang Zai (*NZ Herald*, 18 September).

Republic of the Marshall Islands. Like the FSM, the Marshalls adopted a constitution in 1979 and entered into a compact of free association with the United States in 1986. The Marshalls became a full member of the South Pacific Forum in 1987. The United States retains full defense responsibilities for the islands. Of great importance to the United States is the Kwajalein missile range, which is under the control of the Ballistic Missile Defense Systems Command at Huntsville, Alabama. The command controls a number of islands in the Kwajalein atoll as well as the area of the lagoon where the missiles splash down. The presence of Soviet intelligence-gathering vessels is not uncommon in the region, especially when missile tests are being conducted. However, information was released in 1989 that suggested that the Soviets, using a miniature submarine, may have entered Kwajalein lagoon in July 1987 to steal the flight recorder from a missile launched at Vandenberg Air Force Base. The *New York Times* reported that five searches failed to find the flight recorder, but that a further search "turned up [a] sailors hat, . . . vodka bottles, packs of Soviet-made cigarettes and bug spray of Soviet manufacture" (*NYT*, 12 January). No further information has come to light.

In September the Marshalls turned down an offer from the PRC to establish full diplomatic relations. The Marshalls have had relations with Taiwan since the 1970s. Beijing's offer can best be interpreted in the light of a PRC-Taiwan competition—developing over a number of years now—for influence in the region.

Republic of Palau. The sorry tale of Palauan attempts to adopt a compact of free association with the United States continues. Palau's 1981 constitution contains antinuclear clauses that ban port access for nuclear-powered vessels as well as those carrying nuclear weapons. The constitution also prohibits the storage of nuclear weapons on Palauan soil. The United States will not agree to the compact of free association—with its attendant defense commitments—until the constitution is amended. The problem is that to alter the constitution a 75 percent affirmative popular vote is required. Experts maintain that it would be difficult to get 75 percent of Palau's eleven thousand electors to agree on anything. The six referenda thus far held on the question demonstrate this point. Votes in favor of amending the constitution to secure the compact have ranged from 61 to 72 percent, but never more. Other attempts have been made to alter the process of constitutional change. Thus far, these have been blocked by the Palau High Court.

Palau needs the compact to get assured access to U.S. aid programs. However, a U.S. General Accounting Office report issued in mid-1989 has indicated a considerable level of incompetence and even corruption on the part of Palau's administrators. Between 1981 and 1988 some US$156 million was given to the island state, despite which the economy is reported to be on the point of collapse. (*Pacific Islands Monthly*, October.)

As the last of the territories under the U.N.-mandated TTPI, Palau's troubled relationship with the United States has provided the Soviet Union with an opportunity to discomfit Washington. As a member of the U.N. Trusteeship Council—which will oversee Palau's transition to independence—the Soviet Union has accused the United States of "annexationist plans" and seeking to develop military or nuclear bases on Palau. (*FBIS-SOV*, 5 June.) These objections notwithstanding, the council accepted a report (with Soviet dissent) in June that argued that "free association with the US remains the preferred future status option of the overwhelming majority of the people of Palau." (*Pacific Research*, August.) It remains to be seen how this preference will be implemented in practice. In 1990 a further attempt will be made to change the constitution and ratify the compact. However, Palau's antinuclear constitution has become something of a cause célèbre with the regional peace movement. Attempts to change it will no doubt be subject to protest of an anti-American variety.

Peter Jennings
Australian Defence Academy, Canberra

Sri Lanka

Population. 16,881,130 (July 1988)
Parties. Communist Party of Sri Lanka (CPSL, pro-Moscow); Janatha Vimukthi Peramuna (JVP, Maoist)
Founded. CPSL: 1943; JVP: 1968
Membership. CPSL: 5,000 estimated; JVP: unknown
General Secretary. CPSL: Kattorge P. Silva
Politburo. CPSL: 11 members including Silva and

Pieter Keuneman (president); JVP: Rohana Wijeweera (leader); Upatissa Gamanayake (deputy leader); both killed November 1989.

Status. Both legal

Last Congress. CPSL: Thirteenth, 22–26 March 1987; Extraordinary Congress, 9–11 December 1989

Last Election. CPSL: presidential, 1982: did not run a candidate; presidential, 1988: did not run a candidate but supported a coalition (United Socialist Alliance) candidate, Ossie Abeygoonasekera, who received 4.6 percent of the vote; parliamentary, 1989: ran with 3 other parties as United Socialist Alliance; 2.9 percent (3 members elected). JVP: presidential, 1982: 4.2 percent; presidential, 1988: did not contest; parliamentary, 1989: did not contest.

Auxiliary Organizations. CPSL: Federation of Trade Unions (24 affiliated unions), Public Service Workers' Trade Union Federation (100 affiliated unions), Communist Youth Federation, Kantha (women's) Peramuna; JVP: Deshapremi Janatha Vimukthi (military wing)

Publication. *Aththa* (major daily newspaper, editor A.U.M. Abeyratne, 28,000 circulation)

Both the old and the new left in Sri Lanka experienced a bad year in 1989. The old left lost in the parliamentary elections, and most of the new left's leaders were either captured or killed by government security forces in November.

In the presidential elections held late in December 1988, the old left, represented by the United Socialist Alliance (USA) candidate Ossie Abeygoonasekera, received only 4.6 percent of the total votes cast. The USA consists of four left-wing parties: the Communist Party of Sri Lanka, the Lanka Sama Samaja party (Equal Society party), the Nava Sama Samaja party (New Equal Society party), and the Sri Lanka Mahajana party (People's party). They did even worse in the parliamentary elections held on 17 February. Their alliance won only 3 of 225 seats in the parliament and received only 2.9 percent of the total votes.

The United National Party (UNP) won the election and 125 seats. It did, however, lose its two-thirds majority in parliament when the Sri Lanka Freedom party won 67 seats. The other 30 seats were split among Tamil and Muslim parties and a small leftist party, the Mahajana Eksath Peramuna (People's United Front). All but one of the 23 seats won by the Tamil parties were captured by former guerrilla groups that had been in rebellion against

the government until the Indo-Lanka peace accord in 1987. An independent slate of electors representing the Eelam Revolutionary Organization of Students (EROS) won thirteen seats and dominated the voting in the Tamil heartland in the northern Jaffna Peninsula. The EROS slate allegedly had the backing of the Liberation Tigers of Tamil Eelam (LTTE), the last Tamil rebel group fighting the government. The Eelam People's Revolutionary Front (EPRLF), which ran under the Tamil United Liberation Front banner, won seven seats. The EPRLF and EROS are two of the most left-wing parties among the Tamils, although both claim that they are not now and never were Marxist parties.

To end the ethnic conflict, the new UNP president, Ranasinghe Premadasa, began negotiations with the LTTE in May and reached an agreement that their military actions cease and that some authority devolve to the Tamil regions of the country. As a result of these negotiations, President Premadasa asked the Indian government to remove its troops by the end of July, the second year since their arrival in Sri Lanka. The Indian government refused to pull out or to cease its military actions against the LTTE. It feared that its departure would result in a bloodbath because the LTTE had attacked and killed members of the former Tamil guerrilla organizations who supported the Indo-Lanka accords. Those units belonged to the EPRLF, the People's Liberation Organization of Tamil Eelam, and the Tamil Eelam Liberation Organization.

The People's Liberation Front (Janatha Vimukthi Peramuna, JVP) represents the new left of Sri Lankan politics and has been assassinating government supporters. The front intensified its attacks after the Indians refused to leave the country. From late June through August some 225 people per week were killed, the highest death level the country had experienced since violence worsened in 1983. Many of these killings were carried out by death squads of off-duty security personnel and supporters of the UNP. The death squads began killing suspected JVP sympathizers in two areas previously untouched by the violence, the Anuradhapura and Kandy districts.

On 12 November the charismatic leader of the JVP, Rohana Wijeweera, was captured near Gampola in Kandy district by government forces. After being interrogated he informed the government about the JVP and led government security forces to a JVP hideout in Colombo where he was allegedly shot by one of his own men. The next day the government reported that the second in command of the JVP, Upatissa Gamanayake, was captured and later killed trying to escape. Both JVP leaders' bodies were cremated within hours of their deaths. Over the next two weeks the entire JVP Politburo was captured or killed along with each party's district leader including the head of the JVP's military wing, S.S.P. Fernando, who went by the name of Keerti Vijaybahu, an ancient Sri Lankan king who expelled the Chola invaders from India in the eleventh century.

The JVP party is organized around small cells of around five members and supposedly had more than ten thousand active supporters. By December the JVP seems to have reorganized and again launched violent attacks.

By the end of the year the LTTE was still at war with the Indians and was already attacking the Tamils as soon as Indian troops withdrew from any area. To protect their allies, Indian forces began training and arming a Tamil militia called the Tamil National Army, made up of EPRLF and TELO supporters and Tamil youths. The Tamil National army fought with the Sri Lankan army and the LTTE forces throughout much of November and December.

By year's end the JVP and its ten thousand supporters were still active. The old left, the Sri Lankan Communist party and its allies, appear to have lost their influence in Sri Lankan politics and been replaced by the JVP.

Robert C. Oberst
Nebraska Wesleyan University

Thailand

Population. 55,524,352 (July)
Party. Communist Party of Thailand (CPT)
Founded. 1942
Membership. 250–500 members (estimated); armed communist insurgents total 300–500 (estimated).
General Secretary. Thong Jaensri (unconfirmed; pseudonym?)
Politburo, Secretariat, and Central Committee. No data

Status. Illegal
Last Congress. Fourth, March–April 1984 (clandestine, met in four regions of the country).
Last Election. No communist party candidates allowed to participate in the most recent (1988) election.
Publications. *Thong Thai* (Thai Flag); *Prakai Fai* (The Flame) (intermittent underground publications)

The most vivid sign of democratization in contemporary Thai politics is the rise to power of Chatichai Choonhavan, the first elected member of Parliament to become prime minister since 1976 (during the three-year democratic period). Chatichai became prime minister following the 24 July 1988 parliamentary elections, when he was elected a member of Parliament from Khorat province representing the Chat Thai party. As leader of the political party with the largest plurality in parliament, Chatichai formed a coalition government of five leading political parties.

Chatichai moved quickly to consolidate his administration through appointments to the cabinet of influential politicians and business leaders. His reputation for being in league with big business grew when he appointed wealthy industrialists to cabinet positions controlling the nation's economic policies. He also shored up military support by giving army Commander in Chief Chavalit Yongchaiyut a free hand in determining military policies and personnel decisions despite Chatichai's self-appointment as minister of defense. Chatichai had important contacts with leading military officers because, 30 years previously, he had retired from the military, where he had reached the rank of army general.

Contributing to the wide support of the present government is the fact that for three decades the Thai economy has grown at an average annual rate of 7 percent. Since 1986 the growth rates have been the highest in the world, averaging almost 10 percent. These spectacular percentages were achieved while inflation was kept under 3 to 4 percent. Although the gap between Thailand's rich and poor increased during this period of growth, virtually every socioeconomic group in the kingdom enjoyed an improvement in its standard of living.

The greatest obstacle to continued economic growth is the poor state of infrastructural facilities including roads, electricity, and telecommunications. A second problem is the depletion of Thailand's natural resources, especially its forests. Moreover, foreign investment and foreign trade have made the Thai economy vulnerable to the vagaries of the world's capitalist system.

Government Anticommunist Activities. Because insurgency in Thailand has been all but ended, the Chatichai administration in 1989 moved to abrogate the 37-year-old anticommunist act. Thai army Commander in Chief Chavalit proposed that the act be replaced by a wider security law that also covered economic and social crimes (*FEER*, 7 September). Thailand's improved relations with neighboring socialist countries was cited as a further reason for abrogating the act.

Under the existing act, suspected communists can be indefinitely detained by a military tribunal. The few suspects detained at present are former members of the CPT. Many suspected subversives have been allowed limited freedom under the act, and an amnesty act passed by Parliament in 1989 will allow many of the detainees to be released.

Communist Party Activity. As in the past decade, Thai civilian and military leaders continued to proclaim the demise of the CPT. Deputy army Commander in Chief General Wanchai Ruangtrakun announced in March that the CPT must soon dissolve. Speaking in his capacity as assistant general director of communist suppression, Wanchai explained that the CPT has run out of qualified leaders because many former leaders have been arrested or died. Only 9 of the original 35 Central Committee members are still active.

Communist terrorism has almost ceased. In 1978, 774 government officials were assassinated by terrorists, but only 7 in 1989. Members of the Laos-based Thai communist movement began returning home to Thailand in 1989 because of improved conditions between Laos and Thailand. Laotian authorities stopped providing assistance to the pro-Soviet Phak Mai movement, which is a splinter group of the CPT.

The Phak Mai movement had formed because of an ideological conflict within the pro-China CPT. Vietnam and Laos financially supported it. The *Lak Thai* newspaper reported that the Phak Mai is now known as the Sayam Mai (New Siam) party and/or the Green Star party because its members have a green, five-pointed star tattooed on their left arms. The party, made up of Hmong hill tribesmen and former members of the CPT, operates in the northern and northeastern part of Thailand, especially in Nan province (*Lak Thai*, in Thai, 9 October; *FBIS-EAS*, 23 October).

In early 1989 some one thousand members of the Communist Party of Malaya (CPM) living along the Thai-Malaysian border surrendered to the Fourth Army Command, thereby undermining the CPM's ability to carry out armed struggle against the Malaysian government in Kuala Lumpur. The insurgents were to be resettled on Thai territory in Songkhla and Yala provinces. The CPM members and Thai government officials reached agreements assuring that the Thai and Malaysian governments would guarantee the safety of the CPM members, that there be no harassment once they agree to end their armed struggle, and that CPM members be allowed to permanently resettle in Thailand.

On 2 December the CPM and Thai and Malaysian officials agreed to end more than 40 years of armed struggle. The legendary leader of the CPM, Chin Peng, who signed the pact in Thailand's Had Yai, had fought for 41 years, first against the Japanese during World War II. He became general secretary of the communist party and led the twelve-year insurgency against the Malaysian government from 1948 to 1960.

All parties pledged to end armed struggle, dissolve the CPM, and agree that half of the former CPM members return to Malaysia while the other half resettle along the Thai border. General Chavalit announced that efforts to defeat the CPT must be continued, arguing that communism has still not been wiped out. He stated that if the communists who leave the jungle have no intention of overthrowing the country and the royal institution, then the country welcomes them. He warned that the communists could still emerge in the next decade.

General Chavalit attributed the communist problem to two factors: national problems and the democratic problem. In his view Thailand was at a crucial point because most people believed that full democracy had been attained. That belief made people forget that national problems exist that can still be exploited by the communists (*FBIS-EAS*, 11 August).

Relations with Communist Neighbors. Chatichai has called for better relations with Vietnam, Laos, and Cambodia. He invited Cambodian premier Hun Sen to visit Bangkok and moved to improve ties with Laos after decades of intermittent border skirmishes and diplomatic conflicts.

Chatichai's new nationalism emphasizes economic rather than security relations. He wants the United States to be an equal rather than a patron. Thai foreign policy has lessened security dependence on the United States, asserted a policy of equidistance in its relations with allies and adversaries, and launched a new Indochina policy without seeking the support of the United States.

In January, Foreign Minister Sitthi Sawetsila led a Thai delegation on an official visit to Vietnam. The visit was the first of its kind in thirteen years by a high-ranking Thai official. The visit followed the announcement of the Vietnamese plan to withdraw all troops from Cambodia. The purpose of the visit was to expand economic relations between the two countries and to "build mutual trust" and open a "new chapter in Thai-Vietnamese relations." Talks were also scheduled to focus on a future peace settlement for Cambodia.

Relations with Laos were also improved in 1989 with a series of visits by top officials including army commanders in chief and prime ministers. These meetings included negotiations regarding border camps, which hold about 80,000 refugees, and the building of a bridge between the two nations near Vientiane.

Most momentous of the many visits between leaders of Thailand and the regional communist nations was the meeting between Prime Minister Chatichai and Cambodian premier Hun Sen. Because Thailand did not recognize the Phnom Penh regime, Hun Sen came as leader of a Cambodian faction rather than as a head of government.

No new ground was broken at the January meeting, although the Phnom Penh administration's legitimacy was strengthened and a "psychological breakthrough" occurred between the two countries. Prince Sihanouk and the leaders of the Association of Southeast Asian Nations expressed dismay at the reversal of Thai policy vis-à-vis Cambodia. The meeting did not lead to the re-establishment of diplomatic relations between Thailand and the People's Republic of Kampuchea.

Hun Sen returned to Bangkok in May for talks with Chatichai regarding Thai aid to the Khmer opposition factions and preparations for the peace negotiations to be held in Djakarta. Chatichai agreed to end Thailand's military support of the Cambodian resistance and called for a cease-fire on the parts of all the Cambodian groups.

Prime Minister Chatichai visited China in March and October. As former foreign minister he had extensive ties with Chinese officials. His trips were planned to increase government-to-government trade and economic cooperation and to discuss means to resolve the Cambodian crisis. The leaders of the two nations also discussed the possibility of

China's selling tanks, armored personnel carriers, artillery pieces, and ammunition to Thailand at special "friendship prices" to aid the Thai military's modernization and diversification of arms supply sources. The Thai air force began negotiations on the purchase of Chinese F-7M jet fighters, but by the end of the year no decision was made. Thai ambassador to Beijing Tet Bunnak announced in November that Sino-Thai relations were at their best since the two countries established diplomatic relations fourteen years ago (*FBIS-EAS*, 2 November).

Clark D. Neher
Northern Illinois University

Vietnam

Population. 66,820,544 (*World Factbook* 1989)
Party. Vietnam Communist Party (Viet Nam Cong San, VCP)
Founded. 1930 (as Indochina Communist Party)
Membership. 2,195,824 (*Nhan Dan*, 3 February); 80 percent male; 99 percent ethnic Vietnamese; average age: early 50s (est.); 40 percent *ban co* (poor peasant); 25 percent peasant/farm laborer; 15 percent proletariat; 20 percent other
General Secretary. Nguyen Van Linh (b. 1915)
Politburo. Nguyen Van Linh, Vo Chi Cong (b. 1912), Do Muoi (b. 1917), Vo Van Kiet (b. 1922), Le Duc Anh (b. 1910?), Nguyen Duc Tam (b. 1920), Nguyen Co Thach (b. 1920), Dong Sy Nguyen (b. 1920?), Tran Xuan Bach, Nguyen Thanh Binh, Doan Khue, Mai Chi Tho (b. 1922), Dao Duy Tung
Secretariat. Nguyen Van Linh, Nguyen Duc Tam, Tran Xuan Bach, Dao Duy Tung, Tran Kien, Le Phuoc Tho, Nguyen Quyet, Dam Quang Trung, Vo Oanh, Nguyen Khanh, Tran Quyet, Tran Quoc Hoang, Pham The Duyet
Central Committee. 124 full and 49 alternate members
Status. Ruling party
Last Congress. Sixth, 15–18 December 1986
Last Election. 19 April 1987, Eighth National As-

sembly, 98.8 percent, 496 seats, all VCP-endorsed (*Indochina Chronology*)

Auxiliary Organizations. Vietnam Fatherland Front, Nguyen Huu Tho, chairman; Ho Chi Minh Communist Youth Union, Ha Quang Du, general secretary

Publications. *Nhan Dan* (The People), VCP daily (cir. 500,000), editor, Ha Dang (also Central Committee member); *Tap Chi Cong San* (Communist Review), VCP theoretical monthly; *Quan Doi Nhan Dan* (People's Army), army newspaper

The year 1989 probably will be remembered by Vietnamese historians as the year the VCP went to the ideological barricades to preserve orthodox communism. Its grim struggle took place in a world where most other Leninist systems were undergoing revolutionary changes.

It was the intent of the Hanoi leadership to hold back the tide of change and defend the ideological status quo: the rest of the Leninist world might foolishly be dismantling what was an eminent, wholly admirable governing system, but this was not going to happen in Vietnam. However, the same intent had been entertained by other leaderships in Eastern Europe, but to no avail. Thus the question posed at year's end was whether party Secretary Nguyen Van Linh and his ruling thirteen-man Politburo would be able to hold back the tide of history. It seemed unlikely that they could do so permanently. However, standing against such a judgment was the record of the past: the Hanoi leadership had frequently gone against the previous trend of events and against conventional wisdom and succeeded. Indeed Vietnam's long history is filled with improbable occurrences, unanticipated successes, and victories few had predicted.

The challenges thrown down, the dilemmas faced, the anxieties raised, the contradictions posed—within a leadership attempting to fix workable party and state policies under conditions of extreme ambiguity and flux—all appeared with admirable clarity at the party's two Sixth Congress's plenums during the year: the Sixth Plenum in May, whose agenda was chiefly concerned with economic reform, and the Seventh Plenum in August, devoted to the stunning changes under way in the USSR and Eastern Europe and what these portended for Vietnam. Published materials, particularly speeches by party chief Secretary Nguyen Van Linh with his frank admissions of shortcoming and anxiety, provide a clear, authoritative picture of the leadership's assessment of the internal and external scenes and how it intends to deal with these.

The plan of the reform process fixed the parameters of the plenum's activities and all of the debate and had been in place since the meeting of the seminal Sixth Plenum (Fifth Congress) in December 1986. It drew on the example of the USSR, although exactly how much of a model the USSR was remains a subject of debate among outside observers. Certainly in terms of rhetoric there was great similarity. Major Moscow concepts involved are *glasnost'*, or openness; *perestroika*, or restructuring the system; *novoie mislenie*, or new thinking; and *demokratizazia*, or democratization. There is no exact linguistic equivalent of *perestroika* in Vietnamese; two terms are employed meaning *renovation*: *do moi* and *canh tan*. *Glasnost'* is translated as *coi mo*, but its meaning is as vague in Vietnamese as it is in Russian (or in English for that matter). *Novoie myshlenie*, or new thinking, is translated into Vietnamese as *tu duy moi*, but is little used except by party theoretical journals. The concept of democratization is carefully prescribed when it is discussed at all.

Leadership and Party Organization. The highest-level leadership in Vietnam had been involved in an intense and complex political struggle beginning with the death of Le Duan (July 1986). Initially it was anticipated that out of the factional infighting that characterizes Vietnamese politics would quickly come a new leadership, that is, the struggle would work itself out in a matter of months, as had been the case earlier when party leadership realignment was required. Instead it became protracted and as of the end of 1989 had not resolved itself. The prolongation of the political struggle was partly because it involved a lugubrious generational transfer of political power. (See *YICA*, 1989, for detailed discussion of the existing factions and the issues that divide them.) All of this contributed to another year of leadership disarray and indecision.

This is not to suggest that the party leadership was or would become self-destructive. Politburo membership was based on decades-long associations, and although individuals might strongly disagree on policies, there was an overriding sense of unity that bonded them together.

Conservative sentiment continued to dominate Politburo thinking, particularly in terms of taking risks in the name of social change. In the factional struggle between the reformers and the conservatives, the latter held a slight predominance. Because the rule of collective leadership continued to prevail, however, the operative rule remained that all decisions had to represent a consensus.

Official Politburo statements early in the year clearly indicated the top leadership's assessment of where the party and the society stood. This viewpoint was reinforced by the official documentation from the two party Central Committee plenary sessions during the year. Chief elements of this consensual view were the following:

• The party in Vietnam, being part of the international communist movement, has come under an unprecedented onslaught from two forces, one external, one internal. Externally are the forces of imperialism led by the United States and directed against both the socialist world and the national liberation movements in Third World countries. Internally are the reactionary forces, those within Vietnam directed against both the party and the state.

• The ultimate goal of the Vietnamese society remained "to advance toward socialism," and existing "widespread and distorted notions to the contrary" in Vietnam were to be rectified. It would be permissible to borrow science and technology from capitalist countries, but not institutions, ideas, or methods that counter orthodox Marxism-Leninism. That ideological reaffirmation in effect fixed the outer limits of *coi mo* (openness) in Vietnam.

• Progress had been made in the effort to reform and overhaul the economy and parts of the society. However, most sectors remained "rife with numerous difficulties." This was by way of general assessment of the Vietnamese current conditions. The Politburo's judgment was that mixed results had been achieved: some commendable progress in agriculture, in economic decentralization, and in the various motivation and mobilization campaigns; less success in increasing productivity either on the farm or in the factory. Institutional revitalization of the CPV continued to fall short. Most seriously, the ideological task of persuading both party members and the general public that Marxism-Leninism has the solutions to Vietnam's various problems made little progress.

• The campaign against negativism (a catchall term for what is wrong with the society) had not met expectations and must be pursued more vigorously. In addition to the party, this is also the task of the mass media, mass organizations such as the Fatherland Front, and the National Assembly. Essentially the antinegativism campaign became a moral exhortation effort by all communication institutions, which are charged with exposing and denouncing "typical cases of negativism such as degenerate and deviate cadres, unhealthy lifestyles, the bad practices of hooligans, thugs and dishonest merchants" as well as the more abstract "obsolete mechanisms of management," all of which perpetuate negativism.

• Absent, and badly needed, was some party-supplied comprehensive, unifying concept for organizing and administering the renovation process. Essentially this is a statement of need for some plausible and attractive ideological construct that will prove to be workable. However, this was not seen as a call for an intellectual statement or doctrinal explanation so much as for a generalized procedure to mobilize and motivate party members and the general public. Chiefly it involves the major existing institutions serving those purposes: the mass social organizations, the agitprop cadre corps, the *khiem-thao* (criticism/self-criticism) mechanism, the mass media, educational institutions, and the cultural sector.

• The responsibility for reform through renovation must be broadly spread within the society, not simply vested in party and high-level state leaders. This requirement appears directed chiefly at the National Assembly as part of a concerted effort to grant the assembly more responsibility and authority. This concept is akin to the so-called democratization process in the USSR because it extends political involvement beyond the party. The Politburo made a direct appeal to Vietnamese intellectuals, artists, and other creative influentials to support the renovation effort, offering as incentive greater artistic freedom or at least a reduction of coercive state and party controls. There was an affective quality about this call for a "democratic atmosphere" in meeting "people's legitimate demands" and in the importance of "listening to the opinions of upright people in settling problems at the grassroots level in fair, reasonable, orderly and law-abiding ways." But behind the forthcoming rhetoric one heard a note of hesitancy, a sense of uncertainty that reflected the thinking of the still-powerful conservatives in the Politburo as to exactly how far the people can be trusted in assuming authority and responsibility for their own affairs.

• The mass media were to be enlarged, improved, and energized in the task of achieving reform through moral exhortation. More resources were to be devoted to agitprop work, education, the press-information sector, and party schools. Said Linh in his Sixth Plenum report, "The entire people, the Party and the population, must be educated in the persistence of socialist ideals and objectives . . . we will not take the capitalist road."

• To supervise all this, a special committee reporting to the Central Committee Secretariat was established and charged with monitoring progress in renovation. The committee was also to evaluate systematically the "ideological status of both Party cadres and Party members," meaning that the party's semipurge, under way for several years, probably would continue. And the committee was ordered "systematically to evaluate the political mood of the people." This was indeed a new and innovative move, a serious effort to take the political pulse of Vietnam nationwide.

None of this was meant to suggest a basic philosophical change in the Vietnamese ruling system. The sense of the official pronouncements was that the party must better supervise the two administrative institutions—the state bureaucracy and the National Assembly–mass organization matrix. Above all it was constantly stressed that the party must continue to monopolize political power. The long-standing dictum, "the party holds power," was constantly reiterated. It was not Marxism that needed to be defended. Marxism in Vietnam was vague enough to include virtually any government policy. Rather it was Leninism and the concept of the party as vanguard of the proletarian dictatorship. The party, in the name of the workers monopolizing political power, would be willing to permit criticism under certain circumstances, would even tolerate limited dissent, but it would not share political power. It is at that point that the barricade is reached.

The Seventh Plenum (August) witnessed the frankest assessment of the current threats to the system's fundamental stability. Secretary Nguyen Van Linh's speech (August 28) reported that "ideological deviationism had emerged among a large number of Party cadres and rank and file members," which had given rise to specific "deviant ideological viewpoints." He did not describe these, saying only that although "held by only a handful of cadres and Party members we cannot disregard them, for they can spread, becoming a breeding ground for venom." Linh did blame the problem in part on "wrong ideological currents coming from the outside." However, his chief point was that deviationism was due to failed party leadership. Good

leadership, he said, would "create unanimity of viewpoint within the Party and among the people and hence stabilize the situation."

The "reactionary forces" within Vietnam to which the plenum rhetoric alluded appeared to be chiefly from older southern party members. Some observers perceived a growing challenge from the military, both from the People's Army of Vietnam (PAVN) High Command and from the military retirees.

Drawing considerable notice from the foreign press during the year was the Club of Former Resistance Fighters (informally, the Old Revolutionaries Club) headquartered in Ho Chi Minh City, which included retired General Tran Van Tra; Tran Bach Dang, former Ho Chi Minh City party committee secretary; Ha Huy Giap, former Socialist Republic of Vietnam (SRV) minister of education; Nguyen Van Tran, former SRV ambassador to the USSR; and others. Some one hundred members of the club sent an open letter to the Central Committee in June calling for true elections rather than elections manipulated by the party. Those involved appeared to be chiefly southerners; all were former prominent members of the party. Although they backed Nguyen Van Linh in his struggle with the conservatives, their policy recommendations went far beyond what Linh would endorse.

The PAVN, given its size (2.9 million including militia) and its centrality in Vietnamese life, represented the major potential political challenge to party leadership. Top generals in the PAVN had been restive over the state of affairs for nearly a decade, judging by editorials in the military newspaper *Quan Doi Nhan Dan*. One discontent, until it was resolved this year, was the no-win policy of the war in Cambodia. The PAVN High Command's more central concern, however, was that it might not in the future be able to perform its assigned duty, to defend Vietnam. The sense of this view was that Vietnam's "economic inferiority," its economic weakness, meant that the society could not support PAVN and that the PAVN should not be as dependent as it now is on the USSR for most of its military hardware because that source in the future could become unreliable. What was required, the generals argued, was more research and development work, serving both the PAVN and the society in general, to lift the country by its technological bootstraps. What was also required, the generals contended, was to develop a new strategic concept for the defense of Vietnam, one not built on the requirement of sophisticated hardware but rooted in the older, more traditional *dau tranh* (struggle) strategy of people's war.

Party Domestic Affairs. The chief routine party activity during the year was a series of district-level party elections followed by district-level congresses. Agenda of the latter largely concerned overhauling the grass roots–level party administration and redefining local cadre tasks and responsibilities. The semipurge, weeding out the incompetent and disciplining or expelling the corrupt, continued as it had in the past decade. The rate of party recruitment slowed during the year chiefly, it appeared, because higher standards for membership were imposed, recruitment efforts being concentrated on the young, educated professionals rather than among proletarians. *Nhan Dan* (3 February) said the number of party members admitted in 1988 was 82,824, which was 20 percent less than the previous year.

There were also a series of upper-level, or leading, cadre conferences during the year. One of these in Hanoi (14–19 September) was a gathering of PAVN upper-level cadres, which was also attended by "old revolutionary generals" from the South. Nguyen Van Linh made a determined effort to set down a philosophical statement as to what the true believer in Vietnam should now believe. The sense of his explanation was this:

The conceptual foundation of the Vietnamese society was to be seen as firm, reliable, and not to be questioned. Basic ideology remained the same. There was to be no change in the fundamental doctrinal principles: dictatorship of the proletariat, monopoly of political power exercised by the party, adherence to proletarian internationalism as far as possible, and, above all, continued total faith in communism as the wave of the future. "Marxism-Leninism," he said, "will always serve as the ideological foundation of the Party and the guide for the Revolution. It is not to be abandoned, although it may be interpreted creatively and enriched." Above all nothing must weaken the doctrinal rationale of the dictatorship of the proletariat because that would strike at the party's legitimacy and diminish the authority of the party leadership.

However, Linh continued, there is room, indeed imperative need, for reform within both party and state. Reform he defined as overcoming erroneous concepts and enriching correct concepts, not breaking away from Marxism-Leninism. Political reform meant strengthening the party's leading role in guiding the society, not in sharing political power. The economic system was not to be changed so much as it was to be made to work better, more efficiently, in a more dynamic manner.

The ideological dilemma faced by the party in this reform-without-change approach was graphically illustrated by the efforts of Linh and other party theoreticians to fit the concept of democracy into the general scheme of things. On the one hand, the party must be a *dau tranh* (struggle) institution, able to act quickly and forcefully when required in both political *dau tranh* and armed *dau tranh* arenas. This requires centralized control, a party hierarchial structure modeled after the armed forces, and a population motivated to iron self-discipline and unquestioning obedience to the Politburo. On the other hand, *dau tranh* was represented as an egalitarian, nonelitist, people's movement, horizontal in construct rather than vertical. The masses were to lead themselves using the mechanism of the party as the vanguard. Resolution of this contradiction was to be found in the idea of democratic centralism as defined by Lenin: unfettered discussion and deliberation on pending questions, monolithic unity in action once policy is fixed. Democratic centralism was actually practiced in the 1930s, but gradually gave way to party cadre manipulation. In later years the VCP had wrestled with the doctrinal issue of the proper concept of democracy because it was central to all of the major issues it faced and still faces.

Plenum reports and party theoretical literature all made frequent references to the term *democracy*. These allusions were carefully stated. Vietnam was committed to socialist democracy, or guided democracy, the two terms being used interchangeably. There was the need to "bring the spirit of democracy into play"; the reform effort required "social democratization"; there must be "general democratization of the social life in Vietnam"; and so on. It was stressed that care must be taken to distinguish socialist democracy from Vietnam's ideological enemy, bourgeois democracy. Any definition that connoted "pluralism, political plurality and multiparty opposition parties" was suspect. Such forms deny the idea of the party monopolizing political power and are "merely cunning schemes by imperialists and reactionaries who are enemies of class and the nation."

This concept equated democracy with justice but not with freedom. Furthering the democratic spirit meant eliminating unjust practices by party cadres and others, such as "mandarinism," meaning imperious behavior. Bringing the "spirit of democracy into play" did not mean power sharing but better mobilizational and motivational campaigns to persuade the masses to accept party decision making as being democratic. Usage clearly skirted the concept of democracy rooted in individual freedom; nowhere in the literature was linkage made between democracy and freedom. The best that could be offered was to define individual freedom as a "corridor within democratic centralism." Hence democracy as employed by the party in Vietnam was contained, proscribed, limited, manipulated, the antithesis of the essence of the true spirit of democracy, which is freedom of choice.

Implicit in the party's treatment of the concept of democracy during 1989 was that there might be at work influences within the party seeking to restore the original, pre-Lenin concept of democracy in party affairs, that is, genuine freedom in debating policies, but still with unquestioned support once fixed. The sense of this seemed to be that true democratic centralism could be made to work in Vietnam.

At the less theoretical level the energies of the party cadres and rank and file during the year were devoted to efforts to improve the party's leadership over the economic sector and over the political sector to the extent it impinged on economic reform and improved economic performance. The focus here was on the three major immediate economic needs: to increase rice and other food production, to deliver more necessities of life to the Vietnamese consumer, and to increase hard currency holdings through increased exports to the capitalist world.

Sixth Plenum criticism of the economic sector was heavy and specific: "unsteady" grain production, a "confused" domestic trade sector, fluctuating prices, serious underemployment and unemployment, high inflation, a huge state budget deficit, interest on foreign debts that could not be paid, low reserves of hard currency, too many subsidies being paid workers, a population increasing at too rapid a rate (est. 2.5 percent per year), a weak economic infrastructure, and an excessively dense bureaucracy.

Death in 1989 claimed a number of major party figures:

• Le Thanh Nghi. This retired Politburo member died 16 August in Hanoi at the age of 78. Nghi was an economic agitprop cadre turned foreign aid fundraiser. A trained economist in the 1950s, he moved into motivational work in the economic sector, running party emulation campaigns to increase production; in the 1960s he devoted his efforts to

soliciting economic and military aid from abroad. He retired in the mid-1980s.

• Huynh Tan Phat. The chief theoretician of the National Liberation Front (of South Vietnam) and one of the few Viet Cong to make the lateral transfer to authority in Hanoi after the war, he died 30 September in Ho Chi Minh City at age 76. At the time of his death he was a vice-chairman of the SRV Council of State.

• Nguyen Huu Chinh (alias Nguyen Xuan Huu). Central Committee member (Fourth to Sixth congresses) from Quang Nam-Da Nang province, he died 29 October "of a serious illness" at the age of 67. Before his retirement Chinh had been in the National Assembly and a member of the SRV Council of State.

• Hoang Truong Minh. Central Committee member, National Assembly vice-chairman, and major figure in the Fatherland Front, he died 12 October of a "serious illness" at the age of 67. Minh had also been a leader in the Lao-Vietnam friendship organizations.

As a footnote to history, Hanoi officials in 1989 acknowledged that they had falsified the day of Ho Chi Minh's death so that his death date would not fall on Vietnam's National Day. Ho died on 2 September 1969 rather than on 3 September, as reports announced at the time. Officials also said they had ignored the provision of Ho's last will and testament that he be cremated (he was enshrined in a Soviet tomb instead). And they ignored Ho's instruction that there be a one-year moratorium on agricultural taxes after his death. For years there had been speculation that Ho's will was doctored because the original handwritten text was never displayed. This was corrected in 1989 with the publication of *President Ho Chi Minh's Testament* by Su That Publishing House.

During the year the party observed the 40th anniversary of the founding of its highest-level school, the Nguyen Ai Quoc Institute in Hanoi. The school was founded in February 1949 in Luong village, Dinh Hoa district, Bac Thai province. Ceremonies were held at the institute 29 September with its director, Nguyen Duc Binh, and most Politburo members in attendance. Since its inception the school has graduated 19,076 persons.

Front Organizations. The institutional triangle of control in Vietnam, as in other Leninist systems, has been the troika of party, state, and mass organizations. In Vietnam the mass organization—the Fatherland Front—has worked as an integral part of the National Assembly to mobilize and motivate, not as an electorate-legislative function. Beginning in 1986 the nature of the mass organization began to change. The party began a concerted effort to transfer more responsibility to the Fatherland Front and the National Assembly, offering as inducement increased authority. This trend continued during 1989.

International Views, Positions, Activities. As with its treatment of other orthodox Marxist-Leninist influences in Vietnam, the party leadership in dealing with external problems also struggled to assert that what was past was prologue. Constantly maintained was the contention that the two principles of the external relationship—Vietnamese patriotism coupled with proletarian-socialist internationalism and Vietnam's national strength allied with "strength of the epoch" (i.e., communism's "wave of the future")—remained unchanged and as powerful as ever. Nguyen Van Linh at the Seventh Plenum declared that "the fact is communist parties (around the world) are firm and strong. The world revolutionary movement is developing. Socialism is constantly maturing."

The "end of communism" issue was the chief agenda item at an August high-level party cadre conference in Ho Chi Minh City. Linh offered a frank assessment of unfolding events as he saw them: an "unprecedented onslaught against socialism by the imperialist forces headed by the United States . . . insidious schemes and tricks of imperialism putting a number of fraternal socialist countries under threat . . . a matter of acute political sensitivity" for the entire Leninist world. Although "misled comrades in Warsaw" and elsewhere were partly to blame for this condition, chief villain was the United States: "Bush arrogantly pledges to destroy Socialism . . . acts frantically and intensively to do so . . . thus revealing proof of the U.S. imperialists' wolfish nature."

Focal point of this phenomenon was seen as Poland. Said a *Nhan Dan* editorial (25 August):

> The crisis in Poland is a struggle between the revolutionary and prosocialist forces and the counterrevolutionary and anti-socialist forces such as the Solidarity Trade Union and other reactionary organizations. . . . Opposing forces have deliberately caused and aggravated and increased political difficulties when allowed to operate legally, aided by the U.S. and the West as well as by the Church with the Communist

Party in Poland trying to carry out political reform as state pluralism with a multiparty and multi-trade union society.

The essence of the party's official evaluation of the world scene was that nothing basic had changed. Two contending camps still existed: socialism and capitalism, with the same contradictions: between exploiter and exploited, between worker and bourgeois, and between national liberation movements and imperialism. The struggle itself remained as defined long ago by Lenin, a matter of who will defeat whom.

There was in this assessment a perverse unwillingness by the party leadership to recognize the fact of stunning change under way in the Leninist world, a change in which old assumptions were disintegrating. Acknowledging that fact required, if nothing else, development and application of new doctrinal and policy guides. Official Hanoi pronouncements portrayed the world scene as simply a continuation of past imperialist and reactionary efforts to undermine Marxism-Leninism, not as a from-the-bottom revolution. They persisted in seeing a philosophical division that no longer existed.

In the world of party and state diplomatic relations the chief concern during the year was the Cambodian peace process, an issue tied to virtually all of Vietnam's bilateral relations as well as to most of its external problems. Beginning in early 1989 feverish regional activity began to find ways and means to bring the forlorn little country of Cambodia back to peace and stability. The effort reached a climax in Paris in late July at an eighteen-nation French-sponsored conference. By any measure the conference accomplished little, hardly keeping the peace process alive.

Hanoi's chief purpose at the conference was to extract such benefits as it could from its decision to withdraw the last of its troops from Cambodia. Rather than expressions of appreciation, many conference speakers asserted that Vietnam should never have invaded Cambodia in the first place and now was simply rectifying that error. Throughout the conference there was also steady criticism of Vietnam for its use of "settlers" (ethnic Vietnamese civilians living in Cambodia—estimates vary from 100,000 to possibly 500,000), a code term to mean continued Vietnamese influence and control of Cambodia after the departure of its troops.

The decision to disengage militarily from Cambodia was bold and decisive and not one that could have been made easily in Hanoi. At stake were genuine Vietnamese national security concerns, principally the fear of a hostile government coming to power in Phnom Penh. Vietnam is a long, narrow country and highly vulnerable to threat on its flank. The decision to withdraw its troops amid uncertainties as to what would result in Cambodia appears to have resulted from a changed view by the three military members of the Politburo—Le Duc Anh, Doan Khue, and Dong Sy Nguyen—who decided that Vietnam must bite the bullet and disengage from Cambodia and apparently were confident that this would not seriously threaten Vietnam's national security.

There was little other change during the year in Vietnamese foreign relations. The cold war with China continued despite high-level talks by officials from the two foreign ministries. Vietnam remained diplomatically isolated in the region and throughout the world. Excessively dependent on the USSR and the Council for Mutual Economic Assistance, it was unable to attract little more than token foreign economic investment and aid from capitalist countries. There was during the year no significant change in the nominal relationship that Vietnam had with the United States.

Douglas Pike
University of California at Berkeley

EASTERN EUROPE AND THE SOVIET UNION

Introduction

The late summer and fall of 1989 will go down in history as the time when the last colonial empire began to lose control over its dependencies in Eastern Europe. This disintegration was recognized by Mikhail S. Gorbachev in his 9 December speech before the Communist Party of the Soviet Union (CPSU) Central Committee, when he admitted that

- Communist parties no longer ruled in either Poland or Hungary.
- "Friends" in East Germany and Czechoslovakia largely had lost their positions.
- New political forces were seeking other ways of social development.

These statements recognized that the revolution throughout the outer part of the imperium was irreversible. Only five days before Gorbachev's address, the political-consultative committee of the Warsaw Treaty Organization (WTO) issued a communiqué condemning the 1968 invasion of Czechoslovakia.

The Soviet Union. Gorbachev appeared to be more successful in foreign affairs than he was on the domestic front. He made several spectacular arms control proposals in support of a "common European home." Withdrawing the last combat units from Afghanistan on 15 February created a certain degree of euphoria among elites in the West. *Time* magazine selected Gorbachev as its "man of the year."

Despite *perestroika* in the USSR, economic indicators continued to decline. Official Soviet spokesmen admitted a budget deficit totaling 11 percent of gross national product, subsequently raised to 165 billion rubles (*NYT*, 15 March 1990). Demands for outright independence or local autonomy spread from the Baltic states through the republics facing West into the Caucasus and Central Asia. As a result, troops sent by Moscow killed demonstrators in Tbilisi and Baku as well as in other localities. Wildcat miners' strikes developed into major ones between Siberia and the Ukraine.

National elections under *demokratizatsiia* in March 1989 resulted in a new Congress of People's Deputies that did not include many prominent CPSU functionaries. A smaller, working legislature, or Supreme Soviet, was elected in May by the above body and soon manifested its independence. It continued to modify draft legislation and exercise oversight responsibilities, both new to the Soviet system of government.

The CPSU Central Committee plenum in April removed 110 "dead souls" from its own ranks as well as from the Central Auditing Commission. At the September plenum, Gorbachev succeeded in ousting V. M. Chebrikov and V. V. Shcherbitskii from the Politburo, replacing them with KGB chairman V. A. Kriuchkov and First Deputy Premier Iu. D. Masliukov.

Soon thereafter, developments in Eastern Europe seemed to be spinning out of Soviet control: communist leaders fell from power in one country after another, the Berlin Wall opened, and both Germanies appeared to be heading toward unification regardless of what the major powers wanted. Gorbachev himself appeared to be exerting his influence, in person or through his chiefs of mission attached to USSR embassies, for the purpose of eliminating old and conservative leaders from their positions of power.

Eastern Europe. With the overthrow of Nicolae Ceauşescu in Romania on 22 December, all six of the bloc communist parties had acquired new leaders. Noteworthy also has been the acceleration of change from a political power monopoly to pluralism. Elections in Poland brought a noncommunist into the premiership as head of a coalition government in August. Other national elections were scheduled to take place between March and

June of 1990, most of which should follow the Polish example.

Eastern Europe is gravitating toward the West in its search for new political and economic models. After more than 70 years, the Soviet Union had not produced anything worthy of imitation. Hence the drive by East Europeans to rejoin the mainstream of politics in the West and, eventually, become part of an all-European community.

However, two bloc organizations still remained intact at year's end and are being paid at least lip service by their East European members. The WTO provides the rationale for Soviet troops stationed in East Germany, Czechoslovakia, Hungary, and Poland; by early 1990 all except East Berlin had requested negotiations with Moscow on withdrawal of these armed forces. It is probable that a new German Democratic Republic (GDR) government will do so after the 18 March elections.

The other organization that holds the bloc together is the Council for Mutual Economic Assistance (CMEA), which exchanges raw materials from the USSR for locally manufactured goods. East European factories would close down without the petroleum, natural gas, iron ore, electricity, cotton, and even grain from the East. The prospect of German unification might spell the de facto end of CMEA, with the former GDR becoming a possible conduit for European Community benefits to the rest of Eastern Europe.

• Albania, isolated by choice from the bloc since 1961, continues to remain fearful of change. A shake-up of the ruling party's Secretariat and the Interior Ministry (police) as well as other government agencies suggested that leader Ramiz Alia distrusts young executives. He claims that Albania is the sole country in the world that is building socialism and not looking to anybody else for help.

• Bulgaria ended an era with the ouster on 10 November of Todor Zhivkov, who had headed the ruling party for 35 years. His successor, Petur Mladenov, described the economy as being "on the verge of a heart attack." Within four weeks, all top posts had been cleared of the old guard. However, demonstrators in Sofia and elsewhere called for multiparty elections (which will be held in June 1990) and elimination of the leading role in government, exercised by communists. Nine dissident groups formed a Union of Democratic Forces and entered into negotiations with the regime early in the new year.

• Czechoslovakia's more rapid transition was triggered by the police brutally suppressing a 17 November student demonstration that attracted 100,000 participants in Prague. One week later, all members of the communist party presidium (Politburo) and Secretariat resigned. An extraordinary congress during 21–22 December made further changes that eliminated about 30 senior functionaries from office. Party membership dropped by three-fourths from earlier claims.

Meanwhile, a general strike on 27 November forced the government to accept a coalition cabinet, the resignation of the president two weeks later, and the election of playwright Vaclav Havel to that office before year's end. During this same period, all political prisoners were released. Several thousand strike committees throughout the country began to organize independent labor unions. Apart from dissident groups, a Civic Forum established itself and hitherto subordinate political organizations (e.g., the socialist and people's parties) asserted their independence from communist hegemony.

• East Germany's revolution resulted in dismissal of the communist party leadership, triggered by the mass exodus in the hundreds of thousands (via Czechoslovakia, Hungary, and Poland) to the neighboring Federal Republic during 1989. Mass demonstrations in Dresden and Leipzig seemed to escalate after Gorbachev's visit to East Berlin for the 40th anniversary of the German Democratic Republic. Erich Honecker's resignation on 18 October and the promotion of his protégé did not stem resignations from the ruling party, which lost 600,000 members, or one-fourth of its total, between October and the extraordinary congress.

The first half of this special party session during 8–9 December 1989 resulted in a new leadership under a 41-year-old attorney, Gregor Gysi. Rather than a new name, the communists added to their Socialist Unity Party of Germany a hyphen followed by Party of Democratic Socialism. The next regular congress, in the spring of 1990, would come up with a new designation, program, and statutes.

• Hungary held pride of place in terms of rapid change evolving from a split in the ruling communist movement between party leader Károly Grósz and three reformers on the presidium. The congress voted overwhelmingly on 9 October to change the name from the Hungarian Workers' Socialist Party to the Hungarian Socialist Party (HSP) and give up its ruling status. Two months later the HSP had only 51,000 members, whereas a breakaway group that had retained the original designation claimed

100,000 (later admitted to be only 82,000) at its Fourteenth Congress on 17 December.

A public opinion survey indicated that the HSP would obtain only 16 percent of the vote in the first free national elections scheduled for 25 March 1990. Results of a referendum (58 percent turnout) on when and how the new president would be elected postponed that event until after the above date and decided that the new democratic assembly would select the chief of state. The old National Assembly voted on 21 December to dissolve itself on 16 March 1990.

• Poland has had a majority of noncommunists in the government since September 1989 as a result of semifree elections held three months earlier based on the April roundtable agreement with the regime. Communists retained four key portfolios: defense, interior, foreign trade, and transportation, which undoubtedly will change after the next national elections are held.

Meanwhile, the Polish United Workers' (communist) party, once two million strong, decided to disband and re-emerged under a different name. This was accomplished toward the end of January 1990 and resulted in two new movements: the Social Democracy of the Republic of Poland, with some five thousand members, and a Social Democratic Union that numbered only one hundred persons.

The problem, not unique to Poland, is how to replace the 900,000 communists who belong to the *nomenklatura* and occupy key positions in government, armed forces, police, industry, and even the agricultural bureaucracy. Among other things, it will take time before replacements can be trained.

• Romania shed its communists quicker than any other country in Eastern Europe. The regime of Nicolae and Elena Ceauşescu collapsed on 22 December, when the couple fled Bucharest by helicopter only to be captured and executed three days later. The ruling party of 3.8 million members disappeared; a group of communists who had been removed from important positions by the Ceauşescus seized power and proclaimed themselves the Council of National Salvation. They scheduled parliamentary elections for 20 May 1990.

The Fourteenth (and last) Congress of the Romanian Communist Party was held between 20 and 29 November and served as a platform for rejection of any change. Only when the regime fell was it possible to learn how badly the economy had deteriorated. Fictitious figures on the production of grain, for example, concealed the fact that the population at large suffered for the crash repayment of the country's foreign debt.

• Yugoslavia, never part of the Warsaw Pact and only an associate member of CMEA, remained afflicted with both political and economic problems. A dispute between Serbia and Slovenia threatened to tear the country apart (the former declared an economic boycott of the latter in November). Efforts by Albanians to obtain independence and the ouster of other ethnic groups from Kosovo province added to the tension. Some 400,000 Serbs and Montenegrins have left that province since 1945. Strikes, inflation, and unemployment appeared to be endemic.

Membership in the League of Yugoslav Communists has steadily dropped, even in the armed forces and especially among those under 27 years of age. The Fourteenth Extraordinary Party Congress was scheduled for 20–22 January 1990. Meanwhile, other political movements have been established throughout the country, in effect creating the beginnings of a multiparty system. The country seemed faced with chaos and perhaps a breakup into separate republics.

CMEA still binds all of the East European countries, except Albania, to the USSR. Member states have experienced a notable slowdown in growth as well as other problems. Trade and cooperation within CMEA continued to stagnate, with the regular June council session canceled. Eastern Europe continues to barter shoddily manufactured goods in return for Soviet raw materials.

At the 45th CMEA council session in early January 1990, USSR prime minister N. I. Ryzhkov warned that abandoning the organization would wreck all member economies. He proposed that, beginning in 1991, 10 to 15 percent of intrabloc trade be conducted for hard currency at world market prices. Only the Soviet Union would benefit, however, especially if petroleum and natural gas were sold for what they cost in Western Europe. Purchasing power for the East Europeans would drop by 30 percent, converting a bloc trade surplus into a $10 billion balance-of-payments deficit.

The Warsaw Pact and stationing of Soviet troops on the territories of four allied countries represent a major impediment to national self-determination. The troops totaled 380,000 in East Germany, some 80,000 in Czechoslovakia, another 65,000 in Hungary, and only 50,000 in Poland. Early in 1990 negotiations resulted in agreements to remove all USSR armed forces from Czechoslovakia and Hungary by mid-1991. Gorbachev had announced before the U.N. General Assembly the unilateral withdrawal of 50,000 troops from Eastern Europe, although no verification procedures were offered.

It appears that the Warsaw Pact can no longer be used effectively as an instrument of intervention, and this was acknowledged in a communiqué on 4 December. Member governments stated that the invasion of Czechoslovakia in 1968 had been an error, violating the basic principles of the pact itself. This communiqué disavowed the infamous Brezhnev Doctrine of limited sovereignty and admitted that a Tiananmen Square option would not work in Eastern Europe.

Soviet foreign propaganda continues to be directed against the West and the United States in particular. A report issued in August by the U.S. Department of State on active measures and propaganda is replete with documented examples of disinformation originating in Moscow. The so-called new political thinking does not include a cessation of Soviet propaganda warfare being conducted in the mass media; however, Gorbachev's image and reputation are much higher abroad than at home.

On the eve of the Malta summit, V. V. Zagladin, adviser to President M.S. Gorbachev, explained the aim of people's diplomacy and the common European home as appeals to Western public opinion, which in turn pressures governments on issues where traditional diplomacy has not succeeded. This approach is facilitated by inviting USSR officials to appear on television and write op-ed page pieces in the West.

International communist front organizations represent another vehicle for Soviet foreign propaganda. Financed by the USSR, the supposedly independent *World Marxist Review* (*WMR*, published in Prague) is operated by the International Department of the CPSU central apparatus. A recent defector from the *WMR* staff gave the main purpose of the magazine as coordination of world communist movement activities.

The largest and most important front is the World Peace Council (WPC), which runs a $300,000 per year deficit. This deficit is made up by the Soviet Peace Fund, which contributes 90 percent of the WPC's total income. There are indications that this support is being cut back: WPC headquarters staff in Helsinki has been reduced by at least four technicians and two officers. This may, however, represent an effort by the USSR to make

the fronts more self-sufficient, rather than reduce their worldwide activities.

Richard F. Staar
Hoover Institution

Albania

Population. 3,208,033 (*World Fact Book*, 1989, p. 2)
Party. Albanian Party of Labor (Partia ë Punës e Shqipërisë)
Founded. 8 November 1941
Membership. 147,000 claimed: 39.8 percent laborers; 31.4 percent white-collar workers; 25.5 percent cooperativists. Women constitute 32.2 percent of the membership (*Zeri i popullit*, 4 November 1987).
First Secretary. Ramiz Alia
Politburo. 13 full members, most of whom occupy positions in the executive and legislative bodies of the country: Ramiz Alia, chairman of the People's Assembly, chief of state, commander in chief of the armed forces, and chairman of the defense council; Adil Çarçani, prime minister; Besnik Bekteshi, minister of industry and mines and acting minister of energy; Foto Çami, member of Academy of Sciences, chairman of committee on foreign relations of People's Assembly, member of Secretariat; Lenka Çuko, only woman on Politburo, member of Secretariat; Hekuran Isai, member of Secretariat; Hajredin Çeliku, minister of transportation; Rita Marko, deputy chairman, People's Assembly; Pali Miska, deputy chairman, Council of Ministers, and minister of agriculture; Manush Myftiu, deputy chairman, Council of Ministers, and chairman of state control commission; Prokop Mura, minister of people's defense; Muho Asslani, first secretary, Durrës party district; Simon Stefani, deputy chairman, Council of Ministers, and minister of internal affairs. There are five candidate members of the Politburo: General Kiço Mustaqi, chief of staff, armed forces; Llambi Gjegprifti, chairman of the people's council, Tiranë district; Vangjel Çerava, first sec-

retary, Korcë party district; Qirjako Mihali, director, Albanian state bank; Piro Kondi, first secretary, Tirana party district.

Secretariat. 4 members: Ramiz Alia, first secretary; Foto Çami, Lenka Çuko, Hekuran Isai
Status. Ruling party
Last Congress. 3–8 November 1986
Last Election. 1 February 1987
Auxiliary Organizations. Albanian Democratic Front (ADF), Nexhmije Hoxha, chairwoman; Central Council of Trade Unions of Albania (CCTUA), Sotir Koçallari, chairman; Union of Labor Youth of Albania (ULYA), Mehmet Elezi, first secretary; Albanian War Veterans, Shefqet Peçi, chairman; Pioneers of Enver, elementary school organization
Main State Organ. Council of Ministers, 21 members, inclusive of the new post of secretary to the council of ministers
Publications. *Zeri i popullit*, daily organ of the Central Committee of the APL, founded 25 August 1942; *Zeri i rinisë*, daily organ of ULYA; *Bashkimi*, daily organ of the Democratic Front; *Puna*, weekly organ of CCTUA; *10 Korrik* and *Lluftetari*, biweekly organs of the Ministry of Defense (circulated in the armed forces); *Nentori*, literary monthly organ of the Albanian Writers and Artists League; *Laiko Vema*, organ of the Democratic Front for the Greek minority. The Albanian Telegraphic Agency (ATA) is the official state news service.

The Albanian communist party (renamed Albanian Party of Labor in 1948) was established on 8 November 1941 in Tiranë on the initiative of the Comintern and the Yugoslav communist party. In a sense the party can be viewed as the product of the invasion of the Soviet Union by Nazi Germany. Like their counterparts in neighboring countries, Albanian communists were expected to commence resistance against the Germans, to forget the Hitler-Stalin pact and by all means help the "motherland of socialism," then under Nazi attack. But to do so, they had first to organize. (Before the German invasion of the USSR, there was little organized communist or any other resistance in Albania. In fact, several communist leaders [among them Ramiz Alia, Manush Myftiu, Tahir Demi, Behar Shtyla, Ciri Çarçani, Bedri Spahiu, and Fadil Çuçi] were members of the Albanian fascist movement and ardent supporters of nationalist causes.) (For biographical sketches of some of these communist

leaders see Stavro Skendi, *Albania* [New York: Praeger, 1975], Appendix A, pp. 323–45.)

The creation of the Albanian communist party was announced in illegally distributed pamphlets on 8 November 1941 in Tiranë. But few young people were encouraged by the new party's leadership to demonstrate against the Italian occupation. The party, formed on Comintern instructions, was organically linked to the Yugoslav communist party as indicated by the two Yugoslav emissaries, Dušan Mugoša and Miladin Popovič who were instrumental in the party's creation, remaining in Albania for the duration of the war to assure control over the new party. The overall supervision of Albanian affairs, however, was the responsibility of Svetozar Vukmanovič-Tempo. The Yugoslav role in the formation and organization of the Albanian communist movement is all but omitted from government-sanctioned history books. Enver Hoxha in his personal account of the party's founding—*Kur Lindi Partia: Kujtime* [When the Party Was Born: Memoirs] (Tiranë: Shtëpia Botuese, "8 Nentori," 1983)—attempts to rewrite history to suit his personality cult. In a narrow, nationalistic manner, Hoxha and other Albanian historians emphasize alleged or actual Yugoslav attempts to control domestic Albanian developments, but ignore all other aspects of party-to-party relations. Moreover, they assert that the unification of several warring communist factions in 1941 was the work of Hoxha's "genius." Available documentation disproves these claims. Recent accounts confirm that for the duration of the war and up to the Yugoslav-Soviet break, the leaders of the Albanian communist party, Hoxha included, were eager pawns in Tito's broader Balkan schemes. The late deputy defense minister and Central Committee member, Panayot Pljaku, who defected to Yugoslavia in 1957, revealed with indisputable evidence that, as early as 1942, Albanian communist leaders carried dual party membership cards—Albanian and Yugoslav. (Panayot Pljaku, *Nasilje nad Albanskom Revolucijom* [Tyranny Over the Albanian Revolution] [Priština: Rilindja, 1984], pp. 161–193.)

The Albanian communist party remained technically illegal for the duration of the war. Enver Hoxha, who was selected as the compromise provisional first secretary, heeded the advice of British intelligence operatives as well as the Yugoslavs and submerged communist ideology under nationalism to forge a broad national liberation effort. To achieve that goal, he sought the support of respectable nationalists who were sincere in their opposition to the Nazi-Italian occupation, but whose naïveté helped the communists ride to power on the back of Albanian nationalism. The high point in the communist party's efforts to appropriate national-ism and use it for their own ends occurred on 16 September 1942. In a "unity" conference held under the watchful eyes of the Yugoslavs in the small town of Peza, the National Liberation Front was created and the term *communism* went out of use for the duration of the war. The front, however, was domi-nated from the outset by the communist party. Its apparatchiks branched out into the partisan units, usually beyond harm's way as political commissars, preparing the ground for the hijacking of power as soon as the Germans withdrew from the country.

The first congress of the Albanian communist party, in November 1948, formalized the break with Yugoslavia, changed the name of the party to the Albanian Party of Labor (APL), and unleashed a massive purge of Titoists and "revisionists." The 1976 constitution (article 3) established the APL as the "leading force of state and society" and "Marx-ism-Leninism as the ruling ideology" (*Rruga ë par-tisë*, no. 2 [February 1976].)

A permanent characteristic of the APL is its instability at the top and its propensity to change friends and allies whenever the latter attempt to moderate its policies. Since assuming power in No-vember 1944, the APL has maintained control over the country via the politics of permanent purge, the brutal use of violence by the *Sigurimi* (security police), and a vast network of informers who reach everywhere, including emigré communities. Seven major purges were undertaken by the late dictator and first secretary, Enver Hoxha, beginning in 1948. The last one involved Mehmet Shehu, Al-bania's prime minister for 28 years, and hundreds of his followers. Ramiz Alia, who replaced Hoxha on the latter's death in April 1985, thus far has avoided the type of bloody rule for which his predecessor was famous. Compared with Hoxha, his regime seems moderate, pragmatic, and contradictory. All changes in personnel undertaken since 1985 have stopped short of total political banishment or phys-ical elimination of opponents; but in ideology and relations with Albania's former benefactors, Alia still employs the tone and intensity of Hoxha's pronouncements.

Internal Party and Government Affairs. Major economic issues and a perceptible fear of unmanageable change preoccupied the top APL leaders during 1989. Critical areas of economic

activity, such as agriculture and extractive indus-tries, again fell short of expectations, causing short-ages in consumer goods and foodstuff. Whether the apparent disruption in productivity was the result of Alia's massive cadre rotation (*YICA*, 1989), ordered in June 1988, or other objective factors cannot be ascertained. Press accounts, however, make the point that whatever its purpose, the rotation (which amounted to a minicultural revolution) has been disruptive and stalling. Entrenched bureaucrats have apparently succeeded in analyzing its applica-tion to death and in the process caused problems in the economy (*Zeri i popullit*, 11 February). The party daily, exasperated at the fact that "no sooner is this problem [rotation] mentioned than so-called studies appear" on how to apply it, complained, "We have sentimental analyses and questions: Who will be the first to go on the list? Who are those with fewer family problems? What benefits does the cadre leave behind? . . . What is his pay here and what will it be there?"

Economic problems were openly discussed in the People's Assembly in conjunction with the pre-sentation of the 1989 budget (*Zeri i popullit*, 28 December 1988; *FBIS*, 10 January). The chairman of the state planning commission, Niko Gjyzari, identified areas of deficiencies with unusual blunt-ness and pointed an accusing finger against a spe-cific minister (*Zeri i popullit*, 17 January). Soon thereafter all those criticized by Gjyzari were re-moved from their posts.

At the Seventh Central Committee (CC) Ple-num, convened on 1–2 February to discuss Adil Çarçani's report "On Some Measures for the Fur-ther Development of Agriculture," Alia surprised his colleagues by announcing changes in the com-position of the cabinet and party Secretariat. In all, twelve major changes in cabinet and party posts were involved. Five of those affected are clear de-motions, but all seem to reflect Alia's concern with events in Eastern Europe and the Balkans. The five cabinet posts that changed hands because of short-comings included Llambi Gjegprifti, replaced as minister of industry and mining and returned to his post as chairman of the Tiranë people's council (equivalent to mayor); Luan Babameto, minister of transportation, given the obscure assignment of chairman of the Durrës district people's council; Themie Thomai, a woman, was removed as minis-ter of agriculture and transferred to the district of Ljushna as party chief; Lavdosh Ahmeti, relieved as minister of energy, with no new post announced; and Deputy Premier Vangjel Çerava, transferred to

Korçe as district party secretary. All five who lost their executive positions were full members of the Central Committee, and two of them were candidate Politburo members as well (ATA, 2 February; *FBIS*, 3 February).

More important than the changes at the executive level were those in the party Secretariat and the key Ministry of the Interior. Simon Stefani was removed from the Secretariat and appointed a deputy premier and interior minister. His place in the Secretariat was taken by Hekuran Isai, his predecessor in the same ministry. Isai had lost that position at the Ninth APL Congress. The changes do not seem to have been exercises in musical chairs or exclusively linked to economic problems or even trade of positions. The removal of Hajredin Çeliku from the Secretariat and his appointment as transportation minister is an obvious demotion. The same can be said about Vangjel Çerava's transfer to Korçe. These two actions suggest Alia's distrust of younger people. Several other changes support this interpretation.

The young and able Politburo member Besnik Bekteshi was removed as deputy premier and assigned the troublesome ministries of Industry and Mining (acting minister for energy). Given the failure of extractive industries and energy enterprises to meet their production quotas, these posts are a prescription for failure rather than reward. In contrast the 70-year-old Manush Myftiu (who, between 1940 and 1941, like Alia, was an active member of the fascist Albanian Youth of Lictor) was given the critical post of chairman for the state control commission in addition to being a deputy premier. As indicated earlier, the changes affected the Secretariat as well. It now consists of three members besides Alia: Foto Çami, Lenka Çuko (the only woman), and Hekuran Isai. Similarly, the number of deputy premiers was reduced from four to three: Manush Myftiu, Pali Miska, and Simon Stefani.

Changes in party and government structures indicate Alia's ambivalence about who his allies and enemies might be. Coming on the heels of criticism of party organs for their failure to implement the cadre rotation (*Zeri i popullit*, 11 February), one can surmise that he does not feel secure with the level of control he has achieved over base organizations.

The critical post that changed hands, the Ministry of the Interior, can only be explained by Alia's determination to get a grip on an agency notorious for its unreliability, but critical in its dealing with the

uncertainties that events in Eastern Europe have set in motion, even in hermetically sealed Albania. It should be noted that all ministers of the interior since 1948 (except Isai) have been purged, executed, or banished. The new arrangements in critical posts in the context of a growing ideological debate on the implications of *perestroika* seem to be aimed at improving control over the party apparatus, the security forces, and the cadres. Such control is essential irrespective of the direction that Alia might take in the near future. Tensions between the party hierarchy and *Sigurimi* have been rumored throughout the year in Tiranë and may explain placing a member of the Secretariat with no previous experience in security affairs in charge of the Ministry of the Interior. Indicative of something happening in party-*Sigurimi* relations is that, for the first time, a novel highly critical of the latter was published in Tiranë and, according to Western sources, sold out within days (*RAD Background Report*, no. 203, 15 November).

The novel, titled *Thikat* (Knives), was written by Neshat Tozaj, who was once employed by the *Sigurimi* and knows its inner workings. The central theme of the novel is *Sigurimi's* habit of converting every ordinary antisocial act into a plot to overthrow the regime. Two things surrounding the publication of *Thikat* add to its significance: first, its author, once severely criticized, was praised for his courage by Albania's most famous writer, Ismail Kadare (*Drita*, 15 October), and second, Kadare is a close friend of Alia's.

The central character in the novel is a psychopath who slashed a few tires on cars belonging to foreign diplomats. Even though it was proven that the perpetrator (a woman) was deranged, *Sigurimi* saw this random act as "a plot to harm Albania's good name and relations with foreign governments." Kadare made a bold statement about the potential impact of *Thikat* by predicting that the novel "will disturb the conscience of many people [and] will prove its emancipating effect" (ibid.). Past experience shows that no such statements are committed to print without high-level political backing.

Throughout 1989, Alia's comments on *perestroika* and *glasnost'* often contradicted his policies and actions on domestic and foreign policy issues. He seemed hard-pressed to reconcile Albanian ideological rigidity with the pragmatism required to manage a modern economy, feed the people, and broaden ties with the West without permitting its bourgeois values to penetrate Albanian society.

Alia took pains to stress that personnel changes decided at the Seventh CC Plenum were "not connected with any question concerning the trustworthiness or political position of any comrades; they are dictated," he said, "solely by the intention of providing new stimuli to the work of the party, the state, and the economy" (ATA, 2 February; *FBIS*, 3 February). Regardless of his assurances, a group of younger leaders—Vangjel Çerava, Besnik Bekteshi, Hajredin Çeliku and Qirjako Mihali, along with the technocrats Lavdosh Ahmeti and Luan Babameto—have lost ground, for the time being, to the older generation and the hard-liners.

Party theoreticians and mass organizations spent an inordinate amount of time and ink criticizing the evils of *perestroika* and *glasnost'* at the philosophical/theoretical level.

To express fully his views on developments in Eastern Europe and the Soviet Union and place the Albanian position on solid nationalistic foundations, Alia visited the small town of Peza on the 47th anniversary of the conference considered to be the turning point in the party's efforts to appropriate nationalism for its own ends. Although there to unveil a monument to a respected Albanian nationalist (Myslim Peza, for whose clan the town is named), Alia denounced the Soviet and Eastern European models as bourgeois perversions and irrelevant to Albania's approach toward a socialist society. "We are a small country," he said, "but the sole country that is building socialism and developing without looking to anyone else for help" (*Zeri i popullit*, 17 September). The official APL line vis-à-vis events in Eastern Europe is simple and self-serving: socialism did not fail, but revisionism did. As seen from an Albanian perspective, the cause of all East European problems is traceable to "expansion of private property . . . class oppression and exploitation" (ibid.). A more comprehensive critique of events in Eastern Europe and clear evidence of APL confusion emerged from the proceedings of the Eighth CC Plenum (25–26 September).

Alia's report to the Eighth Plenum tacitly underlined two things: (1) unless something is done with a growing and self-perpetuating bureaucracy, the upheavals of Eastern Europe could very well occur in Albania and (2) the party needs to find a way to deflate the pressures for rapid change and gain time to manage it.

In a deliberate attempt to preempt the cataclysmic events of Eastern Europe and despite his rhetorical bravado, Alia gave his approval to several "ideas that have merit" for further consideration. These "ideas" have been common occurrences among the new regimes in Eastern Europe. Thus elements of restructuring were apparent in party and state pronouncements along with parallel efforts to present them as the logical evolution of party policies initiated without duress or any linkage to what was happening elsewhere.

Thus, Alia told members of the Central Committee at the Eighth Plenum that he would reach outside the party to fill positions if necessary, which sounds like power sharing. On this point, Alia unambiguously warned that "every post, including that of minister, military commander, diplomat, and those in leading bodies, can be entrusted to a son or daughter of the people, quite irrespective of whether he or she is a member of the party" (*Zeri i populit*, 29 September; *RAD Background Report*, no. 191, 16 October). Moreover he also found merit in two ideas in the main report to the plenum delivered by Lenka Çuko: nominating "more than one candidate" for elective party posts of basic organizations and "limiting the tenure of office for secretaries of basic organizations and bureaus to no more than four or five years." Adoption of such ideas, he said, could "assist in the preparation of every communist as a leader." (*Zeri i populit*, 29 September.)

At the same plenum, Alia reiterated his insistence that the APL has no intention of diluting its ideological orthodoxy when he stated:

> No concessions will be made to the bourgeois ideology in any field, either politics, arts and culture, or in economic relations. There must be no concessions to religious ideology in any of its various forms. We take this stand as convinced atheists, but also in order to protect the unity of a people that, over the centuries, have suffered from rifts and divisions inspired by churches and mosques." (*Zeri i popullit*, 29 September.)

In a year-end address to the nation, Alia repeated the APL position that what happened in Romania cannot happen in Albania because the "party had served the people well" and therefore it has no fear of popular uprising. Yet he admitted that events in Eastern Europe "have inspired certain known anti-Albanian forces to resume the campaign of slanders against our country." (*WP*, 2 January 1990.)

Çuko's report at the Eighth CC Plenum, despite its sloganeering title ("On Further Strengthening the Party and Improving Its Work in Accordance with the Demands of the Times"), identified critical party weaknesses that potentially could lead to internal upheavals. Among them were discipline lapses in party organizations, excessive bureaucratization of party and state, and loss of party authority at the local level (*Zeri i popullit*, 27 September). One way to deal with such issues, she said, would be to limit the tenure of elected party cadres to "no longer than four or five years" and to offer more than one candidate for elected positions in basic party organizations. "There is room for improvement in the electoral procedure within the party . . . by including more candidates than will be elected on the list for posts in the bureaus," she stated. "Let us elect those who obtain the most votes in secret ballots, but at least fifty percent of the votes." (ATA, 26 September; *FBIS*, 4 October.) Her report, like Alia's comments, makes no mention of expanding the same principles in the elections of the highest party organs. Yet the notion of multiple candidacies, secret ballots, and nonparty individuals serving in high government positions are new elements in an ongoing public debate about ways to restructure the system without calling it *perestroika*.

Çuko pointed to some serious problems with party organizations in districts that traditionally did not accept central authority with good grace. Forty-three basic organizations in the agricultural district of Kruja "have still not overcome their backwardness," she pointed out (ibid.). In the district of Mat, with 2,484 communists, "there are still problems, shortcomings and failures to meet the general industrial plan." In other regions the basic organizations avoid responsibility and leave everything to be decided at the top. The result is, she said, that "party committees often issue excessive recommendations to the point of paternalism . . . [and] between 60 and 70 percent of the work of basic organizations is in one way or another suggested to them, not to say imposed from above."

Foto Çami, a member of the secretariat and an individual with hidden agendas, continued his well-known habit of providing a contradictory portrait of himself and, by extension, of the higher Albanian leadership. His pronouncements, like Alia's, reveal ideological confusion or calculated efforts to cover all bases in the event that the East European revolutions spread to Albania. Since 1985, Çami has expressed views that could easily define him either as Albania's Gorbachev or as a clone of Enver Hoxha.

At a meeting of writers and artists held in February, Çami called on the members of that influential

group to be more innovative and not to be "afraid to make mistakes" (*Drita*, 19 February). That speech shows him as a serious thinker proposing new approaches to arts and literature and imploring the intelligentsia to "always strive to uncover problems and solve them." Making it clear that he favored open discussion, he told the gathering, "Thought takes form and becomes conviction in the fire of debate; discussion; creative and formative talks; political, scientific, and cultural events; and analyses of our literature and of world literature" (*RAD Background Report*, no. 60, 31 March).

This and several other major pronouncements, however, contrast sharply with Çami's later views on *perestroika*, pluralism, and *glasnost'*. Speaking in his home town of Gjirocaster, he denounced East European reforms as proof of the correctness of the Hoxha line. "The crisis that these countries are experiencing," he said, "is not the crisis of socialism. It is the crisis of the revisionist system itself and the logical end of their anti-Marxist course" (*Zeri i popullit*, 19 September).

Throughout 1989 the mass media and party organizations simultaneously carried out two campaigns vis-à-vis events in Eastern Europe: first, the APL mobilized all resources to reinforce its own ideological rigidity and, second, it used the press to provide sufficient amounts of accurate and timely information to impress those who might harbor ideas of public dissent that it feels secure with its orthodox line.

All party and government changes in Eastern Europe were promptly and factually reported. The resignation of Todor Zhivkov was announced without comment by the official news agency (ATA, 11 November; *FBIS*, 13 November), as were the changes in party and government leadership in Czechoslovakia, the German Democratic Republic (GDR), Hungary, and Romania. In an unusual gesture, Alia warmly congratulated Petur Mladenov of Bulgaria "on the occasion of your election to the high office of chairman of the People's State Council of the People's Republic of Bulgaria" (ATA, 20 November; *FBIS*, 21 November).

By the end of the year, it was clear that the Albanian government (despite events in the Warsaw Pact countries) had not abandoned its quest for normal state-to-state relations with all East European states, but that quest was coupled with an intensified ideological campaign against their revisionist parties. Yet the APL seemed surprised by the intensity of anticommunist feelings among the East European intelligentsia and commenced a renewed effort to find new ideological partners and avoid total isolation. Cuba and Third World splinter groups emerged as potential allies. Castro's foreign minister, Isidoro Malmierca, paid an official four-day visit to Tiranë where "identity of views on foreign policy issues was noted" and an economic and cultural agreement signed (ATA, 8 November; *FBIS*, 16 November). While in the Albanian capital, Malmierca was received by all major political actors, including Alia, but avoided making any statements concerning Albania's brand of Marxism-Leninism. Instead he appeared to be a sympathetic listener to Alia's assurances that "the Albanian people have bound their life to socialism" and that "in the future, too, our stand will remain the same as presently in defense of freedom, independence and sovereignty" (ATA, 11 November; *FBIS*, 16 November).

Events in Eastern Europe were linked to two attempts at public demonstrations against the Albanian regime. In the city of Shkodër students from a technical school went into the streets and denounced party corruption (*Washington Times*, 29 December; Antenna FM radio station, Athens, Domestic Service, 3 January 1990). The Albanian government denied the occurrence of any demonstration in Shkodër; Greek diplomatic sources confirmed it. In the southern city of Gjirocaster, the Prasos brothers, four young men of Greek descent, were dragged behind tractors for allegedly agitating against the regime and attempting to imitate East German youth by trying to cross the border into Greece. It is rumored that at least one of the four died as a result of the torture. (*Typos*, 3 December.) The Greek government instructed its chargé d'affaires in Tiranë to seek information and verify the condition of the young men. The Albanian government denied the request (*Athens News Agency*, 30 December). This prompted the Greek foreign minister, Andonis C. Samaras, to declare that "he will not close his eyes to the brutal violations of the fundamental human rights of our North Epirot compatriots" (Athens News Agency, 28 December). The following day the Greek chargé d'affaires in Tiranë was summoned to the Foreign Ministry and handed a note of protest for "interference in domestic affairs." Escalating the polemics the Greek delegation to the European Parliament tabled a resolution condemning the Albanian government for torture and the alleged death of one of the Prasos brothers and requested the president of that body to "forward the resolution to the Tiranë government, governments

of European Community member states, the United Nations, and the European Commission" (ibid.).

Economic Issues. The economic condition of the country was discussed in stark terms and unusual openness by state and party officials throughout the year. The decline in productivity that marked the previous year continued during 1989. Andrea Nako, minister of finance, frankly admitted that the state budget had begun with a serious deficit from the previous year, during which "some enterprises in agriculture, the energy industry, light industry, construction and mining did not meet their financial targets according to the plan" (*Zeri i popullit*, 28 December 1988). As a result of these failures, he said, "overall state budget earnings were 91 percent fulfilled and were only 81 fulfilled in agriculture" (ibid.).

Serious shortcomings in agriculture were the central topic of the Seventh Central Committee Plenum. Decisions reached at that meeting to make agriculture a top priority were rendered meaningless by the worst drought in 40 years. The drought also affected hydroelectric power production, prompting stern warnings for conservation (*Zeri i popullit*, 14 February; *RAD Background Report*, no. 37, 2 March).

A key decision of the Seventh CC Plenum involved opening up new lands. The problem was that it meant draining marshlands and deforestation, two practices that have a devastating impact on the environment and the climate. But the choices are limited. The plenum noted that from 1980 to 1988 alone there had been an 18 percent decrease in per capita arable land, mostly due to regime encouragement of population growth (*RAD Background Report*, no. 37, 2 March).

The problems in agriculture were exacerbated during 1989 by deteriorating farm machinery and not enough hard currency to purchase spare parts or new equipment. To remedy the situation, the Albanian government turned to the Federal Republic of Germany (FRG) and Holland to obtain new farming equipment. The FRG, according to Yugoslav sources, provided assistance in the form of grants for such purchases (*Politika*, 29 January).

Low labor productivity reached alarming proportions during 1989, prompting Alia and other leaders to go on the road to try to promote cadre enthusiasm. Throughout the year, all the members of the Politburo tried to cope with the problems of a stagnant economy and shortcomings in most areas.

Typical of the message delivered was Alia's address to the cadres of the Tropoje district:

> Losses arising from damages and breaches of financial discipline are not inconsiderable, not to mention absenteeism and failures to realize labor norms, subjects which deserve more attention. In the first six months of 1989, one-fourth of all working people working according to norms failed to meet their targets. In the first six months of 1989, production losses through absenteeism totalled 17,000 days. (*Zeri i popullit*, 7 October.)

A serious problem in keeping track of economic trends was created by the innovative way that bureaucrats have found to "fulfill the plan," but never deliver the goods. Thus, during the first quarter of the year, 22 of the 26 districts supposedly fulfilled the "bulk plan," but none of them met their quotas as "far as range of products" was concerned. What this jargon means is that the districts fulfilled plans in producing raw materials, but failed to convert them into usable goods (*Puna*, 11 April). The result was shortages in consumer goods of all sorts. To spark productivity, the Albanian government reintroduced the "concept of incentives," but as in the past this did not make much difference during 1989. The expected impact of incentives on productivity was canceled out by the government's parallel decision simultaneously to raise productivity quotas, making it impossible for most enterprises to meet criteria for bonuses. As the party daily stated, "it must be realized that increased production above the plan is the basis for benefiting" from incentives, but it left open exactly how far "above the plan" (*Zeri i popullit*, 26 February).

Auxiliary and Mass Organizations. The general council of the Democratic Front of Albania (DFA), an umbrella organization consisting of all eligible voters (minus the "enemies of the people"), met in Tiranë on 10 March to deal with two important matters: the forthcoming elections to the people's councils and people's courts and preparations for the Sixth Congress of the front (ATA, 10 March; *FBIS*, 14 March). The meeting was presided over by Nexhmije Hoxha, widow of the late dictator, who still plays an important behind-the-scenes role in Albanian politics. The general council decided to hold the DFA's Sixth Congress from 26 to 28 June and issued its predictable appeal to the masses to be "vigilant against enemies of Albania and supportive of the unity between party and people" (ATA, 12 March; *FBIS*, 14 March).

The Sixth Congress of the front was attended by Alia and most major figures of the Politburo. Mrs. Hoxha delivered the main report in which she declared the organization to be "an active auxiliary of the party for the education of the new man" (ATA, 26 June; *FBIS*, 28 June). Moreover, she used the opportunity to denounce Yugoslavia's accusations that Albania interferes in its domestic affairs and supported the claims of Kosovo Albanians "who are demanding those rights which they won through their national liberation war" (ibid.). At the conclusion of the congress, a 25-member presidium was elected consisting mostly of new faces and prominent personalities (ATA, 29 June; *FBIS*, 6 July). Mrs. Hoxha was re-elected chairwoman of the front, along with four deputy chairmen, only one of whom (Pilo Peristeri) is a holdover (ibid.).

Elections to the people's councils and people's courts were held on 7 May, under the auspices of the DFA. A total of 43,000 local officials were elected "following discussion on their merits" (*Rruga ë partisë*, no. 7, July). The propaganda machinery presented these elections as "unique" in Albanian history, and Alia suggested at the Eighth APL CC Plenum that they must be examined as a model for elections in basic party organizations. The uniqueness is that "more than one candidate" was considered for the various posts. According to the party's theoretical review, "the merits and the evaluation of 130,000 candidates who, in turn, have been selected out of an even larger number" have been considered (ibid.). This seems to be an effort by the party hierarchy to give the impression that the multiple candidacies principle (a major demand in Eastern Europe) has been applied in Albania. The results of the elections, however, indicate that only the approach has changed.

Of the 1,945,615 registered voters, almost 100 percent participated in the process. "Over 99.99 percent of the voters took part in the elections for the people's councils. Five votes were cast against [candidates]" (ATA, 8 May; *FBIS*, 9 May).

The Union of Labor Youth of Albania (ULYA) held a Central Committee plenum in August to discuss problems facing the younger generation (*Zeri i rinisë*, 30 August). The main report was delivered by the first secretary, Mehmet Elezi, who criticized the narrow-minded manner in which elders attempt to deal with youth problems. In an allusion to reported disturbances at the University of Tiranë by students protesting poor living conditions, Elezi singled out those who take a look at youth problems only when "something unexpected happens" and forget about them soon thereafter (ibid.; *RAD Background Report*, no. 177, 20 September).

A survey of Albanian youth was conducted by researchers who supposedly promised anonymity to respondents. However, when the researchers received answers they did not like, Elezi said, their scientific interest turned to anger and a demand to know "who are these people who like rock? Who have been the persons claiming to like rock? Everything must be done to find out who they are" (*Zeri i rinisë*, 2 September). If the secrecy promise was violated, he asked, "how will we then be able to figure out their thoughts, feelings, and reasoning?" (ibid.). Invited to the youth plenum (a usual occurrence) was Professor Hamid Beqeja, who is popular among university students and who over the years has engaged in a one-man campaign against conservative attitudes toward youth problems. A year ago he raised issues that had been taboo with the publication of an article in *Zeri i popullit* on sex education (*YICA*, 1988).

Elezi and other speakers repeated the problems that Albanian young people face today (alien influences, rote learning, boredom, etc.) and urged a more honest approach to these on the part of their elders. Young people have little to do and spend a lot of time watching Greek, Italian, and Yugoslav television. Thus foreign influences had their impact on the young who, like their counterparts everywhere, are susceptible to fads such as colorful clothes and T-shirts with slogans on them. Among the slogans seen at the Durrës beach, as noted in *Bashkimi* (7 September), were Born to Raise Hell and Surf Club, Australia. An answer to the foreign-made T-shirts with provocative slogans, said a *Bashkimi* editorial, would be to produce them domestically and substitute clean, national slogans.

Social and Human Rights Issues. The Tiranë regime is sensitive to accusations that it violates the human rights of its citizens. In response to repeated criticisms of "gross violations of religious and civil rights," the government took a number of steps to deflate such charges.

After numerous previous attempts to secure a visa had been denied, in August the government allowed Mother Teresa to visit Tiranë (ATA, *FBIS*, 16 August). Earlier refusals of the Albanian authorities to permit her to visit relatives were brought to the attention of the Human Rights Commission in Geneva in February by the International Federation for the Protection of the Rights of Ethnic, Religious and Linguistic Minorities, a nongovernmental organization recognized by the U.N. Although the visit was called "private," Mother Teresa was received by Mrs. Hoxha, Foreign Minister Reis Malile, Minister of Health Ahmet Kamberi, the chairman of the presidency of the People's Assembly, Petro Dode, and other state and party officials (ibid.). Dutifully, the Albanian-born nun and Nobel peace prize laureate placed a wreath at the monument of "Mother Albania" and "paid homage and laid a bouquet of flowers on the grave of Comrade Enver Hoxha" (ATA, 15 August; *FBIS*, 16 August). The world renowned Catholic nun did not utter a word of criticism against the regime for its brutal suppression of religion.

In response to criticism by Greek ethnics for the oppression of their kinsmen in Albania and for the refusal of authorities to permit reunification of families, Deputy Foreign Minister Muhamed Kapllani announced with great fanfare that visas had been granted to Greeks for visits with relatives on the other side of the border (ATA, 24 May; *FBIS*, 30 May). Kapllani said that "his government decided to satisfy the Greek demands in recognition of the excellent level of bilateral relations which the two countries have attained in recent years" (ibid.). In fact it was in response to a "demand" made by then Greek foreign minister Karolos Papoulias. With elections in Greece set for June, Papoulias came under severe criticism by political opponents for spending more time defending the Tiranë regime than defending the human rights of the Greek minority and the Albanian people. Kapllani's gesture was intended to "show results" from Papoulias's policy. Five individuals benefited from the "humanitarian act" of the Albanian government, two of whom were in desperate need of medical attention and entered Greek hospitals on arrival in the city of Yannina (northwest Greece). The New Democracy party denounced the transparent Albanian attempt to influence these June elections. (*Kathimerini*, 27 May.)

On national liberation day the presidium of the National Assembly declared a wide-ranging amnesty for prisoners, mostly violators of the penal code (ATA, *FBIS*, 16 November). The propaganda machinery made maximum use of the amnesty decree and presented it as evidence of "socialist humanism" (*Bashkimi*, 17 November).

A reading of the pertinent decree, however,

shows that no political prisoners were released. Specifically, the decree states that

> exempted are those persons who have been found guilty of crimes against the state according to articles 46–60 of the penal code; illicit appropriation of socialist property, according to articles 61–68 of the penal code; appropriation of private property [euphemism for stealing] according to articles 101–102 of the penal code as well as those persons who have been given incommutable sentences for various repeated penal offenses (*Bashkimi*, 16 November).

Demographic Trends. From 2 through 8 April the Albanian government conducted a census of the population (ATA, 9 July; *FBIS*, 11 July). According to its figures the total population of Albania as of 12 April stood at 3,182,417, an average annual growth of 57,800 and a total growth of 591,800 since the previous census.

The census showed little change in the urbanization process. Of the total population, 64.4 percent still live in the countryside and only 35.5 percent in urban areas. Males constitute 51.5 percent. Of the total, the Albanian authorities stated that only 64,816 are "non-Albanians" (Greeks, Macedonians, Serbs, Montenegrins, and others). In an unusual step (perhaps in response to official Greek claims that the size of the Greek minority is much larger), the Albanian ambassador to the U.N. placed on record the results of the census and gave the size and ethnic breakdown of the population. Contrary to reports by analysts "that official Albanian figures . . . were also accepted by the Greek authorities" (*RAD Background Report*, no. 142, 8 August), the opposite is true. The Greek Foreign Ministry instructed its U.N. mission to challenge the Albanian figures. The alternate chief of the Greek delegation to the U.N., Leonidas Chrysanthopoulos, stated that Albanian authorities underestimated the size of the Greek minority, and he provided statistical evidence from several sources (including the FRG Statistical Service) that places the number of Greeks in Albania as at least 200,000 (Greek Press and Information Office Bulletin, *Proini*, 26 October).

Although at the Seventh CC Plenum it was noted that arable land per capita had decreased by 18 percent during the past eight years, the Albanian government continues its policy of offering incentives to encourage population growth. On 13 November the presidium of the People's Assembly issued Decree No. 7339, which lowers the pension age to 50 for women with six children or more. The decree, intended as an incentive for population growth, reads as follows: "women, members of cooperatives, who have borne and raised six or more children up to the age of eight years, have the right to receive retirement pension after reaching the age of fifty years if they have worked for at least fifteen years" (ATA, 14 November; *FBIS*, 20 November).

Foreign Relations. During 1989 the Albanian diplomatic service and high-ranking party and government officials escalated their attempts to expand relations with the West. For most of the year the Tiranë government attempted to normalize economic and state-to-state relations with Eastern Europe as well. Since the events in Poland, however, caution has replaced eagerness in Tiranë's attempts to deal with such transformed governments.

Relations with Eastern Europe followed the usual Albanian two-track approach: intense criticism of revisionism, *perestroika*, and *glasnost'* and pragmatism in pursuit of predictability in state-to-state dealings. The Albanian government upgraded its diplomatic missions to the ambassadorial level with the GDR, Bulgaria, Czechoslovakia, and Hungary, indicating approval of trends toward independence from Moscow (*NYT*, 13 November). Plans to do the same with Poland were suspended after Solidarity's advent to power.

Albania remained an active and often eager participant in multilateral Balkan gatherings. From 18 to 20 January the Albanian government hosted the "protocol meeting of senior officials of Ministries of Foreign Affairs of Balkan countries" (*Zeri i popullit*, 21 January). In October a meeting of "the Committees for Balkan Understanding and Cooperation and Other Similar Non-Governmental Organizations" met in Tiranë. This group, supposedly a "non-governmental, private entity," was addressed by senior officials, including Foreign Minister Malile, Deputy Premier Pali Miska, and others (ATA, 19 October; *FBIS*, 26 October). That same month, Llambi Gjegprifti traveled to Belgrade to participate in the conference of mayors of Balkan capital cities. His visit coincided with intense Serbian-Albanian polemics over the situation in Kosovo (ATA, 1 October; *FBIS*, 2 October).

The most pronounced growth in relations has been with the FRG, which seemed to be competing with the GDR (before the collapse of the Honecker and Krenz regimes) in pursuing expanded economic ties with Albania.

Bonn and Tiranë broadened their contacts further during 1989, as reflected in multiple visits (in both directions), economic agreements, and cultural exchanges. Siegfried Lengl, secretary of state in the FRG Ministry of Economic Cooperation, visited Tiranë and signed a "cooperation agreement" with his counterpart, Konstantin Hoxha (ATA, 19 March; FBIS, 21 March). Politburo member and academician Foto Çami paid a visit to Bonn, where he was received by Foreign Minister Hans-Dietrich Genscher and other high-ranking federal officials (ATA, 11 May; FBIS, 12 May). A seminar on trade with the FRG was held in Munich (ATA, 27 July; FBIS, 31 July), and later a "Week of Culture of the Federal Republic of Germany" was organized in the Albanian capital (ATA, 27 September; FBIS, 29 September). In this connection, Helmut Schoefer, state minister at the Ministry of Foreign Affairs, visited Tiranë where he also was received by high-ranking government and party officials (ATA, 28 September; FBIS, 29 September). Senior Albanian functionaries paid official visits to France, Turkey, Spain, Italy, Switzerland, Greece, and other West European countries. Most of these visits were reciprocated by their counterparts.

Relations with France were placed on a fast track with Foreign Minister Reis Malile's visit to that country (ATA, 31 March; FBIS, 4 April). In the fall the French minister of labor, Jean-Pierre Soison, visited Tiranë and was given access to most senior party and state officials (ATA, 28 September; FBIS, 30 September). Subsequently the two countries inaugurated Paris to Tiranë air service (ATA, 14 November; FBIS, 20 November).

The first visit by an Albanian foreign minister to Spain also took place in November. Foreign Minister Malile spent four days in Madrid at the invitation of his counterpart, Francisco Fernandez Ordonez (ATA, 1 November; FBIS, 6 November). While there, he signed a cultural agreement and was received by the prime minister and King Juan Carlos (ATA, 2 November; FBIS, 7 November). On the way back, Malile stopped in Rome, where he held talks with Deputy Foreign Minister Claudio Vitallone (ATA, 4 November; FBIS, 6 November). In the same month an Italian economic delegation headed by the minister of foreign trade, Renato Rugierro, visited Tiranë and signed an economic agreement (ATA, 9 November; FBIS, 16 November). The agreement and visits would indicate that the stalemate caused by the Albanian family that sought asylum in the Italian embassy in Tiranë in December 1985 may be on its way to a resolution.

Greek-Albanian relations started off with good prospects in 1989, but deteriorated following the fall from power of Andreas Papandreou and his socialist party. The plurality party of New Democracy, which formed a coalition cabinet after the June elections, is on the record as "not being bound by the unilateral termination of the state of war" between the two countries without a resolution of the status of all prewar treaties governing the rights of the Greek minority in Albania (see YICA, 1988). While PASOK (the socialist party) was in power in Greece, relations were smooth because Papandreou never criticized Stalinist regimes. In February the then Greek foreign minister, Papoulias, received his counterpart in the city of Yannina (where Malile engaged in a little bourgeois shopping) and returned the visit to Gjirocaster, where the two men went hunting (ATA, 18 February; FBIS, 21 February). However, by fall relations had deteriorated, and the conservative Greek foreign minister, Samaras, formally demanded better treatment for the Greek minority in Albania (Athens News Agency, 28 December).

Albanian-Turkish bilateral relations continued to improve during 1989. Early in the year, Malile visited Ankara, where he signed an agreement on telecommunications and promised to "raise the level of political relations even higher" (ATA, 2 February; FBIS, 6 February). In an indirect reference to the Turkish minority's plight in Bulgaria, Malile reiterated his government's policy "on respecting the human rights of ethnic minorities in the Balkans."

The German Democratic Republic maintained a high profile in the Albanian press until communist rule collapsed. GDR foreign minister Oskar Fischer paid an official visit to Tiranë in June (ATA, 19 June; FBIS, 20 June). During his stay in the Albanian capital, all issues affecting cooperation were discussed with an apparent identity of views.

Formal and "correct relations" were maintained with the GDR even after Honecker was replaced by Krenz. In November a GDR delegation headed by Deputy Premier Horst Soelle visited Tiranë and signed a broad economic cooperation agreement (ATA, 7 November; FBIS, 9 November). The Albanian press reported all events related to the collapse of communist rule in the GDR, and Ramiz Alia, in his capacity as president of the republic, sent greetings to Krenz (ATA, 8 November; FBIS, 9 November).

Relations with Hungary were not affected, but the Albanian press was virulent against the "Hungarian counterrevolution." Rehabilitation of the "traitor Nagy" was condemned in harsh terms, as was the removal of the word *people's* from the name of the Hungarian Republic (*Zeri i popullit*, 29 October).

Albanian-Czechoslovak relations improved significantly during the year, with Prague emerging as Tiranë's critical supplier of technology, transportation vehicles, and chemicals. In September (when both belonged to the category of rejectionists), the two countries elevated their diplomatic representations to ambassadorial level. Earlier in the year a comprehensive economic agreement was signed in Prague (*Rude pravo*, 25 May; *FBIS*, 1 June). The autumn developments in Czechoslovakia cooled relations, but changes in Prague were reported accurately and with reserved commentary in the Albanian press. Apparently the Tiranë regime took special care not to burn bridges. Czechoslovakia is "one of the principal trading partners of Albania" according to *World Marxist Review* (September 1989), and Albania can not afford to change suppliers of critical equipment without further disrupting its economy.

Yugoslav-Albanian contacts were affected by the events in Kosovo and massive protests by Albanian nationals in Kosovo expressing their strenuous objections to proposed revisions to Serbia's constitution (*Zeri i popullit*, 29 March). The party organ and numerous officials (among them Çami) denounced "Serbian chauvinism" and lamented the fact that "no law protects the Albanians now; they are in the mercy of tanks; they all are declared counterrevolutionaries and enemies. It is precisely Palestine, precisely South Africa" (ibid.). By fall relations had deteriorated further, with a strike by Albanian miners in Kosovo and arrest of a popular Albanian communist leader, Azem Vlasi, for alleged complicity in instigating the strike (*NYT*, 3 November). During the turmoil and police intervention, several Albanian nationals were killed (ibid.). Despite the tense situation in Kosovo, however, state-to-state relations retained a degree of civility and the two countries cooperated in several inter-Balkan gatherings.

Sino-Albanian relations took another step this year toward growth and normalization, despite events in China. The Albanian press and the propaganda machinery were discreet in their coverage of the brutal Chinese repression of the student and workers' revolt. The use of tanks in Tiananmen Square was reported with strongly worded titles in newspapers and other means of communication, but in a safe way: quoting only Western sources under the rubric "press review." The Albanian Telegraphic Agency reported "nearly 1,400 killed and 10,000 wounded" and dismissed the whole affair as another case of revisionism at its worst.

In late November, an Albanian delegation headed by Konstantin Hoxha visited Peking and signed a significant agreement to form the Joint Commission of Economic and Technical Cooperation as well as a trade protocol that the two countries routinely conclude every year (ATA, 24 November; *FBIS*, 29 November).

Soviet-Albanian relations continued as in years past with two notable changes: (1) the antirevisionist offensive of the Albanian party leadership was much more intense and (2) Moscow's efforts to normalize relations with Tiranë (by blaming the whole dispute on the two dead leaders, Hoxha and Khrushchev) continued unabated and oblivious to the latter's rejections.

More than a dozen favorable items appeared in the Soviet press commending the Albanian people for their commitment to socialism. *Sovetskaia Rossiia* (11 January), in a signed article, called the break in relations "unnatural" and praised the Tiranë leadership for its expansion of ties with the Balkan and other countries (*FBIS*, 11 January). The Soviet-Albanian Friendship Society met again in the autumn to discuss ways of improving relations with the Albanian people (*Pravda*, 7 September), but *Zeri i popullit* denounced Moscow for its oppression of the Baltic republics (ATA, 25 September; *FBIS*, 5 October). Alia, one of the architects of the split with Moscow, continued his attacks on modern revisionism, but the tone of his speeches left an opening for change in his country's relations with the USSR. Because Moscow had thus far avoided intervening in the domestic affairs of East European states, Alia seemed less strident in his comments about state-to-state relations with its East European allies. Speaking to the fiercely nationalistic and independent Gheghs in the districts of Pukes, Tropoje, and Bajram, Çuri pointedly emphasized the value Albania placed on "sovereignty and independence" and only as an afterthought commented on ideological issues (*Bashkimi*, 6, 9 October; *Zeri i popullit*, 7 October).

Soviet-Albanian polemics in 1989 were laden with another issue, the USSR position on Kosovo, that until recently had been kept off their agendas. The Albanian mass media denounced the Soviet Union for allegedly taking the Serbian side on the constitutional disputes over Kosovo. *Izvestiia* published a lengthy article in which "inciters" of separatism were criticized, setting off a barrage of denunciations by the Tiranë state-run media (*Izvestiia*, 7 March; *RAD Background Report*, no. 48, 14 March). The commentaries even raised the specter of the old Russian-Serbian alliance and its implications for the Balkans.

United States–Albanian relations showed no improvement, but at the informal level a number of things happened that suggested the willingness of the Tiranë regime to ignore formalities and pursue wider contacts with Albanian emigrés in the United States, Canada, and West Germany. Numerous visits by Albanian nationals took place, and in some cases prominent emigré leaders were received by high-level party and state officials. A unifying issue for the Tiranë regime and the Albanian diaspora remains the Kosovo issue, and the Albanian regime is adept at exploiting its nationalistic value. *Glasnost'* has also affected Tiranë in religious matters. A monsignor of the Albanian Orthodox Church in the United States visited Tiranë several times, the latest in November (*Washington Times*, 9 January 1990). Contrary to the behavior of Mother Teresa (who kept silent on issues of religious persecution), the Orthodox clergyman claims that he conducted a small service in a hotel lobby (under the watchful eyes of the *Sigurimi* and perhaps for foreign consumption) and performed a grave site ceremony.

Party Relations. The Central Committee of the APL invited all known Marxist-Leninist parties, usually small splinter groups of Western romantics, to attend the 45th anniversary of Albania's liberation from Nazi occupation. Representatives from Portugal, Spain, the Dominican Republic, Canada, Brazil, Denmark, Ecuador, and the Palestine Liberation Organization responded (ATA, 26, 28 November; *FBIS*, 1 December). There were no formal party-to-party contacts with Eastern Europe, China, or the Soviet Union.

Nikolaos A. Stavrou
Howard University

Bulgaria

Population. 8,985,800 (*Rabotnichesko delo*, 23 February)

Party. Bulgarian Communist Party (Bûlgarska komunisticheska partiya; BCP)

Founded. Bulgarian Social Democratic Party founded in 1891; split into Broad and Narrow factions in 1903; the Narrow Socialists became the BCP and joined the Comintern in 1919.

Membership. 984,000 (*Pravda*, 31 January 1990). According to information presented at the Thirteenth Party Congress in April 1986, 44.36 percent of the members are industrial workers, and 16.31 percent are agricultural workers (BCP Central Committee Report to the Thirteenth Congress, BTA, 5 April 1986; *FBIS*, 8 April 1988). Bulgaria has not published data on ethnic minorities since 1965; Turks and Gypsies, the two largest minority groups, are believed to be underrepresented in the BCP in proportion to their numbers in the general population.

General Secretary. Petûr Toshev Mladenov (b. 22 August 1936)

Politburo. 8 full members: Petûr Mladenov (chairman, State Council), Georgi Atanasov (b. 1933, prime minister), Belcho Belchev (b. 1932, minister of finance), Dobri Dzhurov (b. 1916, minister of national defense), Alexander Lilov (b. 1933), Andrey Lukanov (b. 1938), Panteley Pachov (b. 1939, chairman, Plovdiv BCP regional committee), Mincho Yovchev (b. 1942, deputy chairman, council of ministers; minister of industry and technology); 4 candidate members: Petko Danev (b. 1942, first secretary Varna BCP regional committee), Ivan Ivanov (b. 1942, first secretary of Stara Zagora BCP municipal committee), Ivan Stanev (b. 1932), Dimitûr Stanishev (b. 1924, head of the foreign policy and international contacts department of the BCP central committee)

Secretariat. 6 members: Alexander Lilov, Andrey Lukanov, Dimitûr Stanishev, Prodan Stoyanov (b. 1936, head of secretarial department of the BCP central committee), Dimo Uzunov (b. 1941), Kiril Zarev (b. 1926, deputy chairman, National Assembly; minister of the economy and planning)

Central Committee. 185 full and 145 candidate members

Status. Ruling party

Last Congress. Thirteenth, 2–5 April 1986, in Sofia; next congress scheduled for 26 March 1990

Last Election. 8 June 1986. All candidates ran on the ticket of the Fatherland Front, an umbrella organization (4.4 million members) comprising most mass organizations. Fatherland Front candidates received 99.9 percent of the votes cast. Of the National Assembly's 400 members, 276 belong to the BCP and 99 to the Agrarian Union; 25 are unaffiliated (most of these are Komsomol members). The Bulgarian Agrarian National Union (BANU, 120,000 members) formally shares power with the BCP and holds 3 of the 27 seats on the State Council; holds positions in the ministries of justice, public health, and social welfare; and fills about one-sixth of the people's council seats. BANU leader Angel Dimitrov's post as first deputy chairman of the State Council makes him Petûr Mladenov's nominal successor as head of state.

Auxiliary Organizations. Central Council of Trade Unions (CCTU, about 4 million members), led by Petûr Dyulgerov; Dimitrov Communist Youth League (Komsomol, 1.5 million members), led by Rossen Karadimov. Civil Defense Organization (750,000 members), led by Colonel General Tencho Papazov, provides training in paramilitary tactics and disaster relief; Committee of Bulgarian Women (30,000 members), led by Elena Lagadinova, stimulates patriotism and social activism.

Publications. *Rabotnichesko delo* (*RD*, Workers' Cause), BCP daily edited by Radoslav Radov; *Partien zhivot* (Party Life), BCP monthly; *Novo vreme* (New Time), BCP theoretical journal; *Otechestven front* (Fatherland Front), front daily; *Dûrzhaven vestnik* (State Gazette), contains texts of laws and decrees. Bûlgarska Telegrafna Agentsiya (BTA) is the official news agency.

Bulgaria came to the end of an era with the forced resignation of state and party leader Todor Zhivkov. His efforts to resist *perestroika* or at least to confine its effects within narrow limits initially showed some success, but were unable to deter the growth of reformist opposition in the country or in the BCP itself. Bulgaria was also affected by the pace of developments across Eastern Europe and perhaps by direct Soviet pressure. The new leadership headed by Petûr Mladenov began a purge of

Zhivkov's supporters as the year ended and appeared to enjoy a measure of popular support as it undertook the preparation of further political and economic reforms.

The End of the Zhivkov Era. On 10 November, the day after East Germany opened the Berlin Wall, the resignation of Todor Zhivkov as party general secretary and president of the State Council was tersely announced to a meeting of the BCP Central Committee. Zhivkov had headed the BCP for 35 years and had combined state and party leadership for 27. He had been in power longer than any other living Soviet bloc leader, and an entire generation of Bulgarians had come to maturity under his regime. Zhivkov's downfall will probably be seen as the product of changes set in motion by Mikhail Gorbachev in the USSR and throughout Eastern Europe, but there were a number of domestic factors as well.

The economic situation. According to official statistics the Bulgarian economy had few problems. A government report on 1988 economic performance was optimistic, stating that Bulgaria had developed "at a high and stable rate," achieving an increase of 6.2 percent in domestic net material product (*RD*, 23 February). But this report appeared a month later than was customary and contained strange inconsistencies. For example, it stated that industrial production had grown by 5.1 percent and that agricultural production had declined by 0.7 percent. Because those two sectors made up three-quarters of the total domestic net material product and because no remarkable growth was reported in other areas, the overall growth rate of 6.2 percent appears to have been chosen to correspond to the five-year plan targets rather than to reality. A critical analysis of the report appeared in the popular weekly *Pogled* stating that "Our official statistics . . . year after year offer us optimistic reports, while in practice, in everyday life, we are confronted with the severe shortage and declining quality of a large number of goods, with the continuous hidden or open increase in their prices." The article criticized the inconsistent reporting of economic statistics that failed to make clear how categories were defined, to state whether calculations were made on the basis of constant prices, and to examine such issues as the poor quality of manufactured goods (*Pogled*, 8 May; RFE, *Situation Report*, 22 May).

At the beginning of the year, Zhivkov introduced

a new round of economic restructuring. Admitting that past measures had failed owing to "lack of experience," organizational confusion, and the "alienation of the workers," Zhivkov proposed that henceforth the basic unit of production would be the "firm." Firms could be established by state agencies, banks, cooperatives, or individual citizens and would be permitted to issue their own stocks or bonds. Firms operated by private citizens would be permitted to hire up to ten workers on a permanent basis and an unlimited number on temporary contracts. According to predictions in the press, thousands of new firms were expected to appear, but most of these would result simply from changes in terminology. At a BCP Central Committee plenum in July, Zhivkov repeated standard complaints about the economy's low efficiency, poor quality of industrial production, and slow pace of technological change. His solution this time was a reform of the banking system that aimed at turning the Bulgarian National Bank into 60 independent units. Zhivkov also called for steps to make the Bulgarian lev convertible with Western currencies, beginning with the creation of a hard lev backed by gold or high-quality products that could coexist with the present currency (RFE, *Situation Report*, 1 September).

Despite Zhivkov's admissions of economic shortcomings and economic disruption caused by the exodus of Bulgaria's ethnic Turks (see below), official reports through the third quarter continued to maintain that plan targets were being met (RFE, *Situation Report*, 5 October). Following Zhivkov's fall, however, Mladenov described the Bulgarian economy as being "on the verge of a heart attack." The most critical problems he cited were that 40–45 percent of Bulgaria's production facilities were obsolete, that production of many critical goods had actually declined since 1980, that the growth of wages had outstripped the growth of consumer goods available to the population leading to shortages and inflation, and that the state budget had been operating at enormous deficits. Bulgaria's net hard currency debt was said to approach $8 billion ($10 billion gross debt less $2–2.5 billion in gold and other credits), an amount that was described as Bulgaria's "critical limit" (BTA, 11 December; FBIS, 12 December). Kiril Zarev, designated to become the next minister of the economy and planning, also described the Bulgarian economy as in a "catastrophic situation." He blamed Zhivkov and Grisha Filipov for launching grandiose projects without considering how they might be completed

or their effect on the rest of the economy, and he accused them of constantly disregarding the advice of trained economists. As a result the economy experienced a prolonged period of stagnation and even decline and the country's foreign debt soared. The new finance minister, Belcho Belchev, added that the debt situation had grown particularly acute over the past three years, when the bulk of it was accumulated (RD, 25 November; FBIS, 1 December). Shortly afterward, Petûr Dyulgerov, chairman of the Central Council of Trade Unions and candidate Politburo member, admitted in an interview that for years the government had published statistics that had little to do with reality. Independent research conducted by the Trade Union Council showed that two-thirds of the population's monthly wages were below the minimum acceptable standard and that the plight of the country's pensioners was even worse. Dyulgerov blamed the economic situation on the desire of "some people" to amass great wealth through "speculation, corruption, theft, and misappropriation" and to the fact that only 16.6 percent of production funds were devoted to consumer needs while the rest was earmarked for heavy industry by leaders "blindly following dogmas" (Trud, 20 November; FBIS, 30 November).

Party spokesmen also admitted that insufficient attention had been paid to the deterioration of the environment and that correcting the problems resulting from years of neglect would be both slow and expensive. Although extensive blame was heaped on Zhivkov and his cronies, Mladenov and other speakers admitted that problems similar to Bulgaria's were endemic throughout the socialist community and were in part due to the basic structure of socialism as it had developed to this point (BTA, 11 December; FBIS, 12 December).

Dissent. Because Zhivkov appeared to embrace glasnost', perestroika, and "new thinking" in the summer of 1987, a number of independent organizations sprang up to test the limits of government tolerance. One of the most influential was the Discussion Club for the Support of *Glasnost'* and *Perestroika*, which formed in November 1988 and whose members included many of Bulgaria's prominent intellectuals and even important party figures. Its guiding spirit was the sociologist Zheliu Zhelev whose study *Fascism* was suppressed for calling attention to features common to totalitarian regimes. Eco-*Glasnost'*, established during the spring of this year, descended from the organization formed to protest environmental pollution in Russia (see *YICA*, 1989, p. 300). Led by actor Petûr Slabakov and zoologist Petûr Beron, Eco-*Glasnost'* sought to focus attention on the deterioration of the Bulgarian environment and on the political causes of the government's indifference to the problem. Other groups included the Independent Association for the Defense of Human Rights in Bulgaria, formed in January 1988 to bring international attention to human rights abuses; *Podkrepa* (Support), formed in February at Plovdiv, which described itself as an independent trade union representing the scientific, technical, educational, and cultural professions; and the Committee for Religious Rights, Freedom of Conscience, and Spiritual Values, formed at Veliko Tûrnovo in March. Reports of the formation of other independent organizations were also frequent during the year.

Efforts to suppress the growing number of popular independent initiatives seemed only to encourage dissidents. In December 1988 and January expulsion and other sanctions were imposed on party members active in the Club for the Support of *Glasnost'* and *Perestroika*. Many of them, along with nonparty members of the club, were dismissed from their positions. In January the Ministry of Internal Affairs announced the arrest of several leaders of the Independent Association for the Defense of Human Rights on charges of spreading false rumors. Protests from the government of France (President Mitterrand had intended to meet with representatives of the association during his state visit to Bulgaria in February), from intellectuals and human rights groups around the world, and from Bulgaria's own intellectuals led to the release of the dissidents, although several were kept under house arrest in the provinces and all were subjected to a vicious campaign of slander in the press. *RD* and other newspapers featured a letter-writing campaign that denounced many dissidents as "political outcasts, fascists, and extremists" and accused them of wanting to tear down the achievements of Bulgarian socialism (*RD*, 11 February). The poet Petûr Manolov, secretary of the Independent Association, began a hunger strike after the police refused to return his personal archives, which had been seized when he was arrested (*News from Helsinki Watch: News from Bulgaria*, January). A protest to the authorities was signed by 27 of Bulgaria's leading intellectuals; when the Bulgarian media refused to acknowledge it, Blaga Dimitrova, considered by many to be Bulgaria's greatest living writer, read it on a broadcast of Radio Free Europe's Bulgarian service (RFE, *Situation Report*, 3 February). The use of Radio Free Europe and similar stations by Bulgarian dissidents became so frequent during the year that Bulgarian authorities began to refer to their critics as "the correspondents of foreign radio stations."

During 20–21 February the Politburo met with selected "representatives of the intelligentsia," mainly the leaders of the cultural unions, to discuss the role of intellectuals in the reform process. Zhivkov again paid lip service to radical reform and gave a sharp critique of Stalinism, but failed to fill in the "blank spaces" in the BCP's or his own past. He warned that Bulgaria would not tolerate "national nihilism" or expressions of "negative attitudes toward our country or toward socialism." (Sofia Domestic Service [SDS], 20 February; *FBIS*, 21 February; RFE *Situation Report*, 9 March.) Zhivkov's speech seemed to have little effect, as dissident activities continued to expand. Between 23 February and 15 March the country's twelve cultural unions held congresses that were marked by outspoken criticism of the government, of censorship, of repression, and of the slow pace of reform. Most of these congresses voted out their incumbent, conservative leaderships in favor of figures known to be sympathetic to more rapid change. (RFE, *Situation Report*, 22 May.) In May dissident intellectuals gathered signatures for an appeal to the National Assembly that criticized the stagnation in Bulgaria compared with the events in Poland, Hungary, and the Soviet Union and called for the introduction of basic civil rights and an end to the communist party's monopoly of power. Security forces arrested several leading intellectuals in a search for the originators of this appeal. (RFE, *Situation Report*, 22 May.)

During the spring the protest movement also spread among Bulgaria's ethnic Turks, who had been relatively quiet since the brutal assimilation campaign of 1984–1985. A number of ethnic Turks launched hunger strikes apparently to gain attention from the Helsinki follow-up conference on human rights held in Paris on 30 May. These protests escalated to open demonstrations in a number of towns and villages that resulted in violent clashes with the authorities and several deaths. By the end of May the demonstrations included thousands of participants, and hundreds of arrests were reported along with news of substantial movements of police and military units in the regions with heavily Turkish populations. Zhivkov went on national television to quell rumors of massive unrest; denying that

Bulgaria had a substantial Turkish minority, he repeated the fiction that most of the ethnic Turks were in actuality Bulgarians who had been forcibly converted to Islam and a Turkish identity during the Ottoman period. He attributed disturbances among Bulgaria's Muslims to confusion over the terms of a new passport law and to an anti-Bulgarian campaign carried on by Turkey and challenged the Turkish government to open its borders to Bulgarian Muslims so that it would be revealed how few were truly discontent with life in Bulgaria (SDS, 29 May; *FBIS*, 30 May; Sofia press, *Za dobrosûsedski khumani tsivilizovani otnosheniia: iziavlenie na . . . Todor Zhivkov*, undated). At the same time the government began to deport the leaders of the Turkish protests to Yugoslavia and Austria; when Turkey responded to Zhivkov's challenge by declaring that it would accept refugees from Bulgaria, the authorities launched a broad campaign of terror against the ethnic Turks, forcing thousands to cross the border where they were placed in hastily organized camps. Before the Turkish government again closed the border, more than 300,000 ethnic Turks abandoned Bulgaria, an exodus that focused worldwide attention on Bulgaria's human rights record. (Helsinki Watch, *Destroying Ethnic Identity: The Expulsion of the Bulgarian Turks*, October.)

The flight of ethnic Turks also disrupted the economy, particularly the agricultural sector, where natural conditions should have led to an excellent harvest for the first time in several years. However, tobacco, Bulgaria's principal cash crop, was grown almost entirely by members of the Turkish minority. Moreover, when they were deported or fled, many Turks abandoned their livestock, disrupting the collection of dairy products and eggs. Industry was affected as well, with reports of widespread factory shutdowns in areas where the Turkish population was concentrated. The government responded by adopting provisions for the local mobilization of labor that would permit authorities to draft workers for additional jobs. This was apparently intended as an emergency measure only because it reportedly led to demoralization among those affected. Brigades of secondary school and university students were expanded and required to work for longer periods, compulsory Saturday work was reimposed, and pensioners were encouraged to return to jobs where their experience could be utilized (RFE, *Situation Report*, 5 October).

During the spring and summer, at least four samizdat journals were launched to circulate political ideas and literary works still shunned by the official press. The editor of one (*Glas* [Voice]) was Vladimir Levchev, a literary critic and active dissident who is the son of Liubomir Levchev, head of the Bulgarian Writers' Union until this year. In his introductory editorial, the younger Levchev wrote:

> Bulgaria is becoming more and more dirty and untidy; the shops are becoming emptier and emptier; the prices are rising higher and higher; the rivers and even the Black Sea are dying. At the same time, official reports talk of an upsurge, progress, and a qualitatively new stage. We all know the truth . . . If we do not wake up from the big slumber right now, if we do not raise our voices and wake up our state, very soon it will be too late. (RFE, *Situation Report*, 5 December.)

Eco-*Glasnost'* and other groups became particularly active in October when Bulgaria hosted the Conference on Security and Cooperation in Europe forum on environmental protection. The presence of foreign diplomats and journalists for a time allowed dissident groups to operate in the open. The authorities attempted to confine dissident activities to Sofia's southern park on the outskirts of the city, but when they were unable to do so launched a crackdown. Dissident leaders who lacked Sofia residence permits were ordered out of the city, and on 26 October the police arrested and beat up several members of Eco-*Glasnost'*. This produced a wave of diplomatic protests, and on 3 November, when Eco-*Glasnost'* carried a petition on the environment to the National Assembly, Sofia saw its first mass (between five thousand and nine thousand participants) protest demonstration since the consolidation of communist rule (RFE, *Situation Report*, 5 December; *Free Bulgarian Center Newsletter*, November; *NYT*, 4 November).

Internal party conflicts. The erratic leadership of Zhivkov vis-à-vis the economy, dissident intellectuals, and ethnic Turks undoubtedly caused an erosion of support in the party leadership, compounded by resentment of Zhivkov's efforts to promote the careers of his son and other favorites. Vladimir Zhivkov especially was extremely unpopular both among the general public and among the party leadership and possessed a reputation for limited intellectual ability and excessive enjoyment of alcohol and gambling. Bulgaria's academic community had already been alienated by the younger Zhivkov's appointment as a professor in the Academy of Social Sciences and Social Management; in July he was made head of a newly created BCP

Central Committee department on culture. Zhivkov's colleagues expected him to try to raise his son to Politburo membership as he had done with his daughter in the late 1970s. "We all have children," said one of Zhivkov's accusers later, "and so a father's ambitions are understandable, but the children should have some sense, at least some qualifications" (SDS, 17 November; *FBIS*, 27 November). Zhivkov also boosted the career of Petko Danchev, who had become a candidate member of the Politburo in 1988. In July he was made a deputy prime minister, in line to replace Georgi Atanasov. Danchev, born in 1949, is from Todor Zhivkov's native village of Pravets and is rumored to be Zhivkov's illegitimate son. Another Zhivkov protégée, Stanka Shopova, born in 1955 and the former head of the Komsomol, also was moved rapidly forward, being made head of the BCP Central Committee's propaganda and agitation department. In the aftermath of Zhivkov's fall, bitter feelings were expressed against the former leader's favoritism and his tendency to appoint people to offices for which they lacked ability and experience; many of them were rapidly removed from office.

Soviet involvement. The role of the Soviet Union in Zhivkov's downfall is difficult to clarify. Outwardly, Zhivkov did not seem to be in disfavor; he visited the USSR for a meeting with Gorbachev that was said to have taken place in "the warm, friendly atmosphere traditional for Bulgarian-Soviet relations" (*Pravda*, 24 June). It had long been rumored, however, that the Bulgarian and Soviet leaders disliked each other. Zhivkov's bloc diplomacy seemed oriented toward Czechoslovakia, East Germany (see below), and China. One of his critics cited a Zhivkov memorandum of February 1987 that put the Soviet embassy "in a panic" because it stated that Bulgaria had accomplished all the reconstruction that it needed in 1956 (SDS, 17 November; *FBIS*, 27 November). It was also pointed out that Politburo member Milko Balev, described as Zhivkov's chief sycophant, was deliberately shunned by the Soviet leadership. Both Petûr Mladenov, Zhivkov's successor, and Defense Minister Dzhurov are known to enjoy good relationships with Soviet leaders. Mladenov set the coup against Zhivkov in motion following a visit to China, and it was widely rumored that on his way to Beijing he had stopped in Moscow for consultations with Gorbachev. Mladenov denied the Moscow stopover (BTA, 20 November; *FBIS*, 21 November), but from expressions in the Soviet press (*Pravda*, 13,

15, 18, 29 November, 1 December) and from official statements, the replacement of Zhivkov was not unwelcome to Moscow.

Zhivkov's removal. The details surrounding Zhivkov's fall are unclear. According to the official report, the question was discussed by the full and candidate members of the Politburo, BCP Central Committee secretaries, and the chairman of the Central Control-Auditing Commission. Because this body of 21 contained a solid majority of Zhivkov supporters (14 were either fired or soon resigned), Zhivkov's fate was probably not decided by majority vote; there was much speculation about the role of Defense Minister Dobri Dzhurov and the army. According to one account that appeared in the *Financial Times* (16 November), Foreign Minister Mladenov brought the confrontation to a head by stating that he could no longer serve under Zhivkov's leadership and Dzhurov arranged to neutralize Zhivkov's personal security force. However the issue was decided, Prime Minister Georgi Atanasov announced Zhivkov's "resignation" to the plenum of the Central Committee, which voted to extend thanks to the former leader for his years of service and nominated Mladenov as the new leader (SDS, 10 November; *FBIS*, 13 November). But the fiction that Zhivkov had voluntarily retired was quickly dropped as criticism of his former leadership became more intense and was extended to his closest supporters; the Central Committee's vote of thanks was officially rescinded on 8 December (BTA, 8 December; *FBIS*, 11 December).

Six days after Zhivkov's dismissal a second BCP Central Committee plenum removed his three closest allies, Milko Balev, Grisha Filipov, and Dimitûr Stoianov, from the Politburo and expelled them from the Central Committee. Petko Danchev and Stoian Ovcharov were both dropped as candidate members of the Politburo and Danchev was also removed from the Central Committee. BCP Central Committee secretaries Emil Khristov and Vasil Tsanov were pensioned off and Yordan Yotov, the party's chief ideologist, was also relieved of his post as a Central Committee secretary although he temporarily kept his seat on the Politburo (BTA, 16 November; *FBIS*, 17 November). Stanko Todorov, who had been demoted from the Politburo to the presidency of the National Assembly, was nominated to return to the Politburo, but declined, stating that at age 68 his career was nearly over and that younger cadres should assume the leadership (*RD*, 26 November; *FBIS*, 5 December).

On the following day a meeting of the National Assembly broadcast on national television officially removed Zhivkov and his allies from their posts in the government (BTA, 17 November; *FBIS*, 20 November). At this point open denunciations of Zhivkov and his supporters began. The principal indictment was made by Slavcho Trûnski, a respected former partisan commander who had been imprisoned during the Stalinist era. He accused Zhivkov of infinite conceit, of amassing personal wealth exceeding that of the former czars, of grossly mismanaging the economy, and of appointing his incompetent favorites and relatives to critical positions (SDS, 17 November; *FBIS*, 27 November). Meanwhile in the square outside the assembly, a demonstration of more than 100,000 people heard numerous speakers denounce the former leader and posters appeared that caricatured him as Hitler or showed him wearing prison stripes (*RD*, 18 November; *FBIS*, 22 November; *NYT*, 18 November).

On 8 December another plenum of the Central Committee completed the work of clearing the party's top positions of the old guard: Ivan Panev, Yordan Yotov, and Pencho Kubadinski resigned as full members of the Politburo; Georgi Yordanov and Grigor Stoichkov resigned as candidate members. Twenty-two full and four candidate members were also expelled from the Central Committee, including Stoian Ovcharov, Stanka Shopova, and a number of others who held important positions under Zhivkov. An odd development concerned Nacho Papazov, who had formerly headed the party's control-auditing commission. He had been made a Central Committee secretary and a full member of the Politburo when Zhivkov fell and had taken an active role in denouncing the former leader, but suddenly resigned his party positions without explanation (BTA, 8 December; *FBIS*, 11 December).

Zhivkov's further disgrace came on 13 December when the Central Committee expelled him, his son, and Milko Balev from the party altogether. Zhivkov was accused of "gross violations of the laws and gross mistakes in policies that brought the country to a serious crisis." It was also announced that an investigation would be opened into possible financial abuses by Zhivkov and his son. A letter from Vladimir Zhivkov denying all charges and welcoming a full investigation was read on national television (*NYT*, 14 December).

The New Leadership. Petûr Mladenov, who was quickly made head of state by the National Assembly following his rise to party leadership, was not well known despite his long political career. Although he was soon being described as the most liberal of the Zhivkov-era leaders, he had no public record on domestic issues, having specialized entirely in foreign policy. Mladenov was born in 1936 in the village of Toshevtsi near the Danube, the son of a BCP activist who was killed in the partisans. He graduated from Bulgaria's Suvorov Military Academy and then studied philosophy at Sofia University. He graduated from the Moscow State Institute of International Relations in 1963 after which he began a rapid climb in the party bureaucracy, leading to his appointment as foreign minister in 1971. He was made a candidate, then a full, member of the Politburo in 1977. Mladenov is believed to be in fragile health, having undergone a heart bypass operation in Houston several years ago and visiting the United States frequently for follow-up treatments. (*NYT*, 11 November; *WP*, 11 November; BTA, 10 November; *FBIS*, 13 November.) There was some speculation that Mladenov would prove to be a transitional figure and that his election was the result of compromise among other party strongmen, the most important of whom were Politburo member and Prime Minister Georgi Atanasov, Andrei Lukanov (a third-generation party leader), and Alexander Lilov. Lukanov was made a Central Committee secretary and full member of the Politburo and placed in charge of a special party and state commission to investigate "the deformations in social and economic life" during the Zhivkov era. He also seemed to be the government figure with the best ties to the country's dissident groups (BTA, 22 November; *FBIS*, 24 November). Lilov, who holds a doctorate in literature, was once thought to be a likely successor to Zhivkov. He was purged in 1983 when Zhivkov reversed a trend toward cultural liberalization; since that time he has been director of the Institute of Modern Social Theories, an institution that sheltered thinkers whose views were not in line with the leadership. Lilov was added to the Politburo and made a Central Committee secretary on 8 December (BTA, 8 December; *FBIS*, 11 December).

Belcho Belchev was made a member of the Politburo and the Central Committee secretariat and named minister of finance. He had held the finance ministry before, but had been downgraded by Zhivkov two years earlier (BTA, 9 December; *FBIS*, 11 December). Two regional party first secretaries, Panteley Pachov of Plovdiv and Mincho Yovchev of Khaskovo, were also made full Politburo members (BTA, 17 November; *FBIS*, 29 November). With the changes of November and December, the average age of the Politburo has dropped a full decade, from 65 to 55. With the exception of Dobri Dzhurov, all the members were born between 1932 and 1942.

Petûr Dyulgerov and Dimitûr Stanishev remained candidate members of the Politburo and were joined by Petko Danev and Ivan Ivanov, the regional BCP secretaries from Varna and Stara Zagora, and by Ivan Stanev, a member of the BCP Sofia municipal committee, who was described as having made major contributions to Bulgaria's economic efficiency (BTA, 17 November; *FBIS*, 29 November).

Dimitûr Stanishev and Kiril Zarev were the only holdovers on the Central Committee secretariat. Zarev, who was named minister of the economy and planning, was clearly intended to play a central role in shaping the new regime's economic policies. Prodan Stoyanov, head of the Central Committee's administrative department, and Dimo Uzunov, first secretary of the Tolbukhin regional party committee, were also made Central Committee secretaries.

By the end of the year changes at the center began to be reflected in the provinces. In Razgrad the regional BCP committee required two rounds of voting before Boris Anastasov defeated a rival candidate for the post of first secretary (BTA, 14 December; *FBIS*, 15 December). In Burgas an extraordinary plenum of the regional BCP committee ousted First Secretary Nikolai Zhishev owing to "his age and the sociopolitical trends emerging in the region." Two candidates competed for Zhishev's office, with Ivan Chengeliev emerging as winner. The extraordinary plenum was held in response to rallies and demonstrations that demanded the resignation of the entire regional apparatus (SDS, 14 December; *FBIS*, 15 December).

The first steps of the new regime. In his speech to the Central Committee plenum that made him general secretary, Petûr Mladenov stated that there was no alternative to restructuring and that "we should not be frightened by the fact that . . . pluralism can and certainly will emerge" (SDS, 10 November; *FBIS*, 13 November). The Politburo quickly moved to rescind sanctions, reinstating the party memberships of eleven activists, most of them members of the Club for the Support of *Glasnost'* and *Perestroika*, and recommending that they be restored to their former positions (BTA, 13 November; *FBIS*, 14 November). Rehabilitation was also extended to Stoyan Mikhailov and Svetlin Rusev, who were both restored to the Central Committee (BTA, 17 November; *FBIS*, 17 November; on the expulsion of Mikhailov and Rusev, see *YICA*, 1989), and to Nikola Popov, an economist who had been censured by the party and fired as rector of the University of Sofia in 1987 for his criticism of Zhivkov's economic policies. Academician Popov was promptly re-elected rector when the incumbent university administration was toppled (BTA, 18 November; *FBIS*, 20 November).

Mladenov held a four-hour meeting with representatives of the intelligentsia, including many who had been active in the dissident movements, promising to continue to remove Zhivkov's allies and to permit greater freedom of expression (BTA, 14 November; *FBIS*, 15 November). The first meeting of the National Assembly abolished article 273 of the criminal code, which made illegal almost all forms of unauthorized political activity, and amnestied all who had been convicted under it (BTA, 17 November; *FBIS*, 20 November). Mladenov also closed down the department of the Interior Ministry that dealt with ideological subversion (BTA, 25 November; *FBIS*, 27 November), and the Bulgarian Supreme Court reversed a Sofia court's refusal to register the dissident organization Eco-*Glasnost'* on the grounds that the decision had been the result of political interference. Eco-*Glasnost'* was recognized as a legal, independent organization on 10 December (*WP*, 12 December).

The effort of Mladenov and his allies to gain the support of the country's intelligentsia seemed to enjoy a measure of success. A rally called by dissident groups for 17 November was approved by the government and turned into an endorsement of reform, with hostility channeled toward Zhivkov. At later rallies and demonstrations prominent dissident intellectuals appealed for Mladenov to be given time to prove himself, but a growing tone of impatience was evident. The results of a poll published by the newspaper *Trud* (16 November) immediately after Zhivkov's fall indicated that although the new leadership enjoyed general support, one-fifth of the population believed that improvements would not come no matter who stood at the head of the BCP. Moreover, the respondents unanimously agreed that Bulgaria was experiencing a crisis brought on by the nation's leadership, and one-third agreed with the proposition that "in Bulgaria nothing goes as it should." The strongest hostility was expressed against the "privileges and Mafia of relationships" of the country's elite, and strong support was given to the separation of the party from the state, the "rejuvenation of cadres," the pluralism of opinions, and genuinely free elections.

At demonstrations in Sofia and around the country, demands were frequently raised for multiparty elections and the elimination of the constitutional provision that granted the BCP a leading role in the government. Mladenov put such a proposal before the National Assembly, but some deputies pointed out that constitutional amendments require a one-month waiting period. Mladenov promised that the amendment would be passed as soon as it could be done legally and that free elections would be held before June 1990. At a Central Committee plenum 11–12 December, Mladenov also announced that the next BCP congress would be moved up to 26 March 1990. Speakers at the plenum implied that the congress would bring about substantial changes in the composition of the Central Committee and in regional party leaderships (SDS, 11, 12 December; *FBIS*, 12, 13 December).

Although the new leadership recognized major economic difficulties, it had not yet determined the measures it would take to deal with them. Support appeared to be building for the government to undertake a stabilization program involving an attempt to raise living standards by increasing the resources devoted to consumer production and to agriculture while gradually introducing more basic structural reforms. But some economists were calling for immediate, radical changes. In an article published in the party daily, the economist Ivan Kostov argued that Bulgaria's problems were rooted "in the very system of present-day socialism" and that halfway measures to cure them would result in failure and the collapse of public confidence. Kostov called for the complete dismantling of "command-administrative socialism." Although this would result in immediate declines in living standards, dislocations, and inequalities, the government could use its resources to provide a floor of social services and to promote retraining and education aimed at making the Bulgarian labor force competitive in the modern economic world (*RD*, 30 November; *FBIS*, 7 December; BTA, 9 December; *FBIS*, 11 December).

At the end of the year the government also announced an end to the persecution of the ethnic Turks. In an address to about one thousand *pomaks* and ethnic Turks gathered before the National Assembly, Stanko Todorov and Alexander Lilov announced that "everyone in Bulgaria will be able to choose his name, religion, and language freely" and that the National Assembly would pass the appropriate legislation immediately (*WP*, 30 December). Although this policy was supported by dissident groups, it was not popular among ethnic Bulgarians, and anti-Turkish demonstrations were held around the country, some demanding that a national referendum be held on the issue. In a televised address to the nation, Todorov pleaded for tolerance and warned that Bulgaria's reputation in Europe depended on it. Hostility toward the ethnic Turks was still strong, however, and there were reports that local authorities were refusing to follow the government's instructions. It was also suggested that hard-liners in the party were attempting to use the hostility toward the ethnic Turks as a weapon against reformers (*WP*, 6, 7 January 1990).

While the new government was attempting to develop a program, nine dissident groups came together to form a Union of Democratic Forces on 7 December. The constituent assembly of the new organization adopted a program calling for "political pluralism, a multiparty system, a law-respecting state, and a market economy" as well as many other specific reforms. Zheliu Zhelev was elected chairman of the union's coordinating council and Petûr Beron its secretary. The writer Georgi Spasov and Rumen Vodenicharov, head of the Independent Human Rights Society, were designated as spokesmen (BTA, 7 December; *FBIS*, 8 December).

An interview with Zhelev was published in the Defense Ministry's paper *Narodna armiia* (5 December). In it he stated that socialism is a utopian goal and that in the real world there is no economic system superior to capitalism. He described Bulgaria's system as being a degenerate, corrupt form of state capitalism with a totalitarian political superstructure, and he called for the country to move toward a more progressive form of capitalism based on free markets and multiparty democracy. On 3 January 1990 Zhelev, Beron, and Vodenicharov met with Lukanov, Lilov, and Belchev to lay the groundwork for a series of negotiations between the government and the independent groups (*WP*, 4 January 1990).

Social and Political Awakening. Zhivkov's fall, the reforms promised by the new leadership, and developments throughout Eastern Europe stimulated stirrings toward political independence and activism in a number of institutions that had been passive or repressed for decades. The Bulgarian Agrarian National Union (BANU), the principal democratic force in Bulgaria since the early years of the twentieth century, provided the core of the opposition to the communization of the country. Although it continued to exist as an institution under the communist regime, it was thoroughly under the BCP's control. Demands for the restoration of BANU as a genuine political force led to the resignation of the old leadership, headed by Petûr Tanchev, that was distinguished only by its subservience to the BCP. Angel Dimitrov, who had been active in the dissident movement, was elected the new secretary of BANU. Dimitrov stressed that BANU would be fully independent of the BCP and called for the formation of a state commission to rehabilitate the agrarian leaders who had been repressed by the communists. He also stated that BANU should aid those survivors who "had to pass through prisons and camps" as a consequence of their opposition to communism (BTA, 2 December; *FBIS*, 7 December). Before Zhivkov's fall some dissident agrarians founded an independent branch of the union called BANU–Nikola Petkov (NP) after the agrarian leader executed in 1947. BANU-NP chose to retain its independence and joined the Union of Democratic Forces on 7 December (BTA, 7 December; *FBIS*, 8 December).

An expanded plenum of the Central Council of Trade Unions (CCTU) declared Bulgaria's unions independent of state and party control and pledged to wage a genuine battle in defense of the working class (BTA, 23 November; *FBIS*, 4 December). *Trud*, the CCTU's newspaper, perhaps more than any other official publication took advantage of the government's new commitment to *glasnost'* to publish frank and honest discussions of the country's problems and to press for change. At a plenum of the BCP Central Committee on 13 December, Petûr Dyulgerov resigned as a candidate member of the Politburo, saying that it is a conflict of interest for trade union officials to hold executive positions; he called on other union officials at all levels to resign from any positions they might hold in the party, state, or economic bodies (BTA, 14 December; *FBIS*, 14 December). Residual distrust of the CCTU was also apparent as some local unions declared their independence from the national organization and as the membership of the independent *Podkrepa* grew rapidly (BTA, 1 December; *FBIS*, 5 December).

At the University of Sofia a rebellion of reform-minded faculty and students led to the establishment of a Democracy Club to work for genuine autonomy for the country's institutions of higher education. Nikolai Genchev, historian and activist in the

Club for the Support of *Glasnost'* and *Perestroika'*, organized the Democracy Club, which spearheaded a successful drive to remove the university administration and to elect a new rector and academic council (BTA, 23 November; *FBIS*, 27 November). An activist student from the university was elected head of the Dimitrov Communist Youth League (Komsomol) at a boisterous meeting that ousted the old leadership, expelled Zhivkov's granddaughter, and revoked the honorary membership of Zhivkov's son (*NYT*, 21 December).

Elena Lagadinova, chairman of the Committee on Bulgarian Women, reminded a plenum of the BCP Central Committee not to forget the discrimination against women that had become widespread in the country during the Zhivkov period (*RD*, 26 November; *FBIS*, 5 December).

Local communists joined a demonstration of "several thousand" in a village near Vratsa devoted to rehabilitating Ivan Todorov-Gorunia, a general who committed suicide in 1965 following the discovery of his attempt to organize a military coup against Zhivkov. The village petitioned the government to reopen Todorov-Gorunia's case and proposed that a monument be erected to him (*Zemedelsko zname*, 28 November; *FBIS*, 4 December).

Numerous reports appeared in the press on the formation of local independent groups. Information was often fragmentary, but testified to the ferment taking place in society.

Foreign Affairs. *The Soviet bloc.* During the year, Zhivkov's diplomacy focused on strengthening relations with conservative governments and forces in Eastern Europe. Several top-ranking officials exchanged visits with Czechoslovakia, and *Rabotnichesko delo* (21 August) defended the legitimacy of the 1968 Warsaw Pact invasion at a time when the legislatures of Poland and Hungary were condemning it. In its turn, Czechoslovakia defended Bulgaria's campaign against its Turkish minority (BTA, 13 September; *FBIS*, 14 September). Zhivkov's one foreign trip, in addition to his annual visit to the USSR, was to take part in the celebration of the 40th anniversary of the founding of the German Democratic Republic. In addition to the East German leadership, he met with Nicolae Ceauşescu of Romania and President Daniel Ortega of Nicaragua (BTA, 7 October; *FBIS*, 11 October). The Bulgarian press condemned Hungary for opening its border to allow East German citizens to depart to the West (RFE, *Situation Report*, 5 December).

The Zhivkov policy toward conservative or

orthodox communist governments extended to China. Shortly after the massacre in Beijing, the Chinese foreign minister visited Sofia, where the Bulgarian government issued a statement supporting the Chinese action as "meant to restore order" and "protect the socialist gains of the working people." Following the visit a Bulgarian-Chinese Friendship Society was established (BTA, 13 June; FBIS, 14 June). On the very eve of the move against Zhivkov, Mladenov made a goodwill visit to China, meeting with Chinese leaders and signing protocols aimed at improving trade and cooperation (BTA, 6 November; FBIS, 13 November). High-level Bulgarian delegations were also sent to North Korea and to Cuba (RFE, Situation Report, 5 December).

Bulgaria's conservative bloc orientation dissolved with the Zhivkov regime, and Mladenov hastened to stress Bulgaria's solidarity with the USSR and the reformist communist parties (BTA, 14 November; FBIS, 15 November). Soviet foreign minister Shevardnadze told a session of the Supreme Soviet's foreign affairs committee that "we actively support the policy line of the new Bulgarian leadership" (BTA, 17 November; FBIS, 21 November). Mladenov traveled to Moscow during 4–5 December for a meeting with Gorbachev. The two leaders expressed mutual support, and Gorbachev accepted Mladenov's invitation to visit Bulgaria during the coming year (BTA, 5 December; FBIS, 6 December).

Diplomatic activity in the Balkans, with the exception of Bulgaria's relations with Turkey, was quiet during the year as the Balkan states were preoccupied by internal developments and the changes in progress in the rest of Eastern Europe. Yugoslavia did raise again its long-standing concern about Bulgaria's mistreatment of its "Macedonian minority," but Bulgaria, which holds that the inhabitants of Macedonia are not a separate nationality, ignored the issue (RFE, Situation Report, 9 March).

Noncommunist countries. Until Zhivkov's fall, Bulgaria's relations with the noncommunist world were dominated by the issues of human rights abuses and the repression of Bulgaria's Turkish minority. International human rights organizations, such as Amnesty International and Helsinki Watch, consistently focused attention on Bulgaria's repression of dissidents; their efforts were often seconded by Western governments. During a two-day state visit, French president François Mitterrand spoke out strongly in favor of human rights and civil freedoms and met with a group of Bulgarian dissidents (Paris Domestic Service, 18 January; FBIS, 26 January; NYT, 20 January).

The meeting of the Conference on Security and Cooperation in Europe (CSCE) and associated events in Paris in May provided a forum from which the Turkish government and exiled Bulgarian dissidents launched a broad attack on the repression of the Turkish minority and political dissenters (RFE, Situation Report, 29 June).

As part of the justification for its intensified persecution of the ethnic Turks, the Bulgarian government claimed that Turkey was preparing for war and would partition Bulgaria as it had Cyprus. Anti-Bulgarian feeling ran high in Turkey as large-scale public demonstrations were held to protest Bulgaria's conduct. The U.S. Senate unanimously voted to condemn Bulgaria for its treatment of the Turkish minority and voted $10 million to aid the refugees (Congressional Record, 15 June). The United States also recalled its ambassador because of Bulgaria's continuing human rights abuses. The European Parliament, the Council of the Economic Community, and the North Atlantic Treaty Organization also issued condemnations (BBC, 16 August).

The CSCE environmental conference in Sofia in October again focused attention on the suppression of human rights in Bulgaria, and several Western diplomats met with Bulgarian dissidents, visited areas of heavy Turkish population, and were present at demonstrations organized by dissident groups (Free Bulgarian Center Newsletter, November). The fall of the Zhivkov regime soon afterward seemed to offer the opportunity for a rapid improvement in Bulgaria's relations with the West. Bulgarian delegates met with representatives of the European Community in Brussels during 14–15 December after which it was reported that if Bulgaria continued to introduce political and economic reforms it might share in the assistance currently being extended to Poland and Hungary. Further discussions were scheduled to take place early in 1990 (BTA, 15 December; FBIS, 21 December). The announcement of the end of the anti-Turkish campaign was welcomed by the government in Ankara, which stated that Turkish-Bulgarian relations could now be rebuilt on a new foundation (WP, 30 December).

John D. Bell
University of Maryland, Baltimore County

Czechoslovakia

Population. 15,658,079 (July 1989)
Party. Communist Party of Czechoslovakia (Komunistická strana Československa; KSČ)
Founded. 1921
Membership. 1,574,690 (ČTK, 8 January 1990). (See, however, Adamec's statement at plenum [17 February 1990], where he claims that the total is one-fourth of this.)
Chairman. Ladislav Adamec
General Secretary. Vasil Mohorita
Presidium. Ladislav Adamec, Břetislav Benda, Josef Čížek, Miroslav Húsčava, Ignác Janák, Ivan Knotek, Hana Kožežníková, Antonín Mladý, Vasil Mohorita, Valeria Petrincová, Ondřej Saling, Karel Urbánek, Miroslav Válek, Miroslav Zajíc; alternate member: Miroslava Němcová
Secretariat. 5 secretaries: Ivan Knotek, Vasil Mohorita (general secretary), Ondřej Saling, Karel Urbánek, Miroslav Zajíc; 4 Secretariat members: František Hanuš, Zdeněk Hoření, Otto Liška, Josef Mevald
Control and Audit Commission. Josef Trmala, chairman
Central Committee. 135 full and 62 candidate members
Status. Legal
Last Congress. Seventeenth, 24–28 March 1986, in Prague; next regular congress scheduled for 1990 (an extraordinary congress held December 1989)
Slovak Party. Communist Party of Slovakia (Komunistická strana Slovenska; KSS); membership: 436,000 members and candidates; after the resignation of the Presidium and the Secretariat on 6 December, the KSS was governed by an action committee headed by Pavol Bolvanský; extraordinary congress held on 17 December.
Last Election. 1986; 99.94 percent; all 350 were National Front candidates; 66 percent of seats reserved for KSČ candidates; free elections with separate ballots for each political party scheduled June 1990.
Auxiliary Organizations. Revolutionary Trade Union Movement (Eleventh Congress, April 1987); Union of Farmers' Cooperatives; Socialist Youth Union (Fourth Congress, October 1987); Union for Cooperation with the Army; Czechoslovak Union of Women; Union of Fighters for Peace. Most mass organizations began a process of restructuring in December 1989.
Main State Organs. The executive body is the federal government, which is subordinate to the 350-member Federal Assembly, composed of the Chamber of the People (200 members) and the Chamber of the Nations (150 members). Until November 1989, the assembly rubber-stamped all decisions made by the KSČ Presidium and Central Committee. Return to a pluralistic democratic system was promised in December 1989. Since then, the assembly has assumed all legislative initiative. One hundred and twenty communist members ceded their seats to noncommunists.
Publications. Rudé právo, KSČ daily; Pravda (Bratislava), KSS daily; Tribuna, Czech ideological weekly; Predvoj, Slovak ideological weekly; Život strany, fortnightly devoted to organizational and administrative questions; Práce (Czech) and Práca (Slovak), Revolutionary Trade Union dailies; Tvorba, weekly devoted to domestic and international politics; Nová mysl, Marxist-Leninist theoretical weekly. Československá Tisková Kancelář (ČTK) is the official news agency.

The KSČ developed from the left wing of the Czechoslovak Social Democratic party, after having co-opted several radical socialist and leftist groups. Constituted in Prague at a merger congress in November 1921, it was admitted to the Communist International (Comintern) the same year. Its membership in the Comintern, however, was uneasy until 1929, when the so-called Bolshevization process was completed and a leadership of unqualified obedience to the Soviet Union assumed control. During the time of the First Czechoslovak Republic (1918–1939), the KSČ enjoyed legal status, but it was banned following the Munich Agreement in October 1938. After World War II, it emerged as the strongest party in the first postwar elections of 1946 (with 37.9 percent of the vote), but it did not poll an absolute majority. In February 1948, the KSČ seized all power in a coup d'état and transformed Czechoslovakia into a communist party-state. The departure from Stalinist policies and practices started later in Czechoslovakia than in other countries of Central and Eastern Europe, but in 1968 it led to a daring liberalization experiment known as Prague Spring. A Soviet-led military intervention by five Warsaw Pact armies in August of the same year ended that democratization course and imposed on Czechoslovakia the policies of so-called normalization, returning to unreserved subordination to the Soviet Union and the CPSU and consistently emulating the USSR in all areas of social life. However, the leadership put into power by the intervention did not follow the Soviet lead when reforms were initiated there by Mikhail S. Gorbachev, paying only lip service to *perestroika* and refusing to adopt *glasnost'*. This position caused an increasing isolation of Czechoslovakia within the system of the European communist party-states and brought about the collapse of the regime in November 1989.

1989—Annus Mirabilis. The year 1989 saw the most radical change imaginable in the KSČ and in the country hitherto ruled by this party. Before the year ended, the KSČ had ceased to be the party in power and faced the possibility of a thorough transformation, a split, a disintegration, or a combination of all three. Similarly, in December 1989, Czechoslovakia ceased to be a communist party-state. It would be difficult, after the events of 1989, to reclassify the KSČ into any established category; perhaps its performance in the elections scheduled for 8 June 1990 may provide some lead.

The process that resulted in the KSČ losing political control over Czechoslovakia is often referred to, especially in the domestic media, as the "velvet revolution" (*sametová revoluce*), which emphasizes the nonviolent nature of the change. (Absence of violent conflict per se has not been a Czechoslovak specialty.) In almost all countries of the Soviet bloc, the communist parties renounced—or were deprived of—their exclusive power without significant physical clashes with the opposition or deployment of force. Furthermore, as in other communist-dominated countries of Central and Eastern Europe, the reform movement in the CPSU and in the Soviet Union also acted as a catalyst and a safeguard of the ultimate success of the change in Czechoslovakia.

Soviet support, or at least benign acquiescence, represents another novelty of 1989 in international communist affairs. Not only did the KSČ lose the quality of a ruling party and Czechoslovakia the quality of a communist party-state, but the KSČ was no longer dependent on the previously superordinate power center located in the CPSU and Czechoslovakia was freed from the status of a satellite—the obligation for the party to devise its policies in

agreement with those set by its Soviet counterpart and for the country to adopt political, economic, and social institutions fashioned on the model of the Soviet Union (these requirements were articulated in the Brezhnev Doctrine of "limited sovereignty" promulgated after the Soviet-led invasion of Czechoslovakia in August 1968).

Yet we would not be doing justice to the magnitude of the changes that occurred in Czechoslovakia during 1989 if we mentioned only the change in the relationship between the party and the state, or the party and the international communist movement, or the communist party and the recognized headquarters of this movement (the USSR). Czechoslovakia at the threshold of the 1990s was about to embark on a new period of history. One of the first acts of the new government—the request that Soviet troops leave Czechoslovak territory—symbolized this new era and the will to seek a new place in Europe and the world.

The nature of the subject addressed by the present essay, however, requires that we should also focus on communist affairs. In this context, it means dealing with the developments in, and the activities of, the KSČ. What follows, therefore, is a summary account of the party's rule in all major sectors of public life during 1989. We nevertheless must keep in mind that with the surrender of power in early December of that year, the KSČ stopped determining the course of events in domestic and foreign affairs that traditionally constitutes the subdivisions of the individual ruling parties' profiles in this volume.

Party Internal Affairs. The KSČ entered what was to become the most fateful year in its seven decades of history burdened with two serious, virtually unsolvable problems. One, which had plagued the party since the Soviet-led military intervention against the reformist leadership of Alexander Dubček in August 1968, was a deep split in the party between those who had supported Dubček and those who backed, or participated in, the course imposed by the CPSU under Leonid Brezhnev. In addition, a great majority of parties in the international communist movement condemned the invasion and many, such as the Communist Party of Italy, continued to denounce it on every occasion. The party governance, with President Gustáv Husák and General Secretary Miloš Jakeš at the head, suffered throughout most of 1989 from the lack of a mandate in the eyes of the rank and file. This protracted legitimation crisis was considerably aggravated by the second problem, the change of the political line in Moscow in 1985 initiated by CPSU general secretary Mikhail S. Gorbachev. Soviet reforms, as it turned out, were similar to—if not more radical than—those of the 1968 Prague Spring. For more than three years, then, the KSČ policies have been in disagreement with those of its erstwhile model. Husák and his team were reluctant to follow the Soviet example not only because they disapproved of *perestroika* and *glasnost'*, but also— and above all—because they feared that adopting that course would remove the basis of their legitimacy. Opting for disagreement with the current Soviet line appeared to them to be a lesser evil. Nevertheless, it generated difficulties and contradictions of its own, which gradually worsened as the year advanced.

At the start of 1989, the Husák leadership seemed to think that it would be able to live with both problems. It may have also entertained the hope that the liberalization introduced by Gorbachev would soon reach its limits, these limits being the preservation of the communist party monopoly in the USSR as well as in the countries of the Soviet bloc. (They shared this assumption—and the ensuing surprise when it proved wrong—with many a hitherto highly reputed Western "expert" on Soviet and communist matters.) Thus they expected that the Brezhnev Doctrine would eventually be upheld, either by Gorbachev or by whoever replaced him, and that the line followed by the KSČ since April 1969 (when Gustáv Husák was appointed to the office of the general secretary) would be justified. There may have also been a hope that Gorbachev himself would be demoted by the CPSU should he stray too far from established Leninist principles.

The conservative leadership of the KSČ, however, had to face another problem that emerged in 1988 and gradually gained importance as 1989 progressed: the impact on Czechoslovakia of the political, economic, and social changes in the communist party-states in Czechoslovakia's immediate neighborhood (Poland, Hungary, and finally East Germany). From hindsight, it is probably these developments that most surprised the KSČ leaders. At any rate, it can be argued that the collapse of the totalitarian system in the three nations, especially East Germany, was the single most important external factor in the process of political and social change in Czechoslovakia during 1989.

The final outcome of this process—the virtual disappearance of the KSČ as a major force from the Czechoslovak political scene—was also to a considerable degree determined by the immobility of the party leadership in the face of domestic and international problems. Characteristic of the establishment's unwillingness to respond to the quickly deteriorating situation was the tenor of the ceremony commemorating the seizure of power by the KSČ in 1948 ("Victorious February"). The main speaker, Presidium member and head of the Prague party committee, Miroslav Štěpán, insisted in his speech on the respect of the "leading role of the party"— another term for power monopoly—as the condition of any dialogue with other groups or components of Czechoslovak society (*Rudé právo*, 24 February). Shortly afterward it was announced that the president of the republic, Gustáv Husák, had fallen ill (Radio Prague, 7 March). Speculation in the foreign press—that the illness might have been a political one preparing the way for Husák's eventual replacement—was denied by a Foreign Ministry spokesman as "completely unfounded" (ČTK, 9 March). Some observers believed that more significant changes would occur at the forthcoming Eighteenth Party Congress, citing as evidence that its date had been advanced from March 1991 to May 1990. However, events developed too fast to permit confirmation or refutation of this prognosis.

Activities of the party leadership during 1989, however, seemed to indicate the opposite. As late as October, in the draft of new party statutes, the claim to power monopoly was clearly upheld, although in the introduction of multiple candidacy for various party posts, the draft incorporated a few concessions to *perestroika* (*Rudé právo*, 31 October). The three meetings of the party's main governing body, the Central Committee, held in the course of the year did not suggest any willingness of the leaders to embark on a reform path. The first plenary session, during 30–31 March, dealt mainly with the problems of education. On this occasion, General Secretary Miloš Jakeš explicitly refused to rehabilitate or to reintegrate into the party previously expelled communists who had participated in the liberalization policies of 1968, notably Alexander Dubček (*Rudé právo*, 31 March). At the subsequent Central Committee plenum on 15 June, Jakeš reiterated the basically negative position of the KSČ on the idea of restructuring. This time, however, he admitted that among the rank and file there was "a widespread anxiety about the developments in Poland and Hungary" (*Rudé právo*, 14 June). Personnel changes made on this occasion did not modify in any way the conservative elements' control of the party. Even the Central Committee Third Plenum, held during 11–12 October, continued a line hostile to any meaningful change or improvement. Introducing minor changes in the composition of the party organs, the plenum also proposed a cut in the length of obligatory military service from 24 to 18 months, hoping that this would be interpreted as an acknowledgment of Gorbachev's disarmament initiatives (*Rudé právo*, 12 October). Seeking to identify possible representatives of a more liberal course among the KSČ leadership, foreign commentators followed with interest the statements of Presidium member and federal Prime Minister Ladislav Adamec. His view that a "proper assessment of Czechoslovakia's past" could no longer be postponed and that "an accurate picture of its history" was indispensable to future policies (Radio Prague, 22 February); his sharp criticism of the performance of the Council of Mutual Economic Assistance (Czechoslovak Television, 30 March); his candid admission that "most industrial sectors are lagging ten or more years behind the rest of the world" and that "Czechoslovakia has no economic reserves" (Radio Hvězda, 20 June); and his opinion that the Action Program of the liberal leadership under Alexander Dubček in 1968 contained "a whole series of positive elements" (Austrian Television, 20 October) made Adamec, in the eyes of certain observers, a suitable candidate for the role of future reformer. This expectation was only partly borne out by subsequent events.

On the whole, the ossified structures of the party and its leadership, entangled in a web of serious contradictions, proved incapable of adequate reaction to the trends manifest in most of the Soviet bloc. After the brutal repression of a peaceful manifestation by university students in Prague (17 November), on the 50th anniversary of the Nazi massacre of Czech students (see Domestic Affairs), the noncommunist majority rose up in a show of strength. Mass protests in the streets of Prague and other cities, involving hundreds of thousands of people, took place. Under this pressure, reinforced by an impressive two-hour general strike, the conservative leadership collapsed and offered its collective resignation on 24 November. Presidium member Karel Urbánek became general secretary (*Rudé právo*, 25 November). His tenure was short; in December, he was replaced by the chairman of the Socialist Youth Association, KSČ Secretariat member Vasil Mohorita, while Ladislav Adamec assumed the newly established function of party chairman, which had been abolished in the 1950s. The main press organ sadly commented that "the

party had deserted the people" and should therefore not be surprised if "the people turned its back on the party" (*Rudé právo*, 22 December).

The spectacular reshuffling in the party's top organs was followed by the most consequential step since the seizure of power in February 1948: on 29 November, the communist caucus in the Federal Assembly, still representing a two-thirds majority, voted together with the rest of the deputies to abolish the article in the constitution that guaranteed the leading role to the KSČ, thus relinquishing its power monopoly (Radio Prague, 29 November). On the same occasion, the KSČ majority supported elimination from the constitution of the clause requiring education in Czechoslovakia to be based on the principles of Marxism-Leninism.

These two acts profoundly changed the position of the KSČ in the society, as well as its self-image, but the party's woes were far from over. They did not heal the twenty-year split between the protagonists of reform policies in 1968 and the now demoted "normalizers" who owed their positions to Soviet military intervention and the Brezhnev Doctrine. Although offered rehabilitation and the possibility of return, supporters of the Prague Spring refused to come back. Their main representative, Alexander Dubček, was elected chairman of the Federal Assembly (ČTK, 28 December). He and his followers constituted an initiative group called Democratic Forum (as distinct from the Civic Forum, the coordinating platform for noncommunist groups during the November 1989 "velvet revolution"). Dubček's group made public its intention to wait until the Eighteenth Party Congress in May 1990 to make a decision about eventual merger, which would be contingent on KSČ willingness to adopt the most important elements of the Democratic Forum's program. Thus at the end of 1989 the KSČ, with a new leadership but many important seats in its governing organs vacant, faced the prospect of a split not dissimilar from that out of which it had been born nearly 70 years earlier.

Domestic Affairs. The "unassimilated past" of the KSČ, a radical shift in foreign and intrabloc policies of the Soviet Union, and the developments in other communist party-states of Central and Eastern Europe, although important in themselves, were only corollary conditions for a change of regime in Czechoslovakia. For the rest, the velvet revolution was carried out by domestic forces. The extent of the popular movement in November showed how deeply dissatisfied the citizens were with 40 years of communist rule. Reviewing the events of 1989 up to their dramatic climax, an observer might wonder why the power holders had not at least tried to forestall the outburst by making concessions in areas that did not immediately affect the privileged position of the KSČ. Signs of discontent abounded everywhere, but it would not have been impossible to placate some of them without endangering the party power monopoly.

One such instance was public concern over the environment. The ecological movement had grown steadily during the previous decade; its main press organ, *Nika*, was part of the nondaily media with the largest circulation in the country. In the dispute between ecologists and communist authorities, environmental risks connected with a large Czechoslovak-Hungarian power plant project on the Danube, between the towns of Gabčíkovo and Nagymaros (see *YICA*, 1989), provided a test case. After the Hungarian partner, under equal pressure from public opinion, withdrew from the project, a retreat on the Czechoslovak part would most likely not have caused too much harm to the KSČ's domestic image. Yet the regime chose to continue construction of the dam and to dismiss environmentalists' protest as "expressions of ecological hysteria" (*Rudé právo*, 13 April).

In areas where the leadership occasionally did respond to the popular will, its response was either too restricted or came too late. An example was the relationship between the state and the churches. Although an agreement had been reached with the Vatican on filling the vacant bishop seats in both republics (ČTK, 5, 26 July), the essential step—granting greater autonomy to the churches—was relegated to a new constitution, which meant a delay of at least two years in its implementation. More important, "democratization" was promised as part of this constitution (Ladislav Adamec at a railroad workers' rally in Temelín; *Rudé právo*, 21 September); the effect of this promise was greatly weakened for the same reason. "Greater participation in the legislative and governmental process" by noncommunist parties of the National Front was also declared to be a goal of the regime in 1989, but no concrete steps were undertaken (*Svobodné slovo*, 5 May; Prague, AFP, 13 October). Aware of public criticism about the red tape connected with obtaining passports and the allocation of foreign currency for travel, a reform of the relevant legislation was prepared and carried out; however, enforcement of the simplified regulations was postponed to January 1990 (Radio Hvězda, 21 September).

Hesitation, inconsistency, and slow reaction to events paired with intransigence concerning all ideas and initiatives that did not originate with the party or in KSČ-controlled groups and organizations were among the policies of the KSČ leadership. The regime for all practical purposes ignored the petition for religious freedom signed by some 350,000 persons during 1987 and 1988 (see *YICA*, 1989). In a similar way it disregarded a petition for political and economic reforms called "Just a Few Sentences" (*jen několik vět*) released on 29 June with eighteen hundred signatures; the document soon gathered close to twenty thousand supporters (Prague, Reuters, 30 June). Official media claimed that the petition called for the return of state-owned enterprises to their previous private owners, although nothing of the sort had been said in the text (Radio Prague, 30 June). General Secretary Jakeš accused the authors of the various petitions of "using methods of rude terror"; in his view their goal was "to scare society in order to prevent anybody from supporting the policy of the party" (*Rudé právo*, 18 July).

As the year advanced the authorities grew increasingly nervous about all manifestations of dissent. On two occasions, especially, they showed their apprehension by an extraordinary mobilization of all forms of the repressive apparatus: on the anniversaries of the suicide of Jan Palach (a student who on 15 January 1969 burned himself alive in protest against the Soviet invasion) and of the Soviet military intervention on 21 August 1968. A commemoration of the former planned by the Charter '77 group was forbidden by police; when about five thousand people nevertheless gathered in Prague, they were dispersed by force, and 91 demonstrators were apprehended. Police also prevented crowds from visiting Palach's grave in Všetaty, north of Prague. Individuals who later tried to deposit flowers on the spot where Palach had immolated himself were arrested and charged with hooliganism. Brutal acts of the regime provoked further demonstrations that lasted for almost a week (Prague, UPI; Reuters; 16 January; *Večerní Praha*, 17 January; Prague, DPA, 22 January). The 21st anniversary of the invasion, a politically sensitive date because a protest here signified the denial of legitimacy to the government, prompted all possible repressive measures. Yet despite police precautions—preventive custody of known dissidents, restrictions on travel by foreigners to Czechoslovakia, closing off parts of the capital city—about ten thousand people demonstrated against the Soviet intervention and continuing presence of the Red Army in Czechoslovakia (Prague, AFP, 21 August). Regime media abstained from giving the anniversary any prominence, so it was only the opposition that reminded the public of the event. The KSČ press charged that the protest had been instigated and organized by the Voice of America and Radio Free Europe, supposedly seeking "an internationalization of antisocialist provocations in Czechoslovakia" (Rudé právo, 22 August).

In the meantime independent initiative groups, even outspokenly political organizations, proliferated. Among these, three attracted special attention both at home and abroad because in their form and programs they came close to rudimentary political parties, possible bases for future pluralism. In February, Obroda (renewal), subtitled A Club for Socialist Restructuring, was constituted in Prague. Considering its professed goals and names of some of its leaders, it looked as if this group was a nucleus of the Czechoslovak Social Democratic party that had been forcibly absorbed by the KSČ after the coup d'état of 1948. Party-obedient media did not fail to recognize it as such and to denounce it (Rudé právo, 11 February). In October, members of the Czechoslovak People's party, part of the National Front, formed another group called Stream of Rebirth (Øbrodný proud). Its purpose was "to work at reintroducing Christian and democratic principles into political life" (Lidová demokracie, 16 October). Observers believed that Stream of Rebirth wished to replace the traditional People's party organization, tarnished by collaboration with the KSČ during the years of communist rule. Also in October, Democratic Initiative, a group founded in 1987, held a constituent conference in Prague and openly revealed its intention to be "a politically active force in Czechoslovakia" (RFE, Situation Report; Czechoslovakia, no. 20, 6 October). The regime tried to stem the spread of independent groups, threatening them with prosecution and substantial fines, especially for unauthorized publication activities, but to no avail. Party spokesmen admitted that independent groups could no longer be ignored. Jan Fojtík, chief KSČ ideologist, stated that "ideological and political offensives alone would not be sufficient to paralyze antisocialist forces" and that "a well thought-out tactic against these forces" would have to be developed (Radio Prague, 25 January). No such tactic, however,

was in evidence until the final confrontation in November.

The showdown was preceded by a series of demonstrations in Prague and other major cities. Of these, the one on Czechoslovak Independence Day, 28 October, appeared to be the largest; according to various estimates, as many as twenty thousand people participated in this event (Prague, Reuters, 29 October). The demonstrators were dispersed by brutally behaving police. Some 355 persons were arrested, among them 17 foreigners including citizens of neighboring communist-ruled states. When representatives of France, Great Britain, and the United States protested against the use of force, Czechoslovak authorities rejected their protests. Miroslav Štěpán, KSČ Presidium member and head of the Prague party committee, called the arrested individuals bandits and gangsters (Radio Prague, 1 November) and emphasized that any dialogue about democratization must be "conducted exclusively on the basis of party policy." To be sure, none of the official reactions was apt to improve the explosive climate, which some commentators likened to "a pile of firewood awaiting a suitable spark."

As already observed, an important catalyst in the developments at the end of 1989 was the events in neighboring communist-ruled countries, especially East Germany. The fall of the Honecker regime and the opening of the Berlin Wall undoubtedly emboldened the opposition in Czechoslovakia, which experienced the crisis of the East German communist regime on its territory, for it was from Czechoslovakia that large contingents of East German refugees departed for the Federal Republic immediately before the collapse of the Socialist Unity Party of Germany. The Czechoslovak regime made every effort to isolate the refugees in the West German embassy compound, but by early October the mass defections of East Germans via Prague had become a public secret (Czechoslovak Television, 28 September). Members of Czechoslovak dissident groups and others provided the refugees with food and clothing, and some even received them in their apartments, although this was forbidden by the police (Prague, Reuters, 4 October). Feelings among the Prague population were a mixture of sympathy or envy and regret that there was "no West Czechoslovakia for the Czechs and Slovaks to go" (Reuters, ibid.). Nevertheless, the political disintegration of the seemingly most solid Soviet satellite encouraged the independent movement in Czechoslovakia during the decisive days and weeks that followed.

By early November, Czechoslovakia had become the only communist party-state in the northwestern tier of the Soviet bloc that remained committed to the political course set by Leonid Brezhnev. However, not even this circumstance could prod the leaders seriously to consider political reforms. As late as 12 November, at the national conference of the Socialist Youth Union, General Secretary Miloš Jakeš affirmed that the party would never relinquish its "leading role" or tolerate street protests and organized opposition (*Rudé právo*, 13 November). It was, however, from among the young population that the proverbial spark was struck. Two weeks later, after a particularly savage beating of student demonstrators by police with scores of seriously wounded and even dead feared, a number of professional and cultural organizations led by the Union of Dramatic Artists publicly condemned the government. Surprisingly, the main party daily printed their protest on the front page (*Rudé právo*, 18 November). The executive committee of the Youth Union joined the protesters. Hundreds of thousands of people assembled in the streets of Prague calling for resignation of party and government leaders. They were soon followed by tens of thousands in other cities. The official media, especially television, publicized these demonstrations in great detail and thus helped spread the protest into all parts of the country. Under mounting pressure, the entire Presidium of the KSČ placed "its mandate at the disposal of the party" on 24 November. The government resigned after the prime minister, Ladislav Adamec, promised the representatives of the opposition, now formally constituted as the Civic Forum, that a new government would be formed in which the will of the people would be represented. On 27 November, a widely supported two-hour general strike took place (Radio Prague, 27 November). Two days later, the Federal Assembly abolished the article of the constitution giving the KSČ a privileged position ("leading role") (Czechoslovak Television, 29 November).

On 3 December, Ladislav Adamec presented to Gustáv Husák, the president of the republic, a new government in which five members were noncommunists, but sixteen were still appointed by the KSČ. Of the latter, thirteen had been ministers in the previous cabinet. The Civic Forum rejected this government, pointing to the fact that the "leading role" of the communist party had been abolished by the parliament and threatened new demonstrations and strikes if the demand for a cabinet with a noncommunist majority were not met. After several attempts to find a compromise, Adamec resigned as federal prime minister on 7 December (*NYT*, 4, 8 December). President Husák supported Adamec in his refusal to engage in "politics under pressure from the street" and declared that he would not yield to the call of the opposition for his resignation, but would remain in office until his mandate ran out in June 1990. However, an intensified wave of demonstrations coinciding with a declaration at a Warsaw Pact meeting that the military intervention of 1968 had been a violation of international law broke the last opposition of the conservatives. A new government with a noncommunist majority was formed by Marian Čalfa, member and official in the communist party of Slovakia, on 10 December (*NYT*, 11 December). Gustáv Husák resigned the presidency of the republic immediately after he swore in the Čalfa cabinet (Radio Prague, 10 December). About three weeks later, the Federal Assembly, where the KSČ still held a two-thirds majority, elected Václav Havel—the world-renowned playwright, former dissident and political prisoner, and head of the Civic Forum—as the first noncommunist president of Czechoslovakia in 41 years (*NYT*, 30 December).

One of the first acts of the new government was to submit a formal request to the USSR government for a withdrawal of all Soviet troops from Czechoslovakia by the end of 1990. Barbed wire and fortifications on the western borders (the Iron Curtain) were removed. Travel restrictions, censorship, and all limitations on freedom of assembly were rescinded. In the wake of the new freedoms, about 35 groups had registered by the end of the year as political parties. General elections were scheduled for 8 June 1990. The KSČ—or what is left of it by then—will, for the first time in 44 years, compete against other parties on an equal basis for the support of the electorate.

Culture, Youth, and Religion. The events of 1989 in Czechoslovakia testified to the importance of these three areas for politics in a communist party-state. Somewhat ironically, they also justified the apprehension and mistrust that the communist system had from the beginning shown toward these spheres of social life. The representatives of culture, youth, and religion have always been in the forefront of the struggle for more freedom. In 1989 they supplied an important contingent of leaders for the reform movement.

In January, 692 prominent Czechoslovak artists sent an open letter to federal prime minister

Ladislav Adamec protesting the arrest of Václav Havel and other participants in the commemorative ceremony for Jan Palach in Prague (Prague, UPI, 27 January). Another 360 artists joined this protest two weeks later (Prague, Reuters, 11 February). This initiative was countered by five hundred veteran members of the KSČ who claimed that the letter "spoke out against progress" and in favor of "rightist forces who aim at overturning the socialist development of society" (Rudé právo, 18 March). In August a group of Slovak intellectuals protested the trial in Bratislava of known dissidents, among them Miroslav Kusý and Jan Čarnogurský (Prague, PAP, 30 August). In October 110 Czechoslovak journalists petitioned Prime Minister Adamec to discontinue the criminal prosecution against the editors of the samizdat paper Lidové noviny (Prague, AP, 13 October). Film director Jiří Menzel, who signed the January petition of 692 artists in favor of the arrested participants in the Jan Palach ceremony, later gave an interview to the Paris daily Le Monde in which he denounced the persecution of Czech and Slovak writers and declared that he "could not remain silent while somebody like Havel, who deserves more respect than I do, has to be in prison" (Le Monde, 5 April). The funeral of well-known dissident and Slovak writer Dominik Tatarka in May provided an occasion for a great manifestation of solidarity with nonconformist artists. One thousand people, among them former KSČ leader Alexander Dubček, attended the services (Bratislava, AFP, 15 May). The artistic community was outraged when popular musician František Stárek was condemned to 30 months in prison for participating in unauthorized concerts and publishing the samizdat musical periodical Vokno (Window) (Prague, AP, 28 June). Apprised of the persecution of Czech and Slovak musicians, American singer Joan Baez, at a guest concert in Bratislava, performed a piece composed by Petr Cibulka, then awaiting trial for charges similar to those leveled against Stárek (Bratislava, AP, 11 June). It was viewed as a victory for independent music art when in July the authorities consented to register the group Art Forum (Prague, Reuters, 7 July). One of the founders of this group, Karel Srp, had been jailed because of his earlier part in setting up an independent jazz organization in 1984 (see YICA, 1988, 1989). Rock fans in Czechoslovakia were alerted to the interdependence between artistic freedom and civic freedom when Michael Kocáb, head of the band Výběr and publisher of the periodical Melodie, published an interview on this topic

in the samizdat periodical Lidové noviny (no. 6). In 1989 Kocáb started negotiations with the American rock music composer Frank Zappa about producing a joint album and about a proposed visit of Zappa to Prague, which eventually took place in January 1990 (Večerní praha, 19 January 1990). In the summer independent writers scored also when the Czechoslovak section of the International Association of Poets, Playwrights, Editors, Essayists and Novelists was reconstituted, eighteen years after its dissolution by the "normalizers." Many prominent nonconformists and dissidents became members and officials: Jiří Mucha (president), Václav Havel, Ivan Klíma, Karel Šiktanc, Zdeněk Urbánek, and others (Prague, Reuters, 1 August; ČTK, 2 August).

The community of Czech and Slovak writers and artists also actively participated in the "velvet revolution" and provided a pool from which many incumbents of public office were recruited. The role of the Union of Dramatic Artists in the mobilization of the public after the events of 17 November and the election of Václav Havel as president of the republic are two examples. In a similar way, the youth were an important foci of political action in those critical days. Undoubtedly meeting to perform or listen to rock music made it easier for the dissident youth leaders to bring many thousands of young people into the streets. However, even the official regime youth organization, the Socialist Youth Union, served as a basis for protest. Its press organ was the first to break obedience to the party, and its general secretary became the most outspoken critic of the conservative leadership. After the shakeup at the extraordinary congress in December, Vasil Mohorita became the new party leader.

As for religion 1989 brought some notable improvements in the situation of the churches and the believers. The protracted conflict with the Vatican over the nomination of bishops and archbishops had been settled before the November events. The traditional pilgrimages to Levoča in July and to Nitra in August were as impressively attended as ever, but there was much less obstruction and harassment on the part of the communist authorities. It was estimated that some 200,000 pilgrims traveled to Levoča (Kathpress, July 2), whereas about 50,000 believers came to Nitra (Bratislava, Reuters, 13 August). The most important religious event in 1989, however, was the canonization of Blessed Agnes of Bohemia in Rome in November. This ceremony, carried live by Czechoslovak Television, was the first time that official media had publicized such an event (Czechoslovak Television, 12 November). About ten thousand Czechs and Slovaks traveled to Rome for the occasion. Also present were a number of official and diplomatic representatives of Czechoslovakia, as well as the Czechoslovak primate, Cardinal František Tomášek, and other Czech and Slovak prelates. Tomášek was chosen by Pope John Paul II as one of the cocelebrators of the canonization mass (AP, 12 November).

Although the Catholic church was not directly involved in political life before and during the "velvet revolution," individual church dignitaries and believers, as well as clergymen and adherents of other Christian churches, actively participated in these events. The widely respected Cardinal Tomášek, who lived to the age of 90, expressed concern about "dangerous tension" developing in the country and "a growing number of citizens who demand a say in how the state is run" in a letter addressed to government officials that he also made available to various press agencies (East European Information Agency, VIA, 6 August). He also discussed the issue with federal first deputy prime minister Matej Lúčan (Smena, 8 August). When the first noncommunist majority government was formed under Marian Čalfa, one minister without portfolio was Richard Sacher, who represented Stream of Rebirth, the Catholic-inspired revival group in the Czechoslovak People's party (ČTK, in English, 10 December).

Dissidence. The year 1989 witnessed a peak of dissident activities in Czechoslovakia. Dissident initiatives—petitions, protests, memoranda to authorities, street manifestations, and independent publications—were more frequent than ever. Police repression also multiplied, but was rather inconsistent and patently inefficient. Some groups, such as Charter '77, and some individuals, such as playwright Václav Havel, continued to be targets of repressive measures. In addition to being ineffective, however, the persecution of dissidents also became counterproductive. For example, the repeated harassment, arrest, and condemnation of Havel during 1989 not only exacerbated public discontent, but prompted protests from important personalities and groups at home and abroad. The protesters were joined by groups, both official and unofficial, from communist countries such as Poland, Hungary, and East Germany (Budapest, *Mai nap*; DPA; 2 March; *Trybuna ludu*, 4 March). The wave of protests eventually made general secretary

Miloš Jakeš uneasy. At a meeting with party officials in Červený Hrádok in western Slovakia, he admitted that "arresting Havel served no purpose" and that the party "must not direct hits [*sic*] against him" (tape-recording made available to Western media; RFE, *Situation Report, Czechoslovakia*, no. 21). The regime tried various tactics to deal with the opposition during 1989. Although it did not cease labeling Charter '77 as an "anti-State group," it allowed a meeting between five signatories of the charter and the official Czechoslovak Committee for Human Rights. On this occasion committee representatives said that the Independent Peace Association, a dissident pacifist group, could participate in a working group for alternative military service (Radio Prague, 22 February) and could hold its monthly meetings without police interference (Prague, AP, 22 February). Occasionally, demonstrators were allowed to carry out their protests without police intervening: on 18 January, in the aftermath of the brutally repressed memorial demonstration for Jan Palach, a group of five thousand demonstrators gathered around the statue of St. Venceslas shouting "Freedom!" "We want to live like human beings!" and "Where is Havel?" (Prague, AP, 18 January). Yet the overall pattern of the government's reaction to dissidence was inconsistent, with the frequent use of force.

The tactics chosen by the conservative establishment to deal with the dissidence appear inadequate, whereas the strategy adopted by the dissidents proved suitable to the situation. The account of their confrontation in the critical days of November 1989 is the account of the "velvet revolution" itself (see the sections on party internal affairs and on domestic affairs). Those dissident circles then constituted the main source of candidates for governmental posts during the period of transition. The Civic Forum, for example, an umbrella for various dissident groups, was eminently suitable as a human talent reserve to be drawn on in the process of renewing democratic pluralism.

The Economy. Although the economic situation of Czechoslovakia in 1989 was relatively stable and better than in most communist party-states with the exception of East Germany, economic concerns played an important role in the process of political change. Ironically, the Jakeš leadership was willing, however grudgingly, to consider reforms in the economic sphere—where, in comparison with the USSR, they appeared less urgent—and refused to follow the Soviet example in the more crucial political area. In any event, the inseparable connection between the two was all the more so in Czechoslovakia's case because 80 percent of its exports and imports were oriented toward the countries of the Soviet bloc and its economy could not ignore those countries' reforms. Moreover, Czechoslovak economic experts, independent of the considerations of foreign trade, were pessimistic about the future of Czechoslovak industry and agriculture if a swift and vigorous modernization were not embarked on soon. The role of economists in the late 1980s was thus similar to that of their counterparts immediately preceding Prague Spring; however, the problems faced by the former appeared much more serious than those confronted by the latter, and the reforms contemplated by the former were much more radical departures from the economic system and principles of "real socialism" than that envisaged by the latter in 1968.

At the start of the year, Czechoslovak State Bank president Jan Mitro announced that several large Czechoslovak industrial corporations were insolvent and that 38 of them would have to be "restructured." The total insolvency was estimated to be the equivalent of US $1.5 billion (Radio Prague, 10 January). Mitro's statement was confirmed by Prime Minister Ladislav Adamec, who indicated that entire branches of heavy industry would have to be phased out of operation, which might cause unemployment (Czechoslovak Television, 11 January). In an interview with Reuters news agency, Secretary of the Committee for Planned Management Jaromír Matějka made a still more pessimistic assessment: according to him, no less than 30 percent of Czechoslovak industry was "hopelessly uneconomic and fit only for closure or complete overhaul" (Prague, Reuters, 29 August). The general situation of the Czechoslovak economy was also the subject of an extensive report by Prime Minister Adamec to the Federal Assembly in June in which he stated that no substantial improvement of the economic situation could be expected during the current five-year plan (1986–1990) and that the growth in domestic net product would be below the target figures. Adamec also disclosed that financing social programs could become a problem and that the country could not afford to live beyond its means. One main difficulty of the enterprises, according to Adamec, was the underutilization of working time, as little as 75 percent. Adamec, however, did not mention changing the system of ownership and management as a possible remedy (Radio Hvězda, 20 June). Public opinion, in con-

trast, seemed aware of this possible avenue of reform. A government-sponsored opinion poll carried out in 1989 revealed that a majority of Czechoslovak citizens rated capitalism higher than socialism, as far as the ability of the two systems to provide food, industrial goods, science and technology was concerned (Radio Prague, 15 October).

Expert opinion did not differ from that of the general public except it was supported by hard data. In the course of the year several detailed evaluations of Czechoslovakia's economy and its prospects for use by governmental and planning agencies found their way into the media. Two such studies attracted wide attention. The first, developed by a group of economists led by Valtr Komárek, director of the Forecasting Institute of the Academy of Sciences, was titled "Detailed Forecasts About the Czechoslovak Socialist Republic Until 2010," and was later incorporated in a more general document submitted by the State Planning Commission to the Presidium of the KSČ. The criticism of the current economic situation was so sharp and the reforms so radical in this document that the Presidium "suspended its approval" (Radio Hvězda, 23 June), which was tantamount to a rejection. Komárek and his associates argued that unless market forces were allowed to play a role in the Czechoslovak economy, Czechoslovakia would sink to the level of the Third World. Even more provocative was their call for a "division of powers" in the country, allowing for the autonomy of the political and economic spheres (RFE, Research, 21 June, 5 July), a clear recommendation to abandon political criteria in the management of the economy. Their conservative opponents were not far off the mark when they accused Komárek of promoting "a change in the social basis of the society" (East European Market, 7 April). The reformers countered by pointing to the "illusion of pastoral idyll of a secluded Czechoslovakia governed by the economic laws of socialism," an image that in their opinion had already collapsed "under the weight of historic facts" (Politická ekonomie, no. 5).

The second document concerning the Czechoslovak economy to stir professional circles as well as public ones was an analysis by Miloš Zeman, head of the Economic Institute's Department for Forecasting, that appeared in the monthly Technický magazin (no. 8, August). This study became widely known when Zeman explained its main contents in a television interview (Czechoslovak Television, 25 August). Zeman's facts were bleak: during 40 years of communist rule, Czechoslovakia had dropped from 10th place to 40th place among the industrial powers of the world; in the development of professional skills, measured by the pace of change in the educational system, it had dropped to 50th place, behind the Himalayan state of Nepal; it has one of the lowest adult life expectancy rates; and 30 percent of its environment is devastated by pollution. For this nearly catastrophic state of things, Zeman blamed the political system introduced by the KSČ after the coup d'état in 1948. Zeman's criticism transcended the purely economic realm and became a plea for radical political reform as the only means of economic revival. Although the television management called his views "extreme" (Czechoslovak Television, 28 August), their impact was considerable and brought down the wrath of the power holders on his head. Early November, it was reported that Zeman had been dismissed from his post at the Economic Institute (Prague, Reuters, 1 November).

Meanwhile the leadership of the KSČ pursued its own economic reform, little more than cosmetic changes. In October the two houses of the Federal Assembly discussed the implementation of the new economic laws; the economy and the environment were also on the agenda of the KSČ Central Committee plenum, held at the same time (Radio Prague, 10 October; Rudé právo, 12 October). Economic indicators did not suggest much progress; for example, the midyear economic report of the Federal Statistical Office showed that the targets of the economic plan had not been reached in any major sector. Only 47.1 percent of the scientific and technical projects had been completed. Labor productivity increased only by 1.4 percent. The goal of reducing the exports to nonsocialist countries had not been reached (Czechoslovak Television, 19 July). Prime Minister Adamec commented that the government restricted itself to describing the problems instead of solving them. "We are losing our battle," said Adamec. (Rudé právo, 20 July.)

Indeed, within the following four months, the regime lost not only the economic battle but also the political one. Reformist economists were vindicated, and it was from their center that the cadres of the new nation's leadership were partly recruited. Marian Čalfa's cabinet, sworn in 10 December, included Valtr Komárek as first deputy premier and two of his close collaborators, Vladimír Dlouhý and Václav Klaus, as the deputy premier for the State Planning Commission and the federal minister of finance, respectively. They inherited the Herculean task of leading the Czechoslovak economy out of the crisis caused by 40 years of dogmatic experiments (NYT, 12 December).

Foreign Affairs. In 1989, the conservative regime had maneuvered itself into an absurd foreign relations situation. Although contacts with the United States, the European West, and the neutral nations of the world continued to be cool, the relations with the other communist party-states, notably those in Czechoslovakia's neighborhood, deteriorated rapidly, partly because these nations, societies, and communist parties were moving away from the "real Socialism" model of the Brezhnev era. The Jakeš team perceived that its strength depended on the solidarity of the regimes in the northwestern tier of the Soviet bloc and on the Soviet Union. However, increasing disharmony between the political course adopted by the CPSU and the Soviet Union on the one hand and that pursued by the KSČ and the Czechoslovak government on the other was aggravated by the rapid change of the political systems in Poland, Hungary, and, since October 1989, East Germany. Czechoslovak communists were apprehensive lest "anti-Socialist ideas" be smuggled into the country via the "fraternal channels" from Eastern Europe or that "anti-Socialist forces" at home be encouraged by the democratization of the political life in that region. These apprehensions increased the earlier, sometimes economic tensions among the "fraternal nations" of the Warsaw Pact. For example, the disagreement between Czechoslovakia and Hungary about the future of the power plant project Gabčíkovo-Nagymaros (see the section on domestic affairs) and the measures taken by Czechoslovak authorities to restrict purchases of consumer items in Czechoslovakia by visitors from Poland and the Soviet Union fueled the ideological differences (Radio Prague, 12 May; Radio Budapest, 14 May). The conflict became even more serious when Czechoslovakia's allies proceeded to re-evaluate their past, especially their role in the Soviet-led military intervention against the reformist leadership of Alexander Dubček in 1968. When a delegation of the Polish parliament, including representatives of Solidarity, visited Czechoslovakia in July, KSČ media accused the Poles of wishing "to force our country to adopt Polish-style reforms and into economic anarchy" and of aiming "to re-evaluate the period at the end of the 1960s," which could lead only to disorder and chaos (Rudé právo, 27 July). An open crisis in the relations between Czechoslovakia on the one hand and Poland and Hungary on the other broke out when the parliaments of Poland and Hungary voted to condemn the participation of their own troops in the 1968 invasion and presented an apology "to the people of Czechoslovakia." The Presidium of the KSČ and the Federal Assembly responded by a warning that these moves "were helping anti-Socialist forces" (ČTK, 17 August). The party ideological weekly *Tribuna* labeled the political and economic changes in Poland and Hungary—and implicitly those in the Soviet Union—as a "sell-out of Socialism" (nos. 35 and 36, 6, 13 September). The regime was also irritated by the signs of sympathy that were shown to Czechoslovak dissidents by these two countries, not only by independent groups but also by leading personalities such as Polish premier Mazowiecki and the Hungarian party leader Imre Pozsgay (PAP, 8 September; MTI, 9 September).

The contacts with the West and the Third World also suffered from the repercussions of the stormy events in Central Europe. Because Czechoslovakia was for several weeks the theater of the largest exodus from East Germany, negotiations with the Federal Republic of Germany (FRG) on this point were inevitable. Regime spokesmen accused the FRG of trying to "profit from this occurrence to undermine the stability in this region" (Radio Prague, 26 September; Czechoslovak Television, 28 September; ČTK, 29 September). The issue was settled by Foreign Minister Jaromír Johanes in talks in New York with his West German counterpart, Hans-Dietrich Genscher (New York, DPA, 26 September). While in New York, Johanes also met with U.S. secretary of state James Baker. Baker told Johanes that relations between the United States and Czechoslovakia could improve only if there were "a substantial improvement in the human rights situation" (*NYT*, 28 September). The interest of the Bush administration in Czechoslovakia was documented by the appointment of Shirley Temple Black as ambassador to Prague. She presented her credentials to President Husák, observing wryly that her last visit in the Czechoslovak capital had been "under somewhat different circumstances" (i.e., 21 August 1968, the day of the Soviet invasion) (*NYT*, 23 August).

Foreign Trade and Debt. One difficult problem besetting Czechoslovak foreign trade in 1989 was its lopsided orientation, with nearly 80 percent of exchanges being with communist countries out of which more than 60 percent is with member nations of the Council for Mutual Economic Assistance (CMEA). Although this had been an almost explicit goal of foreign trade policies after 1950, in recent years a correction was considered desirable (one reason for the change of mind might have been political: too much dependency on communist party-states might have appeared dangerous to the regime because CMEA members could go the way of "abandoning Socialism" and "contaminate Czechoslovakia with their heresies"). The statistical figures published in the summer indicated that the reorientation was slow in coming: turnover with CMEA dropped by only 0.2 percent, and the CMEA share of Czechoslovak foreign trade was still 61.9 percent, as compared with 64.6 percent in 1988 (*Rudé právo*, 22 July).

Closely connected with the problem of the orientation of foreign trade was that of payment balance. Hard currency, for obvious reasons, had been in short supply for decades. Czechoslovakia's foreign debt, amounting to more than US $12 billion (in all currencies), was relatively low, especially in comparison with Hungary and Poland, but it remained unchanged through 1989 (Radio Prague, 20 June; *Rudé právo*, 11 November). To facilitate the foreign payments situation, either Western credits or the free convertibility of the Czechoslovak koruna would be necessary. The possibility of the latter was discussed in the KSČ Presidium in the spring, when a law about hard currency transactions was being drafted; convertibility was declared to be the ultimate aim (*Rudé právo*, 25 March). Czechoslovakia also started negotiating with the International Monetary Fund and the World Bank about renewing its membership in those two bodies (Radio Prague, 30 May), with a view to applying for credits to modernize industrial production. However, the call of some economists for more direct credits from Western banks and corporations was rejected (*Rudé právo*, 25 July); "world Socialism can consolidate itself and achieve new prosperity without help or direct gifts from capitalism." Estimates of the need of the Czechoslovak economy, however, spoke a different language; a thorough revitalization of industry alone would cost about US $20–$30 billion (*The Economist*, 29 July). Considering that the nation's gross debt to Western banks is about US $4.5 billion (only a fraction of the debt incurred by Poland, for example), there seems to be room for further borrowing. This will have to be decided by the new government.

International Communist Movement. The last year in which the KSČ was a ruling party was also the year of the greatest upheavals not only in the communist parties of Central and Eastern Europe and of the USSR, but also in the parties of the West and the developing countries. The tumultuous transformations were prompted by the change in the perspective and the policies of the recognized center of the movement, the Communist Party of the Soviet Union. As pointed out earlier, this development considerably speeded up the spectacular political and social transformations in Czechoslovakia in 1989. The ongoing change in the communist world, however, also caused a whole series of problems and difficulties for the KSČ, especially because its leadership until November determinedly opposed all reform. In 1989 the KSČ was in conflict with all major communist parties, East and West. Its strategy for survival—which did not work—was built on the assumption that the key component of the northwestern tier of the system, East Germany, would hold. Events belied this theory. The one bright moment for the conservative KSČ leadership may have been when a conservative regime was reinstated in China in June. Official media, although it began with a somewhat balanced coverage of the Beijing demonstrations (*Rudé právo*, 29 May), soon fully adopted the language of the Chinese conservatives and argued that the measures against the students were correct. "The Chinese party leadership had shown more than enough patience. The unrest has aimed at overthrowing the Socialist order." (Czechoslovak Television, 7 June; *Rudé právo*, 14 June.)

Almost simultaneously, a mass demonstration took place in Budapest on the occasion of the reburial of Imre Nagy, Hungarian prime minister in 1956 who was executed by the Soviets in 1958. This climate was not to the liking of the KSČ leadership, which correctly sensed it as a sign of further liberalization in Hungary. Shortly before, at the plenary session of the Central Committee, General Secretary Jakeš expressed his fears about further developments in Poland and Hungary and "negative elements that accompany restructuring" in these two countries (Radio Hvězda, 14 June). Party chief ideologist Jan Fojtík said that "counterrevolutionary forces are standing under the banner proclaiming the regeneration of Socialism" and that "this is happening in neighboring Hungary" (Radio Hvězda, 16 June). Hungarian foreign minister Gyula Horn rejected Fojtík's statement as "an interference in the internal affairs of Hungary" that was incomprehensible and unacceptable (MTI, in English, 17 June). The dispute between the KSČ and the "fraternal

parties" north and south of the Czechoslovak border intensified as the year advanced, reaching its peak with the already mentioned repudiation of the 1968 military intervention on the part of the Polish and Hungarian legislative organs. When the Berlin Wall came down and the conservative KSČ leadership lost its most reliable ally, its strategy was in a disarray. History did not give it a chance, however, to show how it would have handled the tearing down of the Berlin Wall, which happened at the same time (November) that the entire Warsaw Pact Council condemned the 1968 invasion and the Brezhnev Doctrine. In any case it probably would have administered the coup de grace to the "normalization" course; as things turned out, it was only the finishing stroke to the political career of Gustáv Husák.

At the end of the year, the relation of the Communist Party of Czechoslovakia to the rest of the international communist movement had changed profoundly, but was not less complicated. Questions of all kinds emerged: What is the future of the KSČ? With which parties, if any, will it associate in the days to come? Will there be a world radical socialist movement, similar in ideological orientation and internal discipline to the one we have known? The KSČ, if it is to survive, will have to answer these questions and wait to see what others emerge. One thing is certain: it will no longer be a ruling party, but a legal one at best.

Zdeněk Suda
University of Pittsburgh

Germany
German Democratic Republic

Population. 16,586,490 (July 1989)
Note. In December 1989 the Sozialistische Einheitspartei Deutschlands added Partei des Demokratischen Sozialismus to its name. The Politburo, Secretariat, Central Committee, and office of general secretary were abolished at the De-

cember congress and replaced with the structure outlined below.

Party. Socialist Unity Party of Germany–Party of Democratic Socialists (Sozialistische Einheitspartei Deutschlands–Partei des Demokratischen Sozialismus, SED-PDS)

Founded. 1918 (SED, 1946; SED-PDS, 1989)

Membership. 1 million claimed (*Pravda*, 28 January 1990; *FBIS-SOV*, 7 February 1990)

Party Chairman. Dr. Gregor Gysi (41)

Party Deputy Leaders. Hans Modrow (61), prime minister; Wolfgang Berghofer, head of the commission on the political system, mayor of Dresden; Wolfgang Pohl, head of the commission on organization and party life; (to be named) head of the commission on economic and social policy

Presidium of the Party Governing Board. Monika Werner, head of the party delegation in the Volkskammer; Marlies Deneke, head of the commission for youth and women's policy; Lothar Bisky, head of the commission on the press and media, temporary head of the commission for education; Klaus Höpcke, head of the commission for culture and science; Hans-Joachim Willerding, head of the commission for international affairs; Helmar Hegewald, head of the commission for Third World policy

Arbitration Committee. Günter Weiland, chairman. Members: Günter Auerbach, member of a district council; Gisela Braun, collective farm worker; Karl-Heinz Eife, section manager; Steffan Flachs, officer; Ralf Förster, economic manager; Werner Fraenkler, party secretary; Michael Giese, planning head; Manfred Günther, museum director; Jochen Kretchmer, actor; Doris Lange, section manager for post office; Gerhard Lauter, officer; Joachim Lochmann, factory manger; Werner Müller, worker in an agricultural chemical center.

Party Managing Board. 99 full members

Status. Ruling party

Last Congress. Extraordinary Congress, 8 December

Publications. *Neues Deutschland*, Wolfgang Spickermann, editor in chief; *Einheit*; *Neuer Weg*. The official news agency is Allgemeiner Deutscher Nachrichtendienst (ADN).

The flight of hundreds of thousands of East German citizens to the Federal Republic and West Berlin in the last months of 1989, along with mass public protests, overshadowed all other developments in the GDR (German Democratic Republic). At the end of the year the leadership's inability to solve the country's problems led to the collapse of the Socialist Unity Party (SED). The power vacuum that developed was filled by a host of new political organizations and a call for free elections early next year.

At the beginning of the year the Erich Honecker regime continued to deny, as it had throughout 1988, that pressure for change and reform was growing in the GDR. On the surface, especially during the first half of 1989, the party adamantly set its face against reform. The central leadership seemed firmly in control and the major institutions of the country secure and entrenched. The security police force was among the most efficient and ruthless in the communist world. The GDR's economy, although showing some signs of weakness, continued to be the most successful in the Eastern bloc. In Eastern Europe the SED was second only to Romania in the high ratio of party membership to population size.

Despite the obvious strengths of the regime, there were some disturbing signs. Disaffection and pressure for reform had been growing throughout 1988 and continued into the new year. The dissatisfaction centered on shortcomings in the economy, continuing religious persecution, human rights issues, travel and emigration restrictions, and a deteriorating environment. The leadership also found itself increasingly out of step with the pace and direction of change in the Soviet Union and Eastern Europe.

Nonetheless, the difficulties and tensions that faced the regime at the beginning of 1989 provided no indication of the revolutionary and disintegrative events that were to follow. The Honecker leadership well understood the extraordinary dangers that GDR versions of *glasnost'* and *perestroika* posed for the survival of its socialist system. In adopting what must have seemed the necessary hard-line, however, it paid a disastrous price in increasing isolation both at home and abroad. The leadership attempted to maintain its established policy of conservative adaptation to the new situation that was emerging in Eastern Europe. Although it tried to improve its relations with the Federal Republic (FRG) and the European Community, these efforts first faltered and then failed altogether during the course of the year.

The GDR's institutional structure proved fragile to an extent that surprised all observers. The political and social consolidation and growing self-confidence that seemed to characterize the GDR in the years following the erection of the Berlin Wall in 1961 collapsed in a few weeks during October and November. The structure, political culture, and policy agenda of the most successful "developed socialist" society in the communist world all proved shallow and ultimately as dependent on Soviet backing as at any time in the GDR's history. When faced with an internal crisis, an accelerating process of change elsewhere in Eastern Europe, and a Soviet Union unwilling to offer unqualified support, the entire structure was swept away in an astonishingly short time.

In October the leadership of Honecker disintegrated; by the end of the year the party was unable to control events or even to maintain itself in power. Those who had argued that the GDR's version of socialism was too fragile and too poorly rooted to sponsor or even survive far-reaching reform were vindicated. The Berlin Wall symbolized the regime's determination to preserve the identity of the GDR and protect its socialist principles; Honecker had promised it would remain for "fifty or a hundred years" (*ND*, 20 January). When it did come down the future of the GDR was cast into doubt. The last remnants of the old order are likely to be swept away in the free elections now scheduled for 18 March.

Leadership and Party Organization. A drive to improve the quality of the party was announced at the beginning of the year; to that end there was to be a renewal of party cards in December (*FBIS*, 27 January). Although the party had reported losses in membership since 1987 (*FBIS*, 18 January; *Informationen* 2, 27 January), it was not until the crisis of October and November that the SED began its precipitous decline. On 25 November *Neues Deutschland* reported that between the end of September and the end of November the SED had lost 10 percent of its membership. The report went on to warn that the erosion would deepen in the light of the revelations concerning widespread corruption among party officials (*ND*, 25 November). In December defections rose further. Because members simply handed in their cards and walked away from the party, no one could be sure from day to day how much attrition had taken place. Estimates on the losses since September ranged between 600,000 (*LAT*, 10 December) and 1,000,000 (*NYT*, 8 December).

Honecker's leadership was secure at the end of 1988, but the new year saw renewed speculation about the aging general secretary's political future

(*YICA*, 1989). In 1989 there was evidence that the leadership's rejection of *glasnost'* and *perestroika* had become a source of tension in the party (Jörg-Peter Mentzel, "Perestroika in der DDR?" *Beiträge zur Politische Bildung* 10/1), and there were some indications that the issue of reform threatened the coalition of hard-line and pragmatic tendencies that Honecker had so far managed to hold together.

Die Troika, a book by Markus ("Mischa") Wolf, the GDR's former intelligence chief, appeared early in the year and caused something of a sensation. The book indicated that Wolf was an admirer of *glasnost'* and that his surprise resignation in 1988 had been at least partly motivated by his rejection of the SED's cautious approach to reform (*Der Spiegel*, 2 January; *FBIS*, 9 January; RFE, 12 April; *Informationen*, 28 April; *YICA*, 1989). More ominously for the political security of the leadership, other divisions began to appear within the party as many lower-level functionaries openly expressed support for Mikhail Gorbachev's ideas (*NYT*, 8 March). In November 1988 the banning of the Soviet magazine *Sputnik* occasioned demonstrations and strikes in Berlin, Jena, Halle, and Weimar, followed by widespread disaffection within the party and resignations of party officials (*Süddeutsche Zeitung*, 11 January). The on-again, off-again banning of Soviet publications and films during the first half of the year was an indication of differences within the party on the issue of *glasnost'* as well as the leadership's uncertainty as it attempted to maintain a coherent policy. The party's problems with *glasnost'* were also apparent in the pages of the GDR's scholarly and theoretical journals, which failed to support the leadership's rejection of Soviet-style reforms for the GDR (*Warsaw, Polityka*, 31 January; *JPRS*, 15 February).

The slogan for the party was Socialism in the GDR's Own Colors, and the old idea of a "separate German road to socialism," which had been the slogan of the German communists between 1946 and 1948, was dusted off once more (*ND*, 10 July; *Einheit* 1; RFE/RL, 28 July). Honecker's often-repeated claims that the GDR represented the leading edge of the creative development of socialism and that there was no need to follow the course set by the Soviet Union, Poland, and Hungary were greeted by increasing skepticism not only among the population but within the party as well.

Speculation concerning Honecker's political future intensified as it became apparent that his health was deteriorating. On 8 July, during a Warsaw Pact summit in Bucharest, Honecker was suddenly taken to the hospital. The official explanation was that he suffered from a minor gallbladder problem (ADN, 9 July), but this did not quash the rumors, which were current for the rest of his term in office, that he was seriously ill with cancer. A change in leadership appeared imminent when, on 18 August, Honecker re-entered the hospital for major and reportedly unsuccessful abdominal surgery (*NYT*, 31 August).

The prospect of a succession offered little hope for resolving the deepening social, political, and economic problems that faced the party. More than one-third of the membership of the Politburo was made up of men in their 70s, with Erich Mielke, the minister of state security, the most senior at 81. Mielke had been minister of state security in 1953, the time of the Berlin uprising. His continued presence within the leadership symbolized how isolated and inflexible the party had become.

Egon Krenz, Central Committee secretary for state security, had long been considered as the man most likely to take over from Honecker. Although at 52 he was the youngest member of the Politburo, he did not offer new alternatives. In fact many observers considered Krenz even less flexible than Honecker on the question of reform (for a short biography of Egon Krenz, see *RAD Background Report*, RFE/RL, 20 October; *ND*, 19 October) and felt that he would have little chance of restoring the credibility of the system in the eyes of the growing opposition and reform movements. Krenz had a reputation as a tough-minded, shrewd, and able conservative, and events earlier in the year had done nothing to soften his image. In his capacity as chairman of the electoral commission, he allegedly falsified the results of the regional and district elections of 7 May. Going further than any of his colleagues, it was Krenz who sent a message on behalf of the Politburo congratulating the Chinese leaders on their suppression of the prodemocracy movement (*NYT*, 20 November). (All such favorable commentaries on the Chinese events were transparent warnings that draconian measures might be undertaken against the GDR's own opposition.) (On the SED's position on the Beijing events, see also *FBIS*, 9 June; *ND*, 5 June; *Junge Welt*, 6 June.)

As of the middle of September, Günter Schabowski, the first secretary of the East Berlin regional SED executive, was viewed by some as offering hope for a new, more reform-oriented leadership. Although a close supporter of Honecker in the past, of all the principal leaders Schabowski was on the best political and personal terms with the Soviet leaders. During an official visit to Moscow, he openly voiced his approval of Soviet policies and was thought to be Moscow's choice for the leadership. (*NYT*, 20 July; *WSJ*, 5 September.) Moscow's preferences, however, were not necessarily an asset in the crisis that faced the party.

Other possible contenders were Siegfried Lorenz, party secretary for Karl-Marx-Stadt, and Hans Modrow, first secretary in Dresden. Modrow, who enjoyed the confidence of Moscow (*NYT*, 20 July), had gained a reputation as a clear-sighted and flexible leader. Not a member of the Politburo, he was unpopular with Honecker because of his reputation as a party liberal (for a short biography of Modrow, see *NYT*; *ND*, 14 November). At the SED Central Committee's Eighth Plenum 22–23 June in East Berlin, the Dresden party organization was under pressure to work harder to resist reforms and to stick closer to the principles of democratic centralism. (*ND*, 23–25 June.)

The first round in the leadership succession ended in October as the crisis in the country came to a head. At the beginning of the month, Honecker returned to active public life from his convalescence to preside over the festivities marking the GDR's 40th anniversary, scheduled for 6–7 October. The celebrations, which did nothing to alter the atmosphere of social disintegration, were marred by the thousands of people who took to the streets in Berlin, Leipzig, and Dresden. Some of the protests led to violence and brutal police repression (*NYT*, 8 October). The presence of Gorbachev, who had come to Berlin for the anniversary, added to Honecker's difficulties, for the Soviet leader could not disguise his support for those in the party who saw the need for reform (*RAD Background Report*, RFE, 19 October; *WP*, 8 October).

Even after the embarrassments of the 40th anniversary, Honecker appeared set against concessions, and there were intimations that he had decided on a Tiananmen Square solution to the regime's problems. (After the fact, leading SED officials revealed that Honecker had signed an order for the police in Leipzig to use force to break up the demonstrations, which took place on 9 October when an estimated 70,000 people took to the streets. Egon Krenz later claimed that it was his personal intervention that reversed the decision [RFE/RL, 20 October]; however, his reputation as the man who over two years had led the campaign of repression stood in the way of his gaining much from this intervention.)

As further evidence of the possibility of violent

repression, Honecker held talks with visiting Chinese deputy prime minister Yao Yilin on 9 October while the Leipzig demonstrations were under way. According to reports from ADN, the two leaders had agreed that "there was a fundamental lesson to be learned from counter-revolutionary unrest in Beijing for the present campaign against the GDR and other socialist states."

In mid-October, against the background of massive protest rallies in Leipzig and other major centers, Honecker, in a desperate bid to retain the leadership and to find a way out of the crisis, opened a dialogue on social and economic reform with the official minority parties (the Democratic Peasants' party, the Christian Democratic Union, the Liberal Democratic party, and the National party). Honecker promised that new policy proposals would be forthcoming from the Central Committee in November (*NYT*, 14 October). Although this was the first time that Honecker had spoken openly of the need for reform, he stopped short of making overtures to the opposition or suggesting that the party would be willing to share power with noncommunists.

Honecker's belated efforts to restate the SED's strategy did not dampen the public's enthusiasm for reform or consolidate his deteriorating position within the leadership. On 18 October, following what was reported as protracted and heated discussion within the Politburo on the leadership and reform issues, Honecker resigned and named Egon Krenz to succeed him as general secretary, president of the GDR, and chief of the Defense Council. Two of Honecker's closest allies, Günter Mittag, Central Committee secretary for economic affairs, and Joachim Hermann, Central Committee secretary for agitation and propaganda, also stepped down; otherwise there were no Politburo changes. (*ND*, 19 October.)

The stewardship of Egon Krenz was destined to be a short-lived transition on the way to a completely restructured political system. An uncertain but ever-escalating demand for change came directly from the streets in an avalanche of public protest that reached a scale without precedent in modern European history. The disintegrating economy, the continuing flood of emigration, and the refusal of the public to see Krenz as its savior ruled out reconsolidation. During November and early December, a host of regional party leaders resigned and the party's membership shrank, according to the most conservative estimates, by 600,000, or 25 percent, between October and early December

(*LAT*, 10 December). On 7 November, Willi Stoph, chairman of the Council of Ministers, and the entire government resigned (*ND*, 8 November). On 8 November, the Politburo, at the beginning of an emergency meeting of the Central Committee, also resigned. The new Politburo was reduced from 21 full members to 11. Of the sixteen full and candidate members in the restructured Politburo, seven were new appointments. Of these, three—Hans Modrow, Wolfgang Rauchfuss, and Wolfgang Herger—were new full members, and one—Gerhard Schuerer—was promoted from candidate status. (*ND*; *NYT*, 9 November.)

At the end of its emergency meeting, the Central Committee announced a new Action Program that promised

1. A new election law that would guarantee free and democratic elections
2. A guarantee of the free exercise of the constitutional powers of the Volkskammer and all elected bodies
3. The formation of a democratic coalition government
4. The introduction of a new constitutional court system, along with legal and judicial reforms, including laws to protect the freedom of the press
5. The abolition of privileges of SED officials that were not justified by performance
6. The substitution of civilian for military service for all conscientious objectors
7. The introduction of comprehensive economic reforms that were to be guided by market conditions
8. The priority production of consumer goods
9. Revisions of the educational law
10. The restoration of internal democracy within the SED (*ND*, 9 November.)

On 13 November, Hans Modrow was elected prime minister (*ND*, 14 November), and for the first time the Volkskammer elected a noncommunist, Günter Maleuda, leader of the Democratic Peasants' Party, as its president (*ND*, 14 November). On 17 November a new government built on a coalition with the four communist-allied parties was announced. The SED's coalition partners obtained 11 out of 27 seats (down from 44); the communists retained the Defense, Interior, and Foreign ministries. (*ND*, 20 November.)

In the last difficult weeks, the Krenz leadership tried desperately to align itself with the process of democratic renewal, but could do little but react to the storm of popular demands. The center of power had shifted to the streets of Leipzig, Berlin, and other major cities. New political movements and parties formed overnight, and the party made no effort to stand in the way. There was a flood of resignations and dismissals of regional party officials. In Halle, Hans-Joachim Böhme was removed as first secretary; in the district of Cottbus, Werner Waldek was dismissed; the mayor of Stralsund, Horst Lehman, resigned; Gerhard Müller was dismissed as district party chief in Erfurt; the entire Secretariat in Rostock district resigned; and Siegfried Lorenz was removed from his post as first secretary in Karl-Marx-Stadt. (*ND*, 9–15 November.) On 14 November, Annelis Kimmel, the head of the Federation of Trade Unions (FDGB), announced that the FDGB was severing its official ties with the SED and that she wanted the leading role of the party to be abolished (ADN, 14 November). At the end of November the Free German Youth Movement (FDJ) also disassociated itself from the party and embraced democratic reform (*NYT*, 27 November).

The new leadership conceded what would have been unthinkable only a few weeks earlier and announced head-spinning reforms almost daily. The opposition organization, New Forum, was legalized. Restrictions on the press were dismantled, travel restrictions were removed on 9 November, and the Berlin Wall was opened. (*ND*, 9 November.) The SED renounced its monopoly of power, a move legalized by the People's Chamber on 1 December (*NYT*, 1 December). The security police were to be reduced and renamed (*NYT*, 18 November), and an emergency party congress was called for 15–17 December with a mandate to democratize and restructure the SED (*ND*, 9 November).

Krenz survived as general secretary until 3 December, when he was forced to step down as the party's credibility disintegrated amid revelations of widespread corruption of SED officials under Honecker (*ND*, 22–23 November; *Die Junge Welt*, 23 November; *NYT*, 25 November). After 3 December the party was run by a 25-member working group that was responsible for investigating charges of corruption and making the preparations for the emergency congress, the starting date of which was brought forward to 8 December (*ND*, 4 December). As its chief investigator the working group appointed Gregor Gysi, the young lawyer who is chairman of the GDR's bar association. Gysi had earlier acted on behalf of the opposition group New Forum (for a short biography of Gysi, see *NYT*, 16 December).

The working group's investigations into the corruption and abuse of privileges of the former leadership resulted in the arrest, on 3 December, of four former Politburo members: Günter Mittag, Harry Tisch, Gerhard Müller and Hans Albrecht (*ND*, 4 December; see also *ND*, 24 November; *WP*, 9 December), and Erich Honecker and his wife, Margot Honecker, the former education minister, were charged with corruption and placed under house arrest (*LAT*, 24 November; *WP*, 1 December; *WP*, 29 December).

Elections were called for May, and the year ended in the afterglow of the party congress, which saw the election of Gregor Gysi as the new chairman of a party that was attempting to redefine itself. The post of general secretary and the organs of the Politburo and Secretariat were abolished by the congress. The delegates also opted to change the name of the party to the Socialist Unity Party of Germany–Party of Democratic Socialists (SED-PDS). The new leadership pledged itself to a completely de-Stalinized social democratic vision in a new party statute. (*FBIS*, 21 December.)

Domestic Affairs. *Social and political affairs.* January, February, and March were marked by a growing number of illegal assemblies and protest demonstrations in Leipzig, Dresden, and East Berlin. On 14 January, 80 protesters were detained by the police during a civil rights demonstration in Leipzig (*FBIS*, 17 January). On 17 January, 120 protestors were arrested during an official rally commemorating the anniversary of the assassination of Karl Liebknecht and Rosa Luxemburg. In March hundreds demonstrated in Leipzig and Dresden to back demands for exit visas to the West (*FBIS*, 14 March). After the regional elections of 7 May, there were demonstrations and protests centering on allegations of rigged election results (*RAD Background Report*, RFE/RL, 10 May).

The Honecker leadership responded to these protests with an increasingly ineffective mixture of repression and minor concessions. There were shooting incidents at the Wall, and Amnesty International condemned the GDR for human rights violations and arbitrary action over the emigration issue. (WRE, 19–25 January; Hamburg, DPA, 6 February; *FBIS*, 7 February.) Border guards who defected to the West, however, reported in April their units had been ordered not to shoot at escapees (*NYT*, 15 August). There were also promises to ease travel restrictions, and legal emigration was allowed to increase over 1988 levels (RFE/RL, 6 April). In keeping with the contradictory stance of the regime on this issue, many who applied to emigrate were subsequently imprisoned, and Amnesty International reported that "travel and emigration are the number one human-rights problem in East Germany" (*CSM*, 28 February). Demonstrators, although harassed and sometimes brutalized by the police, were often simply detained overnight rather than arrested and sentenced. There was censorship of Western and Soviet publications, but from time to time censored materials reappeared (see *FBIS*, 21 February, on the screening of Soviet films that had been banned in 1988).

During the first half of the year the leadership made great efforts to distance itself and the GDR population from the dangerous reforms in the Soviet Union, Poland, and Hungary, but these efforts were increasingly compromised by the pace of events. From the point of view of the future of the GDR, the most significant development in Eastern Europe in the first months of 1989 was the Hungarian government's decision in May to begin opening its frontiers to the West. In August several hundred East Germans took advantage of the new escape route and left for West Germany via Czechoslovakia, Hungary, and Austria. Between August and November more than 100,000 followed. (*RAD Background Report*, RFE/RL, 4 August; *RAD Background Report*, RFE/RL, 14 September.) Because most of those who left were skilled young workers and professionals, the economy was threatened as was the image of social tranquility and relative economic success that the regime had carefully nurtured and promoted for years. The emigration also fed a growing mood of despair and resentment at home and encouraged the demand for reform both within and outside the party (*NYT*, 15 October). The response of the East German authorities to these developments at first consisted almost entirely of vitriolic attacks on the FRG and Hungary. In a diplomatic note of 12 September, Hungary was condemned for "a clear violation of legal treaties" and " a violation of the basic interests of the GDR" (*NYT*, 13 September; *ND*, 14 September). A press and media campaign was launched against the FRG in a desperate attempt to paint a picture of housing problems, insecure working conditions, and inadequate social services in the West. Reviving slogans from the time of the construction

of the Wall in 1961, *Neues Deutschland* accused the FRG authorities of "trade in human beings" (*Menschenhandel*; *ND*, 19 September) and warned of "revanchist plans" to extend the boundaries of West Germany to those of the Reich in 1937 (*ND*, 13 September). The initial reaction of the opposition was mixed. Some worried that the exodus compromised the chance of true change, that emigration was an easy alternative to staying home and working for the reform of socialism (*NYT*, 15 November). The government's decision on 9 November to allow unrestricted travel to the West and to remove the Wall made all such doubts irrelevant. It would not be possible to reimpose the restrictions. In two weeks, in an explosive increase in travel, more than 6,000,000 East Germans visited West Berlin and the FRG (*NYT*, 23 November).

At the beginning of the year there were an estimated two hundred small opposition groups in the GDR, most of which had been in existence for several years (*RAD Background Report*, RFE/RL, 4 January). By August this number had increased to approximately five hundred (*RAD Background Report*, RFE/RL, 18 August). These groups, most of which had formerly existed under the protective umbrella of the Evangelical church, began to organize nationally, and new organizations formed spontaneously throughout the country. The opposition expressed an interest in reforming rather than dismantling the system and did not at first call for an end to the SED's monopoly of power. They were interested neither in the idea of reunification with the FRG nor in the introduction of market relations for the economy; renewal and national salvation on the basis of a democratized and humanized socialism were the ideas that united all the major reform and opposition groups. (RFE, 3 August; RFE, 18 August; RFE, 25 August.)

The most significant new effort to reorganize and consolidate the opposition was undertaken by Hans-Jürgen Fischbeck, a physicist at the Academy of Sciences in Berlin, who announced in August that plans had been in motion for several months to form a "united opposition for national renewal" (RFE/RL, 18 August). Before the end of the year four major opposition groups —New Forum, Democracy Now, Democratic Awakening, and the Social Democratic Party (SPD)—emerged and absorbed most of the smaller organizations. Of the four, New Forum first emerged as the strongest but by the end of the year was losing ground to the SPD. (RFE/RL, 5 December.) Despite the rationalization and absorption, 28 separate political groups were in existence at the end of the year according to the information service in the GDR embassy in Ottawa.

At first the regime resisted all suggestions of a dialogue with the opposition as a means for reducing tension and addressing the country's problems. The party's leaders and ideologues correctly saw political pluralism as an uncontrollable threat that could destroy the GDR's claims to legitimacy and a separate existence. Speaking in August, Otto Reinhold, the SED's leading ideologist, drew a clear link between the survival of the country and the continuance of the GDR's version of socialism, noting that a "capitalist" GDR would have no meaning alongside a capitalist West Germany (RFE/RL, 25 August; for similar sentiments expressed earlier in the year, see Hermann Axen on intellectual pluralism in *ND*, 18–19 February).

Nowhere in Eastern Europe, except perhaps in the Soviet Union, was the survival of communism linked to the survival of the state. That the regime understood this reality makes their intransigence understandable. However, without Soviet support for a solution through force and suppression, the SED had to face the alternative: by the end of November the party's leadership was compelled to recognize and enter into roundtable discussions with the major groups as well as with the parties that had been allied with the SED. These "official" parties undertook to free themselves from their formal ties with the SED and, after a wave of resignations among their old leaders, declared themselves ready to participate in the political process as independent parties. (RFE, 5 December.) Manfred Gerlach, the leader of the small Liberal Democratic party, was elected acting chairman of the Council of State (acting head of state) by the Volkskammer to replace Krenz (for a short biography of Gerlach, see *NYT*, 7 December).

In December no combination of political forces or coherent party structure had yet emerged to fill the void left by the collapse of the SED. In an important sense the opposition was as much overtaken by events as was the SED. The political agenda has been increasingly set in the streets of Leipzig, Berlin, and Dresden, and the opposition has done little more than reflect, rather than organize and direct, the demand for change. The East German SPD seems in a better position to emerge as a leading political force than any of the other noncommunist parties and groups. Although it was not formed until November and was initially much weaker than New Forum, it has the enormous advantage of organizational links and support from

the SPD in the FRG. Talks opened between the SPD floor leader in the Volkskammer, Ibrahim Boehme, and Hans-Joachim Vogel, the chairman of the SPD's Bundestag parliamentary group, on 13 December. At these meetings extensive organizational and financial support was pledged for the East German party. Structural links in the form of a "contact committee" were also announced. (*FBIS*, 14 December.)

The previously crucial political role of the Evangelical church has been overtaken by events. The church had long acted as the protector and mentor for the opposition, but by late summer the increasing militancy of the opposition had to some extent embarrassed the church and complicated its relations with the SED. As its old role as a mediator between the regime and the opposition became increasingly less relevant, so too did the vague slogan "the church in socialism," and church leaders were forced to rethink their attitudes toward both the regime and socialism. At the end of the year the church continued to be a major force in encouraging the further democratization of the GDR, but it no longer occupied the central place in the GDR's political life that it had earlier in the year. (*Frankfurter Allgemeine*, 13 March; *FBIS*, 17 March; *RAD Background Report*, RFE/RL, 3 August.)

Economic affairs. Before the crisis overtook the economy, the GDR's economic priorities and problems had been little altered from the previous year. For the first six months of 1989, statistics published in the GDR showed that produced national income (the GDR equivalent of gross national product) had risen 4 percent beyond the 1988 level and that industrial production was outstripping the plan requirements (*NYT*, 15 October). Estimates published in the West set the performance much lower, at approximately 2.5 percent real growth (CIA, *World Fact Book*, 1989; *NYT*, 1 April). A more general official claim, which Honecker repeated as late as mid-October, was that the GDR was among the most "productive industrial lands" with one of the highest standards of living in Europe (see, for example, Honecker's survey of the GDR's achievements on the occasion of the GDR's anniversary celebrations, *ND*, 9 October).

The regime pointed with special pride to its record number of housing starts, claiming to have one of the strongest records for new housing construction in Europe (for a generally favorable overview of the GDR's recent record in housing development, see Marilyn Rueschemeyer, "New Towns in the

GDR," in *The Quality of Life in the GDR* [Sharpe, 1989]).

During a Central Committee seminar on the problems of the GDR's economy, Günter Mittag, the SED's principal spokesman on economic questions, offered a sketch of the economic prospects and priorities of the economy. Noting the country's dependence on trade, he stressed that the GDR must expand its bilateral trade. He emphasized the need to further develop high technology, especially the computer and microchip sector, and made much of the GDR's advances in this field (but see Harry Maier, *JPRS*, 28 April). On the question of the structure of the economy, he underlined the importance of the concept of self-financing for the productivity of industry (*ND*, 9 March). This last theme was repeated often during the first half of the year. The self-financing enterprise was regarded as the centerpiece of the GDR's supposedly unique and pioneering experiment with socialist production techniques and thus an important part of the rationale for denying the need for Soviet-style economic reform.

Despite the optimism of the GDR's claims, many Western analysts view the GDR's performance figures with skepticism, as do many economists in the GDR. Harry Maier, dean of the business science faculty of the Nordische Universität Flensburg-Neumünster in the FRG and before 1985 a leading economist in the GDR, provided a very different assessment. In an article written in April, Maier convincingly stated that the economy was already in crisis and that this fact was well understood in the GDR. "The population of the GDR and the majority of SED members recognize the necessity of radical reforms. The claim of the present leadership, that they have initiated far reaching reforms since assuming power in 1971, is considered an embarrassment even by the most faithful party members." (*Die Zeit*, 17 March; *JPRS*, 28 April.)

Although no one disputes that the GDR's economic performance has been superior in per capita production and in the quality of industrial products to the other East European economies (*NYT*, 13 March), many analysts argue that the GDR is further behind West European standards than it has been prepared to admit. After taking into account the international market value of the East German mark as compared with its arbitrarily set value and allowing for shortages and the poor quality of goods and services, it is doubtful whether the more developed Western economies provide a useful comparison for the GDR. Rather it is Mexico, Argentina, or perhaps the German economy of the 1930s that provide appropriate models for comparisons of GDR personal income, purchasing power, and the general quality of life (*NYT*, 1 April).

The specific economic problems that have plagued the economy over recent years remained little nearer solution during 1989 (*YICA*, 1989). The GDR faced serious labor shortages long before the massive hemorrhage of workers during the second half of the year. One consequence of this was an increasing need for guest workers; in 1989 foreign workers were reported to number approximately 85,000, drawn mainly from Vietnam, Cuba, Ethiopia, Angola, Mozambique, the People's Republic of China, and Poland. The presence of these foreign workers gave rise to hostile feelings among some East German workers (*Frankfurter Allgemeine*, 14 February).

The economy was also no nearer to meeting its shortages of quality fuels. The damage to air and water quality due the GDR's heavy reliance on its abundant supplies of lignite continued to be enormous and a major issue for those demanding the overhaul of the system. Some progress was made during 1988 and 1989 in reducing the emissions of sulphur dioxide, but they remained at levels four to five times the standard for European Community countries (*CSM*, 25 July; RFE/RL, 21 February; for an overview of the environmental issue in the GDR, see Joan DeBardeleben, "The Future has Already Begun," in *The Quality of Life in the German Democratic Republic*). The regime was increasingly sensitive to the pollution issue and in the first half of the year concluded a number of environmental protection agreements with Poland, Czechoslovakia, and the FRG (see, for example, *ND*, 2 February; *RAD Background Report*, no. 31).

During the last three months of the year all economic policies were dictated by the crisis and the desperate attempts to restore order. In response to the accelerating demand for change, the regime itself led the attack on the hitherto sacrosanct institutions of the command economy. At the end of the year a host of market-oriented reforms were either under way or promised for the near future.

That the economy was in an uncontrollable tailspin was fully appreciated by the Krenz leadership. The mass emigration of thousands of professionals and skilled workers had hopelessly exacerbated an already acute labor shortage. At the end of the year the solution to the mass exodus was still not in sight. The bold decision to open the frontiers to the West seemed at first to stem the headlong rush to leave, but the exodus soon returned to unmanageable levels. By the end of November approximately 300,000 people had left for the West. The head of Berlin's Office for Labor and Wages reported that more than twelve thousand jobs were vacant in the capital alone and that only a few who had left the country had subsequently returned to work. (*LAT*, 26 November.) The transport, medical services, and construction industries were hit especially hard (*NYT*, 16 November, 30 December). Army and police personnel had to be redeployed to ease the strain on essential services. By the end of November, approximately one-third of the Volksarmee was being employed in civilian jobs. (*LAT*, 26 November.) The effect of emigration and of the revelations concerning the corruption and special privileges of the party elite also took their toll in worker apathy and generally low morale (*WSJ*, 22 November).

With the border open, a currency crisis loomed as millions hurried to purchase luxury consumer goods in the West. Then thousands from West Berlin and the FRG made purchases in the GDR, taking advantage of cheap East German goods and a rapidly deflating East German mark (*NYT*, 24 November). The health of the economy was more dependent than ever on support from and closer ties with the FRG and the European Community. In the last months of 1989, both Krenz and Modrow repeatedly stressed the urgency of establishing closer economic ties with the West as a way out of the morass. (*ND*, 15 November; *Berliner Zeitung*, 16 November; *ND*, 17–18 November; *NYT*, 16, 21 November.) The near hopeless condition of the GDR's economy is forcing the pace of collaboration with the FRG, for the economy has reached a point where massive and direct FRG involvement is the only way out—a powerful argument for reunification. Following agreements reached in December, FRG and GDR bilateral economic relations have already been institutionalized to a considerable extent. In talks between Modrow and Helmut Kohl on 14 December, they agreed to form a joint economic commission to "deepen economic relations" and signed a cooperation agreement to extend economic and industrial cooperation. The joint statement issued by Kohl and Modrow following their meeting in East Berlin on 19 December went even further in extending economic collaboration. This statement outlined plans for direct FRG support for economic cooperation and joint ventures and raised the limit of guaranteed exports from the GDR to the FRG. Joint undertakings on environmental protection were also announced. The statement went on to outline plans for adjusting the convertibility of the East German mark to three to one. Extensive joint efforts in the fields of transportation, postal service, and communication were also outlined. (*FBIS*, 21 December.)

Foreign policy. The brief period in October between the celebration of the GDR's 40th anniversary and the fall of Honecker witnessed the complete collapse of the foreign policy design that the SED had developed after Honecker's visit to the FRG in September 1988 (*YICA*, 1988). The growing domestic crisis meant that relations with the FRG and the Soviet Union came to dominate all else. During that struggle the communist leadership was forced to abandon all the objectives with which it had begun the year.

In the first half of 1989, the major foreign policy goals remained essentially what they had been throughout 1988. Seeking to consolidate its special status in Eastern Europe as the Soviet Union's senior strategic and economic partner, the Honecker leadership tried to insulate its domestic policies and institutional structure against the pressure of reforms in the Soviet Union, Poland, and Hungary. It also set out to continue the orderly and profitable process of gradually improving economic and other ties with the Federal Republic, while preserving and expanding the GDR's legitimacy within the FRG and among the FRG's partners in the European Community and the North Atlantic Treaty Organization (NATO). Beyond these major concerns, the GDR continued to pursue better trading and political relations with Third World countries and with its nonaligned European neighbors.

There was continuity during 1989 with respect to the minor themes of East German foreign policy. In the months leading up to the crisis in October, the GDR succeeded in maintaining its policy toward the Third World. The principal targets of the GDR's attention remained what they had been in 1988 (*YICA*, 1989). In Latin America, Cuba and the Sandinista regime of Nicaragua received special attention (*FBIS*, 17 April; *ND*, 18 May; *FBIS*, 14 August). In Africa the GDR continued to give special attention to Mozambique, Angola, and Ethiopia (*ND*, 25–26 February, 13–14, 18 May). In the Far East new trade initiatives were launched with India (*ND*, 7 February). Efforts to expand collaboration with Austria during 1988 continued into 1989 (*ND*, 16–17 September). High-level talks were also held with Sweden and Finland that resulted in a number of agreements with these countries on bilateral trade and cultural relations (*FBIS*, 24 January; *ND*, 19 May, 8 September). The special relationship that emerged with Belgium continued to be nurtured (*ND*, 13–14 May; *FBIS*, 22 May).

In its relations with the United States and the other major NATO partners, the GDR supported the new initiatives on arms control and troop reductions in Europe; in January the GDR announced its own substantial military reductions (*FBIS*, 24 January). In March, U.S. military inspectors arrived in East Berlin as provided for in the intermediate-range nuclear forces (INF) treaty (*FBIS*, 14 March). In August a congressional delegation from the House of Representatives Armed Forces Committee visited Berlin at the invitation of the Volks-kammer Committee for National Defense. The visit was welcomed as a historic occasion in the relations between the two countries and offered hope for expanded contacts in the future (*ND*, 8 August).

George Bush's administration viewed the crisis in the GDR with deep concern and saw the mass emigration of East Germans to the West as a powerful destabilizing influence for all of Europe and as a threat to the European strategic balance (*NYT*, 7 November; *LAT*, 8 November; *WP*, 9 November). In October and November, U.S. officials were skeptical about the Krenz leadership's ability to restore order and introduce reform (*NYT*, 7 November). Relations between the GDR and the United Sates, despite their increasing importance, remained remote even during the decisive last three months of the year. The Bush administration considered but did not find a formula for intervention to speed the process of reform in the GDR (*CSM*, 1 November). Nonetheless, at the end of the year the United States could look forward to a growing involvement in German affairs as the German question moves to the forefront of the European, NATO, and Four-Power agendas.

Intra-German relations. During the first months of 1989 the SED continued to expand its contacts with the FRG and West Berlin along the same lines as the previous year. The desire to promote the inter-German relationship, which was shared with Bonn, was strong enough to prompt some outside observers to speculate on the eventual union of the two Germanies. (*NYT*, 15 May.) The focus remained on trade and cultural relations as it had during 1988 (*FBIS*, 15 March). There was also a new emphasis on bilateral arrangements with West Berlin and the FRG on pollution control. Between January and March there were numerous

high-level meetings with West German politicians and officials, and in February the first contacts between the Bundeswehr and the Volksarmee took place when a delegation of Bundeswehr officers visited the GDR (*ND*, 7 February). Discussions on environmental protection were held with representatives from Schleswig Holstein (*ND*, 2 February). There were meetings later in the month between Honecker and the prime minister of Baden Würt-temburg, Lothar Spaeth, and the mayor of Hamburg, Henning Voscherau, on trade and transportation issues (*ND*, 25–26 February).

The cordiality between the FRG and the GDR was disrupted briefly in March because of FRG protests over shooting incidents at the Wall (*WRE*, 9–15 March), but a warmer atmosphere was quickly restored. On 6 July the GDR's environmental minister, Hans Reichelt, and his FRG counterpart, Klaus Toepfer, signed a number of important agreements on environmental protection. The FRG agreed to transfer 300,000,000 deutsche marks to finance water quality projects on the Elbe and sulphur dioxide emission controls (*ND*, 6 July).

A high point in the pursuit of the GDR's established objectives came on 19 June when Honecker and Walter Momper, the mayor of West Berlin, held wide-ranging talks on themes in keeping with the SED's inter-German policy. During the course of the talks they stressed the inviolability of present borders as a guarantee of peace in Europe, the positive improvement in relations between West Berlin and the GDR, the easing of travel restrictions, and a mutual concern to cooperate in the protection of the environment. At the end of the talks it was announced that visa and travel restrictions for residents of West Berlin would be eased (*FBIS*, 20 June).

The meeting with Momper took place against a background of disturbing new problems with the FRG, and the whole tenor of the relationship changed rapidly as the GDR grappled with the challenges of an increasingly militant opposition and the flight of large numbers of its citizens. In the West there were more calls for reform and the removal of the Wall. At the SED's Eighth Plenum, 22–23 June, Politburo member Joachim Hermann attacked those who used "revanchist slogans" for German reunification and those who called for antisocialist "bourgeois reform." Referring to the local successes of the right-wing Republican party, he noted that a day would come when those calling for reunification would be glad for a part of Germany that was protected from fascism by the Wall.

The difficulties in the relations between the two Germanies came to a head in the beginning of August when an embarrassed West German government was forced to close its Prague and Budapest embassies and its mission in East Berlin because of overcrowding by the growing number of East Germans (*LAT*, 9 August; *WSJ*, 14 August; *NYT*, 23 August). In September the SED concealed a planned visit by an SPD delegation from Bonn because of SPD criticism of the GDR's handling of the refugee question and refusing to introduce democratic reforms. The visit, which had been planned for 18 September, had been the center of increasing disquiet within the SPD and had only been agreed to after lengthy debate and with the requirement that members of the delegation would meet with representatives of New Forum (*RAD Background Report*, no. 176, RFE/RL, 20 September).

Bonn's embarrassment over the refugee question was coupled with alarm as it saw its German policy disintegrating and as it recognized the threat to stability on its borders. The official response was to urge the SED toward reform as an answer to the flood of refugees. Financial aid was offered to the GDR as a way of helping it bring in the necessary changes, but there was no thought of using the occasion to destabilize the SED regime. (*CSM*, 3 October; *NYT*, 22 October.) The agreement reached on the weekend of 30 September between the FRG, the GDR, Poland, and Czechoslovakia to allow East German refugees to leave the Warsaw and Prague embassies for the West did nothing to ease the situation. Rudolph Seiter, the FRG minister responsible for the West German side in the negotiations, stated at the beginning of the talks that reform was the only viable approach. According to Seiter, the FRG would not close the doors of its embassies to the refugees, but would offer financial help to the GDR if the necessary economic and political reforms were introduced (*CSM*, 3 October). The calls for reform from Bonn grew in frequency and intensity throughout October and November; on 21 October, Kohl called for free elections in the GDR (*CSM*, 22 October).

The negative response in the GDR to the suggestions coming from Bonn changed radically after Honecker's ouster. On 13 October, Honecker had called for a dialogue between the two governments on the refugee issue, but that call was greeted with skepticism in Bonn in view of the hostile and uncompromising tone of the GDR press on the issue (see, for example, *Berliner Zeitung*, 12 October; *NYT*, 13 October). After the formation of the Krenz

leadership, the way seemed open for cooperation in the resolution of the crisis. Krenz moved toward the introduction of dramatic reforms, but the signals from East Berlin were still mixed. Harry Otto, the GDR's deputy foreign minister, saw Bonn's offers of help as "patronizing if not insulting." Krenz asserted that there could be no question of "tutelage" to outside forces. (*NYT*, 22 October.)

In November, as pressure mounted in the GDR and the scope of the reforms undertaken by the Modrow and Krenz leadership pointed to the introduction of a democratic order in the GDR, the initiatives coming from Bonn went much further than they had earlier. On 28 November, Kohl outlined a ten-point plan for ending the division of Germany. The ten points included establishing joint standing committees on economic, environmental, scientific, and cultural affairs and a permanent commission for consultation between the two governments. The plan included a promise of economic aid before any other steps were undertaken. Kohl spoke of "confederative" structures that were to define the new Germany. The exact shape of such a confederation was left for future discussion. (*RAD Background Report*, no. 211, RFE/RL, 30 November.) Given the scope and radical intent of the plan, the response in the GDR was surprisingly positive. Earlier Prime Minister Modrow spoke of the possibility of a "community of treaties" that would govern the relations between the two Germanies in the future; thus it was in the sense of treaty obligations between two separate and sovereign states that the GDR leaders understood the possibilities for a closer and more structured relationship with Bonn. Krenz, in an interview with the *Financial Times* (25–26 November), observed, "if one defines the word confederation as based on two independent, sovereign states, then one can talk about anything." The reaction of the noncommunist parties was mixed, with the dominant attitude being one of caution. The opposition for the most part wanted to ensure the continued survival of the GDR in any new arrangements with the West Germans and thus showed considerable reserve when faced with the Bonn initiatives (*FBIS*, 21 December).

After the resignation of Krenz at the beginning of December, the possibilities for some form of reunification improved. After the talks between West and East SPD parties on 13 December and the establishment of organizational links between them, the SPD was open to the idea of eventual reunification (*FBIS*, 14 December). At the same time, the mood of the public demonstrations suggested that public opinion was shifting toward the idea of one Germany (*NYT*, 19 December) and the attitude of the Modrow government became more accepting of the idea of institutionalized cooperation. The joint statement that followed Kohl's working meeting with Modrow in East Berlin on 19–20 December showed that the East Germans were willing to accept many of the ten points that the federal chancellor had outlined at the end of November (*FBIS*, 21 December).

International party relations. The direction of change in the Soviet Union and elsewhere in the communist world was away from the hard-line stances preferred by the SED. The East German communists had long been uncomfortable with the increasingly open political discussion in the Soviet Union. The open criticism of Stalin, which made its reappearance with the advent of Gorbachev, led to the banning of the Soviet German-language magazine *Sputnik*. (*Süddeutsche Zeitung*, 11 January.) The fear of opening the question of Stalin and Stalinism had not, it should be noted, prevented criticism by GDR historians of Stalin's role in the murder of German communist leaders in the purges of the 1930s (*ND*, 12 January).

Despite the misgivings and tensions that troubled the GDR's relations with the Soviet Union, the SED leadership entered the new year secure in the conviction that they could continue to count on Soviet support for their version of "developed socialism" (*YICA*, 1988). The SED leaders, drawing comfort from the GDR's central place among the Soviet Union's allies, assumed, as did many others, that Soviet strategic and economic interests set limits on how far the Soviets could go in pressuring Honecker for reform. Gorbachev's repeated assurances that each communist party was responsible for designing policies to suit its own circumstances could be interpreted as a further guarantee of the status quo in the GDR, a welcome aspect of Gorbachev's policies in East Berlin (*ND*, 18–19 February).

As the Communist Party of the Soviet Union gave up its role as the center of ideological orthodoxy, the division between reform-oriented and hard-line regimes in Eastern Europe deepened. Early in the year the SED's official line on the reform process under way in Poland and Hungary hardened and became overtly critical. Articles appeared in the East German press attacking departures from the principles of the command economy and central party control (*ND*, 18 February;

Berliner Zeitung, 27 February). At the same time, criticism of the SED's policies was voiced in Hungary and Poland. For example, on 12 February the Hungarian government daily, *Magyar Nemzet*, published an editorial critical of conditions in countries that were resisting reform (*Soviet East European Report*, RFE/RL, VI/7 10 March; for a critical Polish assessment of the GDR's stance on reform, see *Polityka Warsaw*, 31 January; *JPRS*, 15 February). The divisions in Eastern Europe also affected the SED's relations with the nongoverning communist parties. The Italian Communist Party openly sided with the opposition in the GDR; in October, during the anniversary celebrations in the GDR, the Italian party daily, *L'Unita*, featured an interview with New Forum leader Baerbel Bohley (*RAD Background Report*, no. 18, RFE/RL, 13 October). The SED worked hard to avoid being isolated among the West European parties; Honecker and other members of the Politburo held talks with leaders and representatives from many of these parties. The SED press gave extensive coverage to some of the exchanges, especially to talks held between Honecker and Alvaro Cunhal, the general secretary of the large and conservative Portuguese party. (*ND*, 6 July.)

There was a noticeable tendency toward an unofficial restructuring of interparty and interstate relations as ideological differences intensified among the Warsaw Pact partners. Any semblance of a common Warsaw Pact foreign policy broke down, with individual members differing widely on issues such as the prodemocracy movement in China. Efforts to reform and restructure the Council for Mutual Economic Assistance along the lines of a common market for Eastern Europe were increasingly handicapped by the conflicting views among member states on issues such as currency convertibility. At the heart of such difficulties was the increasingly wide divergence of domestic economic policies (*Soviet East European Report*, no. 7, RFE/RL, 10 March; *RAD Background Report*, no. 154, RFE/RL, 23 August; *RAD Background Report*, no. 163, RFE/RL, 7 September).

During the first half of the year, the GDR, Romania, Czechoslovakia, and Bulgaria were working toward an informal alliance to resist the pressure for change. The GDR was the key to any effective hard-line combination because if Prague and Bucharest saw that change could not be resisted in East Germany, they would see it as unlikely to be resisted anywhere.

The GDR sided with the Romanians on the question of the fate of Romania's Hungarian minority. In February, *Neues Deutschland* defended Nicolae Ceaușescu's rural resettlement plans (*ND*, 11–12 February; for GDR attempts to strengthen bilateral ties with Sofia, see *ND*, 15 June). The GDR also showed sympathy for the Czech leaders on the reassessment of the 1968 invasion that had been undertaken in the Soviet Union, Hungary, and Poland. The GDR also took the Czech side in the dispute between Hungary and Czechoslovakia over the Hungarian decision to air a television interview with Alexander Dubček, the former leader of the Communist Party of Czechoslovakia (*RAD Background Report*, RFE/RL, 2 May; *RAD Background Report*, no. 163, RFE/RL, 7 September).

Although their leaders extended their good wishes to the hard-line Czechoslovakian party, protests in the GDR supported Czech dissidents. There were reports that 171 peace and human rights groups had signed a petition demanding the release of Václav Havel. (*JPRS*, 23 January; *FBIS*, 21 March.) The reactions of opposition groups in the GDR to the plight of dissidents elsewhere in Eastern Europe illustrated the difficulties that attended SED attempts to isolate its population from outside influences. The regime nonetheless persisted in its efforts and, given the availability in the GDR of West German television and radio coverage of events in Eastern Europe, was often made to look ridiculous. *Neues Deutschland*, for example, contrived to comment on the Polish elections of 4 June without once mentioning the fact that the communists had been defeated (*ND*, 9 June).

The GDR's efforts to strengthen a common front against radical reforms led the leadership to strengthen bilateral relations with conservative parties outside Eastern Europe, including the parties of North Korea, Cuba, Albania, and the People's Republic of China. Oskar Fischer, the GDR's foreign minister, visited Albania in June, thus becoming the first senior official from Eastern Europe to visit Tiranë since Albania and the Soviet Union severed diplomatic relations in 1961. The visit resulted in two important agreements, one on trade and economic cooperation and the other in the field of health and medicine. Ramiz Alia, the Albanian leader, was especially fulsome in his praise of the GDR's achievements. Fischer noted that "a good basis exists for the broad and dynamic development of interstate cooperation" (*RAD Background Report*, no. 114, RFE/RL; *ND*, 21 June). After the suppression of the prodemocracy movement in the People's Republic of China (PRC), the SED lead-

ership undertook to include the PRC in the common front and was quick to support the decision to use force against the student movement (*ND*; *Die Junge Welt*, 6 June). The SED's expression of moral support for the PRC was matched by a series of high-level talks between the two parties. In July an accord was signed in Beijing between the PRC and the GDR on furthering economic cooperation (*ND*, 7–8 July). Also in July, Politburo member Günter Schabowski flew to Beijing on an official friendship visit during which the Chinese general secretary, Yiang Zemin, thanked the SED for its "deep understanding and support" of the measures undertaken by the PRC to restore order (*ND*, 15–16 July).

The ideological differences in Eastern Europe came into focus after the Hungarian decision on 10 September to allow East German refugees to leave its territory for the FRG. Tension between the GDR and Hungary had been building on the refugee question since May, when Hungary began opening its frontiers to the West. Hungarian officials had become increasingly reluctant to stand in the way of East Germans using the relatively easy access into Hungary as an escape route to the West. Hungarian police stopped stamping the passports of East Germans trying to leave Hungary illegally, and border guards frequently turned a blind eye as refugees fled across the frontier into Austria (*RAD Background Report*, no. 163, RFE/RL, 7 September). The GDR was outraged at the Hungarian decision to break its 1969 treaty obligations and violate the interests of an ally.

The reaction from the GDR's Warsaw Pact allies was mixed. Czechoslovakia and Romania condemned the Hungarian decision. The reaction of the Poles varied from enthusiastic support for the decision by Solidarity to cautious equivocation on the part of Wojciech Jaruzelski, Poland's communist president. (*RAD Background Report*, no. 174, RFE/RL, 15 September.) It was, however, the Soviet reaction that was the most significant for the future of the GDR's relations with its partners, and it was mixed and equivocal. Igor Ligachev used the occasion to condemn the FRG for "slander" of the GDR (*ND*, 13 September). Boris Yeltsin, in contrast, noted that "people have the right to live where they want" (*NYT*, 13 September). The official Soviet media coverage seemed to reflect this ambivalence, for although it was generally supportive of the GDR's complaint, it also betrayed some sympathy with the Hungarian decision (*RAD Background Report*, no. 174, RFE/RL, 15 September).

The Soviet reaction to the GDR's difficulties was

an indication that Soviet backing for the SED leadership could not be taken for granted. Gorbachev's central concern was to preserve predictability and stability in the Soviet Union's relations with Eastern Europe, and it was not clear that the Honecker regime would always be able to meet that concern. The downside of Gorbachev's policy of noninterference in the internal problems of its allies became more apparent to the SED leaders as their problems multiplied and their isolation deepened. Honecker had hoped that Gorbachev's presence at the 40th anniversary celebrations would restore some of the SED's lost credibility, but the result was quite different. Although Gorbachev was careful not to criticize his hosts in public, he made it clear that he saw reform as necessary in the GDR. Gorbachev's visit to Berlin and his firsthand experience of the depth of the resentment of the GDR's population likely brought him to the conclusion that the Honecker regime was a liability to his general European policy (*LAT*, 25 October). Speaking on East German radio (Radio DDR II) on 19 October, Soviet Foreign Ministry spokesman Gennadii Gerasimov noted that the exodus of refugees had "unsettled" the Soviet leaders and repeated Gorbachev's warnings of how important it was "not to lag behind realities" (WRE, 19–25 October). At the end of December, Horst Sindermann, a former member of the Politburo, in an interview with *Die Junge Welt*, stressed that Gorbachev had put behind-the-scenes pressure on Honecker (*Toronto Globe and Mail*, 28 December). At the same time, it might also be true that Gorbachev's failure to be more forthright in his criticisms of the SED made it clear to the opposition that they could not expect changes to come in the GDR merely as a result of Moscow's changed outlook. If change was to come, then it would be as a result of intensified pressure from below. In that sense, Gorbachev may have done more to strengthen the resolve of the opposition than he did either to comfort the SED's leaders or to help them reform their party.

After Honecker's fall on 18 October the question of hard-line and reform orientations in Eastern Europe became increasingly irrelevant. The GDR's shift to the reform-oriented side was decisive for change everywhere in Eastern Europe (at that time only the increasingly isolated and embattled regimes of Czechoslovakia and Romania remained) (*CSM*, 16 November). After 18 October it became clear that much more had been at stake than the fate of a hard-line leadership. The Soviets accepted the logic of the SED argument that reform would lead to the destruction of the GDR, but drew different conclusions than did the SED. The question arose as to whether the Soviet Union under some circumstances might sacrifice its client state. As early as January, Soviet foreign minister, Eduard Shevardnadze, who had been ambivalent about the future of the Wall, observed that a situation could be envisaged where the Wall would no longer be necessary. It was not difficult to infer that under some circumstances the Soviet Union would accept a reunified Germany (*FBIS*, 24 January). In the last three months of the year, as the East German party grappled with an increasingly unmanageable crisis, the Soviet Union moved closer to the idea of a reunified Germany. When the East German people took to the streets in late October, Shevardnadze was assuring the Supreme Soviet in Moscow that the changes taking place in Eastern Europe were "qualitative" and taking place because "people want them," but said nothing about ultimate guarantees for the GDR (*LAT*, 29 October). Egon Krenz rapidly instituted changes that went further than those introduced in the Soviet Union. Throughout, Gorbachev welcomed and encouraged the reforms undertaken by Krenz, Modrow, and Gysi. The Soviet attitude remained positive even though the removal of the Wall, the surrender of the party's monopoly of power, and closer ties with the FRG, and the call for free elections all pointed to the eventual reunification of the two German states, despite the fact that the communists and many of the opposition groups continued to insist on a reformed and separate GDR.

Davis W. Daycock
University of Manitoba

Hungary

Population. 10,566,944 (July 1989)
Parties. Hungarian Socialist Workers' Party (HSWP) and Hungarian Socialist Party (HSP)
Founded. 1918 (HSWP), 1989 (HSP)
Membership. 82,000 (HSWP); 50,000 (HSP)
General Secretary. Gyula Thurmer (HSWP); Rezsö Nyers (HSP)

Status. Ruling party

Last Congress. Fourteenth, 6–10 October (HSWP/HSP); HSWP held the first part of a second Fourteenth Congress 17 December to reconstitute the party (the second part of this congress is scheduled for January 1990).

Last Conference. Second, 20–22 May 1988

Last Election. June 1985; 387 seats (35 nationalist, 352 multicandidate constituencies). Approximately 70 percent of deputies are HSWP members.

Publication. *Népszabadság* (HSP daily)

Party Affairs. The year 1989 marked the final victory of the 1956 revolution over a semi-Stalinist regime that had exhausted itself politically, economically, and spiritually in attempting to usurp the democratic ideals of the Hungarian people.

Accordingly, throughout the month of January, representatives of the various opposition groups and even some leading figures within the HSWP demanded a radical re-evaluation of 1956 in the spirit of truth and justice. As a result of mounting domestic and international pressure, then government spokesman György Marosan announced on 26 January that the Hungarian government had decided to allow the exhumation and reburial of former Prime Minister Imre Nagy, former Minister of Defense Pál Maleter, and three of Imre Nagy's other associates: Miklós Gyimes, József Szilágyi, and Géza Losonczi (*Népszabadság*, 27 January). With the exception of the last man, who was murdered in his prison cell, all were executed on 16 June 1958 after a secret trial for their role in what the Kádár regime had from the start stubbornly termed the *counterrevolution* of 1956.

In his announcement, Marosan stated that the government's decision had been prompted by the leadership's desire to "promote national reconciliation." Yet instead of ending the national debate about 1956 and the role János Kádár had played in it, the government's action opened the floodgate of long-suppressed emotions in Hungary.

In an interview with the "168 Hours" program of Radio Budapest on 28 January, then Politburo member and Minister of State Imre Pozsgay revealed that a special party historical committee had concluded that the 1956 revolution was not counterrevolutionary in its nature (Radio Kossuth, 28 January). Rather, according to Pozsgay, the revolution was a "popular uprising against an oligarchic form of power that debased the nation." To add insult to injury in the eyes of Kádár loyalists, Pozsgay

claimed that a careful re-examination of historical and political documents proved the correctness of Imre Nagy's attitude during the political crisis of 1954 and 1955. Expanding on his statement, Pozsgay pointed out that to correctly evaluate the 1956 revolution, one has to go back to 1948–1949, when Mátyás Rákosi and his clique abolished the multiparty system in Hungary. The "dictatorship of the proletariat" with its obligatory one-party system, Pozsgay concluded, proved to be a "dead-end street" for socialism; this model did not work and led to the crisis of 1956. Going beyond the scope of the interview, Pozsgay added, "From the moment that the dictatorship of the proletariat was proclaimed, the workers' participation in the exercise of power ceased to exist." He also denied charges by the Kádár regime that the workers' councils set up in 1956 were counterrevolutionary bodies. Rather these workers' councils were the re-creation of the democratic councils that existed in factories under capitalism and were eliminated after nationalization. The HSWP, Pozsgay counseled, must give up its monopoly of power and allow the creation of a multiparty system. He also sounded a warning concerning the seriousness of the political, economic, and social crisis. Finally, Pozsgay stated that the committee would periodically publish its findings without submitting them to the party's Central Committee for prior review.

Attesting to the division within the leadership of the HSWP, then party leader Károly Grósz publicly disagreed with Pozsgay's assessment of the 1956 revolution. In an interview with the Hungarian news agency MTI, Grósz stated that "it was not for one person or a task force committee to issue a ruling." According to him the committee was appointed by the Central Committee, which is exclusively authorized to render a final opinion on the events surrounding 1956 (*Népszabadság*, 30 January). In a rejoinder another Politburo member, Prime Minister Miklós Németh, also criticized Pozsgay for his remarks. Németh stated that the committee had only been engaged in "a partial study" and that it was erroneous to describe "complex phenomena" in "one-word terms." (*Magyar Hirlap*, 1 February.)

Sensing that the twin issues of 1956 and multiparty democracy can determine his political future, Pozsgay relentlessly continued to pursue a populist political line. Addressing the party *aktiv* of Hódmezövásárhely on 3 February, he asked the people to trust and follow him toward a democratic system of government in Hungary (*Magyar Nemzet*, 4 February). The next day, Imre Nagy, then first secretary of the Central Committee of the Communist Youth League, stated at the conference of young activists in Zalaegerszeg: "The debated statement of Imre Pozsgay about a popular uprising having taken place in Hungary in 1956 is not far from the truth" (*Népszabadság*, 5 February).

In response to Pozsgay's unexpectedly aggressive campaign against the *nomenklatura*, an extraordinary plenum of the Central Committee of the HSWP was called on 10 February, ten days ahead of schedule. Despite public promises by the leadership, the Central Committee meeting was closed to the media and the public. In addition members of the Central Committee needed a second day to hammer out a compromise position on 1956 and the possibility of a multiparty system. During the session, 47 of the 107 members of the Central Committee spoke and seven more submitted their comments in writing. (*Népszabadság, Magyar Hirlap, Magyar Nemzet*, 12 February.) Then party chairman János Kádár, who had not been at a Central Committee meeting since November 1988, was again asked not to attend the plenum. Excerpts from the final communiqué were broadcast on 12 February. The complete text of the communiqué was not published in the Hungarian newspapers until 13 February (*Népszabadság, Magyar Hirlap*). Finally, on 16 February the party daily *Népszabadság*, published the Central Committee's seven-point statement dealing with the reform of Hungary's political system.

The Central Committee communiqué stated that the HSWP must take urgent actions to end Hungary's "economic, political and moral crisis." The communiqué also stated that the most fundamental condition for progress was the creation of a market economy based on mixed forms of ownership, with state and cooperative ownerships keeping their "determinative role" in the economy. In the communiqué members of the Central Committee reiterated their determination to continue the reform of Hungary's political institutions. Moreover, the Central Committee conceded that political pluralism can only be accomplished within the framework of a multiparty system. However, any transition to a multiparty system must be achieved "gradually" to keep the process of political change within "predictable limits." Both the "forced acceleration" of change and its undue delay "are dangerous." (Ibid.)

The communiqué also dealt with the controversial issue of 1956. The Central Committee voiced its approval of the continuing public debate over the events leading to the revolution, but stressed the need for more scientifically based research into the "national tragedy of 1956." For the first time the Communists admitted that there had been a "genuine popular uprising" in 1956. Concomitantly, however, the Central Committee concluded that those who were aiming at a "bourgeois restoration" and thus committed "counterrevolutionary acts" had gained the upper hand over the leadership of the revolution. (Ibid.)

Finally, the Central Committee termed hasty Imre Pozsgay's decision to release the conclusions of the committee's findings without prior consultation with the Central Committee and called the subsequent debates and accusations "regrettable" (ibid.). Yet the Central Committee reaffirmed its confidence in Imre Pozsgay.

In a lengthy television and radio interview subsequent to the plenum, party leader Károly Grósz warned that multiparty democracy can only operate within the socialist system. He also stated that the requirement that future political parties must function on a "socialist basis" would be laid down in the new constitution. With respect to his public disagreements with Imre Pozsgay, Grósz stated that "there was not, is not, and will not be a Pozsgay affair" (Radio Kossuth, 13 February).

Assessing the importance of the extraordinary plenum, Prime Minister Miklós Németh said that the most significant result of the Central Committee meeting was that it pre-empted a break within the party into orthodox and reform Communists over the evaluation of 1956 (Radio Kossuth, 12 February; *Magyar Hirlap*, 15 February).

Yet a survey published by the party daily *Népszabadság* on 20 February found that 53.7 percent of the Hungarians considered that the 1956 communiqué was "not realistic, obscured the facts, and still protected the interests of those who had a part in suppressing the Revolution."

The reactions of the various noncommunist independent groups and parties were generally balanced. Although they all welcomed the communiqué as an important step toward the establishment of a democratic Hungary, they criticized the ambiguous nature of the Central Committee's statement with regard to 1956. They also deplored the political and economic privileges that the Communists enjoyed, including their control of the media. To achieve real equality and fairness in politics, they proposed a discussion between themselves and the Communists. (*Magyar Nemzet*, 20 February.)

At a follow-up two-day session of the Central Committee on 20 February, the leading body of the

HSWP unanimously approved a draft of the new constitution. The draft report submitted by György Fejti stated that in the new constitution Hungary must be defined as a free, democratic, and socialist state. More important, the HSWP's leading role shall not be mandated in the new constitution, but neither will a multiparty system. Parties whose programs and political objectives do not conform with the new constitution shall not be allowed to function legally. (*Népszabadság*, 22 February.)

Having opted for a multiparty system the HSWP decided to formulate a new political program more attuned to the changing political climate in Hungary. Drafted by János Berecz and published in the *Népszabadság* on 11 March, the new party program was rich in promises but short on specifics. As with previous programs, the new one was designed to appease everybody without offending anybody. At the end it even failed to motivate party members. As Social Democrat György Rudner stated,

The program wants too much and promises too much. It would be much more useful if it gave concrete proposals and did not prompt visions of the Promised Land. For this reason, it has no real credibility for me, especially since the party's principles have, in reality, been the same over the past 40 years. Practice has proved to us that the HSWP has not really taken them seriously. (*Magyar Nemzet*, 12 March.)

In a more practical vein the Central Committee nominated Mátyás Szürös to replace National Assembly chairman István Stadinger, who submitted his resignation on 20 February. Subsequently, Szürös was elected by the National Assembly as its chairman on 10 March.

Amid an increasing malaise within the HSWP and society at large, Hungarians prepared for the first free celebration of 15 March, the anniversary of the Hungarian nation's liberation war against the Hapsburgs in 1848–1849. Testing the willingness of the opposition groups and parties to cooperate with the communists, the HSWP, its youth organization, and the Patriotic Peoples' Front issued a call for a joint celebration of this national holiday (*Népszabadság*, 2 March). Rejecting the communists' offer, the opposition groups and parties pointed out that "as long as the representatives of power do not draw the appropriate conclusions from their past behavior of using police force and other means of intimidation against us, we are not willing to celebrate together" (*Magyar Nemzet*, 10 March).

It was not surprising, therefore, that celebrations followed a certain pattern throughout Hungary. Party and government representatives celebrated early in the morning, whereas the people marched, laid wreaths and, listened to speeches in the afternoon. Apart from these activities, 31 alternative organizations issued a joint twelve-point statement entitled "What Does the Hungarian Nation Want?" The statement demanded the creation of a representative government including a multiparty system; free and fair elections; a constitutional rather than a police state; respect for human rights guaranteed by an independent judiciary; freedom of speech, the press, conscience, and education; the right to strike; equal and proportionate sharing of the tax burden; public control of public spending; an end to privileges for certain groups and individuals; an efficient economy and market; equality for the various types of property ownership; reductions in bureaucracy; elimination of the infamous workers' militia; freedom and sovereignty for the peoples of Central and Eastern Europe; a neutral and independent Hungary; the withdrawal of Soviet troops; a responsible policy on minorities and emigrés; self-respect for the nation; an end to falsification of history; the just treatment of the 1956 revolution and its martyrs; and the designation of 23 October as a work-free national holiday (ibid.).

In both Budapest and provincial cities, people marched peacefully carrying Hungarian national flags without the hated coat of arms of the communist state. Citizens wore buttons bearing the coat of arms of the Hungarian kingdom or that of 1848. Throughout Hungary cries for "independence, democracy and a free Hungary" echoed (Radio Kossuth, 15 March; *Magyar Hirlap, Magyar Nemzet*, 16 March). The Hungarian nation became reunited not on the terms offered by the communists, but on the terms of its own sense of freedom and justice.

In the wake of the 15 March celebration, it became even more apparent that the HSWP was plagued with severe political, structural and ideological problems. Thus, on 12 April the general secretary as well as the entire Politburo tendered their resignations (*Népszabadság*, 13 April). Although Károly Grósz succeeded in saving his position, three orthodox Communists (János Berecz, István Szabó, and János Lukács) were removed from the highest executive body of the party. The fourth, Judit Csehák, lost her seat because of her political insignificance. The new Politburo had only nine members instead of the previous eleven.

Having concluded that the changes in the composition of the Politburo were too little and too late, Prime Minister Miklós Németh called for a separation of power between the party and the government. To demonstrate his independence, Németh proposed changes to his government's Presidential Council without consulting with the party's Central Committee (*Magyar Hirlap*, 30 April). The five new ministers and the new chairman of the planning office were approved by the National Assembly on 10 May without party interference (ibid., 11 May). Unfortunately for Miklós Németh, his reshuffle of the cabinet was greeted with cynical indifference by the Hungarian people and the various opposition parties. Indeed, his appointees could hardly have been described as newcomers to the Hungarian political scene: Four of them were promoted from second-rank positions. Csaba Hutter, the new minister of agriculture, was a National Assembly deputy from Nógrád county and director of a large agricultural cooperative. Ferenc Glatz, who became minister of culture, was editor in chief of the monthly *Historia* and director of the Hungarian Academy of Sciences' Institute of History. Neither did changes in the second echelon of his government indicate that Miklós Németh was embarking on a radically different personnel policy. Instead of reaching outside the ossified party and government bureaucracies, he filled his cabinet with mostly mediocre officials.

The process of disintegration that engulfed the HSWP and the government by the end of April also reached the Hungarian Communist Youth League (KISZ). On 23 April, the league changed its name to Hungarian Democratic Youth League. The new league declared its support only for the reformers within the HSWP (*Népszabadság*, 24 April).

In May support for the HSWP and the government reached a new low. A public opinion poll conducted in March and April by the Hungarian Academy of Sciences' Sociological and Social Science institutes revealed that only 24 percent of those interviewed believed that the HSWP was concerned about, and represented, their interests compared with 66 percent in 1985 (*Magyar Nemzet*, 15 May). Similarly, public confidence in the National Assembly plunged from 70 percent to 44 percent.

In May, undoubtedly concerned about the future of the party and also to dramatize the seriousness of the overall situation in the country, the HSWP's leadership moved to signal a break with the past and thus distance itself from the political and economic mistakes perpetrated by the Kádár regime throughout its 32-year-long reign. Accordingly, on 8 May,

the Central Committee voted to remove János Kádár as chairman of the HSWP. At the same time, Kádár also lost his seat on the Central Committee. At the same session, members of the Central Committee also voted in favor of holding a national party conference in the fall of 1989. In addition, the Central Committee approved a number of other important measures proposed by the Politburo (*Népszabadság*, 9 May). Thus, the HSWP Central Committee surrendered its right to nominate candidates for top government offices previously reserved for members of the *nomenklatura*, ordered the transfer of control over its paramilitary forces to the government, and adopted guidelines for a law on political parties.

To up the ante, on 13 May, Prime Minister Miklós Németh announced that the government was suspending for two months all construction work on its part of the highly controversial and corruption-ridden joint Hungarian-Czechoslovak hydro-electric project at Gabcikovo-Nagymaros on the Danube (*Magyar Hirlap*, 14 May). Predictably, the various opposition groups and parties welcomed the decision as a "significant step toward national reconciliation" (*Magyar Nemzet*, 14 May).

Meanwhile, the internal erosion of the HSWP continued unabated. On 21 and 22 May the first national conference of the HSWP reform circles was held in Szeged. Attesting to the depth of division within the party, the reform circles decided to issue their own manifesto. In this document they demanded that the HSWP reform and take the lead in helping society become a democratic constitutional state by peaceful means. The manifesto also admitted that Imre Nagy had been a victim of a political show trial. Representatives of the reform circles asked for forgiveness from his and other victims' relatives on behalf of those responsible and suggested that the HSWP Central Committee do the same before the reburial on 16 June (ibid., 23 May).

At a subsequent Central Committee session on 29 May, the so-called reformers within the party scored a clear victory over the more orthodox forces headed by Károly Grósz. In what amounted to a major political blow to his prestige, Grósz had to acquiesce in a communiqué that assessed Imre Nagy as a significant historical figure who fought for an end to Stalinism in Hungary. Moreover, Grósz was forced to support the holding of a national party congress as opposed to the party conference that he favored. His defeat, however, did not prevent Grósz from firing a parting shot at the reformers within the party. In his speech he complained that

> there is a petit bourgeois mentality in this party, which is first and foremost the advocate of limitless democracy. This force wants to start everything anew; cast aside even what is valuable; and at times it seems to me that it is led by renewal for its own sake and not by a spirit of conscious construction. (*Népszabadság*, 31 May.)

In personnel matters, two Kádár loyalists resigned from the Central Committee rather than face public investigation of their roles in the execution of Imre Nagy and his colleagues: Sándor Rajnai, the Hungarian ambassador to the Soviet Union, had supervised the arrest and investigation of Imre Nagy. Mihály Korom also played an active role in assisting János Kádár to destroy the opposition after 1956.

Finally, on 16 June, Hungarians of all political persuasions had their chance to come to terms with the national tragedy of 1956 and its aftermath. In spite of Prime Minister Miklós Németh's and National Assembly chairman Mátyás Szürös's presence at the ceremonies, every speaker at Heroes' Square deplored the crimes committed by the Kádár regime against the nation and called for a communist-free government in Hungary (*Magyar Nemzet*, 17 June). Clearly, the Hungarian nation was not willing to extend the olive branch of reconciliation to the so-called reformers within the HSWP.

Strong criticism of Károly Grósz and other leaders of the HSWP intensified throughout June. The increasingly harsh and even uncivilized political struggle within the leadership of the HSWP alarmed the rank and file of the party as well as the nation at large. By the end of June the membership of the HSWP (at one time around 880,000) had fallen to below 750,000 (*Népszabadság*, 2 July). The so-called reform wing of the HSWP believed that only immediate reforms could ensure the political survival of the communists. It criticized Grósz for his indecisiveness and lack of enthusiasm for radical reforms. (Ibid., 23 June.) From the more radical followers of Imre Pozsgay in the provinces, demands for Grósz's resignation became a daily ritual (*Magyar Nemzet*, 16 June; *Petöfi Népe*, 24 June). On the other side of the spectrum, members of the Ferenc Münich Society attacked Grósz for not standing up to Imre Pozsgay and his followers (*Népszabadság*, 25 June). Another newly founded group, which called itself the Marxist Unity Plat-form, labeled Grósz a traitor for ousting Kádár and accused him of replacing democratic centralism and one-party rule with capitalism and bourgeois ideology (ibid.). In this situation a split within the party appeared imminent.

To avert such a fateful occurrence, an emergency meeting of the HSWP Central Committee was called for 23 June. At the end of the two-day meeting—described by the majority of the participants as "heated," "animated," "aimed at clarifying matters," and "seeking party unity"—Rezsö Nyers, a social democrat turned communist, was elected chairman of the HSWP. In addition, a four-man Presidium and a 21-member Political Executive Committee were set up. The Presidium included Rezsö Nyers, Károly Grósz, Miklós Németh, and Imre Pozsgay. To sweeten the bitter pill that Grósz and his followers had to swallow, the Central Committee also decided to nominate Imre Pozsgay for the newly created post of president of Hungary (ibid., 25 June), which would preclude any future leadership role for Pozsgay in the party. Clearly, these changes substantially reduced the powers of HSWP general secretary Grósz and strengthened the positions of his reformist opponents. By the same token, the unity of leadership was preserved and thus a split within the HSWP was, at least for the time being, prevented. At the end of the meeting, party spokesman László Major announced that the next HSWP congress would be convened on 7 October. (Ibid.) The Central Committee also produced a statement on the HSWP's situation and its political objectives that averred that socialism in Hungary could only be achieved through a new political and economic model. According to the Central Committee such a model would be based on the principles of democratic socialism, including a constitutional state, parliamentary democracy based on a multiparty system, and a market economy in which community property must continue to play a decisive role. Moreover, the HSWP would remain loyal to the teachings of Marxism and to "leftist, socialist, and humanist ideas." To further confuse both the membership of the party and the nation, the Central Committee called for "a new synthesis between communist and social-democratic values." (Ibid.)

Efforts by the leadership of the HSWP to improve its image were first put to the test on 22 July. On this day the first multiparty elections in more than 40 years were held in four electoral districts in Hungary. In Gödöllö, a town of about 35,000 just outside Budapest, the 35-year-old Lutheran clergyman Gábor Roszik won 69.2 percent of the ballots cast. His opponent—the HSWP candidate Aladár Körösföi-Kriesch, whose grandfather was a famous painter—received less than 20 percent of the votes. According to newspaper reports the HSWP pumped about a hundred times as much money into the campaign in Gödöllö as did the opposition (*Magyar Nemzet*, 23 July). In the three other electoral districts, the low turnout necessitated runoff elections. These were held on 5 August and resulted in further defeats of HSWP candidates. (Ibid., 6 August.)

The dramatic but long-expected demise of the HSWP happened on 7 October, when the delegates to the HSWP's extraordinary congress voted to terminate the party and establish the new Hungarian Socialist Party (HSP) (*Népszabadság, Magyar Hirlap, Magyar Nemzet*, 10 October). The abolition of the old party and the creation of the new one were approved by an overwhelming majority of the 1,274 delegates at the congress. Out of 1,202 delegates who participated in the vote, only 159 voted against and a mere 38 abstained. On 10 October, Rezsö Nyers, the former chairman of the old HSWP, became the new chairman of the new HSP. After considerable behind-the-scenes bargaining and lobbying reminiscent of the political methods of the Kádár era, the various factions agreed on a joint list of new Presidium members. The two ex officio members were Rezsö Nyers and the would-be faction leader of the HSP in the new Hungarian National Assembly to be elected on 25 March 1990. Others elected to the Presidium were Imre Pozsgay, Miklós Németh (who, however, resigned in protest against the HSP's position on the new state budget on 18 December), Gyula Horn, Jenö Kovács, Mária Ormos, Pál Vastagh, Imre Nagy, Béla Katona, Lajos Menyhárt, György Szabó, Lidia Rácz, Ilona Madl, László Boros, Ferenc Kósa, Iván Vitányi, Csaba Hámori, Csaba Vass, József Géczi, Béla Fabry, László Körösföi, Károly Lakos, and Sándor Szili. In addition to members of the former *nomenklatura* and sympathetic members of the intelligentsia, there are only two active workers (Boros and Szili) in the Presidium. The peasantry has no genuine representative. The old HSWP Central Committee would be replaced by a National Board to be elected in January 1990. No member of the current Presidium would be allowed to serve on the board. Members of the HSWP had until 10 November to opt for membership in the new HSP (*Népszabadság*, 11 October). Since then, this deadline has been extended at least twice because only a few thousand have joined the new party.

Just a week after the close of the fateful HSWP congress, a group of Hungarian communists loyal to the old HSWP denounced the recent transformation of their party into the HSP and pledged to continue to uphold the organizational structure and policies of the old HSWP (ibid., 4 November). As their chief spokesman, Róbert Ribanszki, stated in an interview with the BBC, the communists loyal to the policies of János Kádár are resolved to maintain their political and organizational independence from the new HSP (BBC, "Central Talks and Features," 5 November). On 10 November the former general secretary of the HSWP Central Committee, Károly Grósz, ended weeks of hesitation and declared himself ready to take an active part in the revival of his old party (*Népszabadság*, 11 November). Subsequently, on 17 December, the newly constituted HSWP elected Gyula Thurmer as its general secretary. Displaying his ignorance of the situation in the country, the new HSWP general secretary declared that his party intends to represent the elderly and the various minorities (ibid., 18 December).

Domestic Affairs. Throughout 1989 the domestic agenda was dominated by the important issues of political and economic reform. Following the 10–11 February HSWP Central Committee plenum that endorsed the transition to a multiparty system, the National Assembly unanimously approved the principles of the new constitution at its session of 8–10 March. According to the National Assembly's decision, the new constitution would no longer include any reference to the "leading role of the HSWP," thus opening the door for the establishment of a multiparty system. The principles also called for the establishment of the office of president of the republic, a central auditing office as an arm of the Parliament, and an ombudsman's office (*Magyar Nemzet*, 11 March).

Just a day after the conclusion of the National Assembly's session, the Hungarian Democratic Forum opened its first national congress at Budapest's Karl Marx University of Economic Sciences. The forum, officially established in September 1988, elected a 15-member presidium and issued a 21-point political statement. The statement, entitled "Freedom, Independence, and Democracy," called on all Hungary's democratic forces to join together in rescuing the nation from its moral, political, and economic crisis by turning the country into an independent and democratic state within the framework of European culture and civilization. The statement also stressed that the forum wanted to achieve its political and economic objectives exclusively by peaceful means. (Ibid., 12 March.)

On 19 March the first national congress of the Federation of the Free Democrats was held in Budapest. The federation published the first comprehensive opposition draft program for government based on the political and economic principles of the democratic countries of North America and Western Europe. The draft program, which was subsequently ratified on 16 April, defined the federation's main objective as "enhancing the social processes through which our culture and institutions may be integrated into Europe's culture and its institutional system." At the same time, the program decisively rejected both the "utopia of reform communism" and Pozsgay's and other reformists' favorite concept of "the third road." The federation warned that "paths seeking to avoid what have become known as European values lead to either a right-wing dictatorship or left-wing totalitarianism." The program also called for an entirely new constitution that would end the HSWP's monopoly of power, guarantee the sovereignty of the people, and, instead of limiting the powers of the citizens, limit the powers of the state by separating the three branches of government. The federation's spokesman, Péter Tölgyessy, urged that the new constitution be drawn up by a new democratically elected parliament and not by the present communist-dominated National Assembly. Another important part of the program dealt with the problem of poverty in society. Noting that the number of poor people has increased alarmingly, the program stated that the rapidly deteriorating situation has created untenable social tensions. Claiming that Hungarian society was characterized by a "deep and widening gulf" between a "stable, secure majority" and an "uneducated, unskilled minority," the program called for a social security system that would take care of the people's basic needs. Finally, the program urged the HSWP to "keep its military organizations out of the political arena" and to forego any attempt to limit the activities of independent groups. (Ibid., 21 March.) At its 16 April meeting, the federation issued a declaration stating that the HSWP-dominated government was unable to deal with Hungary's political and economic crisis in a satisfactory manner and should therefore be replaced until the elections of 1990 by an interim government. Another declaration suggested that

property owned by the HSWP and its auxiliary organizations must be seized and placed under public control (ibid., 17 April).

In response to the federation's demand for the resignation of the government and for a dialogue between the HSWP and the opposition forces, the HSWP agreed on 9 June to begin wide-ranging negotiations with Opposition Round Table (ORT), an umbrella organization of independent groups (*Népszabadság, Magyar Hirlap, Magyar Nemzet,* 10 June). The next day representatives of the HSWP and the opposition groups signed an eight-page agreement defining the objectives and the procedures of the negotiations. The two main objectives of the negotiations were to determine "the principles and rules that will promote the realization of a democratic transition" and to discuss "the strategic tasks involved in overcoming the economic and social crisis." The agreement unequivocally stated that these objectives were meant to establish a Western-style, multiparty, democratic political system. The parties to the agreement also pledged to use "all political means at their disposal" to ensure that decisions reached during the negotiations are put into practice (*Magyar Nemzet,* 11 June). An agreement was also reached on the venue of the talks. Accordingly, they were held in the Parliament Building and were presided over by Mátyás Szürös, the new president of the National Assembly.

At the negotiations that commenced on 21 June the HSWP's delegation was headed by Imre Pozsgay. Other members of the delegation were Zoltán Gál, a state minister in the Ministry of Internal Affairs, Géza Kilenyi, a deputy minister in the Ministry of Justice, and Rezsö Nyers. At the start of the meeting ORT made a concession: Under pressure from the HSWP, representatives of ORT agreed that both political and economic issues, in equal proportion, should be the subject of further talks. On behalf of ORT, Iván Petö explained that

> it is difficult in today's economic situation to make people who are less experienced in politics understand why organizations that have no power to influence the economy do not want to negotiate about it. We felt that it was not profitable to adhere so rigidly to our principles that our behavior might be misunderstood. (Ibid., 22 June.)

On the basis of ORT's concession, two committees were designated to deal with the separate issues of political and economic reform. The first committee, which dealt with political questions, focused on the topic of constitutional changes, the establishment of the office of president of the republic, the creation of a constitutional court, the legal regulation of political parties, the forthcoming elections to the National Assembly, revisions to the penal code, a new law on the press, and the creation of legal guarantees that exclude violent solutions to Hungary's present problems. The second committee, which handled economic issues, discussed strategies for dealing with the economic crisis, ways of treating the social consequences of the economic crisis, property reform, and questions related to new laws regulating land ownership and cooperatives (*Magyar Hirlap*, 17 June).

After this promising start, however, the negotiations ran into an impasse over the main political issues of a new constitution, procedures for multiparty elections, the election of a president, and the financing of political parties and their election campaigns. The negotiations were suspended after open conflict erupted at the 27 July sessions. (On that day, the HSWP's delegation was headed by György Fejti in place of Imre Pozsgay [*Magyar Nemzet*, 28 July].) When the talks resumed on 24 August, the HSWP was remarkably inconsistent on the issue of the HSWP's representation in the workplace. Péter Tölgyessy, ORT's spokesman, charged that HSWP's objective at the negotiations was "to hold onto its hegemony by hiding behind a democratic facade." Moreover, he pointed out that HSWP's insistence on including in the constitution "the leading role of the working class, the absolute priority of public ownership, and the education of the young people in a socialist spirit" reflected its true hegemonic intentions. He also accused the HSWP of using these "classical Stalinist tenets" as bargaining chips to pressure ORT into further concessions and of attempting to maintain "the old institutions and the old leaders by faking democracy." (Ibid., 29 August.) During the session, Imre Pozsgay presented ORT with an ultimatum: Unless the opposition was prepared to reach an agreement by 18 September at the latest, the communist-controlled government would submit legislation on the democratic transformation to the equally communist-dominated National Assembly. (*Népszabadság*, 26 August.)

Thus, following three months of hard bargaining, the HSWP and five of the opposition groups represented in ORT, including the Hungarian Democratic Forum, the largest among them, reached an agreement on 18 September on the process of transition from one-party rule to a multiparty system of government (*Magyar Hirlap*, 19 September). Four others, among them the Federation of Free Democrats and the Alliance of Young Democrats, refused to sign the accord. Their reluctance to approve the accord was based on the timing of the proposed elections for the newly created post of president of the republic (*Magyar Nemzet*, 19 September). The HSWP nominated Imre Pozsgay as its candidate and pressed for an early referendum under the auspices of the communist-controlled National Assembly. Initially, ORT remained united and strongly opposed to the HSWP timetable by arguing that it was another device to ensure further HSWP control over the government. In a joint statement, ORT stated that a strong presidency under HSWP member Imre Pozsgay could "carry over the hegemony of the HSWP into a democratic system, even if the HSWP is defeated in the elections." By claiming to move away from the HSWP, Pozsgay succeeded in splitting ORT. At the founding meeting of a Movement for a Democratic Hungary, Pozsgay declared that if elected president of the republic he would listen to the entire nation "rather than subordinate himself to the interests of a party" (*Népszabadság*, 12 July). In addition, using his close personal ties to the then leaders of the Hungarian Democratic Front, Lajos Biró and József Antal, he promised the latter the position of prime minister after the elections.

When an agreement was reached, it was left to the communist-controlled National Assembly to rubber-stamp its provisions, and indeed, on 18 October, the National Assembly adopted by an overwhelming majority a series of amendments to the country's constitution. Accordingly, the amended preamble of the constitution states that Hungary is "an independent, democratic state based on the rule of law, in which the value of bourgeois democracy and democratic socialism are equally recognized." The Hungarian state is defined as a "republic" rather than a "people's republic." The leading role of the HSWP was eliminated, and the term *people's sovereignty*, defined as the people's power exercised by the people both "through its elected representatives and directly," reintroduced into the constitution. The National Assembly also abolished the 21-member Presidential Council and created the office of president of the republic. Pursuant to the new constitutional provisions, the president is to be elected for a four-year term by the National Assembly and he is the commander in chief of the armed forces. The amended constitution further mandates that "political parties can be established freely and are free to operate" provided they observe the constitution. Another amendment states that Hungary's economy shall be based on "a market economy that also makes use of the advantages of planning, and in which public and private property are equal and receive equal protection." (*Magyar Közlöny*, 30 September.)

The National Assembly failed to solve the controversy over the timing of the presidential elections. After requesting a recess and briefly discussing the issue with his cabinet, Prime Minister Miklós Németh proposed, and the National Assembly agreed, to defer action on a call by the Federation of Free Democrats and the Alliance of Young Democrats for a referendum on delaying the vote until after the parliamentary elections (*Magyar Hirlap*, 12 September). At the same time, however, Németh promised that a referendum would be held if the 200,000 signatures collected by the two opposition groups proved to be legally valid.

In other matters the National Assembly voted to ban all political parties from the workplace beginning in January 1990. The National Assembly also passed a law mandating that all parties shall receive subsidies from the state budget and barring any party from accepting money from outside the country or from state agencies or enterprises. (Ibid.)

After bowing to domestic and international pressure, the National Assembly ordered on 30 October that a referendum must be held on 26 November on whether the country's presidential elections should take place before or after the first free parliamentary elections. At the same time three other questions were also placed on the ballot: Should party organizations move out of the workplace? Should the HSWP (now the HSP) give an account of the assets that it owns or administers? Should the Workers' Guard be disbanded? The referendum, by some 6,000 out of the nearly 4.3 million votes cast, gave the Federation of Free Democrats a marginal victory (*Magyar Nemzet*, 29 November). This result assured that presidential elections will not take place until after the 25 March 1990 parliamentary elections.

Paving the way for Hungary's first free parliamentary elections in 42 years, the National Assembly voted on 22 December to dissolve itself. In a roll call vote, 320 deputies voted to end the National Assembly's mandate on 16 March 1990 (*Magyar Hirlap*, 23 December). The elections will be held on 25 March 1990.

Economic Affairs. The 1980s were a decade of mounting foreign indebtedness, rapid economic decline, unemployment, and impoverishment of large segments of the Hungarian population. To set the tone for 1989 and beyond, the then HSWP daily *Népszabadság* reported on 3 January that the average real wage in Hungary had dropped to the level of 1973. According to the author of the article, statistician Mihály Zafir, the gross income in Hungary averaged $160 a month, which amounted to only $127 after tax and pension deductions. In the conclusion of his article, he stated that "if we want to find a year when earnings were worth the same as last year, we would have to go back to 1973."

Despite the worsening economic situation, no fundamental changes were implemented by the government in 1989. The new enterprise law, which was passed by the National Assembly in October 1988, did not fulfill official and private expectations. Vegetating and deficit-ridden state enterprises were hoping for foreign investors to relieve them of their financial and economic miseries. Because of the uncertain political situation and widespread cynicism among the population, however, few viable small or medium-sized enterprises were established. As a result, no real economic alternatives to the rigid and debt-plagued state enterprise system arose, seemingly perpetuating Hungary's industrial stagnation and technological backwardness vis-à-vis the West.

Despite a great deal of rhetoric by the government, no serious actions were taken to solve the problems of the grossly inefficient steel and coal industries. The bankruptcy law was also sparingly used in 1989 (*Heti Világgazdaság*, 11 March). Once again, an entrenched, conservative, professionally inept, and morally corrupt government and economic bureaucracy kept a paralyzing hold on the country's huge state-controlled industrial and agricultural sector. Through the system of over-regulation, various ministries and Hungary's National Bank maintained the same powers they enjoyed before 1989. Thus far, the government has not dared to openly challenge or oppose the large interest groups.

Another major shortcoming of the year 1989 was that the government once again failed to present the National Assembly and the nation with a comprehensive and coherent national economic policy. Thus budget and public finance reform, economic constitutionality, privatization, inflation, and unemployment policy, as well as the complex issue of sociopolitical reform, were only addressed in a fragmented and haphazard fashion.

In 1989 the agricultural sector also continued to face mounting problems. Generally speaking the same macroeconomic problems that plagued the entire economy, such as slow growth, high foreign debt, bad investment, insolvency, an aging and dwindling work force, and mismanagement, combined to create a critical situation. The congress of the National Council of Cooperatives in December only reinforced the powers of those who oppose any radical structural changes in Hungarian agriculture.

On the positive side, Western assistance and steadily growing investment indicated that there were some positive developments in Hungary. President George Bush's visit in July yielded $81 million instead of the originally promised $25 million over the next three years. At the end of September the U.S. government granted permanent most favored nation trade status to Hungary (*WP*, 29 September). Countries of the European Community and member states of the Organization for Economic Cooperation and Development also helped the country with a combination of loan packages and investments. New joint ventures with American, West European, and Japanese partners numbered more than three hundred in 1989.

Yet true changes in the Hungarian economy could only take place when essential reforms in the political life of the country are introduced after the 25 March 1990 elections. The new government must formulate a comprehensive national economic policy, publicize it, and implement it without further delay, for only a well-informed Hungarian people will support any proposed structural transformations in the economy. A mistrusting society will render any attempt to reform a crisis-ridden economy meaningless.

A first step in the right direction came on 22 December when the National Assembly approved the new austerity measures suggested by the International Monetary Fund and proposed by the government. Accordingly, rents of state-owned apartments will be raised by an average of 35 percent starting in February 1990. Prices of basic commodities will increase by an average of 25 percent. Interests on loans will also be taxed retroactively (*NYT*, 23 December). Prime Minister Miklós Németh predicted additional budget cuts and warned of a steep increase in unemployment and a further decline in the standard of living (*Népszabadság*, 23 December). Meanwhile, for the average Hungarian 1990 promises nothing but social tensions and economic misery. His disapproval of the country's economic situation will certainly manifest itself at the ballot boxes on 25 March.

Foreign Affairs. In terms of national interest, Hungary's foreign policy was a success story in 1989. The main objective of this policy was, at the minimum, to prevent criticism of domestic developments by Moscow and, at the maximum, to secure Soviet support for needed political and economic reforms. Hungarian foreign policy also served to demonstrate to the West that the leadership is determined to transform the country into an independent, democratic, and free market–oriented society. In this context, the uniqueness and the higher quality of Hungarian progress, compared with the inferior Polish situation, were constantly emphasized. Last but not least, Hungarian foreign policy aimed at preventing the hard-line leaderships of East Germany, Czechoslovakia, and Romania from organizing against Hungary and thus reviving the specter of the "little entente" that has haunted the Hungarian leadership since 1968.

Speaking on the "Radio Diary" program from Budapest on 30 January, Mátyás Szürös, then HSWP Central Committee secretary and chairman of the National Assembly's foreign affairs committee, profusely praised the Soviet Union for its "outstandingly important role" in the process of global and regional relaxation of international tensions. Paying tribute to the "unilateral Soviet disarmament," he claimed that "it reflects the Soviet Union's feeling of responsibility—its responsibility toward the fate of humanity and the world and, of course toward the Soviet people." (Radio Kossuth, "Radio Napló," 30 January.) Thus having established the Soviet Union and, by implication, its leader Mikhail Gorbachev as the driving forces behind the favorable international changes, Szürös set the tone for Prime Minister Miklós Németh's so-called working visit to Moscow.

The meetings between Németh and Gorbachev and then between Németh and Ryzhkov took place on 2–3 March. Németh emphasized the need to improve coordination of the national economic plans of the Soviet Union and Hungary. He noted with satisfaction that significant efforts were already being made to create new forms of production and scientific and technical cooperation between the two countries. He also revealed that twenty joint enterprises in different branches of the national economy, two international associations, and nineteen joint scientific collectives had been created in the last few years. Clearly courting Soviet favors, Németh promised Moscow new projects in Hungary connected mainly with construction and the expansion of the nuclear power station at Paks. Németh also echoed the Soviet line on the Council for Mutual Economic Assistance (CMEA). Noting that the advantages emerging from the implementation of the decisions of the 44th CMEA session and the international socialist division of labor within this organization were important factors in the development of the Hungarian national economy, he assured his guests that Hungary will in the future strive to improve "the structure of Soviet-Hungarian economic links by raising the technical level and quality of goods supplied to the Soviet Union." (Radio Kossuth, 3 March; *Népszabadság*, 4 March.)

Following closely in Németh's footsteps, Károly Grósz, then still the general secretary of the HSWP Central Committee, visited the Soviet Union on 23–24 March. After paying lip service to *glasnost'* and *perestroika*, he expressed the opinion on Moscow television that "the changes under way in our countries have much in common. The process of society's democratization is currently developing very dynamically in the Soviet Union." Singling out the CPSU Central Committee's decision on the further development of the agricultural sector, he stated that "the efforts to accelerate the course of economic reforms [in the Soviet Union] in my view acquire an extraordinarily great significance." (*Népszabadság*, 25 March.)

In addition to favorably comparing Soviet developments with the reform process in Hungary, the HSWP leadership was eager to portray Hungary as a reliable ally of the Soviet Union. Expanding on this theme, Szürös stated that

we believe that Gorbachev sees the benefit to the Soviet Union of relations with stable allies. The question is not how far we can trust the Soviet Union but how much trust we can gain from a Soviet Union that has changed by abandoning the discredited Brezhnev doctrine.... We must proceed to a new order in constant accord with the Soviets, coordinating the pace of diplomatic action with the growing aspirations of the Hungarian people and other peoples. (Ibid., 29 March.)

The HSWP leadership remained undaunted even by the hypothetical statements of academician Oleg Bogomolov. Presumably not being able to decide whether to qualify Bogomolov's statements on Hungary's neutrality as a provocation or as a trial balloon, both the HSWP and the government maintained their officially pro-Soviet posture. Even the partial Soviet troop withdrawals from Hungary were portrayed by the leadership as part of a greater strategic design by the two superpowers rather than a diplomatic victory for Hungary. (Ibid., 30 March.)

To emphasize the HSWP's loyalty to the Soviet Union, Rezsö Nyers, immediately after his election to the chairmanship of the party, undertook the obligatory pilgrimage to Moscow. In his interview with Budapest television he stated that relations between the two countries are excellent because they are based on mutual interests, problems, and solutions (Magyar Televizió, 14 July).

Hungary's foreign policy strategy toward the West showed a high degree of sophistication and an understanding of both the Western political mind and the modus operandi of the media. In their speeches and frequent interviews, Hungarian politicians consistently hammered away at the theme of the country's desire to become an accepted member of the community of independent and democratic nations. This, they emphasized, could not happen without the political, economic, financial, and moral assistance of the West. At the same time, they asked for understanding for the slow pace of the reform process, pointing to Hungary's delicate geographic and strategic situation in central Europe.

The treatment of President Bush's visit to Hungary in July provided a closer look at the delicate balancing act of the Hungarian leadership. On the one hand, Hungarian citizens were not limited in expressing their spontaneous excitement over the president's presence in their country. On the other hand, the Hungarian leaders kept their distance and refrained from making any statement or expressing any sentiments that could upset or offend Moscow.

In another move to please the United States, on 18 September Hungary restored full diplomatic relations with Israel (*Népszabadság*, 19 September). Almost simultaneously, Hungary applied for membership in the Council of Europe. By taking these symbolic steps toward joining the community of Western European nations, Hungary signaled its intentions to serve as a bridge between the two parts of Europe. Yugoslavia, Poland, and the Soviet Union have already announced that they too might follow Hungary's lead and apply for full membership in the Council of Europe.

In addition to the Soviet Union, Hungary had to

deal with the growing resentments within the East German, Czechoslovak, and Romanian leaderships. Essentially, Hungary and the other three countries were afraid of one another. The Hungarian leadership feared the eventual revival of the "little entente," whereas East Germany, Czechoslovakia, and Romania were afraid that developments in Hungary would undermine their monopoly of power over their subjects. To prevent an alliance, the Hungarian leadership embarked on an international version of the famous salami tactic applied successfully by Rakosi against his domestic opposition in the mid- and late 1940s. In April, for example, when Hungarian-Czechoslovak relations reached a particularly low point, Hungarian television aired a two-part exclusive interview with Alexander Dubček (Magyar Televizió, 11, 12 April). In August a similar interview was aired by Hungarian television with the former Romanian king Michael (ibid., 23, 24 April). Both countries protested and recalled their respective ambassadors for consultations (Rudé pravo, 13 April; Scînteia, 25 August). In the same month, both the Czechoslovak and the Romanian media complained bitterly about the alleged "internationalization of anti-socialist protests" (Scînteia, 28 August; Rudé pravo, 30 August). Indeed, two young Hungarians were fined and expelled for participating in an unauthorized demonstration in Prague to mark the 21st anniversary of the Soviet-led invasion of Czechoslovakia. Since the HSWP, the other opposition groups and parties, and the Hungarian National Assembly had already condemned the invasion and Hungary's participation in it, Hungary launched an official protest against their detention and trial (Magyar Nemzet, 24 August). When the two Hungarian citizens, György Kerényi and Tamás Deutsch, returned to Budapest, they received a hero's welcome by both the leadership and the people (ibid., 30 August).

The potentially most damaging Hungarian move, however, was the leadership's decision, announced on 10 September, to allow East German refugees to leave for the West (Népszabadság, 11 September). To say that the Hungarian leadership was purely motivated by its desire to destabilize the Honecker regime would ignore the complexity and the delicacy of the refugees' refusal to return to East Germany. Most important, the Hungarian leadership had to consider the issue of its domestic and international credibility. Having complained bitterly for years about the inhuman and illegal treatment of the Hungarian minority in Romania, it could not ignore its own standards and international

obligations. Moreover, the leadership could not discriminate in its treatment between the Hungarian and Romanian refugees on the one hand and the refugees from East Germany on the other. Finally, the Federal Republic of Germany, the largest West European donor of financial and economic assistance to Hungary, was closely watching the situation of the Germans in Hungary.

During the crisis the Soviet Union sent mixed signals to all three countries. On the one hand, the official news agency TASS accused "certain political circles and some media" in the Federal Republic of launching a "tendentious campaign" against the GDR (Pravda, 11 September). On the other hand, the Soviet television newscast "Novosty" carried a report showing understanding for Hungary's predicament and subsequent decision (Népszabadság, 14 September). The newscast noted that

> in recent weeks the Hungarian government has been constantly occupying itself with issues connected with the situation of East German citizens in Hungary who wish to go to the Federal Republic of Germany.... The situation on the Austro-Hungarian border became tense, and there were a growing number of illegal border crossings and various crimes. It was in this situation that the Hungarian government was forced to take the decision.

Thus absolved by Moscow of any wrongdoing, the Hungarian leadership notified East Berlin that East Germans who express their desire to go to the West would be allowed to leave Hungary. (Ibid.)

As a result of the Hungarian decision, the Honecker regime collapsed within a month. The events in East Germany were quickly followed by the collapse of the Husak-Jakeš regime in Prague. Finally, just before Christmas, the hated Ceaușescu clan was overthrown in Romania.

Independent Groups and Parties. On the basis of the results of the 26 November referendum, the revived HSWP will only receive about 5 percent of the votes on 25 March 1990. The newly created HSP has faced major difficulties in increasing its membership to twenty thousand. Because of the fading popularity of Imre Pozsgay, the HSP's share of the votes cast on 25 March most likely will not exceed 10 percent. The remaining 85 percent will be divided among Hungary's other political parties.

Among these newly created parties, four have a good chance of receiving more than 5 percent of the votes. The party that has excellent name recognition, political history, and broad-based support at the grass roots level is the Hungarian Independent Smallholders' party (Független Magyar Kisgazda Párt). Founded in 1930 the party was reorganized in Szentendre on 12 November 1988. As of 20 December 1989, the party had an estimated membership of more than 40,000 organized into some three hundred chapters nationwide. The Smallholders' party program, based on the original charter of the party, calls for free elections, a new constitution, and a national referendum on the major issues, such as the nature of the political system and the future of the Soviet troops in Hungary. The main political and economic objectives of the Smallholder's party are the radical reform of the political system, the revitalization of agriculture and related industrial branches, and the rehabilitation of the farmers, the free market, and price reform. The leaders of the Smallholders' party are Isván Prepeliczay, Péter Hardi, Vince Vörös, Sándor Faludy, Tivadar Partay, Dezsö Futó, Pál Dragon, and Géza Zsiros. The Smallholders' party has the best chance of becoming the majority party in the new National Assembly.

The Social Democratic party (Szocialdemokrata Párt, SDP) was founded in 1890 and reorganized on 9 January 1989. The SDP has a well-organized political base in the major cities. Despite the initial bitter feuds within its leadership, it stands a good chance of becoming a major political force in Hungary. The political objective of the SDP is to establish a West European–style democracy in the country. The SDP's leadership consists of Anna Petrasovics, János Bölcskei, András Révész, and Tibor Baranyai.

The Federation of Free Democrats (Szabad Demokraták Szövetsége) was founded on 13 November 1988. This party's strength lies in the urban areas. The Free Democrats have had difficulties establishing a viable political infrastructure in the provinces. Despite this shortcoming, the Free Democrats are one of the key opposition parties in Hungary. Their manifesto, entitled "The Program of Change of the Political System," demonstrates conceptual clarity and a realistic approach and is likely to appeal to most of the intellectuals and some of the farmers and workers. The Free Democrats are led by János Kiss, Gábor Demszky, Imre Mécs, Bálint Magyar, Ottilia Solt, László Rajk, Jr., and Árpád Göncz.

The Alliance of Young Democrats (Fiatal Demokraták Szövetsége) was founded on 30 March 1988 and represents mostly the youth. The Alliance advocates the restoration of Western-style democracy and a total reform of the country's political and economic system and is fiercely opposed to the presence of Soviet troops in Hungary. Its leading members are Zsolt Németh, Viktor Orbán, Miklós Andrássy, Csaba Fodor, Zsuzsa Szelényi, and Tamás Deutsch.

Miklós K. Radványi
McLean, Virginia

Poland

Population. 38,169,800 (July 1989), growth rate is 0.5 percent per annum.
Party. Polish United Workers' Party (Polska Zjednoczona Partia Robotnicza, PZPR)
Founded. 1948
Membership. 2,090,000 (July 1989) claimed; 1,000,000 estimated at end of year.
First Secretary. Mieczysław F. Rakowski
Politburo. Władysław Baka, Kazimierz Cypryniak, Manfred Gorywoda, Wojciech Jaruzelski, Czesław Kiszczak, Janusz Kubasiewicz, Iwona Lubowska, Zbigniew Michałek, Leszek Miller, Marian Orzechowski, Wiktor Pyrkosz, Mieczysław Rakowski, Gabriela Rembisz, Janusz Reykowski, Florian Siwicki, Zdzisław Swiątek
Candidate Members. Zdzisław Balicki, Marek Hodakowski, Zbigniew Sobótka
Secretariat. Marek Król, Zbigniew Michałek, Leszek Miller, Włodzimierz Natorf, Mieczysław Rakowski, Marian Tęspien, Sławomir Wiatr, Zdzisław Balicki
Status. Minority in the ruling government coalition
Last Congress. Tenth, July 1986
Last Election. July; 37.5 percent; 173 of 460 seats
Publications. *Trybuna ludu*, party daily, *Nowe drogi* and *Ideologia i polityka*, party monthlies. Polska Agencja Prasowa (PAP) is the official news agency.

Although it is still premature to place the extraordinary events that took place in Poland during 1989 in the context of a broad historical perspective, it should be emphasized that the scope of freedom recently attained by the Polish nation had been expected immediately after World War II. The right to "free and unfettered" elections guaranteed by the provisions of the Yalta agreement was suspended in Poland for two generations. Not only did the nation lose more than six million of its citizens and half of its prewar territories during World War II, but it had to experience more than four decades of communist totalitarianism.

Liberation from the imperial grip of Moscow came late, and a heavy price has been paid for the newly acquired freedom. Poland suffers from an immense array of intractable social and economic problems that may require another generation to cure. The country is one of the poorest in Europe, and Germany, its traditional Western rival, is the leading European economic power and on its way to being unified. International trends are not favorable because the country may soon face a consolidated German state that far outdistances Poland demographically and economically.

The disintegration of the Soviet state may not be advantageous to the international security of Poland. The poor and troubled Polish state is losing its utility for Moscow as a barrier against the West. Again, Russians may seek closer ties with Germans at the expense of Poles, who, thanks to Moscow's heavy-handed policies, have been reduced to "the sick men of Europe." The developments in East Germany have diverted world attention from Polish to German affairs, despite the fact that Poland initiated and continues to lead an evolution toward democracy and a free market economy. The emerging Europe is in danger of acquiring the political characteristics of the 1930s, including a powerful Germany and an insecure Soviet Russia searching for every possible way to enhance its international standing. Historically, this situation has always proven fatal to Poland.

The Polish nation, however, feels triumphant over the capitulation of communism and the rapid spread of the "Polish disease" throughout Eastern Europe and a good portion of the Soviet state. Despite economic hardships, the Poles have overcome the apathy and resignation that prevailed since martial law was imposed in December 1981. This signals hope for internal recovery and an external search for a new system of security in Europe.

The Party. Activities of the communist party in 1989 began with arrangements for the second part of the Tenth Central Committee Plenum, which took place in Warsaw 16–17 January. The first part

of the plenum met at the end of December 1988 to discuss the rapidly deteriorating political and economic situation, including the party's position on roundtable talks between the authorities and the opposition. It was apparent from the beginning of the plenum that the party was deeply divided on the question of concessions to bridge the political cleavage in the country.

It appears that the authorities had a realistic perspective on the political situation in the country and had already accepted the necessity of negotiations with Solidarity, but remained divided with respect to the country's prospects for a speedy economic recovery and the strength of the opposition. The pessimists—represented by Władysław Bąka, member of the ruling Politburo and Central Committee secretary responsible for economic affairs—were skeptical about the 1989 central plan and, consequently, about the party's ability to lead Poland out of crisis. Wages had risen twice as fast as productivity, becoming the most negative and recurrent economic phenomena. In his address to the plenum, Bąka expressed concern over the economic program of the party and asked "whether the 1989 economic policy principles really constitute an economic breakthrough, whether they will really lead to equilibrium, a stabilization of prices, and an improvement to the market and to shopping conditions" (*Trybuna ludu*, 21 December 1988).

The optimists followed Poland's premier Mieczysław Rakowski. In his view, the roundtable negotiations were just a new form of consultations with the constructive opposition to determine the extent of the joint responsibility for the reforms advocated by the party. Solidarity, in his perspective, was negotiating from a position of weakness, because

unlike the opposition, we hold powerful trump cards, the most powerful of which is an extensive program of socioeconomic reforms. The opposition does not have such a program. Basically, all the opposition is doing is making faces and saying "no" to everything, or repeating objectives already contained in our programs. (*Trybuna ludu*, 22 December 1988.)

Unable to work out a uniform approach to Solidarity, the party decided to postpone any decision until the middle of January 1989, scheduling the second half of the plenum after consultations with the local party organizations and, most likely, with Moscow.

Once the spirit of realism and compromise prevailed, the second half of the Tenth Plenum came out in favor of broadening the national accord, of shaping an extensive proreform coalition open to varied standpoints and opinions, including those of the opposition. This would link all those who strive to get the country out of crisis and want to act with respect for the law and the Polish *raison d'état*. Moreover, the plenum resolution endorsed humanitarian values, including the "good of man, his needs and striving," social justice, "human and civil rights in their socioeconomic and political and spiritual discussion," and the "rights and sovereignty of other states and nations," rather than loyalty to Marxism-Leninism and Moscow. In fact, with its focus on pluralism, a market economy, and condemnation of "Stalinist lawlessness," some sections of the resolution could easily be confused with statements expressed by the Roman Catholic church. Finally, this document endorsed the "leading role of the working class" instead of the traditional support for the leading role for the party. (Warsaw Domestic Service, 18 January; *FBIS-EEU*, 19 January.) After four decades of political monopoly, the party had begun making preparations to share power.

On the day following the Tenth Plenum, General Wojciech Jaruzelski, who at that time was still the first secretary of the PZPR Central Committee, held a press conference with representatives of the Polish and international mass media. Immediately he focused on forthcoming political restructuring, stating that the "turn of 1988 and 1989 will with certainty go down as an exceptionally important moment in our own history" and that the "sociopolitical landscape of Poland will be subject to serious changes." The party accepted the "self-limitation" of its role and decided to cooperate in the "development of parliamentarianism in the socialist state." (Warsaw Domestic Service, 19 January; *FBIS-EEU*, 23 January.)

In short, after seven years of political and economic failure, the party made a decisive step toward a national accord, including the recognition of Solidarity. At the same time, however, General Jaruzelski fully realized that it was a provocative step that, in effect, paralyzed the party and split it into several factions. The most pronounced division included the central party apparatus and the hard-line local party organizations. Especially evident was opposition of the old regime-sponsored union, unaccustomed to competition among the workers, to the prospects of rivalry with Solidarity. Alfred Miodowicz, chairman of the official All-Polish Al-

liance of Trade Unions (Polish acronym, OZPP) and member of the Central Committee, admitted that his organization was not prepared for trade union pluralism in Poland and reacted with "astonishment, protest, dissatisfaction." (Warsaw Domestic Service, 20 January; *FBIS-EEU*, 23 January.)

Confusion among the rank-and-file party members surfaced when the top leadership reversed its uncompromising position toward Solidarity and abandoned Marxism-Leninism and the principle of centralism. Some members of the party even promoted the theory that General Jaruzelski's long-term objective was destruction of the party; the nomination of Mieczysław Rakowski from the position of Poland's premier to party first secretary inadvertently fulfilled these predictions. Without any constituency of his own, Rakowski weakened the party, galvanized the opposition, and ruined the economy to the point where abdication from power was the only alternative left for the communists. Jaruzelski, however, escaped the consequences of his policies when he assumed the position of Poland's president.

Along with the fundamental political changes, the Tenth Plenum mandated a substantial reduction of the party apparatus. Only three departments of the Central Committee were left intact to run daily affairs: the Central Committee office, the party management office, and the cadres' department. The plenum set up fifteen substantive commissions to reduce its political personnel by 45 percent. This change was designed to reduce the operating expenses of the party as well as to shift the center of gravity from central to regional offices and to increase responsibilities of elected party bodies by subordinating the executive apparatus of power to them.

The Eleventh Plenum of the Central Committee met in Warsaw on 31 March to hear the progress report on roundtable negotiations between the regime, represented by Minister of Internal Security Czesław Kiszczak, and the Solidarity organization. The Central Committee approved institutional reforms aimed at establishing a civic society and a "state based on socialist parliamentary democracy." However, special attention was placed on refurbishing the ruling united front, a coalition comprised of the Communists, the United Peasant party, the Democratic party, the lay Catholic and Christian movements, PAX (the Christian-Social Union), and the Polish Catholic-Social Union (*Trybuna ludu*, 1–2 April). Facing the upcoming semifree elections, the party became aware of its dependence on these junior partners, who for decades were treated in an arbitrary manner by the hegemonic PZPR.

The Eleventh Plenum marked the beginning of the party's electoral campaign. The Central Committee became concerned over an accelerated reduction in party ranks. The membership loss in 1988 was 17,000 and in the first month of 1989 amounted to 10,500 members. The average age of 44.6 for a party member and the fact that only 6 percent of the members were under 30 proved equally disturbing. Zygmunt Czarzasty, secretary of the Central Committee, urged an "offensive" geared

> on the one hand, to winning over society, and on the other, to the more effective and intellectually more creative communication of the substance of the 10th Central Committee plenum to party organizations in a way that will restore confidence in the power of the party and the sense of its actions.

The communists hoped to garner public confidence and popularity with the help of an anti-Stalinist platform, that is, the "elimination of the remnants of Stalinism in Poland and redressing the injustices experienced by citizens during the years 1937–1955, including those experienced by Polish Communists." (*Trybuna ludu*, 1–2 April.) The PZPR was still confident that its "prenuptial agreement" with Solidarity on the new political model in Poland would leave the communists as power brokers on the national scene.

The Twelfth Plenum of the Central Committee met two weeks later, on 15 April, for final consultations on the roundtable talks with Solidarity. Its resolution was unusually brief and concerned with matters of secondary importance. (Warsaw, PAP, 15 April; *FBIS-EEU*, 17 April.) In an interview with Finnish television, General Jaruzelski failed to mention the plenum and focused on international issues, implying that the most recent party meeting was just a form of internal consultation that introduced no changes to the line agreed on at the Tenth Plenum. Because nothing could be resolved, the plenum suspended its deliberations until the end of July, when the second half of the meeting was scheduled to take place.

When, on 28 July, the second half of the Thirteenth Plenum convened in Warsaw, political problems facing the party were far more serious than at the Tenth Plenum six months before. The main subjects of debate were an assessment of the politi-

cal situation after the roundtable deliberations, the elections to the *Sejm* and the Senate, and an evaluation of the country's economic situation. After losing the elections the party continued to struggle for a majority in the new government, appealing to the opposition for strict adherence to the roundtable agreement and to the public and the members of the ruling coalition for support.

As publicized speeches testify, the majority of the Central Committee realized that the party was in shambles. Marian Orzechowski, a member of the PZPR Central Committee and a hard-liner known for his frankness, stated,

> The majority of society has had enough of the party as it has been up to now . . . [and] a considerable part of the party base has had enough of the style and effects [of] the action of the present leadership, of the way decisions are taken, of the way [of] communicating with party people.

Turning to an evaluation of the economic situation, Orzechowski admitted that it had "drastically worsened." He continued,

> Statistical assessments, actual practice, and the perceptions of people make clear that not only have we not come close to the aims sketched out a year ago, but, quite the contrary . . . the crisis in house construction has deepened. Inflation is beating all records; the exchange rate for the dollar has reached soaring, utterly absurd levels. The Polish złoty is becoming a scrap of paper. (Warsaw Domestic Service, 28 July; *FBIS-EEU*, 31 July.)

Personnel reshuffles in the party leadership were the only important part of the Thirteenth Plenum and evidence that the center of political gravity in Poland had begun to shift rapidly away from the party. First, General Jaruzelski, elected president of the Polish People's Republic, resigned as party first secretary. He was replaced by Mieczysław Rakowski, the former premier of the government. On the evening of 28 July, after the conclusion of the first day of the Thirteenth Plenum, Jaruzelski had a lengthy discussion with the head of the Roman Catholic church in Poland, Cardinal Józef Glemp, chairman of the Episcopate. Cardinal Glemp congratulated Jaruzelski, endorsed his policies, and symbolically referred to him as the president of the republic, failing to mention people's republic. It is expected that in 1991 a new constitution will return to the historical term used by the cardinal. (Warsaw Domestic Service, 28 July; *FBIS-EEU*, 31 July.)

The Central Committee also accepted the resignation of several other prominent members of the Politburo, or Secretariat, including Kazimierz Barcikowski, Stanisław Ciosek, Józef Czyrek, Alfred Miodowicz, Władysław Baka, Zygmunt Czarzasty, and Marian Orzechowski. The new secretary thus inherited an organization that was intellectually and politically decimated. In his acceptance speech, however, he promised not to "fall on our knees before a political enemy on any occasion" and proclaimed that "alien to me are all concepts oriented toward liquidation of ideological sources of our movement. I reject nonsense talk about Marxism being played out, about the need to replace it with another source of ideological inspiration." (Warsaw, PAP, 30 July; *FBIS-EEU*, 1 August.) Interestingly, the newly appointed first secretary failed to include Leninism in his ideological oath.

Following the Thirteenth Plenum, the party realized that it had become an entirely different organization. Deprived of its leading role, it was no longer synonymous with the government and had to compete for a share of political power. This unprecedented development necessitates intellectual and political adjustments, which are likely to take time for a party apparatus accustomed to a political monopoly and little public accountability. Communists have no experience with political opposition, in particular, how to hold a ruling coalition together.

Immediately following the Thirteenth Plenum, the new first secretary of the Central Committee visited the PZPR parliamentary club to recommend Czesław Kiszczak, a member of the Politburo and minister of the interior, as a candidate for premier. The idea of supporting Kiszczak's candidacy originated at the Thirteenth Plenum, and Rakowski was made responsible for its implementation. The communist deputies invited Kiszczak for a formal interview, questioning him on a number of economic, social, and political issues; following an internal debate the PZPR parliamentary club officially endorsed him for the post of premier. Marian Orzechowski, leader of the club, presented Kiszczak as a successful negotiator of the new social contract with Solidarity and as an experienced politician committed to economic reform, political renewal, and compromise with the opposition. The communist leadership did not realize how unpopular this architect of martial law and political repression in the early and middle 1980s was. This step would soon break up the coalition with other parties and political groups, frustrate Solidarity, and eventually leave the communists isolated from the political scene in Poland. The idea of having a policeman as premier of a coalition representing all political orientations in Poland was unacceptable to everybody except the PZPR, for it appeared that the party intended to continue martial law politics under a facade of the new social accord in Poland. Announcement of Kiszczak's candidacy was immediately opposed by Solidarity and resisted by Solidarity's club of parliamentarians. "I was for President Kiszczak, I am against Premier Kiszczak," declared Lech Wałęsa. (Paris, AFP, 1 August; *FBIS-EEU*, 1 August.)

When the Fourteenth Plenum of the Central Committee was called by emergency procedure in Warsaw on 19 August, the issue was no longer how to create a new government but how to define the party's role in a Solidarity-led coalition government. Deserted by its traditional partners, the party had to consider joining a coalition government in which the leading role would be played by Solidarity. In fact, the PZPR leadership had to formulate a completely new program to fit its new role as a "constructive opposition, guided by the best conceived interest of the people and the state." (Warsaw Domestic Service, 19 August; *FBIS-EEU*, 21 August.)

Bitterness and disappointment prevailed during the meeting as PZPR first secretary Mieczysław Rakowski accused his former allies of "breaking the agreement on the distribution of forces in the *Sejm*" and preferring "opportunistic alliances" and "confrontation" with the communists. Knowing that the political trends were highly unfavorable for the communists, Rakowski used the plenum as a show of force or even as a threat of unilateral action whereby the party would take control of ministries essential to internal and external security and refuse to cooperate in all other political matters. This strategy was aimed at forcing Solidarity and its new allies to accept the idea of a grand coalition that would provide the communists with a sizable share in the government. Poland, according to the party, could never extricate itself from this crisis without the active participation of the communists. In the unsubstantiated view of the Central Committee, the party continued to have solid roots in Polish society and deserved credit for its achievements. Rakowski, aggressive and impatient, concluded that under his leadership the party would become demanding and militant:

I also believe that as a result of the political situation and the government configuration taking precisely this shape, there is a chance that our party will become a party of struggle. I have political struggle in mind. I interpret it as having to defend our program, our ideals, to defy all kinds of rumors, idiotic slanders, and attacks on the historic attainments of People's Poland. For instance, I consider that in spite of all the errors, all lapses, and tight spots that we have gone through. (Warsaw Domestic Service, 19 August; *FBIS-EEU*, 21 August.)

This new political campaign included a telephone conversation between Rakowski and Soviet leader Mikhail Gorbachev. This political move received wide publicity in Poland and abroad because Gorbachev had once stated that "Polish problems could not be solved without the participation of the PZPR." Without strong communist representation in the government, argued Rakowski, Poland would soon be "in conflict with its neighbors, deprived of a real economic infrastructure—I mean the thousands of people who link our economy with the CMEA countries—[and] exposed to unilateral actions by neighboring or more distant countries discussing Poland without Poland's population" (quoted in "The 14th PUWP Plenum and Its Aftermath: The Party Tries to Hold on to Power," by Anna Świdlicka, RFE/RE, Polish SR/4, 12 September).

Rakowski's strategy paid off when the party received several ministries in the new government. The future survival of the party as a political force in Poland is directly tied to its participation in the government, and its popularity is fading. The guarantee that ministries in internal and external security would be in the hands of the party is not sufficient for the survival of this organization, for these ministries are under the direct supervision of President Jaruzelski, who has already distanced himself from the party.

The practice of splitting the Central Committee plenums into two parts persisted during the fifteenth meeting. Internal divisions could no longer be handled at the Central Committee level, but had to be reconciled via consultations with local authorities. The first half of the Fifteenth Plenum met on 18 September in Warsaw to discuss the PZPR's future. For the first time in party history, it no longer had a majority in both legislative and executive bodies; a transition from socialism to capitalism had begun. Following a breakdown of the old coalition, the communists were given only four

ministerial posts in the new government: national defense, internal affairs, foreign economic relations, and transportation, in addition to deputy chairman of the Council of Ministers, which went to General Kiszczak as minister of internal affairs.

The main theme of this plenum revolved around forming a new image and public support for the party, as well as defining its stance vis-à-vis the government. Chosen were a role of "constructive opposition" and a political line "in a spirit of shared responsibility for instituting essential reforms that meet the needs of working people and are in keeping with the Polish *raison d'état* and the spirit of the free roundtable" (*Trybuna ludu*, 20 September).

With power no longer in its hands, the Central Committee advocated unity of action but diversity of views within the party and a reconciliation with pluralism. During the second half of the plenum, First Secretary Rakowski expressed hope for a "rapid intellectual revitalization" and a "down to earth approach" closely reflecting reality (*Trybuna ludu*, 4 October). The leadership realized that the party suffered from bureaucratic sluggishness and frequently failed to respond quickly to a changing political situation. Finally, the communists failed to develop a procedure that would guarantee the best and most active members opportunities to reach leadership positions.

To address this problem, the Fifteenth Plenum accelerated preparations for the Eleventh PZPR Congress, scheduled to begin on 27 January 1990. This general conference would have three tasks: first, to debate the future of socialism in Poland, second, to develop a new and more democratic framework for the party, and, third, to address the problem of the deteriorating socioeconomic situation on the country.

This political campaign of the party includes preparing to pick up the pieces of the political coalition centered around Solidarity if it fails to improve the situation and breaks down in disagreement. Some party officials believe that the present coalition will not last more than two years. (*Polityka*, 1 July.)

Tactics employed by the party emphasize the end of an era in its history. Perception of a centralized, dogmatic, authoritarian, and conservative organization usurping political power and mishandling social and economic affairs is to be substituted by a completely new picture. Reference to communism has almost disappeared from the party's statements. Instead, the PZPR calls itself "the left" and claims to be representing a completely new platform of social equality, democracy, stability, economic prosperity, pragmatism, antibureaucratic attitudes, and a concern for national security in the time of a nationalistic revival in Germany.

One symptom of stagnation in the party was indicated by an opinion poll conducted among members and candidate members on how the delegates to the Eleventh Congress should be elected, how the debates ought to be held, how the congress should be organized, and whether the party's name should be changed. Only 1,114,551 party members and candidates (that is, 50.6 percent) responded; of those who did respond, 80.5 percent expressed a preference for direct elections of delegates to the Eleventh Congress; 84 percent preferred a broad debate on political programs, ideology, organization, and allowing other political groups to participate in preparations for the congress; and 72.1 percent, that the PZPR be transformed into a new party with a new program, statute, and name (*Trybuna ludu*, 4 October).

Ambiguity over the future of the party will persist for the time being, but the possibility that the PZPR will remodel itself to reflect the tradition of the Polish Socialist party, which in 1948 was forcibly merged into the united communist party, dominated by the pro-Soviet members of the old Polish communist party, cannot be ruled out. In this case, the party would adopt the traditions of West European socialism and abandon Russian Marxism-Leninism. It is also possible that the party will break down along ideological lines into socialists, supported by a majority of its current members, and a minority of orthodox and militant communists hanging on to the outdated slogan and practices. The third alternative would involve a peculiarly Polish synthesis of socialism and communism, that is, uniting the liberals and the hard-liners of the party. Political liberals in the party have already established their own identity as the 8 July Movement. In the declaration adopted at a meeting held in Warsaw on 11 October, party liberals stated that

> The Polish United Workers' Party (PZPR) has exhausted its capacity to effectively influence public life and the functioning of the state.
>
> The new party must emerge from a critical reassessment of the achievements of the Polish workers' movement and, in particular, of the legacy of the Polish Socialist Party; a legacy that hitherto has been overlooked.
>
> The highest value for us is the sovereignty of the Polish nation and state, that is, the inalienable right to

decide about our own affairs without interference. We consider the establishment of friendly relations with all Poland's neighbors to be one of the most valuable achievements of People's Poland. At the same time, we support the democratization of the Warsaw Pact and the modernization of CMEA so that they can never again become instruments permitting domination by those who are stronger and interfere in the internal affairs of member states.

> We are seeking to make the 11th Congress produce a party that will bring together people who earn a living through their own work, a party that is capable of operating in a parliamentary democracy, a Socialist Party of Poland. (*Trybuna ludu*, 13 October.)

Dominated by intellectuals, this group perceives the party as a powerful force that is becoming a "dinosaur on the Polish political scene." A solution lies in drawing

> on the rich experiences of Polish socialism, experiences which were brutally and artificially ended in 1948. It is also worth drawing on the experiences of present-day Western social democratic parties, but without the exaggeration and fascination that certain comrades are too easily inclined to display. If we wanted to copy Western social democracy, we would have to begin by restoring capitalism in Poland. Let us leave this task to others, because there is no shortage of advocates of solutions of this kind, whereas we should occupy ourselves with protecting these values which, despite the mistakes, we have managed to introduce and disseminate in Poland over the past 45 years. (From a statement by Tomasz Natecz, lecturer at Warsaw University, delivered before the second half of the Fifteenth Plenum; *Trybuna ludu*, 4 October.)

The Sixteenth Central Committee Plenum met on 7 November and continued the debates that had begun during the Fifteenth Plenum, with sharp disagreements on procedures to elect delegates to the Eleventh Congress. Conservative members who desired to preserve the Leninist character of the party challenged the idea of a direct election of delegates and favored the establishment of minimum wages and a policy to defend public property from foreign capital. The liberals, in contrast, tended to conclude that the "present system had not been socialist" and advised a return to the "achievements and experience of the Polish Socialist Party." The most radical view, however, was expressed by Hieronim Kubiak, a professor of the Jagiellonian University in Kraków and a member of the Politburo in the 1970s, who argued that the PZPR should dissolve itself and be replaced by a completely different party. To the opponents of social democracy he responded, "Social democracy had obtained results not in theory but in practice." (*Trybuna ludu*, 7 November.)

The result was an ambiguous compromise that gives every party member the right to exercise only "*direct influence* [emphasis added] on the process of nominating and electing delegates," but states that the delegates should have the "freedom to seek ideology and programs" for the reformed party (*Trybuna ludu*, 8 November). In conclusion, the Sixteenth Plenum was unable to reconcile differences and postponed a struggle over the future of the party until what, one way or another, is going to be the last congress of the PZPR.

Transfer of Power. A search for a lasting compromise between the ruling communist party and society as represented by Solidarity began at the end of 1988, but was suspended when the Central Committee failed to agree on its approach to the opposition. Two winter months were lost on intraparty struggle until, at the end of January, the second half of the Tenth Central Committee Plenum reluctantly approved a return to negotiations.

The decision to negotiate with the union indicated that the regime intended to recognize Solidarity as a legitimate opposition in the country. Since August 1980 the authorities have learned to coexist with the union, and the issue of its relegalization was no longer the key stumbling block to a new social contract in Poland. The party's primary concern was the prospect of semifree elections. Fears of an open political contest with the union prompted the party to stress the necessity of "national accord" between the government and the union to avoid confrontations at the election booth. The party expressed preference for the joint platform and announced that under no circumstances would it allow the formation of a new political party.

The authorities continued to think in the tradition of the "united front"—political parties dominated and manipulated by the communists. They were ready to invite Solidarity to be a member of the governing coalition without giving the union any higher political status than a political club or association.

Although the authorities were reluctant to share political power with the union, they were looking for an agreement that would give the party new legitimacy to govern and leave Solidarity to manage the economic crisis. The PZPR leadership calculated that for the price of recognition of the union they could purchase its loyalty and cooperation. The only alternative to an agreement legalizing Solidarity was another rigged election boycotted by the union. Such a national boycott would further discredit the party, immobilize the entire state, and provoke a second martial law. A pre-electoral agreement with the union was planned as a way of co-opting the union and giving it the status of a loyal opposition. As one Polish commentator noted, "What they want is for the opposition to give up its autonomy, to define itself as being within the limits of the system" (quoted in *WP*, 20 February).

The party was aware that its political choices were few and unpleasant. General Wojciech Jaruzelski admitted, "Theoretically, there are three choices: Extraordinary measures and an iron fist policy, or capitulation and a wait for clemency, or accord and struggle in constructing a socialist parliamentary democracy that is meant to strengthen Poland in the final reckoning and secure its harmonious and modern development" (*Trybuna ludu*, 13 March).

The inaugural meeting of the roundtable took place on 6 February, when all 57 participants representing the government and the opposition met together for the first time since December 1981 when martial law was imposed. The entire nation was aware that seven years had been wasted in a unilateral attempt by the party to pull the country out of its social and economic crisis. During those years, the party realized that the future political system in Poland would have to be based on democratic principles and respect for human rights. Introductory statements at the roundtable expressed hope that the discussions would lead to a new economic order, self-sufficiency in food, the end of strikes, and political pluralism.

Although General Kiszczak, who represented the government, stressed the authorities' willingness to search for a new social contract in Poland and the responsibility of all political factions to cooperate toward a national accord that would lift the country out of its current status of the "sick man of Europe, a flashpoint constituting a potential threat for itself and for others," Lech Wałęsa focused on the depth of the crisis:

We say words that are festive, but what Poland now needs is facts, courageous decisions, and wise, vigorous action. For the whole period of 40 years there has been a constant flow of words, and what came of it?

Europe and the world are developing at fast pace before our eyes. We are on the spot. We see this in foreign films and the windows of hard currency stores. We work in old factories full of machines that are falling apart.

The catastrophe of the Polish economy is our greatest national complaint. We all know what has been spoiled over the decades cannot be repaired in a moment . . .

There is only one direction: It must lead to a democratic system, to the rule of law, to national security, to civic freedom. Even if this cannot take place immediately, we must start somewhere. (Warsaw Domestic Service, 6 February; *FBIS-EEU*, 7 February.)

The roundtable deliberations were not limited to the party versus Solidarity duel like the one in Gdańsk that resulted in the August 1980 agreement. Besides the old rivals the participants included representatives of the United Peasant party (ZSL) and the Democratic party (SD), both allied with the Communists; the Patriotic Movement for National Rebirth (PRON), a communist-dominated umbrella organization serving as a facade of democracy; the semi-independent Christian Social Union; the semi-independent Association of the Polish Catholics (PAX); and various other social, political, and religious organizations. The roundtable provided national recognition and a chance to acquire a share of power that the communists were about to lose. The PZPR, in contrast, welcomed the opportunity to divide the opposition into a number of small groups that could be played one against another to weaken its main foe, Solidarity. The political role of the official union that in 1982 replaced Solidarity was of special significance. Originally the All-Polish Alliance of Trade Unions (OZPP) was promised a full monopoly of trade union activities throughout the country and to formally become the heir of Solidarity, taking over its property, members, and program. The return of Solidarity as a legitimate political actor in Poland threatened the survival of OZPP and gave it the stigma of subservience to the party. For Alfred Miodowicz—OZPP national chairman, member of the ruling Politburo, and *Sejm* deputy—continuing political existence required a strong assertion of self-identity and independence from the party and Solidarity. He adopted a radical and populist program that projected the image of a defender of the working class from the arbitrary nature of the

communist party and Solidarity's tendency to press economic reforms at the cost of the workers.

In his opening address, Miodowicz noted that "it took us a long time to get to this table. The dispute about Solidarity was taking place. But wasn't it in fact an expression of the fears of those who govern facing the common front of the working people?" He then stated the objectives of his organization at the roundtable discussion:

The issue involved is Poland so that our country can be normal, so that decent people can live decently on their wages, pensions or annuities—decently means without fear about the next day or next month. It means they can hope and be able to believe, and be certain, that Poland is not a wicked stepmother driving out her children to the foreign lands in order to get bread but rather better prospects and a European standard of living.

Finally, came the credo of Miodowicz's address:

We, the working people, have the greatest need for democracy, because this is what we have so far been most deprived of. That is why we favor the upcoming elections to the *Sejm* proceeding in a democratic way. We have no reason to play with marked cards: We want open, frank rivalry. We want an honest struggle for the mandates, between those who represent various interests and arguments. (Warsaw Domestic Service, 6 February; *FBIS-EEU*, 7 February.)

Despite those emotional appeals and skillful maneuverings both before the elections and during the prolonged efforts to organize a new government, Miodowicz and his union were handicapped by their illegitimate origins associated with martial law. As a member of the Politburo and without an independent political status for his organization, Miodowicz could not desert the communist coalition as easily as ZSL and SD could. It was not until the end of 1989, when distintegration of the PZPR had become unavoidable, that Miodowicz admitted his union had made a mistake by associating itself with the Communists and declared his intention to convert OZPP into a political party.

The All-Polish Alliance of Trade Unions transformed itself into a radical organization inciting workers against both the party and Solidarity and thus creating the danger of anarchy. The main weapon in its campaign against Solidarity was the so-called indexation, that is, the automatic cost of living increases to keep up with inflation. Solidarity wanted an 80 percent automatic pay increase; the OZPP, however, publicly argued for a 100 percent increase, combined with advanced payments and bonuses. The OZPP soon became a highly destabilizing element in the domestic political scene, building its identity on opposing austerity measures advanced by Solidarity. This negative stand ensured the OZPP of continuing public attention. In October the OZPP called for another roundtable talk to discuss social affairs and to adopt an efficient program of economic recovery.

During the two-month-long roundtable negotiations, the delegates organized themselves into three working groups on the economy, social policy, and trade union pluralism. Progress toward agreement was reported after every meeting, as all sides were inclined to make concessions while pursuing vigorous struggles for power and influence. Once the PZPR made its historical decision to share political power, negotiations became a political battleground over the fate of the socioeconomic system in Poland.

The agreement was signed on 6 April. "I am of the opinion," declared Lech Wałęsa, "that nobody was defeated by anybody at the roundtable talk because nobody wanted to defeat anybody, all tried to save Poland" (Warsaw Domestic Service, 6 April; *FBIS-EEU*, 7 April). Solidarity emerged victorious, but refused to present the results in terms of a zero-sum game. Only the OZPP expressed opposition to the agreement, calling it a play calculated to implement economic reforms at the expense of the Polish worker. A lengthy document issued at the end of the roundtable cautiously defined pluralism as the right of free association, freedom of speech, independence of the judiciary, local self-government, and trade union pluralism. The union was not given the status of a political party, but this has not stopped Solidarity from behaving as if it were a party. Nevertheless, the agreement included a section on restructuring the political system according to the principle of separation of powers and a bicameral parliament.

First, the agreement stipulated re-establishing the upper legislative chamber, the Senate, with the power to "initiate legislation and consider the decrees passed by the *Sejm* [the lower chamber]; if it objects to a given decree, its second passage by the *Sejm* will require a majority of two-thirds votes in order to be effective." Moreover, "the Senate combined with the *Sejm* into the National Assembly shall elect the first President of the Republic by an absolute majority of votes." Finally, "the Senate, elected by the sovereign will of the nation, shall exercise substantive control over, in particular, human rights, rule of law, and socioeconomic life."

Second, Poland was to acquire a new executive office in line with its pre-war tradition:

The office of the President is warranted by the need for a stable state and to make decisions in the event of a blockage of work at the *Sejm* and the Senate or a protracted government crisis. The President's term of office shall last 6 years. The powers of the President shall be broad as regards to representing the state and exercising executive powers. The President may refuse to sign a law and return it, together with a rationale, for reconsideration by the *Sejm*. The *Sejm* may overturn the President's veto by a majority of two-thirds.

Among the powers of the president is the right to impose martial law for a period of three months and extend it for an additional three months with the agreement of both the *Sejm* and the Senate. During martial law the president may neither disband the legislative bodies nor change the electoral law. The *Sejm* could be disbanded for three months "to form a government or vote on a long-range socioeconomic plan, or if a law passed by the *Sejm* violates the President's constitutional prerogatives."

Third, Poland would receive an independent judiciary guaranteed by granting tenure to judges and "prohibition against the transfer of judges to other jurisdictions contrary to their will." The right to make appointments to judicial posts was granted to the president, who has to select one individual from two candidates submitted by the General Assembly. (*Trybuna ludu*, 7 April.)

This rough draft of the future political order demonstrates the strong influences of Western democratic ideas and is the embodiment of Poland's own democratic tradition dating back to the constitution of 1791. Institutional arrangements proposed by the roundtable agreement were often general, vague, and sketchy, but they left no doubt that Poland had begun an evolution toward Western-like democracy.

More important perhaps than the institutional structure during the period of transition from a one-party to a multiparty system was a short range agreement on elections to the *Sejm* and the Senate. The roundtable agreement authorized all legally existing parties to nominate candidates, as well as "citizens acting independently of these organizations, provided that the number of signatures on the nominating petition is at least 3,000." The number of candidates could also be unlimited.

The pre-electoral agreement stipulated that "60 percent of seats to the *Sejm* will be held by the PZPR-ZSL-SD coalition" and 5 percent by the religious organizations associated with the communist regime. The remaining 35 percent of the seats in the *Sejm* were to be freely competed for. Ten percent of the total number of seats allocated to the ruling coalition were to be filled from a national slate. Elections to the Senate were not to "be curtailed by any agreement on the apportionment of seats." In effect, Poland was due for the first semi-free elections since World War II.

Finally, this new social contract included a section on economy. The most important elements included "qualitative and quantitative improvements in the supply of consumer goods," cutbacks in state expenditures and in military spending, balancing the state budget within two or three years, the sale of state-owned property, reduction in investments, and numerous other detailed measures intended to overcome the economic crisis with minimal negative consequences for the population. Transition to a market-oriented economy was formally given the green light.

Despite its imperfections, the agreement broke through the political deadlock that had paralyzed the country for seven years. It mandated important institutional changes and economic restructuring, bringing hope and optimism after a long period of apathy and distrust. Bronisław Gieremek, one of the main architects of Solidarity's political strategy, concluded that the roundtable could at least "reverse the growing trend toward thinking that things are going to become worse. Arresting this trend is the only thing that we can achieve today" (*Trybuna ludu*, 10 April). This cautious attitude was confirmed by a public opinion poll conducted by a social research center in Poland wherein only 12 percent of the respondents stated that the situation in the country would "definitely" improve, 52 percent answered "rather yes," 22 percent, "rather not," and 6 percent, "definitely not" (*JPRS-EEU*, 8 May).

The open ballot elections agreed on at the roundtable negotiations were scheduled to take place on 4 June. Out of the 460 seats in the lower house, the *Sejm*, 65 percent were allocated to the communist-based coalition and 35 percent of the members were to be elected freely. Moreover, of the 65 percent of the seats reserved for the authorities, 38 percent was set aside for the PZPR and 27 percent for the others. The communists, then, would be a minority entitled

to control slightly more than one-third of the *Sejm*, with no more than veto power over constitutional amendments. The political fortunes of the party became contingent on cohesiveness of the old coalition. The 65 percent also included the so-called national list, 35 individuals, the party's top leadership, who were to be run unopposed. Candidates running from this national electoral list included General Kiszczak, Alfred Miodowicz, Mieczysław Rakowski, and five other prominent members of the Politburo.

The upper chamber of the national assembly, the Senate, would have one hundred members who would be chosen in free and open elections. The Senate would consist of two representatives from each of Poland's 49 voivodships, plus one additional senator each from the capital city of Warsaw and the Katowice voivodship.

The magnitude of the communist defeat exceeded all expectations. During the first stage of the election the Citizens' Committee of Solidarity, a coalition of all opposition candidates, won 92 of 100 seats in the freely elected Senate and 160 of the 161 seats in the *Sejm*. The most humiliating development, however, was that, out of 35 unopposed candidates on the national list, only two received the more than 50 percent required for election to the *Sejm*. Thus only two candidates from the national list and three in contested elections with the 65 percent reserved for the governing coalition managed to obtain more than half the votes. Consequently, 294 undecided contests had to be repeated in a runoff vote. (*LAT*, 10 June.) The elections were a plebiscite on communist rule in Poland and on the program of economic reform.

The other surprise from the election involved voter participation. Only a little more than 62 percent of the eligible citizens participated in the 4 June election, meaning that almost 40 percent of the people could not shake off the feeling of apathy and resignation. The second round of the election was set for 5 July.

The political situation became serious once the party recognized that there was massive national support for Solidarity and that, even without competition, candidates on the national list still had to be approved by more than 50 percent of the voters to win election to the *Sejm*. Aware of the deep and irreparable political damage suffered by the communists, the party leadership proceeded with a tactical move that could undermine the entire structure of the recently concluded agreements. On 12 June Premier Mieczysław Rakowski and several other members of the ruling Politburo who had been rejected by the voters withdrew their candidacies. This step increased political uncertainty in Poland and put pressure on Solidarity to campaign on behalf of the communist candidates to help them secure the required percentage of votes. Eventually, Lech Wałęsa accepted the idea of endorsing candidates representing the communist party, but only according to Solidarity's preference for party liberals and reformers.

The party escaped this trap by having the Council of State issue a decree amending the electoral law for the coming runoff elections to permit the governing coalition to nominate two candidates for each of the 33 unfilled seats, plus two candidates for all others to achieve 65 percent, that is, 264 seats of the 460 seats in the *Sejm*. This guaranteed that one out of two candidates would obtain at least 50 percent support from those who participated in the elections.

Only 28 percent of the eligible voters turned out, but with each candidate opposed, the communists and their allies finally gained a mandate to occupy the 65 percent of the seats in the *Sejm* allocated to them (*LAT*, 20 July). The Solidarity opposition was competing for only nine of the 303 *Sejm* and Senate seats, winning eight and losing only one seat out of 100 in the Senate. One wealthy member of the communist party is believed to have spent two hundred million złoty ($235,000) in the pre-electoral campaign. The final results of the elections, as agreed on during the roundtable talks, gave 65 percent of seats in the *Sejm* to the regime. Within that 65 percent the PZPR gained 37.5 percent, or 173 seats; the United Peasant party, 16.5 percent, or 76 seats; the Democratic party, 6 percent, or 27 seats; the procommunist Catholic PAX group, 2.2 percent, or 10 seats; and the ecumenical Christian-Social Union, 1.1 percent, or 5 seats. Only one seat out of one hundred in the Senate fell into communist hands. (RFE/RL, Polish SR/111, 6 July.)

The first major business of the new Polish parliament was to elect, in a joint session of both houses, a new chief executive—the president of Poland. During the roundtable talks, it was expected that General Kiszczak would be the main contender for this post, but the humiliation of the communists in the national elections necessitated a search for a stronger candidate. Solidarity also favored a strong military figure as president and felt comfortable with General Kiszczak, who was closely identified with the roundtable negotiations and who was described by Wałęsa as "one who promises to continue the reforms and who always keeps his word" (*WP*, 2 July). However, General Wojciech Jaruzelski, still first secretary of the communist party and the only politician enjoying the complete support of the army, appeared as the sole figure in Poland who could prevent chaos and outside intervention.

At the same time, however, the fluid political situation in Poland loosened ties among the members of the governing coalition; the communist party began to rupture into the conservative wing, which accused Jaruzelski of yielding too much power to the opposition, and the liberals, who were accused of leaning toward compromise with the union. Consequently, General Jaruzelski could not expect total support from the communist party and its allies, and his popularity among the opposition was low. The union continued to mistrust him for having imposed martial law in December 1981. Stating a lack of public support as the reason for withdrawing his candidacy for the office of the president, General Jaruzelski first declined to accept a nomination advanced by the PZPR, but reversed this decision as no alternative candidate could preserve internal stability and be acceptable to Moscow. Poland needed a strong executive to set forth a program of deep political and economic change. If the president of Poland were to be elected in universal voting, there was no doubt that Lech Wałęsa would be the winner. (*NYT*, 19 July.)

On 19 July the new National Assembly voted for president. General Jaruzelski ran unopposed, but without the support of Solidarity. The roundtable agreement imposed no such obligation on the union, and although many members of Solidarity favored Jaruzelski's election, they could not afford to alienate their supporters who continued to identify the general with the 1981 crackdown. Solidarity used abstentions, invalid votes, and absent votes to enable Jaruzelski's candidacy to pass. The final results were as shown in the table. Those results demonstrate a breakdown of the governing coalition, as 31 members refused to support the general. Jaruzelski was elected with the lowest possible majority and in a fundamentally nondemocratic manner.

In his inaugural speech, President Jaruzelski promised to "reconstruct the economy," to "shape a new democratic order," and to be a "president of accord, the representative of all Poles . . . [who] wish to gain the trust of those who express opposition or reluctance in relations to me personally." (Warsaw Television Service, 19 July; *FBIS-EEU*, 20 July.)

	Y^1	N^2	A^3	$Inv.^4$	$Ab.^5$
Solidarity	1	222	18	7	11
PZPR	171	1	—	—	1
Peasant party	54	6	13	—	3
Democratic party	20	4	3	—	—
PAX	10	—	—	—	—
Christian Social Union	8	—	—	—	—
Polish Catholics	5	—	—	—	—
Coalition total	269	11	16	—	4
PZPR senators	1	—	—	—	—
Total	270	233	34	7	15

[1] yes, [2] no, [3] abstention, [4] invalid vote, [5] absent or refused to vote. (Taken from Warsaw PAP, 21 July; *FBIS-EEU*, 21 July.)

On behalf of Solidarity, Lech Wałęsa responded in the following manner:

> We are also aware of internal and external political conditioning due to which only a representative of the government-party coalition could have been elected president. We are aware that his choice may not suit many of our compatriots, both because of the procedure of selecting him by votes of the representatives' organ whose composition reflects the round table political agreement but not the true preferences and political options of society.
>
> We expect that the new president will—the more so—use his post for continuing and even accelerating the transformations under way in Poland, that will contribute to implementation of the round table agreements and that he will realize the policy of Polish reason of state reaching beyond particular interests of one party. He is also obliged to create conditions for free parliamentary elections during the coming four years and for a general presidential election for the next term.

The end of one political crisis marked the beginning of another, this time over the choice of the next premier and the political profile of the first semi-freely elected government. Immediately after his election to the office of president, General Jaruzelski recommended his close friend and associate, General Czesław Kiszczak, for the post of premier. Michael T. Kaufman, noted observer of Polish affairs, wrote in the *New York Times* that "in nodding toward General Kiszczak, who does not arouse the same strong emotions from either party hard-liners

or the Solidarity opposition, General Jaruzelski was also extending the 'Bonapartist' course, in which military figures have gained the upper hand over ideologues and tactics have superseded dogma" (*NYT*, 1 July).

General Kiszczak was respected among the governing coalition and the opposition for his organizational abilities, political flexibility, and familiarity with the nation's economic problems. The opposition perceived him as an honest individual who would proceed "along the lines of the roundtable." (*NYT*, 3 August.) The communist party, on the other hand, looked at Kiszczak as one who would reassert the party's ultimate control over the next government.

To win nomination for premier, General Kiszczak had to obtain a simple majority of 460 members of the *Sejm*, where the governing coalition controlled 299 seats. On 2 August, however, the Peasant party revolted by refusing to support Kiszczak's candidacy despite General Jaruzelski's warnings that he would dissolve the *Sejm*. General Kiszczak was confirmed by a majority of 237 votes; 173 legislators voted against him, 10 abstained, 32 Solidarity legislators were absent, and 8 votes were invalid. The significant aspect, however, was that six communist legislators voted against Kiszczak and several more abstained, five members of the Peasant party voted against him, six abstained, and two or three members of the Democratic party voted no. (*NYT*, 3 August.) The governing coalition was rapidly breaking apart.

Kiszczak's election as a premier-designate only magnified the political crisis in Poland. For two weeks he was unable to form either a coalition government based on the old pattern of Communist-Peasant-Democratic party alliance or a grand coalition that would include some members of Solidarity. The communists failed to recognize that the political situation in Poland was completely different from the past 45 years, when they had a monopoly of power and could dictate conditions to other parties, and were unwilling to make a compromise with the Peasants, who controlled 16.5 percent of the seats and could determine which of the two major parties, that is, the PZPR or Solidarity, would obtain a majority in the *Sejm*. Aware of their bargaining power as a swing party in Poland, the Peasants approached Lech Wałęsa about forming a Solidarity-based government.

Under those conditions, Solidarity promoted the alternative presented by the slogan Your President—Our Premier and invited the Peasant and

Democratic parties to negotiations aimed at forming a government of "national trust" based on the union. General Kiszczak resigned as premier, and the possibility of the first noncommunist government since 1944 became real. (*Trybuna ludu*, 7 August.) Solidarity controlled more than 35 percent of the *Sejm*, and this considerable power was greatly amplified by the 99 percent majority in the Senate, which had the power to block any action of the *Sejm* majority. A government controlled by the opposition had a much better chance to stabilize the entire system in Poland and prevent the return to martial law. Still, the issue of whether the Solidarity government would be the so-called small coalition without the PZPR or a grand coalition that would include the communists remained unresolved. Lech Wałęsa's first offer, however, called for a small coalition; the union rejected the idea of a grand coalition, with its role confined to a "decorative" function. As Solidarity's caucus leader Branisław Gieremek explained, the grand coalition would "fail to disturb the existing structures of power but would act to reinforce them" (quoted in RFE/RE, Polish SR/13, 22 August).

The possibility that the communist party would be placed in opposition had an alarming effect in Moscow. The Soviet ambassador in Warsaw, Vladimir I. Borovikov, met with leaders of the Peasant and Democratic parties, but could not persuade them to join the PZPR. (*NYT*, 14 August.) *Pravda* accused Lech Wałęsa of delivering an "unparliamentary" blow to Kiszczak's attempt to organize a governing coalition by holding negotiations with the Peasant and Democratic parties "before Kiszczak had finished forming a new government in accordance with the *Sejm's* instructions, which is contrary to the generally accepted principles of parliamentary democracy" (14 August, 2d edition). Excluding the communists from government in Poland would imply that they were incapable of managing the country, and Moscow was concerned that a noncommunist government in Warsaw might not respect the international obligations of Poland, particularly the country's membership in the Warsaw Pact.

Equally alarmed was the political establishment in Poland. The removal of the communist party from the government meant automatic termination of the *nomenklatura* system of appointments and privileges enjoyed by the PZPR officials. For the political apparatus of the PZPR, Solidarity's ascent to power appeared as a counterrevolutionary coup d'état.

The political situation in Poland gave General Jaruzelski no realistic options. Numerous strikes threatened the stability of the state. In the summer of 1989, prices went up three- to fourfold, and the specter of Tiananmen Square hung over the nation. Transfer of power to the union was unavoidable. A political compromise was worked out at the meeting between President Jaruzelski and Lech Wałęsa where the labor leader agreed that instead of a grand coalition at least two communist ministers would be added to the new government. The interior and defense ministers would then function as a political umbrella over the Solidarity government. With Moscow's approval, the Polish president nominated Tadeusz Mazowiecki to be the first noncommunist premier of Poland in 45 years. On 24 August, Mazowiecki was approved by a huge majority, 378 to 4, with 41 abstentions. Some 130 members of the communist party expressed their support for Mazowiecki. (*WSJ*, 25 August.)

Mazowiecki is a modest, low-profile, Catholic politician. In March 1968 he presented a motion to the *Sejm* condemning the anti-Semitic campaign and the persecution of students. In the middle of the 1970s, he initiated and led the protest against a constitutional amendment guaranteeing the communist party political monopoly in the country. Later he became active in the opposition, protesting communist attacks on workers and the opposition. He was one of the negotiators of the August 1980 agreement, held the post of editor in chief of *Tygodnik Solidarność*, and was arrested during martial law. He is regarded as a pragmatic and courageous politician familiar with facts and the short- and long-term consequences of his actions. (*Gazeta wyborcza*, 21 August.)

Approval of Mazowiecki was instantaneous and included support from both domestic and international leaders. Roman Malinowski, chairman of the Peasant party, and Jerzy Jóźwiak, chairman of the Democratic party, called Mazowiecki's election "a new chapter in our history" and said that "we are convinced that your historical mission will end in a success and that the formed government of national responsibility will meet the expectations of the Polish nation." Archbishop Bronisław Dąbrowski, general secretary of the Conference of the Polish Episcopate stated that "you [Mazowiecki] will be recorded in the postwar history of Poland as the first premier representing genuine Catholic society" (Warsaw, PAP, 24 August; *FBIS-EEU*, 25 August).

Reaction from abroad included congratulations from President Bush, who assured Mazowiecki of

U.S. support for rebuilding Poland's economy. Moscow quickly added its approval of Mazowiecki's commitment to continued good Polish-Soviet relations and to Poland's participation in the Warsaw Pact and CMEA. TASS commentator Aleksandr Kondrashov stated,

> Of course, all are concerned about further developments in Poland. But debating on further ups and downs of the inner political life in the country is a useless task. However, taking into account the imperative of overcoming crisis in the shortest time possible that the country faces, a new government can achieve this only through [a] constructive, creative approach and not through negotiation and confrontation. (Warsaw, PAP, 25 August; *FBIS-EEU*, 29 August.)

Sergei Stankevich, member-coordinator of the international group of USSR people's deputies, also expressed the Soviet perspective, saying,

> International correspondents in Moscow are asking what the attitude of the Soviet Union will be, and what is the likelihood of Soviet interference in the course of events in Poland. As regards us, we must categorically state that the practice of illegal interference in the internal affairs of East European neighbor states should be buried once and for all. (*Gazeta wyborcza*, 23 August.)

The still orthodox Czechoslovakia voiced its disapproval, calling President Jaruzelski's decision to select a noncommunist premier as proof that in "Poland socialism is being dismantled" and that "this choice is the nail in the coffin of socialism in Poland" (*Gazeta wyborcza*, 22 August). Romania went as far as to suggest that the Warsaw Pact rally to stop Solidarity from taking power (Paris, *International Herald Tribune*, 30 September).

The government organized by Premier Mazowiecki is in reality a grand coalition that includes the four communists. The Peasant and the Democratic parties each received positions of deputy premier. The Solidarity coalition had control over fourteen ministerial posts, seven for the union, four for the Peasants, and three for the Democrats.

Moscow made it clear that the Soviet leadership would not approve a Solidarity-based government without communist control over the Defense and Interior ministries. The 40-minute telephone conversation between Mieczysław Rakowski and Mikhail Gorbachev was widely publicized in Poland to convey the Soviet view that "Poland's

problems cannot be resolved without PZPR participation" (*Izvestiia*, 24 August). The Soviets emphasized that the roundtable agreement contained a guarantee that the future government would include the communists, and Moscow insisted that Solidarity respect this provision in its political plans.

Alliance with the communists was an uneasy task, as communist tactics included "blackmail and intimidation" (Lech Wałęsa, as quoted in RFE/RE, Polish SR/14, 12 September). But Wałęsa also recognized that the Solidarity government had to compromise with Moscow and facilitate President Jaruzelski's task of mediating between Solidarity and the Soviet leadership. "Jaruzelski...has made a great gesture in choosing against all...reservations, to nominate [Mazowiecki] as our premier," admitted Wałęsa. The new government was designed to represent political forces committed to socioeconomic reforms. "I certainly do not exclude the Communists," stated Wałęsa. He continued,

> They have most experience in governmental matters and know most about public administration. Whether those who know how to govern have or have not the political will to govern in the way the country wishes is another question, as experience has shown. If, however, the Communists have this will it will be to the benefit of all. If not, we shall be able to do more without them, despite having less experience. A compromise for the sake of reforms is, however, necessary; the struggle now going on is between those who want reforms and those who do not, those who do not feel the challenge of the times. (Ibid.)

When the new government was finally assembled on 12 September it was perhaps the biggest development in Poland since the 1945 Yalta accord. All members of the new cabinet, including General Kiszczak, pledged loyalty to Mazowiecki. One of the first steps of the new authorities was to disband the Motorized Units of the Citizens' Militia (ZOMO), the paramilitary units that had enforced martial law in 1981. This decision was justified as a money-saving measure and a step to remove "irritation" from society. (*Trybuna ludu*, 30 September.)

Premier Mazowiecki promised to refrain from a "witch hunt" of those who owed their jobs to *nomenklatura* and told them not to feel threatened by the transfer of power at the top. The country had been governed by the communists on all its administrative levels, including 80 percent of its provincial administrators, 86 percent of its mayors, and 83 percent of its 55,000 managers of state enterprises.

(*WP*, 3 September.) The new government was thus ready to address Poland's main problem—the grave economic crisis.

The Economy. A general overview of the Polish economy in 1989 showed a continuing deterioration in its performance, despite several attempts to implement economic reform. Until the new government took over political power in September, communist authorities had focused on the following aspects of economic life:

1. The trend toward managerial independence, including self-financing, by various publicly owned enterprises reduced waste, reduced unprofitable production somewhat, and helped to regroup the employees in a more rational manner. This positive trend, however, was neither universal nor significant enough to turn the Polish economy around. The government continued to interfere at will in the operations of enterprises, and demonopolization of production had been slow. Political considerations were still given priority over economic calculations. Economic power in Poland continued to be based on principles of command planning instead of market conditions.

One reason for the slow pace of economic reforms was a lack of equal rights for all sectors of the economy. Neither preference for the public sector nor administrative interference had been removed. A legal foundation for privatization had not been fully established because a great portion of the state-held assets had not been transferred, sold, or leased to local governments and enterprises, and few companies were operating with the participation of cooperative and private capital. The state continued to be directly involved in managing economic operations. Employee self-management had not been implemented, and the influence of the work force on decision making continued to be minor.

2. Restructuring the Polish economy was behind schedule. Reducing the share of raw material and energy in complex and heavy industry in Poland's economy had not been achieved to the point that would affect the overall structure of the economy. Enforcement of the antimonopoly law is weak; the heavy industry sector, functioning outside the market principles, enjoys political privileges. Stalinism continues in the Polish economy because of the *nomenklatura* system of appointments for more than 900,000 upper-level managers, a demand for heavy industry products ordered by the government, and discrimination against light industry, agriculture, and services.

The implementation of economic reforms in Poland had not been subject to social supervision and control. Trade unions and other social organizations were excluded from the coordination of reforms at all administrative levels, and a large portion of critical economic data had been filtered out from public scrutiny or totally concealed. The public thus lacked enthusiasm and support for the communist program of economic reforms.

3. The agricultural potential of Poland had been neglected since the communists took over. Instead of becoming a focal point of the entire economy, the agricultural sector was subjected to politically motivated discrimination in terms of priority of investments. Economic reforms designed by the communist party failed to give high priority to agricultural production, neglected its infrastructure, and encouraged young people from rural areas to flee to the cities.

Another highly negative development affecting agricultural production in Poland is the state of the environment. The communist-sponsored program of economic reform neglected to address the problem of ecological disasters in Poland. Magnified by the poor distribution and service, inadequate food supplies in Poland caused great hardships in daily life. The communist authorities refused to abandon their economic policies that gave priority to unproductive heavy industries, while addressing society's needs in a marginal fashion.

The accumulation of errors and discrepancies in economic policy over the previous four decades have wrought havoc on the Polish economy and social life. The policies of the last communist government, headed by Mieczysław Rakowski, gave rise, in the summer of 1989, to a report from the Main Statistical Office that Poland's economic situation had been deteriorating to a critical point. Industrial production in the second quarter was 2.2 percent lower than in the analogous period for 1988; in the industrial sector of the Polish economy the decline reached 5 percent. Also, the number of completed dwellings had fallen by 11.9 percent, and public construction (hospitals, schools, kindergartens) declined by 80 percent.

In agriculture the procurement of slaughter animals dropped drastically. In June the state was able to purchase 25 percent less meat a day, and in July, 62 percent below the normal level. This decline had a destabilizing effect on the entire economy and social stability in Poland. The government of Mieczysław Rakowski failed to provide incentives for the farmers, making agriculture an unprofitable enterprise.

The weakening of the Polish economy had a negative impact on exports and forced the regime to increase imports. The volume of exports in the first six months of 1989 was only 1.5 percent higher than the year before, whereas imports increased by 19 percent. The surplus of convertible currencies was reduced to $167 million, precluding the possibility of servicing Poland's $40 billion foreign debt.

Meanwhile, inflation in Poland approached 1,000 percent, with the price of the dollar on the free market soaring up to fifteen thousand złoty. As a result, there was a general flight from the national currency to hard foreign exchange and goods, which contributed to the dramatic increase of the central budget deficit in the first half of 1989. Almost half of the state expenditures (44.7 percent) were paid by printing money that had no real value, causing a rapid increase in the market's imbalance. (*Trybuna ludu*, 28 July; RFE/RL, Polish SR/13, 22 August; *WP*, 21 October.)

Premier Rakowski refused to accept responsibility for the economic catastrophe in Poland. Following his resignation on 4 July, he accused society of a lack of patience and refusing to accept his conditions. (*Trybuna ludu*, 25 July.) Independent observers, however, concluded that Premier Rakowski's attitude toward economic problems was dominated by negligence and a lack of understanding of economic reality. In particular, he had refused to introduce changes in the obsolete economic structure of the country or to provide incentives to increase production. Introduced on 30 July, "marketization"—the end of a freeze on prices and wages and termination of central control to redirect the Polish economy toward a free market—was ineffective because the regime refused to encourage structural changes favoring reduction in consumption. (RFE/RL, Polish SR/13, 22 August.)

The most radical solution to Poland's economic problems was proposed by two Harvard specialists—Jeffrey Sachs and David Lipton. Their shock treatment for the Polish economy involves an immediate and simultaneous end to the monopolization of production and distribution, full convertibility of the złoty according to the market rate, immediate elimination of all subsidies and an end to price controls, freedom of export and import, freedom to develop and operate private enterprises, and suspension of the repayment of foreign debts.

Within a six-month period, this Poland could envision the end of inflation, an increase in production, and the beginning of a steady increase in the standard of living.

The main thrust of Sachs's approach to economic problems in Poland centers on the hyperinflation that wrecked the entire economic structure of the country, including the collection of taxes; the initial phase of this approach calls for "corrective inflation" that would allow the regime to discontinue subsidies combined with about a $1 billion foreign loan to support the Polish currency, a $700 million grant from the International Monetary Fund to stabilize the Polish economy, and another $500 million of assistance for the transfer of welfare from the public to the private sector of the economy.

Professor Sachs is optimistic about the economic potential of Poland and sees foreign investments in the Polish economy as sound economics and politics—a "highly productive market economy in the center of Europe . . . Timely assistance will pay for itself many times over by allowing sharp cuts in the hundreds of billions of dollars that we and our allies now pay for the defense of Western Europe" (*NYT*, 11 September). As a pioneer of democracy within the Soviet bloc, Poland is entitled to sympathetic understanding in Western capitals.

Polish economists generally agree that the introduction of free market principles would eventually turn the economy around, but that the country would not survive politically if such harsh economic measures were introduced. Also, Poland has neither the managerial system nor a socioeconomic class capable of providing the expertise and leadership necessary for an instantaneous switch from a socialist to a capitalist economy. Foreign analysts, in addition, do not realize how monopolized the Polish economy is and how immune to market incentives. Most enterprises in Poland are controlled by governmental bureaucracies who react slowly, if at all, to the law of supply and demand, and the work ethic is low. (*Gazeta wyborcza*, 28 August.)

Another weakness of the Sachs program is that it ignores the issue of ownership. The true cause of economic problems in Poland and other socialist countries is public ownership of the means of production. Polish economist Rafał Krawczyk criticized Sachs for failing to address the basic cause of the difficulties. The implementation of his program would place the state sector, which generates 80 percent of national production, in an idling position. (RFE/RL, Polish SR/14, 12 September.)

Transition from socialism to a market-oriented

economy must be gradual and take into account the political realities in Poland. Speaking to the *Sejm*, Tadeusz Mazowiecki looked at Poland's economic problems:

> The most important matter for society is the state of the national economy which today must be regarded as critical. Everything has already been said about how bad it is and why. The problem is how to get out of that. I am fully aware of the great work that will be required of the newly created government and of everyone to restore the economy. The long-term and strategic aim of the government's actions will be to reinstate in Poland the economic institutions that have long been known and proven. By that I understand a return to a market economy as well as the role of a state approaching that of economically developed countries. (Warsaw Television Service, 25 August; *FBIS-EEU*, 25 August.)

One of the first economic moves made by Mazowiecki's government was to reactivate the National Commerce Bank and authorize it to perform three functions: first, to make investments as in a market economy; second, to act as a commercial bank in lending and credit activities; and third, to act as a restructuring bank responsible for increased effectiveness in the national economy. The bank would thus accelerate the economy, assuming the role of the national treasury. (*Rzeczpospolita Reforma Gospodarcza* (supplement), no. 162, 22 June; *JPRS-EEU*, 29 August.)

This step may indicate that the government of Premier Mazowiecki preferred a toned-down version of this economic recovery plan, known in Poland as a "leap into the abyss." The alternative "long staircase" scenario for economic recovery is viewed with great pessimism because it would prolong the crisis over several years. The government has to take risks because, as a Polish columnist observed,

> before a historical undertaking, no one can know in advance what the outcome will be. We do know for sure that cautious measures will change nothing now and that the absence of change means a worsening of the economic catastrophe and the approach of a political one... A leap into rough seas is risky, but the ship is sinking and the engine is about to explode. (Quoted in RFE/RL, Polish SR/14, 12 September.)

Privatization of industry was also one of the top economic priorities of the Solidarity government, but implementation of this program encountered

serious difficulties when members of the *nomenklatura* began to exploit this opportunity to assume control over national assets. The best example of this trend was the highly controversial sale of the Lenin Shipyard in Gdańsk, following the decision of the Rakowski government to close it. Former managers of the shipyard "had either rented out parts of the enterprise or had set up joint stock companies that had appropriated considerable parts of the assets but without taking on any of the outstanding debts" (RFE/RL, Polish SR/14, 12 September).

This reality dampened progress toward privatization, a program that was intended to achieve three main objectives: first, the transformation of the Polish economy into a free market system with a convertible currency; second, creating an extensive stratum of individual owners of capital who would provide a social base for the new socioeconomic order; and third, ensuring that the social costs of this evolution are as low as possible and spread throughout the entire society. (*Gazeta bankowa*, 26 June–2 July; *JPRS-EEU*, 22 September.) Although only partial privatization is likely, the general guidelines toward privatization will probably include distribution of state assets, which cannot be permitted without payment because this does not improve efficiency; selling state assets at market value and, if possible, through an auction system (privatization cannot be used to circumvent tax laws); and parliamentary control over privatization.

The economic recovery plan eventually adopted by the Mazowiecki government is a politically cautious version of the Sachs plan. Premier Mazowiecki extended the length of transition to a free market economy from six months to about two years and divided the strategy into two distinct stages. The first stage would tackle only two issues, namely, inflation and monopolization of the Polish economy. Political risks involved in this stage are high because the regime intends to freeze wages, whereas prices are likely to increase several times. For this reason, the Solidarity-led government requested a moratorium on strikes and limits on indexation, adopting, in effect, the key elements of the previous program. However, the majority government in Poland is in a better political situation to push through harsh economic measures and, having strong support from the West, is in a position to soften the trauma of the Polish consumer. Prices of consumer goods in Poland are expected to reach their real market value, ending subsidies and price control and reducing the central budget deficit. Sale of some state assets would help to generate additional income that would be used to support the state budget.

The second stage of the plan is divided into three separate parts, each designed to foster a structurally different economy in Poland. This process will begin with a *Sejm*-supervised privatization of ownership followed by the introduction of the market sovereignty principle and the full convertibility of the Polish złoty. Poland will also enter the global economy with a Western-like banking system and a new taxation law. The social price of these evolutionary changes include a 20 percent rate of unemployment and the sacrifice of many social programs and benefits. However, Leszek Balcerowicz, deputy premier and finance minister, has "made it clear that they will not sacrifice the integrity of their program in the interest of placating the public and will not compromise economic rationality" (RFE/RL, Polish SR/16, 14 November; *WSJ*, 13 September). This will be a difficult task in a society where in 1988 social service spending grew 71.7 percent, subsidies on prices of consumer goods increased 105.6 percent, and total governmental spending went up 67.1 percent (EIU Country Report, no. 1). Similar increases are expected during 1989.

The reform package also includes draconian price increases ranging from 40 percent for bread to 400 percent for electricity and gas and 600 percent for coal. This "deep surgical cut" calls for a 2–3 percent reduction in gross national product and 20–25 percent unemployment, and the end to subsidies for inefficient state enterprises, which would be forced to declare bankruptcy. (*Newsweek*, 15 January 1990.)

Prospects of major economic dislocation threatened internal stability as the communist and the OZPP deputies launched a campaign of accusations including charges that the Solidarity government was undermining the welfare of the working people and selling Polish land and industry to foreigners. Under such circumstances, Lech Wałęsa called for granting the government "special powers" that would give ministries a free hand in handling economic matters without parliamentary approval. Premier Mazowiecki rejected Wałęsa's recommendation, although expressing appreciation for his "concern in the face of delay," and continued to struggle in the *Sejm* until his program of reforms was approved. (*WP*, 15, 18 December.)

Massive economic aid to Poland from Western countries has become the key element of the entire scheme. The Polish crisis is not merely a short-term problem, but a long-term international issue that requires international attention and Poland's cooperation in attracting foreign capital investment. Commitment of aid to Poland by the end of 1989 included $148.4 million in food assistance and up to $333 million of economic aid from the European Community, $1.6 million in food aid from Austria, $10 million in food aid plus $17 million in short-term credit from Canada, $40 million over two years from Denmark, $640 million over three years from France, $1.62 billion from West Germany, $180 million from Italy, $150 million from Japan, $450 million over five years from South Korea, a $500 million loan for unemployment insurance from the World Bank, and $700 million from the International Monetary Fund (IMF) (*WP*, 3 December). In addition, the U.S. government is likely to contribute up to $1 billion. Also, there are numerous private aid programs, the best known of which is a possible purchase of the Lenin Shipyard in Gdańsk by Barbara Piasecka-Johnson, a rich Polish-American who may provide $100 million to enter the joint venture with the Polish government (*NYT*, 11 June).

Foreign aid to Poland is not limited, however, to financial assistance and a moratorium on debt repayment, but includes technical and managerial expertise, help in the establishment of a modern banking system, improvement of telecommunications, and the building of cold storage facilities, roads, and the rest of the economic infrastructure. To cope with the complexities of foreign aid to Poland, President Bush has named Deputy Secretary of State Lawrence S. Eagleburger as coordinator of U.S. support to Poland and Hungary (*WP*, 8 December).

The postcommunist authorities recognized the primacy of economics over politics. Compliance with IMF rules is of critical importance; unlike the Western governments that support certain policies or programs of the Polish government, the IMF and the World Bank

channel multilateral aid in return for firm commitments to policies leading to economic stabilization. The standard formula for IMF-sustained recovery is for "standby" loans to be provided on the condition that the recipient country carry out the agreed structural changes to its economy and adopt specific policies designed to secure the necessary economic adjustment. If the recipient fails to adhere to such conditions, the loans are discontinued. (RFE/RL, *RAD Background Report*, no. 186, 10 October.)

During 1989 a political stage was set for major economic changes in Poland. If the economic stabilization program is successful, the country may experience economic recovery by 1992. However, considering the fragile social peace in the country, the likelihood that social welfare programs will need to be continued for the sake of political stability is high, prolonging and complicating the evolution to a market economy. Poland will succeed if the tough policies are fully and honestly explained to the public, if the government quickly creates sound legal foundations for economic changes, and if foreign aid promotes structural changes and relief from social dislocation.

Society. The agony of communism and the transition to democratic institutions have extracted a heavy toll from Polish society, but have also enabled the country to address some of its most painful problems, including coming to grips with Poland's past as well as rehabilitating the victims of communism. The Social Committee for Human Rights has been established in Poland to conduct a

> complete and precise elucidation of the entirety of the acts of lawlessness which occurred before 1956 in the operations of the organs of public security, military information, the Ministry of Justice, the prosecutor's office, courts, and the special commission, and preparation of a report on this issue, to be submitted to state authorities and released to the public. (*Polityka*, 4 March.)

Because a statute of limitations makes it impossible to punish crimes after twenty years, "murderers and butchers are among us, they are reaching their senior age, they are receiving retirement benefits and annuities, but the law cannot get them anymore" (ibid.). An investigation of Stalinist crimes in Poland not only would have historical significance, but would rehabilitate a number of political leaders who were imprisoned, executed, or died under questionable circumstances. However, the police and court records of the majority of victims cannot be found; thus the only evidence that can be used for the purpose of rehabilitation is in the possession of the victims and their relatives. Special attention must be given to the notorious Commission for Combating Abuse and Economic Sabotage, which from 1945 to 1954 sentenced thousands of people each

year to labor camps and confiscated property without a trial or giving the accused a chance to defend himself.

Demands that crimes committed against the Polish nation during the Stalinist period be fully accounted for received even stronger attention when the Solidarity-dominated government assumed political power. Public demands that those responsible for carrying out political crimes should not have the benefit of a statute of limitations caused Justice Minister Aleksander Bentkowski to issue a communiqué that stated, "the crimes of the Stalinist period will be revealed, their perpetrators prosecuted, and victims compensated for material and moral losses. There are the requirements of the law, the sense of justice and the principle of non-limitation of war crimes against humanity." (Warsaw, PAP, 3 October; *FBIS-EEU*, 10 October.)

That rehabilitation includes military personnel of the Polish armed forces who fought on the Western front during World War II. In March 1989, Premier Rakowski approached Major General Stanisław Maczek, the 98-year-old former commander of the Second Polish Army, with an invitation to visit Poland during the 50th anniversary of the outbreak of World War II. The invitation read:

> Among the very many issues which I have to attend to is the desire to right the wrongs inflicted on you, Mr. General, in the past by Polish authorities. I regret the way you, Mr. General, and your soldiers were judged then. Despite many unfair judgments and decisions by the Polish authorities at the time, you remained for us, my fellow countryman, the model patriot and soldier.

The invitation was declined "for health reasons, at least," but a full recognition of the contribution made by the Polish armed forces fighting beside British and American troops had been achieved, with patriotism placed higher than ideological preference.

The most emotional and politically significant issue, however, has been Soviet responsibility for the massacre of some 4,300 Polish officers in the Katyn forest near Smolensk in 1940. USSR authorities have always maintained that this crime was committed by German troops, although it was generally known that the killing of the Polish officers occurred before the German invasion of the USSR.

In February 1989, Moscow admitted that the massacre had been carried out by Soviet security forces (NKVD), and six months later the Polish-Soviet historical commission confirmed this conclusion (*Polityka*, 21 August). Moreover, the Polish government concluded that the Katyn massacre had all the earmarks of genocide, and the Polish prosecutor general requested that his Soviet counterpart "initiate and carry out an investigation into the murder at Katyn and other locations, the whereabouts of which have not been established thus far, of Polish officers." The second request concerned full rehabilitation of the Polish military and political leaders who in 1945 were kidnapped from Poland by the NKVD and tried by a military tribunal in Moscow. (*Trybuna ludu*, 13 October.)

The eradication of such blank spots in the history of Polish-Soviet relations meant more than moral satisfaction. Participating in the Katyn memorial service, Zbigniew Brzeziński referred to

> the symbolic nature of Katyn. Russians and Poles, tortured to death, lie together here. It seems very important to me that the truth should be said about what took place for only with the truth can the new Soviet leadership distance itself from the crimes of Stalin and the NKVD. (Moscow Television Service, 30 October; *FBIS-SOV*, 2 November.)

A Polish commentator placed an urn containing soil from Katyn in the tomb of the unknown solider in Warsaw. He concluded that the Katyn tragedy "was perpetrated in circumstances which are difficult to explain, which have no precedent in Polish experience, and which elude logical reasoning." (*Zycie Warszawy*, 21 April.)

It is not surprising, therefore, that anti-Russian demonstrations occurred frequently throughout the year. In May students from the Jagiellonian University in Kraków, a majority of them members of the pacifist-ecological Freedom and Peace movement, organized about a thousand supporters who called for the withdrawal of Soviet troops from Polish territory and the resignation of the local police chief, the party secretary, and the city president. They chanted "Soviets go home" and "commies out" and, according to some sources, attacked a Soviet diplomatic building with stones. Clashes with police resulted in injuries and arrests.

Demonstrations marked a recognition of the "international day for the struggle against militarism." Among the specific demands advanced by the young people were calls for an immediate end to military training in secondary schools, an end to compulsory military training for all students, the abolition of the draft, and political prisoner status for those imprisoned for refusing to undergo military service. The communist newspaper *Trybuna ludu* characterized the Kraków incidents as "scandalous . . . evidence of barbarism and irresponsibility" and expressed a fear that the legalization of the opposition could be harmful to Poland's relations with Moscow (17 May).

Besides bringing the issue of Soviet troops stationed in Poland to the attention of Polish authorities, demonstrations organized by Freedom and Peace contributed to the decision to freeze funds designated for the construction of a nuclear power plant near Lake Żarnowiec. After the Chernobyl accident this project was nicknamed "Żarnobył," a symbol of arbitrary and arrogant conduct by authorities who ignored the opinions of society. (*Słowo powszechne*, 18 September.)

Public controversy over the Żarnowiec nuclear plant is not over; the Rakowski government suspended this project because of lack of money, and the new government has yet to make a decision regarding its future. Supporters of the plant argue that Poland desperately needs this source of energy, that the reactors at Żarnowiec would operate on completely different principles than those at Chernobyl, that there will be no danger of a Chernobyl-type accident, and that there is no alternative to completing the plant. Its opponents, however, point out that if a breakdown should occur, radioactivity would need to travel only twenty kilometers to the populated area of Gdynia-Sopot-Gdańsk, with unthinkable consequences. The building costs are such that the investments would never be recovered, and public displeasure will likely make this project politically unfeasible in the future. The fate of this first nuclear power project in Poland will most likely be contingent on the success or failure of the entire economic system.

In the realm of politics, Poland has undoubtedly achieved a historical breakthrough by concluding the roundtable talks and becoming the first Soviet-bloc country to establish a noncommunist government. The negative side of the Polish political milieu is a growing tendency toward localism and populism, that is, toward politicking, petty rivalries between the regime-sponsored trade unions and Solidarity, and a frequent entry into the political arena of numerous small groups and parties. Weimarization of Polish politics is a possibility, especially in light of the traditional Polish propensity toward political chaos. The OZPP-Solidarity rivalry is steadily growing and threatening the stability of the country, as the All-Polish Alliance of Trade Unions has been drifting toward radicalism to retain its separate identity. The OZPP has adopted a class-oriented approach using its control over numerous fringe benefits, like housing and vacations, to challenge Solidarity. With frequent references to Wałęsa as a king and his group of advisers as the court, the OZPP is fighting its image as an illegitimate child in Polish politics by presenting Solidarity as a well-to-do member of the establishment immune to economic hardships suffered by the average citizen.

The long-term calculations of the OZPP are most likely based on the following: First, legalization of Solidarity did not result in a rapid increase of its membership. In October the union registered only 2.2 million members, which is about one-fifth of its original membership before the introduction of martial law. The current numerical strength of Solidarity is only slightly higher than that of the decimated communist party, whereas the OZPP claims seven million members. Second, Solidarity suffers from deep internal divisions between radicals and moderates, a cleavage that may eventually weaken Solidarity's political power and create conditions for the OZPP to emerge as the main spokesman for the public interest. Third, by taking over political power, Solidarity has de facto ceased to be a trade union and has assumed the functions of a political party. If the trend continues the OZPP may soon be left without a rival. The current political platform followed by the OZPP includes dissociation from the communist party and opposition against partnership with Solidarity and to the sale of state assets. In the future, the OZPP hopes to become a political party whose constituency would include workers and lower-level personnel in state and local bureaucracies. The ranks of the OZPP will be full until the economy shows strong signs of improvement. (Warsaw, PAP, 4 April; *FBIS-EEU*, 4 April, 5 October.) The OZPP has recently opposed Solidarity's request to impose a moratorium on strikes and is waiting for the Mazowiecki government to deploy security forces against demonstrating workers when the possibility of provocation could be ruled out (*Le Monde*, 9 September).

Splintering trends in Polish politics are taking place at a time when the influence of the Roman Catholic church is declining. The church brought the communists and the opposition to roundtable negotiations, but, having accomplished its mission, the church has moved into the shadow of the new noncommunist authorities and assumed its ordinary role as a religious and social institution. The church is now likely to pay attention to its own internal problems, including ideological adaptation to the needs of a modern society and the quality of its national leadership. Addressing this subject, Cardinal Glemp admitted that the "societal triangle" of party-Solidarity-church has ended and that "today the vote of the Church has become a normal one. It corresponds more to the mission of the Church as it exists in the West." (*Sueddeutsche Zeitung*, 28 September; *FBIS-EEU*, 19 December.)

Appointment of Józef Cardinal Glemp in 1980 to replace Stefan Cardinal Wyszyński as the Polish primate has been questioned on numerous occasions by the church hierarchy and the public. Cardinal Glemp reportedly lacks the foresight and appeal of his predecessor, and as a leader he has been out of tune with the majority of Polish clergy and society. His conciliatory approach to the communist authorities earned him the nickname "Comrade Cardinal," and his lack of a broad perspective has impaired the effectiveness of his personal leadership.

His involvement in the controversy concerning the nuns at the Auschwitz death camp was one of the best examples of his questionable leadership skills. In 1987 an agreement was signed in Geneva between Jewish and Catholic representatives regarding the relocation of Catholic nuns out of Auschwitz. The Jews had objected to the nuns' presence in this former Nazi extermination camp where several million Jews had been murdered; when the Polish side suspended implementation of the agreement, Jewish groups organized protests in front of the building. Cardinal Glemp accused the Jews of offending the feelings of Poles, violating Polish sovereignty, and lacking sensitivity to the fact that besides two million Jews, tens of thousands of Christian Poles had also lost their lives at Auschwitz. After concluding that Jewish behavior was "aggressive," Cardinal Glemp refused to honor the agreement. The high cost of relocation, estimated at $2 million, was given as an additional reason for keeping the nuns in the old building. Addressing Jews, Cardinal Glemp stated that "your power lies in the mass media that are easily at your disposal in many countries. Let them not serve to spread anti-Polish feeling." (*NYT*, 29 August.)

International controversy over the convent spread rapidly and soon involved the International Council of Christians and Jews, several Jewish organizations in Western Europe and the United States, and the Holy See. Intervention from the Vatican was needed to end this dispute. The pope offered to assist in moving the nuns to a new location, and a special commission of the Polish church recognized the agreement as binding. Meanwhile, Cardinal Glemp issued another letter stating that the "best solution to the dispute involving the Carmelite convent in Auschwitz would be for work to start as soon as possible. It is my intention that the Geneva Declaration of 1987 should be implemented, and I am therefore keen to work on a friendly dialogue between Christians and Jews." (*NYT*, 3, 22 September.)

The Auschwitz incident did not overshadow the political accomplishments of the church, whose main success before the change of government in Poland was new legislation on guarantees of freedom of conscience and religion. In 1945, when the concordat with the Apostolic See was broken by the communist regime, this most powerful institution in Poland—representing more than 90 percent of the entire nation—lost its legal identity. This was a political as well as a practical issue because the churches are not only the faithful and the clergy, but also charitable organizations, educational institutions, and universities as well as various monuments, buildings, farms, cemeteries, and so forth. Furthermore, there are religious presses, radio, TV, and theater.

The new law, which comprehensively regulates the position of the church in Poland, includes the following key provisions:

• The legal entity of the church on the national level is the Conference of the Episcopate of Poland.
• Discrimination against or privileges on account of religion or convictions about religious matters is prohibited.
• The church has a right to govern itself with respect to its own matters according to its own law.
• The church has the right to conduct religious worship inside or outside churches without applying for permission.
• The Feast of the Blessed Virgin shall be restored as a national holiday.
• The church is authorized to create a charitable organization, the Polish Caritas.
• The church has the right to open up its own radio and television station.
• The church has the right to establish and manage, without obtaining permission, theaters, cinemas, and film studios as well as libraries. (*Kierunki*, 25 June.)

Normalization of the status of the Catholic church in Poland opened the way to re-establishing diplomatic relations between Warsaw and the Vatican. Formally, this happened on 17 July, emphasizing the continuity of such relations between Poland and the Holy See, which date back to 1555. (RFE/RL, Polish SR/12, 28 July.)

The Polish government described this new beginning as a "very important fact that crowns a long process of normalization of relations between the state and the church"; the Vatican, in contrast, issued the following brief statement:

The Holy See and the Polish People's Republic, mindful of the noble tradition, dating several centuries, of ties between the Holy See and the Polish nation, and desirous of developing friendly mutual relations, have decided to re-establish, as of today, diplomatic relations between the Holy See and Poland at the apostolic nuncio level for the Holy See and ambassadorial level for the Polish People's Republic. (*NYT*, 18 July.)

The ideological struggle between Marxism-Leninism and Catholicism was coming to an end. On 26 August, Pope John Paul II issued an apostolic letter marking the 50th anniversary of the outbreak of World War II, which included a statement that "Nazi paganism and Marxist dogma are both basically totalitarian ideologies and tend to become substitute religions." With this attack on Soviet ideology, the pope pronounced the victory of Western values in Poland and a readiness to normalize relations with other East European states and with the USSR. Normalization of relations with Hungary and Soviet leader Mikhail Gorbachev's audience with the pope in early December were the next two steps in this historical mission of the church to reverse the communist tide in Eastern Europe.

Foreign Affairs. With the disappearance of the spheres of influence in Europe, the old security concerns about the future of Polish-Soviet, Polish-German, and Polish-American relations have returned. The communist view of national security called for a tight integration within the Warsaw Pact. At the price of limited sovereignty, Moscow extended assurances to Warsaw that German nationalism and territorial ambitions would not jeopardize Poland's independence. Modern Poland does not want to end up in the backwoods of the continent as a politically unstable and economically backward state living off the largess of the West. Thus the economic success of Poland is of key importance to its national security and self-identity. The basic objective of Warsaw's foreign policy is to strengthen

Poland's position in Europe and in the world and create favorable external conditions for socio-economic development. Poland's international position is no longer measured in military terms, but depends on its internal conditions. If the internal crisis becomes incurable, Poland's independence would be difficult to sustain.

The Soviet Union is Poland's largest neighbor. Polish-Soviet relations which define the extent of Polish independence, are critical to the security and stability of the Polish state. Until 1989, Polish-Soviet relations were dictated by Moscow and presented as a new form of international relations governed by friendship and mutual admiration rather than self-interest and the balance of power. Even before the Solidarity-dominated government surfaced in Warsaw, the Polish authorities reformulated the essence of these relations by emphasizing *raison d'état* and geostrategic calculations. The new government of Premier Mazowiecki has removed ideology from foreign policy and taken a critical view of the last 50 years of Soviet policy toward Poland and of the role of the Warsaw Pact. The sole function of the pact should be to protect the external security of its members, to discuss disarmament, and to maintain relations with NATO, without any interference in the domestic affairs of any country. Until now the Warsaw Pact has been an aggressive instrument of Soviet domination in Eastern Europe.

Political change in Poland necessitated frequent consultations between Jaruzelski and Gorbachev. In May, Jaruzelski visited Moscow to brief Gorbachev on the pace and direction of political restructuring in Poland. The Soviet leader approved the results of the roundtable negotiations and sanctioned removal of the so-called blank spots from the history of Polish-Soviet relations. A joint Polish-Soviet commission of historians was already investigating mutual relations at the advent of World War II, including the questions of Katyn, the Soviet-German treaty of 1939, and compensation for Polish forced labor during Stalinist times. Timing of the visit and the attention given to the blank spots were integral parts of the political campaign organized by the communist party, which was struggling to convey the image of independence and distance from Moscow. Concluding his visit to Moscow, Jaruzelski stated that

another significant step has been made on the road of our cooperation and the strengthening of our friendship. The talks I have had today with Comrade Gorbachev have confirmed our mutual respect and mutual

trust. I think that an honest assessment of the past and resolute looking forward is the basis for such relations. (Warsaw Television Service, 28 April; *Pravda*, 29 April; *FBIS-SOV*, 1 May.)

The communist defeat in the summer elections changed the character of Polish-Soviet relations. As a Soviet commentator noted,

Of course, all are concerned about further developments in Poland. However, taking into account the imperative of overcoming crisis in the shortest time possible that the country faces, a new government can achieve this only through a constructive, creative approach and not through negation and confrontation. A different approach, for instance, appeals "to dismiss a million Communists from work" voiced in some political circles, may lead only to aggravation of confrontation and it would be simply impossible to overcome crisis in such a situation. (Warsaw, PAP, 25 August; *FBIS-EEU*, 29 August.)

Moscow was anxious about the noncommunist government in Poland, but could not change the course of events without force. The first manifestation of a new relationship between the countries was a visit to Moscow by Adam Michnik, a prominent Solidarity activist. In an interview with the Soviet press, he stated, "We must try to understand each other and heal our common wounds in order to avoid trouble." (Moscow World Service, 23 August; *FBIS-SOV*, 24 August.) Describing the significance of this visit, a communist corespondent in Moscow wrote,

Almost four years ago when I started working as PAP's [Polish Press Agency] Moscow correspondent, even in my wildest dreams, I would never have assumed that I would one day be sitting in the hall of the Supreme Soviet among people's deputies, who describe themselves as the opposition, and that in addition, Adam Michnik, the politician and opposition activist, would be sitting among us; someone who has been called a revisionist, ideological saboteur, agent provocateur, and imperialist spy. (*Polityka*, 22 July.)

The Soviet leadership has finally abandoned its long-standing objective of Sovietization and become interested in fostering stability in Poland.

A new understanding between both countries was elaborated during Eduard A. Shevardnadze's visit to Warsaw at the end of October, when the government of Premier Mazowiecki was already in power. Discussions between Polish and Soviet officials centered on three issues: sovereignty of the Polish nation, continuing membership in the Warsaw Pact, and Poland's right to "moral satisfaction" for Soviet crimes committed against the Poles during World War II. (*NYT*, 25 October.)

The Polish side demanded that the USSR end its sphere of influence politics in Eastern Europe and approach international security issues without violating other countries' rights to self-determination. Speaking to the Supreme Soviet, Shevardnadze assured his listeners that the Warsaw Pact has experienced "historic, qualitative changes. We are building relations with them [East European allies] on the basis of sovereign equality, the impermissibility of any intervention and the recognition of each country's absolute freedom of choice" (*NYT*, 25 October). When Premier Mazowiecki arrived in Moscow at the end of November, he assured Soviet officials that "I have not heard a serious-minded politician speaking about the withdrawal of Poland from the Warsaw Pact, or making any calculations on the basis of this" (Moscow Television Service, 26 November; *FBIS-EEU*, 27 November).

Poland will continue to support the Warsaw Pact for as long as it is needed to contain German nationalism. Moscow, in exchange, has agreed to supply 85 percent of Poland's crude oil, 65 percent of its processed petroleum products, and 72 percent of the iron ore and defer a $6 billion loan for ten years. In Moscow, Mazowiecki held talks with Secretary Gorbachev and Premier Ryzhkov and signed a new Polish-Soviet agreement on the protection of the environment. Reassessment of the more serious matters was postponed until some measure of stability is achieved in Poland and the USSR.

It will take a long time for Polish-Soviet relations to be normalized. The gravity of Poland's economic situation precludes threats of invasion like those in 1956, 1968, and 1981 or the Nazi-Soviet occupation of Poland in 1939 or Soviet accusations against Solidarity. For the time being, in the words of Adam Michnik, both governments find it "easier . . . to sail past all the rocks and pitfalls. . . If we do not, we will sink." (*Gazeta wyborcza*, 25 October.)

Also, Soviet relations with Poland are adjusted to and reflect political dualism in Warsaw. With his control over Poland's armed forces, President Jaruzelski has his own close links with Moscow, whereas matters less sensitive to national security are within the jurisdiction of Premier Mazowiecki. As long as the Warsaw Pact continues to exist, this two-tier approach to Polish-Soviet relations will endure and new "blank spots" are likely to appear.

Finally, the new Polish government makes distinctions between Poland's relations with Moscow and with other nations in the USSR. Premier Mazowiecki is developing bilateral ties with three Western republics of the USSR—Lithuania, Belorussia, and the Ukraine—on such mutual problems as the status of Polish minorities and the preservation of Polish cultural monuments. Moscow is no longer seen as the spokesman for all nationalities within the Soviet state.

Polish relations with Germany also have assumed a new character and proportion. During previous decades, Polish submissiveness to Moscow served as a guarantee for the security of the Polish western border. At the same time, Polish insistence on the division of Germany was evident in Poland's support for the East German state. The existence of two Germanies was considered mandatory for territorial integrity, the independence of Poland, and peace and stability in Europe.

All these axioms of post–World War II foreign policy had to be revised to reflect political changes in Europe. First, the Polish government ceased to look at West Germany as an enemy, although Warsaw is deeply apprehensive about revanchist trends in the Federal Republic of Germany (FRG). Second, the East German state lost its utility for Poland once the division of Europe began to erode, whereas the FRG acquired a special role as the main source of economic aid for Poland.

A breakthrough in Polish-German relations was achieved during West German chancellor Helmut Kohl's visit to Warsaw in November. The top issue for Poland is to obtain fresh guarantees for its western borders, whereas the FRG seeks to gain respect for the rights of ethnic Germans living in Poland and to use Polish–West German relations to exert political influence on East Berlin.

Before Kohl's departure for Warsaw, the FRG parliament issued a resolution that reassured the Poles that "their right to live in secure borders will not be questioned now or in the future by territorial claims from us Germans" (*WSJ*, 9 November). The value of the economic package brought by Chancellor Kohl is estimated to approach $2 billion, demonstrating the FRG commitment to the process of democratization in Eastern Europe and the desire to play a crucial role in the region.

The West German guest was disposed to address the moral dimension of Polish-German relations by accepting Germany's responsibility for the invasion of Poland, making a symbolic visit to Auschwitz, and joining Premier Mazowiecki at a Catholic mass in the Silesian town of Krzyżowa, the site of a 1921 Polish uprising against German rule. The mass attended by Polish and German leaders became a sign of reconciliation between the two nations. (*NYT*, 15 November.)

Before his arrival in Poland, Chancellor Kohl stated that "horrific deeds against Poland took place in the name of Germany, but also bad things were done to Germans in the name of Poland—here I have in mind the resettlement of Germans after 1944 and 1945" (Warsaw Television Service, 8 November; *FBIS-EEU*, 9 November). At the conclusion of the visit, a joint statement was signed by Chancellor Kohl and Premier Mazowiecki reaffirming the 1970 Polish-FRG treaty, which provided for the inviolability of Poland's western border. Also, FRG president Richard von Weizsaecker accepted an invitation to visit Poland, and Premier Mazowiecki is to visit Bonn in 1990.

With respect to the German guilt for the war, the joint statement read,

> The 50th anniversary of World War II which was unleashed by the attack of National Socialist Germany on Poland, and the large number of victims that this war claimed are a reminder and an appeal to shape permanently the relations between the two countries and peoples in a peaceful way. This anniversary reminds us of the special historic and moral dimension of the relations between Germans and Poles. (*Rzeczpospolita*, 15 November.)

When, in December, Chancellor Kohl revealed his ten-point program for German reunification, he declared that Germany would not question the Polish western border, but chose to circumvent the issue of explicit guarantees of the so-called Oder-Neisse line. The chancellor apparently cannot risk alienating the right-wing conservative groups in his country.

Changes in Poland and other East European countries were an open invitation for the United States to become involved on behalf of democratic forces. The Polish case is particularly important because of its international and internal implications for Washington. Following the roundtable agreement, President Bush announced that the "Poles are now taking concrete steps that require our active support" and that the new political situation in Poland was "potentially a watershed in the postwar history of Eastern Europe." Speaking at Hamtramck, a suburb of Detroit, to a predominantly Polish-American community, President Bush unveiled the following program for Poland:

1. The United States will grant Poland special tariff exemption under the generalized system of preference.
2. The administration will submit to the Paris Club a motion on rescheduling Poland's foreign debt.
3. The administration will support an agreement with the International Monetary Fund to provide new credits for Poland on a standby basis.
4. The United States will guarantee loans for American business ventures in Poland.
5. The Small Business Administration and other U.S. business organizations will be encouraged to expand private investments in the private sector of the Polish economy.
6. Washington will encourage debt-for-equity trade, involving commercial purchase at a discount of outstanding Polish bank loans.
7. Consideration of loans by the International Finance Corporation to support Poland's private sector would be encouraged.
8. Exploration of new exchange and cooperative programs to support Poland's private sector would be accelerated. (Warsaw PAP, 17 April; *FBIS-EEU*, 26 April.)

During his visit to Warsaw in July 1989, President Bush pledged $100 million from the Economic Support Fund and $15 million for a U.S.-Polish cooperative venture to control air and water pollution in Kraków and construction of a new U.S. cultural center in Warsaw. However, these amounts were declared insufficient once Solidarity assumed political power, and the total amount of direct support is now approaching $1 billion over the next three years, plus a $100 million food shipment delivered in 1989. (Francis T. Miko, "East European Reform and U.S. Policy," *CRS Issue Brief*, Library of Congress, November.) Together with the FRG, the United States became the principal underwriter of Poland's transition to democracy and a free market economy.

Two political events exemplify the new character of Polish-American relations. In summer 1989, President Bush visited Poland and in November, Lech Wałęsa arrived in the United States. In Poland, the U.S. president facilitated an understanding between the party and Solidarity. His personal endorsement of the roundtable agreement and U.S. willingness to invest in the Polish economy generated the enthusiasm and optimism necessary to overcome the crisis. But the most extraordinary event was Lech Wałęsa's visit to the United States. This architect of democratic change in Eastern Europe was only the second foreign visitor without an official governmental position to address a joint session of Congress. (The first was the Marquis de Lafayette, who had been invited to speak to a joint session in 1824.) The Polish labor leader received an enthusiastic welcome and promises that the amount of U.S. aid would be increased. President Bush decorated Wałęsa with the Medal of Freedom for displacing a communist government for the first time in Eastern Europe. (*NYT*, 15 November.)

Relations between the two countries have entered a new era. A democratically elected government in Poland will help build mutually advantageous and comprehensive ties in political, economic, and cultural affairs. A democratic and stable Poland has become an important outpost of democracy in Eastern Europe, projecting its influence on the republics of the USSR and on Moscow.

Conclusion. In less than six months some communist regimes of Eastern Europe had been replaced by prodemocratic forces. Poland assumed the pioneering role in this process, having rebelled frequently in the past against Soviet rule and ideology. Elections that finally took place in the summer of 1989 had been delayed for eight years since the idea was originally advanced in December 1981. This delay inflicted incalculable socioeconomic harm on Poland, but finally convinced the communist leaders in East European capitals and in Moscow that pluralism was unavoidable. Having dismantled the political framework of communism, Poland is now facing the arduous task of economic reorganization and containing the Polish propensity toward anarchy and quarrelsome self-destruction. Political instability in Poland would reverse all progress toward democracy and a free market economy.

By the end of 1989, Poland had entered the second building stage after the country was liberated from the Nazi occupation in 1945. Its success or failure will define Poland's place in a unified Europe.

Arthur R. Rachwald
U.S. Naval Academy

Romania

Population. 23,153,475
Party. Romanian Communist Party (Partidul Communist Român, RCP)
Founded. 8 May 1921
Membership. 3,813,000, as reported at the Fourteenth RCP Congress in November 1989. At that time, party members made up one-sixth of the total population of Romania and one-third of the active population (i.e., excluding pensioners and minors). The social composition of the party remained relatively constant over the last decade— 55 percent workers, 16 percent peasants, and 20 percent intellectuals. Of total party membership, 36 percent were women. (*Scînteia*, 21 November).
Note on party leadership. The party officers listed below are those elected at the fourteenth RCP Congress on 24 November. Only minor changes in leadership were made at the congress, and most individuals were re-elected to posts they held before. One month later, RCP general secretary Nicolae Ceauşescu and his wife, Elena, were executed following a popular uprising. Ten days later the new Romanian government arrested the other top leaders of the RCP. New leaders were not elected following Ceauşescu's death, and there were widespread calls for the dissolution of the party. The National Salvation Front government announced that a popular referendum would be held at the end of January 1990 to decide whether the party should be outlawed.
General Secretary. Nicolae Ceauşescu (until 25 December)
Political Executive Committee (PEC). 21 full members, 8 of whom are members of the Permanent Bureau: Nicolae Ceauşescu, general secretary of the RCP, president of the Socialist Republic of Romania, chairman, National Defense Council, chairman, Supreme Council on Socioeconomic Development; Emil Bobu, Central Committee (CC) secretary for party organization, chairman, Council on Problems of Economic and Social Organization; Elena Ceauşescu, first deputy prime minister, chairman, National Council of Science and Instruction; Constantin Dăscălescu,

prime minister; Ion Dinca, first deputy prime minister, Manea Manescu, vice-president, State Council; Gheorghe Oprea, first deputy prime minister; Gheorghe Radulescu, vice-president, State Council; other full members: Lina Ciobanu, deputy prime minister; Ion Coman, CC secretary for military and security matters; Nicolae Constantin, chairman, Central Collegium of the RCP; Miu Dobrescu, chairman, Central Council of the General Confederation of Trade Unions; Ludovic Fazekas, deputy prime minister; Ilie Matei, CC secretary; Paul Niculescu; Constantin Olteanu, CC secretary for propaganda and media, member, State Council; Gheorghe Pană, chairman, Committee for People's Councils' Affairs; Barbu Petrescu, first secretary of the Bucharest Municipal Party Committee, chairman of the Municipal People's Council (mayor of Bucharest); Dumitru Popescu, rector; Stefan Gheorghiu, RCP Academy; Ion Radu, deputy prime minister; and Ioan Totu, minister of foreign affairs; 26 alternate members: Ştefan Andrei, deputy prime minister; Radu Balan, chairman, State Planning Committee; Bogdan Balauta; Maria Bradea, RCP first secretary of Satu Mare County; Nicu Ceauşescu, RCP first secretary of Sibiu County; Silviu Curticeanu, CC secretary; Gheorghe David, minister of agriculture; Carol Dina; Ion Fratila; Suzana Gădea, chairman, Council of Socialist Culture and Education; Mihai Gere, chairman, Council of Working People of Hungarian Nationality; Maria Ghitulica, vice-president, State Council; Nicolae Giosan, chairman, Grand National Assembly; Mihai Marina; Vasile Milea, minister of national defense; Ioachim Moga; Ana Mureşan, minister of domestic trade, chairman, National Council of Women; Cornel Pacoste, deputy prime minister; Tudor Postelnicu, minister of internal affairs; Petre Preoteasa; Stefan Rab; Ion Traian Stefanescu; Ion Stoian, CC secretary for international relations; Iosif Szasz, CC secretary, vice-chairman, Grand National Assembly; Ioan Toma, first secretary of the CC, Union of Communist Youth and Minister of Youth; Ion Ursu, vice-chairman, National Council of Science and Instruction

Secretariat. 11 members (with presumed areas of responsibility); Nicolae Ceauşescu, general secretary; Vasile Bărbulescu, agriculture; Emil Bobu, party organization; Ion Coman, military and security matters; Silviu Curticeanu, chief of staff; Ilie Matei; Constantin Olteanu, propaganda and media; Ion Sirbu, the economy, control of

party and state bodies, staff activity; Ion Stoian, international relations; Constantin Radu, cadres; Iosif Szasz

Central Committee. 281 full and 186 alternate members elected at the Fourteenth RCP Congress on 24 November

Status. From 1948 until 31 December 1989, the RCP was the only legal political party in Romania. Following the overthrow and execution of Nicolae Ceauşescu in December 1989, the Council of the National Salvation Front (NSF) announced that democratic, multiparty elections would be held in April 1990. On 31 December a decree law was issued on the registration and operation of political parties in preparation for the elections (Radio Bucharest, 31 December). The president of the Council of the National Salvation Front announced that the RCP would be outlawed in response to popular demands, but the following day he announced that a national referendum would be held on whether to ban the RCP (*WP*, 13, 14 January 1990).

Last Congress. Fourteenth, 20–24 November 1989 in Bucharest

Last Elections. 17 March 1985 for members of the Grand National Assembly (parliament). Of the 15,732,095 registered voters who participated in the election, 97.8 percent voted for candidates of the Socialist Democracy and Unity Front (SDUF). In December 1989, the Council of the NSF announced that free and democratic elections for parliament would be held in April 1990, but newly organized opposition parties demanded that the date be postponed to allow the parties more time to organize.

Auxiliary Organizations. SDUF, the RCP's political front organization, selected candidates for local and national government office: Nicolae Ceauşescu, chairman; Manea Manescu, first vice-chairman; Tamara Maria Dobrin, chair of the Executive Bureau. General Confederation of Romanian Trade Unions (7 million members); Miu Dobrescu, chairman of the Central Council. Union of Communist Youth (Union Tiniteretul Comunist, 4 million members): Ioan Toma, first secretary of the CC. National Council of Women: Ana Muresan, chairwoman. Council of Working People of Hungarian and German Nationalities: Mihai Gere, Eduard Eisenberger, respective chairmen. Following the overthrow of Ceauşescu in December 1989, these front organizations became moribund. New democratic organizations have been established that in many cases are similar to these institutions. For example, the National Salvation Front has a number of similarities to the SDUF; the Committee of Free Trade Unions was established at the end of December (AFP, 27 December; Agerpres, 28 December); and organizations for the Hungarian and German ethnic minorities, the Hungarian Democratic Union of Romania (Agerpres, 28 December) and the Democratic Forum of Romanian Germans (DPA, 31 December), have been created.

Publications. *Scînteia*, RCP daily (except Monday), Ion Mitran, editor in chief; *Era socialistă*, RCP theoretical and political biweekly; *România liberă*, SDUF daily (except Sunday); *Lumea*, foreign affairs weekly; *Revista economică*, economic weekly. Agerpres is the official Romanian news agency. Following the popular uprising in December, several of these publications underwent major changes. For example, *Scînteia* (The Spark) became *Adeverul* (The Truth); *Lumea* became *Lumea Azi* (The World Today), and its format was altered to include foreign press commentaries. Agerpres became Rompres, and a new director was named.

The RCP was founded in Bucharest on 8 May 1921, after splitting with the Social Democratic party over the question of affiliation with the Communist International. For the next three years the RCP was subject to police harassment and restrictions on its activities, and in April 1924 it was outlawed. Even before its ban the RCP was unsuccessful in attracting support. In 1922 its membership was reported to be two thousand, the highest estimate of its numbers during the interwar period was only five thousand.

Many factors contributed to its failure to win support. During the first decade of its existence, the RCP suffered from a leadership that was highly fractionalized, and it took a full decade before the Soviet Union was able to establish control over the party. The most serious obstacle was the party's subservience to the USSR and its hostility to Romanian national aspirations. After World War I, Romania acquired Bessarabia from Russia and Transylvania from Hungary, both of which were inhabited by substantial ethnic Romanian populations, but also included significant numbers of minorities. The Soviet Union refused to accept the loss of Bessarabia, and the RCP was forced to adopt policies favoring its return to the USSR. Because the hostility of the Hungarian minority to Romania's annexation of Transylvania was a source of in-

stability the Soviets wanted to exploit, the RCP was required to support "national self-determination" for Transylvania (that is, its separation from Romania). This placed the RCP squarely at odds with Romanian national aspirations. As a result, the small RCP was dominated by ethnic minorities and had little appeal to Romanians.

The party came to power as a result of the occupation of Romania by the Red Army during the final year of World War II. Soviet occupation forces required that the insignificant RCP be included in successive coalition governments. With the support of these foreign troops and with RCP control over a core of militant forces in the major population centers, the party gradually seized the dominant role in the coalition governments. It acquired additional credibility when it won the support of Dr. Petru Groza, a political leader who had participated in Romanian governments during the 1920s. The RCP-dominated government, with the help of the occupying Soviet army, suppressed the traditional political parties and "won" the elections of 1946. When it was fully in power, the RCP banned all other political parties. The final stage was the merger of the RCP with the remnants of the Social Democratic party in 1948. The new organization—the Romanian Workers' party (Partidul Muncitoresc Român, RWP)—was the only legal political organization permitted in Romania. The leaders of the former Social Democratic party took a minor role in the new organization, and RCP leaders quickly completed their total domination of the RWP and the country.

During this period, the communist leadership was involved in a bitter struggle between two principal factions. The Muscovite faction, which spent most of the interwar years in Moscow, was led by Ana Pauker and Vasile Luca; the nativist faction, most of whose members spent those years in Romania, was headed by Gheorghe Gheorghiu-Dej. In 1952 Gheorghiu-Dej gained the upper hand, purged his opponents, and established uncontested control over the party.

Although ethnic Romanians came to play a dominant role in the party's leadership, particularly after the purge of the Jewish Pauker and the Hungarian Luca, the party was still dominated by the Soviet Union and seen by most Romanians as an alien institution inimical to Romanian interests. Gheorghiu-Dej carefully followed the accepted Soviet pattern, and Romania became a model Stalinist satellite. Agriculture was collectivized, at the cost of further alienation of the peasantry, and a program of Stalinist industrialization was implemented at considerable economic and personal cost. Party control was established over intellectual and cultural life, which assumed the drab, gray uniformity of socialist realism.

After Joseph Stalin's death in 1953 and the rise of Nikita S. Khrushchev to power in the Soviet Union in the mid-1950s, Gheorghiu-Dej began to take steps that ultimately led to important economic and political differences with the USSR and to a redefinition of the relationship between the RCP and the Romanian people. Initial Soviet efforts toward the economic integration of Eastern Europe in the late 1950s and the early 1960s were stubbornly resisted by Gheorghiu-Dej. Although the Soviet proposals had a certain economic rationale, the RCP doggedly pursued a Stalinist policy of economic nationalism and proceeded with the construction of a series of heavy industry projects that the USSR strongly opposed.

The development of significant differences between the Soviet Union and China in the early 1960s provided Romanians with the opportunity to expand their autonomy from the USSR in interparty affairs. This reached its high point in the April 1964 statement of the RCP Central Committee, which asserted the sovereignty and independence of each party and affirmed the principle of noninterference of parties in each others' internal affairs. This foreign policy provided an opportunity for the party to develop genuine national support.

These policies were initiated under the leadership of Gheorghiu-Dej, who led the RCP from 1944 until his death in 1965, but they were continued and extended by his successor, Nicolae Ceauşescu, who dominated the RCP and Romania from 1965 until his death in December 1989. Ceauşescu's rise resulted from his long and close association with Gheorghiu-Dej that began at the end of World War II. After the death of Gheorghiu-Dej in 1965, Ceauşescu's leadership of the party was confirmed at the Ninth RCP Congress (at which the RWP was renamed the RCP). In international relations, Ceauşescu continued the policies of autonomy begun under Gheorghiu-Dej. The high point of these policies came in 1967–1968 when Romania maintained diplomatic relations with Israel while the rest of the Warsaw Pact severed those ties, established diplomatic relations with West Germany before the Soviet Union approved *ostpolitik*, and moved closer to the nonaligned bloc. Ceauşescu's vigorous denunciation of the Soviet-led invasion of Czechoslovakia in August 1968 marked

the apogee of Romanian defiance of the Soviet Union, but it also emphasized the limits of deviance. Although the RCP under Ceauşescu continued to pursue an international policy reflecting a degree of autonomy from the Soviet Union, it carefully avoided pushing that policy to the point of provoking Soviet military intervention. Although Soviet threats and actions established clear limits to his foreign policies, Ceauşescu's international policies were the principal source of his legitimacy with the Romanian people.

Between 1965 and 1971, Ceauşescu pursued a certain liberalization in the economy and in cultural policy. After that, however, he pursued a rigid, centralized economic policy involving substantial investment in heavy industry and extremely limited production of consumer goods. This, plus lack of investment and poor organization in agriculture, contributed to periodic food shortages and growing popular dissatisfaction. Under Ceauşescu's economic policies, Romania incurred substantial foreign debts that were extremely difficult to repay. A massive effort to cut imports and expand exports to repay all foreign debt contributed to severe economic hardship. In the cultural and educational sphere, Ceauşescu demanded rigid ideological consistency.

The Soviet Union under the leadership of Mikhail S. Gorbachev began to reform its economic and political system, and Hungary and Poland undertook significant reforms of their own. Ceauşescu, however, vigorously opposed these moves. Initially, his opposition was discreet, but increasingly it became more open and adamant. Ceauşescu's brutal repression of dissent among the Romanian population, his harsh treatment of the large ethnic Hungarian and German minorities, and his suppression of religion resulted in the international isolation of Romania. This decline in international status also contributed to the loss of domestic support, particularly when coupled with Ceauşescu's gross mismanagement of the economy and his rigid, Stalinist internal policies.

Party Leadership and Organization Under Ceauşescu. During 1989 citizens of Poland, Hungary, East Germany, and Czechoslovakia cheered the end of the communist monopoly of power and the end of the communist political and economic system. In Romania, which saw the only violent overthrow of its ancien régime, the change was couched in personal terms—the toppling of the dictatorship of Nicolae Ceauşescu. Unlike the other countries of Eastern Europe, Romania's revolution overthrew a despised tyrant. Romania was unique in Eastern Europe not only in the violence of its revolution, but also in the personal nature of its totalitarian system.

Although Romania's communist party and political institutions were similar to those of its Warsaw Pact allies, there were important differences. Power was concentrated in the hands of the party chief; he was all-powerful, not the first among equals in the Politburo. In many respects Ceauşescu's regime was much more like the totalitarian Stalinism of the 1930s and 1940s than the oligarchic party structure that evolved in the Soviet Union and Eastern Europe after Khrushchev. The party was one of the principal instruments through which Ceauşescu ruled, but it did not temper or limit his power. An instrument for co-opting popular support for the regime, the Romanian party was by far the largest in Eastern Europe—one-third of the working adult population were members. Membership, however, was simply one requirement to get ahead in the system, and party members were not the "vanguard of the proletariat," let alone participants in any kind of decision making.

Rotation of cadres. To prevent any individual from establishing a power base in any particular party or government organization, Ceauşescu adopted a policy of rotating individuals in and out of party and government positions, a practice that became party dogma. Party and government officials were not permitted to remain in the same or similar positions for long periods. Ministers, county party first secretaries, local government leaders, and central party officials were constantly rotated from one position to another. The official reasoning was that this allowed individuals to bring their varied experience to problems. The more important purpose was to prevent any RCP leader from establishing a solid geographic or organizational power base from which to challenge the incumbent party leader. The result was that the only constituent for aspiring RCP officials was Nicolae Ceauşescu.

All power to the family. Reliance on his own family was one of Ceauşescu's key means of maintaining his grip. This was not simply a case of nepotism (spreading the status, benefits, and perquisites of public office among relatives), for trusted members of the clan held key positions and played critical roles in maintaining the power of the regime. The prime example, of course, was Elena

Ceauşescu, wife of the party leader. She became a full member of the party PEC in 1984, as well as first deputy prime minister and chairman of the National Council of Science and Instruction. The most important post, which she held for the last decade, however, was head of the RCP Party and State Cadre Commission, which oversaw all key party and government personnel appointments. Her status as number two was clearly reflected in the obsequious homage paid to her by party and government officials on her 70th birthday (*Scînteia*, 8 January; RFE, *Romanian Situation Report*, no. 1, 2 February).

Other members of Nicolae Ceauşescu's family to hold key party and government positions were his brother Lieutenant General Ilie Ceauşescu, deputy minister of defense responsible for party control of the armed forces; his brother Nicolae A. Ceauşescu, head of the cadres department at the Ministry of Internal Affairs, with responsibility for the secret police; and his brother Ion Ceauşescu, first vice-chairman of the State Planning Committee and a member of the Council of Ministers. A fourth brother, Marin Ceauşescu, was head of the Romanian trade mission in Vienna, where he reportedly was responsible for all secret police (Securitate) activity in Western Europe (Vienna, *Kurier*, 28 December; *NYT*, 29 December). Vasile Bărbulescu, the CC secretary responsible for agriculture, is a brother-in-law of the Romanian president. It is significant that the family members in key positions were mostly responsible for personnel, military, and the secret police. Nicu Ceauşescu, the youngest son of Romania's first couple, was an alternate member of the PEC, a position to which he was re-elected at the Fourteenth Congress in November 1989. Earlier in his career he served as first secretary of the Union of Communist Youth, but in late 1987, he was appointed RCP first secretary of Sibiu County, a key post.

The Securitate. Another key to Ceauşescu's power was the Securitate, the secret police. Almost as large as the military, the Securitate served as an elite praetorian guard for Ceauşescu and the Romanian leadership. Carefully recruited, indoctrinated, and provided with the best, most modern equipment, they were lavished with food, consumer goods, and other perquisites not available to ordinary Romanians. In turn, they were isolated from the population. Their responsibility was to protect Ceauşescu, guarantee the loyalty of the regular military units, and intimidate Romanians into compliance. The Securitate maintained a massive spy surveillance operation in which Romanians were required to inform on one another, all contacts with foreigners were carefully catalogued, and vast dossiers were maintained on hundreds of thousands of individual Romanians. When the extent of this surveillance operation was revealed after the December uprising, it shocked even Romanians who knew of its existence (*NYT*, 25 December, 2 January 1990; *WP*, 30 December). The violence and bloodshed of the Romanian revolution in December 1989 were largely the consequence of Ceauşescu's Securitate forces, who fought on for many days after the military forces had deserted Ceauşescu and joined the uprising against the regime. In fact, one of the principal reasons for executing Nicolae and Elena Ceauşescu was to discourage further Securitate resistance.

Manufactured charisma or the cult of personality. Another part of Ceauşescu's strategy to maintain power was the encouragement of a public ritual of adulation intended to demonstrate his political strength, obscure opposition to his rule, and convey the aura of legitimacy. The personality cult began with his 55th birthday in 1973 and reached a new climax in January of 1988, when Ceauşescu celebrated his 70th birthday. His 71st birthday in January 1989, however, also produced a new round of obsequious affirmations of love for the leader, including the publication of another volume of his collected works and well-publicized birthday greetings from various foreign officials, including Mikhail Gorbachev (*Scînteia*, 25, 26 January; RFE, *Romanian Situation Report*, no. 1, 2 February).

Opposition to Reform. Ceauşescu's outspoken opposition to the economic and political reforms taking place in the Soviet Union, Hungary, and Poland during 1989 was the dominant theme that reverberated through the RCP's domestic and international policies. As massive changes took place in Eastern Europe, Ceauşescu was increasingly locked into ever more rigid antireform positions on every issue. Initially his opposition to Soviet reforms was principally in the economic area, but gradually this broadened and intensified in the ideological sphere as well. The antireform stance became a critical element in Romania's relations with its Warsaw Pact allies. As communist parties in the other East European countries collapsed one by one, however, the antireform stance served only to

isolate Romania further and emphasize Ceauşescu's slipping grasp on reality.

Opposition to market-oriented economic change. Ceauşescu continued his adamant refusal to initiate market-oriented changes in the Romanian economy, which continued to be run in a highly centralized fashion. In a personal speech to top party and government officials marking his birthday in January, Ceauşescu said he could not understand the "theses cropping up in a number of countries that once again the way should be eased to various forms of capitalist ownership" because "handing over the means of production by the working class and the people would be tantamount to the liquidation of the bases of socialism" (*Scînteia*, 27 January). Just before the Warsaw Pact summit at Bucharest in early July, Ceauşescu reiterated that "any diminution of the role of large-scale socialist industrial and agricultural property, . . . even small-scale property holdings, . . . endangers the development of socialism" (*Scînteia*, 29 June). The Fourteenth RCP Congress in November again rejected economic reforms and called for strengthening the party's leading role and of central planning.

No weakening of the communist party's monopoly on power. Ceauşescu strongly opposed anything that would undermine the leading role of the communist party. The party daily editorialized that any theory advocating the reduction of the party's leading role is an "emanation of bourgeois ideology" reflecting "the absence of a deep and lasting attachment to the principles of revolutionary ideology" (*Scînteia*, 18 January). Just before the Warsaw Pact summit in Bucharest, Ceauşescu again expressed "astonishment" and "concern" over "the tendency to weaken the leading role of the party in certain countries" (*Scînteia*, 29 June). In a series of theses issued by the RCP in preparation for its Fourteenth Congress, this position was reiterated in even stronger terms: "Life has demonstrated the profoundly erroneous and harmful nature of the concept that there is no longer a need for the communist party to exercise its leading role in society . . . The communist party cannot share, and even less can it renounce, its role as society's leading political force" (*Scînteia*, 5 July).

Intensification of the class struggle. In view of the success of reform among other communist parties, Ceauşescu called for a fight against all those who favor "de-ideologizing international relations and relaxing the class struggle" (*Scînteia*, 29 June). The RCP theses called on the party "to apply firmly the principles of scientific socialism, to strengthen the ideological and political struggle, and to increase the activity against any attempts—both from the outside and from inside—that might jeopardize the interests of socialism" (*Scînteia*, 5 July). In remarks to economic delegations from the USSR and the Soviet republics participating in the Bucharest International Trade Fair, Ceauşescu said that imperialism has not changed its character and that class struggle will never end as long as there are still exploiting classes (Agerpres, 16 October). This focus on class struggle was increasingly out of step with changes in the Soviet Union and the rest of Eastern Europe and was similar to Stalin's ideological pronouncement that, as the communist revolution succeeds, its class enemies intensify their effort to undermine socialism; thus there is a greater need for class struggle.

Mismanagement of the Economy. The Romanian economy under Ceauşescu was one of the most Stalinist and controlled economies in Eastern Europe. Ceauşescu personally took a direct hand in its management at the highest level as the chairman of the Supreme Council on Socioeconomic Development. The economy suffered greatly from Ceauşescu's penchant for grand schemes and massive undertakings that provided great occasions for speeches, flags, and bands, but that were costly and contributed far less to the national economy than the investment poured into them. One example was the construction of the Danube–Black Sea Canal, a scheme to shorten by a hundred miles or so the distance river vessels had to travel from the northward bend of the Danube River to the Black Sea. The project cost billions, but the contribution to the country's economy was minimal. In 1989, on the fifth anniversary of the opening of the canal, Radio Bucharest (21 May) reported that during its first five years of operation, the canal had carried 35 million tons of traffic, only 8.7 percent of its planned annual capacity of 80 million tons.

Another serious problem was Ceauşescu's reliance on ideological exhortations to work harder to motivate workers, while ignoring economic incentives—salary increases and more food and consumer goods for the workers—which would have been far more effective in increasing productivity and output. Until he was toppled from power at the end of December, Ceauşescu made frequent periodic visits to farms, factories, and retail outlets throughout Romania exhorting workers to work harder, improve their efficiency, and struggle to build up socialism. RCP Political Executive Committee sessions were held monthly to review economic progress, but during 1989 continued serious shortcomings were reported. In June poor economic performance during the first five months of the year was criticized (*Scînteia*, 3 June); in August the PEC deplored the fact that planned production targets were not met for the first seven months of the year, that production costs were higher than projected, and that investment was lagging (*Scînteia*, 5 August). Hortatory language emerged from these sessions but no serious effort to come to grips with the fundamental economic problems facing Romania.

Foreign debt and food shortages. Another element that limited the Romanian economy was Ceauşescu's paranoid insistence on economic autarky. Although most East European states moved beyond the Stalinist concept of economic self-sufficiency, Ceauşescu still pursued economic independence. Romania's substantial foreign debt, incurred in the late 1960s and 1970s to encourage economic growth, became a major problem, and Ceauşescu did not like international lending institutions or foreign bankers. In recent years, he launched a major, centrally directed effort to wipe out Romania's foreign indebtedness. Imports were reduced to the absolute minimum, and all products that could be exported were shipped abroad.

Because agricultural products were a major export, most high-quality meat and produce went out of the country. Romanian consumers were left with bruised, spoiled fruits and vegetables and chicken feet or pork bones. In February a West German government agricultural official reported to the Bundestag that there were fights in Bucharest over the sale of potatoes, that Romanian bread was often inedible, and that rationing of foodstuff was a paper procedure because rationed foods were rarely available (RFE, *Weekly Record of Events; România*, 22 February). *Pravda* (7 July), in a remarkably frank story, reported the problems: "For several years Romanians have not been receiving enough food and manufactured goods. Lines, infamous shortages, ration cards, and the strict conservation of fuel and energy, sometimes contrary to the interests of the people—this is the reality of Romania today."

Between 1981 and the end of 1988, Romania reduced its foreign debt from some U.S. $10 billion to about U.S. $2.5 billion. At an RCP Central

Committee plenum in April, Ceauşescu announced that Romania had completed repaying its foreign debts (Agerpres, 14 April; *Scînteia*, 15 April); an official week of celebration throughout the country followed. Three days later the Romanian parliament adopted legislation barring Romania from accepting foreign loans (*Scînteia*, 19 April).

Party efforts to deal with the food supply. Despite his lack of realism, Ceauşescu apparently knew that the lack of food was a source of serious discontent. His efforts to deal with that problem, however, indicate the extent to which his last year in power was pervaded by a lack of realism. He continued a high level of food exports, even after the foreign debt had been repaid, so as to continue importing capital equipment, and he attempted to deal with the demand for food with unrealistic promises of production. In a speech to the National Council of Agriculture in mid-August, Ceauşescu announced that there would be a record cereal harvest of 40,000,000 tons, a significant increase over the 1988 output of 32,600,000 tons (Agerpres, 11 August; *Scînteia*, 12 August). Two months later, he informed a CC plenum that grain yields would exceed 60 million tons—almost doubling the 1988 output and 50 percent higher than his August estimate. At the same time, he promised substantial increases in other crops over 1988 and forecast high meat consumption quotas for the next year (Agerpres, 25 October, *Scînteia*, 26 October). After Ceauşescu's execution, the National Salvation Front government announced that the 1989 grain harvest was only 18,000,000 tons.

At the same time, Ceauşescu made few changes in food distribution. On 8 October he visited markets and shops in Bucharest and criticized the fact that there were food shortages despite a good harvest. The same day he chaired an RCP CC meeting on the food supply. During the next two days, he visited Bucharest markets and food-processing plants near the capital, where he made suggestions for modernization. The media claimed that the supply of goods had improved significantly thanks to his visits (Agerpres; *Scînteia*, 8, 9, 10, 13 October). Two weeks later, he said that Romania ranked among the first nations in Europe and the world in terms of living standards (Agerpres, 25 October; *Scînteia*, 26 October). After the overthrow of Ceauşescu the pent-up demand for food was evident in the journalists' stories from Romania reporting popular euphoria when foodstuffs previously intended for the export market were made available to the population.

The Growth of Dissent. *Rising expectations.* The serious shortage of food was the most obvious and universal problem that led to the intensification of popular discontent during Ceauşescu's last year in office, but also contributing to rising levels of dissatisfaction was the change in expectations generated by the transformations taking place throughout Eastern Europe during 1989. The Romanian government carefully controlled the domestic news media to limit and sanitize information about the reforms in the Soviet Union, Hungary, and Poland, but international broadcasts by Radio Free Europe, the British Broadcasting Corporation, Voice of America, and even Radio Moscow in Romanian provided information, as did Hungarian radio and television, which by the end of 1989 were operating free of any government or party control. Thus expectations were rising in Romania because of dramatic developments throughout Eastern Europe, whereas conditions inside Romania were the same or growing worse.

Dissidents become more vocal. The Ceauşescu regime had always had its dissident intellectuals— poets, writers, mathematicians, and others who opposed the communist system. In the past these isolated individuals were harassed, imprisoned, and intimidated into silence by the Securitate or eventually fled Romania. In recent years, increased international attention and greater emphasis on human rights as a result of the ongoing Helsinki process gave intellectuals and other dissidents in Romania greater stature and increased the cost to the regime of harassing them. In 1989 the growing openness in Hungary, Poland, and the Soviet Union made dissidents still bolder. The cost of dissent, however, was still high. An Amnesty International report issued in London on 25 October said that Romania had eighteen known prisoners of conscience and several hundred more whose identity was not known. All had been imprisoned for exercising their rights of freedom of expression or attempting to leave the country illegally.

Doina Cornea, a university professor in the Transylvanian city of Cluj and one of Romania's most outspoken dissidents, sent a series of open letters to President Ceauşescu protesting human rights violations in Romania and calling for an end to harassment and repression. Despite isolation and abuse by the Securitate, she continued her struggle and received considerable international attention from French, Belgian, and British diplomats and political leaders. Another visible dissident, poet Mircea Dinescu, protested official harassment against himself and other dissidents in open letters and statements to Romanian officials. (Although Dinescu's work could not be published in Romania, a Soviet Moldavian journal published four of his poems in April.) Another dissident, biophysicist Gabriel Andreescu, one of Romania's hitherto quiescent scientific and technical professionals, sent a letter protesting conditions in Romania to the Paris meeting on human rights of the Conference on Security and Cooperation in Europe. In an interview with French television (10 June), he said authorities told him either to conform or to emigrate, but he chose to defy them and remained in Romania to continue his protests. As conditions worsened and dissidents became bolder, even intellectuals who had been part of the Romanian cultural establishment began to waver. In September, Mircea Iorgulescu, editor of the prestigious Writers' Union journal *România Literara* and a member of the Writers' Union board, requested political asylum in Paris. (See RFE, *Romanian Situation Report*, no. 3, 29 March; no. 4, 4 May; no. 5, 16 June; no. 6, 4 August; no. 8, 8 November.)

The most celebrated religious dissident in Romania was Pastor Laszlo Tökes, an ethnic Hungarian from the city of Timişoara. For some time he had been outspoken in his criticism of the Ceauşescu regime and, as a result, subject to vicious police harassment and intimidation. After giving an interview to Canadian television in August, he was arrested and detained by police. Later he was removed as head of his congregation in Timişoara. Although he was of ethnic Hungarian background, Tökes had a strong following among ethnic Romanians as well. In a letter smuggled out of Romania in October, Tökes urged solidarity between Romanians and ethnic Hungarians to bring about Romania's democratic transformation. The crisis that ultimately precipitated collapse of the Ceauşescu regime was another police effort to arrest Tökes in Timişoara on 16 December (see below).

Treatment of the Hungarian and German minorities. Official Romanian denial of linguistic and cultural rights to nearly two million ethnic Hungarians and 350,000 ethnic Germans living in western Romania was another important source of domestic dissent and international criticism. Romanian policies restricted education in the Hungarian and German languages, limited the publication of materials in those languages, and harassed minority intellectuals. Perhaps the most serious threat to minority culture was the policy of rural systematization, Ceauşescu's grand scheme to reduce by half the number of Romania's rural villages to bring the benefits of "socialist culture and society" to the countryside, to allow easier control of the population, and to increase the land available for cultivation. Although Romanian officials gave assurances that this policy was not intended to undermine minority culture, systematization envisioned the wholesale destruction of Hungarian and German churches, cemeteries, historical buildings, and traditional villages, and the plan would disperse minority communities and merge them with ethnic Romanian villages. Despite massive international protests, Ceauşescu continued with the program. (RFE, *Romanian Situation Report*, no. 4, 4 May; no. 5, 16 June.)

The exodus of Romanian citizens. One of the most dramatic consequences of the deterioration in living conditions and intensification of police repression during 1989 was a massive exodus of Romanian citizens. Because many of those who left were ethnic Hungarians and because of Romania's long common border with Hungary, most Romanian refugees fled to Hungary. From mid-1987 through February 1989, some fourteen thousand persons escaped, an average of about seven hundred per month. As conditions deteriorated in 1989, the numbers increased: In July, the total was 1,600, and in September it increased to 2,600, about one-third of whom were ethnic Romanians (MTI, 10 March, 31 August, 4 October). Through October 1989 the number who had left during the previous two years increased to 24,000, almost one-fifth of whom were Romanian, one-twentieth German, and three-fourths Hungarian. Hungary had to shoulder the substantial burden of caring for the refugees. Radio Budapest (4 August) reported that during the first half of 1989, the Hungarian government had spent U.S. $2.5 million and that the U.N. High Commission for Refugees made a grant to Hungary of more than U.S. $5 million in July to aid in caring for those who fled Romania. Among the many refugees in 1989 was Nadia Comaneci, the world-renowned Olympic gymnast, who had to leave her gold medals behind when she fled Romania.

Leaving Romania was difficult. Exit visas were almost impossible to obtain, the border was heavily fortified with barbed wire and other obstacles, and border guards had instructions to shoot those who attempted to cross illegally. The Polish Foreign Ministry delivered a formal protest to Romania after 30 Polish tourists were attacked with tear gas and beaten by Romanian border guards after being taken off a train from Budapest to Bucharest. Radio Budapest (24 September) reported that Romanian border guards had crossed into Hungarian territory in pursuit of seven Romanian refugees. The motivation to leave, however, was strong, although the price of an attempt to flee could be death. A number of Romanians were killed trying to escape. On one occasion two young children were shot by border guards; several times, Hungarian officials reported bodies that had washed ashore on the Hungarian side of a boundary river.

Prominent communists sign letter criticizing Ceauşescu. Another indication of the growing dissatisfaction was those who were willing to question the regime publicly. In March, in a political move unprecedented in Romania since the communist party came to power, six prominent former members of the RCP sent an open letter to Nicolae Ceauşescu that criticized his failure to observe provisions of the 1975 Helsinki Final Act and accused him of discrediting socialism, destroying the national economy, ignoring the Romanian constitution, violating human rights, and causing the international isolation of Romania. Those who signed the letter were Gheorghe Apostol, former RCP first secretary; Constantin Pirvulescu, former Politburo member and founding member of the RCP; Alexandru Birladeanu, former deputy prime minister and Politburo member; former Foreign Minister Corneliu Manescu, who had made an international reputation as chairman of the U.N. General Assembly; Silviu Brucan, former Romanian ambassador to the United States and the U.N. and former editor of the party daily *Scînteia*; and Grigore Raceanu, veteran RCP member (RFE, *Romanian Situation Report*, no. 3, 29 March; Paris, *The Fight*, no. 118, 22 March).

The initial response of the regime was published in an editorial in *Scînteia* (17 March) that equated criticism of Romania's domestic situation with espionage and treason. Later in the year, Ceauşescu took the same line in an interview with the U.S. magazine *Newsweek* (14 August). He said the six dissidents were agents of foreign countries—the Soviet Union, the United States, Great Britain, and France. The six were not put on trial, according to Ceauşescu, because they had expressed regret for signing the letter.

Securitate forces launched a campaign of harassment and intimidation against the signers as soon as the letter became public. The day after it appeared, the prosecutor general announced the discovery of "a grave act of treason" by Mircea Raceanu, a former diplomat and the son of Grigore Raceanu. Former Hungarian foreign minister Janos Peter reported that Manescu was placed under house arrest in a critical state of health (*Népszabadsag*, 21 April). AFP and Radio Budapest (9 May) reported that Manescu was forcibly moved to a new residence to isolate him from friends who were bringing medicine, and Western diplomatic sources in Bucharest said that both Manescu and Brucan had been moved to small houses with no running water in a slum area of Bucharest. Western governments intervened in an effort to provide some protection from official harassment. The Federal Republic of Germany's (FRG) foreign minister invited Manescu to speak in West Germany, and that country's ambassador to Bucharest was recalled in protest when Romanian police prevented the ambassador from delivering the letter of invitation to Manescu. The FRG and French foreign ministers continued an active campaign to let Romanian officials know of their personal interest in Manescu and the signers of the letter.

Opposition groups. The formation of various opposition groupings was a unique development in communist Romania. Although the groups were established underground and had to be careful to avoid Securitate harassment, there were reports outside Romania of such groups. Radio Budapest (17 August) reported the formation of Romanian Democratic Action, making public a program that criticized the communist leadership of Romania, called for the creation of a democratic state, and urged the adoption by Romania of reforms similar to those being implemented in the Soviet Union, Hungary, and Poland. *Le Monde* (25 October) reported that a number of RCP members had set up a Front of National Safety and issued an appeal to delegates of the forthcoming RCP congress to dismiss Ceauşescu.

Foreign Relations. The last year of Ceauşescu's rule in Romania must have been extremely frustrating. More than any other communist leader, he considered himself an international statesman. During his early years as Romanian leader, he cultivated a wide range of international contacts and prided himself on being able to talk with world leaders on all sides of controversial issues. It was a key element of Romanian policy to develop a broad spectrum of contacts as a means of bolstering the country's independence from the Soviet Union. Because of the domestic repression, human rights abuses, and denial of rights to Hungarians and other minorities, however, Romania faced increasing international isolation. Romania was an embarrassment to the Soviet Union and the reform-minded states of Eastern Europe. Western Europe and the United States shunned Ceauşescu. Third World leaders saw little advantage in cultivating ties with Romania. In two decades, Ceauşescu went from a guest welcomed in all major world capitals for his independence from the Soviet Union to an isolated leader whose international contacts were limited to antireform states in Eastern Europe (until they too collapsed) and other international outcasts such as China, North Korea, and Iran. His vehement opposition to reform, which became a dominant element in Romanian foreign and domestic policy, even led the regime to adopt positions that were dangerously close to endorsing the Brezhnev Doctrine, a major departure in Romanian foreign policy.

Relations with the Soviet Union. Gorbachev's leadership of the reform forces contributed to the strain in Soviet-Romanian relations. The RCP reiterated its firm rejection of the prerogative of any other communist party, including that of the Soviet Union, to prescribe what should be done in Romania:

> It is the specific merit of the RCP, of its general secretary [Ceauşescu], to have struggled decades ago against the dogmatic views of a "common pattern," a "unique model" for building socialism. As there are no patterns for building the new society, there can be no compulsory patterns or recipes for improving socialist construction. (*România Liberă*, 17 January.)

For the most part, however, the Soviet Union was not the principal villain for Romania. Hungary and Poland were plunging ahead with reform much faster than the Soviet Union, and Hungary in particular was close enough that the contagion of reform was much stronger from Budapest than Moscow.

Relations with Moscow were not close, but differences were muted. *Pravda* (7 July) published an article on the eve of the Warsaw Pact summit in Bucharest that implicitly criticized the political and economic situation in Romania under Ceauşescu, but also praised some of the more controversial achievements such as building canals and so forth. In connection with the summit, Ceauşescu and Gorbachev met for bilateral talks in Bucharest. TASS (7 July) reported that they affirmed the sovereignty of individual communist parties to determine their own domestic political agendas, but this did not exclude exchanging experiences and coordinating approaches to problems. In a comment on the Warsaw Pact summit, *România Liberă* (10 July) criticized attempts by "certain participants" to give some countries, including Romania, "advice" and "recommendations" that they should renounce "the basic principles of socialism" and reintroduce private property and Western-style democracy.

The Soviet desire to avoid controversy with Romania included a handsoff policy, even in the face of the sharp deterioration of relations between its two Warsaw Pact allies, Hungary and Romania, over treatment of ethnic minorities in Transylvania. In an interview with the West German newspaper *Bild am Sonntag* (23 July), Hungarian prime minister Miklós Németh said that Gorbachev would not play the role of mediator between Romania and Hungary in their dispute over minority rights.

Despite the generally tranquil relationship with the Soviet Union, there were interesting Soviet barbs at Romania. For example, a journal in the Moldavian Soviet republic published four poems by the prominent Romanian dissident Mircea Dinescu, whose writings were banned in Romania. The Soviet press agency Novosti also published a 113-page booklet in Romanian on reform in the USSR.

Criticism of reform in Hungary and Poland. Romanian displeasure with events in Hungary and Poland was voiced at critical points during the year. The situation in Hungary was of much greater concern to Romania because relations with Hungary had been strained for years, because they shared a common border, and because the existence of the Hungarian minority in Romania increased the probability of the infection of reform reaching Romania. The selection of a Solidarity government in Warsaw and the U.S. president's visit to Poland and Hungary, however, brought Poland into Romania's antireform focus. On the day before the Polish government relegalized Solidarity, *România Liberă* (17 January) warned against undermining the leading role of the party. When President George Bush visited Hungary and Poland in July, Romanian media told of a Warsaw Pact meeting held shortly before in which members countries were warned to "be increasingly vigilant against any attempt to destabilize the situation in their countries" and spoke of "a reappearance of attempts to interfere in the domestic affairs of the socialist countries" (*România Liberă*, 10 July; *Scînteia*, 11 July).

On 16 June the Hungarian government permitted the reburial with honor of Imre Nagy, prime minister during the 1956 Hungarian revolution. The Romanian government made an official diplomatic protest to the Hungarian ambassador in Bucharest, Romanian officials in Hungary boycotted the ceremony (as did those of China, North Korea, and Albania), and mass meetings were held throughout Romania to denounce the "grave anti-socialist, revisionist, and anti-Romanian demonstrations in Budapest" (Agerpres, 17 June). In fact, neither Romania nor Romanian-Hungarian differences were mentioned in the speeches delivered at the Nagy reburial ceremonies, although the fact that Nagy was detained on Romanian territory would have provided an excellent opportunity for such statements (see RFE, *RAD Background Report*, no. 17, 30 June).

In September the Hungarian government permitted thousands of East German tourists to leave Hungary for Austria and West Germany, a decision that ultimately forced the German Democratic Republic to open the Berlin Wall and that led to the weakening of its communist party. Again the Romanian reaction was one of outrage. A statement of the Romanian press agency accused Hungary of "grossly violating international conventions . . . The unconcealed interference in the GDR's internal affairs organized by revanchist, revisionist, and chauvinistic circles against socialist countries and socialism in general constitutes a grave infringement of human rights and of national and international law." (Agerpres, 12 September.) In October, Ceauşescu attended the celebrations marking the 40th anniversary of the GDR in East Berlin and had talks with Erich Honecker. The two leaders agreed that communist states should seek to develop in accordance with both "Marxist-Leninist principles" and specific national conditions, repelling imperialist attempts to de-stabilize them (*Scînteia*; *ND*, 8 October).

The concern with reform in other East European countries caused authoritative Romanian voices to justify the invocation of the Brezhnev Doctrine, which Soviet leaders were in the process of abandoning. This about-face completely reversed the fundamental Romanian position first enunciated in the early 1960s opposing intervention by the Soviet Union or any of its allies in the internal affairs of other countries. The first indication of such a reversal of policy was in an article in a historical journal by Lieutenant General Ilie Ceauşescu, brother of the party chief, that linked the historical struggles to preserve Romania's territorial integrity with the contemporary RCP struggle against Hungary's efforts to call attention to Romanian human rights violations in the international arena. General Ceauşescu wrote, "The overtly revisionist, revanchist attitudes displayed by the neighboring state [Hungary] in its relations with Romania cease to be a problem that interests the Budapest government alone" (*Lupta Intregului Popor*, no. 2; RFE, *RAD Background Report*, no. 86, 17 May).

Similar logic was voiced by the RCP daily *Scînteia* (20 August) when a noncommunist prime minister was nominated in Poland. Romania had made indirect comments disapproving the relegalization of Solidarity and the overwhelming Solidarity victory in the June elections, but an authoritative editorial commented directly on the nomination of Tadeusz Mazowiecki in Warsaw. Developments in Poland placed "in jeopardy the interests of socialism, including those of the Warsaw Pact" and served the "interests of the most reactionary forces." Furthermore, the Romanian press leveled a strong personal attack against Mazowiecki, claiming that he was known for his antisocialist positions and connections with imperialist, reactionary circles. The RCP daily said that everything possible should be done to enable the Polish communist party to form a government.

Polish news media reported an even stronger reaction. The RCP leadership held an urgent meeting about the Mazowiecki nomination, and the Polish ambassador to Bucharest was called in by the RCP CC secretary for international relations, Ion Stoian, who read a statement on behalf of Ceauşescu informing the Poles that the RCP and Romania, "as a socialist country," could not consider the Polish developments "as Poland's purely internal affair" (*Gazeta wyborcza*, 29 September; Reuters; AP, 29 September).

These Romanian statements and actions pointed toward Romanian acceptance of the Brezhnev Doctrine to suppress reform, something that earlier would have been unthinkable. The Soviet Union, however, had already abandoned the Brezhnev Doctrine. Following the Malta summit, the Soviet Union and the Warsaw Pact formally condemned the 1968 invasion of Czechoslovakia and repudiated the Brezhnev Doctrine. In December, ironically, U.S. secretary of state James A. Baker III said the United States would support Soviet intervention in Romania to help democratic forces consolidate their overthrow of the Ceauşescu regime.

Relations with Hungary. Relations with Hungary continued to worsen in 1989. Hungary's role as a leading advocate and example of reform was only one aspect of the growing tension, as Hungary took a more aggressive position in the struggle against Romanian human rights violations, particularly restrictions against the ethnic Hungarian minority in Transylvania. In the ongoing Conference on Security and Cooperation in Europe (CSCE), the Helsinki conference, Hungary was a frequent and outspoken critic of Romanian human rights policies. Hungarian accusations were made at the CSCE follow-up meeting in Vienna, and Hungarian government representatives worked with Western and neutral delegations to secure strong statements on human rights and minority rights in the final document of the conference. Romania was the only government of the 35 participating in the conference to announce that it did not consider itself bound by the human rights provisions adopted at the conference (Agerpres, 15, 18 January; *Scînteia*, 17, 19 January; see RFE, *Romanian Situation Report*, no. 1, 2 February). Later in the year, at the CSCE Paris human rights conference, the Hungarian government again accused Romania of discriminating against the Hungarian minority, restricting Hungarian-language education, limiting radio and TV broadcasts in Hungarian, and closing Hungarian-language publications (MTI, 12 June).

Another forum in which Hungary criticized Romania was the U.N. Commission on Human Rights in Geneva. The Hungarian deputy foreign minister denounced Romania at the annual meeting of the organization in February and supported a Swedish proposal on appointment of a special envoy to investigate human rights in Romania—an unprecedented action by one member of the Warsaw Pact against another (UPI, 27 February). When the Swedish resolution was approved by a vote of 21 to 7, however, not only did Hungary vote for the resolution, but representatives of the USSR, Bulgaria, and East Germany abstained (UPI, March 9).

At Ceauşescu's initiative, talks were held in connection with the Warsaw Pact–PCC meeting in Bucharest with Hungarian party chairman Rezsö Nyers, Prime Minister Miklós Németh, and Foreign Minister Gyula Horn. Radio Bucharest (8 July)

said that the exchange became heated when Nyers asked Ceauşescu to halt the rural systematization program. Ceauşescu rejected that request and also a proposal for a bilateral commission to examine the situation of the ethnic Hungarian minority. Horn told journalists in Bucharest that Hungary's political relations with Romania were at the "bottom point." He also referred to the "emergence of certain military threats in recent months" that seriously affected Hungarian relations with Romania. (MTI, 8, 9 July.)

At a press conference in Budapest on 10 July, Horn expressed concern at Ceauşescu's remarks that Romania had the capability to produce nuclear weapons (*Scînteia*, 16 April; RFE, *Romanian Situation Report*, no. 4, 4 May) and indicated other causes of anxiety about Romania's potential military threat to Hungary (MTI, 10 July). In an interview with the Italian daily *Repubblica* (16 July), Horn said that although Romania did not at present pose a concrete military threat to Hungary, the possibility of a threat should not be underestimated. Horn said that during the Warsaw Pact summit in Bucharest, the Hungarian delegation emphasized that "if a small country were to buy intermediate-range missiles of the type that are now being dismantled by both the Soviet Union and the USA, this would destabilize the security of the whole continent." Romania, Horn added, did not reply. In response to Hungarian concerns, however, the Argentine ambassador to Budapest (Radio Budapest, 27 July) informed the Hungarian government that Romania did not intend to purchase Argentinean medium-range missiles.

The increasingly free news media in Hungary contributed to the deterioration between the two countries. Hungarian television (31 July) aired an interview with former Romanian King Michael, who said that Romania had become an absolute monarchy in which people were the property of the state and were treated like cattle and sold for hard currency if they wanted to emigrate. He also denounced the rural resettlement scheme as a crime against humanity. The Romanian Foreign Ministry tried to prevent airing of the interview, but Hungarian communist officials could only express regret and note that they, too, considered broadcast of the program to be unfortunate (MTI, 4 August). Romania recalled its ambassador to Budapest in protest over the interview; meanwhile, Swiss police in Geneva reported that after the broadcast the former monarch received death threats in phone calls and letters.

Lieutenant General Ilie Ceaușescu, brother of the Romanian president and a deputy minister of national defense, was invited to visit Hungary by the Hungarian minister of defense. Several Hungarian opposition groups publicly protested the invitation, citing the fact that General Ceaușescu had published a number of articles defending Romania's historic claims, many of which attacked Hungarian scholars, Hungarian history, and Hungarian government policies. A week later, the Hungarian Defense Ministry announced cancellation of the visit.

Ties with antireform regimes. As paranoia about reform in Hungary and Poland increased, Romania's ties improved with those communist states in Eastern Europe that opposed reform: East Germany, Czechoslovakia, Bulgaria, and Albania. In fact two of Ceaușescu's few foreign visits in 1989 were to East Germany and Czechoslovakia. Relations between Ceaușescu and Honecker improved significantly as both maintained their opposition to reform. A large number of high-level party and government visits were exchanged during the year, and Ceaușescu attended the celebrations at East Berlin in early October marking the 40th anniversary of the establishment of the German Democratic Republic. After Honecker was removed and the political landscape in the GDR transformed, Ceaușescu's relationship with East Berlin became formal and distant.

Much the same pattern occurred in relations with Czechoslovakia. Before November there were several meetings between senior government and party officials. Despite protests by Charter 77 against Ceaușescu's visit to Prague, Czechoslovak party leader Miloš Jakeš warmly welcomed the Romanian leader for a short visit in May. When Czechoslovak prime minister Adamec met with Ceaușescu in Bucharest, press reports noted that Romania and Czechoslovakia "shared similar positions on socialist construction and the major issues of world political life" (Agerpres, 6 September), but Romanian media did not report that Adamec complained to Romanian officials about problems faced by Czechoslovak tourists, including excessive waiting periods at the border and difficulties in obtaining gasoline and diesel fuel (Radio Prague, 6 September). Romanian media reported little about the upheaval in Czechoslovakia during November.

Relations with nonruling parties. The RCP, which had prided itself on its broad range of contacts with nonruling communist parties, found its interparty relations deteriorating because of its human rights record and its opposition to reform. Although relations deteriorated with most West European communist parties (the Italian, Austrian, and Finnish parties did not send delegations to the Fourteenth RCP Congress in November), relations with the Italian party declined the most during 1989. In the 1960s and 1970s the Italian party and the RCP both opposed Soviet efforts to impose common positions on issues. Now, however, the Italians were embarrassed by Romania. At the Italian party congress in March, General Secretary Achille Occhetto described the situation in Romania as "very grave" and said the country had become "closed and immobile." In September the Italian party did not invite the RCP to its annual festival and in December completely broke off relations with the RCP because of repeated human rights violations. (RFE, *RAD Background Report*, no. 215, 5 December.)

Relations with pariah states. As relations worsened with the Western countries over human rights issues and as the antireform states of Eastern Europe began to fall, Romania had good relations only with those regimes that were international outcasts because of their own repressive internal human rights policies.

Romania's traditionally good ties with China and North Korea remained strong. Romania's state-controlled news media coverage of the Chinese repression of popular protests for democracy in June is a measure of its friendly relations with China. Czechoslovak, Hungarian, and Polish media offered critical factual coverage of the Tiananmen Square massacre in Beijing. Romanian media, however, generally remained silent about the situation. A high-level Romanian delegation visited Beijing less than a month after the massacre, and warm, friendly greetings were exchanged between Ceaușescu and Chinese party leader Jiang Zemin. Ceaușescu told the Chinese that the RCP would remain "the trusted friend" of the Chinese party, and the Chinese leader thanked the RCP for its understanding and support when the Chinese party "was confronted with temporary difficulties" (Agerpres; XINHUA, 10 July). At a reception at Beijing in August for Romania's national holiday, the Romanian ambassador said that his government supported China's "struggle against the sabotaging of socialism" (Agerpres, 19 August). Romania and China continued to exchange high-level delegations.

Ceauşescu's relations with North Korean leader Kim Il Song have been particularly close, and the opposition of both to the Soviet-inspired reform confirmed that friendship. The two also had a common dislike for Hungary—the Romanians because of differences over treatment of the Hungarian minority in Romania and the North Koreans because Hungary had established diplomatic relations with South Korea. Romania's relations with Cuba in the past were cordial, but not particularly close. During 1989, as Fidel Castro's differences with Moscow over reform became increasingly apparent, Cuba's relations with Romania appeared to grow warmer as well (RFE, *Romanian Situation Report*, no. 6, 4 August).

Another pariah state to enjoy close links with Romania was Iran. Romania was anxious to obtain Iranian oil on favorable terms, and both states were anxious to use relations with the other to break out of international isolation. During 1989 there were a number of high-level meetings with Iranian officials. Sayed Ali Khamenei, the president of Iran, visited Bucharest in February. Only three days before the visit, AP (22 February) reported that Iran would export five million metric tons of crude oil to Romania in 1989, more than half the 9.4 million metric tons extracted domestically in Romania during 1988. Ceauşescu also paid a state visit to Iran in December, just as the popular uprising against his rule was beginning. This was his only state visit to a noncommunist country during the year.

Another international outcast who continued to maintain close ties with the increasingly isolated Ceauşescu in 1989 was Palestine Liberation Organization (PLO) chairman Yassir Arafat. In January, Ceauşescu formally recognized the Independent State of Palestine and raised the PLO representation in Bucharest to the rank of embassy (RFE, *Romanian Situation Report*, no. 2, 2 March). Ceauşescu also held talks in Romania with Arafat during July and October, and Arafat was one of the few top foreign dignitaries to attend the Fourteenth RCP Congress in November.

Relations with West European countries and the United States. Romania's flagrant violations of human rights dominated its relations with the countries of Western Europe and the United States, and intransigence in the face of strong Western protests resulted in the further deterioration of relations with Western countries. At the ongoing CSCE follow-up meeting in Vienna, Romania managed to alienate the North Atlantic Treaty Organization and neutral governments with its constant disagreements over human rights language and the announcement that it did not consider itself bound by the human rights provisions adopted at the conference (Agerpres, 15, 18 January; *Scînteia*, 17, 19 January; see RFE, *Romanian Situation Report*, no. 1, 2 February). This pattern was repeated at the CSCE Paris human rights conference and in other multilateral meetings during the year.

The European Community (EC) was also involved in strong actions of protest against Romania because of its human rights policy. The European Parliament adopted a number of strong condemnations of Romania, and the EC foreign ministers group expressed dismay over continuing abuses of fundamental human rights. In protest, the EC subsequently suspended all talks with Romania on an economic agreement.

Individual West European countries made their views on human rights known by sending diplomats to meet with Romanian dissidents and through diplomatic protests to Romania over individual cases. On several occasions, Western ambassadors were recalled: France recalled its ambassador in March, Britain canceled a visit by a high-level Foreign Office official, and the Netherlands canceled scheduled talks on a cultural agreement with Romania. West Germany recalled its ambassador in April and the following month issued a strong protest after an "unbelievable" incident in which Romanian Securitate forces attacked the wife of a West German diplomat in broad daylight while she was taking a walk near her home (DPA, 10 May). There were also a series of strong diplomatic exchanges between the FRG and Romania over the invitation to former Romanian foreign minister Corneliu Manescu to visit West Germany. Belgium recalled its ambassador and made a strong official protest to Romania when a senior Belgian politician was beaten by Romanian police as he tried to visit a Romanian dissident in Cluj. Not to be outdone, Romania recalled its ambassador to Britain in April for "menacing actions" carried out jointly by Britain and Hungary against Romania's territorial integrity.

Because of declining trade with Romania as well as the serious human rights violations, smaller West European countries closed their embassies in Bucharest. Portugal, following the precedent of Norway and Denmark, did so in March. Ceauşescu's denial of reality and the regime's effort to obscure the truth were evident in a Romanian media report on the farewell meeting between Ceauşescu and the departing Portuguese ambassador. Agerpres (30 March) reported that relations between the two countries were expanding and completely failed to mention that the ambassador was leaving because he was closing the embassy.

Western countries also continued to protest Romania's rural systemization program. Rural communities in Europe adopted Romanian villages and sent letters to Romanian officials protesting the regime policy that would destroy these places. The project, Operation Romanian Villages, announced that one thousand European communities had adopted such villages. An official U.N. Educational, Scientific, and Cultural Organization (UNESCO) delegation also visited Romania in June to gather information on the village razing policy, and the issue was put on the agenda of the UNESCO executive committee in September.

A controversy with the U.N. Commission on Human Rights continued over Professor Dumitru Mazilu, a Romanian expert on human rights who was prevented from delivering a report on human rights and youth by Romanian officials. Finally, in August, after several stormy confrontations with Romanian officials, the U.N. published his report, which included a special addendum on Romania that sharply attacked human rights abuses and the deterioration in living conditions. In a letter to the commission, Mazilu said he was prevented from leaving Romania and was being terrorized by the secret police, who warned him that he had to "obey or die." The U.N. Commission on Human Rights appointed a special investigator on human rights in Romania, but Romania refused his request for an entry visa in July. On 1 September, the Subcommission on Prevention of Discrimination and the Protection of Minorities adopted a resolution asking the U.N. secretary general to investigate the situation of Dumitru Mazilu. (Mazilu became a leader in the new Romanian government following the overthrow of Ceauşescu in December.)

The United States was active in criticizing Romanian human rights abuses, particularly in the multilateral forums of the CSCE and the U.N. Commission on Human Rights. The high-profile visits of President Bush to Hungary and Poland during July served to emphasize the isolation of Romania; in earlier days Bucharest had been on the itinerary of U.S. presidents visiting Eastern Europe. Romania harshly criticized the president's trip; Scînteia (14 July) said that visit was aimed at "de-stabilizing the socialist countries," and accused the United States of using a cover of "so-called help" to foster anti-socialist developments. The ending in 1988 of most favored nation status for Romanian exports to the United States resulted in a drop in Romanian-U.S. trade by more than 63 percent, to $204,000,000 during the first six months of 1989, according to figures of the U.S. Department of Commerce.

The Fourteenth RCP Congress. The Fourteenth Congress of the RCP was held in Bucharest during 20–25 November. The event, officially designated Congress of the Great Socialist Victory, only emphasized how out of touch Ceauşescu was. The Polish communists had suffered a crushing defeat in free elections six months earlier and in August had installed the first noncommunist prime minister since World War II. Hungary's communist party had split into two factions, and even party leaders admitted that neither successor party or even the two combined could gain close to a majority of the votes in free elections planned for the following spring. Just a few weeks before the opening of the congress, Ceauşescu's contemporaries in the other Eastern European countries had been deposed in the face of popular discontent. In East Germany, Erich Honecker had been removed from his post as party leader and president and was under house arrest. The new East German government had opened the Berlin Wall, and the party and government were in total disarray. In Bulgaria, Todor Zhivkov had been replaced as president and party leader; in response to popular protests he and several of his close associates had been expelled from the party. Three days before the RCP congress opened, mass demonstrations in Prague had met with violent police repression and mass protests against police brutality were taking place. During the Romanian congress, Czechoslovak party leader Miloš Jakeš was forced to resign and the government went through the first of several reorganizations in response to popular discontent. At the time of the congress, Romania was the sole hard-line, antireform regime remaining in Eastern Europe except Albania.

Ceauşescu and his cronies, in contrast, were celebrating the victory of socialism. Immediately after the congress opened with the singing of the national anthem, the 3,308 delegates burst into an ovation, applauding and chanting "Ceauşescu reelected at the 14th Congress!" "Ceauşescu! RCP!" "Ceauşescu and the people!" "Ceauşescu! Romania!" The first proposal to the congress was that Ceauşescu—"the most beloved and loyal son of our socialist nation, a brilliant and revolutionary militant, and a prominent figure in the contemporary world"—be proclaimed chairman of the congress. By thunderous acclamation the proposal was approved.

During Ceauşescu's six-and-a-half-hour report to the congress, he repeated sixteen times that Romania had reached "new heights of progress and civilization" and six times affirmed that the country was headed for the "golden dream" of communism. According to a Western reporter, he was interrupted 125 times with "thunderous applause" (DPA, 20 November). The speech (Agerpres, 20 November; Scînteia, 21 November) and the other addresses at the congress reiterated themes that had been heard through the year. Reform was denounced in the strongest terms. Ceauşescu condemned market-oriented economic reforms and affirmed that it was "incomprehensible" and "unscientific" to suggest that socialist and capitalist means of production could exist side by side. He also repeated in the strongest terms that the party cannot give up its leadership of society—there could be no end to the RCP's monopoly of power.

One unusual and controversial section of Ceauşescu's speech was his insistence that all agreements concluded in the past with Nazi Germany be condemned and annulled. The significance of that statement is that in 1939 Nazi Germany and the USSR agreed that the Soviet Union should receive the disputed territory of Bessarabia, which Romania held from 1918 to 1940 and 1941–1944. Ceauşescu's statement was an appeal to traditional Romanian nationalism, similar to his many previous efforts to manipulate that issue to his benefit. The statement was seen by some as a warning to Moscow against any effort to impose reforms on Bucharest. A TASS commentator responded "to Western media interpretations" of Ceauşescu's remarks that "no serious or responsible politician" could question postwar borders, "including the Soviet border with Romania" (TASS, 23 November).

The foreign delegations at the congress reflected Romania's growing international isolation. The heads of diplomatic missions to Bucharest of the twelve members of the European Community, the United States, and Canada and several neutral and most Latin American countries boycotted the congress (NYT, 21 November). Several important West European communist parties— including the Italian, Austrian, and Finnish—did not attend. The Hungarian party also refused to send a representative. Delegations from the other East European and Soviet parties attended the congress, but they were of lower rank. The Soviet message to the congress mentioned the need for mutual exchanges of experience to reveal the "humanist potential of socialism," no doubt an unwelcome phrase to the Romanians (Radio Moscow, 20 November). In response to the boycott of foreign representatives, the generally low level of representation, and the criticism implied in some of the party messages to the congress, Ceauşescu mentioned two countries represented at the congress with high-level party delegations as examples of countries that had chosen the proper path of socialist development—China and North Korea. (For reports on the Fourteenth RCP Congress, see RFE, Romanian Situation Report, no. 9, 14 December.)

Popular Uprising and Collapse of the Old Regime. Less than three weeks after the conclusion of the Fourteenth RCP Congress, the series of events began that culminated in the collapse of the Ceauşescu regime and the execution of the president and his wife. The image conveyed at the party congress—that nothing had changed in Romania and that Ceauşescu was firmly in command—was clearly hollow, but the speed of the uprising and the bloody violence that was unleashed were a shocking contrast to the peaceful transformations that took place elsewhere in Eastern Europe.

Unrest in Timişoara. The triggering event took place in the western Romanian provincial city of Timişoara, near the Hungarian border. On the nights of 15–16 December, Romanians and Hungarians formed a human chain around the home of Laszlo Tökes, the dissident pastor of the Hungarian Reformed Church, to prevent his forcible deportation to a remote Transylvanian village by Securitate forces. Those who rallied to prevent Tökes's removal included a large number of ethnic Romanians as well as Hungarians and Germans. Tökes and his pregnant wife were subsequently taken by Securitate forces to the northern part of Transylvania, where they were beaten and abused (Radio Bucharest, 27 December; Hamburg, Bild, 30 December).

The next night (17 December) the demonstration expanded well beyond the crowds gathered around Tökes's house, and the center of the city was filled with antigovernment demonstrators. Eyewitnesses reported Romanians shouting "Liberty! Liberty! Liberty!" as they marched through the streets. Speakers on streetcar platforms repeatedly referred to the collapse of communist governments in Hungary, Poland, Czechoslovakia, and East Germany.

Workers reportedly chanted "we are ready to die," and demonstrators from a factory on the outskirts of Timişoara pulled down, tore up, and trampled on portraits of Ceauşescu (AFP, 20 December). Police, military, and Securitate forces were mobilized to regain control of the situation, but demonstrators actively opposed the troops. As the military brought in tanks and armored vehicles and helicopters flew overhead, demonstrators barricaded the streets in front of and behind the tanks with streetcars.

According to subsequent accounts, Ceauşescu personally gave the order for troops to open fire at the slightest provocation (MTI, 28 December), which they did on a crowd in the center of Timişoara. There were also reports of demonstrators being run down by armored vehicles. Although some reports indicated that the armed forces refused to open fire on the population, Securitate forces, some of whom were wearing military rather than Securitate uniforms, fired on the crowds. Popular feeling against the regime is indicated by an eyewitness report on Budapest television (18 December): "Pregnant women in the crowd were pointing at their stomachs as they shouted to the soldiers, 'Shoot here; kill them now, because once they are born we will not be able to feed them anyway.'" Troops launched a manhunt for participants in the demonstration, searching for houses in the city where demonstrators might have fled. There were reports of protestors being killed in the houses where they were found, and the manhunt continued through the night. The number of those killed is estimated to be as high as two thousand. Medical personnel at hospitals in Timişoara reported caring for large numbers of injured.

The massive show of military force permitted authorities to regain control of the city. Japanese diplomats reported that more than a thousand Securitate men were in control of the center of the city, that armored vehicles were located in the central square, and that machine gun emplacements were set up on major street corners. Virtually every shop in the center of the city had its windows broken; damage was extensive. (Reporting on developments in Timişoara was fragmentary because no foreign journalists were there when events began and Romanian media did not report on the events. The most extensive accounts came from Hungarian media [Radio Budapest; Budapest Television, 17, 18, 19, 20 December]. Also reporting were Tokyo's Kyodo News Service, 20 December; Munich, *Sueddeutsche Zeitung*, 20 December; TANJUG, 19 December; Radio Vienna Domestic, 20 December; Austrian Television, 19 December; *NYT; WP*, 19, 20, 21 December; *WP*, 31 December.)

The response of Romanian officials was to tighten security throughout the country. Military units carefully checked anyone seeking to enter or leave Timişoara, and troops were called out in other locations as well. Tanks and troops were positioned in visible locations in Arad and Oradea, important cities north of Timişoara that are also near the Hungarian border. Eight- to ten-man patrols were seen in Arad (Radio Budapest; Hungarian Television, 19, 20 December). Romania closed all of its borders with Hungary, Yugoslavia, Bulgaria, and the Soviet Union. Officially the reason given was "due to a lack of beds in Romanian hotels, and weather conditions not suitable for tourism." All cross-border trains were stopped "until further notice." (Radio Belgrade, 20 December.)

Nicolae Ceauşescu was scheduled to pay a state visit to Iran beginning on Monday morning 18 December. He left for Teheran on schedule as planned, but Elena Ceauşescu did not join him, which was unusual because she had accompanied him on previous state visits. Elaborate communication arrangements were set up between the Central Committee offices in Bucharest where Elena Ceauşescu was in charge, Nicolae Ceauşescu in Teheran, and local military authorities in Timişoara. On Wednesday afternoon, Ceauşescu returned to Bucharest and that evening made a televised statement with his wife and other leading regime officials at his side. He made no reference to casualties, but said soldiers used their weapons to fire "warning shots" after being "attacked by demonstrators." Ceauşescu said the events had been "incited by chauvinists, irredentists, and espionage organizations" whose aim was to dismember Romania, and he accused Hungary of encouraging the disturbances. Ceauşescu was trying to blame the Hungarian minority in an effort to rally Romanian nationalists against the demonstrators. He announced a state of emergency in the Timişoara region, imposed a series of restrictions on public gatherings, and placed military forces on alert (Bucharest Television, 20 December).

On Thursday (21 December) thousands of demonstrators again converged in central Timişoara and staged a general strike to protest the massacre of civilians by Romanian troops and to call for the end of the Ceauşescu regime. Troops and Patriotic Guards (the paramilitary workers' militia) were ordered to the city, but soldiers now joined the demonstrators. There were reports of high-ranking officials from Bucharest going to Timişoara in an effort to restore order. One report said CC secretary Emil Bobu personally directed military and police operations in the city. Others said that Prime Minister Constantin Dăscălescu and Deputy Defense Minister Ilie Ceauşescu, brother of the Romanian president, were sent to Timişoara. A Committee for Socialist Democracy was established in Timişoara that demanded the resignation of the entire Romanian government and party leadership and the restoration of democracy, free elections, and freedom of the press. (AFP; TANJUG; Radio Budapest; Radio Belgrade; Radio Zagreb, 21 December; Radio Vienna, 22 December; MTI, 28 December.)

Unrest spreads to Bucharest. To demonstrate his strength and bolster his support, Ceauşescu called a mass rally at the Square of the Republic in the center of Bucharest during the day on Thursday (21 December). Shortly after he began speaking, however, protesters in the crowd booed, whistled, shouted, and called for his removal from power. Romanian radio and television, which were carrying the rally live, cut off the sound track and played patriotic music for three or four minutes, but not before it was obvious to viewers and listeners throughout the country that protesters had disrupted the rally. Perhaps the most important impact of the speech was the televised look of shock, surprise, and fear on Ceauşescu's face as the protesters interrupted his address. Although Ceauşescu completed the speech, at the end of the rally columns of demonstrators left the square and went through other parts of the city burning Ceauşescu portraits and chanting anti-Ceauşescu slogans. Diplomats and foreign journalists who attended the speech reported that demonstrators shouted "Freedom," "Down with Ceauşescu," and "Timişoara" to show solidarity with residents of the town where Securitate forces had killed and injured thousands of protesters. Police and Securitate forces threw tear gas and opened fire in an effort to disperse the crowd in Bucharest. Meanwhile, fire trucks and armored vehicles were brought to block all approaches to the presidential palace and the Central Committee headquarters nearby.

The disturbances continued throughout the night, with reports of fighting, tear gas attacks, mass disturbances, and more casualties. Because of their superior equipment, Securitate forces were able to regain control of the central part of Bucharest by morning. At 9:55 A.M. Ceauşescu issued a presidential decree declaring a state of emergency throughout all of Romania and placing all military forces, Patriotic Guards, and other forces on alert. At the same time it was announced that Defense Minister Vasile Milea had committed suicide after having been uncovered as "a traitor against Romania's independence and sovereignty" (Radio Bucharest, 22 December). According to postrevolution accounts, Milea had committed suicide rather than direct the troops to fire on unarmed demonstrators as he was ordered to do by Ceauşescu (Agerpres, 29 December). Another account suggests that it was Elena Ceauşescu who ordered the troops to fire on demonstrators when Nicolae Ceauşescu was in Iran, but that Milea refused, instructing the army not to use force. When Nicolae Ceauşescu returned from Iran, he threatened to put Milea on trial during a stormy confrontation, and Milea committed suicide shortly afterward (AFP, 25 December; Belgrade, *Borba*, 26 December). Milea, honored by the new government for his courage in resisting Ceauşescu's order, was promoted to the rank of general of the army posthumously and given a state funeral (Agerpres, 29 December).

An hour after Ceauşescu's state of emergency decree was announced, the radio and television station was stormed by demonstrators. In a highly emotional and confusing broadcast, some 30 opposition leaders, writers, students, and journalists spoke over national radio and television. They announced Ceauşescu's fall from power, declared that the Front for National Salvation was assuming power and that the Romanian armed forces were joining the people in opposing the regime, and reported heavy fighting in the town of Sibiu, where Ceauşescu's son Nicu was RCP first secretary. Officials at the radio and television offices reported that Nicolae and Elena Ceauşescu had fled, and urgent appeals were broadcast asking military units and the Romanian people to stop them.

Ceauşescu flees Bucharest; unrest spreads. Nicolae and Elena Ceauşescu fled by helicopter from the roof of the Central Committee offices shortly before demonstrators took over the radio and television studios. With the dictator and his wife were Emil Bobu and Manea Mănescu, two of their oldest and closest associates. The helicopter was so overloaded that one of the crew members had to sit on Ceauşescu's lap. The aircraft flew to a Ceauşescu residence at Snagov, twenty miles north of Bucharest, where some items were picked up and where Bobu and Mǎnescu were left because of lack of space. They then headed for a military airport at Boteni. The helicopter had been sighted, however, and the pilot told Ceauşescu that they could be shot down. Ceauşescu demanded that the craft land immediately, and Nicolae and Elena, with two bodyguards, hijacked an automobile and fled toward Tirgoviste. En route, they were recognized and apprehended by military forces (*România Liberă*; AFP, 28 December; *NYT*, 1 January 1990). There were various reports about their intended destination. Some suggested that they were trying to flee to those parts of Romania where Ceauşescu thought he still had support to mount a counterattack. Other reports suggested that he was seeking to flee to China or Iran. One foreign news agency reported that Soviet authorities had denied a request from Ceauşescu to fly through Soviet air space en route to China, but a Soviet Foreign Ministry spokesman called the report "groundless" (AFP, 24 December). Ion Iliescu, chairman of the National Salvation Front, announced publicly that Nicolae and Elena Ceauşescu had been apprehended as they were trying to flee (Radio Bucharest, 23 December).

The announcement of the Ceauşescus' capture did not restore calm to Romania. Although the regular armed forces joined the popular revolution and fought with those seeking the overthrow of Ceauşescu, the Securitate forces continued to fight against the demonstrators and the armed forces. Although outnumbered by the regular military, the elite Securitate forces had the best and most sophisticated military equipment, stockpiles of weapons and ammunition in strategic points in Bucharest and other major cities, and access to a series of secret underground tunnels connecting the major buildings in downtown Bucharest. Because Securitate troops were the major instrument of Ceauşescu's rule and thus hated by the population, they had little hope that they would be well treated if they surrendered. As a result they fought a ferocious rearguard battle and took a heavy toll against the military, Patriotic Guards, and students who were fighting for the revolution. They also caused uncertainty and confusion by wearing regular military uniforms. In addition to the violence in Timişoara and Bucharest, major fighting was reported in Sibiu, Braşov, Cluj, Iasi, and a number of other Romanian cities.

The trial and execution of the Ceauşescus. The fierceness of the fighting and the concern that the Securitate forces would continue fighting if there was any possibility of restoring Ceauşescu to power

were the major reasons for deciding to execute the Ceauşescus. The announcement of the execution was made late in the evening of 25 December. Earlier that day, at a military facility near Tirgoviste, the president and his wife were brought before an "extraordinary military tribunal." The charges against them were

> the genocide of more than 60,000 victims [much too high if it referred to the victims of the popular uprising; apparently it applied to victims of his nearly quarter century of power]; undermining state power; the organization of armed actions against the people; destruction of public assets, including the destruction and damaging of buildings, explosions in towns, and so forth; sabotage of the national economy; and finally, an attempt to flee the country with funds in excess of $1 billion deposited in foreign banks (Radio Bucharest, 25 December).

After the Ceauşescus were questioned at some length by a prosecutor, the court issued a verdict of guilty and pronounced the death sentence. When volunteers were sought for the firing squad, more than three hundred soldiers reportedly volunteered, though only a few were needed. Details on the trial were reported by Radio Bucharest, 26 December and Vienna Television, 27 December. A transcript of the Vienna Television version was published in full in *WP*, 29 December. (See also RFE, *RAD Background Report*, unnumbered, "Nicolae and Elena Ceauşescu Executed After Summary Trial," 27 December.)

Romanian television showed Nicolae and Elena Ceauşescu undergoing a medical examination immediately before they were executed. This was the first time that the two had been shown on television since their arrest. The next day, Romanian television showed a still photograph of the body of Nicolae Ceauşescu after the execution. To emphasize the end of the regime, television continued to rebroadcast that picture throughout the day. The actual execution was not broadcast, but that evening (26 December), the full trial was broadcast on both radio and television.

With Ceauşescu and his wife dead, the Securitate forces were gradually brought under control. Deadlines were announced for the surrender of Securitate troops, and the military forces were consolidated; but there were incidents of crack Securitate snipers firing at military personnel and Romanian civilians for several days. Gradually, however, order was restored, and one week after Ceauşescu was deposed, the new government was in place.

The toll of the Romanian uprising was high. The International Red Cross estimated that ten thousand people were killed in the uprising against Ceauşescu (AFP, 2 January 1990). Many of the victims were unarmed protesters in Timişoara, Bucharest, and other cities; many of them were students who were mowed down by Securitate forces. The number of military personnel who were killed in the fighting was reported to be about three hundred.

The RCP and Romania in the Aftermath of the Revolution. *Calls for the dissolution of the RCP and the establishment of democratic political parties.* Within a week of Ceauşescu's death an "initiative group" of the RCP issued a statement welcoming the uprising of 22 December, dissociating themselves from the previous regime, condemning Ceauşescu and his associates, and calling for the convening of an extraordinary party congress to dissolve the party and place "all of its property in the hands of the people, through the Council of the National Salvation Front" (Agerpres, 30 December; *NYT*, 1 January 1990). A few days later, strong public protests against the RCP led the National Salvation Front (NSF) to announce that the RCP would be banned, but the following day the NSF announced that the party's future would be decided in a national referendum (*WP*, 13, 14 January 1990).

The establishment of political parties suggests that political activity is under way in anticipation of free elections. The Christian National Peasant party began publication of a newspaper on 25 December; the organizers of this party include a number of prominent human rights activists. The following day organizers of the Romanian Democratic party made public the party's draft program. The Liberal Party, the oldest of Romania's political parties, was re-established on 31 December at a constituent conference of former members of the party and younger sympathizers. The National Peasant party, the largest of Romania's interwar political parties, which won an estimated 70 percent of the vote in the last free election in 1946, was re-established on 26 December by party veterans and others. (RFE, *RAD Background Report*, unnumbered, "New and Old Parties Budding in Romania," 27 December; ibid., "Romania's 'Historic Parties' Relaunched; Decree on Party Registration Issued," 2 January 1990.)

The National Salvation Front government. The new government of Romania, the NSF, announced its assumption of power on 22 December when Ceauşescu fled. There is no indication that the NSF existed before the uprising against Ceauşescu. On the evening of 22 December, the day Ceauşescu fled, Ion Iliescu, who was later given the title president of the NSF, read a communiqué from the NSF announcing that "all power structures of the Ceauşescu clan have been dissolved. The government is dismissed. . . . All state power has been assumed by the Council of the National Salvation Front."

The NSF-proposed program called for abandoning "the leading role of a single party"; free elections in April; separate legislative, executive, and judicial powers; limited terms for government officials; changing the country's name from the "Socialist Republic of Romania" to "Romania"; the drafting of a new constitution; restructuring of the national economy "in accordance with the criteria of profitability and efficiency"; an end to the policy of resystematization in the countryside and a return to small-scale peasant production; restructuring education along democratic and humanistic lines and elimination of "ideological dogmas"; "observing the rights and freedoms of national minorities and ensuring their full equality with Romanians"; reorganizing trade to satisfy daily needs of the population, including an end to the export of foodstuffs and an end to exporting oil products; observance of Romania's international commitments, "primarily those to the Warsaw Pact"; and promoting domestic and foreign policies that are subordinate to the interests of the people, including the "complete observance of human rights and freedoms, including the right to free movement" (Radio Bucharest, 22 December).

The leaders of the NSF and the new government it appointed appear to be a self-designated group. Although councils were established locally throughout Romania, the national council in Bucharest was apparently established first and the local organizations developed later to replace local RCP and SDUF organizations. The leadership of the NSF is a combination of former Communists who held prominent positions but then fell out of favor with Ceauşescu, dissident intellectuals, and military leaders appointed by Ceauşescu who joined the revolution. Initially the NSF appeared to be an unstructured agglomeration, but it gradually began to coalesce and developed a more formal structure. Initially it was announced that the NSF was headed by former Romanian foreign minister Manea Mănescu (Radio Budapest and Radio Belgrade, 22 December), but other than this initial announcement Mănescu was not mentioned again and played no role in the organization, probably for reasons of age and health. (Mănescu is 73 and in ill health, as was reported earlier when he signed the letter critical of Ceauşescu.)

The NSF leadership. The leader of the NSF from the beginning was Ion Iliescu. Even before he was named president of the NSF Council on 26 December, he made several key public announcements over national radio and television. He read the communiqué announcing the NSF seizure of power and its program, and he publicly confirmed that Nicolae and Elena Ceauşescu had been captured. Iliescu, 59, was first secretary of the RCP's Union of Communist Youth, minister of youth affairs (1967–1971), and RCP CC secretary for propaganda (1971). He served as a party first secretary in two counties and was an alternate member of the RCP's Political Executive Committee (1974–1979). Iliescu had a good reputation within the party, but apparently was increasingly out of step with Ceauşescu's policies. In 1979 he was dropped as an alternate member of the PEC and in 1984, removed from the CC. He became director of the Bucharest Technical Publishing House. Romanian media reported that Iliescu was a student in Moscow with Mikhail Gorbachev, and he is seen by many to be a reformer in Gorbachev's mold. (AFP, 26, 27 December; Agerpres, 29 December; RFE, *RAD Background Report*, unnumbered, "Membership of Romania's National Salvation Front Council Made Public," 26 December.)

The new prime minister of Romania is Petre Roman, the son of Valter Roman, a prominent Romanian communist until his death in 1983. Petre Roman, 43, received a degree in hydrotechnology from the Bucharest Polytechnic Institute and a doctorate in the same field from the National Polytechnic Institute in Toulouse, France. According to Agerpres (26 December) he returned to the hydraulics department of the hydrotechnology faculty at Bucharest Polytechnic, where he became a professor and department chairman. He has not previously held a government position. Roman is to remain as prime minister until free elections are held in 1990. (Agerpres, 26, 29 December; RFE, *RAD Background Report*, unnumbered, "Biographical Sketches of Romania's New Leaders," 26 December.)

The first deputy president of the NSF Council and chairman of the NSF Working Commission on Constitutional, Juridical, and Human Rights is Dumitru Mazilu, a lawyer and professor of law. He came to the first meeting of the NSF Council directly from prison, where he had been imprisoned by the Ceauşescu regime for criticizing Romania's human rights record. He endured a harrowing eighteen months of police harassment, isolation, and imprisonment in his effort to present to the U.N. Commission on Human Rights a report on human rights and youth which he had been commissioned to prepare. (RFE, *RAD Background Report*, unnumbered, "Biographical Sketches of Romania's New Leaders," 26 December; RFE, *RAD Background Report*, unnumbered, "Membership of Romania's National Salvation Front Council Made Public," 26 December.)

The category of former prominent communist officials who fell from favor under Ceauşescu and who are now members of the NSF Council includes Carol Kiraly, an ethnic Hungarian from Transylvania, who, like Iliescu, was a rising RCP star in the 1970s. Kiraly is vice-president of the NSF Council and chairman of the NSF Commission for National Minorities. Silviu Brucan, 73, was chief editor of the RCP daily *Scînteia*, head of Romanian television, and ambassador to the United States and the U.N. He was dropped from official positions in 1966, one year after Ceauşescu became party leader. Brucan was one of the prominent signers of the letter criticizing Ceauşescu in March 1989; he serves as a member of the council and chairman of its Commission for Foreign Policy. Martian Dan, the secretary of the NSF Council, was Iliescu's successor as first secretary of the Union of Communist Youth (UCY) and minister of youth affairs, but he held these positions for only one year (1971). He was a member of the Central Committee, but was removed in 1974. Apparently he has not held a political position since then. Because he replaced Iliescu at the UCY, the two probably worked together and have known each other for some time.

Military officers who led the fight against the Securitate forces and whose support was critical in establishing the temporary government, now identified as leaders in the NSF Council, include Major General Stefan Gusa, chief of the General Staff, first deputy minister of defense since 1986, and full member of the RCP CC since 1987; Lieutenant General Victor Stanculescu, first deputy minister of defense since 1985, apparently responsible for military industries and arms exports; Major General

Gheorghe Voina, an army officer who had just been promoted to full membership in the RCP CC at the Fourteenth Congress; and Captain of the First Rank Emil Dumitrescu and Captain Mihail Lupoi, neither of whom have held prominent positions previously. (RFE, *RAD Background Report*, unnumbered, "Biographical Sketches of Romania's New Leaders," 26 December; ibid., "Membership of Romania's National Salvation Front Council Made Public," 26 December.)

In addition to Dumitru Mazilu, dissidents who have been prominently identified with the NSF include Doina Cornea, a university lecturer from Cluj who is one of Romania's best-known human rights advocates and who was just released from two years of house arrest; Mircea Dinescu, a dissident poet; Dan Desilu, a poet who strongly denounced Ceauşescu in an open letter; Ana Blandiana, a well-known writer; Pastor Laszlo Tökes, the ethnic Hungarian whose resistance to state interference in church affairs started the protests in Timişoara; Geza Domokos, a writer and editor; and film actor Ion Caramitru, who chairs the NSF Commission for Culture.

The composition of the NSF raises a number of questions about the direction it will take in the future. Prominent former Communists and Ceauşescu military appointees may not be vigilant in weeding out collaborators of the deposed dictator. Because Ceauşescu successfully co-opted individuals in his regime, there is no group of experienced opposition leaders who were not part of the old system; hence, the NSF justifies its dependence on officials and bureaucrats of the old regime. Some question whether the NSF will be tempered or restrained by the disparate group of human rights activists and intellectuals who have never held public office. For the 45 years that the communist party has been in power, Romanians have had no experience with democracy or democratic institutions, and well before that time the governments were hardly democratic. Old habits are difficult to change, particularly when there is little experience with democratic accountability.

Already some troubling signs have appeared. The NSF has taken on some of the appearances of the Socialist Democracy and Unity Front. Questions were raised when an "initiative group" of the Romanian Communist party, composed of relative unknowns, called for the party's dissolution and placing "all of its property in the hands of the people through the Council of the National Salvation Front" (Agerpres, 30 December; *NYT*, 1 January

1990). Already there have been questions from students and others who fear the NSF is too closely identified with the previous regime and who question its ability to lead the country to democracy. Students and others shouting No to Communism! have marched in the streets of Bucharest on several occasions. A student rally at the Bucharest Polytechnic Institute on 7 January 1990 questioned the secretive way the NSF is running the country, the retention of so many people from the old regime, and the front's manipulation of the media. The Romanian media did not report on the political issues raised by the students. A gathering of the newly organized Peasant and Christian Democratic parties complained that state-run television ignored opposition gatherings, but covered NSF activities; one of the front's officers acknowledged that the criticism was justified and that two communists were given time on television. He asked why the Peasant and Christian Democratic parties had not been allowed similar time. (*LAT*, 7 January 1990.) New opposition parties have complained that April elections will not give them adequate time to prepare and that early elections will favor candidates of the NSF. Further questions have been raised about assuring all candidates equality in the upcoming election. The NSF has indicated its willingness to negotiate on these and other issues with the various parties.

The road to democracy and economic reform is a difficult one, even under the best of circumstances. The overthrow of Nicolae Ceauşescu, bloody and violent though it was, may prove to be the easiest step on the road to democracy, for the troubling legacy of Nicolae Ceauşescu will continue to haunt the Romanian people and their new leaders.

Robert R. King
Washington, D.C.

Union of Soviet Socialist Republics

Population. 288,742,342 (*World Fact Book*, 1989)
Party. Communist Party of the Soviet Union (Kommunisticheskaia Partiia Sovetskogo Soiuza, CPSU)
Founded. 1898 (CPSU, 1952)
Membership. 19,487,822 (*Izvestiia TsK KPSS*, no. 2, February); 522,884 admissions in 1988, workers, 45.4 percent; peasants and collective farmers, 11.4 percent; white-collar workers and others, 43.2 percent; women, 29.9 percent
General Secretary. Mikhail S. Gorbachev
Politburo. (Unless otherwise indicated, nationality is Russian; first year is date of birth, second is year of election to present rank.) 12 full members: Mikhail S. Gorbachev (b. 1931, e. 1980), chairman of the Presidium, president, Supreme Soviet; Aleksandr N. Iakovlev (b. 1923, e. 1987), chairman, party commission in international affairs; Vladimir A. Kriuchkov (b. 1924, e. 1989), chairman, Committee for State Security (KGB); Egor K. Ligachev (b. 1920, e. 1985), chairman, party commission on agriculture; Iuri D. Masliukov (b. 1937, e. 1989), first deputy chairman (first deputy prime minister), Council of Ministers; Vadim A. Medvedev (b. 1930, e. 1988), chairman, party commission on ideology; Nikolai I. Ryzhkov (b. 1929, e. 1985), chairman (prime minister), Council of Ministers; Eduard A. Shevardnadze, Georgian (b. 1928, e. 1985), foreign minister; Nikolai N. Sliun'kov, Belorussian (b. 1929, e. 1987), chairman, party commission on social and economic policy; Vitalii I. Vorotnikov (b. 1926, e. 1983), chairman of the Presidium, Supreme Soviet of the Russian Soviet Federated Socialist Republic (RSFSR); Lev N. Zaikov (b. 1923, e. 1986), secretary, Central Committee, CPSU; Vladimir A. Ivashko, Ukrainian (b. 1932, e. 1989), first secretary, Ukrainian Central Committee. 7 candidate members: Aleksandra P. Biriukova (b. 1929, e. 1988), deputy chairman (deputy

prime minister), Council of Ministers; Dmitrii T. Iazov (b. 1923, e. 1987), minister of defense; Anatolii I. Luk'ianov (b. 1930, e. 1988), first deputy chairman of the Presidium, vice-president, Supreme Soviet; Evgenii M. Primakov (b. 1930, e. 1989), chairman, Council of the Union, Supreme Soviet; Boris K. Pugo, Latvian (b. 1937, e. 1989), chairman, Party Control Committee; Georgii P. Razumovskii (b. 1936, e. 1988), chairman, party commission on party building and personnel; Aleksandr V. Vlasov (b. 1932, e. 1988), chairman, RSFSR Council of Ministers.
Secretariat. 13 members (* indicates member of Politburo): *Mikhail S. Gorbachev, general secretary; *Aleksandr N. Iakovlev, international affairs; *Egor K. Ligachev, agriculture; *Vadim A. Medvedev, ideology; *Nikolai N. Sliun'kov, economy; *Lev N. Zaikov, military-industrial complex; *Georgii P. Razumovskii, cadres; Oleg D. Baklanov, Ukrainian (b. 1932, e. 1988), defense industry; Andrei N. Girenko, Ukrainian (b. 1936, e. 1989), legal policy; Iuri A. Manaenkov (b. 1936, e. 1989), RSFSR affairs; Egor S. Stroev (b. 1937, e. 1989), agriculture; Gumer I. Usmanov, Tatar (b. 1932, e. 1989), nationalities issues; Ivan T. Frolov (b. 1929, e. 1989), editor in chief, *Pravda*
Central Committee. 251 full and 109 candidate members. The Central Committee is organized into 6 commissions and 9 departments; key department heads include Valentin M. Falin (b. 1926), international; Ivan I. Skiba, Ukrainian (b. 1937), agriculture; Nikolai E. Kruchina (b. 1928), administration of affairs.
Status. Ruling and only legal party
Last Congress. Twenty-seventh, 25 February–6 March 1986, in Moscow
Last Election. Congress of People's Deputies, March–April 1989; 2,250 members; 87.6 percent of elected candidates were CPSU members against 71.4 percent in the Supreme Soviet elected in 1984. The working legislature, the Supreme Soviet (chosen from the congress membership), was elected in May 1989 and contains 522 members.
Defense Council. This is the inner circle of leadership concerned with national security affairs: chairman, Mikhail S. Gorbachev; deputy chairman, Lev N. Zaikov. Other members include Nikolai Ryzhkov and Eduard A. Shevardnadze; Aleksandr N. Iakovlev is probably a member, as is Dmitrii T. Iazov. Possible members or associates: Vladimir A. Kriuchkov; Valentin M. Falin; Colo-

nel General Mikhail Moiseev (b. 1938), chief of staff and first deputy minister of defense.

Government. 86 members of the Council of Ministers, including 3 first deputy chairmen (first deputy prime ministers), 10 deputy chairmen (deputy prime ministers), 15 ex officio deputy chairmen (prime ministers of the union republics), 57 ministers or chairmen of state committees

Auxiliary Organizations. Communist Youth League (Kommunisticheskii Soiuz Molodezhi, Komsomol), 38 million members, led by Vladimir Mironenko, Ukrainian (b. 1953); All-Union Central Council of Trade Unions (AUC-CTU), 132 million members, led by Stepan A. Shalaev (b. 1929); Voluntary Society for the Promotion of the Army, Air Force, and Navy (DOS-AAF), more than 65 million members; Union of Soviet Societies for Friendship and Cultural Relations with Foreign Countries.

Publications. Main CPSU organs are the daily newspaper *Pravda* (circulation more than 5 million), the theoretical and ideological journal *Kommunist* (appearing 18 times a year, with a circulation of more than 1 million), and the semimonthly *Partiinaia zhizn'*, a journal of internal party affairs and organizational matters (circulation more than 1.1 million). *Kommunist vooruzhennykh sil* is the party theoretical journal for the armed forces. The Komsomol has a newspaper, *Komsomol'skaia pravda* (6 days a week), and a monthly theoretical journal, *Molodaia gvardiia*. Each USSR republic prints similar party newspapers in local languages and usually also in Russian. A reorganization of specialized publications is scheduled for the beginning of 1990: *Rabochaia tribuna* will replace *Stroitel'naia gazeta* and *Sotsialisticheskaia industriia*; *Dialog* will replace *Agitator* and *Politicheskoe samoobrazovanie*; *Ekonomicheskaia gazeta* will become the weekly *Ekonomika i zhizn'* (TASS, 25 August; *Pravda*, 15 September). Telegrafnoe Agentstvo Sovetskogo Soiuza (TASS) is the official news agency.

After assuming office as general secretary of the CPSU in March 1985, Mikhail Gorbachev set in motion a reform program designed to cure or ameliorate the economic and social problems associated with the starkly evident general systemic crisis. The long "period of stagnation," according to Gorbachev, had created a situation that threatened the USSR's ability to function as a Great Power.

There were three major aspects of Gorbachev's program: *perestroika* (restructuring), *glasnost'*

(openness or publicity), and political reform. *Perestroika* was primarily designed to make the economy more efficient; *glasnost'* was aimed toward the dissemination of information needed for the success of *perestroika*, the curbing of bureaucratic opposition to reform, and the enlisting of support for Gorbachev against entrenched officeholders. Political reform was viewed by the party leader as essential for the achievement of other planks in the reform program.

Meanwhile, in foreign affairs, Gorbachev launched initiatives to bring the USSR out of its isolation and to create an international climate conducive to domestic recovery. The international arena proved more malleable than the domestic one, as the Soviet leader became the central figure in world politics, achieving notable success in fostering arms reductions and influencing West European elites and publics. His oft-repeated theme of "our common European home" seemed borne out by his apparent rejection of Soviet belligerence, evidenced by such moves as arms control agreements and Soviet withdrawal from Afghanistan.

At home, the reform program moved slowly. Disasters such as the nuclear explosion at Chernobyl in April 1986 and the December 1988 earthquake in Armenia were setbacks, but the main causes of slow progress ran deeper. Resistance in both party and government to reform was widespread, and the working class generally was suspicious of changes that might undermine the economic security (albeit at unsatisfactory levels of consumption) of socialism. Most important, *glasnost'* set loose long-smoldering national resentments in a country with more than one hundred recognized ethnic groups; the resulting discord provided critics of Gorbachev, led by Central Committee secretary Egor Ligachev, with their strongest ammunition against the party chieftain. Despite these obstacles, Gorbachev steadily consolidated his power within the CPSU and achieved a standing abroad that made him an indispensable figure. Moreover, the constitutional changes approved by the epochal party conference in the summer of 1988 promised more control by Gorbachev, as the newly powerful presidency would presumably be filled by the general secretary.

The year 1989 provided even greater challenges for Gorbachev. *Perestroika* was not working as envisioned. The economy had *declined* from its position four years earlier, and shortage of consumer goods was so extreme that the regime spent several billions of scarce hard currency dollars to attempt some temporary alleviation of hardship and discontent. The budget deficit now stands at 11 percent of gross national product; a top economist close to Gorbachev called it the country's most pressing problem.

The nationalities problem, however, overshadowed all else. Moscow was faced with demands from the Baltic states, Georgia, and Moldavia for extreme autonomy or independence. A revived nationalist movement appeared in the Ukraine, whereas Azerbaijan and Armenia engaged in something resembling civil war, with Azerbaijan blockading rail shipments into Armenia. Georgians and Abkhazians intensified their continuing conflict, and ethnic Russians claimed discrimination by indigenous ethnic groups in the Baltic and elsewhere. Troops killed demonstrators at Tbilisi in April, which led to a purge of the Georgian leadership and hasty attempts to absolve Gorbachev of responsibility for the massacre.

Gorbachev admitted that he had failed to recognize the extent and depth of the nationalities problem. In early July he called for a revamping of the federal system; later in the same month, the Central Committee approved a lengthy policy statement on nationalities issues at a plenum devoted to that topic. But the nationalities cauldron continued to boil, sparked by demands for secession from the USSR by various groups in the outlying union republics. Serious doubts about whether the USSR could survive with its existing territorial boundaries and, if so, by what means, clouded the future of democratization and Gorbachev's leadership.

After a rash of wildcat strikes in the spring, the government proposed a law recognizing the right to strike. This was followed by major strikes by miners in Siberia and the Ukraine in July; opposition leader Boris El'tsin was enlisted to appeal to the striking workers. The strikes were settled by concessions that set a dangerous precedent, given the condition of the economy and the political climate. Gorbachev subsequently called for strong legislation to deal with strikes, but the Supreme Soviet in October agreed to a ban only on stoppages in vital industries.

Ultimately, improvement in the economy depended on rationalization of economic mechanisms and processes (i.e., movement toward a market economy). Gorbachev supported this rhetorically, but in practice, the regime continued to postpone price reform and placed new restrictions on cooperative enterprises. At year's end, the economic outlook remained bleak.

The USSR's experiment in democratization got under way during the year. Elections for the new Congress of People's Deputies in March resulted in some staggering losses for party and other establishment officials, and runoff elections a few weeks later confirmed the trend. Gorbachev chose to interpret the results as a victory for reform rather than as a defeat for the party, but the congress turned out to be a heterogeneous assemblage, including supporters and critics of reform, party hacks, political mavericks, and fervent nationalists.

When the congress met in late May, Gorbachev experienced some rough moments, but was elected to the presidency and apparently succeeded in adding a new instrument of power to his already impressive array. However, the election of the Supreme Soviet (the working legislature) by the larger congress produced considerable controversy, and the Supreme Soviet subsequently proved to be highly independent.

Within the party, Gorbachev's power consolidation continued. A Central Committee (CC) plenum in April ousted 110 officials from the CC and Central Auditing Commission membership, removing a major obstacle to the party leader. However, the events of spring and summer, with all their challenges to Moscow and the leadership, brought discontent more fully into the open, and at the July CC plenum several Politburo members voiced criticisms of Gorbachev's policies. The leader fired back with a call for a purge of the party from bottom to top, including the Politburo. In September, Gorbachev succeeded in shaking up the Politburo again. Full members Chebrikov and Shcherbitskii, both cool to Gorbachev, were replaced by KGB chief Kriuchkov and First Deputy Premier Masliukov. Two Gorbachev protégés were named as candidate members, and four regional party secretaries, all strong supporters of reform, were added to the Secretariat.

Effects of the unsettled domestic situation were felt abroad. The Soviet bloc in Eastern Europe was struck by dramatic developments that the USSR could no longer control. Leaderships toppled in four Warsaw Pact countries, the Berlin Wall was punctured, and a noncommunist was named to head the government in Poland. Some of those situations were clearly in line with Gorbachev's objectives: He had strongly advocated reform in East Europe while maintaining a public stance of noninterference, and his support of closer economic ties with West Europe would be favored by the political changes in East Europe. There were also strong indications that Gorbachev had exerted powerful behind-the-scenes influence in favor of reform and leadership changes in East Europe as late as November and December.

However, events had moved faster than anticipated, and the specter of German reunification suddenly re-emerged, to be emphatically rejected by the Soviet leader. Just as at home, Gorbachev's initiatives appeared to have produced unforeseen consequences. Gorbachev's motives, however, may have made little difference; the crisis in the empire could be traced back to the economic decline of the USSR. The domestic economic crisis led to *glasnost*; *glasnost'* had yielded to the rising of subordinate nationalities. With the USSR seemingly falling apart due to ethnic conflicts, Moscow was in no position to intervene in East Europe, and Gorbachev had no choice but to stand aside or give assent as the winds of change swept the area.

Among other communist party states, Gorbachev encountered strong resistance to his ideas on reform. He received friendly welcomes in Cuba in April and in China in May, but the sequels were vociferous opposition to *perestroika* by Fidel Castro and the brutal suppression of the Chinese democratic protest movement. Gennadii Gerasimov's description of East Europe as subject to the Sinatra doctrine rather than the Brezhnev Doctrine now seemed to apply to the entire communist system.

With the bloc in apparent collapse and the USSR engulfed in domestic turmoil, it appeared that the only remaining sources of national power were Soviet military strength and Gorbachev's magnetic hold on Western publics. But military power no longer counted for so much in the global balance partially because of Gorbachev's earlier foreign policy moves, and the USSR was moving toward military retrenchment. Gorbachev remained popular in the West, but it was increasingly doubtful that this asset could be converted into a level of economic assistance that would shore up the ailing Soviet economy.

Gorbachev was still capable of spectacular foreign policy moves, as when he met Pope John Paul II in early December and initiated diplomatic relations with the Vatican. But when Gorbachev met U.S. president George Bush near Malta, also in December, the two superpowers had perhaps less capacity for influencing world events than at any time since World War II, and the Soviet decline was especially marked. However, skillful diplomacy still held the potential for a Europe more or less in accord with Gorbachev's designs, provided the

USSR could be held together while economic reforms were being implemented and provided Gorbachev could retain power. His hold remained strong on his principal base of power, the party. Local elections had been postponed largely because of possible further embarrassment to local and regional party officials. The Twenty-eighth CPSU Congress had been moved to October 1990 and would almost certainly cap Gorbachev's consolidation of power within the party. But the Soviet leader's greatest advantage was probably the lack of a viable alternative to him, either within or outside of the party.

Leadership. Gorbachev moved to a new stage of power consolidation during the year, eliminating pockets of opposition, removing or disarming opponents, purging recalcitrant or flawed officials in union republic parties, and above all strengthening his hold on the central party apparatus. He again proved to be a master of timing, forging victories by meshing advantageous circumstances with his meticulous amassing of organizational power. The upgrading of the presidency gave him additional leverage in the party, providing a popular source of legitimacy unavailable to his predecessors. But the revised constitutional system and the freewheeling criticism evoked by *glasnost'* brought the role of the party in the Soviet system into question as never before and produced continual grumbling in the ranks of the *nomenklatura*, a governing elite operating under siege. Yet, despite the tremors associated with democratization, the internal structure of the party remained largely untouched; in fact, under Gorbachev democratic centralism appeared to be more fully operative than in the tenures of his post-Stalin predecessors. One negative aspect for Gorbachev and the central leadership was the increasing difficulty of maintaining control over some of the outlying union republic organizations whose leaders were caught between the requirements of Moscow and the demands of rebellious predominant local ethnic groups. Moreover, the attraction of the party appeared sharply diminished, reflected in the lack of entries into and withdrawals from its membership and in the pronounced decline of the Komsomol. All this, plus the signal lack of early success for economic *perestroika*, made the party leader a target for the most open criticism that he had faced, which continued even after his notable political triumphs of the year.

Opponents of Gorbachev in the upper leadership, apparently undeterred by the party leader's sweeping triumph at the September 1988 CC plenum, continued to follow a public line contrary to the general secretary's expressed views. Egor Ligachev, demoted to agriculture commissioner at the September conclave, insisted in late January that existing collective and state farms had "vast potential" for improving Soviet agriculture, in contrast to Gorbachev's scheme for promoting private or semi-private farming. Two weeks later, Viktor Chebrikov, head of the party commission for legal affairs, attacked the informal nonparty associations that had proliferated during the previous two years (BBC-CARIS, 13 February).

Elections for the new Congress of People's Deputies provided an unprecedented test for Gorbachev, for those dissatisfied with his reform program, and for the party as a whole. There seemed to be a built-in safety valve for the party, however, in that one-third (750) of the deputies were reserved for "public organizations," which would presumably be under party control. The one hundred party representatives were elected by the Central Committee, which simply endorsed a list presented by the Politburo with no competition for places. Moreover, about one-fourth of the deputies elected by the public were without opposition in predominantly rural districts, where party machines were in firm control. A major issue of the election campaign arose from charges of machinations by party organization officials to maintain control over the nomination process. The success of such maneuvers in many districts raised fears among reformers that the congress would be dominated by hard-line party bureaucrats to the detriment of Gorbachev.

The election results, however, contained some surprises, with profound consequences for party leadership at all levels up to the Politburo. In the most highly publicized contests, reformers almost invariably emerged victorious against more conservative opponents. A result politically damaging to both Ligachev and Moscow party leader Lev Zaikov was the overwhelming success of Boris El'tsin in Moscow. Running in a district of 6.7 million registered voters, one of the country's largest, El'tsin won more than 90 percent of the vote against his party-backed opponent, factory manager Evgenii Brakov (*WP*, 27 March). Also in Moscow, Mayor Valerii Saikin and Iuri Prokof'ev, deputy city party leader, were both defeated.

The ultraconservative Leningrad party organization was particularly hard hit. Iuri Solov'ev, provincial party first secretary and a candidate member of the Politburo, lost, although he ran unopposed, because a majority of the voters cast ballots against him. Also in Leningrad a former prosecutor, Nikolai Ivanov, who had accused Egor Ligachev of quashing a corruption investigation, won on the second round with 60 percent of the votes (*LAT*, 11 May).

Ukraine party leader Shcherbitskii was also embarrassed by the election outcome. In Kiev, city party leader Konstantin Masik and Mayor Valentin Zgurskii lost although both were unopposed (*WP*, 28 March), and in Kharkov, *Ogonek* editor Vitalii Korotich won 84 percent of the vote despite desperate opposition from local party officials (*LAT*, 11 May).

Premier Ryzhkov was another loser in the congress elections, as establishment candidates fared badly in his political base of Sverdlovsk. Provincial party first secretary Leonid Bobykin, who had joined in the denunciation of El'tsin at the 1988 party conference, lost heavily, and Vladimir Volkov, a party organizer in a factory and the only person who had defended El'tsin at the conference, won by an overwhelming margin (*CSM*, 29 March).

Gorbachev was upbeat about the election results, professing to see the outcome as an indication of popular support for reform, although many veterans in the second level of party leadership remained unconvinced. As nationalities tensions erupted, as the shortage of consumer goods became more pressing, and as the shortcomings of Soviet society continued to be pointed out under *glasnost'*, regional party secretaries who saw their fiefdoms crumbling became increasingly vocal in their protests. At the Central Committee plenum in April, criticism was quite open, and in an unusual move several of the negative speeches were printed in *Pravda*.

Solov'ev, Leningrad's big loser, objected to the new openness about Soviet history, saying that people were led to regard the CPSU as the "party of mistakes and crimes against the people." Ratmir Bobovikov, first secretary of Vladimir *obkom* and believed to have been a protégé of former Politburo member Grigorii Romanov, warned that praise for Soviet reforms by the Western "class opponent" was not a good sign (ibid., 2 May). Vladimir Mel'nikov, Komi party chief, sarcastically denounced "cheerful speeches" about the elections, obviously referring to Gorbachev, and reminded the CC that 30 regional secretaries had lost. Moscow province first secretary Valentin Mesiats echoed Mel'nikov's views and described demonstrators as "scum."

Moscow's defeated mayor Saikin noted that people had "lost their optimism," and Irkutsk's Aleksei Miasnikov said that the political situation was "very worrying." (*Pravda*, 26, 27, 28 April.) Politburo members Iakovlev and Medvedev were attacked by name in the debate. Notably, Solov'ev, Bobovikov, and Mel'nikov all lost their regional posts later in the year.

Despite the verbal barrages at the meeting, Gorbachev was as usual one step ahead of his critics. The party reverses in the first round of the elections had clearly put the old guard on the defensive, and Gorbachev again timed a sudden political thrust to bring off a coup. At the April plenum the general secretary was able to solve the problem of CC members who had been dismissed or had retired from their official posts but retained membership in the CC, accounting for nearly one-fourth of the full members. (One of the original purposes of the 1988 party conference had been a renewal of the CC membership, but Gorbachev had failed to obtain the power to conduct a purge via that method. It was thus assumed that he would continue to face this uncertain if not hostile element in the CC until the next party congress, which would under normal scheduling be held in 1991.)

These expectations were crumpled when at the plenum it was announced that 74 of the 301 full members had "resigned," as had 24 candidate members and 12 members of the party auditing commission (ibid., 26 April). (Nine pensioners were said to be too ill to attend and remained nominal members.) A total of 24 candidate members were promoted to full membership, including such reformist stalwarts as Evgenii Velikhov, vice-president of the Academy of Sciences; Evgenii Primakov, director of the Institute of the World Economy and International Relations; and Iulii Kvitsinskii, ambassador to West Germany.

The official explanation of the purge was not accepted in any quarter; it was implausible that all those CC members would voluntarily renounce their memberships. Ruthless pressure was surely exerted behind the scenes by such figures as CC secretary Iakovlev, Cadres Secretary Razumovskii, and perhaps most important by Nikolai Kruchina, a longtime Gorbachev client. As head of the CC Department for Administration of Affairs, Kruchina controlled the perks that constituted the principal leverage against these retirees.

Despite the dramatic improvement of the CC composition from Gorbachev's standpoint, Party Secretary Medvedev admitted that problems remained. Medvedev pointed out that seven of the fourteen union republic party chiefs and more than half of the regional party first secretaries, all appointees under Gorbachev, were not CC members and that under party rules could not attain that status until the next party congress (*NYT*, 26 April).

Gorbachev was not, however, confining his consolidation of power to the party organization. The new Congress of People's Deputies was designed not only to enhance processes of democratization but also to buttress the leader's personal power; some critics, including supporters of *perestroika*, maintained that the latter motivation was the dominant one.

The powerful presidency was the centerpiece of the constitutional innovation, and Gorbachev could confidently expect to be elected to that post and dominate the legislature as well as gain direct supervision over the government. When the congress assembled, Gorbachev was elected by a nearly unanimous vote, but met some blunt criticism at the conclusion of the first session of the new Supreme Soviet. In the ensuing debate on Gorbachev's election, Andrei Sakharov, although professing to be a Gorbachev supporter, asserted that there should be a full discussion of the leader's record. In a display of *glasnost'*, Gorbachev was criticized from the floor for his personal perks, and one delegate compared him to Napoleon; Raisa Gorbacheva was also a target of criticism (ibid., 27 May). Boris El'tsin declined nomination for the presidency on grounds of party discipline; to protest the uncontested nomination of Gorbachev an obscure delegate, Aleksandr Obolenskii, nominated himself (*Pravda*; *NYT*, 26 May).

On the third day of the session (Saturday, 27 May), the new legislature threatened to get completely out of hand. Following announcement of the previous day's secret voting on Supreme Soviet nominees, Boris El'tsin and several other prominent reformers including Tatiana Zaslavskaia, Gavril Popov, and Sergei Stankovich were defeated in voting for Moscow's 29 deputies. Two provincial Gorbachev clients, Kuibyshev first secretary Veniamin Afonin and Volgograd party chief Vladimir Kalashnikov, were also defeated. When some deputies complained that Gorbachev's longtime friend and protégé Anatolii Luk'ianov was being forced upon them as a vice-presidential nominee, Gorbachev headed off trouble by agreeing to postpone that order of business until the following Monday (Moscow Television, 27 May; *Pravda*; AP, 28 May). Over the weekend, a compromise was worked out, due in part to deft maneuvering by Gorbachev. Delegate Aleksei Kazannik, who had been supported by El'tsin, resigned his Supreme Soviet seat to make way for the controversial former Moscow party chief. With El'tsin assured of a place in the new Supreme Soviet, Luk'ianov easily won election to the vice-presidency (*NYT*, 30 May).

When the newly elected Supreme Soviet held its first session, Gorbachev faced further tests. The principal personnel issue revolved around the nomination of Kazakhstan party leader Gennadii Kolbin for the post of chairman of the People's Control Commission, an agency designed to oversee the government's activities and audit its spending. It was generally recognized that the appointment promised Gorbachev an effective mechanism for tightening his control over the state apparatus. Boris El'tsin was nominated as an alternative candidate but he again bowed to party discipline and withdrew his nomination, accepting Gorbachev's offer of the chairmanship of a commission overseeing capital construction. Gorbachev, presiding, counted 34 votes against Kolbin and 53 abstentions, with the remainder presumed to favor the Kazakhstan leader. However, observers noted that about half of the five hundred deputies present appeared not to have taken part in the voting (*LAT*, 8 June). Kolbin was subsequently replaced in his Alma Ata post by Kazakhstan premier Nursultan Nazarbaev (49), a Kazakh.

In the first meetings of the two legislative bodies, Gorbachev put his prestige on the line by personally presiding and attempting to direct the proceedings along the lines he preferred. He had gained substantial organization power, but open criticism of the leader and the sometimes disorderly activities somewhat dimmed Gorbachev's charismatic image.

Nevertheless, Andrei Sakharov, on a visit to Britain, said that Gorbachev "enjoys practically unlimited power," that nothing in reality had changed in the USSR, and that the state apparatus responsible for the current crisis was still in place (*NYT*, 24 June).

Another step in leadership renewal came on 12 July. In a surprise visit to Leningrad accompanied by Personnel Commission chairman Razumovskii, Gorbachev presided over the dismissal of Iurii Solov'ev, the regional party secretary who had suffered a humiliating defeat in the congress election. Solov'ev was replaced by Boris V. Gidaspov, an industrial chemist and member of the Leningrad party's governing bureau since 1987 (*Pravda*, 13 July). Gidaspov was the only member of the Lenin-

grad leadership elected to the Congress of People's Deputies, but he had been criticized during the campaign for a "somewhat authoritarian management style" as director of Tekhnokhin, a Leningrad chemical conglomerate (*NYT*, 13 July). Gidaspov, who was not a member of the CPSU Central Committee and thus ineligible for Politburo membership, subsequently promised that he would not accept such a national post after he attains CC status (ibid., 29 August).

Despite his losses and the continuing public attacks against him, Egor Ligachev continued to speak out against certain aspects of *glasnost'* and *perestroika*. In a June address at Moscow's Timiriazev Academy of Agriculture, Ligachev was sharply critical of "reformist" or "radical" deputies, saying that "there were attacks on the Communist Party, calls to eliminate its leading role, declarations in favor of political pluralism." He was also critical of the leadership's movement toward more private farming and insisted on the correctness of a collective farm system (*WP*, 20 June).

As Moscow's woes mounted—miners' strikes in Siberia and the Ukraine, the economy generally in disarray, and national discontent erupting on various fronts—Ligachev was joined by other important party members in criticizing the prevailing political course. At a CC plenum on 18 July, Lev Zaikov said that "party committees are losing control." Ligachev blamed the liberated media for election losses. Vitalii Vorotnikov called Gorbachev's economic program a failure and urged that it be scrapped. Premier Ryzhkov warned that the party was losing control of the increasingly independent legislature. Ryzhkov and Gorbachev maintained that the answer to these problems was the acceleration of reform. Ideologist Vadim Medvedev said that the party should reassert control over the media. Ligachev suggested turning back the clock by urging the party "to make use of the valuable experience accumulated during the period of building socialism" (*Pravda*, 21 July).

Despite the criticism, Gorbachev at the plenum called for a purge extending from the work collective to the Politburo and subsequently demonstrated that this was not an idle threat. However, the usual speculation about his future appeared during Gorbachev's summer vacation, and some reformists expressed fears of a conservative backlash that might include military intervention.

Meanwhile, principal critics Chebrikov and Ligachev emphasized the serious dangers inherent in unstemmed nationalist disorder. Ligachev told

Pravda (9 September) that if ethnic discord and strikes continue, "the disintegration of the USSR is inevitable."

On the evening following Ligachev's interview in *Pravda*, Gorbachev made a 25-minute speech on television (his first public appearance since returning from vacation) that blasted nationalists and opponents of reform. He condemned protest strikes in the outlying republics and said conservatives and radicals were trying to push the country into serious instability:

> In this multivoice choir, we can hear threats of approaching chaos and talk of a threatened coup, and even of civil war. It is a fact that some people would like to create in this country an atmosphere of alarm, a feeling that there is no way out, a feeling of uncertainty. We should not fall for this. We should not halt in our tracks but continue along the path of planned change. (*NYT*, 10 September.)

Eleven days after his televised address, Gorbachev made good on his July threat of a purge. At the CC plenum, 19–20 September, a lengthy policy statement on nationalities issues promised greater regional autonomy and several personnel changes were announced.

Legal Affairs Commission chairman Chebrikov, Ukraine party chief Shcherbitskii, and CC agriculture secretary Viktor Nikonov were all ousted as full Politburo members, and Deputy Premier Nikolai Talyzin and Leningrad party first secretary Iurii Solov'ev were dropped as candidate members. Chebrikov and Shcherbitskii were known as sharp critics of some of Gorbachev's policies. Nikonov, one of Gorbachev's earliest appointees in April 1985, had attained full Politburo status in 1987. However, he had failed to measure up to the "new style" of leadership demanded by Gorbachev, exhibiting rudeness and arrogance during a goodwill visit to the American Middle West in 1987. He was apparently an easy target for sacrifice, given the troubles in the consumer sector.

Solov'ev, an extremely conservative leader of Leningrad *obkom* since 1985, was targeted for dismissal after his defeat in the congress elections. Talyzin, Gorbachev's choice as head of Gosplan and first deputy premier in October 1985, had become a scapegoat for the slow pace of economic reform, his political demise prefigured by the loss of the Gosplan portfolio and demotion to deputy premier in 1988.

KGB chairman Vladimir Kriuchkov and First Deputy Premier and Gosplan chairman Iurii Masliukov moved up from candidate to full Politburo membership. Added to candidate membership were Boris Pugo, party leader of Latvia, 1984–1988, and chairman of the Party Control Committee since October 1988, and Evgenii Primakov, since June 1989 chairman of the Council of the Union (the upper house of the Supreme Soviet), and a close adviser to Gorbachev, frequently accompanying the leader on foreign trips (*Pravda*, 21 September). All four Politburo promotees have publicly identified themselves with reform; however, Kriuchkov's long career in the KGB reflected nothing of a liberal background. Pugo also had a history of work in the security arm, having served as head of the Latvian KGB from 1980 to 1984.

Four regional party chiefs were added to the party Secretariat: Egor Stroev, first secretary of Orel *obkom*, succeeded Nikonov in the agriculture slot; Iurii Manaenkov, first secretary of Lipetsk *obkom*, reportedly was given special responsibility for RSFSR affairs; and Gumer Usmanov, Tatar regional party leader, apparently took over duties regarding nationalities issues (*NYT*, 21 September; *Report on the USSR*, 6 October). Andrei Girenko, Crimean party chief, was also named to the Secretariat. Girenko told *Pravda* (27 September) that he would be "dealing with the improvement and *perestroika* of party work" but that "the specific sector may, of course, be named once I start my new job." As a member of the Legal Affairs Commission, Girenko was expected to assume responsibility in that area, making him the immediate Secretariat supervisor of the KGB. The appointments of both Usmanov and Girenko underscored the urgency of the nationalities issue: Usmanov is a Tatar, and Girenko is listed as Ukrainian. However, Girenko's original first name is Adolf, and he is believed to be at least half-German.

Although the results of the plenum reflected Gorbachev's strong hold on the party organization, there were indications that the discord at the July plenum had been taken into account. Premier Ryzhkov had objected to the presence of two men responsible for agriculture on the Politburo, and there had been much criticism of the breakdown of "law and order," Chebrikov's area of responsibility. There had also been expressions of dissatisfaction, in which Manaenkov had joined, with the state of affairs in the central party apparatus and calls for the establishment of a new party organ for the RSFSR (*Report on the USSR*, 11 August). Further, the promotion of Kriuchkov emphasized Gorbachev's continuing reliance on the KGB, and it seemed possible that the weight of the security organization had been influential in the personnel changes in the leadership. However, from Gorbachev's standpoint the KGB's influence was somewhat balanced by the Supreme Soviet's new supervisory role over that organization.

The continuing presence and outspokenness of Ligachev after the plenum was puzzling. On the same day as the Politburo reshuffle, Ligachev was officially cleared of corruption charges brought by Telman Gdlian and Nikolai Ivanov, two former prosecutors (*CSM*, 22 September). In October, Ligachev resumed his verbal sparring with the party leader and, in an interview, said that it was premature to think that the Soviet economy could be removed from party control and urged an increase in government financing for the agricultural sector rather than encouragement of private farming (Radio Moscow, 9 October; RL, *Soviet/East European Report*, 15 October).

As expected, Shcherbitskii also lost his post as head of the Ukrainian party. With Gorbachev present and orchestrating the proceedings, the Ukrainian party CC ousted Shcherbitskii and replaced him with second secretary Vladimir Ivashko (57) (AP, 28 September; *Pravda*; *WP*, 29 September).

Lev Zaikov was relieved of his post as head of the Moscow party organization in late November and replaced by Iurii Prokof'ev, the city deputy leader who had failed badly in the March People's Congress election. Gorbachev said that the change would permit Zaikov to concentrate on his role as Politburo member in charge of military industry. At the same time, it was announced that Zaikov had been appointed deputy chairman of the Defense Council. (*Pravda*, *NYT*, 22 November.)

Despite the upheavals of the year, Gorbachev seemed to have fared better than some of his colleagues on the Politburo, for Ligachev, Zaikov, and Ryzhkov had all witnessed a diminution of their influence. Barring serious setbacks for Gorbachev in the interim, Ligachev, Zaikov, and RSFSR president Vitalii Vorotnikov will most likely be displaced at the Twenty-eighth CPSU Congress, originally scheduled for October 1990. Given the condition of the economy, Ryzhkov's hold on the premiership also may not be very secure. However, an unprecedented phenomenon occurred during the year made possible by the constitutional reforms—the rise of potential leadership outside the party hierarchy. The most obvious was Boris El'tsin, who used electoral politics to stage a political comeback, although

his future prospects were clouded by his erratic behavior and his alleged authoritarian tendencies. Another outsider was the historian Iurii Afanas'ev, who emerged as a leading spokesman for "radical" democrats. Perhaps the most intriguing was Lieutenant General Boris Gromov, commander of the Kiev military district, who took advantage of *glasnost'* and democratization to become a spokesman for the far right; some feared him as a possible future "man on horseback" contender for power.

Semen Grossu (55), head of the Moldavian party since 1980, was replaced by Petr Luchinskii (49), in the first secretaryship. Luchinskii had served as first secretary of the Kishinev party committee and as second secretary in Tadzhikistan (TASS; *FBIS*, 16 November). Grossu had become the Moldavian party leader when Konstantin Chernenko dominated the republican organization; his continuing in the post five and a half years into the Gorbachev era was surprising.

Former President, Foreign Minister, and Politburo member Andrei Gromyko died on 2 July (*NYT*, 4 July).

In an effort to discredit Leonid Brezhnev, the former leader's 1978 Order of Victory award was annulled by the Presidium of the Supreme Soviet as "inconsistent with the statute on the Order of Victory" (*Izvestiia*, 29 September).

Another footnote to the history of the Brezhnev era was provided by former Leningrad leader, CC Secretary, and Politburo member Grigorii Romanov. In a letter to *Pravda* (15 September), Romanov denied borrowing imperial chinaware from the Hermitage Museum in 1979. According to reports at the time, the chinaware, part of a collection that had belonged to Catherine the Great, was smashed by drunken guests at the wedding reception for Romanov's daughter.

At its December plenum, the CC decided to hold an expanded committee meeting in January on speeding up reform and named Ukrainian leader Vladimir A. Ivashko to the Politburo (*NYT*, 10 December). Reportedly, Gorbachev faced heavy criticism from conservatives. Kemerovo party chief Aleksandr Mel'nikov was said to have scorned Gorbachev for "bowing to the capitalists" and "asking a blessing from the Pope." Gorbachev, enraged, supposedly offered to resign and was upheld by the CC, with Mel'nikov forced to apologize. Gorbachev was elected to the new post of party chief of the Russian federation. (AP, 10 December.)

Party Organization and Personnel. As *glasnost'* and democratization proceeded, the party's internal operations received more public scrutiny than ever before. In January it was revealed that party membership fees in 1987 amounted to 1.34 billion rubles, only enough to finance 81 percent of all budget expenditures. The remainder were covered by deductions from the profit of enterprises under party jurisdiction (*Izvestiia TsK KPSS*, no. 1, January; *Argumenty i fakty*, no. 5, 4–10 February). In February a report was issued on the 1989 budget, which totaled 2.7 billion rubles, mostly financed by members' dues (*Pravda*, 10 February).

In July, *Sotsialisticheskaia industriia* (28 July) invited its readers to participate in discussions of "the place and role of the CPSU in contemporary society," and in September an article by G. Belotserkovskii in the same publication complained about the absence of procedures for resignation from the CPSU. Belotserkovskii noted that this had not been a question in the past but that "times are different now. Many taboos have been broken, including the one against self-initiated departure from the CPSU." (*Sotsialisticheskaia industriia*, 10 September; *FBIS*, 20 September.)

In July the Moscow party newspaper published a collection of articles and letters complaining about the loss of party prestige, the decline in enrollment of new party members and resignation of old ones, and the defection of candidates to informal political organizations (*Moskovskaia pravda*, 11 July). An article in *Pravda* (10 July) by a communist couple reported that their 26-year-old daughter had quit the party in disgust and could not be convinced that "there are honest communists." As the new openness pointed up morale problems, the CC revealed data confirming the decline. According to the CC, induction of new members began to fall off in 1987 and in 1988 plunged to 20 percent of that of previous years (*NYT*, 12 July).

The strongest indicator of public discontent with the party was the defeat of a number of prominent party officials in the March elections and the tenuous hold on the outlying republics, particularly in the Baltic states, where party leaders often survived only by establishing a modus vivendi with nationalist organizations. Gorbachev told a meeting of senior Soviet editors that the defeat of scores of CPSU candidates was a natural part of the democratic process and should not be a cause for alarm. He said further that the Soviet people had chosen the candidates they felt were the strongest supporters of reform, whether party members or independents (*WP*, 31 March).

Gorbachev, however, increasingly adopted a public posture of concern about party morale and the party's relation to society. At the July CC plenum, he called for a purge of the party ranks from the shop floor to the ruling Politburo (*Pravda*, 21 July). At the September CC plenum, Gorbachev confirmed postponement of local elections (in which the party was expected to sustain even more devastating losses), announced that the Politburo had approved a proposal to convene the Twenty-eighth CPSU Congress in October 1990 (several months ahead of the expected date), and promised a dramatic reorganization of the party (*LAT*, 20 September).

The controversial editor of *Pravda*, Viktor Afanas'ev, was fired in October shortly after Gorbachev issued a verbal blast at the editor of the popular antiestablishment weekly *Argumenty i fakty* (*WP*, 20 October). Apparently, the leader was venting his displeasure against critics both left and right. *Pravda's* republication in September of an Italian newspaper article that said that Boris El'tsin drank and shopped his way through a tour of the United States and a subsequent forced apology for reprinting the article may have figured in Afanas'ev's dismissal. Probably more important were the decline in *Pravda's* circulation from ten million in 1985 to about half that four years later and Afanas'ev's consistent conservative position on certain reform issues. Ironically, Afanas'ev had almost lost his job in 1979 because of his revelations about corruption in Krasnodar *krai* under Leonid Brezhnev's crony Sergei Medunov; during the first half of the 1980s, Afanas'ev was said to be close to Iurii Andropov and Gorbachev. Afanas'ev was replaced at *Pravda* by Ivan T. Frolov (60), who had been an aide to Gorbachev for two years after serving as editor of *Kommunist* (*NYT*, 20 October).

The ticklish relationship between the party and newly formed nationalist organizations figured in a sharp blast by *Pravda* (1 July) against the leadership of the Belorussian party. The article denounced "intolerance and aloofness" by the Belorussian leadership and mentioned First Secretary Efrem Sokolov. *Pravda* particularly criticized the Belorussian leadership for "continuing rude attacks" on Vasil Bykov, a leader of the Belorussian Popular Front who had accompanied Gorbachev to New York in 1988.

The nationalities issue posed problems for the party in all the outlying republics, particularly

Georgia, where protests and a massacre of protesters led to a purge of the top leadership (see below). But in terms of central control of the republican party organizations, the biggest problems were in the Baltic states, where local party officials were required to seek a balance between Moscow and local national activists. The head of Sajudis, the Lithuanian *perestroika* movement, said in October that the Communist Party of Lithuania would probably secede from the CPSU at its congress in December (Vienna Domestic Service, 2 October; *FBIS*, 3 October). Six weeks later the threat of such action had become serious enough for the Politburo to summon top leaders of the Lithuanian party to Moscow for an urgent conference (AP, 14 November). However, the Lithuanian party carried out its threat in December, leading to an emergency meeting of the CPSU CC (*WP*, 22 December; AP, 26 December) and a subsequent mission by Gorbachev to the rebellious republic.

Numerous changes were made in personnel assignments during the year, some of them resulting from the party's debacle in the congress elections and some reflecting the rise of tensions between nationalities: A. A. Volintsev was elected first secretary of the Maritime Territory Party Committee, replacing D. N. Gagarov, who retired with a pension (*Pravda*, 15 January). I. P. Kochetkov was relieved of his duties as second secretary of the Armenian Central Committee and was succeeded by O. I. Lobov (ibid., 18 January). Former Krasnodar *krai* party first secretary Sergei F. Medunov was expelled from the party for "violations during his term" (ibid., 24 March).

B. V. Adleiba was relieved of his duties as first secretary of Abkhaz province committee of the Georgian party and was replaced by V. F. Khishba, formerly first-vice chairman of the Georgian Republic State Committee for Environmental Protection and Forestry (ibid., 7 April). Anatolii I. Kornienko, deputy head of the CPSU CC Department of Party Construction and Personnel Work, replaced K. I. Masik as first secretary of the Kiev city party committee (ibid., 23 July). I. A. Karimov was named first secretary of the Uzbekistan CC, moving up from his post as first secretary of the Kashka-Daria province party committee. A. R. Atadzhanov, vice-chairman of the Uzbek Republic Council of Ministers, was elected party chief in Kashka-Daria (ibid., 28 July). N. D. Shvirev was relieved of his position as first secretary of the Cheliabinsk party *obkom* and was succeeded by Second Secretary A. P. Litovchenko (ibid., 13 August).

Aleksandr A. Khomiakov was appointed deputy of the RSFSR Council of Ministers. His post as first secretary of the Saratov party *obkom* was taken by K. P. Murenin (ibid., 11 August). Ratmir S. Bobovikov, first secretary of the Vladimir party *obkom*, retired on a pension and was replaced by F. G. Kondriukov, chairman of the province Soviet executive committee. Vladimir I. Mel'nikov was relieved as first secretary of the Komi province party committee, but had a "soft landing," becoming USSR minister of the timber industry. His successor in Komi was I. A. Spiridonov, provincial party second secretary (ibid., 10 August).

Anatolii N. Balandin, first secretary of the Orenburg province party committee, retired on a pension. His place was taken by provincial Second Secretary A. F. Kolinichenko (ibid., 26 August). Dmitrii V. Romanin, first secretary of the Kaliningrad province party committee, also retired on a pension and was succeeded by Second Secretary I. N. Semionov (ibid., 8 September).

Replacements for the regional party secretaries named to the CPSU CC Secretariat at the September CC plenum were as follows: M. S. Shaimiev, chairman of the Tatar Autonomous Republic Council of Ministers, succeeded Gumer I. Usmanov as first secretary of the Tatar province party committee; V. V. Donskikh, chairman of the Lipetsk province Soviet executive committee, replaced Iurii A. Manaenkov as first secretary of Lipetsk party *obkom* (ibid., 24 September); N. A. Volodin, a secretary of the Orel province party *obkom*, moved up to first secretary in place of Egor Stroev; N. V. Bagrov, deputy head of the CPSU CC Department of Party Construction and Personnel Work, filled Andrei N. Girenko's slot as first secretary of the Crimea province party committee (ibid., 26 September).

Government. The Soviet government, caught in the vortex of reform, was frequently chastised for the failures of economic *perestroika*. Unused to the gauntlet of public and legislative censure, top government officials had to readjust their behavior to fit the situation and some fell victim to democratization.

The new openness had led, the previous October, to an admission by Finance Minister Boris Gostev of a budget deficit of $58 billion. In January, Leonid Abalkin, director of the National Institute of the Economy (subsequently appointed deputy premier) and a close adviser to Gorbachev, said that the budget deficit amounted to $165 billion. Western economists estimated that this was about 11 percent of the USSR's gross national product, compared with the U.S. budget deficit, which is about 4 percent of gross national product. Abalkin also predicted that it would be another six years before *perestroika* produced a significant improvement in the Soviet standard of living (*NYT*, 26 January).

The budget deficit and a public backlash against prosperous entrepreneurs accounted for the government's announcement, in April, of a new tax structure. The progressive income tax, to start in January 1990, ranges from 12.2 percent for incomes of $1,120 per month to 50 percent for incomes about $2,400 per month (*Izvestiia*, 18 April).

Some outer limits for *glasnost'* were defined when a government official was fired in May. Aleksandr Aksenov, head of the state committee for radio and television, apologized to the CC plenum for a suggestion on live television by Mark Zakharov, director of Moscow's Leninskii Komsomol Theater, that the body of V. I. Lenin should be removed from public view on Red Square. Three weeks later, Aksenov was "retired." (AP, 17 May.) Although Aksenov, once a KGB official and formerly premier of Belorussia and ambassador to Poland, was 65 and at a convenient retirement age, it was generally believed that his exit was related to the Zakharov controversy.

Premier Ryzhkov got off to a good start with the new Supreme Soviet in June when he announced plans for a government reorganization following his re-election as chairman of the Council of Ministers. Ryzhkov said that eighteen state agencies would be eliminated and the number of cabinet positions reduced and that some managerial functions would be surrendered to the union republics. One ministry slated for elimination was the Ministry of Light Industry, which directed production of consumer goods. According to Ryzhkov the remaining ministries in Moscow would abandon day-to-day management of industry and focus on long-range planning and scientific and technological work (*Izvestiia*, 11 June).

Ryzhkov, who had easily weathered some criticism in the debate over his nomination, encountered harsher critics when he presented his proposed government to the newly empowered legislature. The Supreme Soviet blocked appointments of eight top officials, and Ryzhkov conceded defeat, saying in an interview, "we have to get used to this." Two Gorbachev associates, Vladimir Kalashnikov, Volgograd party first secretary, nominated as first deputy premier for the food sector, and Marat V.

Gramov, named to head the state sports committee, were among the defeated candidates. Environmentalists blocked the confirmation of Gennadii Bogomiakov, party chief of the Tiumen region, as minister of the petroleum industry. Polan A. Poladze was rejected as minister of irrigation, and four top scientists turned down offers to head the state committee on ecology. The incumbent minister of culture, Vasilii G. Zakharov, was blocked by ethnic minorities. Other losers were Vladimir G. Gribov, nominated to head Gosbank, and Lira G. Rosenova, candidate for chairman of the state price-setting committee (*NYT*, 28 June). All these nominees were checked by committees. In the following week, the Supreme Soviet as a whole rejected two nominees on the final vote: Vladimir M. Kamentsev, a close associate of Gorbachev's, was voted out of office as a deputy prime minister and chairman of the Foreign Economic Commission (ibid., 5 July), and Nikolai S. Konarev was ousted as minister of railways (ibid., 6 July).

Defense Minister Dmitrii Iazov was confirmed in his post on 3 July, but only after sharp scrutiny by the Supreme Soviet. The defense minister was attacked from both right and left, with the harshest criticism coming from those who considered him a representative of the military old guard; several delegates, including some serving in the armed forces, called for his resignation. However, Gorbachev intervened in the debate and strongly supported the defense minister. One point of interest in Gorbachev's speech was the public identification for the first time of members of the Defense Council other than the chairman: Gorbachev said that Premier Ryzhkov and Foreign Minister Shevardnadze were members and that the Council included "comrades in charge of the defense industry and selected members of the armed forces" (RFE, *Research*, 24 July).

After much haggling and substitution, Ryzhkov finally got the government confirmed. In his concluding speech at the Supreme Soviet session, Ryzhkov said that "we are profoundly grateful that the members of the government have received a genuine mandate of confidence" and called for the acceleration of *perestroika* to produce "a breakthrough to a new quality of life for the Soviet people." The premier said that a "system of businesslike contacts" had been established between the government and the Supreme Soviet and called the formation of the government under the new circumstances perhaps the most unusual event in the history of the Soviets (*Pravda*, 18 July).

The budget problem continued to be a major concern. Gorbachev, in a nationwide television address on 9 September, said that the government's program "may include unpopular, probably tough, and even painful measures." The government's budget proposal, submitted to the Supreme Soviet later in the month, called for reducing the deficit from $192 billion to $96 billion in one year and for cutting $153.8 billion in capital outlays (30 percent of the expenditures on new factories and production equipment), while increasing production of consumer goods by 6.7 percent (AP, 16 September).

In November, Deputy Premier Leonid Abalkin proposed a plan to gradually introduce price reform, with some wholesale prices and wages to begin rising in 1990, retail prices in 1991, and prices largely decontrolled by the mid-1990s. Abalkin also called for the government to begin selling off unprofitable state-owned businesses to workers or cooperatives, for the sale of shares in industrial enterprises, for the establishment of a stock market, and for competitive bidding for government contracts (ibid., 13 November).

The government introduced landmark legislation in November that would open up the USSR to the outside world. The draft law would allow Soviet citizens to emigrate and travel abroad freely. First Deputy Foreign Minister Anatolii Kovalev told the Supreme Soviet that "adoption of this law will create the legal guarantee of the right of everyone to leave any country, including his own, and to return to his own country, rights that we in various international agreements have committed ourselves to honor."

Fedor Burlatskii, chairman of the Soviet Human Rights Commission, said that between 500,000 and 600,000 people probably would apply to emigrate once the law is adopted and that six to eight million would travel abroad in 1990 on business or tourist trips (LAT, 14 November).

Governmental changes in the union republics included the appointment of Aiaz N. Mutalibov as chairman of the Azerbaizhan Council of Ministers (Izvestiia, 19 February) and the naming of Anatolii S. Morgasov as chairman of the Uzbek republic KGB (Pravda vostoka, 25 February).

In Georgia, O. I. Cherkezia, chairman of the republic Council of Ministers, was elevated to the chairmanship of the republic's Supreme Soviet Presidium. Z. A. Chkheidze was appointed chairman of the Council of Ministers, and O. V. Kvilitaia was named first deputy chairman (Izvestiia, 31 March). In the purge of the Georgian leadership following the killings in Tbilisi, Chkheidze lost the pre-

miership and was replaced by party secretary N. A. Chitanava (Pravda, 15 April).

Sergei V. Bashilov retired as USSR minister for construction in the Urals and western Siberia (Izvestiia, 6 April). Vladimir G. Kliuev (65) former party first secretary of Ivanovo obkom and long associated with the textile industry, retired as USSR minister of light industry (ibid., 15 April).

The Presidium of the USSR Supreme Soviet relieved Boris N. El'tsin of his duties as first vice-chairman of the USSR State Construction Committee and as a USSR minister at his request, in connection with his election as a deputy to the People's Congress (ibid., 24 May).

Vice-president Anatolii Luk'ianov was confirmed as chairman of the Interim Committee for Combating Crime in the USSR (ibid., 17 August).

Congress of People's Deputies and Supreme Soviet. As the USSR began implementing the 1988 constitutional reforms, two major questions raised widespread speculation: would the party control the election of deputies? and how much power would the legislatures—the larger body of the congress and the smaller working legislature, the Supreme Soviet—have?

The aftermath of the elections showed unfamiliarity on all sides with anything approaching democracy, and meetings sponsored by radical groups frequently seemed as authoritarian as those arranged by establishment bureaucrats. Much controversy arose over alleged fixing of elections by local party bosses, and there was considerable criticism of reserving one-third of the congress seats for public organizations. Some disputes were handled by deft maneuvering, as when Andrei Sakharov was named as a candidate by the Academy of Sciences after an earlier rejection (AP, 10 April). The election results stunned old-line party leaders (CSM, 29 March), but the varied composition of the congress that resulted from the March elections and late runoffs indicated that no single group or faction would dominate the legislature. On balance, it was also favorable for Gorbachev, because his dual roles as head of the governing elite and leader of the opposition would presumably be aided by the splintering of the legislature.

These expectations were fulfilled when Gorbachev won victories on votes for major positions. However, he endured perhaps the most severe face-to-face public criticism of any leader in Soviet history and was obliged to speak frankly to the delegates, as when he acknowledged that Soviet military spending amounted to $123 billion—four times higher than previously admitted—and promised to cut back (*Izvestiia*, 31 May). Gorbachev's political skills had not, however, deteriorated, and he was able to deflect opposition to election of his close associate Anatolii Luk'ianov as vice-president and head off an incipient revolt over selection of Supreme Soviet deputies with a behind-the-scenes deal for the seating of Boris El'tsin.

The new Supreme Soviet proved to be highly independent when, by blocking objectionable nominees, it forced a governmental reshuffle (see above). Subsequently, the legislature settled down to a more humdrum operation, but on several occasions acted apparently more or less independently on important matters.

As the strike crisis mounted in July, the Supreme Soviet issued an "Appeal to the Soviet People" that urged calm, made a plea against the spread of strikes, and promised legislation to provide full independence and self-management for work collectives, "real transfer of land to the farmers," "sovereignty and financial autonomy" for the union republics, and "democratic election of people's representatives to local and republican bodies of power" (Radio Moscow; TASS, 25 July; RFE, *Research*, 28 July).

Following up on the promises to the republics, the Supreme Soviet on 27 July approved resolutions to allow Estonia and Lithuania to assume control of their budgets, industry, transportation, trade, and natural resources by the end of the year (*Izvestiia*, 28 July). However, the legislature refused to enact formal laws to grant economic autonomy to the two republics.

The government called for a ban on strikes until 1991; the Supreme Soviet refused to comply but did outlaw strikes in key industries, such as transport, communications, power, and defense. The new law outlined steps—conciliation, mediation, and arbitration—that workers must follow before they can legally strike and made the courts, not the government, the referee if disputes arise over the right to strike (ibid.; *LAT*, 10 October).

Two weeks later, the Supreme Soviet voted (254 to 85) to eliminate the reserved congress seats for public organizations, including the CPSU, but the measure also required the assent of the parent congress (AP, 24 October).

A law on the court system passed in November was generally in line with wishes expressed earlier by Gorbachev. The law provides for trial by jury in those cases where defendants are accused of crimes involving fifteen years imprisonment or the death penalty and allows defense lawyers to participate in cases starting with the preliminary investigation (TASS, 13 November).

When the People's Congress met in December, the big issue was repeal or revision of Article Six of the Constitution, which guarantees the leading role of the CPSU. At Gorbachev's urging, the congress voted (1,139 to 839) against debating the issue. During the debate, Gorbachev unceremoniously cut short Andrei Sakharov, who died two days later at his home (*NYT*, 13, 14 December).

All in all, the new legislatures appear to have made an auspicious beginning in a political system previously bereft of popular participation in the business of government. But both the elites and the public require further adjustments to solidify the early achievements of political reform. This was acknowledged by Fedor Burlatskii in testimony before the Commission on Security and Cooperation in Europe in Washington. Burlatskii said that after "70 years of trying to teach others how to live," the Soviets were now studying the lessons of American democracy (AP, 28 November).

The Economy. At the outset of the year, the regime responded to protests of the high prices charged by private entrepreneurs by announcing that it would give preference in state loans, tax rates, and supplies of raw materials to businesses that sell goods and services at state-controlled prices. Meanwhile, the Politburo made public a plan to give local authorities broader powers to set price ceilings for cooperative restaurants. Justice Ministry spokesman Georgii Golubov said that the restrictions would cover less than 1 percent of the 48,000 private businesses, but other observers predicted that hundreds of fledgling entrepreneurs would be put out of business (TASS, 5 January; *NYT*, 6 January).

High prices would, of course, be charged in the open market for scarce goods and services; moreover, the size of cooperatives ruled out economies of scale. But the highly touted beginning of a legal limited market economy had not solved the general problems of consumers; in fact, the shortages had become more acute. Gorbachev admitted this in a speech during the first week of the year and conceded that the public increasingly blamed his policies for the deteriorating economic situation:

> People are talking about a lack of goods, food, about queues, about the housing problem, about defi-

cits of services and other spheres that touch the everyday lives of people. And the thing is that the criticism is not just of these deficits. People directly connect it with *perestroika*, they say that so far it has promised nothing socially or economically, that in many cases the situation even has gotten worse.

Gorbachev added that the Kremlin's budget problems might require a cut in defense spending and called budget deficits the "gravest heritage" of his predecessors, whom he accused of carefully hiding those deficits from society (*Pravda*, 8 January).

Further admissions came from the party leader in February. On a visit to Kiev, he halted his limousine to wade into a downtown throng, where he was met by a barrage of complaints about living standards, nuclear power, and other matters. Gorbachev told the crowd that if a group of American experts commissioned to study plans for two nuclear reactors in the Crimea concluded the project was unsafe, the facilities would be used only as training installations. He acknowledged that "goods that were in abundance" previously—soap, detergents, and sugar—had become scarce and that the authorities were trying to find out why. On price reform, he promised that food prices would not be raised for two or three years, until food supplies improved (*NYT*, 21 February).

After losses in the oil export trade in 1988, the USSR agreed in March to cooperate with the Organization of Petroleum Exporting Countries and cut its oil exports by 5 percent. In 1988 crude oil and refined product sales to Western nations rose 7.9 percent, but export revenue fell by 11.8 percent (TASS; Reuters, 3 March; *NYT*, 4 March).

The perennial problem of agriculture was the subject of a CC plenum in March. In a major speech on 15 March, Gorbachev introduced a "new agrarian policy" that called for a radical reversal of the policy of centralized farming, the immediate dismantling of the state agricultural bureaucracy, and the gradual introduction of free markets (ibid., 16 March). On the following day, the CC endorsed specific proposals made by the party leader, including lifetime leases by farmers of state land; the abolition of Gosagropom, the superagency responsible for agriculture; more-flexible pricing of some farm products; and the breaking up and selling of some economically inefficient state farms (*Pravda*, 17 March).

Egor Ligachev said that the party endorsed "all the ideas" expressed by Gorbachev, but said that changes in the farm sector would be "on a purely voluntary basis" and that no one in the party favored a wholesale breakup of the collective system (*NYT*, 17 March).

Any major gains from reform in the agricultural sector would likely be long term. The more immediate problems facing the leadership were exacerbated by the restlessness of workers. After a rash of wildcat strikes, the head of the trade unions, Stepan A. Shalaev, announced that the government was submitting to the Supreme Soviet a draft law permitting strikes, except those that were "politically motivated" (*Trud*, 3 May). While the draft law was under consideration by the new Supreme Soviet, strikes broke out in major coal mining areas.

Initially affected were five mines at Mezhdurechensk—in western Siberia's Kuznetsk Basin, with 107,000 workers—and mines in the nearby cities of Novokuznetsk, Osinniki, Prokopievsk, Kiselevsk, Leninsk-Kuznetskii, Berezovskii, and Kemerovo. Demands ranged from a greater share in the profits of mines and a stronger local voice in mine management to more food in stores, warmer winter clothing, improved maternity leave, antipollution measures, and housing improvements (*NYT*, 15 July).

Miners in the Ukraine took their cue from their comrades in Siberia and shut down eight mines in the Donetsk Basin. According to Soviet press reports, two thousand miners demanded more rapid reduction in the bureaucracy running the mines, longer vacations, and improved housing, fewer demands than those of the workers in the Kuznetsk Basin (TASS; AP, 17 July). Premier Ryzhkov reported to the Supreme Soviet on 16 July that 110,000 miners were striking in the Kuznetsk Basin, that a high-level team had been sent to the area to negotiate, and that the national economy would soon begin feeling the effects of the walkout (TASS, 17 July; *NYT*, 18 July).

Gorbachev issued a personal appeal to the miners to end the strike and later confessed that the leadership had been tied up for days dealing with the crisis. Boris El'tsin also urged the miners to return to work; the utilization of the opposition leader demonstrated how critical the situation was in the Kremlin. After hectic negotiation the strikes were settled by extensive local concessions, which set precedents certain to encourage labor strife elsewhere.

Although no other work stoppage during the year was as critical, the recognition that strikes could pay off without the danger of forceful repression by the authorities helped spur worker unrest in various areas. Wildcat strikes hit the Vorkuta mining region in late summer. A transport strike at Baku in September was reported to have a "tangible effect" on operations of the Novo-Bakinskii Vladimir Il'ich oil refinery (*Pravda*, 6 September; *FBIS*, 7 September). An alternative trade union, the Latvian Workers' Union, was set up in Latvia (*Sovetskaia Latviia*, 12 September; *FBIS*, 5 October).

Independent coal miners, at a meeting of the coal miners' union central committee in September, succeeded in ousting several union officials and won a commitment to hold a nationwide coal workers' congress in March 1990. Spokesmen for the dissident workers said the results of the meeting would probably prevent an outbreak of new work stoppages in the fall. However, the trade union establishment turned back a demand to sever connections with the All-Union Council of Trade Unions (AUC-CTU) and create what would have been the first major independent union in the country (*NYT*, 17 September).

In October Gorbachev called for a total ban on strikes for fifteen months. Dealing the leader his first major policy defeat in the new legislature, the Supreme Soviet adopted more-moderate legislation, authorizing strikes except where such action would endanger lives, health, or the national economy and outlining procedures that must be followed before workers can legally strike (*LAT*, 10 October).

The law, which specifically prohibited strikes in certain crucial industries, was quickly challenged. Two weeks after passage of the law, about 16,000 of the 24,000 miners in the Vorkuta region walked out, forcing closure of four of the area's thirteen mines. A workers' spokesman said that promises made in an August collective bargaining session had not been fulfilled. New demands by the miners were political and far beyond the scope of local authorities; the miners wanted a repeal of Article Six of the USSR constitution, which establishes the preeminence of the CPSU in Soviet society, and a requirement that the posts of president and general secretary of the CPSU not be held by the same person (*NYT*, 26 October).

The debate over private entrepreneurship continued. In September, Gorbachev joined other deputies in denouncing the "astronomical prices" charged by cooperatives, and a motion to close down all cooperatives engaged in trading and purchasing was defeated by the narrow margin of 205 votes to 190 (*LAT*; BBC-CARIS, 27 September). In

October the Supreme Soviet authorized local governments to set maximum prices for cooperatives, imposed price controls on all products made from government-supplied materials, and prohibited private firms from selling imported goods. The legislation had Gorbachev's support. (*LAT*, 17 October.)

Although limiting the operations of private entrepreneurs, the Supreme Soviet began to deal with the concept of property. Deputy Aleksei N. Boiko, an economist at the University of Donetsk and a member of the legislature's Committee on Economic Reform, was preparing a draft defining "personal property," "individual property," and "household means of production" (*NYT*, 1 October).

In September, in a major move aimed toward the integration of the USSR's economy into the global one, Gosbank devalued the ruble from $1.60 to sixteen cents. The change applies to foreigners in the USSR and to Soviet citizens traveling abroad. Although the new official rate was still well below that of the black market, it was viewed by some Western economists as a step toward the free convertibility of rubles into foreign currencies (TASS, 25 October; *NYT*, 26 October).

Meanwhile, the economic news was bad. The USSR People's Control Committee revealed that unsatisifed demand for goods and services stood at 70 billion rubles according to one set of figures and 100 billion rubles according to another set (*Pravda*, 23 September). First Deputy Premier Lev Voronin told the Supreme Soviet that, in the first eight months of the year, production of 62 of 178 of the most important types of output was lower than for the corresponding period in 1988 (ibid., 26 September). Oleg Bogomolov, director of the Institute of Economics of the World Socialist System, declared that Moscow had bungled economic reforms and must move quickly to a free market system to stop strikes and ethnic clashes. Bogomolov said the per capita production of food had declined and that "one commodity after another," ranging from soap to refrigerators, had disappeared from the consumer market (*WP*, 20 September).

The shortage of soap and other cleaning materials led to epidemics of lice in hospitals, adding to the ills of the troubled medical industry. A crash program announced in the summer to import consumer goods had made little impact, and coal shortages were expected for the winter due to the summer strikes and resulting disruptions.

One indication of the severity of the economic crisis was Gorbachev's reported remarks to U.S.

president Bush at the Malta summit. According to an American official, Gorbachev suggested that his position as Soviet leader was secure and not threatened by political opposition, but said that his campaign to end the shortage of consumer goods was "the ultimate test" of his leadership. Some U.S. officials were left with the impression that Gorbachev was uncertain about how to solve his economic problems (*NYT*, 6 December).

Nationalities. Ethnic conflicts continued and intensified during the year, posing a greater problem for the leadership than ever before and evoking some doubts about the future of the USSR in its present territorial form. Moscow's longtime confident stance on the nationalities question had proven to be a chimera; now the question was whether any long-term stability could be achieved in the outlying republics.

The nationalities problem had received insufficient attention from the leadership, even after the Alma Ata riots of December 1986. Gorbachev, evidently led by early expressions of support for *glasnost'* and *perestroika* by non-Russian spokesmen, thought of the subordinate nationalities as a reserve army in his drive for reform. But the ethnic groups had agendas of their own that *glasnost'* allowed to be expressed, and discontent was intensified by economic distress. Political reform, crucial for Gorbachev, provided further opportunities for open expression by the disaffected groups.

During 1989 the Soviet leadership devoted considerable attention to the nationalities, including presenting a lengthy program to deal with the problems at the July CC plenum. But Moscow mixed force and compromise in an erratic approach that seemed bereft of long-range realistic planning. One advantage for the CPSU leadership was that hostility between some subordinate nationalities was fiercer than any anti-Russian feeling; nevertheless, popular fronts in outlying areas had begun to cooperate. The long-range problem was to maintain the territorial integrity of the USSR; in the short run, the negative economic consequences may be even more important. Options for the leadership were limited by, among other things, the connection of nationalities problems with broader policy goals. For example, suppression of secessionist movements in the Baltic republics would almost certainly destroy Gorbachev's European policy.

At the year's outset, Nagorno-Karabakh remained a center of contention between Azerbaijanis and Armenians; on 12 January the Soviet government announced the imposition of "a special form of administration" on that predominantly Armenian enclave in Azerbaijan (*LAT*, 13 January). By order of the Supreme Soviet Presidium, as of 20 January, "the plenary powers of the organs of power" were suspended pending new elections and their functions temporarily handed over to the Special Administration Committee (*Trud*, 21 January; *FBIS*, 24 January). Arkadii Vol'skii, chairman of the committee, said three days later that "life in the Nagorno-Karabakh autonomous region is gradually returning to normal" (TASS, 23 January; *FBIS*, 24 January).

In the north, a rally in Lithuania called for all Soviet troops to pull out of the Baltic states (BBC-CARIS, 12 January). The Estonian Supreme Soviet enacted a law on 19 January making Estonian the state language (*Pravda*, 20 January), and Lithuania adopted a similar law one day later (TASS; *FBIS*, 26 January). Latvia was expected to follow suit, and a special commission under the Supreme Soviet of Moldavia moved to make Moldavian that republic's official language (TASS, 20 January; *FBIS*, 24 January).

Some nationalists in Lithuania thought that the legislation did not go far enough. Sajudis reform movement demonstrators picketed the Lithuanian Supreme Soviet building claiming that the draft law left too much room for the use of Russian and made bilingualism legal in the republic (Vilnius Radio, 23 January; *FBIS*, 26 January). Demands for making the main indigenous ethnic group's language the official one soon followed in Tadzhikistan and Uzbekistan (Paris, AFP; *FBIS*, 20 March).

After the regional CC condemned "anti-Soviet and separatist" currents within the Movement for Latvia's National Independence, some 200,000 turned out in Riga for a popular front protest demonstration (Paris, AFP, 12 March; *FBIS*, 13 March).

Troops reportedly used gas against demonstrators on 12 March in the Moldavian capital of Kishinev. It was unclear, however, whether the troops used tear gas or some other, undetermined kind (RFE, *Research*, 20 April).

While attention was concentrated elsewhere, trouble was brewing in Georgia. Thousands of people defied tanks and soldiers and took to the streets of Tbilisi on 8 April in a protest demanding independence for the Republic of Georgia (AP, 8 April). On the following day, when the demonstrations resumed, troops killed nineteen demonstrators, wounded more than two hundred, and allegedly used toxic gas (ibid., 9 April). A general strike had begun on 7 April in support of the protesters; the strike eased up during the following week, and some buses and trolleys were operating by 11 April. Meanwhile, police arrested hundreds of people and seized tens of thousands of hunting rifles in an effort to calm the republic.

President Gorbachev said he considered free expression a "sacred principle," but had some tough words for the Georgian nationalists, expressing his resolve to oppose "extremism, anti-Soviet displays, and the destructive actions of adventurist elements" (ibid., 11 April). Foreign Minister Shevardnadze, former party chief of Georgia, was dispatched to Tbilisi to try to restore calm; as the facts of the massacre became clear, attempts were made to distance Gorbachev. A government report said that Gorbachev did not learn about the killings until six hours after the event, and a subsequent investigation cleared the party leader of responsibility.

Shevardnadze addressed a plenum of the Georgian CC that accepted the resignation of Georgian first secretary Dzhumber I. Patiashvili; a separate meeting of the Presidium of the Georgian Supreme Soviet removed Zurab A. Chkheidze, who had assumed the position in March, from the republic premiership (*Izvestiia*, 15 April). Givi G. Gumbaridze, who had served for two months as chairman of the republic KGB and earlier as first secretary of the Tbilisi city party committee, was elected Patiashvili's successor. Nodari A. Chitanava, a secretary of the Georgian CC, was named chairman of the republic's Council of Ministers.

Five days after the violence in Georgia, tanks rolled into the Estonian cities of Tallinn and Tartu as well as the Latvian capital, Riga, and troops poured into Tashkent, the capital of Uzbekistan, on 10 April, following a nationalist meeting the previous day (AP, 15 April). The show of force may have had local calming effects, but did little to stem the nationwide protests. On 24 April nearly 50,000 people held a rally in Armenia's capital, Erevan, to commemorate the massacre of Armenians by Turkish troops in 1915 and to call for the release of jailed nationalists. The demonstration was held despite a severe warning against it from the republic's Interior Ministry (Paris, AFP; *FBIS*, 24 April). On 23 April, some two thousand members of the Democratic Union held a rally in Moscow's Pushkin Square to protest the killings in Tbilisi, and 47 were arrested; the Soviet media called it "an unauthorized meeting with provocative aims" (TASS, 23 April; *FBIS*, 24 April).

Georgia was reported to be calming down. Foreign Minister Shevardnadze returned to Moscow on 18 April and a midnight to 5 A.M. curfew in Tbilisi was lifted that morning. Troops and armored personnel carriers had left the city, which was being patrolled by four thousand volunteer workers and 750 policemen (AP, 18 April). Despite the outward calm secessionist sentiment grew in the southern republic. In a move to appease nationalist feeling, the authorities in Georgia declared 26 May—the anniversary of the 1918 "restoration of Georgia" as an independent state—a holiday and freed four nationalist leaders arrested following the 9 April demonstrations. On the holiday more than 200,000 people attended a rally in Tbilisi (Paris, AFP, 26 May; *FBIS*, 30 May).

Mass nationalist rallies continued in Moldavia (RFE, *Research*, 5 May), while Russian organizations protested alleged discrimination against non-Moldavians resulting from new language laws (*Sovetskaia Moldavia*, 11 April; *FBIS*, 25 April). In late spring and summer, the Moldavian nationalist movement grew increasingly radical. The Popular Front of Moldavia held a rally of 70,000 to 80,000 people in Kishinev on 25 June to protest the USSR's 1940 annexation of Moldavia. For the first time at a public event, the Romanian province of Bessarabia's incorporation into the USSR was denounced, ouster of the republic's leadership was demanded, and calls were made for the return of territories lost to the Ukrainian republic (RFE, *Research*, 14 July).

Meetings of the Congress of People's Deputies reflected the rise of nationalism in the country. Particularly active were delegates from the Baltic states, who were shaken and angry after Roy Medvedev told the legislature that the Baltic republics were taken by force in 1940 and that the official version—that they joined the USSR voluntarily—was a lie. Gorbachev declared his support for an investigation, and the congress assented without a vote (AP, 1 June). A congress commission declared in July that the occupation of the Baltic states was illegal and admitted that there existed a secret protocol relating to the area in the 1939 Nazi-Soviet pact (Stockholm Domestic Service, 23 July; *FBIS*, 24 July). *Argumenty i fakty* published the secret protocol in August (BBC-CARIS, 14 August).

In the first week of June rioting broke out in Uzbekistan between Uzbeks and members of the Meshki Turk minority. Interior Minister Vadim Bakatin reported that six thousand Interior Ministry troops had been sent to the affected area (Moscow Television, 5 June; *FBIS*, 6 June). Within a week the death toll from violence in the Fergama region had reached 79, and more than eight hundred people had been injured (*Izvestiia*, 9 June). In Kokand mobs stormed police stations and seized three locomotives (*Komsomol'skaia pravda*, 9 June). Many of the Kokand hooligans were reported to have arrived in the city in organized columns from other regions (*Trud*, 9 June). In Tashlak a mob of Uzbeks reportedly "tried several times to occupy an administration building and inflict reprisals on women and children of the Turkish nationality" (*Krasnaia zvezda*, 9 June). Three weeks later, the situation in the area was described as "getting back to normal" (Moscow Television, 1 July; *FBIS*, 3 July).

Rioting was also reported in Tadzhikistan and in Kazakhstan. Rioters in the city of Novii Uzen, in Kazakhstan's oil producing district, demanded that authorities evict all members of Caucasian ethnic groups from the city, complaining that the settlers dominate oil industry jobs. At least four people died in the rioting, and hundreds of Interior Ministry troops were brought in to restore order (AP, 25 June).

Ethnic violence flared in July in Abkhazia. Apparently started by a dispute over whether the local university in Sukhumi should be split into Abkhaz and Georgian sections, eighteen people were reportedly killed in the subsequent riots and 239 injured. Authorities declared a state of emergency and sent three thousand Interior Ministry troops in to end the violence. As news reports reached Moscow of the outbreak in Sukhumi, Soviet television showed troops in riot gear patrolling the streets of Stepanakert, the capital of Nagorno-Karabakh (BBC-CARIS, 19 July).

President Gorbachev in a nationwide television address on 1 July appealed "to people of all our country's nationalities" to "display the greatest responsibility." He promised "the most resolute measures" against "those who provoke interethnic clashes and call for borders to be redrawn and for national minorities to be expelled," but admitted that "many problems have accumulated that demand both close attention and urgent actions" (*Izvestiia*, 2 July).

The July plenum on nationalities issues was well timed, as ethnic discord rose to fever pitch in various parts of the USSR. In his major speech to the plenum, Gorbachev called for "working out an up-to-date strategy of the party on the nationality issue by relying on Leninist principles, realities, and prevalent trends in the world public movement." He called recent criticism of "deformities" in inter-

ethnic relations "justified" and "essential," but said that "any attempts to distort and belittle the real achievements in the sphere of national relations is an outrage against the memory of several generations of Soviet people" (*Pravda*, 20 September). The CC adopted a platform calling for a clear delineation of the division of powers between the central government and the union republics, the transition of the union republics to economic accountability and self-financing, and the full restoration of "the legitimate rights and interests of people living in the autonomous republics, oblasts, and *okrugs*" (ibid., 24 September).

The action of the CC did not alleviate the ethnic turmoil. Thousands of Russian factory and shipyard workers in Tallinn led by the Russian nationalist group Intermovement walked off their jobs on 26 July to protest what they called discriminatory legislation on elections, language, and residence (*WP*, 27 July). Pending before the Estonian legislature was a bill requiring a two-year residency for voters and a ten-year residency in the republic and five years in a district for candidates for local offices. The all-union party youth newspaper said the law would deprive soldiers, students from other republics, and visiting specialists of the right to vote (*Komsomol'skaia pravda*, 26 July). The draft law was passed by the Estonian legislature on 8 August and was followed by scattered protest strikes by Russian workers in factories and shipyards (*LAT*, 10 August). By 16 August more than twenty thousand workers had walked off their jobs, shutting down 51 factories and enterprises (AP, 17 August).

President Gorbachev and the Kremlin leadership rejected the Estonian law, calling it unconstitutional and a violation of human rights. The Presidium of the USSR Supreme Soviet announced that by 1 October, Estonia's government would present the republic's legislature with proposals to bring the law into line with the Soviet constitution (TASS, 16 August).

On the following day the CPSU leadership issued a document offering the union republics more power, including the right to question all-union laws before a high court, and raising the possibility of revision of the 1922 treaty on the formation of the USSR. The draft policy also called for a law banning "nationalist and chauvinist" organizations (*Pravda*, 17 August). Leaders of non-Russian ethnic groups immediately dismissed the proposals as inadequate.

The 50th anniversary of the Nazi-Soviet pact raised Baltic nationalism to new heights. On 23

August activists formed a human chain of protest stretching across the three republics (*NYT*, 24 August), producing additional fears in Moscow about ethnic cooperation, already evident in relations among the Baltic popular fronts and nationalist movements in Belorussia and Moldavia. The CPSU CC responded with a statement that separatists were leading the three republics "into an abyss" (*Pravda*, 27 August). Shortly afterward, *Pravda* (29 August) accused the People's Front of Moldavia, which had supported measures making Moldavian the exclusive official language of that republic, of trying to "take power on the crest of a muddy wave of chauvinism and separatism."

Because Gorbachev was on vacation, there was speculation that these attacks had been launched independently by conservative elements in the CC. It was unlikely, however, that Gorbachev entirely rejected this approach. Lithuanian party first secretary Algirdas Brazauskas reported that Gorbachev had called him on 25 and 27 August to express concern about developments and to reject any further concessions to the nationalists (AP, 28 August).

Elsewhere the picture also remained bleak. Nagorno-Karabakh was racked by strikes and frequent armed clashes, and the main military newspaper said that Armenia and Azerbaijan were "like gunpowder" and that Nagorno-Karabakh was on the point of civil war (*Krasnaia zvezda*, 3 September). Nevertheless in November the Soviet parliament approved a plan that returned control of Nagorno-Karabakh to Azerbaijan, but ordered the Baku government to work closely with the Armenian minority in the region (AP, 28 November). In Sumgait, the site of major violence in 1988, tensions between Armenians and Azerbaijanis were said to be increasing (*WP*, 10 September). On 13 September Azerbaijan CP first secretary Abdul-Rakman K. Vezirov signed a protocol with the Popular Front of Azerbaijan promising to legalize the popular front, lift a military curfew, and convene a session of the republic's parliament to pass a new sovereignty law asserting Azerbaijan's right to defy federal authority. In return the popular front agreed to end the rail embargo against Armenia by calling off the protest strike that had halted traffic (*NYT*, 12 October).

Although the Ukraine had been fairly calm during the ethnic disturbances, in September, the first congress of the Ukrainian Popular Front for *Perestroika* (Rukh), was held in Kiev. Unlike the Baltic popular front movements, Rukh did not demand independence, but called for the USSR to be transformed into a confederation of sovereign republics (*WP*, 9 September). Rukh became highly active during the remainder of the year.

On 13 September, Gorbachev met in Moscow with first secretaries, premiers, and presidents from the three Baltic republics and reportedly offered limited sovereignty and economic independence with the understanding that the three republics would not try to secede from the USSR (ibid., 15 September). Addressing the CPSU CC on 19 September, Gorbachev said that "talk of secession is an irresponsible game" and branded those demanding it as "adventurists." The general secretary upheld one-party rule in the USSR, but gave qualified endorsement to autonomy for the republics (*NYT*, 20 September).

During the fall, Moscow continued to pressure the political leaderships of the Baltic republics trying to avert a head-on confrontation. But in December the Lithuanian legislature voted (243 to 1) to abolish the clause in its constitution giving the communist party a monopoly on power, and the Estonian CC voted to drop the party's leading role (*WP*, 8 December). The actions by the two Baltic states brought to the fore demands in the People's Congress, when it reconvened on 12 December, for a multiparty system (*NYT*, 13 December). This challenge was repelled with difficulty by Gorbachev, who had consistently upheld the one-party system, maintaining that the CPSU was a suitable vehicle for reform.

The Latvian popular front, running on a platform of independence from Moscow, won more than half the vote in Riga and more than 55 percent outside the city in December elections for city and regional councils. Early returns also indicated an impressive showing by the popular front in Estonian elections (*NYT*, 12 December).

Religion played a role in some of the nationalities' tensions, particularly in Lithuania and the Ukraine, and the regime displayed a much more flexible stance in regard to religious toleration during the year. Lithuania's two leading Roman Catholic bishops were returned to head dioceses after a combined 53 years of internal exile, and Belorussia got its first bishop in 63 years (*Time*, 4 December). These moves paved the way for the historic December meeting between Gorbachev and Pope John Paul II in the Vatican. Ukrainian authorities had restored some one thousand churches to the Orthodox religion during the year, but had not committed any buildings to Catholics, apparently because of opposition by the Orthodox hierarchy (*Newsweek*, 11 December). But the cathedral in

Kiev was taken back by Catholic believers in November. The authorities accused the Catholics of forcibly seizing the cathedral but did not try to recover it. Preaching in the cathedral, Uniate priest Iaroslav Chukhnii proclaimed his allegiance to Pope John Paul II (AP, 26 November). Earlier, in September, an outdoor mass in Lvov on the 50th anniversary of Stalin's annexation of the western Ukraine from Poland drew some 100,000 people (*NYT*, 18 September).

Jewish emigration expanded greatly, and in February 50 Jews gathered in Moscow to receive their charter as the first chapter in the USSR of B'nai B'rith (*LAT*, 22 February). The first national conference of Soviet Jews in 70 years was held in December and faced demonstrations by Russian nationalists and Palestinians. Conference leaders warned that anti-Semitism was on the rise in the USSR (*LAT*, 23 December).

Ideology. The "new thinking" of the Gorbachev era in foreign policy was designed, in part, to serve specific domestic purposes. However, certain problems appeared in the elaboration of an ideological platform by the new leadership, and after four years Gorbachev and his associates had still not worked out a consistent, coherent theoretical defense of the new policies.

Gorbachev's equation of *perestroika* with revolution seemed to imply that the USSR had ceased to be revolutionary. Moreover, the rejection of some of Lenin's major tendencies raised serious questions about the validity of Soviet socialism. As to Lenin, Gorbachev followed a highly selective approach, taking certain aspects of regime policy during the New Economic Policy period as guidelines for "democratic socialism." But the new thinking, going beyond any alleged original Leninism, contained two contradictory aspects. On the one hand, Gorbachev defended certain vital ingredients of Leninism—one-party rule, democratic centralism, the ideological supremacy of the communist party—all of which implied a basis in class struggle. On the other hand, Gorbachev, in his book *Perestroika* and elsewhere, and his close associate Aleksandr Iakovlev, in his August 1988 Vilnius speech (see *YICA*, 1989), projected "common human interests" as transcending the class struggle.

The major planks in the leader's platform, *perestroika* and *glasnost'*, utilized well-worn concepts inherited from previous leaders; Gorbachev was seeking to maintain the essentials of the regime and refurbish its operations without sacrificing its basic structure. This required a practical program for moving the system forward and an ideological rationale to justify policies in terms of a Marxist framework. But as chinks in the communist edifice at home and abroad appeared on almost a daily basis, Gorbachev was reduced to ad hoc decision making to meet immediate crises. This made resolving the ideological problems difficult, but Gorbachev stoutly defended his somewhat nebulous theoretical underpinnings. His task was made no easier by attacks during the year from both the right and the left on ideological grounds.

At the outset of the year, Gorbachev blasted those critics in a speech to scientists and cultural figures. He rejected the criticisms of conservatives who claimed that "restructuring is leading to chaos" and that "we have gone astray not only in determining the ways and means of solving problems but also in the very choice and setting of our goal." Such people, said Gorbachev, were beginning to show nostalgia for "the good old days" and were calling for "a firm hand" to rule the country. The party leader also pointed to "radicals" who raised the question of "whether the framework of socialism is too narrow for restructuring" and "sneaked in" ideas of political pluralism, a multiparty system, and "even private property." Such people, said Gorbachev, talked about the supposed impossibility of "disclosing the potential of socialism through restructuring." Both types of critics, he charged, were guilty of "lack of faith in our system, in our people, in the party, and in our socialist institutions." (*Pravda*, 8 January.)

Attitudes toward Stalin and the era of the "cult of personality" were ideological touchstones during the early Gorbachev years. Revelations about Stalin continued, but concern with excesses of the dictator's rule gradually gave way to anxiety about "neo-Stalinism," reflecting the activity of those who, according to Gorbachev, longed for the "good old days."

Expanding on an article that had appeared in *Moscow News* in November 1988, Roy Medvedev wrote in February that about twenty million people had died under Stalin's terror and that the total number repressed was about 40 million; these figures agreed with Western estimates (*Argumenty i fakty*, 4–10 February). In April the party published an official text of Khrushchev's secret speech ("On the Cult of Personality and Its Consequences") denouncing Stalin to the Twentieth CPSU Congress in 1956 (*Izvestiia TsK KPSS*, no. 3).

Commenting on his new book, Major General

Dimitrii Volkogonov, official biographer of Stalin, appeared to touch upon current fears about "neo-Stalinism": "Stalinism can be eliminated by enlightenment, by revealing the truth and by real political and economic change, by real success. We have to find real alternatives to the Stalinist development we have had." (*LAT*, 29 October.)

As in the previous year, Party Secretaries Aleksandr Iakovlev and Egor Ligachev were standard-bearers in the argument about "common human interests" versus "class struggle."

In a speech on 11 July ostensibly about the bicentennial of the French Revolution, Iakovlev questioned Marxism-Leninism's alleged ability to provide guidance in understanding the present and planning the future. He said that one of the lessons to be drawn from the history of revolutions is that "subordination to a dogma...inevitably gives rise to a multitude of 'unfreedoms' in society" and pushes revolutionary ideals into the background (*CSM*, 20 July).

In his speech to the September CC plenum, Ligachev said that "a bitter struggle for power is raging in various parts of the country" and lashed out at those who "stand for turning toward capitalism and bourgeois democracy, for the introduction of private property into the economy and a multiparty political system." Ligachev charged that "the main threat to *perestroika* comes from those pushing us onto the capitalist path. It does not come from those branded as 'conservative' for their belief in socialism and the people and their faith in the principles of internationalism" (*Pravda*, 22 September).

Defending *perestroika* at the September CC plenum, Gorbachev seemed to echo the views of "reformers" in the 1983–1984 "contradictions of socialism" debate: "Refining socialist property is the key issue of *perestroika*... Without changes long overdue in this area, we shall be unable to overcome the alienation of working people from the means of production." (Ibid., 20 September.)

Although acknowledging that alienation exists in the USSR, Gorbachev maintains that the phenomenon is not inherent in the nature of the socialist system. However, precisely this argument was put forward by economist Rair Simonian in a September interview with *Ogonek* (10 September) in which he said that socialism alienates workers and hampers the competition needed for free development of the individual, one of the ideology's stated goals, and that under socialism "generally speaking, a worker is exploited by the state."

The Soviet brand of socialism was under attack from many quarters, and Gorbachev offered a spirited defense of the system in an address to a national student conference in Moscow: "We cannot allow dissatisfaction with ourselves, with how we live now, to be transformed into attempts to question our indisputable, universally recognized achievements and the choice of socialism itself" (Moscow Television; AP, 15 November).

Pravda (26 November) published a synthesis of recent remarks by Gorbachev. In the article the CPSU leader downplayed criticism of capitalism, but also sought to identify his program closely with Marx. Gorbachev argued that socialism must modernize, adopting traits of capitalism if necessary. He said that achievements attained under capitalism, such as "equality of all before the law" and general prosperity, should not be dismissed because of ideology. He also said that "we are building humanitarian socialism" and that the new "human face" of socialism "fully corresponds to the thought of Marx."

Gorbachev continued to hold on to the idea of one-party rule in the USSR, a vital dictate of Marxism-Leninism, but the party appeared to soften its stance on this issue in early December. An unsigned editorial in *Pravda* (8 December) said that "every point in the constitution," including Article 6, which guarantees the leading role of the CPSU, "can be thought through, modernized, or even excluded." However, *Pravda* rejected calls by "ultra-radicals" for an emergency debate in the parliament on the one-party system as "irresponsible."

Auxiliary and front organizations. Affiliated public organizations felt the impact of the rise of unofficial organizations and the growing tendency for political activity to take place outside established channels. Particularly affected were two organizations that had been major transmission belts for the party.

The Komsomol, which had been faring badly in competition with unofficial groups and having difficulties in recruitment, was acknowledged to be in crisis, compounded by organizational problems. In a January interview, the youth affiliate's leader, Vladimir Mironenko, said that the Komsomol was being "resurrected as a political organization" and that the Komsomol's role in the drafting of a law on young people occurred because "about 70 percent of society's social problems are youth problems" (*Izvestiia*, 4 January). The January plenum of the Komsomol CC nominated 102 candidates for people's deputies and elected six new full members and three new candidate members to the committee (*Komsomol'skaia pravda*, 15 January; *FBIS*, 18 January).

During a May plenum of the Komsomol CC, the committee voted to approve the proposed draft law on young people, but only after what was described as "rather heated" discussion (Moscow Television, 19 May; *FBIS*, 26 May). Komsomol leader Mironenko was criticized on personnel questions and was forced to defend himself in his closing speech (*Komsomol'skaia pravda*, 24 May; *FBIS*, 8 June). Viktor Chebrikov, Politburo member and chairman of the Legal Affairs Commission, represented the CPSU CC at the meeting, an indication that the Komsomol was expected to assume a greater role in the maintenance of "law and order." Another meeting of the Komsomol CC in October covered much the same ground as the May session (*Komsomol'skaia pravda*, 27 October; *FBIS*, 9 November).

The All-Union Central Council of Trade Unions (AUCCTU) was busy dealing with strikes and threats of work stoppages and trying to fend off attempts to form independent unions. The organization also apparently played a major role in preparation of the "Draft Law on the Rights of Trade Unions," which included a qualified right to strike (*Trud*, 3 March, 29 April). A regular plenum of the council was held in September to discuss the draft law and "urgent tasks" of the trade unions in the current phase of *perestroika* (Moscow Domestic Service, 5 September; *FBIS*, 6 September).

The plenum of the USSR Writers' Union Board in January was devoted to ecological questions. Much criticism was directed at the continuation of environmentally damaging projects. V. K. Egorov, deputy head of the Ideological Department, represented the CC at the meeting (*Sovetskaia Rossiia*; *FBIS*, 18 January).

International Views, Positions, and Activities. When Mikhail Gorbachev addressed the U.N. General Assembly promising reductions of Soviet forces in East Europe and held a farewell meeting with U.S. president Ronald Reagan in December 1988, he seemed at the top of his game. His major initiatives had made him the central figure in world politics, and events seemed to be moving in directions favorable to his plans. The tumultuous developments of the new year, however, served to diminish the Soviet leader's role, as well as the superpower stature of the USSR. It was possible that unforeseen circumstances could be incorpo-

rated into Gorbachev's apparent grand design, albeit with some tactical modifications. Much would depend on the impact of Soviet domestic turmoil and on external affairs over which the USSR now had sharply curtailed influence.

Shortly after his accession in 1985 it was evident that Gorbachev was preparing for an increasingly multipolar world in which the superpowers would no longer be able to guarantee the tenuous peace that had prevailed for 40 years. Two contrasting approaches concerning USSR policy emerged in the Soviet leadership. One—represented by Anatolii Dobrynin, from March 1986 secretary of the CC for international affairs—emphasized relations between the superpowers. The other—advocated by Aleksandr Iakovlev, also a CC secretary—stressed relations with Western Europe and "borderlands" areas adjoining or in close proximity to the USSR and downplayed the American connection.

Gorbachev was able to combine the two approaches using a thaw in relations with the United States as a means for inducing greater cooperation from Western Europe. But the American connection took primacy because a thaw between the superpowers was an essential condition for "normalization" in Europe. Gorbachev's meetings with Reagan, capped by the May 1988 Moscow summit, seemed to signal an end to the cold war or at least a general lessening of international tension and a reduction of the Soviet military threat. But the détente between the superpowers also marked the diminution of superpower clout in world politics; once the overt hostility between the two was removed, the military basis for domination of their respective blocs also evaporated. Logically, the next step was to establish stable relationships with those powers that figured to gain in the developing balance of power. When Dobrynin was dropped as a CC secretary and Iakovlev became head of the new CC Commission on International Affairs in September 1988, Gorbachev viewed the first phase of his grand design as complete.

In the new year the borderlands strategy was much in evidence. Moscow sought to follow up on Foreign Minister Shevardnadze's December 1988 visit to Japan and moved much closer to Iran. A February visit by Shevardnadze to Beijing prepared the way for the Sino-Soviet summit in May, when Gorbachev re-established the high-level party-to-party contacts with the Chinese Communist Party that had been suspended for a quarter-century. Soviet criticism of the subsequent brutal suppression of the democracy movement in China was muted, and the new relationship between Moscow and Beijing helped motivate the U.S. mission to China under National Security adviser Brent Scowcroft in December.

But the main target remained Western Europe. Aid from the capitalist countries was important for overcoming economic stagnation in East Europe, and Gorbachev urged closer economic ties in his July speech to the European parliament at Strasbourg. Given the setting and the circumstances, "our common European home" no longer seemed a lofty or distant objective.

The USSR appeared set on a course to meet the military and political preconditions for closer cooperation between the two sections of the continent. The pullout from Afghanistan had a profound influence on West European elites and the public; the impression of a nonbelligerent USSR was bolstered by the promised reduction of forces in East Europe. On several occasions during the year, notably in Gorbachev's address to the European parliament and in his speech at the Warsaw Pact meeting in Bucharest a few days later, the USSR indicated a renunciation of the Brezhnev Doctrine. Moreover, the rhetoric was backed by Soviet action, or inaction, as Moscow made no moves to utilize its considerable military forces in East Europe to halt the spreading breakdown of communist rule in the area.

Gorbachev, in fact, worked behind the scenes to spur reforms and personnel changes in the bloc regimes. This gambit presumably did not anticipate the early end of communist domination in these states, but when Poland installed a noncommunist premier in August, the new government was endorsed by the Kremlin. Subsequent moves toward pluralist political systems in Czechoslovakia, Hungary, and East Germany also met no outward opposition from the Soviet leadership. However, the puncturing of the Berlin Wall on 9 November created a starkly different situation, with enormous implications for the long-run and perhaps short-run balance of power in Europe.

Gorbachev sought to stem the tidal wave of change by expressing firm opposition to German reunification, but the East European bloc as a political entity had, in effect, collapsed. If "our common European home" were to fit Gorbachev's needs, it would have to be remodeled. One immediate result of the overwhelming flood of dramatic events was a further shift in Moscow's attitude toward the United States; priorities had to be rearranged.

Gorbachev's early moves in foreign policy had probably been designed in part to get U.S. troops out of Europe, presumably leaving the USSR as the strongest power on the continent and perhaps leading to a variant of "Finlandization" for the West European countries. Now it seemed that Gorbachev needed a U.S. presence in Europe, including contingents of U.S. troops, to manage the transition to a new European order. The ultimate nightmare of Soviet foreign policy planners for a generation—a strong united Germany in the center of the continent—suddenly emerged as a possibility, and U.S. aid was needed to help balance the thrust of a potentially dominant German state. (Washington had its own reasons for joining in to slow down the coalescence between the two Germanies.)

This was the background for the summit between Bush and Gorbachev at Malta in December. Before that meeting, Gorbachev made an epochal visit to Pope John Paul II at the Vatican and agreed to establish diplomatic relations. This unprecedented and amicable conference reportedly led to a backlash of criticism at the December CC plenum, but further solidified Gorbachev's image in Western Europe and offered the possibility of calming some nationalist tensions in Lithuania and the Ukraine.

At Malta, Bush and Gorbachev disagreed over Central America, but were in general accord on Soviet internal reforms, international economic cooperation with the USSR, arms control, and other matters. The perception of common interests was apparent; the unspoken unifying factor was events in Germany. For more than 40 years, Germany has been the center of world stability, the tripwire that guaranteed mutual forbearance by the nuclear-armed superpowers. Now it was an arena of significant instability, and both superpowers were disconcerted by the prospects, even though all the unexpected peaceful changes in Germany and elsewhere in the bloc were triumphs of democracy and vindications of U.S. rhetoric over four decades. Bush's comments after the summit indicated that his position on early German reunification was virtually indistinguishable from Gorbachev's.

Although both superpowers' influence have been eroded by domestic problems and the rise of other global power centers, they still possess enough residual power to exert a major impact on European politics in the foreseeable future. The probability of major troop reductions in Europe by both sides will presumably lead, within a few years, to a further diminution of the two countries' impact on continental affairs, but such reductions are dictated by the European policies of each. In the meantime, management of and lengthening the transition to a non-bipolar arrangement of Europe required the collaboration of the United States and the USSR. Because Moscow's concerns in the area are more urgent than those of Washington, it seems likely that the USSR would face a bargaining disadvantage in its relations with the United States. This, however, was perhaps the least of Gorbachev's problems.

Gorbachev apparently had a vision of evolving multipolarity earlier than any other major world leader and shaped his overall strategy accordingly. His dazzling successes had helped solidify his domestic power by making him an indispensable figure in the conduct of foreign policy. In 1989, however, reality suddenly outstripped strategy. As crisis management became the order of the day in European affairs, as well as in domestic economy and politics, the Kremlin was threatened with system overload in its decision-making processes. Nevertheless, the long-run outlook was not necessarily unfavorable for the USSR. The euphoria in the West during the year over the "end of history" may have been premature; the USSR was still far from being a democratic state in the Western sense and possessed enormous reserves of power potential, despite its current difficulties. Moreover, even after arms control agreements, the Soviet military machine was probably stronger at the end of 1989 than it had been in March 1985. Thus barring internal political upheaval the USSR would continue to be a major player on the world stage, not just another state, and its aims would be fundamentally different from those of other major powers. Some alteration of the world scene in 1989 did appear irreversible, but changes in the USSR had less of an air of finality than those elsewhere (thus the atmosphere of caution in certain quarters in the West).

Eastern Europe. During the early months of the year, there were few outward manifestations of the undercurrents that would sweep the area. Moscow was working to keep change within bounds in some places, but its main thrust was toward the encouragement of reform, stoutly resisted by several regimes. East Germany's Erich Honecker was particularly adamant in his opposition to restructuring in the German Democratic Republic (GDR), and in the winter of 1988–1989 he and his hard-line associates gave every indication of being in control of East Germany (*CSM*, 24 February).

In February internal changes in Poland were reflected by the publication, in a Polish journal, of an article charging the USSR with responsibility for the massacre of four thousand Polish officers in the Katyn Forest in 1940 and by an announcement by the Polish government that the wording on Warsaw's monument to the victims was to be changed (BBC-CARIS, 22 February).

When President Gorbachev received Hungary's premier Miklós Németh and party leader Károly Grósz in separate meetings at Moscow during March, he reportedly gave the green light to Hungary's internal reforms, including introduction of a multiparty system. Attending the congress of the Italian communist party in Rome, Aleksandr Iakovlev joined Hungarian reformer Imre Pozsgai in warning of threats to reforms in their countries posed by conservative forces (ibid., 6, 24 March).

In May, Defense Minister Dmitrii Iazov represented the Kremlin in talks with Czech party leader Miloš Jakeš and Czech president Gustáv Husák. The official communiqué on the visit indicated that Iazov discussed restructuring in both countries with Jakeš and dealt with military matters relating to "the defensive military doctrine" and "the decisions on the unilateral reduction of the armed forces" with President Husák (TASS, 11 May; *FBIS*, 15 May).

July was a busy month for Gorbachev in matters of the bloc. In Strasbourg on 6 July, speaking to the Council of Europe, the Soviet leader suggested that the 35 nations that drafted the 1975 Helsinki Final Act should meet again to lay down another grand design for the future of the continent, one "open for trade and minds open to ideas." Gorbachev also gave another sign of renouncing the Brezhnev Doctrine with an implied promise of Soviet noninterference in Eastern Europe:

> Any interference in domestic affairs and any attempts to restrict the sovereignty of states—friends, allies, or any others—are inadmissable. . . . Social and political orders in one country or another changed in the past and may change in the future. But this change is the exclusive affair of the people in that country and is their choice. (*NYT*, 7 July.)

Before the Strasbourg speech the Soviet leader met with French president François Mitterrand in Paris and at a joint press conference was asked about the possibility that communist parties might be ousted from power in Poland and Hungary. He replied that "how the Polish people and the Hungarian people will decide to structure their societies and lives will be their affair," but he predicted that "the process of democratization" would ultimately transform not only Poland and Hungary but all of Eastern Europe (ibid., 6 July).

Both in Paris and in Strasbourg, Gorbachev warned against efforts to overcome the division of Europe by "the overcoming of socialism," saying that this was "a course toward confrontation, if not worse" (ibid., 7 July).

The Warsaw Pact meeting in Bucharest immediately after Gorbachev's trip to France dealt with adapting the alliance to the evolving East-West relationship, including formulating a response to U.S. president Bush's proposal of 29 May for a joint reduction in U.S. and Soviet troops to 275,000 for each side by 1993. The Soviet news agency Novosti reported that the leaders of the seven states also discussed creating a Warsaw Treaty Organization (WTO) political commission to arbitrate disputes between members. Gorbachev again promised non-interference in bloc members' internal affairs: "Each country and each party has its own specifics and can continue its own individual road to socialist democracy and progress," he said in a dinner toast after the first day of the meeting (AP, 8 July).

Before his return to Moscow, Gorbachev told Soviet television that he looked toward resolution of "the final task, the breakup of military blocs" and that the alliance would probably "transform itself from a military-political to a political-military one" (TASS, 9 July; WP, 10 July).

Although Gorbachev adhered firmly to the stance of no overt interference in Eastern Europe, he continued to exert pressure behind the scenes. In Hungary the pace of change was accelerating, and in late July Gorbachev held his third top-level meeting with Hungarian leaders in four months, conferring with party chairman Rezsö Nyers and General Secretary Károly Grósz. Reportedly, in their various meetings, the Hungarian officials sought to reassure Gorbachev on the continuation of reform without establishment of a "bourgeois system" and on adherence to the Warsaw Pact. In the late July meeting the two sides agreed to later discussions on "the further withdrawal of Soviet troops" (BBC-CARIS, 25 July).

Soviet troop withdrawal was a centerpiece of Gorbachev's strategy for Central Europe, and in the spring the small pullout from East Germany was reportedly on schedule (CSM, 22 May). In August, however, a U.S. congressional delegation visiting East Germany and Moscow concluded that a shell game was at work, a reshuffling of troops designed to make the withdrawal appear larger than it was. The U.S. legislators concluded that the equivalent of three Soviet divisions would be removed from the GDR rather than the four promised by Gorbachev (RFE, Research, 11 August).

The pace of change in Eastern Europe accelerated in late summer. The changes as well as the pace surely worried the Soviet leadership, but Moscow maintained an outward calm. When Tadeusz Mazowiecki was named prime minister of Poland, the first noncommunist to head a government in the bloc in more than four decades, the Soviet government sent him a message of congratulation (TASS, 24 August; RFE, Research, 20 September); and KGB chief Vladimir Kriuchkov was dispatched to Warsaw to endorse the move.

Moscow reacted favorably to the GDR agreement on the departure of East German refugees from Federal Republic of Germany (FRG) embassies in Poland and Czechoslovakia (Moscow World Service, 2 October; FBIS, 3 October), and CC International Department head Valentin Falin said that "matters in the GDR" had been "partly exaggerated" by the Western media (Die Welt, Hamburg, 2 October; FBIS, 3 October). Soviet media avoided criticism of Hungary, which had allowed thousands of East Germans to cross its borders into the FRG; TASS called the exodus a "propaganda hullabaloo" that was part of "a tendentious campaign against the German Democratic Republic" (CSM, 3 October).

Despite the steady resistance of the East German leadership to reform, Gorbachev journeyed to Berlin for the 6 October celebration of the 40th anniversary of the GDR. In his major speech at the festivities, Gorbachev said that "as in any other country, the GDR has its own problems of development, which require consideration and resolution," but implied noninterference in GDR affairs with the affirmation that "equality of rights, independence, solidarity determines the content of relations among the socialist countries" (Pravda, 7 October).

Five days after his Berlin speech, Gorbachev received Poland's party chief Mieczysław Rakowski in Moscow. Rakowski said after the meeting that Gorbachev had no objection to the Polish party following the example of the Hungarian party, which on 7 October voted to dissolve itself and form a Western-style socialist organization (WP, 12 October).

When Gorbachev visited Finland in late October seeking an injection of expertise and capital to aid perestroika, he assured Finnish leaders that the USSR has "no moral or political right" to interfere with East Europe's moves toward democracy, according to spokesman Gennadii Gerasimov (AP, 25 October).

After the opening of the Berlin Wall on 9 November (*NYT*, 10 November), Gorbachev continued to follow his public hands-off policy, but a radically different situation had been created, with early German reunification now looming as a possibility. During the remainder of the year, Gorbachev on several occasions sternly asserted that the question of German reunification was not "on the agenda."

Further recognition of the new noncommunist leadership in Poland was forthcoming from Gorbachev when he welcomed Premier Mazowiecki to Moscow in late November. According to TASS, Gorbachev told Mazowiecki that the USSR is ready for "close interaction with the new Polish leadership and with all Polish political forces, public and religious figures, trade unions, and religious organizations" (*WP*, 25 November). At a news conference, however, the Polish premier could cite no progress on a number of economic issues he raised with Soviet officials, including increasing deliveries of Soviet oil and gas, cutting the Polish share of the expense of USSR troops in Poland, postponing repayment of Poland's large debt to the USSR, and compensating Poles deported to the USSR during and after World War II. Mazowiecki also could obtain no change in the official Soviet position on the Katyn Forest massacre (*NYT*, 26 November).

When Warsaw Pact leaders assembled in Moscow on 4 December to hear Gorbachev's report on his summit meeting with U.S. president Bush, the alliance had become heterogeneous, its representatives ranging from the noncommunist Mazowiecki to Romania's hard-line communist Nicolae Ceauşescu (who was, however, to be deposed and killed before the month was out). A major action at the meeting reflected the new political realities of the region. The USSR joined with Bulgaria, Hungary, the GDR, and Poland in condemning their combined 1968 invasion of Czechoslovakia. TASS said that the Soviet and Czechoslovak leaderships would begin talks on possible reduction of Soviet troops still based in Czechoslovakia (AP, 5 December).

Western Europe. Despite the mounting difficulties at home, the Soviet leadership was able to devote much attention to Western Europe, which remained in the forefront of Moscow's diplomatic planning. Keenly aware of the potential contribution by the Western democracies to the sagging USSR economy, Soviet officials expended great efforts to promote closer economic ties, and some of these had an immediate payoff. Gorbachev's personal popularity remained high with the West European public, an asset fully exploited by the Soviet leader. Toward the end of the year the emphasis switched to politics, as the startling developments in the GDR raised the "German question" to a critical concern. Although the breakdown of communist rule in East Germany created complex problems for the Soviet leadership, it had its advantages for Gorbachev's European strategy. The FRG would need Moscow's help in revising the status of the two German states, and other West European countries would feel some commonality of interests with the USSR on the German question.

An economic setback opened the year. Spain imposed a ban on the import of four-wheel-drive Soviet vehicles until April. Before the ban, Soviet all-terrain vehicles held a 16 percent share of the Spanish market, and European (Economic) Community officials said that without the ban the entire Spanish industry in this sector would be wiped out (*Insight*, 16 January). Other developments were more promising. A Soviet delegation led by Deputy Premier Vladimir Kamentsev concluded several agreements on economic cooperation in London, including one for a joint British-Soviet enterprise to build a polymer plant in Budennovsk and to produce polyethylene in Kazan (*Pravda*, 9 February). Deputy Premier Lev Voronin visited Paris and pushed expanded trade at the 23d session of the Soviet-French Commission on Scientific, Technical, and Economic Cooperation (*Izvestiia*, 17 February). FRG minister of economics Helmut Haussmann met top USSR government officials in Moscow during the first week of March for talks on trade and economic cooperation (*Sotsialisticheskaia industriia*, 2 March; *FBIS*, 7 March).

President Gorbachev met British prime minister Margaret Thatcher in London in early April for talks described by *Pravda* (7 April) as "businesslike." As usual, the two leaders exchanged views frankly; a British spokesman said they "argued energetically" over the Soviets' reported sale of long-range bombers to Libya and a possible negotiated ban on nuclear weapons. They also disagreed about existing nuclear weapons in Europe. Thatcher repeated her oft-stated view that, given the Soviet superiority on the ground even after projected conventional arms cuts, some nuclear weapons were necessary for deterrence; Gorbachev disagreed (AP, 6 April). Queen Elizabeth II, with the approval of the Thatcher government, accepted

Gorbachev's invitation to visit Moscow at an undetermined future date.

The big news of the visit came when, in another unilateral disarmament gesture, Gorbachev announced a halt in Soviet production of nuclear weapons–grade uranium and the closing by 1991 of two reactors used to make weapons-grade plutonium. The move was dismissed by independent experts and the Bush administration as meaningless in military terms. Coupled with the peaceful gesture came a warning by Gorbachev that a North Atlantic Treaty Organization (NATO) plan to modernize short-range nuclear weaponry could force the USSR to respond in kind and would jeopardize conventional arms reductions in Central Europe (*LAT*, 8 April).

The mostly convivial atmosphere of the Gorbachev United Kingdom trip gave way the following month to the common pattern of Soviet-British relations. The British Foreign Office announced on 19 May expulsion of eleven Soviet citizens—diplomats, trade mission officials, military attachés, and journalists—"for activities incompatible with their status" (TASS, 21 May; *FBIS*, 22 May). The USSR retaliated by expelling eight British diplomats and three journalists (London Press Association, 21 May; *FBIS*, 22 May). The new thinking had evidently not altered some traditional Soviet international behavior; two months earlier, the Swiss government accused a Soviet diplomat of spying and banned him from re-entering Switzerland (Berne International Service, 4 February; *FBIS*, 7 February).

More-important concerns were evident on both sides of the already rusting iron curtain. Moscow was strenuously pushing efforts to convince West European elites, more wary than the masses, of the sincerity of Soviet intentions under the new thinking. Vitalii Zhurkin, director of the Institute for Europe of the USSR Academy of Sciences, stressed to the Italian Socialist party congress in May that the Soviets took, on balance, a positive view of the process of West European integration (RFE, *Research*, 30 May). An article by A. Grachev in *Pravda* (26 May) vehemently denied that Soviet peace initiatives were efforts to split NATO or that the "common European home" was "an operation to undermine the program of West European integration."

Gorbachev and his wife, Raisa, were given a rousing reception by enthusiastic crowds in Bonn, Stuttgart, and Dortmund during their visit to West Germany, 12–15 June. Gorbachev met with FRG chancellor Helmut Kohl and Foreign Minister Hans-Dietrich Genscher (*Pravda*; *NYT*, 13–16 June). The leaders issued a joint declaration long on rhetoric and short on substance that indicated agreement on general principles of "new political thinking," security matters, and bilateral relations (*Pravda*, 14 June), but avoided any change in the status of Berlin or any mention of German reunification. The visit's impact was mainly symbolic, indicating a new closeness in relations between Moscow and Bonn (RFE, *Research*, 19, 20 June). At this point the FRG was clearly at the center of European strategy for Gorbachev; the situation in the GDR was still stable enough that the approach could be relatively simple.

Pravda (16 June) hailed the visit as a "landmark event" in FRG-USSR relations, and the Soviet media noted one immediate result of the visit, an agreement, signed in Moscow on the day following Gorbachev's departure from the FRG, making the West German Siemens company a supplier of computers to the USSR (TASS, 16 June; *FBIS*, 17 June).

The USSR was granted the status of observer at the Council of Europe Parliamentary Assembly, along with Hungary, Poland, and Yugoslavia. Cementing the new relationship, Anders Bjoerk, president of the assembly, led a delegation to Moscow in late June for talks he described as "very concrete and constructive." Bjoerk said that matters discussed included human rights, environmental protection, culture, regional conflicts in areas adjacent to Europe, and efforts to combat international terrorism (TASS, 29 June; *FBIS*, 30 June).

The Moscow talks were followed by Gorbachev's appearance before the Council of Europe in Strasbourg. Before that historic appearance, he conferred with French president François Mitterrand in Paris. The two presidents held a joint press conference during which Gorbachev was upbeat about democratization in East Europe and reticent about recent events in China. The Soviet leader emphatically denied that the processes of change in the USSR involved "abandoning our values, socialism, and the people's power" (*Pravda*, 7 July).

At Strasbourg, Gorbachev made a bid for closer relations between East and West in line with his concept of a common European home. He sought to reassure West Europeans by again affirming his opposition to "any interference in domestic affairs and any attempts to restrict the sovereignty of states" and by urging that "competition between the different types of society" be "directed at creating better material and living conditions for all people." Gorbachev said that the USSR and the United States constitute a "natural part" of the European international-political structure and that "their participation in its evolution is not only justified, but is also historically determined." The Soviet leader acknowledged differences between East and West on matters of nuclear disarmament but said that if NATO were willing to enter into negotiations on tactical nuclear weapons, the USSR could "make further unilateral cuts in our tactical nuclear missiles in Europe without delay" (TASS, 6 July; *NYT*, 7 July).

Gorbachev made a further major move on East-West relations in mid-July when he sent the Group of Seven meeting in Paris a letter calling for greatly expanded economic cooperation between Eastern Europe and the West to promote worldwide growth and ease the Third World's debt problems. "Multilateral East-West cooperation on global economic problems," he said, "is far behind the development of bilateral ties. This state of things does not appear justified, taking account of the weight that our countries have in the world economy" (ibid., 16 July).

Pushing the drive for economic links, Gorbachev sent Deputy Premier Aleksandra Biriukova to Britain for talks in late July. She conferred with Prime Minister Thatcher about cooperation in the modernization of light and textile industry, in the production of medicines and medical equipment, and in the training of Soviet management personnel in Britain (*Pravda*, 28 July).

Thatcher returned Gorbachev's April visit in September. Following their meeting in Moscow she voiced strong support for the "historic changes which are taking place in the Soviet Union" and said that she and Gorbachev had agreed that a treaty scaling down conventional armed forces and armaments in Europe could be ready before the end of 1990. On the economic front, however, the prime minister opposed Soviet admission to the International Monetary Fund (IMF) and to the General Agreement on Trade and Tariffs (GATT), explaining that the USSR should first make its economy more open (TASS, 23 September; *FBIS*, 25 September).

Meanwhile, FRG foreign minister Genscher was optimistic about possibilities for further "specific results" on disarmament in 1990 and said that West Germany would support any accord between the USSR and the United States on banning chemical weapons (*Pravda*, 19 September). USSR foreign minister Shevardnadze met with Genscher at the U.N. in September to discuss Soviet–West German relations and disarmament issues related to the recent meeting in Wyoming between Shevardnadze and U.S. secretary of state James Baker (TASS, 28 September; *FBIS*, 29 September).

Gorbachev made another flashy gesture on unilateral disarmament when he visited Finland in October and pledged to eliminate a class of Soviet nuclear submarines operating in the Baltic Sea as part of a plan to drastically reduce the USSR's military presence in northern Europe. He called on Finland and other Nordic countries to pressure the United States and NATO to make similar weapons reductions. U.S. spokesman Marlin Fitzwater dismissed the proposal, and Finnish officials also seemed unimpressed (Knight-Ridder newspapers, 27 October).

Perhaps the most impressive demonstration of Gorbachev's determination to break down barriers and influence Western opinion was his unprecedented meeting with Pope John Paul II on the eve of the Malta summit. The Soviet leader and the pontiff talked for an hour and a half in the Vatican. It was agreed that the USSR and the Vatican would establish official bilateral relations as a first step toward normal diplomatic relations, and Gorbachev pledged that the Ukrainian Catholic church would be legalized when the Soviet parliament passed a freedom-of-conscience law (*NYT*, 2 December).

Two weeks after Gorbachev's meeting with the pope, the Soviets scored their most important success to date on cooperation with Western Europe. Shevardnadze signed a ten-year trade agreement with the European Community (EC) providing for the gradual lifting of EC import quotas on Soviet industrial goods by 1995 and closer cooperation in areas including nuclear energy and safety, financial services, environmental protection, and management training. In return the USSR promised to give West European businesses greater access to the Soviet market. France's foreign minister, Roland Dumas, hailed the agreement as "facilitating the integration of the Soviet Union into the world economy" (AP, 18 December). In another symbolic move, Shevardnadze visited NATO headquarters for a talk with NATO secretary general Manfred Woerner (*NYT*, 20 December).

U.S.-Soviet Relations. Confronting a new leadership in Washington, Moscow was unable to accelerate the momentum of U.S.-USSR détente, and Soviet media comment indicated dissatisfaction with the "distrust" and caution displayed by the Bush administration (Moscow Domestic Service,

20 January; Moscow World Service; *FBIS*, 23 January; *Pravda*; *FBIS*, 24 January). However, various contacts continued. U.S. House of Representatives Armed Services Committee chairman Les Aspin met Marshal Sergei Akhromeev in Moscow; Soviet and U.S. antiterrorism experts held a seminar in Moscow; and a U.S.-Soviet economic conference assembled at the U.N. in New York (*Pravda*, 23 January; TASS, 25 January; *FBIS*, 26 January).

The dynamics of change on both sides propelled further moves toward détente, and gradually the Bush administration warmed to Moscow. Secretary of State Baker visited Moscow in May (*Pravda*, 12 May), and in the last week of that month Bush proposed a joint reduction in U.S. and Soviet troops stationed in Europe to 275,000 for each side by 1993, accompanied by cuts in combat aircraft and other conventional weapons (*NYT*, 30 May). Gorbachev offered to scrap five hundred tactical nuclear warheads during Baker's Moscow visit. At Strasbourg in July Gorbachev tried to induce NATO to participate in talks on short-range weapons by offering the possibility of unilateral cuts in Soviet tactical nuclear weapons (see above).

While the two sides exchanged arms control tentatives, other business went forward. Six major U.S. corporations — Mercator Corp., RJR Nabisco, Eastman Kodak, Chevron, Archer-Daniels-Midland Co., and Johnson and Johnson — signed a trade agreement with the Soviet government that was expected to lead to the creation of at least 25 U.S. joint ventures in the USSR and eventually inject up to $10 billion into the Soviet economy. Western observers anticipated that the trade pact would increase pressure on the Bush administration to loosen restrictions on trade with the Soviet bloc (*WestWatch*, May).

Admiral William J. Crowe, chairman of the U.S. Joint Chiefs of Staff, visited Moscow in July at the invitation of USSR chief of staff Colonel General Mikhail Moiseev and conferred with Gorbachev. The main result of the meeting was a "dangerous activities agreement" for the avoidance of hostilities due to accidents or untoward incidents (TASS, 8 July; *FBIS*, 10 July).

A laser in south Kazakhstan said earlier by the Pentagon to be capable of damaging U.S. satellites was examined in July by a group of U.S. congressmen and scientists who concluded that the laser was too weak to cause such damage (*WP*, 9 July).

Another irritant in bilateral relations came to the fore in August. Despite two private appeals by the

United States, the Soviets conducted an intercontinental missile test with a splashdown between two remote Hawaiian islands (AP, 14 August).

In September discussions of considerable importance for the future of the U.S.-Soviet relationship were held, first in Washington between Shevardnadze and U.S. president Bush and then in Jackson Hole, Wyoming, between Shevardnadze and U.S. secretary of state Baker. Gone was the slight chill of the previous winter; now the two sides were moving more or less in tandem. Following the meeting with President Bush, Shevardnadze said that they had "discussed questions on a large scale, including Soviet-American relations, disarmament, arms control, and other international issues (TASS, 21 September; *FBIS*, 22 September). After the Washington talk on broad issues, the two foreign ministers journeyed to the remote location in Wyoming for quiet exchanges on the technical details of achieving agreement on a number of matters. The major concern of the Wyoming conference was arms control negotiation, but some delegation members on both sides expressed the view that solution of the USSR's economic crisis would be more important than arms control for Soviet-American relations in the near future (*WSJ*, 25 September).

Agreement was reached on several thorny problems related to arms control. Shevardnadze expressed Soviet willingness to sign and ratify a treaty on strategic offensive weapons "even if no agreement has been reached on the antiballistic missile problem by the time it has been fully drawn up." The United States agreed to withdraw its proposed ban on mobile intercontinental ballistic missiles and some progress was reported on submarine-launched ballistic missiles. The Soviets announced that they were completely dismantling the Krasnoiarsk radar station, and the United Sates agreed to consider the USSR's concern over U.S. radar stations in Greenland and Britain. Baker and Shevardnadze signed an agreement on nuclear weapons verification measures to guide the Geneva negotiators in working out specific measures. Progress was reported on reaching an agreement on chemical weapons, and the Soviets made a proposal for inclusion of all tactical aircraft and a mutual limitation of 4,700 planes that provided some promise for unlocking the negotiations on conventional weapons at Vienna. Baker and Shevardnadze also agreed on a summit meeting between Presidents Bush and Gorbachev in late spring or early summer of 1990 (*Pravda*, 25 September).

Other contacts that would have been unthinkable five years earlier continued. An unofficial meeting of U.S. and Soviet counterterrorism experts was held in Los Angeles (ibid., 27 September), and USSR defense minister Iazov made a week-long visit to the United States, where he conferred with President Bush and gave a joint press conference with U.S. secretary of defense Richard Cheney at the Pentagon (*Krasnaia zvezda*, 4 October; *FBIS*, 5, 10 October; TASS, 7 October; *Pravda*, 8 October). For the first time, U.S. and Soviet diplomats held a joint press conference at the U.N. after cosponsoring a resolution pledging to work together to strengthen the organization's specialized agencies (*NYT*, 4 November).

A major foreign policy speech by Shevardnadze in October promised further improvement in Soviet-U.S. relations. The Soviet foreign minister admitted that the Soviet radar station in Krasnoiarsk violated the U.S.-Soviet antiballistic missile treaty and said that the invasion of Afghanistan had violated international law (AP, 23 October). On the same day, U.S. secretary of state Baker delivered a speech expounding an unusually positive view of the possibilities for far-reaching understandings with Moscow. The Soviet concession on strategic defense at Jackson Hole was depicted by Baker as a major move that could facilitate completion of a strategic arms reduction treaty (START). Baker said that although Gorbachev's domestic reforms were still in midpassage, "the political face of Soviet power is being changed already" and that the "historic political transformations" in Eastern Europe required reassessment of European security relationships and the U.S.-Soviet strategic relationship (*NYT*, 24 October).

While the diplomats pushed détente, the U.S. military was involved in a reassessment of the Soviet "threat." On 18 November, U.S. secretary of defense Cheney said there was evidence that the USSR had cut military spending in 1989 (AP, 18 November). On the following day, Cheney said the Pentagon planned to cut military spending in 1990 because "the likelihood of all-out conflict between the U.S. and the Soviet Union . . . is probably lower now than it's been at just about any time since the end of World War II" (ibid., 19 November). American intelligence experts concluded that the United States would likely have a month or more of warning before a full-scale Soviet attack in Europe, far more than previously thought (*NYT*, 26 November). However, a Pentagon report warned that many frontline U.S. weapons had "been rendered poten-

tially obsolete" by Soviet missiles designed to exploit the Defense Department's heavy reliance on radar (Knight-Ridder newspapers, 7 December).

The Bush-Gorbachev summit at Malta in December had more atmosphere than specific agreements. Bush did signal an openly cooperative political and economic relationship with the USSR and active support of Gorbachev and his policies at home and in Eastern Europe (*WP*, 4 December). Both presidents expressed hope that START could be signed at the June 1990 summit in the United States and that differences could be settled to reduce conventional forces in Europe. Bush complained about Soviet arms in Central America; Gorbachev said that such weapons were not being sent to the area. Bush offered to end U.S. production of binary chemical weapons when an international agreement is reached banning them. In economic matters the U.S. president tendered a waiver of the Jackson-Vanik amendment restricting trade when the Supreme Soviet passed legislation permitting free emigration and support for observer status for the USSR at GATT meetings (*Pravda*; *NYT*, 4 December).

Five days after the Malta meeting, the Bush administration rebuffed a Soviet offer to join in a pact for arms reduction in Central America (Knight-Ridder newspapers, 9 December), and U.S. vice-president Dan Quayle called Central America " a contentious issue" (*Izvestiia*, 9 December).

The improved relationship with the United States obviously influenced Shevardnadze's optimistic outlook when he visited NATO on 19 December. Viewing prospects as favorable for reaching agreements in 1990 on reduction of conventional forces in Europe and for progress in talks on nuclear arms and chemical weapons, the Soviet foreign minister called for cooperation between NATO and WTO and seemed to imply that the two alliances should cooperate to prevent an early reunification of Germany (*NYT*, 20 December).

A fresh irritant in relations between Washington and Moscow appeared immediately after Shevardnadze's NATO visit. When the United States intervened in Panama, the Kremlin predictably denounced the move as "gunboat diplomacy" (TASS, 20 December; *NYT*, 21 December).

China. Re-establishment of relations with Beijing was the paramount event of the year and indeed of the decade in Soviet Asian policy. The way for the May summit in Beijing was prepared during a February visit to the Chinese capital by Foreign Minister Shevardnadze (*NYT*, 2 February).

When Gorbachev arrived in Beijing for the historic meeting, the student demonstrations were in progress. The Soviet leader steered carefully between the democracy movement and the Chinese leadership as several events had to be canceled or rerouted because of the occupation of Tiananmen Square by the protesters. The two leaderships agreed to restore regular state-to-state and party-to-party relations with regular meetings between the parties, to work toward demilitarizing their border, to step up economic and cultural exchanges, and to raise talks on the border to the foreign ministerial level to speed up a settlement. However, differences over Cambodia were unresolved. (*Pravda*; *NYT*, 18 May; TASS, *Pravda*, 19 May.)

The brutal crackdown on demonstrators after Gorbachev's departure did not sidetrack the new relationship with China's rulers. USSR spokesman Gennadii Gerasimov said that the Soviet leadership had not expected the repressive move and was "extremely dismayed" at Beijing's actions (AP, 9 June). However, this was an isolated reaction. Soviet television, unlike that of the West, did not depict the violence in Beijing, and Soviet newspapers reprinted the People's Republic accounts of "reactionary forces" spurred by foreigners' incitement. Gorbachev refused to be drawn into criticism of the Chinese leadership (*NYT*, 13 June) and attracted Western criticism for his reticence during the visit to Bonn.

The hands-off policy vis-à-vis China's internal turmoil evidently paid off for Moscow in the continuing rapprochement. Gorbachev's deputy Anatolii Luk'ianov headed a delegation to Beijing in September for discussions on "normalization" with top Chinese leaders (*Izvestiia*, 11 September; Moscow Television, 12 September; *FBIS*, 13 September). At the same time, Zhy Liang, head of the International Liaison Department of the Chinese CC was in the USSR for a meeting with Aleksandr Iakovlev (TASS, 12 September; *FBIS*, 13 September). Foreign Minister Shevardnadze met with Foreign Minister Qian Qichen at the U.N. in New York for discussions on Cambodia, Afghanistan, the Near East, and southern Africa and for a report on the Soviet-U.S. talks in Wyoming (*Izvestiia*, 2 October).

The USSR Supreme Soviet Presidium and the USSR Council of Ministers sent friendly greetings to Chinese leaders on the 40th anniversary of the Chinese communist regime (*Pravda*, 1 October);

the occasion was marked in Moscow by a ceremony attended by Politburo member Vadim Medvedev (*Izvestiia*, 1 October). The People's Republic leaders returned greetings, sending a warm message to Gorbachev and Premier Ryzhkov on the occasion of the 40th anniversary of the establishment of diplomatic relations between the two countries (*Pravda*, 3 October).

One concrete result of the closer relationship between Moscow and Beijing was the beginning in September of construction of a railway to connect Kazakhstan and the northwest section of China's Sinkiang Uighur Autonomous Region. The railway is scheduled for completion by 1992 (Moscow International Service, 27 August, *FBIS*, 13 September; *Insight*, 9 October). Another result was a third new air route between the USSR and China, from Khabarovsk to Harbin (Moscow Radio, 23 September; *FBIS*, 28 September).

Further indications of normalization came in the fall. A Chinese party and government delegation headed by Vice-Premier Yao Yilin stopped in Moscow en route to Berlin for the 40th anniversary of the GDR (*Pravda*, 3 October). A delegation from the Heilongjiang Provincial People's Government led by Governor Shao Qihui visited the USSR in November and met with Vladimir Vorotnikov, chairman of the RSFSR Supreme Soviet Presidium (*Sovetskaia Rossiia*, 18 November; *FBIS*, 22 November), and with Aleksandr Vlasov, premier of the RSFSR (TASS, 20 November; *FBIS*, 21 November). Also in November, Iurii Melentev, minister of culture of the RSFSR, visited China at the invitation of the governments of Liaoning and Jilin provinces (Moscow Radio, 14 November; *FBIS*, 22 November).

It was unlikely that interaction between the two communist giants would have major practical consequences, particularly in economic matters, although cross-border trade was already important on both sides. Further, the Cambodia issue remained sensitive. But the lowering of tension was significant in itself. Major aims of the borderlands strategy had been reduced hostility toward the USSR by adjoining or neighboring states and avoiding the specter of "encirclement." From that perspective, Gorbachev's China policy appeared successful at year's end.

Japan. The USSR sought to build on Foreign Minister Shevardnadze's December 1988 visit to Tokyo to promote relations with Japan. Some success was achieved in the vitally important economic sphere, and the tone of the relationship seemed to improve. Serious differences, however, remained throughout the year, particularly over the Northern Territories.

Agreement had been reached in December between Shevardnadze and Japanese leaders on a proposed visit to Japan by Gorbachev. When former Japanese premier Yasuhiro Nakasone visited Moscow in January, Gorbachev said that consultations were under way concerning the specific date of the visit. Nakasone indicated that the purpose of his visit was to sound out the Soviet leader on the USSR's intentions regarding the Northern Territories (Tokyo, NHK Television, 18 January; *FBIS*, 19 January). Japan's prime minister, Noboru Takeshita, in a speech to the diet in February, said that Tokyo "consistently advocates establishing relations of genuine mutual understanding with the Soviet Union and signing a peace treaty," but that this could be achieved only by return of the Northern Territories (*Krasnaia zvezda*, 11 February; *FBIS*, 16 February).

Talks at the deputy foreign minister level were held in Tokyo, 19–20 March, on a wide range of issues (Moscow Radio, 21 March; *FBIS*, 22 March). These were followed by a meeting of the permanent working group on a peace treaty; Deputy Foreign Minister Igor Rogachev headed the Soviet delegation. Again, the issue of the Northern Territories was reportedly the central point of contention (TASS, 21 March; *FBIS*, 22 March). Japan's foreign minister, Sosuke Uno, described the discussions as "frank" (TASS; *FBIS*, 22 March).

One week after the Tokyo talks, an agreement was signed in Moscow for a Japanese cosmonaut to participate as a crew member of the Soviet orbital station *Mir* no later than mid-1991 (TASS, 27 March; *FBIS*, 30 March). Pushing for closer economic ties, Moscow stressed the potential of joint ventures on Sakhalin (Moscow Radio, 30 April; *FBIS*, 10 May), and played up Soviet-Japanese joint ventures in lumber and chemicals in Siberia (Moscow Radio, 16 April; *FBIS*, 21 April). However, an *Izvestiia* article (11 May) by A. Anichkin reflected some dissatisfaction with the state of relations, despite the flurry of increased contacts. The article concluded that "too much potential remains unrealized—in politics, the economy, culture."

Gorbachev's visit to Beijing drew a favorable response from Tokyo. A spokesman for the Japanese government welcomed initiatives on further reduction of Soviet troops in the Far East and Gorbachev's call that Beijing have broader ties with Japan (TASS, 17 May; *FBIS*, 18 May).

Economic links drew Moscow's attention during the spring and summer. The Gosteleradio TV and Radio Committee and the Japanese Nishi-Nihon company signed a contract for the exchange of television programs (TASS, 22 May; *FBIS*, 25 May). In August, Premier Ryzhkov welcomed a Japanese business delegation attending the Twelfth Joint Soviet-Japanese Economic Committee meeting in Moscow and made a strong appeal for closer economic ties (Moscow Radio, 26 August; *FBIS*, 5 September).

Military considerations play a major role in Soviet-Japanese tensions, and at another foreign ministers' meeting in May, the Soviets indicated a new tolerance of the U.S.-Japan security treaty. Colonel General Mikhail Moiseev, chief of the General Staff, became the first military leader to acknowledge acceptance of the special U.S.-Japanese military relationship in a July interview with Tokyo television (Tokyo, NHK Television, 19 July; *FBIS*, 21 July). However, in a written reply to the Japanese news service, Moiseev made it clear that the plan to withdraw 120,000 troops from the Soviet Far East did not include those deployed on the four Soviet-held islands off Hokkaido (Tokyo, KYODO, 19 July; *FBIS*, 21 July).

Two economic conferences were held at the end of summer. The first, held in Moscow during 23–25 August, concentrated on regional cooperation in the Soviet Far East and the creation of consumer goods production there with the participation of Japanese capital (*Izvestiia*, 27 August). The second, held at Vladivostok in early September, dealt with the development of economic exchanges and joint ventures and the establishment of free economic zones in the USSR (Moscow Radio, 7 September; *FBIS*, 13 September). An economic cooperation agreement was signed on 14 September between the USSR Ministry of Foreign Economic Relations and the Socialist Research Institute of the Japanese Society for Trade with Socialist Countries (TASS, 14 September; *FBIS*, 15 September).

Foreign Minister Shevardnadze and Japanese foreign minister Taro Nakayama met at the U.N. in September and agreed on a 1991 visit by Gorbachev to Japan. A spokesman for the Japanese Foreign Ministry said that Tokyo welcomed the idea of Gorbachev's visit and "expects good results from summit talks" (TASS, 29 September; *FBIS*, 2 October).

Southeast Asia and the Pacific. As in other areas, economics figured prominently in Soviet activities. A USSR parliamentary delegation visiting Manila in January met Filipino governmental ministers concerned with the economy and made a proposal for increased trade and economic cooperation (TASS, 17 January; *FBIS*, 18 January). In February, the Soviet ambassador to the Philippines, Oleg Sokolov, announced a forthcoming agreement on economic and technical cooperation between the two countries. Efforts were being made to increase the annual trade volume from $40 million to $200 million (Moscow Radio, 24 February; *FBIS*, 1 March).

Fishing is of crucial importance for the Soviet food industry, and the USSR made efforts during the year to expand its fleet area, reportedly offering a higher fee than Japan for fishing rights. The USSR, renegotiating its agreements with Vanuatu and New Zealand, also made an offer to Papua New Guinea. Australia, earlier a strong critic of Soviet incursions into the South Pacific, was reportedly also close to an agreement under which Soviet fishing vessels operating in Antarctica would have port access (London, *Daily Telegraph*, 4 April).

Two Soviet representatives, Iurii Akhremenko and Vladimir Ivanov, became the first USSR officials to visit the Republic of China on Taiwan in 40 years when they attended the 22nd annual meeting of the Pacific Basin Economic Council to promote Soviet economic and trade activities in the Asia-Pacific region (*Insight*, 19 June).

Prospects for trade were highlighted during the visit of Indonesia's president, Suharto, to the USSR in September. While Suharto was in the USSR, four joint Soviet-Indonesian ventures were announced for production of tea, furniture, and palm oil (TASS, 7, 8 September; *FBIS*, 11 September).

Politically, the main issue of the region was Cambodia, which complicated the USSR's relations with China, the United States, Thailand, and other states. Moscow hailed Hanoi's announcement that withdrawal of Vietnamese troops from Cambodia would be completed by September 1989 (Moscow Radio, 11 January; *FBIS*, 13 January). But this was only the first step toward a comprehensive settlement. Some movement was evident during Shevardnadze's visit to Beijing in February. A joint communiqué called for a "speedy, just, and rational resolution of the Cambodian problem" without "external interference." The foreign ministers said that the U.N. could play an "appropriate role" in a political settlement and agreed that the USSR and

the PRC would be willing to take part in international guarantees of Cambodia as an "independent, peaceful, neutral, and nonaligned state" (*Pravda*, 6 February).

Laotian foreign minister Soulivong Phasitthidet met with Soviet deputy foreign minister Igor Rogachev in Moscow, 30 March–3 April, on the Cambodian problem and stressed the importance of "political means" and negotiations to secure an early settlement. But the core of the problem remained the composition of a postsettlement government in Cambodia, with the position of the Khmer Rouge the most difficult aspect. The Sino-Soviet summit in May was apparently inconclusive on the issue, and an international conference, attended by twenty delegations representing eighteen countries and two international organizations, convened in Paris in July to discuss a Cambodian settlement (TASS, 30 July; *FBIS*, 1 August). The conference was marked by wrangling and a divergence of viewpoints (TASS, 31 July; *FBIS*, 1 August).

When Vietnam completed its withdrawal from Cambodia, "total and as scheduled," the USSR Ministry of Foreign Affairs hailed the step as creating "a condition favorable to national reconciliation and the search for a solution to the Cambodian problem (Moscow Radio, 28 September; *FBIS*, 29 September).

Whereas the Kremlin concentrated on Vietnam's position in Southeast Asia, "guest workers" in the Soviet capital were involved in disturbances that suggested underlying ethnic animosities inimical to the USSR-Vietnam relationship. Soviet youths and Vietnamese workers at the Likhachev Automobile Plant engaged in a fight on 20 September said to involve 70 people, and there was reportedly an attack by one hundred Vietnamese on a police station on 23 September. The Soviet press account said that Vietnamese stabbed a policeman in the 20 September fight, as well as another policeman and a passerby in a separate incident the following day, and wounded five members of the militia in the 23 September disturbance (*Moskovskaia pravda*, 26 September; *FBIS*, 5 October).

India. India had not been a primary target of the borderlands strategy, because it had been the only major country on the periphery that had mostly friendly relations with the USSR during the time of the Soviets' extreme isolation (1983–1985). However, with the opening to China, it was necessary to reassure India on the special relationship between the two countries, and normal contacts were maintained during the year.

Deputy Premier Biriukova visited New Delhi in February for talks with Prime Minister Rajiv Gandhi and other Indian officials. A major focus of the talks was the development of joint enterprises (TASS, 18 February; *FBIS*, 22 February), and an agreement was signed in early March on a joint venture for the export of Soviet-made software and the manufacture of personal computers (TASS, 6 March; *FBIS*, 7 March).

Following Gorbachev's visit to China, Deputy Foreign Minister Rogachev was sent to New Delhi to report on the Beijing meeting and to assure Gandhi that the normalization with China would not adversely affect Soviet-Indian ties. Gandhi approved the results of the Beijing meeting and also praised Soviet actions on Afghanistan and progress toward a settlement in Cambodia (TASS, 24 May; *FBIS*, 25 May).

Gandhi visited Moscow in July and had a long session with Gorbachev. Their talk covered Pakistan, the north-south dialogue, Iran, and other issues (Delhi Domestic Service, 16 July; *FBIS*, 17 July).

The USSR has been a major supplier of arms for India, and military cooperation was enhanced by the August visit of India's army chief of staff, Nishwa Nath Sharma. While in the USSR, General Sharma conferred with Defense Minister Iazov, visited Leningrad, and toured the Kiev military district (TASS, 30 August; *FBIS*, 31 August).

Afghanistan. The Soviet agreement to withdraw from Afghanistan had been a major factor in the USSR's improving relations with the United States and Western European countries and a precondition for rapprochement with China. During the year, Moscow collected diplomatic dividends from the move, but problems remained.

Deputy Foreign Minister and Ambassador to Afghanistan Iulii Vorontsov warned on 10 January that the pullout of the remaining 50,000 Soviet troops by the 15 February deadline set in the Geneva accords depended on the Afghan guerrillas' willingness to accept a cease-fire and the outcome of negotiations on forming a new government in Kabul (*NYT*, 11 January). The threat followed a Vorontsov meeting in Islamabad with Pakistan's prime minister, Benazir Bhutto (TASS, 8 January; *FBIS*, 9 January). However, on the same day as Vorontsov's warning, Major General Lev Serebrov, a member of the Soviet army's high command in

Afghanistan, gave assurances that the second phase of the withdrawal would be completed on 15 February (Belgrade, TANJUG, 10 January; *FBIS*, 11 January).

A week later, it was reported that Soviet troops had left 26 of Afghanistan's 32 provinces (*Pravda*, 18 January). Meanwhile, Foreign Minister Shevardnadze vowed that the USSR would supply the Afghan government with arms if the war continued and expressed confidence in survival of the Kabul regime (AP, 15 January). In late January rebels fired rockets at Kabul as more Soviet soldiers left the country, and a guerrilla leader said that war planes bombed villages and killed hundreds to clear a path for the withdrawal. As the fighting intensified, USSR defense minister Iazov discussed withdrawal plans with President Najib and other Afghan officials in Kabul (ibid., 28 January). Fearing the worst, the Soviets tried a last-ditch effort to cobble together a coalition government in Kabul, and Foreign Minister Shevardnadze made a hurried trip to Pakistan with that end in view, but to no avail (*CSM*, 6 February).

Despite extreme difficulties, the Soviet withdrawal was completed on schedule (*Pravda*, 15 February). As the Kabul regime held on desperately, *Pravda* (17 March) said that the People's Democratic Party of Afghanistan was essential for Afghanistan's future, and the continued fierce fighting was blamed on "outside interference." Launching a charge that was to become familiar during the year, *Pravda* (20 March) accused the United States and Pakistan of violating the Geneva agreements. Those countries were also charged with responsibility for failure to reach a negotiated settlement, and, following U.S.-Pakistani negotiations in Washington in June, Moscow accused them of continuing to pursue a "tough course" on Afghanistan (TASS, 20 June; *FBIS*, 21 June).

Soviet negotiations with the *mujahideen* on prisoners of war reportedly showed progress in June (Hong Kong, AFP, 26 June; *FBIS*, 27 June; *Izvestiia*, 29 June), and in July a breakthrough was reported in the task of finding Soviet servicemen imprisoned in Afghanistan (*Pravda*, 23 July). But Moscow saw no prospect for an early Afghan peace and blamed "outright sabotage" by Pakistan and the United States for continuation of the "fratricidal" war in Afghanistan (ibid., 3 August).

Negotiations on various fronts for a political settlement continued, and the much-traveled Shevardnadze flew into Kabul on 6 August for talks with Afghan leaders. Shevardnadze expressed confidence in the process of negotiations, pointing to movement in the "inter-Afghan dialogue," the "very constructive position" adopted by Iran toward the Afghan question and an Afghan settlement, and the role of the U.N. He charged that Pakistan's shipment of military supplies to the Afghan rebels violated the Geneva accords. The USSR, he said, would continue to supply Kabul with arms on "a legitimate basis" without violation of the Geneva accords, but was prepared at any time to cease all military supplies to Afghanistan on a reciprocal basis (ibid., 8 August).

While both fighting and negotiations continued inconclusively, Shevardnadze issued a sensational confession to the Soviet parliament in October. He said that the invasion of Afghanistan had violated Soviet law and norms of international behavior and that the decision to intervene "was taken behind the backs of the party and the people" (*NYT*, 24 October). Although Shevardnadze no doubt scored points with "radical" Soviet legislators and with Western public opinion, his declaration tended to undermine whatever legitimacy remained for the Kabul regime.

Middle East. The Soviets made a major attempt to get back into the Middle East peace process in February. Foreign Minister Shevardnadze met separately in Cairo with Egypt's president, Hosni Mubarak, Israeli foreign minister Moshe Arens, and Palestine Liberation Organization (PLO) leader Yassir Arafat, following meetings in Damascus with Syria's president, Hafez Assad, and in Amman with King Hussein (*Pravda*, 21–23 February). Shevardnadze carried with him a four-point peace plan: formation of a preparatory committee representing Egypt, Jordan, Syria, Lebanon, and the PLO to come up with a coordinated Arab stance for an international conference; revival of Gorbachev's proposal for formation of a committee from the five permanent members of the U.N. Security Council to organize an international conference; holding a U.N. Security Council session at the foreign minister level; and arranging a direct meeting between Israel and the PLO within the framework of an international conference (London, *Al-Sharq al-Awsat*, 25 February; *FBIS*, 1 March).

The Middle East imbroglio was too complicated for a solution from a single initiative, but Shevardnadze did succeed in achieving a more realistic goal—the expansion of Soviet diplomatic influence in the region. The foreign minister was the first high-level Soviet official to visit Cairo since 1972,

and it was apparent that Mubarak shared most of his views on a Middle East peace initiative. Shevardnadze conveyed an invitation from Gorbachev for Mubarak to visit Moscow, which the Egyptian president accepted (*WP*, 22 February). The meeting with Arens also evidently went smoothly. The Israeli foreign minister said that the two sides agreed to open a bilateral dialogue between Soviet and Israeli experts and that "we made as much progress as we had a right to expect." However, Arens restated Israel's rejection of any PLO role at the bargaining table and said that "anybody who meets with Arafat legitimizes violence" (Knight-Ridder newspapers, 24 February).

One purpose of Shevardnadze's trip to Damascus had been to try to improve relations with Syria, which was apparently disenchanted with Moscow's "new thinking" for the region. Assad was reportedly particularly adamant against any Soviet yielding to U.S. positions on an international peace conference for the region (*Insight*, 6 February). Shevardnadze probably offered a significant inducement to make Damascus more flexible during his February visit, for it was learned in May that the USSR would supply Syria with MiG-31 fighter planes to replace its MiG-25s and also with airborne warning and control system planes derived from the Iliushin 11-76 *Mainstay* aircraft (Abu Dhabi, *al-Ittihad*, 22 May; *FBIS*, 24 May).

The regional target showing the most positive results for Moscow during the year was Iran. Ayatollah Javadi Amoli, Ayatollah Ruhollah Khomeini's personal representative, arrived in Moscow on 3 January (TASS; *FBIS*, 3 January). Thereafter, the Moscow-Teheran rapprochement, which had had a modest beginning in the previous year, gained momentum. A few days later, Iran's minister of economic affairs and finance, Mohammed Javadi Iravani, said that he expected economic ties with the USSR to expand "remarkably" (*Insight*, 16 January). Iran's deputy foreign minister, M. Larijani, said that relations between the two countries had recently reached a high level and that Iran would assist in resolving the basic questions on the Soviet pullout from Afghanistan (*Pravda*, 19 January).

The pace quickened when Shevardnadze journeyed to Teheran in February. In conversations with Iranian parliament speaker A. A. Hashemi-Rafsanjani and with Premier M. Musavi, Shevardnadze dealt mainly with issues relating to the Iran-Iraq conflict, Afghanistan, and the Persian Gulf (ibid., 28 February). Shevardnadze also met with Khomeini, who stressed to the Soviet foreign minister the importance of "the expansion of strong ties in various dimensions to confront the devilish acts of the West." The meeting came two days after Khomeini declared that Iran does not need the West, and Shevardnadze did not raise the issue of Khomeini's 14 February order for the assassination of the author Salman Rushdie, an intercession reportedly requested by Britain (AP, 26 February).

Iranian deputy foreign minister Mohammad Hoseyn Lavasani visited Moscow on 17 March (TASS, 17 March; FBIS, 20 March), followed two weeks later by Foreign Minister Ali Akbar Velayati. Afghanistan held center stage in Velayati's talks with Shevardnadze. It was agreed that Rafsanjani would visit Moscow later in the year, and, indicative of the economic motivations behind the diplomatic thaw, the talks were joined by Foreign Economic Relations Minister Konstantin Katushev and Nikolai Konarev, USSR minister of railways and cochairman of the Soviet-Iranian commission for economic cooperation (TASS, 31 March; FBIS, 3 April).

Further discussions on economic matters were held in Teheran during April focusing on gas exports from Iran and Soviet assistance to Iran in the building of power plants and developing a metallurgical industry (Moscow World Service, 23 April; FBIS, 24 April).

The Soviet-Iranian rapprochement peaked in June with the visit of Rafsanjani to Moscow, two and a half weeks after the death of Khomeini. Gorbachev greeted the Iranian leader warmly, saying that "we favor a political dialogue, regular contacts, and mutual links" (NYT, 21 June). Reportedly, there was some friction over alleged Islamic fundamentalist influence as a source of the USSR's troubles in Uzbekistan, but Rafsanjani followed his visit to Moscow with a stop in Baku, heavily populated with devotees of Islam, where there were pledges on the exchange of religious leaders. Gorbachev announced the restoration of railroad service across the Soviet-Iranian border and the likely reopening of the Iranian natural gas pipeline to the USSR (ibid., 22 June). In a joint communiqué, Gorbachev pledged that he was "ready to cooperate with the Iranian side in strengthening the defense capability." At a postmeeting press conference, Rafsanjani rejected any notion of a similar détente with the United States and indicated that Khomeini's death sentence against Salman Rushdie was still in effect (ibid., 23 June). It was perhaps a sign of the deftness of the new Soviet diplomacy that the overtures to Teheran, coming at a time of intense con-

cern about Iranian support for terrorism, elicited no perceptible backlash in the West.

Two weeks after the Gorbachev-Rafsanjani meeting, it was announced that joint Soviet-Iranian drilling for oil would begin in the southern shelf of the Caspian Sea, the geological prospecting study having been completed (TASS, 8 July; Reuters, 9 July; FBIS; NYT, 10 July). Meanwhile, Moscow sought to reassure Arab leaders unsettled by the new relationship between the USSR and Iran. In talks with Iraqi and Gulf states' officials and with Arab League secretary general Chedli Klibi, Soviet representatives gave assurances that the USSR had not concluded a major arms deal with Iran that would disrupt the military balance of the region or destabilize the area and that the USSR would not supply Iran with sophisticated offensive weapons (Kuwait, al-Qabas, 26 July; FBIS, 28 July).

Shevardnadze went back to Teheran in August. Afghanistan was again reportedly the main focus of discussion, with Iran's help in regard to a political settlement still a matter of vital concern to Moscow (Moscow World Service, 1 August; NYT; TASS; FBIS, 2 August).

Economic ties were further strengthened in November. An agreement signed in Teheran provided for the export of two billion cubic meters of natural gas to the USSR between 1 April and 31 December 1990, with annual volume increasing to three billion cubic meters in 1991. In exchange, the USSR agreed to send supplies of equipment and machines and to participate in the construction of nineteen important economic installations in Iran (TASS, 4 November; FBIS, 6 November).

Somewhat balancing the Teheran connection, the Kremlin sent Foreign Economic Relations minister Konstantin Katushev to Baghdad in July. Katushev brought back an accord on trade and technical cooperation. Under the agreement, the USSR pledged to assist with several vital economic projects in Iraq (TASS, 12 June; FBIS, 13 June; Insight, 17 July).

Shevardnadze continued his dialogue with Israel's Arens at the U.N. in September (TASS, 28, 29 September; FBIS, 29 September). However, any further normalization of relations with Israel appeared to be on hold. In September, Israeli agriculture minister Katz-Oz was denied a visa for an unofficial visit to Estonia (Paris, AFP, 6 September; FBIS, 7 September), and in December, the Soviets opposed a U.S. effort at the U.N. to repeal a General Assembly resolution equating Zionism with racism (NYT, 16 December).

Africa South of the Sahara. The Soviets continued their cautious approach to events in Africa by pursuing a policy of "constructive disengagement" (*CSM*, 27 April) based on economic calculations of Soviet interests and poor prospects for Marxist regimes in the area. Although most Soviet aid continued to socialist states, there was a tendency to aid countries, regardless of ideology, that were seen as good financial investments (*Insight*, 27 February). However, Moscow maintained regular contacts with the Marxist regimes and kept a close watch on the peace process in Namibia.

In February the USSR donated a ship with two thousand tons of cargo capacity as part of its emergency assistance to Mozambique (Maputo Radio, 21 February; *FBIS*, 1 March), and documents on trade and economic relations were signed following the fifth session of the Soviet-Mozambican intergovernmental commission on economic and technical cooperation and trade on 3 March (*Pravda*, 4 March). USSR deputy foreign minister Anatolii Adamishin stopped in Harare later that month on a tour of southern Africa and conferred with Zimbabwe's president, Robert Mugabe, on the possibilities for ending hostilities in Mozambique and other matters (TASS, 31 March; *FBIS*, 3 April). In October a delegation of political workers from Mozambique's armed forces was in Moscow, where it was received by General Aleksei Lizichev, head of the Main Political Directorate, and General Dmitrii Iazov, USSR minister of defense (*Krasnaia zvezda*, 26 October; *FBIS*, 27 October).

A delegation from the Popular Movement for the Liberation of Angola was in Moscow 17–21 January to study economic reform (*Pravda*, 22 January). In June, Moscow hailed the signing of a cease-fire between the Angolan government and the National Union for the Total Independence of Angola (UNITA). *Pravda* (24 June) saw good prospects for peace if the accords in Namibia were honored and if outside interference, "primarily by the United States," in Angola's internal affairs ceased. In August, Deputy Foreign Minister Adamishin charged that UNITA had started violating the agreements after two days (Moscow Radio, 26 August; *FBIS*, 30 August).

Namibia and Angola had been covered in the December 1988 Brazzaville agreement on disengagement in southwest Africa sponsored by the United States and the USSR, with Adamishin playing a key role (see *YICA*, 1989). UNITA had not been a party to that pact; thus the June cease-fire agreement had been a major step forward. But

Moscow, relishing its role as a promoter of liberation and peaceful change, appeared to devote more attention to Namibia.

Pravda (7 March) charged that South Africa had unleashed "psychological warfare" against the South-West Africa People's Organization in a desperate attempt to assure a friendly state on its borders. Adamishin acknowledged in April that Soviet representatives had been meeting with South African officials, but only "to attain a settlement in the region." He admitted that past Soviet policies had not worked and said that a stop to armed conflict in the area would permit the USSR to reduce expenditures and "to steer things toward mutually profitable economic cooperation" (Moscow Radio, 23 April; *FBIS*, 25 April).

Adamishin in an August interview was generally optimistic about the prospects for a peaceful transition in Namibia, scheduled for independence in April 1990 (Moscow Radio, 26 August; *FBIS*, 30 August). Moscow warned in October that continuing U.S. assistance to the National Union for the Total Independence of Angola posed a danger for the settlement in Namibia (Moscow Radio, 16 October; *FBIS*, 18 October). When elections in Namibia were held as scheduled, Foreign Minister Shevardnadze praised the efforts of the U.N., the Organization of African Unity, and South Africa, but warned that "as long as apartheid exists, there will be a conflict situation in the region" (TASS, 22 November; *FBIS*, 24 November).

Foreign Economic Relations Minister Konstantin Katushev led the Soviet delegation at the eighth session of the Soviet-Ethiopian commission on economic, scientific, and technical cooperation and trade (TASS, 13 January; *FBIS*, 18 January). In subsequent weeks, the Soviets reportedly exerted pressure on Ethiopia's leader, Mengistu Haile Mariam, to negotiate with his domestic opponents, but to no avail. After some reported progress late in the summer on negotiations with the Eritrean rebels, Deputy Defense Minister General V. I. Varennikov was dispatched to Addis Ababa for talks with Ethiopian military leaders (Addis Ababa Radio, 21, 22 September; *FBIS*, 26 September). The Soviets also sought to promote a peaceful solution within Somalia when that country's deputy premier, Ahmed Mohamed Farrah, visited Moscow in February (Moscow International Service, 27 February; *FBIS*, 3 March).

The new leader of the Sudan, Umar al-Bashir, said that the Sudanese government hoped to improve cooperation with the USSR in various fields

(Moscow Television, 17 July; *FBIS*, 20 July); the statement came two weeks after a successful military coup in Khartoum.

The commander of Ghana's ground forces, Major General W. M. Mensah-Wood, received a warm welcome in Moscow from top officials of the Defense Ministry when he visited in November (*Krasnaia zvezda*, 16 November).

In October Mali ratified an agreement setting up a joint Malian-Soviet air transport company. The pact had been negotiated in June; the delay in ratification was attributed by diplomatic sources to French objections (*Insight*, 16 October).

Relations between the USSR and Sierra Leone were strained early in the year. Two Soviet journalists were expelled from that country in January, and a Soviet scientific vessel was detained in February (*Sovetskaia Rossia*, 24 February; *FBIS*, 1 March). However, the frictions were overcome (*Insight*, 26 June), and in the fall talks were under way in Moscow on implementation of the USSR–Sierra Leone fishing protocol (Freetown Domestic Service, 23 September; *FBIS*, 26 September).

Latin America. Cuba and Nicaragua, Moscow's allies in the region, remained the central focus of Soviet attention, as the Marxist regimes in both countries posed difficulties for détente with the United States. Fidel Castro was a source of additional problems.

The Soviets were still subsidizing the Cuban economy by more than $5 billion per year, but could make little headway in influencing Castro. On the contrary, the Cuban leader remained firmly opposed to Soviet-style reforms and maintained a belligerent attitude toward the United States in the face of the growing closeness between Washington and Moscow (*NYT*, 6 January).

P. I. Kormilitsin, Soviet trade representative in Cuba, implicitly admitted that Cuba was a serious economic liability for Moscow when he pointed out major difficulties in the relationship during a March interview (*Izvestiia*, 29 March). However, Cuba was still a political asset, giving the Soviets at least a toehold in the Caribbean. When Gorbachev visited Cuba in early April, he trod warily in public, although Castro bluntly opposed major Soviet policies.

The Cuban leader told the National Assembly that Moscow's approach to economic and political change did not apply to Cuba because of differences in size, ethnic diversity, and history and pointedly said that "if a socialist country wants to construct capitalism, we have to respect its right to construct capitalism" (*NYT*, 7 April). In contrast to Gorbachev's more conciliatory approach, Castro delivered a fierce denunciation of American imperialism. The two leaders did sign a largely meaningless friendship treaty that condemned the use of force as an instrument of foreign policy (ibid., 6 April).

Gorbachev promised in May to halt Soviet weapons shipments to Nicaragua, but U.S. spokesman Marlin Fitzwater said there was evidence that Soviet arms were still going to Nicaragua (ibid., 17 May). This issue remained a vexing one between Washington and Moscow and, after the crash of a Nicaraguan plane loaded with Soviet-made weapons inside El Salvador, a major focus of U.S. president Bush's complaints at the Malta summit. Gorbachev continued to deny that the Soviets were shipping weapons to the Caribbean area (ibid., 4 December).

Shevardnadze visited Nicaragua and Cuba after attending the 44th session of the U.N. General Assembly in New York. In Managua, Shevardnadze said that the USSR had temporarily suspended arms shipments to Nicaragua and that economic exchanges must be reoriented to aim at social and development goals (*Pravda*, 6 October). In Havana, the Soviet foreign minister said that he had "interesting and detailed talks" with Fidel Castro and referred to Soviet-Cuban relations as very good (TASS; *FBIS*, 6 October).

Cuba was also involved directly, as well as an alleged indirect conduit for the flow of weapons, in the U.S.-Soviet tension over arms. The USSR Foreign Ministry said that U.S. complaints about the delivery of MiG-29 warplanes to Cuba were an attempt to worsen relations on the eve of the Malta summit. Spokesman Gennadii Gerasimov claimed that the delivery of two training MiGs was part of an agreement signed several years previously (AP, 17 November).

Shevardnadze's visit in October did nothing to moderate Castro's resistance to Gorbachev's policies. Only days after the Malta summit, Castro was at his most vitriolic in a speech in Havana. He blasted the "Yankee empire" as embodying "Hitler's dream of world domination" and again roughly rejected any idea of Soviet-style reform. He complained of the difficulty in building communism when others are "slandering socialism, destroying its values, discrediting the party and liquidating its leading role, doing away with social discipline and sowing chaos and anarchy everywhere" (*NYT*, 9 December).

When the United States invaded Panama some two weeks after the Malta summit, the Soviets denounced the action in the strongest terms (ibid., 21 December). It was not clear how this action would affect Soviet willingness to cooperate on Central American issues. Earlier, the Bush administration had rebuffed a call for the United States and the USSR to join in a pact for arms reductions in Central America (Knight-Ridder newspapers, 9 December). However, there were indications that the U.S. intervention in Panama would not be allowed to disrupt other aspects of the developing Soviet-American relationship.

Party International Contacts. The greater flexibility of the CPSU on all fronts made relations with other communist parties easier during the year, but the turn to pragmatism, with uncertain ideological grounding, rendered cohesion of the heterogeneous communist movement even more problematical. Within the East European bloc, the CPSU leadership sought to encourage reform without altering the fundamental characteristics of the party-states, But Moscow's forswearing of overt interference diminished its leverage. As communist rule in the area unraveled during the latter months of the year, the CPSU sought to put the best face possible on developments, but had little control over the course of events. Outside the base bloc, major parties in China, Cuba, and Nicaragua were even more independent of Moscow. China turned back the clock on internal reform, and Cuba's Castro sharply rejected both domestic and foreign policy approaches of the CPSU. Nevertheless, the CPSU during the year maintained contacts with parties representing a wide diversity of views, seeking to preserve some semblance of a leadership position among the world's communist parties.

East Germany's Socialist Unity Party (SED) was a special target, but its leadership was highly resistant to Soviet-type reforms. When the SED leadership collapsed under the weight of suddenly unleashed protests, the CPSU tacitly approved the new ambiguous arrangement of power in the GDR. Foreign Minister and Politburo member Shevardnadze visited East Berlin in June for talks with SED leader Erich Honecker. The official communiqué on the visit highlighted their mutual "satisfaction at the high level and the active shaping of relations between the SED and the CPSU" (*Pravda*, 10 June), a statement that failed to account for the CPSU's views on SED internal policy. Later in the month, Honecker journeyed to Moscow, where he was at least publicly warmly welcomed by Gorbachev and CPSU CC secretary Aleksandr Iakovlev (*ND*, 28 June).

As long as East Germany was relatively stable, its strategic importance tended to override any dissatisfaction with the SED leadership's domestic hard line, and the CPSU continued to follow its public hands-off policy. In September, Honecker's kindred spirit Egor Ligachev was dispatched to East Berlin for talks (TASS; *FBIS*, 12 September), but he was soon followed by CC secretary Vadim Medvedev, who attended a bloc ideological secretaries' conference in the GDR capital (TASS, 20 September; *FBIS*, 22 September).

The situation by the time of Gorbachev's October visit to Berlin for the 40th anniversary of the GDR had become uncertain. There were already indications of slippage of control by the SED, and Gorbachev adopted a restrained, balanced approach at the ceremonies. He mildly admonished the SED on the need for "consideration and resolution" in regard to problems of development, but strongly implied that he would not interfere in the domestic affairs of the GDR and SED (*Pravda*, 7 October). The official hands-off policy continued in subsequent weeks as the SED leadership collapsed.

Relations with the Hungarian party were evidently more cordial. Several meetings were held with top officials of the Hungarian party and government (see above), and the CPSU leadership, although endorsing domestic reform, was clearly concerned about the Hungarians' movement toward a market economy and disturbed about the prospects for a multiparty system in the country. However, when representatives of the Hungarian Socialist Workers' party reached an accord with other groups on a multiparty system, the move was endorsed by Moscow (*Izvestiia*, 23 September).

The CPSU was remarkably supportive in public of the dramatic changes in Poland. When party chief Mieczysław Rakowski conferred with Gorbachev at Moscow in October, the Polish United Workers' party leader said that Gorbachev had no objection to the Polish party's following the example of the Hungarian party and dissolving itself to form a Western-style socialist organization (*WP*, 12 October).

Czechoslovakia attracted less public attention from Moscow, but the CPSU maintained close contacts, notably a February meeting in Moscow between Josef Lenart, Politburo member and secretary of the CPCZ CC, and Nikolai Sliun'kov,

Politburo member and secretary of the CPSU CC (*Pravda*, 10 February).

A delegation of the Sofia city committee of the Bulgarian party led by Ivan Panev, member of the Politburo and first secretary of the Sofia city party committee, met with Lev Zaikov, CPSU Politburo member and first secretary of the Moscow city party committee, on prospects for expansion of interaction between the party organizations and labor collectives of the two capitals (Moscow Domestic Service, 26 September; *FBIS*, 28 September).

Leaders of the bloc parties had the opportunity for private discussions on interparty matters in July at the Bucharest Warsaw Pact summit, which was mainly devoted to questions of the changing East-West relationship (AP, 7 July).

Bloc parties held a conference of CC secretaries for international questions in Bulgaria during the last week of September. The conference was attended by party representatives from Bulgaria, Vietnam, East Germany, North Korea, Cuba, Laos, Mongolia, Poland, Romania, Czechoslovakia, and the USSR. CPSU representative Aleksandr Iakovlev said that the conference participants discussed the position of socialism in the world, the situation in the socialist world, and the "all-European process and its prospects" (*Pravda*, 29 September).

Soviet concern over ethnic tensions and a willingness to learn from Yugoslavia's experience as a multiethnic society were apparent when a delegation from the League of Communists of Yugoslavia (LCY) was welcomed by the CPSU CC and the Academy of Sciences for "consultation on urgent problems of interethnic relations under socialist conditions" during 17–18 April. Delegation head Ivica Racan, member of the LCY CC presidium, was welcomed by CPSU Politburo member and CC secretary Viktor Chebrikov (ibid., 19 April). Alternate Politburo member Aleksandr Vlasov visited Belgrade in September for talks on economic cooperation (TASS, 25 September; *FBIS*, 26 September).

Interparty "reformist" cooperation was apparent at the congress of the Italian Communist Party (PCI) in March when Aleksandr Iakovlev, representing the CPSU, joined with Hungarian reformer Imre Pozsgay in warning of the threat posed to reforms by conservative forces in their countries (BBC-CARIS, 24 March). When PCI head Achille Ochetto met Gorbachev in Moscow earlier in March, the CPSU leader expressed the wish to develop with the West European social democratic parties the same sort of relationship the CPSU has with the PCI (RFE, *Research*, 8 March).

Iakovlev also represented the CPSU at the Ninth Congress of the German Communist Party (DKP) in Frankfurt am Main in January (TASS, 5 January; *FBIS*, 6 January). In June, DKP leader Herbert Mies met with CPSU leader Gorbachev during the latter's official visit to West Germany (TASS, 15 June; *FBIS*, 16 June).

Vladimir Kalashnikov, first secretary of the Volgograd *obkom*, represented the CPSU at the Nineteenth Congress of the Swedish Communist Workers' party at Stockholm in May (*Pravda*, 5 May). V. N. Sharkov, deputy chief of the CPSU CC Party Building and Cadre Work Department, represented the CPSU at the Twenty-fourth Congress of the Communist Party of Belgium (ibid., 18 March).

Veteran leader of the French Communist Party (PCF), Georges Marchais, visited Moscow in September and met with CPSU CC secretary Vadim Medvedev for talks on "certain issues of cooperation between the CPSU and the PCF" (TASS, 26 September; *FBIS*, 27 September).

A delegation headed by V. S. Babichev, deputy chief of the CPSU CC Party Building and Cadre Work Department, visited Cyprus in January at the invitation of the Progressive Party of the Working People of Cyprus (TASS, 17 January; *Pravda*, 18 January).

Jambyn Batmonh, general secretary of the Mongolian People's Revolutionary Party, met CPSU general secretary Gorbachev in Moscow in July (TASS, 26 July; *FBIS*, 27 July). Ho Tam, Politburo member and CC secretary of the Workers' Party of Korea (WPK) conferred with CC secretary Iakovlev in September to plan interparty contacts in accord with an earlier meeting between Gorbachev and WPK leader Kim Il-sung (ibid., 23 September).

Kakhar Makhkamov, first secretary of the Tajikistan CC, led the CPSU delegation at the Fourteenth Congress of the Indian Communist Party in March (TASS, 6 March; *FBIS*, 7 March).

The CPSU was represented at two African parties' congresses during the summer. V. S. Baltrunas, secretary of the Lithuanian CC, led the CPSU contingent at the Fourteenth Congress of the Congolese Party of Labor (TASS, 26 July; *FBIS*, 28 July), and V. P. Sobolev, second secretary of the Latvian party, headed the CPSU delegation at the Fifth Congress of the Mozambique Liberation Front (*Pravda*, 4 August).

General Secretary Gorbachev traveled to Havana in May for talks with Fidel Castro, and Politburo

member and Foreign Minister Eduard Shevardnadze visited both Nicaragua and Cuba in October
(see above). In January, Politburo member and
Chairman of the RSFSR Supreme Soviet Presidium
Vitalii Vorotnikov visited Cuba (ibid., 5 January),
where he had formerly served as ambassador; candidate Politburo member Iurii Masliukov made the
trip to Havana later that month for talks on economic matters with party and government officials
(ibid., 19 January).

A delegation of workers from the Association for
the Unity of Australian Communists was in the
USSR, 26 March–4 April, at the invitation of the
CPSU CC to study economic reform (ibid.,
6 April).

Biographies. *Iurii Dmitrievich Masliukov.*
Masliukov, a Russian, was born in 1937 at
Leninabad, Kirghizia. After graduating in 1962
from the Leningrad Institute of Mechanics, he became an engineer at a military research institute and
joined the CPSU in 1966.

In the 1970s, Masliukov served as chief engineer
at a major military plant and then as deputy minister
of the defense industry. In November 1982, when
Nikolai Ryzhkov moved from Gosplan to the CC
Secretariat, Masliukov succeeded him as a first
deputy chairman of the planning agency. After
Ryzhkov assumed the premiership, Masliukov was
appointed, in November 1985, as a deputy prime
minister. In 1986, at the Twenty-eighth CPSU Congress, Masliukov was elected a member of the
CPSU Central Committee.

In February 1988, when Gosplan head Nikolai
Talyzin was dismissed because of steady criticism
of that agency, Masliukov was named as his replacement, appointed as a first deputy prime minister,
and elected a candidate member of the Politburo.

In the leadership reshuffle of September 1989,
Masliukov was elevated to full membership on the
Politburo, becoming the youngest full member of
that body.

(Sources: *RL, Research,* 1 April 1986; *Pravda,*
7 February 1988; *Izvestiia,* 8 February 1988;
Pravda; NYT, 21 September.)

Boris Karlovich Pugo. A Latvian, Pugo was
born in 1937 at Kalinin, northern Russia. A 1960
graduate of Riga Polytechnic Institute, Pugo started
his career in the Komsomol and then moved to
regular party work, rising to the post of first secretary of the Riga city organization. In 1980, he was
named to the chairmanship of the Latvian KGB.

When Latvia's longtime party boss August E.

Voss was elevated to the honorific post of chairman
of the USSR Supreme Soviet Council of Nationalities in April 1984, Pugo was chosen as his
successor. As first secretary of the Latvian party,
Pugo became one of the most outspoken defenders
of Gorbachev's reform program in the outlying republics and was rewarded in September 1988 when
he was transferred to Moscow to head the CPSU
Party Control Committee, in place of the deposed
Mikhail Solomentsev. At the Central Committee
plenum of September 1989 Pugo was elected as a
candidate member of the Politburo. Pugo has been a
member of the Central Committee since the Twenty-
seventh CPSU Congress in March 1986.

(Sources: *Sovetskaia Latviia,* 15 April 1984;
FBIS, 1 April 1984; *RL, Research,* 1 April 1986;
Pravda, 1 October 1988; *Pravda; NYT,* 21
September.)

R. Judson Mitchell
University of New Orleans

Yugoslavia

Population. 23,724,919

Party. League of Communists of Yugoslavia (Savez
Komunista Jugoslavije, LCY). Throughout 1989
the LCY remained the only constitutionally legal
party in the Socialist Federal Republic of Yugoslavia (SFRY). However, there are regional communist party organizations in the six republics—
Slovenia, Croatia, Bosnia-Hercegovina, Montenegro, Macedonia, Serbia—and the two Serbian
autonomous provinces, Kosovo and Vojvodina, as
well as a party organization in the Yugoslav armed
forces, (JNA).

Founded. April 1919 as the Socialist Workers
Party of Yugoslavia; disbanded and replaced by
the Communist Party of Yugoslavia (CPY) in June
1920. After being expelled from the Cominform
in 1948, the CPY changed its name to the League
of Communists of Yugoslavia at the Sixth Party
Congress in 1952.

Membership. 1,868,000 claimed before emergency congress (*Pravda,* 21 January 1990; *FBIS-
SOV,* 25 January 1990).

President of the Presidium. Dr. Stipe Šuvar (53), a Croat from Croatia; replaced in May 1989 by Milan Pančevski (54), a Macedonian from Macedonia.

Secretary of the Presidium. Stefan Korošec, a Slovene from Slovenia, whose two-year term began in June 1988. The number of executive secretaries steadily declined from seven in November 1988 to two, Dr. Stanislav Stojanović and Ljubomir Varošlija, by the end of 1989. This number varies as needed.

Presidium. 23 members representing the republics, autonomous provinces, and the LCY organization in the armed forces. Officially, 14 members hold that job between party congresses. There are 9 ex officio members who take part in Presidium meetings by virtue of being presidents of their own territorial League of Communists (LC) or the head of the JNA party organization. Because these presidencies rotate on different schedules—one- or two-year rotations—these members of the Presidium change on a staggered schedule. That process was complicated in 1989 because Dr. Stipe Šuvar (Croatia) and Dr. Vasil Tupurkovski (Macedonia) were elected to the collective state presidency and by the republic/provincial party congresses held prior to the LCY Fourteenth Extraordinary Party Congress, scheduled to begin 20 January 1990. Members: Slovenia, Stefan Korošec and Boris Muževič; Croatia, Ivica Račan, Stipe Šuvar (resigned), and Marko Lolić; Bosnia-Hercegovina, Ivan Brigić and Ugljesa Uzelac; Montenegro, Momir Grbovic and Petro Vukotic; Macedonia, Milan Pancevski and Vasil Tupurkovski (resigned); Serbia, Dusan Čkrebić and Petar Skundrić; Kosovo, Jusuf Zeljnulahu; Vojvodina, Stanko Radmilović. Ex officio members: Slovenia, Milan Kučan; Croatia, Stanko Stojčević, replaced by Ivica Račan; Bosnia-Hercegovina, Dr. Abdulah Mutapčić, replaced by Dr. Nijaz Duraković; Montenegro, Momir Bulatović; Macedonia, Jakov Lazaroski, replaced by Petar Grosev; Serbia, Dr. Bogdan Trifunović; Kosovo, Rahman Morina; Vojvodina, Stanko Radulović; JNA, Vice-Admiral Petar Šimić.

Central Committee. 165 members: 20 from each republic, 15 from each of the two Serbian autonomous provinces, and 15 from the army's party organization

Status. Ruling party

Last Congress. Thirteenth, June 1986

Last Elections. May 1986. The Yugoslav parliament has two chambers: a 220-member Federal Chamber and an 88-member Chamber of Republics and Provinces. Elections are conducted by the Socialist Alliance of Working People of Yugoslavia via a complex delegate system. Dusan Popovski, president of the Assembly, was replaced in May by Slobodan Gligorijević. The term of office is currently one year.

Auxiliary Organizations. The Socialist Alliance of Working People of Yugoslavia (Socijalistički savez radnog naroda Jugoslavije, SAWPY) is a mass umbrella organization that includes major political/social organizations as well as individuals. SAWPY provides the political machinery for conducting elections and mirrors the national/regional tensions that conflict the LCY. There is also the Confederation of Trade Unions (Savez Sindikata Jugoslavije, CTUY); the League of Socialist Youth of Yugoslavia, Savez socijalističke omladine Jugoslavije, LSYY), and the veterans' organization.

Government Bodies. An 8-member collective state presidency was elected in May 1989 for a five-year term. The president and vice-president serve for one year, and these positions rotate among the membership. Raif Dizdarević was replaced in May 1989 by Dr. Janez Drnovšek (39), Slovenia, as president of the SFRY; Dr. Borislav Jović, Serbia, became vice-president. Although internal republic factionalism delayed the selection of representatives from Bosnia-Hercegovina and Macedonia, by the end of the year the state presidency was in place. Other members of the presidency are Bogic Bogičević, Bosnia-Hercegovina; Nenad Bućin (55), Montenegro; Dr. Stipe Šuvar, Croatia; Dr. Vasil Tupurkovski, Macedonia; Riza Sapundziju, Kosovo; Dr. Dragutin Zelenović (61), Vojvodina. The general secretary of the presidency is Ljubiša Korać. Day-to-day government is in the hands of the Federal Executive Council (FEC) headed by its president, 64-year-old Prime Minister Ante Marković (Croatia), who was chosen in March to replace Branko Mikulić, who stayed on in an interim capacity after his government resigned 30 December 1988. Vice-presidents of the FEC are Aleksandar Mitrović and Zivko Pregl. Among the most important federal secretaries are Budimir Lončar, foreign affairs; Colonel General Veljko Kadijević, defense; and Petar Gračanin, internal affairs.

Publications. The main LCY publications are *Komunist* (weekly) and *Socijalizam* (monthly); other major publications include daily newspapers: *Borba* (SAWPY), *Politika* (Serbian strongman Slobodan Milošević's party line), *Vjesnik* (Zagreb), *Delo* (Ljubljana), *Oslobod-jenije* (Sarajevo), *Nova Makedonija* (Skopje), and *Rilinda* (Priština). Prominent weeklies are *NIN* (*Nedeljne informativene novine*, Belgrade) and *Danas* (Zagreb). The boldest youth weekly newspapers are the Slovene Youth Organization's *Mladina*, the Belgrade University's *Student*, and the Zagreb University's *Studentski list*. Much controversial religious material appears in the biweekly Catholic journal *Glas Koncila*. Philosophical and social controversy is often covered by the Belgrade biweekly *Književne novine*. Military views are often expressed in the JNA weekly *Narodna armija*.

Leadership and Party Organization. Throughout 1989 the LCY leadership was full of polemical pronouncements at virtually perpetual party plenums. As a way of coming to grips with the country's economic/political crisis, however, these tactics were not very successful as seen by their increasingly alienated constituency. At the beginning of the year LCY Central Committee member Ivo Druzić (Croatia) pled with LCY president Stipe Šuvar, Croatia, and Serbian LC president Slobodan Milošević to bury the hatchet and stop sniping at one another. As he put it:

> I have had enough of our talking in codes, wearing kid gloves here in public yesterday and today, but ruthlessly kicking each in the shins under the table. I have had enough of our sitting on a cart careening into the abyss and doing nothing to stop it, but instead hitting at each other. I want something better because I know that Yugoslavia can again become a decent place to live. (Belgrade Domestic Service, 31 January; *FBIS*, February 1.)

His appeal fell on deaf ears, although once it was clear that it was impossible to remove Šuvar as president of the party, direct polemics subsided. At the end of March the LCY presidency rejected calls from Vojvodina and Serbia to remove Šuvar as president; those calls were based on there being an unprincipled coalition at the top of the LCY and that Šuvar was responsible for Albanian nationalism and should be dismissed for his criticisms about mass rallies as a tactic for relieving leaderships. (TAN-JUG, 30 March; *FBIS*, 31 March.)

A Zagreb headline, "Continuation of Cold War," summed up the Twentieth LCY Plenum. This Croa-

tian analysis warned that aborting the search for a Yugoslav synthesis might result in "two types of social organization, two national geographic groupings" and that "the Polish way," a military solution, waited in the wings (*Vjesnik*, 12 February; *FBIS*, 17 February). At this point Serbs did not appear unduly worried about criticism by Slovenes. As one Slovene observer put it, Milošević and his supporters tolerated such criticism, "obviously reckoning that it is not yet time for the clash between Slovenia and Serbia" (Ljubljana, *Delo*, 4 February; *FBIS*, 9 February).

The plenum closed with a ringing call for eliminating conflicts and restoring unity in the party and the country. Reiterating the party's commitment to socialist self-management and a nonaligned Yugoslavia founded on federal principles, it insisted that all controversial issues within the party could be resolved in a democratic way (TANJUG, 1 February; *FBIS*, 2 February). Suggestions on how to accomplish this, however, were conspicuously absent.

The response was openly skeptical. According to one Montenegrin commentator, the Twentieth LCY Central Committee plenum was memorable "only for its length" (Titograd, *Pobjeda*, 3 February; *FBIS*, 10 February), while a Slovene assessment likened the Central Committee to "marathon runners running in a vicious circle" (Ljubljana, *Delo*, 4 February; *FBIS*, 9 February).

Thus as the year began there was general agreement within the party that the economy and the political system were in crisis. Everyone agreed that to dig out of the political/economic quagmire required a three-pronged reform of the economy, the political system, and the party itself. There agreement ended. The differences centered on the nature of the political/economic crises facing Yugoslavia and involved conflicting priorities and competing agendas.

There was no agreement on where to start and how to go about such reforms. Although politicians emphasized the need for democracy and pluralism, they had very different things in mind than the range of expectations those words created at the level of mass politics.

Simultaneously, a generational change was under way. Notwithstanding the party leadership's differences on Slobodan Milošević's manipulation of mass popular protest in his struggle to reverse the "parcelization" of Serbia and to reintegrate the autonomous provinces into Serbia proper, the 1988 toppling of the provincial leaderships in Kosovo and

Vojvodina inevitably changed faces at the top of the federal party. That process continued with the fall of the Montenegrin leaders after two days of mass protest in early January. (TANJUG; *FBIS*, 11 January.)

Although cadre changes at Twentieth LCY Plenum, 30 January–1 February, were not as extensive as some hoped or feared, eight new members came on board to replace those from Vojvodina who had resigned. Other dismissals and resignations followed: Azem Vlasi and Svetislav Dolasević (charged by the Serbian Central Committee with responsibility for Albanian nationalism in Kosovo), as well as Munir Mešihović (president of the Bosnian-Hercegovinan party, held responsible for the Agrokomerc financial scandal). Kolj Siroka (Kosovo) was given a vote of confidence. Montenegrin representatives Marko Orlandić and Vidoje Žarković resigned from the LCY presidency as a result of the January demonstrations that brought down the entire Montenegrin leadership.

Fifteen members were relieved of their posts in accord with personal requests or the principle of separating party and state functions (Belgrade Domestic Service; *FBIS*, 2 February). These included former presidents of the presidency of Yugoslavia Lazar Mojsov (Macedonia), Sinan Hasani (Kosovo), Radovan Vlajković (Vojvodina); former Interior Minister Stane Dolanc (Slovenia); and former Prime Minister Branko Mikulić (Bosnia-Hercegovina). The dismissal of Ivan Stojanović and Borisav Srebrić (Serbia) because they were "frequently criticized by some forums and press in Serbia" is a euphemism for having fallen into disfavor with Milošević and raises some doubt about resolving controversial issues in "the most democratic way."

The changeover continued at the Twenty-first LCY Central Committee Plenum, 17 February. Thirty-three new members were elected to the LCY Central Committee: 11 from Bosnia-Hercegovina; 6 from Montenegro; 5 from Macedonia; 4 from Kosovo; 2 each from Serbia, Slovenia, and Croatia; and 1 from Vojvodina (TANJUG, 17 February; *FBIS*, 21 February). President of the State Presidency Raif Dizdarević resigned from the LCY Central Committee in accordance with the principle of separation of party and state functions.

Four members were dismissed from Central Committee membership on grounds of their lack of ideological/political responsibility: Mate Andrić, Hrvoje Istuk, Milanko Renovica, and Nikola Stojanovic, spent social means improperly in a scandal

involving summerhouses and other leisure objects in Neum. General Petar Matić, a prewar Communist and a military hero of the War of Liberation, resigned in the face of charges that he had an improper attitude regarding "the excessive autonomy policy" of Vojvodina, although there were not enough votes to dismiss him.

Thus by the end of the Twenty-first Plenum a total of 44 new members had joined the LCY Central Committee since the Thirteenth Party Congress in 1986, eight under the one-third maximum change between congresses allowed by party statute (TANJUG, 17 February; *FBIS*, 21 February). In May seven more new members were elected: four from Croatia, two from Vojvodina, and one from the party organization in the JNA. Whether that process was due to the success of Serbian centralism/expansionism or to popular demand in Vojvodina, Kosovo, and Montenegro, sweeping cadre changes were under way. Municipal and communal politicians were also swept out of office in the wake of these leadership reshuffles.

At the Twenty-fifth LCY Plenum, Vasil Tupurkovski, recently elected to the SFRY presidency from Macedonia, resigned in line with the rule on separation of state and party functions. No explanation was forthcoming of the decision to reduce the LCY Central Committee from 165 to 129 and the Statutory Commission from 24 to 15 or the one to keep the membership of the supervisory commission to 15, but to drop the ex officio membership of the heads of such commissions in the republics/provinces and the JNA. (TANJUG, 31 July; *FBIS*, 1 August.) In any case this streamlining of top party bodies was contingent on the approval of the star-crossed Fourteenth Extraordinary LCY Congress, which had been moved from December 1989 to January 1990 to allow the republic/provincial/JNA party congresses to meet before the federal congress.

The movement at the top of the party was paralleled by a steady decline in LCY membership and morale. The number of young people (under 27 years old) dropped from 33.1 percent of LCY members in 1980 to 18.1 percent by June 1988. Figures on recruitment in 69,028 basic party organizations in 1986 were discouraging—71 percent of them did not recruit one new member, and there was no sign that the downward trend was being reversed on the eve of the 1990s. (*Borba*, 21, 22 January.) The only regional party to record an increase for 1988 was Kosovo—from 106,172 to 107,301. Even the party organization in the armed forces dropped from

81,551 in 1987 to 77,878 mid-1988. (*Borba*, 21, 22 January; *FBIS*, 9 February.)

Fourteenth Extraordinary LCY Congress. Demands for a special LCY congress came first from Montenegro, were upheld by party organizations throughout Serbia by a special conference of the Vojvodina LCY, and supported by the Central Committee of the Bosnia-Hercegovina LCY and the party leadership in Macedonia. LCY president Stipe Šuvar opposed the idea that the congress be special or extraordinary on the grounds that this was just another strategy of the campaign of "individual sections of the party" (read Milošević and the Serbian leadership) to condemn the federal party leadership and take it over in the name of the "so called anti-bureaucratic revolution." (TANJUG, 12 April; *FBIS*, 13 April.)

The Twentieth LCY Central Committee Plenum endorsed the idea of holding a congress before the end of the year, but did not resolve the issue of whether the congress would be special, extraordinary, or early. Subsequently the 22 April LCY Central Committee Plenum adopted a face-saving compromise: the congress would be called both the Fourteenth *and* an Extraordinary Congress. More important, the decision that this congress would be run according to the rules of a regular congress and be prepared by a 63-member committee (regional plus JNA and top federal party members) headed by LCY president Stipe Šuvar made including extraordinary in its name a largely empty victory for those in Serbia who hoped to either control the agenda or gain increased delegates.

During the heated debate over this issue, one delegate from Bosnia-Hercegovina declared himself against a special congress and noted that some leaders and leaderships were behaving "like arsonists rather than fire-fighters" in debates over the deepening divisions between republic/provincial parties. A delegate from Montenegro who had favored a special congress summed up the feeling of public exhaustion with the wrangling at the plenum when he suggested that the energy spent on debating the congress's name might better go to solving development problems. (TANJUG, 19 April; *FBIS*, 20 April.)

Congress delegates were to be selected by an elaborate voting formula that took into account both size of the regional parties (i.e., number of rank-and-file members) and parity among parties. On the basis of membership the ratio was one delegate for each two thousand members, a total of 994. According to the parity principle, there would be 60 delegates from each republic, 40 from each autonomous province, and 30 from the party organization in the army for a total of 470, plus 204 members of LCY organs. These totals meant that 629 delegates would come from Serbia, 278 from Bosnia-Hercegovina, 240 from Croatia, 166 from Macedonia, 157 from Vojvodina, 139 from Slovenia, 123 from Montenegro, 112 from Kosovo, 86 from the LCY in JNA, and 7 from the basic LCY organizations of the federal organs. (TANJUG, 19 April; *FBIS*, 21 April.) Election rules required regional party organizations and the party organization in the JNA to have more candidates than delegates to be selected and to vote by secret ballot.

Because of the difficulty of scheduling the republic/provincial and JNA party conferences, the congress was postponed until January. The battle lines, however, were drawn from the beginning. The draft document on party reform, which was to serve as the basis for public debate before the party congress, was accepted by the LCY Presidium in early April. This draft had been produced by a Commission on Party Transformation set up at the October 1989 Seventeenth Central Committee Plenum. Disagreement centered over party or non-party pluralism.

The Slovene position was a stronger orientation toward the market economy and acceptance of political pluralism outside the LCY; Croatia initially had serious reservations. Šuvar made his opinion clear: noting that before the war Yugoslavia had 39 parties, he said that he feared "the multiparty system would produce a hyperpolarized, blocked and divided society in which the production of clashes would replace the production of goods." (*Borba*, 1, 2 January; *FBIS*, 18 January.) Yet by the time of the Croatian LCY congress, movements and parties were multiplying in Croatia, and the party leadership decided to embrace the inevitable.

The Serbian leadership was especially negative to retaining decision making by consensus and hostile to the idea of pluralism outside the party. Milošević personally criticized the draft document for not offering explicit answers to the reform of the political system, "not saying what kind of Yugoslavia we want." He disagreed with the document's protection of the constitutional duties and obligations of republics and provinces. However, somewhat ironically, given the subsequent Serbian break of economic relations with Slovenia, the Serbian strongman insisted that monetary, fiscal, and foreign economic relations must be under the jurisdiction of the federation. (TANJUG; *FBIS*, 7 April.)

Despite his success in re-establishing Serbian dominance over the autonomous provinces of Kosovo and Vojvodina via the amendments to the Serbian constitution, Milošević was overtaken by events. Serbia began the year on a steamroller of Serbian nationalism that successfully mobilized Serbs in Kosovo, Vojvodina, and Montenegro to sweep those who opposed Milošević out of power; by the end of the year the backlash not only in Slovenia and Croatia but in Macedonia and Bosnia-Hercegovina had virtually isolated the Serbian leadership. As one prominent political scientist in Belgrade said of the Macedonian party leadership election, "It is enough for us to support a candidate to make sure he will lose."

This internal isolation of Serbia contrasted sharply with the dramatic transformation of neighboring East and Central European communist regimes. With the crumbling of the Berlin Wall, communist parties and governments collapsed. As the 1990s approached, the Yugoslav and the Albanian Communists were the only ruling parties left.

The handwriting was on the wall. In December the Serbian party congress reluctantly agreed not to prevent the development of opposition parties. Notwithstanding the cynicism in Slovenia concerning this step on the road to a multiparty system, this shift in the Serbian position paved the way for a compromise at the upcoming party congress.

Domestic Affairs. *The government.* Although Branko Mikulić and his entire government resigned on 30 December 1988, the prime minister stayed on until his successor, Ante Marković, took over in March. The former prime minister defended the policy of his government and strongly implied that party interference had contributed to his difficulties. Appealing for increased separation of functions, he emphasized that it would be better for both the LCY Central Committee Presidium and the FEC if "each did its own work," that is, the party leadership should limit itself to the ideological/political question of socioeconomic relations and let the FEC perform the executive role of the assembly. The FEC should be accountable to the assembly and to the public. (Sarajevo, *Večernje novine*, 16 January; *FBIS*, 24 January.)

On 19 January the SFRY presidency proposed Ante Marković (64), Croatia, as the candidate for FEC president by a vote of five to two (*Borba*, 21, 22 January; *FBIS*, 26 January). Marković, a politi-

cian with an entrepreneurial spirit and substantial economic experience, was a supporter of the market economy.

Marković streamlined the FEC by dropping from 29 members to 19. The new government was selected from 85 candidates proposed by the republics and provinces. Nationality composition was represented in the FEC nominations as a whole, but was not the criterion when republics and provinces did not present Marković with "suitable candidates" for the posts he offered them (TANJUG, 15 March; *FBIS*, 22 March).

No sooner was the Marković team in place than sharp outbursts of nationalism erupted throughout the country due to the acceptance of amendments to the Serbian constitution legally reintegrating the autonomous provinces of Kosovo and Vojvodina into the republic. Serbs rejoiced. Emergency measures contained but did not control Albanian protests. Demonstrations in Slovenia protested violations of Albanian human rights and publicly supported Kosovar Albanian provincial autonomy and self-determination. The Serbian leadership stopped sniping at LCY president Stipe Šuvar, Croat, and began aiming heavy polemical volleys against Slovene government/party leaders for not bringing the truth as perceived in Belgrade to Ljubljana.

In a major horizontal rotation, key party/state leaders rotated not out but into another high-level position in a different bureaucracy. Party president Šuvar was elected to represent Croatia on the collective state presidency as was LCY presidium member Vasil Tupurkovski after a runoff in Macedonia. Slobodan Milošević gave up his position as head of the Serbian party and became republic president.

Much of the drama surrounding governmental politics centered on the elections for the new state presidency. It was Slovenia's turn to select the president of the presidency. To the consternation of some political observers in Belgrade, 56 percent of the 87.5 percent of the Slovene voters who went to the polls voted for a relatively unknown 39-year-old candidate, Dr. Janez Drnovšek. (TANJUG; *FBIS*, 3 April.)

The deadlocked contest in Bosnia-Hercegovina was particularly acrimonious. There was a considerable outcry over Dr. Nenad Kečmanović's withdrawal as a candidate for the SFRY presidency because of his "contacts with foreigners." This issue raised the ominous question of the role of security forces in Bosnia-Hercegovina and delayed the selection of the Bosnian representative to the state presidency while charges and countercharges were exchanged.

Drnovšek's difficult job was further complicated in September by the Slovene decision to ignore warnings from the state presidency and adopt an amendment to the Slovene constitution proclaiming the republic's right to secede from the country (*NYT*, 17 September).

Serbian suggestions that there be one popularly elected state president, this time from Serbia because Tito had been a Croat (*Borba*, 1, 2 April; *FBIS*, 6 April), were unacceptable to the leaderships of Slovenia and Croatia. A public opinion poll taken in the six republics, however, showed that of those questioned 61 percent (Serbia, 95 percent; Macedonia, 65 percent; Bosnia-Hercegovina, 60 percent; Slovenia, 55 percent; Croatia, 50 percent; and Montenegro, 45 percent) favored a one-person state president, even if there was disagreement about the method of selecting such a person. The same poll showed the preference for a four-year president at 40 percent for Bosnia-Hercegovina and 80 percent in Serbia with the other four republics ranging between 60 percent and 70 percent (*Borba*, 8 May; *FBIS*, 2 June).

The economy. The Mikulić government had had a negative economic performance rating. During its eighteen months in office, inflation galloped from 90 to 250 percent. The $20 billion foreign debt grew to an estimated $23 billion. The internal debt (what enterprises owe to one another) was officially put at $20 billion, although some economists said it could be double that figure. (RFE, *Research*, 10 January.) According to the Federal Institute for Statistics, the social product fell by 2 percent in 1988 (*Politika*, 9 January; *FBIS*, 26 January).

This economic crisis, however, was due to far more than federal mismanagement, for there was much republican/provincial fiscal irresponsibility as well. With some justice the former prime minister complained that

> The biggest problems are caused by disunity in the economic system . . . The SFRY Assembly adopts an act on the basis of the Constitution; then the Presidium of a republican LC CC says that the act has not been adopted on the basis of the Constitution and that it supports a stance on this question adopted by its own assembly . . . The organs of the federation are constantly under fire, not only by . . . the media but by organs of republics and provinces. That is why the

public has the impression that the federal organs are to blame for such things as failed investments about which republics and provinces usually decide. (*Večernje novine*, 16 January; *FBIS*, 24 January.)

Mikulić's replacement inherited a probationary economic policy propped up by temporary measures adopted by the SFRY presidency because there was no agreement between republic/provincial delegates in the federal assembly (Belgrade, TANJUG, 9 March; *FBIS*, 10 March). By the time Marković had put together a government and presented his program to the assembly, inflation was at 346.3 percent (Yugoslav Institute for Market Research, Belgrade, TANJUG, 13 March; *FBIS*, 20 March). Unemployment officially increased to 15 percent although many thought it was actually closer to 20 percent. Personal incomes had fallen 25 percent since 1980 and fell another 7.8 percent during 1988. (Belgrade Domestic Service, 16 March; *FBIS*, 20 March.)

Initially the new prime minister's long-term program for tackling the economic crisis by striking at the roots of inflation received widespread support; however, it could not withstand the austerity measures needed to put such a program into place. Exhausted by economic hardship and social unrest, the underdeveloped parts of the country demanded concrete anti-inflation measures to give them some relief. (Belgrade, TANJUG, 22 May; *FBIS*, 24 May.)

Despite skyrocketing inflation, Marković defended the government's policy and presented the federal assembly with laws necessary to establish the legal infrastructure of market socialism (*Borba*, 26 July; *FBIS*, 2 August), with predictable results.

Weary commuters came to view demonstrations in front of the assembly primarily as a traffic hazard and strikes as increasingly normal manifestations of political discontent. According to a report of the Republic/Provincial Council of the TU Federation, 1,194 strikes took place between January and August involving 273,543 workers. The largest number was 376 in Croatia; the smallest number was 34 in Vojvodina. (Belgrade, TANJUG, 1 October; *FBIS*, 6 October.) The main reasons for these work stoppages were salary payments that were too low or delayed. Belgrade trade unions insisted on anti-inflationary measures, reminding the federal and republican politicians that every 50th citizen in Belgrade was on some kind of social assistance. (Belgrade, TANJUG, 18 August; *FBIS*, 22 August.)

As the summer wore on, Yugoslav farmers got into the act. Basing the price of wheat on world market prices was sound economic policy, but unacceptable to domestic farmers, who would receive less than $1 per hour for their labor. Between three thousand and ten thousand outraged farmers marched in the rain to demand that the federal assembly stop discriminating against agriculture in favor of industry, increase their access to the policy process, and adopt specific reforms ranging from elimination of harmful taxes to "healthy competition and anti-monopoly laws." The cornerstone of the workers and farmers' demands was an end to inflation. (Belgrade, TANJUG, 28 August; *FBIS*, 29 August.)

The government responded with promises to prepare additional anti-inflation measures. However, although there was total agreement that inflation, officially edging toward 800 percent, was unbearable, there was no agreement on what to do about it.

The core of the reforms—independent enterprises without strong state influence, market criteria, equal status of enterprises under all forms of ownership, "profit as the ultimate objective" (Belgrade, TANJUG, 12 March; *FBIS*, 13 March)—remained acceptable. Yet demands for market socialism were combined with the contradictory insistence that the means for getting there (i.e., the instruments of economic reform) not be put into place before "equalization of all economic sectors; private to social, foreign to domestic, agricultural to everyone else." As one Croatian daily summed up the government's dilemma, "The tragedy of Ante Marković's government lies in the fact that its term belongs to a time when there is no economic policy measure which equally hits and benefits everybody" (*Vjesnik*, 20 August; *FBIS*, 31 August). The Sarajevo newspaper *Oslobojenje* attacked the prime minister's program as a sellout to capitalism with the prediction that his government was doomed in any case (*Borba*, 25 August; *FBIS*, 1 September).

Like the aborted campaign for market socialism in 1965, there was deep disagreement on who would pay for the cost of change. The northern, relatively developed republics are more willing to accept the market's verdict than their less-developed southern neighbors because genuine economic reform means closing down some 10 percent of Slovene firms. In Montenegro as many as 80 percent of the enterprises could go bankrupt. Thus a Belgrade political scientist flatly concluded that "no Montenegrin politician can accept that sacrifice no matter what he believes about market economies" (*CSM*, 16 May).

The Marković government held that anti-inflation measures could not succeed without creating a legal foundation for a market economy and the "material conditions" for reforms. Piece by piece the scaffolding went up. Fought through the assembly were amendments to existing laws on accounting enterprises, banks, and other financial institutions and new laws on labor relations, foreign trade, commodity reserves, securities, and money and capital markets.

By the end of the year laws before the federal assembly on foreign currency, prices, and taxation had become deadlocked by republic/provincial disagreements. Nonetheless, Marković insisted that sufficient preconditions had been met to move forward in the war against inflation.

Indeed, the prime minister's report to the assembly contained many favorable economic indicators. Exports were up. There was a $2.3 billion balance of payments surplus. Foreign exchange reserves had reached $5.8 billion. The foreign debt had dropped to $16.6 billion. Only 16 percent of the foreign currency went to debt servicing as compared with 45 percent "in the most difficult periods." Industrial production was up 1.9 percent, and agricultural production, by 6 percent.

Marković's shock treatments were in line with the theories of Harvard Professor Jeffery Sachs or what in December 1989 might be called the Polish road to capitalism. The dinar was to become convertible, pegged to the deutschmark at a seven to one ratio (the U.S. dollar would be twelve to one) and not changed until June 1990. Yugoslavs would have the right to exchange dinars for foreign currency at the official rate.

Convertibility would be combined with a tight monetary policy, a balanced budget, a floating interest rate, and market-determined prices (with the exception of some infrastructural services such as energy and utilities, where prices would be frozen until June 1990). Most painful for the alienated, increasingly desperate Yugoslav population was that wages would be frozen at the November 1989 rate until June. (*Borba*, 19 December.)

There were many complaints: the Serbs condemned the program out of hand, and the Slovenes resisted the taxation measures. Yet during the infighting, it became clear that Serbian detractors were largely isolated. When agreement could not be reached, the federal assembly resorted to temporary emergency measures and gave Marković the green light. Ordinary Yugoslavs who were being asked to pay the price were at least relieved something was being done to deal with the estimated 2,000 to 5,000 percent inflation. (TANJUG, 29 December.)

Thus in 1989 the Yugoslav government set out on what many viewed as its last chance to salvage the economy. On the plus side the economy had made enough progress to gain support from the International Monetary Fund. This plan, the only strategy that had any current credibility among international lenders, had been worked out with the power players in the international financial community, would facilitate debt rescheduling, and would receive the maximum of available new resources.

On the minus side, given the dramatic transformation of the rest of Eastern Europe, Yugoslavia had fallen to the bottom of the visibility charts, never a good position from which to seek funding. Still worse the Marković government had little control over the political preconditions for success. As one commentator warned when the LCY Presidium joined the chorus of those demanding anti-inflation measures: "Everybody knows that inflation cannot be crushed in a country in an atmosphere dominated by interethnic quarrels, confrontations, swindles, suspicions and aggressive nationalist revivals... Reason and expertise have virtually no chance in such a climate and must make room for the irrational craziness which is uninhibitedly spreading." (*Borba*, 26, 27 August; *FBIS*, 7 September.)

In short, the success or failure of economic reform in Yugoslavia is less a matter of the economic soundness of the plan than of the willingness of republic/provincial leaders to implement it. Serbian president Slobodan Milošević has the power to make or break the move to a market economy.

As a former banker, Milošević has supported many of Marković's plans. Indeed, in a September interview with a *New York Times* journalist, Milošević called for a unified market economy, central control over a unified monetary system, taxation, relations with foreign countries, and a central bank to operate along the lines of the federal reserve. He advocates a market of capital, labor, and technological knowledge and accepts the full economic independence of enterprises. (*Politika*, 10 September; *FBIS*, 18 September.)

Unfortunately, whether intentionally, as charged in Slovenia and Croatia, or inadvertently, the Milošević personality cult created a climate in which his economic common sense could not withstand Serbian anger at the refusal of Slovene au-

thorities to allow a mass meeting in the Slovene capital, Ljubljana, by Serbs intent on bringing their version of the "truth about Kosovo" to Slovenia. The response—breaking Serbian political and economic relations with Slovenia and pressure by Milošević's supporters to cut off existing contracts with Slovene partners—undermined the united market, enterprise independence, and the Serbian economy.

As the year ended there were signs that the Serbian economic boycott of Slovenia was quietly lapsing. However, it was still unclear whether Serbia would accept the prime minister's emergency measures and allow him to put the Yugoslav economy on the road to recovery.

The nationalities question. During 1989 national/ethnic tensions in Yugoslavia skyrocketed in tandem with inflation. Questions proliferated, but there was a shortage of agreed-upon answers. National feelings were inflamed by confrontational polemics among regional politicians who substituted populist appeals to national identity for economic performance in their search for legitimacy.

Republic media hurled charges of national separatism at Kosovar Albanians who did not accept the diminished autonomy of the province enshrined in Serbian constitutional amendments and Slovene determination to protect government by consensus and charges of national unitarianism against the Serbian drive to reintegrate both autonomous provinces into Serbia proper and attempts to use mass meetings of Serbs in other republics as an instrument of Serbian policy.

Slobodan Milošević, the Serbian party leader/then president, struggled with Azem Vlasi, former president of the provincial party, throughout February as striking Albanian miners and students protested Vlasi's removal from his federal party posts and demanded rejection of the centralizing Serbian constitutional amendments and the resignation of what they viewed as a Serbian puppet leadership of the provincial party/government. (Priština, *Rilindja*, 5 February; *FBIS*, 10 February.)

These protests climaxed in an eight-day hunger strike by thirteen hundred miners from the Stari Trg zinc mine in Titova Mitrovica. Students at Priština University joined the hunger strike in solidarity with the miners, and an estimated 40,000 Albanians went on a general strike in support of the Stari Trg miners (TANJUG, 9 March; *FBIS*, 10 March). The three targeted members of the Albanian leadership—Rahman Morina, president of the provincial party committee; Husamedin Azemi, Priština's municipal party president; and longtime Kosovo leader Ali Sukrija—resigned, thereby getting the Albanian miners out of the mines, but setting off a protest hunger strike by an estimated eight hundred Serbian and Montenegrin miners in another Trepca mine in Leposavic (RFE, *Report*, 8 March).

Once the Albanian miners were safely hospitalized, the resignations of the ethnic Albanian Kosovo leaders were reversed by the LCY CC Presidium. The state presidency declared emergency measures in Kosovo, reinforced the federal militia, partially mobilized the army, banned all public protests, put restrictions on press coverage, and declared a curfew. Vlasi and other former Albanian leaders were arrested for "counterrevolutionary" activity, allegedly organizing or at least encouraging the striking miners. According to Lazar Mojsov, the Macedonian representative on the state presidency, security services had uncovered a "blueprint" for a three-stage ethnic Albanian uprising in the province. (*Borba*, 2 March; RFE, 8 March.)

Although the emergency measures did not eliminate the Albanian protests, they did make it possible to hold the much-heralded six hundredth anniversary celebration of the 1389 battle of Kosovo without violence. In Serbia there was much satisfaction with the perceived benefits of Milošević's firmhanded approach; the hope there was that the amendments to the Serbian constitution would prevent the out-migration of Serbs and Montenegrins from the province and, from the Serbian perspective, equalize the position of Serbia within Yugoslavia.

Yet those steps considered by Serbs so necessary to equalize Serbia were seen by many Kosovar Albanians as a means of reducing provincial autonomy to an in name only proposition, abandoning the 1974 constitution and condemning them to permanent second-class citizenship. Although striking miners had been coaxed out of the mine by subsequently unkept promises, their complaint—equating "the entire Albanian nationality with nationalists and separatists" (*Borba*, 4, 5 February)—had not been dealt with.

Moreover, the handling of the Stari Trg strike and the imposition of emergency measures further polarized the republican leaderships, for within Slovenia and Croatia there was substantial open support for what many in the northern republics viewed as a justified demand for political dialogue rather than a separatist movement on the part of Kosovar Albanians. Reportedly, 245,000 Slovenes signed a petition against the introduction of emergency mea-

sures in Kosovo. (Ljubljana, *Delo*, 28 February; *FBIS*, 3 March.) Their dismay was articulated dramatically when more than a thousand Slovenes gathered at Canker Cultural Hall in Ljubljana to plea for reason, peace, and cooperation over what they viewed as repression of ethnic Albanians. The Canker Hall meeting was carried live by Ljubljana radio and television. Slovene party leader Milan Kučan and the head of the Slovene Socialist Alliance joined the president of the Slovenian Farmers Alliance, Ivan Omam, and the president of the Slovenian Democratic Alliance, Dimitrij Rupel, on the platform.

Predictably, the Serbs were hurt, offended, and furious. In their view the Slovene leadership had sold out to separatism and was undermining Yugoslavia as well as unfairly attacking Serbia. Thus following the Canker Hall meeting, the contest fluctuated between Milošević and Slovenian party president Milan Kučan and between Slovene and Serbian leaderships, all of which further fanned the flames of national passions. The Kosovo situation was intensely significant for Serbia and Slovenia alike. To even think about republic status for the province was, for the Serbs, to destroy historical Serbia. The Serbian warriors who died trying to hold back the Turks had made the Field of the Blackbirds, Kosovo Polje, sacred; the home of the Serbian church was in Peč, in Kosovo. For the Slovenes, 1.7 million Albanians were being deprived of their constitutional status for what Slovenes saw as endemic Serbian hegemonic ambitions. Mass meetings had toppled the governments of Kosovo, Vojvodina, and Montenegro in a steamroller of Serbian nationalism that must be stopped or there would be no place for the 1.7 million Slovenes in Yugoslavia.

Serbs resented what they saw as Slovene insensitivity, elitism, presumption of superiority, and economic exploitation of Serbian resources. Slovenes felt that Serbs were blind to the fears created by "greater Serbia" rhetoric and that they had no understanding of the democratic process. Slovenes experienced Serbian nationalism as a primitive assault on reason, considered Serbian law and order measures in Kosovo repressive, and believed that Serbs boycotted Slovene goods because the less efficient Serbian enterprises did not want to pay their bills. Reported acts of vandalism against Slovenes working in Belgrade and Serbs vacationing in Slovenia made matters worse.

In May the Slovene presidency, in an effort to deescalate, sent a letter to the Serbian presidency saying that notwithstanding Milošević's attacks on Slovenia there were some grounds for agreement with respect to the Serbian leader's more-positive goals. The letter suggested that the leaderships of Slovenia and Serbia meet to iron out their differences "for the sake of the Yugoslav federation." (*Borba*, 31 May; *FBIS*, 6 June.) The Serbian leadership, however, was not interested in talking unless its Slovene counterpart was willing to admit the error of its ways.

At this point those who feared that Yugoslavia might not survive what was increasingly seen as a no-win contest began to allow other Yugoslav republics to get into the act. In Bosnia-Hercegovina, *Oslobodjenje* analyzed the Serb-Slovene confrontation as the outcome not of different views on Kosovo but of "two diametrically opposed political concepts" and warned that ultimatums are not the answer to "this bone stuck in the Yugoslav throat." The Sarajevo newspaper then criticized Milošević for responding to the Slovene presidency request for dialogue with a political ultimatum and suggested that the conclusions of the European parliamentary delegation after their visit to Kosovo supported the Slovene call for a political solution to the problems of the province and that Serbs should take this into account. It went on to call on the Yugoslav federal presidency to bring about a reconciliation to Slovene-Serb bickering. (*Borba*, 8 June; *FBIS*, 19 June.)

Others took sides more openly. In Vojvodina, *Dnevnik* (Novi Sad) blamed "the self-invited guest" (Slovenia) for closing the door to dialogue. In Croatia, *Vjesnik* (Zagreb) strongly supported the Slovene position, while the Montenegrin *Pobjeda* (Titograd) contented itself with warning of the consequences of continued nationalist polarization (TANJUG, 5 June; *FBIS*, 6 June).

Before the end of the month, Slovenia made it clear that if compromises could not be reached, the Slovenes were not willing to play by Serbian rules. The Slovene Assembly Commission on the Right to Secede stressed that Slovenia was a part of Yugoslavia on the basis of *the Slovene nation's right to make its own decisions*, which included the *right to secede or join*. (TANJUG, 16 June; *FBIS*, 19 June.) Not surprisingly, this wording later reappeared in the controversial amendment to the Slovene constitution.

Milan Kučan, president of the Slovene LC, spelled out the implications for Slovene participation in the proposed Fourteenth Extraordinary LCY Congress by asserting that either the congress would be pledged to a democratic dialogue on equal footing or the Slovenes would boycott it (*Delo*, 20 June; *FBIS*, 22 June). The Slovene LC Presidium was even more explicit, threatening that if Slovenia was outvoted on the key questions concerning the LCY program and statute, they would convene an extraordinary Slovene congress to decide whether to unilaterally cancel compliance with democratic centralism or declare complete organizational independence of the Slovene LC (*Borba*, 21 June; *FBIS*, 27 June).

The City Committee of the Belgrade League of Communists then accused *Borba* of conducting an anti-Serbian policy against the president of the Serbian presidency, Slobodan Milošević. In response the SAWPY newspaper's editorial collegium denied being anti-Serb, anti-Croatian, anti-Slovene, anti-Macedonian, or anti-Montenegrin and maintained that *Borba* was a Yugoslav, socialist, democratic discussion forum for critical open dialogue. (*Borba*, 12 July; *FBIS*, 14 July.)

Meanwhile, the Serbian LC CC session devoted to international relations defended changes in the Serbian constitution that would allow more control over the autonomous provinces as being in the interest of Albanians in Kosovo as well as of Serbs and Montenegrins. The session insisted that Serbs fight against nationalism and that the hysteria in the Slovene and Croat press concerning Serbian nationalism was only to frighten people. (TANJUG, 13 July; *FBIS*, 14 July.)

The depth of Serbian frustration was captured by Mirko Stojić's claim to the LCY CC Commission for International Relations that Yugoslavia was in a "war" in which all means were used against one republic to prevent it from constituting itself as agreed (reintegrating Kosovo) and his demand to know how the Slovenes would feel if Italy raised the question of the Slovene coast and Serbia supported Rome (*Borba*, 21 July; *FBIS*, 27 July).

The view from Zagreb (like that from Ljubljana) was in direct opposition to the view prevailing in Belgrade. Dragutin Dimitrović, secretary of the Presidium of Croatian LC, dismissed Milošević's thesis about the Serbs being an endangered nation in Yugoslavia as

an attempt to rally Serbs throughout Yugoslavia, redefine the postwar rules of the game, and redraw the borders of republics. We will not be provoked . . . We are reacting with increasing legality, keeping cool, and enabling the system's institutions to act correctly in preserving the SFRY . . . For a year this thing was swirling around Yugoslavia, was tolerated, and ran unchecked . . . We have drawn the line. It remains for federal institutions to see that laws are implemented. (*Borba*, 24 July; *FBIS*, 28 July.)

According to Slovene interpretations, the recall of U.S. ambassador Zivorad Kovačević from Washington had sinister overtones. A "capable and responsible ambassador whose works were highly respected at home and abroad" had been sacrificed to the forces of growing nationalism by "those who want to tailor Yugoslavia according to their own blueprint" (Maribor, *Večer*, quoted in *Borba*, 3 August; *FBIS*, 9 August).

Reported Belgrade police brutality against Boris Muževič—an LCY CC Presidium member from Slovenia who had spoken out against Serbian nationalism—when he was arrested for speeding, confirmed the worst fears in Ljubljana. Muževič admitted the traffic offense and described the beating on Slovene radio. (Radio Ljubljana, 24 August; *FBIS*, 25 August.) Subsequently, the LCY Presidium condemned the behavior of the Belgrade police and regretted that all sides had blown the incident out of proportion in view of worsening international relations (TANJUG, 23 August; *FBIS*, 24 August).

In this politicized climate the announced intention of Kosovar Serbs to bus 40,000–100,000 of their dedicated supporters into Ljubljana on 1 December to bring the "truth about Kosovo" to Slovenia elicited rejection and still more hostility from Slovenes. When the Slovene counteroffer—that a delegation of Serbs and Montenegrins come and make their case to the Slovene parliament or on Slovenia television—was ignored, the Slovene leadership banned all meetings on that day, and the uninvited guests stayed home. This, in turn, precipitated the Serbian break of political and economic relations with Slovenia.

As the year ended, other republics, worried and fed up, aimed increasingly strident criticism at Serbs and Slovenes alike. In his speech to the Bosnian-Hercegovian LC congress, Nijaz Duraković, republic president, expressed the widely shared opinion that such interrepublic squabbles were not the way to get the country out of crisis.

We can see where the conflicts between the leaderships of Serbia and Slovenia have led to. . . . No leadership will have political legitimacy if they take measures . . . limiting the functioning of Yugoslavia as a united country. . . . Neither the leadership in the SR

of Serbia nor that in the SR of Slovenia has the right to risk in such a drastic manner not only the integrity and independence, but the very survival of Yugoslavia. (TANJUG, 5 December; *FBIS*, 15 December.)

Bosnian fears of a spreading Milošević movement were heightened by reports of a Serbian Orthodox feast in Bosnia at which pictures of Milošević were surrounded by pictures of saints. An estimated 23 buses arrived from Kosovo, and it was alleged that all passengers traveled free. (Zagreb, *Vjesnik*, 14 August; *FBIS*, 22 August.)

The federal chamber of the Yugoslavia parliament requested that Serbian and Slovene assemblies move into the breach left by the party presidencies that were still not speaking and called for an end to interethnic and interrepublic conflicts. The parliament characterized such conflicts as "in violation of the Constitution and the law, of human rights, and freedoms" and deplored disruption of the Yugoslav united market. (TANJUG, 21 December; *FBIS*, 22 December.)

Whether in response to the federal governmental intervention or because the warring republican leaders were exhausted, there did seem to be some movement in both Ljubljana and Belgrade. Kučan stressed that the amendments to the republic constitution were not a screen for Slovene separatism, but a safeguard of the democratic nature of the Yugoslav federation. Warning that "ultimatum-style policies" had brought the country to the brink of civil war, he insisted that the consequences of such policies did not have to be the destiny of Yugoslavia. (TANJUG; *FBIS*, 22 December.)

For his part, Milošević described the dispute as one "between conservative and progressive forces and not between the two leaderships." He maintained that there was "a way out of the current situation" and that "conditions exist for a settlement." (TANJUG, 21 December; *FBIS*, 22 December.)

Grudging acceptance of multiparty participation (albeit after republic elections in November) at the Serbian LC congress narrowed political differences between Serbia and Slovenia and set the stage for a temporary end to their differences. Serbia was now largely isolated, whereas Milošević's apparent victory over Azem Vlasi resulted in international and domestic criticism of the treatment of imprisoned Kosovar Albanians (*Amnesty International Newsletter*, July). Indeed, there were even signs that Vlasi might be pardoned by the federal presidency (*Borba*, 28 July; RFE, *Research*, 17 August).

The year that had started with Serbian strongman Slobodan Milošević on an apparent political roll ended with increasing questions about his cadre policy, his ability to deliver on the economy, and even payoffs in Kosovo. Such questions would probably have been still more insistent had not his supporters felt obligated to defend him against the barrage of attacks from other republics; ironically, Milošević's Slovene and Croat detractors served him well. Likewise Stipe Šuvar's most vocal Serbian opponents were as important as his admirers in assuring the former LCY president his seat as the Croatian representative on the SFRY presidency.

Alternative Movements and Parties. Throughout the year alternative movements and parties proliferated because they could legally exist under the umbrella of the Socialist Alliance. Although some were willing to work within that framework, others were not. In March the SFRY presidency tried to ease the situation with a statement that founding political parties was incompatible with the Yugoslav constitution. This opinion was promptly rejected by the Presidium of the Socialist Democratic Alliance of Slovenia on the grounds that only the constitutional court of Slovenia could decide on an organization's legality. (*Delo*, 22 March; *FBIS*, 23 March.)

The alternative movements and organizations ranged from the twenty thousand protesting environmentalists from the industrial town of Zenica who claimed that "Zenica is Chernobyl in monthly repayments" (TANJUG, 20 January; *FBIS*, 27 January) to associations for the return of Serbs and Montenegrins to Kosovo to Social Democrats, nationalist organizations, human rights committees, and support groups for a united Europe. The following is a list of these organizations:

Association for Yugoslav Democratic Initiative, Zagreb. According to its Manifesto its purpose is "political and cultural activity on behalf of democratic institutionalization and integration of Yugoslavia." The association's bylaws were published (*Borba*, 8 June; JPRS-EEU, 89-077) at the founding meeting 1 February (Belgrade Domestic Service, 2 February; *FBIS*, 9 February). According to Branko Horvat the association does not intend to become a political party, but plans to remain a movement for the democratic transformation of Yugoslavia through creating a community of citizens and federal units. Advocating continuity with the Korcula Philosophy School and Praxis, the association does not want to have anything to do with

SAWPY. Therefore the Croatian Secretariat for Internal Affairs refused to register it on 3 April (*Borba*, 8 June; JPRS-EEU, 89-077). In March the alliance began publishing the country's first unofficial newspaper, *Republika* (Paris, AFP; *FBIS*, 13 April).

Croatian Social Liberal Alliance. Registered with SAWPY, this alliance's stated goals include a national referendum on issues of political pluralism, multiparty systems, elimination of landholding limits, the free market, federalism founded on consensus with self-determination and right of secession (confederation) and transformation of the Socialist Alliance of Croatia into the Mass Alliance of Equal Political Organizations (*Vjesnik*, Saturday supplement, 27 May; *JPRS-EEU*, 89-079).

Green Action (split). This association of citizens is dedicated to ecological initiatives to spread knowledge about global, Yugoslav, Croatian, Dalmatian, and local environmental problems. A movement, not a party, its bylaws appeared in *Borba*, 8 June (*JPRS-EEU*, 89-079).

Croatian Democratic Community. Not a separate political organization, but a "rallying point" for citizens committed to democracy, this group favors an independent Socialist Alliance as an umbrella for differing ideological aspirations, not a transmission belt of the LCY, and emphasizes Croatia and Yugoslavia joining the European Community (*Borba*, 8 June; *JPRS-EEU*, 89-079).

Citizens' League for a United Europe (split). The league, a member of SAWPY, advocates a European community and a united Europe to include Yugoslavia and emphasizes human rights and culture (ibid.).

Committee for Protection of Human Rights. Made up of some twenty thousand individual members and three hundred collective members, the committee was originally founded to protect the rights of journalists being tried in a military court in Ljubljana (Zagreb, *Danas*, 1 November 1988; *FBIS*, 26 January).

Slovene Peasant Alliance. This alliance's stated goal is to make it possible for peasants and farm workers to participate in shaping political decisions. Favoring the development of family holdings as basic production units, the abolition of maximum landholding, and a tax policy to give incentives for efficient farming, it is a member of Socialist Alliance program (*JPRS-EEU*, 7 July). Founded 1988, its first annual general meeting reported twenty branches and a membership of twenty thousand. (*Delo*, 16 March; *FBIS*, 27 March.)

Slovene Democratic Union. The program statement advocates political pluralism, parliamentary democracy, and a new constitution to protect the sovereignty of Slovenia in its contractual relationship with the Yugoslav community. Founded in Ljubljana 11 January, the union wants civilian control and equality of languages in the JNA and agrees to exist within SAWPY as long as the Socialist Alliance takes democratizing itself seriously. Rejecting party political monopoly, the union emphasizes the rights of citizens to public service regardless of origin, sex, conviction, religion, or sexual orientation. (Ljubljana, *Mladina*, 23 December 1988; *FBIS*, 5 January.)

Academic Anarchist Anti-Federal Alliance. Its program asserts that it is the second illegal party in Yugoslavia (the LCY is the first one) and that it has two aims: legalization of the LC and scrapping SAWPY (*Borba*, 26 January; *FBIS*, 9 February).

Social Democratic Alliance of Slovenia. This alliance supports a multiparty system and a parliamentary democracy, demanding a new Slovene constitution to protect Slovene sovereignty and statehood and redefine Slovene defense policy. Committed to a Yugoslavia that allows all republics to express their differences and developmental needs (i.e., federalism based on self-determination and mutual advantage) its foreign policy orientation is Slovene and Yugoslav inclusion in Europe's economic, technical, and cultural milieu. Its annual meeting was scheduled for 16 February. (Ljubljana, *Mladina*, 3 February; *FBIS*, 13 February; text of program, *Borba*, 8 June; *JPRS-EEU*, 89-077.)

Slovene Christian Social Movement. Not a political party, but a movement in favor of all social forces desiring "constructive development of the Slovenian nation," it has a critical attitude to socialist reality, but does not consider itself anticommunist (*Borba*, 8 June; *JPRS-EEU*, 89-077).

Yugoslav Alliance (Ljubljana). Working for the cultural, political, and economic integration of southern Slav peoples respecting their particu-

larities, the alliance's platform is a state based on law, human rights, protection of the environment, and rapid transformation of the political and economic system in the sense of strengthening Yugoslav statehood (ibid.).

New Democratic Circle (Novi Sad). The circle focuses on sociopolitical issues, particularly human rights in all parts of Yugoslavia (Novi Sad, *Dnevnik*, 24 January; reported in *Borba*, 26 January).

Democratic party (Titograd). This is the first party in opposition to the League of Communists (Zagreb Domestic Service, 15 December; *FBIS*, 18 December).

These new political actors combined with the sobering Romanian example undoubtedly contributed to the LCY CC year-end recommendation that the party give up its 45-year monopoly of power "to prove," as party secretary Stefan Korošec put it, "that we do not find ourselves at the tail of reforms in socialism" (*NYT*, 27 December).

Soldiers in politics. National and ethnic tensions, violence in Kosovo, and disagreement over emergency measures meant the continued role of the Yugoslav military/political actors in the arena of internal security as well as on issues of economic reform and political pluralism. Taking the form of a running battle between Slovene critics and federal defenders of the Yugoslav armed forces, on the most extreme end of the spectrum there were statements such as the following:

> Yugoslavia has joined the famous club of military dictatorship states . . . by a march of generals through institutions. Uniformed apparatchiks can now topple anybody in the party oligarchy: Marković, Milošević, or Kučan. It is also obvious that the civilian party top leadership has not even a minimum of influence on the dirty business of the Yugoslav military industry." (*Mladina*, 14 April; *FBIS*, 15 May.)

Dobroslav Paraga, founder of the Croatian Human Rights Committee who now lives in Ljubljana, asserted that army and intelligence services were forming a state within a state in Yugoslavia. He speculated that if multiethnic conflict escalated, an army coup was possible. (*Frankfurter Rundschau*, 24 June; *FBIS*, 25 July.)

Conversely, Janez Drnovšek, state president, dismissed the suggestion that, if Yugoslav politicians cannot get together, a general might take power and insisted that the army had supported all trends for normalization and stabilization of the political/economic situation (interview with *Der Spiegel*, 22 May; *FBIS*, 23 May). In June the FEC issued a report criticizing the attacks on the army as "a weapon in the hands of enemies of this country, enemies of our integrity, our federal organization" (*Politika*, 30 June; *FBIS*, 5 July).

The army's message was unambiguous. Concerning Kosovo, General Mirković, chief of the JNA general staff, stressed that emergency measures were necessary for the stability of the province and the security of Yugoslavia. In his view it was "illusory and extremely unrealistic" to assume that those measures could be quickly rescinded. However, Mirković also rejected the idea that such measures could be a lasting situation: "the military leadership has always believed and continues to believe that the key to the Kosovo lock is political action and the economic prosperity of the province." (*Narodna armija*, 20 April; *FBIS*, 3 May.)

On the issue of reform, Secretary of Defense Veljko Kadijević assured his civilian colleagues that the army supported a modern, efficient federal state; a modern, socialist market economy; and the further democratization of society. He opposed "anti-socialist forces for the restoration of capitalism as well as those who are disintegrating and destroying Yugoslavia" and said that the army was ready to defend the country's territorial integrity and constitutional order.

Along with these general statements concerning the military mission were complaints of increasing nationalist sentiments among conscripts and pledges to protect the standard of living for members of the JNA, especially those whose duties "expose them to long-term increased efforts caused predominantly by unfavorable trends in society" (a euphemism for dangerous duty in Kosovo). (TANJUG, 26 May; *FBIS*, 30 May.)

This raises the fundamental conflict between the corporate interests of the armed forces on the one hand and the desperate need for resources in non-military sectors of the economy on the other. General Svetislav Popović, in his appeal for the stable, timely financing of armed forces, promoted the case of the JNA. According to his figures, over the last fifteen years funds set aside for the army had dropped from 6.17 percent to 4.6 percent of the national income and there had been a 15.8 percent fall in real army pay over the last year. (TANJUG,

14 June; *FBIS*, 15 June.) These are legitimate concerns; however, even at 4.6 percent of the national income, the armed forces gets 57 percent of the Yugoslav federal budget (TANJUG; *FBIS*, 19 July). Another 11.4 percent of that budget also goes to army-related spending for disability and veterans' pensions. Compare this with the 6.6 percent for the insufficiently developed republics and Kosovo and 6.5 percent for the work of running the government. (*Borba*, 19 July; *FBIS*, 25 July.)

General Simeon Bunčič may have been right in warning the Twenty-fifth LCY CC Plenum that the Yugoslav revolution is in more danger from interethnic quarrels led by republicans than from enemies of socialism and self-management (Belgrade Domestic Service, 30 July; *FBIS*, 31 July). Apart from civilian mismanagement, these questions remain: Where are the funds to come from to finance a political solution to the agony of Kosovo? What political role will the JNA play should the "unsuitable" party pluralism of today (in the eyes of the Yugoslav chief of staff, Lt. Gen. Slagoje Adzic) (TANJUG, 6 December; *FBIS*, 7 December) become the reality of tomorrow?

Foreign Policy. Throughout the year Yugoslav foreign policymakers had four primary tasks:

1. Preparing for the Ninth Summit of the Nonaligned Movement (NAM) in Belgrade in 4–7 September
2. Positioning Yugoslavia so as to minimize costs and maximize benefits associated with the European integration process on the road to a united Europe in 1992
3. Mobilizing external resources and the understanding of international financial circles to save the country from economic disaster
4. Containing the damage to Yugoslavia's image and prestige caused by ethnic violence and human rights violations in Kosovo

Foreign Minister Lončar spelled out Yugoslav foreign policy objectives in Ljubljana. He stressed Yugoslav commitment to modernizing the NAM and adapting it to the transformation of Soviet–U.S. relations, the new Europe, and the imperatives of the twenty-first century. This endeavor, the *perestroika* of NAM's political style, focused on the need for short documents that could serve as a basis for dialogue with those outside the movement. There was an effort to recast the north-south dialogue into a less confrontational mode that would emphasize mutual advantage and partnership.

With respect to Europe, the foreign minister cautioned that the need to move closer to the European community must not come at the expense of Yugoslavia's political integrity. Nonetheless, he recommended moving from third group relations with the European Community (EC) to special status and expanding technological and financial cooperation. This process was directly related to the health of the Yugoslav economy, which would undoubtedly benefit if the EC could be convinced to take part in infrastructure projects in Yugoslavia as a part of Europe's own infrastructure needs. Lončar's concrete program included dialogue with the European Council and intensified cooperation with the European parliament. (TANJUG, 14 February; *FBIS*, 16 February.)

These objectives dovetailed with those put forward by Prime Minister Ante Marković when he took the job as head of the government in March. Marković reassured those who feared that Yugoslav chairmanship of the NAM would slow down the move to Europe, insisting that the importance of the nonaligned summit and Yugoslavia's role in modernizing the NAM strengthened "our possibilities for firmer relations with Europe." He put Dzevad Muježinović, minister without portfolio, in charge of organizing the summit.

Marković referred to specific forms of regional cooperation such as the Ale-Adria working community and inter-Balkan cooperation. Expressing impatience with the pace of Yugoslav European policy, the prime minister spoke of the "need to avoid endless discussion and engage in functional links to Europe." He pointed to the fact that *perestroika* opened new possibilities for economic ties with the Council for Mutual Economic Assistance as well. (Belgrade Domestic Service, 16 March; *FBIS*, 20 March.)

The Nonaligned Movement. In April, SFRY president-elect Janez Drnovšek addressed Slovene concerns about the Yugoslav role in the ninth nonaligned summit given Yugoslavia's current economic and political difficulties. Drnovšek linked supporting a summit with concrete economic objectives, especially a settlement of the debtor crisis plaguing developing countries, to Yugoslavia's own indebtedness problem. At the same time he spoke of his vision of Yugoslavia as a democratic state with an independent and fair legal system, included in other organizations besides NAM and "with its

place in the European Common Market." (TANJUG, 7 April; *FBIS*, 10 April.)

The Yugoslav foreign policy/government establishment, then, did not see the trade-off between Yugoslavia's commitment to nonalignment and its need for Europe that appeared obvious to many Yugoslavs in Belgrade as well as in Ljubljana. Yugoslav preparations for the ninth summit provided an opportunity for numerous economic discussions. By mid-August there had been 80 high-level consultations, and Lončar personally met with representatives of some 50 nonaligned countries. (TANJUG, 17 August; *FBIS*, 22 August.)

This second Belgrade summit of the nonaligned was more than four times the size of the movement's founding Belgrade summit in 1961, which was attended by 25 member states and three observers. In 1989 Belgrade hosted delegates and journalists from 102 member countries, ten observer countries, ten observing international organizations and liberation movements, nineteen guest countries, and 33 guest international organizations. If Western analysis had paid more attention to the guest list, Washington might not have been caught so flat-footed by the dramatic changes in East Central Europe that followed. For the first time delegations from Bulgaria, Czechoslovakia, East Germany, Hungary, and Poland attended. The extravaganza went remarkably smoothly despite Col. Moammar Khadafy's insistence on bringing his camels (subsequently donated to the Belgrade zoo) and some differences between Yugoslav and Libyan security.

On the substantive side, the extensive presummit networking paid off. Although there was a hardening of the Yugoslav draft document on South Africa, for the most part an evenhanded approach and a moderate tone survived in the final documents of the summit. (Belgrade, *Review of International Affairs*, 20 September.) To the extent that these documents were vehicles for communicating with those outside the movement, the modernized NAM communication was the crucial first step in making the movement's economic objectives more obtainable.

The Yugoslav foreign policy establishment considered the summit a success. Even in Ljubljana, where the strongest reservations had been expressed, there was a sense that, notwithstanding Yugoslavia's responsibility for chairing the movement, the Foreign Ministry had at last turned its attention to what Slovenes perceived as their number one problem: how not to be sitting on the sidelines in 1992.

Relations with the West. Yugoslav relations with the West centered on a search for resources to help deal with the country's economic crisis, attempts to establish channels of access to the integration processes associated with Europe in 1992, and damage control of the negative press associated with the situation in Kosovo.

Borislav Jović, president of the Serbian assembly and subsequently elected to the federal collective presidency, insisted to a trade union delegation from West Germany that any outside support for ethnic Albanian separatists in Kosovo whether deliberate or not represented a plan that would break up Yugoslavia. Jović considered recent criticism by the European parliament to be based on ignorance rather than on bad intentions and stressed that in his view the changes in the Serbian constitution do not take away rights from ethnic Albanians who "still enjoy the best treatment of any national minority in the world." (Belgrade, TANJUG, 19 April; *FBIS*, 20 April.) Although his opinion was shared by many Serbs in and out of political life, it was not how Slovene and Croat politicians and politically concerned citizens saw the status of the Kosovar Albanians.

Throughout the year the issue of Kosovo was also a constant irritant between the federal assembly and the Foreign Ministry. The foreign minister spelled out the domestic/foreign policy linkage in this regard in no uncertain terms: "Yugoslav diplomacy invests daily efforts towards eliminating negative effects which events in the province of Kosovo and divisions in the country have on Yugoslavia's international position." (TANJUG, 7 April; *FBIS*, 10 April.)

That such efforts were a sensitive area could be seen during the visit of the European parliamentary delegation to Yugoslavia 28 May–1 June to see the situation in Kosovo. In response to attacks in the assembly for "inadequate efforts" by Yugoslavia to present the true state of affairs, Deputy Secretary for Foreign Affairs Milivoje Maksić defended the Foreign Ministry's handling of this matter: "Kosovo is the absolute priority for the federal secretariat for foreign affairs. [However,] times are changing. Visits such as these are normal for an open society and not a matter of interference in internal affairs or of any alleged encroachment of sovereignty." (TANJUG, 13 June; *FBIS*, 14 June.) This interpretation found support in the northern republics of Slovenia and Croatia, but was viewed as something of a federal copout by many Serbs.

On the economic front, notwithstanding the implications for the upcoming nonaligned summit, one of departing Prime Minister Mikulić's last initiatives was in the form of expressed Yugoslav interest in developing cultural and economic ties with Israel, although he considered that conditions were not yet ripe for full diplomatic relations (Tel Aviv, *Ha'aretz*; *FBIS*, 13 March). However, the issue of such relations was on the agenda by the end of the year.

Another breakthrough materialized just as the Marković government came in. On 15 March, Yugoslavia and Taiwan signed a mutual cooperation agreement focused on opening trade offices in Yugoslavia and Taiwan; this move reopened trade ties after a 40-year break in economic relations.

In general the emphasis was on improving the economic infrastructure rather than on increased credits. Prime Minister Marković underlined this economic development strategy to U.S. businessmen in Cavtat, stressing that joint investments that contributed to a new Yugoslav economy, new technology, and new market were more important for Yugoslavia than new loans. (Radio Belgrade, May 29; *FBIS*, 31 May.)

In line with this policy a second investment agreement was signed with West Germany (much like an earlier agreement with Austria) that guaranteed that the investor would have the same protections as at home. This agreement could increase West German penetration of the Yugoslavia economy, for it was already Yugoslavia's second-largest trading partner and most important partner in joint ventures and import of technology. (Belgrade, TANJUG, 23 June; *FBIS*, 27 June.)

The Austrian-Yugoslav Commission for Economic Cooperation agreed that both sides would decrease customs duties and discussed the need to do something about Yugoslavia's $170 million trade deficit with Austria, the Yugoslav desire to conclude a separate agreement on economic cooperation with the European Free Trade Association (EFTA), and a proposal that the EFTA countries set up a special fund to support structural and reform-minded changes in Europe. (Belgrade, TANJUG, 23 June; *FBIS*, 27 June.)

Notwithstanding tensions in the U.S.-Yugoslav relationship generated by the arrest of the Yugoslav consul general in Chicago for laundering money during a sting operation and by U.S. congressional resolutions condemning human rights violations in Kosovo (*Borba*, 19 June; *FBIS*, 22 June), a U.S. congressional committee for energy and commerce visited Yugoslavia to discuss bilateral economic cooperation and expanding opportunities under the new law on foreign investments. Given that Slovene exports to the United States account for 25 percent of total Yugoslav exports, it is not surprising that the delegation visited Slovenia as well as Belgrade. (*Borba*, 12, 13 August; *FBIS*, 17 August.)

Overall there was satisfaction concerning Lončar's June visit to Washington (TANJUG, 16 June; *FBIS*, 19 June) and Prime Minister Marković's October trek to the U.S. capital. In both cases the dialogue centered on economic reform, the Yugoslav role in the nonaligned movement, and the situation in Kosovo. From the Yugoslav perspective the results in the first two categories were satisfactory; in the third one, less so. (*Borba*, 19 June; *FBIS*, 22 June.) A secondary but nonetheless serious problem was the lack of media attention and popular understanding of Yugoslav reform dynamics in circumstances where the revolutionary transformations cracking the once-solid Soviet bloc upstaged the efforts of the Yugoslav government to undergo its own *perestroika*.

State president Janez Drnovšek played a substantial role in economic talks with potential Western partners. While in Paris for the two hundredth anniversary of the French revolution in July, he discussed international political and economic issues with West German chancellor Helmut Kohl, British prime minister Margaret Thatcher, U.S. president George Bush, Canadian prime minister Brian Mulroney, and European Commission president Jacques Delors. The next month the Yugoslav president was in Italy for a working visit on bilateral relations, especially economic cooperation. At this time Foreign Minister Lončar met with his Italian counterpart, who stressed the value of the contribution to international cooperation and stability that Yugoslavia would make as chair of the nonaligned movement. (TANJUG, 8 August; *FBIS*, 10 August.)

A range of nationality issues also affected relations with Yugoslavia's neighbors. There were Yugoslav protests to the Greek ambassador that a Yugoslav folklore group from Skopje had to return from Athens without giving its concert because the organizers had failed to get the permit from the Greek authorities (TANJUG, 15 June; *FBIS*, 16 June).

Soviet-Yugoslav relations. Politically Yugoslavia's relations with the Soviet Union were on an even keel, although the pace of *perestroika* in Moscow and the dramatic developments within the former Soviet bloc had a range of unsettling implications for Yugoslavia's lagging party/political reform. LCY president Stipe Šuvar put forward the Yugoslav perspective in an interview in *Pravda* (3 March) (*FBIS*, 7 March). There were no longer any political problems between the USSR and Yugoslavia, but some problems in the economic sphere continued to leave their mark. Šuvar emphasized Soviet recognition of Yugoslavia's nonaligned foreign policy, the upcoming ninth nonaligned summit in Belgrade, and the need for a more important role for Yugoslavia in Europe.

The problem that the Yugoslav party president referred to was a substantial imbalance in Yugoslav-Soviet trade. In November 1988 the 26th meeting of a Yugoslav-Soviet committee announced that $555 million of the trade imbalance had been converted into credit to be repaid between January 1991 and June 1994. However, as the year opened, Yugoslavs were concerned that so little had been done about the $1.7 billion trade imbalance that had grown since 1985 because of the price of petroleum, which made up a substantial part of the 85 percent of Yugoslav imports of raw materials from the USSR (*Ekonomska politika*, 28 November 1988; *FBIS*, 8 February).

The Yugoslav side increasingly viewed this imbalance as a subsidy to the Soviets that the Yugoslav economy could ill afford. Given that the national bank paid exporters within days, whereas Soviet payments could take months, exporting eastward fueled inflation even though there were enterprise advantages. Who gained and lost was less clear. According to some reports, Yugoslav exports to the Soviet Union were relatively evenly distributed: Serbia, $590 million; Croatia, $662 million; Slovenia, $401 million. (Ibid.) Others insisted that "Serbia suffers most" because some 40 percent of exports to the clearinghouse area are from Serbia (Belgrade Domestic Service, 21 July; *FBIS*, 24 July).

In principle, Soviet-Yugoslav trade talks agreed to a completely balanced and equal rate of trade in goods and services valued at about $6 billion for 1989. This was about a $200 million increase over 1988. However, the existing trade imbalance was passed on to a working group for a medium-term trade agreement for 1991–1995. Reports of a trade protocol signed 1 March made no reference to solving the delicate question (TANJUG, 1 March; *FBIS*, 8 March), and Yugoslav complaints continued on this score notwithstanding a $196 million decrease in June from the peak balance in mid-May of $1.67 billion (Belgrade, TANJUG, 21 July; *FBIS*, 24 July).

The more forthcoming Soviet view of nonalignment was reiterated by Boris Smelnov, vice-president of the Soviet Academy of Sciences, during his visit to Belgrade when he assured his Yugoslav hosts that the Soviet Union no longer believed the nonaligned were "natural allies" of the socialist countries, but had accepted that they are "a global independent factor in international relations" (TANJUG, 10 May; *FBIS*, 11 May).

The SFRY also targeted areas of mutual advantage by supporting the Warsaw Pact initiative to abolish military blocs (TANJUG, 25 May; *FBIS*, 30 May) and by a note from Yugoslav state president Janez Drnovšek to Gorbachev and Bush during their December summit welcoming their get-together as promoting a favorable political climate and peace in the world as called for in the documents of the ninth nonaligned summit. Drnovšek expressed his hope that the Soviet-U.S. dialogue might extend to the serious economic problems that, as he saw it, were integral to political solutions (TANJUG, 24 November; *FBIS*, 4 December).

Intracommunist politics. Yugoslavia's reaction to the fate of the friends and foes of reform varied. Officially, Yugoslavia expressed "great concern" over the massacre of prodemocracy forces in Tiananmen Square. However, in the realm of practical politics there was an effort to salvage developing economic cooperation with China, and no obstacles were seen to the meeting of the Yugoslav-Chinese Committee for Cooperation in the Sphere of Economy, Trade, Technology, and Science set for 6 June. (*Politika*, 4 June; *FBIS*, 6 June.) Reportedly it was the Chinese side that postponed Prime Minister Marković's visit scheduled for the end of the month.

The mildness of SFRY official reaction was attacked by the Human Rights Committee of the Serbian Writers' Association (*Borba*, 23 June; *FBIS*, 29 June). The Croatian LC strongly condemned Chinese "bloody repression" (Belgrade, TANJUG, 12 June; *FBIS*, 13 June), and warnings were sounded that the Chinese solution could occur in Yugoslavia (*Borba*, 15 June; *FBIS*, 20 June)—a thinly veiled reference to the volatile situation in Kosovo.

This pattern of ambivalent response reflecting rejection in principle of the use of force, an attempt to limit the economic fallout to Yugoslavia's already staggering economy, and lessons drawn by those engaged in domestic political struggle continued as neighboring East Central European parties and governments toppled during October and November. The winds of change that swept out the Erich Honecker era and pushed Egon Krenz to one side also shattered Yugoslav hopes of expanded cooperation in machine building and mining that had been under discussion in Belgrade days before Honecker fell. (*ND*, 13 October; *FBIS*, 19 October.) The fate of the 1990 trade protocol with Czechoslovakia signed on 28 November was somewhat more hopeful but still unclear (TANJUG, 28 November; *FBIS*, 6 December).

Politicians undoubtedly worried about their jobs, while in the media and the popular mind there was a feeling of being left behind. Many agreed with the assessment that Yugoslavia was falling apart as the bloc reformed (*Borba*, 24 November; *FBIS*, 4 December). The mood in Yugoslavia was on the side of change.

In this environment the response to Nicolae Ceauşescu's last stand was much stronger than the reaction to party/state violence in China. The LCY halted official cooperation with the Romanian Communist Party and withdrew its invitation for a Romanian delegation to attend the LCY Fourteenth Extraordinary Party Congress in January. (Belgrade Domestic Service; *FBIS*, 20 December.) During the last weeks of December many Yugoslavs watched the television coverage of the Romanian revolution until the early hours of the morning. The popular revulsion at the level of corruption—symbolized by the golden scales on which Elena Ceauşescu weighed the imported meat she fed her small dogs while Romanian children suffering from malnutrition were given AIDS-infected blood—had repercussions for Yugoslav reform. Demands for clean government at home intensified, and more and more among the privileged political elite began to fear the handwriting on the wall.

Auxiliary Organizations. Like the LCY the auxiliary organizations were convulsed by national/ethnic confrontations and caught up in the struggle of competing reform strategies and agendas. The most dramatic impact was on the Socialist Alliance, for the proliferating alternative movements and parties became a potential alternative to the alliance in some kind of ill-defined loyal opposition. The tensions created by these conflicting pressures could be seen at the beginning of the year in warnings from the SAWPY leadership that if the LCY did not stop patronizing the SAWPY and allow genuine pluralism, a radical reform of the political system would be unavoidable. (*Politika Ekspres*, 4 January; *FBIS*, 10 January.)

Meanwhile the routine of bureaucratic reorganization went forward. The SAWPY federal conference was reduced from 243 to 125 members and its presidium from 34 to 30. In a move that made bureaucratic sense but inevitably increased conflict, the coordinating committee for safeguarding Tito's name and work merged with the coordinating committee for marking important anniversaries and the history of Yugoslavia's nations and nationalities. (TANJUG, 8 February; *FBIS*, 9 February.)

As for the government's program for restoring the economy, there was considerable ambivalence. As Marković took over, Bozidar Čolaković, the president of the SAWPY federal conference, warned of the need for a safety net to protect those who would bear the greatest burden of reform. His qualified support for free market activity was balanced by the objection that the consumer must put up with shortages and prices that "impoverish and humiliate him" (TANJUG, 15 March; *FBIS*, 17 March).

Čolaković handled the issue of political pluralism gingerly, calling for "respecting the boundaries" set up by the constitution as a first step in reform of the Socialist Alliance (Belgrade, TANJUG, 6 April; *FBIS*, 7 April). He initially rejected a multiparty system for Yugoslavia as too dangerous in view of Yugoslavia's past experiences with interethnic strife and insisted that only the LCY could "secure cohesion and maximum unity in Yugoslavia" (Belgrade, TANJUG, 7 April; *FBIS*, 10 April).

In May, Čolaković was replaced by the first woman president of the SAWPY federal conference, Jelena Milojević, from Vojvodina. From her discussion of the problems inherent in legalizing political pluralism, it was clear that the organizational hesitation to take the plunge remained. (*Borba*, 10, 11 June; *FBIS*, 22 June.)

The problem was that the federal Socialist Alliance had no more control over its republic/provincial branches than the LCY had over the party's regional organizations. It was the Serbian Socialist Alliance that called for breaking economic relations with Slovenia in response to the Slovene refusal to allow the Kosovo "Truth" rally in Ljubljana. The federal SAWPY conference warned about the dangers of national/ethnic divisions and demanded that SAWPY regional organizations "critically examine" the activity of republic/provincial media and stop the "media war" within Yugoslavia (TANJUG, 15 December; *FBIS*, 18 December). But apparently it would or could do nothing to keep those regional organizations from randomly undermining the united market as a means of political retaliation. Therefore, SAWPY was not a realistic alternative to the LCY because the Socialist Alliance suffered from the same political paralysis that had infected the party.

The same problem could be seen in the relationship between the presidium of the federal youth organization and republic/provincial youth organizations. The federal organization tried and failed to mediate conflicting republic/provincial conflicts and demands. It unanimously supported both Ante Marković and Borislav Jović as candidates for prime minister and rejected the Slovene proposal that the secretary of defense be a civilian as not of "the utmost importance." These fence-sitting efforts satisfied no one, and within the Slovene youth organization serious discussion of abolishing the official youth organization continued. (Belgrade, *Mladost*, 7 November 1988; *JPRS-EEU*, 26 January.)

There was, however, an interesting initiative in the foreign policy arena. The Youth Federation Commission for International Relations and Cooperation sharply criticized Yugoslav foreign policy for being conducted as "if we were still in the cold war" and failing to keep up with the changes in the world. Charging that there was no united policy on relations with neighboring countries, it recommended that the youth federation examine the doctrine of Yugoslav foreign policy and strive to establish contact with representatives of the youth of the Albanian party with a view to organizing a youth summit by the end of the year. The problem of the Macedonian minority in Greece was also discussed. (*Borba*, 16 February; *FBIS*, 24 February.)

As for trade unions, Andejelko Vasić, 52, who took over as president of the Confederation of Trade Unions in May, inherited an organization in equal disarray. Trade unions were understandably concerned with inflation and unemployment. The response to the Marković anti-inflation package at the end of the year paralleled the positions of republic/party government leaders, although even in that regard there was not complete discipline in the ranks. The *Borba* trade union ignored the call of the Belgrade trade union council for a half hour warning strike to protest the government program. (Belgrade Domestic Service, 20 December; *FBIS*, 21 December.)

Robin A. Remington
University of Missouri at Columbia

Council for Mutual Economic Assistance

Disintegrating Tendencies

A combination of deteriorating economic performance and burgeoning political developments in 1989 challenged the very existence of the Council for Mutual Economic Assistance (CMEA). Based on command planning and on the rejection of contacts with the West, CMEA-imposed institutional links on Eastern European countries significantly weakened in the 1980s because of the Soviet incapacity to assure unlimited supplies of energy and raw materials. The professed goals of the new governments—opening to the West, free market economies, and democracy—make CMEA, which was established as a result of popular rebellions in Eastern Europe, increasingly obsolete. Trade and cooperation within the bloc stagnated during 1989. Because of internal tensions and disagreements, the regular June session of the CMEA council in Sofia was postponed until early January 1990.

Because of domestic political and economic pressures, the new governments began to reassess their links with CMEA. Despite numerous calls for dissolution, representatives of the ten countries attending the Sofia session pledged to work together to infuse new vitality into CMEA. The compromise in Sofia demonstrates the hard realities underlying political changes in Eastern Europe: because of dependence on the Soviet Union, members cannot afford to withdraw from CMEA, but they cannot afford to observe the CMEA rules because the latter represent an impediment to the transition to market economies. The search to solve this dilemma will shape intra-CMEA relations in the future.

Background. Established in January 1949, CMEA is an international governmental organiza-tion. Its active members include the Soviet Union, Bulgaria, Czechoslovakia, the German Democratic Republic (GDR), Hungary, Poland, Romania, and three non-European countries: Cuba, Mongolia, and Vietnam. Albania, although originally a member, has not participated in CMEA since December 1966. The supreme policy-making body is the council, which is convened once a year. The CMEA Executive Committee and Secretariat are responsible for day-to-day management.

Because of its unique features—a highly uneven distribution of power and domestic command planning systems—it is not easy to compare CMEA with other international economic organizations. It is not a customs union because tariffs have no impact on the foreign trade of its members. Because planning is the mechanism for allocation, stimulation, and coordination of economic activity in individual member countries, CMEA does not qualify as a common market. Because member countries have not transferred their national rights of sovereignty to the CMEA, it is not a supranational organization empowered to make and interpret rules. Andrei Lukanov, chairman of the CMEA Executive Committee, stated that each member "retains full sovereignty in the field of its economic policy and in its economic decisions and the ways and means of managing economic life" (Moscow Television Service, 25 January; *FBIS-SOV*, 26 January).

CMEA can be compared with international governmental organizations such as the United Nations but CMEA's purpose is not universal. Instead, it focuses on providing a framework for economic interaction among its member countries and the rules that they have agreed to observe in their economic transactions (see, for example, Jozef M. van Brabant, *Socialist Economic Integration* [Cambridge, Eng.: Cambridge University Press, 1980]).

The creation of CMEA reflected Joseph Stalin's concept of a separate "world socialist market" as a viable alternative to the capitalist one that was doomed to disintegrate (Stalin, *Economic Problems of Socialism in the USSR* [New York, 1952], pp. 24–27). This, however, was only one component of the Soviet policy aimed at preventing the West from controlling political developments in Eastern Europe and at decoupling the area from the world economy.

The communiqué issued at the time of CMEA's formation explicitly mentioned the need for integrating newly established communist regimes in

Central Europe with the Soviet Union in response to the Western boycott of

> trade relations with the countries of people's democracy and the USSR because these countries did not consider it appropriate that they should submit themselves to the dictatorship of the Marshall Plan...In light of these circumstances, [to] establish...wider economic cooperation between the countries of people's democracy and the USSR, the conference considered it necessary to create the Council for Mutual Economic Assistance. (Michael Kaiser, *Comecon: Integration Problems of the Planned Economies* [London, 1965], pp. 1–12.)

The communiqué, however, did not stipulate a mechanism for integration nor was there any mention of coordinating economic policy and development programs, which indicates that Moscow at that time did not attribute any practical significance to CMEA. A formal charter was not adopted until the twelfth council session in 1959, ten years after CMEA had been established.

Economic Underpinnings. CMEA has been shaped by the political and economic dominance of the Soviet Union, the great disparity in the economic and technological levels among member economies, and the institutional traits of individual domestic economic systems. Soviet dominance accounts for a radial pattern of economic interaction; the developmental gap contributes to internal tensions; and the domestic economic system is largely accountable for parallelism of economic structure and a bias in favor of autarky. Because of drastic deteriorations in the performance of CMEA economies during the 1980s and political changes in those countries, these underpinnings of political economy are under stress.

The Soviet Union accounts for about 70 percent of the total gross domestic product (GDP) within CMEA, and most transactions in goods and services by members are with the USSR. As the Soviet Union towers over other countries in the "socialist community," the pattern of intra-CMEA interaction is radial, that is, bilateral ties between individual members and the USSR overshadow multilateral links. Moscow's hegemonic position rests on its military and economic dominance, which has been exercised inter alia through the Warsaw Treaty Organization and CMEA, both of which provide the Soviet Union with mechanisms for fostering the alliance.

The USSR, one of the largest producers and net exporters of natural resources in the world, has traditionally been the major supplier of energy and raw materials to other CMEA countries. As a result of industrialization—characterized by a complete disregard of their endowment in natural resources and by excessive consumption of energy and raw materials (see Paul Marer, "The Political Economy of Soviet Relations with Eastern Europe," in Sarah Meiklejohn Terry, ed., *Soviet Policy in Eastern Europe* [New Haven, Conn.: Yale University Press 1984], pp. 158–60)—the East European CMEA members have become critically dependent on Soviet resources. Thus a political and military dependence has been complemented by an economic one.

The parallelism of economic development is an outcome of similar institutional arrangements in communist-ruled societies and Soviet demands on its junior allies. The East European CMEA members depend on supplies of raw materials from the Soviet Union and on access to the West for technology to produce manufactured goods of better quality. This may satisfy the USSR demand, but is often not sufficient to meet world standards. Eastern Europe thus obtains from the Soviet Union natural resources that can be sold for hard currency in international markets, paying for them with goods that are often noncompetitive in those markets. This arrangement has been increasingly criticized by Moscow.

CMEA members have neither incentives nor opportunities to develop multilateral ties with any country other than the USSR. CMEA's striking feature has been the growth of integration along the lines of the radial pattern centered around Moscow and, in contrast, the dependence of smaller East European CMEA members on the West.

The shares of trade of smaller East European countries with one another have significantly decreased over the last twenty years. For instance, the average (unweighted) share of their mutual imports fell from 46 percent in 1971–1975 to 38 percent in 1981–1985, whereas imports from the Soviet Union increased from 54 to 62 percent. The share of noncommunist trade partners in their total exports increased in the same period from 33 to 38 percent.

The Soviet Union's share of the trade of the non-European CMEA members increased even though Cuba and Mongolia increased their supplies of raw materials to the Eastern European countries (see Horst Brzezinski, "Economic Relations between European and the Less-Developed CMEA Countries," in *East European Economies: Slow Growth in the 1980's*, vol. 2 [Washington, D.C.: Joint Economic Committee, U.S. Government Printing Office, 1986], pp. 302–28). Trade turnover with the CMEA economies also accounts for a significantly larger portion of the non-European CMEA economies' trade, ranging in the 1980s between 70 percent (Cuba) and 97 percent (Mongolia).

The second unique trait of CMEA is the gap between technological and economic levels of the European and the non-European members that reflects the north-south division in the international political economy. No economic grouping in the world is characterized by such disparities, and the objective of CMEA (Article 1 of its charter) is the gradual evening out of development levels in all participating countries. At the Forty-fourth CMEA Council session (Prague, 1988), the delegate from Vietnam called for "making conditions and the level of development even for all members" (Belgrade, *Borba*, 12 July 1988; *FBIS-EEU*, 19 July 1988). Because of the absence of reliable estimates for per capita gross national product (GNP) in the non-European member countries, it is difficult to assess to what degree this objective is being met. Judging by the fact that there has been little progress in evening out the level of East European economies, it is inconceivable that the gap was reduced between them and Cuba or Vietnam.

CMEA membership introduces potential areas for conflict similar to those between north and south in other international fora. Non-Europeans are encouraged to specialize in subtropical products and raw materials. Bilateral agreements signed with Cuba in 1988 promise CMEA assistance in developing the engineering industry and consumer goods production in exchange for sugar, citrus fruits, and nickel. Similar arrangements exist between other CMEA countries and Vietnam. The CMEA Committee on Cooperation in Planning, which met in Havana on 17 January, considered special comprehensive programs for multilateral cooperation between European CMEA member countries and Vietnam, Cuba, and Mongolia. Participants in the 130th session of the CMEA Executive Committee reportedly discussed the results of multilateral cooperation between the European CMEA countries and the Socialist Republic of Vietnam (SRV), Cuba, and Mongolia in machine building, development of specialized and cooperative production of tools, instruments, ships, and sailing vessels in the SRV and of transport and agricultural machine building in Cuba. However, no details concerning economic

assistance extended by European CMEA members were given.

Eastern Europe has been under considerable pressure from Moscow to pick up part of the Soviet burden. New governments in Eastern Europe are unlikely to provide assistance to Cuba, Mongolia, or the SRV, particularly under the guise of higher (than world) prices paid for their exports. They can no longer afford it, and there is a significant domestic political opposition to giving aid to Third World communist regimes.

The third general factor that makes CMEA unique is the absence of market mechanisms. Command planning, which emerged in the Soviet Union during the 1930s and was adopted by other communist-ruled countries, is void of contractual relationships, interdependencies between buyers and sellers, and autonomous economic agents responding to price signals. Its logic is politics—the primacy of political considerations over those of economic efficiency. Rather than autonomous activities geared to finding the most efficient ways to produce goods and services, as is the case in market economies, its modus operandi is state control. Therefore in contrast to societies where interaction of state and market pushes toward international integration, the politically dominated communist system confines economic activity to its national boundaries.

The logic of this economic system, which is based on administrative directives, has been extended to relations among communist-ruled countries. As the Soviet economist R. Grinberg noted, "the administration-by-edict system of economic management that has grown up in each of the socialist countries has been accurately reproduced in relations within CMEA too" (*Izvestiia*; *FBIS-SOV*, 16 January 1988). However, this reproduction has never been completed, as there is no supranational planner. The decisions concerning intra-CMEA relations are thus an outcome of bargaining among its member governments. Bargaining, a dominant mechanism of allocation, is constrained by the primacy of security interests and the use of world market prices in intra-CMEA transactions. It is also critically dependent on the Soviet ability to suppress national interests of smaller CMEA members.

That the communist economic system is devoid of market competition has profoundly affected the organization of inter-CMEA relationships. From the point of view of external economic interaction, the system displays a strong bias in favor of autarky. Uninformed planners cannot identify areas in which they have comparative advantage. Domestic producers insulated from both foreign and domestic consumers have no incentive to look actively for marketing opportunities. The absence of financial and commodity convertibility in turn fosters a propensity toward structural bilateralism in intra-CMEA relations, to borrow an apt term from Jozef van Brabant (*Bilateralism and Structural Bilateralism in Intra-CMEA Trade* [Rotterdam: Rotterdam University Press, 1973]).

Structural bilateralism is the result of the state's foreign trade monopoly or, more generally, restricting public economic policy instruments in both the national and the CMEA arenas to the use of administrative tools. As a result, there are few effective mechanisms to encourage specialization and active participation in the international economy because specialization within CMEA would entail unbalanced trade flows, which would run counter to the economic interests of the trading partners. Credits and other financial devices using the transferable ruble cannot provide this kind of incentive. Iurii Shiriaev, director of the International Institute of Economic Problems of the World Socialist System, noted, "A guiding principle in such cases [bilateral cooperation agreements] was not effectiveness [efficiency], but the formal need to balance mutual deliveries. A feeble link-up between the value sides of cooperation curtailed the possibilities of taking advantage of international [CMEA] credits." (Shiriaev, "New Strategy of Cooperation and Development of CMEA Countries," *Social Sciences* (Moscow), no. 3, 1988, p. 12.)

Under such institutional constraints, there is little incentive to open the economies, even to intra-CMEA trade. Thus the volume of intra-CMEA exports increased about 20 percent between 1980 and 1986, whereas total exports of highly developed Western economies increased by more than 30 percent in the same period (Warsaw, *Życie gospodarcze*, no. 35, 1988).

The extremely low mobility of factors of production should stimulate larger trade than occurs in economies characterized by relatively unfettered movement of capital and labor. Except for unplanned trade deficits, which have to be financed ex post facto, and credit transactions limited to some jointly undertaken projects, there is little capital flow. Labor mobility is also limited. The only exception is import of labor by Czechoslovakia and the GDR, mainly from Vietnam and—to a lesser extent—from Poland, but the magnitudes involved are rather limited. This low mobility of capital and labor has not been conducive to increased intra-CMEA trade (Paul Marer and John M. Montias, "CMEA Integration: Theory and Practice," in *East European Economic Assessment*, part 2, *Regional Assessments* [Washington, D.C.: Joint Economic Committee, U.S. Government Printing Office, 1981], p. 168). The trade intensity of the CMEA economies is well below the levels of market economies at a similar per capita GNP. Thus even the low mobility of factors of production does not compensate for the antitrade bias of centrally planned economies.

Without the introduction of convertibility of national currencies and a market mechanism in domestic economic systems, this antitrade bias cannot be overcome unless national sovereign rights over all areas of economic policy are transferred to a supranational planning authority. There has been, however, no political will among the CMEA members to integrate along those lines. Except for Nikita S. Khrushchev's ill-fated attempt at supranational planning and Mikhail S. Gorbachev's short-lived hopes to revive CMEA, the Soviet Union has not sought to subjugate its client states to a single, all-encompassing plan, but apparently has sought to strike a balance between the region's viability and the capacity to control its "junior allies." The result is that the organization "has never succeeded in developing an economically coherent or politically feasible plan for promoting increased interaction on a multilateral basis." (Karen Dawisha, "Eastern Europe and Perestroika under Gorbachev: Options for the West," in *Pressures for Reform in the East European Economies*, vol. 2 [Washington, D.C.: Joint Economic Committee, Congress of the United States, U.S. Government Printing Office, 1989], p. 529.)

The alternative to supranational planning would be organizing intra-CMEA interaction on a market basis, that is, with a price mechanism and convertibility of national currencies. In this vein, the pro-reform shift in Moscow has also affected CMEA. The last five years have witnessed a spate of public policy declarations from CMEA sessions that promise an overhaul of the administrative mechanism for cooperation and efforts toward gradual introduction of conditions for the unfettered movement of production factors and goods among member countries. It remains to be seen whether this goal will be vigorously pursued by all CMEA members.

The scope for transforming CMEA is limited by the necessity of assuring a link between the pace of domestic change and that of CMEA. The organiza-

Table 1: Growth Rates of Net Material Products in 1981–1989
(in percent)

	1981–1985	1986–1989	1986	1987	1988	1989
Bulgaria	3.7	4.3–4.6	5.3	5.0	6.2	0.0–1.0
Czechoslovakia	1.7	2.1–2.3	2.6	2.2	2.5	1.0–1.5
GDR	4.5	3.1–3.4	4.3	3.6	3.0	1.0–2.0
Hungary	1.3	1.0	0.9	3.0	0.0	0.0
Poland	−0.8	2.2	4.9	1.9	4.2	−2.2
Romania	4.4	4.6–4.9	7.3	4.8	3.2	2.0–3.0
USSR	3.6	2.8–3.1	4.1	2.3	4.4	0.0–1.0

SOURCE: Derived from data in Piotr Cyburt, "Economy Worse than Politics," *Życie gospodarcze*, 14 January 1990.

tional structure of CMEA is not flexible enough to accommodate fully market and nonmarket economies. If planning is abolished, as will be the case in Poland as of 1990, then there is no room for coordination of plans, which has been the hallmark of CMEA. If the state withdraws from direct control over enterprise activities, then it can no longer make any delivery commitments to other CMEA partners. If what is to be produced is decided by enterprises, not directly by central authorities, then the existing CMEA mechanism becomes incompatible with the domestic economic system and an impediment to change. Hungarian deputy finance minister Zsigmond Járai observed that CMEA is "the main reason for the rigidity of Hungary's economy, since 45 percent of Hungarian foreign trade must be done by cutting out the role of money" (Budapest, MTI, 21 July; *FBIS-EEU*, 89-140).

The wave of democratization sweeping Eastern Europe has raised the question of reformability. Leaving aside domestic constraints, the transition to a market economy cannot succeed unless CMEA applies similar principles to those employed in national reforms in member CMEA economies. As of January 1990, no consensus could be reached as to the pace and direction of radical economic change. The Polish experiment of going directly from administrative planning to a market economy is to be followed by Czechoslovakia. Hungarian planners have already allowed some free enterprise within a planned economy and abolished the state monopoly over foreign trade. The directions to be taken by other CMEA countries are as yet unclear. The intensity of cooperation will depend on the similarities of institutional change in economic systems. The recent discussions about creating a mini-integration bloc encompassing the "reformed"

economies of Czechoslovakia, Hungary, and Poland (Tony Smith, "Comecon Future," AP, 11 January 1990) demonstrate that Eastern European economists and policymakers are aware of the necessity for corresponding institutional changes in member countries.

Cohesion of the arrangements underlying CMEA is considerably weakened by a rapid deterioration of the Soviet economy, particularly the fall in output of oil and other raw materials, as well as symptoms of economic crisis in other CMEA European economies. Although the average growth rates during the 1986–1989 period were slightly higher for most CMEA economies than for 1981–1985, there was a steep deterioration in 1989 even in the usually inflated official data (see table 1). Western estimates are lower. Swedish economist Ånders Åslund, for instance, argued that the Soviet national income fell last year by 5 percent, and it could decline by another 10 percent in 1990 ("Gorbachev: Governing on the Razor's Edge," *WP*, Outlook section, 28 January 1990).

Because of the radial pattern and East European dependence on the USSR, the Soviet economic disturbances are being transmitted to other countries. The growth of intra-CMEA trade during 1987 and 1988 lagged behind the growth of trade of CMEA countries with other partners (*Gospodarka światowa i gospodarka Polska w 1988 roku*, [Warsaw: Central School of Planning and Statistics, 1989], p. 42). Although the contraction stems in part from improved East European terms of trade with the Soviet Union (e.g., the latter's exports in value terms fell by 4 percent in 1988), the major reasons have been a decline in output and the energy crisis exacerbated by strikes in coal mines last year. Complete data are not available for 1989, but those disclosed suggest a further decline: for instance, the value of Polish imports from the Soviet Union during the first nine months was ten percent lower than in the same period of 1988 (*Foreign Trade during the First Three Quarters of 1989* [Warsaw: Ministry of Economic Cooperation with Countries Abroad, 26 October]), and all Eastern European economies ran trade surpluses with the USSR in part because of cuts in Soviet exports. Trade surpluses exacerbate domestic economic disequilibria, that is, generate shortages and inflationary pressures.

Domestic imbalances significantly increased in the European CMEA countries during 1989. According to the latest estimate, the Soviet budget deficit of 120 billion rubles amounted to about 20 percent of the national income produced in 1988 (*Życie gospodarcze*, no. 2, 14 January 1990). Even in the allegedly well-managed East German economy, the domestic debt last year reached about 50 percent of the national income. In both Czechoslovakia and East Germany, the two most developed CMEA economies, there occurred a significant decline in the availability and quality of consumer goods. Shortages of consumer goods dramatically expanded in 1989 as compared with 1988 in Bulgaria, the USSR, and Romania. Authorities in Poland, Bulgaria, and the Soviet Union lost control over the growth of personal incomes, which exacerbated inflationary pressures. This loss of control, combined with deregulation of prices for agricultural products, produced hyperinflation in Poland.

Other symptoms of economic crisis included rapidly declining rates of capital formation; falling exports with the exception of Czechoslovakia, Hungary, and Poland; and growing indebtedness to the West.

The fall of Soviet exports and limited opportunity for the expansion of intra-CMEA trade produced a growing frustration among policymakers. Former Polish deputy prime minister Ireneusz Sekula complained that "mutual transactions within CMEA are falling, and it is very often easier to trade outside CMEA than within it" (Warsaw, *Trybuna ludu*, 19 May). Czechoslovakia's new government declared the old communist trading bloc dead, and its outspoken finance minister Vaclav Klaus argued in favor of scrapping CMEA trade agreements because "the economic crisis gripping the Soviet Union and all six Eastern European member states had made it obsolete in its present form" (*NYT*, 5 January 1990).

Institutions and Scope of Activity. The communiqué from the founding meeting of CMEA (Moscow, 1949) indicated that the following countries participated: the Soviet Union, Bulgaria, Czechoslovakia, Hungary, Poland, and Romania. It also contained the provision that all other European countries were invited to join (Zbigniew M. Fallenbuchl, Toronto, *International Journal*, no. 1). This provision was removed at the Sixteenth Council session held in Moscow during mid-1962.

As of January 1990, there were eleven full members of the CMEA. Albania joined in 1949, but since the Fifteenth Council session (Warsaw, December 1961) has not participated in any activity or paid its dues (Richard F. Staar, *Communist Regimes in Eastern Europe*, 5th rev. ed. [Stanford: Hoover Institution Press, 1988], p. 292). The newly established German Democratic Republic (GDR) joined the organization in 1950, and Mongolia, in 1962. During the 1970s, two communist-ruled Third World countries became full members of CMEA: Cuba (1972) and the Socialist Republic of Vietnam (1978). Despite the strong support of the GDR, the application of Mozambique was rejected in 1981. Probably because the economic cost has exceeded political and military benefits to the Soviet Union, other allies in the Third World were discouraged from applying for full membership. Contrary to the expectations of some analysts in the 1970s, three other Marxist-Leninist regimes (Laos, Afghanistan, and Cambodia) were not incorporated as full members to CMEA.

The organizing principle underlying membership is that of the "interested party," that is, members retain full discretion over their participation in CMEA programs. Full membership, however, is not the only affiliation status envisaged by the CMEA charter. The other forms include limited participant, cooperant, and observer. The only country that has limited membership status is Yugoslavia: the agreement was signed in 1965 at the Nineteenth Council session in Prague. Yugoslavia participates in several programs, and its representatives attend policy-making CMEA Council meetings.

Three countries—Finland (1973), Mexico (1975), and Iraq (1976)—ratified cooperant status agreements with CMEA. These countries do not have centrally planned economies and are not empowered to conclude foreign trade agreements on behalf of private corporations. For this reason their involvement in CMEA activity consists of sending mixed government-business delegations to explore business opportunities. They may sign directional agreements with various bodies of CMEA, but their implementation is not binding. These countries do not participate in council meetings.

Another designation for interest in developing interaction with the CMEA is observer status. Since 1978 this group has included the following nine countries: Afghanistan, Angola, Cambodia, Ethiopia, Laos, Mozambique, Nicaragua, North Korea, and South Yemen. Apparently not all of them have retained this status. Among the observers of the Forty-fourth (Prague, July 1988) and Forty-fifth (Sofia, January 1990) Council sessions, there were no representatives from either Cambodia or North Korea; the other seven sent official delegations. The status of Afghanistan is not clear, but the signing of a protocol by the CMEA Commission on Cooperation with Afghanistan in Kabul on 2 April 1988 may indicate its upgrading to a cooperant status. According to this agreement, "concrete objects and fields of cooperation between the CMEA and Afghanistan were defined." (TASS; *FBIS-SOV*, 5 April 1988.)

Granting status within CMEA tends to reflect the relations between a country's government and the Soviet Union. The People's Republic of China, for example, held observer status at one time. Others, like Guyana, Chile under Salvador Allende, and Egypt, were said to have been considering obtaining this status (Marer and Montias, "CMEA Integration," p. 150). Because CMEA is not a supranational organ, a special status governing an affiliation of a country with the CMEA remains secondary to its already established political or economic links with the Soviet Union.

The institutional framework of CMEA is not a carbon copy of command planning hierarchies in the Soviet Union or most other CMEA members, although it has many of the same traits. In the absence of markets and autonomous activity to establish links across borders, interdependence can only be promoted and coordinated by explicit action of the states involved. As a result, there is a myriad of functional and branch organs within a centrally administered framework.

At the top of the organizational pyramid is the session of the council, the supreme policy-making body that has been convened over the last twenty years at least once a year except for 1989. CMEA members are represented by prime ministers or communist party first secretaries. The resolutions of the council are reviewed by members. If approved, they serve as a framework for bilateral or multilateral negotiations. The agreements set the stage for implementation, which is monitored and supervised by appropriate permanent commissions or committees. Given the "self-interested" party provision, CMEA is structured in such a way as to provide the framework and facilities for bilateral negotiations.

The Executive Committee, Secretariat, committees, permanent commissions, and functional organizations form the core of CMEA planning and negotiating machinery. The Executive Committee (established in 1962), whose members are permanent representatives with the rank of deputy prime minister, is in charge of cooperation within CMEA. The Moscow-based Secretariat, which meets four times a year, supervises and is responsible for implementing council recommendations. It also provides policy input for council sessions.

Council committees, the organizational innovation of the 1971 Integration Program, are designed to promote coordination of research and development efforts and to develop productive structures in member countries by establishing organizational facilities for joint planning. Following are the seven committees that now exist and the year in which they were established: (1) Planning, 1971, (2) Science & Technology, 1972, (3) Foreign Economic Relations, 1988, (4) Agro-Industrial Complex, 1988, (5) Engineering, 1985, (6) Electronics, 1988, (7) Fuels and Materials, 1988. (Staar, *Communist Regimes in Eastern Europe*, p. 301; Vlad Sobell, *Red Market* [Aldershot, Eng.: 1984]; *RAD Background Report*, no. 37; Munich, RFE:RL, 1988; Prague, *Hospodarské noviny*, no. 106, 1988.) Five committees were established during the 1980s.

Permanent commissions are the regional equivalent of branch ministries in member countries, although some of them are in charge of functional issue areas, such as environmental protection and public health. Permanent commissions include the following: (1) Coal Industry (Warsaw), 1956, (2) Chemical Industry (East Berlin), 1956, (3) Transportation and Civil Aviation (Moscow), 1988, (4) Light Industry (Prague), 1963, (5) Telecommunications and Posts (Moscow), 1971, (6) Environmental Protection (Moscow), (7) Electrical and Atomic Energy Agency (Moscow), 1988, (8) Statistics (Moscow), 1988, (9) Legal Affairs (Moscow), 1988, (10) Standardization (East Berlin), 1962. (Ibid.)

Although permanent commissions (also known as standing committees) are responsible for creating international economic associations, they are not empowered to make decisions binding on all CMEA members unless a country becomes a member of a CMEA international economic association. INTERMETAL, the CMEA equivalent of the West European Coal and Steel Community, for example, can pass resolutions binding on all members (Staar, *Communist Regimes*, p. 298). Because the international economic organizations are subject to the national jurisdiction of the country in which their headquarters are located, they are not part of the CMEA institutional structure. However, they do have a close relationship with permanent commissions.

The following are functional organizations: (1) International Bank for Economic Cooperation (Moscow), 1964, (2) International Investment Bank (Moscow), 1971, (3) Institute for Standardization (Moscow), 1962, (4) Institute for Economic Problems (Moscow), 1972, (5) Administration for the Electric Power System (Prague), 1964, (6) Freight Bureau (Moscow), 1963, (7) Railroad Car Pool (Prague), 1964 (Staar, *Communist Regimes*, p. 301; Sobell, *Red Market*, p. 19; *RAD Background Report*, no. 37; Munich, RFE:RL, 1988; *Hospodárské noviny*, no. 106, 1988).

The scope of activities of functional organizations is indicated by their names. The two CMEA banks deserve a short comment, however. Although the original purpose of the International Bank for Economic Cooperation (IBEC) was to effect intra-CMEA settlements and to provide short-term loans (Jozef van Brabant, *East-European Cooperation— The Role of Money and Finance* [New York: Praeger, 1977], p. 125), it mainly performs bookkeeping operations associated with transactions among members. Because of low interest rates and a limited resource base, the IBEC cannot act as a significant financial intermediary.

Nor can the International Investment Bank (IIB), which was established to help finance investment in member countries as well as in joint CMEA projects. Its scope of credit activity has not been impressive. The IIB's loans amounted to TR 5.5 billion between 1971 and 1988 (Berlin, *Aussenwirtschaft*; *JPRS-EEU*, 29 August). Credits are mainly in transferable rubles that are worthless outside bilateral CMEA relations. Thanks to IIB's borrowing in the international capital markets, however, some loans are in convertible currencies. Beginning in 1988, the IIB became involved in financing micro-integration, that is, joint ventures and direct pro-

duction contracts among enterprises (TASS; *FBIS-SOV*, 83-034).

In addition to the organizations discussed, there are various institutionalized activities such as conferences of nongovernmental organizations with some ties to the CMEA; the seven annual CMEA conferences to consult on trade, patents, and so forth, which reportedly were abolished in 1988; and various intragovernmental ad hoc groups. According to one estimate, about 100,000 people were involved in CMEA and CMEA-related activity during the 1970s (Marer and Montias, "CMEA Integration," p. 151).

The institutional structure of CMEA has evolved considerably since the 1950s, mirroring the changing priorities and areas targeted for regional coordination. Until the adoption of the Comprehensive Program in 1971, the CMEA bureaucratic apparatus had been enlarged by adding new organizational bodies that were to foster coordination along branch lines.

With the adoption of the Integration Program in 1971, however, the thrust of organizational activity shifted to functional issues of integration. Three Council committees charged to perform key line functions were established: the Committee on Cooperation in Planning, the Committee on Scientific Technological Cooperation, and, in 1974, the Committee on Cooperation in Material and Technical Supply. The first two still exist; the third was reportedly closed down in 1987–1988. (Munich, *RAD Background Report*, no. 37; RFE:RL, 8 March 1988.)

Committees with wider responsibilities replaced permanent commissions or bureaus. For example, the Permanent Commission on Research and Development was transformed into the Committee on Cooperation in Research and Technology, whereas the Bureau of the Executive Committee was upgraded to the Committee on Cooperation in Planning. Its members were the chairmen of the national planning commissions, thus introducing an extra link between the Executive Committee and the national economic decision-making process. This enhanced the notion of a single super plan for the CMEA, yet it "fell well short of being a supranational planning agency," as Sobell observed (*Red Market*, p. 17). Member governments apparently were unwilling to transfer their decision authorities to the CMEA.

Neither the organizational reform that followed adoption of the Integration Program nor the proliferation of various intragovernmental commissions and bilateral cooperation agreements led to increased coordination of development plans or contributed in any measurable way to production specialization and multilateral trade. Miklós Németh, secretary of the Hungarian communist party in an interview with the Soviet weekly *Ekonomicheskaia gazeta* (no. 6, 1988), gave the following assessment:

> We feel that the stabilizing influence of CMEA countries' cooperation has declined over the last decade. In their mutual ties, most countries strove not to increase exports but to solve the balance problems on the basis of additional imports. Nor has there been a proper solution to questions of the development, production, and reciprocal deliveries of the latest equipment and technology needed to reduce energy- and materials-intensiveness and to improve the structure of production in general. (*FBIS-SOV*, 18 February 1988.)

That CMEA is in need of repair has become a recurrent theme since the Forty-third Extraordinary Session of the Council in Moscow, 13–14 October 1987, convened specifically to address this issue. The session called for restructuring the mechanism of public economic policy coordination and specialization and cooperation in production. The final communiqué called for fostering direct ties among enterprises and research institutions from different countries and for an increased effort to change the financial arrangements underpinning intra-CMEA trade and specialization.

However, the focus of reforming activities was on organizational changes, not financial restructuring. The permanent commissions were streamlined so that their number went from 24 in 1987 to 13 by the end of 1988. Some of them were abolished altogether, and others were merged and their functions assumed by new committees. However, full information is not available as to their current status, for the communiqués on funding new CMEA organs do not provide details as to which permanent commissions have been affected by the reorganization. Two new permanent commissions were established: one for cooperation in environmental protection and the other on cooperation in electricity and nuclear power. The latter was the result of a merger of two former commissions dealing with these matters (Sobell, *Red Market*, p. 3). The resolution of the 44th session also called for fusing the CMEA permanent commissions for the oil, gas, and coal industries, as well as for geology. It is not clear whether these have already been merged.

As part of the reorganization, two new committees were established: one for cooperation in foreign economic relations and the other for cooperation in the sphere of the agro-industrial complex. The former is to supervise "work on perfecting price formation, contractual standards and general terms of reciprocal trade." (TASS; *FBIS-SOV*, 15 February 1988.) The latter's main function includes "coordinating economic and scientific and technical policy . . . on the most important problems of scientific and technical progress in the agro-industrial complex for the entire cycle from scientific research work to the production and sale of output" (*Sel'skaia zhizn*; *FBIS-SOV*, 21 January 1988). This committee convened a meeting at Prague in 1988 during which decisions were reached to establish a new system of scientific information—the so-called Agroproinform for agriculture, forestry, and the food industry.

Streamlining also affected the CMEA Secretariat. At its 126th session in Moscow (February 1988), the Executive Committee approved measures for reorganizing that body. According to the final communiqué, "Secretariat activity is to focus on the ongoing analysis of the state of cooperation, the preparation of economic analyses and forecasts" (*Pravda*, 8 February 1988). Other documents also emphasized that the Secretariat would pay more attention to "fulfillment of adopted resolutions." Some departments were to be enlarged, in particular those responsible for intersectoral matters, and "new departments, for example the fuel-and-power and metallurgy ones, will be formed," said Viacheslav V. Sychev, secretary of the CMEA, in an interview with Soviet journalists. (TASS; *FBIS-SOV*, 5 February 1988.)

Some of these organizational measures had already been implemented. The CMEA Executive Committee's report that was submitted to the 44th session in Prague (July 1988) informed participants that the CMEA apparatus had been "organizationally simplified, and the number of tenured positions for employees of the CMEA Secretariat . . . reduced by almost one-third" (Prague, *Rudé pravo*, 6 July 1988; *FBIS-EEU*, 15 July 1988).

The institutional changes were designed to improve information flow, to make CMEA organs more active in encouraging cooperation, and to monitor actual implementation of resolutions adopted at the sessions. Thus far they have fallen short, and any progress achieved in streamlining and reducing the CMEA bureaucracy may be illusory. Former prime minister of Romania, Constantin Dăscălescu asserted that there was a tendency "of some ministries and central bodies in our countries to replace the dissolved CMEA bodies by new organizational forms outside the Council, which should actually examine the same problems that were examined by the former bodies" (Bucharest, *Scînteia*; *FBIS-EEU*, 14 July 1988). One bureaucracy had been replaced by another.

Areas of Integration and Restructuring. According to its charter, CMEA is charged with coordinating efforts to promote socialist economic integration, stimulate economic and technological progress, and gradually even out the level of economic development among CMEA country members (*Osnovnye dokumenty Soveta Ekonomicheskoi Vzaimopomoschchi*, vol. 1 [Moscow, 1981], pp. 10–11). Because of the absence of supranationality and the limitations inherent in the administrative mechanisms for coordinating and stimulating economic activity, the organization faces several obstacles in the pursuit of these objectives. It has to seek consensus among members or limit its efforts to interested member countries. The implementation of adopted agreements is not a grass roots spontaneous process in response to economic stimuli, as is the case in the West, but requires an explicit *administrative* action by the state.

The institutional devices and public economic policy instruments that have evolved over the past four decades represent attempts to overcome the difficulties of opening centrally planned systems. The tools used to achieve CMEA's declared objectives belong to the realm of administrative planning and management: preplan frameworks or programs, five-year trade agreements, joint investment projects, target plans, cooperation and specialization agreements, joint ventures, and five-year plan coordination. In view of a reassessment regarding the economic role of Eastern Europe by the Soviet Union, these tools have been carefully scrutinized by CMEA organs since 1985.

One of the first instruments was exchange of information between chairmen of planning agencies and other party and government officials on the content of five-year plans to reduce parallelism in capital projects (industrial development strategies remained highly similar in CMEA economies). However, because it is impossible to demonstrate that development strategies would produce even more parallelism without this type of coordination than has been actually observed, the effectiveness of this instrument is difficult to assess. As was pointed out earlier, the institutional body in charge of coordination—the CMEA Committee for Cooperation in Planning (founded in 1971)—does not have supranational authority.

Other mechanisms are the direct ties among firms and joint ventures. Although the first enterprise jointly owned by member countries' firms was established in 1959 (Marer and Montias, "CMEA Integration," p. 151), joint ventures remained rare until recently. Promotion of direct ties and joint ventures has been a hallmark of Soviet policy toward CMEA since Mikhail S. Gorbachev was appointed CPSU general secretary in March 1985. The IIB was to promote this form of economic integration in its lending policies. For example, the bank financed the Bulgarian-Soviet Avtoelektronika plant and the Bulgarian-Soviet knitwear factory—both located in Bulgaria.

In 1986–1989 such microties were established mainly between the Soviet Union and other countries, thus reproducing the radial pattern characteristic of CMEA. In 1987, for instance, 116 Hungarian and Soviet enterprises established direct ties and nineteen joint enterprises and two associations were set up (*Ekonomicheskaia gazeta*, no. 6, February 1988; *FBIS-SOV*, 88-032). According to former Polish prime minister Zbigniew Messner, "more than 200 production enterprises, 190 trade organizations, and 100 R&D organizations established direct links with the Soviet partners" (Warsaw, *Rzeczpospolita*, 6 July 1988). Coal and energy enterprises from the GDR concluded agreements with twelve Soviet enterprises during 1987–1988 (East Berlin, *Presse-Informationen*, 6 May 1988; *JPRS-EEU*, 15 July 1988).

The effectiveness of this instrument, which removes direct control of a CMEA member government over some areas of an enterprise activity, hinges on the compatibility between bilateral arrangements and the domestic system of enterprise performance appraisal. Because in most CMEA countries bonuses and rewards are linked to enterprise financial performance, lack of convertibility hinders cooperation. A partial solution is the use of domestic currencies. Recently, several CMEA countries (Bulgaria, Czechoslovakia, Hungary, Poland, Mongolia, and the Soviet Union) negotiated bilateral agreements to settle accounts in their respective domestic currencies. Except for one Bulgarian agreement with Czechoslovakia, all other agreements are with the Soviet Union. These agreements, however, are not likely to promote microties unless domestic currencies are domestically convertible, that is, an enterprise having a surplus can directly purchase goods on the domestic market of its partner.

The alternative is to use Western convertible currencies. This form of organizing intra-CMEA transactions was discussed at the 130th session of the CMEA Executive Committee in Moscow (*Trybuna ludu*, 19 May) and during the Forty-fifth Council session in Sofia (*LAT*, 10 January 1990). The shift to convertible currencies has been supported by the Soviet Union and, in principle, by other CMEA members. Soviet deputy prime minister Stefan A. Sitarian announced at the conclusion of the Sofia summit meeting that Moscow "would agree on pricing and payment conditions with each country on a bilateral basis" (*NYT*, 11 January 1990). It is likely that trade deficits will be settled with convertible currencies in 1991.

Although agreements on specialization date back to the early 1950s, a major step to make them a leading tool of integration began after the adoption of the 1971 Complex Program. Having carefully examined empirical data on these agreements, specialists at the Rand Corporation concluded that they have neither increased multilateralization of economic ties nor improved technological innovativeness (Keith Crane and Deborah Skoller, *Specialization Agreements in the Council for Mutual Economic Assistance* [Santa Monica, Calif.: Rand Corporation, 1988], pp. 59–60).

Despite these shortcomings, specialization agreements are a part of CMEA interaction. As the Polish deputy to the permanent representative at CMEA, Stanisław Wyłupek, noted, "although only 17 percent of deliveries of Polish capital equipment to CMEA countries are the result of specialization or coproduction agreements, the value of this export (TR 1.8 billion) is very important in our foreign trade" (*Trybuna ludu*, 6 January).

Long-term target plans designed for selected sectors of the economy have been developed in an attempt to integrate the prospective plans of the member countries on a sectoral basis. These plans are similar to the comprehensive programs discussed below in that they provide a framework for bilateral and multilateral agreements concerning trade within these sectors, joint projects, specialization, and cooperation in production, science and technology, and other areas.

During the 1970s joint investment projects were the core of integration efforts to develop supplies of important industrial raw materials. The largest undertaking so far was the Orenburg project (con-

struction of a natural gas complex at Orenburg and a 1,700-mile pipeline to the Soviet western border). Its total cost of $6 billion absorbed about half the expenditures on joint projects during the 1976–1980 period (Marer, "Political Economy of Soviet Relations with Eastern Europe," p. 163). The second largest undertaking was a pulp mill at Ust Ilim. These two endeavors were jointly planned and built by the participating countries. The project belongs to the country in which it is located, and, in exchange for secured supplies at negotiated prices, the participants provide equipment as well as labor and hard currency. Joint projects are often financed through the IIB. No undertakings on the scale of the Orenburg project were undertaken during the 1980s.

Major programs set the long-term priorities that CMEA members are to incorporate in their developmental plans and specify the basic rules and procedures to be established in their interaction. CMEA had two such programs; the third one—the Collective Concept of International Socialist Division of Labor in the Years 1991–2005 (hereafter, DL)—is still in a conceptual phase. The first—the Comprehensive Program for the Further Extension and Improvement of Cooperation and the Development of Socialist Economic Integration by the CMEA Member-Countries (hereafter, CP)—was adopted at the 25th session of the Council at Bucharest in July 1971. Although the document referred to "improvement of commodity money relations," its thrust centered on cooperation in planning in selected spheres of the economy. It laid the framework for joint resource development projects, mainly in the Soviet Union, with participation of interested countries.

The second project was the Comprehensive Program for the CMEA Country Members' Scientific and Technical Progress through the Year 2000 (hereafter, STP). On the basis of a decision taken by the CMEA meeting at Moscow in June 1984, the Soviet Union pushed STP through the extraordinary Forty-first Council session at Moscow in December 1985. Its preparations started during early 1984 in response to external developments like the launching of the Strategic Defense Initiative (SDI) in the United States, the Eureka program in the European Community (EC), and the sanctions on the Soviet Union in the aftermath of the imposition of martial law in Poland. The basic priorities of STP are similar to those of the Eureka program. STP focuses on five major areas whose development aims at making CMEA a technological community. These areas, ranked according to their priority in the program, include the following:

1. Computerization and "electronization" of the economy
2. Increased automation of production processes
3. Acceleration in the development of nuclear energy
4. Development of new materials and technologies for their production
5. Biotechnology

STP was conceived of as a vehicle that would assist CMEA economies in the transition from an extensive to an intensive pattern of economic growth and aid the Soviet Union in changing the composition of its exports to CMEA economies by increasing the share of manufactured goods at the expense of oil, whose price had been declining. The program—initially consisting of 93 (later expanded to 94) projects in which all full members and Yugoslavia were to participate—had two special features. First, it directly addressed the structural inability of centrally planned economic systems to convert research and technical knowledge into efficient technologies and new products. The program called for the development of agreements that would "encompass all stages of the process—science-technology-production-marketing." (Sofia, *Robotnichesko delo*; *FBIS-SOV*, 7 March 1988.)

Second, it called for microintegration, that is, establishment of direct across-the-border links between research institutes and among enterprises. Projects were supervised and coordinated by so-called head organizations, usually research institutions with no links to the industrial sector.

By mid-1989 the following six projects had been prepared: (1) modern, highly efficient automated equipment for production of new materials, (2) thermal protection on temperature regulated and hardened coatings, (3) ceramic materials, technologies, and specialized equipment for parts of combustion engines and gas turbines, (4) equipment and diagnostic instruments for immuno-fermentational analysis of viral and bacterial diseases of potatoes, (5) preparations from nitrogen-fixing microorganisms for basic agriculture, (6) veterinary preparations and their cooperative production (Prague, *Rudé pravo*; *FBIS-EEU*, 29 July).

Implementation of STP has run into a problem familiar to bureaucratically managed economic ac-

tivities; its complexity has exceeded the management capacity of CMEA organs. By the end of 1987, only 285 cooperation agreements and nine hundred contracts for specific research projects had been signed by the ten participating countries (*Rudé pravo*; *FBIS-EEU*, 6 May 1988); about nineteen hundred organizations were involved last year (*Rudé pravo*; *FBIS-EEU*, 29 July). Given this complexity, it is not surprising that most contracts were either not fulfilled at all or fell behind schedule. In addition, products were well below international technical standards. It was estimated that 30 percent of all products developed were not equal to world standards (ibid.).

The often-insurmountable coordination problem has been magnified by the necessity to control all stages of technology or product development processes under different national jurisdictions. To make things worse, there was little willingness among CMEA members to become seriously involved in STP. As former Czechoslovak deputy prime minister Jaromir Obžina noted,

The *retarding* factor in the current realization of both the Comprehensive and the large target-oriented scientific-technical and technological projects is *our weak knowledge and experience in organizing and managing extensive and demanding programs, and the failure to comprehend the fact that without earmarking clearly delineated financial and foreign exchange funds for individual programs one can expect neither rapid results nor the end of superfluous administrative work.* Papers and goodwill, even in the form of concluded agreements, can be no substitute for the necessary resources dedicated to resolving research tasks and applying the results in social practice. (Emphasis in original, ibid.)

Even assigning priority to STP projects "in the plans of individual countries so that these projects receive 'most favored treatment' in the mechanism of CMEA cooperation," as Soviet official Nikolai Sliun'kov, CPSU Politburo member, argued (Budapest, *Népszabadság*; *FBIS-EEU*, 24 June 1988), would not prevent STP from faltering. The program was too broad (*Planovane hospodarstvi*, no. 2, 1988), and therefore preferential treatment came down to "most favored treatment," which did not bode well for implementation. In addition, the absence of convertibility and well-defined procedures for pricing research and development undermined the program and gave preference to bilateral rather than multilateral cooperation. (Ibid.)

The problems with STP were acknowledged in official documents of CMEA Council sessions at Moscow (1987) and Prague (1988) as well as of the CMEA Executive Committee. In its report to participants at the 44th session in Prague, for instance, the CMEA Executive Committee frankly admitted that "thus far, we have not succeeded in overcoming the serious difficulties which have for a long time accompanied cooperation in production. . .based on the outputs of the Comprehensive Program for Scientific-Technical Progress and agreements on direct relations" (*Rudé pravo*; *FBIS-EEU*, 15 July 1988).

To cope with these shortcomings, several solutions were suggested: (1) pooling R&D resources of the member countries, (2) establishing large international institutions, staffed on a competitive basis and endowed with up-to-date scientific equipment (*Rudé pravo*; *FBIS-EEU*, 16 June 1988), and (3) selecting head organizations on the basis of competitive bidding. These measures so far have not infused STP with vitality. Although a CMEA official recently asserted that "all the program's targets will be fulfilled by the year 2000, and more than 1,500 kinds of new equipment. . .and much else will be created" (Moscow, *Sel'skaia zhizn*, 25 January), it is unlikely that CMEA will become a world technological leader in the foreseeable future.

The winds of reform blowing from Moscow and growing frustration with STP implementation triggered a thorough examination of the factors accountable for the problems of organizing interaction among CMEA members. The Forty-third CMEA Council session directed the Secretariat to develop a new approach to socialist integration. A comprehensive program, which became known as the Collective Concept of International Socialist Division of Labor in the Years 1991–2005 (DL), was submitted and adopted at the 44th session. In contrast to two previous programs, DL included not only general statements calling for intrabranch specialization and new forms of cooperation, but also "proposals for dividing into stages the restructuring of the mechanism of multilateral cooperation and the integration of socialist economy."

DL seeks to extend the ties among CMEA members beyond governments. It identifies three levels of cooperation: (1) the governmental level, where a framework for public economic and scientific-technological policies is set, (2) the intermediate level of negotiations between representatives of the leading sectors, and (3) the enterprise level. Although the first and, to a lesser extent, the second have been the core of the traditional mechanisms, the third one revives the idea of the 1971 Integration Program. By granting enterprise management the authority to deal with foreign firms, DL challenges the sacrosanct principle of state monopoly over foreign economic relations.

The DL program recognizes the existing constraints; to alleviate them it promises gradual introduction of decentralizing measures that should result in a "joint socialist market." Direct administrative tools of control are thus to be supplemented by indirect tools of public economic policy. The objective is to establish economic mechanisms of integration that "will be able to combine the planning of cooperation with the growing role of economic instruments." (*Trybuna ludu*, 6 January 1989.) By the end of 1990, currency exchange, legal, and organizational problems are to be solved.

Proposals for restructuring do not require elimination of planning. Instead they recommend fusing plan with market and call for concerted economic policy and coordination of plans in industrial firms that would be made possible by "upgrading of the methods of pricing, widening of monetary functions of the transferable ruble, and the use of national currencies to service direct ties" (TASS; *FBIS-SOV*, 12 July 1988).

The concept of DL is internally inconsistent and conceptually flawed. First, the call for enterprise autonomy and contractual relations with other economic actors is not compatible with a requirement—extensively discussed in 1989 by the CMEA Executive Committee—of a "three-level system of plan coordination" (Warsaw, PAP, 25 January; *FBIS-SOV*, 26 January) because enterprises would remain subject to a plan.

Second, the principle of integration underlying DL whereby each country is to retain full sovereignty in the field of economic policy (*Rzeczpospolita*, 18 August) is not reconcilable with economic integration. Therefore, it is scarcely surprising that—as former Polish official Stanisław Długosz put it—"we have not worked out theoretical principles of an integrated socialist market, although in many areas work is already in its advanced stages, for example, in the area of the multilateral settlement of accounts in CMEA" (ibid.). The principles of such a market cannot be developed because the institution of market cannot exist when fully fused with the state, that is, when economic actors are subordinated to the plan.

Third, linking the implementation of DL to significant improvement in technologies demonstrates a total misunderstanding of the market economy. CMEA secretary Viacheslav Sychev stated that DL will be implemented gradually because "national markets need to be considerably more saturated with high-quality goods and services than now, of course, and radical changes in the technical level of production are also needed" (Moscow, *Komsomol'-skaia pravda*; *FBIS-SOV*, 15 June). Sychev believes that administrative planning will bring about a technological explosion and an abundance of high-quality goods and services. But these are the very areas where central planning has failed.

Because of formidable technical and political obstacles, the joint socialist market will not emerge soon (if at all). It must be preceded by the emergence of market economies in all member countries, the convertibility of currencies, and the removal of administrative barriers to free movement of capital. Political obstacles are likely to emerge as governments that were brought about in 1989 by popular rebellions make the transition away from the communist economic system. Because of domestic political and economic pressures, some CMEA members—in particular, Czechoslovakia, Hungary, and Poland—will work hard to reorient their economies toward the West and may lose interest in CMEA.

The economic reform measures already implemented make some components of the traditional "integration" mechanism obsolete. In some countries plans are either no longer prepared or are not compulsory for economic actors. Two countries—Hungary and Poland—seek to expand the private sector. Therefore, at the Forty-fifth Council session in Sofia, East European and Asian leaders committed themselves to scrap procedures for coordinating five-year plans (*LAT*, 10 January 1990). The dissenting voice came from Cuba's vice-president, Carlos Rodrigues, who warned that "introducing the market should in no way mean a move towards anarchy in production. Recognizing a certain degree of private ownership does not mean this should have a main role in society." (Ibid.) Nonetheless, delegates to the 45th session agreed that "the bloc was not working and needed an overhaul" (Sofia, AP, 11 January 1990). The final outcome of institutional tinkering will be shaped by the political evolution in Soviet–East European relations, as was the case in the past.

Oil, Foreign Debt, and Cohesion of CMEA.

The current Soviet economic crisis has changed the major components that shape CMEA activity, that is, the Soviet economic posture toward CMEA countries. Its evolution was marked by transfers of resources to the Soviet Union during the 1950s, more equitable relations in the 1960s, and increased Soviet opportunity costs in the 1970s. There was little political risk in tapping East European resources to offset the impact of the Western embargo in the 1950s. Opportunity costs of providing Eastern Europe with energy and raw materials were minimal when buyers dominated the international commodity markets in the 1960s. These costs substantially increased during the 1970s, but were compensated for by several favorable developments in world markets. The trade pattern, involving the exchange of Soviet hard currency exportables for internationally noncompetitive East European manufactured goods, was then acceptable to Moscow. As viewed from the Kremlin, this was "an effective but cumbersome" arrangement, to paraphrase Michael Marrese ("CMEA: Effective but Cumbersome Political Economy," *International Organization*, no. 2, Spring 1986). By the late 1980s, this arrangement had become both ineffective and unwieldy.

The oil shock of 1974, combined with an expanding demand by smaller CMEA members for Soviet raw materials and energy, significantly changed the matrix of intrabloc relations. During the 1960s, when the prices of raw materials and energy were either falling or stagnating, the Soviet Union was ready and willing to meet the East European demand that arose from inefficient industrial use and an investment bias in favor of raw materials–intensive and energy-intensive sectors. The situation changed in late 1973 when the Organization of Petroleum Exporting Countries (OPEC) successfully effected an almost fivefold increase in oil prices (Persian Gulf oil rose from $2.48 per barrel in 1972 to $11.65 per barrel on 1 January 1974). Between 1972 and 1974 the price of manufactured goods rose by 43 percent; that of energy and raw materials rose by 250 percent.

Given the Soviet emphasis on raw materials/energy and East European specialization in manufactured goods, this dramatic reversal in the terms of trade between raw materials and manufactures changed priorities in commercial policies. The USSR wanted to reap hard currency benefits from the sale of oil and other raw materials on international markets, whereas the East Europeans desired to secure their supply. As a consequence of the oil shock, the opportunity cost of oil exports to CMEA significantly increased for the Soviet Union. At

USSR insistence, the 1975 Moscow agreement amended one provision of the 1958 Bucharest arrangement: the prices were to be revised every year instead of every five years. This new arrangement provided CMEA members with a protective shield against worldwide energy scarcities at Soviet expense because the sale of oil to non-CMEA countries would generate several-times-higher foreign revenues.

Leaving aside the consequences of overhauling the Bucharest formula on political stability and CMEA's cohesion, the Soviet "lost revenues" were compensated for by several developments. First, thanks to its improved terms of trade with the noncommunist world, the USSR enjoyed large windfall gains estimated at $50 billion for 1973–1980 (Paul Marer, *The Economies and Trade of Eastern Europe*, discussion paper #6 [Bloomington: Indiana Center for Global Business, Indiana University, 1988]). Second, the Soviet Union garnered a large share of the dramatically expanding arms market in the OPEC countries. Third, it curtailed growth rates of its oil supplies in the 1970s, which fell to zero in the 1980s. Fourth, taking advantage of its newly acquired bargaining strength, the USSR was in position to sway East European CMEA members to increase their assistance to non-European members—Mongolia, Cuba and Vietnam—as well as some pro-Soviet regimes in the Third World (ibid.). Finally, under pressure of the declining availability of Soviet supplies of raw materials, some CMEA countries became interested in carrying out provisions of the Comprehensive Program concerning joint investment programs.

These programs, which consisted of developing a USSR resource base and the infrastructure to transport basic fuels and raw materials—cofinanced by interested CMEA countries—became the nucleus of regional integration in the 1970s and were advantageous both to the Soviets and to the East Europeans (John Hannigan and Carl McMillan, "Joint Investment in Resource Development," in *East European Economic Assessment*, p. 265). The latter would obtain secure, long-term access to raw materials that otherwise would have to be purchased for scarce hard currency. The USSR, in turn, would receive much-needed assistance in developing resource bases and transport facilities in the remote Siberian regions. A significant part of the output would be used for domestic consumption and export to the West.

This change in CMEA priorities also served Soviet political objectives. The joint investment projects added a seemingly permanent dimension to the existing radial network of bilateral arrangements that tie CMEA countries to the USSR. On top of increased East European diversion of exports from other markets—mainly domestic and potentially from other CMEA countries—to the Soviet Union, triggered by their declining terms of trade, the new pattern locked the CMEA economies even tighter to the USSR. As the authors of a U.N. report noted, "The expansion of exports [to the Soviet Union] necessitated new industrial capacities, often designed to meet the demand of the expanding Soviet market" (*Economic Survey of Europe in 1988–1989* [New York, 1989], p. 196). In a similar vein, Hungarian prime minister Miklós Németh wryly observed, "we carried out investments worth many tens, even hundreds of billions of forint which did not shift the structure of Hungarian production in a modern direction, for at the time these were based on a secure [Soviet] market" (Budapest, *Népszabadság*, 7 July 1988; *JPRS-EEU*, 10 August 1988).

The Soviet demand—because of the size of its market—exceeded supply capacities of the East European economies. As a result, the propensity of East European planners to develop the same lines of production was not offset by constraints of the Soviet import demand. The resulting lack of coordination regarding purchases of Western technology and know-how reduced the potential for development of multilateral ties. This in turn exacerbated structural dependence on the USSR, as the East Europeans sought to adjust their development plans to meet Soviet requirements. Pressures to introduce economic reforms to adjust to the international economy were thus considerably weakened because of the Soviet "protective shield," revealed in energy supplies and tolerance for East European manufactures of low quality. This lack of incentives to adjust to non-CMEA markets was also fueled by USSR resistance to decentralizing economic reforms, as illustrated by the case of Hungary in the 1970s. The other reason was the newly gained access of East European countries to Western private financial markets, the consequence of petrodollar recycling after the first oil shock. The paradox was that Western credits provided another disincentive to East European regimes to develop high-value manufactured goods because during the 1970s their "lagging capacity to expand the export of high-value manufactured goods to the West was bridged by credits" (Marer, "Foreign Trade Strategies in Eastern Europe," pp. 19–20).

Under these circumstances, it is scarcely surprising that "not a single one of the important provisions [of the Comprehensive Program] proclaimed there [Bucharest] has been carried out thus far," as Polish economist Jerzy Kleer observed (Warsaw, *Polityka-Eksport-Import*, no. 8, 1988). Indeed, with the exception of joint projects in the Soviet Union, provisions for innovative, market-oriented financial and currency settlements were not implemented because that would have entailed economic reforms in the Soviet Union. Neither short-term incentives nor the political willingness to promote multilateral links existed when Soviet domination was not in danger.

The circumstances shaping the posture of the Soviet Union and other members toward the issue of regional integration changed during the 1980s. Because of expanding costs for servicing the international debt and the Western credit squeeze, the economic situation of East European countries deteriorated. Recession in the West and the increased cost of Soviet oil—only party mitigated by USSR willingness to run trade deficits with its CMEA partners—exacerbated their balance-of-payments problems during the 1981–1986 period.

The East European balance-of-payments crisis of the early 1980s revealed the weaknesses of the intra-CMEA framework. As a result of the absence of coordination for purchases of capital equipment and technology from the West during the 1970s, a "secondary [imported] parallelism emerged," to borrow an apt description from Soviet economist Shiriaev ("New Strategy of Cooperation and Development of CMEA Countries," Moscow, *Social Sciences*, no. 3 [1988]). Neither coordination of economic policies, designed to cope with external financial problems among CMEA members, nor "mutual" economic assistance in the time of crisis could be detected. Cuts in Western imports and the stagnation of Soviet deliveries of basic fuels and raw materials dampened export other than to the USSR or other CMEA member economies. Among the first casualties of these economic problems were the CMEA specialization agreements, as a Rand study noted (Crane and Skoller, *Specialization Agreements*). CMEA did not provide a buffer that would dampen the impact of external disturbances. As one author observed, the organization proved irrelevant during this period (Fallenbuchl, *International Journal*, no. 1). This realization became widespread among policymakers, particularly from those countries that were hit hardest, namely, Hungary and Poland.

It was not until Gorbachev's ascension to power, coinciding with deterioration of the Soviet economy, that the issue of socialist integration re-entered Moscow's political agenda. This new interest in CMEA was also triggered by a growing technological gap between CMEA economies and the West and declining Soviet hard currency revenues. As a result of depressed world prices for oil and other raw materials, USSR terms of trade with the West sharply decreased. In addition, Middle East importers of Soviet arms curtailed their purchases because of significantly reduced oil revenues. In consequence, the buffer that had allowed the Brezhnev regime to cushion the political impact of the stagnating domestic economy vanished. It became apparent to the new USSR leadership that only significant changes in managing the economy and modernizing the productive structure would prevent a crisis.

Seeking assistance for the modernization drive, the Soviet leadership turned to CMEA for support. STP—the first example of the USSR commitment to increase economic integration among CMEA countries in the field of scientific-technical development—was designed to counter the technological warfare allegedly launched by the United States against socialist countries. Although there was little progress in STP implementation, Moscow's verbal commitment increased. At the Council session in Bucharest (1986), USSR prime minister Nikolai I. Ryzhkov declared, "The Central Committee of our Party directs all state organs, all links of the Soviet economic mechanism towards all considerable extension of the cooperation with the CMEA countries, for all the utmost utilization of the advantages of the international socialist division of labor in order to intensify production" (Ånders Åslund, "The New Soviet Policy Towards International Economic Organizations," London, *The World Today*, February 1988).

Thus in stark contrast to the de facto benign neglect of the 1970s, the USSR became committed to restructuring the mechanism of coordination and cooperation within the bloc. Five sessions of the Council held between 1985 and 1988 were devoted to a critical appraisal of every aspect of CMEA. They did not result in any significant change, as various CMEA documents readily admit; for instance, the final communiqué of the 44th session reads inter alia, "The economic cooperation of the CMEA countries does not as yet properly encourage a greater efficiency of their economies" (*Pravda*, 8 July 1988).

All the drawbacks and obstacles to integration were revealed in the new spirit of *glasnost'*, although information concerning intra-CMEA agreements remained secret until early 1990—that is, if a decision to publish the Executive Committee's report to the Forty-fifth Council session is sustained. The market ideas that had been circulating among East European economists, particularly Hungarians and Poles, since the Khrushchevian debate on a socialist international division of labor were given an official seal of approval during the Forty-third Extraordinary Council session, convened at Moscow during 13–14 October 1987, and the 44th session, at Prague, 6–8 July 1988. USSR prime minister Ryzhkov declared that "to us, the integrated market is not a fashionable buzzword but an important direction of development of the integrative process" (Warsaw, *Polityka*, no. 29, 1988).

However, there are indications that official Soviet enthusiasm for the integrated socialist market evaporated in 1989. The idea of a CMEA market disappeared from the official CPSU daily, *Pravda*, a fact noted in proreform CMEA countries (Warsaw, *Życie gospodarcze*, 5 November 1989). A former Polish official in the CMEA, Stanisław Długosz, went on record to say that "the Soviet interest in implementing decisions of the Forty-third and Forty-fourth CMEA Council sessions has visibly declined" (*Życie gospodarcze*, 6 August).

The change in Moscow's approach to CMEA stems from the realization that a stranglehold over Eastern Europe does not assure the Soviet Union any greater stability, that policing the region would undermine Gorbachev's policies of *glasnost'* and *perestroika*, and that the integrated socialist market is not an attractive alternative for either the Soviet Union or other East European economies toward integration with the world economy. The security costs to Moscow of loosening its grip on the "junior allies" are not prohibitive. As one author observed, "Geostrategic realities give the majority of East European nations no alternative but to maintain close security links with Moscow. Domestic changes taking place within the region will not jeopardize the Soviet position in Europe, but will substantially reduce the cost of the empire." (Arthur Rachwald, "Soviet-East European Relations," *Current History*, November.) As a result, political and economic ramifications of Soviet–East European relations recently have changed and exacerbated disintegrating tendencies within CMEA.

Disintegrating Tendencies in CMEA.
CMEA is in crisis. Although participants in the Forty-fifth Council session held at Sofia in January 1990 agreed that CMEA needs a drastic overhaul, no agreement was reached on the rules to dismantle or how soon specific changes should be introduced. In contrast to the Council sessions during the 1980s, the view that CMEA is crisis-ridden was shared at Sofia by all its European members, the Soviet Union included. The Hungarian prime minister stated that "this meeting will lead to a turning point for our organization. A period of more than forty years is coming to an end." (*LAT*, 10 January 1990.)

Soviet delegate Stefan Sitarian supported the idea: "We need a new type of Comecon [CMEA] built on new principles and approaches" (*WP*, 10 January 1990). The future institutional shape of CMEA remains to be seen. It is certain, however, that the traditional economic underpinnings of CMEA are beyond repair. CMEA is not likely to become a "council of mutual economic development" soon.

The disintegration is the result of processes that date back to the 1960s and 1970s. The original concept of CMEA, which was predicated on decoupling the Soviet bloc from the world economy and integrating East European economies with the USSR, has been achieved, although to varying degrees. The "success," however, has largely contributed to economic collapse and disintegration of communist regimes in Eastern Europe during 1989. The paradox of the current situation is that neither can the Soviet Union afford to underwrite the "deal" that has maintained the cohesion of the grouping, nor can other CMEA members afford to leave the organization.

CMEA has achieved a high level of sufficiency. It is estimated that member countries obtain 68 percent of their imported capital equipment, 96 percent of their petroleum and ferrous raw materials, and 65–80 percent of nonferrous metals through mutual deliveries (*Trybuna ludu*, 6 January). Despite these impressive figures, CMEA economies have been unable to keep up with technological progress without Western imports. Sluggish economic performance as well as the necessity of generating trade surpluses to service Western debts compel CMEA members to seek ways of reintegrating with the world economy. Almost half a century of a communist economic system, artificially sustained by CMEA trade patterns, has made a return to West European markets difficult.

Economic cohesion of the bloc has been assured by an unwritten contract according to which the USSR supplies oil, gas, and other raw materials in exchange for East European manufactured goods. This contract has been breached by the Soviet Union on two counts. First, it was unable or unwilling to meet the growing demand for oil by CMEA partners because of the increase in production and transportation costs and, more recently, because of economic recession. For example, Soviet oil exports during 1989 dropped to about 50 percent of plan targets (*Życie gospodarcze*, 14 January 1990). In addition, falling oil prices in world markets have forced the USSR to expand its export to the West to prevent a decline in hard currency revenues. Although between 1960 and the late 1970s the volume of Soviet oil deliveries to Eastern Europe increased by 50 percent (Paul Marer, "Foreign Trade Strategies in Eastern Europe: Determinants, Outcomes, Prospects" [Paper delivered at the Twelfth International Workshop on East-West Economic Interaction, Athens, Georgia, 1–5 April]), it stagnated during the 1980s except for a 6 percent upswing in 1986 stemming from a sharp increase of exports to Romania (*Economic Survey of Europe in 1987–1988*, p. 198).

USSR unwillingness to abide by rules that it imposed on CMEA has exacerbated economic problems of smaller CMEA countries and has been a source of frustration in Soviet-East European relations. The USSR first slightly changed the price-setting code in 1975 to take advantage of the 1974 oil shock. Faced with steeply deteriorating terms of trade and a reduced Soviet supply of primary materials, East European regimes adjusted to worsening terms of trade by simultaneously increasing exports and cutting imports from the USSR. Had there been no second oil shock (1979–1981), the East European adjustment would have been smooth. The East European aggregate trade balance for the period 1970–1980 moved from a deficit of about TR 4 billion (in current CMEA prices) to an aggregate surplus in the 1981–1988 period of about TR 15.7 billion (in 1980 CMEA oil prices), as compared with a total deficit of TR 1 billion in current CMEA prices over the same period (calculated from data in *Economic Survey of Europe in 1988–1989*, pp. 196–201). Improved terms of trade—the result of the falling CMEA oil prices—in East Europe generated a TR 3.5 billion surplus in its trade with the Soviet Union during 1988 and at least a TR 5 billion surplus in 1989 according to preliminary estimates (*Życie gospodarcze*, 14 January 1990). In the case of Bulgaria and Poland surpluses were used to pay their Soviet debts, but the Czechoslovak and Hungarian surpluses (in 1989, about TR 1 billion each) amounted to forced credits to the Soviet Union. In contrast with earlier East European efforts to adjust to USSR demands through transfer of resources to the foreign sector and away from domestic use, no similar action has been taken by the Soviet Union; domestic concerns about the crisis-ridden economy have prevailed over obligations to CMEA junior partners. The problem is, however, that surpluses, although beneficial to the Soviet Union, contribute to convertible currency balance-of-payments problems, inflationary pressures, and shortages—particularly of consumer goods—in Eastern Europe. In consequence, the Soviet economic crisis contributes to the deterioration of other CMEA economies.

Second, in another departure from the established CMEA code of conduct, Moscow has forced the East European countries to supply it with increased amounts of food products and consumer goods. These products often have significant convertible currency value and can be sold easily in international markets. Although this change in composition of the Soviet import demand from Eastern Europe has not yet produced a full symmetry in the proportion of hard goods (i.e., goods easily sold in Western markets) that are mutually traded, it has further eroded the foundations of intra-CMEA relations and released disintegrating tendencies.

There are two other areas where the traditional arrangement that kept the CMEA bloc together is under growing pressure for change. First, the USSR would like to see a prompt shift from transferable rubles to convertible currency and wants to expand dramatically its exports of manufactured goods to Eastern Europe. The Soviet proposals to replace transferable rubles, which are worthless except for bilateral transactions within CMEA, with Western convertible currencies and to change the Bucharest price-setting code produce ambivalent feelings among East European policymakers. On the one hand, they realize that those measures are undoubtedly necessary to remove the insulation of CMEA from the world economy: Because of the incompatibility between enterprise autonomy in foreign trade and the administrative straitjacket of CMEA, they are an impediment to changes in the economic system that are either contemplated (Czechoslovakia) or already implemented (Hungary and Poland).

On the other hand, "when the oil price rose, Eastern Europe had to increase significantly its exports to obtain the same amount of oil and raw materials" (Piotr Cyburt, "What Will Happen to CMEA?" *Życie gospodarcze*, 5 November). According to this line of argument, the USSR should pay back the windfall profits it accrued between 1975 and 1986 (Stanisław Długosz, "CMEA: Is a Radical Transformation Feasible?" *Życie gospodarcze*, 6 August).

If intra-CMEA trade were immediately put on a convertible currency basis, East European countries would lose, at least over the short run, because their transferable ruble exports can purchase more oil in the Soviet Union than in convertible currency markets. According to one estimate, Soviet oil is about 50 percent cheaper for Poland than oil imported from elsewhere (Jan Danielewski, "Trade with the USSR," *Polityka-Eksport-Import*, 9 December). It has been estimated that Hungary and Poland would each lose about $1.5 billion a year. At the 45th CMEA session at Sofia in January 1990, the icy reaction of Czechoslovak delegates to a Soviet suggestion that a switch be made to a convertible currency basis also suggests significant losses to the Czechoslovak economy.

Second, the program approved by the CPSU Politburo in 1988 calls for radical changes in economic relations between the USSR and other CMEA countries (TASS, 3 November 1988); namely, fuel and raw materials that now account for about two-thirds of Soviet exports to other CMEA countries are to be increasingly replaced by a dramatically expanding share of finished products, machinery, and equipment. The statement by USSR prime minister Nikolai Ryzhkov in a speech at the Moscow CMEA session—that all future increases in the Soviet exports to other CMEA partners should come from the sale of capital equipment—has been incorporated in a CMEA draft for a collective long-term plan. According to this draft, the USSR is to increase machine building exports by 400 percent by the year 2005.

Under present circumstances these Soviet demands will only accelerate the disintegration of CMEA. Eastern Europeans are in no position to improve the quality of their exports to the USSR for at least three interrelated reasons. First, seeking an adjustment to balance-of-payments disequilibria in the early 1980s, most of them drastically curtailed investment and imports of Western technology. As a result, the technological quality of their manufactures and their international competitiveness is lower than it was in the 1970s (Kazimierz Poznanski, "The Competitiveness of Polish Industry and Indebtedness," in Paul Marer and Włodzimierz Siwinski, eds., *Creditworthiness and Reform in Poland* [Bloomington: Indiana University, 1988], pp. 46–52).

East Europe sends mainly raw materials and low-processed goods to the nonsocialist world, which account for about 70 percent of its total exports. For example, the share of high-technology products being exported to the West fell from 1.2 percent in 1980 to 0.6 percent in 1986; this share in exports to the Third World increased from 9.8 percent to 13.2 percent (*Życie gospodarcze*, no. 35, 27 August). Thus highly processed products are in short supply throughout Eastern Europe.

Second, USSR pressure for higher-quality products may lead to cuts in East European imports of low-quality products from the Soviet Union. For instance, Hungary wants to replace the USSR as its major iron ore supplier because the low-grade content of Soviet steel allegedly accounts for their steel products' lack of competitiveness (*NYT*, 4 January 1988). Many other areas offer East Europeans the possibility of retaliation by demanding low-processed products from the Soviet Union that meet international standards. Their bargaining position will certainly improve if the USSR insists on increasing the share of capital equipment in its exports to Eastern Europe.

Third, meeting the Soviet request for high-quality products would entail a significant restructuring of East European economies. Over a period of 40 years, their investment programs have been designed to replace hard currency imports and to pay for USSR deliveries of raw materials. Changing this structure would require stepping up investment outlays and Western imports. Most CMEA countries are now free to gravitate openly toward Western Europe. Given their strenuous balance of payments position and domestic political tension, none of these options is within easy grasp. Yet more active use of economic statecraft by Western governments in response to the fall of communist regimes in some CMEA countries may ease the process of their reintegration with the world economy.

Whatever the prospects for reintegration, CMEA could no longer ignore the European Community (EC). In line with Gorbachev's concept of a "common European home," the Soviet Union dropped its demand that CMEA be treated as an equal partner of the EC (Ånders Åslund, "The New Soviet Policy Towards International Economic Organizations," *World Today*, February 1988). Gorbachev's discussions, first with Italian prime minister Bettino Craxi in May 1985 and later with President François Mitterrand in October 1985, removed obstacles to the signing of a joint declaration on the establishment of official relations between the EC and the CMEA in Luxembourg on 25 June 1988. Although "a joint declaration with the EC last year created prerequisites for trade and economic cooperation" (Moscow TASS, 23 January; *FBIS-SOV*, 24 January), the agreements that had been signed were between individual CMEA countries and the EC and not between the two groups. Sergei Ugarov, an adviser on CMEA-EC relations at the CMEA Secretariat, complained that

> although two meetings of the two organizations' experts have been held since the signing of the joint declaration, as is stipulated by the document, although CMEA proposed seven concrete areas of possible cooperation, the matter has not come as yet to a detailed discussion of the methods and forms of interaction in each of these areas (TASS, 24 June; *FBIS-SOV*, 89-123).

Because CMEA is not a supranational organization and therefore is not in a position to sign agreements that would be binding for its members, it is hardly surprising that negotiations for a multilateral EC-CMEA agreement proceeded slowly (the first round of talks took place in November 1988 and the second in April 1989).

Although attempts to seek better trade relations with the EC prompted CMEA countries to reach several agreements on specific sectors, such as steel and textiles, no other CMEA government except Romania signed a comprehensive agreement before the 1988 CMEA-EC joint declaration. According to this agreement, the EC commission has become empowered to negotiate agreements with individual CMEA countries. During 1989 a scramble took place among Eastern European governments to negotiate the best agreement. Several were signed: the trade and cooperation agreement between the EC and Hungary promises elimination of all protectionist measures imposed on Hungarian exports by 1995, both agricultural goods and manufactures, in return for better conditions for Western business; the agreement with Czechoslovakia will reduce considerably the list of products subject to EC quantitative restrictions (the value of Western concessions is put at $10 million, according to Philip Hanson and Vlad Sobell, "The Changing Relations

between the EC and the CMEA," Munich, *RAD Background Report*, no. 73, 3 May); the agreement with Poland calls for abolishing all import quotas on a fixed timetable. Negotiations for a new comprehensive agreement with Romania were suspended because of human rights violations under the Ceauçescu regime, and Bulgaria is involved in negotiating a trade and cooperation agreement.

It remains to be seen what impact this new drift toward the West and the multibillion dollar aid and loan programs that are currently being developed by Western governments will have on intra-CMEA relations. Whatever impact these have, the East European CMEA economies will find it extremely costly to reorient their trade away from one another and the Soviet Union. The latter absorbs almost 60 percent of their foreign trade, whereas the corresponding figure for Western Europe is about 20 percent.

Conclusion. The CMEA institutional framework, although designed to extend domestic planning activity to a regional level, does not delegate directly to CMEA the authority to execute plans. Most interaction is subject to bilateral controls by the respective national planning bodies, whereas calls for multilateral cooperation and coordination are subject to CMEA institutions. Introduced changes may improve the organization's ability to track new opportunities, but can do little to create sustained interest in cooperation among economic actors. These will become another source of frustration to those keen on socialist integration unless they are assisted by the measures enabling integration at the level of firms. Meaningful integration would entirely scrap the existing administrative planning system.

Despite various organizational changes introduced during 1988–1989, the debate at the Forty-fifth Council session in January 1990 showed that CMEA is still in need of a major overhaul. The wave of democratization sweeping Eastern Europe has brought to power politicians and experts who are aware that CMEA is not reformable. Czechoslovak and Hungarian delegates to the Forty-fifth Council session wanted a thorough dismantling of CMEA. This did not happen. Instead, session participants endorsed a committee that would formulate proposals within two months for bringing the integration mechanism in line with economic reforms in Eastern Europe (*WP*, 10 January 1990).

Bartlomiej Kaminski
University of Maryland at College Park

Warsaw Treaty Organization

By the end of 1989 the Warsaw Pact had surrendered to the people of Eastern Europe. In response to the unanticipated formation of the Solidarity government in Poland in late August, Gorbachev announced in late October the revocation of the Warsaw Treaty Organization (WTO) security guarantee to the ruling communist parties of Eastern Europe (*Izvestiia*, 27 October). Within weeks, WTO parties had in effect conceded power to their alienated societies by entering into roundtable negotiations with ad hoc sociopolitical groups, by bringing noncommunists into national governments, and by promising free elections in the first half of 1990.

The new military reality of Eastern Europe was that the fraternal parties could no longer rely on USSR/WTO forces to enforce the Brezhnev Doctrine—the WTO commitment to "joint defense of the gains of socialism against internal and external reaction" (V. G. Kulikov, *Kollektivnaia zashchita sotsializma* [Moscow, 1982], pp. 21, 31). All that was left of the 1955 Warsaw Treaty was the Article 4 requirement that the newly sovereign states of Eastern Europe consult with one another in the event that any one of them faced an external security threat.

As an alliance of ruling communist parties, the Warsaw Pact had been bound together by the parties' common dependence on a highly visible USSR/WTO capability for military intervention. In exchange for the Soviet security guarantee, the ruling parties integrated their national armed forces into a USSR-dominated command system structured for military actions in both East and West Europe.

By revoking the Soviet security guarantee to the fraternal parties, Gorbachev destroyed the capability of these parties to maintain the elaborate bilateral links between national defense ministries and WTO/USSR agencies that had constituted the actual command and control structure of the WTO. Without these linkages, the unified doctrine, common programs, and pre-1989 style joint exercises of the alliance would soon disappear.

The year 1989 began with Gorbachev and his Warsaw Pact allies defining the East-West arms control agenda by a series of dramatic unilateral Soviet and WTO force reductions. Gorbachev initiated these cutbacks in a December 1988 address to the United Nations in which he elaborated a program for drawing Western and Eastern Europe into a "common European home" (*Pravda*, 8 December 1988). In this common home, Gorbachev urged the elimination of nuclear weapons, especially U.S. nuclear weapons.

The year ended with Gorbachev reporting to the USSR Congress of People's Deputies as follows:

> Fraternal parties are no longer ruling in Poland and Hungary. Our friends in the German Democratic Republic and Czechoslovakia have largely lost their positions.
>
> New political forces have emerged in the arena. They include both those who support the socialist idea and those who seek other ways of social development...
>
> We proceed from the fact that any nation has the right to decide its fate by itself, including the choice of a system and the ways, pace, and methods of its development. (*Pravda*, 12 December.)

In Romania the disappearance of the Soviet intervention threat removed the sole justification for society's continued acceptance of the Ceaușescu dynasty. The only policy of the regime that enjoyed popular support was the assertion of national independence by withholding Romania's armed forces from participation in the bilateral integration mechanisms of the Warsaw Pact. Deprived of their nationalist justification, Ceaușescu's Securitate forces responded to popular revolt with a brief but bloody defense of the ancien régime before surrendering to the army, which no longer had the mission of preparing to resist a possible Soviet intervention.

The new governments in Poland, Hungary, and Czechoslovakia quickly began exploratory discussions with the USSR over the rapid withdrawal of Soviet garrisons from their countries. Even the new head of the East German communist party called for removal of Soviet troops from East Germany by 1999. (*NYT*, 7 January 1990.)

The Soviet negotiator at the Vienna talks on Conventional Forces in Europe (CFE) informally approached the Americans about the possibility of rapidly drawing down USSR and U.S. forces in Europe to no more than 275,000 on each side (*NYT*, 5 January 1990). In the CFE negotiations, the Soviets had previously rejected U.S. proposals to limit U.S. and USSR forces based in Europe to the previously mentioned totals, limits that would probably leave the Bundeswehr as the largest national force in Central Europe proper.

American intelligence estimates that were leaked to the press concluded that by late 1989 the Soviets had virtually no capability to lead their allies or even their own forces for a surprise attack on the North Atlantic Treaty Organization (NATO) (*WP*, 2 December). In the course of a few months the Warsaw Pact threat, which for 35 years had driven a neverending NATO debate over how to deter a conventional attack by superior WTO forces, had withered away.

The future course of CFE negotiations will no longer be over the military-technical intricacies of asymmetrical conventional force reductions by the WTO and NATO. The new military issues will be managing an orderly Soviet withdrawal from Eastern Europe, defining the national missions of newly independent East European forces, and redefining the purposes of Soviet, U.S., French, and British nuclear arsenals.

The most important item on Gorbachev's 1990 European security agenda became his urgent appeal, first made during October in Finland and repeated on his way to the U.S.-USSR summit in Malta, for a Helsinki Two conference that would redefine political, economic, and military relationships from the Atlantic to the Urals (*Pravda*, 27 October).

At the end of 1989 Gorbachev wanted a Europe that would include two Germanies, a USSR comprised of all its present non-Russian union republics, and a Warsaw Pact. But by endorsing the principle of national self-determination and renouncing the use of armed force in interstate relations (*Pravda*, 26 October), Gorbachev had put himself on a collision course with the dynamics of national self-determination in the Germanies and in the USSR itself.

When Gorbachev first proposed Helsinki Two, he suggested a conference for 1992. The chain reaction set off by the revocation of the Soviet security guarantee to ruling East European parties exploded so quickly that within a month Gorbachev had moved the proposed date back to 1990.

Whether or not a new Conference on Security and Cooperation in Europe (CSCE) is held, the issues involved will have to be faced. In comparison with the questions Gorbachev raised about the future of Germany and the USSR, the question of the formal survival of the Warsaw Pact became almost trivial.

The Self-Destruction of the Warsaw Pact. The self-destruction of the Warsaw Pact as an alliance of ruling communist parties in 1989 resulted from the unanticipated interaction of a series of policies launched by Gorbachev shortly after he came to power in 1985. He had evidently intended these policies to be mutually complementary; instead, they proved mutually contradictory. Gorbachev's original intent appears to have been to substitute political solutions for military solutions to the linked problems of political instability in Eastern Europe, German reunification, NATO/European Community (EC) political support for anti-communist/anti-Soviet movements within Eastern Europe, and a runaway East-West arms race based on exotic and expensive technologies. The unanticipated result of Gorbachev's reform policies was to multiply the number and severity of the political problems faced by the Soviet leadership from the Atlantic to the Urals and virtually to decommission the armed forces of the WTO.

The first set of policies leading to the disintegration of the WTO was Gorbachev's attempt to export *perestroika* from the USSR to Eastern Europe. Adoption of Gorbachev-style reforms in the WTO states had the effect of linking the irreversibility of *perestroika* in the USSR to the continuation of reform programs in Eastern Europe.

During early 1989 only two of the six ruling East European parties embraced the Gorbachev reform program. In Poland and Hungary—countries experiencing accelerating socioeconomic decay—the local parties decided to follow Gorbachev's lead down the fine line between sharing power and surrendering power.

Gorbachev offered a special incentive to the rulers and ruled of East Europe to walk such a fine line. The incentive—implicit in his endorsement of the Polish roundtable agreement in the spring of 1989 and explicit in his July speech to the Council of Europe at Strasbourg—was a pledge not to resort to Soviet military interventions against ruling communist parties engaged in radical reform programs.

In Poland the fine line between sharing power with Polish society and surrendering power led to the creation of a Solidarity government in late August. In this government the communists were junior partners (holding the Ministries of Defense, Interior, Transportation, and Foreign Trade) and more than ever dependent on their silent partner in Moscow.

A second group of policies set in motion by Gorbachev was a European arms control program focused on the CFE talks that began at Vienna in March. These negotiations were limited to the complex issues of asymmetrical reductions of conventional forces. In addition, the USSR also participated in a parallel Vienna conference on military confidence-building measures, held under the auspices of the 35-nation CSCE.

The primary goal of the overall WTO arms control program was to free the Warsaw Pact states from the ruinous economic costs of a high-tech arms race against an opposing alliance with four or five times the economic resources of the Council for Mutual Economic Assistance (CMEA) bloc.

The overall WTO arms control program also sought NATO reductions in nuclear forces, in U.S. naval forces, and in U.S.-based air forces, although most of these elements were not on the formal agenda at either of the Vienna conferences. The overall NATO force reductions sought by the WTO would have in effect undercut the NATO doctrines of forward defense of the West German border and flexible response.

Forward defense required not only NATO forces based in West Germany, but a massive U.S. reinforcement capability. Flexible response required a range of U.S. nuclear forces from the tactical to the strategic. As Marshal Kulikov complained in his valedictory volume as WTO commander, the combined effect of the doctrines of forward defense and flexible response was to make the inner-German border a potential site for the eruption of a global nuclear war (V. G. Kulikov, *Doktrina zashchita mira i sotsializma* [Moscow, 1988], pp. 65–69).

The credibility of the WTO arms control program for conventional weapons came to rest in part on the implementation of a defensive WTO posture first announced in May 1987. This doctrine sought to restructure WTO forces so that they would not threaten NATO with a continental war. The WTO conventional arms control program also came to depend on the restored credibility of long-standing Soviet pledges not to resort to the first use of nuclear, chemical, or conventional weapons under any circumstances. Gorbachev reaffirmed these pledges in his July speech at Strasbourg.

The third set of policies that led to the disintegration of the WTO were those intended to build a "common European home" on the twin pillars of *perestroika* in the CMEA and arms control in the

European theater. In both halves of Europe, the requirements of building a common Europe imposed political constraints on the use of Soviet conventional military power for protecting ruling parties against domestic opponents.

The NATO states were expected to finance the construction of this common European home from the peace dividends of the arms control process. Western investment in the CMEA states would grant the subjects of the Soviet empire honorary citizenship in a Europe from the Atlantic to the Urals, provided they learned to meet Western economic and technological standards.

In meeting these standards, they would revitalize their socioeconomic systems and thus grant legitimacy to the ruling communist parties that had built the common European home. Such enhanced legitimacy would in turn preclude the need to resort to Soviet military interventions to sustain the East European regimes.

At the same time, the ruling parties of Eastern Europe were to enlist their societies in grandiose Soviet schemes for the intensified integration of East bloc agencies at every level, including the military structures of the Warsaw Pact, the economic enterprises of the CMEA, and the cultural and scientific institutions of the USSR and Eastern Europe. Gorbachev made clear that in the common European home there were to be *two* socioeconomic blocs, each obliged to respect the right of the other to internal consolidation.

The policies of *perestroika*, arms control, and the common European home were intended to stabilize the crumbling regimes of Eastern Europe. This objective was summed up accurately, if awkwardly, in the July 1989 declaration of the WTO Political Consultative Committee (PCC): "For a Stable and Secure Europe, Free of Nuclear and Chemical Weapons, For a Substantial Reduction in Armed Forces, Armaments and Military Spending." The text of this declaration explained how all these policies were mutually complementary. (*FBIS-SOV*, 89-130, 10 July.)

However, Gorbachev also wanted the Warsaw Pact to reissue a security guarantee to the ruling parties of East Europe by preserving a "counteroffensive" capability. The 1987 PCC statement on military doctrine had required such a capability to "defend socialism" (*FBIS-SOV*, 87-104, 1 June 1987). In his initial commentary on the new WTO doctrine, Soviet defense minister D. Iazov declared the following: "The Warsaw Treaty Organization is a qualitatively new sociopolitical entity, having arisen as a natural phenomenon for the defense of the socialist gains of workers from the intrigues of aggressive imperialist forces" (*Pravda*, 27 July 1987).

In this commentary the Soviet defense minister also accused NATO of "plotting schemes for the dismantling of the social system in the countries of socialism." Invoking the all-encompassing concept of "the socialist fatherland," General Iazov had declared in a passage specifically directed at the latent domestic opponents of the ruling East European parties,

The defensive military doctrine of the Warsaw Pact, designed exclusively for the repulsing of a military threat, all the same does not signify that our actions have a passive character.

They will be based on the unshakable fundamental of the Leninist teaching on the defense of the socialist fatherland.

In the case of aggression, our armed forces together with the fraternal socialist armies will defend our socialist gains with all decisiveness. (Ibid.)

Before his honorable retirement in early 1989 as the WTO commander in chief, Marshal V. G. Kulikov declared, in a pamphlet addressed to the West, "the necessity to preserve peace should not be made conditional on the socialist countries' renunciation of their socio-moral achievements . . . The socialist countries will never go back on their ideals." (*The Military Doctrine of the Warsaw Pact Has a Defensive Character* [Moscow, 1988], p. 32.)

In a Russian-language book aimed at an East bloc audience, Kulikov was more specific: "In the doctrine of the member states of the Warsaw Pact, the task of the prevention of war is closely linked with the task of defending the socialist gains of the fraternal peoples and of giving a rebuff to an aggressor" (Kulikov, *Doktrina* [1988], p. 93).

In his public statements the new WTO commander, P. G. Lushev, confirmed the arguments of the Kulikov testament on the need for a "counteroffensive" capability (*FBIS-SOV*, 89-031, 16 February). The following is a TASS report of General Lushev's position:

The Warsaw Pact countries believe that there is no guarantee of the irreversibility of the current positive [arms control] processes. Therefore, in the course of their restructuring, their armed forces are invariably kept at the required fighting efficiency and combat readiness level.

The peoples of the allied countries can be sure that the defense capability of our states is being maintained at a reasonable level of sufficiency so that no one will be tempted to encroach on our security. (Ibid.)

The 1989 PCC statement also affirmed the need for a counteroffensive capability by insisting that the WTO remain prepared "to repulse decisively any manifestation of revanchism and chauvinism" and to preserve "the territorial and political realities which have taken shape" (*FBIS-SOV*, 89-130, 10 July "Declaration" and also "Communiqué").

As in Poland during 1981, the expectation was that the USSR/WTO security guarantee would enable local security forces to manage local crises without requiring direct Soviet intervention. In his speech at Strasbourg, Gorbachev warned the West against any attempts at "overcoming socialism . . . this is a policy of confrontation if not worse" (*Current Digest of the Soviet Press* [*CDSP*], 2 August).

But in 1989 the use of the WTO counteroffensive capability became hostage to the irreversibility of *perestroika* at home and abroad, to the momentum of the East-West arms control process, and to the requirements of building the common European home. The credibility of these policies came to rest on observing the long-standing Soviet rhetorical commitment to the principles of sovereignty and noninterference in relations among the WTO states. The Warsaw Treaty itself had endorsed these principles.

During August Gorbachev faced this dilemma in Poland with the formation of a government dominated by noncommunists, but still retaining a limited communist role. In September the Hungarian party appeared to be on the verge of a similar surrender. These two situations required Gorbachev to decide if he would, in effect, revoke the Soviet security guarantee to all the ruling parties of East Europe by honoring his pledges not to intervene.

To use armed force against Solidarity or to intervene in Hungary would have destroyed the arms control process, the common European home, and the policy of *perestroika* at home and abroad.

Gorbachev revoked the Soviet security guarantee to the East European parties in a joint statement with the Finnish government at Helsinki on 26 October that authorized the Finlandization of Eastern Europe. Both signatories pledged "Unconditional respect for the principle of freedom of socio-political choice, the de-idolization and humanization of international relations, the subordination of all foreign policy activities to international law and the supremacy of all human values and interests" (*Izvestiia*, 27 October).

The WTO Committee of Foreign Ministers confirmed the revocation of the Soviet security guarantee in a statement on the following day:

> Despite all the ambiguities of the situation, the conditions in Europe have ripened for a radical turning point in relations among the countries of the continent and for a gradual overcoming of its divisions and for a final eradication of the Cold War.
>
> One of the basic conditions for the construction of a secure, peaceful and undivided Europe is recognition of the rights of each nation to independent determination of its fate, to the free choice of the path of its social, political and economic development without interference from outside." (*Pravda*, 28 October.)

Gorbachev's press spokesman, Gennadii Gerasimov, described the new policy to Western reporters as the "Sinatra Doctrine," referring to the classic Frank Sinatra song "My Way." The new policy, he said, was intended to allow East European states to manage their affairs "their way" (*NYT*, 26 October).

But in avoiding a Soviet conflict with the Poles and Hungarians, Gorbachev's endorsement of the principle of national self-determination set in motion two linked processes that promised even greater crises: the possible unification of the two Germanies and the possible disintegration of the USSR.

In calling for a Helsinki Two conference (*Pravda*, 26 October) to codify the application of the Sinatra Doctrine, Gorbachev was calling on the members of NATO, the WTO, and the European neutrals to define a Europe with two Germanies and a USSR including all its present non-Russian republics.

Other profiles in *YICA* examine the internal developments in Poland, other East European states, and the USSR that underlie the crises of the Warsaw Pact countries. The sections below focus on two issues: the evolution of WTO arms control policy toward NATO during 1989 and the process by which Gorbachev came to revoke the Soviet security guarantee to the ruling parties of Eastern Europe.

The interaction of these two elements with the processes of domestic reform in the Soviet bloc forced Gorbachev to recognize that peace with Western Europe required peace with Eastern Europe and that peace with both halves of Europe

eliminated the requirement for the Warsaw Pact as it had been structured from 1955 to 1989.

The WTO had been structured for offensive actions against all possible opponents of the postwar status quo in Eastern Europe, the two Germanies, and NATO. This offensive posture had compelled a grudging acceptance of a status quo lacking legitimacy in either half of Europe. Since May 1987, Gorbachev had attempted to secure Western subsidies for the Soviet empire by trying to exchange the offensive posture of the WTO toward NATO as a whole for a Western commitment to underwrite the economic restructuring of Eastern Europe.

When Gorbachev declined to use the residual counteroffensive capability to preserve collapsing parties in Poland and Hungary, he removed the rationale for retaining the WTO counteroffensive capability. He also removed the rationale for the arms control policies of 1985–1989 that sought to undermine the NATO doctrines of forward defense and flexible response, two doctrines that had challenged both the pre-1987 WTO offensive posture and the post-1987 counteroffensive posture. In 1990, the Soviet Defense Ministry faced the new task of articulating a genuinely "defensive doctrine" at all levels—regional and strategic.

The Warsaw Pact Arms Control Agenda in 1989. During 1989 the WTO, in a carryover from 1988, supplemented a wide-ranging and contradictory arms control program that focused on Europe but also included global Soviet-American issues. This agenda contained unilateral WTO force reductions, specific proposals at the CFE talks, and offers of confidence-building measures at the Vienna session of CSCE. It also involved measures aimed at aggravating an internal NATO debate over the modernization of short-range nuclear systems. The WTO agenda also had long-term declaratory objectives ranging from propagandistic to utopian.

By early 1990 entirely different security dynamics had emerged in Europe. The development of new European security arrangements may include elements that were part of the 1989 WTO formal agenda. Tracing the emerging system back to the WTO arms control agenda of 1989, however, would require an ex post facto identification of WTO priorities that may not coincide with the de facto objectives of that year.

Assessing the true objectives of the 1989 agenda may be an impossible exercise, given the interest of the Gorbachev leadership in stressing (mainly for domestic audiences) the continuity of Soviet policy in the two very different eras on either side of the historic changes of late 1989. Assessing the true agenda through the summer is a problematic exercise because most major USSR/WTO statements on European security issues contained highly contradictory proposals and positions.

A typical example is the Appeal Adopted by the Council of Foreign Ministers of the Warsaw Pact States (*Pravda*, 13 April), which combined a call for "a world without weapons and wars" with the following analysis of the immediate security problems facing the WTO:

> The ministers...emphasized the need for decisively rebuffing any manifestation of revanchism, chauvinism and nationalism, any forms of enmity among nations and attempts to question the territorial integrity of states.
>
> They note with special concern the growing spread of neofascism in a number of European countries. Regardless of where such events take place and what form they assume, they pose a threat to international peace and security. (Ibid.)

This ritual warning about the German threat and the need of the WTO to rebuff it links the policies of early 1989 with those of 1968 and 1956, when the revanchist threat was invoked to justify Soviet military interventions. This warning also reconfirmed the axiom of the post-1987 doctrine that the WTO had to maintain a counteroffensive capability to rebuff challenges to "existing territorial and political realities."

It may be that the true content of the 1989 European security proposals was ambiguous and contradictory. In retrospect, the price of these ambiguities and contradictions appears to have been the disintegration of the Warsaw Pact.

Below is a brief list of the major arms control initiatives of the Warsaw Pact in 1989. These selections support the conclusion that the Soviets wanted to (1) disengage from the overall NATO/WTO arms race by eliminating the capacity of either alliance to launch a surprise attack and fight a continental war without a very lengthy mobilization, (2) maintain the capacity for limited military action in Central Europe for the purposes of keeping the Germanies divided and keeping East European regimes in power, (3) undercut the credibility of the NATO doctrines of forward defense and flexible response to ensure the Soviet capability for limited actions in Central Europe.

Unilateral Arms Control Measures.

• *December 1988 Gorbachev speech to the United Nations:*

Reduction of 500,000 personnel from the Soviet Armed Forces, including 240,000 in the European theater, with associated European theater cuts of ten thousand tanks, 8,500 artillery pieces, plus a 14.2 percent cut in overall Soviet defense spending.

In Eastern Europe itself, a cut of 50,000 Soviet military personnel, five thousand tanks, and six tank divisions (four from East Germany, one each from Hungary and Czechoslovakia).

• *January–February 1989, associated unilateral WTO cuts as follows* (*FBIS-SOV*, 89-027):

Bulgaria: 12 percent cut in defense spending, some ten thousand military personnel, two hundred tanks.

Czechoslovakia: 15 percent budget cut, twelve thousand troops, 850 tanks, 165 armored personnel carriers, 51 aircraft.

East Germany: cut of ten thousand military personnel, six tank regiments, one air squadron, 50 aircraft.

Hungary: 17 percent budget cut, 9,800 personnel.

Poland: budget cut of 5.5 to 7.7 percent, fifteen thousand personnel.

Romania: no announced cuts in conjunction with the WTO arms control program.

WTO commentaries on the unilateral Warsaw Pact force reductions invariably called on NATO to respond in kind. (For instance, the 13 April session of the WTO Committee of Foreign Ministers; the 9 July PCC statement, "For a Stable Europe.")

One Western analyst dubbed the Gorbachev cuts "pre-emptive concessions" intended to leave the U.S. and NATO in the position of responding to an agenda set by the East (Jack Mendlesohn, *Arms Control Today*, March).

• *30 January "Statement of the Committee of Defense Ministers...on the relative numerical strength of the armed forces of NATO and the Warsaw Pact"* (*FBIS-SOV*, 89-018, 30 January):

This was by far the most detailed public comparison of WTO and NATO armaments ever provided by the WTO. As one observer noted the only area of agreement between opposing NATO and WTO inventories of the European military balance was that Luxembourg had six antitank missile launchers. (Douglas Clarke, RFE, *Background Report*, 1 February.)

The significance of the document consisted in the willingness of the WTO to engage in public debate over the number of weapons to be counted in the Vienna negotiations on CFE.

By including NATO naval and air force assets based in North America and by acknowledging that "the WTO has superiority in tanks, tactical missile launchers, air defense interceptors, infantry fighting vehicles, armored personnel carriers, and artillery," the WTO defense ministers were able to claim an overall balance: "Taking into account all the components of the military balance in Europe, it may be characterized as a rough parity which denies either side any hope of achieving a decisive military superiority."

The ministers also summed up a position dating back to the announcement of a new military doctrine in 1987: their desire to deprive each alliance of an "offensive" capability while allowing each alliance to preserve a "defensive" capability. "Neither of these alliances, while reliably ensuring its defenses, should have the resources for a surprise attack against the other or for launching offensive operations in general."

The policy implications of this analysis were that the WTO should forfeit its superiorities (tanks, artillery, and armored personnel carriers) and that NATO should forfeit its superiorities (U.S. naval and air forces).

• *Late May announcement by the USSR that it would withdraw 500 nuclear warheads from tactical nuclear weapons systems based in Eastern Europe:* (*FBIS-SOV*, 89-098, 23 May).

In addition, the USSR offered to withdraw all its tactical nuclear systems from Eastern Europe by the end of 1991 if the United States withdrew all its tactical nuclear forces from Western Europe.

The Soviet unilateral nuclear withdrawal of five hundred warheads in effect demanded a reciprocal action on the part of the United States; the United States and West Germany were facing the politically delicate issue of the modernization of U.S. tactical nuclear forces as called for by a NATO decision.

Nuclear Arms Control Proposals.

• *The 12 April session of the WTO Committee of Foreign Ministers issued a statement summarizing*

all WTO European nuclear arms control proposals (*FBIS-EEU*, 89-070, 13 April):

A separate set of negotiations on tactical European nuclear weapons systems with less than a 500-km range.

The elimination of all tactical nuclear missiles from Europe.

The creation of a series of denuclearized zones: a 300-km-wide zone along the FRG border with the East; a Baltic nuclear-free zone; a Balkan nuclear-free zone; and other zones such as the Mediterranean.

• *Other WTO statements called for long-standing proposals:*

The signing of a Soviet-U.S. treaty cutting strategic nuclear weapons systems by 50 percent.

The elimination of all nuclear weapons by the year 2000.

Other Arms Control Measures Proposed by the WTO.

The eventual withdrawal of all foreign military bases on a global scale, including Europe (Eduard Shevardnadze, *International Affairs* [Moscow], September 1988, from his address to the Special U.N. Session on Disarmament).

The disbanding of NATO and the Warsaw Pact, and as a first step the dismantling of their military organizations (1987 PCC Statement, *FBIS-SOV*, 87-104, 1 June 1987; also 1989 PCC statements).

The elimination of all chemical weapons (PCC, 1989).

The creation of international verification agencies to monitor all arms control agreements, including those requiring the destruction of armaments, disbanding military units, etc. (PCC, 1989, 1988).

Elaborate confidence-building measures focusing on the exchange of military delegations and inspections (PCC, 1989, 1988).

Special confidence-building zones along the East-West border (PCC, 1989, 1988).

Associated Nonmilitary Measures.

• *Since the announcement of the 1987 new doctrine, the WTO has regularly called for a great increase in economic, technological, and scientific ties between East and West. For instance, the 1989 PCC Statement* (*FBIS-SOV*, 89-130, 10 July):

The states represented at the conference attach great importance to increasing mutually advantageous economic and scientific-technical cooperation among CSCE participant countries.

It is essential to remove the obstacles and restrictions on the path of developing trade, scientific, technical, and production contacts, and to expand reciprocal access to modern technologies.

Such appeals clearly stated the USSR/WTO policy of inviting the European Community to finance the economic and technological renovation of the CMEA system.

Warsaw Pact Proposals at CFE.

• *In May at the Vienna negotiations on CFE, the WTO proposed limiting personnel and armaments in three corresponding zones on each side:*

The WTO modified this proposal with a 29 June program for limits on forces in a four-zone system. In each set of proposals, the critical area was the central zone.

In the case of each of the three other zones—southern, northern, and rear—of the 29 June proposal, the size and structure of Soviet forces would be such that they could not sustain on short notice an all-European continental war in which the crucial battle would still be fought on the central front.

These proposals were attempts to disengage corresponding parts of the NATO alliance from possible conflict on the central front in exchange for reducing the capacity of the USSR to conduct flank operations in support of a conflict on the central front.

The essence of the WTO security proposals, as restated at the July PCC sessions, was "ruling out the possibility of a sudden attack and of conducting large-scale offensive operations" (*FBIS-SOV*, 89-130).

However, the WTO never claimed to seek a purely "military" solution to the problem of the use of armed force. The PCC noted that "the objective is to reduce armaments until the threat of war is totally eliminated. This objective can be obtained only as a result of mutual efforts, with the utmost reinforcement of the political rather than the military elements of security and stability." (Ibid.)

In retrospect the main significance of the May proposal was in the conception of the first zone, a central zone, consisting on the WTO side of the GDR, Poland, Czechoslovakia, and Hungary. On the western side, the zone consisted of the FRG, the Benelux countries, and Denmark.

The central zone proposed in May was a slightly expanded version of the zone covered in the inconclusive Mutual and Balanced Force Reduction (MBFR) talks, which had not covered forces in Denmark or Hungary.

By including Hungary, with its 1988 garrison of 65,000 Soviet troops, the central zone proposed in May politically offset the effect of Gorbachev's 50,000-man cut of Soviet troops from East Europe as a whole.

Put another way, NATO confronted, on the central front of the central zone proposed in May, roughly the same number of troops that it would have faced on the central front of the previous MBFR zone, even after the unilateral cut of 50,000 Soviet troops.

The difference was that the Soviet garrison in Hungary was no longer assigned, for military-political purposes, to the southwestern front of Europe.

The central zone proposed in May would permit each alliance a total of 570,000 personnel, 8,700 tanks, 7,600 artillery pieces, 14,500 armored personnel carriers, 420 aircraft, and eight hundred helicopters. The Soviets would contribute 350,000 of the Warsaw Pact's manpower in the central zone.

Such a force could bring considerable military power to bear against West Germany and against Warsaw Pact members.

Such a force met WTO requirements for a "counteroffensive" capability justified by the need to "rebuff" any challenges to "existing territorial and political realities" (PCC, July).

• *On 29 June the WTO proposed a different system of zones and force limits. There were to be four zones on each side—central, north, south, and rear:*

The proposed central zone on the WTO side was to consist of the GDR, Poland, Czechoslovakia, Hungary, and four military districts of the USSR: the Kiev, Carpathian, Belorussian, and Baltic.

At the same time the troop and armament limitations for the smaller central zone proposed in May would be retained as a subsystem of the enlarged central zone proposed in June.

By including Soviet forces based in the USSR in the central zone, the new proposal of 29 June made the "defense" of East European territory synonymous with the "defense" of Soviet territory.

On the Western side the central zone was to

consist of the FRG, Denmark, the Benelux states, France, and Britain.

The enlarged central zone proposed in June would permit each alliance 910,000 personnel, 13,300 tanks, 11,500 artillery pieces, 20,750 armored personnel carriers, 1,120 aircraft, and 1,250 helicopters.

Within this central zone, the Soviets proposed to maintain in the GDR, Poland, Czechoslovakia, and Hungary the same number of Soviet forces first proposed in the May version of a central zone.

The Soviet proposal would have permitted the USSR to maintain 350,000 Soviet troops in Eastern Europe plus 4,500 tanks, four thousand artillery pieces, 7,500 armored personnel carriers, 350 aircraft, and six hundred helicopters. These limits covered all the "foreign" forces based on WTO territory.

The WTO proposal would impose similar limits on the total of all foreign NATO forces based in West Germany and the other NATO states of the proposed zone. Such limits would thus permit the Soviets a continued numerical superiority over U.S. forces in Europe because other foreign forces were also based in the FRG.

Such limits would make the total size of the Bundeswehr less than that of the Soviet garrison in the proposed central zone.

That is, the Soviet forces in the revised central zone would have been larger than either the total of U.S. forces or the total of West German forces. Soviet forces would have the largest national military force in the central zone.

Given the troop levels proposed in the other three zones, the Soviet proposals would have denied each alliance the capacity for a theaterwide offensive against the other side.

On the central front, the Soviets would forfeit a capability to strike deep into Western Europe, but they would retain a capability to strike at opponents in Eastern Europe or the two Germanies. In other words, the Soviets would retain a counteroffensive capability to defend "the gains of socialism."

The thrust of the WTO proposals, as applied to the NATO forces, would compromise the credibility of the existing NATO doctrines of forward defense of the West German border and flexible response.

WTO statements specifically declared that NATO attempts to maintain the forces necessary to support these two doctrines were incompatible with the arms control system envisioned by the WTO.

The 1989 PCC communiqué declared that "the strategy of nuclear deterrence which was confirmed afresh at the recent [spring] session of the NATO Council remains a dangerous anachronism which is at variance with the interests of universal security."

The Revocation of the Soviet Security Guarantee to the East European Communist Parties. The argument here is that Gorbachev unintentionally revoked the long-standing Soviet security guarantee to the ruling parties of East Europe by making his East-West arms control agenda conditional on the unilateral Soviet renunciation of the use of force in East-West relations and in relations between ruling communist parties.

These two self-imposed restraints made it politically difficult to intervene in Poland and Hungary, where the communist parties themselves had agreed to partial surrenders of power. Gorbachev publicly acknowledged the self-imposed restraints in July during his speeches to the Council of Europe in Strasbourg and before the PCC session in Bucharest. Technically, all Gorbachev did was endorse the principles of sovereignty and noninterference in internal affairs—rhetorical positions frequently taken by previous Soviet leaders and enshrined in the text of the Warsaw Treaty itself. Gorbachev, however, deliberately left his audience with the distinct impression that in the future reality would conform to rhetoric.

At the same time, Gorbachev's statements at Strasbourg and to the PCC made it clear that the Soviets expected the WTO/CMEA system to endure and that the people of East and West Europe had a common responsibility to see to it that the Soviet bloc survived intact in the common European home. This responsibility included the lifting of barriers to East-West trade and technology transfer. Furthermore, both Gorbachev and the PCC reaffirmed the role of the Warsaw Pact in preserving the Eastern bloc status quo.

The statements listed below from Gorbachev's speech in Strasbourg and at the PCC 10–11 July attempt to document this interpretation.

Statements on the Nonuse of Force by the WTO against NATO or against Ruling Communist Parties.

• *Gorbachev in Strasbourg, 6 July (CDSP, 2 August):*

The philosophy of the concept of a "common European home" rules out the probability of an armed clash and the very possibility of using force or the threat of force, above all, military force—alliance against alliance, within alliance or wherever.

To replace the doctrine of deterrence, it offers a doctrine of restraint.

• *The WTO PCC Declaration, 7–8 July (FBIS-SOV, 89-130):*

Stability presupposes the renunciation of confrontational doctrines and of the gamble on force, and the inadmissibility of direct and indirect interference in the internal affairs of other states.

Statements on the Permanence of the WTO/CMEA System.

• *Gorbachev in Strasbourg, July:*

Many in the West see the existence of two social systems as the major difficulty. But the difficulty actually lies elsewhere—in the widespread conviction (sometimes even a policy objective) whereby overcoming the split in Europe means "overcoming socialism."

But this is a policy of confrontation, if not worse. No European unity will result from such approaches.

The fact that European states belong to different social systems is a reality.

• *The PCC, 7–8 July:*

The Warsaw Pact participant states accord paramount importance to...moving forward along the road of building an indivisible Europe of stable peace and cooperation, a common European home with a diversity of social and state systems in countries, with respect for the territorial and political realities which have taken shape.

Endorsement of the Right of Each Ruling Party to Carry out Its Own Domestic Reforms without Outside Interference.

• *Gorbachev in Strasbourg:*

Social and political orders in one or another country have changed in the past and may change in the future.

However, this is exclusively the affair of the peoples themselves, it is their choice.

Any interference in internal affairs and any attempts to restrict the sovereignty of states—either friends or allies or anyone else—are inadmissible.

Differences between states cannot be eliminated. They are, as I have said on more than one occasion, even beneficial—provided, of course, that the competition between the different types of societies is oriented toward creating better material and spiritual conditions for people.

• *PCC, 7–8 July:*

The conference reaffirmed the common desire to act in the interests of socialism, to improve cooperation among the allied states and to make reliable provision for their security.

Confidence was expressed in the ability of the socialist states and of the leading forces of society to solve the problems that have arisen at the current stage of their development.

Emphasis was also placed on the need to develop relations among them on a basis of equality, independence and the right of each to develop independently its own political line, strategy and tactics without outside interference.

The Necessity for Removing East-West Trade Barriers.

• *Gorbachev in Strasbourg:*

Now for the economic content of the common European home. We consider the formation of a vast economic expanse from the Atlantic to the Urals with a high level of interconnection between its eastern and western parts, to be a realistic prospect...

...in our age, economic ties apart from scientific-technical ties are something not quite normal. But in East-West relations, the latter have been significantly enfeebled by Cocom [the Coordinating Committee on East-West trade].

• *The PCC, 7–8 July:*

The states represented at the conference attach great importance to increasing mutually advantageous economic and scientific-technical cooperation among CSCE participant countries.

...It is essential to remove the obstacles and restrictions on the path of developing trade, scientific, technical and production contacts, and to expand reciprocal access to modern technologies.

The Maintenance of the WTO as the Agency for Preserving East Bloc Socio-Economic Systems.

- *Gorbachev speech to PCC, 8 July (FBIS-SOV, 89-131):*

At the same time, assessing the situation realistically, we cannot fail to see that the movement toward peace has still not become irreversible or reached the point where the force of momentum comes into play.

Threats—and considerable threats at that—persist.

Psychological confrontation has been by no means overcome either, nor has its material base been dismantled.

Under these conditions our organization [the WTO] continues to act as guarantor of the socialist state's security and all European stability.

- *PCC, 7–8 July:*

The conference participants were unanimous that the Warsaw Pact is reliably serving to provide for the security of its member-states and is an important factor for peace and stability in the entire world.

Assessing the Contradictory Elements of the WTO Program. East European observers of the ambiguous elements in the July statements by Gorbachev and the PCC could reach contradictory conclusions. A Hungarian journalist wrote that the Brezhnev Doctrine had been buried at the PCC session (*FBIS-SOV*, 89-138, 20 July). If he meant by this the doctrine of WTO intervention against ruling communist parties, as in 1968 Czechoslovakia, he was undoubtedly correct. But the initial Soviet response to the unexpected possibility of a noncommunist government in Poland suggests that Gorbachev did not intend his renunciation of the use of armed force against NATO or against ruling parties to be taken by East or West as a revocation of the traditional Soviet military security guarantee to ruling parties.

A high-ranking member of Solidarity informed Western journalists that Poland's General Wojciech Jaruzelski had warned the Polish opposition in late July that the Warsaw Pact would not tolerate the formation of a Solidarity government (*NYT*, 27 July). Another Solidarity official declared that if Jaruzelski did offer Solidarity some token cabinet posts, the portfolios would be those of "death, industrial shortages, and food deficits" (ibid.).

But as the crisis in Poland continued through August, Gorbachev evidently came to realize that the use of armed force to preserve the leading role of the communist party in Poland would destroy *perestroika* not only in Poland but throughout the bloc. The use of armed force would also destroy the policies of encouraging arms control, building a common European home, and obtaining Western economic and technological aid for the Soviet economy. The price for the ambiguous and contradictory positions taken on the use of armed force was the immobilization of the Warsaw Pact.

The change in the practical implications of Gorbachev's policies can be seen in the contrast between an analysis presented during May by Vitaly Zhurkin, director of Moscow's Institute of European Affairs, and an October speech by Eduard Shevardnadze just before the formal renunciation of the Soviet security guarantee. Zhurkin wrote about NATO–Warsaw pact relations in the following terms:

The complex of relations that has been established in the West is an important element in the stability of the situation as a whole.

Therefore, the East must conduct itself in such a way that this stability is not disturbed; it must proceed from the premise that the status and development of relations among the Atlantic states are the West's concern.

This applies equally to stability in Eastern Europe. And we in turn have a right to expect the same attitude on the part of the West. (*Pravda*, 17 May.)

The Zhurkin statement politely warned the West not to object to unilateral Soviet actions within the Eastern bloc. But in October, Foreign Minister Shevardnadze disavowed such a position in a speech to the Supreme Soviet. Before delivering the address Shevardnadze and other high-ranking officials held consultations with East European officials in late September and early October, probably to inform them of the impending shift in Soviet policy (*FBIS-SOV*, 89, 191/193/206). In addition, in early October the Soviet journal *New Times* published an article speculating about a drastic overhaul of the WTO (*FBIS-SOV*, 89-206, 26 October).

In his 23 October speech to the Supreme Soviet, Foreign Minister Shevardnadze, just before the formal revocation of the Soviet security guarantee to ruling parties, discussed the long-term costs of the use of Soviet armed force. In this speech he mentioned not only Eastern Europe but Afghanistan and the ruinous costs of the East-West arms race.

He specifically noted that the programs for restructuring in the USSR, pursuing arms control, and gaining access to Western technology and credits had become dependent on avoiding the use of armed force. In the passages cited below, he presented a justification for not intervening in the developing crises in Poland and Hungary:

> Our people and socialism paid a high price in the past for the notion that we could ignore the world around us and disregard the interests of others...
>
> Restructuring...predetermines the need for a fundamentally different foreign policy. But the perception of this policy, the foreign response to it, depends directly on the consistency and irreversibility of restructuring...
>
> ...In some of these [WTO] countries, new alternative forces are entering the political arena. No one is bringing them in. They are coming in because that is what the people want.
>
> These states continue to be our neighbors, allies and friends. All our commitments remain in force.
>
> One thing is clear: we can no longer operate within the old structures that took shape in the past.
>
> Economic, scientific-technical and cultural cooperation must be shifted to a new basis.
>
> We understand the desire of our friends to have diverse and broad ties with the whole world...We are taking this path ourselves. (*Pravda*, 24 October.)

After making this speech, Shevardnadze went to Warsaw to attend a session of the Warsaw Pact Committee of Foreign Ministers (CFM). The host for the meeting was Krzysztof Skubiszewski, the first noncommunist foreign minister in Eastern Europe since 1948. On 27 October, Shevardnadze signed a communiqué that declared that each European state had a right to "independent determination of its fate, to the free choice of the path of its social, political and economic development without interference from outside" (*Pravda*, 28 October).

The CFM communiqué represented the obituary of the Warsaw Pact as it had been structured from 1955 to 1989. It seemed both political and poetic justice that the fate of the Warsaw Pact was decided in Warsaw.

Christopher D. Jones
University of Washington

International Communist Organizations

WORLD MARXIST REVIEW

The Prague-based *World Marxist Review* (*WMR*), the Soviet-controlled international communist theoretical monthly, is the only permanent institutional symbol of unity for the world's pro-Moscow and independent communist parties (see *YICA*, 1984 for a fuller treatment). A Soviet defector and former *WMR* staff member Ievgenii Novikov revealed that it is specifically the International Department (ID) of the Communist Party of the Soviet Union (CPSU) that operates the magazine (*Washington Times*, 3 May). Its chief editor has always been a Soviet; the person currently occupying the position is Aleksandr Subbotin. (Note that the number two Soviet on the staff, Managing Editor Sergei Tsukasov, died in 1989.)

Novikov also stated that "the main purpose of the publication is to help coordinate the activities of the international communist movement" (ibid.). Such coordination is facilitated by the fact that 68 communist parties and a single "vanguard revolutionary democratic" party (see below) have representatives on the WMR's Editorial Council. These are offset, however, by a body of Soviet staffers who apparently see to it that nothing antithetical to the CPSU is printed (see *YICA*, 1984). The wide range of such coordination activities in 1989 could be seen by the magazine being represented at the Budapest meeting in May of "closely coordinating nongovernmental organizations" (the major Soviet international communist front organizations—see below) and by Subbotin himself participating in the September meeting at Varna of international secretaries from ruling communist parties (Prague, *IOJ Newsletter*, no 11; *Pravda*, 30 September). What the exact *WMR* function was at these two meetings is not known.

More obvious in its intent is a *WMR* spin-off, *First Hand Information*, which came to our attention during the year and whose purpose is described in its subtitle: *Communists and Revolutionary Democrats of the World Presenting Their Parties*. This directory of communist and "vanguard revolutionary democratic parties" (near-communist parties deficient in organizational discipline and/or ideological development) claims to be based largely on contributions by the parties themselves and is a valuable indicator of which parties in this category are officially recognized by the Soviets. It was published by the *WMR*'s Peace and Socialism Publishers and edited by Subbotin. At least one of the two compilers, Vladimir Shelepin, is or had been a WMR staffer (London, *WMR*, May 1987). The first appearance of *First Hand*, in August 1988, was followed in June by Peace and Socialism Publishers' announcement that it was discontinuing *Information Bulletin*, the long-standing journal of communist party statements, meetings, and the like (Prague, *Information Bulletin*, December).

FRONT ORGANIZATIONS

Control and Coordination. The Soviet-line international communist front organizations that have been operating since World War II are counterparts of organizations established by the Comintern after World War I, and their function is the same: to unite communists with persons of other political persuasions to support, strengthen, and lend respectability to Soviet foreign policy objectives. Moscow's control is evidenced by the fronts' faithful adherence to the Soviet policy line and by the withdrawal patterns of member organizations (certain pro-Western groups withdrew after the cold war began, Yugoslav affiliates left after the Stalin-Tito break, and Chinese and Albanian representatives departed after the Sino-Soviet split developed).

The CPSU controls the fronts through its International Department (ID) (U.S. Congress, *The CIA and the Media*, Washington, D.C., 1978, p. 574), and ID sector chiefs have been publicly involved with front affairs—Iuliy F. Kharlamov in the World Peace Council (WPC) and Georgi V. Shumeiko in the World Federation of Trade Unions (WFTU) and the Afro-Asian People's Solidarity Organization (AAPSO) (*Problems of Communism*, September–October 1984, p. 73). Such officials appear to operate, however, through the Soviet national affiliate, which usually has a representative at the front's international headquarters. This individual is usu-

ally one of the secretaries, but in some cases he or she may be a vice-president (*YICA*, 1981).

In addition to the ultimate coordination afforded by the CPSU through the ID and the appropriate Soviet national affiliate, there are more direct means. First, the WPC, the largest and most important of the international fronts, provides positions in its top organs for leaders of the other main fronts (*YICA*, 1988, see also chart 1). Second, the *WMR* has a Peace and Democratic Movements Commission that apparently furnishes representatives to the collective meetings of the major fronts (see below) and supervises front participation in the magazine's seminars and articles (see *YICA*, 1989). Note that during 1989 the *WMR* carried articles by the leaders of the WPC, AAPSO, Asian Buddhist Conference for Peace (ABCP), Christian Peace Conference (CPC), International Institute for Peace (IIP), and the International Organization of Journalists (IOJ). Third, since 1978 these fronts, defining themselves as "closely coordinating nongovernmental organizations," have been meeting together at least once a year to coordinate policy (*YICA*, 1987; Clive Rose, *The Soviet Propaganda Network*, London: n.p., 1988, p. 55). The published attendance at these meetings is used as the criterion for consideration here as a major front, and one more was noted in this context during May: the Latin American Continental Students' Organization (OCLAE) (Prague, *IOJ Newsletter*, no. 11).

A few additional points should be made regarding coordination. The meetings of closely coordinating nongovernmental organizations appear to have stepped up recently; meetings were held in October 1988 (Cairo, AAPSO-hosted), January (Prague, International Union of Students [IUS]-hosted), and May (Budapest, World Federation of Democratic Youth [WFDY]-hosted) (ibid., no. 22, 1988 and no. 11; Prague, *CPC Information*, 13 January). Although the total number of organizations represented at any one of these meetings has varied between eight and seventeen, the tally for the seven meetings for which we have attendance records shows that the WPC, WFTU, CPC, IOJ, IUS, and the Women's International Democratic Federation (WIDF) have never missed; the AAPSO and WFDY each was absent only once; and the World Federation of Teachers' Unions (FISE), only twice (Rose, *Soviet Propaganda Network*; *YICA*, 1987; Prague, *IOJ Newsletter*, no. 11). Also, various large front gatherings provide the opportunity for coordination—for example, the World Youth Festival at Pyongyang in July (see below) was attended

Chart 1: Major International Communist Front Organizations

Organization (president, general secretary, or equivalent)	Year founded	Headquarters	Claimed membership	Affiliates	Countries
Afro-Asian Peoples' Solidarity Organization (AAPSO) (Murad Ghalib,* Nuri Abd-al-Razzaq Husayn*)	1957	Cairo	no data	87	no data
Asian Buddhist Conference for Peace (ABCP) (Kharkhuu Gaadan,* G. Lubsan Tseren*)	1970	Ulan Bator	no data	15	12
Berlin Conference of European Catholics (BCEC) (Franco Leonori,* Hubertus Guske)	1964	East Berlin	no data	no data	45
Christian Peace Conference (CPC) (Károly Tóth,* Lubomir Mirejovsky)	1958	Prague	no data	no data	ca. 80
Continental Organization of Latin American Students (OCLAE) (Jorge Arias Diaz,[2] Angel Arzuaga Reyes*[3])	1966	Havana	no data	34[1]	26[1]
International Association of Democratic Lawyers (IADL) (Joe Nordmann, Amar Bentoumi)	1946	Brussels	25,000	no data	ca. 80
International Federation of Resistance Movements (FIR) (Arialdo Banfi, Alix Lhote)	1951	Vienna	5,000,000	78[4]	27[4]
International Institute for Peace (IIP) (Erwin Lanc,[5] Max Schmidt[5])	1957	Vienna	no data	no data	no data
International Organization of Journalists (IOJ) (Kaare Nordenstreng, Dušan Ulčak*)	1946	Prague	ca. 250,000	no data	120+
International Radio and Television Organization (OIRT) (Karel Kvapil,[6] Gennadij Codr)	1946	Prague	no data	29[7]	23[7]
International Union of Students (IUS) (Josef Scala,* Georgios Michaelides*)	1946	Prague	40,000,000[8]	117	110
Organization of Solidarity of the Peoples of Africa, Asia, and Latin America (OSPAAAL) (Susumu Ozaki? Rene Anillo Capote*)	1966	Havana	no data	no data	no data
Women's International Democratic Federation (WIDF) (Freda Brown,* vacant?[13])	1945	East Berlin	200,000,000	142	124
World Federation of Democratic Youth (WFDY) (Walid Masri,* György Szabó*)[4]	1945	Budapest	150,000,000	ca. 270	123
World Federation of Scientific Workers (WFSW) (Jean-Marie Legay, Stan Davison)	1946	London	1,000,000+[9]	ca. 46	70+
World Federation of Teachers' Unions (FISE) (Lesturuge Ariyawansa, Gerard Montant)	1946	East Berlin	26,000,000+	ca. 150[12]	79
World Federation of Trade Unions (WFTU) (vacant,[10] Ibrahim Zakariya*)	1945	Prague	ca. 214,000,000	92	81
World Peace Council (WPC) (Romesh Chandra,* vacant[11])	1950	Helsinki	no data	no data	145[14]

* World Peace Council Presidential Committee member (Helsinki, *New Perspectives*, June).

1. Prague, *World Student News*, no. 8.
2. Ibid.
3. Helsinki, *New Perspectives*, June.
4. East Berlin, *Neues Deutschland*, 26–27 August.
5. Ibid., 10 January. Schmidt is director of the Scientific Council.
6. Prague, *IOJ Newsletter*, no. 11.
7. *Yearbook of International Organizations, 1989/90* (Munich: K. G. Saur, 1989), entry CC2391.
8. Prague TV, 15 November; *FBIS*, 16 November.

9. Sofia, BTA, 7 October; *FBIS*, 13 October.
10. Budapest, MTI, 24 March; *FBIS*, 3 April.
11. Helsinki, *Peace Courier*, no. 7/8.
12. East Berlin, *Teachers of the Whole World*, special edition, September, p. 4.
13. Helsinki, *Kansan Uutiset*, 20 September; *Helsinggin Sanomat*, 21 September.
14. Prague, ČTK, 18 March 1988; *FBIS-EEU*, 21 March 1988.

by the presidents of the WFDY and the IUS; the general secretaries of the WFTU, the International Association of Democratic Lawyers (IADL), and the Organization of Solidarity of the Peoples of Africa, Asia, and Latin America (OSPAAAL); and lesser-ranking members of the WPC, AAPSO, IOJ, OCLAE, WIDF, and perhaps others (our listing was not complete) (*Pyongyang Times*, 1, 3, 9 July; Prague, *Flashes from the Trade Unions*, 28 July). An eight-member delegation from Saudi Arabia (*World Student News*, no. 11) and representatives from Bahrain also attended (ibid.). In 1988 such an opportunity had been afforded by the June nuclear-free zones meeting at East Berlin (*YICA*, 1989).

Techniques. Events surrounding the WPC, the World Youth Festival (the largest front event of the year), and to some extent the WFTU gave an idea of the new directions the Soviets wished certain traditional front activities to take. The WPC headquarters staff was reduced by at least four technicians and two officers during the year (Helsinki, *Tiedonantaja*, 3 February; Helsinki, *New Perspectives*, no. 6/88, no. 6/89). As for the WPC policy organ, its bureau meeting in June approved proposals to replace the present 54-man bureau by an up to ten-man presidential board and the nearly three hundred strong presidential committee by a new, 40-person bureau (Helsinki, *Peace Courier*, no. 7/8). As for meetings, the WPC canceled its Disarmament Commission meeting, scheduled for April, failed to hold either its normal yearly presidential committee meeting or a projected one between NATO and Warsaw Pact soldiers, and apparently did not even plan a triennial congress (habitually held the same year as the council meeting, in this case 1990) (ibid., nos. 4, 11).

These organizational cutbacks can be partially attributed to a financial crisis: the WPC was said to be running a deficit of around $300,000 a year, the bureau had to appeal to WPC national affiliates for financing the 1990 council meeting, and fundraising was slated to be a theme at one of the ten working groups during the latter (ibid., nos. 7/8, 11). That the crisis would only get worse was indicated by WPC staffer Mark Waller, when he said in the middle of the year that the Soviet Peace Committee [SPC], the WPC's "biggest financial backer," was going to "slash" its dollar contribution (ibid., no. 7/8). (Earlier, WPC vice-president James Lamond revealed that the Soviet Peace Fund [SPF] had been contributing about 90 percent of the WPC's

total income, but that this might change in the near future [ibid., no. 4]).

At first glance, it would appear that at least the projected future cutbacks (no policy organ, no future congress) are the result of Soviet financial policy changes brought on by a worsening economic situation. It does not appear, however, that either the SPC or the SPF, through which monies are channeled to carry out the former's policies, is or had been in the process of reducing its overall activities or expenditures—quite the contrary. In August SPC chairman Genrikh A. Borovik announced that SPC contacts had increased tenfold "in recent years" (*Pravda*, 28 August). In October the SPF sent an unprecedentedly large (320 plus) delegation to France and the SPC, a 53-member one to Japan; earlier, in May, the SPC sent a hundred-man delegation to West Germany. In December the SPF and SP were cosponsors of a new University of Peace and Human Rights in Moscow.

In April two SPC leaders, then First Vice-Chairman Vladimir N. Orel and Secretary Grigory Lokshin, suggested that WPC decision making be diffused in two ways: transferred from the center more to the regional and national levels within the organization and become less directing and more cooperative and consensual vis-à-vis other peace movements (Moscow, *New Times*, April, no. 15; Moscow, *XX Century and Peace*, no. 4). These points were made again toward the end of the year by SPC chairman Borovik (Helsinki, *Peace Courier*, no. 11). During September–December at least five regional meetings of WPC affiliates were held as scheduled (albeit in preparation for the February 1990 council meeting); internal squabbling within the WPC and upheavals within the bloc put the organization in no position to be directive or authoritative toward any of the other peace movements. This call for diffusion of decision making was apparently brought about in part by a Soviet perception that the WPC had lost credibility in the West. Vladimir Orel admitted that the organization suffered from an image "as Moscow's stooge," that its actions had often enhanced this stereotype, and that "all this did not happen without our [the Soviets] having a hand in it to put it mildly" (Moscow, *New Times*, April, no. 15). (A similar type of admission was made by Soviet and East German trade union leaders at the general council meeting of the WFTU in November when they stated that their unions had often acted as instruments of state and party policy rather than as independent workers' organizations [London, *Morning Star*, 21 November]. It was a great year for self-criticism!)

That a smaller but more broadminded and decentralized WPC might concentrate on information activities was suggested by both SPC secretary Lokshin in April and the WPC bureau in June (Moscow, *XX Century and Peace*, no. 4; Helsinki, *Peace Courier*, no. 7/8). When the schedule for the WPC council meeting was published in September, it noted that working group eight would be devoted to "the new dimension in the peace movement's information activities" (*Peace Courier*, no. 9). Lokshin stressed that such WPC informational activity should be undertaken on behalf of the entire peace movement and might be carried out at the regional level as well as from the center, thus tying the idea to previously noted suggestions (Moscow, *XX Century and Peace*, no. 4).

Another suggestion for the WPC (as well as the other international fronts) centered on increased activity within the U.N. framework. Although this was an area of previous WPC (and other front) successes, it also seemed tied to getting WPC president Romesh Chandra out of Helsinki. In September 1988 the WPC had been re-elected (after a three-year hiatus) as a vice-president of the Conference of Non-Governmental Organizations in Consultation with the U.N. Economic and Social Council (CONGO), the most important nongovernmental organization (NGO) structure unofficially but influentially associated with the U.N. (Washington, *Up Front*, March; U.S. Department of State, *Soviet Influence Activities*, August 1979, p. 44; Rose, *Soviet Propaganda Network*, p. 65). This election allowed Chandra to retake a job in which he had previously served influentially for more than ten years (Rose, *Soviet Propaganda Network*, p. 65); it also resulted in a slight improvement in the overall position of the pro-Soviet forces in CONGO (see chart 2). Next, Gorbachev called for a series of NGO meetings sponsored by the U.N. in his December 1988 speech to that body (Washington, *Up Front*, March). The aforenoted January meeting of closely coordinating NGOs was specifically devoted to apportioning out specific U.N. tasks to the various organizations of the group (Prague, *CPC Information*, 13 January). In February the WPC (Chandra) was re-elected as vice-president of the Geneva-based NGO Special Committee for Disarmament; WPC ally Edith Ballantyne was re-elected president, six of the twelve elected board members represented closely coordinating NGOs (an increase of one), and the SPC was elected one of two

observers (Helsinki, *Peace News Bulletin*, no. 10, March). Finally, working group ten of the forthcoming WPC meeting will be concerned with "cooperation with the U.N., the Non-Aligned Movement and other intergovernmental organizations and with international NGO's" (Helsinki, *Peace Courier*, no. 9).

Helsinki's *Kansan Uutiset* of 30 June carried an article by American WPC secretary Robert Prince stating that Chandra would be made honorary WPC president at the forthcoming council meeting; Chandra will then set off to Geneva to supervise the WPC's U.N. work (CONGO is colocated in New York and Geneva). Chandra either does now or did until recently chair two other Geneva-based NGO bodies—the Special Transnational Committee and the Special Subcommittee on Apartheid, Racism, and Racial Discrimination—and the WPC serves/served on the board of the Geneva-based Special NGO Committee on Development (U.S. Department of State, *Soviet Influence Activities*, p. 44; Rose, *Soviet Propaganda Network*, p. 65; R. Herbert, *An International NGO and the UN System* [Cairo: Afro-Asian Publications, undated], appendix). Chandra's willingness to step down from the WPC presidency is open to question: up until now he has been able to do this U.N. work while retaining the top WPC post; the Soviets have belabored Chandra's offhand remarks that he would retire at the forthcoming council meeting (e.g., Orel, Lokshin, and Borovik each mention the subject in their aforenoted statements on the WPC); and, most important, Chandra seems not to have publicly disavowed a campaign by Latin American WPC leaders, with claimed support from their African counterparts, to have him re-elected as president (Porto Alegre, Centro Brasileiro de Defensa da Paz e da Ecologia, *Paz*, undated). Chandra is generally regarded as having the support of the Third World; with respect to the opening statement of this paragraph, *Kansan Uutiset* (on 12 January) blamed Chandra for ousting Johannes Pakaslahti from the WPC secretary generalship and painted the latter as a pluralistic reformer.

As with the peace movement, Soviet attitudes and actions regarding the Pyongyang World Youth Festival in July implied the same approaches: antipathy to large, costly meetings, fears of downgrading Third World issues, advocacy of more use of the U.N., and the involvement of a wider political spectrum. According to London's *Guardian* of 4 April, the Soviet spokesmen at the then recently concluded fourth festival preparatory committee meeting pro-

**Chart 2: Conference of Non-Governmental Organizations in Consultation with the
U.N. Economic and Social Council (CONGO) Board***

Office	Before September 1988	After September 1988
President	Marek Hagmajer (World Federation of U.N. Associations)	Marek Hagmajer
First vice-president	Victor Hsu (World Council of Churches)	Ralston Deffenbaugh (Lutheran World Federation)
Vice-president	Baha'i International Community	World Union of Catholic Women's Organizations
Vice-president	*Afro-Asian Peoples' Solidarity Organization*[1]	*World Peace Council*
Secretary	International Alliance of Women	Baha'i International Community
Treasurer	World Jewish Congress	World Jewish Congress
Other board members	*Christian Peace Conference*	*Christian Peace Conference*
	International Association of Democratic Lawyers	*International Association of Democratic Lawyers*
	Women's International Democratic Federation	*Women's International Democratic Federation*
	International Confederation of Free Trade Unions	International Confederation of Free Trade Unions
	Muslim World League	Muslim World League
	Pax Romana	Pax Romana
	Women's International League for Peace and Freedom[2]	Women's International League for Peace and Freedom
	World Federation of Trade Unions	*World Federation of Democratic Youth*
	Amnesty International	*World Federation of Scientific Workers*
	Anti-Slavery Society for the Protection of Human Rights	Arab Lawyers Union[3]
	Associated Countrywomen of the World	International Federation of Business and Professional Women
	International Commission of Jurists	International Federation of Women Lawyers
	International Federation of University Women	International Movement for Fraternal Union Among Races and Peoples
	World Veterans Federation	International Planned Parenthood Federation
	Union of Arab Jurists	World Federation of Methodist Women

* Of the 829 nongovernmental organizations having consultative status with the U.N. Economic and Social Council, 201 are members of CONGO (*Directory of U.N. Systems Databases on NGO's* [New York: U.N., 1988], p. 29).

1. Closely coordinating nongovernmental organizations are in italics. Additional such members of CONGO are the International Federation of Resistance Movements, International Institute for Peace, International Organization of Journalists, and International Union of Students (IUS) (*Yearbook of International Organizations, 1989/90* [Munich: Saur, 1989], entry no. EE0409y). With the exception of the IUS, these are the same twelve that have consultative status with the U.N. Educational, Scientific, and Cultural Organization, the twelfth in the latter case being the Asian Buddhist Conference for Peace (U.S. Department of State, *Soviet Influence Activities*, p. 48).

2. Women's International League for Peace and Freedom is a close ally of the World Peace Council (see *YICA*, 1986).

3. The Arab Lawyers Union (ALU) is a regional extension of the International Association of Democratic Lawyers (IADL): the ALU president is an IADL vice-president, the ALU secretary general is an IADL secretary, and the IADL secretary general is an ALU deputy secretary general (Brussels, *Information Bulletin of the Activities of the IADL in 1987*).

posed that future festivals be less extravagant (as the Soviets "could no longer afford the cost involved"), that they be less preoccupied with anti-imperialist rhetoric, and that they be brought under the U.N. umbrella with more countries involved. This broadening of the festival movement had been specifically spelled out by IUS secretary general Georgios Michaelides at the third preparatory committee meeting (November 1988) when he called for a broader platform, range of opinion, "forces," and range of venue (Prague, *World Student News*, March). In retrospect, he appears to have been promoting the Soviet line.

The contention might be made that the Soviets, in addition to wanting to change the nature of future festivals, failed to support the North Koreans to the extent they had expected. Unconfirmed reports indicated that the Soviets were to provide $32–$35 million but ended up giving only $20 million (*FEER*, 27 April; Munich, *Guardian of Liberty*, September–October). (This may not have had too much overall effect, however, because the North Koreans spent an estimated $4–$5 *billion* on the festival, much of which was spent on erecting more than two hundred buildings; this reportedly caused them to halt repayment of their foreign debts. [Munich, *Guardian of Liberty*, September–October; Moscow, *New Times*, July, no. 28; *NYT*, 9 July].)

Failure of the Soviets to furnish the requisite number of Aeroflot tickets may have produced a decline in festival attendance. Roughly twelve thousand rooms with a capacity of from two to six per room were said to have been built to house festival delegates; even at the minimum capacity this would have housed about 24,000 (*New Times*, July, no. 28; Comite Preparatorio Coreano del XIII FMJE, *Boletin del Festival*, no. 11). Yet statistics for foreign attendance were in the fifteen to twenty thousand range, with the bulk of Western estimates tending toward the lower end (Munich, *Guardian of Liberty*, July–August; *Washington Times*, 7 July; *WP*, 10 July; Wellington, *Unity*, 6 October). North Korean accounts stressed that 180 countries were represented (the largest ever) rather than emphasizing total attendance, for at fifteen thousand it would have been the smallest festival ever, according to IUS statistics (*Pyongyang Times*, 7, 9, 15 July; Prague, *World Student News*, no. 2). According to the latter, attendance at previous festivals had ranged from 17,000 to 34,000, and a rather jaundiced Soviet view of the festival in the aforenoted

New Times commented on the diminishing number of participants at the festivals.

Just as the apparently diminishing Soviet support for the WPC was being paralleled by an upsurge in SPC and SPF activity, so a similar lack of enthusiasm for the WFDY/IUS-sponsored World Youth Festival was being paralleled by apparent Soviet support for the formation and continued development of newer, nontraditional fronts. Chart 3 (presumably incomplete) is a list of such activity from November 1988 to October 1989.

In sum, then, the Soviets appear merely to be shifting their priorities within the field of "people's" or "citizen" diplomacy, as they now call it, rather than drastically reducing such activity overall.

Although no curtailment was noted at the WFTU General Council meeting in November, there was the same emphasis on broadening contacts (in the speech by General Secretary Ibrahim Zakariia, the appeal regarding the forthcoming Twelfth World Trade Union Congress, and a message to the World Confederation of Labor) (Prague, *Flashes from the Trade Unions*, 1 December). Just as the WPC had regional meetings in preparation for the forthcoming 1990 council meeting, the WFTU held five of them the day before its general council meeting (ibid.).

Themes. After deleting the functional topics mentioned above under techniques (information activities, financial problems, cooperating with the U.N. and NGOs), the proposed working groups (WGs) for the forthcoming WPC session cover the same five general topics as did the organization's 1988 *Programme of Action* noted in last year's *YICA* (1) peace, security, and disarmament (WG one "new comprehension of security concepts for the 90's"; WG two "concepts, ways, and means for the complete elimination of nuclear weapons and of chemical and other weapons of mass destruction"; WG three "promotion of peaceful political solutions to regional conflicts; solidarity with movements for liberation"); (2) socioeconomic development (WG five "development and economic security"); (3) human rights (WG six "the human dimension of global security"); (4) environmental concerns (WG four "ecological security—a global challenge for humanity"); and (5) culture and education for peace (WG seven "new concepts for peace, culture, and education") (*YICA*, 1989; Helsinki, *Peace Courier*, no. 9). The WPC's 1989 *Programme of Action*, published in late 1988, also followed the same lines as its 1988 predecessor, but gave less prominence to

Chart 3: Activities of Nontraditional Fronts

Month	Organization	Meeting	Year founded	First year noted (YICA)
November	International Foundation for the Survival and Development of Humanity	First board meeting (Washington)	1988	1989
March	International Trade Union Committee for Peace and Disarmament	First drafting group meeting (Prague)	1982	1986
June	International Center for Trade Union Rights	Fourth administrative committee meeting (Geneva)	1987	1988
July	International Liaison Office for Nuclear Free Zones	First meeting (East Berlin)	1988	not noted
August	Generals for Peace and Disarmament	Seventh meeting (Warsaw)	1981	1982
September	International Association of Lawyers Against Nuclear War	First world congress (The Hague)	1987	1988
October	International Physicians for the Prevention of Nuclear War	Ninth annual congress (Hiroshima/ Nagasaki)	1980	1988

racism and apartheid and more to "peace as a basic human right" and the environment ("ecological security—a challenge for humanity's survival" was the caption rather than simply an "environment"); the first change appears as a movement away from a Third World issue, the second a movement toward a developed world issue.

The selection of subject matter for the eight dialogue centers (DCs) at the World Youth Festival in July showed a more Third World approach than the WPC programs, hardly surprising in view of the undoubted North Korean influence. Although "peace, disarmament, and a nuclear free world and security" were apparently top priority (DC number one), "anti-imperialist solidarity" (DC number two) and "the nonaligned movement" (DC number three) had separate centers (subsumed under WGs three and ten, respectively, in the WPC schema). Whereas DC number four, "the new international economic order, the external debt, disarmament for development," covered virtually the same ground as the WPC's WG six, DC number five coupled "the protection of nature and the environment" with "a new international order in information and communication" (NIOIC), something the WPC agenda seemed to have ignored. (Among other things, NIOIC gives Third World governments control over their news media so as to eliminate "distortions" regarding their countries put out by the wire services and other instrumentalities of the United

States, Western Europe, and Japan—see *YICA*, 1985, 1987.) Two human rights DCs, one for youth (number six) and women (number seven) were established at the festival; education was coupled with science and technology (number eight) rather than culture. These differences were not particularly revealing except to underline an increasing human rights emphasis (note conferences devoted to this subject sponsored by the IADL at Paris in March and the IOJ at Geneva in April, as well as the aforenoted December establishment of a Peace and Human Rights University) (Prague, *World Trade Union Movement*, no. 9; Helsinki, *New Perspectives*, no. 9).

The general council meeting of the WFTU in November, its major conference of the year, had an apparently even stronger Third World orientation. Although its May Day centenary declaration had the normal "peace-development-rights" line, environment seems to have been ignored (also an omission at the Third World AAPSO the previous year—see *YICA*, 1989) (Prague, *Flashes from the Trade Unions*, 1 December). Even more surprisingly, of the 21 messages, telegrams, and statements coming out of the council meeting, 14 dealt with Third World political issues (Palestine, South Africa, Panama, El Salvador, Afghanistan, Lebanon, Ethiopia, Sudan, Bahrain, Saudi Arabia, Oman, Chile, Iran, and Korea) (ibid.). All this occurred despite the momentous events in the Soviet

Union and Eastern Europe, which were much more trade union oriented, and despite the emphasis on this very subject at the meeting by Soviet WFTU vice-president Stepan A. Shalaev (London, *Morning Star*, 21 November). This very impact on bloc trade unionism, however, may have prevented normal control by the affected organizations over the course of the meeting, thus allowing Third World unions to have more of a voice.

Personnel. The most interesting personnel development in the front field during 1989 was the creation of three vacancies. Sándor Gáspár (Hungary) resigned the WFTU presidency in March, with the position not having been filled by the end of the year. It appears that Johannes Pakaslahti (Finland) has vacated the WPC general secretaryship and that this position has been abolished (Budapest, MTI, 24 March; *FBIS*, 3 April; Helsinki, *Peace Courier*, nos. 7/8; *YICA*, 1989). (It is rumored that Ray Stewart from New Zealand will be taking over the presumably less powerful position of WPC executive secretary at the time of the February 1990 council meeting in Athens [ibid.].) Finally, Inger Hirvela (Finland) refused the WIDF general secretaryship when elected in September (Helsinki, *Kansan Uutiset*, 20 September).

The newly elected World Federation of Teachers Unions (FISE) leadership, as of the organization's Fourteenth Congress in September, is as follows: *Bureau*: president: Lesturuge Ariyawansa (Sri Lanka); vice-presidents: Michele Baracat (France), Abani Boral (India), Elba Esther Gordillo (Mexico), Helga Labs (GDR), Mamadou N'Doye (Senegal), Rimm Papilov (USSR), and Jamil Shihada (Palestine); *Secretariat*: general secretary: Gerard Montant (France); secretaries: Hans Christoph (GDR), Mikhail Kolesnikov (USSR), Carlos Poblets Avila (Chile) (East Berlin, *Teachers of the Whole World*, special edition, September).

The Fifteenth General Assembly of the WFSW, held in October, re-elected Jean-Marie Legay (France) as president, N. P. Gupta (India) as a vice-president, and Stan Davison (UK) as general secretary. Newly noted vice-presidents coming out of this meeting were Maurice Wilkins (UK), Oleg Nefedov (USSR), Aleksander Yankov (Bulgaria), M. Hasegawa (Japan), and H. Boutaleb (France?) (London, *Scientific World*, no. 4). Earlier, the top leaders of the IIP had been identified as Erwin Lanc (Austria), president; Klaus von Dohnanyi (FRG) and Vitaly Zhurkin (USSR), vice-presidents; and

Max Schmidt (GDR), director of the Scientific Council (*ND*, 10 January).

Materials published following the 1988 AAPSO congress in November give us the most complete picture yet of that organization's leadership: *Presidential Board*: president: Murad Ghalib (Egypt); vice-presidents: Aziz Sharif (Iraq), Vassos Lyssarides (Cyprus), Abdul Aziz (Sri Lanka), Alfred Nzo (South Africa), Tramos Makombe (Zimbabwe), Abdallah Hurani (Palestine), Aaron Shihepo (Namibia), Muhammad Abd-al-Fattah (Western Sahara), Vital Balla (Congo), Mahdi al-Hafiz (Iraq), Ali Amir Muhammad (Tanzania), Joseph Musole (Zambia), Ousmane Camara (Guinea), Sherif Messadia (Algeria), Walid Jumblat (Lebanon), Mikhail Kapitsa (USSR), Nguyen Thi Binh (Vietnam), Miraj Khalid (Pakistan), Kim Bong Gu (North Korea), Abdul Basir Ranjar (Afghanistan), plus unfilled slots for Madagascar, Syria, Libya, Bangladesh, and India (*VII AAPSO Congress*, New Delhi, 1988, p. 178); *Secretariat*: general secretary: Nuri Abd-al-Razzaq Husayn (Iraq); deputy general secretaries: Chitta Biswas (India), Mirpasha Zeinalov (USSR), S. al-Khamri (possibly S. al-Gampi—see *YICA*, 1989) (South Yemen), Nestor Embubulli (Namibia?); secretaries: Sidney Molifi (South Africa), Muhammad Sobyah (Palestine), Nguyen Trung Hieu (Vietnam), E. A. Vidyasekera (Sri Lanka), Daniel Kouyella (Congo), Julien Randriamasivelo (Madagascar), Zubayr Sayf-al-Islam (Algeria), Fathi Abd-al-Fattah (Egypt), G. Nassar (Lebanon), Thomas Schubert (GDR), Panteley Spassov (Bulgaria), A. Rogh (Afghanistan), plus unfilled slot for Ghana (Cairo, *Afro-Asian Solidarity*, no. 1, inside front cover).

Personnel overlaps are such as to make the AAPSO especially close to the WPC. Of the twenty AAPSO vice-presidents noted above, six are also WPC vice-presidents (Sharif, Nzo, Hurani, Balla, Muhammad, and Ranjbar), whereas the president, general secretary, and three more vice-presidents (Musole, Camara, and Jumblat) are members of the WPC presidential committee (Helsinki, *New Perspectives*, no. 5). Another vice-president (Aziz) and a deputy general secretary (Biswas) were also members of the WPC during 1983–1986 at least (World Peace Council, *List of Members*, 1983–1986, Helsinki, n.d., pp. 96, 144). By contrast, some effort seems to have been made to distance the IIP from the WPC. Whereas Zhurkin and Schmidt were members of the 1983–1986 WPC, Lanc and von Dohnanyi were not (ibid., pp. 82, 156). The latter two are well-known mainline socialists, a contrast to their respective predecessors, Georg Fuchs (Austria) and Gerhard Kade (FRG), both members of the 1983–1986 WPC (ibid., pp. 74, 166).

Materials recently received but dating back to 1987 added the formerly unknown IADL officers to the list: Vice-Presidents Gonzalo Taborga (Chile), Babacar Niang (Senegal), and Beinusz Szmulker (Argentina); and Secretaries Faruq Abu Issa (Sudan), Monique Chemillier-Gendreau (France?), and Eduard Rabofsky (country unknown) (*Information Bulletin of the Activities of the I.A.D.L. in 1987*, Brussels, n.d., pp. 34, 122, 126, 131, 132, 146). Other front leaders newly elected this year were OIRT president Karel Kvapil (Czechoslovakia); WPC vice-presidents Abdul Basir Ranjar (Afghanistan), Johannes Pakaslahti (Finland), and Hasan Maki (North Yemen); IOJ vice-president Chun Jun Guk (North Korea); and WPC secretary Vladimir Orel (USSR) (Prague, *IOJ Newsletter*, no. 11; Helsinki, *New Perspectives*, no. 6; Prague, *Democratic Journalist*, no. 10). Newly noted this year were IUS vice-president Vesselin Valchev (Bulgaria), FIR secretary Oskar Wiesflecker (GDR?), and WFDY secretary Thierry Angles (France), the last one also having been the coordinator of the World Youth Festival at Pyongyang (Prague, *World Student News*, no. 4; *ND*, 31 March, 26–27 August; Paris, *L'Humanité*, 4 July).

The following newly noted *World Student News* staff members may be IUS secretaries because their countries were previously noted as having persons in such positions: Hector Ortiz (Puerto Rico), Felix Andriantsoavina (Madagascar) and Danica Lacova-Nadova (Czechoslovakia) (Prague, *World Student News*, no. 9–10). Similarly, newly noted *World Youth* staffers A. Skvortsov (USSR), R. Khalafalla (Sudan), and C. Gutierrez (Chile) are probably WFDY vice-presidents; S. Herrman (GDR) appears to be a secretary of that organization (Budapest, *World Youth*, no. 6). Finally, of the newly noted faces on the *Democratic Journalist* staff, Belay Feleke (Ethiopia) and Mazin Husayni (Palestine) are probably IOJ vice-presidents. Antonio Ma. Nieva (Philippines) and P. Sainath (India) are probably IOJ secretaries; Miguel Rivero (Cuba) might be either (his country is slotted for both positions) (Prague, *Democratic Journalist*, January 1990).

Wallace H. Spaulding
McLean, Virginia

Soviet Foreign Propaganda

The decade of the 1980s ended with a U.S. weekly magazine proclaiming Mikhail Gorbachev its Man of the Decade (*Time*, 1 January 1990). In France, he received a similar designation. Other awards included one from the U.N., and he was nominated for the Nobel Peace Prize for the third time. In the history of Marxism-Leninism no other communist leader has been so honored, certainly not in capitalist countries. "Snowing the West," *Time* pronounced, "has been easy for Gorbachev." Observing that "Gorbachev has adopted many of the West's favored buzz words: stability, reasonable sufficiency, mutual security, the unwinnability of nuclear war, interdependence, human values, a civil society, the fate of the earth, the endangered planet," Western officials and the public characterized him in superlatives. He was viewed as a "political genius." (ibid.)

USSR policies of *glasnost'* and *perestroika* have become part of the international lexicon. Add to these new political thinking, democratization, unilateral military reductions, withdrawal from Afghanistan, equality, reform, dialogue, détente, self-determination, disarmament, peace, cooperation, as well as admission of past sins and current problems, and the world, particularly in the West, is impressed.

As proof of the Kremlin's new policies, Soviet publicists cited innumerable political, economic, social, cultural, ethnic, military, and even ideological changes. Marxism-Leninism was being modernized. Socialism was developing with a "human face." Associations were formed and strikes allowed. Churches were reopened, and Gorbachev even visited the Pope. The gulag system was detailed, dissidents were freed, and citizenship of expellees restored. A new legal system, press law, CPSU rules, and constitution were drafted and discussed. Demonstrators and the media voiced injustices and demanded reforms. Failures in all fields were acknowledged. The somewhat democratic elections for the Congress of People's Deputies

(CPD) were hailed. Criticism of the CPSU included its general secretary, its perks, and its *nomenklatura* system. Neither the dreaded KGB nor the military were spared. In addition to continued de-Stalinization and attacks against Krushchev as well as Brezhnev's stagnation, questions were raised about the hitherto sacrosanct Lenin. Ideological controversy raged between party reformers and conservatives, as the regime sought to minimize such problems as opposition to Gorbachev.

Media Developments. During the year the parameters of freedom in the media were unclear. Certainly there was more freedom of expression but there were limitations as well. An indication of the latter could be seen in a Central Committee pronouncement that strongly criticized some publications for excessive criticism of the Soviet military (*Krasnaia zvezda*, 6 July). Several unresolved developments during 1989 are likely to have an effect on foreign propaganda. The Law on the Press and Other Mass Information Media faced serious difficulties, and the year ended with only a first draft. The subject as well as the draft were widely discussed in the media and heatedly debated by the Supreme Soviet. Among the most controversial problems are those for ownership and censorship (*Izvestiia*, 25 November, 5 December). During the second part of the year especially, the official censorship body, *Glavlit*, and its agents appeared uncertain about their role and were often cautious.

However, high-ranking officials exercised unconcealed pressure for conformity with official policy, criticizing those who strayed left or right. Gorbachev engineered the dismissal of several newspaper editors; in a televised address to journalists at *Pravda*, he emphasized the requirement of media support for his policies and criticized recalcitrants. He introduced Ivan T. Frolov as the new editor in chief, replacing Viktor F. Afanasiev. Earlier Frolov had served on the editorial board of *World Marxist Review* and as chief editor successively of *Voprosy filosofii* and *Kommunist*. The last two years, he worked as an assistant to Gorbachev (see Frolov's profile in *Izvestiia*, 24 October). In December he was elected a Central Committee secretary (*Pravda*, 10 December).

Propaganda. *Propaganda*, which continued to be an important instrument of Soviet foreign policy, can be defined as "information that reflects the perceptions or perspectives of a government" (U.S. Department of State, *Soviet Influence Activities: A*

Report on Active Measures and Propaganda, 1987–1988, August, p. iii). Gorbachev's policies of *glasnost'*, *perestroika*, and new political thinking dedicated to peace have created a receptive international environment unprecedented in the 72-year history of the USSR. He propagates his own policies, expertly and effectively, aided by a vast bureaucracy. The latter operates worldwide and, together with "active measures" (*aktivnyie meropriiatiia*), has been endowed with a budget of approximately $4 billion annually (U.S. Congress, House, Permanent Select Committee on Intelligence, *Soviet Active Measures*, 1982). Although official U.S. sources have been reluctant to publish new figures, they see no significant diminution of the level of either activities or budgetary allocations.

Active measures are defined as "deceptive operations that attempt to manipulate the opinions or actions of individuals, publics, or governments." They are generally covert and include the use of front organizations and disinformation. The most recent State Department report, cited above, observed that Soviet covert operations had not decreased against the United States. The only perceptible difference between 1989 and previous years has been a decrease in the more egregious reporting by the Soviet media, possibly the result of high-level official U.S. protests (Charles Z. Wick, *Soviet Active Measures in the Era of Glasnost*, Washington, D.C.: U.S. Information Agency, July 1988, p. 6; *Soviet Influence Activities*, p. 1).

Organization. Soviet active measures and propaganda cannot be easily separated, but the focus of this essay is on propaganda (for an earlier summary of Soviet propaganda themes, see *YICA*, 1985). Under Gorbachev several changes were made over the last two years in the structure and leadership of the propaganda apparatus. Six commissions were established in the Central Committee on 30 September 1988, and they oversee all spheres of domestic and foreign state and party activities. One in particular has a direct responsibility for propaganda: the Ideology Commission, headed by Vadim A. Medvedev. Also of importance, but involved less directly, is the International Policy Commission, directed by Aleksandr N. Iakovlev. A third, the Legal Policy Commission, is heavily involved in active measures that implement propaganda themes. The first two control, respectively, the Ideology and the International departments. Both Medvedev and Iakovlev are Politburo members and veteran propagandists who continued in their positions throughout 1989.

Medvedev had been deputy chief of the Propaganda Department during 1970–1978. A secretary of the Central Committee since 1986, he also served as chief of the Department for Liaison with Communist and Workers' Parties of Socialist Countries until 1988. Iakovlev worked in various media and propaganda positions from the 1950s until his appointment as ambassador to Canada (1973–83). He was chief of the Propaganda Department (1985–86), then became a secretary (1986) in charge of propaganda, culture, and, since 1988, foreign affairs. His publications are clearly anti-American. Iakovlev, who was an exchange student at Columbia University in 1959, is considered to be a trusted adviser to Gorbachev. Both Medvedev and Iakovlev are enthusiastic proponents of *glasnost'*, *perestroika*, and new political thinking.

Consisting of 25 members, Medvedev's Ideology Commission includes, in addition to the head of the Ideology Department, the chief editors of CPSU organs *Pravda* and *Sovetskaia kultura*; the chairman of the State Committee for Television and Radio Broadcasting; the first secretary and a secretary from the board of the USSR Union of Writers; the USSR minister of culture; the president of the USSR Academy of Sciences; the chairman of the USSR State Committee for Publishing Houses, Printing Plants, and the Book Trade; the director of the Institute of Marxism-Leninism; the chairman of the board of the Russian Soviet Federated Socialist Republic Union of Theater Workers; an aide to the CPSU general secretary; the first secretary of the board of the USSR Union of Composers; the chairman of the USSR State Committee for Public Education; and the rector of the CPSU Academy of Social Sciences.

In addition to the International Department, Iakovlev's International Policy Commission consists of 23 members, including an aide to the general secretary; the chairman of the Union of Soviet Societies for Friendship and Cultural Relations with Foreign Countries; the director of the Institute of World Economics and International Relations; the first deputy and a deputy minister of foreign affairs; the chief editor of the government organ, *Izvestiia*; the chairman of the KGB; a deputy chairman of the Council of Ministers; a vice-president of the USSR Academy of Sciences; a former chief of the general staff of the USSR Armed Forces and a first deputy USSR defense minister; and the director of the Institute of the USA and Canada.

These and others are all high-ranking members of the CPSU in addition to their government or institutional positions, and all are active supporters of current policies. The Ideology and International departments contribute to the Politburo's formulation of foreign policies as well as oversee the implementation and dissemination of those policies. The Ideology Department formulates policy proposals, including propaganda themes, for the mass media. Its head since 1988 has been Aleksandr S. Kapto, a Ukrainian and the secretary responsible for ideology of the Ukrainian party during 1979–1986. He became a full member of the Central Committee in 1986 when he was named ambassador to Cuba. He is a member of the Ideology Commission. Under the Ideology Department, the International Information subdepartment disseminates Soviet propaganda externally through TASS, Radio Moscow, and Novosti, as well as through the embassies and consulates. The USSR continued its traditionally heavy investment in foreign language publications.

Under the International Commission, the International Department has been headed since 1988 by Valentin M. Falin, a veteran specialist on foreign affairs who was ambassador to the Federal Republic of Germany during 1971–1978, first deputy chief of the International Department (1978–1983), editor of *Izvestiia* (1983–1986), and chairman of the Novosti Press Agency (APN) during 1986–1988. A candidate member of the Central Committee since 1986, Falin became a full member in April 1989. Among responsibilities of the International Department are foreign communist parties, front organizations, friendship societies, international departments of Soviet mass organizations, and foreign affairs institutes at the Academy of Sciences. Falin and his department provide foreign policy guidance to other party and government agencies.

The Ideology and International commissions, through their Ideological and Information departments, direct the Soviet propaganda apparatus. They exercise control through the government, which is headed by officials who are simultaneously members of the commissions. As noted above these include high-level officials of the Council of Ministers, the chairman of the State Committee for Television and Radio Broadcasting (A. N. Aksenov), and the chairman of the State Committee for Publishing Houses, Printing Plants, and Book Trade (M. F. Nenashev).

TASS and Novosti. Moscow fully employed the instruments at its command—radio, television, film, newspapers, journals, books, personnel (CPSU, government, journalists, academics), delegations, cultural exchanges, and foreign aid—in support of its foreign policy objectives. Operating under the Ideology Department, the print medium has been the flagship of Soviet propaganda since Lenin's time. The press, he said, is "a collective propagandist and a collective agitator."

TASS (Telegraphic [News] Agency of the Soviet Union) is the government news agency with correspondents in 127 countries. It receives and transmits more than ten thousand typed pages daily and distributes more than five million photographs annually (*USSR Yearbook '89*, Novosti). Leonid Kravchenko, its general director, revealed that TASS has about five thousand employees (*Literaturnaia gazeta*, 15 March). At a media conference in Munich, Kravchenko inaccurately predicted that a new press law providing for extensive freedoms would be enacted before the end of the year (DPA, 9 October).

Of particular importance in disseminating foreign-language propaganda materials abroad is Novosti, or APN, which claims to be "an information agency of Soviet public organizations," but is in fact controlled by the CPSU and propagates its policies. An enormous foreign propaganda enterprise, Novosti has a network of 130 information centers, press bureaus, and correspondents' stations in about 115 foreign countries. APN produces press releases and bulletins in numerous languages and has an active placement service that has increased in recent years in Western countries. It provides videocassettes in applicable languages to its field representatives and renders journalistic assistance to more than two thousand foreign media representatives, claiming a high rate of "positive" reports on the USSR. Also, APN has established association with numerous publishers, news agencies, and periodicals. Its chairman of the board since October 1988 has been Albert I. Vlasov who previously had been first deputy chief of the CPSU propaganda department.

APN publishes books, brochures, newspapers, and magazines (weeklies, biweeklies, and monthlies) totaling approximately 35 million copies per year. Developing countries are especially targeted for dissemination. Among APN journals are *Asia and Africa Today* (two languages), *Culture and Life* (five), *New Times* (ten), *Soviet Union* (twenty), and *Soviet Woman* (fourteen). The well-known *Moscow News*, which began in 1930, is published weekly in seven languages and distributed in more than one

hundred countries. APN has printing plants in twelve countries publishing magazines in 45 foreign languages on a variety of subjects, including Soviet foreign policy and international affairs. It issues a yearbook on the Soviet Union in English, French, German, Spanish, and Italian (*USSR Yearbook '89*; *The Art of Democracy*, APN). Thousands of titles are published annually with tens of millions of copies distributed around the world. Most are brochures, such as the following published in 1989 (the number of foreign languages and for whom the brochure is intended are in parentheses):

- *Lenin on the Revolutionary Creativity of the People* (13, for developing countries and socialist countries of Asia)
- *Marxism and Africa* (4, for developing countries)
- *A Pocket Encyclopedia* (11, for youths in all countries)
- *To Restructure and Humanize International Relations* (13, for all areas)
- *Nuclear Deterrence: Retrospects and Prospects* (5, for capitalist and developing countries)
- *Looking toward the Future* (6, for capitalist countries)
- *What Kind of World Will Our Children Inherit* (6, for capitalist and socialist countries)
- *On the Concept of Humanitarian Survival* (6, for all countries)
- *Geopolitics of Imperialism* (4, for developing countries)
- *On the U.S. Military-Industrial Complex* (5, for developing countries)
- *NATO: History and Our Time* (10, for capitalist and developing countries)
- *Human Rights in the Capitalist World* (4, for all areas)
- *USIA's Propaganda Activities* (6 for developing countries)
- *Welcome to My Home* (4, a coloring booklet for children about hospitality of Soviet boys and girls who wish to make friends in capitalist and developing countries)

(Source: APN, *New Publications*, 1989).

APN publishes a series entitled *Documents and Materials*, with speeches and reports, by Gorbachev, Foreign Minister Eduard Shevardnadze,

Iakovlev, Medvedev, and others. Booklets on the peoples of the USSR, cultural life, and other topics positively portray Soviet society and policies. *STP (Socialism: Theory and Practice)* is a monthly published in English, French, German, and Spanish with distribution in more than one hundred countries.

Other Soviet activities intended to influence foreign public opinion are educational, cultural, technical, and scientific exchanges; festivals; and exhibitions. For many years Moscow has invested heavily in subsidized education for students of Third World countries. During 1988–1989 there were more than 100,000 foreign students from 149 countries studying in the Soviet Union. The Patrice Lumumba University at Moscow, founded in 1960, is one of more than five hundred educational institutions where foreign students are placed. About fifteen hundred Soviet teachers were at work in some 30 developing countries (*USSR Yearbook 1989*).

A joint U.S.-Soviet venture conducted by *Literaturnaia gazeta* outside of TASS or APN jurisdiction was an attempt to market an international edition of that Russian-language periodical. According to Yuri Izylumov, first deputy editor in chief, an English-language *Literaturnaia gazeta International* (LGI) was to be published during 1989 in the United States and made available to other English-speaking countries. A pilot issue came out during the Reagan-Gorbachev summit in 1987 that "aroused a lot of interest in the U.S.," Izylumov claimed. He also claimed that there were 100,000 foreign subscribers to the Russian journal, the number they presumably hope to obtain for the English version. LGI would "fill a void," he said, that exists in the West for information "written by Soviets for Soviets" (*Soviet Life*, July). An inquiry to LGI's American sponsor in Washington, D.C., revealed that the venture is "on hold," perhaps to commence during 1990. Several serious problems delayed publication, including technical, editorial, and political ones. The American partner said that although he had turned over 60,000 names and addresses to the LGI, because of the difficulties he was withdrawing from the venture, but that another U.S. firm would undertake it (telephone interview, January 1990).

In addition to the foregoing activities, APN and other agencies and officials attach great significance to personal appearances. Appreciating the tremendous value for their cause of exposure on national radio or, preferably, national television, during 1989 Soviet representatives were given unprecedented opportunities as guests on the major networks and were thus viewed by many millions of Americans and other Western publics. In addition to Gorbachev, Shevardnadze, and Foreign Ministry spokesman Genadii Gerasimov, a widely recognizable Moscow personality was Georgii Arbatov, the long-time director at the Institute of the USA and Canada, and a highly regarded Soviet propagandist.

External Radio Broadcasting. Modest changes were made in external broadcasting by the USSR. As of 31 December, it totaled 2,178 hours per week in 84 languages to more than one hundred countries. This was 73 hours per week less than the previous year, the decrease due primarily to reductions in Russian-language broadcasts. With repeats the figure surpasses three thousand hours weekly, maintaining its status as the world's largest international broadcaster. Radio Peace and Progress (RPP) broadcasts 67 hours weekly. Established in 1964 as a "public organization," RPP has been promoted as the voice of Soviet public opinion. Broadcasting to all regions of the world, RPP depends on Radio Moscow for facilities and is controlled by the Soviet government and the CPSU. Recently tempered, RPP's record has been one of great stridency.

In addition to Moscow, republic radio stations broadcast externally as follows: Radio Baku (45 hours per week), Dushanbe (28), Alma Ata (21), Kiev (49), Minsk (10), Riga (16), Tallin (53), Tashkent (71), Tbilisi (6), Vilnius (14), and Yerevan (57). At the beginning of the year Radio Moscow initiated broadcasts in Tagalog and Malay. Although RPP ceased broadcasts to China, the same program was continued by Radio Moscow (telephone interview with U.S. Information Agency specialist, 6 January 1990).

Over the years the Soviet Union's clandestine radio stations, located in the USSR and Eastern Europe, were targeted primarily against China, Iran, Turkey, Greece, Spain, and Portugal. Some were discontinued when local communist parties were legalized. However, with Gorbachev's leadership seeking to improve relations with the above countries, clandestine broadcasts have essentially ceased operation. In an obvious gesture toward Turkey, Moscow suspended carrying political messages promoting the Turkish United Communist Party on the Turkish-language "Our Radio" program. The USSR transmitter in East Germany stopped broadcasting completely; the one in Romania continued programming with music but not news or political commentaries. "Our Radio" was probably the last clandestine radio to sign off (*FBIS Trends*, 6 June). The Soviet jamming of foreign broadcasts—BBC, Voice of America (VOA), Deutsche Welle, Radio Liberty—which began in 1948, finally ended in November 1988. Dismantling of the jamming facilities began at Minsk (TASS, 26 May; *FBIS*, 30 May).

New Political Thinking. Gorbachev apparently concluded that past USSR foreign military ventures had been both economically draining and negatively viewed internationally. Often appearing as a peacemaker if only rhetorically, he sought to repair the considerable damage, increase Soviet involvement in world affairs, and in the process elevate his government's prestige. Largely because of the economic crisis, major Soviet instruments supported high-level diplomatic forays in conjunction with traditional propaganda. The regime recognized that the Stalinist-type abrasive, bellicose, and threatening tone of the past was counterproductive, resulting in suspicions of Soviet intentions, strong reactions to continual charges of "imperialism," and characterization of the USSR as the "evil empire." The substance, to some degree, and the tone moderated, thus becoming more effective. For the Kremlin the results were astounding, probably surprising both Gorbachev and his detractors. He was unquestionably the key player, often seizing initiatives and upstaging American leaders. His prestige abroad soared, and opinion surveys revealed him to be the most popular world leader in Western Europe. Even in the United States, *Time* called him a "political genius."

Soviet officials and propagandists continued to portray the policies of *glasnost'*, *perestroika*, and new political thinking as fundamentally altering domestic policies and foreign relations. At the Nineteenth All-Union Party Conference (1988) Gorbachev criticized "command methods" of conducting not only domestic but also foreign relations. Ideology Commission chief Medvedev emphasized that "the leading role [of the CPSU] cannot be reduced. On the contrary its influence will grow but not only by command and administrative methods but through influencing public opinion" (Medvedev, *The Ideology of Restructuring: Principles and Practical Actions* [Novosti, 1989], p. 20). Publicly, Gorbachev distanced himself from previous regimes and modified the former Soviet policy of militarism. However, Moscow blamed "countering imperialism" (and thus the West) rather than earlier Soviet leaders.

Gorbachev's rationale for his "new political thinking" included the inordinate increase in nuclear weapons and a changed international situation resulting in greater interdependence. A further admission was that the previous peaceful coexistence of states with different social and political systems involved a "particular form of class struggle." Although this was not entirely concealed in past decades, neither was it widely publicized nor, except for some specialists, taken seriously in the West. Peaceful coexistence continues to be the keystone of USSR policy, applicable to all states and considered "the only possible and absolutely necessary" policy for East-West relations. Moscow also claimed that "universally human values are indisputably of prime importance" in the new political thinking (*USSR Yearbook 1989*, p. 51). Peaceful coexistence and humanism have been continually called for by Soviet officials and the mass media.

To achieve its goals, Moscow advocated the following: phased elimination of nuclear weapons by the year 2000, an international security system, confidence-building and verification measures for the military, withdrawal of troops and elimination of all overseas bases, international economic security, and direct involvement of science in world politics (ibid., pp. 51–52). The intermediate-range nuclear forces (INF) treaty was frequently mentioned as a success, but only as a first step, the next being a 50 percent reduction in strategic nuclear weapons. Gorbachev and others promoted these positions, as they have their bilateral negotiations on nuclear testing, the multilateral talks on conventional forces in Europe, and others.

Efforts to Improve Image. USSR authorities publicized the worldwide transformation of Soviet society and foreign policies resulting from *glasnost'*, *perestroika*, and the new political thinking. The objective was to persuade foreign governments and publics that the changes are real, that the Kremlin has divorced itself from Stalinist totalitarianism, and that it is developing democracy at home and leading the world toward peace. Internal progress was promoted in the following fields:

- Open society:
  —Greater information on party and government activities, including the KGB and the preparation of accurate maps
- Human rights and civil liberties:
  —Permission for demonstrations

—Release of political prisoners

—Opening of churches, rehabilitation of priests, and importation of bibles

—Freer expression in the mass media and preparation of a new press law

—Release of human rights activists, including Sakharov, and restoring citizenship to exiles

- Publishing previously banned works by Aleksandr Solzhenitzyn, including his *Gulag Archipelago*, and others such as Roy Medvedev

- Legislating greater legal freedom and preparing a new legal system

- Admitting past shortcomings and crimes by Stalin, Khrushchev, and Brezhnev

- Reviewing the history of the Soviet Union, including policies involving the Hungarian uprising (1956), the Warsaw Pact occupation of Czechoslovakia (1968), and the invasion of Afghanistan (1979)

- Permitting associations and groups to organize, as well as hints of allowing political parties

- Modernizing and humanizing Marxism-Leninism and the "leading role" of the CPSU (Article 6 of the constitution)

- Reorganizing the government by establishing the Congress of People's Deputies, upgrading the Supreme Soviet into a more meaningful legislative body, and providing for more democratic elections

- Extending *perestroika* to the Soviet armed forces, the KGB, and relations with the nationalities

- Allowing, even encouraging, changes in Eastern Europe

- Withdrawing from Afghanistan

- Disarming unilaterally and reducing the military budget

- Reconstructing the economy and developing social programs for a better life for Soviet citizens

Foreign Policy. In the spirit of *glasnost'* past Soviet policy decisions have been scrutinized, especially relating to the 1979 Soviet invasion of Afghanistan, the Soviet-led 1968 Warsaw Pact occupation of Czechoslovakia, and the 1962 Cuban missile crisis. Some new information has surfaced, but definitive accounts are still awaited. In a new

nonsecretive and more open foreign policy mechanism, the foreign minister declared that such a system will prevent future "senseless expenses" like Afghanistan (*New Times*, 7 July 1988). The important change in Soviet and Warsaw Treaty Organization (WTO) policy was characterized by Gorbachev at the conference of the Political Consultative Committee in Bucharest as a shift in emphasis from "military-political to political-military" (*Pravda*, 10 July). This meant diminishing confrontation, continuation with the Helsinki process, and more intense dialogue especially with Western Europe, including the United States and Canada.

At the July 1988 conference on foreign affairs, cited above, Shevardnadze acknowledged that foreign policy is not the province of the Foreign Ministry alone but of several foreign policy agencies "under the guidance of the party" (*International Affairs*, no. 10, 1988). The following year he said that "defining and shaping the country's foreign policy is the function of the party and state leadership" and that at no time in its history "has the CC CPSU Politburo dealt with foreign policy issues as intensively, scientifically and collectively as now." For 1989 he added the Congress of People's Deputies, the Supreme Soviet, and the latter's Committee for International Affairs to those with competence in foreign affairs (*The World Has Become a Safer Place*, pp. 7–8, 14).

With new political thinking came the question of possible abandonment of Marxism-Leninism. Leading ideologues have put that question to rest. Vadim Zagladin, who had been first deputy chief of the International Department (1975–88) and who currently is an adviser to Gorbachev as well as chairman of the Supreme Soviet, reflected the views of all officials: "Our course toward peace, toward peaceful coexistence and competition between the two systems does not at all imply abandonment of our revolutionary goals" (Vadim Zagladin, *To Restructure and Humanize International Relations* [Novosti, 1989], p. 87).

Propaganda Themes. May Day and Great October Revolution slogans prepared by the Propaganda Department represent general policy guidance for domestic and foreign propaganda. The 1989 slogans were fewer in number (22 and 16 respectively, a drop of eight each from 1988) and less militant in tone, reflecting changes under Gorbachev. *Perestroika* and new political thinking appeared in speeches and articles dealing with foreign affairs during the year. In May and October exhortation for *perestroika*—"the continuation of the great cause of Lenin"—was cited in a total of nine slogans.

Among the others were calls for "revolutionary renewal of socialism," "socialist internationalism and Soviet patriotism," "Soviet servicemen! strengthen combat organization and discipline," "strengthen the collaboration of the peoples of socialist states," "people of the planet! Fight for a nuclear-free and nonviolent world," "fervent salute to the communists and democratic forces of all countries," and "peoples of the earth! let us jointly secure peace and preserve our planet for future generations." Gorbachev's policy of a common European home was among the May Day slogans, and the new political thinking was in the October slogans (*Pravda*, 16 April, 1 November).

The following propaganda themes were clearly discernible during the year:

- Peace
  —In Europe, on the planet
  —Aim: to secure a nuclear-free and non-violent world community
- Disarmament ("socialism's goal")
  —Unilateral disarmament
  —Defensive military doctrine
  —Withdrawal from Eastern Europe
  —Policy of reasonable sufficiency
- Humanizing and expanding international relations
  —Apply *perestroika* to foreign affairs
  —Respect sovereignty, independence, and territorial integrity of countries
  —Follow a policy of noninterference in internal affairs of other countries
  —Renounce force and threat of force
  —Work toward long-term peaceful coexistence
  —Increase contacts in all fields
  —Deideologize relations
  —Work for ecological security
  —Step up activities at the U.N.
- Improve and expand East-West relations
  —End the Cold War
  —Go from confrontation to cooperation
  —Go from military-political to political-military
  —Achieve a balance of interests
  —Work for closer East-West economic ties
- Improve and expand U.S.-Soviet relations
  —Intensify disarmament negotiations

  —Expand dialogue, contacts, exchanges
- *Perestroika* for Eastern Europe
- Our common European home
  —Historical ties
  —For present, include United States and Canada
- Solving regional problems
  —Withdraw from Afghanistan
  —Work for peace in Persian Gulf, South Africa, Southeast Asia

The themes are comprehensive, reflecting current USSR foreign policy that emphasizes, as noted above, moving from a military and confrontational posture to a more political and cooperative orientation. Propagation of the Soviet new thinking was conducted by scores of Soviet officials and orchestrated by the ubiquitous media. In addition to traditional diplomatic machinery, which includes non-diplomatic operatives, Moscow employed a campaign of "public diplomacy" on a substantially increased scale.

People's Diplomacy. A clear exposition of this "diplomacy" and the "common European home" was given by Zagladin over Moscow television. Timed to appear before the Malta summit, Zagladin said that the aim of "people's diplomacy" is for the Soviet Union to appeal to Western public opinion, which would respond by pressuring governments on issues where traditional diplomacy is not succeeding.

Zagladin recalled that people's diplomacy was practiced by nineteenth-century European socialists, with the First International addressing the masses directly. The current Soviet policymakers are especially impressed with the Bolsheviks' use of this tactic during 1917 in developing sympathy from the masses abroad. According to Zagladin, the most significant factor in the Bolshevik campaign was the attractive symbol of "peace," which is desired by everyone.

Applied to current USSR policies, people's diplomacy is intended to persuade the masses that because "their survival is at stake" they have a right to intervene in their government's diplomacy to determine what causes people to act, to "internationalize the struggle for peace," to create a favorable general atmosphere, and to involve the entire political spectrum, including political antagonists and conservatives, for opportunities to suggest useful arguments to defeat the opponents. Zagladin declared that the area of emphasis for people's diplomacy is Europe (Moscow Television, 11 November; RL, *Report on the USSR*, 29 December; and response to personal query). In 1989 Novosti published a booklet in four languages entitled *Soviet People's Movement and People's Diplomacy* by S. Khudiakov from Moscow State University's Institute of International Relations.

Disarmament. The Gorbachev regime came to realize that the Soviet military buildup caused the West to upgrade its own armed forces. In addition, past USSR resistance to verification measures, especially on-site inspection, and published U.S. documentation of Soviet treaty violations created suspicion and loss of credibility in Moscow's arms control and disarmament proposals. The USSR had a tarnished image.

Faced with failed policies of military intimidation and debilitating costs, the Soviet leadership recognized the futility of continuing a policy of overpowering militarism and made a conscious decision to pursue demilitarization on a scale beyond the rhetoric of past regimes. In his comprehensive report to the Congress of the USSR People's Deputies, Gorbachev reiterated the direction of foreign policy as taken by among others, the Twenty-seventh Party Congress and the Nineteenth Party Conference. He emphasized that "the country's security should be maintained above all by political means as an integral part of universal and equal security" and that "the use of force and the threat of force . . . is impermissible" (Moscow Television, 30 May; *FBIS*, 31 May).

This policy is intended to recoup economic benefits, gain international prestige as "peacemaker," influence Western public opinion to undertake disarmament programs, and, in the process, cause a rift between the United States and its Western allies. The Soviet Union, after all, had a preponderance in military forces, was constantly modernizing, and even with impressive quantitative reductions, would become "leaner but meaner." Moscow touted its new policy of "reasonable sufficiency" and its military doctrine as being defensive.

The December 1987 INF treaty was hailed by both sides and their allies. In the foreign minister's eyes, although the Soviet Union destroyed more missiles, it was because "we [had] installed more" and the result was "the removal of American missiles from our frontiers" (Eduard Shevardnadze, *The World Has Become a Safer Place* [Novosti, 1989], p. 4). The INF treaty was followed by Gor-

bachev's announcement before the U.N. General Assembly on 7 December 1988 of unilateral Soviet force reductions over the next two years of 500,000 troops, including 50,000 from Eastern Europe; ten thousand tanks and eight hundred aircraft from the European USSR and Eastern Europe; and 8,500 artillery systems. In May 1989, Gorbachev announced additional unilateral reductions of five hundred "tactical nuclear weapons" targeted against Western Europe.

These moves, Soviet publicists reflected, were "to accelerate" the disarmament process (*Socialism*, May). Along with reducing the danger of war, Moscow said that all other activities should be subordinated to ecological security (from *Nauchnyi kommunizm* in ibid., p. 14). The international movement Eco Forum for Peace held a meeting in Moscow to discuss "the struggle for peace" and "the struggle to conserve nature" (*Pravda*, 29 September).

The Soviet Union portrayed itself as a leading voice for disarmament. Continuing to claim "a rough balance" of forces between the North Atlantic Treaty Organization (NATO) and the WTO, Moscow pointed to its willingness to reduce its conventional forces, navies and air forces as it "warily gazes at the high seas, with the U.S. maintaining the bulk of its strategic arms on submarines." However, times and "global attitudes" are changing, so that the United States and Great Britain "no longer object to Moscow as the venue for the 1991 International Conference on Humanitarian Issues" (*Soviet Life*, June).

Our Common European Home. In his 30 May address to the Congress of People's Deputies, Gorbachev said that "a major area of our foreign policy work is participation in the building of a common European home" (ibid.). When he went to France in October 1985 (the first Western country he visited after becoming general secretary), it showed a renewed interest of Soviet foreign policy in Western Europe. In France, as he had in 1984 in London, Gorbachev made a favorable impression on his official hosts and the public. A major foreign policy conference, held at the USSR Foreign Ministry in July 1988, designated Europe as the principal region for exploitation (*Mezhdunarodnaia zhizn*, nos. 9, 10, 1988). However, Gorbachev's personal intense involvement came in 1989, the logical result of his "new political thinking" being to establish a "common European home."

In Gorbachev's foreign travels he employed a

public relations style not previously observed in a Soviet leader. Official visits to Western Europe in 1989 included Great Britain (April), West Germany (June), France (July), and Italy (November). In October, Gorbachev visited Finland. While in Rome he had an historic meeting with Pope John Paul II, breaking a 70-year Soviet record of antipathy toward the Roman Catholic church. He was the first CPSU leader to meet with the pope, appearing more a religious person than an atheist when he spoke of the "need" for "spiritual values."

Even before Gorbachev's formal meeting with the pope, a high-level Vatican delegation headed by Secretary of State Agostino Cardinal Casaroli, attended the Russian Orthodox millennium celebration, and the cardinal met with Gorbachev. In his brief but conciliatory remarks to Pope John Paul II, Gorbachev characterized the meeting as a "remarkable event." He said that an "agreement in principle" was reached for official relations and promised that "in the near future a law regarding freedom of conscience is to be passed in our country." Also, the two leaders discussed a future visit of Pope John Paul to the Soviet Union (*Visit of Mikhail Gorbachev to Italy* [Novosti, 1989], pp. 63–64). The event made a positive impact not only on Roman Catholics but on people throughout the world.

Gorbachev envisioned Europe as "a commonwealth of sovereign democratic states." As though to soothe lingering doubts about Soviet messianism, he declared that "we have abandoned the claim to have a monopoly on the truth." In all visits, Gorbachev in various ways promoted Soviet policies of denouncing nuclear war, struggling for peace through disarmament and the Helsinki process, and developing closer relations between WTO countries and the West European countries. He received an abundance of favorable publicity for himself and for Soviet policies.

Mindful of Western suspicions that the Soviet Union's objective was to drive a wedge between the United States and its allies, Gorbachev sought to allay such fears. Addressing the Council of Europe, he said that the "realities of the present day and the prospects for the visible future are obvious." The United States, like the Soviet Union, is "a natural part of the European international political structure." He said that the Cold War and confrontation should be placed in the archives and that the "European idea" should be pursued, citing Victor Hugo's dream of "a higher society," a European fraternity (Moscow Television, 6 July; *FBIS*, 7 July).

An English-language publication for American readers phrased the Gorbachev comment as follows: the United States is "a factor in the European process, and it would be primitive or, frankly speaking, even absurd to underestimate this reality, and all the more so to build plans along that line" (*Soviet Life*, October). The publication commented that "the preparation to build the European home showed that, in a sense, the U.S. is part of Europe and will remain part of it in the foreseeable future." Therefore, all talk of driving a wedge "is so blatantly wrong that it does not deserve even the name of a propaganda cliche" (ibid.).

Gorbachev reported on his visits to Great Britain, West Germany, and France to the Supreme Soviet on 1 August. Characterizing these countries as among the "world's foremost powers," he said that "all three have tremendous influence over European and global politics." He observed greater mutual trust and greater content in Soviet-European relations. He said that "personal contacts are tremendously significant in modern politics" and that barriers are toppling, especially with West Germany. National elections, the People's Congress, and the Supreme Soviet impressed the Europeans. He said that for the Europeans, the nuclear threat has receded and the fear of war is gone, with the public giving credit for this to the Soviet Union.

Gorbachev noted that as a result of the INF treaty the United States had not increased its military budget over the last three years. As he told the Council of Europe ("to the world") in Strasbourg, the West increasingly sympathizes with the USSR's "renewed socialist state," and hostile speculation is evaporating. He sounded euphoric at the opportunity of speaking to such an assemblage as the Council of Europe—"one of the pillars of the European home and a body in which to work jointly on important initiatives." The "humanization" of Soviet relations "creates a favorable public opinion and encourages millions of Europeans to bolster the peace process on the continent." He mentioned the importance of contacts, such as youth ("an investment in the future"), parliamentarians, and the military, among others. (*Mikhail Gorbachev's Address* [Novosti, 1989].)

Foreign Minister Shevardnadze confirmed the purpose of Gorbachev's visits to West European countries and his address to the Council of Europe, saying that "all fit into the concept of a common European home with room available for the USA and Canada there." The architectural design of the common European home, he said, is "developing into a structure with a clear outline, one resting on trust and expanding ties between states at all levels and in all areas." (*The World Has Become a Safer Place*, p. 23).

Reflecting on Gorbachev's U.N. address was an article in London's *Financial Times* entitled "Can NATO Survive Détente?" for there was now in Western Europe the prospect of no "enemy" (i.e., the USSR) to maintain unity in NATO. The article pointed out that the "large majority" of the West German public, polls showed, oppose nuclear modernization and that up to 80 percent favor removing all nuclear weapons from their territory (*World Press Review*, February). The next month, this same source cited the Hamburg weekly *Die Zeit* as reporting that for many West Germans it is the United States that threatens their sovereignty. On the eve of Gorbachev's visit to West Germany, an ABC News survey revealed that most citizens of that country believed that the USSR and its leader were more interested in making progress on arms control than were the United States and President Bush (*WP*, 30 May).

The Soviet media gave the upcoming NATO summit substantial coverage, citing "sharp differences" (TASS, 27 May), the "deepest crisis in NATO's history" (Moscow Television, 29 May; *FBIS*, 30 May), and "serious controversy" (Moscow Radio, 29 May; *FBIS*, 30 May). Attacks against NATO continued during the year. For example, Army General Vladimir Lobov, chief of staff for the WTO Joint Armed Forces, charged that whereas the two alliances are negotiating for reduction of conventional forces, "the U.S. and NATO armed forces are continuing completely in accordance with their doctrines of 'direct confrontation' and 'flexible response,' which have a clearly offensive, aggressive thrust and visualize the possibility of mounting military operations through a surprise attack" (*Krasnaia zvezda*, 29 April). The Soviet-West German political declaration was characterized by Foreign Minister Hans-Dietrich Genscher as a "milestone" in the countries' relations (DPA, 13 June). Other officials and media were less euphoric, but in general the document was viewed enthusiastically. For example *Die Welt* (14 June) declared "seldom has a foreign policy document been welcomed so unanimously," but concluded that "now, deeds must follow words." While in Bonn, Gorbachev met with local communist leader Herbert Mies. TASS (15 June) reported that both agreed that the "warm welcome" given Gorbachev "reflects deep-going changes in the minds of citizens under the influence of the Soviet peace policy,

democratization and *glasnost'*." At the same time Supreme Soviet International Commission chairman Iakovlev met with leaders of the German Green party. Among other things, the talks concerned interparty contacts (TASS, 15 June).

Gorbachev met with President François Mitterrand a second time, at the latter's initiative, in Kiev. The two leaders held a joint press conference following their "working summit." Their discussion concentrated on European affairs. According to TASS (6 December), they agreed to maintain permanent contacts and to intensify their dialogue. Gorbachev told the press that, as previously, the two presidents regard the United States as an "indispensable element" in the European building (Moscow Radio, 6 December; *FBIS*, 7 December). Mitterrand reportedly gave his support to Gorbachev's call for an all-European summit meeting in 1990.

In line with its policy of expanding relations, especially with European countries, Moscow among numerous other activities established with Switzerland a management school at Kiev. Along the same path, it signed a management training agreement with France. In pursuit of "ecological security," Moscow concluded a treaty with Sweden to reduce pollution in the Baltic Sea. Among the Soviet delegates to the West European–USSR dialogue in Austria (5–8 July) was Pitrim, the Russian Orthodox metropolitan and People's Deputy.

On balance the West Europeans exhibited caution about Soviet policies and the role of the United States in their future. As the London *Economist* (11 November) said, the American presence is needed at a time when "Europeans are filled with a curious mixture of exhilaration and unease about their future."

Our common European home was one of the most heavily promoted themes. A government journalist spoke of "bridges" between the Council of Europe and the Council for Mutual Economic Assistance countries, quoting President Mitterrand as saying "I believe that the time has come to establish closer ties between the two Europes, without any preliminary conditions" (*Izvestiia*, 22 June). Gorbachev pointed to a record of agreements signed during his visits to West Germany and France, 12 and 22, respectively, which "have provided an unprecedented foundation for mutually beneficial cooperation" (*Mikhail Gorbachev's Address*, p. 12). New West European consulates were opened in Munich and Kiev. In line with its expanding relations, Moscow increasingly involved foreigners in its space program. A French-USSR agreement provided for a long-term program of manned flights (*Izvestiia*, 23 December), the latest in a full series of cooperative ventures involving Britain and Austria as well as the United States and Japan (TASS, 28 December).

United States: Friend and Foe. For Soviet officials and propagandists, the United States was at once a cooperative partner and the traditional enemy. Moscow perceived U.S.-Soviet relations as so markedly changed that a rapprochement could be established. In the Gallup poll of "most admired men," Gorbachev was second only to Presidents Reagan and Bush in 1988 and 1989. U.S.-Soviet relations have improved over the last several years, especially in arms control negotiations. Gorbachev's new political thinking has altered the Soviet attitude toward various negotiations, and he met with President Reagan as follows: at Geneva in 1985, Reykjavik in 1986, and Washington, D.C., where on 7 December 1987 the INF treaty was signed. INF is cited as a positive beginning for further reductions. Negotiations on strategic, conventional, and other arms continued during the year under review.

Gorbachev met once more with President Reagan, during 20 May–2 June 1988 in Moscow, where several agreements were signed including one on exchanges for 1989–1991 that would extend the U.S.-Soviet General Exchanges Agreement, covering 1986–1991, originally signed on 21 November 1985 at the first Reagan-Gorbachev summit. (This five-year hiatus stemmed from the Soviet invasion of Afghanistan.)

Improvement of relations between the two countries (the United States now led by President Bush) appeared brighter than perhaps at any time since the October Revolution. Ministerial-level contacts were frequent, and the presidents met at their first summit in early December. No agreements were signed, but the leaders agreed to meet again in June 1990. Meanwhile, their negotiators were pursuing talks on strategic, conventional, and other arms reductions. President Bush pledged to support observer status for Moscow at the General Agreement on Tariffs and Trade meeting and a movement to waive the Jackson-Vanik amendment.

Public expressions were perhaps most important. President Bush said in December 1989, "With reform under way in the Soviet Union, we stand at the threshold of a brand-new era of U.S.-Soviet relations. It is within our grasp . . . to overcome the division of Europe and end the military confrontation there." Gorbachev declared that "the arms race, mistrust, psychological and ideological struggle, all those should be things of the past."

The U.S.-Soviet exchange agreement includes projects in education, the performing arts, exhibits, and television and film, as well as professional and citizen exchanges. Reagan and Gorbachev approved a new, broad-based people-to-people initiative to expand contact between citizens of the two countries. The U.S. Information Agency (USIA) implements both the agreement and the initiative (USIA, *U.S.-Soviet Exchange Initiative Fact Sheet*, September).

Since 1956 the United States and the Soviet Union have distributed, on a reciprocal basis, the monthly magazines *America Illustrated* and *Soviet Life* (previously, *USSR*). The Russian-language *America Illustrated*, published by USIA, is intended "to create a better understanding of the United States" and is distributed in about 80 Soviet cities. The number of copies distributed is controlled by agreement. In 1989 sales of 100,000 were permitted, plus two thousand to the American embassy in Moscow for complimentary mailing (USIA, *Facts about* America Illustrated, January 1990). *America Illustrated* was always in great demand; however, copies in varying numbers, higher during periods of poor bilateral relations, were returned to the U.S. embassy as "unsold," and some subscribers failed to receive their copies. In recent years this situation has improved.

The English-language *Soviet Life*, also illustrated, is published by the Soviet embassy in Washington and printed by an American firm. Material is provided by the Novosti Press Agency in Moscow. The December issue stated that the average monthly number of copies sold or distributed during the preceding year was 66,500. According to editor in chief Robert Tsfasman, subscriptions increased from 50,000 to 58,000 during the year for an increased readership of 30,000 (*Soviet Life*, December). The range of topics is extensive, portraying Soviet life and foreign affairs.

The year of favorable relations was capped by Presidents Bush and Gorbachev videotaping New Year's greetings, done yearly since 1986, except for 1987. The U.S. president offered "warm greetings" for the New Year and said "we should redouble our efforts to forge a new century of peace and freedom." He praised Gorbachev as "a good partner in peace" and told the Soviet people that the United States, with NATO allies, "seeks no advantage from the extraordinary changes under way" in Eastern

Europe. Gorbachev told the American people that the world is "forging ahead in pursuit of happiness, freedom, and democracy." He added that it would be "naive, preposterous and dangerous to try to stop the quest." The Soviet leader envisioned a "real watershed" in 1990 in "arms control and arms reductions." He predicted that the 1990s would be "a decade of great closeness between the U.S. and the Soviet Union" on the basis of a balance of interests. (*WP*, 1 January 1990; *Facts on File*, 1–5 January 1990.)

In the positive portrayal of developments, Moscow played on "improved U.S.-Soviet relations," citing the INF treaty, the ongoing strategic arms reduction talks and other negotiations, the Afghanistan agreement, the bilateral approach to Lebanon, and the attitude toward President Bush's visit to Poland and Hungary as "calm, dignified, and constructive evaluations...from all levels," in contrast to past reactions (*Soviet Life*, October).

Anti-U.S. Propaganda. In line with Zagladin's authoritative declaration, noted above, that the Soviet course "does not at all imply abandonment of our revolutionary goals," Moscow has not abandoned its propaganda against the United States. Although there is a lessening in stridency and perhaps quantity, the present campaign is appreciably more effective. The targets of attack are the United States as the leader of NATO and international imperialism; the Strategic Defense Initiative (SDI); and the offensive U.S. military doctrine: producing nuclear, biological, and chemical weapons and continuing support of the war in Afghanistan; encircling the USSR with military bases; threatening naval operations in the Indian Ocean and the Mediterranean; supporting international terrorism in Third World countries; and interference in Central America.

Moscow continued to attack the Central Intelligence Agency (CIA), the Federal Bureau of Investigation, and Radio Liberty and VOA broadcasts. It continued its disinformation and active measure campaigns against the U.S. government (for the latter, see U.S. Department of State, *Soviet Influence Activities*, August).

During the year, in addition to television as noted above, USSR officials appeared in the U.S. media in unprecedented numbers. For example, Viktor Karpov, deputy minister of foreign affairs, had an article in the *NYT* (12 June) on "Moscow's View: The Bush Proposal on European Arms," and Genrikh Trofimenko, head of the foreign policy depart-

ment of the USA and Canada Institute, wrote one entitled "Malta Summit a Prelude to Bigger Things Ahead" (*CSM*, 30 November).

Moscow began attacking SDI from its inception (see U.S. Arms Control and Disarmament Agency, *The Soviet Propaganda Campaign against the U.S. Strategic Defense Initiative* [Washington, D.C., August 1986]). These Soviet attacks have continued. According to TASS (14 March), the Pentagon's "leakage of confidential information" about a new version of SDI, the "Brilliant Pebbles," was done to bolster the program. The news agency said that the new version, like the previous one, "is absolutely senseless" and "will not protect the U.S.A. from a retaliatory strike." The military observer's article was published by the Defense Ministry organ, *Krasnaia zvezda*, two days later. *Pravda* (20 March) said that SDI proponents had attempted to influence the White House to bolster the SDI program. The CPSU organ charged that this was another instance of "pressure" on the Soviet Union, "still trying to speak from a position of strength." *Pravda* (21 October) also charged that SDI is "a stimulus for a qualitative arms race" and that the aim of the so-called U.S. military-technical leadership is to "gain military superiority." Major General Vladimir Belous called SDI "notorious" and an obstacle to U.S.-Soviet negotiations. According to that officer, President Bush adheres to the "policy of strength" and supports SDI. He threatened that weapons in space would have "fatal consequences" (Vladimir Belous, "SDI: The Strategy of Doom," *Socialism*, November).

The CIA has been a special target of Soviet active measures, disinformation, and propaganda activities. Novosti and Progress Publishers published books alleging CIA covert operations against India and Afghanistan (Rustem Galiulin, *The CIA in Asia* [Progress Publishers, 1988]) and in the 1978 Jonestown tragedy (*Once Again about the CIA* [Novosti, 1988]). *Izvestiia* (20 April) perpetuated the allegations, saying that evidence points to CIA involvement in the Guyana massacre. *USA: Economics, Politics, Ideology* (June), published by the Institute for the USA and Canada, perpetuated false charges of the U.S. government's role in the 1977 killing of the American ambassador in Afghanistan. In an article titled "The CIA against Panama" (*Ekho Planety*, 17–23 June), the Soviet writer charges the United States with "destabilization" in the area and says that the CIA supplied American media with information intended to discredit Noriega. On 18 August, *Pravda* published a piece based on an "investigation" of the 1981 death of General Omar Torrijos, the writer claiming that the general's brother has evidence of CIA involvement in the death. Moscow also attempted to discredit CIA analyses of the Soviet Union, for example, on defense outlays and *perestroika* (*Literaturnaia gazeta*, 6 December).

The USSR frequently denounced U.S. involvement in regional problems while claiming for itself the role of peacemaker, mediator, and initiator of the settlement of such conflicts. Further, the USSR claimed that it and Afghanistan have been from the beginning of agreements "strictly complying with their obligations," charging Pakistan with an "obstructionist line which hinders the Afghan settlement" on the refugees. Nevertheless, Afghanistan was said to have marked a "new phase" in settling regional conflicts in the Persian Gulf, in South Africa, and in Southeast Asia, with the Soviet Union "doing everything in its power to achieve progress" (*USSR Yearbook 1989*, p. 54).

Moscow cited an NBC report about forthcoming deliveries to the Afghan opposition of "large-scale military and civilian cargoes," which, the commentator charged, "is a sign that in practice no radical reassessment of American policy toward Afghanistan is taking place" (Radio Moscow, 15 June; *FBIS*, 23 June). The Soviet Union continued to support the Kabul regime and, allegedly to counter U.S. and Pakistani aid to the insurgents, threatened to "offer . . . its most sophisticated military aircraft" (*Izvestiia*, 12 July). As the conflict intensified, so

did Moscow's diplomatic and propaganda campaigns to achieve, in the words of Foreign Minister Shevardnadze, "a final political settlement of the Afghan problems" (*Izvestiia*, 8 August).

The Soviet Union has consistently criticized U.S. involvement in Latin America, in recent years especially that in Central America. Gorbachev visited Cuba in April, signing a Treaty of Friendship and Cooperation with Fidel Castro. Writing in *Socialism* (November), Yuri Alexandrov, a specialist in international law, reported Gorbachev's characterization of the United States as having "regarded Latin America as its anteroom and behaved accordingly." After enumerating U.S. military activities in Latin America, Alexandrov attributed to Gorbachev's speech in Havana the comment that "the USSR was not seeking nor had ever sought military, naval, and air force bases in Latin America. Nor has it ever intended to deploy nuclear or other weapons of mass destruction there." At the Malta summit Gorbachev gave President Bush assurances that the Soviet Union was not supplying military arms directly to the Sandinistas in Nicaragua.

The Soviet Union had supported the Noriega regime. When U.S. forces deposed Noriega in December, Moscow's reaction was immediate and sharp, the media characterizing the American action as "aggression" (Radio Moscow; *FBIS*, 20 December; TASS, 21 December), "invasion" (*Sovetskaia rossiia*, 21 December), and "imperial thinking" (*Pravda*, 21 December).

John J. Karch
Falls Church, Virginia

THE MIDDLE EAST AND NORTH AFRICA

Introduction

For the Middle East and North African communist parties and their allies the principal events of 1989 piled disaster upon misfortune. First, the successive collapse of East European governments virtually eliminated the crucial network of alliances that had provided political support and logistic backing for radical causes in the region for decades. Lost was not merely the constant exchange of visits reducing the isolation and frustration of the rejectionist and radical Arab states and the shadowy movements of banned parties. More important, tangible security support had come in the form of extensive East German, Bulgarian and other secret police, espionage, and special forces training. Moreover, Eastern Europe's sales of military equipment had grown ever more critical as détente reduced the outflow of the Soviet arms-supply spigot. Iran's mounting dependence on Eastern bloc weapons was dramatized in March by two major military agreements—with Romania and Czechoslovakia—relating to base construction, arms-factories management, the delivery of 180 Soviet tanks assembled in Czechoslovakia, and technology for antitank and air-to-air missiles. (KEYHAN, London, in Persian, 30 March; FBIS-NES, 4 May). For Iran and other anti-Western states like the People's Democratic Republic of South Yemen (PDRY), East Europe's stunning changes shifted the political balance adversely in a situation where the tide of world events was already flowing negatively. Iran repeatedly protested West Germany's "growing tendency...toward arrogance and counterrevolution against the Islamic revolution," accusing the FRG of allowing its companies to assist Iraq with the manufacture of medium-range missiles with chemical warheads. (Tehran Domestic Service, in Persian, 2 May; FBIS-NES, 4 May.) Regardless of its validity, the charge made by Iran illustrates the general loss of leverage by Third World countries who looked to Eastern Europe for support, a loss embarrassingly dramatized for Iran at the year's end by Ceauşescu's gory demise only two days after he had returned from a heavily publicized state visit to Tehran. Iran's tightly controlled media has studiously ignored the wave of dramatic changes toppling regimes in the Eastern bloc.

The completed withdrawal of Soviet troops from Afghanistan early in the year failed to precipitate the mujahideen military victory over the Moscow-supported People's Democratic Party of Afghanistan (PDPA) that many observers had expected. Nor did another year of formal cease-fire between Iran and Iraq see movement in stalled negotiations over even the least controversial issues, such as the exchange of prisoners. But these stalemates seemed to ripen Moscow's prospects for greater political advances in the region, particularly in conjunction with the less rigid ideological posture in Iran following the Ayatollah Khomeini's death. President Hashemi-Rafsanjani's visit to the USSR in June dramatized what appeared to be a major improvement in relations between the two states. Announcements of major economic and trade agreements followed, embellished with extravagant rhetoric like that displayed in Rafsanjani's comment on the result of his visit: "One of perhaps the most favorable situations—unprecedented in the history of...Iranian-Soviet relations—has arisen now" (Pravda, 22 June; FBIS-SOV, 22 June). Moscow's open-armed response to Tehran's hectic courtship was reminiscent of several periods during the war when Iran's isolation was greatest and its military fortunes at lowest ebb.

For Iran's communist Tudeh Party this improving relationship was a painful reminder of the low priority Moscow assigns to indigenous parties relative to its major strategic designs. The Tudeh continued its campaign against the previous year's executions by the revolutionary government and in February succeeded in mobilizing over 30 communist parties in countries ranging from Argentina to Turkey to join in condemnation of the executions in Iran and in demands for the release of all political prisoners there. (*Tudeh News*, 1 February.) In its 48th anniversary statement, the Tudeh Central Committee bemoaned its losses under Khomeini's "mass killing" and acknowledged that "one party or one organization cannot replace the present regime," and that all opposition forces need to "uproot the greedy way of thinking that they alone can be an alternative" (Radio of the Iranian Toilers, in Persian, 2 October; *FBIS-NES*, 6 October).

Moscow's expression of token loyalty on the occasion of the Tudeh's 48th year of faithful devotion came in a Moscow Radio editorial on 14 September which defended the party and denied charges that it had spied for Moscow. The foreseeable reaction of the Tehran press exemplified the reality of numerous remaining imperfections behind the ballyhoo extolling a USSR-Iran honeymoon, as Moscow was accused of "meddling in our internal affairs in a very naive way by...defending the Tudeh Party [and] bringing back memories of that country's...past as a meddling government" (Tehran, *Keyhan Havai*, 27 September; *FBIS-NES*, 6 October). The paper explained the dichotomy of Soviet policy as evidence of a split between the Gorbachevian forces and those "who are still faithful to the old ways," perhaps missing the irony of a similar opposition within Iran's polity between pragmatists bent on normalizing Iran's international relations and those wanting to spread its revolution covertly to Muslims everywhere, including the Muslim parts of the USSR.

Other fundamental problems between Moscow and Tehran were noted by Iran's media throughout the year. A leading newspaper, for instance, after elaborating on the many areas of shared policy—such as "the non-presence of foreign fleets in the region...and the timely and gradual increase of the price of crude oil"—said that Soviet pursuit of détente with the West comes before cooperation with Third World countries; that "In other words, the two sides' different outlook toward the west, the nature of Afghanistan's future government and the method of resolving the Zionist problem, make the arena for action limited" (Iran National News Agency, 3 March, quoting *Ettela'at* daily, 2 March). "Moscow's steady arms supply to Baghdad as an obstacle in the peace efforts" was also highlighted.

Moscow was not without its own complaints about its partner in the relationship. Long after Rafsanjani's visit to the USSR, Radio Moscow complained of continued Iranian efforts to export the Islamic revolution as a Khomeini legacy "nobody has changed," and which added "an Iranian element

to an already complex and bloody Lebanese crisis...[in which] Iran seemed to be supporting creation of an Islamic republic in the half-Christian Lebanon" (Moscow Radio, Peace and Progress, in Arabic, 30 October; *FBIS-SOV*, 2 November).

Also troubling to Iran was Iraq's participation in one of the two major unions in the Arab world notable during the year. The long Gulf war resulted in the marked strengthening of the Gulf Cooperation Council (GCC), which links the states of the Arabian peninsula, and also was responsible in part for the political realignments preceding formation in February of the Arab Cooperation Council (ACC), comprising Iraq, Jordan, Egypt, and the Yemen Arab Republic. Of major significance were Egypt's reintegration into the Arab world and the fact that the ACC was unified as a moderate bloc, similar to the GCC in its international posture. Holding the potential for continuation of the important wartime cooperation between Iraq and Egypt, the ACC's creation appeared economically motivated as much as politically pragmatic in orientation, much in contrast to earlier attempts at Arab unity founded on grandiose political and military designs.

Iraq's cautious flirtation with political pluralism—national assembly elections in April—categorically excluded the already banned Iraqi Communist Party (ICP) on the grounds of their support for Iran during the war. Only politically tame electoral candidates were allowed to participate, and from exile in Damascus the ICP growled that "these forged elections will only bring about a forged assembly, which does not represent...the will of the Arab people in Iraq" (Radio Damascus, 1 April; *FBIS-NES*, 4 April). While realizing the need for change, Iraq's leadership appears stalled on its implementation. First Deputy Prime Minister Taha Yasin Ramadan admitted this need during a December interview, in which he declared: "The Ba'th Party needs competition to rejuvenate it and stop it from growing old, as in the case of the communist parties in Eastern Europe" (London, *al-Tadamun*, 4 December; *FBIS-NES*, 7 December). The end of the year still saw only Ba'thist political groups tolerated and even within party confines no evidence that President Saddam Hussein had initiated a truly collegial dialogue. Notwithstanding Moscow's high-profile diplomatic efforts to mediate the unyielding disputes between Iran and Iraq, the flow of sophisticated weapons to Baghdad continued, witness completed delivery of fifty MiG-29s during the two-year period ending in December. (*Middle East Economic Digest*, 24 November.)

The People's Democratic Republic of South Yemen's ruling (Marxist) Yemeni Socialist Party (YSP) fought its regional and international isolation, which became noticeably more pronounced because of developments in the Arab world as well as in Eastern Europe and the USSR. In December, the YSP Central Committee announced approval of a multiparty system, ordering the Politburo to prepare procedural guidelines for allowing other parties. This step followed earlier decisions to encourage the private sector, attract Western investment, and allow independent candidates to run for local government elections. All unprecedented in the rigid PDRY political environment, these steps all appear partly due to the formation of the Arab Cooperation Council. The mounting credibility of the Gulf Cooperation Council (GCC), which joins Saudi Arabia with the Arab states of the gulf, had left the PDRY dangling. This situation was undoubtedly a major cause of the two Yemeni presidents' November announcement of an agreement on unity made with obvious serious intent as opposed to previous declarations often made while the two countries were on the brink of war. (*Middle East International*, 15 December.) While the process of achieving unity will undoubtedly span years rather than months, its very existence at least opens a door out of the PDRY's isolation and is a hedge against the unknowns of rapid developments in the USSR and Eastern Europe. Ironically, just as the YSP was busily trying to change its spots by accepting pluralism, a new Marxist party, the Yemeni Popular Unity Party (YPUP), surfaced in the YAR, apparently composed of a small group of merged revolutionary parties and organizations which split from the opposition National Democratic Front in 1979 (*WMR*, June).

Another member of the ACC, Jordan, was compelled by events to offer economic and political reforms following serious riots throughout the country in April, which forced the resignation of Prime Minister Zaid Rifai. Although the government principally blamed Muslim fundamentalists for the riots, members of the Communist Party of Jordan (CPJ) were also arrested. (*CSM*, 21 April.) By early September, the majority of detainees had been released, and the badly divided CPJ made frantic efforts to prepare for November general parliamentary elections, the first in 22 years. Only one communist, 'Isa Madanat, won a seat in elections noteworthy for the Islamic movement's capture of 20 out of 80 seats. (Amman TV Service, 10 November; *FBIS*, 13 November.) The elections were universally regarded as free and honestly administered, although as members of a still officially banned though tolerated party, CPJ members had to run as individuals.

In the neighboring Israeli-occupied West Bank, by contrast, the conditions of the *intifada* have enhanced the role of the Palestine Communist Party (PCP), some analysts assert, to the point where it is the most successful communist party in the Arab world today, an achievement whose magnitude is much diminished by the woeful status of the PCP's competition (Alain Gresh, "Palestinian Communists and the Intifada," *Middle East Report*, March–April). As is the CPJ in Jordan, the PCP, although illegal, is generally tolerated, undoubtedly because of its emphasis on political as opposed to physical struggle and its presumed value in dividing the strength of the PLO. The PCP's general secretary (unnamed) claimed in an August interview that his party's "leading role" in the uprising was evidenced by the fact that two-thirds of the Palestinians "who have died in Israeli prisons" have been communists (*WMR*, August). In Israel proper, the legal Communist Party of Israel (CPI) draws its strength primarily from Israeli Arabs. Having 4 seats (with the Democratic Front for Peace and Equality) out of 120 in the legislature, the CPI has a forum for attacking both the Likud on the right and Labor in the center. Compatible with Arab political trends elsewhere, local elections in February brought important victories for Islamic candidates, including the winning of 6 out of 19 seats on the Nazareth Council. (*CSM*, 13 March, 12 September.)

In Lebanon, the Lebanese Communist Party (LCP) continued to exploit the freedom of action occasioned by that tragic country's lack of effective central government. Maneuvering carefully in the maze of warring political factions and their militias, the LCP remained within the coalition of Nationalist Parties that includes the important Druze forces and supports political reform and the expulsion of Israeli forces from South Lebanon and asserts the necessity of close cooperation with Syria. The LCP claimed responsibility for an infiltration across the Israeli border in September which brought heavy casualties to each side (Sawt al-Shaab [LCP Radio], 10 September; *FBIS-NES*, 12 September). Three months later, Israel retaliated with a tank and helicopter-gunship raid of 100 commandos, and claimed destruction of two LCP bases in South Lebanon (*NYT*, 27 December). In all party statements, the LCP continued its complete approval of USSR policy, ignoring the massive wave of change sweeping through what was once called the Eastern bloc. In a behind-the-times fashion, the neighboring Syrian Communist Party (SCP) continued to extol Marxist virtues, blaming Syria's economic crisis on "close economic ties with the world capitalist market" (*WMR*, May). Given the SCP's history of slavish attachment to Moscow's line, its eventual catch-up gymnastics will provide that party with a tough intellectual exercise. For Moscow, Iraq's new involvement in Lebanon in support of the anti-Syrian forces of General Michel 'Aun was a further complication deepening the split between its allies in Baghdad and Damascus.

For the USSR, however, the re-establishment of relations between Syria and Egypt as the year ended offered the potential for increased diplomatic opportunities in Lebanon and elsewhere. The badly splintered communist movement in Egypt, though, has long been of no or little use to Moscow, particularly as the Islamic militants have come to represent the major opposition force. The Egyptian Communist Party (ECP) and its various communist allies apparently work primarily "through professional unions, clubs, and organizations," according to the Ministry of Interior (*al-Ahram*, 15 April; *FBIS-NES*, 17 April). The ministry made sporadic arrests of ECP members during the year and confiscated tons of leaflets. In general, however, the ECP and its allies are permitted to function, leading some to speculate that the Mubarak government finds the "mainstream left" of use in offsetting Islamic extremists. (*The Middle East*, November.) If that is true, the use of such a tactic would be an ironic twist of history. During some periods in Nasser's Egypt, the Islamic fundamentalists were tacitly encouraged in order to dilute the power of the communists.

The countries of North Africa resemble those of the Middle East, as the communist and allied parties of the Maghreb now must swim upstream against two powerful currents: (1) the strong thrust of the governments in power toward the West and freer economic systems; and (2) the rising force of religious revivalism. The Socialist Vanguard Party (PAGS) of Algeria, proscribed since 1962 as a Marxist organization, was officially recognized in September, and its general secretary, Sadiq Hadjeres, met with Algerian president Chadli Benjedid. But Benjedid's moves toward a market-oriented economy and accommodation with the IMF create far less scope for cooperation between the party and the government than might have existed under the

state-capital programs of Benjedid's predecessor, Boumedienne. The apparent solution of the quarrel between Algeria and Morocco over the Western Sahara greatly lessened tensions in the region and made the outlook for the success of the Arab Maghreb Union, declared during the year (linking Libya, Tunisia, Morocco, Mauritania and Algeria), far more favorable (Oussama Romdhani, "The Arab Maghreb Union: Toward North African Integration," *American-Arab Affairs*, Spring 1989). Morocco's Party of Progress and Socialism, a legal communist organization, appeared to be preoccupied with adjusting to the union and seeking opportunities to consolidate party programs. The Tunisian Communist Party's (PCT) situation, again, is representative of the plight of many of its fellow communist parties throughout the region. The PCT rejects President Ben Ali's push toward more reliance on market forces and greater orientation toward the international economy. Yet the political mood of Tunisia seems to favor such a shift. To the extent that the country's poor are in opposition to the government, their backing apparently has been captured by the Islamic movement.

James H. Noyes
Hoover Institution

Afghanistan

Population. Unknown but estimated at 14.8 million (*Americana Annual*, 1989); exodus of refugees plus wartime casualties have reduced significantly a population that in 1978 was thought to number about 17 million.

Party. People's Democratic Party of Afghanistan (Jamiyat-e-Demokrati Khalq-e-Afghanistan, literally Democratic Party of the Afghan Masses; PDPA). The party has two basic and mutually antagonistic wings, Parcham (Banner) and Khalq (Masses), as well as numerous smaller factions that have developed since 1986.

Founded. 1965

Membership. Party-membership claims were contradictory in 1989. The highest figure given was

230,000 (*FEER*, 13 July), yet only a few days later President Najibullah said there were 200,000 members (Radio Kabul, 21 July; *FBIS*, 26 July). In fact, neither figure is realistic in terms of popular support. According to a PDPA spokesman in January, 62 percent of the membership are "active in the armed forces," and Defense Minister Tanai later declared that 60 percent of the armed forces are party members (Hong Kong, *Standard*, 9 January; AFP, 16 August; *FBIS*, 17 August). Estimates of the Republic of Afghanistan (RA) armed forces' strength have varied from a Soviet observer's low of 40,000 (*FEER*, 23 February) to the unrealistically high 500,000 claimed by the regime. But party affiliation in the armed forces, where enlisted men are pressured to join, does not constitute ideological commitment; another Soviet observer's estimate of only perhaps 30,000 dedicated party members (*FEER*, 13 April) is probably closer to the truth but still high.

The qualitative and intellectual decline in membership noted in *YICA*, 1989, received further confirmation when a regime collaborator told a Soviet interviewer that "it is regrettable that there are very few representatives of the intelligentsia among party and government leaders" (*Selskaya Zhizn*, 27 January; *FBIS*, 1 February).

General Secretary. Lt. Gen. Najibullah, also known as Dr. Najib, Mohammed Najibullah, Mohammed Najibullah Ahmadzai, and other variations (age about 44, Pashtun, studied but never practiced medicine) (*YICA*, 1987); in 1989 almost never addressed or listed by his party title but by the politically neutral honorific "The Esteemed."

Politburo. 14 members: Najibullah, Sayed Mohammed Gulabzoi (about 45, Pashtun, airforce background, former minister of interior, informal head of Khalqi faction, as of 1988 in polite exile as Afghan ambassador to Moscow), Mir Saheb Karwal (Pashtun, member of Supreme Defense Council [SDC], Secretary of Kabul Provincial Party Committee since 1981, promoted from Alternate Politburo in October [Bakhtar, 25 October; *FBIS*, 26 October]), Najmuddin Kawiani (about 40, pre-party background unknown, in charge of the Central Committee [CC] International Relations Department, House of Representatives [HR] delegate from Balkh, chief of HR standing committee on international relations), Sultan Ali Keshtmand (54, Hazara, intellectual, reappointed prime minister in February [*San Francisco Chronicle*, 22 February], SDC deputy chief, long-time economist/administrator for Ka-

bul regimes since 1980), Suleiman Laeq (60, Pashtun, writer/media, minister of tribal affairs), Dr. Haider Masoud (51, Tajik[?], SDC member, CC publicity and extension department, HR delegate), Farid Ahmad Mazdak (30, Tajik, SDC member, long-time chief of the Democratic Youth Organization of Afghanistan [DYOA], HR member from Kabul City [Radio Kabul, 19 February; *FBIS*, 21 February], promoted from alternate to full Politburo [Bakhtar, 25 October; *FBIS*, 26 October]), Niaz Mohammed Mohmand (Pashtun, economics expert, HR delegate for Kunar, chief of HR's agriculture, land reform and water commission), Nur Ahmad Nur (53, Pashtun, intellectual, ambassador to the U.N.), Gen. Mohammed Rafi (about 44, Pashtun, SDC member [Radio Kabul, 19 February; *FBIS*, 21 February], vice-president), Abdul Wakil (43, economist/teacher, SDC member, foreign minister [ibid.]), Gen. Mohammed Aslam Watanjar (44, Pashtun military officer, minister of interior, SDC member [ibid.]), Lt. Gen. Ghulam Farouq Yaqubi (Pashtun, minister of state security, SDC member [ibid.]). There are two alternate members: Lt. Gen. Nazar Mohammed (55, Pashtun, military officer), and Lt. Gen. Shahnawaz Tanai (40, Pashtun, military officer, SDC member, minister of defense).

Secretariat. 14 members: Najibullah, Karwal (Bakhtar, 25 October, *FBIS*, 26 October), Kawiani, Keshtmand, Laeq (ibid.), Masoud, Mazdak (ibid.), Nur, Nazar Mohammed (minister of construction) (ibid.), Mohmand, Ahmad Nabi (secretary of the Kandahar Province Party Committee), Mohammed Daoud Razmyar (secretary of the Kabul City Party Committee and HR delegate), Mohammed Khalil Sepahi (HR representative from Herat and secretary of the Herat Province Party Committee), Mohammed Sharif (governor of Balkh and secretary of the Balkh Province Party Committee). Note: Karwal was not mentioned in the secretariat in 1988 but was included in 1989.

Central Committee. Up to 134 full members and 55 candidate members. (One CC member was killed in April, and in October 19 new full members and one new alternate were identified, and two unnamed former full members were dropped [ibid.]. It is not known how much attrition the CC may have suffered due to party purges, war casualties, or natural causes.)

Status. Ruling party

Last Congress. First, 1 January 1965, in Kabul;

National Conferences: 14–15 March 1982 and 18–19 October 1987. Only one party plenum was recorded in 1989, on 25–26 October (Radio Kabul, 26 October; *FBIS*, 26 October).

Last Election. Despite promises of general elections, none was held in 1989, but a Grand Assembly (*Loya Jirga*) was convened in May. In one of the swiftest electoral processes ever seen, the rules for electing *jirga* delegates were published on 14 May, the elections were held three days later, and some 732 delegates then reportedly convened on 20 May for several weeks of deliberations (Radio Kabul, 14, 17, and 20 May; *FBIS*, 17 and 22 May). In spite of suspicions that the speed implied a measure of rigging, some 65 delegates were reportedly arrested for opposing Najibullah (AFP, 2 June; *FBIS*, 6 June).

Auxiliary Organizations. Information about the party and fronts was relatively sparse in 1989. Najibullah's used the euphemism of "social organization workers" when referring to a claimed membership of one million in the National Front (NF), presided over by Abdul Rahim Hatef (Radio Kabul, 21 July; *FBIS*, 21 July). The Union of Journalists (president: Hassan Bareq Shafiee) claims 1,900 members (*Pakistan Times*, 21 July). Earlier claims that trade unions had more than 300,000 members (*YICA*, 1989) were belied when Kawiani admitted to a Soviet interviewer that the Afghan working class numbered "no more than 60,000" (*Argumenty i Fakty*, 28 April to 5 May; *FBIS*, 9 May), a figure that is itself probably an exaggeration. The DYOA launched "Social Order Brigades" totaling 220 youths in two northern provinces, Jauzjan and Kunduz, perhaps as a form of militia not unlike the old Soviet Komsomol *druzhina* (*Kabul Times*, 18 September).

In the absence of new data, some figures from 1988 were: trade unions (president: Abdus Sattar Purdeli), 304,899 members; DYOA (first secretary: Mazdak), 280,000 members; All-Afghan Women's Association (AAWA; chairperson: Masooma Esmati Wardak), 125,000 members; Association of Lawyers (chairman: Prof. Ghulam Sakhi Masoon), 1,045 members (*YICA*, 1989). For further, if now dated, information on fronts, see *YICA*, 1988 and 1989.

A new organization called the National Salvation Society was formed in October under the presidency of one Mohammed Asghar and vice-presidency of Mohammed Aman. Under King Zahir, Asghar had been minister of justice and Aman minister of finance. Consisting of only some 15 "neutral and liberal-thinking" members, the group claimed to be apolitical and intent only on bringing peace to Afghanistan.

Publications. New in 1989: *Payam* (Message), replacing *Haqiqat-e-Enqelab-e-Saur* (The Saur revolution truth) as the PDPA CC's official daily organ, Bareq Shafiee, editor (*Kabul Times*, 1 January); and *Hafta*, a weekly that achieved brief prominence when it was banned for suggesting better ballot box procedures for future elections (AFP, 28 August; *FBIS*, 29 August). Old publications: *Heywad* (Homeland), Hamid Rokh, editor, organ of the presidency; *Anis*, daily, NF organ; *Jamhuriat*, daily; Bakhtar, official news agency, Sarwar Yuresh, chief; *Sarbaz* (Soldier), twice weekly (renamed from *Haqiqat-e-Sarbaz* [The soldier's truth]), Gen. Fakhri, editor; *Darafsh-e-Jawanan* (The banner of youth), Pashtu and Dari daily; *Dehqan* (Peasant); *Kabul Times*, English-language daily, Mohammed Sediq Rahpoe, editor; *Storai* (Story), DYOA monthly; *Peshahang* (Pioneer), Pioneer monthly; *Zindagi Hezbi* (Party life), biweekly magazine of the CC, possibly shut down with the founding of *Payam*, Abdul Rahim, editor (*YICA*, 1989). The regime also maintains a radio station and has a limited television network.

Background. In 1967, two years after its founding, the PDPA split into opposing wings: Parcham and Khalq. Both kept the PDPA name, and both were loyal to Moscow, but each maintained a separate organization and recruitment program. Khalq, led by Nur Mohammed Taraki, the PDPA's founder, drew its support from the relatively poor rural intelligentsia and recruited almost solely among the Pashtuns, then the dominant Afghan ethnic group (about 50 percent of the population). Parcham, more broadly represented ethnically, was urban-oriented and appealed to a wealthier group of educated Afghans. It was led by Babrak Karmal, son of an Afghan general. Both groups focused their initial recruitment efforts on intellectuals, media employees, and especially teachers. When Mohammed Daoud overthrew the Afghan monarchy in 1973, the Parchamis at first collaborated with him and were obliged to refrain from aggressive recruiting. The Khalqis, however, remained in opposition and began an intense recruitment campaign among the military in preparation for the PDPA coup that was to follow five years later. During this period, the Khalqis moved from numerical parity with the Parchamis to significant superiority.

Under Soviet pressure, Parcham and Khalq formally reunited in mid-1977, and their combined strength was enough to overthrow Daoud and inaugurate the Democratic Republic of Afghanistan (DRA) in April 1978. They almost immediately fissioned again, however, with Taraki sending the most prominent Parchamis into diplomatic exile as ambassadors and jailing or demoting most of those who remained in Afghanistan. When a Parchami plot to unseat Taraki was discovered in the summer of 1978, the ambassadors were recalled but disobeyed the order and fled into exile in Eastern Europe.

Meanwhile, popular resistance to Khalq's rigorous Marxist-Leninist rule grew rapidly and soon threatened to topple the new regime in spite of massive Soviet military aid. In September 1979, the Soviets attempted to force another artificial reconciliation between Parcham and Khalq, but their plan to place all the blame for the schism on Taraki's deputy, Hafizullah Amin, backfired when Amin himself seized power and murdered Taraki. But Amin could not pacify his rebellious people, and on 27 December 1979, Soviet troops invaded, shot Amin, and restored the Parchamis to power. Babrak became the new leader and tried to heal the breach with the Khalqis on the one side and the Afghan population on the other. In neither effort was he successful, and in May 1986 he suffered the first of several demotions from power. His successor, Najibullah, performed no better, and the regime maintained a tenuous hold on power only in a few main Afghan towns during daylight hours, thanks to a Soviet presence that slowly swelled from 85,000 combat troops in 1980 to about 120,000 by the end of 1984. Thereafter, the strength of the Soviet occupation forces remained fairly constant until May 1988, when the first true withdrawals began.

Since the Soviet invasion, the PDPA technically has not been a communist or even a socialist (by Soviet definition) party, but merely the ruling party in a country undergoing the "national democratic stage of revolution." In 1987, with the probable knowledge that they would soon no longer enjoy Soviet military protection, regime spokesmen began emphasizing the nonsocialist nature of this regime, and these denials have persisted ever since. Unmistakably, but privately, loyal to Marxism-Leninism as a creed (and by extension to whatever ideology Moscow espouses at any given time), the Afghan communist leaders have been driven to distance themselves ever further from traditional Leninist rhetoric and practices.

During the period from 1987 to 1989, there was a wholesale renaming of institutions, journals, the nation itself (which became the Republic of Afghanistan), and even the leader, who added the religious suffix *ullah* to his secular name, Najib. Pseudo-democratic institutions were set up, including a parliament to replace the old rubber-stamp Revolutionary Council, and a program of "national reconciliation" was launched, with the proclaimed goal of permitting groupings not controlled by the PDPA to share in political power. A new constitution was promulgated.

The achievement of legitimacy became urgent when Soviet leader Mikhail Gorbachev declared in early 1988 that his troops would be out of Afghanistan by 15 February 1989. By the end of 1988, it was clear that Gorbachev fully intended to meet his self-imposed deadline, and it appeared that the days of the unpopular pro-Soviet regime were numbered.

Party Leadership and Organization. In 1988, reporting in Afghan media on party activities became rarer. This trend continued and became even more noticeable in 1989. Not until October was any mention made of a party plenum, normally an at-least thrice-annual event. Normally a rich source of information about party affairs, the *Kabul Times* all but ceased to mention the organization. Party leaders almost invariably were referred to by their state ranks, the one exception being Kawiani, whose Politburo and Secretariat positions were always listed, with or without mention of his Supreme Defense Council membership. Even when Najibullah addressed greetings to other general secretaries, *e.g.*, to Mikhail Gorbachev on the occasion of the anniversary of the October Revolution, only his own state rank of Afghan president, not PDPA general secretary, went with the signature. His last peptalk to party cadres was broadcast just before the Soviet withdrawal (Radio Kabul, 5 February; *FBIS*, 6 February); thereafter the party was in virtually total eclipse until October.

Shortly before the last Soviet troops were due to leave, it was reported that Najibullah was on the point of changing the PDPA's name to the Liberal Democratic Party of Afghanistan, but two months later he specifically denied this intention, without, however, ruling it out as a future option (AFP, 10 January; *FBIS*, 11 January; *Pravda*, 26 April; *FBIS*, 26 April). It was alleged that he had been overruled by outraged hard-line party members and army officers.

There was one departure from the unspoken party line on anonymity. In August, the message sent by the Ministry of State Security (WAD) to Najibullah on Afghanistan's Independence Day addressed him by his party title at three different points and concluded, "... we have learned patriotism from our beloved party. We are proud of our patriotic party and proud of our membership of [sic] this party" (*Kabul Times*, 23 August). This message, which would have been unremarkable only a few years before, contrasted sharply with those sent to Najibullah by other Afghan organs and with the general tenor of the press, which remained mute about the PDPA. WAD's importance as the regime's strongest bulwark and Najib's own parent service, lends added significance to the text.

With this one exception, the PDPA's self-effacing attitude remained consistent and appeared designed to present a minimum profile to a citizenry that was literally up in arms against it. It was characteristic of the new trend that the tinted issue of the *Kabul Times* that came out in honor of the 70th anniversary of Afghanistan's independence from British rule was colored blue rather than red (ibid.).

None of this, however, signified a reduction of the party's real role in running the part of the country that remained under Kabul's control. In fact, the party found it expedient to abandon the camouflage of the ostensibly uncommitted Hassan Sharq government, installed in 1988 shortly after the Soviet Union began to withdraw its troops, in favor of a new council of ministers whose orientation was unmistakable. Seven noncommunist ministers were dismissed, along with four communists whose loyalty may have been suspect, to be replaced by seven full members of the CC, one alternate member of the CC, one probable KGB agent, and two ostensible noncommunists (a medical doctor and a mullah), whose party connections could only be inferred from the rest of the council (*Kabul Times*, 19 February).

Najibullah seems to have defined his main problem here as circling the party's wagons in preparation for a last, desperate fight, hoping to heal splits in the PDPA by including representatives of all intraparty factions as members of the new government. Ismail Danesh, a member of the Khalqi faction who had been banished to a diplomatic post in Libya, was recalled and became minister of higher and vocational education. Danesh had collaborated with Najibullah's Parchami faction, and his rehabilitation was less surprising than that of Shah Wali, foreign minister and third-ranking member of the hated Khalqi regime of Hafizullah Amin, who in April was named a minister counselor of the council

of ministers (Radio Kabul, 4 April; *FBIS*, 5 April). In June, the Parchami Mahmud Baryalai, a half-brother of deposed party leader Babrak Karmal and still in jail for factionalism earlier in 1989, was appointed first deputy prime minister (Radio Kabul, 24 June; *FBIS*, 26 June).

On 19 July, Danesh was fired, ostensibly for poor performance, and ten days later Najibullah appointed an old party stalwart, Nur Ahmad Nur, as ambassador to the United Nations (Radio Kabul, 19 and 29 July; *FBIS*, 21 and 31 July). These actions may possibly have been connected with an internal coup attempt that was supposed to have occurred about this time, but a more likely explanation is that they resulted from the inherent contradictions in Najibullah's policies. On the one hand, he had to reabsorb the Khalqi hard-liners into the party leadership to project an image of unity and an ability to negotiate from a position of strength; yet on the other, he had to present a façade of sweet reasonableness to the mujahideen with whom he wished to have those negotiations. His solution, which can only be inferred, appears to have been dismissal for the most intransigent Khalqis, suppression of all information about the factional struggle, and a campaign of forceful persuasion.

Media coverage in July of Najibullah's "new military doctrine" (never spelled out) that had to be explained personally to the military and police by Defense Minister Tanai and Interior Minister Watanjar, respectively, add weight to this interpretation. Both the military and police are strongholds of Khalqi sentiment, and the implication is that the new doctrine was not going down well with the hard-liners.

Najibullah appears to have succeeded well enough—or become desperate enough—to include still more Khalqis in the upper reaches of the party apparatus at the October plenum. Of the nineteen new CC members, five were identified party apparatchiks (four provincial party secretaries and one assistant city secretary); four were members of the intelligentsia (two doctors, a teacher, and a media specialist); three were of unknown background; three were connected with the police or military; and four had vanished in 1979 when they had been members of Amin's last CC. Only six of the nineteen had been alternate CC members before their new appointment. The lone new alternate member was a provincial secretary.

The simultaneous rehabilitation of four prominent Khalqis was unprecedented, and it is likely that the army and police appointees were also Khalqis.

Although the newly anointed may feel some temporary gratitude toward Najibullah, it is not in the Afghan tradition to allow such sentiments to stand in the way of an established feud, and new dissension within the ranks of the CC is almost inevitable. Najibullah has moved personnel adroitly while fostering a façade of unity, but the factionalism that has dogged the PDPA since its founding is hardier than any leader who has yet appeared.

Domestic Affairs. The new year dawned inauspiciously for Kabul as the Soviet troops were completing their withdrawal. Amidst widespread predictions that his regime was doomed (an opinion shared by many Soviet observers), Najibullah dug in for what could have been his final battle.

A new conscription decree was endorsed by the Council of the Constitution Secretariat on 26 January. Although the details remained unclear, by 1 February more than 5,000 PDPA and DYOA members from Kabul city were reportedly mobilized to defend the capital. Many of these (the figures ranged from 1,300 to 3,200) opted for a Special Guards unit, made up of the most ideologically committed party and DYOA members. The fact that 2,300 of the Special Guards, whose total membership has not been revealed, were reportedly enrolled in literacy courses, however, sheds some doubt on the depth of their ideological comprehension.

Meanwhile, the Indian embassy had been issuing visas at the rate of 200 per day since October 1988, and among the applicants were supposed to be several Politburo members and the dependents of Prime Minister Hassan Sharq (AFP, 6 February; *FBIS*, 6 February).

The last Soviet troops reportedly left Afghan soil on 15 February. Three days later Najibullah declared a state of national emergency that suspended the nation's largely cosmetic civil rights for six months, revamped the council of ministers, and appointed a twenty-man Supreme Defense Council (SDC) "with the aim of implementing central leadership in conditions of the state of emergency" (TASS, 20 February; *FBIS*, 22 February). With the exception of the ostensibly nonparty civilian vice-president, Abdul Rahim Hatef, all SDC members were ranking members of the party and/or the military/security hierarchies.

Najibullah's first test came in the battle for Jalalabad, a provincial capital about halfway between Kabul and the Pakistani border. The mujahideen (holy warrior) resistance had set its sight on Ja-

lalabad as the future seat of a government-in-exile that had been set up in Pakistan. But the mujahideen were not equipped, trained, or organized to fight a conventional battle, and they suffered from internal rivalries as intense as those among the various PDPA factions. The only hope for victory lay in mass defections from the government ranks, but the ill-advised execution of prisoners by one mujahideen group led to a stiffening of the government troops' resolve, and after a seesaw battle that might have gone either way, the Kabul forces were able to drive off the besiegers.

Had the mujahideen prevailed at Jalalabad, it is unlikely that the Najibullah government could have survived to the end of 1989. Instead, however, the government gained a reprieve, and the morale of the mujahideen and their supporters dipped. As the summer progressed, things continued to go badly for the resistance. Its political arm, the exile Afghan Interim Government (AIG), was a shaky, bickering coalition that proved unable to mobilize either internal or external support; mujahideen field commanders had little respect for it, and only four countries (Saudi Arabia, Bahrain, Malaysia, and Sudan) recognized it. The flow of weapons from the United States had begun tapering off in September 1988 and only began to pick up a year later in response to massive arms shipments by the USSR to the Kabul regime. And in July 1989, the most effective mujahideen field commander, Ahmad Shah Massoud, had his top deputies wiped out in an ambush by a rival group (Gulbuddin Hekmatyar's Hezbe Islami), thus postponing a large-scale, possibly decisive offensive planned for late 1989.

Nevertheless, neither the victory of its forces at Jalalabad nor the mujahideen's misfortunes altered the basic vulnerability of a government that had been installed by the Soviets. A number of measures taken by the regime indirectly revealed its basic insecurity.

For example, in late April, Najibullah passed out 120 promotions to the rank of general. Two days later, the triumphal Saur Revolution Day military parade was held one day early at dawn with no warning, apparently out of fear that mujahideen attacks would disrupt it. Throughout the year, medals were handed out in profusion, and periodic amnesties were declared. During the summer, the Afghan media began reporting the "voluntary" re-enlistment of entire units to fight the "extremists." By September, Najibullah's personality cult was reaching new heights, with half or more of all front page articles in the *Kabul Times* devoted to his various activities and speeches. In October, the state of emergency was declared ended because of the improved security situation in the country, but five weeks later it was reimposed for another six months (Radio Kabul, 14 October and 21 November; *FBIS*, 16 October and 22 November). In November, a food-supply commission was established "to launch a serious struggle against crimes of sabotage and hoarding" (Radio Kabul, 21 November; *FBIS*, 22 November). Finally, Najibullah persisted in presenting his regime and himself as independent, nationalist, and especially Islamic, contrary to all evidence and his own earlier admission that professions of religious belief were merely a political expedient.

Many of Najibullah's measures recalled those taken by Hafizullah Amin in 1979, just before the Soviets invaded to prevent the collapse of Afghan socialism. But not even Amin had been driven to downplay socialism and espouse religion, survival measures last seen in a Marxist-Leninist state when Stalin used them as a necessary last resort to turn back the Nazis in World War II.

The depth of the regime's crisis was revealed in December, when the state prosecutor revealed that 127 officials had been arrested for a mujahideen-inspired coup plot. The conspiracy involved not only officers (including three generals) of the artillery, the air defense, and the Ministry of Defense, but also civilians from the Ministry of Interior and the Ministry of State Security. Both "prominent" and middle-level officials were involved in the aborted putsch, which was barely averted (*Pravda*, 19 December; *FBIS*, 22 December).

Nevertheless, although his position was anything but secure, Najibullah maneuvered adroitly in the arena of political/psychological warfare. The departure of Soviet troops gave him an opportunity to present himself and his party as the true Afghan patriots and the resistance as the "foreign hirelings." Seizing on an alleged statement by Pakistani president Ghulam Ishaq Khan, he claimed that Pakistan planned to absorb Afghanistan into a confederation. As part of his campaign of "national reconciliation," he offered mujahideen commanders not only government-sanctioned full autonomy, but also heavy weapons and financial aid, provided they promised to permit unhindered passage of government convoys through their territories. There were conflicting reports as to the success of this ploy and widespread doubt that it could succeed in the long run; Afghan regional leaders have a tradition of entering into such agreements with Kabul for short-

term profit and without any intention of holding to them (*FEER*, 26 October).

The regime's efforts to gain credibility through the Afghan version of *glasnost'* provided at least one revealing statistic: the claimed loss of 40,000 PDPA lives since the party came to power in 1978, as a result of "serious mistakes." This acknowledgment, by Kawiani to a Soviet interviewer, was not intended for Afghan audiences, nor was Kawiani's further admission that "our party . . . is Marxist in terms of its ideology," an assertion that other Afghan leaders had taken some pains to deny for the preceding two years (*Argumenty i Fakty*, 28 April–5 May; *FBIS*, 9 May).

In an address to the *loya jirga* in May, Najibullah proposed a comprehensive peace plan that included a conference to set up a "leadership council" that in turn would form a "broadbased government" whose duty would be to prepare a new constitution (subject to approval by the *loya jirga*), which would then be followed by general elections. This proposal met with outright rejection by the mujahideen (Radio Kabul, 20 May; *FBIS*, 23 May).

Government efforts to convince refugees to return from foreign exile, though unflagging, were generally unsuccessful. The net flow if anything continued to be outward. The city of Kabul, its population swollen during the war by refugees from the countryside to more than two million, was losing 40,000 per month in the summer of 1989, in part due to mujahideen rocket attacks. Although estimates of the city's population made from Pakistan continued to claim two million inhabitants, Soviet estimates of the population dropped to 900,000 (TASS, 31 July; *FBIS*, 1 August).

Front Activities. As with the PDPA, the fronts in 1989 continued to maintain a very low profile. On rare occasions the DYOA, AAWA, and trade-union officials would send telegrams or meet with corresponding delegations from other countries, but it appeared that visits to war-torn Kabul had become less attractive to leftists since the departure of Soviet troops.

In March, the NF was reorganized and "a number of executive board members were released" (Radio Kabul, 16 March; *FBIS*, 21 March). A new vice-chairman, Abdul Qudus Ghorbandi, and a new secretary, Feda Mohammed Dehnishin, were appointed. Ghorbandi was a member of the Khalqi faction who had been under arrest from 1980 to 1987, and Dehnishin was a Parchami with publicity/propaganda experience who, however, was fired from the CC in 1987. The reorganization took place when the recently appointed ministers, most of them CC members, were receiving maximum publicity, and it may have signified a quiet tightening of party control over the NF.

In April, the DYOA was given credit for the "mobilization of 195,334 youths," perhaps a euphemistic way of referring to its total membership (Bakhtar, 27 April; *FBIS*, 1 May). If so, it would signify a considerable drop from the 280,000 members claimed by DYOA in 1988 (*YICA*, 1989).

The fairly extensive coverage in Afghan media given to "opposition parties" in 1988 (*YICA*, 1989) had largely disappeared by 1989. The Alliance of Leftist Democratic Parties, which in 1988 had consisted of the PDPA, the Organization of Working People of Afghanistan (OWPA), the Revolutionary Organization of Working People of Afghanistan (ROWPA), the Peasants Justice Party (PJP), and the Islamic Party (IP), in its two 1989 meetings (January and August) appeared to have slimmed down to just the PDPA, OWPA, and ROWPA. The PJP was mentioned briefly in March, but not in connection with the Alliance. No word was heard of the IP, and of the other, supposedly more truly oppositional parties, only the Ansarullah Union received one brief mention in August, claiming a membership of 2,000. Its membership in the NF casts doubt on its alleged independence. (*Afghan Information Centre Monthly Bulletin* 101, August 1989.)

One new party, the Organization of Young Workers of Afghanistan, was supposedly formed in June, but no names were released in association with it, and after one mention no more was heard of it (*Kabul Times*, 26 June). The National Salvation Society was formed in October by persons mostly associated with governments under the monarchy. Although the identifiable members have no known connection with the PDPA, the fact that the new group was formed with the tacit blessing of Najibullah's government seemed bound to discredit it in mujahideen eyes.

The foregoing may indicate that the day of the rump political party and front group has passed in Afghanistan, at least while the regime has only a tenuous hold on power.

International Views, Positions, and Activities. In keeping with its low profile with regard to internal matters, the PDPA as an organization was not much active in international affairs. Kawiani, the only high Afghan official invariably listed by his party rank while operating internally, appeared to be the party's main foreign envoy as well. In January, he represented the PDPA at the Thirteenth Congress of the Communist Party of India (Marxist) and was probably responsible for that party's vocal support of the RA in February. He visited Czechoslovakia's General Secretary Jakeš in July, went on to Austria in early August, and was received in Moscow en route home.

The USSR sent alternate Politburo member and chief planner V. Maslyukov to visit Afghanistan in January, and in May dispatched the deputy secretary of the Moscow City Party Committee to visit his opposite numbers in Kabul. Moscow apparently remained steadfast in its insistence that the PDPA have a role in any future Afghan government. By August, however, the CPSU seemed less eager to lend its own dwindling stock of prestige to its discredited Afghan offspring, and Kawiani was received in Moscow not by the CPSU's International Department but by the International Affairs Committee of the Supreme Soviet, a state organ (*Izvestiya*, 5 August; *FBIS*, 11 August).

In September, Najibullah and Kawiani, the former as president and the latter as PDPA Politburo member and CC secretary, hosted a representative of India's Congress Party, and it was Kawiani who signed the resulting party-to-party cooperation protocol that was to extend to 1991 (*Kabul Times*, 12 September). Earlier, Foreign Minister Wakil had paid a working visit to Delhi in March and had helped cement Indian support for the RA. Subsequent reports, vigorously denied by New Delhi, that the Indians had agreed to furnish 600 military advisers to help the RA troops could not be verified (*The Muslim*, 26 March; *FBIS*, 4 April).

Also in September, Najibullah attended the Non-Aligned Movement (NAM) in Belgrade and used it as a forum to push his policies. The absence of any triumphant coverage in Afghan media, however, indicates that he did not receive warm endorsements from the other member states.

RA state relations with the USSR, though much stronger than PDPA-CPSU relations and apparently improving through much of 1989, also seemed to be showing some strain by year's end. Moscow's initial confidence was shown in several ways. Diplomatically, Soviet First Deputy Foreign Minister Yuliy Vorontsov remained as ambassador to Kabul after the Soviet troop withdrawal. Foreign Minister Shevardnadze visited Kabul in January and August.

Militarily, between early March and the end of August, a massive Soviet airlift delivered an estimated 550 SCUD surface-to-surface missiles, 160

T-55 and T-62 tanks, 615 armored personnel carriers, and 1,600 5-ton trucks (*Washington Post*, 2 September). Senior U.S. officials estimated that the total value of Soviet arms deliveries to the RA during this time were between $250 and $300 million per month (*NYT*, 3 November). In April, Defense Minister Tanai boasted that if the mujahideen were to score successes, "we can always call on our great friend the USSR for assistance" (Radio Kabul, 21 April; *FBIS*, 26 April).

In addition to the military aid, the USSR was providing a limited supply of consumer goods for the hard-hit civilian population. Thanks to the restrained policy of the mujahideen controlling the northern approaches to Kabul, nonmilitary relief convoys were permitted to pass unscathed (save for a traditional Afghan "road tax" of goods) into the capital. In addition to this centrally administered aid, various Soviet cities continued their "direct cooperation" programs of aid to individual Afghan communities: Gorky to Mazar-e-Sharif, Leningrad to Herat, Omsk to Pul-e-Khumri, Barnaul to Kunduz, Volgagrad to Shiberghan, Krasnodar to Faizabad, and Moscow to Kabul (*Kabul Times*, 25 January). In all, the USSR was credited with supplying Afghanistan with 85–90 percent of all foreign aid received (*Kabul Times*, 5 August).

Direct cross-border trade with Soviet Central Asia was reported to have grown dramatically, from 5.3 million rubles in 1987 to 27 million rubles in just nine months of 1988–1989 (*Afghanistan Forum* XVII #2, March 1989). Delegations from Soviet Central Asia visited Afghanistan in February, April, and October to discuss direct trade, and an Afghan-Uzbek agreement for gas and oil exploration was signed in February. On the Afghan side, Ahmad Lmar, as the head of a chief directorate attached to the Council of Ministers, handled matters concerning direct trade. During the summer, visits to the northern provinces by ranking PDPA and RA officials, including Kawiani, Mazdooryar, Keshtmand, and Baryalai, probably indicated continued interest in preserving that corner of Afghanistan as a fall-back redoubt in case Kabul were to fall.

In education, the process of Sovietization via study in the USSR continued. In February, some 6,000 Afghans were reported to have received diplomas from Soviet institutions of higher education, and between 1984 and 1988, 1,800 orphans and deprived children between the ages of 6 and 12 had been brought to Soviet boarding schools "for sound training and studies." About 400 more are enrolled in similar orphanages in Czechoslovakia, Hungary, and Mongolia. These children are housed and fed at Soviet expense, and 45 Afghan teachers have been sent to instruct them in Afghan languages, history, geography, and even "religious sciences." Contacts with their families in Afghanistan are "maintained through letters" (*Kabul Times*, 16 August).

But in April the first indications of strain could be found in an article by an Afghan writing in a Soviet magazine and blaming some Soviet advisers from the "period of stagnation" for contributing to the PDPA's too-rapid push for socialism in 1978–1979 (*Sovetskaya Rossiya*, 27 April; *FBIS*, 3 May).

In September, the Afghan foreign ministry denied that there were any Soviet advisers remaining in the country, only to have the claim refuted the next day by a Soviet diplomat who said there were 300 advisers still there (AFP, 3 and 4 September; *FBIS*, 5 September).

Meanwhile, Soviet deputies were objecting ever more strenuously to the expense of maintaining Najibullah in power. Since September, 1988, the natural-gas lines from Afghanistan into the USSR had been capped for fear of sabotage or destruction by the mujahideen, thus blocking the only source of money for Moscow in Afghanistan.

In September, Ambassador Vorontsov was recalled. He was replaced in October by a man with a more modest career, Boris N. Pastukhov, a foreign-service officer whose last post had been that of ambassador to Denmark.

Although Soviet spokesmen put up a brave front of claiming that Najibullah had to be part of any future Afghan government, some analysts detected a softening of their position on this matter (*NYT*, 16 December). Meanwhile, a suggestion on Soviet television by M. Leshchinskiy, a well-known Soviet journalist and former defender of Soviet actions in Afghanistan, that Soviet aid to Kabul be curtailed provoked a furiously incoherent reaction from Bakhtar. "He in his reportage repeatedly made jugglery with a boiled water teapot," fumed the press agency's English-language report (Bakhtar, 12 December; *FBIS*, 13 December). Prospects for smooth Soviet-Afghan relations in 1990 did not appear fair as the new decade dawned.

Najibullah had confounded the world by holding onto power through 1989, but his survival probably had been due more to the ineptitude, internal dissension, and diminishing foreign support found among the resistance than to any improvement in his own credibility. Regardless of his efforts to appear religious, nationalistic, and independent, to most

Afghans his image was still that of a secret policeman and a Quisling. Nevertheless, he seemed to be the most effective of the PDPA leaders, and it appeared that the party's prospects for clinging to power would be even poorer if he were replaced.

Ruth and Anthony Arnold
Novato, California

Algeria

Population. 24,946,073
Party. Socialist Vanguard Party (Parti de l'avant-garde socialiste; PAGS)
Founded. Founding Congress of Algerian Communist Party in 1936 (renamed PAGS in 1966)
Membership. Unknown; estimates vary from a few hundred to a few thousand
First Secretary. Sadiq Hadjeres
Politburo. No data available
Secretariat. No data available
Status. Officially recognized in September 1989
Last Congress. Sixth, February 1952
Last Election. N/a
Auxiliary Organizations. No data
Publications. *Sawt ash-Sha'b* (Voice of the people), issued intermittently

Background. The Algerian Communist Party was founded originally in 1920 as a branch of the French Communist Party. It has existed as an independent party since 1936. Although the PCA was one of the major participants in the war of independence against France (1954–1962), the party was quickly proscribed in November 1962. Since then members of the party have clandestinely organized, renaming the PCA in 1966 the Socialist Vanguard Party. PAGS has held no regular party congress, but has at least twice (in 1969 and 1981) issued broad programs. Several younger members of PAGS assumed positions of leadership in the Algerian National Youth Organization (UNJA) by 1980; the student union has remained one of the main sources of recruitment for PAGS since then. They have also taken part in the organization and policymaking functions of the country's national workers' union,

the Union Générale des Travailleurs Algériens (UGTA). Until its recognition this year, PAGS was unofficially tolerated by the government, even though periodic repression occurred.

Leadership and Party Organization. Despite its assumed relatively small size, PAGS is thought to be highly organized. The 1988 riots in Algiers and other major cities in Algeria showed the ability of PAGS to mobilize on short notice and join large crowds of students and unemployed youth. It is also thought to have sympathizers inside many of the country's trade unions and mass organizations, perhaps a result of its anticolonialist stance, which was part and parcel of Algeria's official rhetoric until recently.

Domestic Party Affairs. The recognition of PAGS in September 1989 and a meeting between its first secretary Sadiq Hadjeres and the Algerian president Chadli Benjedid undoubtedly marked the high points of the party's good fortunes. Hadjeres's remarks after his meeting with Benjedid indicate that PAGS is aware both of its relative strength inside the country and of its responsibility to form a viable opposition party. For most of former president Houari Boumedienne's tenure in office (1965–1978), PAGS members supported his state-capitalist experiment, in which the state shouldered most of the responsibilities of providing for development in Algeria.

His successor, Chadli Benjedid, was viewed as much less of a revolutionary. When he steadily turned toward a more market-oriented economy, PAGS saw its fears confirmed; the new president was what they called a member of Algeria's "comprador class." According to PAGS, and many members of a loose coalition of supporters, Boumedienne's experiment in state capitalism should have continued and been brought to a successful conclusion. Hadjeres remains opposed to the contention that the Algerian state was no longer able to manage the country's economy and continues to view the worsening socioeconomic conditions inside the country as a result of Benjedid's economic experimentation.

It is therefore not surprising that PAGS was intimately involved in the riots that shook Algeria in the fall of 1988. Although it seems clear that it had no part in instigating the troubles, PAGS—and the Islamists—quickly aligned themselves with those in the streets. The riots were the most serious disturbances Algeria had faced since independence in

1962 and briefly threatened to bring down the regime. In several communiqués issued during and after the riots, PAGS castigated the Army of National Liberation (ALN) for having killed hundreds of young people at the orders of an elite class of politicians who had profited extraordinarily from the new economic direction taken by Benjedid. Its criticisms echoed those made by its counterparts in Tunisia and Morocco against the economic liberalization policies of their respective governments.

The outcome of the riots, which led to well-publicized reforms that included plans for a multiparty system, emboldened PAGS to openly state its positions in the nation's newspapers and to take part in public debates on the political direction Algeria should take. In 1989, PAGS repeatedly stated what it views as the basic incongruities of the Algerian economy. It rejects the government's position that difficult international economic circumstances made the draconian belt-tightening imposed since 1986 a necessity. Rather, they argued that nepotism and bad management had contributed to the problem, and pointed to the growing disparity between rich and poor in Algeria. The political system came under particularly severe attack. The National Liberation Front (FLN), the country's only official party prior to the riots, was described as morally and politically corrupt. PAGS pointed out several officials, including Muhammad Shariff Messaadiya, one of the FLN's top leaders, who had enriched themselves to an extent previously unknown in the country.

The political reforms that followed in 1989 strengthened even further PAGS's contentions that the government should be forced to share power and to reconsider the pace and direction of economic and political reform. The government's decision to quietly seek an accommodation with the International Monetary Fund, and with relatively few conditionality clauses attached, was decried by PAGS as a sell-out to capitalist interests; but the criticism was muted, perhaps because PAGS realized that if it ever became part of a coalition government it would have little choice but to endorse the agreement, given the dismal economic conditions Algeria labors under. Much of this criticism may only be for rhetorical purposes: PAGS has to contend inside Algeria with the Trotskyist Organisation socialiste de travailleurs (OST), one of whose senior members (Louise Hannoune) was interviewed in one of Algeria's leading publications. OST consistently outflanked PAGS in 1989 in delivering well articulated criticisms of the country's economic policies.

Observers have wondered whether the recognition of PAGS and some of the other opposition groups by the government is not meant to reduce the influence of the Islamist movement. PAGS itself seems to have given some thought to a possible governmental strategy of "divide and rule" and has attempted to keep its relations with the newly created Islamist party intact. Although they differ on several important issues, the two parties share a history of oppression and of championing the rights of the poor in Algeria. At the end of the year the unlikely alliance showed no sign yet of breaking down.

International Views, Positions and Activities. Like its counterparts in Tunisia and Morocco, PAGS has been largely preoccupied with internal affairs in 1989. It has apparently judged them to be at a critical stage, so much so that *Sawt ash-Sha'b* referred only perfunctorily to what are normally its international concerns. In general, its positions and views on international matters have been predictable: support for the *intifadah* in Palestine; support for the rapprochement between the United States and the Soviet Union; and a continued call for Algeria's neutrality in international politics.

Dirk Vandewalle
Dartmouth College

Bahrain

Population. 496,759
Party. National Liberation Front of Bahrain (NLF/B)
Founded. 1955
Membership. Unknown but believed negligible
Chairman. Yusuf al-Hasan al-Ajajai (not noted since 1983)
General Secretary. Saif ben Ali (noted from 1987)
Governing Committee. (List of names incomplete): Yusuf al-Hasan al-Ajajai (last noted 1983), Saif ben Ali, Abdallah Ali Muhammad al-Rashid (also member of World Peace Council Presidium), Muhammad Ali, Ali Nagi Abdallah, Badir Malik,

Aziz Mahmud (last noted 1983), Yusuf al-Hasan (alternate member only)
Status. Illegal
Last Election. N/a
Auxiliary Organizations. Bahrain Peace and Solidarity Committee (affiliated with the World Peace Council and Afro-Asian Peoples' Solidarity Organization), Democratic Youth League of Bahrain (affiliated with the World Federation of Democratic Youth), National Union of Bahraini Students (affiliated with the International Union of Students), Women's Organization of the NLF/B (affiliated with the Women's International Democratic Federation), Federation of Bahraini Workers (affiliated with the World Federation of Trade Unions)
Publications. *Al-Jamahir* (The masses), newspaper; *al-Fajr* (The dawn), theoretical quarterly; *al-Sharara* (The spark), internal news bulletin

The NLF/B is apparently regarded by the Soviets as one of thirteen "vanguard revolutionary democratic parties," a category of organization falling just short of full-fledged communist parties because of ideological and disciplinary shortcomings (*Problems of Communism*, March–April 1982). This assessment of the NLF/B was given in the authoritative *First Hand Information*, which had been "signed for printing" on 16 August 1988 (Alexander Subbotin, ed., *First Hand Information*, Prague: Peace and Socialism International Publishers, 1988, pp. 9 and 63). Note that the party has habitually participated in meetings where all the other groups had full communist party status, as well as in those where there were other "nonkosher" parties present (see *YICA*, 1989).

The article in *First Hand Information*, as well as one written by NLF/B spokesman Abdallah al-Rashid published in the November *World Marxist Review*, stressed that the immediate domestic goal of the organization is to restore the parliamentary regime and democratic freedoms that the country had until 1975 (Subbotin, p. 64; *WMR*, November). (The NLF/B sees itself subjected to increasing repression justified by "fictitious charges" that it is attempting to "overthrow the regime and establish socialism" [ibid.].) As for foreign policy, both articles call for the removal of "imperialist," especially U.S., military presences from Bahrain, and the Persian Gulf in general. The article by al-Rashid decries the economic "exploitation" of Bahrain by the transnational corporations as well (ibid.).

Some forward movement appears to have been made in the NLF/B's policy on alliances. Whereas in early 1988 it claimed to have been "working to establish cooperation with" the People's and Islamic Fronts for the Liberation of Bahrain, in late 1989 it claimed an alliance with the former and a dialogue with the latter, and made a joint statement with both to the Gulf Cooperation Council (*YICA*, 1989; *WMR*, November).

In fact, this emphasis on a "united front from above" contrasted somewhat with the mid-1988 stress in *First Hand Information* on "mass organizations," in which the NLF/B claimed to be both cooperating with the Popular Front and recruiting members for itself (Subbotin, p. 64). And whereas *First Hand Information* mentioned positively underground activity in all the fields covered by the "auxiliary organizations" listed above (ibid.), the November article talked only of the party's trade-union activity, and this information was coupled with a complaint that the government had set up a rival, legal Workers Committee of Bahrain (*WMR*, November). It would appear that the NLF/B's domestic activities in the field of mass organizations might not be going well at all.

Internationally, the party's undertakings encountered fewer obstacles. A Bahrain National Preparatory Committee, presumably including members of the aforenoted Democratic Youth League and National Union of Students, was reported to have sent a delegation to the Pyongyang World Youth Festival in July (*Pyongyang Times*, 1 July). Earlier, in November 1988, Husayn Musa and Abd-al-Hadi (not further identified) were listed as having represented the Peace and Solidarity Committee at the New Delhi Seventh Congress of the Afro-Asian People's Solidarity Organization (*VII AAPSO Congress*, New Delhi: Reception Committee, undated, p. 195). Given the situation in Bahrain, all or part of either delegation might well have come from the possible site of the NLF/B headquarters in Damascus or from elsewhere abroad (*YICA*, 1989).

Wallace H. Spaulding
McLean, Virginia

Egypt

Population. 54,777,615
Party. Egyptian Communist Party (al-Hizb al-Shuyu'i al-Misri; ECP)
Founded. 1921; revived in 1975
Membership. 500 (estimated)
General Secretary. Farid Mujahid (apparently)
Politburo. Michel Kamil (chief of foreign relations), Najib Kamil, Kamal Muhammad Magdi (representative to the WMR); Magheed Ibrahim; other names unknown
Central Committee. Farid Mujahid; Yusif Darwish; Magheed Ibrahim; other names unknown
Status. Proscribed
Last Congress. Second, 1984
Last Election. 1987 (no Communists elected)
Auxiliary Organizations. Union of Egyptian Peasants; participation in other groups (see below)
Publications. *Al-Intisar* (Victory), main ECP newspaper, published about nine times a year, beginning in 1973; *al-Wa'i* (Consciousness), dealing with intraparty issues; *Hayat al-Hizb* (Party life), primarily concerned with party work; *Kadaya Fikriya* (Questions of ideology), a theoretical journal; *Aurak Ummaliya* (Workers' gazette). In the recent past, Egyptian Communists in Paris have published *al-Yasar al-Arabi* (The Arab left).

Background. The Egyptian communist movement remains as splintered as ever. Besides the ECP, several groups have surfaced in recent years. These include the Revolutionary Current, the Egyptian Communist Party–8 January, the Egyptian Communist Workers' Party (Hizb al-Ummal al-Shuyu'i al-Misri; ECWP), the Popular Movement, the Armed Communist Organization, the Egyptian Communist Party-Congress Faction, a Trotskyist organization called the Revolutionary Communist League, and the Revolutionary Progressive Party. It is possible that some of these are merely descriptive labels rather than formal names of organizations, and it is not known whether there is any relationship between any of these groups and the ECP (or, in most cases, whether they continue to exist). An article in the leftist newspaper, *al-Ahali* (30 August;

FBIS, 5 September), questioned whether the ECWP exists at all or is merely "something that the state organs imagined had been created, following the workers' movement in the iron and steel factories which moved to defend their means of subsistence and against the aggressions on their standard of life." On the other hand, the Cairo newspaper *al-Jumhuriya* even claimed that the ECWP was "an offshoot of a communist organization in an [unnamed] Islamic country in which communist principles were not in favor" (MENA, 26 August; *FBIS*, 28 August).

All evidence points to the relative insignificance of communist groups in comparison with the threat posed by militant religious movements. Some even point out that the regime finds the "mainstream left" useful in combating Islamic militant groups (*The Middle East*, November).

In August, the government announced that tons of leaflets had been seized and that 52 members of the ECWP had been arrested "on the charge of belonging to an illegal, clandestine organization," along with members of "a Shiite ring" apparently made up of non-Egyptian Arabs (MENA, 26 August; *FBIS*, 28 August). Interior Minister Zaki Badr alleged that the two "subversive organizations . . . intended to breach security, commit sabotage and incite the masses of the population against the government" (ibid.). These arrests followed a metal-workers' strike in the industrial town of Helwan, south of Cairo. At least some of the detained individuals, among whom were "many educated people, and workers . . . : some respectable journalists and known lawyers; some critics, writers, and artists and other members of Egyptian and Arab committees defending human rights" (*al-Ahali*, 30 August; *FBIS*, 5 September), were later released, allegedly after being tortured. The Egyptian Human Rights Organization, two of whose Executive Council members were among the detainees, called them "prisoners of conscience" (AFP, 5 September; *FBIS*, 5 September). *Al-Ahali* (30 August; *FBIS*, 5 September) asked whether the arrests were "a 'precautionary' step to frighten and terrorize" people who might want to support workers' demands at a time of governmental demands to accept IMF and World Bank guidelines on ending subsidies. Even Western diplomats in Cairo were said to be puzzled about the whole matter, considering the fact that most of the detainees were respected human-rights activists (*The Middle East*, November).

In October, the State Investigation Department

in Gharbiyah Governate reported that it had discovered the existence of another communist organization in the city of al-Mahallah al-Kubra. Thirteen people were "arrested and severely tortured" in an attempt to elicit confessions of affiliation with the group. (*al-Wafd*, 19 October; *FBIS*, 23 October.) No name for the new communist organization was mentioned.

Leadership and Party Organization. Little is known about the ECP's leadership and organization. Few party officials have been mentioned in available publications. Official statements of ECP leaders published abroad are mostly anonymous. The names most often mentioned are those of two Politburo members: Michel Kamil, obviously because of his position as the party's chief of foreign relations; and Kamal Muhammad Magdi, representative to the *WMR*. All indications point to the typical pattern of "democratic centralism," albeit in a rudimentary form resulting from the group's small membership and clandestine character.

According to *First-Hand Information: Communists and Revolutionary Democrats of the World Presenting Their Parties* (Prague: Peace and Socialism International Publishers, 1988), divisions within the ECP are resolved through "dialogue on a democratic basis," with "divergent views" aired in "the intra-party news bulletin" (p. 124). The first party congress, which met in Egypt in September 1980, adopted the party's Program and Rules, while the second congress met in September 1984, presumably outside the country (p. 124). More than 30 percent of the members of the party are said to be workers, while more than half of the total membership is made up of people under 30 years of age. Members may recommend others as candidate members for determination by "one of the party organisations." This status lasts for four months in the case of workers and six months for nonworkers, but nine months "for members of non-Marxist political organisations." The party organizes courses throughout Egypt for "educating its members and training its cadres." (p. 125.)

The interior minister announced in April that members of an ECP cell in al-Mansurah, some of whom resided in Alexandria, were arrested. They allegedly possessed leaflets calling for revolt. (Cairo, *al-Ahram*, 15 April; *FBIS*, 17 April). In addition to the leaflets, other articles were confiscated, including typewriters and cameras (*al-Wafd*, 16 April; *FBIS*, 18 April).

The state security police allegedly uncovered another ECP cell in May, arresting six leaders of the party. They were accused of possessing many leaflets and copies of *al-Wa'i* and *al-Intisar*, and also the ECP's bylaws and "provocative leaflets." (Cairo, *al-Jumhuriyah*, 31 May; *FBIS*, 2 June.) And yet the police are said to "turn a blind eye" to official ECP publications available at newsstands (*The Middle East*, November).

For a review of contents of *Kadaya Fikriya*, which has been published twice annually since 1985 under the editorship of Mahmud Amin al-Alim, see *World Marxist Review* (Toronto), January, pp. 91–92.

No ECP statements are available on domestic issues during the year. In the issue of *Information Bulletin* for November 1988, Politburo member Magheed Ibrahim analyzed "religious extremism," maintaining that the way to combat it is "by expanding class-based activities."

Auxiliary and Front Organizations. Little information has come to light about auxiliary organizations of the ECP. *First-Hand Information* (p. 125) asserts that the party "took an active part in the creation of a Union of Peasants, which in 1987 held its 3rd Congress." This publication further informs us of the ECP's "important role" in such trade unions as those of lawyers and journalists and "in the creation and activity of the Progressive Union of Women, the Progressive Union of Youth and the Democratic Union of Youth, and in the work of the Egyptian Peace and Disarmament Committee," in addition to its being "actively involved in the mass movements in defence of the legitimate rights of the Arab people of Palestine." All of this is generally confirmed by the Interior Ministry's claim that the ECP acts "through professional unions, clubs, and organizations" (*al-Ahram*, 15 April; *FBIS*, 17 April) and by reports from security organs that "intransigent communist elements" as well as religious militants "played a part in kindling the Egyptian Lawyers Association crisis" that began on 19 January (London, *al-Sharq al-Awsat*, 30 January; *FBIS*, 2 February).

It is also possible that the ECP is involved in the Egyptian Committee for Afro-Asian Solidarity. The committee is headed by Ahmad Hamrush (MENA, 6 January; *FBIS*, 6 January). One of its members, Fuad Mursi, participated in the meeting of the Afro-Asian Peoples' Solidarity Organization Congress, held in Delhi in 1988 (Prague, *WMR*, July).

Together with other leftist groups, the ECP ran

1,500 candidates in the 1987 trade-union elections; 650 of these were elected (ibid.).

Much more important than the ECP—which recurrently calls for the establishment of an even broader national front—or any other communist organization is the broad, legal leftist opposition front, the National Progressive Unionist Party (NPUP), whose general secretary is longtime Marxist Khalid Muhyi al-Din. (For a biography of Muhyi al-Din, see *YICA*, 1984.) Its deputy general secretary is Rif'at Sa'id. Some of the members of the NPUP are Marxists; some of these come from the ranks of the ECP, which is described as "mak[ing] a weighty contribution to [the NPUP's] work" (ibid.); others are Nasserites or other opponents of the nonsocialist, pro-Western direction of the regime. The NPUP publishes the widely circulated weekly newspaper *al-Ahali* (edited by Muhyi al-Din, with Muhammad Sid-Ahmad as managing editor). Having gained only 2.2 percent of the vote in the most recent general elections (1987), the NPUP does not have any seats in the People's Assembly.

An "extraordinary congress" of the NPUP met on 23 February and adopted amendments to the party's constitution. According to Central Committee Secretary Abdel Gaffar Shukr, the party wishes to give "special attention" to such goals as "broadening of the ideological base," greater "inner-party democracy," and more "mass involvement, democracy and effectiveness." (*WMR*, Toronto, September.)

In January, Assistant General Secretary Sa'id joined with leaders of other opposition parties in a call to their fellow Egyptians to push for legislation allowing truly free elections. Their exhortation stressed, *inter alia*, the importance of judicial supervision of the whole electoral process, cancellation of current voter registration lists, and severe punishments for vote rigging, as well as cancellation of emergency laws, or at least their suspension, during elections. In this statement they also called upon the Egyptians to "confront all the economic and political challenges facing the country." (*al-Wafd*, 9 January; *FBIS*, 11 January.) Together with the Wafd Party, the NPUP decided to boycott the elections for the advisory Consultative Council. General Secretary Muhyi al-Din and Wafdist leader Fu'ad Siraj al-Din explained that this decision had been made because the council is not a legislative body. This decision followed a meeting with the other opposition parties. (*al-Ahram*, 1 May; *FBIS*, 4 May.)

In an interview in Libya in June, Muhyi al-Din opined that it is not desirable to attack "religious reformists and extremists . . . head on." He suggested that it is, rather, necessary for the "democratic, nationalist, and progressive forces," whose weakness has allowed the Islamic groups to gain ground, to "counter their influence by reaching out to the masses and their concerns [about] . . . democracy, bread and inflation." He explained that the Islamic groups "were giving all of their attention to students and professionals, ignoring the concerns of workers and peasants." He added that it is necessary to continue working with other political parties to achieve democracy, for "economic reform cannot be achieved without political reform." (Kuwait, *al-Watan*, 26 June; *FBIS*, 30 June.)

Following the arrest of strikers in the Helwan steel plant in August, the NPUP condemned such "repressive methods . . . under the emergency law." The NPUP's expression of solidarity with the workers led to the arrest of several members of the party. (Paris, Radio Monte Carlo, 24 August; *FBIS*, 25 August.) As for the arrest of people accused of belonging to a communist organization, an article by Muhammad Sayyid Ahmad in *al-Ahali* (30 August; *FBIS*, 5 September) argued that, even if such a charge is true, it is "the old rotten justification which says that believing in communism or joining a communist organization definitely, and automatically means believing in the use of violence."

General Secretary Muhyi al-Din characterized "the ruling circles" as "lavishing privileges on Big Capital" and "impoverishing most of the people" (*WMR*, Prague, November).

With regard to international affairs, Muhyi al-Din noted that although his party opposes "Camp David," it could not be abrogated without "the ability to expel the United States." Thus, since Egypt's inclusion in the Arab fold is in the interest of "Egypt and common Arab action," any demand that the peace with Israel be abrogated before Egypt is brought back into the Arab League would be impractical. (Kuwait, *al-Watan*, 26 June; *FBIS*, 30 June.)

Muhyi al-Din traveled to Moscow in May at the invitation of the Soviet Academy of Science to participate in a debate on the Middle East (MENA, 10 May; *FBIS*, 11 May).

International Views, Positions, and Activities. Politburo member Magdi participated in an international symposium organized by the *World Marxist Review* on "the dialectics of the struggle for peace and social progress in the late 20th century."

The symposium presumably took place during 1988. (*WMR*, Toronto, February.)

Glenn E. Perry
Indiana State University

Iran

Population. 53,866,523 (July 1989)
Party. Communist Party of Iran (Tudeh Party)
Membership. 1,000 to 2,000 hard-core members; 15,000 to 20,000 sympathizers
First Secretary. Ali Khavari
Leading Bodies. No data
Status. Illegal
Last Congress. 1986, National Conference
Last Election. N/a
Publications. *Rahe Tudeh* (Tudeh path), *Mardom* (People) and *Tudeh News* (in English)

Domestic Affairs. Given the truly unprecedented developments in Soviet-Iranian relations in 1989, the Tudeh Party's virtual silence betrayed its deep resentment of the prospects of an improvement of relations between Moscow and Tehran. Since the dawn of the revolution a decade earlier, these developments not only surpassed all others in both quality and quantity, but also presaged better relations between the two countries to the end of the twentieth century. Hashemi-Rafsanjani's visit to the Soviet Union in June 1989 was the single most important event of that year in Soviet-Iranian relations. Yet the Tudeh Party merely used it as an occasion for registering its deep reservations. The Central Committee of the party, in its letter to Mikhail Gorbachev, did not overtly object to the establishment of friendly relations between the Soviet Union and Iran because, it said, it viewed such relations as being in keeping with "the principle of new thinking." But it showed its disapproval nonetheless by saying that it "expects you [Gorbachev] to do all in your power to prevent the execution of tens of women political prisoners using your moral and political influence" (*Tudeh News*, 19 July).

No doubt the fate of Tudeh political prisoners had been a matter of great concern ever since the 1983

crackdown on the party. In 1989, however, it would appear that the party organs were using this concern as a smokescreen to avoid commentary on the unmistakable thaw in the relations of Moscow with Tehran. To be sure, those killed in the wave of executions of captured leftists included members of Tudeh, but the wave had stopped before 1989 (see *YICA*, 1986–1989). Yet, several months into the year the party continued to confirm the names of those who had been executed in 1988. In January, the Politburo of the Central Committee strongly condemned the "barbaric crimes" of the revolutionary government and appealed to "all democratic parties and organizations to intensify their struggle against the inhumane regime" (*Tudeh News*, 18 January). In February, more than 30 communist parties from countries ranging from Argentina to Turkey were persuaded to join the Tudeh Party in condemning the executions in Iran and in demanding the immediate release of all political prisoners (ibid., 1 February). In March, the party charged that the revolutionary regime was "planning to kill hundreds more of the revolutionary and progressive forces while talking a great deal about a sham general amnesty" (ibid., 1 March). By April, the party was scraping the bottom of the barrel in the information it was giving about the executions of 1988 to avoid commenting on the dramatic changes in Soviet-Iranian relations. For example, it gave much space to a letter of protest written in December 1988 by a certain psychiatrist to the Iranian ambassador in GDR on behalf of 500 psychologists regarding the executions of previous months (ibid., 12 April).

Besides ignoring the warming of relations between Moscow and Tehran, the Tudeh Party paid little attention to the implications of the fate of the communist parties in Eastern Europe for its own historically subservient position in relation to the Soviet Union. It is interesting to note that the party's own former leading ideologue, Ehsan Tabari, told a "thousand Islamic scholars" from Iran and several other countries in a conference held in Tehran in January that Marxism had "no future" in Iran (IRNA [Islamic Republic News Agency], in English, 31 January; *FBIS-NES*, 3 February). Such an assessment cannot be discredited simply on the basis of his having said so while a political prisoner in Iran. It showed that he, whose death on 29 April was mourned by the Tudeh Party, was ahead of his comrades in recognizing the fate of traditional communist ideology. The party's statement on the occasion of its 48th anniversary revealed that it continued to hew to its previous orthodox line. It acknowledged that its anniversary was taking place "in the wake of important changes . . . in different areas of the world," and that it was duty-bound to take into account these developments in formulating its policies. But at the same time it "emphasized that the party remains steadfast to its basic principles and beliefs; and it will not surrender to those who are trying—on the pretext of being progressive and reformist—to separate the party from its inner revolutionary stance" (Radio of the Iranian Toilers, in Persian, 2 October; *FBIS-NES*, 6 October).

Iranian sources attributed the weakening of the Tudeh party to changes in the Soviet Union and Eastern Europe as well as to its own divided leadership. They believed that Gorbachev's reforms entailed relative independence for such communist parties as the Tudeh. Furthermore, they believed such parties, which had been all supplied in the past with policies as well as resources from the Eastern bloc, could no longer expect such support. Added to the party's own "weak leadership," these developments meant "more shortcomings" for the party (Tehran, *Keyhan Hava'i*, 21 December 1988; *FBIS-NES*, 13 January).

The dismissal in March of Ayatollah Montazeri, the designated successor to Ayatollah Khomeini, and the death of Khomeini in June, raised the Tudeh Party's hope that the revolutionary regime would soon collapse. Not without good reason, the party attributed Montazeri's misfortune to his protest against the wave of executions in late 1988. The party published the texts of two letters of protest from Montazeri, one addressed to Khomeini, dated 31 July, and the other to high officials, dated 15 August 1988. In his letter to Khomeini, Montazeri had said that the "execution of prisoners who have already been given sentences other than executions and have had no new convictions undermines all judicial norms and judges' rulings; these do not have favorable consequences. . ." In the other letter, he told the officials that this "form of massacre, especially of prisoners and captives, without trial, in the long run benefits our opponents and the world will condemn us. . . It is wrong to combat beliefs and ideology by killing [those who hold them]" (*Tudeh News*, 12 April). The party compared Montazeri favorably with Khomeini, asserting that the latter was "ruthless, bloodthirsty and authoritarian" (ibid., 26 April). Nevertheless, from the party's perspective, the mere fact of "Montazeri's dismissal further exposes regime's instability" (ibid.).

The death of Khomeini, the party believed, all the more revealed the underlying instability of the regime. The party announced unequivocally that "Khomeini's death is the beginning of the collapse of this inhumane regime. . ." (*Tudeh News*, 21 June). The party also predicted that "the agreement within the main factions in the ruling hierarchy will not be long-lived." Nevertheless, the regime's downfall would not take place automatically. It must be brought about by the force of a united front. The party called on "all opposition parties and organizations" to unite and to mobilize the "discontented masses," otherwise " a major historic opportunity will be missed" (ibid.)—that is, the opportunity to destroy the regime.

To the Tudeh Party, as to many others, the swift succession of Khomeini by President Ali Khamenei was only a temporary solution, reflecting merely factional compromise rather than a durable political arrangement to fill the "vacuum of a singular leadership." The referendum on the new and amended articles of the Constitution, also, was about "the issue of separating the religious leadership from the political leadership in order to facilitate the selection of a successor to Khomeini. . ." (ibid., 2 August). The referendum and the election of a new president were scheduled to take place simultaneously at the end of July. The party declaration of 11 July commanded categorically, "We prohibit participation in the referendum on constitutional amendments and in the presidential election" (Radio of the Iranian Toilers, in Persian, 27 July; *FBIS-NES*, 31 July). The party argued that since the outcome of the election of Rafsanjani, like that of Khamenei, was a foregone conclusion "in our opinion, participation in the referendum and election, the results of which have already been decided, will be pointless. . ." (*Tudeh News*, 21 June; see also *Tudeh News*, 2 August).

After Khomeini's death, the Tudeh Party's Iran policy was, as before, flawed by contradictions. On the one hand, the party appeared to take note of momentous changes in the Soviet Union and the rest of the communist world. In fact, it did more, crediting the policy of "restructuring and more openness and democratization" adopted by communist governments to the leadership of the communist parties (*Tudeh News*, 15 February). More specifically, the party appeared to redefine the very concept of freedom. Instead of considering communist parties as the only purveyors of freedom, the party said that "we consider freedom as political pluralism and ultimately free expression of views and ideas. In our opinion, freedom must not and cannot be the monopoly of this or that class or stratum. . ." (ibid., 19

June). On the other hand, it repeatedly claimed that the only viable alternative to the "existing inhumane regime" was "a United Front" of "progressive and democratic forces," hostile to the revolutionary regime whose destruction it advocated by any and all means, including the use of force. One such example cited was the Mojahedin-e Khalq, whose military operations against the Tehran government from bases inside Iraqi territory in July 1988 had unleashed the revengeful and ruthless execution of leftist political prisoners (see *YICA*, 1989).

Foreign Relations. The initiative to improve relations with the Soviet Union in 1989 was Iran's, or more specifically, Khomeini's. Hashemi-Rafsanjani claims that Khomeini told him during his "last days," when his trip to Moscow had become "definite": "Try to have good relations with our great northern neighbor" (Tehran Television Service, 8 June; *FBIS-NES*, 12 June). On 21 June in a speech at a Kremlin dinner in his honor he added that "Imam Khomeyni's message to M.S. Gorbachev constituted the point of departure for the new process" (*Pravda*, 22 June; *FBIS-SOV*, 22 June). The Soviet Union subscribed to the proposition that the improvement in Soviet-Iranian relations was triggered by the Iranian initiative. In its commentary on Rafsanjani's visit to Moscow, Radio Moscow said that the "process of normalization between the Soviet Union and Iran began early this year [1989] when Imam Khomeyni's special envoy came to our country to deliver the imam's message to Soviet leader Mikhail Gorbachev" (Radio Moscow, broadcast in Persian to Iran; *FBIS-SOV*, 22 June).

Ironically, Khomeini's message of 1 January to Gorbachev was in the main an attempt on his part to export the Islamic revolution to the Soviet Union by means of philosophical discussion. He told Soviet Foreign Minister Eduard Shevardnadze on 25 February that "the main point of my message [to Gorbachev]" was "to open a window to the great world—that is, the world in the afterlife, the eternal world" (Tehran, IRNA, in English, 25 February; *FBIS-NES*, 27 February). In attempting to open this window, he told Gorbachev in no uncertain terms that both the East and the West were ideologically bankrupt because they lacked spiritual values, and offered to fill this "ideological vacuum." He added: "Your Excellency Mr. Gorbachev. One should turn to truth. The main difficulty of your country is not the issue of ownership, economics, or freedom. Your difficulty is the lack of true faith in God, the same difficulty which has also dragged the West

toward decadence and dead end. Your principal problem is a long and futile combat with God, the origin of existence and creation." (Tehran Domestic Service, in Persian, 8 January; *FBIS-NES*, 9 January.)

The fact that normalization of Soviet-Iranian relations was triggered by the Iranian initiative, however, does not negate the significant contribution of Soviet diplomacy in paving the way for the progress of the process. From all that is known, Gorbachev's response to Khomeini was both frank and tactful. Without rejecting Khomeini's attempted proselytizing out of hand, the Soviet leader stood his ground by insisting on the premise of "live and let live." Gorbachev wrote to Khomeini that "we follow a fundamental principle: the principle of respect for the freedom of choice for each individual and nation. Consequently, our country and our entire nation has welcomed your great revolution... Your revolution was the choice of your nation and we always have and will continue to support that choice... Our nation too has made her choice in the year 1917..." In delivering Gorbachev's response to Khomeini, Shevardnadze hinted shrewdly that perhaps Iran could follow the example of Soviet ideological flexibility. He said, "We ask ourselves which path should we choose for the future. Is our road to be an old and dogmatic path, or a new and revolutionary path. Our choice is the second path." (Tehran, IRNA, in English, 25 February; *FBIS-NES*, 27 February.) He also told Khomeini frankly, "No doubt we agree on a number of major points, but there are certain points on which we disagree" (ibid.).

Despite disagreements, both Iran and the Soviet Union were determined to normalize and expand relations. Iran warmly received Foreign Minister Shevardnadze from 25 to 27 February, making him the first member of the ruling Soviet Politburo to call on Khomeini. The timing of the visit was clever in two respects. It took place shortly after the last Russian soldier had left Afghanistan. It also coincided with the anniversary of the Soviet-Iranian friendship treaty of 1921. That it came at the end of Shevardnadze's five-country courtesy tour of the Middle East, including such pro-Western countries as Jordan and Egypt, did not in the least detract from its importance. In return, the Soviet Union cordially received the Iranian foreign minister, Ali Akbar Velayati, on a two-day working visit on 31 March and 1 April. Contrary to his first visit to Moscow in February 1987, which was marred by sharp differences between Moscow and Tehran over the Iraq-Iran war, this second visit went smoothly. More important, the two foreign ministers agreed that Hashemi-Rafsanjani's visit to the Soviet Union at the invitation of Gorbachev would take place "in the first half of this year" (TASS, in English, 31 March; *FBIS-SOV*, 3 April).

Multifaceted Iranian and Soviet interests underpinned the political will of their leaders to improve relations. On the Iranian side, such relations would aid the following objectives: political consolidation by the pragmatic factions, economic and military reconstruction, withdrawal of Iraqi forces from Iranian territory, withdrawal of U.S. naval forces from the Persian Gulf, formation of a nonaligned and Islamic government in Afghanistan, and resistance to U.S. political and economic pressures. On the Soviet side, the following objectives figured prominently: containment of Iran's export of the Islamic revolution to the Soviet Union; import of Iranian natural gas; export of Soviet technical and military know-how; maintenance of balanced relations with Baghdad and Tehran; Iranian cooperation for a political settlement in Afghanistan; withdrawal of Western naval forces from the Persian Gulf; and expansion of Soviet economic and political influence in the Middle East, including a major Soviet role in the Arab-Israeli peace process.

By no means a Russophile, Hashemi-Rafsanjani in effect breached the wall of Iranian isolation from the international community by his visit to the Soviet Union on 20–23 June. Although he had been invited to Moscow by the speakers of the Soviet parliaments two years earlier, at the time he considered such a visit "to be rather ceremonial" for a number of reasons: the Iran-Iraq war had not ended; the Soviet Union could not be considered "neutral" in the war; Soviet forces had not withdrawn from Afghanistan; and "the internal situation in the Soviet Union was not favorable for us" (Tehran, IRNA, in English, 20 June; *FBIS-NES*, 20 June). Besides, it is clear that the invitation by Gorbachev himself had a significant effect on Rafsanjani's conviction that "a completely new situation" had emerged and hence, he said, "We took the matter seriously" (ibid.).

The reception the Soviets accorded Rafsanjani confirmed that he was right in taking their invitation seriously. In his welcoming address, Gorbachev reportedly said, "We heard that your visit is the realization of the will of the late imam. For us this is an indisputable confirmation of the seriousness of your intentions. We respond with a friendly and sincere striving to build relations on a new founda-

tion... During the visit we will sign documents on principles of relations and on cooperation for a period ending in 2000... This is why I regard your visit as a landmark event." (*Pravda*, 21 June; *FBIS-SOV*, 21 June.)

Gorbachev's remarks were extremely nuanced to please Rafsanjani and the rest of the Iranian delegation. His deferential attitude toward the Iranian leader was marked by significant assurances about the Soviet support for Iran's independence and revolution. He emphasized the importance of the concept of interdependence as the foundation of foreign policy, saying, "the balancing of interests... is undoubtedly a reasonable principle of conducting international affairs, also settling conflicts..." (*Pravda*, 22 June; *FBIS-SOV*, 22 June).

Rafsanjani was deeply touched by the warmth and respect the Soviet leaders showed him during his visit, making him feel "almost at home" (ibid.). During the first round of talks at the Kremlin, Rafsanjani nailed down what is all-important to Iranian revolutionaries. He said, "the important development in our country after the revolution is that the people and the authorities decide for themselves without [allowing] the intervention of any foreign elements" (Tehran, IRNA, in English, 20 June; *FBIS-NES*, 20 June). The same theme of Iran's independence since the revolution prefaced his dinner speech at the Kremlin. He told Gorbachev that in the past the great powers (meaning Britain and Russia) had tried to "enslave" Iran and "open the way to India. Our country was not regarded as an independent state with which equitable and friendly relations could be maintained" (*Pravda*, 22 June; *FBIS-SOV*, 22 June). Against this background, he told Gorbachev, "One of perhaps the most favorable situations—unprecedented in the history of... Iranian-Soviet relations—has arisen now." That situation was brought about not only by Iran's greater control of its destiny since the revolution, but also by "the policy of restructuring and new thinking," which is of "immense significance" for Soviet-Iranian relations and for "the positive processes in the region and the international arena." (*Pravda*, 21 June; *FBIS-SOV*, 21 June.)

The Soviets' remarkable alertness to Iranian sensitivities and the Iranian leaders' pragmatic ability to try to bury their age-old distrust of Russia, both tsarist and Soviet, resulted in 1989 in their setting the foundations for future political and economic relations. The results of many months of preparatory work were endorsed during Rafsanjani's trip to Moscow, where a variety of documents were signed by the two parties. Gorbachev and Rafsanjani signed declarations on "the principles of relations and friendly cooperation" between their two countries, while the ministers of the two parties signed "a commercial agreement and an agreement for the construction of the Mashhad-Serakhs-Tedzhen railway line." Moreover, the two sides also signed "a memorandum of mutual understanding" on consular affairs. Finally, on 23 June Iran and the Soviet Union issued a joint communiqué.

On the basis of both what was said and done and not said and done in 1989 in regard to the relations of the two countries before, during, and after the Gorbachev-Rafsanjani meetings in Moscow, seven major issues will be discussed below.

1. The foundation of relations. Did Iran and the Soviet Union build a new foundation for their future relations other than, or in addition to their treaty of 1921? Considering the fact that both parties have historically considered this treaty the basic framework of their relations, it is remarkable that nothing was said about it. The reason must be their differences over controversial Articles V and VI, which the revolutionary regime canceled on 5 March and 10 November 1979, as the Pahlavi shahs had tried previously to do. Over the decades, the Soviets had interpreted these articles as allowing them to intervene in Iran militarily if Moscow believed that Soviet security was threatened from Iranian territory. The Soviet Union had repeatedly considered the Iranian unilateral abrogation of these articles as "null and void." Will it continue to do so in the future?

If one were to read between the lines of the first section of the declaration of principles, the answer may be no for two reasons. First, the two sides decided to build their future relations "invariably on the basis of the aims and principles of the UN Charter" (for the text of the declaration, see TASS International Service, in Russian, 22 June; *FBIS-SOV*, 22 June). These aims and principles may indeed be said to supersede the Soviet interpretation of its unilateral right of military intervention in Iran. Second, Iran and the Soviet Union based their future relations on "a vigorous observance of [their] equality, mutual respect for national sovereignty and territorial integrity, non-aggression, non-interference in each other's internal affairs, *the non-use of force and the inadmissibility of the threat of its use in any circumstances, and the resolution of all problems by peaceful means*" (emphasis added). Thirty years earlier the shah had tried during the

course of discussing a nonaggression pact with the Soviet Union to acquire such a Soviet commitment as a means of overriding Articles V and VI, but had failed. The Soviets' "new thinking" appears to have made it possible for the revolutionary regime to achieve that objective at last, either now or in the future, by means of a new treaty of friendship to replace the 1921 treaty in part or in whole.

2. The export of the Islamic revolution. Ever since the dawn of the Iranian revolution Soviet leaders have tried to contain the contagion of the Islamic revolution. Gorbachev, too, has been resolutely opposed to the spread of Islamic revolutionary fundamentalism to such volatile neighboring Soviet republics as Azerbaijan and Turkmenistan. And yet, the export of the Islamic revolution has been considered as a principle of Iranian foreign policy, although the means by which this principle is realized is the subject of vigorous disagreement in Iranian politics. As already noted, in response to Khomeini's proselytizing message, the Soviets insisted on the principle of "freedom of choice." Did Iran and the Soviet Union, then, settle in 1989 their disagreement on the export of revolution?

No categoric answer was possible at the end of 1989. But one could say that while the gap between the divergent views of the two sides on this issue had been narrowed at least rhetorically, in practice the disagreement persists. The Iranians agreed in principle with the Soviets in their declaration that in the religious field they would strive for a "deeper knowledge of the spiritual values of each other's countries" by facilitating visits by delegations and the "establishing of contacts between religious figures of the two countries." In both the declaration of principles and the final communiqué, the commitment to the exchange of religious delegations appeared side by side with the agreement on the broader familiarization of the Soviet and Iranian peoples with "the life, culture, religious beliefs, and traditions and customs of mutual friendship..." (for the text of the final communiqué see *Pravda*, 24 June; *FBIS-SOV*, 26 June). Such mutual commitment to religious familiarization was obviously in keeping with modern norms of international behavior. More important, when Rafsanjani was asked in a press conference in Moscow on 22 June whether there had been "a discussion of the question of events in the Soviet Republic of Uzbekistan," where Iran had been accused of interfering, he replied: "We agreed with the Soviet leaders that we would

not interfere in one another's internal affairs..."
(*Izvestia*, 23 June; *FBIS-SOV*, 26 June).

However, the Soviets were not completely happy
with Iran's continued efforts to export its revolution.
On the one hand, they were pleased to see that
President Rafsanjani condemned, together with
Foreign Minister Shevardnadze, "any act of terrorist kind," and that he also specifically regretted
deeply the execution of Colonel Higgins in Lebanon
(TASS International Service, in Russian, 1 August;
FBIS-SOV, 2 August). On the other hand, the Soviets continued to complain about Iran's revolutionary
activities in Lebanon. Radio Moscow commented
critically on 30 October, months after Rafsanjani's
visit to Moscow, that the principle of the exportation
of the Islamic Revolution was a legacy of Khomeini,
and "nobody has changed this legacy yet," implying
that Iran was trying to create "an Islamic republic in
the half-Christian Lebanon," and thus "the Iranian
element is added to an already complex and bloody
Lebanese crisis..." (Moscow Radio, Peace and
Progress, in Arabic, 30 October; *FBIS-SOV*, 2 November). While Iran's contradictory stance on the
export of the revolution reflected the inconclusive
struggle between the pragmatic realists and radical
idealists in Iranian domestic politics, the Soviet
refusal to condemn Khomeini's death sentence on
novelist Salman Rushdie reflected Moscow's desire
not to rock the boat of Moscow's budding relations
with Tehran, even if the Soviet opposition to the
export of revolution might appear to be ambivalent.

While Rafsanjani's categoric statement in Moscow, "We cannot repeal Shari'a prescriptions made
in Allah's name" (*Izvestia*, 22 June; *FBIS-SOV*, 26
June) left no doubt that he could not lift Khomeini's
death sentence on Rushdie while the radical mullahs
back home were looking over his shoulder, his pre-
departure statement was a better indication of what
might be expected of Iran regarding the export of
revolution in the future if the pragmatic realists
could consolidate power. In responding on 20 June
to the question of an unidentified correspondent
about his objectives in visiting Moscow, he said that
an issue that "is significant to us is the fact that a
large group of the people in the USSR are Muslims,
and we would like to see that the relations we establish with our neighbor leave a positive impact on the
living conditions of the Muslims, too... In practice, the existence of such a large population of
Muslims in our big neighboring country is one of
the motives that can bring the two countries even
closer and can also strengthen our cooperation on
the basis of religious sentiment" (Tehran Domestic

Service, 20 June; *FBIS-NES*, 21 June). By the end
of 1989, such cooperation took the form of the
announced readiness of the Iranian Foreign Ministry to organize pilgrimages of Soviet Muslims to
Iranian shrines (Tehran Domestic Service, 11 December; *FBIS-NES*, 12 December). Such examples
might occasion a constructive redefinition of the
export of the revolution in Iran's foreign policy in
general, and in its relations with the Soviet Union in
particular.

3. The Tudeh Party. While the Soviets complained of continued Iranian efforts to export the
Islamic revolution, the Iranians denounced a kind of
Soviet export of revolution to Iran: support of the
Soviet-backed Tudeh Party. Despite improved relations in 1989, Soviet-Iranian tensions over the
Tudeh Party persisted. The Soviet press and radio
continued, even after Rafsanjani's visit to Moscow,
to speak up for the Tudeh Party, defending it as "one
of the most active participants in the Iranian revolution," which "carried out immense organizational
activity in workshops and factories... A year after
the Tudeh Party surfaced, 170,000 Iranians voted
for it..." (Radio Moscow, broadcast in Persian to
Iran, 6 October; *FBIS-SOV*, 10 October).

This kind of praise for the Tudeh Party infuriated
the Iranians. They denounced Radio Moscow for
defending the Tudeh "at a time when the Kremlin
leaders are attempting to polish their image before
the world..." For the people of Iran, anyone serving the foreigner is a traitor, whether he is, like
Rajavi (leader of Mojahedin-e Khalq), in the service of the United States, or like Kiyanuri (the
former Tudeh leader), in the service of the USSR
and the Soviet Communist Party" (Tehran, *Keyhan
Hava'i*, 18 October; *FBIS-NES*, 31 October). More
important, from the Iranian perspective such support for the Tudeh Party amounted to interfering in
Iran's internal affairs and was contrary to the recent
Soviet-Iranian declaration of principles on their relations. For example, an Iranian newspaper stated
categorically that in defending the Tudeh Party
"Moscow Radio has in effect meddled in our internal affairs..." Naturally, if this is repeated it could
affect the expansion of ties between the two countries at a time when officials from both sides are
trying to expand ties..." (Tehran, *Keyhan Hava'i*,
27 September; *FBIS-NES*, 6 October).

4. The settlement in Afghanistan. The year
1989 witnessed the drawing together of the positions of Iran and the Soviet Union on Afghanistan.

The withdrawal of Soviet troops from Afghanistan paved the way for the development of a Soviet-Iranian dialogue on the formation of a future government in Afghanistan. Toward this end Iran and the Soviet Union tried to bring about a degree of unity between the Peshawar-based alliance of seven Afghan factions and the Tehran-based alliance of eight, although the latter did not participate in the formation of the Interim Afghan Government. Soon after the withdrawal of Soviet forces, Iran condemned "the big powers' interference" in Afghanistan, presumably including the Soviet Union, and urged that "Afghanistan should be left to its people so that an independent, popular and Islamic government comes to power in Kabul" (Tehran, IRNA, in English, 28 March; *FBIS-NES*, 29 March). But after Shevardnadze's visit to Tehran and Velayati's visit to Moscow, despite its nonparticipation in the Geneva agreements, Iran's position drew closer to the Soviet Union's inasmuch as it sought a political rather than a military solution to the problem of Afghanistan. Shevardnadze and Velayati both expressed the desire to see an end to the bloodshed in Afghanistan and to "find a solution to the Afghan problem on the basis of aspirations of the Afghan people" (TASS, in English, 31 March; *FBIS-SOV*, 3 April).

During Rafsanjani's visit to the Soviet Union, the Afghan question figured prominently in the discussions. In welcoming Rafsanjani, Gorbachev said that the Soviet Union was doing "everything possible so that the Afghan people . . . could decide its own destiny in the framework of a neutral, non-aligned, and independent state by political means through national reconciliation, and not through a fratricidal war" (*Pravda*, 22 June; *FBIS-SOV*, 22 June). While in Moscow, Rafsanjani was quoted as saying that the Afghan settlement was "in its entirety a prerogative of the Afghan people and Iran has no right to interfere in its internal affairs. Iran, Pakistan, the PRC, the USSR should help the Afghan people arrive independently at a decision on their country's destiny." (TASS, 22 June; *FBIS-SOV*, 22 June.) Opposed to the Kabul government, Rafsanjani skirted the issue of "national reconciliation," which in the Soviet view entailed the need for forming a coalition government consisting of the Afghan mojahedin and the Soviet-supported Kabul government. Hence, Gorbachev's idea of national reconciliation was not mentioned in the final communiqué. Nor was Iran's idea of an "Islamic government" in Afghanistan. The two countries affirmed instead "the legitimate right of the people of

Afghanistan to preserve that country's *historical Islamic identity* and its territorial integrity," and expressed "the joint opinion of the right of the people of that country to determine their fate without external interference." The two sides also announced their support for "an independent, non-aligned and *Islamic Afghanistan* which will maintain friendly relations with its neighbors." (Emphasis added; *Pravda*, 24 June; *FBIS-SOV*, 26 June.) Rafsanjani said that Iran and the Soviet Union were in "complete agreement" on the question of Afghanistan (Tehran, IRNA, 23 June; *FBIS-NES*, 26 June), but the limits of their agreement were revealed both by the compromises they made and those which remained to be made.

5. The Iran-Iraq settlement and the Persian Gulf. Compared to the Afghan settlement issue, the positions of the Soviet Union and Iran on the Iran-Iraq settlement were relatively close in 1989, as they were also on the related issue of the withdrawal of U.S. naval forces from the Persian Gulf. After the cease-fire became effective on 20 August 1988 and the Iran-Iraq peace negotiations under U.N. auspices began on 25 August, Iran and the Soviet Union intensified their campaign against the presence of Western naval forces in the Persian Gulf. During Velayati's visit to Moscow in late March 1989, both sides reportedly favored "the earliest withdrawal from the Persian Gulf of the warships of states that do not belong to that region, which would facilitate the establishment of peace and security in that part of the world" (TASS, 31 March; *FBIS-SOV*, 3 April).

In his welcoming remarks, Gorbachev told Rafsanjani, "We wish most sincerely success to the Iran-Iraq negotiating process on the basis of the U.N. Security Council resolution 598" (*Pravda*, 22 June; *FBIS-SOV*, 22 June). Rafsanjani did not even mention either the Afghan or the Iraq issue in his dinner speech at the Kremlin. Both sides confined themselves to safe generalities. But the final communiqué revealed that the Soviet position on the Iran-Iraq settlement had drawn closer to that of the Iranians. The Soviets went beyond their usual support of Resolution 598 by joining Iran in expressing "their support for the four-point plan of the UN secretary general, dated 1 October 1988, for speeding up the implementation of this [598] resolution" (*Pravda*, 22 June; *FBIS-SOV*, 26 June). The Iranians, on the other hand, appeared to go beyond their usual demand for the withdrawal of foreign forces from the Persian Gulf. They agreed with the long-time Soviet stance on the Gulf and the Indian Ocean. They joined the Soviet Union in the belief that "the Persian Gulf and the Indian Ocean should be changed into a region of peace and calm, free from all weapons of mass annihilation, including nuclear and chemical weapons; and as a first step in this direction, there should be a complete withdrawal of all the navies of foreign states, and that the security and calm of the region should be provided by the littoral states" (ibid.).

Although Rafsanjani said afterwards that the Soviet Union was "very serious" about the implementation of the U.N. resolution and supported Iran's stance on the establishment of "a just and durable peace" (Tehran, IRNA, 23 June; *FBIS-NES*, 26 June), he did not explain why, in supporting Iran, the Soviets confined themselves to endorsing the U.N. secretary general's four-point plan. This plan had been intended to break the deadlock in the peace negotiations. The Iraqis refused to withdraw their forces to internationally recognized borders because to do so would have implied their acceptance of the Algiers agreement of 1975, which they had scrapped on 17 September 1980 before invading Iran. The Iranians resolutely insisted on the continued validity of the agreement. The secretary general's plan made no mention of either the dispute about the validity of the Algiers agreement or the dispute about the sovereignty over the Shatt al-Arab boundary river, but it called for reopening of the waterway and suggested that the issue of sovereignty over the river be put off until after a peace treaty had been signed.

The absence of any specific mention of the Soviet support for the Algiers agreement in the joint Soviet-Iranian communiqué was rationalized by Foreign Minister Velayati. He said that before Rafsanjani's visit to the Soviet Union, the Soviet Foreign Ministry spokesman Gerasimov had stated in a news conference that "the forces of the two sides should withdraw to the international borders which were clarified in the 1975 Algiers agreement," adding that "we do not have any problem with that country [the Soviet Union] on this issue" (Tehran Television Service, 28 June; *FBIS-NES*, 30 June). The truth is that the Soviets were leaving themselves room to maneuver by being as neutral as the U.N. secretary general, except that in the Soviet case, this neutrality reflected a desire to maintain balanced relations with both Baghdad and Tehran.

6. *Soviet defense aid*. The secrecy surrounding the issue of Soviet defense aid does not lend itself to a detailed discussion at this time, but it is important enough to be considered briefly. For the first time in the history of revolutionary Iran's relations with the Soviet Union, the two countries publicly agreed on a major defense relationship, which, according to Rafsanjani, was one of the "immensely fruitful" areas of agreement between the two states (Kuwait, *al-Qabas*, 26 June; *FBIS-SOV*, 29 June). Although the joint communiqué made no mention of this agreement, it was included in the declaration of principles, which said, "The Soviet side agrees to cooperate with the Iranian side with regard to strengthening its defense capability" (TASS, 22 June; *FBIS-SOV*, 22 June). The nature of this Soviet commitment, which especially worried U.S. circles, remained ambiguous. While in Moscow, Rafsanjani emphasized Iran's drive toward military self-sufficiency, claiming that Iran was "an independent producer of aircraft, missiles, electronics equipment, armored vehicles, and artillery hardware" (ibid.). But he also admitted that in these areas of defense equipment "we do have certain technical needs. We hope to satisfy them from various sources. But Iran will remain independent, including in questions of securing its defense" (*Izvestia*, 23 June; *FBIS-SOV*, 26 June).

From these remarks and others prior to Rafsanjani's visit to the Soviet Union, it would appear that Soviet defense aid would respect Iran's determination to diversify its sources of arms purchases, that the Soviet aid would be mainly technical in nature, and that it would not include the sale of sophisticated arms to Iran. Nearly two months before the Soviet-Iran defense-aid agreement, Iran's first deputy foreign minister, Ali Mohammad Besharati, admitted that Iran was negotiating an arms-purchase agreement with the Soviet Union, but he said, "We have gone into negotiations with various countries *except the Soviet Union for the purchase of fighter bombers*... Very soon you will see fighter bombers flying in the air which are *other than those of the United Sates and the Soviet Union*" (emphasis added; *Tehran Times*, in English, 1 May; *FBIS-NES*, 11 May).

Unofficial and non-Iranian sources were more specific and differed from Iranian accounts on the nature of the arms to be supplied and the conditions involved. A source in Abu Dhabi reported that Moscow and Tehran had initialed a military agreement during Rafsanjani's visit, according to which Moscow would supply Tehran with "about 100 advanced tanks of those recently withdrawn from GDR and CSSR . . . a number of warships, [and] an advanced radar network." The Soviets also agreed to "train Iranian military cadres in the Soviet military academies... It is not likely that the Soviet Union will provide Iran with MiG-29 aircraft, but it is possible for Iran to obtain advanced Soviet planes provided that it agrees to an irreversible end to its dispute with Iraq" (Abu Dhabi, *al-Ittihad*, 26 June; *FBIS-SOV*, 27 June). But another source reported that the Soviets had agreed to provide Iran with "sophisticated weapons in return for a promise from [Iran] not to interfere in the Soviet Muslim areas..." (Kuwait, *al-Qabas*, 26 June; *FBIS-SOV*, 29 June). By the end of 1989 it was claimed that "informed diplomatic sources" believed that the Soviet Union would supply Iran with "civil Ilyushin and Tupolev aircraft" and would help to refurbish Iran's "military and civil airports" (Abu Dhabi, *al-Ittihad*, 2 September; *FBIS-SOV*, 5 September).

The Soviet arms sales to such volatile regions of the world as the Middle East raised wider questions than bilateral relations between Moscow and Tehran. In the Soviet Union, some asked whether the Soviet military cooperation with Iran would help improve the relations of the Soviet Union with Iraq and with the United States; whether it would destabilize the international system; and whether it would be an ethically responsible act. The Soviets answered these questions to their own satisfaction. Pointing to the peaceful objectives of Iran and the Soviet Union, as expressed in their declaration of principles, particularly the objective of peaceful settlement of the Iran-Iraq conflict, they asserted that Soviet-Iranian military cooperation, including arms trade, would hardly destabilize the international system or threaten Iraq and the United States. Furthermore, to prove their point they quoted Gorbachev's reply, at the first session of the Supreme Soviet, to those who criticized the ethical aspect of the Soviet-Iranian military cooperation. Reportedly Gorbachev had said, "We are engaging in arms trade, although we are substantially reducing it. This exists in respect of both socialist and other countries. In this case we are doing business with a neighboring country with which we wish to build normal relations. It turned to us with certain inquiries concerning arms deliveries to ensure its own security. We have taken certain steps. I believe that they do not clash with our ideas about responsibility for the development of international relations, for imparting to them contemporaneous direction aimed at normalizing international affairs, not only at preserving but also at strengthening peace."

(Moscow Domestic Service, 27 October; *FBIS-SOV*, 2 November.)

7. Economic relations. Even before the Russian soldiers left Afghanistan, the Soviets seized on the cease-fire in the Iran-Iraq war to deepen their commercial, economic, and technical relations with Iran (see *YICA*, 1989). As a result, the work of the eleventh meeting of the Iranian and Soviet intergovernmental commission in late 1988 prepared the ground for the unprecedented commitment of the two countries in regard to these relations in 1989. They not only tried to consolidate the piecemeal agreements reached previously, but also to enter agreements in new areas of economic activities. Against the backdrop of constant fluctuations in, and the short-term nature of, Soviet-Iranian relations since the dawn of the Iranian revolution, the long-term and comprehensive agreements in the economic field in 1989 must be considered as a turning point. During the Gorbachev-Rafsanjani summit meeting, Iran and the Soviet Union committed themselves to all-encompassing cooperation in the economic, trade, technical, and industrial spheres, including the peaceful use of atomic energy, and also to cooperation in the spheres of science, space, and education, including the establishment of links between Soviet and Iranian universities. Their cooperation in the trade, economic, scientific, and technical fields was to last to the year 2000, and would involve fifteen sectors of the Iranian national economy.

The resumption of Iranian natural-gas exports to the Soviet Union figured prominently in the negotiations between the two countries in 1989, as it had in previous years, but in 1989 this issue attained a new importance. It was envisaged that Iran would export up to 30 billion cubic meters of gas to the Soviet Union in return for technical equipment and services for industrial projects, transportation, and excavation activities in the Caspian Sea, and for increasing the productive capability of Iran's heavy industries, especially Isfahan's steel industry. The Soviets were also willing and ready to extend some $2 billion worth of credit to Iran for such purposes. (Tehran Domestic Service, 19 June; *FBIS-NES*, 20 June.)

A list of major economic and technical projects agreed upon by the Soviet and Iranian ministers during Rafsanjani's visit to Moscow was presented to the Iranian cabinet for approval on 2 August. It included the following items:

1. Shahid Montazeri and Ramin power plants in Isfahan and Ahvaz with a capacity of 1,430 megawatts;

2. Khoda Afarin and Dez Qal'eh-si water and power installations with a total capacity of 140 megawatts;

3. Two power plants on the Karun river with a capacity of 3,670 megawatts;

4. Other power plants with a combined capacity of 2,000 megawatts;

5. Expansion of the Isfahan steel mill with annual productive capability of four million tons of steel;

6. Steel-rolling mills in Khorasan, Hormozgan, and Azerbaijan provinces;

7. Gas-pressure relay station (s-1) for the second nationwide pipeline and completion of this line; and

8. Mashhad-Sarakhs and Mashhad-Bafq railroads.

It is obvious that the construction of power plants figured importantly in the above list (Tehran, IRNA, in English, 2 August; *FBIS-NES*, 7 August). It was estimated that once completed they would have a total capacity of 8,000 megawatts (Tehran Domestic Service, 19 June; *FBIS-NES*, 20 June). The export of Iran's natural gas to the Soviet Union, which was to finance a number of technical and industrial projects was scheduled to start at the beginning of the Iranian calendar year 1369 (21 March 1990 C.E.). As the year 1989 ended, it remained to be seen whether the two countries would be able to reach a final agreement on the gas issue by that date. Although such an agreement had been anticipated during Rafsanjani's visit to Moscow (Tehran, IRNA, in English, 1 June; *FBIS-NES*, 2 June), it did not come to pass. Nor did the drilling of an oil well in the southern part of the Caspian Sea begin, although Moscow agreed to Tehran's purchasing and renting of off-shore oil platforms for use in the Caspian Sea (ibid.).

Bilateral and transit trade had consistently been the most unstable area of Soviet-Iranian economic relations. The decision to conclude a long-term commercial agreement during the Gorbachev-Rafsanjani summit would not only help stabilize trade relations, but could also remove a persistent source of Soviet complaints against Iran's far greater commercial relations with the West. The value of Iran's trade with West Germany alone was about ten times larger than that with the Soviet Union in 1987: $2.5 billion as compared with

$250 million. It was hoped that Iran's trade with the USSR would reach the $1 billion mark in 1989. Besides the important agreement on the Mashhad-Sarakhs-Tedzhen railway, which has already been mentioned, other agreements on shipping and on transportation by truck were intended to boost trade.

Shipping in the Caspian Sea and the adjacent waterways increased in 1989. In May, it was expected that a joint shipping line would start operations in the sea simultaneously with Rafsanjani's visit to Moscow in June (Tehran, IRNA, 17 May; *FBIS-NES*, 18 May). After the establishment of this line between Anzali and Baku, Iran and the Soviet Union managed, within two months, to transport more than 22,000 tons of goods between these two ports (Tehran Domestic Service, 24 October; *FBIS-NES*, 26 October). In keeping with their agreement at the summit to call the border between the two countries "a border of friendship and cooperation," Iran and the Soviet Union aimed at expanding the exchange of goods, especially between on the one hand, Iranian East Azerbaijan and West Azerbaijan provinces and, on the other hand, Soviet Azerbaijan and Turkmenistan. From the Soviet perspective, trade contacts might help dampen the effects of Iran's propaganda for the export of the Islamic Revolution. By the end of 1989, besides increased trade contacts between Anzali and Baku, contacts across the border between Turkmenistan and Iran were expanding once more after years of stagnation. According to the first deputy prime minister of Turkmenistan, one specific new development would be that shops selling the goods of the other country would open in Iran and in the Turkmen capital Ashkhabad (TASS, 5 July; *Central Asia and Caucasus Chronicle*, October 1989).

There is little doubt that in 1989 new foundations were laid for the expansion of Soviet-Iranian relations in the 1990s, and that Soviet leaders hoped that this development would lead to increasing Soviet influence in Iran and beyond. But it would be a mistake to consider the prospects of greater Soviet influence simply in terms of the zero-sum game of the U.S.-Soviet competition. As I have argued elsewhere, Rafsanjani's visit to the Soviet Union might well signify the beginning of Iran's re-entry into the international community, and signal the desire of Iran's pragmatic leaders to base their country's future relations with other nations, including the United States, more on the concept of national interest than on the idea of a struggle between good and evil (see my article in the "Outlook" section of *WP*, 2 July 1989).

R.K. Ramazani
University of Virginia

Iraq

Population. 18,073,969
Party. Iraqi Communist Party (ICP)
Founded. 1934
Membership. No data
First Secretary. 'Aziz Muhammad (65, Kurd, worker)
Politburo. (Incomplete): Zaki Khayri (79, Arab/Kurd, journalist), Fakhri Karim, 'Abd al-Razzaq al-Safi (59, Shia Arab, lawyer)
Status. Proscribed
Last Congress. Fourth, 10–15 November 1985
Last Election. 2 April 1989; 250-seat National Assembly, no communists
Auxiliary Organizations. No data
Publications. *Tariq al-Sha'b* (People's road), clandestine; *Al-Thaqafah al-Jadidah* (The new culture), an ideological journal; *Iraq Letter*, published abroad

Background. The past year has brought no improvement in the dire straits in which the ICP, along with its Kurdish allies, found itself after the Iraqi armed forces had destroyed guerrilla resistance in northern Iraq in the fall of 1988. The government has cleared a twenty-mile-deep zone along its border with Iran and Turkey to interdict supplies and support for Kurdish guerrillas. The population has been relocated, primarily to non-Kurdish areas distant from this zone. This population shift and Iraqi government security controls have had severe adverse effects on the ICP's organization and functioning.

Leadership and Organization. The principal leaders continue to direct the ICP from outside Iraq. In the spring, First Secretary 'Aziz Muhammad visited Damascus, where he was received by Syrian vice-president Zuhayr Mushari-qah (Damascus,

Syrian Arab News Agency, 19 April; *FBIS-NES*, 20 April). 'Abd al-Razzaq al-Safi, identified as a Politburo member, participated in an international symposium in Prague at the end of 1988 (*WMR*, February), and at a meeting in the offices of the *World Marxist Review* sometime in 1989, he discussed the decisions of the plenum of the ICP's Central Committee in March 1989 (*WMR*, June). Other spokesmen and representatives, *e.g.*, Kadhim Habib and Bilal Samir, were also living outside Iraq (*WMR*, April and July). No news of ICP activities within Iraq has been heard since the Iraqi military operation of 1988, a silence implying inaction.

Domestic Affairs. The Saddam Husayn regime's success in outlasting Iran over eight years of war allowed the Iraqi leader to claim victory in the conflict. This put the ICP in an untenable position because it had opposed the war and had sought to overturn the regime. Support for the war has been made a litmus test of patriotism for Iraqis. Candidates for seats in the national-assembly elections that were held in April had to be able to demonstrate participation in, or support for the war against Iran, a requirement which effectively excluded ICP members even if the party had not been proscribed. The vice-chairman of Iraq's Revolutionary Command Council, Izzat al-Duri, stated that the ICP had "betrayed the homeland" (Paris, Radio Monte Carlo, 30 March; *FBIS-NES*, 31 March). Candidates were scrutinized by the Council, and only those judged safe by the regime were allowed to stand for election. The ICP, in a statement issued in Damascus, denounced the national-assembly elections as farcical, saying that "these forged elections will only bring about a forged assembly, which does not represent any part of the will of the Arab people in Iraq." It asserted "that the Iraqi people will continue to struggle to topple the dictatorship." (Radio Damascus, 1 April; *FBIS-NES*, 4 April.) While the regime has promised that non-Ba'thist political groups and parties will be permitted to organize, none had appeared by the end of 1989. In any event, the ICP was specifically excluded from this promise in statements by Minister of Information Latif Jasim (London, *al-Tadamun*, 28 August; *FBIS-NES*, 6 September) and the speaker of the assembly, who grouped the ICP with two of its Kurdish allies as having "no place among . . . honorable Iraqis because they denied their homeland . . . during . . . [its] ordeal." (Kuwait, *al-Siyasah*, 1 October; *FBIS-NES*, 4 October.)

Under current conditions in Iraq under the dictatorial regime of Saddam Husayn, the ICP has been pushed to the margins of political life. Only the Ba'th Party and a tame Kurdish movement are legal. The Ba'th Party itself is Saddam Husayn's instrument, taking all its cues for statements or action from him. The ICP, linked to Kurdish groups opposed to Husayn's regime, continues to work for a broad national front. The risks which citizens would incur by associating with the ICP are formidable. Antiregime activities have taken place in Baghdad, but the ICP has not claimed responsibility for any of them.

The ICP welcomed the end of the Iraq-Iran war, blaming both sides for the delay in coming to agreement on a cease-fire. It supports implementation of the provisions of U.N. Security Council Resolution 598, which is the instrument under which hostilities were brought to a close. It has tilted toward the Iraqi position in regard to the international border in the Shatt al-'Arab waterway (Iraq claims the entire waterway; Iran wants the line to be the center of the channel) by recommending revision of "the 1975 Algiers agreement in the light of earlier international agreements." (The earlier agreements generally favor the current Iraqi position on the border.) Nonetheless, "our party has not relaxed its struggle for the solution of its own people's basic problems, including genuine autonomy for the Kurds." (*WMR*, April.)

International Relations. The tone of the ICP's pronouncements on international issues has become less strident than in the past. It sees a need for "efforts on the part of the entire world community" to seek solutions to the "socioeconomic problems of the Third World states." A party spokesman has also referred favorably to the Helsinki accords. (*WMR*, August and July.)

Relations between Iraq and the USSR have remained much the same over the past year as earlier. The Soviet Union remains a major source of sophisticated weaponry. Up to fifty MiG-29s were supplied by Moscow to Iraq in 1988–1989 (*Middle East Economic Digest*, 24 November). Contacts in the economic and technical spheres continued at about the same level as in recent years. Visits were exchanged with most East European countries, but none have taken place since the changes of regime in many of those states.

John F. Devlin
Swarthmore, Pennsylvania

Israel

Population. 4,371,478 (not including territories occupied in 1967, except for Jewish settlers)
Party. Communist Party of Israel (CPI); also called New Communist List (Rashima Kommunistit Hadasha: RAKAH)
Founded. 1922 (a short-lived organization in 1920)
Membership. 2,000 (estimated)
General Secretary. Meir Vilner (70; member of the Knesset [parliament])
Politburo. 9 members, including Meir Vilner, David (Uzi) Burnstein, Benjamin Gonen, Wolf Erlich, Emile Habibi, David Khenin, Tawfiq Tubi (deputy general secretary and member of the Knesset), Tawfiq Zayyad (member of the Knesset and mayor of Nazareth); 4 alternates, including Zahi Karkabi
Secretariat. 7 members, including Meir Vilner, Salim Jubran, Salibi Khamis, David Khenin, George Tubi (chief of the Central Committee's international section), Tawfiq Tubi, Jamal Musa
Central Committee. 31 members, including Nimer Marcus and L. Zakhavi; 5 candidates (data on organs not necessarily up to date)
Status. Legal
Last Congress. Twentieth, 4–7 December 1985
Last Election. 1 November 1988; 3.7 percent of the vote, winning 4 seats (with the Democratic Front for Peace and Equality [DFPE]), total number of seats in the legislature: 120
Auxiliary Organizations. Young Communist League, Young Pioneers, Democratic Women's Movement
Publications. *Al-Ittihad* (Emile Habibi, editor; Salim Jubran, deputy editor); *Zo Ha-Derekh* (Meir Vilner, editor); *al-Jadid* (Samih al-Qasim, editor); *Information Bulletin, Communist Party of Israel* (sporadically); *al-Didd; al-Darb; Arahim; Der Weq*

Background. The CPI dates its origin back to 1919, when the partially communist ("proletarian Zionist") Socialist Workers' Party was founded (in 1920, according to other sources). The Palestinian Communist Party was established in 1922 (in 1921, according to current CPI claims), becoming the

Israeli Communist Party after 1948. Following a split in the Israeli communist movement in 1965 largely along ethnic lines, the disappearance of the heavily Jewish Israeli Communist Party (Miflaga Kommunistit Isra'elit; MAKI) left the mainly Arab, pro-Moscow RAKAH as the undisputed claimant to being the Communist Party of Israel (CPI). With Arab nationalist parties not permitted (although the joint Arab-Jewish Progressive List for Peace [PLP] emerged in 1984 to espouse the cause of Palestinian self-determination and thus to compete for the Arab vote), RAKAH has served mainly as an outlet for the grievances of the Arab (Palestinian) minority. It is estimated that about 75–85 percent of the party's vote comes from this sector of the population. The CPI-dominated DFPE got about 50 percent of the Arab vote in 1977, and 38 and 34 percent in 1981 and 1984, respectively. Starting in the 1970s, the DFPE dominated most Arab town councils.

Leadership and Party Organization. The organization of the CPI is typical of communist parties in general and is described by party leaders as based on the principle of "democratic centralism." The Congress normally meets at four-year intervals and chooses the members of the Central Committee and the Central Control Commission, while the Presidium, Secretariat, and general secretary are chosen by the Central Committee. There are also regional committees, local branches (90), and cells. Cells are based on both residence and place of work. The CPI is said to be the best organized party in Israel, which gives it an important advantage in its rivalry with the PLP for Arab votes.

Despite previous vague complaints by at least one CPI leader about the impact of *perestroika* within the party structure (see *YICA*, 1989), another analyst (a member of Shashi, a rival Israeli leftist group) reports that rigidity—demonstrated by the fact that the same two individuals have headed the party list in every election during the past three decades—has "limited the mobilization of many activists." He quotes "one young Arab communist activist," who complained that "We are members of a Brezhnevist party in the era of Gorbachev." (Asher Davidi, "The Elections, the Peace Camp and the Left," *Middle East Report*, March–April).

About 80 percent of the members of the CPI are Arabs, although it claims that the two ethnic groups are represented in it about equally. But Jews predominate in the top party organs, with a slight majority in the Politburo and the Central Committee. In recent years, the Jewish general secretary

has been balanced by an Arab deputy general secretary. Similarly, a Jew, Wolf Erlich, heads the Central Control Commission, while the deputy chairman of that body is Ramzi Khouri, an Arab. Despite Muslim representation during the past two decades, Christians (largely Greek Orthodox) predominate among the Arab leaders. Although the party has been noted as a nearly unique arena of Arab-Jewish amity, there are reports of dissatisfaction on the part of Arabs because of their inadequate representation at the top.

Domestic Party Affairs. The Central Committee met in January and set the date for the Twenty-first Party Congress in April of 1990 (*Neues Deutschland*, 23 January). There was a report of another Central Committee meeting in June (*Neues Deutschland*, 10 June). Aside from one mention of a Politburo meeting in January (*Jerusalem Post*, 17 January; *FBIS*, 18 January), there is no available information on meetings of this or other party organs. In keeping with past statements, General Secretary Vilner emphasized the "pernicious influence [of military spending] on the country's economy" (TASS, 14 February; *FBIS*, 15 February).

In an article in the March issue of the *World Marxist Review* (Prague), Deputy General Secretary Tubi analyzed the results of the November 1988 general elections. He spoke of the coalition of the "extremist-nationalist" Likud and the "right social democratic Labour Alignment" that had "crowned its term with a most grave economic crisis" in which production is declining and unemployment has reached 8 percent. The "prolonged occupation" of Arab territories was said to have left "negative marks on Israeli society," as shown by the "further rise of the extreme nationalist racist forces." But, while noting the "continued shift to the right," he denied "that the people voted against peace," claiming that many Likud voters were protesting against the Labor Alignment's detrimental socioeconomic policy and thus were "more the victims of the social demagogy of the Likud than supporters of its extremist programme."

Tubi maintained that the DFPE's "vote gain was an indisputable success" since it "was shown among the Jewish and Arab population in every town and village." He pointed to "important"—though "modest"—gains among Jewish voters in development townships and reported that the DFPE had obtained 35 percent of the Arab vote (which is only one percent more than in the 1984 elections), getting majorities in Nazareth and "all other important

Arab townships." (The DFPE's percentage of the Arab vote was actually 34.5, compared with 34.4 percent in 1984 [Asher Davidi, "The Elections, the Peace Camp and the Left," *Middle East Report*, March–April].)

The CPI continued to champion the cause of the Arab minority. As has been the case since 1976, the CPI was actively involved in celebrating the Day of the Land (March 30), which involved peaceful demonstrations among the Arab population of Israel proper (*CSM*, 5 April). In November, the Arab population staged a one-day strike protesting the demolition of homes that are illegally built, since the failure of the authorities to allow legal homes to be built apparently leaves the Arabs no other alternative. Although the destruction of homes in the town of Taibe had resulted in riots earlier in the month, the strike—the fourth in four years—was free of violence, as the organizers had hoped it would be (*Jerusalem Post*, international edition, 20–26 November).

In the local elections in February, the communists faced unprecedented opposition from slates of Islamist candidates. Apparently in large part as a result of dissatisfaction over the services previously provided by municipal governments (and owing to the remarkable array of services, ranging from nursery schools to drug-treatment centers, privately funded by the Islamists), an Islamist candidate won the race for mayor of Israel's previously DFPE-dominated second-largest village, Umm al-Fahm, as well as getting twelve of its fifteen council seats. There were also mayoral or council victories by the Islamists in seven other Arab localities, including six out of nineteen seats on the Nazareth council. (*CSM*, 13 March, 12 September.) Since, in large part, this represents the continuing decline of Zionist parties among the Arab population, there is no available data on the degree to which these victories cut into the previous domination by the CPI. Nor is there any way of predicting the consequences for the communists of future national elections being contested by Islamists, a possibility alluded to by one of the movement's leaders. The former DFPE mayor of Umm al-Fahm, Hashim Mahamid, accused the Islamists who defeated him of not being "concerned about what's happening in the West Bank and Gaza" or about "political" as opposed to merely "local" issues. He warned about divisions between Muslim and Christian Arabs that emphasis on religion might bring, and asked: "How can we unify against Israel if they [the Islamists] see the main enemy as nonbelievers?" A fight that left ten people injured occurred in the village of Dayr Hanna between Islamists and communists during the celebration of the Day of the Land (*CSM*, 12 September; Tel Aviv IDF Radio, 30 March; *FBIS*, 31 March).

The CPI conducted a celebration of the 70th anniversary of its founding, held in the city of Acre on 22 and 23 September (*Neues Deutschland*, 23 January, 21 and 25 September).

Auxiliary and Front Organizations. The CPI dominates the DFPE, which includes noncommunist partners: the Black Panthers (a group of Afro-Asian or Oriental Jews protesting discrimination against them by Jews of European origin), whose leader, Charlie Biton, is a member of the DFPE delegation in the Knesset; the Committee of Arab Local Council Heads, whose candidate, as number five on the DFPE list in 1988 barely missed getting elected, but who was scheduled to take his seat in the Knesset in October (*CSM*, 12 September; it was not said which of the previous deputies he would replace); and the Nitzotz-Ashara organization, whose newspaper is *Derech Ha Nitzotz* (Way of the spark), with an Arabic counterpart named *Tariq al-Sharara*. The trial of several journalists working for these newspapers (which had been banned for six months, starting in February 1988), including Managing Editor Assaf Adib and Editor in Chief Michal Shwartz, began in September 1988; a newly established organization called the 21-Year Movement began publication of *Haris ash-Sharara* (Guardian of the spark) (*WMR*, Toronto, January). In addition to its delegation in the Knesset, the DFPE is particularly well organized in Arab towns and villages.

Another leftist group, the Israeli Socialist Left (SHASHI), broke away from the DFPE in 1984, but recommended that its members vote for that list in 1988. SHASHI and some other leftist individuals tried unsuccessfully in 1988 to bring together a broader slate that would have included the DFPE and the PLP, and which some say could have won as many as eight seats. (Davidi, "The Elections, the Peace Camp and the Left.")

The DFPE concluded an agreement with the PLP and the Arab Democratic Party to run a joint list in the Histradut (General Federation of Labor) elections in November, with the DFPE allotted 60 percent of the seats. The PLP accepted the DFPE demand that CPI Politburo member Benjamin Gonen head the joint list. (Jerusalem Domestic Service, 21 August; *FBIS*, 29 August.) This "Joint

Arab List" got 36,182 out of 821,592 votes (4.49 percent) (Tel Aviv, *Davar*, 3 December; *FBIS*, 4 December).

The CPI sponsors the active Young Pioneers and the Young Communist League. At least in the past, it sponsored or actively participated in the Committee against the War in Lebanon, There is a Limit (an organization calling on Israeli soldiers to refuse to serve in Lebanon and the other occupied territories), the Committee for the Defense of Arab Land, Mothers against the War, Soldiers against Silence, Women for Peace, the Israel-USSR Friendship Society, the Israeli Association of Anti-Fascist Fighters and Victims of Nazism, and Arab student committees, notably CAMPUS. Other groups which *First Hand Information: Communists and Revolutionary Democrats of the World Presenting Their Parties* (Prague: Peace and Socialism International Publishers, 1988) lists as including members of the CPI are the Movement of Democratic Women in Israel, the Initiative Committee for the Improvement of Relations with the Soviet Union, the Israel-Cuba Friendship Committee, the Israel-Bulgaria Friendship Committee, the Israel Peace Committee, the League for Human and Civil Rights in Israel, the Druze Initiative Committee, and the Committee against Racism.

In November 1988, CAMPUS and two other Arab student groups, the Arab Student Committee and Students Against the Occupation, were temporarily denied the right to conduct activities at the Hebrew University in Jerusalem following demonstrations protesting the destruction of Arab homes (*Chronicle of Higher Education*, 23 November 1988).

International Views, Positions, and Activities. Ali Ashur was the CPI representative at an international symposium in Prague on "Peace and Revolution in the Nuclear Age," organized by the Commission on General Theoretical and Global Problems of *World Marxist Review* (*WMR*, Prague, February).

In March, the CPSU Central Committee sent "cordial greetings" to its CPI counterpart on the occasion of the latter party's 70th anniversary (*Pravda*, 26 March; *FBIS*, 27 March). On March 18, an article appeared in the Mongolian daily, *Unen*, praising the CPI's 70 years of uniting Arabs and Jews in opposition to "fascism, racism, and aggression," and stressing the continuing growth of relations between it and the Mongolian People's Revolutionary Party since their contacts with each other began in 1956 (Ulan Bator, *Montsame*, 18 March; *FBIS*, 21 March).

General Secretary Vilner sent greetings to the Central Committee of the Romanian Communist Party on the 45th anniversary of Romania's "liberation from the fascist yoke" (Bucharest, *Scinteia*, 30 August; *FBIS*, 5 September). That party's general secretary, Nicolae Ceaușescu, sent greetings and congratulations to the CPI on the occasion of its 70th anniversary (*Scinteia*, 23 September; *FBIS*, 26 September).

Politburo member Wolf Erlich was a guest of the Central Committee of the Socialist Unity Party of Germany (SED) (German Democratic Republic) in September (*Neues Deutschland*, 19 September). The SED Central Committee also sent a telegram of congratulations to Vilner on the 70th anniversary of his party (*Neues Deutschland*, 22 September). The CPI received a similar congratulatory telegram from its counterpart in the Communist Party of Czechoslovakia (Prague, *Rudé Právo*, 23 September; *FBIS*, 29 September).

The CPI calls for peace based on self-determination for the Palestinians, the withdrawal of Israel from all the territories occupied in 1967, and an international peace conference in which the PLO as well as Israel would participate as the road to such a "two states for two peoples" settlement. Its spokesmen characterize the Labor-Likud "bi-party rule" as being united precisely in rejecting all of those principles (*WMR*, Prague, March). Deputy General Secretary Tubi spoke of his government's "brutal and bloody but abortive suppressive measures against the heroic Intifada" and warned against the growth of extremist groups openly calling for "transfer" of the Palestinian population. Vilner maintained that a majority of Israelis want "a dialogue" with the PLO and stressed the "importance" of recent decisions of the Palestine National Council (TASS, 14 February; *FBIS*, 15 February).

Some members of the DFPE and other dovish Israeli groups were detained after they had visited the West Bank village of Nahhalin to express regret for an incident in which five people had been killed (Jerusalem Domestic Service, 25 April; *FBIS*, 26 April).

The CPI has always been strongly aligned with Moscow, toward which it maintains an uncritical stance. Vilner repeatedly called on his government to resume diplomatic ties with Moscow (*Jerusalem Post*, 17 January; *FBIS*, 18 January; TASS, 14 February; *FBIS*, 15 February). A CPI statement in response to Israel's renewal of ties with Hungary suggested that resumption of relations with the USSR and other socialist countries might follow if the Israeli government works toward peace (Tel Aviv, IDF Radio, 18 September; *FBIS*, 22 September). (In December, General Secretary Mikhail Gorbachev rejected a suggestion that the USSR refuse to renew diplomatic relations with Israel unless the latter "makes steps forward in the dialogue with the Palestine Liberation Organisation," a condition which a spokesman for Prime Minister Yitzhak Shamir called unacceptable [*Jerusalem Post*, 1 December; *FBIS*, 1 December]).

Other Marxist Organizations. For background information on the Israeli Socialist Organization (Matzpen) and groups that broke away from it, including the Revolutionary Communist League, see *YICA*, 1982 and 1984.

Glenn E. Perry
Indiana State University

PALESTINE COMMUNIST PARTY

Population. Over 4.5 million (estimated) Palestinians, including 1.6 million in the West Bank and Gaza Strip, about 700,000 in Israel, and more than 1.4 million in Jordan (estimated)
Party. Palestinian Communist Party (al-Hizb al-Shuyu'i; PCP)
Founded. 1982
Membership. Accurate estimate not available
General Secretary. (Presumably) Bashir al-Barghuti (journalist); deputy general secretary: Sulayman al-Najjab
Politburo. Sulayman al-Najjab (member of the PLO Executive Committee), Na'im Abbas al-Ashhab; others not known
Secretariat. Sulayman al-Najjab; others not known
Central Committee. Dhamin Awdah, Mahir al-Sharif, Sulayman al-Nashhab, Ali Ahmad, Mahmud al-Rawwaq, Na'im Abbas al-Ashhab, Mahmud Abu-Shamas, Mahmud Shuqayr (representative of the PCP to the *WMR*); others not known (names on various lists not necessarily up to date)
Status. Illegal, but tolerated to a large extent in Israeli-occupied areas
Last Congress. First, late in 1983
Last Election. N/a
Auxiliary Organizations. Progressive Workers' Bloc (PWB)
Publications. *Al-Tali'ah* (The vanguard), weekly newspaper, Bashir al-Barghuti, editor; *al-Watan* (The homeland); *al-Katib* (The writer), monthly magazine

Background. With the approval of the Communist Party of Jordan (CPJ), the PCP was organized in February 1982, although its statements identify it with the pre-1948 Palestinian Communist Party. The new party was to include former members of the Palestinian Communist Organization of the West Bank and the Gaza Strip, previously a section of the CPJ, as well as members of the Palestinian Communist Organization in Lebanon and all other Palestinian members of the CPJ, except for those living in Jordan, that is, the East Bank.

Leadership and Party Organization. Relatively little is known about the organization of the PCP. The First (constituent) Congress met late in 1983 and adopted a program and rules for the party, as well as selecting the members of the Politburo, Secretariat, and Central Committee. Several non-PCP publications refer to Barghuti as the party's leader (or as its leader in the occupied territories), but there is no evidence that he is necessarily the general secretary. Most of the members of these top organs of the party, which describes itself as being "organised on the basis of democratic centralism," are said to reside in the occupied territories (*First-Hand Information: Communists and Revolutionary Democrats of the World Presenting Their Parties* [Prague: Peace and Socialism International Publishers, 1988], p. 101).

The Palestinian communists' failure to engage in armed struggle seems to have saved their party structure from dismantlement by the Israelis in the early years of the occupation and thus to have enhanced their position in the West Bank and Gaza today, while weakening their appeal in the Palestinian diaspora. Their "long experience with mass movements" has further given them an advantage during the current uprising. All of this is said to make the PCP the most successful communist party in the Arab world today—at a time when communism has reached its nadir elsewhere in that region. (Alain Gresh, "Palestinian Communists and the Intifadah," *Middle East Report*, March–April, pp. 35–36, reviewing [PCP Central Committee member] Mahir al-Sharif, *Al-Shuyu'iyun wa Qadaya al-Nidal al-Watani al-Rahin* [The communists and the issues in the current national struggle] [Damascus: Center for Socialist Research and Study in the Arab World, 1988].)

Palestinian Affairs. The PCP has been particularly active in the Israeli-occupied territories, where it "organizes mass actions against" the occupation (ibid.), but its activities extend to the Palestinian diaspora as well, though not to Israel proper. The party is (or at least was) based in Damascus, as shown by statements issued from there.

Although the PCP is illegal in the occupied territories, it is in fact generally tolerated. But sometimes there are crackdowns, and people are arrested for possessing communist literature. At least in the past, this toleration has been explained in terms of Israel's wish to limit other groups and not to provoke the Soviet Union, as well as the influence of the CPI (which is doubtful) and the PCP's emphasis on political rather than military struggle. Unlike other organizations affiliated with the Palestine Liberation Organization (PLO), the PCP apparently lacks a military force. The inclusion of such a non-guerrilla group and one that unambiguously proclaimed its adherence to the "two-state" idea from the beginning has been called "a double deviation" (Gresh, "Palestinian Communists and the Intifadah," p. 35).

Barghuti, who was once imprisoned by the Jordanians and was subjected to town arrest by the Israelis during the early 1980s, edits the weekly party newspaper al-Tali'a in East Jerusalem. Published since 1976, it has "a high circulation among West Bank intelligentsia and students." The PCP has also published "a monthly literary and political magazine" entitled al-Katib (The writer) since 1980, in addition to its underground "official organ," al-Watan (The homeland), which has appeared sporadically during the past decade.

In an interview with the World Marxist Review, the PCP's general secretary (whose name is not mentioned) reported a recent rapid increase in the party's membership, mainly from among "18 to 22 year-olds participating in the uprising." In fact, he maintained that the "large influx" of new members, together with "a lack of skilled cadres," at first created a difficult problem of educating "these comrades." But he added that the uprising also served to bring out "genuine leaders at all levels," making it "now easier for us to fill the vacuum caused by the campaign of mass arrests" and also allowing "greater decentralisation," with much "propaganda and agitation" conducted by local bodies. (WMR, Toronto, August.)

As evidence of his party's "leading role" in the uprising, the general secretary asserted that two-thirds of the Palestinians "who have died in Israeli prisons" are communists (ibid.).

There has been much rivalry between the communists and other Palestinian organizations. Politburo member Na'im al-Ashhab argued that the Islamists' role in the uprising "is being exaggerated," and suggested that they were in collusion with Jordan's King Hussein (IB, February). The general secretary accused the Israelis of repeatedly trying to create conflict between his party and Islamic organizations by "issuing fake leaflets, circulating false rumours," and like maneuvers, but he reported that all such attempts had failed. He also maintained that the Israelis had tried to disrupt Palestinian unity by playing the "working class and the national bourgeoisie" off against each other, but that the PCP had resisted such class conflict even to the extent of using its position in trade unions to act "as an arbiter" in labor disputes. (Ibid.)

While the uprising in the Israeli-occupied territories began spontaneously in December 1987, a Unified National Leadership soon emerged that included representatives of the PCP along with those of other Palestinian organizations. The PCP also participates in the underground local committees, whose composition, however, seems to vary from place to place. Local "branch commissions" are said to provide assistance in dealing with curfews and in helping to teach methods of food production and craftsmanship aimed at allowing the people to dispense with Israeli-made goods (ibid.). According to the general secretary, it was the PCP that, "Early in the uprising ... proposed and led an initiative to set up people's committees," and such committees "have been playing a leading role in organising and guiding popular resistance" (ibid.).

The PCP has consistently called for a two-state settlement of the Palestine question, with Israel withdrawing from all the territories it occupied in 1967 and the creation of an independent Palestinian state in the West Bank and the Gaza Strip. This would come about as the result of an international peace conference in which all parties, including the PLO, would participate. In keeping with this outlook, Politburo member Na'im Ashhab praised the outcome of the session of the Palestine National Council (PNC) held in Algiers in November 1988, which he described as having "crowned all the previous moments of positive value in the movement" and as having "brought the PLO's stand into line with international law, something that had earlier been present only in the PCP's views." He further praised the session's proclamation of a Palestinian state, whose creation will be " a weighty contribution to the advancement of the civilisation of the region's peoples" and a contrast to "despotic regimes and . . . neighboring Israel, where discrimination prevails," despite "the fact that this decision [to declare a state] looks premature," and he spoke favorably of the renunciation of terrorism, referring to Israel's longtime practice of "state terrorism." (*WMR*, Toronto, February.)

Central Committee member Mahmud Shuqayr attributed "many political shifts" to "the organic combination of . . . the intifada [uprising] and the Palestinian peace plan." Pointing to decisions of the Arab summit and the EEC summit, Shuqayr concluded that they confirm "the fact that the PLO peace plan is the only viable way of settling" the Palestine conflict. He enumerated the objectives of "our struggle" as follows: continuing the uprising, with "autarky" reducing dependence on Israel; accelerating PLO activity and international pressure on the United States and Israel to accept an international peace conference; "improved coordination between the PLO and the national liberation forces in the region" in order to make the Arab regimes implement decisions already reached at Arab summit conferences"; and "broader contacts between the PLO and . . . realistic quarters in Israel." (*WMR*, Prague, November.) A PCP manifesto opposed Israeli proposals for elections in the occupied territories and any Camp David type of autonomy (Tel Aviv, *Hadashot*, 3 January; *FBIS*, 11 January). Shuqayr pointed to several objectionable features of Israeli prime minister Yitzhak Shamir's proposals for elections (see *WMR*, Prague, November).

Writing during his one-year term in prison "for political activity," PCP member (and Bir Zeit physics lecturer) Taysir Aruri outlined the requirements for a peace settlement. He stressed "that the main objectives of each [side must] be realized" and that "a military solution" is no longer an option for anyone. He called for "full political, diplomatic, economic and other relations between the two states, Israel and Palestine," and cited "the experience of European states," in which "common interests, especially in the economic sphere" overshadow any possible conflict, as a model for emulation. (*Jerusalem Post*, 25 August; *FBIS*, 29 August.)

Auxiliary and Front Organizations. The PWB, which is closely tied to the PCP, has long dominated the General Federation of Trade Unions in the occupied areas. Communists have also been involved in student, professional, youth, and women's groups. This is in addition to the organizations created during the uprising (see above).

The PLO, which the PCP recognizes as the sole legitimate representative of the Palestinian people, has long been the equivalent of a government in exile, although the formality of declaring a Palestinian state did not come until the end of 1988. Its supporters and its leadership span the political spectrum, and the inclusion of a PCP representative in its Executive Committee, which is analogous to a cabinet, as well as representation in the PNC since 1987, would seem to qualify it as a popular front (or government of national unity) despite the peripheral role of the communists in the organization. The PLO's dominant component, Fatah, might itself be called a united front, since it avoids ideology in favor of pursuing a national cause. Its members are ideologically diverse, but it is dominated by centrists like Yasir Arafat. Fatah and the communists struggled with each other to control the Palestine National Front, which was formed in 1973 in the occupied areas, and each has blamed the other for its disintegration. The communists have accused Fatah of being dominated by rightists and of dependence on the support of conservative regimes in the Arab world. Small groups like the Popular Front for the Liberation of Palestine and the Democratic Front for the Liberation of Palestine—both of which are represented in the PLO institutions—are Marxist, but are not considered communist.

An additional reason for the PCP's success, together with an absence of sectarianism, is said to have been its avoidance of "dissipation in large popular fronts and the resultant loss of party identity" (Gresh, "Palestinian Communists and the Intifadah," p. 36).

International Views, Positions, and Activities. Only spotty information is available on the PCP's international activities during the year. Shuqayr participated in the Seventh Afro-Asian Peoples' Solidarity Organization Congress in New Delhi in 1988 (*WMR*, Prague, July); an interview with Mourad Ghaleb, the president of the organization, published in the April issue of *World Marxist Review* (Prague), was conducted by Shuqayr. Politburo (and PLO Executive Committee) member Sulayman al-Najjab was a member of a PLO delegation headed by Yasir Arafat that visited Moscow in January and met with Vladimir Buljakov, head of the Middle East Department of the Soviet Foreign Ministry (Sanaa, Voice of Palestine, 17 January;

FBIS, 18 January). A PCP delegation visited Moscow at the end of April (*Pravda*, 1 May). According to the PCP's general secretary, his party's "external activity" has been "invigorated" by the uprising and also by its representation in PLO institutions. He spoke of the "spirit of solidarity and cooperation" with other communist parties in the region, particularly the Communist Party of Israel (CPI), to which he expressed his party's gratefulness because of its "support" for "our struggle." (*WMR*, Toronto, August). Shuqayr also noted the existence of "contacts with some other realistic organisations in Israel," which he described as "fragmented" and as lacking a clear program (*WMR*, Toronto, February).

Recognizing that there has been some progress in the position of the United States on the Palestine question, Shuqayr accused it nevertheless of "manoeuvring in various ways" and of "playing for time" in the hope that Israel would suppress the uprising (*WMR*, Prague, November).

In an article in *World Marxist Review* (Toronto, December 1988), jointly written by Shuqayr and Lumir Hanak, a member of the Central Committee of the Communist Party of Czechoslovakia, a number of international developments, particularly the Soviet-American summit and the INF Treaty, were hailed as representing the beginning of "improvement in the international climate." The article also cited the importance of the Geneva accords on Afghanistan, despite the United States' and Pakistan's flaunting of "their unwillingness to honour their obligations." Giving most of the credit for the improvement to the USSR and the socialist countries generally, as well as to the nonaligned movement, the authors spoke of "those [in the United States] who would like to perpetuate the arms race and international tensions," and of continuing interference by imperialism throughout the world. Recent adoption by several communist parties of "the principles of openness, democracy and independence" was cited as beneficial to their activities and prestige.

Revolutionary Palestinian Communist Party (RPCP).

A breakaway faction called the RPCP, in existence since 1988 (possibly 1987), rejects the PCP's moderate position on the Palestine question. Based in Damascus, the RPCP is associated with the pro-Syrian Palestine National Salvation Front (see *Background Brief*, Foreign and Commonwealth Office, London, September). Its general secretary is Arabi Awwad, and the members of its Politburo include Jiryis Qawwas and Abdullah Nimir. Nothing else about its organizational structure and leadership is known.

A statement issued by the RPCP in May condemned Arafat for his recent abandonment of the Palestine National Charter. The statement specified "new political concessions" Arafat had made "as the price of his visit to France and his meeting with Mitterrand when he announced, with all impunity, his disavowal of the PLO charter, which he considers null and void; and when he declared his approval of elections in the occupied territories under the Shamir plan." Besides condemning these concessions, the statement warned that Arafat would try to stop the uprising "in response to the imperialist and Zionist pressure and conditions." The statement called on Palestinians to "escalate their intifadah and to foil the elections plot," as well as "to express their strong condemnations of . . . 'Arafatist concessions." (al-Quds Palestinian Arab Radio [clandestine], 3 May; *FBIS*, 4 May.) Condemning Prime Minister Shamir's proposals for elections, the RPCP warned against "the world-wide campaign carried out by the Zionist occupiers along with the American imperialism and all its supporters to impose Shamir's project" (Damascus, SANA, 16 May; *FBIS*, 17 May). Another statement by the RPCP leadership called Arafat's suggestion of an economic federation that would include Israel, Palestine, Lebanon, and Jordan, an indication of "the level reached by the rightist leadership which dominates the PLO," and warned that this represents "a readiness for brokering in favor of the Zionist ambition to spread economic hegemony over the region." The statement called the PLO leadership's behavior "humiliating" and "shameful" and "a stigma" to the Palestinian people (al-Quds Palestinian Arab Radio [clandestine], 20 February; *FBIS*, 21 February).

In August, an RPCP statement "condemned the French buildup off the Lebanese coast" (al-Quds Palestinian Arab Radio [clandestine], 24 August; *FBIS*, 25 August).

A communiqué issued by the RPCP reported that its "martyr Fahid 'Awwad group" had attacked Israeli forces and their allies of the South Lebanon Army in southern Lebanon on 12 April. It was stated that this action included an attack with missiles and automatic weapons on a radar station. (al-Quds Palestinian Arab Radio [clandestine], 12 April; *FBIS*, 13 April.) There is no confirmation either of this particular action or of the existence of any military force organized by the RPCP.

Glenn E. Perry
Indiana State University

Jordan

Population. 2,955,660 (World Factbook). West Bank is not included. After 31 July 1988, residents of the West Bank were no longer considered Jordanian citizens, nor the West Bank considered to be part of Jordan.
Party. Communist Party of Jordan (al-Hizb al-Shiyu'i al-Urduni; CPJ)
Date Founded. 1951
Membership. Accurate estimate not available
General Secretary. Dr. Ya'qub Zayadin
Politburo. No data
Secretariat. No data
Central Committee. 'Isa Madanat, Amal Naffa', Fa'iq Warrad, Ishaq al-Khatib, 'Awni Fakhir, 'Abd al-'Aziz al-'Ata, Fawwaz al-Zu'bi, Hashim Gharaybah, Ahmad Jaradat (partial list only)
Status. Illegal
Last Congress. Second, December 1983
Last Election. November 1989. 'Isa Madanat won a seat in an 80-seat parliament. Percentage of votes that went to other communist candidates is not available.
Auxiliary Organizations. None
Publications. *Al-Jamahir* (The masses); *al-'Amil* (The worker); *al-Haqiqah* (The truth)

Background. The origins of communist activity in Transjordan are to be found in labor-organizing efforts which culminated in 1932 in the establishment of a 2,000-member-strong Union of Jordanian Workers. However, Jordan's working class and intelligentsia were quite small in size, and after a few months the union collapsed. In general, the British-installed amir, 'Abdallah, attempted to neutralize most political parties in Transjordan: the communist party was never recognized, and in May 1948 it was proscribed by the Anti-Communist Law. Across the Jordan River, in the British mandate of Palestine, on the other hand, political parties were regulated by the Ottoman Organizations Law of 1907, and the communist movement was known as the National Liberation League ('Usbat al-Taharrur al-Watani).

Subsequent political developments—the incorporation by 'Abdallah into Jordan of the part of east central Palestine that had not become part of the state of Israel—eventually led to the merger of the two communist movements. The National Liberation League, headed by Fu'ad Nassar, had opposed 'Abdallah's moves, calling instead for the establishment of an independent Palestinian state in accordance with the U.N. General Assembly's partition resolution of 29 November 1947. However, in June 1951, the communists on both banks in effect recognized the reality of the annexation of the West Bank by merging their two movements and naming the new organization the Communist Party of Jordan.

In order to evade proscription and participate in the parliamentary elections of 1951, the party adopted the name of the Popular Front (al-Jabhah al-Sha'biyyah). Like most other parties in Jordan at that time, the Popular Front called for the abrogation of the Anglo-Jordanian Treaty and for the legalization of political parties and labor unions. In addition, it called for land distribution and industrialization to increase employment opportunities. Despite intimidation and arrest of candidates by the regime, three Front candidates, from Nablus and Hebron, were elected.

The Partisans for Peace (Jama'at Ansar al-Salam), associated with the Soviet-directed antinuclear movement, provided another forum for CPJ activity in the 1950s, in this case a forum that also attracted a variety of nationalists and establishment figures. The authorities restricted the activities of the Partisans, but were more concerned with the CPJ's covert organizational and propaganda activities on both banks. In the early 1950s, the party published an official organ, *al-Muqawimah al-Sha'biyyah* (Popular resistance), and, in 1952, *al-Jabhah* (The front) and *al-Ra'y* (Opinion). In order to cripple the party, the government arrested Fu'ad Nassar and four other key activists in December 1951.

Despite this blow and the subsequent 1953 amendment of the Law to Combat Communism, which made any association with party activities illegal and punishable by three to fifteen years in jail, the CPJ nevertheless entered the 1954 elections, this time under the name the National Front. More significant historically were the 1956 elections in which the communists with a variety of nationalist and pan-Arab parties called for the abrogation of the Anglo-Jordanian Treaty and protested the regime's rumored inclination to join the U.S.-British–sponsored Baghdad regional security pact. The CPJ received 13 percent of the 1956 vote and thereby became the first communist party in the

Arab East to be represented in a government cabinet. However, a foiled coup attempt in April 1957 led King Hussein to declare martial law, dissolve the parliament, outlaw political parties, and round up hundreds of activists, including hundreds of communists (most of whom remained in prison until the general amnesty of April 1965).

The decade between the 1957 crackdown and the 1967 war was a difficult one for the CPJ. It aligned itself with Egypt and Syria in accordance with the prevailing Soviet policy of cooperating with the national-bourgeois regimes in the Third World, and it benefitted from the Jordanian government's decision to establish full diplomatic relations with the Soviet Union, but as an outlawed organization it continued to operate clandestinely.

The party program issued in 1964 called for rapid industrialization, social-welfare legislation, and a nonaligned foreign policy for Jordan. In a move with longer-term implications for the integrity of Jordan, the CPJ endorsed the creation of the Palestine Liberation Organization (PLO) in May 1964. However, the then-burning issue of pan-Arabism raised potentially divisive problems for the party, and when the new official organ *al-Taqaddum* (Progress), published a front-page article that called Arab solidarity a positive trend and Jordan progressive, the party suffered its first serious internal split. Those responsible for the article were purged as right-wing deviationists.

The devastating defeat suffered in June 1967 by Jordan, Egypt, and Syria at the hands of Israel led not only to the occupation by Israel of substantial areas of Arab land, including Jordan's West Bank, but also served to discredit the Arab regimes involved. Jordan's economy was thrown into recession, and its military destroyed and discredited. It was in this atmosphere that the Palestinian Resistance Movement (PRM), based on Jordan's East Bank, began to attract large numbers of volunteers. The regime's loss of legitimacy provided a political opening for the resurfacing of various political movements, including the communists, and the period between 1967 and 1970 witnessed a flowering of political-organizational activity. However, since these still officially illegal organizations depended on the Palestinian resistance's protective umbrella, when the Jordanian regime moved against the PRM in 1970–1971, the defeat of the resistance meant the end of the period of relatively open political activity.

Illegal political activity re-emerged cautiously after the expulsion of the PRM from Jordan. The approach of the CPJ was given a boost to the extent that following 1971 many Palestinians realized the necessity of working in a larger Jordanian framework, rather than separately as Palestinians (independent of native East Bankers). The communist party had long pushed for political activity organized along class, rather than communal lines. The party remained illegal, as did all parties, but continued to operate, interrupted by periodic crackdowns, usually following major domestic or foreign policy problems. For example, following the student demonstrations in may 1986 at Yarmuk University in Irbid, the entire leadership of the CPJ was arrested, charged with responsibility for the unrest. The charge was unfounded—the unrest was the direct result of university-fee increases and student expulsions which took place against the background of growing dissatisfaction with U.S. Middle East policy (particularly following the bombing raid against Libya in April 1986) and frustration with domestic economic and political developments—but the seventeen detainees were not released until 4 September 1986. Activists from the CPJ, the Marxist Popular Front for the Liberation of Palestine (PFLP), and the Marxist Democratic Front for the Liberation of Palestine (DFLP) have continued to be the most frequently rounded-up suspects on such occasions.

Domestic Attitudes and Activities. Like other countries in the region, Jordan has witnessed an economic slow-down since the mid-1980s. However, beginning in late summer 1988, about the time of King Hussein's announcement of Jordan's legal and administrative disengagement from the West Bank, the value of the Jordanian dinar began to drop precipitously. The downward economic spiral along with increasing pressures for political liberalization led to growing discontent among various sectors in the country. Pressures grew until, as part of a debt-rescheduling agreement with the IMF, the government decided to reduce subsidies on certain items. The decision sparked the outbreak of riots on 18 April in Ma'an, a southern city and a traditional preserve of Hashemite support. The disturbances, called by some Jordan's intifadah (referring to the ongoing uprising in the West Bank and the Gaza Strip), soon spread to other cities, eventually reaching as far north as Salt and ultimately forcing the resignation of Prime Minister Zayd al-Rifa'i. Crown Prince Hasan blamed the riots on "extremist exploitation" and identified the instigators as Muslim fundamentalists (*CSM*, 21 April). Several hundred people were arrested in connection with the riots, among them doctors, writers, journalists, lawyers, engineers, trade-unionists, and students, many alleged to be members of the CPJ, as well as of the PFLP and the DFLP. Some of the detainees were released in two waves in the first and second weeks of May, the majority of the others (60) in early September (Amman Television Service, in English, 2 September; *FBIS*, 5 September). Immediately following the release orders, a number of prominent CPJ leaders who had been in hiding appeared in public. Most prominent among them were Ya'qub Zayadin (CPJ general secretary), 'Isa Madanat (Political Bureau member of the central committee of the CPJ), Imili Naffa', Amal Naffa', Dr. Munir Hamarnah, and Dr. Khalid Hamshawi. (*Al-Muharrir*, 9 September; *FBIS*, 12 September.)

In the wake of the April riots, the Jordanian government announced that general parliamentary elections, the first in 22 years, would be held on 8 November 1989. A new election law was also drafted, increasing the number of seats in the House of Representatives from 72 to 80, and taking into account the severing on 31 July 1988 of legal and administrative ties with the West Bank. As a result, West Bank representation in the Jordanian parliament was terminated, but the division of electoral districts continues to be based on sectarian and tribal concerns rather than the principle of proportional representation.

In the absence of any significant press freedom (the government completely reorganized the already closely controlled press in late August 1988), scores of political leaflets appeared in the kingdom in the wake of the riots. During the Muslim holy month of Ramadan, it was reported that communists had distributed pamphlets while Jordanians had been eating their meal breaking the fast (*Arab Times*, 5 June; *FBIS*, 8 June). Many leaflets, unsigned or signed with pseudonyms, attacked the government for corruption, secrecy, and financial mismanagement. Others, signed by former ministers and officials, called for ending martial law (in effect since 1967), legalizing political parties banned in 1957, and lifting a ban on the nomination of candidates who belong to "illegal organizations," a provision that applies mainly to members of the CPJ, Bathists, and adherents of various Palestinian factions. The king finally lifted this ban in late October 1989, thus allowing such candidates to stand for election, although not as representatives of the still-illegal parties.

Given the prospect of elections, there was a flurry of CPJ activity to unite the party, despite the fact that much of the party leadership had spent the previous five months in jail. As the party prepared for the elections, three strands were visible, that of CPJ general secretary Ya'qub Zayadin, that of former general secretary Fa'iq Warrad, as well as that of a group called the Lenin Cadre (which had first emerged during the CPJ's 1970 split). (*Al-Yawm al-Sabi'*, 6 October.)

CPJ member Imili Naffa' was among four prominent Jordanian women who participated in a public seminar and discussion of both the role of women in the elections and the political and economic decisionmaking process in Jordan. Naffa' had played a leading role in calling for the participation of women in the 1957 elections (the last relatively free elections in the country), and she is considered one of Jordan's most important female political figures. During the seminar, Naffa' argued that the current economic crisis constitutes a basic obstacle to political and social development, especially in matters relating to women. She stated, "We have before us an opportunity to participate effectively in addressing the factors that plague our society and stunt its development. Through women's societies and federations women must raise their consciousness to join the battle, and reject any tribal or religious factor that represents an element of influence on her decision." When asked on what basis Jordanian women should choose a candidate for whom to vote, she replied, "The best candidate is the one who is capable of safeguarding our rights as citizens and who exerts all of his or her efforts to terminate martial law." (*Al-Yawm al-Sabi'*, 9 October.)

Also as part of what was termed the general atmosphere of a "festival of democracy" sweeping the country, following the king's lifting of the ban on communists and others, a rally held for Zayadin attracted some 2,000 supporters, although many more were unable to squeeze into the theater where the event was held (*Middle East International*, 3 November).

Among the most important elements in Zayadin's election platform were calls for the following:

1. Greater freedom for citizens, including freedom of expression, freedom to organize political parties and trade unions, freedom of the press and writing;

2. An end to the application of the Defense Regulations; the release of political prisoners; respect for the authority and independence of the judiciary; and the cancellation of

all laws that limit these freedoms like the anticommunist law, the emergency regulations, arbitrary and administrative arrest, martial law, withholding passports, and forbidding citizens to work;

3. The repeal of the current election law and the drafting of a new one based on democracy and equality;

4. The opening up of Jordan's universities and the establishment of new universities capable of absorbing all Jordanian students; allowing students the right to form their own unions and societies;

5. The preservation of national independence and the termination of all remnants of imperialism; the dissolution of the American-Jordanian joint military committee and the cancellation of joint military maneuvers with the United States;

6. Providing all forms of aid and assistance to the Palestinian people, under the leadership of the PLO, on the basis of the program adopted by the nineteenth session of the Palestine National Council;

7. Providing all aid and assistance to the Palestinian uprising;

8. Standing firm against all plots and pressures of imperialism and Zionism that seek to bypass an international conference, and that seek to end the Palestinian problem through the "Jordanian option." (*Al-Yawm al-Sabi'*, 30 October.)

In a letter to the editor, Zayadin also underlined his rejection of the economic program Jordan had agreed upon earlier in the year with the IMF and called for its cancellation (*al-Ra'y*, 7 November; *FBIS*, 8 November).

Despite the CPJ's efforts, the only communist to win a seat in the new parliament was 'Isa Madanat (Kerak). Another candidate, associated with, but not a member of the CPJ, Fakhri Qa'war (Amman), also won a seat, but he did so at the expense of Zayadin, beating the CPJ general secretary by 600 votes. (*Al-Yawm al-Sabi'*, 2 November.) The Islamic movement won 20 of the 80 parliamentary seats (Amman Television Service, 10 November; *FBIS*, 13 November). The elections were regarded across the board as truly free and open, unprecedented in Jordan's history.

Party Internal Affairs. The CPJ has been plagued by numerous splits since 1970, the most recent of which, in 1987, came in the wake of several organizational measures taken by Zayadin and led a number of members of the Central Committee to form an independent wing of the party. Amal Naffa', a Central Committee Political Bureau member, published an article in February (*WMR*) in which he discussed some of the differences the party had experienced in the past. The broad social spectrum of the party's membership was given partial responsibility for past splits. Naffa' also stressed that the CPJ realizes it cannot succeed single-handedly: it must be willing to make alliances with other class forces, but at the same time be careful to preserve its identity. Naffa' mentioned two of the major sources of intraparty disagreement. The first concerned the role of the Ba'th Party: can the Ba'th be considered an ally, when in Syria it occasionally cooperates with the communists, but in Iraq kills communists? A second source of tension is the party's relationship with the PLO. The PLO at times cooperates with King Hussein or makes concessions to the United States, yet it has also rejected a U.S.-imposed Middle East settlement; it leads the struggle of the Palestinian people; and in 1988 declared an independent Palestinian state. Given these apparent contradictions what should be the CPJ's stance with regard to the PLO?

General Secretary Zayadin published an article in April (*WMR*) entitled "We Want Arab Unity." In the piece, Zayadin discussed the various factors that help shape a nation. He examined the role of imperialism and then went on to discuss the relationship between Islam and Arab nationalism, noting that there is no contradiction between the two. He drew a distinction between the nationalism of the oppressor and the nationalism of the oppressed, insisting that Arab nationalism "has a general democratic, progressive character which it is important to preserve and develop." He also stated, however, that "Arab unity has no final formula, but it must, in any case, be viable, democratic, and open, and must not provide the axis for an alliance aimed against others."

In early October, Zayadin held a meeting in an Amman suburb, in which the reasons for the party's past divisions were discussed. The meeting included a critique by Zayadin of himself and of his group and ended with the announcement of the reunification of the party and the return of a number of Central Committee members to their previous positions: Fa'iq Warrad, Ishaq al-Khatib, 'Awni

Fakhir, 'Abd al-'Aziz al-'Ata, Fawwaz al-Zu'bi, Hashim Gharaybah, and Ahmad Jaradat. Also as a result of the meeting, the party named eight candidates who would stand for elections: Zayadin (Amman's third district), Fawwaz al-Zu'bi (Amman's first district), 'Abd al-'Aziz al-'Ata (Zarqa' district), 'Isa Madanat (Karak district), Sa'ud Qubaylat (Madaba district), Ahmad Jaradat (Irbid district), Walid 'Atiwi (Tafilah district), and Dr. Mustafa Shunaykat (Balqa'-Salt district). (*Al-Yawm al-Sabi'*, 16 October.)

Also in response to the scheduling of elections was the formation of a new party, the Popular Democratic Party (al-Hizb al-Dimuqrati al-Sha'bi), affiliated with the Marxist DFLP. The party will reportedly work to protect human rights and alleviate the suffering of Jordan's poor. (Jerusalem Television Service, in Arabic, 26 July; *FBIS*, 28 July.)

No additional information is available on auxiliary or mass organizations.

International Views, Positions, and Activities. The year 1989 witnessed an unusual amount of interaction between Jordan and the Soviet Union, in part, no doubt, because of its deteriorating economic situation, and in part perhaps because of Jordan's frustration with the United States' position on peace in the Middle East, its continuing massive economic and military support of Israel, and its hesitancy to provide sophisticated weapons systems to its Arab allies.

In mid-January, it was announced that the USSR would import its first consignment of Jordanian phosphate, in implementation of an agreement signed the previous month. This announcement came after a meeting between Prime Minister Rifa'i and the Soviet ambassador to Jordan, Alexander Zinchuk, during which they reviewed cooperation in a number of fields. The two sides agreed that a Soviet technical committee should visit Jordan during January to pave the way for a joint Jordanian-Soviet ministerial committee meeting that would convene in March in Moscow. (*Jordan Times*, 12–13 January; *FBIS*, 19 January.)

As part of a major trip to the Middle East in February 1989 that included stops in Syria, Egypt, Iraq, and Iran, Soviet foreign minister Eduard Shevardnadze also stopped in Amman in what was viewed as a new Soviet diplomatic push for peace in the region. During his two-day visit to the Jordanian capital, the first such visit ever by a Soviet foreign minister, Shevardnadze stressed the importance the Soviet leadership placed on his visit to Jordan as well as the virtually identical positions on peace in the Middle East held by the two parties (Amman Television Service, in Arabic, 19 February; *FBIS*, 21 February).

In late April, Gennadiy Tarasov, USSR envoy to the Middle East, spent several days in Jordan, meeting with Deputy Prime Minister and Foreign Minister Marwan al-Qasim and King Hussein. Agreement was reached to step up bilateral contacts and strengthen the overall effort to end the Arab-Israeli conflict. Tarasov stated at a press conference at the airport before his departure that "it appears [from discussions with Jordanian officials] that Jordan and the Soviet Union have a common stand on the peace process" (*Jordan Times*, 3 May; *FBIS*, 3 May).

May was a particularly busy month for Jordanian-Soviet relations. On 23 May, a Soviet friendship delegation arrived, headed by Nikolay Tsakh, deputy minister in the Ministry of the USSR Maritime Fleet and chairman of the Soviet-Jordanian Friendship Society (Amman-Petra-JNA, 23 May; *FBIS*, 24 May). The following day, the experts' committee entrusted with preparations for the first session of the Jordanian-Soviet joint committee, began meetings in Amman at the Ministry of Trade and Industry. The Jordanian side was headed by Muhammad al-Saqqaf, secretary general of the Ministry of Industry and Trade, and the Soviet side by Mr. N. G. Yakubov, chief of economic relations with the Asian countries' main administration in the Ministry of Foreign Economic Relations. During the meetings Jordan urged the Soviet Union to open its markets to Jordanian products to balance trade between the two countries. (Jordan's imports of Soviet goods continue to increase annually at a time when Jordan has not been able to penetrate the Soviet market.) Also on 24 May, Jordanian minister of tourism Y. Hikmat and Nikolay Tsakh discussed cooperation in tourism; later, members of the visiting Soviet delegation met with Jordan's minister of culture and information, Nasuh al-Majali, to discuss bolstering bilateral relations and exchange in the cultural field (Amman Domestic Service, in Arabic, 24 May; *FBIS*, 25 May). In a related matter, the Jordanian cultural attaché in Moscow reported that nearly 3,000 Jordanian students were enrolled in Soviet universities in January 1989, and that nearly 120 are enrolling annually in various educational institutions in the Soviet Union. Most are studying medicine, and mechanical and aeronautical engineering. (*Jordan Times*, 14 January; *FBIS*, 19 January).

On 30 May, a cooperation agreement was signed

between Bahjat al-Talhuni, member of the Jordanian Senate and chairman of the Jordanian-Soviet Friendship Society and Nikolay Tsakh. The agreement provides for continuing the exchange of visits, holding friendship days on national and official occasions in both countries, continuing to grant scholarships to Jordanian students to study in the Soviet Union, exchanging motion pictures, exhibitions, information, publications, and the like. (*Sawt al-Sha'b*, 30 May; *FBIS*, 30 May.) Talhuni subsequently met in late October with Alfred Chipanis, deputy prime minister of the Latvian Soviet Socialist Republic and member of the Supreme Soviet Presidium, to review the existing relationship between Jordan and the Soviet Union and to continue discussions of regional issues (24 October, Amman Television Service; *FBIS*, 26 October).

On 30 May, a committee of Jordanian and Soviet experts signed minutes of talks held in Amman regarding a project to produce phosphoric acid with Jordanian raw materials, as well as the possibility of cooperation to reopen the timber factory in Aqabah. The minutes also included a discussion of means to promote and bolster bilateral trade, establishing commercial centers and fairs, and expanding tourism. (Amman-Petra-JNA, 30 May; *FBIS*, 1 June.)

On 4 July, King Hussein sent a cable to Soviet president Mikhail Gorbachev expressing his condolences on the death of former Soviet leader Andrei Gromyko (Amman Domestic Service, in Arabic, 4 July; *FBIS*, 11 July).

Jordan's deputy prime minister and minister of state for economic affairs Tahir al-Masri traveled to the Soviet Union on 8 August in order to arrange for a rescheduling of Jordan's debt to the Soviet Union. It is estimated that the installments due to be paid by Jordan to the USSR during the years 1989 and 1990 total approximately $100 million. (Radio Monte Carlo, 2 August; *FBIS*, 4 August.) The total debt is believed to be $200 million (*al-Muharrir*, 29 July; *FBIS*, 2 August). The debts are primarily those incurred by Jordan in purchasing air-defense systems from the Soviets after the United States balked at selling Stinger surface-to-air missiles to Amman (*Insight*, 4 September). As a result of al-Masri's talks with Konstantin Katushev, Soviet minister of foreign economic relations, the two countries agreed to exchange annually, and in equal amounts, products worth $50 million. The two sides also agreed to consolidate bilateral relations of cooperation in various industrial and technological fields: two projects to produce phosphoric acid and tim-

ber; joint agricultural projects; setting up of trade centers; and tourist and cultural exchange (*Sawt al-Sha'b*, 21 August; *FBIS*, 25 August).

Gennadiy Tarasov returned to Jordan on 27 August after meetings in Damascus and discussed a number of bilateral issues, including Moscow's role in achieving stability in the region, especially with regard to the situation in Lebanon. During the visit, Marwan al-Qasim met with Tarasov and expressed Jordan's appreciation for the Soviet support of Arab causes, especially its stand on the Lebanese crisis and its constant support in the Palestine question. (Amman Domestic Service, 27 August; *FBIS*, 28 August.)

On 7 October, King Hussein sent a cable to Erich Honecker, president of the Democratic Republic of Germany, congratulating him on his country's national day (Amman Domestic Service, 7 October; *FBIS*, 11 October).

In the field of relations with Soviet clients in the region, Jordan received the foreign minister of the People's Democratic Republic of Yemen (PDRY; South Yemen) in late February 1989. During his stay, PDRY foreign minister Dr. 'Abd al-'Aziz al-Dali met with Marwan al-Qasim and Zayd al-Rifa'i. Foremost among the topics discussed was the recent formation of the Arab Cooperation Council, whose members include Egypt, Iraq, Jordan, and the Republic of Yemen (North Yemen). (*Al-Ra'y*, 27 February; *FBIS*, 28 February.)

On the heels of this visit came a five-day visit of an industry delegation from the People's Republic of China, headed by Wang Rulin, PRC minister of metallurgical industry. In addition to meetings with various officials, Rulin was scheduled to visit the al-Hasan Sports City project near Irbid, which is being financed by China and built by a Chinese company. (Amman-Petra-JNA, 1 March; *FBIS*, 1 March). PRC foreign minister Qian Qichen arrived in Amman on 16 September for a visit which included talks on peace in the Middle East and on bilateral cooperation in the agricultural, industrial, commercial, and economic fields (Amman Domestic Service, 16 September; *FBIS*, 18 September).

Laurie A. Brand
University of Southern California

Lebanon

Population. 3,300,802 (*World Fact Book*, 1989)
Parties. Lebanese Communist Party (al-Hizb al-Shuyu'i al-Lubnani; LCP); Organization of Communist Action in Lebanon (Munazzamat al-'Amal al-Shuyu'i; OCAL)
Founded. LCP: 1924; OCAL: 1970
Membership. LCP: 14,000–16,000 (claimed); 2,000–3,000 (CIA estimate, *World Fact Book*, 1989); OCAL: 1,500 (see *YICA*, 1989)
General Secretary. LCP: George Hawi; OCAL: Muhsin Ibrahim
Politburo. LCP: 11 members
Central Committee. LCP: 24 members
Status. Legal
Last Congress. LCP: Fifth, February 1987; OCAL: First, 1971
Last Election. 1972, no representatives
Auxiliary Organizations. LCP: Communist Labor Organization, World Peace Council in Lebanon, and a number of student unions and movements
Publications. LCP: *al-Nida'* (The call), daily, publishers are 'Abd al-Karim Muruwwa and George Hawi; *al-Akhbar* (The news) weekly; *al-Tariq* (The road) quarterly. OCAL: *al-Hurriya* (Freedom) weekly, publisher is Muhsin Ibrahim

Background. In 1989 the situation in Lebanon reached another climax in the fourteen-year-old conflict which began in 1975. Local and regional factors led to a major explosion in March when General Michel 'Awn (see *YICA*, 1989) launched a "war of liberation" against Syrian troops in Lebanon. General 'Awn vowed to crush the militias and blockade their illegal ports. As a result Syrian-backed militias blockaded the Christian enclave, touching off six months of artillery battles that left more than 900 people dead. In South Lebanon, the LCP pursued its guerrilla activity against the Israeli-backed South Lebanon Army (for more information see *YICA*, 1988 and 1989). In September, the LCP claimed responsibility for an attempt to infiltrate northern Israel which resulted in heavy casualties on both sides (*FBIS*, 12 September). In late December, about 100 Israeli commandos backed by tanks and helicopter gunships destroyed two bases belonging to the LCP in South Lebanon (*NYT*, 27 December). As a result of the fighting in Lebanon, and at the initiative of Kuwait, the Arab League's Council of Foreign Ministers, designated a seven-member committee to find a solution to the conflict in Lebanon.

Leadership and Organization. The LCP's highest organ is the congress which convenes every five years and elects the Central Committee. Since 1924, the LCP has held only five congresses. Since 1979, George Hawi has served as the general secretary of the LCP. Since its foundation in 1970, OCAL was and is still led by Muhsin Ibrahim.

Domestic Views and Activities. In February, George Batal, member of the Politburo, wrote that "Imperialism and the Zionist circles have been laboring to split Lebanon and to extend the same disunity to other neighboring states" (*WMR*, February). Among the major tasks facing the LCP and its allies was that of ensuring that "military-fascist rule is opposed throughout the nation."

In Damascus, a political and military agreement was reached between the pro-Iranian Hizb Allah and the Shi'ite Amal Movement (for background information see *YICA*, 1988 and 1989). A spokesperson for the Politburo declared that the LCP welcomed the accords between the two Shi'ite militias. However, the LCP urged that this agreement be consolidated at a national, nonsectarian level, given that the fate of South Lebanon is not solely limited to the Shi'ite community but should be perceived in the wider context of resistance to the Israeli occupation (*al-Nida'*, 3 February).

Since the beginning of the conflict in Lebanon the LCP has advocated political reforms as a fundamental condition for stopping the bloodshed in the country. Political reforms were part and parcel of any agreement to elect a new president of Lebanon. Furthermore, the LCP has constantly stressed the issue of the Israeli occupation of South Lebanon and denounced Israel's policy of expelling residents of the "Security Zone" from their villages and houses.

These stands adopted by the LCP were reaffirmed in a statement issued by the Politburo following meetings in Damascus between Syrian vice-president Abdel-Halim Khaddam and George Hawi (*al-Nida'*, 7 February). The LCP praised also the assessment made by the Arab ministerial committee. The committee underlined Lebanon's Arab identity and that it was part of the Arab world, and stressed that political reforms should be implemented concurrently with the holding of presidential elections. The LCP's statement clarified the conditions for a possible success in the execution of the Arab committee's task. For the LCP, Lebanon's unity, sovereignty, and territorial integrity must be taken into consideration. In addition, the LCP called on the Arab ministerial committee to support the Lebanese resistance forces in South Lebanon and the Western Bekaa. According to the Politburo's communiqué, resistance to Israeli occupation in South Lebanon is the fundamental issue in any attempt to find a solution to the Lebanese crisis (*al-Nida'*, 7 February).

In its mediation efforts the Arab League's ministerial committee faced the daunting task of reconciling the opposing stands taken by the various parties in Lebanon. General 'Awn and his allies in the Christian enclave had different priorities from those of the LCP and the Syrian-backed groups in Lebanon. For 'Awn and the Lebanese Forces, the main issue in Lebanon was the presence of Syrian troops on Lebanese soil. Syria's policies and meddling in Lebanon had become the main target of the Christian Lebanese conservative forces. For General 'Awn, Lebanon had to be freed from foreign occupation before any talks on reforms and presidential elections (see interview with General 'Awn, *FBIS*, 31 October).

In the aftermath of the Israeli invasion of Lebanon in 1982, numerous Christian families fled their houses and properties in the Druze-dominated Shuf Mountains. Early in the year, Walid Joumblatt, leader of the Progressive Socialist Party (PSP), had proposed a plan to repatriate the Christian refugees back to the Shuf. This initiative was foiled when one of the most prominent personalities in the PSP, Anwar al-Fata'iri, was assassinated (see *al-Nida'*, 10 February). The LCP and the PSP have been close allies since the eruption of the strife in Lebanon, and are both members of the Nationalist Parties, a coalition of progressive forces formed in the early days of the war in Lebanon. In April, meeting at the residence of 'Asim Qansuh, head of the pro-Syrian segment of the Ba'th Party, the Nationalist Parties set their conditions for a solution to the conflict in Lebanon. First, they called for the "abolition of political sectarianism, the amendment of the Constitution and all legislation, and the purge of the Lebanese Army." Second, the Nationalist Parties called for the liberation of Lebanon from Israeli occupation; and third, they called for the "confirmation of Lebanon's Arabism, which can

only be attained through its distinguished relations with Syria." (*FBIS*, 4 April.) Representatives of the Nationalist Parties, including George Hawi, met in Damascus with Kuwait's deputy premier and the Arab League's general secretary, Chedli Klibi (*FBIS*, 6 April).

By late April, the situation in Lebanon had reached a new height in violence. Heavy bombardments occurred on both sides of the Green Line dividing East from West Beirut. On 23 April, and at the initiative of the Maronite Patriarch, Nasrallah Butros Sfeir, 23 Christian deputies called for a cease-fire and dialogue to end the conflict in Lebanon. In West Beirut, Lebanese parliamentarians and Syrian-backed political forces met to call for a cease-fire and show their support of the Arab League's initiative. General 'Awn reacted negatively to all these attempts at dialogue and emphasized again his intention to free Lebanon from the Syrian presence. In an interview with *L'Humanité*, Hawi described 'Awn's stand as "suicidal" and said that there were three reasons for the general's attitude. "The first is ambition." The second reason according to Hawi was the encouragement of Iraq's Saddam Hussein, who supplied money and weapons to 'Awn and the Lebanese Forces of Samir Ja'ja'. The third reason was that "'Awn and the other reactionary forces knew that the Arab League Commission was going to propose political reforms." For Hawi, 'Awn and his allies' behavior must be explained in light of their total opposition to any proposals for political reforms before the liberation of the country (see *FBIS*, 10 May).

An important characteristic of the Lebanese conflict is the recourse to political assassinations to eliminate prominent figures. This was the case of the Druze leader Kamal Joumblatt who was assassinated in March 1977; Bashir Gemayel, the founder of the Lebanese Forces, who was killed in September 1982; and Lebanon's former prime minister, Rashid Karameh, who was killed in June 1987, on his way to Beirut from his hometown of Tripoli. On 16 May 1989, another prominent figure fell victim to the wanton violence that had engulfed Lebanon since March of that year. Sheikh Hassan Khaled, the Sunni Mufti of the Republic, was blown up in his car in one of the suburbs in West Beirut. As a result of this tragic assassination, a spokesman for the LCP stated that the killing of Khaled was "part of a series of heinous crimes perpetrated by the enemies of Lebanon, the purpose of which was to hit Lebanon's vital symbols in order to provoke further divisions and strife" (al-Nida', 17 May). The Mufti's assassination was perceived by the LCP and its allies as another attempt to undermine efforts to end the latest battles which had erupted in the early part of the year. In the meantime, preparations were afoot for the convening of the eighteenth Arab summit, which was held in Casablanca in the last week of May.

At that meeting, the Arab heads of states asserted that in Lebanon priority must be given to political reforms, which must be effected before the election of a new president. The other resolution adopted at the Casablanca summit included the dispatching of Arab observers to Lebanon to monitor the implementation of the cease-fire and the creation of a Tripartite Committee, which included King Hassan II of Morocco, King Fahd of Saudi Arabia, and Algeria's President Shazli Ben Jadid (see al-Nida', 28 May).

In July, Israeli commandos mounted an operation in the southern Lebanese village of Jibsheet and kidnapped Sheikh 'Abd-al-Karim 'Ubayd, a pro-Iranian religious leader. The Israeli raid was linked to the kidnapping of Lieutenant Colonel Richard Higgins, an American officer attached to the United Nations observation troops in South Lebanon. The abduction of 'Ubayd was denounced by Hizb Allah and Amal. The Israeli action coincided also with the faltering of Arab efforts two months after the summit in Casablanca. The foreign ministers of Algeria, Morocco, and Saudi Arabia issued a statement declaring their inability to convince the parties in Lebanon to implement a plan for reforms they had prepared after extensive consultations.

In early August, the LCP issued a statement in reaction to the rapid succession of events since the Casablanca summit. The LCP Politburo accused Israel and the United States of responsibility for the abduction of Sheikh 'Ubayd. The LCP statement went on to say that the massing of the U.S. fleet near Lebanon's territorial waters, the Israeli actions in South Lebanon, the military escalation by General 'Awn and his "isolationist alliance," the Iraqi escalation, and the failure of the Arab committee's efforts "reveal the extent of the danger of the American-Israeli-Arab reactionary onslaught against Lebanon and its forces resisting the Israeli occupation and sectarian hegemony" (al-Nida', 6 August; FBIS, 8 August). By mid-August major battles had taken place in Souk-el-Gharb, a key position for the defense of the presidential palace in Baabda, where 'Awn had been residing since September 1988. The Politburo issued a statement praising the battles that

had occurred in Souk-el-Gharb between the popular liberation army—in which LCP forces participated—and the soldiers of General 'Awn. The LCP called for the expansion of the war of confrontation and the creation of an enlarged Lebanese front "to wage the battle of national salvation in defense of the interests of the majority of the Lebanese people" (al-Nida', 18 August).

The Arab-sponsored peace efforts were given a major boost when members of the Lebanese parliament convened in al-Ta'if (in Saudi Arabia) and adopted the Arab League's plan of reforms (NYT, 23 November). The peace plan was rejected by General 'Awn because it did not specify a precise timetable for Syrian withdrawal from Lebanon. The Arab plan was also rejected on the grounds that it reduced the control of the Maronite Christians over the levers of power in Lebanon and gave a major role in government to the Muslims (CSM, 21 November). By early December, Lebanon saw the election of René Mu'awwad, a Maronite, as president. He was assassinated after only seventeen days in power. Mu'awwad was immediately replaced by Ilyas al-Hirawi, who was elected in a hastily called session of the Lebanese parliament in the Syrian-controlled Bekaa Valley (Time, 4 December).

International Views and Contacts. At the regional level, the LCP maintained and consolidated its relations with other communist and progressive parties and forces in the Middle East. In February, the Central Committee sent a letter of congratulations to the Iranian leadership on the tenth anniversary of the Iranian Revolution (al-Nida', 14 February). After the death of Ayatollah Khomeini, George Hawi visited Teheran to present his condolences to Khomeini's successor, Ayatollah Khamene'i. This close relationship between the LCP and Iran and the heavy criticisms leveled against Iraq's involvement and support of General 'Awn led to tensions between the LCP and the Ba'th regime in Baghdad. In an analysis published in al-Thawrah, the official daily of the Ba'th Party, Hawi's visit to Teheran was harshly criticized. The Iraqi newspaper in fact wrote that Hawi's visit can be explained in light "of the crisis not only in Hawi's party but also of the other Arab communist parties that are desperately seeking to escape from the dire consequences awaiting them." The Iraqi newspaper criticized the Arab communist parties of total subservience to the USSR "at the expense of basic national and pan-Arab interests" (FBIS, 17 August).

In 1989, al-Nida' celebrated the 30th anniversary of its first publication. Several congratulatory dispatches were sent by, among others, the Cuban newspaper *Granma*, the Soviet news agency Novosti, the East German newspaper *Neues Deutschland*, the Palestinian Communist Party, and the head of the Popular Front for the Liberation of Palestine (PFLP), George Habbash (see *al-Nida'*, 12, 18, 19, and 21, February and 11 March).

In March, and at the invitation of the Central Committee of the Yemen Socialist Party, LCP officials Karim Muruwwa, Yusif Mortada, and Iqbal Saba, visited the People's Democratic Republic of Yemen (*al-Nida'*, 11 March). This visit was followed later in the year by that of the secretary general of OCAL, Muhsin Ibrahim (*FBIS*, 17 October).

The LCP's George Hawi met with Georges Marchais, general secretary of the French Communist Party (PCF). In the course of the encounter, Marchais expressed his solidarity and "supported the appeal made by the Arab League commission in its efforts to create the right conditions for a political solution based on the democratic reforms which guarantee a sovereign, independent, united and democratic Lebanon, free from any foreign presence" (*FBIS*, 4 May).

In 1989, the LCP participated also in the tenth Lebanese National Labor Union Congress. Several foreign trade union representatives attended, including Giorgio Cremaschi, a member of the Italian Confederation of Labor (CGIL) (see interview with Cremaschi in *al-Nida'*, 28 February).

In January a joint delegation of the PSP and the LCP visited Bulgaria and were received by Milko Balev, Politburo member and secretary of the Central Committee of the Bulgarian Communist Party. The two sides emphasized that "as a result of the favorable impact of new political thinking on international affairs," the time was ripe to convene an international conference on the Middle East. The participants in the meeting "welcomed the heroic uprising of the Palestinian people in the Israeli occupied territories" (*FBIS*, 27 January). In May, LCP officials George Hawi, George Batal, and Rafiq Shamun met in Prague with Miloš Jakeš, general secretary of the Communist Party of Czechoslovakia (*FBIS*, 18 May).

The advent of *perestroika* and *glasnost'* did not alter the strong and consistent support of the LCP for the Soviet Union (see *YICA*, 1988 and 1989). Reacting to Gorbachev's new political thinking, Hawi wrote that "new thinking is an integral part of perestroika... We can claim to be Communists only when we are the most resolute champions of democracy and humanism." Hawi went on to assert that the major challenge facing *perestroika* was to find a solution to the fact that "although the working class and its party are in power, people do not feel that it is they who are running the country" (*WMR*, August).

The impact of *glasnost'* on Soviet policy in the Middle East was illustrated by the USSR's ambassador to Syria, Alexander Zotov. In an interview with Milton Viorst, Zotov stated that the Soviet Union is "embarked on a period of cooperation with the United States, the depth of which is yet to be established... Each of us knows that we can't push the other out of the area. To use (George) Bush's term, we are beyond containment." Another important point raised by Zotov is the status of the relationship between Syria and the Soviet Union. In light of the Syrian role and presence in Lebanon, it is important to report the Soviet diplomat's remarks. Zotov said that Syria's president Assad agreed with the USSR that a "military solution to Middle East problems is not in the cards." Zotov explained that the USSR's approach to peace "is not a strict military balance." Syria, according to the Soviet diplomat, had to abandon its concept of "strategic parity with Israel." (For details see Milton Viorst, "The Shadow of Saladin," in *The New Yorker*, 8 January 1990.)

In Lebanon itself, while continuing its support of the LCP, the USSR expanded the scope of its diplomatic activity to find a settlement to the strife in the country. In May, following a meeting in Moscow between U.S. secretary of state James Baker and his Soviet counterpart, Eduard Shevardnadze, a joint statement was issued regarding the situation in Lebanon. In it the two superpowers called for an immediate cease-fire and expressed their support for the Arab League's efforts to find a solution to the Lebanese conflict. Reacting to the Baker-Shevardnadze statement, 'Abd al-Karim Muruwwa, publisher of *al-Nida'*, declared that it was of "great importance," given that it was the first statement to be issued by the two superpowers for a long time. Muruwwa underlined that the joint U.S.-Soviet statement did not address certain matters raised by Shevardnadze, namely the call for Israeli withdrawal from South Lebanon and the implementation of United Nations Security Council resolutions regarding the sovereignty and territorial integrity of Lebanon (*al-Nida'*, 14 May).

Since the crisis began in March, the Soviet ambassador in Lebanon, Vasily Kolotusha, maintained his contacts with the contending parties in the

Lebanese conflict (see *YICA*, 1989). In August, Gennadiy Tarasov, a special Soviet envoy to the Mideast visited Syria and Lebanon. In Damascus, Tarasov met with the Syrian foreign minister, Faruq al Shar', and both agreed to set up a committee to monitor the cease-fire in Lebanon (*FBIS*, 24 August). In Lebanon, Tarasov met with Prime Minister Dr. Salim al-Huss, the speaker of the Chamber of Deputies Husayn al-Husayni, the Maronite Patriarch Sfeir, and General Michel 'Awn. In the course of his meetings the Soviet envoy stressed the USSR's support for the "revival of the tripartite committee's activities." The purpose of the Soviet initiative was to "reactivate the practical efforts for initiating the real national dialogue and to reactivate the Arab and international efforts." Regarding the plan for reforms adopted in al-Ta'if, Kolotusha stated that the Soviet Union would work for the implementation of the al-Ta'if accord because it contains a "common denominator" shared by the Lebanese parties, and that this accord "is what could be achieved after 14 years of war." (*FBIS*, 25 August.)

Publications. Publications of the LCP include the daily Arabic language *al-Nida'*, the weekly *al-Akhbar*, and the journals *al-Tariq* (The road), *al-Thaqafa al Wataniyya* (National culture), *al-Wakt* (The time), and *Sawt al-'Amil* (The worker's voice). The LCP has also a publication in the Armenian language, the weekly *Kanch* (The call). The LCP-operated radio station Sawt al-Sha'b (Voice of the people) has been broadcasting since 1987 (*WMR*, August).

George Emile Irani
Guilderland, New York

Morocco

Population. 25,605,579
Party. Party of Progress and Socialism (Parti du progres et du socialisme, PPS)
Founded. 1943 (PPS, 1974)
Membership. An estimated 4–5,000; the PPS and *World Marxist Review* claim membership in excess of 50,000.

Composition. Unknown
General Secretary. 'Ali Yata
Politburo. 'Ali Yata, Ismail Alaoui, Muhammad Ben Bella, Abdessalam Bourquia, Muhammad Rifi Chouaib, Abdelmajid Bouieb, Umar al-Fassi, Thami Khyari, Abdallah Layachi, Mohamed Moucharik, Abdelwahab Souhail, Amina Lemrini
Secretariat. Umar al-Fassi, Abdallah Layachi, Mohamed Moucharik, Abdelwahab Souhail
Central Committee. An estimated 65–70 members
Status. Legal
Last Congress. Fourth, National Congress, 17–19 July 1987, in Casablanca; meets every four years; total number of delegates at congress: 1,339
Last Election. 14 September 1984. PPS obtained 2 out of 306 seats in the country's parliament.
Auxiliary Organizations. Moroccan Youth of Progress and Socialism (Jeunesse marocaine du progres et du socialisme; JMPS)
Publications. *Al-Bayan* (The manifesto) in both Arabic and French; *al-Bayan al-Taqafi* (The cultural manifesto); *al-Iqtisadi wa al-Mujtama'* (Economy and society; in French and Arabic); *Nisa' al-Maghrib* (Women of Morocco); and *al-Wujud* (Presence)

Background. The Parti communiste marocain (PCM) was founded in 1943 as a branch of its French counterpart, the French Communist Party. It was subsequently banned in 1952 by the French government during the protectorate period. Although legalized when the country gained independence in 1956, it was again banned in 1959 and reemerged fifteen years later in 1974 under the name of the Party of Progress and Socialism (PPS). Since then the PPS has participated in all municipal and national elections, garnering marginal support at the local and regional level (two seats on the Casablanca city council in 1983; two seats in national elections in 1984).

Leadership and Party Organization. The latest PPS national congress, held in July 1987, reelected 'Ali Yata as general secretary of the party, along with most of the old members of the Central Committee. At the same time, the congress elected a thirteen-member Politburo and a number of new members to its Secretariat and its financial commission. The election did not show the infusion of a substantial number of new members into the party, an indication that it has not been able to attract a growing number of Moroccans to its programs.

Domestic Party Affairs. The year 1989 was marked in Morocco overwhelmingly by an attempt to move toward a settlement of the question of the Western Sahara, almost to the exclusion of any other political initiative inside the country. The result has been that the PPS, as have all other opposition movements, has been forced to spend a considerable amount of time and energy formulating a stand on the Sahrawi problem. In general, this has again made two things abundantly clear regarding the PPS's role and standing inside the kingdom.

The first is that, as General Secretary Yata conceded, the PPS has no chance of unilaterally bringing about change in the country's political system. As in the past, the PPS has carefully sought to coordinate—or at least to echo— the positions taken by other organizations. Yata's observation was prompted by the unsuccessful attempts made in Parliament to introduce a number of amendments to regular legislation and to the submitted budget proposals, a repeat of what happened last year. The more or less formal opposition coalition that had been formed at the end of 1987 continued to press jointly for changes, but it was clear that it had lost some of its initial cohesion, and that the king's policies had undercut much of its original rationale. The government continued to reject the PPS and other opposition intervention out of hand, which led Yata to repeat his views that Morocco's leadership was not interested in moving toward a more pluralist, democratic form of government.

The second circumstance clearly shown in 1989 was Morocco's continued commitment to economic liberalization. The PPS, in conjunction with the Istiqlal party—now the country's leading political opposition party, but once the torchbearer during the struggle for independence—have taken similar stands on safeguarding the rights of poorer Moroccans by preventing privatization of certain elements of the state sector. At the same time, the PPS has also stressed its commitment to a "national" education that is simultaneously universal and Arabized. While the government has moved cautiously in regard to the latter, emphasizing its broad commitment to a "culturally valid" education, it is clear that its commitment to a more pronounced market-oriented economy remains strong. The PPS was not able this year, as in the past, to disseminate its message clearly to the country's workers. Although there were some isolated incidents involving the

country's labor force, there is no evidence that they are linked in any way to the PPS; they seem rather to have been spontaneous expressions of dissatisfaction. Despite what the PPS has claimed, there is not in Morocco a clearly articulated feeling of economic disenfranchisement that can be channeled into a forceful opposition movement. Yata himself has in the past been forced to admit on several occasions that the PPS has no clear political or economic platform to replace that of the government, and certainly does not have either the political organization or charisma and political skills of King Hassan II.

Yata and his supporters have pointed out the fragile bases on which the Moroccan economy rests—it is in part a rentier economy dependent on internationally determined prices for phosphates and phosphoric acid, over which it has no control—and have singled out the growing international debt crisis as an indication of a mounting economic and financial dependence. All of this has been linked to what Yata sees as an unavoidable phenomenon under such circumstances: the complete political disenfranchisement of a large section of the population, whose living conditions, housing, employment problems, and social provisions continue to deteriorate as economic privatization creates an even greater social bifurcation. For Yata, the economic direction will clearly mean greater prosperity for a few, at the expense of the greater part of Morocco's population. As in the past, the PPS has been particularly vocal in demanding adequate housing and health provisions for Moroccans—two sectors in which they see the intrusions of the new economic policies leading to speculation, great profits for the local bourgeoisie, and little or no control by the government over potential abuses. Education finally also has been singled out as a target for the PPS's accusation that the government is no longer committed to providing a decent education for all Moroccans. The result, according to the PPS, will inevitably be even greater unemployment and even more pronounced socio-economic divisions, which can only lead to increased tension inside the country.

Auxiliary Organizations. The Moroccan Youth of Progress and Socialism (JMPS) has continued to stress a number of issues in *al-Bayan*. Most important among these in 1989 have been solidarity with the Palestinian intifadah and the right of Moroccan youth to obtain meaningful work. The most important statements, however, have centered on the creation of the Arab Maghreb Union, and the opportunities it offers to extend and consolidate the common concerns of the region's communist parties into one coherent program. The JMPS has called on their counterparts in Algeria and Tunisia to take a unified stand on the Arabization process and on a whole range of social and political issues. It noted with satisfaction that the problems of the past (that is, the tensions between Morocco and Algeria over the Western Sahara) had been removed, and that true progress toward a unified position was now possible.

International Views, Positions, and Activities. The possibility of greater interaction between the Maghribi countries and the lessening of regional tensions continued to absorb much of the energy of the PPS. It has clearly perceived—much like its counterparts in Algeria and Tunisia—that unity among the communist parties may perhaps afford an amount of leverage they have not possessed individually in the past. Although it remains hampered by organizational obstacles, the PPS has forcefully argued that the best way to achieve regional cooperation is to create mass organizations and professional organizations whose activities extend beyond national boundaries. Yata has identified these potential large mass-based organizations as possible foci for popular membership that would allow them simultaneously to reduce the impact of the region's official or officially-sponsored parties. While Yata has been supportive of a regional parliament, he has argued for the creation of these grass-roots organizations that could then influence the overarching political instruments created by those in power in each country. Caught up in the enthusiasm for the promises of the Arab Maghreb Union, the PPS has paid relatively little attention to the remainder of the world, only cautiously praising the developments in Eastern Europe.

Dirk Vandewalle
Dartmouth College

Saudi Arabia

Population. 16,108,539
Party. Communist Party of Saudi Arabia (CPSA)
Founded. 1975
Membership. Number unknown but believed negligible
General Secretary. Mahdi Habib
Other Spokesmen Noted Since 1979. Abd-al-Rahman Salih, Salim Hamid, Abu Abdallah, Muhsin Abdallah, Hamad al-Mubarak (Politburo member)
Status. Illegal
Last Congress. Third, August 1989
Last Election. N/a
Auxiliary Organizations. Saudi Peace and Solidarity Committee (affiliate of the World Peace Council and Afro-Asian Peoples' Solidarity Organization), Saudi Democratic Youth (affiliate of World Federation of Democratic Youth), Workers' Federation of Saudi Arabia (associate member of World Federation of Trade Unions), Democratic Women's League of Saudi Arabia (affiliate of Women's International Democratic Federation), Committee for the Defense of Human Rights–Saudi Arabia
Publication. *Tariq al-Qadyhin* (The road of the working people)

In a sketch, presumably submitted by the party itself, the CPSA claimed to be active in "democratic organizations" in each of the fields covered by the list above plus the "movement of progressive democratic intellectuals." It highlights its "traditional" strength among the oil workers and notes its efforts to form a broad "patriotic" front to overthrow the Saudi monarchy. This assessment was given in *First Hand Information* (Alexander Subbotin, editor; Prague: Peace and Socialism International Publishers, p. 105), which had been made available to the press on 16 August 1988.

General Secretary Mahdi Habib's article in the March issue of *World Marxist Review* went into detail describing the "progressive" elements which he felt had the potential for membership in the aforenoted "patriotic front," elaborating on the pro-modernization sector of the "national bourgeoisie" (as contrasted with the "parasitic, bureaucratic and compradore strata" of that socioeconomic grouping), and identifying the "modernist" intelligentsia (both the "realistic/progressive/democratic" and the "structural liberal bourgeois"—as contrasted with the "doctrinaire and traditionalist" portion of this grouping). Habib alleges that the Saudi government tries to mollify each of these potential elements of a "patriotic front" without making any significant concessions to them and often uses Islamic fundamentalist "pressures" as an excuse. Meanwhile, those already committed to a "democratic" course are said to be suffering under "a wave of terror and repression." (*WMR*, Toronto, March.) Interestingly, in the July issue of *World Marxist Review* it is noted that the bulk of the CPSA members are "believers," and that this is entirely consistent with the party's statutes, a position that would certainly be necessary for any serious attempt to establish a united front in the country.

The available accounts of the CPSA's Third Congress, said to have been held in August (place not given), reiterate the stress on building up a broad "patriotic" front. They also seem to imply that propaganda is a major vehicle for doing this (an emphasis to be found in the aforenoted *First Hand Information* article as well; p. 105). Foreign-policy themes coming out of this meeting were the elimination of foreign military bases in the Near East, peace between Iraq and Iran, withdrawal of all Israeli troops from Arab territories occupied in 1967, creation of an independent Palestinian state, and support for all the various reforms taking place in the USSR. (*Pravda*, 2 September; *Neues Deutschland*, 5 September.)

The National Preparatory Committee of Saudi Arabia, presumably including members of the aforenoted Saudi Democratic Youth, was reported to have sent a delegation to the Pyongyang World Youth Festival in July (*Pyongyang Times*, 1 July).

Wallace H. Spaulding
McLean, Virginia

Syria

Population. 12,010,546
Party. Syrian Communist Party (al-Hizb al-Shuyu'i al-Suri; SCP)
Founded. 1924 (officially as a separate party in 1944)
Membership. 5,000 (estimated)
General Secretary. Khalid Bakhdash (77); deputy general secretary: Yusuf Faysal (63)
Politburo. Khalid Bakhdash, Yusuf Faysal, Ibrahim Bahri, Khalid Hammami (SCP representative to the *World Marxist Review*), Maurice Salibi, Umar Siba'i, Daniel Ni'mah, Zuhayr Abd al-Sammad, Ramu Farkha, Ramu Shaykhu (list of names not necessarily complete or up to date)
Secretariat. No data
Central Committee. Nabih Rushaydat, Muhammad Khabbad, Issa Khuri, R. Kurdi. A.W. Rashwani (not necessarily up to date; other names unknown)
Status. Component of the ruling National Progressive Front (NPF)
Last Congress. Sixth, July 1986
Last Election. February 1986; 8 out of 195 members of the parliament
Auxiliary Organizations. No data
Publications. *Nidal al-Sha'b*

Background. Seemingly no longer a serious threat and following a foreign policy often paralleling that of the Ba'thist regime, the SCP gained quasi-legal status after 1966 and finally joined the Ba'th-dominated NPF in 1972.

The Syrian communist movement has undergone several schisms in recent years. Riyad al-Turk, who was chosen general secretary of one breakaway group in 1974, has been imprisoned without trial since 1980 and subjected to beatings and torture. Dozens of members of the proscribed Communist Party Political Bureau have been imprisoned without trial since the early 1980s, although many others were released in the mid-1980s. Yusuf Murad, a former member of the SCP Central Committee, formed another group, the Base Organization, in 1980. Many members of the Party for Communist Action and others suspected of having ties to that group were imprisoned without charges during the 1980s. Another illegal organization, at least one of whose alleged founders was imprisoned for a while during the 1980s, was called the Union for Communist Struggle. It is not known whether these organizations continue to exist.

Leadership and Party Organization.

Little is known about the dynamics of the SCP's leadership, except that General Secretary Khalid Bakhdash has long been the dominant figure. There have been divisions among the top leaders; for example, Politburo member Ni'mah (now a representative of the SCP on the Central Command of the NPF) broke with the party temporarily during the early 1970s. There were also reports of dissent within the party during 1986. No information is available on meetings of party organs during the past three years.

Domestic Party Affairs.

The only available report of domestic activities during the year relates to a meeting in May of Deputy General Secretary Yusuf Faysal and members of the SCP Politburo with President Hafiz al-Asad (Damascus Domestic Service, 2 May; FBIS, 3 May).

Spokesmen for the SCP in international forums have regularly proclaimed their distaste for the socioeconomic aspects of the Ba'thist regime. One example of this is Politburo member Khalil Hammami's article in the World Marxist Review in May, which noted that although some "ambitious five-year development plans have been implemented to some extent or other" during the past two decades, the country is now in a serious crisis. Among the reasons for the economic crisis, Hammami pointed to continuing "close economic ties with the world capitalist market" and "ignoring the conditions that ensure stronger economic independence," leading to the emergence of "a sizeable parasitic bourgeoisie that has further enriched itself through various kinds of "graft, speculation, smuggling, deception and fraud, profit-tax evasion, etc." in cooperation with high-level bureaucrats, who in turn try to push the regime in a "reactionary" direction. This has resulted, he continued, in "new deprivations for workers, the village poor, and all of those who live on wages." He reiterated his party's solutions as involving an expansion of the public sector, promotion of small-scale private production, setting up state farms, bringing embezzlers to account, and greater economic self-reliance.

Auxiliary and Front Organizations.

Little information (none of it current) is available on auxiliary organizations. According to First-Hand Information: Communists and Revolutionary Democrats of the World Presenting Their Parties (Prague: Peace and Socialism International Publishers, 1988), the SCP participates in labor unions and in "mass organisations," particularly "youth and women's organisations." The party presumably participates in such groups as the Arab-Soviet Friendship Society; the Syrian Committee for Solidarity with Asian and African Countries; the National Council of Peace Partisans in Syria; the Syrian-GDR Friendship Society, and the Syrian-Bulgarian Friendship Society.

The present Syrian regime is officially based on the NPF, which includes the SCP, the Arab Socialist Party, and the Socialist Union, in addition to the dominant Ba'th party, which is non-Marxist. The cabinet includes two members of the SCP, which is also represented in the central leadership of the NPF and, according to First-Hand Information, in local governmental bodies. This does not mean that the SCP has any significant influence, but rather that it has for the time being more or less abandoned revolution in favor of a largely formal role. The quiet position of the regime's partner also conforms to the wishes of the USSR.

As the recipient during the 1980s of massive arms supplies from the USSR, with which it is tied by a treaty of friendship and cooperation, Syria was apparently worried—despite recurring pronouncements about the firm foundations of the Damascus-Moscow relationship—about Soviet general secretary Mikhail Gorbachev's seeming signs of weakness in dealing with the West, his efforts to get President Hafiz al-Asad to improve his relationship with the PLO, and his reported unwillingness to provide the kind of offensive weapons needed for Syria to gain strategic parity with Israel (NYT, 22 February; 23 July). Fearing a deterioration of the two countries' mutual relations, Soviet foreign minister Eduard Shevardnadze visited Damascus at the beginning of his trip to the Middle East in February and met with President Asad for six hours. Agreement was reached on the continuation of high-level visits. (NYT, 23 July.) The joint communiqué at the end of the meeting emphasized its "cordiality" and the two parties' agreement on a wide range of issues, including those related to Palestine, Lebanon, and Afghanistan, and announced that an invitation had been extended to Gorbachev to visit Damascus

(Damascus Television Service, 19 February; *FBIS*, 21 February).

Soviet defense minister Dimitriy Yazov headed a delegation that visited Damascus in March for talks with his Syrian counterpart, Mustafa Talas, and also met with President Asad (Damascus Domestic Service, 30 March; *FBIS*, 31 March). According to "East European diplomatic sources in Damascus," this visit was of great importance in "confirm[ing] and entrench[ing] Soviet-Syrian military relationships" (Abu Dhabi, *al-Ittihad*, 28 March; *FBIS*, 30 March). "Arab diplomatic sources" reported that the main disagreement related to weapons supplies, particularly the Soviet Union's failure to provide Sukhoi-24s to Syria because the latter owed a military debt to the USSR in the amount of $15 billion (London, *al-Majallah*, 5–11 April; *FBIS*, 6 April).

In October, it was revealed that the USSR planned to begin furnishing Sukhoi-24 fighter bombers, beginning with a delivery of 22 of them (Kuwait, *al-Ra'i*, 26 October; *FBIS*, 30 October). Warning about the "strain of military expenditures," Soviet ambassador Alexander Zotov stated a future Soviet policy of limiting arms supplies to those needed for "reasonable self-sufficiency" (*The Middle East*, January 1990).

Numerous other official contacts were announced during the year. A Soviet trade-union delegation visited Syria in March and met with the president of the Syrian General Federation of Trade Unions (Damascus Domestic Service, 29 March; *FBIS*, 30 March). Viktor Chernomydrin, Soviet minister of the gas industry, visited Damascus in April to discuss cooperation in matters related to the gas industry (SANA, 17 April; *FBIS*, 18 April). A delegation headed by "Comrade Ponomarev" of the CPSU Central Committee was received by Ba'thist assistant secretary general Abdullah al-Ahmar during the same month (Damascus Domestic Service, 5 April; *FBIS*, 6 April). Soviet first deputy foreign minister Aleksandr Bessmertnykh and Vladimir Polyakov, chief of the USSR Foreign Ministry's Near Eastern and North African Countries Administration, visited Damascus in July (Damascus Domestic Service, 2 July; *FBIS*, 3 July). In December, Defense Minister Talas met with a Soviet air-defense delegation led by General Ivan Tret'yak, commander in chief of the Soviet Air Defense Forces, while President Asad met with a Soviet parliamentary delegation (Damascus Domestic Service, 3 December; *FBIS*, 4 December). The significance of most of these visits is unclear, and there were presumably others, material on which was unavailable at the time of writing.

There were also numerous contacts with East European governments. Lyubomir Popov, Bulgarian deputy minister of foreign affairs and chairman of the Bulgarian Religious Cults Committee, and a delegation headed by the regional mufti of Bulgarian Muslims met with Syrian vice-president Muhammad Mashariqah in Damascus in February (SANA, 21 February; *FBIS*, 24 February). Velco Palin of the Bulgarian Central Committee headed a delegation that met with Syrian officials in Damascus in October (SANA, 23 October; *FBIS*, 15 October). The Ba'th Party's assistant general secretary, Abdullah al-Ahmar, headed a delegation that participated in the fourteenth Romanian Communist Party Congress in November (Damascus Domestic Service, 18 November; *FBIS*, 22 November). President Asad sent a telegram congratulating President Nicolae Ceauşescu on his re-election as general secretary and expressing "sincere wishes for success" (Damascus Domestic Service, 25 November; *FBIS*, 27 November). In February, Syrian defense minister Mustafa Talas received Jan Sterba, Czechoslovak minister of foreign trade, and Jan Sedik, deputy chief of staff of the Czechoslovak People's Army (Damascus Television Service, 14 February; *FBIS*, 24 February). Miloš Jakeš, general secretary of the Communist Party of Czechoslovakia, as head of a delegation of state and party officials, was a guest of President Asad in April amid many statements about the solid friendship between the two governments (Damascus Television Service, 10 April; *FBIS*, 11 April). President Asad cabled his congratulations to Mieczysław Rakowski following his election as first secretary of the Polish United Workers' Party (SANA, 30 July; *FBIS*, 1 August).

Several Syrian officials visited the German Democratic Republic during the year. These included Deputy Prime Minister Salim Yasin (for economic affairs) in January (*Neues Deutschland*, 27 January); Deputy Foreign Minister Dhia Allah Fattal in April (*Neues Deutschland*, 15–16 April); Ba'th regional command member—and chairman of the Syrian-GDR Friendship Society—Sa'id Hammada in April (*Neues Deutschland*, 26 April); Deputy Prime Minister Mahmud Qaddour (for public services) in July (*Neues Deutschland*, 14 July); and Grand Mufti Sheikh Ahmad Kaftarou in August (*Neues Deutschland*, 24 August).

Rodolfo Puentes Ferro, a member of the Cuban Communist Party Central Committee and deputy chairman of the Foreign Relations Department, headed a delegation that visited Syria in October. Talks with Assistant General Secretary al-Ahmar concerned cooperation between the two parties, and various statements from each side praised the other government's foreign policies (Damascus Domestic Service, 8, 9, and 14 October; *FBIS*, 11 and 16 October).

According to one report, Syria asked China to provide it with M-9 missiles after the Soviet refusal to provide advanced missiles (Kuwait, *al-Qabas*, 27 July; *FBIS*, 28 July). A delegation from the Chinese People's Political Consultative Conference, headed by Han Kehua, held talks in Damascus with members of the NPF Central Command in December (Damascus Television Service, 3 December; *FBIS*, 4 December).

The Iraqi Communist Party's general secretary, Aziz Muhammad, was received by PNF Deputy Chairman Muhammad Mashariqah in April. They discussed the Lebanese situation and described the "clique" headed by General 'Awn as "dependent on the Israeli enemy and the fascist regime in Iraq." (SANA, 19 April; *FBIS*, 20 April.)

International Views, Positions, and Activities. Little information is available on the SCP's international activities. A statement of the SCP Central Committee in January called U.S. "aggression [against Libya] a criminal act" and "part of the imperialist scheme to strike at liberation movements throughout the world" (Damascus Domestic Service, 5 January; *FBIS*, 6 January). In a joint statement issued in Damascus in November, SCP Deputy General Secretary Yusuf Faysal and General Secretary George Hawi of the Lebanese Communist Party praised President Asad's "important role" in the conclusion of the Ta'if agreement on Lebanon. They also discussed "means to support the valiant intifadah [uprising]" in the Israeli-occupied territories. (SANA, 26 November; *FBIS*, 27 November.)

Hammami's article in the *World Marxist Review* (Prague, May) spoke favorably of the Asad regime's development of "wider cooperation with the USSR and other socialist states." Hammami also referred to Damascus's "staunchly anti-imperialist and anti-Zionist stance," which explains the hatred for it on the part of "US imperialism and its strategic ally Israel," and pointed to the latter power's "aggressive actions . . . to which local, Arab and international reaction has made its contribution."

Glenn E. Perry
Indiana State University

Tunisia

Population. 7,916,104
Party. Tunisian Communist Party (Parti communiste tunisien; PCT)
Founded. 1934
Membership. 2,000 (estimated); PCT claims 4,000
Composition. Unknown
General Secretary. Muhammad Harmel
Politburo. 9 members: Muhammad Harmel, Muhammad Ennafaa, Hichem Sekik, Adbelhamid Ben Mustapha, Junaidi Adbeljawad, Bujuma Remili, Ahmed Ibrahim, Abdelmajid Triki, Rachid Mcharek
Secretariat. No data available
Central Committee. 22 members: Ahmed Ben Younes, Junaidi Abdeljawad, Bujuma Remili, Ahmed Ibrahim, Habib Kasdaghli, Rachid Mcharek, Sadik Labidi, Tarak Chaabani, Abdelhamid Larguech, Abdelhamid Ben Mustapha, Abdelmajid Triki, Ali Khmira, Abdelwahab Abassi, Muhammad Ben Della, Muhammad Harmel, Muhammad Ennafaa, Muhammad Lahkdar, Muhammad Kallel, Muhammad Khelifi, Mustapha Ouannen, Noureddine Metoui, Hichem Sekik
Status. Legal
Last Congress. June 1989
Last Election. 2 April 1989 (presidential and legislative)
Auxiliary Organization. Tunisian Communist Youth
Publications. *Al-Tariq al-Jadid* (The new path), weekly. An additional publication was planned for publication in 1989 but has not yet appeared.

Background. The Tunisian Communist Party was founded in 1920 as an offshoot of the French Communist Party and established itself as an independent organization in 1939. It joined the other Tunisian parties in struggling for independence from France, but was quickly eviscerated after 1956 when Habib Bourguiba and his Destour (Constitutional) Party established themselves as the leading political organization. By 1963 Tunisia had emerged as a one-party country, led by the Destour, and the PCT was formally banned that year. It was resurrected in July 1981 during a period of political liberalization in the country. Between July 1981 and November 1983, the PCT functioned as the only legal opposition party in Tunisia. (See *YICA*, 1984, for details on additional parties created that year.)

Leadership and Party Organization. The PCT has local and regional cells, coordinated from its central headquarters in Tunis. All have very limited membership and are overwhelmed by the long-standing organization of the country's major party, the Constitutional Democratic Rally (RCD) headed by President Zine el-Abidine Ben Ali.

Domestic Party Affairs. In several ways 1989 was a crucial year in Tunisian politics, a state of affairs well understood by the PCT's leadership. In an effort to extend his earlier political liberalization measures, President Ben Ali attempted to create a political consensus behind his reforms. After having participated as the only opposition party in the parliamentary by-elections of 24 January 1988, in 1989 the PCT distanced itself from Ben Ali's reforms. In the wake of the 1988 elections, the PCT had made several accusations of election fraud and declared itself unable to participate any further until guarantees were provided for fair elections. Despite this, the PCT joined the other Tunisian opposition movements in signing the National Pact, an attempt by Ben Ali to rally all parties behind his plans for an economic and political renewal in the country. The National Pact was signed symbolically on 1 November 1988, one year after Ben Ali's takeover from former president-for-life Habib Bourguiba. Harmel participated in the ceremony at the Carthage palace.

The PCT has remained suspicious of both the National Pact and the RCD. Although tacitly participating during the early months of 1989 in the new measures announced by Ben Ali, Muhammad Harmel repeatedly stressed that they were insufficient to guarantee a real opposition in the country. The presidential and parliamentary elections of 2 April 1989 marked a break between the PCT (and most of the opposition parties) and the ruling RCD. President Ben Ali's attempt to create a broad coalition for the elections, which would guarantee the opposition parties a share in power, floundered for a number of reasons that the PCT clearly pointed out as almost insurmountable problems to a rejuvenated political life in the country. In the aftermath of the elections, President Ben Ali was overwhelmingly elected president of the country; he had faced no

opposition, and the PCT had supported him as sole candidate, much like all other opposition parties. The parliamentary elections, however, proved to be the real stumbling block. Because of Tunisia's electoral system, all 141 seats went to the RCD. Harmel singled out the electoral procedure as an indication of Ben Ali's inability to reform the country's political system, and pointed out that for all practical purposes an opposition in Tunisia was nonexistent. His argument was bolstered by the fact that the Islamist opposition—not officially recognized and organized for the elections as the Renaissance Party (Hizb al-Nahdha)—managed to obtain almost 14 percent of the popular vote and as much as one quarter of the vote in several cities, without receiving a single seat in parliament.

Since the parliamentary elections, the PCT has kept up this uneasy stance, supporting the ongoing reforms in Tunisia, but skeptical that they will ever lead to real power-sharing by the RCD. Harmel has viewed the role of the PCT in this regard as an organization that must pressure the government to make those changes that are necessary to bring about an effective reform. Harmel has been particularly critical of Ben Ali's attempt to entice several opposition figures to join the government. He specifically decried the defection of Dali Jazy, a founding member of Ahmed Mestiri's Mouvement des Democrates Socialistes (MDS). Jazy was first appointed ambassador to Austria and subsequently became a minister in the current government. The PCT has been equally critical of a number of other defections, including several from Tunisian human-rights organizations. Not surprisingly, when the Tunisian president attempted to invigorate the mechanisms of the National Pact in late 1989, the PCT shied away from endorsing them. And the PCT considered the resignation of Ahmed Mestiri from the MDS, because of what Mestiri called an inability to maintain a credible opposition under the current political circumstances in Tunisia, as proof that the evisceration of the country's political opposition followed logically from the government's exclusionary policies.

The party's position within the country, however, has been seriously affected by a number of different factors. Although the PCT has never been a real threat to any of the government's programs, its ability to act as a spoiler in the political process diminished even further after the April elections. The main reason has been the growing importance of the Islamist movement, which, by its nature, is opposed to Harmel's philosophy. On several occasions in

1988 and 1989, figures in the Islamic movement have targeted the party as "infidel" and unworthy of participating in the country's political life. The PCT's response has been sharp, in essence reiterating the government's position that no single organization (i.e., the Renaissance Party) can claim to represent Islam, and that Islam should not be exploited for political purposes. It is almost ironic that the PCT had long been the defender of the Islamic movement during its repression under President Bourguiba. But the April elections clearly showed that it was the Islamists and not the PCT that have been gaining rapidly in allegiance among the Tunisian population. Even more ironical was the fact that the PCT was forced a few months later to criticize the government's decision not to grant the Islamist movement a permit to function as a legitimate opposition party. It viewed the voluntary political exile of the Islamist movement's leader, Rachid al-Ghanoushi, in much the same light as Ahmed Mestiri's resignation. Both, according to Harmel, result from the RCD's continued stranglehold on the country.

A further difficulty for the PCT has been the continued economic liberalization of the Ben Ali government. Although in principle opposed to an economic system that relies primarily on market forces, and that is oriented toward the international economy, the PCT has had little success in convincing Tunisians of its pernicious effect. Reduced to standing on the sidelines, the PCT has argued for greater protection of the country's poor, but much of its demands have been incorporated very skillfully by the Islamists, who continue to enjoy a greater attraction among the population at large. Its attempts to organize union officials and membership have been equally unsuccessful, a continuation of the PCT's historical inability to attract a substantial number of organizers at the local and regional level.

International Views, Positions, and Activities. Preoccupied with events in Tunisia, the PCT has shown little activity in international settings. The Arab Maghreb Union (AMU) continues to absorb its attention; Muhammad Harmel has repeatedly stressed that the AMU remains an important political framework for fostering relations between the different North African countries. The PCT has vocally supported the creation of several new committees to strengthen the regional organization. Although there are no signs yet that the PCT has taken any steps, it is clear that its leadership has, with great interest, watched the official recognition of the

Algerian communist party and seems poised to attempt a coordination of the Maghrebi communist parties in Tunisia, Algeria, and Morocco.

Dirk Vandewalle
Dartmouth College

Yemen
People's Democratic Republic of Yemen

Population. 2,503,641
Party. Yemeni Socialist Party (al-Hizb al-Ishtirakiya al-Yamaniya; YSP)
Founded. 1978
Membership. 31,000 (including candidate members)
Chairman of the Presidium of the Supreme People's Council (president and head of state). Haydar Abu Bakr al-'Attas (elected November 1986)
Chairman of the Council of Ministers (prime minister and head of government). Yasin Sa'id Nu'man (elected 8 February 1986)
General Secretary of the Yemeni Socialist Party. 'Ali Salim al-Bayd (elected 7 February 1986)
Assistant General Secretary. Salim Salih Muhammad (elected 7 February 1986)
Politburo. 11 members: Salih Munassar al-Siyayli, Salim Salih Muhammad, Haydar Abu Bakr al-'Attas, 'Ali Salim al-Bayd, Yasin Sa'id Nu'man, Muhammad Sa'id 'Abdullah, Sa'id Salih Salim, Fadl Muhsin 'Abdullah, 'Abdullah Ahmad al-Khamiri, Salih 'Ubayd Ahmad, and Muhammad Haydara Masdus. 3 candidate members: Haytham Qasim Tahir, Sayf Sa'il Khalid, and Salim Muhammad Jubran
Central Committee. 77 members
Status. Ruling party
Last Congress. Fourth, 20–21 June 1987
Last Election. 1986, all candidates approved by YSP
Publication. *Al-Thawra*, YSP Central Committee weekly

The winds of reform and liberalization sweeping through Eastern Europe and the Soviet Union during 1989 stirred the People's Democratic Republic of Yemen (PDRY), also known as South Yemen, Southern Yemen, or (as is preferred by its government) Democratic Yemen, in the latter part of the year. Significant changes were promised or became apparent in three arenas: economic and political reform; a perceptible shift closer to moderate Arab states and the West in foreign policy; and accelerating steps toward achieving long-mooted unity with the Yemen Arab Republic (YAR; North Yemen).

Since independence in 1967, Democratic Yemen has pursued a path of "scientific socialism" in domestic policy and close alignment with the Soviet Union and other Eastern bloc countries in foreign affairs. Until 1989 the Yemeni Socialist Party (YSP), heir to the independence-winning National Liberation Front (NLF), was the only legal party in the state; it has had no significant opposition since independence in 1967. The party itself, however, has been riven with factionalism and infighting. Internal power struggles reached climaxes in 1969, 1971, 1978, 1980, and the civil war of January 1986.

The constitution (adopted in 1970 and amended in 1978) specifies that the Supreme People's Council (SPC) is the highest authority. Elections to the council were first held in 1978; members are elected for five-year terms. The SPC elects the president and eleven to seventeen members of the Presidium, to which the SPC's authority is delegated when the SPC is not in session. At first, the Presidium exercised considerable influence as a collegial body, but the president assumed unchallenged predominance as a result of the power struggle of 1971. The SPC also elects the prime minister, the Council of Ministers, and the members of the Supreme Court.

As in other socialist states, real power rests with the party. The superiority of the party was firmly established as a result of events in 1978 which culminated in the execution of President Salim Rubayyi' 'Ali and assumption of his position by a rival and the head of the party, 'Abd al-Fattah Isma'il. During the 1970s, several efforts were made to transform the ruling NLF into a true Marxist organization, and several other small legal parties were incorporated into it. Neither the Popular Democratic Union, a local communist party founded in Aden in 1961, nor the Vanguard Party (Baathist) had seriously challenged the NLF for power.

The First Congress of the YSP was held in October 1972, following the ouster of the party's moderates, and another was held in October 1980, after the defeat of the ultraradical faction. The Third Congress took place in October 1985 amidst considerable tension and the Fourth Congress had to be postponed until June 1987 because of continuing fundamental differences.

Successive struggles for supremacy within the party have eliminated factions from both the right and the far left, as well as most of the original party leaders who fought in the war for independence. In January 1986, the country's pragmatic leader, 'Ali Nasir Muhammad (al-Hasani; prime minister, 1971–1985, and president, 1980–1986), sought to check his deteriorating authority by eliminating his doctrinaire left-wing rivals. Although his supporters managed to kill four of the last five prominent founding members of the party, including former president and former party leader 'Abd al-Fattah Isma'il (al-Jawfi; ousted from power in 1980), 'Ali Nasir's opponents eventually won the resultant civil war. 'Ali Nasir, the fifth of these historic leaders, was forced to flee with his supporters; he maintains homes in the Yemen Arab Republic, Ethiopia, and Damascus.

The remaining nucleus of the Adeni regime, reduced to party lightweights and relatively unknown technocrats, adopted a pragmatic course and pursued many of 'Ali Nasir's policies, especially in foreign affairs, while refusing any dialogue with the exiled president.

Political and Economic Reform. Neither the Yemeni Socialist Party nor the PDRY government appears to have made any direct reference to the process of *perestroika* or to the collapse of communist governments in Eastern Europe. Nevertheless, the Arab world's most doctrinaire political system has committed itself to a similar trend toward liberalization. This continues a process fitfully begun by former President 'Ali Nasir Muhammad and somewhat more energetically pursued by the post–civil war leadership. Suggestions of reform were made at a faster rate after the summer, presumably owing to developments in the Soviet Union and its neighbors. The Council of Ministers, meeting in August, admitted that mistakes had been made in the past and emphasized the essential need for reform, especially in government administration, the trade unions, and mass organizations.

Significant progress came out of the sixteenth ordinary session of the YSP Central Committee on 30 September and 1 October 1989. Taking note of discussions held in regional party organizations and the Politburo's report on the matter, the committee announced that it intended to introduce structural changes in the economy, especially to encourage private-sector involvement, to reduce red tape, to improve marketing procedures, and to promote export industries. Noting the success of liberalization in local government elections (in which independent candidates were allowed to stand for the first time), the committee stressed the need to encourage electoral pluralism and independent thinking within the party itself. Other steps were taken to merge duplicative departments and committees, eliminate unnecessary courses and overstaffing in the party and government, and to permit expression of divergent opinions in the media.

A month later, the Politburo lifted all restrictions on foreign travel and made journeys to the North easier by eliminating forms and requiring just the presentation of identity cards. On the economic side, the government increased its efforts to revitalize the lagging economy by looking to the private sector, officially discouraged for decades, to play a stronger role. By the end of the year, the government had approved construction of the country's first private hotel; this followed the development of privately owned bakeries, small factories, and a chicken farm. A new investment law permitting foreigners to own local ventures was said to be near completion, and plans were underway to encourage investment in tourism, oil exploration, and development of the port of Aden.

Perhaps the most dramatic step came on 11 December when the YSP Central Committee, after two days of debate, declared itself in favor of a multiparty system and ordered the Politburo to draw up guidelines for a law permitting the formation of other parties. This decision reversed a policy of centralization by which several small rival parties to the old National Liberation Front had lost their separate identities when the YSP was created. Potentially, this development marked a major shift in the regime's attitude toward dissident political opinion.

In part, it seemed to represent a culmination of the steps taken towards burying the long-standing antagonisms left over from the 1986 civil war. The PDRY government had announced in March an amnesty of 35 political prisoners convicted at the end of 1987 and said it would permit the return of 30,000 of 'Ali Nasir Muhammad's followers. For his part, the former president renounced any claim to leadership and noted that his supporters had just

met senior PDRY officials for talks on reconciliation. He also urged the Soviet Union to resume mediation efforts and announced that he had ordered his supporters to close their radio station as a goodwill gesture. A successful conclusion to this conciliatory process would solve two nagging problems at a single stroke: it would help defuse remaining ideological and regional/tribal tension in South Yemen; and it would remove a principal source of dissension between North Yemen and South Yemen. By the end of the year, however, no explicit agreement on reconciliation had been reached, although the YSP Central Committee did announce in December that it would accept the return of all opposition elements willing to "abandon wrong approaches."

A second implication was that the socialist system was prepared to embrace greater pluralism. In this sense, the decision announced on 11 December was another aspect of political reform, following on the heels of the new local election law. Shortly after the announcement, three new parties appeared to be formed: the Unifying Democratic Party, consisting of former supporters of 'Ali Nasir Muhammad; the Popular Union Party (communist), led by Jarallah 'Umar; and the National Democratic Party (Baathist), under the leadership of Yahya al-Shami. The appearance of the latter seemed to mark a transformation of the North Yemeni faction in Aden from an exile group (the National Democratic Front) seeking to overthrow the YAR government into an element of PDRY politics. The same may be true for the Popular Union Party, whose leader was also said to be from the YAR, but this party also raised echoes of the old (communist) Popular Democratic Union, which had been merged into the YSP at the beginning of the 1980s.

These changes were all the more remarkable in a state accustomed to reliance on an omnipresent security apparatus. 'Ali Salim al-Bayd chose the occasion of the twentieth anniversary of the establishment of the state-security organization to hint that the climate of reform would also include security. Undoubtedly, the abolition of East Germany's secret police, hitherto ubiquitous in the PDRY's state-security apparatus, would have some effect. It was perhaps significant that some reports suggested that Cuban advisers, who had played a similar role in the party-controlled militia, had been kicked out.

In a cautionary note, it might be argued that the regime emerging in Aden after the chaos of January 1986 had represented a fairly even balance among the remaining ideological, regional and tribal factions. The process of liberalization easily could produce an unintended effect of accentuating these divisions and fragmenting power further. Challenges to power in South Yemen have not been handled very well in the past and a re-emergence of unchecked rivalries as a result of Aden's version of *perestroika* could invite the intervention of the army, whose leadership has been thought to be a stronghold of the Fattahiyin, the confirmed ideologues in the mold of the late 'Abd al-Fattah Isma'il.

Foreign Affairs. There was a rather bifurcated quality to Aden's foreign policy in 1989. A familiar pattern of exchanging visits and contacts with the Eastern bloc dominated the first half of the year, while the second half was marked more by rapprochement with the West and, in particular, detailed negotiations with North Yemen about unification.

The PDRY's most prominent foreign partner continued to be the Soviet Union, with increasing emphasis placed on development of South Yemen's nascent oil industry. In January, Soviet deputy foreign minister Vladimir Petrovskiy stopped at Aden Airport on his return to Moscow from Nairobi. The Soviet minister of construction of petroleum and gas industries led a delegation to Aden in March for a meeting of the Permanent Committee for Economic and Technical Cooperation. The committee held further talks in Moscow in late September, when the PDRY delegation was led by Energy Minister Salih Abu Bakr ibn Husaynun.

The Yemeni-Soviet Joint Planning Subcommittee met in Aden in May and produced a long agenda of areas for cooperation, including water and soil utilization, development of fisheries resources, power, building materials and the construction industry, mapping for potential minerals, the development of transport and communications, and food programs up to the year 2005, as well as the PDRY's economic and social development until that year.

In August, Dr. 'Abdullah al-Khamiri, Politburo member and chairman of the Yemeni Council for Peace, Solidarity and Friendship, met with the Soviet Solidarity Committee in Moscow to discuss Soviet participation in the international symposium on the security of the Indian Ocean, Arabian Gulf, and Red Sea, scheduled to be held in Aden in early 1990 under the auspices of the Afro-Asian Solidarity Organization. YSP deputy general secretary Salim Salih Muhammad also made an official visit to Moscow in October at the invitation of the CPSU Central Committee. That same month, the fifteenth session of the Joint Yemeni-Soviet Committee on Marine Fisheries was held in Aden.

By the end of the year, the Soviet Union's Tyumen Pipeline Construction Association was hurrying to complete the new 204-kilometer-long oil pipeline linking the oilfields of Shabwa governorate to a coastal terminal at Balhaf. The Soviet Union also donated building materials, trucks, tractors, and pumps as a contribution to relief aid after the eastern half of South Yemen was devastated by floods in the spring.

In other Eastern bloc contacts, YSP general secretary 'Ali Salim al-Bayd led a high-level party and government delegation to Czechoslovakia in January; a Bulgarian group visited in June; and then al-Bayd met in East Berlin in October with Nicaraguan president Daniel Ortega, then-Czechoslovak communist party general secretary Miloš Jakeš, and then-Romanian communist party general secretary Nicolae Ceauşescu. Visits were also received from delegations of the Spanish communist party in May and the French communist party in September.

Continuing close ties with the People's Republic of China were marked by a meeting of the Joint Yemeni-PRC Economic, Technical and Trade Committee in September, and the PRC deputy minister for foreign economic and trade relations visited in October. Chinese aid was highlighted by the inauguration of the 5.48-kilometer Aden beltway, linking Crater Pass with al-Rawda, on national day, 30 November.

Third-World visitors to Aden included the Cuban vice–foreign minister in July, a North Korean economic delegation, also in July, and Burkina Faso's head of government in September. President Haydar Abu Bakr al-'Attas headed the PDRY delegation to the summit of the Nonaligned Movement in Belgrade in September.

The initial contacts between the PDRY and the United States in 1988 regarding the resumption of diplomatic relations were taken up again with the assistance of Kuwait. (Aden abruptly broke off ties in 1969 and a scheduled visit by a State Department team in 1978 never took place due to an outbreak of fighting in Aden.) In October, Prime Minister Yasin Sa'id Nu'man disclosed that direct discussions had taken place a few weeks earlier between the two countries' U.N. representatives, 'Abdullah al-Ashtal and Thomas Pickering. According to Foreign Minister 'Abd al-'Aziz al-Dali, the negotiations had run into obstacles over U.S. allegations of South Yemeni support for terrorists and compensation for the former U.S. embassy property in Aden.

Aden also moved to improve its relations with Western Europe. In December, Foreign Office minister William Waldegrave became the first British official of ministerial rank to visit Aden since South Yemen had received its independence. A few weeks later, Italian prime minister Giulio Andreotti became the first West European head of government to travel to the PDRY when he returned a visit paid to Rome in May by Foreign Minister 'Abd al-'Aziz al-Dali, itself the first official visit by a South Yemeni foreign minister to a European country. Rather ingenuously, al-Dali remarked that "It seems that after 20 years [the Western countries] have come to the conclusion that our government is moving in a good and steady direction."

One motive for South Yemen's willingness to improve relations with the West may lie in its search for oil. While the Shabwa field, developed by the Soviet Union's Technoexport, was expected to fulfill the country's domestic needs, exploration in other areas continued. France's Total began exploratory drilling east of the Soviet concession and Elf-Aquitaine held other concessions in Aden, Abyan Province, and west of Shabwa. France was also expected to provide $30 million for refurbishment of the Aden refinery.

Within the Arab world, the PDRY's ties with Syria were particularly pronounced. Defense Minister Salih Ahmad 'Ubayd went to Damascus in March, apparently in search of additional military aid for the PDRY air force (equipped like Syria's by the Soviet Union) and to secure places for Yemeni officers in the Syrian military academy and staff college. Agreement for Syrian aid in other spheres was reached during the visit of Syrian prime minister Mahmud al-Zu'bi in June, and Syrian vice-president 'Abd al-Halim Khaddam went to Aden in September to seek South Yemen's support for Syrian policy in Lebanon.

Perhaps in reaction to Syrian wooing, Palestinian president Yasir 'Arafat traveled to Aden on three occasions (January, August, and October), and also met with YSP general secretary 'Ali Salim al-Bayd in East Berlin in October. A delegation from the Popular Front for the Liberation of Palestine–General Command visited Aden in April, and Lebanese communist party general secretary Muhsin Ibrahim came in October. The presence of President 'Attas at Libya's celebrations of its national day (1 September) followed on the heels of his foreign minister's trip to Tripoli. A few weeks later, al-Khuwaylidi al-Hamid, a member of the Libyan

Revolutionary Command Council, arrived in Aden, his visit being part of a regional tour.

But indications of Aden's apparent desire for more balance in its Arab relations were provided by the establishment of diplomatic relations with Morocco in February, Prime Minister Nu'man's trip to Kuwait in October, and the reception in November of Sudanese president 'Umar Hasan Ahmad al-Bashir in Aden. The PDRY government continued to emphasize strong links with the Gulf states, and its relations with neighboring Saudi Arabia and Oman (despite another border flareup in the autumn) continued to improve.

Foreign Minister 'Abd al-'Aziz al-Dali's visit to Jordan in March fueled speculation that the PDRY might seek admission to the new Arab Cooperation Council (ACC), particularly since North Yemen was a founding member (along with Jordan, Egypt, and Iraq). This idea gained additional currency because of the proliferation of Aden's contacts with all four ACC members. In April, the foreign minister became the first PDRY cabinet member to visit Cairo since Egypt's 1979 peace treaty with Israel, and President Haydar al-'Attas made an official visit to Jordan in September. YAR foreign minister 'Abd al-Karim al-Iryani added another twist with his remark in December that the proposed new unified Yemeni state would adhere to all treaties and obligations to which the PDRY and the YAR were committed, including those relating to the ACC.

Ties with Iraq seemed to regain the warmth they had had before the two countries' relations soured at the beginning of the decade. Iraqi oil minister 'Isam 'Abd al-Rahman al-Chalabi signed an oil-cooperation agreement in Aden in March. This not only provided for the training of Yemeni officials in Iraq, but also increased the amount of crude oil Iraq provides for refining in Aden from the previous level of 15,000 barrels per day. Further economic assistance was signaled by the visit of Iraqi first deputy prime minister Taha Yasin Ramadan in April, who announced that Baghdad would allow Aden to postpone repayment of outstanding Iraqi loans and promised to increase trade between the two countries. An Iraqi minister of state arrived in Aden in June, and, in September, the YSP held talks with a delegation from the Iraq Arab Baath Socialist Party delegation.

Yemeni Unity. Perhaps the most significant development in South Yemen during 1989 concerned the long and erratic efforts to achieve Yemeni unity, which toward the end of the year suddenly began to look as though they might finally bear fruit. As was the case with earlier agreements on unification, which had followed both the 1972 and 1979 border war, the latest bout of pro-unity fever followed a period of tension between the two Yemeni states (official statements by both North and South Yemeni governments invariably refer to "the two parts [*shatrayn*] of the homeland").

The principal cause of strained relations between Aden and Sanaa had been complications arising from the South's civil war in January 1986 and the flight of perhaps as many as 50,000 refugees to the North, among them the defeated president, 'Ali Nasir Muhammad. Both states had a history of providing refuge to the other's dissident groups and allowing these exiles to carry out provocations against the other state; this happened again with 'Ali Nasir Muhammad's followers. At the same time, the prospect of oil discoveries in the two Yemens' disputed border area provided another source of tension. Rumors of aerial dogfights at the beginning of 1987 were followed by serious clashes in November of the same year. Following emergency meetings between the two countries' chiefs of staff in December 1987, the situation appeared to have been defused.

Still, rekindling the fire with substantive moves toward the goal of unification was a slow process. The first trip of YSP general secretary 'Ali Salim al-Bayd to North Yemen since the civil war, a visit to Sanaa in July 1987, was not a success, and his departure without the issuance of a communiqué pointed to the existence of basic disagreements. Similarly, meetings between the two presidents in September in Sanaa 1987 and at the Amman Arab summit shortly thereafter produced no visible results.

Later, however, the unification process began to gather momentum as the two countries moved toward cooperation on energy. Steps were taken toward implementation of the agreement made in January 1985 on a joint petroleum development zone along their unmarked border. YAR deputy prime minister and minister of development Dr. Muhammad Sa'id al-'Attar discussed economic integration and joint oil-investment programs while representing Sanaa at the celebrations of the PDRY's national day on 30 November 1987. This was soon followed by consultations between the two oil ministers.

In late March 1988, Prime Minister 'Abd al-'Aziz 'Abd al-Ghani arrived in Aden at the head of a high-powered YAR delegation, which included the army's chief of staff, the ministers of the interior, oil, and unity affairs, and the governor of the border province. Apparently as a result of Northern pressure, a subsequent meeting between YAR president 'Ali 'Abdullah Salih and YSP general secretary 'Ali Salim al-Bayd in Ta'izz in April resulted in their agreement that the unification process should be revived, as well as confirmation of their commitment to establish the Joint Yemeni Oil Investment Company, originally agreed upon in 1985.

A month later, still another summit between 'Ali Salim al-Bayd and 'Ali 'Abdullah Salih resulted in the pivotal Sanaa communiqué of 4 May 1988. By this statement, the two leaders agreed: (1) to reactivate the Supreme Yemeni Council (SYC), the Joint Ministerial Council, and other unity committees; (2) to instruct the SYC secretariat to prepare a timetable for submission of the unified state's draft constitution to the two parliamentary bodies and then to popular referenda; (3) to revive the Unified Political Organization as provided in the 1972 unification agreement; (4) to find a way to dissipate the lingering obstacles left by the events of 13 January 1986; and (5) to resolve their border dispute by withdrawing military forces from the area in question and setting up the joint petroleum-investment corporation.

The first tangible product of the communiqué of May 1988 came a few weeks later when the two interior ministers announced that border checkpoints were to be abolished and Yemeni citizens of one state would be allowed to travel freely in the other, the agreement becoming effective on 1 September 1988. Then, following the submission of additional unity proposals in September 1988, the Joint Ministerial Council began meeting regularly in the second half of 1988 to discuss joint programs in such areas as trade, public works, transport and communications, agriculture and fisheries, and education and culture. At its meeting in early 1989, the council was unable to reach a decision on a joint currency, but said it looked favorably on a joint Yemeni fund for development.

During other meetings in 1989, the interior ministers discussed means of jointly dealing with criminals and the status of travelers between the two states; the ministers of foreign affairs decided to unify consular work at embassies to handle the affairs of expatriate Yemeni workers; and the ministers of information and culture agreed to share and jointly produce programs for radio and television. Other bilateral meetings were held between the ministers of oil, economy, and information and culture. In August, the board of directors of the joint oil-investment company authorized the company's officials to open negotiations with international oil companies.

The climax of this activity came in the unity agreement of 30 November 1989. Meeting in Aden on the occasion of the 22d anniversary of the PDRY's independence, the two Yemeni presidents announced that the draft constitution of the Republic of Yemen was being referred to the two countries' legislative bodies. In addition, they declared the imminent formation of a single presidential council, to be chaired in rotation by the two presidents. There was to be a single Yemeni representation internationally, the two armies were to merge, and a combined parliament was to be created. Individual agencies were gradually to join in federal ministries, except for four key ministries, which were to retain their separate identities until comprehensive unity had been achieved. Within weeks, a joint delegation, composed of the two ministers of state for unity affairs, was on its way to ACC capitals to explain the new situation.

Further amplification of the agreement of 30 November was provided by the YAR's foreign minister, 'Abd al-Karim al-Iryani, in a subsequent interview. He pointed out that the Cairo agreement of 1972 (following the border war of that year) stipulated that the constitution must be endorsed by the legislative councils within six months after it has been referred to them. Then popular referenda must be held to approve the constitution within an additional six months. This would require declaration of a single state by 30 November 1990. According to the draft constitution, leadership of the federal state is to be invested in a five-member command council, which will in turn elect a chairman to a five-year term.

Some observers made much of the differing viewpoints over whether the new state was to have a multiparty system or would allow only a single party, noting ironically that the PDRY was now pressing for a multiparty system against the resistance of the YAR government. This would appear to be one of the proposed union's lesser obstacles, however. Undeniably, popular emotions in both regions of Yemen run high on the issue of unity, and gains were achieved as a result of the increased activity of 1988 and 1989, particularly the freer movement of citizens and goods and the defusing of the sensitive border issue. Nevertheless, it was still too early to judge whether a true confederation was finally in view, or whether the flurry of activity in late 1989 had produced yet another round of patriotic rhetoric with few tangible achievements behind it.

J.E. Peterson
Muscat, Sultanate of Oman

WESTERN EUROPE

Introduction

The continent saw a dramatic ending to the decade of the 1980s. Not only did the power and position of the communist parties of Central and Eastern Europe collapse, but the structures of Western Europe's communist parties underwent dramatic changes as well. The opening of the Berlin Wall on 9 November 1989 not only signified a symbolic end to the cold war, but gave visible and emotional meaning to the power of the idea of freedom, the democratic ideal, and the strength of the free marketplace.

In 1981 the French Communist Party (PCF) scored a major electoral victory in France. It became a member of the coalition government led by socialist François Mitterrand and held four cabinet posts in one of the most important countries of Western Europe. The prognosis for the future led the *World Marxist Review* to conclude in November of 1983 that "the ideas advanced by Europe's communists meet the innermost interests of the people." The coalition government interpreted those needs as requiring nationalization of major parts of French industry, including its leading banks. The PCF enjoyed legitimacy as a member of a democratically elected government, and provided the example to be followed by its West European counterparts.

Just one year later, however, the cohesion of Western Europe's communist parties was breaking up. In France the programs of economic regulation and social engineering alienated the French electorate and seriously threatened the stability of the French economy. The result was the decision by the French president and his prime minister to curtail the government's programs of socialization, and the PCF resigned from the coalition government. By the end of 1988 the French communists were torn by internal strife—the PCF had suffered its worst election defeat in 60 years in 1986, when it polled only 9.8 percent of the vote in elections to the French National Assembly. In 1988 it was able to capture only 11.3 percent of the vote in the French national election, following Mitterrand's re-election to the presidency for a second seven-year term.

The PCF had proved unable to meet successfully the challenge presented to any legitimate party of government, namely, that of embracing compromise in the interest of the common weal. It had been confronted with a contradiction impossible to resolve: to achieve its goal of "socialism in French colors" while a member of a coalition government. Whether the PCF compromised its own party program or resigned, it would lose credibility. This experience adversely affected the popularity of its counterparts elsewhere in Europe, and it weakened the confidence of Western Europe's voters in the assurances of the communist parties that they were capable of acting as responsible members of democratic governments.

From the mid-1980s to the end of the decade, the PCF experience had challenged other communist parties to demonstrate what constructive role they could play in their respective countries in the future. The result was reflected clearly in the outcome of national elections in Western Europe between 1985 and 1989. In each of the seven national elections held during 1985, the communist parties received fewer votes than they had in previous years. This trend continued during 1986, 1987, and 1988. In 1989, seven national elections were held in Western Europe; they took place in Greece, Ireland, Luxembourg, the Netherlands, Norway, Spain, and West Berlin. Of the thirteen parties with legislative representation, that of San Marino held the highest percentage of seats based on votes received (28.7), followed by Cyprus (27.4), Italy (26.6), Iceland (13.2), France (11.3), Portugal (11.0), Greece (10.97), Finland (9.4), Spain (9.05), Sweden (5.8), the Netherlands (4.1), Luxembourg (3.6), and Switzerland (0.8). The eleven parties without legislative representation received less than one percent of the vote, respectively.

One of the most interesting of the changing and conflicting tides engulfing the continent was the election to the European parliament in Strasbourg, held in June. In the third direct election in the twelve EC countries for 518 seats in the European Parliament, with approximately 242 million people entitled to vote, the Socialists and Social Democrats won 182 seats, and the communist parties obtained 42 seats. The remainder are held by the Greens (48), the Christian Democrats (107), the Liberals (45), the Conservatives (50), parties of the far right (16), and other parties (38). This outcome assumes increasing significance as the 1992 program to establish the European Community's internal market moves forward. The "left" won a two-seat majority, which gives it "oversight over most new European Community legislation" (*Insight*, 10 July). This result led, in turn, to speculation that the 1990s may see an effort to develop "what [EC] commission President Jacques Delors has called 'Social Europe'" (ibid.). As former French prime minister and head of the French socialist slate, Laurent Fabius, observed, "The new Parliament will be more to the left than the preceding one. This will allow us to act with more force to construct the Europe we want" (*NYT*, 19 June). While it was far from certain that the left would be able to dominate the social, economic, and political agenda in the future, the shift to the left was ironic in view of the dramatic social, economic, and political changes in Eastern Europe that occurred several months after the elections. But the election nonetheless pointed to the potential significance of the changes sweeping across Europe in 1989. As the foreign editor of Munich's *Süddeutsche Zeitung* wrote in June:

As "1992" becomes reality, protected markets will crumble even more quickly, cross-migration and competition will accelerate, and resentments will soar— throughout Europe. The recent European elections and the swings to the left and the right are but a taste of things to come. (Josef Joffe, "Europe's Grand Parties in a Tightening Vise," *WSJ*, 26 June.)

While the elections to the European Parliament may have offered a ray of hope to the European left, developments on the continent as a whole did not portend a future of easy solutions to complicated problems.

By the end of 1989 strong leadership in the West European communist movement had almost disappeared, and had been decisively affected by the crumbling of every single communist regime in Central and Eastern Europe (with the exception of Albania) within a matter of weeks, between September and the death of Romania's communist party leader on 25 December. In September the dilemma was described very well by the director of the Center for Strategic Studies at the Free University of Rome:

. . . the majority of Communist leaders in Western Europe now celebrate the marvels of market economy, private entrepreneurship and individual profit, although they know this is the ideological patrimony of their adversaries: liberal, Christian Democratic and—enriched with large doses of social-welfare policies—Social Democratic parties.

Rationally, it seems suicidal for a political party to emphasize the ideological values of its adversaries. The fact is that Communists have learned painful lessons: A modern state cannot be run by central planning; but they also know that without central planning the Communist Party will become irrelevant . . . [the communist parties] in Western European democracies are trying to ride two ponies in opposite directions. Theirs is a fascinating, perilous, exceedingly difficult—and probably hopeless—endeavor. (Enrico Jacchia, "Western Europe Communists: Being Left Without Ideology," *LAT*, 3 September.)

Throughout the decade of the 1980s, time and technology systematically passed by the outdated ideology of Western Europe's communist parties. As the last decade of the twentieth century begins, the crumbling of the Berlin Wall must symbolize for them the crumbling of the tenet they have been preaching for decades: "the belief that free enterprise is evil and profit is its sinful product" (ibid.). They face a future that will be "shaken by painful soul-searching and bitter infighting as they struggle to survive the collapse of traditional Communist governments in Eastern Europe" (Alan Riding, *NYT*, 9 January 1990). They will be very likely to embrace the rebirth of socialism, with a democratic face, and they will extol the virtues of individual liberty and political and economic freedom, as they seek to ally themselves with socialist parties. But, in their heart, their ideological commitment to communism will remain. They are caught in a classic contradiction. How they will resolve their dilemma in relation to their respective electorates will be the history of the 1990s.

The role of the PCF in French political life, and the challenges that party faces, are among the most interesting of those of the communist parties of Western Europe. While its popularity waxed, and then waned during the decade of the 1980s, it nonetheless remained a real if not always influential force in French politics. Party life was affected by internal division during 1987 and 1988. Debates within the PCF included charges that Stalinism had returned to plague the party, public demands for the resignation of General Secretary Georges Marchais, and accusations that the party leadership refused to adjust its policies and programs to reflect fundamental changes in French society.

In the election for the French presidency in 1988, the PCF remained fragmented. The party's candidate, conservative André Lajoinie, polled only 6.8 percent of the vote, the worst performance in the PCF's 68-year history (in 1981 Marchais received 15.5 percent). A second member of the PCF, however, also ran for the office, former party spokesman and reformer Pierre Juquin. While Juquin's showing of 2.1 percent was widely regarded as insufficient to bolster reformist strength within the party, it was also an omen of increasing dissent. The party's leadership claims that the poor electoral results were not an accurate reflection of the PCF's real influence in French political life. Yet the party had strongly supported participation in the democratic process in 1981. Thus, Marchais's conclusion that "the election of the President by universal suffrage is the most undemocratic of elections" stood in stark contrast to its previous position.

At the end of 1988, the PCF held 25 of 577 seats in the French National Assembly as a result of elections in June. They arrived at a legislative modus vivendi with the French Socialist Party (PSF), following a change in the assembly's rules, engineered by the Socialists, which reduced from 30 to 20 the minimum number of seats required for recognition as an official parliamentary group; thus PCF deputies voted with the French Socialist Party (PSF) to elect former socialist Prime Minister Laurent Fabius as president of the National Assembly. This example of leftist unity was short-lived. The PCF continued to experience factionalism and electoral failure in 1989. Frustrated French communists outside the party and determined critics within developed a stronger organization with which to pressure the party leadership for open debate and systemic reforms. One result was the formation of the "New Left, for Socialism, Self-Management, and Ecology" (NG), under the leadership of Pierre Juquin. Out of the NG emerged another group of dissident communists that called itself the "Movement of Communist Renewalists" (MRC). Finally, a third group remained within the PCF and pressed Marchais throughout the year for internal reforms; this group called itself the Communist Reconstructionist Initiative.

The PCF leadership, however, under Georges Marchais, did not share the view that internal reforms were necessary. The seriousness of this division did not escape the French electorate, and the PCF suffered major losses in municipal elections held in March. The party's reaction was to claim that "we are on the rise again," and that membership was increasing. In the elections to the European Parliament, held in June, the PCF received 7.7 percent of the vote, which was an improvement over the 6.7 percent polled in the presidential elections in 1988 (but amounted to a loss of three seats in comparison with the results of the previous election). This result led Marchais to conclude that "we are the future" (*Le Figaro*, 23 June).

Internal dissension and poor electoral showings increased media pressure on the PCF to explain why the party's domestic problems should not be seen as a direct parallel to the collapse of communist regimes in Eastern Europe. Marchais responded that the performance of East European communism was "globally positive" and that capitalism was in the throes of a "systemic crisis" (*Le Point*, 18 September, 20 November). This blatant distortion of European realities was continued at the PCF's Central Committee plenum in October. Marchais virtually ignored the disintegration of communist regimes in Eastern Europe, mounted a scathing attack on the policies of Prime Minister Michel Rocard's government, and condemned the European Community's 1992 program as a surrender of national sovereignty in the interest of promoting a "European pillar of the Atlantic Alliance." This performance evoked an acrimonious response and criticism of the PCF leadership as reactionary, and weakened substantially the position and power of the PCF in French political life. It also alienated those members of the party who hoped for and expected responsible leadership from the party's senior members. Unlike the majority of Western Europe's communist parties, the PCF indicated no intention of revising its own policies and programs to reflect changing political and economic realities in Europe. Thus, division and dissension within the PCF, and increasing criticism from without, were virtually assured throughout 1990 by the announcement that the 27th Party Congress would be held at the end of that year.

The Communist Party of Italy (PCI) has argued since 1986 "that the old differences between the communist and socialist movements are not sustainable" (*YICA*, 1987). The efforts to set aside these differences did not produce a victory at the polls in 1987 of the magnitude the party expected. It won only 177 of 630 parliamentary seats (26.6 percent of the vote). Nonetheless, the PCI remains one of the most influential communist parties in Western Europe in a country of major importance.

In the course of the 1980s, the PCI has increasingly championed a united European left that would transcend the historical division between communists and socialists (or social democrats). Any lingering "Eurocommunist" ambitions or claims to be seeking a "Third Way" (that is, one between Eastern state socialism and Western social democracy) have been abandoned. The party leadership is gambling that its political future will be brighter if it can be viewed as "an integral part of the European left."

In 1988, following a further decline in party fortunes in the municipal elections of May and June, the debate focused on how to chart a "new course" and to redefine the identity of the PCI. Under the new leadership of General Secretary Achille Occhetto, the PCI was charged with "the conquest of the center" in Italian politics. In the October 1988 issue of *World Marxist Review*, party member Gianni Cervetti emphasized the PCI's position that "there is no point in speaking about a communist movement," but that the "forces of progress and renewal" in Western Europe supported the Soviet government's policies of *glasnost'* (openness) and *perestroika* (restructuring). Thus, while the PCF considered the latter policies with antipathy, the PCI welcomed them; for these policies gave the party considerably greater flexibility on the Italian political stage.

The PCI's showing in elections to the European Parliament in June exceeded the party's expectations. It received 27.7 percent of the vote, to the Italian Socialists' (PS) 14.8 percent. The election's real importance to the PCI was that it represented a moral victory after ten years of consistent electoral decline; but it did not thrust the party to the forefront of Italian political life, despite the party's membership of approximately 1,500,000 just after the March 1989 congress.

Throughout the year the PCI struggled to establish its own identity. These efforts ranged from Occhetto's remark that he felt himself to be more a child of the French than of the Russian Revolution, to his open pursuit of closer alliance with the Italian socialists, and to affiliation with the socialist parties of Western Europe in general through the Socialist International. Debate within the party was extensive and concerned a multitude of party organizational questions, as well as domestic-policy posi-

tions. The most interesting development, however, occurred toward the end of the year, and had to be seen as linked to changes in Eastern Europe. In December, the PCI set the date for the nineteenth congress for March 1990, in Bologna. Almost simultaneously Occhetto introduced the proposal that the congress consider establishing "a new democratic political formation, reformist, open to progressive lay and Catholic components," and therewith, after months of debate, endorsed the proposal to drop the "communist" label from the Italian Communist Party, as well as to eliminate the hammer and sickle as its symbol.

The first year of the new decade will see continued debate within the PCI, as it considers what kind of party it wishes to become. But unlike the highly destructive acerbity that has plagued the PCF, the Italian debate may produce positive results for the party's position in relation to the Italian electorate. To do so will require that the party agree on clear domestic policies at its coming congress. The party must also continue to develop its image as a responsible member of the European left, as Europe moves toward 1992. A major step in this direction was Occhetto's visit to the United States in May— the first such visit by a PCI general secretary—"to dispel old, mistaken ideas about Italian Communists," and to present himself "as an exponent of the new European left." In this aim the PCI is not alone. As the collapse of the communist regimes of Eastern Europe continues to discredit the communist idea, the European left may gain, in the process, a new opportunity to earn legitimacy. It is certain that the PCI is pursuing this goal.

The Spanish Communist Party (PCE) has operated legally within Spain since 1977, and claims a membership of 83,000. It was the leading advocate of Eurocommunism until 1981, under the leadership of Santiago Carrillo. Gerardo Iglesias succeeded Carrillo in 1982, at the age of 37, and served as general secretary of the party until 1988. Last year, amid growing anxiety over a "lack of leadership," Iglesias was replaced as general secretary by Julio Anguita (age 49). Led by Ignacio Gallego, pro-Soviet dissidents withdrew from the PCE in 1983 to form in 1984 the Communist Party of the Peoples of Spain (PCPE), with a claimed membership of 16,000 to 17,000. In 1988 Gallego was replaced by Juan Ramos. A second group, led by Carrillo, was created in 1982 following his failure to be reconfirmed as the PCE's general secretary. Carrillo formally resigned from the PCE in 1986 and in 1987 officially formed the Spanish Workers'

Party-Communist Unity (PTE-UC), with a claimed membership of 14,000.

At the beginning of 1989, the PCE pursued a policy of "ideological renewal" in an effort to bring together all communist groups in Spain in a coalition of the United Left. These efforts were supported during 1988 by PCPE chairman Ramos, while Carrillo, as the spokesman for the PTE-UC, rejected unity as advocated by the PCE and endorsed the concept of a federation of communist groups in Spain. In January 1989, at a special unification congress, the PCPE chairman Ramos persuaded a sizable contingent of his party to rejoin the PCE; PCE general secretary Anguita confirmed that approximately 80 percent of the PCPE members had rallied to the PCE and further, that numerous members of the PTE-UC were prepared to follow suit.

The fruits of these efforts were seen first in June, when the United Left coalition received 6.1 percent of the vote and 4 of Spain's 60 seats in the European Parliament. In Spain's national elections in October, the United Left coalition garnered 9.05 percent of the vote and 18 of 350 parliamentary seats (in 1986: 4.6 percent of the vote and 7 seats). This result marked a notable improvement in the political fortunes of Spain's communist parties, despite the Spanish government's assertion that the United Left coalition was merely "a front for the PCE, though they do not dare say so because communism has failed throughout the world" (*Diario 16*, 13 September; *FBIS*, 15 October). Although this was undoubtedly correct, it was also clear that the PCE was seeking to re-establish itself as a credible political force in Spain after a decade of turmoil, and thus enthusiastically endorsed the political changes in Eastern Europe because "they derive from the will of the people." At the same time it was unclear whether the PCE will pursue political and economic goals which are compatible with the economic and political freedoms sought by the peoples of Eastern Europe.

The Portuguese Communist Party (PCP) claims a membership of almost 200,000 in a country with a population of approximately 10.5 million. The party has been led by Álvaro Cunhal since 1961 and holds 30 of 250 parliamentary seats. The party's political influence, however, has declined significantly since it won 19 percent of the vote in 1979 (in 1987 it won 11 percent). The Portuguese communist movement and much of the unionized labor force are controlled by the PCP, one of the most Stalinist parties in Western Europe. Although it

formally supports Soviet domestic and foreign policy, internally it has resisted the kind of reforms that are being discussed within the PCF and undertaken by the PCI.

The primary focus of attention within the party during the year was the division of opinion over Cunhal's successor. In ill health, Cunhal encouraged the debate that centered on the merits of Stalinist Domingos Abrantes versus those of José Luís Judas, a moderate and charismatic leader within the party. Argument within the party was intensified by Cunhal's criticism of changes taking place in Eastern Europe, and his insistence that communist ideology held the solution to the problems of the modern world. At the end of the year, it seemed clear that 1990 would see continued debate over Cunhal's eventual successor, and that until this problem was resolved the eventual place of the PCP in Portuguese political life would remain uncertain.

In Cyprus, Greece, Malta, San Marino, and Turkey, the communist parties do not play influential roles in the design of domestic and foreign policy. The Communist Party of San Marino (PCS) is an extension of the Italian Communist Party, just as the country's other political parties reflect the views of their Italian counterparts. General secretary of the PCS is Gilberto Ghiotti, and party membership is claimed to be 1,200. In national elections in 1988, the PCS received 28.71 percent of the vote and holds 18 of 60 parliamentary seats. This victory allowed the PCS to continue its coalition with the Christian Democratic Party (PDCS) in 1989; between them they hold approximately 75 percent of the country's parliamentary seats. The government is headed by two captains-regent, elected for six-month terms, selected from the 60-member parliament. The PCS was represented by Reves Salvatore (1 October 1988 to 31 March 1989), and by Mauro Fiorini (1 April 1989 to 30 September 1989). The next party congress is scheduled for 1990. At that time, changes in PCS attitudes and programs may result, as a consequence of the political changes taking place throughout Europe.

The Communist Party of Malta (CPM), established in 1969, has an estimated membership of 300, and is led by General Secretary Anthony Vassallo (age 70). It did not participate in a national election until 1987, and its most recent congress was held in July 1988. In the 1987 election the CPM received .08 percent of the vote, and since that time the party has been in decline. In 1989 the CPM ceased publishing the Malta edition of *World Marxist Review*, and its monthly publication, *Zmini-*

jietna, was circulated in only three issues. Despite its efforts to do so, the party has been unable to increase its membership or its influence. Evidence suggested that Malta's Labour Party sought to increase its contacts with communist parties abroad, most notably in Italy, the Soviet Union, and Czechoslovakia. Of particular interest were the Labour Party's discussions with members of the Soviet Academy of Sciences concerning Malta's position with regard to the European Community. The Maltese government itself, however, made it clear that it intended to apply for membership in the EC in 1990. While it maintained cordial relations with the Soviet government and emphasized its policy of neutrality and nonalignment, it also made clear that it was committed to the principles of democratic government. Acting in the spirit of neutrality and nonalignment, it hosted the meeting in December between the leaders of the Soviet Union and the United States.

In Turkey the communist party (UCPT) is proscribed, and is the only communist party of Western Europe to operate illegally. In 1988, it changed its name to the United Communist Party of Turkey following the merger of the Communist Party of Turkey (TCP) with the Workers' Party of Turkey (WPT). Its direct influence in Turkish politics is negligible, but it does seek to support a wide range of leftist activities throughout the country.

In Cyprus, the Progressive Party of the Working People (AKEL) continues to be led by General Secretary Dimitris Christofias (age 43), and claims a membership of 15,000. In the most recent elections held in 1985 the AKEL received 27.4 percent of the vote and holds 15 of 56 seats in the Cypriot parliament. The party's popular support is drawn primarily from the Greek Cypriot majority, which makes up approximately 80 percent of the island's estimated population of 700,009. As was the case for many other communist parties in Western Europe, developments in the Soviet Union and in Eastern Europe also affected the AKEL. Discontent within the party focused on the rigidity of its ideological views and positions that had produced little "real change in policy" (*Cyprus Mail*, 24 November) since the introduction of *perestroika* and *glasnost'* in the Soviet Union. Debate also centered on the Soviet invasion of Czechoslovakia in 1968, and at the end of the year the party declared its previous support of the invasion "mistaken and invalid." It also endorsed the principles of sovereignty, independence and nonintervention in the internal affairs of other countries, and maintained

that "new political thinking" governed the entire system of international relations. The AKEL leadership continued to call for a resolution of constitutional and territorial issues in negotiations between Greek and Turkish Cypriots, presumably in the expectation that it would generate support for the AKEL among the island's voters, and called for the settlement of local and international disputes by peaceful means. The party's reversal of its previous stance condoning the invasion of Czechoslovakia was another example of the parroting of a position taken by the CPSU, but the party remained stagnant, clad in political cliché.

The affairs of the Communist Party of Greece (KKE) were decisively affected by the political fortunes of the country's socialist prime minister, Andreas Papandreou. KKE has been divided between pro-Soviet and Eurocommunist factions since the period of military government in Greece (1967–1974). In the 1980s, rivalries within the Greek communist party became not only intense, but also extremely complex. The pro-Soviet KKE has an estimated membership of 50,000, while the smaller Eurocommunist faction, known as KKE-Interior (KKE-I), divided itself into two groups in 1987. The stronger of the two is known as the Greek Left and is led by Leonidas Kyrkos. The second, and much weaker group, retained the name KKE-I and added the title of Renovating Left under the leadership of Giannis Banias.

In 1989, the KKE moved to the forefront of the political stage. The talks between KKE and the Greek Left (E.AR), which had started in 1988, resulted in February in the formation of a "Coalition of the Left and Progress," with KKE's general secretary, Kharilaos Florakis, as its chairman. The Coalition of the Left adopted a position highly critical of the economic scandals allegedly caused by members of Papandreou's governing Panhellenic Socialist Movement (PASOK), a viewpoint also shared by the conservative New Democracy Party (ND), led by Constantine Mitsotakis. The result was a stunning defeat for PASOK, which won only 125 parliamentary seats (in 1985 it had won 165 seats) and 39.1 percent of the votes. At the same time the Coalition of the Left won 28 seats, of which the KKE held 21, thereby doubling its representation in parliament. Mitsotakis's party received a plurality of 44.37 percent of the vote and obtained 144 seats, just seven seats less than an absolute majority of 151 in the 300 seat parliament. Postelectoral negotiations produced a coalition government of the Coalition of the Left and the conservative ND, which set as its initial task a thorough investigation of the economic scandals that had emerged under Papandreou's government.

Of more striking significance, however, was the fact that the governing coalition legitimized the communist left as a full-fledged and equal participant in the Greek political process. While KKE's participation in the coalition government generated considerable opposition within the party, the Coalition of the Left began to play a legitimate role in Greek politics, reminiscent of the PCF's governmental role in French politics in the early 1980s. Whether or not this will lead to a change in KKE's official name or to a unified party, with the identities of KKE and E.AR submerged in the process, is uncertain. But the Coalition of the Left, following special national elections held in November, lost 7 of the 28 seats it had won in June. This outcome produced an "all-party" coalition government comprised of the Coalition of the Left, ND, and PASOK as the year ended. If the three members of the coalition cannot agree on the election of a new president of the republic in March 1990, it is likely that new parliamentary elections will take place in the spring. Whatever the outcome, however, it is probable that the Coalition of the Left will continue to play an influential role in Greek politics in the new year.

At its peak in 1942, the Communist Party of Great Britain (CPGB) commanded a membership of 42,000 and has never played a major role in Britain's political process. Since 1980 party membership has been declining; in 1988 it stood at less than 10,000 members, and in 1989 it was reported to be approximately 8,000. The decline in electoral support was most graphically illustrated in Britain's last general elections (1987), in which the CPGB's nineteen candidates polled 6,078 votes. The party is represented in the House of Lords by one member, Lord Milford, and has been without representation in the British parliament since 1950.

The rapid changes occurring in Eastern Europe and the Soviet Union exerted a strong influence on the communist movement in Great Britain as well. Throughout the 1980s, the party has been divided by a rift between the Eurocommunist CPGB and more Stalinist factions. The main focus of CPGB activity during late 1989 was the 41st Party Congress, held in London in late November. The party delegates felt vindicated by their long and consistent criticism of the 1968 Soviet suppression of reform in Czechoslovakia, as compared to the pro-Soviet views of their dissident rivals: the Communist Party of Britain and the New Communist Party.

The congress produced a new strategic document, "Manifesto for New Times," which concluded that "Stalinism is dead, and Leninism—its theory of the state, its concept of the party, the absence of civil society, its notion of revolution—has also had its day." Thus, the manifesto argued for a new flexibility, a willingness to recast the communist movement as part of the social-democratic tradition and therefore a willingness to work within a pluralistic democratic system. Consistent with this position, the party elected a new general secretary in January 1990, Nina Temple. At 33 years of age, she is the youngest leader of the CPGB, and she immediately sought to define the path to be followed by the party in the new decade: "If we are arguing that the era of 1917 failed and that that is over, it seems right to look at ourselves and look at what it is we still maintain from that approach and what should go so that we can be part of the contribution to new progressive politics in Britain" (*International Herald Tribune*, 3–4 February 1990).

Irish political life is not influenced to any significant degree by the activities of the Communist Party of Ireland (CPI). Party membership is under 500, and it is without representation in Ireland's parliament. The party's primary bases of support are in Belfast and Dublin. The party advocates creation of a united socialist Ireland by means of working-class solidarity and opposes the use of violence. Like its European counterparts, the CPI is assessing the ideological implications of events in Eastern Europe and the Soviet Union. It is more closely allied with the views of the Communist Party of Britain than with the Eurocommunist CPGB, but there were indications during the year that it would endorse Gorbachev's policy views at a party congress in 1990 convened to debate the significance of developments in the communist movement.

The communist parties of Belgium, Denmark, Luxembourg, and the Netherlands exercised marginal influence on the political life of their respective countries in 1989. The Communist Party of Luxembourg (CPL), headed by René Urbany, won one seat in the Luxembourg parliament in elections held in June and received less than 4 percent of the vote (in 1984 it had obtained 4.9 percent of the vote and 2 of 64 seats). The party claims a membership of 600, and plays no significant role in the European communist movement. It has traditionally maintained close ties with the SED of East Germany, but the value of those ties for the future is negligible.

Within Luxembourg, the CPL has continued to support a coalition of left-wing forces, but has not achieved success at the polls as a consequence of that stance. In a reflection of the political turmoil engulfing Eastern Europe's communist parties, René Urbany acknowledged that "the building of a socialist society in Western Europe is not an immediate prospect" (*World Marxist Review*, July). While the party seeks a broader political following, it is much more likely to remain an unimpressive political entity in 1990.

The Communist Party of Denmark (DKP) has been without representation in the Danish parliament since 1979, and in the most recent national election, held in 1988, the DKP polled only 0.8 percent of the vote. The party's membership is estimated at 7,400.

The year was a tumultuous one for the DKP, which saw continued strife within the party. Financial difficulties resulted in staff reduction, and confrontation with its younger members occupied the DKP's leadership at a time when rapid changes in Eastern Europe demanded its close attention. The DKP sought to form a broad coalition of leftist parties during the year, but this effort proved largely unsuccessful. With the Conservative-led government of Prime Minister Poul Schlueter entering its ninth year in 1990, the Danish left continues its longest period of opposition. As a consequence, DKP chairman Ole Sohn, 35 years of age, has called for an extraordinary party congress in the new year. Whether the congress will be able to inject into the party a new unity of purpose is highly questionable. But it is clear that unless the DKP is able to define new and credible political and economic goals, the political changes sweeping across Europe will assure that the party remains on the fringe of Danish political life.

The Communist Party of Belgium (PCB) is organized within the Union of Communists in Belgium and consists of two groups, one operating in French-speaking Belgium and the other in Dutch-speaking Belgium. In the last national election, held in December 1988, the PCB received 0.8 percent of the vote, and the party has an estimated membership of 5,000.

The most significant event during the year was the party's 26th congress, held in March. While the principal purpose of the congress was to develop the theme of a "Europe of Freedom," its primary result was a reorganization of the PCB under a new name: the Union of the Communists of Belgium. This effort was designed not only to improve coordina-

tion among the party's different organizational groups, but also to provide a new platform from which to deal with the effect of events in Eastern Europe and the Soviet Union on Western Europe's communist movement. Thus, the PCB will seek to design new policies to deal with the challenges presented by the collapse of the ruling communist parties. But the challenges will not be easily met, and the PCB, like its Danish counterpart, is likely to remain on the periphery of Belgian politics.

The Communist Party of The Netherlands (CPN), with an estimated membership of 3,000–5,000, became in 1989 the first of the small communist parties of northwestern Europe to draw the consequences of the changing international situation, as well as of the sociocultural changes in Dutch society that were making a distinct communist program irrelevant. In national elections held in the latter half of the year, the CPN formed the Green Left alliance with three small new-left parties: the Pacifist Socialists (PSP), the Radical Party (PPR), and the Evangelical People's Party (EVP). These four parties have not merged their organizations and claim to maintain their respective identities. The alliance won 4.1 percent of the vote and 6 seats in the Dutch legislature. But at the same time, the CPN also lost its raison d'être and entered the 1990s as a communist party without its former Leninist trappings. Where this would lead it in the new decade was uncertain.

In the Nordic countries of Iceland, Norway, Sweden, and Finland, the communist parties were active, but without major influence. The People's Alliance of Iceland (PA) was founded in 1968, and continues to be led by Olafur Ragnar Grimsson. Membership is estimated at 3,000, out of Iceland's population of approximately 249,000. In the 1987 national elections the party polled 13.2 percent of the vote and holds 8 of 63 seats in the Icelandic parliament.

As the new year began, the PA was a member of a four-party coalition with the agrarian Progressive Party (PP), the reformist Social Democratic Party (SDP), and a splinter parliamentarian group from the Progressives elected to the parliament as the Association for Equality and Justice. With an even split in the lower house of the Althing and only a one-vote majority, the coalition was weak from the beginning. As the economic downturn that had undermined the previous government moved into its third year and inflation continued at over 20 percent, pressure on the coalition mounted. In September, the government was forced to invite the moderate Citizen's Party (CP), headed by PP chairman Steingrimur Hermannsson, to join the coalition. Within the cabinet, PA chairman Grimsson holds the finance ministry, and party members Steingrimur Sigfusson and Svavar Gestsson hold the ministries of communications and agriculture, and of education and culture, respectively. As the year ended, political analysts predicted that the coalition would not survive until the next national elections, which are scheduled for April 1991.

The Norwegian Communist Party (NKP) is without representation in the Norwegian parliament, and has an estimated membership of from 1,500 to 2,000 in a country with a population of approximately 4,203,000. It competes with several small parties of the left, especially the Socialist Left Party (SV), established in the mid-1970s by former members of the NKP, as well as with the Workers' Communist Party (AKP), both of which are larger than the NKP (with 11,000 and 5,000 to 7,000 members, respectively).

The NKP has not held a seat in the Norwegian parliament since 1973, and the party split in 1975, when moderate elements formed the SV. Since that time, the NKP has sought "an alliance of the working-class parties that is able to unite all those who are objective opponents of monopoly capital and imperialism," a position that stands in sharp contrast to its conclusion that the "Social Democrats are our most important alliance partners on all the major political issues today" (*Friheten*, 30 April 1987). The significance of this contradiction was highlighted again in 1989 during Norway's general election in September.

In that election, the Norwegian Labour Party, headed by prime minister Gro Harlem Brundtland, suffered its worse defeat since 1930, receiving 34.3 percent of the vote. The share of the vote garnered by Norway's Conservatives declined from 30.4 to 22.2 percent. The major winners were the libertarian Progress Party, which won 22 seats (it had previously held 2) and the Socialist Left Party (SV), which increased its representation from 6 seats to 17. The NKP, in an electoral alliance with the AKP, received 0.84 percent of the vote and holds no parliamentary seats. It is uncertain how the NKP will react to the dismantling of the communist system in Eastern Europe, but it certainly cannot look forward to 1990 with confidence.

The Left Party Communists (VPK) in Sweden have been represented in the Swedish parliament throughout the 1980s. It continues to hold 21 of 349 seats and remains under the leadership of Lars Werner; membership figures remain constant at approximately 17,000 to 18,000. While the VPK enjoyed modest electoral support in 1988, it too was nonetheless affected by the political events in Eastern Europe. In late November, after the dramatic opening of the Berlin Wall, party chairman Werner gave an interview to the *Svenska Dagbladet* (23 November), in which he acknowledged that the VPK was analyzing its policies and even considering changing its name by removing the word "communist." He seemed to be advocating a broad-based left-wing party that could present a new socialist alternative: "The question is whether developments in East Europe and the process of democratization do not occasion a change of program" (ibid.).

The real question that Werner, as well as his counterparts elsewhere in Western Europe, will face in the new decade is how to explain their sudden and abrupt revision of views they have held for decades, and to make their explanations credible. An excellent illustration of the peculiar relationship to power and politics that has been well developed by the communist parties, was Werner's observation on the use of force in East Germany. It was made in the context of the Swedish government's awarding of the Olof Palme Prize to President Vaclav Havel of Czechoslovakia in November, for his "consistent and courageous work for truth and democracy." Werner recounted, "I froze when I read that Honecker had intended to order the military onto the streets of Leipzig before he was removed" (*Svenska Dagbladet*, 23 and 25 November). At least some Swedish voters must have wondered whether the Berlin Wall had represented a legitimate state border for 28 years, in Werner's view.

Since 1969, the internal affairs of the Finnish Communist Party (SKP) have been dominated by factional strife, which led to a major party split in 1985 resulting from disagreement on the merits of a new party program, "Socialism with a Finnish Face." In 1988, a new generation of leaders emerged in the Finnish communist movement, and immediately moved publicly to support efforts to overcome the party's division and heal its attendant wounds. The SKP split into two groups. The SKP, under the leadership of Jarmo Wahlström (he became chairman in 1988), claims a membership of 21,000 and the Stalinist wing of the party (SKP-Y) claims approximately 13,500 members; until October its chairman was Jouko Kajanoja; he was succeeded by Esko-Juhani Tennilä on October 14.

The year began with broad discussion concerning formation of a Left Alliance composed of individuals and not particular parties. This proposal generated a debate that continued throughout the year because it threatened, if adopted by the SKP, to destroy the party's electoral identity. By the end of the year, the party's Central Committee had adopted a resolution calling on communists to join the Left Alliance following its formal creation in 1990. Thus, a motion to approve the Central Committee's decision to dissolve the party and transfer assets and personnel to the Left Alliance was placed on the agenda of the SKP's 22nd congress, scheduled to convene in early 1990. The future of the party, at least in name, will presumably be determined in the new year. But it was clear at year's end that the SKP, like its West European counterparts, was undergoing a crisis of identity in the wake of the dramatic political changes elsewhere on the continent.

The Communist Party of Austria (KPÖ) and the Swiss Labor Party (PdAS) play minimal roles in the political arenas of their countries. The KPÖ has an estimated membership of 15,000, and in 1989 its chairman continued to be Franz Muhri (age 66). The party received less than one percent of the vote in the most recent national election, held in 1986, and also polled less than one percent of the vote in provincial elections held in Carinthia, Salzburg, and Tyrol in March. The KPÖ's 27th congress was held in early 1990, and Walter Silbermayr succeeded Muhri as party chairman.

Throughout the year the party maintained its pro-Soviet position, and while it endorsed *perestroika*, it also emphasized the necessity to continue the class struggle. Its primary activity early in the year was opposition to Austria's application for membership in the European Common Market, based on the claim that Austria's neutrality would be thereby violated. The party also was sharply critical of the Hungarian government's political reforms, and condemned the decision to allow East German refugees to travel unimpeded to Austria via Hungary. By the end of the year the KPÖ was in a quandary. It would face, in 1990, the dilemma of how to react to the systematic breakdown of the communist system in Eastern Europe. Whether it endorsed the process or condemned it, it would lose credibility with the Austrian electorate—a problem faced by every other communist party in Western Europe as well.

In Switzerland, the PdAS has not played a significant role in Swiss political life for many years. In the last national elections, held in 1987, the party received less than one percent of the vote, and holds one seat in parliament. Since 1987 the party has sought to increase its membership, and 39 percent of the Central Committee is under the age of 40; however, the party adheres to its class-conscious ideology, vocabulary, and slogans. The major change within the party occurred in March with the death of long-time chairman Jean Vincent. Whether his successors will be able to give the party new vitality in 1990 is unclear; but they will have to struggle with reconciling their calls for the freedom of the working classes with the reality that the so-called class struggle has been overtaken by economic reality.

The Socialist Unity Party of West Berlin (SEW) claims a membership of 7,000, in a city with a population of 1.9 million. Party chairman is Dietmar Ahrens, who succeeded Horst Schmitt following the latter's death in April. The SEW holds no seats in West Berlin's parliament, and received 0.6 percent of the vote in the city's election in 1989. In a city that has been divided by the Berlin Wall and surrounded by mine fields, the party has never appealed to the citizens, who have defended their freedom successfully since 1945. The year 1989, however, brought dramatic changes and contrasts to West Berlin, as it did to Germany as a whole.

In 1987, at the party's last congress, the SEW maintained that "our future lies in our Marxist-Leninist firmness in principle, in our undeviating orientation to the interests of the working people, and in our indestructible alliance with the CPSU, with the SED, and with the entire world communist movement" (*Neues Deutschland*, 16–17 May 1987). In 1989, however, the SEW concluded that "*glasnost'* and *perestroika* must be recognized as principles of socialism" (DPA, 23 January; *RAD Background Report/14*, 27 January). As the communist regime in East Germany showed signs of disintegration in the autumn, the SEW made adjustments accordingly. The party newspaper, *Die Wahrheit* (The truth), changed its name to *Neue Zeitung* (New newspaper) in the hope that it would appeal to "the growing need of the leftist, democratic, trade-union spectrum" (*Frankfurter Allgemeine Zeitung*, 16 October), and publication was completely suspended one week later. Following the opening of the Berlin Wall on 9 November, the SEW's entire Politburo resigned. At the end of November, Klaus-Dieter Heiser, an SEW leader, acknowledged that the party had idealized the achievements in East Germany and concluded the SEW "had believed that the collective human rights developed in socialism were to be valued above the individual human rights, such as freedom of movement, which had been fought for in the bourgeois revolution" (*Neues Deutschland*, 28 November). The challenge in 1990 will be how the SEW, if it still exists, can effectively address new problems (without the financial subsidies formerly received from the SED) and survive in a radically altered political environment. The prognosis is pessimistic. The party leadership recommended the dissolution of the party in November. The debate on the party's future will take place at an extraordinary congress scheduled for February 1990.

In the Federal Republic of Germany (FRG), the German Communist Party (DKP) is not represented in the Bundestag and received only 0.5 percent of the vote in the national elections held in January 1987. In 1988, for the first time in fifteen years, party membership dropped below 38,000. Characterized by dogmatism and opposition to change, the DKP was plagued by internal dissension that in 1989 deepened the divisions within the party. The disintegration of the SED in East Germany has brought financial ruin to the DKP (as well as to the SEW). While the party has declared an income of approximately 22 million DM, it has also been receiving in excess of 70 million DM from East Germany, and its entire party program has been systematically coordinated with the SED. The seriousness of its predicament was acknowledged by the DKP at a meeting of its Central Committee on 16 December. It not only announced a continuing decline in membership, but dismissal of more than 80 percent of its employees, termination of many of its leases for buildings and offices, and the transformation of its daily publication, *Unsere Zeit* (Our time), from a daily into a weekly (Kevin Devlin, *RAD Background Report/222*, 19 December). At the end of the year the party was facing a crisis from which it may not recover.

At its Ninth Party Congress, held in Frankfurt in January, party chairman Herbert Mies acknowledged that "the party is beset by hitherto unparalleled inner contradictions" (*RAD Background Report/4*, 11 January), and that the party was threatened by a split. As thousands of refugees from East Germany crossed into the Federal Republic in the latter half of 1989, DKP member Ellen Weber followed the SED accusation by publicly deploring West German "interference" in the GDR's internal affairs (*RAD Background Report/178*, 20 September). While the opening of the Berlin Wall on 9 November slowed the flood of refugees, over one-sixth of the GDR's population visited West Germany on 10 and 11 November. It was a deeply emotional

experience that bore witness to the increasingly rapid collapse of communist rule in the GDR. In a move that posed a direct threat to the credibility of the DKP, the SED changed its name to "SED–Party of Democratic Socialism" in December. In October, a minority wing of the DKP reacted to the events unfolding in Central Europe by convening a "Renewal Congress" which called for a "break with the traditional socialism and party conceptions of the DKP" (*Neues Deutschland*, 24 October). Party chairman Mies and his deputy, Ellen Weber, announced that they would resign their posts at an extraordinary party congress scheduled for February 1990. The announcement in November that the party would no longer be receiving its subsidies from the SED dealt a severe blow to the party's organizational structure; no other West European communist party was so reliant upon a foreign party as was the DKP on the SED. The collapse of communist power and ideology in the German Democratic Republic and the Soviet Union's encouragement of reform in Eastern Europe present a potentially fatal threat to the DKP. At the end of the year, the DKP's leadership was not capable of responding to the changes sweeping across Central Europe, changes that have brought the party to the brink of fragmentation and bankruptcy. As the process of political change in Germany develops in 1990, the fortunes of the DKP will continue to decline; the unanswered questions are how rapidly and to what extent.

Dennis L. Bark
Hoover Institution

Austria

Population. 7,585,766
Party. Communist Party of Austria (Kommunistische Partei Österreichs; KPÖ)
Founded. 3 November 1918
Membership. 15,000 (1986 estimate)
Party Chairman. Franz Muhri (b. 1924)
Politburo. 13 members: Walter Baier, Willi Gaisch, Michael Graber, Franz Hager, Anton

Hofer, Hans Kalt (secretary of Central Committee), Franz Muhri, Otto Podolsky (Vienna party secretary), Irma Schwager, Walter Silbermayr (secretary of Central Committee), Rudolf Slavik, Susanne Sohn, Ernst Wimmer

Secretariat. 2 members: Hans Kalt and Walter Silbermayr

Central Committee. 72 members

Status. Legal

Last Congress. Twenty-sixth, 25–28 March 1987, in Vienna

Last Election. Federal, 23 November 1986, 0.72 percent, no representation

Publications. *Volksstimme* (People's voice), Michael Graber, editor, KPÖ daily organ, Vienna; *Weg und Ziel* (Path and goal), Erwin Scharf, editor, KPÖ theoretical monthly, Vienna

Austria's economy performed well in 1989, and the KPÖ concentrated on its weakest sector, the nationalized industries. Efforts at rationalization or privatization were strongly opposed. International affairs, however, constituted the more important sector of the party's 1989 activities. In midyear, Austria applied for membership in the European Common Market, over the KPÖ's strenuous but totally ignored opposition. Later in the year, the party had to come to grips with the momentous changes in Eastern Europe. Materials available at the time of writing are more interesting than conclusive.

The most important elections of 1989 were the provincial elections of Carinthia, Salzburg, and Tyrol, held simultaneously on 12 March. Everywhere, Communists polled less than 1 percent; in Tyrol, their vote went up from 0.6 to 0.8 percent (*Volksstimme*, 14 March). Results of the provincial election in Vorarlberg on 8 October were equally meager (*Volksstimme*, 10 October). On the other hand, the KPÖ repeated its showing of 6 percent in 1984 in the municipal election in Hallein near Salzburg on 8 October (*Volksstimme*, 10 October). On 24 September, the KPÖ doubled its vote share in the Tyrolean capital of Innsbruck to almost 1.5 percent (*Tiroler Tageszeitung*, 25 September). University elections in May brought the communist students— generally polling between 1 and 2.5 percent—7 percent in Salzburg and 4 percent in Linz (*Volksstimme*, 13 May).

In 1989, *World Marxist Review* published a number of articles by Austrians. In "Class-based and Universal Human Values," Ernst Wimmer pleads that communism's and especially *per-*

estroika's concern with human values not lead to an abandonment of class-based thinking (*WMR*, Prague, May). In the Prague issue for June, Ulrich Perzinger glorifies the role of German Communists in the struggle against Hitler. Lutz Holzinger, in the Toronto issue for September, discusses lingering neo-Nazism in Austria. Manfred Gross was one of ten participants in a symposium in West Germany's Ruhr region dealing with the de-industrialization of Europe (*WMR*, Toronto, January). Franz Hager took part in a symposium on Communists in municipal politics, held in Vienna (*WMR*, Prague, June). It is of interest that two Austrian left Socialists were asked to contribute to *World Marxist Review*: Josef Hindels (Toronto, February) and Erwin Lanc (Prague, July).

Leadership and Organization. On 9 March, the Central Committee of the KPÖ, in a press conference, announced preparations for the party's 27th congress in January 1990. Muhri said: "There is no other party that discusses political content and questions of personnel so early before a Congress. Therefore, the Central Committee has already acknowledged my and the Politburo's proposal, to nominate Walter Silbermayr as new party chairman" (*Volksstimme*, 10 March; see also *Pravda*, 11 March; *WMR*, Prague, May).

The Vienna provincial party congress in late January was held in the afterglow of the nearly 2 percent the KPÖ had polled in the provincial/municipal election of late 1987 (*Volksstimme*, 28 and 29 January). The Styrian congress took place in Graz in April (*Volksstimme*, 16 April). The Tyrolean congress, in April, planned the partially successful Innsbruck municipal election of 24 September (*Volksstimme*, 25 April).

The KPÖ's Central Committee met on 25 February and 11 April. In the first meeting, Walter Silbermayr and Susanne Sohn reported on the scientific-technical revolution (*Volksstimme*, 2 March). Speaking to the second meeting, Franz Muhri pointed to the weakening of the leading parties, the People's Party and the Socialists. He pointed out that Austria's high growth rate serves profits, not people. With regard to the European Community he pointed to the schizoid position of the Socialists (*Volksstimme*, 19 April).

In late January, the Communist Youth of Austria (KJÖ) held a federal congress in Vienna. The main tenor of the congress was that the youth movement had not been much of a success and must do better (*Volksstimme*, 18 and 24 January). In April,

Vienna's KPÖ held a conference on communal affairs. Many planks for a communal program were introduced. The formula: "Think globally, act locally" was adopted (*Volksstimme*, 16, 18, and 21 April). A women's conference in Vienna, in early October, came to the conclusion that thinking class struggle without a consideration of feminism was no longer satisfactory (*Volksstimme*, 3 October).

On 1 May, the KPÖ commemorated the 200th anniversary of the French Revolution and the 100th anniversary of the founding of the Second International. Silbermayr spoke mainly against privatization, corruption, and joining the European Common Market. According to *Volksstimme* (3 May), cold and bad weather could not dampen the spirit of the Vienna parade. The *Volksstimme* festival in early September also met with bad weather (*Volksstimme*, 29 August, 2, 3–4, and 5 September). On 29 August, the party celebrated the 75th birthday of Erwin Scharf, the grand old former Socialist (*Volksstimme*, 29 August).

Domestic Affairs. The KPÖ's concern with the fate of Austria's nationalized industries continued in 1989. The party's voice was directed primarily against privatization, rationalization, layoffs, endangering of pensions, and cutting of amenities for workers. Involved was primarily, but by no means solely, the steel industry (*Volksstimme*, 3, 10, 27, and 29 January; 2, 4, and 22 February; 1, 9, and 22 March; 30 June; 20 July; 19 August; 11 September; 3 November).

In the field of health *Volksstimme* pointed to the shortage of physicians in a Viennese workers' district (2 April) and of medical specialists in Styria (26 August). The People's Party and the Socialists were accused of playing politics with home care for senior citizens (*Volksstimme*, 24–25 September).

In the housing sector, the KPÖ claimed that its city councilor in Graz was instrumental in the condemning of substandard apartments (*Volksstimme*, 21 March). *Volksstimme* strongly opposed turning housing legislation over to the *Länder* (provinces) (21 May) and attacked the privatization of some public housing in Graz (12 July), claiming credit when the Socialists appeared to change course in the matter (3–4 September). The Linz KPÖ demanded making empty apartments available to those needing them (*Volksstimme*, 3–4 September).

Volksstimme (28 September) celebrated 100 years of social insurance in Austria by opposing the partial privatization of the system and formulating demands for its extension.

An interesting initiative came from Ernst Kaltenegger, the communist city councilor in Graz: to erect a monument to those who refused to fight in Hitler's war (*Volksstimme*, 16 September).

Women's rights were one of the party's concerns in 1989. Prominent communist women wrote on it in *Volksstimme*: Irma Schwager (31 January), B. Löw-Radeschnigg (3 March), and Susanne Sohn (5 and 8 March). A conference in September prepared the party's first program for women, to be submitted to the 27th congress and not free of self-criticism (*Volksstimme*, 24–25 September).

Early in the year, the KPÖ called for giving foreign workers in Austria the vote. *Volksstimme* made much of the fact that Vienna's Socialist mayor opposed their enfranchisement, often in opposition to some local Socialist groups in Vienna (23 February; 2, 4, and 9 March).

In August, Muhri advocated a minimum annual income of about $10,000 (*Volksstimme*, 18 August). Throughout the year, the KPÖ spoke out for the rights of refugees, especially those not from communist countries, and of foreign workers (*Volksstimme*, 2 April, 26 October, 4 November).

The Socialists were attacked primarily early in the year. Muhri commemorated the Socialists' 100th anniversary by emphasizing that the principles of 1889 were still good, but not the party's subsequent practices. He called on the Socialists to discontinue enmity against Communists, limits to the left, and opening to the right (*Volksstimme*, 1 January). The Socialists were accused of having abandoned educational reform (*Volksstimme*, 5 January). Michael Graber bemoaned the fact that Socialist leaders were as prone as others to capitalist corruption (*Volksstimme*, 29 January). Both the Socialists and the People's Party were accused of having developed internal political espionage through the Austria state police (*Volksstimme*, 24 January).

When Austria's controversial antifascist monument was dedicated, Alfred Hrdlicka, the famous sculptor, was reported by *Volksstimme* to have made several procommunist remarks (10 May).

Volksstimme gave a fair amount of publicity to a suit brought first against Hrdlicka, then against *Volksstimme* itself, by Austria's highest circulation tabloid *Kronen-Zeitung* (7 and 9 July). In its issue of 20–21 August, *Volksstimme* complained that ORF, Austria's public broadcasting system, would not represent the KPÖ's point of view on matters relating to Austria's internal politics.

International Views. On 17 July, the Austrian government applied for membership in the European Common Market (*CSM*, 19 July). Up to that date, the fight against this application had been the KPÖ's chief activity in 1989. The rear-guard action after that date was almost as fierce.

The KPÖ's 1989 fight began with a New Year's proclamation, "Resistance Makes Sense!" (*Volksstimme*, 1 January). Early in the year, *Volksstimme* attacked Socialist voices contemplating Austria's application (3 and 4 January). A few weeks later, Muhri stated that EC membership was not important because of the community's friendlier attitude toward the nations of the European Free Trade Association, including Austria (*Volksstimme*, 29 January). *Volksstimme* (3 March) attempted to make the EC problem the focus of the provincial election of 12 March. Later in March, *Volksstimme* spared no efforts to emphasize that Austrian enthusiasm toward the community was weakening (21, 24, 25, 26, and 31 March). On 6 April, the Vienna KPÖ staged a "day of action" against the EC (*Volksstimme*, 8 April). Silbermayr demanded that Austria think about the jeopardy to its neutrality from joining the EC and decide on a delay until 1992 (*Volksstimme*, 14 April). *Volksstimme* (20 April) warned that joining the community would jeopardize Austria's social safety net.

As soon as Alois Mock, foreign minister and former leader of the People's Party, delivered Austria's letter of application to the commission in Brussels, Silbermayr demanded his resignation for placing at risk Austria's neutrality (*Volksstimme*, 21 July). A front-page article in *Volksstimme* (3 August) quoted a representative of the food industry as saying that Austria's strict codes may have to be relaxed, should it acquire EC membership; *Volksstimme* added that the health of Austrians and the survival of food-producing firms could be at risk. Later in August, *Volksstimme* reported worries by the USSR about Austria's application (11 August) and a statement by Chancellor Franz Vranitzky that Austria's neutrality could prevent its gaining EC membership (13–14 August). *Volksstimme* called a possible EC membership Austria's "EG-Anschluss" (18 August, 23 September). On 17 October, *Volksstimme* reported that Rudolf Kirchschläger, former president and foreign minister, had worries about an EC membership that had to do with Austria's neutrality. Austria and the KPÖ seemingly were at odds about the implication for Austria's membership of Gorbachev's remarks in Helsinki about the European Common Market (*Volksstimme*, 29–30 October, 1 and 4 November; *Presse*, 10 November).

When the alleged espionage case against Felix Bloch, former official of the U.S. embassy in Vienna, broke, *Volksstimme* inveighed against FBI activity in Austria (30–31 July). In October, the KPÖ sued Robert Lichal, Austria's defense minister, for alleged espionage activity on behalf of NATO (*Volksstimme*, 26 October). In February, *Volksstimme* alleged breaches of the Geneva accord on Afghanistan by the United States and other anticommunist governments (3 and 26 February, 2 August). *Volksstimme* cheered Greece's communist leader, Harilaos Florakis, for joining Conservatives in a government to investigate corruption in the Socialist government of Papandreou (2 July).

When Austria got into trouble with EC countries for trying to regulate truck traffic through Tyrol, *Volksstimme* criticized the Austrian government for not having a basic policy on transportation (9 and 11 July).

First reports about the crisis in China were between neutral and friendly in tone, with emphasis on the historic understanding between Gorbachev and Deng Xiaoping (*Volksstimme*, 28 April, 17 and 19 May). Government intervention against the demonstrators in Tiananmen Square found *Volksstimme* in some confusion (21 and 23 May). On 23 June, *Volksstimme* quoted Muhri as saying that the death penalty was not the answer to China's difficulty. A four-part *Volksstimme* series, entitled "Peking under Martial Law" (18, 19, 20, and 21 July), reads a bit painfully and inconclusively. No wonder the editors refer to "readers who, in the most varied ways, have exercised very vehement criticism of this series, with regard to the editors or the party" (21 July). *Volksstimme* of 11 August gives a terse report of further progress. Michael Graber commented on the 40th anniversary of the Chinese revolution (*Volksstimme*, 1–2 October):

Li Peng and other top officials admitted in recent days and weeks the justification of the mass protest against corruption, inflation, and growing inequities in income. The brutality of the suppression of this protest movement, preceded by an intraparty power struggle, rests on the reputation of the political leadership.

It is of decisive importance that the PRC, despite continuing differences of opinion and interests stands, especially since Gorbachev's visit to Peking, no longer in confrontation with the USSR. This should make those think who prophesy no future for Communism in the world.

The Soviet elections of 26 March were praised by *Volksstimme* before they took place ("Democracy Pure," 16 and 25 March), though the paper warned against El'tsin's demagoguery. Results were acclaimed, but with reservations about El'tsin and ethnic nationalists (*Volksstimme*, 29 March). Werner Pirker's comment on the retirement of 122 members and alternates of the CPSU's Central Committee adumbrates a stronger role of the government in relation to the CPSU (*Volksstimme*, 27 April).

Reports of further changes in the USSR were reported in *Volksstimme* without comment (20 July, 22 September, 6 October). *Volksstimme* of 19 October reported, without comment, on the controversy between Gorbachev and El'tsin. On 18 November, *Volksstimme* predicted, with some warning, the formation of a Social Democratic party in the USSR in 1990.

In February, *Volksstimme* began to warn of developments in Hungary. Prime Minister Nemeth was attacked for contemplating the necessity of some unemployment (3 February). On 24 February, Imre Pozsgay was attacked sharply for calling 1956 a "people's uprising." The same issue reported a *Magyar Hirlap* interview with Otto Habsburg.

In a *Standard* (Vienna) interview of 10 March, Silbermayr expressed hope that progressive forces in Hungary would fight threatening reaction. On 15 March, *Volksstimme* reported, without comment, the new program of the Hungarian Socialist Labor Party. On the same day, the papers ran an interview with a spokesman of the Hungarian government, whose liberalizing views were not condemned, but clearly questioned. The next day, *Volksstimme* politely laughed at Hungarians on a shopping spree in Vienna. On 30 March, *Volksstimme* warned of the legalization of nonsocialist parties in Hungary. *Volksstimme* was alarmed by efforts to de-ideologize Hungary's army (23 May). It also reported prominently about the bitterness of the German Democratic Republic (GDR) over Hungary's letting East German refugees cross the Hungarian-Austrian border (12 September).

Volksstimme voiced serious reservations about the new draft program of the Hungarian Socialist Labor Party, calling it social democrat rather than Marxist (23 September). A lengthy *Volksstimme* article of 25 October bemoaned the practical liquidation of the Hungarian communist party at its congress of 6 October, the change of name from the Socialist Republic to the Republic of Hungary of 23 October, the removal of the red star from the Parliament building, and, as the article claims, the de facto re-institution of exploitation.

A *Volksstimme* story on GDR refugees who had fled to the Federal Republic of Germany (10 August) contains the remarkable sentence: "When tens of thousands of citizens want to leave their homeland this is certainly also a sign that there is something wrong in the country." Several *Volksstimme* articles dealt with pitfalls awaiting refugees in West Germany (22 August, 2, 10–11, and 12 September).

Volksstimme's first reports on demonstrations in the GDR were peculiar, either submerged in a story about Gorbachev or in an anticapitalist editorial (10 October). The next day, reports were objective and expressed gladness over police restraint (11 October). On 13 October, *Volksstimme* reports on the demonstrations were more positive. Media commentator Eduard Schnitzler was almost derided for calling demonstrators "crying throats without heads," and the readiness for dialogue of the leadership of the GDR's Socialist Unity Party (SED) was appreciated. Ulrich Perzinger wrote: "The change in attitude of the SED leadership comes late, but not too late. It results from pressure from below, and not last from the SED ranks themselves." Willi Gaisch, the Styrian secretary, reported from a trip to Magdeburg that there was a genuine desire for more freedom, especially freedom to travel (*Volksstimme*, 15–16 October).

Erich Honecker's replacement by Egon Krenz was welcomed by *Volksstimme* (19 October). Muhri and Silbermayr wished Krenz "empathy" (*Volksstimme*, 20 October). *Volksstimme* (4 November) reported on the media revolution in the GDR ("When TV Is Fun Again"). The same issue reported a steady stream of returning refugees. The issue of 5–6 November headlines the quote from writer Stefan Heym that GDR citizens were about to learn "to walk erect." On 18 November, *Volksstimme* quoted the GDR historian Jürgen Kuczynski: "Lenin would have sent home any organization arriving at unanimous decisions, because it consists either of idiots or of cowards."

When Vaclav Havel, now the president of Czechoslovakia, was sentenced in February to nine months of imprisonment for demonstrating against the Czech regime, *Volksstimme* (23 February) sided with the Austrian government and against the SED, by protesting Havel's conviction and sentence. The anniversary of the suppression of the "Prague spring" of 1968 was reported by *Volksstimme* (22 August) as having been quiet, to the disappointment of the Western media. Czech prime minister Adamec's visit to Vienna was reported as a governmental, not a party, visit (*Volksstimme*, 24 and 25 October).

While visiting Sofia, Muhri said that Turks in Bulgaria were incited from the outside. With regard to Austria and *perestroika*, Muhri said: "Mr. Mikhail Gorbachev is extremely popular in our society" (*FBIS*, 31 July).

In April, *Volksstimme* (8 April) attacked Ceauşescu's cult of personality. Because of this cult of personality, the KPÖ Politburo decided not to send a representative to the Romanian party congress (*Volksstimme*, 18 November).

Early in the year, Ernst Wimmer reported to the thirteenth plenary session of the KPÖ's Central Committee on the situation of international communism (*Volksstimme*, 1989). Wimmer praised competitive elections in the USSR, but attacked capitalistic pluralism, warning that Hungary was coming close to it.

After the "Summit of the Seven" in Paris, Hans Kalt wondered, in *Volksstimme* (18 July), how the United States, having become a debtor nation, could possibly launch a "Second Marshall Plan" for Poland and Hungary.

On the occasion of the 50th anniversary of the Hitler-Stalin Pact, *Volksstimme* (15–16 August) raised the question whether a re-examination of the pact by the USSR might shed new light on the turning over, by Moscow, of Austrian Communists to the Nazis.

Volksstimme (6 October) was wondering whether the major Austrian parties, the Socialist Party and the People's Party, were not misunderstanding *perestroika* by advocating, in fact, a new capitalist bourgeois Europe.

Silbermayr (*Volksstimme*, 26 October) praised *perestroika* and ongoing reforms in the GDR. In Poland and Hungary, he stated, socialist forces seem to be in the minority and the sobering effect of capitalism was yet to be experienced. In this contribution, Silbermayr reflects the KPÖ's view of East Europe as of the end of October: the USSR and the GDR, *si*, Poland and Hungary, *no*.

International Activities. Irma Schwager represented the KPÖ at the 30th anniversary of the Cuban Revolution (*Volksstimme*, 3 and 12 January). At about the same time, Ernst Wimmer represented the party at the Frankfurt congress of the West German DKP (*Volksstimme*, 13 January). On 20 and 21 January, the KPÖ hosted a meeting of communist parties of the European Free Trade Association, with delegates from Finland, Norway, Sweden, and Switzerland attending (*Volksstimme*, 17 and 21 January).

In May, Valentin Falin, chairman of the international division of the Central Committee of the CPSU, visited Vienna and had a meeting with Muhri, which was attended also by Silbermayr, Hans Steiner, and the Soviet ambassador to Austria (*Volksstimme*, 11 May). On 25 May, Muhri visited the Slovak CP in Bratislava (*FBIS*, 30 May). In July, a delegation of the Popular Front for the Liberation of Palestine visited the KPÖ, thanking the party and conferring with Erwin Scharf, Hans Steiner, and Peter Reimair, secretary of the KPÖ's Anti-Imperialist Solidarity Commission (*Volksstimme*, 6 July). Erwin Scharf received birthday greetings from the Central Committee of the Czechoslovak CP (*FBIS*, 31 August). The celebration of the 40th anniversary of the GDR was attended by Hans Kalt and Haslinger, a shop steward of the VOEST steel works (*Volksstimme*, 7 October).

Muhri was congratulated on the occasion of his 65th birthday by Nicolae Ceauşescu (*FBIS*, 30 October) and Egon Krenz (*Volksstimme*, 21–22 October).

On 30 and 31 October, Muhri, Silbermayr, and Steiner visited Moscow, where they met with Falin and had a brief meeting with Gorbachev (*Pravda*, 31 October, 1 November; *FBIS*, 1 November; *Volksstimme*, 5–6 November).

Publications. In 1988, *Volksstimme* counted 1000 new subscribers. A survey showed that two-thirds of the readers were below 50 years of age, 22 percent were employees, 15 percent workers, and 13 percent students. The paper now claims to be a leftist daily as well as the party organ. Distribution of the paper will be improved (*Volksstimme*, 12 March).

Frederick C. Engelmann
University of Alberta

Belgium

Population. 9,887,998
Party. Union of the Communists of Belgium, organized linguistically into the Parti communiste de Belgique (PCB) and the Kommunistische Partij van Belgie (KPB)
Founded. 1921
Membership. Under 5,000
National Leadership. President: Louis Van Geyt; vice-president: Marcel Levaux
National Bureau. Pierre Beauvois, Claude Renard, Robert Dussart, Ludo Loose, Dirk Vonckx
Council General of the Union. 33 members; 5 candidates. Francophone members: Pierre Beauvois, Robert Dussart, Marcel Levaux, Jacques Moins, Jacques Nagels, Claude Renard, Marcel Couteau, Anne Herscovici, Jules Pirlot, Hubert Cambier, Jean-Claude Raillon, Jean-Marie Simon (Liège), Jean-Pierre Michels, Susa Nudelhole, Jean-Marie Simon (Borinage), Jean-Paul Brilmaker, Maurice G. Magis, Daniel Fedrigo, Robert Houtain. Dutch-speaking members: Ludo Loose, Dirk Vonckx, Jos Gijbels, Willy Minnebo, Louis Van Geyt, Miel Dullaert, Filip Delmotte, Jos Wolles, Luk Dombrecht, Bernard Claeys, Robert Crivit, Roger Broos, Marc De Smet, Michel Vanderborght. Francophone candidates: Jacques Coupez, Marcel Bergen, Michel Godard; Dutch-speaking candidates: Bert Vermeiren, Jos De Geyter
Parti communiste de Belgique Leadership. President: Claude Renard; secretary: Pierre Beauvois; president for Brussels region: Anne Herscovici
Francophone Bureau. Pierre Beauvois, Marcel Bergen, Marcel Couteau, Robert Dussart, Daniel Fedrigo, Michel Godard, Anne Herscovici, Marcel Levaux, Maurice G. Magis, Jean-Pierre Michels, Jacques Moins, Jacques Nagels, Susa Nudelhole, Jules Pirlot, Claude Renard, Jean-Marie Simon (Liège), Jean-Marie Simon (Borinage), Josiane Vrand
Kommunistische Partij van Belgie Leadership. President: Ludo Loose
Dutch-speaking Bureau. Bernard Claeys, Jos De Geyter, Filip Delmotte, Hugo De Witte, Miel Dul-

laert, Jos Gijbels, Ludo Loose, Willy Minnebo, Dirk Vonckx
Status. Legal
Last Congress. Twenty-sixth National, 18–19 March 1989
Last Election. 13 December 1987, 0.8 percent, no representation
Publications. *Drapeau Rouge*, daily party organ in French, André Gerardin, editor; *Rode Vaan*, Dutch-language weekly, Miel Dullaert, political director, Jef Turf, editor. The party also publishes in French a periodical of broad theoretical and political commentary, *Cahiers Marxistes*.

For the decade of the eighties, Belgium's history may be generally written around three themes. First, there was the country's persistent economic difficulty, which during the 1980s began to affect even the Flemish north, which had previously prospered while the economy of the French-speaking, Walloon south deteriorated and that of the essentially francophone Brussels area slipped relative to the north's. Second, there was the continuing tension between the two linguistic and three ethnoterritorial communities in Belgium, which—as in previous decades—often paralyzed governments at the center and forced new elections. And third, there was the center's ongoing effort to alleviate the cultural roadblocks to economic reforms and other policy action by further regionalizing power within the Belgian state—a process which formally began with the 1970–1971 revision of the Belgian Constitution.

For the same period, the history of the Belgian Communist Party may also be sketched in terms of three themes. First, the party's belated willingness to adapt its centralized, unitary structure to the "federal" nature of Belgian society or to collaborate with noncommunist parties, and its consequent inability to capitalize on the economic and cultural grievances of Belgian voters. Second, the party's continuing political decline: by the late 1980s the PCB/KPB had dropped from a highly visible actor in Belgian politics, receiving approximately 3 percent of the national and nearly 10 percent of the Walloon vote as late as 1965, to a nearly invisible political observer receiving less than 1 percent of the national vote and 3 percent of the vote in its Walloon base. And finally, the party's efforts in the late 1980s to reverse its political fortunes by regionalizing its structure and by actively pursuing alliances with such other progressive, leftist forces in Belgium as the peace groups, environmentalists, feminists, youth groups, and the socialist party and socialist unions in the country.

The last year of the decade saw the Belgian state begin to reverse its economic misfortune and complete the process of regionalizing political authority, and the Belgian Communist Party accelerate its own regional restructuring and alliance-building efforts and become, if not a more significant force in Belgian politics, a much more visible one.

Party Organization and Structure. The most important event to occur in 1989 was the party's 26th National Congress, held on 18 and 19 March. Although the congress was dedicated to exploring the theme of a Europe of Freedom, its principal item of business was to reorganize and, indeed, rename the Belgian Communist Party.

Prior to the national congress "federative" conferences were held by the party's Dutch- and French-speaking wings and, in early March, by the party's Central Committee. In these conferences, resolutions were prepared for introduction at the national congress in order to complete the party's federalization process by restructuring its Flemish and especially its francophone (Brussels and Walloon) branches into highly autonomous parties in their own right and to rename the national party the Union of the Communists of Belgium. (*Drapeau Rouge*, 20 February, 7 March.) With its approval of these resolutions the National Congress recast the Belgian communist party into a new, federal structure composed of two distinct parties, each with its own governing bodies, joined at the center by a common president and vice-president, a five-member governing bureau, and a 33-member Council General of the Union, which replaced the party's Central Committee.

The center is now charged with facilitating the union's international contacts and remains responsible for the union's foreign-policy pronouncements, including those pertaining to arrival of the single-market stage of Europe's integration, scheduled for 1992. It is also responsible for coordinating the positions of the party's component parts on national-policy matters, for leading the debate on such national issues as arms control and the budget, and for assisting the formation of common campaign strategies where it is desirable to do so. However, in addition to having their own governing bodies, the constituent units were given the authority to define specific policy positions on local and regional matters and to choose specific campaign strategies, including what to do in the June election of repre-

sentatives to the European Parliament. (*Drapeau Rouge*, 18–19, 22 March; *Rode Vaan*, 24 March; *WMR*, Prague, June.)

The party's restructuring was foreshadowed at an extraordinary party congress in June 1988, when the Belgian Communist Party was reorganized internally along regional lines. The action was justified on the grounds that the federalist trends in the state and in its ethnoterritorial communities required a more flexible party structure at the intermediate, regional level between the party's grassroots organizations and its national leadership. A Brussels section was thus added to the party's Flemish and francophone divisions. (See *YICA*, 1989.) And these developments, in turn, had their antecedents in a 1982 meeting, in which the party first adopted a federal structure permitting regional congresses to be held by its Flemish and francophone sections, and in the party's 1986 congress, which recognized the right of the party's wings to adapt to regional issues (see *YICA*, 1987). In sum, the 1989 restructuring of the party represented more of a continuation—or, more precisely, culmination—of previous developments than a radical shift in party policy. On the other hand, previous changes essentially involved organizational decentralization within a single party structure. By contrast, the party's new shape and name indicate a major change in the nature of the party in the direction of a rather peripheral form of federal association between the center and its linguistically organized units.

Activities. Beyond preparing for and hosting its national congress, the party's principal activities in 1989 focused on participation in the direct election of Belgium's representatives to the European Parliament in June and responding to the final stages of the regionalization of decisionmaking authority in the state during the second half of the year.

During the election to the European Parliament, the party's new structure allowed its central organs to focus on the broad issues raised by the further integration of Western Europe, and to speculate on alternatives to the single-market approach to achieving economic, political, cultural, and social democracy in Europe (*Cahiers Marxistes*, March, April–May; *WMR*, Prague, March; *Drapeau Rouge*, 10–11 June). Noting the confusion and breadth of viewpoints on European integration present within the communist parties of Western Europe, the union's leadership chose to stress the broad themes of a social, democratic, peaceful, and ecologically sound Europe rather than particular issues. The emphasis to be given to these goals and the choice of campaign strategy and tactics were left to the party's federative units, the PCB and the KPB.

The PCB, in its own conference in February 1989, decided to follow the decision made by its governing board in the previous November, and chose not to run its own candidates for the European Parliament so as not to split the "movement of the masses" with all of its progressive components. (*Drapeau Rouge*, 20 February.) Consequently, PCB organs tended to stress a general, leftist program and concentrated on urging a leftist vote. In much of Wallonia, this translated into a vote for the Socialist Party and its candidates, including the leader of the nominally nonpartisan but basically socialist movement "Wallonia, a Region of Europe," Jose Happart, whom the francophone Socialist Party had put at the top of its list in return for his agreement to desist from seeking to become mayor of the francophone Fourons enclave in Flanders, despite his alleged inability to speak Flemish. In the past, the PCB has urged support of Happart's movement and even of his cause, which has more than once led to the collapse of the Belgian government. (*YICA*, 1988; *Drapeau Rouge*, 18 April, 31 May, 1 June.)

For its part, the KPB elected to run its own candidates for the European Parliament in a "limited but nevertheless significant manner" by joining with a variety of leftist socialists, Trotskyists, splinter groups, syndicalists, Greens, and independent progressives under the *Regenboog* ("Rainbow" coalition) banner. Even on this list, the KPB's candidates were not especially well placed. Of them, the KPB's president, Ludo Loose, was ranked the highest, but was only fifth. (*Drapeau Rouge*, 21 and 22 March, 16 June.) It mattered little, however. The Regenboog coalition attracted fewer than 25,000 votes in Flanders—approximately 0.7 percent of the Flemish vote—and won no seats (*Drapeau Rouge*, 20 June). As a consequence, the KPB was less able to celebrate the left's general gains in the elections than the PCB, which could rejoice somewhat in both the gains of the ecological group, which increased the number of its representatives from Belgium from one to two, and the Socialists, whose candidates held their party's five seats in French-speaking Belgium, and whose first listed candidate, Jose Happart, received substantially more votes in the country than any other candidate—indeed, more than six times the number of votes that the Regenboog coalition received

throughout all of Dutch-speaking Belgium. (*Drapeau Rouge*, 20 and 24–25 July.)

The party's reconstituted form also gave its regional/linguistic units an opportunity to adapt rapidly to what the *Drapeau Rouge* called "the new face of Belgium" resulting from the state's process of regionalization (*Drapeau Rouge*, 11 January). This "new face" had two major components. First, a directly elected regional assembly with its own executive was finally created for Brussels, equivalent in jurisdiction and autonomy to the regional bodies created nine years earlier for Belgium's francophone/Walloon and Flemish communities. (The first members of the Brussels council were elected at the same time as the vote for the European Parliament; the PCB and KPB fielded no candidates of their own.) Second, consistent with the regionalization plan, shortly thereafter vast powers were transferred from the center to the regional bodies, including control over such matters as public works, housing, transportation, and most energy and environmental policy. Combined, these developments dramatically changed the nature of politics in Belgium: they gave the country the weakest central government of any state in the European Community, necessitated the establishment of protocols linking the three regional bodies, and substantially enlarged the political agenda at the regional level that would be debated by regional political actors.

Both the regionalization process and many of its consequences became the subject of communist commentary and activity in 1989. Much of this reaction took place in the context of broad debate on such domestic issues as the environment and medical care—a debate which often allowed local and regional components of the Union of the Communists of Belgium to respond in alliance with such other progressive forces as the Greens. On other occasions the party chose to focus on specific facets of Belgium's changing political map; for example, the growing strength of the right-wing, nationalist Vlaams Blok in Dutch-speaking Belgium. (*Drapeau Rouge*, 7–9 February, 5 May, 1 June.) Most often, however, party debate and action tended to focus on local problems of concern to Belgians living in sections affected by the state's changing regional structure: the dangers posed to Charleroi's riversides by a development plan proposed in the Walloon Assembly, which led to a public statement against the proposal by the Charleroi communist party in early July; the need for a cultural center for the Huy area, etc. In this context, no issue commanded the attention of the PCB more than the plight of the long-troubled city of Liège, especially in the aftermath of the further devolution of powers in midyear, when the city (once again) found it impossible to meet its obligations and was forced to redefine its public services and accept an austerity plan which cut its payroll by 1240 employees. The *Drapeau Rouge* attacked this plan as an effort to assassinate the city, and reported on events there almost daily for two months, while the PCB federation in Liège joined with socialist trade-union groups and ecologists in protesting the action, complete with Common Front demonstrations at the city hall. (*Drapeau Rouge*, 29 September, 30 September–1 October, 3 October.)

Finally, throughout the year the party's newspapers provided their readers with a steady flow of information, keeping their pages open to all progressive forces while giving their audiences what the political director of *Rode Vaan* called an interpretation of the "facts . . . guided by Marxist convictions and the overall principles of communist policy laid down by the party" (*WMR*, Toronto, November). In addition, party organs also offered a range of activities to entertain as well as educate the community. Thus, both *Rode Vaan* and *Drapeau Rouge* held national festivals, the latter's being a two-day spectacular on 7–8 October, complete with jazz concerts, folk events, expositions, and a ball, and drawing participants from the Ukraine, Hungary, Moldavia, Bolivia, and elsewhere. The *Drapeau Rouge* also continued its practice of sponsoring vacation trips at home and abroad, including trips to Prague and Moscow, and *Rode Vaan*—following feedback from a survey on how to improve itself—began the new year with a revamped layout. On the other hand, despite the party's reorganization, *Drapeau Rouge* continued to operate as the only daily of the Union of the Communists of Belgium, as well as the principal organ of the PCB—an arrangement not without potential difficulties, given a federal party structure designed to allow maximum flexibility to the union's regional/linguistic components in formulating and articulating policy in many areas.

Domestic Policy. The party's small membership, low electoral support, and lack of parliamentary representation since 1985 continues to relegate the union to the role of onlooker and commentator with respect to domestic and foreign policy–making in Belgium. In 1989, however, the party did not want for political issues or visibility. Many of the party's pronouncements and direct actions, beyond those pertaining to institutional change, had to do with matters important either to the party's ideological position on certain issues or to its ongoing efforts to advance its network of alliances with the unions, foreign workers/ immigrants, environmentalists, feminists, and— continuing its efforts of the previous year to narrow the gap between the older and younger members of the party—youth groups. Thus, in a year which saw Belgium grapple both domestically and internationally with arms issues, and in particular with the future of short-range nuclear weapons on Belgian soil, military commitments to NATO, the proper length of military service, and the presence of the arms industry in the economy, the party adhered steadfastly to its president's emphasis on the desirability of a peace economy and the importance of arms reductions to domestic welfare. (*Drapeau Rouge*, 18–19 and 24 February, 12 and 17 April.) Even in these areas, though, the party's new structure provided some breathing space, with respect to emphasis, to components of the party caught in contradictory reactions to the consequences of complex decisions regarding military policy; for example, the PC-Liège, which in July was caught between the union's approval of the Belgian decision to end the presence of Trident missiles in the country and its own aversion to the collateral decision to cease production in Belgium of some elements important to the missile, at the cost of several hundred jobs in Liège (*Drapeau Rouge*, 27 July).

The party's emphasis on a peace economy and zero arms gave it a natural link to the peace groups in Belgium, and the union actively supported their demonstrations against the Trident. In other areas, too, the party was successful in advancing on its agenda issues linking it with other "forces of progress." Its commitment to the migrant workers and foreign workers residing in Belgium, and, more broadly, its condemnation of racism in Belgium and Europe not only led to a series of reports in *Drapeau Rouge* on these workers and the problem of racism in the European Community, but to specific feature articles at the time of the murder in March of moderate Islamic clergy in Belgium (which evoked a sharp editorial attack on a proposal by the Vlaams Blok to suppress Islam in the country) and the assassination in October of a major Jewish spokesman in Belgium (*Drapeau Rouge*, 5 April, 5 October). As a category, political refugees received similar attention even before the westward flight of large numbers from Eastern Europe near the year's end, and political groups like "Wallonia, a Region of Europe" had nearly as much attention devoted to their conferences as *Drapeau Rouge* gave to the union's own congress.

Topics of interest to the leftist Greens were also featured prominently in the union's daily. Here, too, international reports were often carried—articles on the Hague Conference on acid rain in March, for example, or on EC action concerning chemical wastes. However, the stories more often had a domestic thrust, such as those covering a protest in Flanders against waste disposal, the deteriorating condition of the waters of the Meuse in eastern Belgium, and Greenpeace's opposition to an incinerator in Namur.

Perhaps the group which received the greatest attention was women. Reports appeared regularly on the political status of women in Europe, the problems of women living on pensions, and the importance of the contraceptive pill and child-care facilities to the liberation of women. In addition, except for the plight of Liège, no single issue commanded more attention in the party's press in 1989 than Belgium's efforts to amend its abortion laws. As early as January the party was noting that Belgium had become one of the two last states in the European Community (the other being Ireland) to consider amending its "archaic legislation" and decriminalize abortion, a step deemed essential if women and couples were to be able to practice their right to responsible parenthood. (*Drapeau Rouge*, 24 January, 4 and 27 July.) Not surprisingly, the Senate's decision in May to "quasi-depenalize" abortion—reaffirmed in definitive form in June— was heralded as a decisive step toward this right (*Drapeau Rouge*, 11 June).

Elsewhere, the party continued to stress the importance of youth to the party and to Belgium, and to widen its agenda of topics for discussion beyond the traditional workers' issues of job security and nationalization (which in 1989 converged in the threat to jobs posed by schemes to privatize Sabena, the Belgian national airline) to include such social issues as the increased use of drugs among the young, the social evil of battered children, the problems of education in Belgium, and the growing menace of AIDS.

Foreign Policy. Beyond its coverage of Belgian foreign policy (in particular the rift between Brussels and Zaïre in 1989) and events pertaining to the European Community (especially the June conference in Madrid on monetary union, which provoked a sharp critique of Thatcher for her op-

position to such a union), the party's press continued to give attention to issues related to oppressed peoples around the world. Hence, such topics as South Africa, the Palestinians, Third World poverty, and Nicaragua received frequent treatment, especially when interest in them was heightened by such events as the visit of Arafat to Paris and of Ortega to Brussels. Nevertheless, the foreign developments to which the party gave primary attention were those in the communist world, especially Eastern Europe and the Soviet Union.

Responding to events in Eastern Europe might have been particularly vexing since they occurred against a backdrop of two years of efforts on the part of the party and Belgium alike to increase contacts with existing leaderships in Eastern Europe. In 1989 these efforts included a meeting between Louis Van Geyt and Erich Honecker in January, a series of visits by members of the Belgian government and East German officials between February and September, and the visit of Belgium's foreign minister to Poland in April. (*ND*, 30 January, 5 September.) In fact, however, formulating a response to the growing tensions between what were depicted as progressive forces of the democratic left, on the one hand, and the communist parties with monopolistic holds on politics in the Soviet Union, the states of Eastern Europe, and China, on the other, did not cause the Belgian communist party any apparent difficulty.

As early as February, *Drapeau Rouge*, in step with the more progressive communist parties in Western Europe, ran an editorial approving of Poland's steps toward power sharing as a move toward further democratization. Expanding on this theme, the paper further argued that the processes of change in Hungary, Poland, and the USSR required more than mere encouragement because they would not only advance democracy, but bring nearer the day of better relations between Eastern and Western Europe and of a passage from the current Europe of military blocs. (14 February.) Later developments were generally assessed from this perspective. The Soviet elections of April, which resulted in the emergence of opposition inside the assembly, were heralded as a victory of *glasnost'* (*Drapeau Rouge*, 12 April, 19 July). *Perestroika* continued to be touted as "a veritable national movement" and "a socialism to be realized"—becoming the subject of a lengthy article in *Cahiers Marxistes* in March and a series of articles in *Drapeau Rouge* in August (*Drapeau Rouge*, 28 April, 11–13 and 22 August). Even the miners' strike in the Soviet Union was analyzed from this vantage point, as were subsequent events in Eastern Europe. Thus, the often acrimonious political negotiations in Poland in late summer were seen as a natural product of the diverse components of a socialist system raising legitimate questions among themselves, and the exodus of large numbers of East Germans from Germany into Hungary and Austria was interpreted as a result of "the lack of liberty and democracy in East Germany as in other countries of Eastern Europe." Hungary's assistance to those refugees was praised. (*Drapeau Rouge*, 21 August, 12 and 15 September.)

Coverage of events in China was similarly tilted toward the progressive elements. Reports and editorials thus ranged from expressing initial pleasure in seeing "Gorbymania" among the students (*Drapeau Rouge*, 16 May) to statements of concern about the safety of the protesters (*Drapeau Rouge*, 22 May), to a statement of "indignation" by Louis Van Geyt on behalf of the Union of the Communists of Belgium over the dramatic events in Beijing and a call upon the Chinese to stop military intervention and to respect the liberty of the people (*Drapeau Rouge*, 5 June), to highly negative follow-up stories on the subsequent executions in China and sharply worded communiqués from Van Geyt to China's ambassador to Belgium expressing the profound concern of the Belgian communists over the executions in Shanghai and Beijing (*Drapeau Rouge*, 23 June).

The union's leadership had more difficulty in finding an appropriate response to another struggle in the communist world in 1989—the struggle between the unifying structure of the party and nationalist groups threatening the peace and stability of multinational communist countries. In part, this may be because the Belgian communist party itself just reorganized in a fashion which suggests the primacy of national diversity over unitary structure (and perhaps provides a glimpse of the future structure of communist parties in other multinational countries). For whatever reason, in this area the party's press largely limited itself to reporting the events in Bulgaria, Yugoslavia, and the Soviet Union. Although the articles often acknowledged the legitimacy of the causes of such groups as the Estonians and Lithuanians, there were no editorials on behalf of the separatists or minorities except in the case of Bulgaria's repression of Turks, where the issue increasingly appeared to involve a choice less between monolithic communism or chaos, than between repression or democracy and pluralism (*Drapeau Rouge*, 19–20 August).

Finally, in its own diplomatic activities during 1989, the party continued not only to engage in bilateral meetings with representatives of communist states whenever possible, but to sponsor and participate in international communist gatherings. In 1989 the latter included Ludo Loose's attendance at a January symposium in West Germany on communist activities in the workplace in capitalist European countries (*WMR*, Toronto, January), the party's participation in a February conference in Copenhagen, which drew representatives from all states of the EC and focused on questions arising from the contemplated creation of a single market in Europe in 1992, a May meeting of representatives of the Belgian Socialist and Communist (francophone) parties and the Italian Communist Party with a socialist member of the European Parliament on the topic of the Euroleft, and a June conference in Mons, in which the Hainaut (Province) communist organization hosted representatives of the northern wing of the Communist Party of France in a gathering designed to strengthen the ties between the communists in these adjoining areas. Meanwhile, for its part, Belgium continued its policy of establishing relations with communist states, and rapidly adjusted to changes in the East—in particular, to the reconstitution of Hungary's communist party as the Hungarian Socialist Party. Indeed, when in November Hungary and Belgium signed an agreement in Budapest, Belgium became the first NATO state ever to sign a military accord with a member of the Warsaw Pact, albeit in this case essentially a pact concerned with facilitating military and academic visits and exchanges.

Joseph R. Rudolph, Jr.
Towson State University

Cyprus

Population. 700,009 (80 percent Greek; 18 percent Turkish)
Party. Progressive Party of the Working People (Anorthotikon Komma Ergazomenou Laou; AKEL)
Date Founded. 1926 (AKEL, 1941)

Membership. 15,000 (Source: Official AKEL statement, 1988)

Composition. Sex: 24 percent women; nationality: all from Greek Cypriot community; age: 30 percent under 30 years old; occupation: 67 percent industrial workers and employees; 20 percent peasants and middle class

General Secretary. Dimitris Christofias

Politburo. 13 members: Dimitris Christofias, Dinos Constantinou, Andreas Fantis, George Christodoulides, Michalis Poumpouris, Donis Christofinis, Loucas Aletras, Andreas Ziartides, Christos Petas, Kyriacos Christou, Andreas Michaelides, Lakis Theodoulou, Antonis Christodoulou

Secretariat. Dimitris Christofias, Dinos Constantinou, Andreas Fantis, George Christodoulides, Michalis Poumpouris, Donis Christofinis, Loucas Aletras

Control Commission. Made up of three members from the Central Committee; the current chairman is Michaelis Olympios.

Central Committee. 88 members, 10 alternates

Status. Legal

Last Congress. Sixteenth, 26–30 November 1986; extraordinary, 20 December 1987, to endorse George Vassiliou as presidential candidate

Last Election. 1985, 27.4 percent, 15 of 56 seats in Parliament

Auxiliary Organizations. Pan-Cyprian Workers' Federation (PEO), 75,000 members, Andreas Ziartidis, president, Pavlos Digglis, general secretary; United Democratic Youth Organization (EDON), 14,000 members; Confederation of Women's Organizations (POGO); Pan-Cyprian Peace Council; Pan-Cyprian Federation of Students and Young Professionals; Union of Greek Cypriots in England, 1,200 members (considered London branch of AKEL); Pan-Cypriot National Organization of Secondary Students (PEOM); Cypriot Farmers' Union (EKA)

Publications. *Kharavyi* (Dawn), AKEL daily newspaper; *AKEL News Letter* (in English), periodically; *Neos Democratis*, AKEL monthly theoretical magazine; *Ergatiko Vima* (Workers' stride), PEO weekly; *Neolaia* (Youth), EDON weekly; *Parikiaki* (Ethnic community), AKEL weekly (London); *Kyria* (Mrs.), POGO bimonthly; *Yeni Duzen* (New order), Turkish Cypriot pro-AKEL daily newspaper

Background. Cyprus has been effectively partitioned since 1974, when Turkey landed troops on the northern part of the island. The Turkish Cypriots called Ankara's long-awaited action their "liberation" from their encirclement in enclaves since the outbreak of ethnic violence eleven years earlier. On the other hand, the Greek Cypriots insist that it was an illegal invasion which brought about the seizure and occupation of over one-third of the island. The removal of the Turkish troops, as well as of thousands of subsequent settlers from mainland Turkey, is an issue which confounds the ongoing intercommunal talks between the Turkish Cypriot leader, Rauf Denktash, and the newly elected president of the Republic of Cyprus, George Vassiliou. In 1983, Denktash unilaterally declared the independent Turkish Republic of Northern Cyprus (TRNC), which is recognized only by Turkey. The mainland and island Greeks refuse to recognize the existence of a legitimate state north of the "green line," the buffer zone, which has been patrolled by a United Nations peacekeeping force for the past 25 years. The Republic of Cyprus has maintained an economic boycott of the occupied northern part of Cyprus, but the Turkish Cypriots are determined to make the best of what they have.

The leaders of the two communities agreed to resume the stalled negotiations for a settlement of the Cyprus problem in August of 1988. but the target date of June 1989 for finding a solution came and passed without any agreement. The United Nations–sponsored talks broke down in July because Denktash denied the secretary general the right to offer proposals, saying that these should come from the two principals instead. The Greek Cypriots rejected that idea because it would be tantamount to the recognition of Denktash and his "pseudo-state." The two men did meet separately with the U.N. secretary general in New York in late November and early December, but those encounters did not result in any breakthroughs. Further United Nations–sponsored talks will be held in 1990.

Although the AKEL is not banned in the Turkish Cypriot community, the party has chosen not to be active because of the criticism it would engender among the Greek Cypriots. There are now two left-wing political parties in the TRNC: the Communal Liberation Party (TKP) and the Republican Turkish Party (CTP). Of the two, the CTP most consistently parrots the AKEL line in the TRNC, under its chairman Osker Ozgur, who has a permanent column in the party's newspaper *Yeni Duzen*. The CTP, founded in 1970, is the oldest political party in the Turkish community; it polled 22 percent of the vote in the 1976 elections in the north and has been a consistent critic of the Denktash administration. Leaders of both the TKP and the CTP met with the five Greek Cypriot parties twice during the year, once in Prague and the other time on the "green line." The meetings had no fixed agendas, but were intended to make everyone better acquainted and to create a climate of mutual understanding between the two communities. If the north and south of Cyprus were one day reunited in a "federated republic," it is conceivable that the combined electoral strength of the left-wing parties of the two communities could produce a majority of votes in a presidential election.

Leadership and Organization. While the AKEL was reputed to be a tightly controlled apparatus, there was growing discontent in the party ranks that despite the *perestroika* and *glasnost'* movements, there had been "no real change in policy" (*Cyprus Mail*, 24 November). Because of its traditionally close ties to the Soviet Union, the AKEL has tried to adapt to the ways of Gorbachev, but this has not been an easy task. Two senior members of the AKEL took a public stand against what they termed the party's "undemocratic method of operation." The president and the general secretary of the communist labor union, PEO, tried to reform the party from within by declaring at a seminar that the AKEL's support for the Soviet invasion of Czechoslovakia was wrong. They further accused the AKEL leadership of "only paying lip-service to *perestroika*." General Secretary Christofias then stated that he would "not follow the misguided road of analyzing the party through the press and meetings" (*Kharavyi*, 23 November). The party, he continued, has "views" and "will develop them within the guiding organs of the party." Christofias defended the party's record on democratic procedures by saying "party decisions were taken collectively by AKEL members" (ibid.). A statement from the Politburo emphasized the position, and "for the sake of party unity, the questions which have arisen must be discussed and resolved within the party and not in public" (*Kharavyi*, 2 December).

After Gorbachev had condemned the 1968 intervention publicly in December, the PEO leaders suggested that "it is time that our party turned its attention to reforming its own methods" (*Kharavyi*, 3 December). However, it took a plenary of the party's Central Committee in a marathon four-day-long meeting to reappraise its position on the Czech

invasion. The AKEL leadership declared that its previous support of the 1968 Soviet invasion was considered "mistaken and invalid" (*Kharavyi*, 19 December). The party reiterated its commitment to the principles of sovereignty, independence and nonintervention in the internal affairs of other countries. This decision, nonetheless, was not enough for Central Committee member Michalis Papapetrou, who is also an AKEL member of Parliament. Even though he supported the vote, he resigned from the Central Committee and served notice that he would also resign from the Parliament. Papapetrou resigned for "reasons of conscience" following the party's warning that members would "run the risk of disciplinary measures" if they made their disagreements with the party line public. Still, Papapetrou, a 42-year-old lawyer, said that he would "remain faithful to the ideology and principles of the party he has served for 25 years." He also stated that he would be "willing to help in every effort of the party in the direction of democratic socialism and the defense of the working class of Cyprus" (*Kharavyi*, 20 December). This crisis for the AKEL leadership will no doubt spur further action toward positive steps "in the renewal and development of democracy in the party."

Domestic Party Affairs. The AKEL leadership is committed to the continuation of the intercommunal dialog between Denktash and Vassiliou, even though eighteen months have elapsed without visible progress toward unification of the island's two ethnic communities. Commenting on the notion that the Greek and Turkish Cypriots are afraid of one another and are better off living apart, General Secretary Christofias stated that this "fatal incompatibility of Greeks and Turks is just eyewash [*sic*]" (*WMR*, October). Despite the religious, language, and ethnic differences, he feels that the two communities "are united by a common historical and cultural heritage that is more than four centuries old." Moreover, both consider themselves Cypriots first and "the long-suffering island their common homeland." He concluded that the goals of the shared struggle for a "new Cyprus are the evacuation of the occupation troops and Turkish settlers, the dismantling of foreign military bases, and total demilitarization." (Ibid.)

The U.S. State Department's report on human rights which was issued in February gave the AKEL the provocation to accuse the United States of being "hostile" to the Greek Cypriots (Nicosia Domestic Service, 10 February). The authors of the report "inadmissibly equate the victim with the victimizer, equate the way in which human rights function in the free areas of Cyprus with the way in which they function in the occupied areas, and distort the question of missing persons." The AKEL called upon the United States "to reconsider its stand...and exert pressure so that Turkish intransigence in the Cyprus issue may yield." The AKEL attack concluded with the comment that "the U.S. Government stand clearly proves that a correct and just solution of the Cyprus issue cannot be found within the tight framework of NATO and the EEC, but only within the UN framework." The AKEL then returned to its familiar theme of "the need to convene an international conference for the solution of the problem." (Ibid.)

At the beginning of the third round of intercommunal talks in May, the AKEL Central Committee issued a press release that stressed that "the U.S. must do much more to assist in a Cyprus solution than make statements" (*Kharavyi*, 11 May). The release then listed three specific steps the United States should take. First, it "should stop being an obstacle in the way of efforts to achieve a more active intervention by the Security Council." This position, by the way, was advocated by the USSR for the first time only one month earlier (Nicosia, *Filelevtheros*, 5 April). Second, the United States "should stop objecting to the convening of an international conference on the Cyprus issue," which would obviously bring the USSR into a leading role in the deliberations. And third, the United States should urge "both sides to display patience, decisiveness, and a spirit of cooperation." But particularly, the United States "must exert its influence on Turkey and Denktash to abandon their partitionist philosophy so that the road may be opened for a fair and viable Cyprus solution based upon U.N. principles." (*Kharavyi*, 11 May.) The December report of the U.N. secretary general was also criticized for its failure to blame Turkey for "the continuing deadlock in the Cyprus peace talks" (*Cyprus Mail*, 15 December).

International Views, Positions, and Activities. General Secretary Christofias maintains that a "new political thinking" exists under the entire system of international relations. This is based upon two salient features of our age: first, "the growing diversity of our world and the multiple forms in which its component parts are developing"; and second, the "increasing unity and interdependence" of the nation states of the world. This new political thinking must help "to lessen international tensions, settle local conflicts and 'cool' what we call 'hotbeds.'" In short, "practice shows that any conflict can be settled politically, by peaceful means if there are perseverance, patience and goodwill." (*WMR*, October.) He applies this approach to the Cyprus problem by saying that "the key to the resolution of the internal problems is a settlement through reconciliation," while the external problems are settled "through international agreements on the basis of new political thinking." (Ibid.) The nations of the world are in "one boat, and can get drowned or keep afloat only together." That is why "recognition of the priority of common human values, or rather human survival, is the core of new thinking." (Ibid.)

The AKEL continued its fraternal meeting with other communist parties, both on the island and abroad. In January, a cadre of the Salvadoran Liberation Front visited Cyprus at the invitation of AKEL, and received AKEL's "full solidarity" (*Kharavyi*, 15 January). Later that month, an AKEL delegation visited Syria for five days, where its members concluded a two-year "program of cooperation" between themselves and the Arab Socialist Ba'th Party (Damascus Domestic Service, 26 January). The Socialist Party of South Yemen sent a delegation to Cyprus in February and pledged full support for "the struggle by AKEL and the Cypriot people" (*Kharavyi*, 25 February). On the occasion of the third anniversary of the "U.S. aggression against Libya," the AKEL general secretary sent greetings to that country denouncing "U.S. imperialism" and thanking Libya for its support of "the Cypriot people's just struggle" (*Kharavyi*, 16 April). In May, General Secretary Christofias led a delegation to Prague at the invitation of the then–general secretary of the Czech CP, Miloš Jakeš. The two leaders "exchanged opinions on the general development of the international situation, paying the greatest attention to its European and Mediterranean aspects" (ČTK, 23 May). In October, Nicaraguan president Daniel Ortega visited Cyprus at the invitation of President Vassiliou. Ortega said that "the entire Nonaligned Movement has expressed solidarity with the Cypriot people's struggle." Ortega concluded that he and Vassiliou had discussed "with great sincerity" the problems of Cyprus and Nicaragua. They agreed "on the need for closer cooperation" between the two countries "in order to achieve results and conclude their struggle auspiciously" (Nicosia Domestic Service, 10 October).

T. W. Adams
Washington, D.C.

Denmark

Population. 5,129,659 (July 1989)
Party. Communist Party of Denmark (Danmarks Kommunistiske Parti; DKP)
Founded. 1919
Membership. 7,400 (*Jyllands-Posten*, 26 November)
Chairman. Ole Sohn
General Secretary. Poul Emanuel
Executive Committee. 16 members: Ole Sohn, Ib Nørlund, Poul Emanuel, Bernard Jeune, Kurt Kristensen, Dan Lundrup, Jorgen Madsen, Anette Nielsen, Bo Rosschou, Frank Aaen (editor of *Land og Folk*), Anker Schjerning, Rita Sørenson, Inger Rasmussen, Sten Parker Sørensen, Harry Osborn (1 vacancy)
Secretariat. 6 members: Ole Sohn, Poul Emanuel, Frank Aaen, Bo Rosschou (1 vacancy)
Central Committee. 50 members, 17 candidate members
Status. Legal
Last Congress. Twenty-eighth, April 1987
Last Election. 10 May 1988, 0.8 percent, no representation
Auxiliary Organizations. Communist Youth of Denmark (Danmarks Kommunistiske Ungdom; DKU), Communist Students of Denmark (Danmarks Kommunistiske Studenter; KOMM.S.)
Publications. *Land og Folk* (Nation and people), daily circulation 6,500 weekdays and 13,000 weekends; *Tiden-Verden Rund* (Times around the world), theoretical monthly; *Fremad* (Forward), DKU monthly

The year 1989 was a tumultuous one for communism worldwide, and Denmark's far left was no exception. The continuing decline of the Danish Communist Party (DKP) precipitated divisive infighting that led to the temporary dislodgement of its longtime leader, Ole Sohn. Financial difficulties prompting staff layoffs and confrontations with its youth wing also tied up the DKP's leadership at a time when rapid changes in Eastern Europe demanded its close attention. The largely unsuccessful electoral cooperation among the DKP, Left Socialists (Venstresocialisterne; VS), and Socialist Worker's Party (Socialistisk Arbejderparti; SAP) was renegotiated under the banner of the Unity List. As the Conservative-led government headed into its ninth year, Denmark's Communists seem to be continuing their steady slide into oblivion.

The DKP's long-term goal continues to be representation in the Folketing, the Danish parliament, where it would likely support a government led by the mainline Social Democratic Party. Having captured only 0.8 percent of the popular vote in the Folketing election of May 1988, the DKP is highly unlikely to reach alone the 2 percent minimum of the vote necessary to secure a seat. This reality led to a hastily arranged electoral alliance with the VS and SAP, which nonetheless polled just 1.4 percent of the vote. In February, the DKP extended a broad invitation for electoral cooperation to a number of leftist parties, including the VS, the SAP, the Humanist Party (Det Humanistisk Parti; HP), and Common Course (Arbejderpartiet Faelles Kurs; FK), the latter of which lost its Folketing representation in May 1988 by one-tenth of 1 percent. It was clear in August that only the VS and SAP would enter into a formal pact with the DKP. By November, they had collected 24,000 signatures, 1,000 shy of the minimum necessary to register their Unity List for the next Folketing election. Their common program calls for the removal of the nonsocialist government, an active peace and environmental policy, and withdrawal from the EC. They have yet to decide how the ticket's candidates would be nominated from the three parties. (*JPRS-WEU*, 25 September; *FBIS-WEU*, 6 February and 8 December.)

With the Conservative-led government of Prime Minister Poul Schlueter entering its ninth year, the Danish left continues its longest period in opposition. The Social Democratic Party (Socialdemokraterne Parti; SDP) is nevertheless still the largest party in Denmark with 55 seats in the Folketing. Traditional consensus politics, a matter of practical necessity for the minority coalition, has ensured the SDP a continued role in policy formation. During 1989 this included extensive cooperation on social and labor policy and a defense-budget compromise that nominally froze military spending. Toward the end of the year, however, some chinks in this consensus policy emerged. SDP chairman Sven Auken suggested that aid for reforming East European countries would have to come from cuts in the defense budget. The SDP also broke tradition by refusing to support the 1990 government budget, which nevertheless passed in December with the support of the growing right-wing Progress Party (PP). The SDP's calls for official ties with the Baltic states further soured its image because of public sensitivity to the illegal incorporation of those states into the Soviet Union. The increasing isolation of the SDP limits not only its future influence on government policy, but also that of the far-left parties, which rely on the SDP's influence in parliament to advance their initiatives.

Leadership and Organization. After a year of relative stability in 1988, DKP chairman Sohn faced a strong challenge in 1989 from the old-guard, Stalinist wing of the party, which was able to remove him temporarily from office in late November. Sohn's fight for control of the party was the first major factional battle for the 35-year-old former union leader. He was elected to the party's Central Committee in 1980 and three years later to the Executive Committee. He was then chosen to share the party chairmanship with Jan Andersen in 1987, but the latter's early death in July of that year left Sohn alone at the top. (*JPRS-WEU*, 15 December.)

Financial problems occupied much of Sohn's time in the first half of the year. By 1989 the DKP's debts had grown to around 50 million kroner. Losses on the party's day-to-day accounts and from its daily newspaper, *Land og Folk*, had in the past been covered by loans against the DKP's headquarters at Dronningens Tvaergade. The DKP faced the necessity of selling a portion of its party building and firing at least ten staff employees to obtain some liquidity in its accounts. DKP secretary Poul Emanuel, business manager John Poulsen, and Executive Committee member Bo Rosschou took the most criticism for the party's economic problems, and many have predicted that the crisis will end Emanuel's 30-year career with the DKP. (*JPRS-WEU*, 6 June; *JPRS-WEU*, 15 December.)

A dispute with the communist youth group (DKU) in June raised questions about the group's future relationship with the DKP. A student group called the Tiananmen Committee, established in solidarity with the Chinese students who demonstrated for democracy in Beijing, received permission from the DKP to set up a tent at the *Land og Folk* summer festival in Faelledpark. Shortly before the opening of the festival, the DKP withdrew its invitation to the Tiananmen Committee. The DKU responded by giving the committee a corner of its tent and promised the DKP that committee members would not stray from this area. However, when the mid-day heat drove a few committee members outside, they were rounded up by the event organizers and expelled from the festival grounds. The incident prompted DKU's co-chairman John Norbo and international secretary Søren Brostrom to threaten resignation from the party. In an attempt to calm the DKU, Sohn published an apology in *Land og Folk* on 23 August and for the first time formally disassociated the DKP from the Chinese military action in Tiananmen Square two months earlier. (*FBIS-WEU*, 4 October.)

This episode exacerbated existing strains in the DKP-DKU relationship. Continued declines in its membership rolls prompted the DKU's executive committee to consider broadening the organization along more "socialist" lines. The DKU discussed at its October national convention establishing relations with other leftist parties to parallel those with the DKP. By disassociating itself from its image as a feeder organization for the DKP, the DKU hoped to tap a broader segment of the student population. Sohn, who himself rose up through the ranks of the DKU, tried to quell this development by emphasizing the common goals the DKU shared with the DKP. If the DKU continues its drift away from the DKP, this would remove a major source of new party members and hurt efforts to rejuvenate the ranks of the DKP's aging leadership. (*JPRS-WEU*, 17 August; *JPRS-WEU*, 4 October.)

Struggling with these internal problems and the dramatic changes sweeping over Eastern Europe in 1989, Sohn felt compelled to call an extraordinary congress in November to deal with the mounting opposition to the party leadership. When the Central Committee turned down Sohn's request by a vote of 24 to 20, Sohn increased the ante. He declared his intention to resign if a congress were not called. Sohn then sought support from local party organizations, one-third of which could together force the Central Committee's hand. In response, Central Committee member Anker Schjerning organized a group to remove Sohn from office, which he accomplished on 29 November. Schjerning was concerned that an extraordinary congress would split the DKP, especially if Emanuel and Rosschou were forced to resign because of the party's financial crisis. Schjerning had open support for his "coup" from Emanuel, Rosschou, Frank Aaen, Rita Sørensen, Harry Osborn, and Jørgen Madsen. This group represented the old-guard, Stalinist faction of the DKP, which had been particularly critical of Sohn's embracing of the political upheavals in the Soviet Union and Eastern Europe. (*FBIS-WEU*, 20 December; *JPRS-WEU*, 15 December.)

The coup against Sohn proved short-lived, as almost three-quarters of the party's local organizations moved to support him and his call for an extraordinary congress in January 1990. In a quick about-face, Schjerning, who had assumed the chairmanship, announced he would resign and call for Sohn's reinstatement. In Schjerning's apology for his action, he stressed that he was only trying to preserve party unity and was confident that the party could return to the status quo ante without any more upheavals. However the extraordinary congress turns out, the considerable amount of negative press the DKP received during the crisis will undoubtedly further contribute to the party's image as an anachronism in modern Danish society. (*FBIS-WEU*, 20 December.)

Domestic Affairs. Since the 1979 Folketing election in which the DKP lost all seven of its parliamentary seats, the DKP has become an increasingly irrelevant observer and critic of Danish domestic affairs. In an effort to regain influence on the political scene, the DKP has focused on three primary areas of action: electoral campaigns, labor union activism, and general leftist propaganda. Elections are the most important venue because government posts not only confer a direct influence on policy, but also give the party a platform and resources with which to promote its program. Moreover, mere participation in electoral campaigns allows a party exceptionally generous access to radio and television time (all without expense), as long as it appears on the ballot. Given the frequency of Danish parliamentary campaigns (seven since 1973), the DKP considers it essential to secure a place on the ballot. The electoral pact formed by the DKP with the VS and SAP was a first step to ensuring a place on national ballots and increasing the chance of attaining the 2 percent minimum of the popular vote required to gain Folketing representation.

Labor activism continues to absorb a large part of the DKP's attention, albeit recent party struggles have been a considerable distraction. The DKP has had considerable difficulty establishing a role for itself in industrial labor relations. Consensus politics has ensured cooperation between the SDP and the Conservative-led government on labor questions, and the SDP's size has enabled it to take the leading role in the protection of labor's interests. The factions of the labor movement the SDP does not control have tended to associate with the Socialist People's Party (Socialistisk Folkeparti; SF),

a left-wing party with 24 seats in the Folketing. The SAP and the VS are also in competition for labor's ear, limiting the DKP's influence to the extreme fringes of labor.

The DKP's main propaganda vehicle continues to be its party daily, *Land og Folk*. With a circulation of 6,500 on weekdays and 13,000 on weekends, the paper and events sponsored by it are the DKP's only steady access to the public. This summer's *Land og Folk* festival in Faelledpark drew 150,000, a considerable crowd given the limited electoral support the DKP received in the 1988 election. *Land og Folk*, however, has suffered from the same splits and financial difficulties the party itself has experienced. More objective reporting on the changes in Eastern Europe and on party matters drew heavy criticism in 1989 from the DKP's old guard. The attacks drove the paper's political editor, Bernard Jeune, to challenge the party's Central Committee to either condemn *Land og Folk* or reaffirm its editorial independence. In the end, the Central Committee refused to take sides, leaving the issue unresolved. Although its greater objectivity has helped *Land og Folk* increase its number of subscriptions for the first time in ten years, it has nevertheless continued to run a deficit. After losing five million kroner in 1988, the projected deficit was 3.8 million for 1989 and forced heavy staff cuts during the year. (*FBIS-WEU*, 27 April.)

While struggling to gain representation in the Folketing, the DKP backs in principle a socialist alternative government against the nonsocialist coalition. While the VS and SAP have also followed this pragmatic line, it is only germane to the SF, which has the only leftist representation in the Folketing aside from the SDP. Across the board the leftist parties have criticized the nonsocialists for their austerity program. The DKP supports proposals for shorter working hours (without reductions in wages), increased business taxation, restoration of the automatic cost-of-living adjustments, and restrictions on the movement of capital in and out of Denmark. Where the DKP differs from the mainline Social Democrats is in its stand on the nationalization of large industrial and financial concerns. The DKP program also calls for sharp cuts in military spending, which even the SDP renounced upon reaching a defense budget consensus with the government this year. On the whole, the DKP's program shows little change over the past few years. Much of this has to do with its long absence from power and lack of any real influence on the SDP. It is also a reflection of the strong influence of the party's stalwart Stalinists who have greeted *glasnost'*, *perestroika*, and the changes in Eastern Europe with only the deepest of suspicion.

Foreign Affairs. Under Sohn's leadership, the DKP has begun to break out of its strict pro-Moscow orientation. On the Danish left, the DKP has traditionally been the only Danish party to follow a policy of uncritical support of the Soviet Union. When *Land og Folk* began to take a more objective view of Soviet foreign policy in 1988, the sole remarks on the situation from the DKP leadership concerned the paper's editorial conduct. Sohn and a few others in the Central Committee have recently spoken more openly and positively about liberalization in Eastern Europe, but it took the ghost of Danish Communist Arne Munch-Petersen to spark a confrontation with Moscow. A Soviet historian recently uncovered evidence that Munch-Petersen, assigned in 1935 to the Comintern in Moscow, was jailed by Stalin in 1937 and died in a Soviet prison three years later. Munch-Petersen's widow immediately called for her husband's exoneration, and Sohn contacted the Soviet embassy in Copenhagen to demand the facts in the case. Worldwide publicity concerning the case of Swedish diplomat Raoul Wallenberg, who apparently died in a Soviet prison shortly after World War II, undoubtedly influenced Sohn's action, and it appears likely the party will also demand Munch-Petersen's rehabilitation. (*FBIS-WEU*, 4 August.)

If this incident is an indication of the party's growing willingness to criticize Moscow, it has not influenced its basic foreign- and security-policy platform. The DKP remains strongly anti-NATO and anti-EC, cooperating with like-minded activists throughout Europe. But with two-thirds of Denmark supportive of NATO membership and strong business endorsement of EC membership, the DKP has remained largely on the fringes of debate. Only its early support for a Nordic Nuclear Weapons–Free Zone and other antinuclear positions have gained it significant attention, but the INF Treaty and delay in modernization of the SNF in Europe have largely silenced the DKP's bread-and-butter rhetoric. (*FBIS-WEU*, 5 May.)

International Party Contacts. The DKP's internationalism distinguishes it from other Marxist parties. It identifies closely with the "proletarian internationalism" of the CPSU. But, as the latter has retreated from its rhetoric and activism of the past, the DKP has become increasingly isolated. Political upheaval in Eastern Europe and the Soviet Union over the past year limited contacts between the DKP and the communist parties in these countries. The DKP's leadership struggles have also cut into efforts to maintain its international contacts, particularly with East Germany and Poland.

Other Marxist/Leftist Groups. The DKP is only one of several left-wing parties currently active in Danish politics. The elections in May 1988 left only the SF, by far the most powerful of these parties, in parliament. Originally a splinter from the DKP (in 1958), the SF steadily gained ground despite a decade of internal splits and electoral setbacks from 1968 to 1977. Ever since it first gained parliamentary representation in 1960, the SF has courted the SDP in an effort to pull it left-ward. In 1966–1967 and 1971–1973, SF votes kept the Social Democrats in power. The first experiment in formal SF-SDP collaboration (the so-called Red Cabinet) ended when the SF's left wing broke off to form the VS. The SDP has also been wary of too much collaboration with the Marxist left, particularly after several moderate Social Democrats abandoned the party to form the Center Democrats in 1973. Although neither the SF nor SDP have excluded political collaboration in the future, recent SDP collaboration with the government on security policy and labor issues has reduced the SF's influence on its big brother. (*FBIS-WEU*, 9 March.)

The SF's program is at least part of the problem. Preferring firm ideological stances, it has tended to reject negotiation as a method to influence policy. Its platform positions are rigid and largely unacceptable to the SDP. They include a reduction of the workday to seven hours (without wage cuts), compulsory employee profit-sharing and codetermination ("economic democracy"), fiscal and monetary policies free from EC control, and the declaration of Denmark as a nuclear-free zone. One instance of the SF's hardline conviction is its attack on Danish membership in NATO's Nuclear Planning Group (NPG), where the SDP believes membership allows Denmark to influence policy. On the EC, there is some evidence that the SF has moderated its opposition to Danish membership and some party officials are even planning to use the EC Parliament as a source of political power. (*FBIS-WEU*, 9 March.)

The SF is explicitly non-Leninist in its internal governance and attitudes toward Danish parliamentary democracy. Its earlier feuds and schisms have largely faded under the leadership of its veteran chairman, Gert Petersen, although its position as an opposition party has allowed it somewhat greater internal pluralism. With just under 10,000 members, nearly a sixth of the parliamentary vote, and a substantial presence in local government and labor unions, it is an attractive alternative to the SDP and other leftist parties, including the DKP. The SF's generally independent stance, however, did not stop it from opening up direct contact with Moscow in 1988, when Petersen led an SF delegation to the Soviet Union to meet with CPSU, government, and labor officials. (Ritzau's Bureau, 27 September 1988.)

Preben Moller Hansen's Common Course party (FK) disappeared from the parliament in the May 1988 election, having polled one-tenth of one percent under the required minimum for representation. Its program follows the same themes of nationalization and confiscation that characterize the programs of the other leftist parties, especially the DKP, on whose Executive Committee Hansen sat until his feud with the DKP's old guard. Unique to FK are its anti-immigrant proposals and those regarding refugees. Both immigrants and refugees entered Denmark in large numbers in the 1980s. Over the protests of the other Danish leftists, Danish laws have been tightened and the FK supported these changes. Its populist views had provided some entertainment in the normally staid Danish parliament, but they have done little to help the party's credibility. Polls show the FK hovering around 2 percent of the vote, but as few other parties take the FK seriously, it is unlikely to have any impact on national policy even if it re-entered parliament (FBIS-WEU, 21 June).

The VS has continued its sharp decline since its loss of half its parliamentary vote in the 1988 election. In the process of this decline, the party's Leninist faction, under the leadership of Keld Albrechtsen, took over the Executive Committee. Although the decline of its more pragmatic leadership has relegated the VS even more to the fringes of the political scene, its electoral alliance with the DKP and SAP may allow it to recoup its losses in future municipal and possibly parliamentary races.

Two other small parties inhabit the far left of the political spectrum. SAP, a Trotskyist Marxist party, has no permanent political base. It is the Danish branch of the Trotskyist Fourth International, and its weekly paper *Klassekampen* (Class struggle) is well informed on Danish leftist politics and the international Trotskyist movement. In the last municipal elections, it was able to gather little more

than 400 votes and polled only 0.1 percent in the May 1988 parliamentary election. Its electoral alliance with the DKP and VS has given SAP somewhat more exposure, but it is by far the junior partner of the three. The Marxist-Leninist Party (Marxistisk-Leninistiske Parti; MLP) models itself after Enver Hoxha's Albanian Communist Party and is usually ignored by the press and the electorate.

Another small radical leftist movement, the Communist Labor Circle (Kommunistiske Arbejderkreis; KAK) entered the news in 1989 not for its politics, but rather its criminal activities. Created in 1963 by former DKP member and *Land og Folk* journalist Gotfred Appel, KAK espoused sympathies with the Chinese Communists after the Sino-Soviet split. KAK and its youth group, the Communist Youth League (KUF), turned their attentions to the Middle East in the late 1960s, first organizing assistance programs and later sending members for terrorist training in radical Palestinian camps. Members of the group were recently implicated in a string of postal and bank robberies in Denmark and the caching of weapons stolen from Swedish defense-mobilization centers. (Copenhagen, *Information*, 13–14 May.)

Neither the DKP nor other Danish leftist groups have direct ties to parties in Denmark's autonomous territories: Greenland and the Faeroe Islands. While the Faeroes have no significant Marxist movement, Greenland's politics have shown a significant left-wing character since the island obtained home rule from Denmark in 1979. A coalition of the pan-Eskimo Inuit Ataqatigiit (IA) and socialist Simuit parties presided over the withdrawal of Greenland from the EC in 1982. The coalition broke apart in 1988, in part over IA chairman Arqaluk Lynge's strong opposition to Greenland's NATO membership via Denmark. Lynge has also established close ties with the CPSU to promote contacts between the Inuits (Eskimos) in the Soviet Union and those in Greenland, Canada, and Alaska, a move the Soviets capitalized on through their first attendance at the Inuit Circumpolar Conference (ICC) in July. (*Berlingske Titende*, 21 July; Copenhagen, *Information*, 7 March.)

Randolph McNeely
Washington, D.C.

Finland

Population. 4,963,359 (1989)

Parties. Finnish Communist Party (Suomen Kommunistinen Puolue; SKP), contests elections as part of the Finnish People's Democratic League (Suomen Kansan Demokraattinen Liitto; SKDL); Finnish Communist Party-Unity (Suomen Kommunistinen Puolue-Yhtenäisyys; SKP-Y), claims to be legitimate representative of communist movement and runs candidates through an electoral front group, the Democratic Alternative (Demokraattinen Vaihtoehto; DEVA); Communist Workers' Party (Kommunistinen Tyoekansan Puolue; KTP), "revolutionary" splinter from SKP-Y

Founded. SKP: 1918; SKP-Y: 1986; KTP: 1988

Membership. SKP: 21,000; SKDL: 45,000; SKP-Y: 13,500; KTP: est. 200

Chairmen. SKP: Jarmo Wahlström (51, teacher); SKDL: Reijo Käkelä (47, theologian); SKP-Y: Jouko Kajanoja (47, civil servant), resigned 14 Oct., was succeeded by Esko-Juhani Tennilä, 22 Oct.; DEVA: Kristiina Halkola (actress); KTP: Timo Lahdenmaeki (computer technician)

General Secretaries. SKP: Helja Tammisola (43, computer technician); SKDL: Salme Kandolin (41, civil servant); SKP-Y: Yrjö Häkanen; KTP: Heikki Mannikko

Politburo. SKP: includes Aarno Aitamurto, vice-chair (53, lawyer, union official), Tapanie Elgland (journalist), Timo Laaksonen (politician), Tanja Lehmuskoski (party worker), Erkki Kauppila (journalist), Heikki Kiviaho (shipyard worker, union official), Jarmo Wahlström; SKP-Y: includes Marya-Liisa Löyttyjärvi, vice-chair, Esko-Juhani Tennilä (politician), Taisto Sinisalo (party official), Ensio Laine (politician); KTP: includes Juhani Eero, vice-chair (businessman, editor), Hannu Tuominen (toolfitter, party official), Markus Kainulainen (party official), Pekka Tiainen (research technician)

Central Committee. SKP: 20 full members; SKP-Y: 50 full and 15 alternate members

Status. Legal; SKP, SKDL, and DEVA registered as political parties and eligible for public subsidies

Last Congress. SKP: Twenty-first Congress (12–15 June 1987), Helsinki, legitimacy contested, court decision pending (22nd Congress will be held 23–25 Feb. 1990); SKP-Y: First Congress (5–7 June 1987), Espoo; SKDL: Fifteenth Congress (23–25 May 1988), Helsinki; KTP: Founding Congress (23–24 May 1988), Vantaa; First Congress 17–18 June, Vantaa

Last Election. General election for 200-seat Eduskunta, 15–16 March 1987; SKDL: 9.4 percent of vote, 16 seats (including 11 SKP); DEVA: 4.3 percent of vote, 4 seats; next scheduled general election March 1991; presidential election, 31 January–1 February 1988 (popular election), 15 February 1988 (electoral college); Kalevi Kivistö ("Action 88," candidacy endorsed by SKP/ SKDL), 10.5 percent of popular vote, 26 (of 301) seats in electoral college; Jouko Kajanoja (DEVA), 1.4 percent of popular vote, no electoral college seats. Local elections, October 1988; SKDL: 10.3 percent of overall vote; DEVA: 2.5 percent

Auxiliary Organizations. SKP: Finnish Democratic Youth League (SDNL), Finnish Women's Democratic League (SNDL); SKP-Y sponsors parallel organizations

Publications. SKP: *Kansan Uutiset* (daily); *Ny Tid* (Swedish-language weekly); SKP-Y: *Tiedonantaja* (daily); *Kommunisti* (monthly journal), all published in Helsinki; *Kansat Tahto* (local daily), Oulu; *Kansan Sana* (periodical), Pori

The Finnish Communist Party (SKP) was legalized in 1944, following the armistice with the Soviet Union that ended the Continuation War. Communist candidates in local and parliamentary elections stand for office on slates offered by the Finnish People's Democratic League (SKDL), an electoral coalition that includes the SKP as well as socialists and other "progressive" groups committed to a leftist agenda. In 1969, the SKP formally adopted a reformist line that was promoted by its pragmatic and nationalist "majority" wing in the face of opposition from a significant dogmatic and Soviet-oriented "minority" wing. In protest against the majority's "revisionism," the minority, led by Taisto Sinisalo, excluded the majority from eight minority-controlled district organizations. In 1985, a special party congress authorized the SKP central committee to expel these organizations. The SKP subsequently purged party members linked to the minority. The minority refused to accept their expulsion, and, in 1986, Sinisalo's faction set up a parallel party apparatus, the Finnish Communist

Party-Unity (SKP-Y). The minority organization is not registered as a political party but claims to be the "true" SKP. Minority candidates contest elections through a front organization, the Democratic Alternative (DEVA). (For historical background and discussion of intraparty and party/front relations, see *YICA*, 1989.)

Finnish communists took stock of their divided movement in wide-ranging end-of-decade debates on ideology, historical interpretation, procedures, and the nature and future of the party itself. The formation of the Left Alliance (Vasemmistoliitto), envisioned as a completely new, more broadly-based party than the SKDL which it would replace, was set in motion. Led by SKP chairman Jarmo Wahlström and Reijo Käkelä, the communist chairman of the SKDL, both of whom were elected to their posts in 1988, supporters of the plan argued that the new party, appealing to minority communists and noncommunists alike, would shift the center of gravity of Finnish politics to the left and open the way for socialist participation in the government. They optimistically predicted that the Left Alliance could win 15 percent of the vote in the 1991 general election (*Hufvudstadsbladet* [*Hb*], 15 March).

Sharp divisions in the SKP/SKDL soon became apparent, however, on issues such as group vs. individual applications for membership, open vs. qualified membership, terms for accepting minority communists, dual membership in other parties, and whether the SKP should be abolished or continue as a separate cooperating party. Wahlström hammered through Central Committee acceptance of the scenario devised by Käkelä and himself according to which the SKP would read itself out of existence to fuse with the SKDL in a Left Alliance composed of individual members who accepted what amounted to the majority line.

As a result, the proposed Left Alliance and the SKP leadership began to lose credibility both with the public opinion and among grass-roots communists. The latter complained that Marxism would be diluted if the SKP allowed itself to be swallowed up by a new party that was largely noncommunist, while many noncommunist leftists wondered if the Wahlström-Käkelä program meant that, in fact, the Left Alliance would be swallowed up by the communists and become the SKP under a different name. It was noted, for example, that the new party would be completely dependent financially on the SKP's assets. The erosion of Käkelä's position in the SKDL by the end of the year indicated that plans to fuse the SKP and SKDL were not going according to the script he had prepared.

In the Eduskunta (national parliament), the SKDL maintained a tactical alliance with the Finnish Center (KESH) in opposition to the four-party "red-blue" government led by the National Coalition (KOK) and the Social Democratic Party (SDP). Both the SKDL and DEVA cooperated with the Greens (VIRH) in support of stronger legislation to protect the environment. The two communist fronts frequently made common cause in the Eduskunta in 1989, but split on the vote to ratify Finland's accession to the Council of Europe. DEVA opposed membership in an organization which, it argued, was too closely identified with the West, while the SKDL supported the measure, although with reservations.

Events in Central Europe made a deep impact on Finnish communists and added pressure on the SKP to redefine, and on the minority to clarify their ideological and policy positions. Both branches were concerned to consolidate ties with the Communist Party of the Soviet Union (CPSU) and to keep abreast of the fast-moving developments that were appearing to change its role. Formerly, the SKP had a unique relationship among Finnish parties with the CPSU and, therefore, with the Soviet Union. Today, all political parties in Finland maintain some sort of formal ties with the CPSU.

Finland has a special cultural and historical affinity with Estonia. The Finns conduct a number of joint economic ventures in Estonia and, in 1989, expanded the operations of the branch office of their consulate in Tallinn to meet increased demands for consular services there. Developments in Estonia and in the other Baltic republics were given wide coverage in the Finnish press, and individual Finns were outspoken in their support for Estonian national aspirations. The Finnish government continued, however, to keep a low official profile in the region.

President Mikhail Gorbachev made a three-day (25–27 October) state visit to Finland. The Soviet leader held talks with President Mauno Koivisto and Finnish government officials that included such topics as implementation of confidence-building measures in the Arctic and Baltic Sea regions and the creation of free-market economic zones between the two countries. Gorbachev also assured the Finns that the Soviet Union would not put obstacles in the way of their participation in the European integration process. Gorbachev and Koivisto signed a protocol approving increased political, economic, technical, environmental, and cultural cooperation between the two countries. The high point of the visit was Gorbachev's address on 27 October in Finlandia Hall. Of particular significance to the Finns was his unreserved recognition of Finland's neutrality. Previously, Soviet spokesmen had always chosen to emphasize neutral Finland's "special relationship" with the Soviet Union. (Numerous articles in the Finnish press; but see *FBIS-WEU-89-206*, 26 October, and *FBIS-WEU-89-207*, 27 October.)

On 8 April, the SKP Central Committee adopted a new platform that committed the party to support the creation of the Left Alliance. Formal approval of procedures for forming the new party was left to the 22nd Congress, scheduled for February 1990. The Central Committee instructed the Political Committee to make practical proposals for the Left Alliance that would sharpen its profile and clearly differentiate the broadly based party from the SDP. It also agreed to a reduction of the number of its members from 50 to 20. (*Helsingen Sanomat* [*HS*], 9 April.)

Weeks of debate that focused on terms of membership in the Left Alliance and the future role of the SKP accompanied the drafting of the party platform. Wahlström laid out plans for the party's fusion in a broadly based Left Alliance open only to individual membership. Although approved by a three-fourths majority of the Central Committee members, his proposal was challenged by Pertti Lahtinen and Esko Seppanen, both SKDL delegates to the Eduskunta, as well as by Claes Andersson, who had opposed Wahlström for the chairmanship in 1988, former SKP chairman Arvo Aalto, and Kari Uotila, a young shipyard shop steward from Helsinki regarded as a potential party leader. Lahtinen, for example, argued for a loose leftist union of progressive groups that would include a separately constituted SKP. He accused Wahlström of resorting to "Stalinist" tactics and demanded to know on what authority the merger initiative had been undertaken. Wahlström asked in reply by what authority Seppanen had shared lecture platforms with minority communist Esko-Juhani Tennilä to promote reunification of the SKP on terms that had not been approved by the Central Committee. (*HS*, 17 March and 9 April; *Hb*, 19 March.)

The SKP's general secretary, Helja Tammisola, counseled a slower pace in setting up the Left Alliance that would allow more time for discussion of the SKP's role in it. She warned that, if the new party was not recognizably Marxist, many commu-

nists would feel excluded. Tammisola suggested that the Left Alliance could adhere to Marxism without having it as its sole theoretical frame of reference. While agreeing that the new party should admit individual members, she did not see the need for the communists among them to give up their separate SKP affiliation. (*HS*, 29 May.)

SKP-Y chairman Jouko Kajanoja entered the debate, favoring creation of the Left Alliance but urging the SKP to continue as a political party in order that the SKP-Y could be disbanded and the minority reintegrated with the majority. His reasoning mirrored Tammisola's argument for retaining a separate communist organization. The issue of the terms of reintegration divided both the SKP-Y leadership and the party's rank and file. Vice-chair Marya-Liisa Löyttyjärvi agreed with Kajanoja, but General Secretary Yrjö Häkanen was skeptical about prospects for unifying the party. He doubted that the minority could be reconciled within the proposed Left Alliance, which he predicted would become another social-democratic party. (*Hb*, 28 August; *HS*, 5 June.)

On 4 June, Wahlström and Käkelä introduced plans for forming the Left Alliance from a fusion of the SKP and SKDL to their respective party organizations. They asserted that the Left Alliance would be established as a completely new political party, and that it was not to be regarded as a re-packaged SKDL marketed under a new label. The Left Alliance was described as a "member-dominant" party: a party that accepted applications for membership from individual applicants rather than from affiliated groups. (*HS*, 5 June.)

A draft platform for the Left Alliance was presented at a conference in Kuopio in early September. The platform contained notably strong planks on environmental and gender-related issues. The term "socialist movement," used earlier to describe the proposed new party, was omitted from the draft and replaced by "leftist movement," because, it was explained, in a Finnish political context, a "socialist" was a noncommunist. Käkelä added, however, that "in international terms [the Left Alliance is] a socialist party." References to Marxism in the platform were also reduced to a passing statement that the "Marxist tradition of social science research and analysis [is] a component of leftist activities." Critics dismissed the draft platform as a "convenient wish list." (*HS*, 8 and 17 September.)

The emphasis on environmental issues in the platform was intended to appeal to Greens, whom

Käkelä and Wahlström were anxious to attract into the Left Alliance. The Greens had collaborated, for instance, in Action 88, the coalition campaign organization for Kalevi Kivisto's presidential bid that served as a model for the Left Alliance. But their overtures to her party's members had been dismissed from the start by Heidi Hautala, chairman of the Greens. "We are a movement of a different generation," she responded. Hautala put no faith in the "greening" of the SKP, observing that the communists remained "ecologically illiterate." (*Kansan Uutiset*, 14 June.)

On 19 November, the SKP central committee ratified both the draft platform and a resolution calling on communists to join the new party when it was established. A motion to approve the central committee's decision to dissolve the party and transfer assets and personnel to the Left Alliance was added to the agenda of the 22nd Congress, scheduled to convene in February 1990. (*HS*, 20 November.)

In 1988, the SKP-Y had proposed that the 1990 party congress be held as a "reparatory" assembly at which minority-controlled district organizations would be represented. At the same time, however, the SKP-Y rejected the notion of merging a re-unified SKP into a broadly based leftist party. The Supreme Court subsequently upheld the decision of the appeals court that the procedure employed in the expulsion of the minority-controlled district organizations in 1985 was invalid. A lower court later ruled in a separate suit that the SKP's attempt at the 21st Congress in 1987 to legitimize the expulsions after the fact was likewise invalid. (See *YICA*, 1989.) Although the SKP had an appeal pending on the second ruling, representatives from the expelled organizations were invited to Kulttuuritalo (SKP headquarters in Helsinki) in early September, together with a delegation from the Trade Union Confederation (SAK), to hear Wahlström outline plans for the 22nd Congress and the formation of the Left Alliance (*HS*, 6 September).

Later in the month, the SKP central committee agreed to invite the minority organizations to send delegates to the party congress once the SKP-Y had turned over its membership data for inspection. The SKP-Y quickly complied, but the SKP accused the minority of submitting inflated lists. (According to SKP procedures, each district organization is allowed one voting delegate for every 1,000 registered party members. The SKP-Y claims 9,500 members in the eight expelled organizations and an estimated 4,000 members in parallel organizations set up in majority-controlled districts.) The SKP-Y also wondered how many of the 21,000 party members registered in majority-controlled district organizations could be found in cemeteries. (*Hb*, 30 September; *HS*, 6 October.)

The Communist Workers' Party (KTB) was formally registered as a political party in June and held its First Congress in Vantaa on 17 and 18 June. The congress was attended by 180 delegates, who approved a platform that called for the establishment of "socialism by democratic means" and nationalization of large firms. They also confirmed Timo Lahdenmaeki as chairman and Heikki Mannikko as general secretary, posts to which they had been appointed at the KTB's "founding congress" in May 1988. (*HS*, 18 June; see *YICA*, 1989.)

Although registration required collecting the signatures of at least 5,000 sponsors, actual membership in the KTP is estimated at only "several hundred." Despite its small size, the KTP is taken seriously as a sounding board for "orthodox" dissatisfaction with SKP-Y policies. The core of KTP support is located in Helsinki and Uusimaa (the province surrounding Helsinki), among followers of former Uusimaa party boss Markus Kainulainen, who refused to cooperate with either the SKP-Y leadership or the SKP, and who condemned the minority's discussion of reunification with the "revisionist" SKP.

Lahdenmaeki plans to offer KTP lists in several districts in the 1991 general election. The new party's chairman announced that he would seek working partnerships with DEVA and the Greens in those districts.

Majority communists like to consider that a "Eurocommunist" SKP anticipated *glasnost'* by nearly twenty years. The open re-evaluation of ideological values that characterized discussion within Finnish communism in 1989 were reflected in the internal debate on the place of Marxism in the Left Alliance. Not even Karl Marx escaped criticism by Finnish communists.

In an essay on socialist theory and practice published early in the year, Arvo Aalto argued that Marx himself, along with Stalin and Lenin, was a culprit in the crisis of confidence in the communist camp because of inconsistencies in his thought. Aalto, who, as SKP chairman, had ordered the minority's expulsion from the party, questioned Marx's concept of the person as a victim of society, a basic tenet of his thought, observing that, in practice, more workers had been alienated under socialism than under capitalism. He condemned the "ideological dogmatism" of Marx's disciples that had "buried the individual." Although he believed that there was still a role for communism in today's world, Aalto wrote that ideas of a single-value class struggle and one-party system had to be replaced by an active acceptance of individual self-determination and political pluralism. Aalto's essay was severely attacked by a reviewer writing in the SKP-Y daily, *Tiedonantaja*. (*HS*, 1 May and 21 June; *Tiedonantaja*, 23 May.)

Speaking in April at a meeting of the SKP Central Committee, Jarmo Wahlström conceded that so many "downright crimes" were associated with the communist experiment in the Soviet Union that the whole idea of socialism had been given a bad name. He expressed the hope that *perestroika* would "correct the distortions" in the system and lead to "genuine socialism" in the Soviet Union and elsewhere. With a nod to the proposed Left Alliance, Wahlström looked forward to the development of an independent Finnish socialism that would flourish in his country's pluralistic, democratic environment. (*HS*, 9 April.)

In June, while he was still SKP-Y chairman, Jouko Kajanoja wrote in a short article in *Tiedonantaja* that he would hold leaders of the SKP to their word on the necessity for political pluralism when he negotiated terms for reunification of the party with them. Concluding that Leninism was outdated, he called for discarding democratic centralism and urged open elections for the Politburo in a reunited party. Although his statement was given prominence in the national press, Kajanoja's piece was relegated to an obscure notes-and-comments column in the minority-run newspaper. Sinisalo replied to Kajanoja in an autobiographical defense of his Leninism, entitled "To the Main Line." (*HS*, 8 June.)

At a conference of the Left Alliance in December, Reijo Käkelä admitted that a market system was more efficient than a planned economy, although he considered that the state should have a role in managing a market-oriented economy. He saw *perestroika* as an indication that the Soviet Union was moving in that direction. (*HS*, 8 December.) Esko-Juhani Tennilä, recently named SKP-Y chairman to succeed Kajanoja, countered in an interview several days later that *perestroika* did not imply an approval of capitalism. Whenever something did not go well in the Soviet Union, he replied, the majority always laid the blame on socialism and recommended the watering down of Marxism as a cure. Tennilä called instead for a

frank discussion to decide what was basic and usable in Marxism as a guide to future action. (*HS*, 11 December.)

The upheaval in Central Europe posed a serious intellectual challenge for Finnish communists, according to Käkelä (*HS*, 8 December). Political changes there were a "positive development," said Wahlström, who alleged that governments in those countries were implementing the same principles that the SKP had written into its 1969 party program. Wahlström affirmed the SKP's solidarity with communist countries that were renewing themselves. (*HS*, 15 December.)

Developments in Czechoslovakia were of particular relevance to Finnish communists who were attempting to develop the means of reconciling their own differences. The SKP majority leadership's negative reaction to the Warsaw Pact intervention in Czechoslovakia in 1968 was a factor in splitting the party the following year. At a meeting of the SKP-Y's Central Committee, Tennilä admitted that the intervention had been a mistake. The minority had consistently defended the Warsaw Pact's actions, he said, but Tennilä explained that the wrongness of the Soviet occupation had become "clear to us all after we had received new information . . ." He proposed increased contacts with the Czech and other Central European Communist parties "to preserve close connections within the party of Lenin." (*HS*, 11 December.)

Finnish communists also reconsidered their received interpretation of the Winter War (1939–1940). Nearly a half-century after the Red Army invaded Finland, the chairman of the SKP branded the Soviets as "aggressors," who, Wahlström charged, had attacked a neutral country and trampled on "socialist ideals." (*HS*, 9 March.)

By contrast, Timo Lahdenmaeki told the KTP congress that the Winter War had resulted from Finland's hostile policy toward the Soviet Union. He also complained that Finnish communism was operating in an "ideological vacuum," cut off from its Marxist-Leninist roots. (*HS*, 18 June.) Lahdenmaeki also saw no reason to reassess the Warsaw Pact intervention in Czechoslovakia, and he criticized Tennilä for going back on opinions that he, like the rest of the minority, had once held. The revisionist position on Czechoslovakia, he said, had been adopted by the SKP-Y leadership under the pressure of public opinion, and he concluded that "there is no scientific basis for it." (*HS*, 15 December.)

On 7 October, Kristiina Halkola resigned from

the chairmanship of DEVA, to which she had been re-elected in January. Despite criticism from some members of the SKP-Y that she was a political dilettante, Halkola's decision to step down as nominal leader of the hard-pressed minority electoral front was unanticipated. Halkola, identified as a "deep green" noncommunist, was a popular actress when she was named to the post in 1985. Known for her very personal approach to politics, Halkola cited personal reasons rather than political differences for her departure. She explained that she was leaving politics to return to another branch of the theater and recoup some of the income she had lost as unpaid party chairman. Few disagreed with Halkola's contention that DEVA had exploited her profile as a media personality. "I unquestionably think that I am more beautiful [on TV] than Jarmo Wahlström," she said. (HS, 8 October.)

Marya-Liisa Löyttyjärvi, SKP-Y vice-chair, was elected to succeed Halkola three weeks later, at a time when support of DEVA had dropped below 2 percent in opinion polls. A professional politician, she represented the minority with Kajanoja on the planning committee for the Left Alliance and was regarded as the minority's bridge to the new party. She told interviewers that she envisioned the Left Alliance as an "internally loose but externally compact coalition," and that she did not see dual membership in the Left Alliance and a communist party as a contradiction. (HS, 29 October.)

One week after Halkola had quit her post as DEVA chairman, Kajanoja announced his resignation as chairman of the SKP-Y, citing as his reason profound differences within the party leadership over the terms of minority participation in the Left Alliance. For some months, Kajanoja had been urging a joint party congress, at which full and equal membership in the SKP would be restored to the minority, and at which the reunification of the SKP could be sealed. Initially, he had counted Löyttyjärvi and Pentti Stenius-Kaukonen, who was also a member of DEVA's executive committee, as allies, but Kajanoja's position was strongly challenged by Sinisalo, who continued to exercise a decisive influence on the Politburo. General Secretary Yrjö Häkanen and Urho Jokinen, editor of Tiedonantaja, joined Sinisalo in openly opposing Kajanoja. Several days prior to Kajanoja's resignation, the SKP-Y Central Committee overrode the party chairman's objections and decided to prepare for a separate congress, which members of the majority would be invited to attend, that would be held if the 22nd Congress did not accept the minor-

ity delegations. (Hb, 15 October; HS, 6 and 10 October.)

Tennilä, whom Kajanoja had defeated for the party chairmanship in 1988, was elected on 22 October to succeed him in that office. The new SKP-Y chairman confirmed that the expelled minority districts would participate in the SKP congress in February 1990, even though at the time of his announcement formal invitations had not yet been issued. Tennilä said that he looked forward to the 22nd Congress as a "meeting of conciliation." He expressed his readiness to participate with the minority in the Left Alliance, but he conditioned his support on agreement to retain a separate communist party. Tennilä complained that the left had spent most of its energy in 1989 in procedural disputes. The most important task for communists and their allies, he argued, was to remove the KOK from government. (Hb, 23 October; HS, 23 October and 19 November.)

In April, Wahlström conferred with Soviet deputy premier Nikolai V. Talyzin during the latter's visit to Helsinki as head of his country's Friendship, Cooperation and Mutual Assistance (FCMA) Treaty delegation. Talyzin briefed Wahlström on the restructuring of the CPSU. He also met separately with Kajanoja. The Soviet deputy premier reportedly stressed to both Wahlström and Kajanoja that the Finns should have a united communist movement. (Hb, 11 April.)

A CPSU delegation visited Finland at the invitation of KESH in May for a celebration of the fifteenth anniversary of formal contacts between the two parties. In their joint communiqué, the leader of the Soviet delegation, B.K. Pugo, and his host, KESH chairman Paavo Väyrynen, stressed the importance of the Paasikivi-Kekkonen Line in promoting Soviet-Finnish cooperation in the postwar period. Interparty discussions covered such topics as President Gorbachev's 1987 Murmansk proposals on arms reduction in the Arctic and prospects for Finnish participation in the European integration process. (KESH has urged caution on involvement in the process that would undercut existing ties with the Soviet Union.) The CPSU delegation was received by President Mauno Koivisto. (FBIS-SOV-89-097, 22 May.)

CPSU Politburo member Aleksandr Yakovlev held separate interviews with representatives of the SKP and SKP-Y while accompanying President Gorbachev on his state visit in October. Party unity and plans for a conference of European leftist parties in Helsinki in 1990 were discussed. Yakovlev also met with representatives of other Finnish political parties. (*FBIS-WEU-89-207*, 27 October.)

Oiva Bjorkbacka attended the Romanian Communist Party (RCP) congress in Bucharest in November as an "observer" rather than as an SKP representative. In 1988, the SKP had called off all official trips to Romania to protest violations of human rights committed by the Ceauşescu regime against the Hungarian minority there. Bjorkbacka carried the SKP's fraternal greetings to the RCP, which was celebrating the 45th anniversary of its founding. (*HS*, 9 November.)

The SDP maintained established contacts with communist parties in Central European countries, even though fraternal social-democratic parties had arisen to oppose them in 1989. During the year, the SDP exchanged delegations with the communist parties in Czechoslovakia, Hungary, Poland, and the GDR. An SDP delegation paid a working visit to the Soviet Union in December as guests of the CPSU. The SKP, together with the SKDL, has extended invitations to members of European social-democratic and communist parliamentary delegations to attend the "leftist forum" to be held in Tampere in 1990. (*HS*, 19 December.)

A 37-member planning committee for the Left Alliance was appointed in October. Of its members, 18 were communists drawn from both factions. Kajanoja, who had, only a week earlier, stepped down as SKP-Y chairman, was among those representing the minority. The committee held an organizational meeting in Helsinki on Finland's Independence Day (7 December). Its deliberations were dominated by arguments over the terms of membership in the new party. Kajanoja, who had only recently stepped down as SKP-Y chairman, accepted the majority leadership's line virtually without qualification. He accepted the abolition of the SKP as a separate party and opposed further participation in planning by communists who refused to accept the condition of individual membership in the Left Alliance. Kajanoja saw a fusion party as the best vehicle for carrying on the communist agenda and accepted that communists would probably organize a caucus within the Left Alliance. His minority colleague on the committee, Marya-Liisa Löyttyjärvi, favored preserving a communist party outside the Left Alliance to give ideological guidance, but she recognized that dual membership would pose problems for the new party. DEVA, she added, could be abolished once an agreement was reached on the future of the SKP. Löyttyjärvi appeared to assume that the SKP would be reunified

and that the Left Alliance would be composed of individual members. (*HS*, 8 December.)

Reijo Käkelä conceded no options on the question of dissolution and said that the issue was closed, but he seemed to give some ground on open membership. He responded to Löyttyjärvi that any problems regarding the future of DEVA should be resolved when the Left Alliance had proved itself to be the only responsible political force to the left of the SDP. He appealed to minority communists, Greens, and left-wing Social Democrats to come into the Left Alliance, adding that it would be "a matter of conscience" whether an individual wished to participate in the new party while continuing affiliation with another political organization. Käkelä also seized the occasion to reject the "prepackaged dogmas that have outlived their usefulness," among them centralized, planned economies. (Ibid.)

The conference communiqué stated that the aim of the Left Alliance would be to achieve a "more open and more democratic Finland" in a Europe "no longer divided by walls." It was agreed that signatures in support of registering the new party would be collected on May Day 1990 and a founding congress held in June. An eight-member executive committee was empanelled to handle arrangements for inaugurating the Left Alliance. In addition to Käkelä, they included Tammisola and Kari Uutila from the SKP, Löyttyjärvi and Stenius-Kaukonen from the minority. (Ibid.)

The factional struggle between majority and minority communists continued to complicate the appointment of a general secretary of the Finland-USSR Society (SNS). The society, which has 100,000 members, is one of Finland's largest civic organizations. It is dedicated to improving Soviet-Finnish relations at the nongovernmental level. Although all parties are represented among its members, the SKP/SKDL has been particularly influential in the selection of officers. When minority communists and some noncommunists in the SNS blocked the nomination of another majority communist, Oiva Bjorkbacka, to succeed Erkki Kivimaki as general secretary, and when other parties refused to nominate an alternative candidate to the SKP nominee, Kivimaki postponed his retirement until an acceptable replacement could be found. Matters were further complicated when it was alleged that Leonid Laakso, director of the Novosti Press Agency (APN) in Helsinki, had tried to influence Bjorkbacka's election. Laakso firmly denied any intervention on his part in the SNS's internal affairs. In March, Merja Hannus of the SKP, was chosen general secretary in an undisputed election. Observers remarked, however, that intra-party communist squabbles had badly tarnished the society's prestige and limited its future effectiveness. (See *YICA*, 1989; *HS*, 6, 14, 20, and 21 January, 7 and 16 March.)

In June, the SKDL withdrew from membership in the Finnish Peace Defenders, a branch of the World Peace Council (WPC). Headquartered in Helsinki since 1968, the WPC is an international communist-front organization that has continued to follow the "Brezhnev line." Käkelä explained that the SKDL's action was a result of party reorganization and not a matter of principle, but he had been critical of a speech by Matti Ruokala, in which the organization's noncommunist chairman had cautioned against threats to peace posed by the Federal Republic of Germany. SKDL members were advised that they were free to join the Finnish Peace Defenders as individuals. Although communists have been the leading activists in this civic organization, members are drawn from all political parties, and spokesmen for it have included prominent noncommunists. Many members, however, are nonactive, and the SKDL's withdrawal threatens the organization's continued existence. The future of the WPC is also uncertain. In Central European countries, new peace movements emerged in 1989 that refuse to collaborate with the communist-dominated WPC. Other factors cited for declining interest are the cut-back in Soviet funding for the WPC and the elimination of free airline tickets formerly given members for tours and conferences. (See *YICA*, 1989; *HS*, 22 May, 8 June, and 15 and 24 December.)

(On 2 February 1990, Reijo Käkelä resigned as chairman of the SKDL. He announced his resignation to the executive committee of the Left Alliance which had decided, contrary to his recommendation, to allow completely open admission to the inaugural congress in June. Käkelä informed the committee that he did not intend to be a candidate for chairman of the Left Alliance. His departure was regarded as a setback for Wahlström and the SKP leadership.

The expelled minority districts were represented in the 22nd Congress of the SKP meeting in Helsinki from 23 to 25 February 1990. Delegates approved a plan for phasing out operations of the SKP over a three-year period, leaving responsibility for the formal dissolution of the party to the next congress. This procedure was the result of a com-promise between the leadership, who backed quick fusion into the Left Alliance at its inception, and both majority and minority grass-roots opinion that favored keeping a separate SKP organization in existence.)

Biographies. *Jouko Kajanoja* was born in the Tammela area of Häme in 1942. He has a degree in political science and began his career as a civil servant in the Helsinki municipal government before transferring to the Ministry of Interior. He was minister of labor (1981–1982) in the Sorsa government. Kajanoja was closely identified with the "Third Line" in the SKP that attempted to mediate between the majority and minority wings of the party. He was elected party chairman in 1982 with minority support, succeeding Aarne Saarinen. In 1984, he was ousted from that post by his former mentor, Arvo Aalto and was expelled from the SKP with the minority the next year. Kajanoja was named first general secretary of the SKP-Y in 1986 and ran as DEVA's candidate in the 1987 presidential election, winning only 1.4 percent of the popular vote. He succeeded Taisto Sinisalo as SKP-Y chairman in 1988. He is a member of the executive committee of DEVA and sat on the planning committee of the Left Alliance.

Esko-Juhani Tennilä, aged 43, is a 17-year veteran of the Eduskunta, where he has sat in the SKDL and, since 1986, in the DEVA delegation. Tennilä entered politics, however, as a Social Democrat, and his entire political career has been marked by restlessness. He attempted to oust Sinisalo as leader of the minority in 1986, and, in 1988, he unsuccessfully challenged Kajanoja for the SKP-Y chairmanship, calling for a special congress to discuss terms for reunifying the party. Tennilä was named vice-chairman as a consolation. He was a contender for DEVA's presidential nomination in 1989 and subsequently declined to be a candidate for a seat on the Electoral College that was committed to Kajanoja.

Tennilä is viewed by critics as an opportunistic "populist," unpredictable and lacking in principles, and is described as a maverick "Yeltsin-like" personality. Few would deny, however, that he is a popular figure who has his own constituency and is not dependent on a position in the party to keep his name before the public. Tennilä conducted well-publicized speaking tours with SKDL deputy Esko Seppanen to campaign for party reunification, remarking on one occasion that it was his personal wish to sit again in the Eduskunta with the SKDL.

There was a suspicion at the time that he was ready to defect to the majority. In the weeks following his election as SKP-Y chairman, however, he strongly advocated retaining an independent minority line in any talk of reunification or participation in the Left Alliance.

Jarmo Wahlström was "unanimously" elected SKP chairman at the party's conference in Tampere in May 1988. Although regarded as a "moderate" interested in mediating disputes among the tendencies within the party, Wahlström also gained a reputation as a political "hatchet-man" for Aalto and Saarinen in intraparty disputes. As chairman guiding the SKP through a difficult transitional period, he has been an efficient administrator but a colorless leader.

Wahlström was born in Vaasa in 1938 and was raised in a working-class milieu. His parents were active communists. He received pedagogical training and was a teacher before becoming a full-time party official and politician. Wahlström joined the SKP in 1960 and was appointed first chairman of the communist-front Academic Socialist Society in 1964. He was admitted to the Central Committee in 1975 and was named to the Politburo at the 21st Congress in 1987. He was an SKDL deputy in the Eduskunta from 1975 to 1984 and was re-elected in 1987, when he became leader of the SKDL parliamentary group. He was outspoken on environmental issues and opposed the use of nuclear energy in Finland. He was minister of communications (1982–1983) in the Social Democrat-led Sorsa government.

Robert Rinehart
Washington, D.C.

France

Population. 55,994,085 (*World Fact Book*, 1989)
Party. French Communist Party (Parti communiste français; PCF)
Founded. 1920
Membership. 200,000 (*FBIS-WEU*, 30 January 1989)
General Secretary. Georges Marchais

Politburo. 22 members: Georges Marchais, Charles Fiterman (propaganda and communications), Jean-Claude Gayssot (party organization), Maxime Gremetz (foreign affairs), André Lajoinie (president of the Communist group in the National Assembly), Paul Laurent (liaison with party federations), Gisèle Moreau (women's activities and family politics), Gaston Plissonnier (coordination of the work of the Politburo and Secretariat), Gustave Ansart (president of the Central Commission of Political Control), François Duteil (urbanism, environment, and consumption associations), Claude Billard (party activity in business and immigration), Pierre Blotin (education of Communists), Philippe Herzog (economy), Francette Lazard (director of the Marxist Research Institute), René Le Guen (science, research, and technology), Roland Leroy (director of *l'Humanité*), René Piquet (leads French Communists in the European Parliament), Madélaine Vincent (local communities, elections), Henri Krasucki (secretary of the CGT), Louis Viannet (Mail Workers' Federation), Antoine Casanova (intellectual, cultural, educational, and university affairs; also director of the review *La Pensée*), Jackie Hoffman (women's issues)
Secretariat. 7 members: Maxime Gremetz, Jean-Claude Gayssot, André Lajoinie, Paul Laurent, Gisèle Moreau, Gaston Plissonnier, Charles Fiterman
Central Committee. 145 members
Status. Legal
Last Congress. Twenty-sixth, 2–6 December 1987; next congress planned for December 1990
Last Election. 1989, European Parliament, 7.7 percent
Auxiliary Organizations. General Confederation of Labor (CGT); World Peace Council; Movement of Communist Youth of France (MCJF); Committee for the Defense of Freedom in France and the World; Association of Communist and Republican Representatives
Publications. *L'Humanité* (Paris: Roland Leroy, director; daily national organ); *L'Echo du centre* (Limoges, daily); *Liberté* (Lille, daily); *La Marseillaise* (Marseille, daily); *L'Humanité-Dimanche* (Paris: weekly); *La Révolution* (Guy Hermier, director; weekly publication of the Central Committee); *La Terre* (weekly); *Cahiers du Communisme* (monthly, theoretical journal); *Europe* (literary journal); *Economie et politique* (economic journal); 5 journals published by the Marx-

ist Research Institute; 4 monthly magazines; other periodicals on sports, children's themes, and the like, and books on political, economic and social topics published by Editions sociales, the PCF publishing house in Paris.

The year 1989 was yet another bad one for French Communists. The leadership and dwindling faithful remained mired in bitter factionalism, feckless foreign initiatives, and near record-setting electoral failures. The few bright spots in the party's year were more than shaded by continuation of the internecine bloodlettings, political muggings, and stonewalling by the leadership that have become a longrunning comic opera in much of the French media. Communist renegades outside the party and determined critics within became better organized in 1989 to pressure PCF bosses for open debate and systemic reforms. Party leaders, however, hewed to the line that the PCF's problems are behind it, and that a fair reading of the evidence indicates that French communism is "on the rise." The party's general secretary, Georges Marchais, and Politburo hard-liners redoubled their international activities in 1989, partly to mend fences with Moscow over the PCF's widely reported doubts about *perestroika* and partly to deal with the burgeoning specter of implosions of communist parties in Eastern Europe. Meanwhile, French voters again twice devastated communist candidates at the polls, the spastic fits and starts of the PCF's campaigns yielding fresh evidence of what one pundit described as the party's self-induced "political autism."

Leadership and Internal Activities. The months after the PCF's national conference at Nanterre (12–13 November 1988) saw communist leaders attempting to walk the thin line between supporting trade-union strikes against the public sector—a position that led to a fierce standoff with the socialist government of Michel Rocard—and the refusal of the communist deputies in the National Assembly to use their voting strength to join with the right in a vote of censure to bring down the Rocard government. The refusal of party leaders to use their parliamentary clout drew sharp criticism throughout the year, especially from the right, but most media believed that General Secretary Marchais drew back from using "the death penalty" against the Socialists in order to drive the hardest possible bargain in forging leftist "unity" lists in the coming municipal elections. In opposition to the hard line emanating from Nanterre, which essen-

tially blamed the Socialists for rising unemployment, national policies calculated to advance the interests of big capital, austerity that caused worker suffering, and a bloated defense budget in support of NATO militarism, Marchais and other leaders constantly asserted publicly that the object of Communists in forthcoming elections would be to prevent the success of the right, especially the extreme right National Front.

While PCF leaders were locked in several months of negotiations with Socialists on the technicalities of running joint lists in the 1989 municipal elections, dissident Communists both outside and inside the party were organizing to build additional pressure on the PCF hard-line leadership to initiate fundamental changes in the direction and management of the party. The recently expelled former party spokesman Pierre Juquin—who had stood against the party's official candidate in the 1988 presidential balloting—announced the formation of a long-discussed organizational alternative for disgruntled rank-and-file members of the PCF. Juquin's alternative billed itself more as a "movement" than a party. Born out of the ragtag National Coordinating Committee of Communist Renewalists, which had been Juquin's electoral coalition, the "New Left, for Socialism, Self-Management, and Ecology" met for the first time at Plaine-Saint-Denis near Paris in early December 1988. Although Juquin and his allies threatened to participate as independent leftists in coming elections, they clearly had in mind the formation of joint lists with Antoine Waechter's French Greens (Ecologists). In addition, their attention was already more focused on the elections for the European Parliament, set for June (in which proportional voting would give them a better chance of electing deputies) than on the upcoming French municipal elections, in which majority voting and lack of concentrated local support would probably dissipate their strength. It is important that Juquin's New Left (NG) alliance absorbed groups that had been around for some time—notably the Federation for an Alternative Left and the Unified Socialist Party (PSU), which had been a perennial orphan of the French left. (*Libération*, 5 December 1988.)

However, squabbling broke out when it appeared that Alain Krivine's Trotskyist Communist Revolutionary League (LCR) would join Juquin's New Left. Many of the renovators who had followed Juquin out of the PCF and had been the backbone of his presidential bid rejected merger if it meant they would "become Trotskyized," while Krivine equally resisted the notion that his troops would come under the influence of communist "re-newalists." The result was that renegade reno-vators—minus their leader, Juquin—met at Vitrolles (in the dissident Bouches-du-Rhone federation) and formed themselves into the Move-ment of Communist Renewalists (MRC). The MRC, headed by Toulousian and former PCF Cen-tral Committee member Claude Llabres, self-consciously determined to wait for Claude Poperen and Marcel Rigout—dissident former communist ministers still on the Central Committee—to leave the PCF in order to take the lead of the movement, but both remained all year in the PCF as leaders of the "reconstructionist" faction—identified in some of the centrist and conservative press as the "Gor-bachevian tendency" in the PCF. (*Le Quotidien de Paris*, 25 October 1988.)

Meanwhile, the growing group of senior PCF officials whom Marchais had earlier branded as "malcontents" continued to organize themselves as the *reconstructeurs* (rebuilders) of the party. This group—led by Marcel Rigout, former minister in the socialist-communist government of Pierre Mauroy, Claude Poperen, Félix Damette, and Mar-tial Bourquin—had earlier appeared to support Ju-quin's criticisms of the hard-line leadership around Marchais, but refused to follow Juquin into the wilderness of renegade opposition. Throughout 1989, their line continued to be that the PCF is salvageable and can be reformed from within, and at the beginning of the year they banded together in the Communist Reconstructionist Initiative, a movement devoted to spreading the message of in-ternal renewal to communist cells by means of a "temporary bulletin" called *Réconstruction Com-muniste*. (*Le Monde*, 27 December 1988.)

Parallel with the massive but largely ineffective midwinter strikes of the communist-controlled General Confederation of Labor, the PCF Politburo decided to use the "momentum" from the Nanterre conference as a mandate for disciplining dissident departmental federations (*l'Evénément du Jeudi*, 8–14 December 1988; *Le Monde*, 18 October 1988). The leadership's efforts to dissolve and pre-sumably reconstitute the Doubs federation along conservative lines—spearheaded by Politburo member Paul Laurent—met with strong resistance from the renovators' group, backed by four sons of former leaders of the PCF: Pierre Thorez, Serge Rochet, Jerôme Knapa, and André Prenant, who issued a statement condemning the Central Com-mittee's use of "administrative methods" that smacked of "Stalinism" (*Le Monde*, 28 October

1988). Meanwhile, Claude Poperen and other Cen-tral Committee opponents of Marchais railed against the Politburo's subversion of democratic centralism (*l'Humanité*, 17 October 1988). Even Lucien Sève, philosopher and last bona fide intel-lectual of national stature in the Communist Party, also questioned the leadership's resort to "organiza-tional measures" to bring the Doubs to heel.

In the months before the municipal elections, two things became clear: the recent purges of reno-vators and dissidents from major department federations (such as the Seine–Saint-Denis and the Val-de-Marne) had left a more hard-line, intran-sigent element in charge at the local level, and party leaders intended to use the formation of the new lists at least in part to further purge or punish dissidents who remained in the party. The focus of hard-liners at both the national and local levels was the PCF's demand that lists for the upcoming elections be based on the leftist unity agreement of the 1983 municipal elections, that is, Socialists and Commu-nists would each leave the field clear for the other in all those cities and towns where they had agreed to do so in 1983. Of course, Socialists scoffed at this suggestion, arguing that diminished communist strength required the party to take a smaller cut of the action. But, the PCF leadership persisted, spurred on by hard-line local leaders in communist bastions—known as "Red Guards"—some of whom were in former dissident federations and cells that had been recently "normalized" by the leadership and left with a rump of hard-as-nails militants in the majority. (*Le Monde*, 29–30 January.)

According to various press reports, communist leaders cynically offered to take a cut of 10 to 15 percent in some areas if Socialists would agree to lists that would preserve the pre-1983 communist bastions. According to leading political analysts, this "strategy of bastions" had three tactical advan-tages: it would make it possible for PCF leaders to eliminate Socialists and other outsiders who had made inroads into their traditional strongholds; it would make the Socialists appear to stand in the way of unity if they refused; and it would, if successful, promote the claim made by the leadership that the party was on the road to "recovery." (*Le Monde*, 29–30 January.)

The PCF-socialist negotiations for united lists went against the Communists, largely because President Mitterrand ordered the Socialist (PS) offi-cials to drive hard bargains (*Le Point*, 13 February). In the end, agreement was not reached on a large number of seats, and in the first-round "primaries"

Communists and Socialists faced each other. More-over, socialist officials annoyed PCF leaders by sticking to their view that communist renovators were "participating on the left" and should not be excluded from the leftist lists when they were representative of leftist sentiment in the communes (*l'Humanité*, 20 January; *Le Monde*, 18 October 1988). Ultimately these misadventures cost the PCF leadership dearly in the March elections. Not only did they lose ground to Socialists but some of the dissident PCF mayors whom Marchais and Politburo bosses had hoped to dump—Robert Jarry of Le Mans, Jean Ooghe of Saint-Geneviève-les-Bois, and Gaston Viens of Orly—survived the contests, thanks to the pervasiveness of communist dissent at the local level and their own local strength (*Le Point*, 24 April).

The staggering losses in the March municipal elections were the most serious blow to the PCF leadership since the fiasco of the 26th Congress. The party suffered a staggering erosion of the very bedrock of communist power and influence: control of the local offices and city halls that were the wellsprings of the jobs, patronage, and contracts that form the basis of the PCF's national strength. Now deprived of a significant number of such goldmines, the PCF leadership faced a situation of dwindling revenues and therefore membership, similar to the losses it had suffered since the rupture of its alliance with the Socialists after the 1983 municipal elections. At the very least, this made the party more dependent on its other sources of income: so-called red businesses, international investments, and probably shaky contributions from the Soviet Union. (*Le Point*, 27 March.)

On this occasion, even near-record abstentions of French voters—usually a plus for the PCF, since its disciplined militants turn out regularly—did not save the leadership from embarrassment. In the face of events that most political analysts predicted would accelerate the party's tailspin, leaders clung to the assessment, announced in *l'Humanité*, that their strategy and election management had enabled the PCF to "preserve the essentials of its force" (*Le Point*, 27 March).

Electoral disaster also caused the leadership to proclaim even more loudly that the party's strength was returning, that a recovery was in full swing. To support Marchais's numerous declarations, which were variations on the theme "We are on the rise again," PCF officials made frequent claims of membership increases, returning members, and swelling sales of party publications. Officials began the year

by noting that 60,000 new members had joined the PCF in the previous year. Jean-Claude Gayssot, Politburo enforcer and heir-apparent to Marchais, declared proudly in the first issue of *Cahiers du Communisme* (January 1989) that the party had recently won 62,000 converts and that it would reach the goal set at its Nanterre conference of establishing 1,000 new cells by the next party congress, set for December 1990. (*WMR*, Toronto, February.) Meanwhile, at midyear and in the wake of losses in the municipal elections, André Lajoinie—the PCF's standard-bearer in the 1988 presidential contest—maintained that the "conquering spirit" of the party had caused "almost twenty thousand men and women" to "rejoin the Communist Party since the beginning of the year." ("Pour les luttes sociales et politiques une force qui compte," *Cahiers du Communisme*, April.) Marchais also reinforced his claims of a resurgence with figures on new membership. For example, in the wake of the PCF's annual and predictable ritual chestbeating at the September "Fête de *l'Humanité*," he told *Pravda* that the leadership had sold 647,000 tickets to the festival (reinforcing party claims of over 610,000 adherents), that 9,900 persons had "joined our party during the festival, and 7,700 joined the French Communist Youth Movement" (*Pravda*, 20 September). Additional evidence of the party's comeback was deduced from the reported increase in sales of the PCF's daily newspaper, *l'Humanité*. Thanks to the success of local circulation-promotion committees, said Henri Martin (Central Committee member in charge of promoting *l'Humanité*), the circulation of the party's premier newspaper and guarantor of its "pluralism" had increased by 30 and even 35 percent in some areas of France. To reinforce the implication that new readers equaled new PCF militants, Martin cited the evidence of 53 new subscribers in Chalette, in the Loiret, 23 of whom "expressed a desire to participate more actively in the activities of the Party." ("*l'Humanité*, un média pas comme les autres," *Cahiers du Communisme*, January.)

Defeat in the municipal elections made even more important the party's performance in the elections for the European Parliament, set for July. Continuing his recent tactic of distancing himself from election disasters, Marchais again chose a surrogate to lead the communist ticket. Lajoinie had taken the blame for the PCF's poor showing in the last presidential balloting, though no one really held him personally responsible for the party's defeat; this time out the party's economic guru and professor of the University of Paris Philippe Herzog headed the PCF's national list. Herzog's chances of sparking a reversal of the PCF's recent failures were better than at any time since the legislative elections of 1986, largely because the European Community elections gave proportional representation at the national level. Proportional voting—in contrast with the majority system of France—would better allow any small party with a nationwide organization to assert its full strength.

As the Europarliament contests neared, PCF leaders turned up the heat on their erstwhile leftist-unity partners of the Socialist Party, but continued also to attack the reconstructors within their own party who threatened to make the coming elections more difficult. The Socialists were lambasted above all for their tactics in the recent municipal elections. In the first place, communist bosses blamed them for the party's poor showing, especially because they had steadfastly refused to observe the 1983 division of spoils and had insisted that in almost 40 percent of the contests there would be a face-off, that is, "primaries," in which both PS and PCF candidates would compete. Going into the municipal elections, communist spokeswoman Madélaine Vincent had warned, in a report adopted at the January plenum of the Central Committee, that "primaries" would diminish communist chances at the polls. As Socialists held to their demands, and communist leaders eventually had to accept half a loaf, attitudes toward Mitterrand's PS grew noticeably bitter. The forced congeniality of the period prior to the elections eventually gave way to hostility, as communist leaders charged that the PS tactics had caused rightists to be elected in some places, and that the Socialists had even violated their electoral agreement with the PCF. The communist drubbing was probably more difficult to swallow and their attacks on the Socialists were probably all the more bitter because the socialist tactics had paid off handsomely, netting Mitterrand and Prime Minister Rocard almost all the local offices they had lost in the leftist defeat of 1983. (*l'Humanité*, 20 January; Madélaine Vincent, "Municipales: partout rassembler à gauche," *Cahiers du Communisme*, January; *Pravda*, 21 March.)

In the two months between the municipal and the European elections, PCF hard-liners, notably Gayssot, Herzog, and Lajoinie, brandished the prospect of a communist motion of censure in the National Assembly that would surely bring down the Rocard government. Jackie Hoffman, recently installed Politburo conservative, made Socialist

treachery a prominent theme of electioneering for the Euroballoting, as it was in the aftermath of the municipal defeats ("L'avenir est à un parti communiste confiant, lucide, conquérant," *Cahiers du Communisme*, June). In contrast, the PCF reconstructors apparently decided that communists had nothing to gain by goading Socialists, and therefore they participated in a joint colloquium with the PS on 4 May. Meanwhile, Marcel Rosette, former leader of the communist deputies in the National Assembly, wrote to each member of the Central Committee condemning the leadership's general policies, especially its continued use of "administrative methods" to punish dissident cells and federations (*Le Monde*, 15–16 October; *Le Point*, 24 April).

PCF leaders admitted at the Central Committee meeting of 22 June that their performance in the Euroelections had been "disappointing," but Marchais and other Politburo spinmasters took refuge in the analysis that any score bettering their miserable 6.7 percent in the 1988 presidential election would demonstrate "the rising power is the PCF." Or, as Marchais put it almost unbelievably on several occasions, "We are the future." (*Le Figaro*, 23 June; *NYT*, 23 January.) In contrast, reconstructionist leaders, including Poperen, Rigout, and Gaston Viens, declared on the eve of the Central Committee meeting that the leadership's claims of recovery in the face of such apparent electoral disaster was nothing short of a "scuttling process." The Euroelections provided an occasion for dissidents to repeat for the noncommunist media their full litany of demands and charges against the leadership, including the refrain from their manifesto that "the leadership of our party bears the historical responsibility for the decline of our influence." They further drove home the point that the usual Politburo excuses would not explain away the defeat in the European election (7.7 percent for Communists nationwide), since the PCF had declared that national proportional representation would be the optimum process for translating the party's grass-roots strength into offices.

The summer defeats fueled media pressure to explain why the domestic problems of the PCF were not a direct parallel with the collapse of communist regimes in Eastern Europe. Marchais responded with time-honored PCF assertions that everywhere socialism was proving its superiority to capitalism, that the bottom line on the performance of East European communism was "globally positive," and that it was capitalism that was in the throes of a "systemic crisis." (*Le Point*, 20 November and 18 September.) These claims reportedly only magnified pressures from within the party for Marchais's ouster and abandonment of the current leadership line (*Le Point*, 20 November).

Disaffection broke into an open rift in the leadership at the October Central Committee plenum, the atmosphere of which was pervaded by massive coverage in the French media of the further collapse of communism in Central and Eastern Europe. Marchais's report to the session, intended to set the tone for the PCF political *rentrée*, was a scathing attack on the "big stick" social policies of the Rocard government. Instead of rousing the faithful, however, this portent of yet another "hot autumn" drew a heated retort from Central Committee reconstructionists, notably the former ministers Anicet Le Pors and Jack Ralite, and from Lucien Sève. (*Le Monde*, 14 and 15–16 October.) Most devastating, however, former PCF transport minister Charles Fiterman finally came down from the fence and blasted Politburo hard-liners with accusations of "messianism" and self-portrayal as "repositories of revealed wisdom." Although Fiterman was absent from the session (still hospitalized following an auto accident), his written strictures caused consternation in the leadership and what one noncommunist observer called a giant "crack" in the PCF, especially by their strong implication that the Politburo's current strategy was essentially similar to the defunct Stalinist strategy of class war, exclusion, and the "dictatorship of the proletariat." (*Le Monde*, 18 October.) Striking back on national radio (Radio Luxembourg, "Grand Jury," 15 October), Marchais claimed to still enjoy the support of an "overwhelming majority of the party," and he implied strongly (but did not say outright) that both Fiterman and Le Pors had criticized the party's line so thoroughly as to virtually put themselves outside the PCF (*Le Monde*, 17 October; *Le Point*, 23 October).

In the final months of the year, the leadership's attention was increasingly focused on preparations, just getting under way, for the PCF's 27th Congress, set for 1990. As Politburo hard-liners contended with the fallout from recent election reversals, the "softening" of other Eurocommunist parties toward internal reform, and the deterioration of fraternal parties in Eastern Europe, few were unaware that the party's progress toward the next December's congress would be enlivened and excited by increasing dissident attacks on the unrecalcitrant "Brezhnevism" of the leadership and by stepped-up demands for "new thinking" and a new strategy for confronting the party's future ("Marchais: Le dernier carré," *Le Point*, 10 November). Perhaps as a result of the stresses related to successive election defeats and the leadership's more intense factionalism, Marchais (who had a fifteen-year history of cardiac problems) entered a Paris hospital on 10 December, suffering from "irregular heart rhythms." This circumstance guaranteed that the PCF would begin the year of its 27th Congress with speculation about the durability of its beleaguered general secretary (Reuter, 11 December).

Domestic Affairs. The PCF's domestic efforts focused almost entirely on prosecution of municipal- and European Parliament–election campaigns—the ninth and tenth times French voters were called to the polls in less than a year—and on disintegrating relations with the Socialists over a long list of domestic social and economic issues, in particular, the continuation of the Rocard government's austerity budgets. The thrust of the Communists' efforts, both in and outside of election campaigns, was to blame the government and the PS for almost every malady facing France, ranging from the decline of real income among workers to the dramatic upswing in the suicide rate among the nation's young. (*NYT*, 20 March; *l'Humanité*, 12 September.)

Top priority on the domestic agenda for Politburo members was preservation of the party's control of critical municipal strongholds. Seats on the councils of all 36,763 French communes were on the line in the balloting of 12 and 19 March, and Communists aimed to safeguard especially their control of the 81 cities having a population of over 20,000 and of the 53 cities with a population of more than 30,000 where they still held sway. According to various press reports, PCF leaders were especially determined to hold the 43 communist cities with a population over 20,000 located in the five departments around Paris. (*Le Monde*, 29–30 January.) In particular, they were determined to forestall a repeat of what had happened in the last municipal elections, when candidates of the united right, composed of the Neo-Gaullist Party and the Union for French Democracy, ran up gains of 31 towns with a population over 30,000, 16 of them formerly controlled by Communists. (*NYT*, 14 and 20 March; *Financial Times*, 12 January.) In the joint agreement signed by the PS and PCF, the Communists relaxed their earlier demands that Socialists should not oppose them in any of the towns they had lost or won in 1983. The "leftist-unity" strategy announced on 12 January agreed to take the 1983 accords "into account." As political and social goals, the PS and the PCF called jointly for more modern and efficient municipal services; low-cost housing in a good environment; improved education; access to culture, sports, and leisure; improved security, healthcare, and environment; action on economic development; and the energetic defense of jobs. (*l'Humanité*, 13 January; *Financial Times*, 7 and 12 January; Paris Domestic Service, 12 January; *FBIS-WEU*, 13 January; *Cahiers du Communisme*, February; *Le Figaro*, 13 January.)

The details of the unity lists, worked out at the local level and supervised by Marcel Debarge (PS) and Paul Laurent (PCF), left a gaping hole in the PCF's goal of preserving its bastions (*Le Point*, 27 February). January's agreement in principal gave way to failure to reach agreement in practice, as it became clear by early March that there would be PS-PCF "primaries" in 40 percent of the 390 towns with a population of over 20,000. In the 280 largest towns controlled by the right, PS-PCF cooperation was especially dismal; local leftists agreed to joint lists in only 90, leaving 190 to be decided by face-offs. Nîmes, a city of almost 250,000 in the far south Midi, was typical of such failures. Traditionally a communist stronghold, Nîmes was lost to the right in 1983. In 1989, the contest became a three-way battle between the conservative deputy mayor, Jean Bousquet, the former communist mayor, Emile Jourdan, and the town's leading Socialist, François Brugueirolle. Bousquet won outright on the first round, the separate PCF and PS lists polling fewer votes even than they had in 1983. (*Financial Times*, 10 March; *Libération*, 10 February; *l'Humanité*, 14 March.) The façade erected by the PS-PCF negotiations turned out to have so many cracks that much of the noncommunist press called the leftist unity an "electoral fiction" and the negotiations an "electoral pantomime" (*Le Point*, 16 January; *Le Figaro*, 13 January).

While PCF leaders were thus failing to win any advantage in working out grass-roots electoral agreements with the Socialists, according to much of the noncommunist media, they were also sacrificing the political momentum created by their fierce strike activity against the Rocard government in the early winter. Not only did they refrain from the threat of voting to censure Rocard in the months before the elections, they apparently guaranteed not to speak out against the government during the campaigns. (*Le Figaro*, 13 January; *Le Point*, 9 January.)

In the second and decisive round of voting (on 19 March), in which 121 towns with a population of over 30,000 were at stake, Communists who ran alone polled only 2.2 percent of the vote, while PS-PCF unity lists gained only a little more than 16 percent (Paris Domestic Service, 19 March). (It was incorrect, as *Pravda* reported on 5 May, in an obvious effort to help PCF leaders put the best face on their fiasco, that the Communists had polled 15 percent of the total vote—an increase over the 13.5 percent they had polled in the legislative elections.) Suffering what one centrist newspaper called a "flattening," the PCF plummeted in the number of towns it controlled for the third time in successive elections (1977, 1983, 1989), this time losing control of 13 big towns, including a net loss of control of 7 governments (from 53 to 46) in cities with a population over 30,000—i.e., they lost 8 and gained only one. Postelection analysis showed that the party's defeat was across the board: it had lost ground in places of every size, from hamlets to major cities, and notably had suffered a net loss of 15 governments in cities of 20,000 (from 83 in 1983 to 68 in 1989). The most stinging losses came in large, traditional PCF fortresses such as Amiens—one of France's major northern industrial cities—La Ciotat, and St-Dizier. In other strongholds, renovators and reconstructors rolled up impressive, independent victories—like those of Robert Jarry in Le Mans and Gaston Viens in Orly. (*Le Quotidien de Paris*, 21 March; *Pravda*, 21 March; APF, 19 March; *Le Point*, 27 March.) Moreover, Lucien Vassal, a renovator running on an independent socialist ticket headed by Robert Vigouroux, unseated Guy Hermier in the eighth district of Marseille. Hermier, a Politburo member, deputy from the Bouches-du-Rhône, and political director of the PCF's theoretical organ, *Révolution*, had long shown sympathy with dissident views, but paid the price of having sat on the fence long enough to alienate both PCF bosses and dissidents. The depressing outcome for the party was that its strength was more than ever before in its history isolated in "bunker cities," almost two-thirds of them in the Paris region. Communist losses in recent years have made it difficult to argue that there is still a "Red Belt" around Paris, but after the 1989 municipal elections the PCF appeared more than ever to have become a regional party. (*NYT*, 14 March; *Le Point*, 27 March and 3 April.)

Four features of the elections might have been especially alarming to PCF leaders. The first of these was the stunning comeback of the PS, which regained almost all the cities it had lost to the right in 1983. Second, and more portentous, the exit polls conducted by one of France's leading survey firms (IFOP-RTL) showed that only 6 percent of those voting in the municipal elections intended to vote Communist in the forthcoming Euroelections (*Le Figaro*, 23 March; *NYT*, 20 March). Third, the PCF's ace in the hole—record-high abstentions of noncommunist voters—failed this time to save the party from an embarrassing, clear-cut setback (AFP, 19 March). Moreover, disaffected leftists who wanted to vote against the PS did not—as the PCF believes they invariably will—decide to vote Communist. Instead, they found a home among the swelling legions of French Greens, who scored a surprising victory. (*WP*, 21 March; *Le Quotidien de Paris*, 11 July.) Not surprisingly, however, PCF leaders showed no concern at all about these features of their recent disaster; they adopted instead the optimistic line—proclaimed in *l'Humanité*'s banner headlines—that the party still has "Forces Vives" (*l'Humanité*, 21 March).

Marching to the anti-American/anti-NATO slogan "Europe yes, but from the Atlantic to the Urals," PCF leaders almost immediately began preparations for the elections to the European Parliament, scheduled for 18 June, and blanketed the country with five million leaflets proclaiming "The rising power of the PCF" (*Le Point*, 28 November 1988; *Le Figaro*, 23 January). The election campaign included use of the PCF's time-honored anti-European theme of "national independence," and it showcased the party's visceral hostility to the EC's plan for full economic integration by the end of 1992, which communist candidates portrayed as a socialist sellout of France's national sovereignty. EC-92, in the leadership's political lexicon, was no more than a direct attack by big capital on jobs and the social net, and PCF hard-liners portrayed Mitterrand and Rocard as the agents of this dirty trick.

Running against European integration, an exceptionally popular process throughout the EC, netted the PCF barely 7.8 percent of the vote and a loss of three seats in the Strasbourg parliament (a fall from ten to seven). Aside from the loss of seats in a proportional voting contest, probably the most embarrassing aspect of this defeat was the fact that with only seven seats the PCF was required to ask its hated Eurocommunist rival, the larger Italian Communist Party, to take it in as a part of the PCI parliamentary group. (Paris Domestic Service, 18 and 19 June; *Pravda*, 23 June; *Le Figaro*, 23 June.)

PCF leaders blamed their defeat on working-class abstentions, on the drift of the socialist electorate to the right, and on events in China, which had given Communists everywhere a black eye (see Paul Laurent's report of 22 June to the Central Committee on the reasons for the party's defeat, *Le Figaro*, 23 June; *l'Humanité*, 23 June). *Pravda* chimed in with sympathetic variations on the same theme, arguing that the PCF candidates had lost "because of a whole series of internal and external circumstances beyond their control" (*Pravda*, 23 June).

In the aftermath of the municipal elections, PCF hard-liners had opened fire on the Socialists with both barrels; the defeats in the Euroelections only convinced Politburo stalwarts that they had nothing to lose by stepping up such attacks. For the remainder of the year, they waved, but did not use, the threat of censure to bring down the Rocard government. They often made this threat in connection with the passage in the National Assembly of directives relating to the EC-92 program, reserving their harshest criticisms for the lack of a social charter to accompany the program and the planned harmonization of the member states' tax systems, which in the PCF's view threatened to impose even tighter austerity on France. (*Le Point*, 24 April.) Moreover, PCF spokesmen regularly challenged the Socialists to surrender the slavish deference to NATO by shifting 40 billion francs from the military budget to the schools and by abandoning conscription. Marchais's favorite theme in these months was that Rocard was carrying out the policies of the right, in league with the right, using a "big-stick policy" in industrial disputes. At the Central Committee meeting of 14 October, which touched off the disputes with Fiterman, Marchais characterized the PS government's policy as "More money, power, and privilege for Capital's forces; more austerity for the majority of the people." (*Le Monde*, 14 October; Gisèle Moreau, "Le rassemblement porteur de possibilités nouvelles," *Cahiers du Communisme*, February; *Le Point*, 24 April; Guy Poussy, "La lutte pour les salaires et la conscience politique," *Cahiers du Communisme*, April.)

The policy of relentless attacks on the Socialists was in part calculated to take advantage of indications in public-opinion polls that Frenchmen were tiring of Mitterrand, Rocard, and the socialist government. Amid polls showing, for example, that job performance ratings of both the president and prime minister were falling for the first time in many months, party bosses used the celebrations on Bastille Day (14 July) of the bicentennial of the French

Revolution to both intimidate and embarrass Mitterrand. As a counterpoint to Mitterrand's decision to make the festivities a backdrop for the annual summit of the world's seven leading industrialized nations (G-7), PCF officials staged a rock-music concert, which attracted 100,000 to the Place de la Bastille, to protest the "summit of the rich." Moreover, the council of trade unions affiliated with the PCF, the General Confederation of Labor (CGT), threatened strikes and disruptions during the celebrations if Mitterrand continued to refuse to grant an amnesty to ten CGT organizers who had been dismissed by Renault after they had held several company executives hostage during a recent labor dispute. (*NYT*, 13 July; *Le Quotidien de Paris*, 22–23 July.)

Impressions from Bastille Day notwithstanding, the communist-controlled CGT was less active in 1989, and it was especially and uncharacteristically quiet in the autumn and early winter. Despite claims at the end of 1988 that it would create 700 new company cells in the coming year (*Le Point*, 12 December 1988), evidence emerged in the course of 1989—some of it directly from official CGT publications—that the union's membership had undergone a stark decline. The centrist and conservative press, which interpreted the decline as a by-product of the discrediting of ideology among Frenchmen and the sour aftertaste of the CGT's recent strike failures, led the exposure of the CGT's problem, citing the testimony of trade-union dropouts from the previous fall's strikes, a think-tank study of French organizational behavior, and analyses by the Ministry of Labor based on elections to so-called enterprise committees in French industry. (*Le Figaro*, 11 January; *l'Expansion*, 20 January–2 February; *Figaro-Magazine*, 26 November 1988.)

On the eve of its 43rd Congress (on 21 May, at Montreuil), the CGT leadership confirmed the worst suppositions of the hostile conservative media. Official figures published in the union's weekly, *Le Peuple* (2 March 1989), admitted that in the decade between 1977 and 1987 the CGT had lost a staggering 55.61 percent of its members, a total decline of almost 1.3 million workers. Moreover, the decline of the number of active members (the most important segment) was both drastic and steady: from 2.0 million members in 1977 to 1.1 million in 1984, to .9 million in 1985, to .8 million in 1986, to .7 million in 1987. There were similar but less important declines in the numbers of retired members. (*Le Monde*, 8 March.)

The CGT congress was a mixed success for the hard-liners, who paid a price for their ineffective strikes of the previous fall. CGT general secretary Henri Krasucki, widely rumored to have at least one foot on a banana peel because of his soft attitude toward Socialists within the union's leadership, was re-elected to a third term—a rejection of Krasucki's hard-line deputy, Louis Viannet, who was widely seen as the architect of the intense fall strikes and leader of the *pur et dur* faction of the CGT known as the *Khamir Rouge* (the CGT counterparts of the local communist "Red Guards"). Although Krasucki retained his post, CGT hard-liners (probably encouraged by the PCF Politburo) demanded and won the elimination of half the Socialists from the CGT's executive commission. Moreover, knowledgeable observers predicted that Viannet's rising star within the CGT leadership and within the Marchais-dominated Politburo would eventually force Krasucki to give way. (*Le Quotidien de Paris*, 6 March; *Libération*, 10 February; *Le Point*, 13 February and 29 May.) In an oblique reference to probable socialist rank-and-file reaction to the removal of socialist leaders, one CGT militant from a public-sector company complained publicly that "The party is in the process of purposely destroying the CGT" (*Le Quotidien de Paris*, 6 March). At year's end, however, it was still unclear whether the dumping of socialist leaders from the executive commission would have the expected effect of driving large numbers of Socialists from the union.

Foreign Affairs and Security Issues. The PCF's foreign policy was a study in continuity between 1988 and 1989, featuring the same familiar themes. It focused largely on implacable hostility to the European Community's program of market integration by 1992 and distant acceptance of Soviet president Gorbachev's restructuring of Soviet political and economic life. In 1989, however, the PCF also had to face the hard reality of the collapse of communist parties in Central and Eastern Europe and ultimately the unthinkable disintegration, with apparent Soviet complicity, of the East German party (SED) and the arrest of its leadership, including Erich Honecker, for corruption. Meanwhile, the PCF's security policies were again dominated by support for Soviet arms-control and disarmament themes, including the total denuclearization of Europe, the disbanding of the alliances, rapid progress toward reductions of conventional weapons, elimination of the production of chemical weapons and of their stockpiles, and a negotiated settlement in

Afghanistan. In addition, party bosses stepped up pressure on the PS government to return to a policy of national independence, an end to conscription, and the transfer of 40 billion francs from the defense budget to education. Pressure for the last of these steps seemed to bear fruit, and the Communists increased their propaganda when the approaching autumn legislative debate on the socialist government's Military Program Law prompted an open squabble between Prime Minister Rocard and Defense Minister Chevènement over Rocard's plan to shift 11 percent of budgeted defense funds to the PS educational policy (Reuter, 8 October).

Fretting under continued claims in the noncommunist media (*Le Monde*, 25–26 and 28 December 1988) that the PCF openly espoused *perestroika* but privately condemned it, Marchais and Politburo colleagues like *l'Humanité* chief Roland Leroy and Polex foreign affairs boss Maxime Gremetz sought every opportunity during 1989 to publicly declare the party's enthusiasm for Gorbachev's restructuring efforts. They treated readers of *l'Humanité* and *Cahiers du Communisme* to lavish praise of *perestroika* as "a revolution within a revolution," as the "second youth of Socialism," and as the great hope of post-Stalinist communist societies and the global working class. (*l'Humanité*, 6 July; *Pravda*, 18 January, 1 March, 6 July; TASS International Service, 22 September; *FBIS-SOV*, 25 September; François Cohen, "La peréstroika à quatre ans," *Cahiers du Communisme*, January and May.) The leadership's refrain, repeated at every opportunity, was that *perestroika* was terrific for the CPSU (and other parties that needed to break with Stalinism and Brezhnevism), but the French party had rejected those models in 1975 and had no need to adopt another, however useful it might be in the USSR or Eastern Europe (*Le Figaro*, 3 August). Marchais made such arguments the centerpiece of his two, fairly chilly, encounters with Gorbachev in 1989—once during the Soviet leader's visit to Paris and Strasbourg in July, but especially during the French party leader's visit to Moscow in September (*Pravda*, 18 January, 23 September, 14 October; TASS International Service, 22 September; Moscow Domestic Service, 22 September; *FBIS-SOV*, 25 September). Predictably, hard-liner efforts to make a virtue of the necessity of admiring *perestroika* from a distance was grist for reconstructors' mills. Said leading dissident Félix Damette, "The originality of the PCF lies in its repeated declarations of support for the Soviet *perestroika*, whereas its basic activity is diametrically

opposed. Innovative speeches are attempts to conceal a deeply conservative position." (*Le Figaro*, 3–4 August, quoting *l'Humanité*.) At the more specific level of new thinking, prominent "Gorbachevians" challenged Marchais after his return from Moscow to admit that his 1980 support for the Soviet invasion of Afghanistan had been "an error" (*Le Point*, 13 November). Coming as it did on the heels of Marchais's visit and in the context of the building ferment in Eastern Europe, Fiterman's spectacular appeal for new directions and new thinking in the PCF was also widely interpreted as a challenge to Marchais and the Politburo faithful to adopt more "Gorbachevian" attitudes toward self-criticism and self-reform (*Le Point*, 20 November; *Le Monde*, 25–26 and 28 December).

Relations between the PCF and other major European communist parties remained stranded between fragile and deteriorating in 1989. Although hissing between the PCF and PCI did not reach the levels of two years ago, occasional sniping in the press and maintenance of a discreet physical distance showed that there was no improvement, however slight, to report. When PCI chief Occhetto visited France in April, as a guest of the PS, he pointedly did not visit French Communists, and when asked about this, he replied that differences between the two parties "are a secret to no one." (*Le Monde*, 13 April.)

The PCF agreed most with Greek Communists and differed most with Spanish Communists in its attitudes toward the European Community's 1992 program. Traditionally hostile to the EC, and more vehement than any other European communist party regarding the disadvantages of EC-92, French Communists aired public disagreements with Spanish counterparts during the April visit to France by PCE's international-policy secretary Gomez (*Mundo Obrero*, 26 April–2 May). The positive tone of the Spanish attitude stood in marked contrast to the high level of hostility to EC-92 evinced by the Greek communist leader Florakis during his visit, also in April. Marchais and the Greeks cudgeled the EC program as a potential aggravation to the austerity policies that both Greek and French workers had already suffered enough and as a surrender of national identity and sovereignty in the interest of promoting "a European pillar of the Atlantic Alliance." (*l'Humanité*, 18 April.) These strains on their relations notwithstanding, both Greek and Spanish Communists reportedly agreed with PCF leaders to increase efforts in 1989 toward the demilitarization and denuclearization of Europe. In such promotions, French Communists joined twice with elements of the peace movement and German Communists in protests against nuclear weapons—once in a demonstration of late March at Strasbourg, and again in late April in an antinuclear protest near the Albion Plateau, the launching area for France's *force de frappe*. (*Le Point*, 20 March; *l'Humanité*, 18 April; *WMR*, February.)

The most nettlesome foreign-policy issue for the PCF in 1989 was the deterioration and collapse of communist rule in Central and Eastern Europe. Caught flat-footed by the precipitous fall of such rocks of international communism as Erich Honecker, French communist leaders at first defended the beleaguered regimes against the efforts of a "vast campaign of incitement" waged from outside, but later somewhat accepted their fall as a long overdue and salutary "reform" of unreconstructed Stalinist regimes. (Quoted in Kevin Devlin, "Western Communist Reaction to East German Exodus," *RAD Background Report/178*, 20 September.) The key to this modest transformation was apparently the summer junkets, visits, and vacations that many PCF leaders spent in Eastern Europe. French comrades reportedly returned home to formulate a more sober analysis of the future of Eastern Europe. (*Le Point*, 13 November.) However, except for taking a noticeably harder line with Romania—described by PCF officials as "a new Albania"—party spokesmen continued to softpedal the consequences for communism of the events that were splashing across television screens throughout Europe. For example, *l'Humanité* explained the nosedive of close PCF friend Zhivkov and his regime and the anticommunism sweeping Bulgaria as "Socialism . . . changing in order to be more Socialist. It can only demonstrate its superiority by making far-reaching reforms characterized by freedom and democracy." At any rate, "capitalism cannot provide the answers." (AFP, 21 November 1989; *Le Monde*, 14 November; *FBIS-WEU*, 22 November; *Le Point*, 13 February 1989, p. 28; *L'Humanité*, 7 August 1989, p. 10.) Later, far from facing up to the ever more apparent bankruptcy of communism in reforming East European states, PCF spokesmen continued to portray events as "changes [that are] a necessary precondition of the development of Socialism" (*Pravda*, 14 November). The almost surreal quality of this line reached its most extreme degree in November, when Jean-Claude Gayssot announced publicly that events in Eastern Europe were unfolding pretty much as the PCF had expected and predicted. This refrain prompted dissident Claude

Poperen to announce, "The PCF leadership has no answer, faced with the reforms in Eastern Europe." (*Le Monde*, 12–13 November.)

Although preoccupied with EC-92 and Eastern Europe, the PCF included among its other foreign-policy initiatives continued support and propaganda for the nomination of Nelson Mandela for the Nobel Peace Prize—the mainstay of the party's image-burnishing campaign in Africa—and subsequent condemnation of the Nobel Committee for awarding the honor instead to the Dalai Lama. Marchais and colleagues also supported Cuban and Nicaraguan comrades, with Marchais's visit to Havana providing an opportunity to bludgeon U.S. imperialism and militarism in the Western Hemisphere and to meet with Sandinista director Ortega. However, events in Tiananmen Square drew bitter and prolonged reproaches from PCF leaders. (*l'Humanité*, 6 January, 25 April, 5 and 7 June, 28 September; Jean Hermet, "Cuba–Trente ans de Révolution," *Cahiers du Communisme*, February; Beijing Renmin Ribao, 10 October; *FBIS-CHI*, 11 October; Dakar, Pana, 15 January.)

In still other actions, French Communists found time to support the need of the Soviet military to acquire strategic technology when Philippe Herzog criticized the CoCom's prohibition of the sale of strategic technologies to the Soviet Union and Eastern Europe as an unseemly vestige of Cold War thinking. (Sofia, Otechestven Front, 9 August; *FBIS-EEU*, 15 August.) Moreover, PCF leaders joined North Korean counterparts in renewed calls on Western creditors to cut drastically the debts of the Third World (Pyongyang, KCNA, 18 November; *FBIS-EAS*, 21 November).

International Activities. The PCF's international activity quickened substantially in 1989, largely due to the pace of global changes affecting the future of communist regimes, but also probably because fewer elections and other domestic events took up the party leaders' time. French communist delegations made visits to Mozambique (led by André Lajoinie) for Maputo's Fifth Party Congress, to Havana (led by Georges Marchais) for the 30th anniversary of the Cuban Revolution, to Bucharest for the Romanian Communist Party's Fourteenth Congress, and to East Berlin for the 40th anniversary of the SED (Havana Television Service, 7 January; *FBIS-LAT*, 9 January; *Le Point*, 20 February; Maputo Domestic Service, 29 July; Bucharest, Agerpres, 21 November; ADN, 6 October; *FBIS-EEU*, 6 October). Politburo veteran Gaston

Plissonnier led comrades on a visit to Yemen, during which discussion apparently focused on economic development and exploitation of mineral resources (Aden Domestic Service, 28 September; *FBIS-NES*, 20 October). In addition to Marchais's September visit and meetings with Gorbachev, PCF groups visited the USSR several times during 1989, notably in November to familiarize themselves with the workings of *perestroika*, again in November to visit Soviet newspapers, and in October to study Soviet agriculture, and yet another delegation of legislators visited the Supreme Soviet in July (TASS, 19 November; *Pravda*, 24 October, 10 November; *Izvestiia*, 22 July). Marchais led a large PCF delegation to Bulgaria during early August. Although the long visit was a wide-ranging celebration of the PCF-Bulgarian friendship, talks apparently focused on changes and ferment in Eastern Europe, the progress of *perestroika* in the USSR, and—in public at least—Marchais's unabashed admiration for Todor Zhivkov (Sofia Domestic Service, 26 July, 2, 4, and 16 August; *FBIS-EEU*, 3 August; Sofia BTA, 3 August; *FBIS-EEU*, 4 August; *l'Humanité*, 7 August).

A delegation of more than 300 Soviet "partisans of perestroika" visited France in late September, but not under the sponsorship of the PCF. Meanwhile, contacts with East German party officials picked up in 1989, partly because of the incipient changes in the GDR. SED theoretician Otto Reinhold exchanged views with Gremetz in April, while post-Honecker general secretary Günter Schabowski gave a lengthy interview in November to *l'Humanité* on recent reforms (APF, 27 September, 18 November; *Neues Deutschland*, 29–30 April). Marchais also received delegations from parties of less interest to the PCF; these were the Lebanese, North Korean, and North Vietnamese communist parties. In addition, he received a low-level delegation of party officials from Czechoslovakia and a delegation from the Chilean Socialist Party. (*l'Humanité*, 18 February, 22 April; Hanoi, VNA, 26 April; Pyongyang, KCNA, 28 July; *Pravda*, 23 April; *Rudé právo*, 9 September; *FBIS-EEU*, 15 September.) But no visit during the year said more about the PCF leadership's standing with Moscow than did Gorbachev's July stops in Paris and Strasbourg. Although Gorbachev's meeting with Marchais was played up in the PCF press as a major event of the visit, it actually was little more than a photo opportunity. The Soviet president kept Marchais waiting for over half an hour, the meeting took place on neutral territory—the home of the

Turkish ambassador—and it lasted hardly more than 30 minutes. (*l'Humanité*, 6 July; *Le Figaro*, 3 August; Beijing, Xinhua, 6 July.)

Edward A. Allen
Washington, D.C.

Germany
Federal Republic of Germany

Population. 60,977,195, excl. West Berlin (July 1989)

Party. German Communist Party (Deutsche Kommunistische Partei; DKP)

Founded. 1968

Membership. Ca. 40,000 (claimed, 1989); Federal Office for the Protection of the Constitution (BfV) estimates its membership in late 1989 to be only 25–30,000.

Chairman. Herbert Mies (since 1973, but announced retirement in March 1990)

Presidium. 20 members; because of party's turmoil, the entire leadership is to be elected March 1990.

Secretariat. 9 members, to be elected March 1990

Executive. 98 members

Status. Legal

Last Congress. Ninth, 6–9 January 1989, in Frankfurt am Main

Last Election. 1987, ca. .5 percent for "Peace List," in which DKP participated; no representation in federal parliament or parliament of any Land (state)

Auxiliary Organizations. Socialist German Workers' Youth (Sozialistische Deutsche Arbeiter Jugend; SDAJ), ca. 6,000 members in 1989, Birgit Radow, chair; Marxist Student Union–Spartakus (Marxistischer Studentenbund–Spartakus; MSB–Spartakus); Young Pioneers (Junge Pioniere; JP).

Publications. *Unsere Zeit* (Our time), Düsseldorf, DKP organ (editor: Conrad Schuhler), until 1989

daily circulation 23,000, weekend edition ca. 44,000. Because of the party's financial crisis, weekly since late 1989. Many issues were distributed to socialist states through East Berlin. *Elan–Das Jugendmagazin*, SDAJ monthly organ, circulation ca. 19,000; *Rote Blätter* (Red pages), MSB–Spartakus monthly organ, circulation ca. 11,500; *Pionier* (Pioneer), JP monthly organ, circulation 5,000

History. The DKP, which has traditionally been unswervingly loyal to Moscow and East Berlin, grew out of the Communist Party of Germany (Kommunistische Partei Deutschlands; KPD). The KPD was officially founded on 31 December 1918 by left-wing Spartakists, who had broken away from the Social Democratic Party of Germany (SPD) following the Bolshevik revolution in Russia a year earlier.

After the war, the KPD was the first party to be legalized. It became legal on 11 June 1945. It toned down its revolutionary rhetoric and advocated the creation of an "anti-fascist democratic order" and a popular front. It sought to merge with the SPD as a unified German workers' party, something which actually happened in the Soviet zone of occupation on 22 April 1946, when the Socialist Unity Party of Germany (Sozialistische Einheitspartei Deutschlands; SED) was formed. Because of bitter opposition to such merger by leading Social Democrats in the Western zones, especially Kurt Schumacher, no unification took place in the West. The KPD had 2 representatives (out of a total of 65) on the Parliamentary Council, which existed from September 1948 to May 1949 to produce a Basic Law (constitution) for the Federal Republic of Germany (FRG). In the end, the KPD decided to oppose the Basic Law, which came into effect in 1949.

In the first federal elections in 1949, the KPD won 5.7 percent of the votes and gained fifteen members in the Bundestag (lower house of the parliament). In the next election, in 1953, its share of the votes plummeted to 2.2 percent, far short of the minimum 5 percent required for seats in Bundestag. Communists never again won seats, and the party's percentage of the votes declined steadily. The weakening popular support for the KPD merely increased its dependence upon a foreign patron, notably the SED in the German Democratic Republic (GDR). Such dependence contributed to the Constitutional Court's outlawing of the KPD in August 1956.

By the time the party was renamed the DKP and,

as a concession by Chancellor Willy Brandt to the Kremlin, again legalized in 1968 (with new statutes and statements of purpose carefully crafted to be compatible with the Basic Law), two important developments had occurred: first, the party's membership had shrunk to about 7,000; second, the tumultuous 1960s had produced in the FRG scores of radical and independent communist or radical leftist groups which compete with the traditional orthodox party. The DKP does not regard itself as having supplanted the KPD, which in theory continues to exist underground. Indeed, the DKP continues to demand that the decision to ban the KPD be rescinded, something which the West German government assures will not be done. Most of the DKP's present leaders and about half its members once belonged to the KPD.

Crisis Within the Party. The year 1989 brought a crisis upon the entire DKP from which it may never recover. The collapse of communist power and ideology in the German Democratic Republic and the Soviet Union's encouragement of reform in Eastern Europe present a potentially fatal threat to a party like the DKP, which was always studiously servile to the Socialist Unity party of Germany and the Soviet rulers. The DKP's leadership was in no way capable of responding to these changes, which have brought the party to the brink of fragmentation and bankruptcy.

Intraparty tensions had already reached the point of explosion several years before the Berlin Wall came tumbling down on 9 November 1989. Former leader Herbert Mies admitted in 1988 that "profound changes had taken place," including changes "in the internal development of the party." Therefore, the party leadership drew up for approval by the party's ninth congress a report called "Bundesrepublik 2000" (Federal Republic 2000), which contained suggestions for a "peace-oriented and democratic reform alternative for the 1990s." The chairman declared that socialism remained the party's goal, but that urgent questions could not wait until a fundamental restructuring of society had occurred. His party should be able to draw conclusions useful to itself from the process of *perestroika* in the Soviet Union, for which the report contained restrained praise, and free itself from all that is obsolete. In advance of its approval by the ninth congress, this report, which addressed the question of how the party should proceed in the future, was widely discussed within the DKP. Although Mies criticized the attempts made by some party members to turn the DKP into a pluralistic party, he noted that the report was to be presented "for discussion to all forces of the working-class movement, all leftist forces, the peace movement, and social and solidarity movements." (*ND*,1 July 1988; *FBIS*, 7 September 1988.) However, the ninth congress was so divided that adoption of the report had to be postponed.

In the past, the DKP's total loyalty to both East Berlin and Moscow created few problems for the party, except that it reduced the DKP's electoral strength in the FRG to practically zero. Just as the SED, it had consistently pointed to the Soviet Union as the exalted model of "real socialism" and as the country to be emulated. The Communist Party of the Soviet Union (CPSU) was seen as an almost unerring party, and the DKP's motto was "To learn from the Soviet Union means to learn to be victorious." Both the DKP and SED had almost always lined up behind the Soviet Union's foreign- and defense-policy objectives and lent their full weight to their accomplishment. However, the emergence in the Soviet Union of a party leader from a new generation, Mikhail Gorbachev, who attacks corruption and self-serving privilege within the party and advocates intraparty democracy, openness (*glasnost'*), and general restructuring (*perestroika*), has for several years created a serious dilemma for the DKP.

On the one hand, Gorbachev's calls for more democracy were avidly embraced by the DKP's rank and file, who have long been restive because of the "lack of possibilities for intraparty influence and participation," to use the words of party author Erasmus Schöfer. The possibility of embarking upon a new path has its risks, Schöfer admits, but "Communists in the FRG have nothing to lose but their lack of success!" (*Spiegel*, 7 September 1987). Thomas Riecke, a top functionary of the MSB-Spartakus, declared in regard to *glasnost'* that "we must know everything and be able to decide about everything" (*Die Zeit*, 16 October 1987). There were calls for free election of cadres, who are now appointed by the party leadership.

Mies had to admit in an interview that appeared in *Unsere Zeit* (*UZ*) in May 1987 that "there is hardly another topic on which so many party functions, and with such a large number of participants, have been held over the past several years . . . The sympathy for the changes in the Soviet Union is unanimous." He recognized that "the attractive power of existing socialism has been growing" under Gorbachev, who, as polls continue to indicate,

enjoys enormous popularity in the FRG. An overwhelming percentage of West German respondents consider him to be a "man who can be trusted." Only 11 percent (down from 71 percent in 1980!) believed in 1988 that the Soviet Union threatens world peace, while the United States does not. Gorbachev's welcome disarmament proposals present the DKP with "fresh opportunities in, among other things, our united action and alliance policy." It "made it easier for Communists to act as respected and equal partners in the peace movement and other democratic movements. Not least important among the fresh opportunities is the possibility of using the growing sympathy for Soviet policy to spread the influence of the DKP as the party of socialism." (*UZ*, 20 May 1987.)

Gorbachev's dramatic announcement at the U.N. on 7 December 1988 that the Soviet Union would unilaterally reduce its manpower and weapons in the USSR and Eastern Europe, and the Soviets' declaration in Paris on 7 January 1989 that the USSR would begin unilaterally to destroy its stocks of chemical weapons, are the kind of dramatic initiatives on which the DKP would like to capitalize. Throughout 1988 and at the ninth party congress, DKP leaders repeatedly praised the Soviet Union's arms-reduction proposals and called for nuclear- and chemical-free zones, a "zone of trust and security in Central Europe," conventional-force reductions from the Atlantic to the Urals, a Western response to unilateral Soviet withdrawal of some short-range missiles from the GDR and Czechoslovakia, and a rejection of NATO plans to modernize its nuclear forces in Western Europe.

On the other hand, the SED remained cool toward the Gorbachev reforms. In August 1987, Max Schmidt, director of the International Institute for Economics and Politics in East Berlin, told a DKP delegation that "much has yet to reach fruition" and "much will perhaps be undone." The SED prevented *Unsere Zeit* from publishing a speech given in January 1987 in which Gorbachev asserted that "we need democracy as air to breathe." It threatened not to distribute any copies via East Berlin to other socialist countries. (*Spiegel*, 7 September 1987.) The SED's message was: "Go slowly, and wait and see!" It did not want to be exposed to the bacillus of *glasnost'* from both West and East.

The DKP could not ignore these warnings from East Berlin. Confronted with what the relatively liberal Hamburg DKP organization calls "a crisis in the party," the DKP leadership tried to dampen the enthusiasm caused by the "strong impulses" coming from Moscow. In *Unsere Zeit*, a cautious Mies warned that in a capitalist country like the FRG "there can be no imitation of the Soviet approach," and that the party must be careful "not to throw the baby out with the bathwater." One should not "reduce the splendid history of the Soviet Union...to economic and moral problems." DKP members should inform themselves through reports by "fraternal parties," not by "reading tea leaves or using the slanders cooked up by the bourgeois mass media." While there is much need for "invigoration of intraparty life, encouragement of intraparty discussions, and broader involvement of the party membership in the decisionmaking process," "it is not a matter of weakening the principles of democratic centralism in the CPSU...Intraparty democracy for us is not a game, not an end in itself. It is designed to mobilize the party's collective knowledge and strength, and to unite it for the purposeful and centralized actions in the fight against the highly-organized class enemy facing us. We need to have a further development of intraparty democracy, while keeping our communist principles intact." (*UZ*, 20 May 1987.)

Thus the party resorted to censorship to try to silence the enthusiasm for the reform impulses coming from Moscow. When the party poet and a member of the party executive, Peter Schütt, wrote a poem in 1987 with the lines: "After decades of radio silence, the red star is again sending signals," and "there are comrades who have held their hands in front of their faces for so long that they have unlearned how to understand the new radio code," he was encouraged by the chief party ideologue, Willi Gerns, not to publish the poem. To Schütt's surprise, the poem was published by the moderately conservative *Frankfurter Allgemeine Zeitung*. The DKP leadership was reportedly embarrassed by this and especially by the fact that the editors of the Moscow publication *New Time* thanked Schütt for supporting *perestroika*. (*Spiegel*, 7 September 1987.) Schütt remained an ardent reformer, saying in March 1989: "We must move away from the old cadre party and become a modern membership party, by shifting the weight of communist activity and decisionmaking back to the rank and file" (*FBIS*, 15 May).

In 1988, the DKP faced its hitherto most serious crisis in two decades of existence. For the first time in fifteen years, its membership dropped to 38,000, and its members' average age rose. Half of those who left the party cited political and ideological reasons for leaving. Many of those who remained were disillusioned or unmotivated, as the party leaders were increasingly reproached for having "a tendency toward dogmatism," and for encouraging "conformist behavior and closed, inflexible, and authority-minded thinking." (*FBIS*, 15 September 1988.)

Pronouncements, such as that made by Mies in November 1987, went unheeded by many members: "It would be irresponsible, precisely in times of radical change, to eliminate something of the Marxist, revolutionary character of our organizational principles. Precisely in such times,...not less, but more Marxism, not less, but more Leninism is required." (*Infodienst* [*ID*], 30 August 1988.) The party leadership was always proud of having resisted "Eurocommunism," on the grounds that communist parties which had tolerated some pluralism within their ranks had been weakened or split. Ellen Weber tried in 1988 to argue that all the talk of *glasnost'* and *perestroika* was merely "the effort of the bourgeois media and politicians to drive wedges and organize dissension." But Hamburg party chief Wolfgang Gehrcke stated forthrightly that "there are fissures which one must work on. Everyone is looking toward Moscow." (*Stern*, July 1988.)

By early 1988, however, Mies had to admit that for the first time in the party's history there were, in fact, differences of opinion within the party which were extremely difficult to reconcile. In his speech before the meeting of the Presidium in Düsseldorf on 3 and 4 September, he acknowledged "two directions or lines within the party." Alongside a majority wing of *Bewahrer* (maintainers) was a minority of *Erneuer* (renewers) that were calling certain party principles into question: "A break with essential principles of democratic centralism is appearing in outlines." (*FBIS*, 15 September 1988.)

The DKP tried to cope with this challenge in two ways: first, it departed from its customary practice by indeed permitting open discussion within the party and permitted the party news organs to report those disagreements. Never before had there been so much frankness in the party's publications and discussions at party gatherings. At the Presidium meeting of September 1988, two contradictory discussion papers were allowed for the first time; 18 out of 94 members could not agree with the top party leadership, and therefore no agreement could be reached on a common text.

At the same time, the DKP tried to place limits on discussions, declaring that they may show a diversity of opinion, but "not lead to political confrontation or to splintering of forces." They always had to serve "the conscious unity and strengthening of the fighting power of the party." (*Die Welt*, 23 June 1988.) That is, criticism had to remain subordinate to the principles and goals of the party. In Mies's words, it was important to "withstand a trend which would not lead to a renewed, but to a ruined DKP."

The second way of trying to erect a dam against the flood of demands for more "democratization" and a more public party was to discipline those Renewers who had crossed the vague line which the top leaders had tried to draw between permissible and impermissible criticism. In March 1988 the DKP issued a warning to Andreas Müller-Goldenstedt, a Hamburg district leader, for demanding that the DKP primarily operate "for our own country," and that the comrades in the GDR be told once and for all that "we don't want this and that here" [in the FRG]. Disciplinary action was also taken against Helmut Krebs, former member of the Karlsruhe leadership, for writing a discussion paper entitled "How Should the DKP Proceed?" in which he faulted the DKP for underestimating the economic strength of the FRG. The deficiencies of socialism could no longer be denied, he wrote, and the West German working class would tolerate a socialist order only if it did not bring a reduction in their living standard or a diminution in their freedom and human rights. Therefore the party should renounce all unconstitutional means of struggle. (*ID*, 27 May 1988.)

The DKP leadership could have no illusions that the ninth party congress, which took place in Frankfurt am Main from 6 to 9 January, would be like no other before it. It was attended by approximately 700 DKP delegates, and by numerous guests from affiliated and communist-influenced organizations, fraternal communist and workers' parties, "anti-imperialist liberation movements," and socialist embassies. According to the DKP's own information, almost all of the delegates were trade-union members, and close to half were women. The most important statistic, however, was the one-third consisting of "reformer" delegates who came to make things difficult for the conservatives, whom they called "concrete heads." The Renewers mounted an unprecedented challenge against the leaders and demanded more internal democracy, freedom of debate and toleration of dissent. They also explicitly invoked the reform spirit of Gorbachev, a point well supported by Alexander Yakovlev, who pleaded with the party "to let the human face of

socialism emerge again." The SED's delegate, Hermann Axen, did not even mention *perestroika* and sounded the call to traditional militancy. (*RAD Background Report 4*, 11 January.)

Mies admitted to the congress that "the party is beset by hitherto unparalleled inner contradictions" (ibid.), and that the had learned from some of his own mistakes (which he did not specify). He also acknowledged an 18 percent loss in party membership in the past three years. But he insisted that the only way to overcome this drift was to strengthen the unity of the party. Ever the good Leninist, he adamantly rejected the formation of factions within the party.

Under the slogan "For the Renewal of the Federal Republic," bitter and divisive debates took place in a charged atmosphere of personal attacks. Many observers left with mixed feelings and asked what had happened to comradely solidarity. One delegate described the "personal debate" as "no holds barred." In fact, the election question was so hot that, for the first time ever, it had to be postponed for a week. Also for the first time, 110 candidates ran for only 98 seats. When the leaders were finally selected, Herbert Mies had to settle for only 71.8 percent of the votes, and his deputy, Ellen Weber, failed to receive a third of the votes. Nevertheless, the top leadership was able to prevent all but a handful of Renewers from gaining seats in the Presidium and Secretariat. Two of them (youth leaders Birgit Radow and Werner Stuermann) were purged from these bodies in May because they had participated in the organization of "trend meetings" by DKP Renewers; the leadership wanted any talk of party renewal to take place inside, rather than outside, the existing party structures. Also, the conservative majority voted down all the Renewers' motions during the congress. But approval of the two most important documents, "Federal Republic 2000" and "On the DKP's Situation and Future Development," had to be postponed. The congress's concluding session, in an unprecedented move, was put off for six weeks. Mies admitted ruefully that the DKP had "possibly come within seconds of a split." (*RAD Background Report 14*, 27 January.)

The intraparty perils which the DKP faced at its party congress in January pale in comparison with those brought on by the political earthquake that struck the party's exalted models—the GDR and the SED—in the second half of 1989. In late summer a human hemorrhage westward commenced, as East German vacationers began crossing the newly opened border between Hungary and Austria. The next avenue of escape was through Czechoslovakia, from which "freedom trains" took thousands of East Germans through the GDR into the West. The stampede grew when Czechoslovakia opened its western borders. The GDR's media accused the FRG of provoking the crisis, and then-deputy Ellen Weber followed the SED line by publicly deploring West German "interference" in the GDR's internal affairs. (*RAD Background Report 178*, 20 September.) Weber's response was in true DKP character, despite the party's first departure ever from the SED line in June. In the aftermath of the violent crackdown against demonstrators in China on 4 June, the DKP distanced itself from the SED by declaring that "we condemn the death sentences and executions of people, for reasons of humanity, as well as political reasons." (*FBIS-WEU*, 27 June.)

Under enormous stress, the GDR celebrated its 40th anniversary in October. The SED's slogan for the event was "Ever Forward—Never Backward!" The prediction was accurate, but SED chiefs were badly mistaken about which direction was forward. On 18 October, Honecker was ousted from power. He had reportedly wanted to use force against demonstrators in Leipzig, but he was restrained by subordinates, including Egon Krenz, who took over the reins of power for six weeks (*Time*, 11 December). It was obvious to the clear-headed that communist rule without the backing of Soviet troops could not survive anywhere in Germany.

On 9 November, the Berlin Wall came down. It is ironic that a wall which had been constructed in 1961 to keep East Germans in was opened in 1989 for the same reason! The new leadership calculated that a people which was free to go would come back. Within minutes millions of East Germans began pouring over the border. In the first two days, one-sixth of the GDR's population went West for a visit, and almost all of them returned home. Germans, who for decades had suppressed displays of national feeling, experienced a deeply emotional outpouring. While millions sat in front of their televisions and wept, Berliners danced together on top of the Wall, embraced each other on the streets, and chiseled away at the ugly barrier. Suddenly German reunification was back on the agenda, and developments toward it raced faster than any government's ability to react. Demonstrators in the GDR unfurled banners bearing "Germany—One Fatherland!" while support began to grow in both Germanies for unity of some kind. This was a genuine revolution in the streets, quite unlike the revolution which the DKP had hoped for.

It was excruciating for the DKP to witness the rapid collapse of communist rule in the GDR because communism was being thoroughly discredited in Germany—the events "shock us!" (*FBIS-WEU*, 21 November 1989.) Honecker and many other leading SED figures were not only removed from office, but arrested and charged with corruption and enriching themselves while in office. Enraged East German citizens watched television images of the "proletarian" leaders' luxury compound in Wandlitz, estates with as many as 22 staff members, hunting lodges, deer parks, well-stocked wine cellars, and satellite dishes for better reception of Western broadcasts. All were signs of living standards totally removed from the meager everyday existence of normal GDR citizens long fed on exhortations to austerity. Even worse were revelations of shady financial dealings totaling millions of marks, involving illegal arms sales to Third World countries and foreign currency maneuvers, the profits of which ended up in Swiss bank accounts. Said one rank-and-file SED member, "We did not expect this of Communists and their creed of equality." (*Time*, 18 December.)

The entire SED Politburo and Central Committee resigned, and the party decided to abolish these institutions altogether. Honecker's replacement, Egon Krenz, was also forced to step down, to be replaced by a peripheral party member, Gregor Gysi. Gysi is a lawyer who had made a name by defending East German dissidents and the opposition New Forum and by heading the prosecution of former SED leaders accused of corruption. Upon accepting the leadership, he admitted that a complete break with Stalinism and a new form of socialism was needed, and that the SED was responsible for plunging the GDR into crisis. Feeling betrayed, 700,000 of the 2.3 million members left the party within two months. The party initiated a change in the GDR's constitution eliminating the Communists' monopoly on power.

Prime Minister Hans Modrow, former head of the Dresden party and one of the few leading Communists untainted by corruption scandals, announced that free elections would be held 6 May 1990. He estimated that the Communists would win no more than 20 percent of the votes, far behind the opposition groupings. Overnight the parliament (People's Chamber) began acting in an assertive and independent way. Modrow promised that his government would take its direction from parliament, which will be freely elected, a practice which many traditional Communists have decried as "bourgeois democracy." A non-Communist, Manfred Gerlach, became head of state. Even the name of the party was changed to the cumbersome "SED-Party of Democratic Socialism." The term, by emphasizing democratic socialism, was bound to make hard-line DKP members cringe. But the double name reflected an attempt to accommodate those party members who want to break with the past and those who do not; this is an effort which the DKP also must make.

The hated state security forces (Stasi) were defanged and ceased being an instrument of fear. Many agents were reassigned to other duties, and crowds of citizens entered Stasi installations to protect files for later prosecution. The Office of National Security, which directed Stasi, was abolished in December, and the Defense Council resigned, leaving the armed forces under the control of the government, not the SED. The armed militia units (Kampfgruppen) were also disbanded; they were hated by many citizens because they had sometimes been used to put down demonstrations or labor unrest.

Finally, on the occasion of Chancellor Helmut Kohl's historic visit to Dresden on 19 December, when he was greeted by throngs of enthusiastic East Germans, the leaders of both Germanies announced many new agreements that will bring the two closer together. They include massive West German economic assistance, which is contingent upon free elections. Modrow also agreed to dramatic changes in the GDR's stifling economic system which permit joint ventures and direct contacts between state-owned East German and private West German firms. In myriad ways, the two countries tightened their contacts over a broad range of issues, from environmental protection, rebuilding roads and the telecommunications system in the GDR, to swapping spies.

It is an understatement to say that the DKP was overwhelmed by this peaceful revolution in the GDR. A few diehards asserted that it was a "betrayal of the working class" and "democracy flim-flam" when the "class enemy" was given free rein to eject Communists from power through elections (*FBIS-WEU*, 21 November). But the minority wing of the party seized the opportunity to convene a "Renewal Congress" in Frankfurt am Main in October. The central topic was the division within the DKP. The Renewers decided to create their own structures which would enable them to prepare separately for the DKP's future congresses, including the extraordinary party congress in the spring of

1990. A "break with the traditional socialism and party conceptions of the DKP," the allowance of factions within the party, and the resignation of the entire leadership were demanded as necessary preconditions for the wing's further work within the party. The Renewers further decided to create their own office in Cologne and to publish a monthly information letter. For the first time, the split in the DKP was described in *Neues Deutschland* (24 October).

Although they initially decried these demands as an ultimatum, Mies and his deputy Weber conceded that they had to draw conclusions from the "breathtaking" changes in the GDR and the DKP's ruinous internal crisis; they announced that they would step down at the spring 1990 congress. Further changes would have to be decided at that meeting. (*FBIS-WEU*, 3 November; *ND*, 24 November.)

Despite an unconvincing public applauding of the changes which the SED had announced, disaster struck the DKP in late November: the SED informed it that all foreign currency support (which, despite DKP's denials, have amounted to an estimated 50–70 million West Marks annually, sent through conspiratorial channels) would be terminated. SED subsidies had always been essential to the financing of the high costs of maintaining party headquarters in Düsseldorf, an office in Bonn, and more than 200 local offices, the production and distribution of propaganda materials, mass rallies and election campaigns, and subsidies to DKP-affiliated or influenced organizations. DKP functionaries were kept on the payrolls of communist firms and travel agencies directed by the SED. The DKP had few other financial sources, particularly membership dues and income from the sale of party publications. Clandestine subsidies from the SED were about three times higher than the DKP's revenues from within the FRG.

No other Western communist party was so reliant on a foreign party as was the DKP on the SED. The DKP was controlled by the Department of International Politics and Economics (which until 1984 was known as "West Department") of the SED's Central Committee. Leaders of both the SED and DKP had to agree on an annual plan for the West German Communists, and the DKP leadership regularly reported to the SED. Even the DKP personnel files were kept in East Berlin.

Although promising further collaboration, as of the end of 1989 both parties would operate "completely on their own responsibility." No financial help could be expected from the Soviet Union. Contributions by GDR firms operating in the FRG have almost completely dried up. The split in the party has prompted members either to stop making their contributions altogether or to direct them to one or the other of the two wings in the DKP. Renewer Dieter Gautier, DKP chief in Bremen, stated the obvious: "The party stands on the brink of bankruptcy." An estimated 90 percent of the party's bloated staff will have to be dismissed. The party's publications will be severely affected, and East German advertising in DKP publications will almost completely disappear. Faced with the catastrophe which has befallen his party, Mies put on a stiff upper lip in a conversation with the Soviet ambassador in Bonn. Mies spoke of revival through a "purification process." The Renewers would have to leave the party, and a small but fine DKP would remain. (*FBIS-WEU*, 30 November; *Spiegel*, 4 December.)

Ideological Training and Propaganda. The GDR and the Soviet Union always provided vital educational support for the DKP. Over a third of its members had attended courses in the GDR and USSR. The DKP also maintains long-established institutions for this purpose. Founded in 1968, the Institute for Marxist Studies and Research (IMSF) in Frankfurt am Main cooperates closely with the institutes for Marxism-Leninism of the central committees of both the SED and CPSU. The Marx-Engels Foundation in Wuppertal serves as a venue for seminars and conferences. The Marxist Workers' Education (MAB), founded in Frankfurt in 1969, organizes courses and lectures throughout the FRG for politically active Germans who are not members of the DKP, and provides instructors from both Germanies. The DKP annually organizes approximately 8,000 educational lectures, seminars, and courses on such subjects as security in the atomic age, Communists' roles in economic policies, global affairs and culture, and electoral alliances and strategy.

It also lays great stress on contacts with fraternal parties. Until the democratic revolution which occurred in most Eastern European countries in the fall of 1989, the DKP had maintained close contacts with all ruling parties in Eastern Europe, especially with the Soviet Union and the GDR. It sent high-level delegations to their party congresses and received such delegations to its own. Sometimes communist leaders come to the FRG. On the occasion of Gorbachev's visit to the FRG in June 1989, the DKP organized a festival in Bonn, and Mies met with him

for half of an hour in the Soviet embassy before Gorbachev and his wife left for a gala dinner with the West German chancellor.

DKP delegations also travel east. Just days before the January 1989 congress Mies sped to Moscow on an image building trip to see Gorbachev. Also, both Mies and Ellen Weber met with deposed East German leader Egon Krenz in November, and Karl Heinz Schroeder flew to Moscow in November to meet Valentin Falin. Communist leaders in the East have wanted to know what the minuscule DKP is doing and want to use it for whatever support it might muster for Soviet policies, especially regarding security matters. However, there is absolutely no doubt that Soviet and East European communist leaders place far more value on their contacts with influential noncommunist parties in the West and give them far more coverage in their press.

Party publications. The DKP is so insignificant in the FRG that it receives very little attention in the noncommunist press. East German publications, such as the SED party organ *Neues Deutschland*, give it much broader coverage, but until Honecker was replaced in October 1989 they did not report on disagreements or problems within the DKP or with the SED; nor did they report precisely how little electoral support the DKP receives within the FRG. Now the East German media report DKP activities more accurately.

The DKP produces many publications of its own. They include the daily party organ *Unsere Zeit* (*UZ*), founded in April 1969 as a weekly. It has appeared five times a week since October 1973; until the end of 1989 the eight-page daily had a circulation of 23,000. Its 16-page weekend edition, published Fridays, had a circulation of 44,000. It sometimes publishes special editions of up to 300,000 copies called *Extra Blätter*. The editor claims that the FRG's "professional/occupational proscription" (which places legal restrictions on members of antidemocratic parties serving in public service) discourages some potential subscribers; in some cases, this is probably true. *UZ* is guided by party decisions and operates in close contact with the party leadership, who appoint the editor in chief and editorial board. It strives to uphold the tradition of the German communist press begun by *Rote Fahne* (Red banner), founded by Rosa Luxemburg and Karl Liebknecht, and continued by *Freies Volk* (A free people). In response to the turmoil within the DKP, the party leadership permits more open discussions in the party press than ever before. Nevertheless, an internal survey revealed that 94 percent of DKP members do not regularly read *UZ* (*Spiegel*, 7 September 1987). Half of all new readers cancel their subscriptions within one year, and overall circulation is declining (*ID*, 27 May 1988). By 1990 the party's press faced financial ruin and extreme uncertainty about its future.

There are other party publications: The *Volkszeitung* (earlier the *Deutsche Volkszeitung/Die Tat*—German people's newspaper/The deed) had a circulation of about 30,000. However, it ran out of money by 1990 and faced closure. The *Illustrierte Volkszeitung* (Illustrated people's newspaper) appears quarterly. The *DKP Pressedienst* (DKP press service), *Infodienst* (Info service—which provides print for the party's factory, residential area and student newspapers), and the *DKP-Landreview* (DKP rural review) all appear at irregular intervals. On a bimonthly basis, the DKP presidium produces *Praxis—Erfahrungen aus dem Leben und der Arbeit der Partei* (Practice—Knowledge gained from the life and work of the party), with a circulation of 7,500. The *Marxistische Blätter*, published eleven times per year with a circulation of 7,300, is the party's theoretical organ. The party also publishes approximately 340 factory and 450 local newspapers, some of which annually have a dozen editions with as many as 120,000 copies.

These publications are provided with news by two principal news agencies. The Progressive Press Agency (PPA), with headquarters in Düsseldorf and offices in Bonn, Mannheim, Munich, and Kiel, has approximately fifteen editors and correspondents and publishes five times weekly the *PPA Daily Service*, which reports on party activities and offers selected articles from the noncommunist press. About one-third of the material in DKP publications comes from the Allgemeiner Deutscher Nachrichtendienst (ADN), the news agency of the GDR.

Youth organizations. The largest group is the SDAJ, whose membership has plummeted from approximately 15,000 to 6,000, and the number of whose local groups has declined in number from 1,088 to only 674. Its traditional self-image is that of a "revolutionary young workers' organization" devoted to "the teachings of Marx, Engels and Lenin" and fighting for a "socialist Federal Republic," with a planned, socialist economy and power being exercised by the workers. Birgit Radow is the SDAJ's chairperson; she was also a member of the DKP presidium and executive until she was purged in 1989 for supporting the Renewal faction within the DKP. Most followers and functionaries in the SDAJ were calling in 1989 for party reform involving the recognition of pluralism of opinion and autonomy from the DKP. In these uncertain times, the SDAJ faces the danger of a split. Most of the Land chairmen are members of the DKP's Land presidia.

On 2–3 May 1987, the SDAJ held a federal congress in Frankfurt am Main. It was attended by 750 delegates with an average age of 21 years; 14 percent represented school groups, and 34 percent had functions in labor unions or youth councils in factories. DKP chairman Mies spoke of "a common struggle" with the DKP, and the first secretary of the central council of East German Free German Youth (FDJ), Eberhard Aurich, spoke of an "indestructible alliance" between the two youth organizations and asserted: "We have the same ideals and goals. We have the same friends and we hate the same enemies." Radow assured the Soviet Komsomol representative, Nikolai Palzew, that the SDAJ was "enthusiastic" about the "revolutionary restructuring" in the Soviet Union and that its effect in the FRG was to strengthen "the appeal of socialism." To both the Russian and East German visitors, Radow said: "We are proud of our friendship with the GDR and with the young revolutionaries in the FDJ, who make socialism strong in our neighboring country . . . We are spreading far and wide in the FRG the example of the Soviet Union, the GDR, and the other socialist countries. There the new social order is being built for which we want to fight in our own country." (*ID*, 24 July 1987.)

The group's activities are supposed to support those of the parent party and aim particularly at students, apprentices, and soldiers. It seeks contacts with Young Socialists (Jusos), Greens and various groups within the peace movement. To be appealing to those groups, the FDAJ calls for peace and disarmament and for the shutting down of all nuclear energy plants in capitalist countries (but not in socialist countries for the time being because they are "indispensable" there). (*ID*, 24 July 1987.) It maintains ties with communist youth groups in the GDR and other countries. Contacts between the FDJ and FDAJ include regular planning councils, training sessions, exchanges of delegations, and invitations to "friendship camps" in the GDR. SDAJ members participate in such organizations as the Solidarity Brigade in Nicaragua and the Soviet-controlled World Federation of Democratic Youth. It sponsors evening courses, group-leader schools at the Land level, and courses lasting a week at the Youth Education Center at Burg Wahrburg. It also publishes a variety of materials: *Elan—Das Jugendmagazin* is a monthly with a circulation of about 19,000. Every month it puts out an issue of *Artikeldienst für Betriebs-, Lehrlings, Stadtteil- and Schülerzeitungen* (Article service for plant, apprentice, neighborhood and pupils' newspapers). The SDAJ also publishes *Jugendpolitische Blätter* (Pages on youth politics), which appears in approximately 2,500 copies.

The Young Pioneers (JP) is for children and counts 4,000 members. Its functionaries are trained at the Youth Education Center at Burg Wahrburg, and many, including its chairman, Gerd Hertel, belong to the SDAJ and/or DKP. Its executive publishes a monthly *Pionierleiter Info* (Pioneer leader info); a child's newspaper, *Pionier* (circulation 5,000); as well as *Diskussionsmaterial für Pionierleiter* (Discussion material for Pioneer leaders). It has ties with children's groups in the GDR and other socialist countries and with the International Commission of Children's and Adolescents' Movements (CIMEA), an auxiliary of the World Federation of Democratic Youth. The FDJ supervises a JP vacation program in the GDR.

Represented at more than a hundred postsecondary institutions is the MSB-Spartakus, which has about 6,000 members and publishes monthly *Rote Blätter* (Red pages), with a circulation of 11,500, as well as a newspaper, *Avanti*. It is the largest and most powerful left-extremist organization at the university level, and it cooperates with all left-wing groups, including the Liberal Students' League (affiliated with, but to the left of the Free Democratic Party; FDP) and Jusos. MSB-Spartakus and its permanent alliance partner, the Socialist University League (SHB), occupy about a fifth of the seats in student parliaments and have representation in about half of such assemblies. All leftist extremist groups and groups influenced by them occupied a third of such seats in 1987. (*Verfassungsschutzbericht 1987*, published in 1988 and hereafter referred to as *VSB 87*). The MSB-Spartakus represents the United German Students' Association (Vereinigte Deutsche Studentenschaft; VDS) in diverse coordinating committees for protest and peace movements. Most top MSB-Spartakus leaders are DKP members. It regards "the struggle for peace" as one aspect of the class struggle and as a revolutionary objective. It works feverishly to undercut NATO and SDI and to gain support for nuclear-free zones and other objectives which have

a high priority for Kremlin leaders. Unlike the DKP, however, many MSB activists and leaders unreservedly support the Soviet Union's present reform course. The DKP considers its well-organized students to be the essential contact point between the intelligentsia and the working class.

The DKP regards the intelligentsia in the FRG as a potentially rich source of influence. Former Presidium and Secretariat member Gerd Deumlich wrote that "past and present experience shows that the intelligentsia in the FRG is largely in opposition to the ruling circles" because of the ignominy of fascism and the guilt of German capital in starting World War II," even though "the views of many intellectuals can hardly be regarded as consistently progressive, and while their thinking is under the influence of bourgeois illusions and anti-communism." He continued: "The FRG is a visual example of the crisis of capitalism permeating and interweaving every aspect of life in the society: economics, politics, ideology, morality and culture." (*WMR*, September 1987.)

Cover groups and citizens' action groups. For decades the DKP and other communist groups have faced mistrust and rejection by the FRG's general population. For this reason, it has operated through a wide variety of cover groups and has sought to cooperate with protest groups which enjoy greater respectability. It is supported by approximately 50 organizations and action groups, which it heavily influences, but which outwardly appear to be independent; the majority of their members and leaders does not belong to the DKP. Party members are indeed appointed to certain high positions, but the key to these groups' effectiveness is that the DKP's role be as underplayed as possible. Many of the larger of these cover groups are also affiliated with Moscow-directed front groups, such as the World Peace Council (WPC).

Among the more important DKP front groups is the Association of Victims of the Nazi Regime/League of Antifascists (VVN/BdA), with ca. 14,000 members and a monthly publication, *Antifaschistische Rundschau* (Antifascist review), having a circulation of 12,000. The German Peace Union (DFU), with ca. 1,000 members and a monthly publication *Abrüstungs-Info* (Disarmament-info; circulation 4,000), tries to break down anticommunist sentiments and gain support for the DKP's objectives within bourgeois and Christian circles. It was able to mobilize 85,000 protesters in April 1988 (225,000 according to DFU claims) for its annual "Easter Marches." As usual, the central manifestos and accounts for contributions were almost exclusively traceable to functionaries of the DKP and DFU. The number of demonstrators in the 1988 marches was lower than in earlier years because of the Intermediate-range Nuclear Forces (INF) Treaty of December 1987, which robbed the peace movement of its most important rallying point. The continued decline in the perceived military threat to Western Europe and the greatly improved relations between the superpowers, as displayed by Presidents Bush and Gorbachev on warships off Malta in December 1989, make dramatic arms-reduction agreements likely. This fact and another surprise threaten to pull the rug entirely out from under the DFU's feet: the GDR completely cut off its funding (*Der Spiegel*, 4 December 1989).

The German Peace Society/United War Resisters (DFG/VK), with ca. 11,000 members, is the largest DKP front group and has the greatest number of non-Communists, but it is plagued by declining membership and revenues and has had to reduce spending for its quarterly publication *Civil Courage* (circulation: 10,000). Communist influence within the DFG/VK is uneven; some groups and individuals have repeatedly criticized the DKP's power at the highest level, without being able to do anything about it. Other groups are the Union of Democratic Doctors; the Committee for Peace, Disarmament and Cooperation (KFAZ), which publishes *Friedensjournal* and *Friedensschnelldienst* (Peace journal and Peace express service); the Democratic Women's Initiative (DFI), which publishes *Wir Frauen* (We women) and focuses on women's issues on which the DKP has a firm position, such as opposition to military service for women; the Association of Democratic Jurists (VDJ), with ca. 1,000 members and a publication, *VDJ-Forum*, which is a section of the Soviet-controlled International Union of Democratic Jurists (IVDJ). The Anti-imperialistic Solidarity Committee for Africa, Asia, and Latin America (ASK) serves as the framework for joint efforts on behalf of "liberation movements" and in opposition to such U.S. objectives as SDI. The ASK publishes about 5,000 copies of a monthly *Anti-imperialist Information Bulletin*. The Patron Circle of the *Darmstädter Signal* was founded by the DKP, the SPD, the Greens, and Protestant and Catholic clergymen in 1983 to dissuade Federal Army (Bundeswehr) soldiers from taking part in nuclear warfare.

Domestic Attitudes and Activities. A party which has never received more than .3 percent of the votes in federal elections has an obvious problem. Mies openly acknowledges this. As he explained in an interview in the Polish newspaper *Trybuna Ludu* on 20 July 1987, "the DKP has not been able to win a suitable place among representative bodies; its influence on the working class as a whole does not suit today's needs. The party realizes this . . . and right now it is at a stage of productive unrest, involving the seeking of ways generally to increase our influence on the working class."

How can the DKP try to break out of its isolation? It forms electoral alliances, trying thereby to contribute in some way to parliamentary life, and jumps on the bandwagon of extraparliamentary movements, whose momentum stems from dealing with issues of broad concern in the FRG. Looking back over Land (state) elections in 1986, the party saw nothing but dismal failures: .1 percent in Lower Saxony in June and .2 percent in Hamburg in November; it did not even enter the Bavarian election in October. Thus, facing the January 1987 Bundestag elections, it decided to form an electoral alliance in order that its demands "be represented in an alliance more effectively" and "in that way to establish contact with more people, with people whom we Communists do not yet reach." (*UZ*, September 1986). Its "Peace List" invited the Greens to join in a common front, an invitation which the ambitious Greens rejected (*Frankfurter Allgemeine Zeitung*, 12 March 1986). Nevertheless, the DKP decided to ask its supporters to cast their first vote to the direct candidates of the Peace List and their second vote to either the Greens or the SPD, in an attempt to create a "majority left of the CDU" (*ID*, 3 April 1987). (Every voter has two votes: the first is for a candidate in an electoral constituency elected by plurality; the second is for a specific party and determines the percentage and number of seats the party will receive in the lower house. To win any seats at all, though, the party must win at least 5 percent of second votes in the entire FRG; this is a hurdle which the Communists have not come close to clearing since 1949; for this reason it was no genuine sacrifice to recommend that the Communists cast their second ballots for other parties.) This electoral-alliance approach is not new for the DKP. It formed a "Peace List" for the 1969 elections, as it did in the 1984 European Parliament elections, when it won 1.3 percent of the votes. In the North Rhine-Westphalia Land election in 1985 a "Peace List NRW" won .7 percent.

More than 40 percent of the Peace List candidates in 1987 were DKP members or functionaries, and a further 30 percent were in the DFU. Two-thirds of the Federal Governing Board are members either of the DKP or of the organizations which the DKP influences. The DKP and its affiliated organizations, the MSB-Spartakus, the SDAJ and the DFU, bore the brunt of the work and expense for the campaign. However, knowing the average voter's antipathy toward the DKP, it went to great pains to blur the role of the DKP and DFU in the Peace List. The three top candidates were not Communists, and in party publications, only selections of candidates' pictures were published in which Communists were a small minority (*ID*, 3 April 1987).

Peace List candidates received 188,602 or .5 percent of the first votes. Its best Land results were in the city-states of Bremen (1.3 percent) and Hamburg (.8 percent). In various university towns it topped its country-wide average: Tübingen, 3.8 percent; Freiburg, 1.8 percent; Marburg, 1.7 percent; Münster, 1.6 percent. The DKP found these meager results to be "relatively satisfactory." In the party leadership's view, the DKP had helped to "debilitate the right-wing parties," particularly the "Steel Helmet faction of arch-conservatives," and to reverse the slide to the right which the FRG had experienced since 1985. It claimed to have "made the issue of peace and détente the focus and touchstone of its electoral effort" and to have "forced each party to speak up on it too," and to "reject the policy of subjecting West Germany to the interests of the Washington administration." (*WMR*, vol. 17, no. 2, 1987.) In the words of one Presidium member, the DKP's electoral strategy had given

> an uplift to the forces of the left of the CDU/CSU, stimulated positive changes in the SPD, reinforced the position of the Greens in the Bundestag, and raised our party's own prestige in the nation at large and particularly among the Social Democrats, the Greens, and activists of the peace movement and of the working class movement. All this provided an immense incentive for future joint or parallel actions in the common front and in the democratic alliances. (*WMR*, May 1987.)

In actual fact, there is very little evidence that the DKP made significant contributions to or progress toward any of these goals. There are a few instances of cooperation on the local level. For example, *Neues Deutschland* reported on 18 July 1989 the formation of an SPD-Green-DKP alliance in the village of Dietzenbach. However, both the SPD and Greens are aware that their electoral performance would be harmed, not helped, by collaboration with the Communists and that the DKP's minuscule vote-getting potential would be irrelevant to any electoral outcome. This was made clear again in the June 1989 elections to the European Parliament, in which the DKP won .1 percent of the votes in the Rhineland Palatinate and Bavaria, .2 percent in North Rhine-Westphalia, and .4 percent in the Saar. There are indeed discussions within the SPD and Green parties concerning possible alliances, but these discussions revolve around alliances with each other, not with the DKP. Nor are the SPD or Greens dealing with defense issues because they have been prodded by the DKP. Defense and arms-control questions are very much on the political agenda in the FRG, an exposed country in the middle of Europe located along the border with the Warsaw Pact nations, and in which there are a million troops from six different countries and thousands of nuclear warheads. All parties therefore pay close attention to defense issues.

The DKP will continue, as its Presidium announced after the 1987 Bundestag elections, to follow "its line, adopted by its eighth congress, to broaden extra-parliamentary action, its policy of alliances and unity of action, and to enhance on this basis its own political role as a mobilizing and motive force, and increase its membership" (*IB*, May 1987). Nevertheless, its leader announced on 15 October 1989 that the DKP would orient itself toward running its own candidates in the December 1990 federal elections, in order to preserve and strengthen itself. Its membership plummeted in 1989 to 25–30,000, a matter of great concern for the leadership. But an earlier paper published by the party's executive warned about the potential risks of bringing in new members from extraparliamentary alliances. The danger is that

> the allies' ideological and organizational attitudes also have an influence on the Communists. . . When working in the alliances, they [Communists] use the tactics of compromise, but often also carry it over to relations within their own party, so ignoring the fundamental distinction between a patchwork association and the Marxist-Leninist vanguard of the working class.

The report notes that "there is a change in the social make-up of the DKP." The DKP is also recruiting from social strata other than the working class. Indeed, only 20 percent of Communists now work in "large-scale material production." For instance, the biggest DKP plant group in North Rhine-Westphalia, the FRG's most populous Land, is not to be found in the coal and steel industry, but in the city hospitals (*Spiegel*, 7 September 1987). Thus, concluded the DKP report, "it is not right to forget that most of the new members lack what the workers acquire in fighting for their rights at enterprises and in the trade unions, namely, the conscious need for organized and collective action" (*WMR*, January 1987).

The DKP tries to appeal to workers, a steadily declining class in the FRG's modern economy, by demanding such measures as a 35-hour work week without pay cuts, job-creation programs, job security, higher real wages, saving the declining steel and shipbuilding industries, protecting the right of participation in the management of mining and steel-producing facilities, and an end to mass layoffs and social-welfare cuts. but it faces an unmistakable problem in recruiting workers at a time of high unemployment in the FRG. *Neues Deutschland* publicized several cases in 1989 of persons being fired on the grounds that their activities with the DKP were not compatible with their "obligation to loyalty" to the state: an elementary teacher in Stuttgart, a postal employee in Giessen, and a city administrator in Osnabrück. These were not the first instances of such firings, and a dismissed DKP member has great difficulty getting another job. As one such person remarked bitterly, "the alleged black mark of DKP membership is an insurmountable hurdle." (*Spiegel*, 19 October 1987.) Thus, a new recruit must be prepared to sacrifice his livelihood. It is no wonder that the DKP calls for an end to "professional bar/occupational proscription" (*Berufsverbot*, the term used by those who oppose this law; the official title is *Radikalenerlass*— Radicals Decree) against those deemed to be risks to the state. After the January 1989 elections in West Berlin, in which the right-wing Republicans won 7.5 percent of the votes and seats in the city's Senate (entitling them to two seats in the Bundestag after the 1990 elections), the DKP and the Socialist Unity Party of West Berlin strengthened their calls for an end to the Radicals Decree and for the prohibition of right-wing political parties. Its point of view was expressed on a placard unfurled outside the Federal Administrative Court in West Berlin: "Look at this city: Neo-Nazis in the Senate and occupational proscription for Communists!" (*ND*, 2 February 1989.)

The party orders its members to take an active role in trade unions, with the goal of persuading trade unionists that workers' interests are only served by class struggle. It places great value on its "educational work," particularly for the union youth organizations; many union instructors are products of the student movement and advocate orthodox Marxism. Even though few DKP members have risen to leading positions in the unions, three-fourths of them belong to unions, and they exercise influence in some, particularly those of printers, journalists, and the mass media. (*VSB 87.*) In 1985 a Mass Media Trade Union was set up to include the Union of Printworkers, the Union of Journalists, the Union of Writers, the Union of Radio and Television Workers, and the main unions in music, drama, and the plastic and graphic arts. Gerd Deumlich claims that this new union "wants to put an end to the power of the monopolies" in the media and is "a strong response to those who have been conducting a reactionary policy in the mass media and who want to limit the sphere of union political activity." (*WMR*, September 1987.) According to the 1987 BfV report, the number of communist workers' groups has risen to about 400, about one-third of which are active in the metal industry and about a fourth in the public-service sector, principally in communal and Land administrations. Some have only a few members and engage in action only irregularly. The number of DKP factory newspapers has declined to 340, each with a circulation of several hundred to several thousand and most appearing irregularly. (*Handelsblatt*, 22–23 May 1987.)

Despite any possible dangers, the party does work toward the formation of broad alliances. These have the form of "working-class united actions," namely DKP cooperation with trade unionists, workers not affiliated with any party, Christian workers, and Social Democrats. The alliances can also be with intellectuals and the bourgeoisie. Such "prudential coalitions" can seek broader objectives, such as foiling SDI. DKP members need not occupy the leading offices, and they can use "political flexibility" while maintaining "ideological conviction." That is, cooperation should be based on common interests and should not be brought about through compromises with reformist positions. (*ID*, 12 May 1986.)

The DKP leadership believes it sees the wall breaking down between Social Democrats and Communists, a wall which has existed since the foundation of the KPD in 1918, and which was strengthened by the effort of the KPD to absorb the SPD after the Second World War. Serious disagreement continues to exist between the two parties on the "system question"; that is, what kind of regime and economic order is best for the FRG. It has long sought to eliminate or lessen the "fears of contact" (*Berührungsängste*) which have made most groups in the FRG disinclined to deal with the DKP. While there are no high-level party-to-party contacts and absolutely no talk within the national SPD of any form of alliance or formal cooperation with the DKP, some Social Democrats serve on governing boards of DKP-influenced organizations, as well as on "citizens' action groups" and societies that promote friendship with certain socialist countries. Speakers from both parties sometimes appear at the same discussions or meetings. Also, some interviews with Social Democrats are printed in *UZ*. Such speeches and interviews are seldom given by prominent Social Democrats, though. In 1988 the DKP adopted the slogan: "Continue on this path: toward Social Democrats—for unity of action!" (*VSB 87*.) At the university level, the predominantly leftist social-democratic SHB has for years joined in "united actions" with the MSB-Spartakus and, unlike the larger SPD, favors an SPD-DKP alliance. (*ID*, 12 May 1987.)

The DKP also joins the broad-based protest efforts which bring it into contact with a wide spectrum of noncommunist groups and, it hopes, widens its appeal. It now opposes nuclear power or reprocessing plants and is present at the often bloody protests against such installations as the Wackersdorf nuclear reprocessing plant. The DKP claims to have helped expose the true purpose of Wackersdorf: "to be a center for the manufacture of West Germany's own nuclear weapons" (*WMR*, September 1987). In fact, no responsible West German leader advocates the FRG's acquisition of such weapons. In 1988, the DKP demanded that all atomic plants be completely nationalized and placed under strict democratic control (*ND*, 1 February 1988). The DKP advocates protection of the environment and cleaning up the polluted Rhine River. It joined in the movement against the taking of a census. It reasoned that the information thereby gained would strengthen the FRG's character as an "authoritarian surveillance state," as well as support the FRG's "antidemocratic security laws," and thereby serve ultimately "the preparation for war." (*ID*, 15 May 1987.)

Perhaps most important in the party's efforts to reach out to other groups has been its participation in the peace movement. Kurt Schacht, a member of the DKP executive, maintained that "the participa-

tion of DKP members in the peace forums has unquestionably given the party valuable experience and . . . has had a positive effect on the peace movement itself. Cooperation between the Communists, Social Democrats, and Greens has been fostered by the considerable concurrence of their views on questions of war and peace." (*WMR*, March 1987.) Operating within the peace movement is particularly comfortable for the DKP because it is thereby able to devote its energies to supporting Soviet and GDR security objectives. In the aftermath of the INF Treaty, the DKP demanded in 1988 that all trials of participants in peace pickets at U.S. missile bases be stopped, and that all convicted peace activists be given an amnesty, on the grounds that the legitimacy of their efforts had been confirmed by the treaty. (*FBIS*, 18 February 1988.) Throughout 1989 the party also attacked tentative NATO plans to modernize short-range nuclear weapons in Europe, but these plans were quietly forgotten in a year of dramatically improved superpower relations and promises of arms reduction.

Neither the DKP nor the many communist splinter parties (called K-Groups) are the initiators or string-pullers of the peace movement, within which they remain a small minority. For a while, their active role was willingly accepted by the noncommunist majority, which in the early 1980s rallied behind such proclamations as the largely communist-inspired "Krefeld Appeal" of 1980. However, by spring of 1982 tensions between Communists and non-Communists within the movement became obvious. Robert Steigerwald, a DKP leader, scorned ecological and religious elements as "upper-level salaried employees and intellectuals" because they demanded, in the words of Petra Kelly, a "peace movement which thinks and acts in a bloc-free manner." Heinrich Böll commented that "inasmuch as the Communists are controlled from Moscow, their orders are to destroy what is meaningful in these movements by taking part in them and indeed by forcing their way into them." The noncommunist elements within the peace movement did not reject all forms of logistical support, which is probably the Communists' greatest contribution to the movement; the DKP and its affiliated organizations had a disproportionately large representation in many of the movement's operational coordinating committees. For example, DKP delegates regularly attended meetings of the Coordinating Committee of the Peace Movement (KA), despite the fact that the party did not formally belong. Nevertheless, the Greens and other noncommunist activists in the peace movement intensified efforts to distance themselves from Communists. Clearly, the peace movement has in the 1980s been far too large and heterogeneous to be controlled by outside powers or the DKP. (*Armed Forces and Society*, Spring 1984; VSB 87.)

Communists have no reason to be happy about their attempts to work together with the badly divided Greens. They were able to recommend to DKP members to give their second vote in the 1987 elections to the Greens (or the Social Democrats) on the grounds that the Greens are a consistently radical-democratic force that supports the extraparliamentary struggle. Although there are former Communists within the Greens, these former Communists are from the militant communist splinter parties which tend to be hostile or uncooperative toward the DKP.

The fundamentalists (Fundis) had a majority within the Greens' leadership and were fiercely independent, rejecting arguments made by the realists (Realos) that coalitions with the SPD had to be formed. But at the Greens' Karlsruhe congress in December 1988 the pragmatic wing toppled the fundamentalist party executive and thereby gathered the reins of decisionmaking power into its own hands (*Die Zeit*, N. Amer. edition, 16 December 1988). The Realos' domination in Bonn and in the federal organization was strengthened in 1989. Greens still command the allegiance of one in ten voters, as was demonstrated in elections in West Berlin and Frankfurt, where they won 11.8 percent and 10.1 percent respectively, and became coalition partners with the SPD. Even an SPD-Green federal coalition after the 1990 elections is possible. The Greens have never discussed coalitions with the Communists, even though the DKP agreed with the Fundis' position on violence in demonstrations: that there should be an end to the state's "monopoly on the use of force" (*CSM*, 24 November 1987). Responding to a statement by Chancellor Kohl, the DKP Presidium declared that "Kohl's stinging attack on those who allegedly resort to 'violence' during demonstrations disguises the intention to curtail still more the right to meetings and demonstrations" (*IB*, June 1987). It should be said, though, that few, if any, of the several hundred militant demonstrators who travel throughout the FRG to turn every demonstration possible into a violent conflict with the police are following orders from the DKP. Such "chaotists" (*Cháoten*) are not suited for the kind of disciplined party which the DKP tries hard to be.

An obviously exasperated Robert Steigerwald noted that the DKP is

> working hard to secure a political alliance with its [the Green Party's] representatives while criticizing the erroneous and sometimes reactionary views of the latter... Most of the Greens keep aloof from the working class, asserting that it is unable to bring about a revolutionary transformation of society. Marxism is dismissed as a nineteenth-century theory; political economy is replaced with ecology. Marxists and those who worship economic development are equally presented as prisoners of an obsession with economic growth and consumption. (*WMR*, November 1986.)

The DKP's hope to gain advantages by riding the wave of extraparliamentary protest and participating in the peace movement is bound to be disappointed because the momentum and drive of the movement had largely vanished by 1990. There are several reasons for this. The most important is the INF agreement signed in December 1987 between the Soviet and U.S. leaders, calling for the removal from Europe of all U.S. and Soviet medium- and short-range missiles, and the prospect of further steps to reduce strategic arsenals by half. This agreement was made possible by party chief Gorbachev's implicit admission that Soviet missiles are not purely defensive in nature and are part of the problem. This admission undercuts the DKP's persistent efforts to show that the United States and its president were the sole obstacles to disarmament. Also, in contrast with the early 1980s, the peace movement's demands are now incorporated into the SPD and Green manifestos. Thus, the former extraparliamentary opposition to the arms race has been brought directly into parliament. This has eliminated much of the raison d'être of the extraparliamentary peace movement. (*Frankfurter Allgemeine Zeitung*, 27 May 1987.) Gorbachev's dramatic announcement of unilateral conventional-arms cuts at the U.N. on 7 December 1988 was seen by NATO foreign ministers who were meeting in Brussels as "among the most promising developments" and a basis for further negotiations aiming at a military balance at a much lower level of armaments. In 1989, the Conventional Forces Talks in Europe (CFE) showed good prospects for success, and the United States and FRG announced preliminary plans to reduce the size of their armed forces in Europe if those talks achieved successful results. Thus, the subject of arms reductions is in the air, with or without the peace movement's encouragement.

International Views and Party Contacts.

The DKP's statements on foreign policy were always in perfect harmony with those made by the GDR and the USSR. It followed Moscow's and East Berlin's lead in supporting whatever groups they defined as liberation movements. One of these was the Sandinista government in Nicaragua. It invariably supported all aspects of the Soviet Union's peace propaganda, including demands for ending SDI and for removal of U.S. atomic weapons from Europe. It applauded the SPD's party contacts with ruling parties in Eastern Europe and the SPD-SED security-policy talks which resulted in calls for a "security partnership" between both Germanies and the Soviet Union and for the creation in Europe of corridors or zones free of nuclear and chemical weapons. It demanded cuts of 10 percent in the FRG's defense budget and an ultimate end to arms exports. The DKP roundly criticized the Bonn government for making "a big issue of the mythical 'military threat' from the East" and for its position "that there is no alternative to the deterrence doctrine in the foreseeable future and that a continued peace will still require armed forces with well-balanced conventional and nuclear weapons." Finally, the DKP supported unflaggingly the SED's interpretations of the GDR's legal status. It criticized Bonn's "resurgent fiction of a 'single German nation' and hackneyed contentions that the German question 'remains open in the legal, political and historical sense' and that it is still necessary to maintain the concept of single citizenship." It called for "a definitive renunciation of great Germany dreams." (*IB*, June 1987.)

Other Leftist Groups.

In addition to the DKP, there are many small left-extremist groups and parties, action groups, and New Left revolutionary organizations which are active. All disavowed the DKP's pro-Soviet, pro-SED policies and are ideologically deeply divided from one another, even though most of them are willing to cooperate in action alliances. Total membership in these organizations, after allowing for multiple affiliations, declined in 1987 to approximately 62,000, with an additional 49,000 in organizations influenced by left-extremists. They produce about 200 publications with a total circulation of more than four million. They also operate a few pirate radio stations. (VSB 87; *Frankfurter Allgemeine Zeitung*, 27

May 1988.) By far, the favored cause for cooperation is to protest against atomic power. About one-third of all terrorist acts were attributed to the struggle against the peaceful use of nuclear energy. NATO also provided important targets. (*ID*, 24 July 1987.)

The New Left, composed of Marxist-Leninists, Trotskyists, anarchists, autonomists, and antidogmatic revolutionaries, preaches class struggle. It identifies the proletariat as the essential revolutionary force leading the fight to tarnish the image of the FRG's political order in the eyes of its citizens and to overthrow the bourgeois state and capitalist system. Most advocate establishing a dictatorship of the proletariat, culminating in a socialist and ultimately communist social order. They are confident that the bureaucratic failures in communist-ruled regimes can be prevented. The autonomous anarchist groups advocate the eradication of the state, to be superseded by a "free" society. Most New Leftists unabashedly advocate using violence to achieve their aims.

Dogmatic new left. There are a variety of Marxist-Leninist groups, loosely called "K-groups." The strongest of these groups is the Marxist-Leninist Party of Germany (Marxistisch-Leninistische Partei Deutschlands; MLPD), which has about 1,300 members organized in twelve districts and approximately 100 local units. It regards itself as the only Marxist-Leninist party in the FRG. Its chairman is Stefan Engel, and its official organ is *Rote Fahne* (Red banner), whose weekly circulation is about 10,000. It participated in the 1987 Bundestag election, winning 13,821 second votes. This 0.0 percent of the total vote indicates how little electoral hope there is for the K-groups. Nevertheless party spokesman Klaus Vowe called this result "satisfactory," considering that the party had expected to receive only 10,000. Vowe noted that the party would have gotten more votes, were it not for the "falsification" of the party's arguments by the bourgeois media. (*ID*, 3 April 1987.)

The MLPD has three ineffective affiliated organizations with about 300 members. They are the Marxist-Leninist Workers' Youth Association (AJV/ML), which has a press organ, *Rebell*, and a children's group, *Rotfüchse* (Red foxes); the Marxist-Leninist Pupils' and Students' Association, whose organ is *Roter Pfeil* (Red arrow); and an active Marxist-Leninist League of Intellectuals.

The United Socialist Party (Vereinigte Sozialistische Partei; VSP) was born from the 1986 merger of the Communist Party of Germany-Marxist Leninist (KPD, earlier known as KPD-ML) and the Trotskyist Group International Marxists (GIM). The VSP, with about 500 members, is led by Horst-Dieter Koch and has its headquarters in Cologne. Its biweekly publication, *Sozialistische Zeitung* (Socialist newspaper; circulation 2,400), replaced in 1986 the KPD's earlier *Roter Morgen* (Red morning) and the GIM's *Was Tun* (What is to be done). Its youth group is the Autonomous Socialist Youth Group (ASJG).

Members of the KPD who opposed the merger which resulted in the VSP reconfirmed their adherence to the old party statutes and program. Calling themselves the "correct KPD," they maintain headquarters in West Berlin. A separate Workers' League for the Reconstruction of the KPD claims about 300 members, maintains a Communist University League in Bavaria, and published two editions of the *Kommunistische Arbeiterzeitung* (Communist worker's newspaper; KAZ).

The League of West German Communists (Bund Westdeutscher Kommunisten; BWK), which emerged in 1980 from a split in the now defunct Communist League of West Germany (KBW), counts approximately 300 members, organized in groups in seven Lands. It publishes the biweekly *Politische Berichte* (Political reports), with a circulation of about 1,300 copies, and the *Nachrichtenhefte* (News booklets), with a circulation of about 1,000. The BWK is the dominant member of the People's Front, whose business office is in the BWK's main office in Cologne. The People's Front, with about 700 members and a biweekly *Antifaschistische Nachrichten* (Antifascist news; circulation 700) is an instrument for an alliance of left-extremists, and the BWK is willing to cooperate with the DKP and organizations affiliated with it or influenced by it.

The Communist League (Kommunistischer Bund; KB) has its headquarters in Hamburg, where about half of its ca. 400 followers live. Demanding "confrontation with the state" and abolition of the "capitalist republic," it has considerable influence within the Green-Alternative List (GAL). The KB publishes a monthly *Arbeiterkampf* (Workers' struggle), which has a circulation of about 4,800. The "Group Z" split from the KB in 1979 and joined the Greens, with many of its members rising to top positions in the Greens' federal and Land organizations.

About a dozen Trotskyist groups, some existing only in certain regions, have a total of about 500 members. Advocating "permanent revolution" and the "dictatorship of the proletariat," they decry "actually existing socialism" in communist-ruled countries as "bureaucratic" or "revisionist decadence." The League of Socialist Workers is the German section of the International Committee of the Fourth International in London. Together with its Socialist Youth League, it counts fewer than 100 members, and its weekly organ, *Neue Arbeiterpresse*, (New workers' press) has advocated a general strike to overthrow the government. The smaller Trotskyist groups, such as the Trotskyist League of Germany, the International Socialist Workers' Organization, the International Communist Movement, the Socialist Workers' Group, and the Posadistic Communist Party, protest against animosity directed toward foreign workers in the FRG and support revolutionary struggles in the Third World.

The Marxist Group (MG) is a Marxist-Leninist cadre party with a rigidly hierarchical structure, severe discipline, intensive indoctrination and secrecy. Its 1,800 members and several thousand sympathizers are mainly students and academics, and the focus of its efforts is Bavaria. It is convinced that trained agitators must spark a class-conscious proletariat to engage in class struggle. It advocates "thoroughly destructive criticism of all existing conditions." (*VSB 87.*) It communicates through its monthly *MSZ-Marxistische Streit und Zeitschrift-Gegen die Kosten der Freiheit* (Marxist controversy and news magazine–Against the costs of freedom; 12,000 copies); the *Marxistische Arbeiterzeitung* (Marxist Workers' Newspaper; MAZ, which appears irregularly); and the *Marxistische Schulzeitung* (Marxist school newspaper). According to the Federal Office for the Protection of the Constitution, the MG has expanded to the point where it now has more members than did the "K-Groups" at their zenith in the 1970s; its publications have a wider distribution than all other groups in the "New Left" category put together. (*ID*, 30 May.)

Autonomous anarchist groups of the undogmatic left. These groups reject strict organizational structures and are extremely divided over aims and whether to utilize violent or nonviolent action in order to change society.

The Free Workers' Union (FAU), which has 200 members in 22 local groups, is a member of the anarchosyndicalist International Workers' Association (IAA) and publishes bimonthly *Direkte Aktion* in Dieburg. It founded Schwarze Hilfe (Black help) to assist imprisoned anarchosyndicalists, anarchists, and autonomists. It also maintains contact with the international coordinating office of the anarchist Black Cross in London. The principles espoused by anarchosyndicalists can be summarized as opposition to the state, to parliament, and to the military. FAU adherents oppose both Western capitalism and the "state capitalism" practiced in communist countries. They see as their supreme task revolutionary work in factories to create collective resistance against capitalism. They dream of a society characterized by decentralization and self-administration. There are some independent opposition FAU organizations that wish to work also outside the factory arena.

Violence-Free Action Groups—Grass-Roots counts about 800 followers in ca. 70 groups and collectives. The contact and coordinating body for them is the Grass-Roots Revolution—Federation of Violence-Free Action Groups (FoGA), which advocates a nonviolent revolution and creation of a decentralized society based on anarchy and self-administration to replace present state power. Their aims, as indicated by their actions and monthly publication, *Grasswürzelrevolution* (Grass roots revolution), which has a circulation of about 4,000, are primarily antimilitarism, peace, and "social defense." Protection of the environment, especially against nuclear power and reprocessing plants, is also important.

The diverse autonomous anarchist groupings within the undogmatic New Left tend to be tiny, loosely organized, short-lived, and prone to violence. They attract several thousand predominantly young people, who engage in "solidarity actions" to support Third World liberation movements. But their contacts with like-minded left-extremist groups outside the FRG were sporadic and generally limited to specific actions.

Unfortunately, the FRG has many foreign extremist organizations which operate within the country. Their numbers grow as the FRG becomes a haven for more and more refugees from the Third World. The presence of so many visibly alien people creates domestic political tensions and provides a convenient scapegoat and target for right-wing West German extremist circles. The BfV estimates that about 81,600 foreigners belong to leftist extremist organizations (more than twice as many as belong to corresponding right-wing extremist groups). The most active and violence-oriented is the orthodox-communist Workers' Party of Kurdistan (PKK). The Liberation Tigers of Tamil Ealam (LTTE) makes its presence felt, as do violent Palestinian, Iranian, Turkish, and Yugoslavian groups. (*VSB 87.*)

Hard-core terrorist groups. Deadly and destructive terrorist actions continue, although their numbers declined from 1,902 in 1986 to 1,497 in 1987 (*ID*, 30 August 1988). The hard-core, command level (Kommandobereich) of the Red Army Faction (Rote Armee Faction; RAF) is still composed of about 20 underground killers, approximately the same number as in the mid-1970s. They engage in political assassinations and dramatic bombings and claimed responsibility for the attempted assassination of Hans Tietmeyer in September 1988 (*FBIS*, 22 September 1988). On 30 November 1989, RAF assassins killed Deutsche Bank chairman Alfred Herrhausen by means of a remote-controlled bomb. The RAF, which has murdered more than 20 West German business and political leaders since the early 1970s, claimed that changes in Europe require a "new chapter" for the "revolutionary movement." (*Washington Post*, 6 December 1989.) Closely supporting the RAF terrorists is a second echelon of "RAF Militants," numbering approximately 250 persons. Recruited from the anti-imperialist resistance circles, they handle logistics for the command level, such as documents, vehicles, weapons, explosives, and secret housing. These militants reportedly engage in destructive actions against material targets, but not in violence against human beings. A further echelon is composed of "RAF sympathizers," who number around 2,000. They engage in propaganda and public relations for the terrorists and assist those who are in prison. (*ID*, 24 July 1987; *VSB 87.*) Herrhausen's murder was, according to an RAF letter, partly intended to support a hunger strike by faction members in prison, who demanded an end of isolation and the right to be housed together. That strike had also been supported by the Italian Red Brigades. (*FBIS-WEU*, 29 March.) As was proven in 1987, when French police captured four leaders of Action Directe on a farm near Orleans, the RAF maintains close political collaboration with like-minded foreign terrorist groups, such as Action Directe in France, the Fighting Communist Cells in Belgium, the Red Brigades in Italy, and GRAPO in Spain, despite serious setbacks in 1987.

The Red Cells (Rote Zellen; RZ), their female affiliate Rote Zora, and various "autonomist groups" also carry out terrorist attacks. The RZ find themselves in basic ideological agreement with the RAF's "socialist revolutionary and anti-imperialist" aims. The various other groupings and individuals lumped together as "autonomists" also choose their victims in the same basic way as the RAF and RZ and give the same rationales for their attacks as are expressed in the "letters taking responsibility" sent by the RAF and RZ. The common characteristics of all these groups are hatred of the political, social, and economic systems of the FRG and a rigorous readiness to use violence, no matter what it may cost in life and limb.

Die Tageszeitung (The daily newspaper; *TAZ*) is a daily publication close to the alternative milieu and has a circulation of up to 33,000. Its slant is revealed by letters to the editor praising terrorist actions, such as those printed after the nuclear engineer Karl-Heinz Beckurts and his driver had been gunned down in 1986: "Bravo RAF!"; "This was a spy!"; "Now there is one imperialist swine fewer!"; and "I have no pity for the liquidated manager of the nuclear industry of death!" (*Deutschland-Union Dienst*, 16 July 1986.) *De Knipselkrant*, which is published periodically in the Netherlands, also serves as a discussion forum for the "armed struggle." (*VSB 87*.)

The Greens and the SPD's youth, student, and women's organizations are not left-radical groups. Some of their members do share some of the views of the extreme left in an abstract way, and some have been willing to take part in "united actions" with leftists and Communists. Common ground can often be found in support of the Soviet Union's disarmament campaigns, in advocacy of nuclear- or chemical-free zones in Central Europe, or in efforts to reduce the power of the U.S. military, the Bundeswehr, or NATO.

Wayne C. Thompson
Virginia Military Institute

WEST BERLIN

Population. 1,869,000 (1988)
Party. Socialist Unity Party of West Berlin (Sozialistische Einheitspartei Westberlins; SEW)
Membership. 7,000 (SEW's figures; the Federal Office for the Protection of the Constitution [BfV] estimates 4,500). 70 percent joined after 1966.
Chairman. Dietmar Ahrens, acting chairman following death of Horst Schmitt in April 1989
Politburo. Collectively resigned in November 1989
Secretariat. Collectively resigned in November 1989

Executive. 65 members
Status. Legal
Last Congress. Eighth, 15–17 May 1987
Last Election. 1989, 0.6 percent, no representation
Auxiliary Organizations. Socialist Youth League Karl Liebknecht (Sozialistischer Jugendverband Karl Liebknecht; SJ Karl Liebknecht), ca. 600 members; Young Pioneers (Junge Pioniere; JP), ca. 200 members; SEW-University Groups, ca. 400 members
Publications. *Neue Zeitung* (until end of 1989 called *Die Wahrheit*—Truth), SEW daily organ, circulation ca. 13,000; the party also publishes a quarterly magazine *Konsequent* (Consistent; circulation 2,500) for its propaganda work, and its university groups publish *Rote Wochen* (Red weeks) for their agitation activities.

Background. West Berlin remains under formal Allied occupation by the armed forces of the United States, the United Kingdom, and France, which maintain about 10,000 troops there. West Berlin is under the NATO defense umbrella. The 1971 Quadripartite Agreement, signed by the three powers above and the Soviet Union, confirms Berlin's special status. It states that West Berlin is not a part of the Federal Republic of Germany (FRG), but that it has links with the FRG. Despite the fact that this agreement was intended to cover the entire area of greater Berlin, the Soviet-occupied eastern sector of the city has been declared as the capital of the German Democratic Republic (GDR), which refers to the eastern part simply as "Berlin."

West Berlin is, for all practical purposes, ruled by its own elected Senate (parliament), but the three allied powers can and sometimes do veto a law or action of the Senate. Both West Berlin and the FRG seek to maintain close ties with each other; these ties are a diplomatic and economic necessity for West Berlin and a political imperative for Bonn. West Berlin is represented in the federal parliament in Bonn by nonvoting deputies. Residents of West Berlin are not required to serve in the Federal Army (Bundeswehr), a fact which, as is often cited, prompts many young German dissidents to resettle there and thereby greatly enlivens the alternative scene in the city. Indeed, many New Left, left-extremist, and terrorist groups are active in West Berlin.

Membership and Organization. The SEW has, according to its own sources, about 7,000 members, which is about how many votes it re-

ceived in the last Senate elections in January 1989
(6,875). Its 0.6 percent of the total vote was far
short of the 5 percent minimum required for seats in
the city parliament.

The SEW is broken down into twelve sub-
organizations (Kreisparteiorganisationen) and has a
number of affiliated organizations: Communist
youth are organized in the SJ Karl Liebknecht,
which has about 600 members, and which publishes
a monthly journal, *Signal*, having a circulation of
1,000. The Young Pioneers (JP) have about 200. Its
university organizations consist of around 400 students. The SEW-influenced Action Group of Democrats and Socialists (ADS-Westberlin) embraces
approximately 300 persons and publishes the biweekly *ads-info*. Most of its members belong also to
the SEW university groups and agitate against government plans to reform the universities. Its Democratic Women's League Berlin (DFB) has about 600
members and publishes about 600 copies of the
monthly *Im Blickpunkt der Berlinerin* (From the
perspective of the Berlin woman). The German-
Soviet Friendship Society—Berlin has about 500
members. The West Berlin organization of the Victims of the Nazi Regime/League of Antifascists
(VVN/BdA) also has about 500 and publishes a
quarterly antifascist magazine, *Der Mahnruf* (The
warning). The SEW exercises considerable influence over the Berliner Mietergemeinschaft e.V.
(Berlin Renters' Community), whose 8,000 members oppose the elimination of rent controls. It publishes a bimonthly *Mieterecho* (Renters' echo), with
a circulation of 8,000. (*VSB 87*.) The SEW publishes its own newspaper: *Neue Zeitung*.

Traditional Policy Stance. One can better understand the party's daunting challenges and need
for change in the 1990s by looking back on its older
policy positions. The Eighth Party Congress took
place from 15 to 17 May 1987 under the slogan:
"With the SEW for Peace, Work, Democracy, and
Social Progress." There were 587 delegates and
guests from 37 foreign parties and organizations,
including delegations from the Communist Party of
Germany (DKP), the Communist Party of the Soviet Union (CPSU), led by Central Committee secretary Vadim Medvedev, and the SED, led by Neumann. Former SED chairman, Erich Honecker,
sent a telegram to the re-elected SEW leader, the
late Horst Schmitt, wishing him "success,
creativity, and health in implementing the decisions
of the Eighth SEW Congress." (ADN, 15 May
1987.) The only major newspaper which provided

extensive coverage of this congress was the SED's
official organ *Neues Deutschland* (New Germany).
Perhaps the only unusual thing that occurred at the
congress was that Chairman Schmitt was re-elected
with fewer than 94 percent of the delegates' votes, a
very low percentage for an orthodox communist
party (*VSB 87*).

The demands and resolutions produced by the
congress provide an accurate picture of what the
SEW's overall policies and positions were. In defense, it totally backed Soviet and GDR demands,
something about which party chairman Schmitt
makes no bones: "We—the Communists of West
Berlin—support with all our strength the peace
policy of the Soviet Union, the GDR and the other
socialist states." It favored all disarmament proposals made by the Soviet Union, asserting that
"this is ever more necessary because the most aggressive quarters in the U.S. and Western Europe
bound up with the military-industrial complex are
concocting ever more pretexts to frustrate disarmament moves." It called for a replacement of deterrence by "a security partnership with the socialist
states." Nuclear and chemical weapons–free zones
in Central Europe should be created, nuclear tests
stopped, SDI terminated, and no SDI research permitted in West Berlin, and the city should not be
"illegally" involved in NATO strategy or "as a
NATO policy tool." (*ND*, 17 May 1987; *IB*, September 1987.)

In foreign affairs the party was an unfailing
spokesman for the SED's policies, especially with
regard to the status of West Berlin. It stated that it is
time to end the backward-looking "myth of a metropolis," that is, of one Berlin. "West Berlin is not
'part' of a whole city; it is a large city developed in
nearly 40 years under the special conditions of an
occupied territory." Schmitt asked rhetorically "if it
is not time for the governing mayor [of West Berlin]
to state publicly that his competence is confined to
West Berlin and nothing else." West Berlin's need
for broad contacts with the GDR requires that its
government recognize the GDR and "stop interfering with the internal affairs of the GDR. Indeed, it
corresponds to the spirit of the present for the Senate to recognize the GDR borders as state borders.
It is time for all West Berlin authorities at least to
respect the GDR citizenship." In 1988 the SEW
again called for "strict implementation" of the four-
power agreement on West Berlin, ignoring the fact
that that agreement applies to *all* of Berlin. It also
proposed a reduction of U.S., British and French

occupation forces in West Berlin "to symbolic dimensions." (*FBIS*, 13 October 1988.)

Schmitt specifically criticized speeches made on 30 April 1987 by Chancellor Helmut Kohl and former Mayor Diepgen on the occasion of the 750th anniversary of Berlin, which, in Schmitt's words, were "slanderous attacks against the GDR." The GDR officially denies that reunification is a future possibility or that Berlin is "in a waiting mode to become the German capital." The SEW agreed entirely with the SED's rationale for the Berlin Wall, which it called "the secured state border of the GDR vis-à-vis West Berlin: it has led to stability in the area and will remain in place until the reasons for which it was erected in the first place disappear" (i.e., Western meddling). (*ND*, 16–17 May 1987; *IB*, September 1987; ADN, 25 May 1987.)

Like the DKP in West Germany, the SEW is open to "united action" with Social Democrats, the Alternative List (in which the West Berlin Greens participate), and trade unions, especially in the "fight for peace." It joined in the opposition to the census, invoking the "right of resistance" on the grounds that the census violated "basic constitutional rights." It joined many other groups in a demonstration protesting against "police terror and for democratic rights" on the occasion of President Ronald Reagan's visit to West Berlin 12 June 1987, when he demanded that the wall be torn down. (*ND*, 29 and 30 June 1987.) It struggles against unemployment, "poverty caused by social dismantling," "hopelessness," denial of renters' rights, capitalist application of education and technology which harms workers, destruction of the environment, especially the "continuing liquidation of small gardens, fields and forests for the profit-oriented housing development policy," relegation of thousands of artists to a minimal standard of living, and discrimination against women and foreigners. "Our party takes the view that the foreign workers are part of the working class and that we have a common enemy: monopoly capital." (*ND*, 16–17 May 1987; *ID*, 15 May 1987.)

Despite its efforts to become a part of a broad front of "progressive" groups, the SEW's collaboration has never been sought by the ruling SPD-AL coalition, which had emerged victorious from the elections of January 1989. In 1989, the SEW joined with the DKP and SED to condemn the right-wing Republicans, who in January 1989 won 7.5 percent of the votes and entered the Senate (which success will entitle them to two seats in the Bundestag after the federal elections of December 1990). Together the three parties demanded the dissolution of all neo-Nazi parties.

The SEW shares in the "spirit of proletarian internationalism" and sends delegations to fraternal party congresses, especially in the GDR and Soviet Union. For the first time, it sent a representative to a congress of the Communist Party of the USA. Schmitt concluded his address at the SEW's Eighth Party Congress with the words: "Our future lies in our Marxist-Leninist firmness in principle, in our undeviating orientation to the interests of the working people, and in our indestructible alliance with the CPSU, with the SED, and with the entire world communist movement." (*ND*, 16–17 May 1987.)

Search for a New Policy Direction. The year 1989 brought the SEW so many bitter shocks and setbacks that its only alternatives were to attempt to reform itself or to perish. Campaigning under the banners of the rights to work and to live in peace and democracy, the SEW's performance in the January 29, 1989, elections were dismal. The party's public claims that it had made an important contribution to the defeat of the CDU-FDP coalition were not credible, given the SEW's extremely low vote count. More and more SEW activists realized that such poor electoral performances were likely to continue as long as the SEW retained its character as an unswervingly pro-SED and Moscow-oriented party, tightly organized along standard Marxist-Leninist lines, financially dependent on East Berlin, and internally divided over *glasnost'* and *perestroika*. West Berlin voters had not forgotten the gist of the message which former SED Politburo member Alfred Neumann had brought from the SED to the SEW's party congress in May 1987: "The SED and the SEW are linked not only by common roots, traditions, and the same goals and class interests, but also by the socialist worldview and the Communists' confidence in victory." (ADN, 16 May 1987.)

In January 1989, the SEW's official organ reported on the heated discussions within the party concerning its future direction. Unlike the DKP majority, which was rejecting the applicability of Gorbachev's *perestroika* in Germany and voting down the reformist faction within the party, the SEW concluded that "*glasnost'* and *perestroika* must be recognized as principles of socialism," and that "new thinking over the SEW's relationship with the SED must be developed." The SEW began a process of shifting its ideological loyalties from the GDR to the Soviet Union. (DPA, 23 January; *RAD*

Background Report 14, 27 January 1989.) Like the DKP, the SEW departed from the SED line for the first time in June by expressing West Berlin Communists' "shock [at] and opposition" to the Chinese communist leadership for its brutal suppression of demonstrators in Beijing. "We belong to a party that is characterized by profound humanism, the broadest democracy, and a firm class position." SEW members were annoyed and angered by the SED's pressure to make the SEW change this position. (*FBIS-WEU*, 22 June, 12 July, 14 August 1989.)

The dramatic changes which occurred in the GDR and the rest of Europe (see the preceding essay on the FRG) in the fall of 1989 surprised and overwhelmed the SEW, which had historically been so servile to and dependent on the discredited SED. On 15 October the SEW changed the name of its newspaper from *Die Wahrheit* (The truth) to the less arrogant and offensive *Neue Zeitung* (New newspaper). The first issue under the new name asserted that "the times today call for new thinking, new acting—nothing remains as it is." The SEW Communists hope that the *Neue Zeitung* will appeal to readers outside their own tiny circle and will serve "the growing need of the leftist, democratic, trade-union spectrum for a dialogue toward a common new orientation." (*Frankfurter Allgemeine Zeitung*, 16 October.)

In the wake of this political hurricane, which blew down the Berlin Wall on 9 November, the SEW's entire Politburo and Secretariat announced its resignation in order to prevent "unjustified tensions from emerging within the party" (*ND*, 15 November). A committee was formed to plan a meeting of all party members early in 1990. A unanimous resolution recognized that the massive pressure of the GDR's population had forced a change toward a renewal of socialism, but it pointed to risks that the momentous events could be misused by "class enemies" bent upon creating a reunified Germany in the capitalists' image. The nationalist outburst could wipe away "progressive positions" which had been achieved in West Berlin. (*ND*, 21 November.)

Nevertheless, Klaus-Dieter Heiser, an SEW leader, emphasized that "the process of renewal within the SEW was accelerated by the development in the GDR," and that there would be a personal, programmatic, and political renewal of the SEW. He admitted that in the past, the SEW had idealized the achievements and situation in the GDR and had therefore been blind to, or had not wanted to see the growing alienation between the people and the leaders of the SED and the state. "We had believed that the collective human rights developed in socialism were to be valued above the individual human rights, such as freedom of movement, which had been fought for in the bourgeois revolution." What is astounding about Heiser's admissions is not only their self-critical openness, but the fact that they were reported in *Neues Deutschland*! (*ND*, 28 November.)

The SEW now struggles to survive in a city which became very different after 9 November 1989. The former SEW chairman had spoken in 1987 about the "myth of a metropolis"—that there is one Berlin—and had asserted that "West Berlin is not part of a whole city." But Berliners now undergo only cursory security checks when passing through the border for shopping and visiting. By Christmas 1989 they could even stroll through the Brandenburg Gate. West Berliners also shop on the eastern side of the border, and some are even looking for apartments or real estate there. West Berlin's mayor, Walter Momper, regularly meets with his East Berlin counterpart to deal with the urban problems presented by the disappearing border, such as merging transport, garbage-removal or telephone systems. West German businessmen are working out joint ventures with East German firms, since such undertakings were legalized for early 1990. With some kind of unity in the offing, with the SED in disarray, and with noticeable shifts in the political architecture in Europe, the SEW and DKP are having to learn to address new kinds of problems and to survive in a radically changed political environment.

Wayne C. Thompson
Virginia Military Institute

Great Britain

Population. 57,028,169
Party. Communist Party of Great Britain (CPGB)
Founded. 1920
Membership. 8,000 (*Radio Free Europe Research*, 20 December 1989); 7,500 (*NYT*, 2 February 1990)
General Secretary. Gordon McLennan

Political Committee. Ron Halvarson (chairman), Gordon McLennan (general secretary), Ian McKay, Gary Pocock, Martin Jacques, Jack Ashton, Kerin Halpin, Vishnu Sharma, Nina Temple (*Morning Star*, 21 May 1985)
Executive Committee. 45 members
Status. Legal
Last Congress. Forty-first, 25–28 November 1989
Last Election. June 1987, 0.1 percent, no representation
Auxiliary Organizations. Young Communist League (YCL); Liaison Committee for the Defense of Trade Unions (LCDTU)
Publications. *Morning Star, Marxism Today, Communist Focus, Challenge Spark, Our History Journal, Economic Bulletin, Medicine in Society, Education Today and Tomorrow, The New Worker, Seven Days.*

The CPGB is a recognized political party and contests both local and national elections. It does not, however, operate in Northern Ireland, which it does not recognize as British territory. The party has had no members in the House of Commons since 1950, but has one member, Lord Milford, in the non-elected House of Lords.

Leadership and Party Organization. The CPGB is divided into four divisions: the National Congress; the Executive Committee and its departments; districts; and local and factory branches. Constitutionally, the biennial National Congress is the party's supreme authority and, during most of its history—but not in recent years—rubber-stamped the decisions of the Political Committee. Responsibility for overseeing the party's activities rests with the 45-member Executive Committee, which is elected by the National Congress and meets every two months. The Executive Committee is made up of members of special committees, full-time departmental heads, and the sixteen members of the Political Committee, the party's innermost controlling conclave.

Party leaders are deeply preoccupied with the continuing decline in support for the party. Electorally, the party is so battered that it no longer contests as many seats as it once did. Membership, at fewer than 8,000 (only some 50 percent of whom have actually paid their fees), is at its lowest point since World War II. The decline in electoral support was most graphically illustrated in Britain's last general elections (1987) when the party's nineteen candidates polled a mere 6,078 votes.

However, the poor showing of the CPGB at the polls belies the party's still important strength in the trade-union movement and in influencing opinion. Although it does not directly control any individual trade union, the party is represented on most union executive committees and has played a major role in most government-union confrontations of recent years. The CPGB's influence is partly attributable to low turnouts in most union elections, to the fact that it is the only party seeking to control the outcome of these elections, and to its close interest in industrial affairs, which ensures support from workers who might not support other aspects of the party's program.

Domestic Affairs. The rapid change occurring in Eastern Europe and the Soviet Union during the last months of 1989 strongly affected the CPGB, as well as the entire communist movement in Britain. For years, the Communists in Britain have been seriously divided as their electoral support has faded. A bitter internecine struggle intensified throughout the last decade between the Eurocommunist CPGB and other more Stalinist breakaway groups who were unstinting in their support of the ideology and policies of the Soviet Union and the East European bloc.

The crumbling of ruling parties in Eastern Europe as well as in the Soviet Union humiliated the entire communist movement in Britain and led during the last months of 1989 to a quickening decline in membership. The Eurocommunist CPGB, more liberal and reform-minded, took some solace in finding itself more in the mainstream of events than any of its competitor groups within the communist movement. Yet this was small comfort when the CPGB reflected on how the tumultuous events in the East would affect its future.

The main focus of CPGB activity during late 1989 was the Forty-first Party Congress which was held in London in late November. The congress was a regularly scheduled biennial session, but it could hardly have come at a more momentous time, occurring as it did while the Czechoslovakian regime was collapsing.

Speaker after speaker at the congress, including General Secretary Gordon McLennan (who will retire in 1990), welcomed the changes occurring in Czechoslovakia and in the other East European nations. The tone of the comments was both biting and "I told you so." It was clear that the CPGB leadership and delegates felt vindicated by their long and consistent criticism of the 1968 Soviet suppression of the Prague Spring and in their criticism, however mild, of these regimes for their suppression of human rights. They also displayed great satisfaction with their longtime support of Eurocommunism as compared to the hard-line views of their breakaway rivals, the Communist Party of Britain and the New Communist Party.

Yet, the congress also evinced a strong mood of despair. Delegate after delegate acknowledged that however pleased they were at being proved "correct" over the last decades, their pleasure was sharply tempered by the danger which their party now faced.

Martin Jacques, the party's leading ideologue, member of the CPGB Executive Committee, and editor of the party monthly, *Marxism Today*, took the lead in offering the leadership's reaction to the crisis. Jacques introduced and the delegates approved, a document, *Manifesto for New Times*, that set forth a new strategy for the party. Drafted by Jacques, the document declares that the communist system as it has been during the century is finished:

This is the end of the road for the communist system as we have known it: the central plan, the authoritarian state, the single-party system, the subjugated civil society. Stalinism is dead, and Leninism—its theory of the state, its concept of the party, the absence of civil society, its notion of revolution—has also had its day.

Jacques went on to add that the international communist movement was also at an end, a victim of its own inflexibility and isolation from a democratic mandate. In place of the old ways, the *Manifesto* argued for a new flexibility, a willingness to recast the communist movement as part of the social-democratic tradition and therefore a willingness to work within a pluralistic democratic system.

Ironically, while arguing in its *Manifesto* for new flexibility, the CPGB leadership, strongly supported by the party congress, "decisively rejected" any move to make peace with the breakaway "Stalinist" groups, such as the New Communist Party or the Communist Party of Britain. In refusing to promote unity in the face of its crisis, the CPGB was continuing the long-standing conflict within the British communist movement which has been building for some years.

The main dispute has been and continues to be mainly between the CPGB's Executive Committee and the newspaper, *Morning Star*, once recognized by the communist, but separate, People's Press

Printing Society (PPPS). Throughout 1989, the PPPS continued to be in the hands of Stalinist opponents of the Executive Committee's Eurocommunist policies. The *Morning Star* group has historically been bitterly opposed to the leadership's criticisms (muted though they were), of the Soviet Union and to the transformation of the party's theoretical journal, *Marxism Today*, into a popular, but broad-based magazine.

Intraparty conflict during 1989 occurred in the context of, and as a reaction to, several consecutive years of stinging defeats for the political left in Britain. Most important of these have been the miners' strike of 1984–1985, the left's debacle in controlling the Liverpool city government during 1985–1986, together with the years of unsuccessful struggle with the Thatcher government on a whole range of issues. As a result, the already fractured communist movement drifted into an even sharper debate within itself. Who was to blame for these defeats? How should they proceed to bolster the party's position, along with the position of the left? Should the party adopt a more cooperative relationship with the Labour Party and even parties to the right? How should it deal with the British union movement?

The Eurocommunist majority in control of the CPGB has tended to answer these questions by advocating broad alliances with less ideological leftist parties and groups. This has infuriated the harder left, which has reacted angrily through *Morning Star* and its political group, the Communist Campaign Group, as well as the breakaway New Communist Party. To be sure, there have been fractious problems within this opposition, but there is vocal agreement in charging that the Eurocommunist leadership is guilty of soft-headed thinking that has caused the movement to lose its leadership of the working class.

A pattern of vicious attacks from each side against the other, together with Eurocommunist actions to expel rebels from the CPGB have almost completely dominated the time of all the participants, a circumstance which has further hurt the appeal of the party. The 1987 election results graphically showed how extensive the damage has become. Whereas the party fielded 35 candidates and won more than 11,000 votes in 1983, it only offered 19 candidates and won less than 7,000 votes in 1987.

The split seemed to become permanent in 1988, when *Morning Star* and its political group held their own congress. About 150 delegates representing

1,600 dissident Communists met in London and agreed to "re-establish" the Communist Party. They took the name "Communist Party of Britain," as compared to the name "Communist Party of Great Britain," which is used by the Eurocommunists. Predictably, they claimed that they had finally recreated the true communist party, and that socialism would be "firmly" on its agenda.

The CPGB continued to support campaigns including demonstrations against most aspects of government policy. The main CPGB efforts were directed toward the nurses-pay dispute; funding and administration of the National Health Service, which had become a major national political issue during the 1987 election campaign; the government's efforts to pass legislation adopting a new individual poll tax in place of property taxes; and major educational reforms. The CPGB has also strongly supported the resurgence of union militancy, and this advocacy has resulted in an upsurge in strike activity.

Auxiliary Organizations. In industry, CPGB activity centers on its approximately 200 workplace branches. Its umbrella organization in industry is the LCDTU. Although the CPGB is riven by internal disputes, its trade-union structure can still command considerable support from prominent trade union leaders.

The YCL is the youth wing of the party, but has only about 500 members.

The party retains a number of financial interests, including Central Books, Lawrence and Wishart Publisher, Farleigh Press, London Caledonian Printers, Rodell Properties, the Labour Research Department, and the Marx Memorial Library.

International Views and Activities. The CPGB is vocally supporting the upheavals in the Soviet Union and Eastern Europe. It is arguing in favor of multiparty systems, free elections, adherence to human-rights guarantees, an end to the secret-police institutions, and a broader European integration. During 1989 the party has also adopted a more pro-EC stance, reversing years of opposition. The CPGB strongly supports antigovernment activity in South Africa and condemns the apartheid policy.

The Gorbachev reforms in the Soviet Union have naturally attracted the CPGB's intense interest. During 1989, the CPGB became much more openly supportive of those reforms, especially in the wake of Gorbachev's visit to Britain. For their part, *Morn-*

ing Star and its Communist Party of Britain, as well as the New Communist Party, are more tentative in their support for Gorbachev and the changes in Eastern Europe. While supportive of a more humane socialism, these groups seem to be more edgy than the CPGB, as they continue to fret over what they regard as a "revisionist" danger.

Other Marxist Groups. Besides the CPGB, several small, mainly Trotskyist groups are also active. Although some of these groups were growing swiftly in the 1970s, their memberships are now waning.

The most important of the Trotskyist groups is Militant Tendency, which derives its name from its paper of the same name. Militant Tendency claims to be merely a loose tendency of opinion within the Labour Party, but there is no doubt that it possesses its own distinctive organization, and for some years has been pursuing a policy of "entryism" (the tactic of penetrating the larger, more moderate Labour Party). Militant Tendency controls about 50 Labour Party constituencies.

The other significant Trotskyist organizations are the Socialist Workers' Party (SWP) and the Workers' Revolutionary Party (WRP). The SWP has been particularly active in single-issue campaigns, notably the anti-unemployment campaign. It gave active support to striking miners' families, but, in fact, enjoys little support in the coal-mining industry. The WRP's activities are more secretive, but are known to center in the engineering, mining, theater, and auto industries. It focuses its attention on the young and has set up six Youth Training Centres, which are primarily concerned with recruitment.

Gerald A. Dorfman
Hoover Institution

Greece

Population. 10,041,414
Party. Communist Party of Greece (Kommunistikon Komma Ellados; KKE)
Founded.1921
Membership. 50,000 (est.)
General Secretary. Grigoris Farakos (65, Greek, electrical engineer, former editor of *Rizospastis*)

Politburo. Kharilaos Florakis, Grigoris Farakos (65), Nikos Kaloudis (71), Loula Logara (61), Kostas Tsolakis (61), Orestis Kolozof (56), Dimitris Gondikas (48), Aleka Papariga (43), Takis Mamatsis (63); candidate members: Dimitris Kostopoulos (49), Spyros Khalvatzis (43), Dimitris Androulakis (37), Dimitris Karagoules (37), P. Lafazanis, G. Oragasakis, Thanasis Karteros (44)

Secretariat. Giannis Mavrakis (36), Kostas Voulgaropoulos (49)

Chairman. Kharilaos Florakis

Status. Legal

Last Congress. Twelfth, 12–16 May 1987, Athens

Last Election. 5 November 1989, 10.97 percent (as part of the "Coalition of the Left and Progress"), 21 of 300 seats

Auxiliary Organization. Communist Youth of Greece (KNE)

Publications. *Rizospastis* (daily); *Kommunistiki Epitheorisi* (Communist review, KOMEP) monthly theoretical review

In 1989, the communist party (KKE) moved to the forefront of the political stage. The talks between the KKE and the Greek Left (E.AR), which had started in the previous year, and which were intensified in November of that year, reached a conclusion in February 1989 when the two parties formed the "Coalition of the Left and Progress," with Kharilaos Florakis, the then general secretary of the KKE, as its chairman.

The Coalition of the Left adopted a highly critical stance toward the economic scandals allegedly perpetrated by certain leaders of the Panhellenic Socialist Movement (PASOK), including Andreas Papandreou himself (premier, 1981–1989). The cleaning up (*katharsis*) of the scandals became a key plank in the Coalition's electoral platform as the parliamentary election of 18 June approached. The punishment of those involved in the scandals was also the objective of the conservative New Democracy (N.D.) Party. Thus, by a strange twist of political expediency, the conservative N.D. and the Coalition of the Left found themselves traveling the same road. While the charges concerning the scandals were not without foundation, one may suspect that the two parties—the N.D. and the Coalition—focused heavily on the issue of *katharsis* because they hoped to score electoral gains at the expense of PASOK. The Coalition, in particular, expected that many left-leaning PASOK voters would desert their

party in disgust and shift their electoral support to the Coalition.

In the parliamentary election, PASOK lost heavily. From the 2,916,735 votes it received in June 1985, its electoral strength fell to 2,550,402. The number of PASOK's seats in the Chamber of Deputies went from 165 down to 125. On the other hand, the Coalition candidates received 855,559 votes, as compared to 746,660 received in June 1985 by both KKE and E.AR candidates, who ran separately at that time. This increase for the Coalition was partly due to a sizable shift of PASOK voters. The Coalition elected 28 deputies, a marked increase from the 14 seats its two member parties had held in the previous legislature, an increase which was due in part to a new, more proportional electoral system enacted shortly before the election by PASOK and KKE votes, with the rather transparent goal of preventing the New Democracy Party from winning a clear majority of seats in the legislature.

Because no party gained such a majority in the Chamber of Deputies, N.D. and the Coalition of the Left eventually agreed to form jointly a coalition government so that the statute of limitations would not prevent prosecution of those responsible for the scandals. This government, led by Tzanis Tzanetakis, an N.D. deputy as the premier, set as its principal task the *katharsis* of the scandals.

This move completely legitimized the communist left as a full-fledged and equal participant in the political process. For its part, the KKE, as a member of the coalition government, moderated its positions at least rhetorically. The New Democracy and the Coalition of the Left continued to disagree on the future of the U.S. military installations in Greece, on privatization, on the electoral system (N.D. wants a reinforced proportional, the Coalition of the Left a purely proportional one), and on certain economic issues; but on the whole they managed to work together harmoniously by pushing under the rug the divisive issues and concentrating instead on the *katharsis* of the scandals, the one issue on which they were in agreement. During the summer, they pushed forward the parliamentary procedure leading to the indictment of the accused, including A. Papandreou.

The KKE's participation in the Tzanetakis government met considerable opposition within the party and especially within the youth organization (KNE). Kostas Kappos, the party's parliamentary spokesman, voiced strong criticism and resigned from his party posts. His resignation was followed by the resignation of at least twelve members of the party's Central Committee. The editor of *Odigitis*, the KNE's official organ, openly attacked Florakis and his move to join the conservative New Democracy Party in a coalition government, and this sparked a serious clash between KKE and KNE. In late September, the entire KNE leadership was dismissed.

To differentiate the party from the Coalition of the Left, Florakis relinquished in July his post of KKE general secretary and assumed the largely honorific title of chairman, a post created by the twelfth party congress in 1987 but left vacant. Grigoris Farakos, a Politburo member since 1961 and the editor of *Rizospastis*, was elected general secretary. It is widely believed that this is an interim step until the election of Dimitris Androulakis, a candidate member of the Politburo at the present time.

Florakis remains chairman of the Coalition of the Left and Progress and is working closely, and apparently in tandem, with the E.AR's secretary Leonidas Kyrkos. At the same time, Florakis participates in the deliberations of the KKE Politburo, where he exerts considerable influence. Under the Florakis leadership, the Coalition of the Left has begun to play a rather constructive, nonrevolutionary role in Greek politics. In fact, the traditional revolutionary rhetoric—and action—have been taken over by the terrorist organizations "17 November," "1st of May," "Greek Peoples Resistance" (ELA), and certain small, extremist groups embracing a more dogmatic form of Marxist-Leninist ideology. The electoral results indicate that all these groups do not represent more than 1 percent of the electorate. The trend toward moderation displayed by the Coalition of the Left and the KKE may lead to a change in the KKE's official name, as some already advocate. A more likely development is the transformation of the Coalition of the Left and Progress into a permanent, unified party, with the identities of the KKE and the E.AR submerged in the process. In late December, the Coalition leadership took two steps which seem to point in this direction. It established a Political Secretariat and instituted the category of "member of the Coalition," which is distinct from membership in the KKE and the E.AR. The Coalition already espouses a fairly moderate socialist ideology without revolutionary overtones. Currently, it sees its principal role as being the defender of the economic interests of the lower-income groups.

In the election of 5 November—held before the PASOK leaders were brought to trial—the Coalition of the Left lost approximately 121,000 votes, as compared to its showing in June, and ended with 21 seats in the Chamber of Deputies, a decrease from the 28 it held in the legislature elected in June. Most of the lost votes were those of PASOK followers who in June had left their party because of the scandals. For the second time within six months, no political party gained a clear majority of seats in the legislature. Florakis, as the leader of the Coalition of the Left, rejected overtures by PASOK leader A. Papandreou to form jointly a coalition government, apparently because he continued to feel committed to the *katharsis*. Eventually, to break the deadlock, all three parties—N.D., PASOK, and the Coalition of the Left—formed an "all-party" government under veteran economist Xenophon Zolotas, aged 85. This move effectively neutralized the "scandals issue," since it will be rather difficult to prosecute A. Papandreou while PASOK participates in the Zolotas government. Because of the participation of PASOK and the Coalition of the Left in the "all-party" government, the issue of the scandals, which previously prevented their cooperation, has lost much of its political force, and for this reason the chances for a PASOK-Caoliton of the Left government after the next election in April 1990 are very real, since N.D. is not likely to win a clear majority of seats under the present electoral system. An election next April may become inevitable because of the need to elect a new president of the republic in March. Under the constitution, to obtain that position a candidate must receive at least 180 positive votes in the Chamber of Deputies. With the chamber's current composition, no party or political camp can muster 180 votes for its candidate. Barring agreement among the three parties (or at least between PASOK and N.D.) on a common candidate, and such agreement is unlikely, a new election will be necessary in April.

In brief, the major development in 1989 is the emergence of the KKE and the Coalition of the Left as the "king maker" in Greek politics.

Leadership and Organization. The KKE has not changed its organizational structure since the days when it was illegal—except that now it practices less secrecy about the identity of members and cadres. The party members are organized in cells (*pyrines*) in factories, workplaces, and schools, or in neighborhoods for those not gainfully employed, such as housewives or retired persons. Party factions (*fraxies*) are organized by party members within trade unions, professional organizations, and cooperatives in the countryside. Within many professional associations, the party has a separate entity which presents its own slate of candidates during internal elections. The same applies to PASOK and the New Democracy Party. Smaller towns and villages have local KKE organizations headed by a party secretary. This also applies to the various sections of the larger cities, such as Piraeus, Salonika, and Athens. These major cities have, in addition, "city committees" headed by secretaries who are also members of the Central Committee. Each *nomos* (prefecture) has its own "*nomos* committee," headed by a secretary. In addition, the country is divided into major regions such as Crete, the Peloponnesus, Thessaly, Epirus, Macedonia, and Thrace, each headed by a regional party secretary.

The most powerful organ of the party is the Politburo, whose members are elected by the Central Committee. The CC is elected by the party congress, which statutorily meets every four years. The Central Committee has approximately 100 members. The highest executive official in the party is its general secretary, a post now occupied by Grigoris Farakos, a graduate of the Polytechnical School and a party member since 1941. Elected to the Central Committee for the first time in 1961, he became a member of the Politburo in 1968. Before his elevation to the post of general secretary, Farakos was the editor of the KKE daily *Rizospastis*. The twelfth congress, in 1987, created a new post, that of chairman, which is now occupied by Kharilaos Florakis, the former general secretary.

The Greek Left (E.AR) was formerly known as KKE-Interior, a splinter group which separated from KKE in 1968. E.AR has abandoned Marxism-Leninism, together with its original designation. For the record, we note that E.AR has a 101-member Central Committee and an Executive Bureau of which Leonidas Kyrkos is the first secretary and Gr. Giannaros, D. Giatzoglou, Petros Kounalakis, Sp. Likoudis, Ar. Manolakos, Mikh. Papagiannakis, Stergios Pitsiorlas, Giannis Toundas, M. Tandalidis, D. Khatzisocratis, and D. Psikhoyios are members. E.AR follows a moderate Marxist view, and its main support comes from leftist intellectuals and professionals. A splinter group from the original KKE-Interior exists now under the leadership of G. Banias and uses the title "KKE-Interior/Renovating Left," but its following is very limited, as shown by recent electoral results.

Views and Positions. In 1989, the KKE, as the major partner in the Coalition of Left and Progress, intensified its criticism of and opposition to PASOK, its criticism focusing primarily on the economic scandals allegedly committed by the PASOK leadership. Since PASOK's inception in 1974, the KKE has taken a rather supportive stand toward PASOK because of the latter's anti-Western, anti-capitalist views. When PASOK came to power in 1981, the KKE cooperated and supported the government's extensive programs of social benefits for the lower-income groups, its emphasis on the public sector and rather negative attitude toward private enterprise, hostility to NATO and the EC, its call for the removal of the U.S. military installations in Greece, and its call for the "socialist transformation" of society. In March and April 1985, the KKE supported with its votes in the legislature the revision of the Constitution and the election of a new president of the republic favored by PASOK. In the following years, the KKE had reasons to regret its support for the revision of the Constitution.

The relations between the KKE and PASOK cooled off considerably after the 1985 election because of the economic austerity policies PASOK was forced to impose owing to the deteriorating economic conditions. The estrangement between the two parties intensified after 1988, when the first hints about serious economic scandals began to surface. Public-opinion polls conducted during the year indicated that a large percentage of voters (ranging from 15 to 20 percent) was "undecided" as to which party to support in the next parliamentary election. The polls also showed that the vast majority of the "undecided" were former PASOK supporters. The KKE assumed that many of them would seek a new political home within a broader entity of the left. This wider alliance was formed by the KKE and the E.AR in February 1989.

As a result of this alliance and of the subsequent political developments, which for the first time brought the KKE into the government, the KKE has considerably toned down its rhetoric against the EC and NATO and against "capitalism" and free enterprise. While it continues to call for the removal of all U.S. military installations from Greece, it has not allowed this issue to prevent its participation in the Tzanetakis government (June–October 1989) or in the present "all-party" Zolotas government (November 1989–). Symbolic of the party's less strident anti-Americanism were two visits within the last few months of 1989 by the U.S. ambassador, newly appointed Michael Sotirkhos, to the KKE head-quarters in Perissos for the first time in history.

After a rather long period of confusion and un-certainty, the KKE has accepted Gorbachev's pol-icies. In dealing with the collapse of the communist regimes in Eastern Europe, the KKE has adopted the view that the era of a "wrong" socialist model has now come to end, opening the way for a humane and democratic model. It may be noted that the party leadership upholds firmly the practices of "democratic centralism," as G. Farakos clearly stated in a recent (9 December) speech to a con-ference of party cadres. In December, the KKE condemned the 1968 Soviet invasion of Czechoslo-vakia as a "product of the Cold War which emanated from the West but was not limited to it."

The somewhat more moderate views of the party leadership are not shared fully by many of the rank and file who remain attached to their traditional Marxist-Leninist views and regard with dismay the policies of the party leadership and its cooperation with the "class enemy." This is particularly true among the younger members and in the KNE rank and file. They appear to be equally uneasy about Gorbachev's policies and the dismantling of the communist regimes in Europe. The KKE lead-ership tries to walk a path between the traditional views of the rank and file and its new perception of its role as a full-fledged participant in a multiparty democratic system.

Without openly renouncing any of its ideological staples, the party leadership tries to avoid any pro-nounced references to the dictatorship of the pro-letariat, the class struggle, and the revolution. Dur-ing the recent discussions which President of the Republic Khristos Sartzetakis held with the leaders of New Democracy (Kon. Mitsotakis), PASOK (A. Papandreou), and Coalition of the Left (Kh. Flo-rakis), Florakis focused primarily on efforts to pro-tect the "automatic cost of living adjustment" and to obtain assurances that social programs benefiting the lower-income groups will not be severely cur-tailed by the "all-party" government in its efforts to achieve economic stabilization. His comments and overall attitude during the discussion that led to the "all-party" Zolotas government were moderate and constructive.

A major issue for the KKE and the Coalition of the Left is the electoral system, which they wish to change into a purely proportional one. Such a change will enable the Coalition of the Left to increase the number of its seats in the legislature (possibly to 30 or 33), and at the same time make it impossible for the New Democracy Party to win a majority of seats and form a government. Currently, PASOK and the Coalition of the Left (together rep-resenting the leftist, socialist camp) account for 53 to 54 percent of the popular vote.

During 1989, the KKE and the Coalition of the Left made the scandals one of their major issues, to the extent that because of the scandals, they twice refused to form a joint government with PASOK (in June 1989 and again in November 1989), although such a coalition government would have enabled the leftist, socialist camp to continue governing Greece even after PASOK had lost its own majority in the legislature. The issue of the scandals, however, may not be an insurmountable obstacle next April if the New Democracy Party fails to win a majority and PASOK issues a call to the Coalition of the Left for cooperation.

The KKE and the Coalition of the Left strongly denounced the assassination in September of Pavlos Bakoyiannis, a New Democracy deputy and the son-in-law of Kon. Mitsotakis, by "17 November." The party has also been critical of other terrorist actions by "17 November" or ELA.

The traditional revolutionary, anticapitalist views are now being advocated openly by two clan-destine terrorist groups with political pretensions, namely, "17 November" and ELA. These two orga-nizations have engaged in bombings and assassina-tions. Each such action is accompanied by long political statements sent to the newspapers. The statements show extensive familiarity with Marxist-Leninist ideology and with Greek economic and political conditions, current and past. The group "17 November" recently called on all like-minded individuals to form a new revolutionary movement, but its efforts are seriously handicapped by its need for secrecy. In any event, the call was rejected by ELA in December, when this organization placed bombs at the EC office in Athens and at a police station in the suburb of Kalithea. In separate state-ments both organizations have denounced the KKE as an instrument of the capitalist establishment.

Domestic Activities. During the year, the party sought to promote its objectives mostly through the Coalition of the Left and Progress. The leader of the Coalition of the Left is Kharilaos Florakis who was general secretary of the communist party until July, when he became its chairman. For all practical purposes, Florakis continues to speak for the KKE, since no evidence exists as of this essay's composition that he has lost his influence within the KKE's Politburo.

In the early months after its inception, the Coalition of the Left focused on the preparation of its electoral campaign in anticipation of the election of 18 June. The major thrust of its campaign was directed against PASOK, which had "betrayed" the cause of "change"—a rather nebulous concept presumably meaning a socialist transformation of Greek society—with its "antipeople" economic measures and above all with its "plundering of the public treasury" of sums allegedly amounting to hundreds of millions of dollars.

In spite of its criticism of PASOK, the KKE refused to support a motion of nonconfidence introduced in the legislature by N.D. in February, and two months later voted for a bill to change the electoral system introduced by PASOK. Of course, the new electoral system favored the KKE.

In June, the party, as a member of the Coalition of the Left, supported a coalition government formed with the party of New Democracy. In the legislature, the Coalition's deputies and particularly the KKE spokesman, Kostas Kappos, focused heavily on the prosecution of the scandals. (The divisive issue of the U.S. bases was temporarily put aside to allow smooth cooperation within the coalition government.) The Coalition's deputies participated actively in the parliamentary moves for the establishment of the constitutionally required Special Court for former cabinet ministers, and for the indictment of A. Papandreou and of several other key PASOK ministers. In the fall, the party concentrated its efforts on the electoral campaign for the election of 5 November.

Following the election of 18 June and the decision to join the New Democracy Party in a coalition government, the KKE faced a serious internal crisis. Several Central Committee members expressed strong reservations about the decision and eventually twelve of them resigned. Opposition was also voiced by some Politburo members, one of whom was Khalvatzis, but they were persuaded to accept the decision by Florakis, who gained unanimous support for his moves. The crisis did not lead to a split. Somewhat more vexing for the leadership was the opposition within the youth organization (KNE). The KKE's Politburo made efforts to effect reconciliation, but it finally applied the principle of democratic centralism and summarily dismissed the entire executive bureau of the KNE and replaced the editor of the KNE organ *Odigitis*. Nevertheless, the KNE rank and file, who are emotionally attached to the revolutionary rhetoric, and who lack the sobering experiences of their elders, continue to be restless and confused.

As a participant in the Zolotas government, the party now faces a problem because it cannot openly encourage strikes and demonstrations against the economic measures the government has been forced to take. On the other hand, it fears that it may lose its influence in the trade unions to the benefit of more radical elements. Strikes and demonstrations have taken place nonetheless, with or without the party's overt encouragement.

The major challenge facing the party as 1989 came to an end was the need to retain the confidence of its following while shifting from the image and the practices of a revolutionary party to those of a party operating within a multiparty democratic system and having as its objective, not the violent overthrow of the capitalist system, but the defense of the economic interests of the lower-income groups.

International Contacts. In 1989, Florakis continued his visits to foreign countries and his contacts with other communist parties, but not as much as in years past. From 10 to 13 April, Florakis visited Beijing and Tianjin, and a week later, on 18 April, he visited the communist leadership in Paris. On 3 May, he met with Daniel Ortega of Nicaragua, who was visiting Greece at the invitation of A. Papandreou (who was still premier at the time). On 7 May, Florakis met with an Afghan delegation visiting Athens. On 18 September, Florakis visited Todor Zhivkov in Sofia, Bulgaria.

Other Marxist-Leninist Organizations. Several such organizations exist, but they are marginal groups with insignificant influence. Their members are mostly young unemployed university graduates, unemployed laborers, university students, and some young workers, especially in the construction trade. Of these fringe organizations, we mention the Greek International Union–Trotskyists, the Revolutionary Communist Party of Greece (EKKE), the Communist Party of Marxist-Leninists (KK-ML), the Organization of Marxist-Leninists of Greece (OMLE), the Socialist Revolutionary Union, the Greek Leninist Revolutionary Movement (ELEM), the Organization of Communists–Peoples Power (OK-LE), the Organization of Communist Internationalists of Greece (OKDE), and the Revolutionary Communist Party–Greek Section of the Fourth International. There are also a number of anarchist groups, and, of course, one should mention the terrorist organizations: "17 November," "1st of May," and ELA. These three organizations, and in particular "17 November," seem to have highly educated and well-informed individuals in their small and clandestine membership, judging from the proclamations they issue after every terrorist act.

D. G. Kousoulas
Professor Emeritus
Howard University

Iceland

Population. 248,501 (July 1989)
Party. People's Alliance (Althydubandalag; PA)
Founded. 1968
Membership. 3,000 (estimated)
Chairman. Olafur Ragnar Grimsson
Executive Committee. 14 members: Olafur Ragnar Grimsson (finance minister and professor of political science; 46), Steingrimur Sigfusson (minister of communications and agriculture and deputy party chairman), Svavar Gestsson (minister of education and former party chairman), Svanfridur Jonasdottir (ca. 40), Bjorn Sveinsson (PA party secretary; 40), Bjargey Einarsdottir (PA treasurer; 39), Alfheidur Ingadottir (managing director of a salmon farm; 41), Sigurjon Petursson (Reykjavik city council member; 52), Gudrun Agustsdottir (special assistant to the minister of education and Reykjavik city council member; 42), Ottar Proppe (civil servant, Hafnarfjordur Port Authority; 41), Asmundur Stefansson (economist and president of the Icelandic Federation of Labor; 44), Armann Magnusson (Icelandic Federation of Labor official; 40), Stephania Traustadottir (Office of Equal Rights Council; ca. 40), Kristin Olafsdottir (Reykjavik city council member, folksinger, and actress; 41)
Party Secretary. Bjorn Sveinsson
Central Committee. 70 members, 20 deputies
Status. Legal
Last Congress. 16–20 November 1989
Last Election. 1987, 13.3 percent, 8 of 63 seats

Auxiliary Organizations. Organization of Base Opponents (OBO; organizer of peace demonstrations against the U.S.-NATO bases)
Publications. *Thyodviljinn* (daily), Reykjavik; *Verkamadhurinn* (weekly), Akureyri; *Mjolnir* (weekly), Siglufjordhur

Iceland is a land of fire and ice, and its politics are known for their mixture of extremes. Not since the eleventh century, when the world's first parliament (the Althing, established in 930) voted unanimously to embrace Christianity, have Icelanders practiced the consensus politics of their Nordic brethren. In fact, few of the rules of European politics apply on this remote island, where personality plays a larger role in government than parties or institutions. Iceland is the only West European country to have a party with recent communist origins in government, but the People's Alliance (PA) fits few traditional communist molds and has largely discarded Marxist-Leninist rhetoric. It is currently in a broad center-left coalition of five parties and holds three cabinet portfolios.

The PA occupies the left flank of Icelandic politics. It is the successor to a long line of leftist parties dating back to 1930, when the Icelandic Communist Party (Kommunistaflokkur Islands) was formed out of a left-wing splinter group of the Social Democratic Party (Althuduflokkur; SDP). In 1938, the SDP split again, and one faction joined with the communists to create the United People's Party-Socialist Party (Sameingingar flokkur althydu-Sosialista flokkurinn; UPP-SP). In keeping with Iceland's tradition of setting its own course in history, this new amalgamation broke early with the Comintern, establishing the precedent of independent radical socialism without foreign ties. Still another faction from the SDP merged with the UPP-SP in 1956. The PA emerged in its present incarnation from the ashes of the then Socialist Unity Party in December 1968 (*RFE Research Report*, 12 January 1970). Before its inclusion in the current government, the PA last participated in a governing coalition with the agrarian Progressive Party (PP) from 1980 to 1983. That government dissolved after the parliamentary elections of April 1983, in which the PA netted little over 17 percent of the vote.

The PA's decline continued through the elections of April 1987, when it polled 13.4 percent and received only eight seats in the 63-seat Althing. For the first time, the reformist SDP, which received 15.2 percent of the vote and ten seats, outpolled the

PA. The chairman of the SDP and current foreign minister, Jon Baldvin Hannibalsson, outflanked the PA with his strong stump speaking and effective, if idiosyncratic leadership. But the PA lost votes to more than the SDP. An unconventional radical feminist party, the Women's List (Samtok um kvinnalista or Kvennalisti; WL), also continued to surge in the polls at the expense of the PA (*JPRS-WEU*, 29 September 1988).

When the center-right coalition government led by the Independence Party (Sjalfstaedisflokkur; IP) collapsed in September 1988, the PA entered a four-party coalition with the PP, the reformist SDP, and a splinter parliamentarian from the Progressives elected under the banner of the Association for Equality and Justice. With an even split in the lower house of the Althing and only a one-vote majority overall, the coalition was weak from the start. As the economic downturn that undermined the previous government moved into its third year and inflation continued at over 20 percent, pressure on the coalition mounted. Already a group of disparate parties spanning a wide spectrum of outlooks, the government was forced in September 1989 to invite the moderate Citizen's Party (Borgaraflokkur; CP) into the coalition.

The coalition formed by PP chairman and current prime minister Steingrimur Hermannsson was a major tactical coup both for him and for PA leader Olafur Ragnar Grimsson. Hermannsson, whose party commanded only 13 of 63 seats in the Althing, was able to put together a broad platform which all four parties could accept. Grimsson, who failed to win a parliamentary seat, desperately wanted a cabinet ministry. This would not only allow him to speak and present bills in the Althing (though not vote), but also would give him a leading role in Icelandic politics. He fought strong opposition within the PA to bring the party into the coalition and secured the strategic Finance Ministry for himself. He also landed two other portfolios for the PA, both of which have been strategic positions from which it has pursued its objectives. Steingrimur Sigfusson became the minister of communications and agriculture, a post from which he has so far been able to block a feasibility study of a proposed NATO North Atlantic Alternate Airfield and open discussions on an air-traffic agreement with the Soviet Union. Svavar Gestsson received the Ministry of Education and Culture at a time of concern that taking part in the European integration process would threaten Icelandic customs and traditions.

One Icelandic tradition that appears to be holding on strong is the fall in popularity of whatever parties are in power. The current government is, however, breaking all the records. After just over a year, the government has the support of less than a quarter of the public. The PA's popularity sank to an all-time low of 9.3 percent in December (poll conducted by SKAIS), a further drop of 4 percent from its share of the votes cast in the last election. These figures led Foreign Minister Hannibalsson to comment that governing was not a popularity contest. If the serious economic downturn continues unabated, many doubt that the coalition will last until the next election, due to take place by April 1991.

Leadership and Organization. The broad composition of the PA's Central Committee and the PA's history of factionalism have worked to maintain an open, democratic character within a party apparatus that has never followed a strict Leninist organizational model. The intense infighting following the 1987 election, Grimsson's election as party chairman, and the decision to join the coalition in 1988 continues at the local and national level. By negotiating the culture and education portfolio for former party chairman Gestsson, Grimsson temporarily coopted his strongest rival. Gudrun Agustsdottir, a member of the Reykjavik town council and vocal opponent of the PA's participation in the government, became Gestsson's special assistant. Other major PA figures who opposed the coalition, such as Asmundur Stefansson, president of the Icelandic Federation of Labor, have distanced themselves from the PA rather than speak out publicly against it.

The first major challenge to Grimsson's continued leadership occurred in elections to the board of a local party organ, the PA Society in Reykjavik. At a general meeting in late May, Grimsson's supporters were swept off the board and replaced by more conservative PA members who had opposed Grimsson's appointment as party chairman. This defeat for Grimsson was facilitated by his general absence from party functions since assuming his duties as finance minister. A few Grimsson supporters immediately took steps to form a splinter PA organization in Reykjavik, which was later dubbed the "Birting" Society. This split has not only complicated the PA's efforts to form a joint electoral slate with other parties, but also set the stage for a divisive party congress in November. (*Morgunbladid*, 2 June; *Thjodviljinn*, 1 June; *Timinn*, 28 September.)

The party congress from 16 to 19 November was

fraught with leadership and policy disputes. From the beginning, the rank and file rallied behind either the reformist Grimsson or hard-line former party chairman Gestsson. Gestsson attacked Grimsson for selling out low-wage workers and trying to relax restrictions on foreign ownership of industry. In an unprecedented move, Sigfusson, a Gestsson supporter, ran against and defeated sitting deputy party chairman Jonasdottir. In so doing, Sigfusson placed himself firmly in a position to challenge Grimsson at the next party congress, which will take place in two years. The only moment of unity came in the resolution on foreign policy which reiterated the PA's call for the removal of U.S. troops, no new military construction on Iceland, and the establishment of a Nordic Nuclear Weapons–Free Zone (NNWFZ). (*Thjodviljinn*, 20–22 November.)

The recent struggles within the PA are rooted in continuing friction between its academic and labor wings. Grimsson is himself a professor of political science and has been trying to reform the party under more social-democratic lines. His new deputy, Sigfusson, is a hard-line Marxist with a strong labor background. Atlantic Trade Union Federation head Gudmundur Gudmundsson actually resigned his seat in the Althing in protest of the PA's white-collar orientation and openly proposed that a labor-oriented splinter party be formed by a split from the PA. Particularly troublesome for labor during the debate over the PA's participation in a coalition government was a provisional law enacted in May 1988 that suspended the right to bargain collectively and strike. The PA had to accept this law as a condition for entering the government. Furthermore, it was forced to support a temporary wage and price freeze and sales taxes on food that it had earlier opposed on the grounds that these measures were regressive. By making these concessions, the PA further alienated its labor constituency, which accounts for the lion's share of its voting support.

Leadership challenges at the top are also likely to regain momentum as women in the PA become more assertive. The political challenge of the Women's List (WL) has focused attention on the all-male composition of the PA's ministerial appointments. Party rules call for at least 40 percent of all posts to go to women. Gudrun Helgadottir, a leader of the reform faction, felt particularly slighted in not being chosen for one of the three cabinet positions and was only partially mollified when she was elected the first female speaker of the Althing in October 1988. Jonasdottir's defeat in the election of the deputy party chairman in November will also

harden criticism of the PA as an all-male club. If the WL continues to steal votes from the PA, the latter will sooner or later be forced to address this issue of female representation in party and government posts. (*Thjodviljinn*, 22 November; *Nordisk Kontakt*, no. 14–15, 1988.)

The PA's inclusion in the current government has led to some speculation of a rapprochement with the SDP. Grimsson and SDP chairman Hannibalsson have discussed joint speaking tours. Some type of unity slate in the 1990 municipal elections might also enable the two to challenge the Independence Party's (IP) hold on some local posts. In the long run, however, the PA's cooperation with other, more centrist parties, particularly at a time of difficult fiscal and economic decisions, would probably exacerbate frictions within the party. The conservative daily, *Morgunbladid*, speculated that the coalition will encourage more liberal PA members to join forces with the SDP because of the PA's potential for schism and its sagging popularity (2 June).

Domestic Affairs. The poor performance of the economy continues to dominate Icelandic politics and is primarily responsible for the current government's low showing in the polls. The government's national economic program announced in October that the GDP would probably fall by 1.1 percent in 1990, the third straight year of decline. It also predicted 16 percent inflation, an estimate considered optimistic by many private forecasters who are counting on 20–25 percent. Government and central bank predictions of unemployment in 1990 range from 2.5 to 3 percent, which, though low by U.S. standards, are unacceptably high for most Icelanders. A further devaluation of the Icelandic kronur is likely. (*FBIS-WEU*, 27 April; *Nordic Economic Outlook*, Autumn.)

The PA had consistently opposed the previous government's fiscal austerity measures and is currently in the position of extending the very policies it had earlier fought. The government's wage controls were effective for their limited duration, but they angered the PA's labor constituency, and the PA was forced to call for their early repeal. The inflation rate doubled in March after the controls were removed. As finance minister, Grimsson has the difficult task of finding new sources of government revenue without further deepening the recession. In July, he cracked down heavily on businesses that did not pay sales taxes and temporarily closed more than 100 firms in a broadly popular move. The scale of cheating on sales-tax payments was, however, smaller than he made it out to be, and he netted little additional revenue. In the end, he endeared himself little to business at a time when an increased number of bankruptcies threatened to fuel unemployment. With the PA's future tied to Grimsson's coattails, his first year was hardly a boon to the party. (*News from Iceland*, August.)

Grimsson had joined the coalition knowing that Iceland faced some difficult choices. It was his belief, and the focus of his arguments to the PA's membership, that only if it were in power could the PA affect where budget cuts would be made. He has in fact successfully fended off some austerity measures that would have fallen more heavily on labor, but in doing so, he crippled the fight against inflation. The result is that wage earners' buying power continues to drop. Grimsson pushed forward a new, more progressive tax-revenue package, which raised personal income tax to 38 percent and corporate tax to 50 percent. He also secured greater individual tax exemptions and increases for old-age and disability pensions. The PA's inclusion in the government and its chairman's position as finance minister have put a pragmatic face on its policy orientation. But its practical approach has done little to solve Iceland's major economic problems or the party's declining popularity.

Foreign Affairs. The persisting emotional issue in Icelandic foreign policy and one the PA has kept at center stage is East-West relations. NATO membership, the NATO military sites on the island, and naval arms control have received increased attention under the center-left government. The PA has consistently pushed for Iceland's withdrawal from NATO and the removal of all armed forces from the island. The publication of *Red Storm Rising* by Tom Clancy did nothing to ease Icelanders' fears that Keflavik would make them a target in wartime. It is significant that the PA signed a coalition policy statement that does not call for any reductions in military activity on the island, but the party has forced a freeze on new military projects and urged a review of the U.S.-manned Icelandic Defense Force (IDF). In Central Committee meetings, the PA continues to pass resolutions that call for a nuclear freeze as a first step to an eventual Nordic Nuclear Weapons–Free Zone (NNWFZ).

The PA has used the Organization of Base Opponents (OBO) and its control of the Communications Ministry to keep pressure on Keflavik and thwart study of an alternate airfield on the east side of Iceland. The PA supported calls for the cancelation of last summer's NATO exercise, Northern Viking '89, and the OBO staged numerous protests around and, in one case, inside the military base at Keflavik during the exercises. An oil leak at a remote radar station manned by Icelanders also prompted the PA to raise questions about environmental damage caused by the U.S.-NATO military presence. Efforts to conduct a feasibility study on an Icelandic site for the North Atlantic Alternate Airfield (NAAA) were blocked by Communications Minister Sigfusson despite Foreign Minister Hannibalsson's support for the study. Aside from its anti-NATO orientation, the PA is also fundamentally concerned with Iceland's dependence on the employment and purchases that the military presence provides.

The success of the current disarmament talks, particularly CFE and START, has focused debate on naval arms control. The PA has tried to publicize problems raised by growing superpower reliance on naval forces, particularly nuclear submarines. The Soviet nuclear submarine accidents off Norway in 1989 prompted concern about environmental damage and economic loss, if Iceland's fishing grounds, the source of three-quarters of its exports, were damaged. The PA has encouraged Prime Minister Hermannsson, the most vocal proponent of naval arms control, and drowned out Foreign Minister Hannibalsson's advice to be more cautious.

As economic integration in Europe accelerates with the approach of 1992, Iceland has focused increased attention on maintaining access to European markets for its fish products. Iceland has remained outside of the European Community (EC), primarily because of its requirement that Iceland open up its fishing grounds in exchange for the benefits of the single market. The PA has fought EC membership and is concerned with the current negotiations between the European Free Trade Association (EFTA), in which Iceland is a member, and the EC. The PA does not want to accept the single-market requirements of free movement of labor and capital that would allow foreign ownership of Icelandic companies and otherwise change the country's cultural identity.

Icelandic relations with the Soviet Union are largely economic, with the Soviets purchasing large amounts of wool and low-quality fish products in exchange for oil. Iceland is one of the few Western countries that run a trade deficit with the USSR. This may be less a matter of policy than a result of Soviet failures to fulfill purchasing contracts, an issue that has caused some consternation among

Iceland's export businesses. PA officials generally have little involvement in trade or foreign relations with the Soviet Union. The only recent exception to this were discussions in November between Communications Minister Sigfusson and Aeroflot officials on an air-traffic agreement. The agreement would allow Aeroflot flights from the Soviet Union to the United States to make stopovers at Keflavik instead of Ireland's Shannon airport. (*Morgunbladid*, 5 November.)

International Party Contacts. The PA and its predecessors have always remained aloof from international communist movements. As the first to disassociate itself from Stalin's Comintern and denounce Soviet intervention in Eastern Europe, the PA maintains the Icelandic tradition of self-reliance and political independence from Europe. What little contact does exist is mainly with radical socialist parties in the other Nordic countries, namely Norway's Socialist Left and Denmark's Socialist People's Party.

Other Marxist and Leftist Groups. The PA's internal pluralism has discouraged the formation of independent leftist groups, even though the PA itself has often resembled an organized argument more than a political party. Although there were brief flurries of interest in them in the 1970s, Maoism and Trotskyism are not represented in Iceland by organizational structures. The PA remains a divided party, but its ability to maintain some degree of party discipline in coalition with far more moderate parties shows that it combines flexibility with ideology, a mixture that has in recent history discouraged the formation of splinter groups.

The Women's List (WL) is a phenomenon peculiar to Iceland. Women continue to be prominent in Icelandic politics and public life. Their participation is symbolized by the republic's president and most popular politician, Vigdis Finnbogadottir (whose powers are largely ceremonial, but not irrelevant in a cabinet crisis). The WL itself is a radical feminist group, but has a pragmatic domestic program that attracts wide support in this highly egalitarian society. Given its electoral gains in the last election and strong continued popularity, the WL might have been a logical candidate for the current coalition, but aspects of its party program hampered serious consideration of its inclusion by Hermannsson.

All of the other parties accord the WL's parliamentary leaders considerable respect. Neverthe-

less, given the requirements for economic austerity that faced the new government, the WL's demands for massive wage increases for low-paid employees, the majority of whom are women, would have made it a problematic coalition partner in this time of austerity. The WL's general line emphasizes redistributional and social-welfare policies over economic growth and investment. On foreign affairs, its position is strongly pacifistic and opposed to Icelandic commitments to NATO. The party's internal organization is very loose, with annual rotation of the top positions. The WL has clearly attracted many voters who may otherwise have been inclined to support the PA. (*JPRS-WEU*, 4 October 1988.)

Randolph McNeely
Washington, D.C.

Ireland

Population. 3,550,352 (July 1989)
Party. Communist Party of Ireland (CPI)
Founded. 1933 (date of record)
Membership. Under 500
General Secretary. James Stewart
Executive Committee. Includes Michael O'Riordan (chairman), Andrew Barr, Sean Nolan, Tom Redmond, Edwina Stewart, Eddie Glackin
Status. Legal
Last Congress. Twentieth, 28–29 October 1989, in Dublin.
Last Election. June 1989, no representation
Auxiliary Organizations. Connelly Youth Movement
Publications. *Unity, Irish Socialist, Irish Workers' Voice, Irish Bulletin*

The CPI was founded in 1921, when the Socialist Party of Ireland expelled moderates and decided to join the Comintern. During the Civil War, the party became largely irrelevant and virtually disappeared, although very small communist cells remained intact. The CPI was refounded in June 1933, the date the Communists now adopt as the founding date of their party.

The party organization was badly disrupted during World War II because of the neutrality of the South and the belligerent status of the North. In 1948, the Communists in the South founded the Irish Workers' Party and those in the North, the Communist Party of Northern Ireland. At a specially convened "unity congress" held in Belfast on 15 March 1970, the two groups reunited.

The CPI is a recognized political party on both sides of the border and contests both local and national elections. It has, however, no significant support and no elected representatives.

Leadership and Organization. The CPI is divided into two geographical branches, north and south, corresponding to the political division of the country. In theory, the congress is the supreme constitutional authority of the party, but in practice it tends to serve as a rubber stamp for the national executive. The innermost controlling conclave is the National Political Committee. Such little support as the CPI enjoys tends to be based in Dublin and Belfast.

Domestic Affairs. The continuing political division of the country and Ireland's economic problems remained the main issues in 1989. The CPI views the United Kingdom as an imperialist power that gains economically from holding Ireland in a subordinate position. Although continuing to advocate the creation of a single, united socialist Ireland, the party remains opposed to the use of violence and denounces the use of force by armed gangs on either side of the communal divide. For example, it was particularly vehement in its denunciation of the Provisional Irish Republican Army's bombing of the Grand Hotel in Brighton in 1984, which nearly killed several members of the British cabinet including Prime Minister Margaret Thatcher.

The party believes Irish unification can be achieved only by promoting working-class solidarity and thus overcoming the communal divide between Protestants and Catholics. Executive Committee member Morrissey put the CPI view succinctly: "As long as the working class is divided along religions or other lines, the exploiting classes will dominate the political stage and Ireland will remain subordinate to imperialism."

The Twentieth Congress of the CPI met in late October 1989. The main political resolution agreed on by the delegates reaffirmed the party's condemnation of the Anglo-Irish Agreement. The CPI continued to deplore the agreement as a form of British imperialism which allows a continued British pres-

ence in Ireland with consequent violence. The congress also reconfirmed its long-standing opposition to Irish membership in the EC. It warned of the further dangers posed by the creation of a fully integrated common market by 1992.

Addressing the upheaval in the international communist movement, the congress decided to reconvene in early 1990 to discuss the ideological implications of unfolding events in Eastern Europe and the Soviet Union. The CPI leadership expects, at that time, to offer plans for a thorough restructuring of the CPI.

International Views and Activities. The CPI historically has remained staunchly pro-Soviet and outside the Eurocommunist movement. As events in Eastern Europe and the Soviet Union unfolded during late 1989, the CPI began to take first and tentative steps to follow President Gorbachev's leadership toward reformist policies. It was clear, however, that the CPI was not enthusiastic about these changes. In the important relationship with its British comrades, the CPI feels much closer to the views of the breakaway Communist Party of Britain (CPB) than to the mainstream and much larger, but Eurocommunist, Communist Party of Great Britain (CPGB).

The CPI remains strongly anti-American and denounces U.S. policy in Central America, the Middle East, and elsewhere. It favors arms-reduction talks in Europe and opposes the deployment of missiles and former President Reagan's Strategic Defense Initiative.

Gerald Dorfman
Hoover Institution

Italy

Population. 57,557,767
Party. Italian Communist Party (Partito Comunista Italiano; PCI)
Founded. 1921
Membership. 800,000 claimed (*FBIS-WEU*, 11 January 1990).
Chairman. Alessandro Natta (71)

General Secretary. Achille Occhetto (53)

Secretariat. Achille Occhetto, Antonio Bassolino (42; labor and masses), Piero Fassino (40; organization), Fabio Mussi (41; culture, environment and territory), Claudio Petruccioli (48; special tasks), Livia Turco (34; women), Walter Veltroni (34; information and propaganda)

Directorate. 52 members

Central Committee. Approximately 300 members

Guarantees Commission. 60 members; Gian Carlo Pajetta (78), President

Status. Legal

Last Congress. Eighteenth, 17–22 March 1989, in Rome

Last Election. 1987, 26.6 percent, 177 of 630 seats in the Chamber of Deputies, and 28.3 percent, 100 of 315 seats, in the Senate (1983, 29.9 percent, 198 seats, in the Chamber, and 30.8 percent, 107 seats, in the Senate)

Auxiliary Organizations. Italian Communist Youth Federation (FGCI), Italian General Confederation of Labor (CGIL), National League of Cooperatives

Publications. *L'Unità*, daily, Massimo D'Alema (40), editor; *Rinascita*, weekly, Alberto Asor Rosa, editor; *Critica marxista*, bimonthly theoretical journal, Aldo Zanardo, editor; numerous specialized journals and a publishing house, Editori Riuniti

The PCI was founded in 1921 when a heterogeneous grouping of the most radical elements seceded from the Italian Socialist Party (PSI) and joined the Comintern. The party was led by Amadeo Bordiga, who was purged by the Comintern in 1926 and replaced by Antonio Gramsci. In the same year, the fascist dictatorship outlawed the PCI: the organization was forced underground, party headquarters were moved to France, and Gramsci was imprisoned. He was replaced by Palmiro Togliatti, who then led the party until his death in 1964 and who, more than anyone else, was responsible for many of the PCI's most unique features.

Relentlessly persecuted under fascism, the party organization had been reduced to, at most, five thousand members by 1943. The collapse of the regime, followed by the Resistance (in which Communists played an important role) provided the PCI with broad legitimacy by war's end. In coalitions with the Socialists, it regularly received a majority of the vote in the "red belt" of North-Central Italy, and was initially very strong in the industrial north-

west as well. The PCI participated in governments of national unity from 1944 to 1947, until it was expelled from the coalition (along with the PSI, with which it was to maintain very strong links until 1956). Togliatti ignored strict Leninist principles and insisted on building a mass party, present everywhere in society. By the time the PCI was expelled from the government, it claimed over two million members. Membership would gradually decline from the mid-1950s onward, but the party still had over 1.5 million members at the start of the 1970s. The total rose to 1.8 million in the late 1970s, but has declined steadily since then.

Under the leadership of Togliatti and a younger generation of "renovators," the middle and upper reaches of the party organization were de-Stalinized in the latter half of the 1950s. The late 1950s and 1960s also saw an increasing tolerance of internal dissent and a very loose form of democratic centralism, even after Togliatti had died and the helm had passed to Luigi Longo. By the 1960s, a general consensus had emerged throughout the leadership and in much of the rank and file around the Togliattian "Italian Road to Socialism." Some ambiguities about the party's complete commitment to Western democratic values and institutions persisted into the 1970s, when they were dispelled under Longo's successor, Enrico Berlinguer, who became general secretary in 1972 and led the party until 1984.

Although Togliatti always remained close to Moscow, he staked out increasingly autonomous positions in the 1950s and 1960s. He criticized the limits of de-Stalinization in the USSR and called the communist movement "polycentric." He deplored the Sino-Soviet rift and refused to join in condemnations of the Chinese. The highly competitive Italian political arena, in which numerous forces lay claim to left-wing credentials, accelerated the PCI's evolution in the 1960s. By 1968, Longo was able to condemn the invasion of Czechoslovakia in far stronger terms than almost all other nonruling CPs. By the end of the 1970s, stimulated by the desire for democratic legitimacy domestically and by Brezhnev's repressiveness and adventurism externally, Berlinguer had staked out extremely critical positions. Following the imposition of martial law in Poland in 1981, Berlinguer declared that the October Revolution has lost its propulsive energy and no longer had anything to offer Western progressive forces. He also denied that the international communist movement was something distinct from other forces on the left. Following these pronouncements, relations with the Soviets reached the point of a *strappo* (tear or break). Although relations gradually improved in the post-Brezhnev era, the PCI remained totally committed to its position of complete autonomy.

Electorally, the PCI obtained 19 percent of the vote in the first postwar elections in 1946, compared to 21 percent for the PSI and 35 percent for the Christian Democrats (DC). By 1948, after the Socialists had lost their right wing, the Communists became the largest party on the left. They grew to 27 percent by the end of the 1960s. By then, the PSI had been reduced to roughly 10 percent, and was floundering between the PCI and the DC. During the 1970s, the PCI effectively wrote off the PSI and proposed an "historic compromise" with the DC: when the communist vote reached 34.4 percent in 1976, the PCI, already in power in Italy's largest cities, became part of the governmental majority, but was denied cabinet posts. By the end of the 1970s, the PSI indicated its willingness to form majorities without the PCI; this act relegated the Communists back into the opposition, where they have remained since 1979. In the three general elections since 1979, the PCI's share of the vote slipped steadily downward: it obtained just under 27 percent in 1987, leaving it where it had been at the end of the 1960s. The party's share of the vote in local elections also declined steadily through the 1980s, although its immense strength in its strongholds has kept it in power in most of the red belt. A seeming exception to the party's steady decline was the 1984 election to the European Parliament, when the PCI's total jumped to a third of all votes cast, and it outpolled the DC for the only time in postwar Italian history. But this turned out to have been a sympathy vote for Berlinguer, who had died in the midst of the campaign.

The 1980s have witnessed a politically isolated PCI threatened by new formations like the Greens on the one hand and by an increasingly assertive PSI on the other. Relations between the PCI and PSI have been strained as the Socialists, now with nearly 15 percent of the vote, appear willing to countenance an eventual alliance with the Communists only if the PCI is reduced to the status of junior partner. The PCI has responded with relatively vague programmatic proposals and a sometimes desperate effort to resolve what is acknowledged to be a severe identity crisis. In the course of the 1980s, it has increasingly championed a united European left that would transcend the historical division between Communists and Socialists (or social-democrats). Any lingering "Eurocommunist" ambitions or claims to be seeking a "Third Way" (*i.e.*, between Eastern state socialism and Western social democracy) have been abandoned. The party leadership is gambling that its political future will be brighter if it can be viewed as "an integral part of the European left," to use the phrase introduced in the mid-1980s.

Domestic Politics and the PCI. With a nationwide test in the form of elections for the European Parliament scheduled for June, there was considerable speculation as to whether the PCI's ten-year decline would continue. In spite of General Secretary Achille Occhetto's nonstop activities, the portents on the eve of the European elections were extremely discouraging for the PCI. At the end of May, albeit in partial local elections that only involved 3 percent of the electorate, the PCI actually slipped below the total of the PSI: 17 percent vs. 19 percent (*NYT*, 1 June). During this same period, the events in Tiananmen Square generated an attitude of doom in PCI headquarters, for the European vote was less than two weeks away. Even the fact that the Italian government had fallen, and that intense disagreement between the PSI and DC marked the campaign, did not seem to help the PCI's standing in the polls. Everyone, including the communist leadership, expected the party to fall below 25 percent, and there was considerable discussion as to how much over 16–17 percent the PSI would rise (*L'Espresso*, 25 June). The gap between the two parties, over 20 percent in the European elections of 1984 and down to 12 percent in the 1987 general elections, threatened to dip below 10 percent.

To general astonishment, the PCI actually rose a full percentage point over its 1987 general-election total, arriving at 27.7 percent. The Socialists, in contrast, obtained 14.8 percent, a bare half-point above their 1987 result (*l'Unità*, 19 June). The Communists reacted with a mixture of exhilaration and relief. The significance of the European vote is not entirely clear—one need only recall the PCI's astonishingly high 33 percent in 1984—but this was a great moral victory for the party, and it abruptly ended discussions of the PCI's inevitably continuing decline.

These results could not, however, change the fact that the PCI remained as isolated as ever. The Communists were, effectively, bystanders in the governmental crisis that began in May and ended in July with the constitution of Italy's 49th postwar government (*NYT*, 23 July). Christian Democrat Ciriaco De Mita, the outgoing prime minister, was increasingly isolated within his own party, but he was driven from office by the constant criticism of his socialist coalition partners, spearheaded by Bettino Craxi, the PSI's forceful leader. It was widely agreed that the PSI had forced the crisis before the European elections in the expectation that it would be the big (relative) winner. That would have given it more leverage in coalition negotiations, and perhaps even emboldened the Socialists enough to force new general elections (*NYT*, 20 May; *WP*, 20 May). When things did not turn out as Craxi had hoped, Giulio Andreotti, a perennial DC power broker, became prime minister for the sixth time. As generally happens after Italian government crises, the new government consisted of the same five-party coalition as the old one, with very few new faces in the cabinet.

The PCI's role in all this was limited to criticism from the sidelines. It denounced coalition squabbling and governmental paralysis, but its major effort was directed at the PSI. The essence of the communist critique is that the PSI is unique among socialist parties in Europe in that it governs in coalition with conservative forces. It continues to participate in governments that are inherently unstable and incapable of serious reforms, whereas it ought to be moving toward the construction of a future alternative government with the PCI and other progressive and laical forces. In the wake of the European electoral results, some leaders of the PSI suggested that more attention should be paid to the PCI, whose evolution was continuing rapidly (*La Repubblica*, 23 June). But this attention to the PCI was largely part of the infighting between the DC and PSI, aimed at worrying the DC and perhaps gaining some negotiating leverage. It promptly disappeared after the new government had been formed.

In fact, as the PCI has accelerated its own changes, and openly moved away from any distinctive communist identity, relations with the PSI have remained strained and, in some regards, have degenerated. This degeneration was very much in evidence in 1989. Prior to the PCI's eighteenth congress late in March, Occhetto took a number of high-profile trips to underscore the PCI's commitment to its idea of a broad European left that eschewed traditional divisions. It was increasingly clear that the PCI wanted to join, or at least seek some affiliation with, the Socialist International as a way of emphasizing its commitment. A critical step in that direction was to be a meeting in Brussels with the socialist and social-democratic parties of the

European Community to discuss a possible common electoral program in the European elections. The meeting, carefully worked out with Craxi's involvement, was set for early March, just a few weeks before the opening of the PCI's eighteenth congress (Kevin Devlin, *RFE Research*, 23 March).

The meeting never took place. When Occhetto was asked by a journalist whether his party intended to request membership in the Socialist International, he is reported to have responded that formal membership might be premature, but everyone knew that the real obstacle was Craxi (*Corriere della sera*, 2 March). Although Occhetto heatedly denied having made this remark, Craxi used it as a reason to cancel the scheduled meeting. At the congress itself (see next section), the relationship worsened, and Craxi actually led a walkout of the PSI delegation in response to what he considered to be Occhetto's insults.

By the end of the year, the PCI once again had to confront an ambiguous result in a local election. This election was for the city council of Rome and therefore attracted considerable attention. The real story was that the Christian Democrats weathered more scandals and maintained their dominance with a third of the vote. The PCI fell dramatically (-4.7 percent) to 26.1 percent compared with the local elections four years earlier; the PSI's support increased ($+2.2$ percent) to 13.5 percent. But, as has become commonplace by now, observers compared these results to the most recent contests, not the most comparable ones. That sort of analysis showed that the PCI had actually gained (less than one percent) as compared to the 1987 general elections, indicating that the unstoppable decline had apparently been halted. Yet the PCI's total number of votes was down by just over a point as compared with the European vote just four months earlier (*La Repubblica*, 31 October). The year had provided some reassuring signs, but there was not yet enough evidence to say whether Occhetto's boldness had reversed or merely arrested the party's electoral erosion.

Party Leadership, Organization, and Debates. The bicentennial of the French Revolution occurred in 1989, and Occhetto used this as another occasion to underscore the PCI's western roots. He remarked that he personally felt himself to be more a child of the French than the Russian Revolution. The comment generated considerable attention in the national press, and some people called this Occhetto's "final break" with the October Revolution (*Panorama*, 26 November). The remark also generated dissent from some unexpected quarters of the PCI. Luciano Lama, former trade-union head and a prominent spokesman for the most moderate, or right, wing of the party, publicly disagreed with Occhetto. An outspoken proponent of unity with the PSI, Lama nevertheless affirmed that his political roots were Marxist. He went on, "even a reformist can have a strong class-based analysis" (*L'Espresso*, 19 February).

The most significant event in the internal life of the PCI scheduled for 1989 was the eighteenth national congress in March. Occhetto had only succeeded Alessandro Natta as general secretary in mid-1988, after Natta had suffered a heart attack. (The 71-year-old Natta would be elected to the honorific post of party chairman at the congress.) At that time, all tendencies in the party recognized the need for firm, fresh leadership, and Occhetto spent the rest of 1988 consolidating his position and guiding the party toward a congress that was eagerly awaited for the clarifications of the party's identity and strategy it might bring. It would also represent the ratification of Occhetto's leadership by the entire party, and hence would provide him with a real as well as a symbolic mandate.

The congress was held in Rome from 18 to 22 March. The months leading up to the congress were filled with extensive debate about, as well as constant revision of, a precongressional document. Thus there was little that was really surprising in Occhetto's opening and closing remarks to the congress, as well as in the final document approved by the delegates. However, the emphasis given to various themes did furnish a clearer indication of where Occhetto hoped to go—which was already evident in large measure from his emphasis on the PCI's firmly European vocation.

The broader picture was overwhelmed by more immediate political considerations, though, especially by the deteriorating relationship between the PCI and the PSI. Because Craxi had vetoed the PCI's meeting with European Socialists less than two weeks before the congress opened, it was inevitable that harsh criticism of the socialist leader would find its way into Occhetto's opening address. Referring throughout simply to "Craxi," without either a title or the customary "comrade," Occhetto blamed him for constantly seeking disagreement and polemics, and for rebuffing the PCI's proposals on the flimsiest of pretexts. Craxi's behavior showed, Occhetto continued, that he feared "not the

PCI's closed sectarianism, but, on the contrary, its policy of openness," which the PSI could not control or manipulate (*l'Unità*, 19 March). The PSI, he said, was only interested in an alternative in which all other forces of the left dissolved themselves and joined the Socialist Party. Craxi and his colleagues walked out of the conference hall, and told the press that the PCI continued to follow a well-trod, unproductive path that did not bode well for the future.

Polemics with the Socialists not only drove other issues into the background; they also clearly conditioned Occhetto's address. In the period immediately preceding the congress, the party's overtures to the rest of the European left were both high-level and incessant. The question of joining the Socialist International had been put on the agenda, and even the suggestion that the party should drop "Communist" from its name—an issue raised with increasing frequency in the 1980s—was once more in the air (editorial, *La Repubblica*, 18 March).

But Occhetto's address to the eighteenth congress flatly rejected the idea of a name change: "...we say that we do not know why we should change our name. Ours has been, and is, a glorious name that must be respected" (*l'Unità*, 19 March). He went on to reiterate the party's international positions: that an international communist movement no longer existed, and that the PCI sought broad cooperation with all the forces of the democratic left in Europe, but the thrust of this part of his speech was in the direction of a reaffirmation of the PCI's historical identity. Such assertions of autonomy and what the Communists call *patriotismo di partito* (party patriotism) brought frequent applause from the assembled delegates. But they also put the entire leadership in a difficult position, as would become evident by the end of the year when a name change finally was proposed. Instead of broaching, or even opening the way, to the topic at the congress, the short-term need to stake out a stronger position with regard to the PSI prevailed, and rendered the leaders' ultimate tasks more complicated.

Beyond the headline-grabbing polemics, the eighteenth congress of the PCI reaffirmed and consolidated the "new course" that had been spoken of continuously since Occhetto's accession to the top office of the party. In spite of terrible relations with the other major party of the left, the PCI's commitment to a genuine alternative to the DC's system of power was reaffirmed. So was its complete support of reforms in Eastern Europe, with emphasis on the need for political pluralism and market mechanisms. Its desire for increased collaboration and broad convergence among all the components of the European left was reasserted. Underlining the party's more recent sensitivity to issues and actors outside its historic constituencies, both Occhetto's address and the final Political Document (*l'Unità*, 23 March) also emphasized civil liberties, the environment, North-South relations, and women's rights. The party even passed an amendment banning smoking in party meetings at all levels (*NYT*, 25 March), a truly radical measure given the smoking habits of the European left and labor movement.

Most of the final document of the congress passed with relative ease, although several items were amended. A few items were heavily debated and only passed after extensive discussion. The most problematic and conflictual of all was an amendment proposed by the Communist Youth Federation (FGCI), calling for a guaranteed minimum income, which itself was extensively altered before it was finally passed. Opposition to the FGCI's proposal was expressed from both sides of the spectrum in the PCI. The more moderate wing, represented by such leaders as Giorgio Napolitano and Luciano Barca, spoke against the extension of indiscriminate welfare statism and profligate spending. The more radical left wing, especially those closest to the labor movement, such as Bruno Trentin, head of the major confederation of unions (CGIL), argued that payments should be linked to a job-training program. Proponents of the measure, in contrast, argued that it reflected a new cultural outlook that did not see an automatic linkage between money and employment (*l'Unità*, 23 March; *La Repubblica*, 23 March).

The PCI's sensitivity to this issue, which would have been unthinkable several years earlier, indicates the party's awareness of how relatively weak is its standing among young people in Italy. Blunt comments by Occhetto, as well as by top leaders like Fabio Mussi, head of the Culture and Environment Department (*WMR*, Toronto, August), and Massimo D'Alema, editor in chief of *l'Unità* (*L'Espresso*, 13 August), acknowledged the party's inability to attract youth. D'Alema indicated that the party daily was discussing promotional items such as musical cassettes and publishing the lyrics of favored folk singers. In fact, for many years the party and the FGCI have sponsored musical concerts (usually, but not always, involving more politically committed artists) in an effort to draw young people into their orbit.

The PCI's effort to increase its appeal to young people also led it to dramatically reverse its commitment to a universal military draft. Late in 1988 Occhetto, addressing the FGCI, argued that the draft should be reduced to six months. Two weeks later, the party was calling for the outright abolition of compulsory military service. In an article in *l'Unità*, Ugo Pecchioli, a veteran leader with specific expertise in the stability of Italian democratic institutions, asserted that only a small military that could adequately be staffed by professionals was required (*La Repubblica*, 20 December 1988; *FBIS-WEU*, 24 February).

The eighteenth congress also witnessed a number of refinements of the PCI's organizational practices, already much modified in the 1980s. The term "democratic centralism" was dropped altogether from the Party Statute, for since 1986, members have in any case not been bound to agree with a decision once it is taken by a majority. Indeed, they remain free to publish their dissent openly. The only remnant of the past remains the ban on formally organized factions (Mussi in *WMR*, August), and even that stricture would in practice be superseded by the end of the year. Because of some dissatisfaction at the way Occhetto was chosen as general secretary the previous year, electoral procedures were modified to make secret ballots the norm in voting for all leadership positions except membership in the Central Committee (CC) and the Federal Committees, which are the provincial equivalent of the CC. But even in these cases, it only requires 10 percent of the delegates to force a secret ballot (*l'Unità*, 23 March). In yet another symbolic departure, the Central Control Commission (and its provincial counterparts) was renamed the Guarantees Commission (CG).

In the preparations for the congress, the party established its own affirmative-action program after intensive pressure from Livia Turco, the head of the PCI's Women's Commission and a member of the Secretariat. Joining Turco in this effort was Tiziana Arista, the current regional secretary of the Abruzzo and, several years earlier, the first woman ever to be named a federation secretary in the South (*Panorama*, 7 January 1990). The party eventually agreed that a third of the delegates to the eighteenth congress would be women. Moreover, the party also undertook to elect women to 30 percent of all positions in leadership organs (e.g., the CC and Federal Committees). It actually kept this promise, for the CC elected by the congress was 31 percent female. This was achieved by immensely expanding the size of the CC, from 215 to 300 members, more than doubling the number of women (from 40 to 93), while avoiding the painful exercise of cutting dozens of established male leaders.

The new CC (in an enlarged plenum that included the CG) met early in April to elect the true leadership, the seven-member Secretariat and the fifty-member *Direzione* (Executive, literally Directorate). The Secretariat's youthful profile was reinforced as its oldest member, Gianni Pellicani (57), was dropped and two younger leaders closely identified with Occhetto's New Course were added: Walter Veltroni (34), who heads the Information and Propaganda Department, and Antonio Bassolino (42), who is in charge of Labor and Masses. With this shift, the oldest member of the Secretariat became the 53-year-old Occhetto. Returning to the Secretariat were Piero Fassino (40), Turco (34), Fabio Mussi (41), and Claudio Petruccioli (48).

Elections to the *Direzione*, as to the Secretariat, were by secret ballot, with the results published in the party paper. But whereas the Secretariat nominations went smoothly, this was not the case for the *Direzione*. One of the elder statesmen of the party's moderate wing, and once one of Enrico Berlinguer's closest collaborators, Paolo Bufalini, refused to accept his nomination (*l'Unità*, 6 April). Another moderate, Gianni Cervetti—a top-ranking leader of the 1970s and early 1980s—was the only person on the fifty-member list who failed (by a single vote) to receive the required 50 percent plus one, and hence was not elected (*l'Unità*, 7 April). Moreover, the elected leaders who received the fewest votes were all easily identifiable as part of the party's moderate or right wing, those most in favor of rapprochement with the PSI and much more extensive changes in the PCI.

These results troubled PCI moderates. Giorgio Napolitano, often called the PCI's "foreign minister" and one of the most respected leaders of the party, as well as the acknowledged spokesman of its right wing, was deeply troubled. He noted that the congress had ended on a unitary note, with appreciation for the contribution of all viewpoints within the party. Now, part of the CC was going against this unitary spirit in reprehensible ways: Cervetti (and those who had obtained embarrassingly low totals) had not been challenged in the discussion prior to the vote. Instead, secretly, they had been punished. This smacked of "organized unilateral pressure to force and distort the political choices of the congress, and to introduce surreptitiously into the life of the party a fractionistic (*correntizia*) practice

aimed at striking comrades engaged in a responsible unitary dialectic" (*l'Unità*, 7 April). Other moderate exponents, including *Direzione* member Gianfranco Borghini and prominent figures like Guido Fanti and Antonio Pizzinato (ex-secretary of the CGIL) complained that a legitimate part of the party had rudely been "brushed aside" (*l'Unità*, 9 April).

The composition of the *Direzione* generated other complaints within the party concerning which groups or categories had been systematically underrepresented. The Socialists, quick to capitalize on the PCI's internal difficulties, emphasized the humiliation of the right wingers in an editorial in their daily entitled "Massacre of the Reformists" (ibid.). The situation was serious enough to require a communiqué from the Secretariat, which stated that the new *Direzione* "fully represents the party's wealth of positions and orientations," although it did note the "important fact" of Cervetti's exclusion (ibid.).

By far the most intense debate of 1989—and of the entire decade—took place long after the congress, and, ironically, found Occhetto being charged with having policies that were far too moderate. In the aftermath of the congress, and especially on the occasion of his trip to the United States and during the European elections, Occhetto was constantly queried about the likelihood of the PCI's changing its name. He repeatedly resisted the suggestion, which was openly supported by the moderates. On the eve of his trip to the United States, pressed by foreign and Italian journalists on the subject, he responded, "We do not agree to change our name on outside orders," in an unmistakable reference to the PSI. He also echoed the point made at the congress: "for millions of Italians, that name has been a symbol of great struggles for democracy and freedom" (*L'Espresso*, 14 May). He then left the door open, adding that "if the Italian political scene changes and it is possible to create another political formation, the name change could be discussed . . ." (ibid.).

A month later, in the heat of the electoral campaign, he emphasized the party's distinctiveness, which he viewed as a powerful advantage. "Some of our adversaries," he noted, "want to nullify the major novelty in Italian politics—the presence of a Western socialist party that, because of the way Italian history has evolved over the past seventy years, happens to be called the Italian Communist Party" (*La Repubblica*, 15 June). The PCI's showing in the elections seemed to confirm Occhetto's arguments. The electoral result was widely viewed, inside and outside the PCI, as a vindication of his leadership. Postelectoral analyses pointed out that there was near-unanimity in the party concerning affiliation with the Socialist International: only the hard-line left wing, led by Armando Cossutta, was opposed, but this group was increasingly isolated as events in the USSR and Eastern Europe undercut the appeal of their orthodoxy. Yet observers noted that considerable resistance existed, among leaders and militants, to a change of name (*L'Espresso*, 25 June). Still, even many leaders identified as *occhettiani* had begun lobbying for a change, and it was rumored that Occhetto himself favored something like *Democrazia Socialista* (ibid.).

The summer brought no dramatic developments on the Italian left of the sort Occhetto had indicated would be necessary to set in motion the kind of dramatic alterations implied in changing the party's name. But the summer and fall did bring revolutionary changes to Eastern Europe, and it was apparently these changes (particularly those in Hungary) that moved him to act in November. After telling a gathering of veteran partisans that a dramatic change was in store, Occhetto used the occasion of a meeting of the *Direzione* a few days later to announce what was immediately dubbed a *svolta* (dramatic turn). The time had come, he said, to undertake the complete restructuring of the Italian left. The PCI should put itself forward as a unifying pole in this reconstruction, open to all progressive forces in Italy. To underline the constituent nature of this new phase in Italian history, which obviously would take a long time, the PCI would have to change its name and its entire organizational way of life (*l'Unità*, 15 November). The organization implications of this new formation would, among other things, include organized factions, according to Occhetto: "Of course, a new grouping embracing different experiences entails the possibility of different platforms which would manifest themselves as in all other European socialist parties" (*La Repubblica*, 15 November).

The delicate balancing act that followed the congress was over, and even many of those favorable to a name change were shocked at the suddenness of the turn of events. Fully 45 of the 52 members of the *Direzione* spoke at that tumultuous meeting, and many expressed reservations about its timing. Although the shift had not been imposed by Craxi, it was clearly the product of external forces, and many leaders did not think it was very well thought out. In the end, however, the *Direzione* approved Occhetto's proposal and a meeting of the enlarged CC-CG was called for the end of the month (*L'Espresso*, 26 November).

An extremely lively, but increasingly bitter, debate immediately erupted in the PCI. The plenum of the CC-CG was even more tumultuous than that of the *Direzione*, lasted a full five days (20–24 November), and was eventually addressed by a record-setting 159 people, with another 96 submitting written comments (*l'Unità*, 25 November). Placard-waving militants stood outside party headquarters during the meetings, imploring their leaders to remember the party's glorious traditions. In the course of the debates, as well as during heated exchanges outside the meeting room, it became clear that Occhetto was putting his own future on the line: his own and his collaborators' comments predicted that the leadership would resign if rebuffed. On the final day, 326 members voted on the resolution to "begin the founding process for the creation of a new political organization." Moreover, under intense pressure from the opposition, the proposal for a new organization was to be placed before an extraordinary congress—the first in the history of the PCI. Occhetto and those around him made it clear that they would have preferred a longer time frame, but their hand was forced by the opposition (*L'Espresso*, 10 December). The congress was tentatively set for early 1990, which meant that the new formation would almost immediately have to contest the nationwide local elections scheduled for early summer. The vote was 219 in favor of the resolution, with 73 opposed, and 34 abstentions (*l'Unità*, 25 November). Another plenum was called for December, at which time the date of the congress would be fixed, and competing documents on the subject of a new organization would be voted on.

The broad lines of division within the party emerged in the November debates, and they did not obey a neat organizational or ideological logic, save for the extreme right and left on the PCI's spectrum. Occhetto and most of those associated with his leadership felt that events in the East demanded dramatic initiatives from the PCI. Fabio Mussi of the Secretariat used revealing language when he remarked, "We want to create a *perestroika* of the Italian left" (*WP*, 25 November). For the various components of the party's most moderate wing, these changes were coming, if anything, late in the game. Among these centrists and rightists, many had reservations about the vagueness and peremptory timing of Occhetto's initiative, but almost all agreed that decisive action was called for under the extraordinary circumstances in Hungary and, by the end of November, in Czechoslovakia and East Germany as well. It was immediately clear, however, that this was a heterogeneous, if quite large, coalition. Many *occhettiani* were known to be highly critical of the moderates, whom they consider far too accommodating toward the PSI. The *occhettiani* are also generally quite close to the *ingraiani* in their sensitivity to the so-called new movements like feminism and ecology, whereas the moderates in the PCI have always tended to be suspicious of nontraditional or extrainstitutional forces.

Opposing the *svolta*, or at least abstaining, were some centrists who were offended by the suddenness of the move, or its awkward timing, which, in their view, made the party once more appear to be reacting to events rather than presenting well-reasoned proposals. Most of the party's elder statesmen were also reported to be deeply offended that Occhetto had not even consulted them before making his dramatic announcements (*Corriere della sera*, 10 December). The most notable members of this group were party chairman Alessandro Natta and CG president Gian Carlo Pajetta. Other prominent figures who announced their opposition included the highly respected veteran and long-time former editor of *l'Unità*, Aldo Tortorella.

But the most predictable opposition to the *svolta* came from the various components of the party's left wing. The hard-line left, prominently represented by Cossutta, has never accepted the party's Euro-left orientation. The more radical left's opposition was also a foregone conclusion. Critical of repression in the East, and sensitive to new movements and actions based on mass mobilization more than institutional maneuvering, the radicals have been especially notable in the 1980s for their extreme suspicion of too rapid an embrace of Craxi and the PSI. Historically associated with 74-year-old Pietro Ingrao, but strongly present among the generation of the 1960s and younger leaders as well, many radicals framed their opposition in terms strikingly reminiscent of Occhetto's own comments during and immediately after the eighteenth congress. At the November plenum, for instance, Ingrao himself emphasized that Italian communism "has been and remains something different from the communist parties and dictatorial regimes of the East. Millions of Italians have not only waged battles for freedom around the word 'communism,' but they have seen in it the protection of the weaker as a patrimony to be cherished" (*NYT*, 26 Novem-

ber). The members of the *Direzione* siding with Ingrao were Gavino Angius, who runs the party's department charged with local governmental affairs, Giuseppe Chiarante, a noted intellectual, and Lucio Magri and Luciana Castellina, former leaders of Il Manifesto who had been expelled in 1969, but were readmitted in the late 1970s. Other prominent top-level dissidents, whose left leanings have never been a secret in the PCI, included ex-union leader Sergio Garavini and Adalberto Minucci.

The voting at the November plenum, as well as the heated and extensive debate following it, showed that Occhetto had widespread support, especially among most of the current leadership at all levels. But there was anguish and doubt even at the very summit of the PCI: two of six members of the Secretariat (Bassolino and Turco) openly admitted that their allegiances were torn because of their strong identification with much of what the *ingraiani* had always stood for. Bassolino expressed the discomfort he felt in the company of the moderates, with whom he had little in common (*Corriere della sera*, 12 December). And in the immediate aftermath of the plenum, as provincial federations met and expressed their immediate reactions to the proposal, deep divisions were evident up and down the peninsula: Florence and Bari were reported to be evenly divided between Ingrao's and Occhetto's positions; Rome actually voted by a 60 percent majority in favor of Ingrao, while more moderate strongholds like Milan and Bologna were safely in the secretary's column (*Corriere della sera*, 3 and 4 December).

As the December plenum approached, the debate in the party grew polarized and acrimonious. The targets of the opposition's attacks increasingly included the way the party was being run, not simply specific proposals. And these attacks came not only from leftists like Lucio Magri, but also from highly respected elder statesmen like Pajetta and Natta (*La Repubblica*, 6 December). At the *Direzione's* last meeting of the year, these leaders denounced what they called the personalistic way the debate was being carried out (while almost never mentioning Occhetto by name) in the pages of the daily paper, but also the way top-ranking leaders were being sent to the federations to manage the discussion. Magri called this "majority factionalism," and Natta and Occhetto are reported to have exchanged heated remarks (*Corriere della sera*, 6 December). The *cossuttiani* published a "dossier" denouncing "twenty days of disinformation and mystification" on the part of the leadership, particularly its use of *l'Unità* (*Corriere della sera*, 7 and 8 December).

The unexpected depth of the hostility, as well as the breadth of the resistance he encountered, made Occhetto backtrack as he tried to appeal to more sectors of the party. Events would soon show that he was particularly concerned not to show himself in too close an alliance with the right. As he and his closest collaborators worked on successive drafts of the document they would present to the plenum, considerable maneuvering took place as various spokesmen announced their satisfaction or dissatisfaction with the draft they had seen (*La Repubblica*, 17 December). A few days before the plenum, obviously sensitive to many of his own vacillating supporters as well as those he still hoped to win over, Occhetto made a considerable concession and announced that neither the name nor the symbol of the PCI would be put into question at the next congress; this meant that the party would contest the upcoming elections with its traditional logo, which contains a hammer and sickle as well as the letters "P.C.I." (ibid.). The document explicitly criticized Craxi's approach to the unity of the left, and also put any eventual unity fairly far into the future.

In the December plenum of the CC-CG, the nineteenth congress was set for 7–10 March 1990 in Bologna. Following procedural rules adopted in the mid-1980s, the contending documents that would serve as the basis for debate in the lower levels of the party—and which would eventually be voted on in all the lower-level congresses—were presented. Three contending motions were formally accepted at the plenum. The importance of this formal acceptance is that it gives each motion's sponsors and representatives equal access to the party press and to all party organizations and locales. Delegates will be elected to the nineteenth congress in proportion to the support received by each motion.

Not surprisingly, Occhetto's motion garnered a strong majority, including almost all national leaders with positions of responsibility in the party organization, and all but one of the party's twenty regional secretaries (*L'Espresso*, 7 January 1990). Without proposing an immediate change of name, it called for "a new democratic political formation, reformist, open to progressive lay and Catholic components." The opposition motion with the strongest support was sponsored by Natta, Ingrao, and Tortorella, and was signed by 63 leaders; the Cossutta motion obtained ten signatures. These 73 opposition votes corresponded precisely to the number of votes cast against Occhetto's resolution in November, but the identity of the number hid the shifting of numerous individuals. For example, eight original abstainers signed the Natta-Ingrao motion, and about a dozen original "no" votes signed Occhetto's motion (ibid.).

If Occhetto's motion reflected some compromises, so did that of Natta et al. The fact that its very harsh tone represented a dilution of earlier, even more brutal language, was widely reported (ibid.; *Corriere della sera*, 21 December). It objects to the proposed "dissolution" of the party, emphasizing that the PCI has nothing to be ashamed of with regard to its past; broader unity can be sought, it argues, without denying the party's own distinct identity. Above all, the document attacks what it calls the vagueness, confusion, and desperation of the *svolta*. The leadership's "illusory search for an insertion at any cost into the governing area" has already caused extremely serious damage to the party. It calls for a more explicit political program, and an end to excessive top-down leadership (*verticismo*) in the PCI. It also criticizes the party's slowness to react to new forces, lamenting that this caused it to miss a golden opportunity when there was a more progressive thrust in society. And, while applauding the PCI's criticism of Stalinism and dogmatism in the East, it castigates the party for having moved too slowly on these matters in the past as well. Many observers noted the irony of these last points, which are expressions of the radical left's long-standing critique. Some of the most prominent signatories of the document were, after all, at the very summit of the party when it was missing these important opportunities (*Corriere della sera*, 21 December; *La Repubblica*, 21 and 22 December).

Cossutta's motion is of course critical of the PCI's stance on the East for entirely different reasons: for this group, the party has been far too hasty to condemn what remains a valid experience. The hard-liners' document also denounces what it sees as the proposed liquidation and dissolution of the PCI, and adds its own harsh criticism of the way the party has been run. As with the *ingraiani* and other oppositionists, however, the *cossuttiani* almost never mention Occhetto by name—a pointed way of avoiding what they consider the personalization that has taken place in the party. As the year ended, the top party leadership was bracing for what it knew would be a rough battle, but it remained convinced that the opposition motions would obtain no more than 25 percent of the delegates to the upcoming congress (*L'Espresso*, 9 January 1990).

International Views and Contacts. The PCI was more active on the international front in 1989 than it had been for some time. Among other things, Occhetto visited both the USSR and the United States in the first half of the year. This activism reflected the press of important developments: in Western Europe, the elections to the European Parliament; in Eastern Europe, the increasing pace of change. But it also reflected a desire to underscore aggressively the PCI's independence, commitment to democratic values, and entitlement to full membership in the European left. At the same time, as conditions in the USSR and Eastern Europe evolved in directions applauded by the Italians, relations between the PCI and the forces of reform in the East were increasingly friendly. In contrast, where events evolved more slowly (Czechoslovakia, East Germany, and Romania, until late in the year), or where they regressed (China), the PCI was unsparing in its already harsh criticism.

One clear reason for the Italians' improved attitude toward the Soviets was the latter's continuing admission of earlier errors in connection with the PCI. Referring to the nadir of relations between the PCI and the CPSU in the early 1980s, an article that appeared in *Kommunist* early in 1989 admitted that the PCI's criticisms of that period had been warranted, and that the Soviets had been wrong to attack then–general secretary Enrico Berlinguer and the entire party leadership. In a heavy dose of self-criticism, it was now admitted that PCI criticism of the socialist systems' weaknesses in the wake of the coup in Poland was correct. The Soviets were now claiming that much can be learned from the PCI (translation in *Rinascita*, 28 January).

This mea culpa may have been a gesture to ensure that Occhetto's scheduled visit to Moscow, just two weeks before the PCI's eighteenth congress, went smoothly. By Occhetto's own account of a five-hour meeting with Gorbachev, "the results even exceeded our expectations" (*l'Unità*, 2 March). The Italian leader reported that the topics discussed—in a conversation variously described as "open," "useful," and "lively"—included changes and reforms under way in both parties, as well as events in both Western and Eastern Europe. He made clear that while he had applauded developments in some Eastern countries—singling out multiparty experiments in Hungary—he was highly critical of foot-dragging in Czechoslovakia and, especially, in Romania. When asked by journalists how Gorbachev had reacted to some of his more forceful assertions (especially those concerning Czechoslovakia and

Alexander Dubček, a key symbol for the PCI), Occhetto was more evasive. He limited himself to saying he was sure that Gorbachev understood what the Italians meant (*Corriere della sera*, 1 March; *La Stampa*, 1 March).

Occhetto was less reticent about the Soviet leader's expressed views on Western Europe. He portrayed Gorbachev as highly receptive to the PCI's desire to overcome historical divisions between European Communists and Socialists. He also took some pains to ensure that Gorbachev's overtures to Western Europe and his references to "a common European home" should not be seen as a ploy to drive a wedge between the United States and its West European allies (*l'Unità*, 2 March). The PCI was clearly taking advantage of the general thaw in Europe, and was pressing its special qualifications to act as a bridge between the Western left and a rapidly evolving East. Occhetto's first meeting as party leader with Gorbachev had obviously served both domestic and broader international purposes.

Additional evidence that Occhetto viewed his warm relationship with Gorbachev as an asset came at the PCI's eighteenth congress, when a videotaped greeting from the Soviet leader was played to the assembly. Gorbachev stated that he sent the message at Occhetto's urging. The event was notable less for what the Soviet leader said than because it happened at all. For a party as sensitive about its perceived independence as the PCI, this was an interesting symbolic development.

The eighteenth congress was marked by additional symbolism concerning developments in Eastern Europe, in the figure of Alexander Dubček. The deposed symbol of the Prague Spring of 1968 had long been treated with great respect by PCI leaders, who had condemned the invasion when it happened and consistently criticized repression in Czechoslovakia ever since. Attention to that country had escalated in 1988, which marked both the twentieth anniversary of the Prague Spring and a journey by Dubček to Italy to receive an honorary degree from the University of Bologna. After receiving his honor, Dubček was publicly fêted by the PCI. In 1989, the party continued to repeat that the entire Soviet bloc should admit it had been wrong to crush the Czech experiment, and Dubček should be completely rehabilitated.

Early in the year the PCI prominently featured an interview with Dubček, in which he mercilessly assailed the hard-line leaders of his country (*l'Unità*, 10 January). Combined with the glowing reception he had received a few months earlier, it is not surprising that the rulers of Czechoslovakia denied Dubček a visa to travel to Italy when the PCI invited him to attend the eighteenth congress. This act spurred the PCI to even more extensive criticism of the regime, and a clear highlight of the fourth day of the congress was an outpouring of affection for the man who would in fact be rehabilitated and elected president of the Czech parliament before 1989 was over. Dubček, in any event, sent a warm message to the congress (*l'Unità*, 22 March). Later in the year, he authored a long article entitled "Czechoslovak Apartheid" (*l'Unità*, 3 September) denouncing the regime's attempts to justify the 1968 invasion after the Hungarians and Poles had openly admitted that it had been a mistake.

Developments in Eastern Europe naturally kept the PCI very busy all year, ultimately vindicating many of the positions it had long held, but occasionally leaving Italian Communists, like everyone else, breathless at their rapidity (see the earlier discussion of the proposed change of the PCI's name). Throughout the year, the PCI consistently lauded developments in Hungary and Poland, while continuing to criticize East Germany, Romania, and Czechoslovakia. To make its displeasure with the latter two regimes as obvious as possible, the PCI openly did not invite them to its annual National Festival of *l'Unità* in September. In previous years, the Italians had been much more diplomatic, inviting everyone and leaving it to the "fraternal party" (to use a term no longer used by the PCI itself) to decide whether to attend or not (Kevin Devlin, *RFE Research*, 5 September).

On numerous occasions throughout the year, until events in the aforementioned countries also began to change, the PCI provided a forum for exiled activists, while constantly condemning the immobilism of the entrenched regimes. For example, after the East German regime banned New Forum, an interview with one of its leaders (Bärbel Bohley) was featured in the party's daily newspaper. To drive the point home, the interview appeared on the 40th anniversary of the German Democratic Republic, accompanied by a stinging editorial denouncing the regime's isolation and resistance to the changes occurring in Eastern Europe (*l'Unità*, 7 October). A few weeks later, the PCI openly declined an invitation to attend the Romanian Communist Party's congress, and informed the Romanian ambassador that the party found continuing violations of human rights in his country to be unacceptable (*Izvestiia*, 15 November; *FBIS-SOV*, 16 November).

Italian Communists also felt strongly vindicated by events in Hungary in 1989, and alternately applauded the Hungarians for their courage and the Soviets for their forbearance. In June, Occhetto went to Budapest for Imre Nagy's reburial, and laid a wreath on his grave on behalf of the PCI. In October, following the momentous congress at which the Hungarian Socialist Workers' Party changed its name, Occhetto (and Giorgio Napolitano) were invited for talks with the leaders of the newly renamed Hungarian Socialist Party. The PCI was the first Western party of the left to be so honored, and the Hungarians (including president-to-be Imre Pozsgay) told the Italians that the PCI had been a great inspiration, and indeed contributor, to the process of change in that country. The PCI gave these accolades extensive coverage, underscoring how the Hungarians, like the Italians, were interested in building bridges to all forces on the European left and eventually seeking an "organic relationship" with the Socialist International (*l'Unità*, 17 October).

With respect to the Soviet Union itself, the PCI continued to give favorable coverage to Gorbachev, as it has since he rose to power. Another meeting with Occhetto took place late in the year in Rome, on the occasion of Gorbachev's summit with U.S. president George Bush in Malta (*l'Unità*, 1 December). This encounter was preceded by a visit of Antonio Rubbi to Moscow, where the head of the PCI's International Relations Department met with the Soviet leader (*l'Unità*, 1 November).

While the PCI's coverage of domestic affairs in the USSR was inevitably supportive of the changes under way, it continued to emphasize the internal resistance and difficulties Soviet reformers faced. Coverage of the increasingly complex situation in the Baltic states was extensive but diplomatic, that is, events were generally reported in straightforward fashion, with considerable empathy for the difficulties confronting the Soviet leadership. A partial exception was the front-page article in the party daily in which Senator Luciano Lama explicitly said that the Baltic countries were correct to denounce their annexation in 1940. Whatever justifications may have existed half a century ago, Lama went on, were certainly no longer valid today. He then immediately added that while everyone "takes as given" these countries' national rights, the *real* issue is how to go about restoring them in light of the difficulties currently confronting the USSR (*l'Unità*, 24 August).

For the PCI, as undoubtedly for many others, by

far the most distressing developments in the communist world took place in the People's Republic of China, in early June, when the regime violently crushed the prodemocracy demonstrations in Tiananmen Square and elsewhere. As events were coming to a head late in May, Occhetto and Antonio Rubbi went to the Chinese embassy to urge restraint on the PRC's government (*l'Unità*, 24 May). A few days later, the party formally issued a statement supporting the demonstrators (*l'Unità*, 30 May). As the situation grew increasingly tense, a group of PCI activists constructed their own version of the "Goddess of Liberty" statue in one of Milan's major squares.

Immediately following news of the bloodbath, the PCI condemned the acts of the regime in the strongest possible terms. Occhetto personally called a demonstration in front of the Chinese embassy, and then led a sit-down protest at the embassy's gates, along with a group estimated at between 1,500 and 2,000. Denouncing the "criminal acts" carried out in China, he said that those responsible had no right to associate themselves with socialist ideals (*l'Unità*, 5 June). In an interview the next day, he said "we no longer recognize these regimes as socialist" (*Corriere della sera*, 6 June). On the same day, the editor in chief of *l'Unità*, Massimo D'Alema, wrote a front-page editorial denouncing "the failure and indefensibility of authoritarian systems like those found in the countries of so-called 'real socialism'" (6 June). Occhetto immediately announced that he had canceled his plans to visit China later in the year, and that the PCI "disinvited" the Chinese to their National Festival of *l'Unità*. The party also demanded that the Italian government freeze economic relations with the People's Republic of China, starting with all military matters (*l'Unità*, 10 June).

The speed and depth of the PCI's initiatives and denunciations were rooted in the party's sincere revulsion at the events in China, but they were aggravated by the fact that this all took place during the electoral campaign for the European Parliament. As the *New York Times* correctly noted, Italian communist leaders were escalating their criticism, reflecting their anguish at the thought of voters going to the polls with fresh impressions of a communist government shooting down its young people (*NYT*, 9 June). Judging from the PCI's showing in the elections (see earlier discussion), the party did manage to distance itself from the Chinese regime relatively well.

These were the major activities involving the PCI and the established socialist states in 1989. In a more minor key, but still worthy of mention, was a conference in Trieste in February that was jointly hosted by the PCI's Gramsci Institute of Friuli-Venezia Giulia (Italy's northeasternmost region) and the Marxist Center of the Slovenian League of Communists. This gathering analyzed the reforms under way in Eastern Europe, focusing on Poland, Hungary, and Yugoslavia. Although the bulk of the participants were members of the Italian or Slovenian parties, various Hungarian and Polish contributions added to an often lively three-day meeting (Kevin Devlin, *RFE Research*, 17 February). Not surprisingly, there was extensive discussion of the need and desirability of political pluralism in all these societies, and the PCI was again able to demonstrate that it was well situated to play an important mediating role between East and West.

The PCI's *West* European vocation as the champion of a broad "Euro-left" was also very much in evidence throughout 1989, as we have already noted earlier. This took two main forms in the year of the elections to the European Parliament. Before and after the elections, the PCI sought out the widest possible range of contacts with major European socialist parties, particularly the German Social Democratic Party (SPD)—a favored interlocutor for many years—the French Socialists (PS), and British Labour. Rivalry and conflict between the PCI and the PSI, as we have seen, destroyed what obviously would have been a major coup for Occhetto: a March meeting, in Brussels, with the Union of Socialist and Social-Democratic Parties of the European Community to discuss a common program for the June elections. But this major disappointment did not prevent the Italian leadership from maintaining and intensifying already strong bilateral links with key European socialist parties.

The PCI has never hidden the fact that its overtures to European Socialists have been viewed most favorably by the SPD and PS, and the party was able to reinforce this impression during the campaign for the European Parliament. It invited Maurice Duverger, a famous French political scientist and jurist, to stand as an independent candidate in its electoral list. Duverger, a prominent adviser and friend of President François Mitterrand, agreed, and praised the PCI's "truly European perspective" as well as its courage in undertaking a "complete cultural revolution" in *Le Monde* (text in *La Repubblica*, 7/8 May).

The SPD, given its own ambitions, is especially interested in the PCI's mediating potential between the USSR and the West in an era of greatly reduced international tensions (interview with Karsten Voigt, *l'Espresso*, 19 March). In January, Occhetto visited Germany for talks with leaders of the SPD. And in April, he met with PS leader Pierre Mauroy, whom he found in agreement with him about the need to reorganize the entire European left, and create "a Euro-Left extending beyond Eurocommunism and Eurosocialism, transcending the old boundaries of the debate on the left" (*l'Unità*, 13 April). In a pointed reference to Craxi and the PSI, Occhetto went on to note that the PCI's socialist interlocutors outside Italy, "unconcerned by matters of rivalry, are able to perceive the value and importance of these positions" (ibid.).

In April, Occhetto visited leaders of Spain's United Left Party, and in May the head of the Danish Socialist People's Party, Gert Petersen, came to Rome. The significance of these encounters became clear after the European elections. In July, in Brussels, Occhetto presented a new "United European Left" caucus that would sit in the European Parliament apart from the communist group. The 28 members of the new grouping, 22 of whom were elected in the PCI's lists, included the entire Spanish United Left and Danish Socialist People's delegations, along with a single Greek Communist (*l'Unità*, 21 July). The new alignment was twice the size of the Communist Caucus, which included the French, Portuguese, and Irish delegations, as well as three of the four Greek Communists. Occhetto proposed the new group as "the nucleus of a real European left" (ibid.).

Many observers saw this move as a prelude to seeking membership in the Socialist Caucus of the European Parliament in Strasbourg and, eventually, as a way for the PCI to breach the question of joining the Socialist International. A month before the announcement in Brussels, there had been hints from a member of the Secretariat, Piero Fassino, that the PCI might well take a fairly dramatic step in the European Parliament. Fassino reiterated that the party's ultimate goal was membership in the Socialist International (*L'Espresso*, 25 June). The pace of high-level contacts continued until late in the year, when Occhetto met with Neil Kinnock, leader of Britain's Labour Party, in Brussels (*La Repubblica*, 11 November).

Finally, one of the most significant international activities of the PCI in 1989 was the visit of Occhetto (accompanied by Napolitano) to the United States in May. This was the first such visit by a PCI general secretary, and it was undertaken during the campaign for the European elections. Occhetto was quite explicit that the purpose of the trip was not only "to dispel old, mistaken ideas about Italian Communists," but to present himself "as an exponent of the new European left" (*La Repubblica*, 16 May). Although official U.S. reserve toward the PCI ruled out any formal government contacts, Occhetto and Napolitano did meet with a variety of congressional leaders from both houses of Congress, including conservative Republican Alan Simpson of Wyoming as well as House majority leader Tom Foley. Many other prominent figures were met at a dinner hosted by the Italian ambassador (Kevin Devlin, *RFE Research*, 22 May). The visit also included numerous roundtables, interviews, and speeches and seminars of the type that PCI leaders have carried on over the past decade. Although it was primarily of symbolic value, this visit represented a breakthrough in that it did, finally, involve the head of the PCI. The party's patient diplomacy, often thwarted by the State Department as well as various political events (such as Italian elections), had finally paid off.

Stephen M. Hellman
York University
North York, Ontario, Canada

Luxembourg

Population. 366,329 (July 1989)
Party. Communist Party of Luxembourg (Parti communiste luxembourgeois; CPL)
Founded. 1921
Membership. More than 600
Chairman. René Urbany (re-elected)
Executive Committee. 10 members: Aloyse Bisdorff, François Hoffmann, Fernand Hübsch, André Moes, Marianne Passeri, Marcel Putz, Babette Ruckert, René Urbany, Serge Urbany
Secretariat. 1 member: René Urbany
Central Committee. 33 full and 6 candidate members
Status. Legal
Last Congress. Twenty-fifth, 23–24 April 1988; held in Differdange

Last Election. 1989, under 4 percent, 1 of 64 seats
Auxiliary Organizations. Jeunesse communiste luxembourgeoise; Union des femmes luxembourgeoises
Publications. *Zeitung vum Letzebürger Vollek* (Newspaper of the Luxembourgian people), daily, 1,500–2,000 copies (CPL claims up to 20,000)

It almost sounded pathetic when René Urbany, chairman of the tiny CPL, as late as July 1989, proudly announced that his party organizes "coach tours to other *socialist countries*: The GDR, Czechoslovakia and Bulgaria," and considered it even necessary to explain that "the building of a socialist society in *Western Europe* is not an immediate prospect. . . ." (*WMR*, July; my emphasis.)

Because of the country's size, which barely equals that of Rhode Island, and partly because its government is a constitutional monarchy (Luxembourg has been an independent Grand Duchy since 1868), the orthodox pro-Soviet CPL plays no significant role in the European communist movement and only a minor domestic political role. In the last federal election to the Chamber of Deputies (June 1989), the communist voting strength in that body was reduced to one seat.

Leadership and Organization. The CPL almost seems to be a family operation, as the political as well as the theoretical leadership of this active party is dominated by the Urbany family. The chairman's father, Dominique Urbany, was one of the party's founders, and led it until 1977. He remained in the CPL as honorary chairman until his death in October 1986 (*Neues Deutschland*, 27 October 1986). Many key positions within the party and its auxiliaries are occupied by members of this family. Jaqueline, René, and Serge Urbany are members of the new Central Committee, and René and Serge Urbany are also in the Executive Committee. Jaqueline Urbany is a member of the important Finance and Control Commission. In addition, René Urbany is director of the party press, which is heavily subsidized by the Society for the Development of the Press and Printing Industry, an organization founded by the SED (the East German communist party). The CPL's publishing company, COPE, not only prints and distributes the French edition of the *World Marxist Review*, but also serves other communist parties abroad. Since 1976, René Urbany has held a seat in the Luxembourg parliament. Although the party's positions have become somewhat stronger in the capital and in some municipalities of the industrialized south, its political influence has seemed to continue to decline since 1968.

Domestic Affairs. Probably the single most important event of 1989 for the CPL was that it lost one of its two seats in the election in June. This turn of events is not surprising. Last year's congress was held under the vague motto "Let's get going," and the main points discussed were the rapid de-industrialization of Luxembourg, the major shifts in the country's social structure, and the appeal for world peace and nuclear-free zones. In his opening report, René Urbany then lamented that the mining industries' collapse and the complete disappearance of the miners' trade in Luxembourg caused disappointment among many potential followers, and apparently dissuaded them from joining the old-fashioned party. Furthermore, according to René Urbany, the number of workers in Luxembourg's steel industry has diminished by 50 percent over the past fifteen years: "In 1970, the steel industry accounted for over 28 percent of the Gross Domestic Product, and for 12 percent of all jobs: today the figures are 11 and 9 percent, respectively" (*WMR*, July 1988). These profound changes have had a tremendous impact on the structure of the industrial proletariat, which has constituted the backbone of the communist party, and cost the CPL one of its two seats in the parliament.

According to the *World Marxist Review* (July), the CPL again offered to work with the Socialist Workers' Party (POSL) and all other left-wing forces. The POSL and the People's Christian Social Party form a coalition having 40 seats in the parliament. Although it was repeatedly denied last year, the CPL and the POSL were already cooperating in three regions.

In view of the fact that the majority of the citizens receive their information mainly through TV, the party continued to give its newspaper a more attractive format. The *Zeitung vum Letzebürger Vollek* is now emphasizing more strongly commentaries, ideology, and interpretation to balance the allegedly bourgeois information given over TV.

International Affairs. One of the major events of 1989 for the CPL certainly was the "comradely" visit in January of an official SED delegation under the leadership of Werner Eberlein, a member of the East German party's Central Committee. As usual, topics of mutual interest, such as international solidarity, disarmament, and peace, were on the agenda. (*ND*, 26, 27, 28 January.) In return, a CPL delegation, led by René Urbany, was invited to East Berlin in February to discuss "questions of the common European home" (*ND*, 21 February). In April, Nikolay Ryzhkov, a member of the Politburo of the CPSU's Central Committee, met with Urbany in Luxembourg. The conversation apparently was marked by a comradely atmosphere (*FBIS*, 20 April). The party's international activities in 1989 culminated in the traditional *Pressefest* in September in Schifflingen, at which René Urbany, in his opening address, pathetically accused West Germany of blackmailing the GDR and of oppressing the international socialist movement (*ND*, 18 September). On 14 April, a delegation of the Luxembourg-China Friendship Association led by Franco, president of the group, traveled to Shanghai. Jiang Zemin, a president of the Shanghai Association for the Promotion of Friendship with Foreign Countries, extended a warm welcome to the delegation. (*FBIS*, 18 April.)

Besides these modest international activities of the CPL and potential sympathizers, there were again a few additional indications of intensified contacts between the CPL and the SED. But this state of affairs might have changed by the time this is published.

Kurt R. Leube

California State University, Hayward

Malta

Population. 351,307 (September 1989, Malta Central Office of Statistics)
Party. Communist Party of Malta (*Partit Komunista Malti*; CPM)
Date Founded. 1969
Membership. 300 (estimated)
General Secretary. Anthony Vassallo (70, on full-time party work)
Central Committee. 13 members: C. Zammit (president), A. Vassallo (general secretary), V. Degiovanni (Central Committee and international secretary), R. J. Mifsud (propaganda secretary), D. Mallia (organizational secretary), J. Attard, L.

Attard-Bezzina, J. M. Cachia, A. Caruana, A. Cordina, K. Gerada, M. Mifsud
Status. Legal
Last Congress. Fourth Congress, 15–17 July 1988
Last Elections. 9 May 1987
Auxiliary Organizations. Malta-USSR Friendship and Cultural Society; Malta-Czechoslovakia Friendship Society; Malta-Cuba Friendship and Cultural Society; Malta-Korean Friendship and Cultural Society; Young Communist League (*Ghaqda Zghazagh Komnisti*); Union of Progressive Youth; Peace and Solidarity Council of Malta; Women for Peace; Association of Progressive Journalists
Publications. *Zminijietna* (Our times), tabloid published irregularly, partly in English and partly in Maltese; *Bandiera Hamra* (Red flag), issued by Young Communist League; *Bridge of Friendship and Culture*, quarterly journal of the Malta-USSR Friendship and Cultural Society

The CPM has been in decline since its sorry performance in the May 1987 general elections. The party has reduced its activities, and it appears that its sources of finance have dried up substantially, to the extent that it has ceased to publish the monthly Malta edition of the *World Marxist Review* entitled *International Political Review*. During 1989, the CPM's local publication *Zminijietna* published only three issues, although it is supposed to be a monthly publication. The party contented itself with the issue of a few formal press releases on matters of topical interest. One expressed concern about a government computer data base on public-service employees (*Orizzont*, 7 February). Others dealt with police intervention and the use of CS gas following incidents during the Republic Day celebrations (*Zminijietna*, May) and the increase of airfares by the Maltese National Airline (*Orizzont*, 12 September). One condemned the U.S. intervention in Panama (*Orizzont*, 23 December).

The CPM membership merged with other left-wing forces to sustain Malta's neutral and non-aligned status. Meanwhile, the Soviet Union filled the vacuum left by the CPM's slight activity through a wide range of initiatives calculated to project a benevolent image. The dramatic turn of events in Eastern Europe, leading up to the Malta Summit and beyond, as well as President Gorbachev's visit to the island—the first ever by a Soviet leader, and one who, incidentally, had just met the pope with maximum television exposure—amply compensated for the loss of face by the CPM.

The CPM's Central Committee secretary, Victor Degiovanni, reported in the March issue of the *World Marxist Review* that the CPM had made an examination of conscience after the 1987 electoral defeat to reassess its work and effectiveness. He charged that the sixteen-year rule by the Malta Labour Party "had left the workers in dismay," and that the social-democratic MLP was unable to retain power "due to lack of contact with workers' realities." He expressed the view that this alienated the workers and resulted in their shift to the right. In this new situation, the CPM planned to increase its numerical strength as well as its effectiveness. This it proposed to do by relaxing its criteria regulating membership. Moreover, new members will no longer be required to undergo a probationary period.

The CPM decided to open a research and documentation center to help educate new members, who were to be reorganized in a system of cells in workplaces and in the various electoral districts. The setting up of these cells is the responsibility of the organizational secretary. In order to overcome problems that may arise from the dilution of ideological fervor of new members, it was decided to reconstitute the Executive Committee within the Central Committee. This name is a euphemism for an old-fashioned Politburo.

By the end of 1989, there was no tangible evidence that these decisions had led to a qualitative change in party work. The CPM has all but gone to earth and remained silent on the major issues that have been sweeping across the communist world, from Tiananmen Square in China to the Berlin Wall and Romania.

While the CPM's decline continued, there has been increasing evidence of new contacts between the Malta Labour Party and foreign communist organizations and governments. The party's international secretary, Leo Brincat, attended the congress of the Italian Communist Party in Rome, where he was also reported to have had bilateral talks with Alexander Yakovlev, Politburo member of the CPSU (*Orizzont*, 3 March). A few days earlier, on 6 March, Antonio Rubbi, member of the PCI Directorate for international relations, met Leo Brincat and the MLP's leader, Dr. Carmelo Mifsud Bonnici (*The Democrat*, 1 April).

The MLP's deputy leader, Joe Debono Grech, attended a conference in Lisbon on the unification of Korea, as guest of the North Korean government (*Orizzont*, 7 March). Debono Grech and another Labour MP, Dr. John Attard-Montalto, were the special guests of the Kim Il-Sung regime for the Thirteenth World Youth Festival in Pyongyang (*Sunday Chronicle*, 16 July). A party of twenty Maltese youths from communist youth groups and the youth movements of the MLP and the General Workers' Union (GWU) were among the participants in the festival (*It-Torca*, 6 August).

The general secretary of the MLP Youth Movement, Raymond Tabone, attended a conference dealing with disarmament and security in Czechoslovakia, organized by the Czech Communist Youth Organization for 500 delegates from all over the world (*Orizzont*, 6 June). Two members of the IMEMO Institute for World Economy and International Relations of the Soviet Academy of Sciences, V. Zuiv and I. Abratova, visited Malta as guests of the MLP to discuss, among other things, Malta's position in relation to the European Community. They had four meetings with the leader and other representatives of the party. The nature of their conclusions was not disclosed. (*Orizzont*, 5 and 9 June.)

In the course of the year, a Labour Party candidate who had unsuccessfully contested the 1987 election, and who had since been expelled as a dissident, Carmen Spiteri, claimed that the MLP had been infiltrated by Communists. She said she was prepared to provide the names of the people in question and demanded their resignation. She made vague allegations about persons in the leadership being aware of such infiltration and failing to do anything about it. (Malta, *The Times*, 8 August.) After her expulsion, she wrote and published a letter to the Party Executive reiterating the same allegations (*In-Nazzjon Taghna*, 10 October).

Meanwhile the Soviet embassy increased its visibility by a substantial degree, with the ambassador, Vladimir Ya Pletchko, and his numerous staff adopting new-style tactics and exploiting to the maximum the new atmosphere of détente.

After failing to meet a number of deadlines, the Marsa Shipyard delivered the first of eight timber carriers ordered by the Soviet Union (Malta, *The Times*, 1 July). Because of this delay, the shipyard had to pay a penalty of 1,750,000 U.S. dollars. When Prime Minister Fenech Adami was in New York to address the U.N. General Assembly, he met the Soviet foreign minister, Edouard Shevardnadze and asked that this penalty be waived. (Malta, *The Times*, 3 October). Shevardnadze undertook to have this matter considered by the appropriate authorities, and the Soviets renounced their penalty rights as a gesture of good will a few days before the

Bush-Gorbachev summit meeting. The order of the eight timber carriers formed part of the current five-year Malta-USSR trade protocol, which expires at the end of 1990.

Negotiations have been opened for the subsequent trade protocol, and the program for the delivery of the remaining seven ships may have to be rephased.

The existing trade protocol covering the period from 1987 to 1990 proved to be a disappointment also to the Maltese side in that the targets set were far from achieved. The protocol made provision for the purchase of Maltese goods by the Soviets in the amount of 40 million U.S. dollars each year (*Orizzont*, 26 November 1986). During 1987 and 1988, Maltese exports to the Soviet Union declined progressively to the point that in 1988 Malta had an unfavorable trade balance of nine million dollars (Malta, *The Times*, 7 April), having sold six million U.S. dollars worth of visible exports and imported 15.2 million dollars worth of Soviet products (*Malta Trade Statistics*).

Throughout 1989, the Soviet ambassador and his Commercial Office made strenuous efforts to reverse the trend. They were supported by high-level Moscow dignitaries who visited the island in the course of the year. The deputy minister of trade of the RSFSR, B. Tichanov, headed a trade delegation to discuss the deteriorating situation (*Orizzont*, 8 March). A high-powered delegation from the Chamber of Commerce of the USSR, led by Vice-President Igor Kanaev, paid a five-day-long call on the Maltese Chamber of Commerce. This provided the visitors with an opportunity for extensive contacts with private sector representatives (*Commercial Courier*, August). The Soviet minister of trade, Kondrad Terech, made a fleeting follow-up visit and went out of his way during a busy 24-hour program to call on the Maltese Chamber of Commerce (*Orizzont*, 2 September). Another buying delegation arrived from Moscow in early November under the leadership of the minister of trade of the Soviet Republic of Dagestan, B. U. Gudijev (*Commercial Courier*, December). The Soviets attributed to their domestic difficulties and the shortage of hard currency, as well as the upheavals brought about by the process of *perestroika*, the slower tempo of trade. Nevertheless, the intense Soviet initiatives led to a substantial increase of Maltese exports to the USSR during 1989. The final official figures were not available at the end of 1989, but Maltese government sources estimated that they would exceed

twenty million U.S. dollars (Malta, *The Times*, 29 May).

The Soviet embassy had an intense program in cultural and other areas of cooperation, maintaining its visibility through the media practically the entire year. There were book donations to the University of Malta, photographic and postage-stamp exhibitions, visits by folkdancing and musical groups, a Komsomol troop, and a ballet ensemble. The *pièce de résistance* was a visit by a 160-member-strong Red Army Ensemble, whose dazzling performance was compered by a Maltese-speaking Soviet officer.

To the foregoing, one must add separate visits by two Soviet cadet training ships, visits by eye specialists, and invitations extended to Maltese artists, students, and others to travel to the Soviet Union.

Aeroflot, which has been using Malta as a transit point for the past six years (*Orizzont*, 6 January), flies in tons of Soviet literature, which are steadily thrown into Maltese hands like confetti. The embassy places a substantial amount of film and radio material with the Maltese broadcasting media.

A director of the Novosti Press Agency, Yevgeny A. Roumiantsev, visited Malta in August and called on various media editors to discuss "measures for further cooperation between Maltese and Soviet newspapers" (*The Democrat*, 19 August).

As can be seen, during 1989 the activities of the Soviets were even more insistent than before, but they were also manifestly more slick, more soft, and more effective.

They were supplemented by other initiatives from Eastern-bloc countries. Czechoslovakia signed a cultural protocol with the Maltese government (*Nazzjon Taghna*, 14 January) and a health protocol (Malta, *The Times*, 4 April). The Maltese ambassador to Czechoslovakia, F. E. Amato Gauci, presented his credentials in February and had talks with various Czech government ministries (*Nazzjon Taghna*, 25 February).

The parliamentary secretary for health, Dr. George Hyzler, visited Sofia for "final discussions leading to the signing of a plan on cooperation in the health care field" between Malta and Bulgaria (Malta, *The Times*, 9 September). A GWU delegation was invited to Bulgaria (*Orizzont*, 22 May). A program of cooperation in the arts was launched (*The Democrat*, 15 April), and the Bulgarian national airline was offered incentives to encourage Maltese visitors to Bulgaria. A total of 1,400 Maltese took advantage of these opportunities during 1989 (*Nazzjon Taghna*, 20 December).

North Korea has reduced its activities in Malta substantially since the change of government.

Auxiliary Organizations. The only auxiliary organization of the CPM which maintained its usual tempo of activity during 1989 was the Malta-USSR Friendship and Cultural Society. The society observed the fifteenth anniversary of its foundation this year. It organized a public forum on Malta-USSR relationships and a number of cultural events (*Orizzont*, 27 July). The Soviet ambassador presented special diplomas to four of its founders, namely Geraldu Azzopardi, Paul Agius, Anton Agius, and Anthony Ciappara, in recognition of their pioneering efforts. The minister of education, Dr. Ugo Mifsud Bonnici, presented another diploma of appreciation to a Dominican friar, Father Marius Zerafa, on the same occasion. (*Orizzont*, 7 October.)

Apart from undertaking its routine annual activities, which include the offer of scholarships for study in the USSR, Russian language lessons, and conducted group tours to the Soviet Union, the society mounted a public forum on Lenin (Malta, *The Times*, 26 April). The Soviet ambassador presented a range of audiovisual equipment to the society to facilitate the work of the Russian language classes (*Orizzont*, 9 August).

The Peace and Solidarity Council issued a public statement warning that "efforts are in hand to change Malta's neutral and nonaligned status" leading to Maltese accession to "the Western bloc" (*Zminijietna*, June).

The Malta-China Friendship Society, which observed a stony silence on the suppression of the prodemocracy movement in Tiananmen Square and throughout China, surfaced during September to hold an exhibition of photographs "illustrating progress in China during the last 40 years." The exhibition was opened by the new Chinese ambassador to Malta, Mr. Mei Ping (Malta, *The Times*, 25 September).

All of the CPM's other auxiliary organizations showed no signs of movement throughout 1989.

Policies of the Maltese Government. The Maltese government repeatedly professed its adherence to Western democratic principles at the United Nations and elsewhere, publicly declaring its intention to apply for full membership in the European Community next year. Prime Minister Fenech Adami paid official visits to the United States, Great Britain, Italy, and West Germany dur-

ing 1989. At the same time, the Maltese government continued its relations with the Soviet Union on a nonideological basis, maintaining its neutral and nonaligned status.

The president of Malta, Dr. Vincent Tabone, was interviewed by *World Marxist Review*, presumably when he was still minister of foreign affairs. The interview was carried verbatim in the July issue. Dr. Tabone spelled out Maltese official policy in fairly precise terms as follows:

I believe that a small independent nation can only maintain its independence if it is a neutral country. We are attached to a neutrality policy based on the principles of non-alignment. On the other hand, we have some specific ideas with regard to the concept of freedom and democracy. We believe in a multi-party system. We believe in individual freedom and the freedom of everyone to express his or her views and in that respect we are Western-oriented as regards the type of democracy we follow. But we also acknowledge that we have always been and felt European.

With specific reference to the Mediterranean, Dr. Tabone said in the course of the same interview:

My belief is that peace has been kept in the global dimension since the last war because there has been a military balance between East and West. Balance has been the essence of peace. And even in the very positive reduction of armaments so far agreed between the USSR and the USA—it is balance they speak about. Therefore I feel that shifting this balance is not a step towards peace. This is my view, and therefore I do not subscribe to the request for the Superpowers to leave the Mediterranean without ensuring that the military balance remains.

It seems that Soviet policy and that of its sympathizers in Malta is to encourage the Maltese government to maintain a neutral and nonaligned stance. It also appears that the intense and relatively expensive program of Soviet presence and activity in this 100-square-mile island is primarily intended to ensure that Malta does not diverge from its path.

In a briefing paper distributed by the Novosti Press Agency to journalists attending the Malta summit in December, it is stated that "on the whole, Soviet-Maltese relations are at a good level and steadily developing. The Soviet Union states with satisfaction that since the Nationalist Party came to power in 1987, after an interval of 16 years, Malta's course for friendly, equitable and mutually advantageous relations with the Soviet Union has not changed." (APN, 2 December.)

J. G. E. Hugh
Valletta, Malta

The Netherlands

Population. 14,790,125

Party. Communist Party of the Netherlands (Communistische Partij van Nederland; CPN), since 1989 allied with Radicals, Socialist-Pacifists, Evangelical People's Party in so-called Green Left

Founded. 1909

Membership. CPN: 3–5,000 (estimated). Social composition of delegates to 1984 congress: 10 percent manual workers, 10 percent teachers, 22 percent civil servants (including teachers), 10 percent social workers, 20 percent unemployed, 5 percent nurses (Fennema, "The End of Dutch Bolshevism?" in Waller and Fennema, eds., *Communist Parties in Western Europe*, Oxford: Blackwell, 1988)

Chairman. Elli Izeboud

Politburo. 55 members, including Elli Izeboud, Ina Brouwer, Marius Ernsting, Nico Scouten, Jan Berghuis, Leo Molenaar, Jan de Book, Ton van Hoek, Geert Lameris

Central Committee. 46 members, including Henk Hoekstra, secretary; Ton van Hoek, international secretary; Joop Morriën, Jon Geelen, Wemke Ketting-Jager, Edward Koen

Status. Legal

Last Congress. Thirty-first, 8–11 April 1989, in Amersfoort

Last Election. 1989, Green Left wins 4.1 percent, 6 of 150 seats in Second Chamber (lower house); 1987, CPN wins 1 of 75 seats in First Chamber (senate)

Auxiliary Organizations. CPN Women, General Netherlands Youth Organization (ANJV), Stop the Bomb/Stop the Nuclear Arms Race, CPN Youth Platform, Scholing en Onderwijs, Women Against Nuclear Weapons

Publications. *De Waarheid* (Truth), official CPN daily, circulation about 10,000; *CPN-leden krant* (Bulletin for party members), appears 10 times annually; *Politiek en cultuur*, theoretical journal published 10 times annually; *Komma*, quarterly published by the CPN's Institute for Political and Social Research; CPN owns Pegasus Publishers.

In 1988, a Dutch political scientist predicted "the end of Dutch Bolshevism" (Meindert Fennema, "The End of Dutch Bolshevism?" in Michael Waller and Meindert Fennema, eds., *Communist Parties in Western Europe: Decline or Adaptation?* Oxford: Blackwell, 1988, pp. 158–78). In 1989, the prediction effectively came true. The CPN leadership, realizing that the party would never again win parliamentary representation by itself and was sliding swiftly toward total extinction, formed the Green Left alliance with three small new left parties: the Pacifist Socialists (PSP), the Radical Party (PPR), and the Evangelical People's Party (EVP) (*NRC Handelsblad*, 3 July; *FBIS-WEU*, 7 July). The constituent parties of the Green Left have not merged their organizations and claim to maintain their respective identities. For example, the CPN will doubtless continue to hold party congresses and elect a Central Committee and a Politburo, at least for a while, since doing so takes only a few dozen people. Moreover, the last Communists are precisely those who will least of all want to admit that their historic role has ended. Yet this residual existence is mainly a way of saving face, since the party no longer has a viable separate function or identity in Dutch politics.

The Dutch Communist Party thus became the first of the small Northwest European parties to draw the consequences of the changing international situation. It was aware as well of the sociocultural changes in Dutch society that were making a distinct communist identity irrelevant. In 1989, after a long illness, Dutch Bolshevism as a living ideology and strategy of political mobilization came to an end. How far personalities and sociocultural elements of Dutch communism may survive in its new guise as ecological-feminist leftism is a question for future editions of this yearbook.

The epoch that ended in 1989 began in 1909, when radical Marxists from the revolutionary left wing of the labor movement and the Labor Party (PvdA) founded the Social Democratic Party. In 1919, as the Communist Party of Holland, it affiliated with the Comintern, and in 1935 took its present name. It won representation in the Staaten Generaal (parliament) in 1918 and remained there until 1986. In 1940, Nazi Germany occupied the Netherlands, but the party remained legal as long as Germany was allied with the Soviet Union. It was suppressed, and lost its parliamentary membership, from 1941 to 1945.

In its ideological and social composition, the CPN resembled other Northwest European communist parties. Like them, it was a small party that never captured more than a few percent of the vote, with the partial exception of the immediate postwar years. In 1946, 11 percent of Dutch voters supported the CPN, a figure that fell to 6 in 1951 and 2.4 in 1959. In 1945, likewise, the party newspaper *De Waarheid* briefly enjoyed a circulation of 300,000—more than any other paper in the Netherlands. This temporary upswing reflected popular respect for the CPN's role in the Resistance and sympathy for Stalin and the Soviet Union, rather than any penetration of communist ideology into the Dutch left or Dutch political culture as a whole.

When Nikita Khrushchev gave his Secret Speech in 1956 denouncing Stalin, the CPN did not undertake any process of de-Stalinization in its own ranks or methods. Nevertheless, starting in 1960, the CPN gradually distanced itself from Moscow on a range of issues, while retaining a Stalinist internal structure and remaining loyal to Marxism-Leninism and the Moscow-led international communist movement. From the early 1960s on, CPN leaders considered revisionism in various forms as the best strategy to widen their base of support. In 1963, for example, they declared a policy of "autonomy" in relation to Moscow and gave some support to China in the Sino-Soviet dispute. In 1968, they denounced the invasion of Czechoslovakia by Warsaw Pact troops. Simultaneously, the CPN pursued "autonomy" at home by opening a dialogue with the growing noncommunist intellectual left and with progressive Catholic and Protestant thinkers. This campaign encouraged some 5,000 members of the fast-growing student generation to join the party between 1968 and 1975 and gave it 4.5 of the vote in the 1972 elections. As part of this change, the social composition of party congresses and, presumably, of the membership as a whole changed radically. By 1977, students, social workers, and teachers—the classic core groups of the "1968 generation"— formed a third of the delegates and outnumbered manual workers, the traditional core of the party. Despite these changes, the CPN organization remained rigidly Stalinist. (Marcel van der Linden and Joost Wormer, "The End of a Tradition: Structural Developments and Trends in Dutch Communism," *Journal of Communist Studies* 4 [1988]:78–87; Fennema, "The End of Dutch Bolshevism?")

Emboldened by the prospect of success in recruiting members of the 1968 generation, younger CPN leaders began arguing in the early 1970s that if the party would develop a broad left strategy using the new themes of pacifism, feminism, and environmentalism, it would be even better placed to attract elements of the progressive middle class and thus turn itself into a serious rival of the PvdA. It was important to make this effort because if the CPN missed that chance, it would be seized by other radical parties that were then springing up—the PSP and the RPP—with which it finally merged in 1989. At the time, these arguments failed to convince the powerful CPN chairman, Paul de Groot, an old-style Bolshevik of the purest type. In the 1977 elections, the PvdA recaptured most of the votes previously lost to the extreme left, including the CPN, which won only 1.7 percent and two seats. De Groot maintained that the CPN had lost ground because it was no longer Bolshevik enough, had become disloyal to the Soviet Union, and had lost contact with manual workers. His opponents, naturally enough, argued the opposite position, namely that the CPN was doomed to disappear unless it pursed a New Left strategy far more vigorously.

The result of this internal struggle was a compromise. The CPN rejected Eurocommunism and returned, temporarily, to full loyalty to the Soviet Union, which it had not displayed so completely since 1960. On the other hand, the Central Committee refused to accept that the party's future lay with manual workers, fast disappearing in the Netherlands. Followers and opponents of the pro-Soviet line continued to fight each other as CPN support in the country declined, until the anti-Stalinist feminists, pacifists, and environmentalists won in 1982.

Two currents in Dutch society contributed to the change in the CPN in the 1980s, both growing out of the progressive cultural revolution of the 1960s: feminism and antinuclearism. The feminists accused the party of being male-dominated and obsessed with ideology and demanded equal representation in party organs. Unlike all earlier oppositional movements, the feminists did not represent a coherent ideological position that the Stalinists could easily attack; moreover, the cultural climate made it difficult for them to resist the feminist agenda as such, as they could then be accused of male chauvinism.

Antinuclearism began in earnest in 1978 and accelerated from 1979 to 1983, when the Netherlands was party to the NATO decision to modernize nuclear weapons in Europe. Both currents affected large parts of Dutch society, including the center-right parties. The CPN theoretically stood to benefit from adopting the new progressive agenda, as it did when it adopted a new program in 1984, the first since 1952, which replaced Marxism-Leninism by Marxism-feminism. In 1984, the party officially abolished democratic centralism in its own ranks and announced that it now fully accepted parliamentary democracy. Unfortunately for the CPN, its reorientation availed it very little, if at all. Some pro-Soviet Bolsheviks, mostly in Amsterdam, left the party in 1982 and formed a splinter group, the Union of Communists in the Netherlands (VCN). On the other side, many feminists and pacifists, who had supported the CPN in the hope that it was about to adopt their agenda completely, left again in 1985 because change was not coming about quickly enough. Membership, which had risen from some 11,000 during most of the 1960s to 15,500 in 1980, plummeted again to 6,000 in 1986, a smaller number than at any time since the 1930s.

These developments on both flanks weakened the CPN as the 1986 elections drew near. Despite attempts to build electoral alliances with the PSP and the RPP, the CPN competed on its own in these elections, which were a disaster for the party. In the municipal elections in March, it lost a third of its seats on municipal councils. In the parliamentary elections in May, it won only a third of the vote of 1982, namely 0.6 percent. As a result, there were no Communists in the Second Chamber of parliament for the first time since 1918. As in 1977, the PvdA took votes and seats from all three of the small radical parties. It nevertheless failed to oust the coalition government of the Christian-Democratic Appeal (Christen-Democratisch Appel; CDA) and the liberal People's Party for Freedom and Democracy (Volkspartij voor Vrijheid en Democratie; VVD) led by Ruud Lubbers, which continued in office with 81 out of 150 seats.

Apart from internal divisions, another reason that the CPN lost ground was that its new agenda was indistinguishable not only from that of the PSP or the RPP, but even, in many respects, from that of the dominant left wing of the PvdA. The CPN could offer no fresh solutions to the questions raised by radicals inside or outside the working class. Dutch voters sympathetic to antinuclearism or feminism might well ask why they should vote for the CPN if the PSP, the RPP, or another fringe grouping without the taint of a Stalinist past was equally open to their views. In short, the turn to feminism and pacifism in the 1980s served only to make the CPN irrelevant. It was to preempt this fate that the CPN decided to join the Green Left in 1989.

Internal Party Affairs. The CPN held its Thirty-first Congress in Amersfoort in April 1989 "to discuss tasks facing Dutch Communists in domestic and foreign policies, work out a programme of action until 1991, and elect the party's leadership" (TASS, 8 April; *FBIS-SOV*, 17 April). On the latter point, the congress re-elected Elli Izeboud as chairman as well as most of the existing members of the Politburo and Central Committee. On the nuclear issue, the congress issued a predictable declaration denouncing NATO nuclear weapons and alleged nuclear-war plans in Europe, calling for a completely nuclear-free Europe, and praising the peace policy of the Soviet Union. This declaration continued what was, in the 1980s, the most important public activity of the CPN, namely its intense involvement in the peace movement against NATO's nuclear modernization plans. Communists dominated large parts of the movement's organizational framework, including its most important element, the Interdenominational Peace Council (IKV). In 1983, a Soviet diplomat reportedly bragged to a Western journalist that the Soviet Union could put 50,000 Dutchmen on the streets against NATO missiles within 24 hours. The transmission belt for such an order must presumably have been the CPN. When U.S.-Soviet negotiations ended in the INF treaty of December 1987 that mandated the removal of all land-based intermediate-range nuclear weapons from the arsenals of both superpowers, however, the CPN found itself with a much less contentious issue in the peace arena.

In 1988, NATO revived plans to modernize U.S. tactical nuclear weapons, that is, missiles with a range of less than 330 miles, in West Germany. These were designed to deter the vast Soviet superiority in such missiles, of which the United States had 72 and the Soviets several hundred in Central Europe. The CPN congress denounced this proposal, even though it did not directly involve the Netherlands, and the issue was therefore of far less concern to Dutch public opinion. In the spring of 1989, politicians in most NATO countries, as well as most observers, still considered it viable, and NATO leaders tentatively reaffirmed it at the regular biennial NATO summit in May 1989. When the new democratic leaders and aspiring leaders of East Central Europe began demanding that the Soviets withdraw all forces from Poland, Czechoslovakia, Hungary, and East Germany, the modernization proposal lost all attractiveness. By the end of 1990 no serious observer any longer considered it either relevant or realistic.

The CPN congress also criticized the Dutch center-right government's "attacks on social achievements and democratic rights," by which it meant government attempts to limit unemployment benefits and restrain wage inflation (*Neues Deutschland*, 8–9 April). Most important, however, was the matter of election strategy. At the time, the next Second Chamber elections were scheduled for May 1990. Elections to the European Parliament in Strasbourg, however, were taking place in June, and Izeboud and the party decided to join forces with the RPP in a Green Left alliance for this election. Despite high hopes, the alliance failed to win a seat in the elections for its leading candidate, a leftist Catholic priest (Kevin Devlin, "The Elections to the European Parliament: United Europe's Disunited Communist Parties," *RAD Background Report 105*, 19 June 1989; *NRC Handelsblad*, 19 June; *FBIS-WEU*, 26 June). In late May, a crisis in the VVD, the CDA's coalition partner in government, made early elections likely. If the CPN were to have any sort of showing at all, it would have to be via a strengthened Green Left. Accordingly, the CPN and RPP began wooing two other small leftist parties, the PSP and the EVP, whose leaders decided on 1 July to join the Green Left. The Green Left received high support in the polls leading up to the election, as much as 7–8 percent, though in fact the alliance vote was 4.1 percent. In the outgoing parliament, the RPP and the PSP had three seats; in the new parliament, the Green Left obtained six seats.

Prime Minister Ruud Lubbers's CDA held its own in the elections. The liberal leader, Joris Voorhoeve, had declared before the elections that he expected the VVD to go into opposition. This left Lubbers the choice of governing alone, with the support of the VVD, or in a broad left-right coalition with the PvdA, which was the option he finally chose. The PvdA had been adopting more centrist fiscal, social, and industrial policy stances during the later 1980s, so the coalition with the CDA was by no means unexpected. The PvdA leaders clearly calculated that the chance of political influence in government outweighed any possible loss of voters on their left flank. On the other hand, this very slight rightward drift of the PvdA did undoubtedly yield some marginal voters to the Green Left, thus assuring its parliamentary representation, and indirectly contributing to the ghostly survival of the CPN.

With the nuclear issue out of the way, it was easier than ever before for the conservative-led Dutch government to continue its own strategy of maintaining power, a strategy that made it frustratingly difficult not only for the CPN, but for its partners in the Green Left, to present themselves as the apostles of peace. This strategy consisted in adopting the peace rhetoric of the left and welcoming Mikhail Gorbachev's "new thinking" about a "common European house" as the sign of a new era, while pursuing nonsocialist domestic fiscal and economic policies.

Conclusion. The CPN and the other Green Left parties had started the 1980s with feminism and antinuclearism as their two main themes. More than ideologies, these themes were rather social and cultural rallying points for a certain small but vociferous sector of the Dutch middle class, the "pink bourgeoisie" of teachers, journalists, progressivist doctors and bureaucrats, and other urban intellectuals. Antinuclearism lost most of its relevance in 1989, but, as its name indicated, the Green Left entered the 1990s with a useful replacement: environmentalism. Of course, all Dutch political parties—indeed, all political parties anywhere in the world—professed to be in favor of the environment. The question was not whether to protect it, but how. In fact, environmentalism as an issue was undergoing a process similar to, but even more thorough than, that of the peace issue in the early 1980s. What happened to the peace issue was that it was overtly depoliticized, that is, removed from the possibility of political argument, for who could be against peace? In fact, of course, clever ideologues and manipulators used this apparent depoliticization to enforce a rigid version of what peace was supposed to mean. As a result, to be for peace came to mean to be against NATO's nuclear weapons, that is, to be for a quite specific form of peace, namely Soviet power.

Thanks to the vigor of pro-NATO liberal and conservative critics, this depoliticization of the peace issue stopped short of complete success. So far, the ideologues of environmentalism have prevented the depoliticization (and hidden politicization) of that issue from facing a similar limit. In both European and American politics, the universal position in favor of the environment is rapidly taking the shape of a specific position in favor of certain policies, all of them involving state action and regulation, whose benefit to the environment is doubtful indeed.

The Netherlands is a crowded country. Most Dutchmen see environmental problems, and most believe that the solution lies in state action. The specific contribution of the Green Left to this situation is to provide a cultural and social environment for those groups in Dutch society that require intimate and demanding political associations for what they consider moral causes. The personality type that requires such associations is a constant in all modern societies. Therefore the Green Left will probably live, though the CPN as we have known it may die.

David R. Gress
Hoover Institution

Norway

Population. 4,202,502
Parties. Norwegian Communist Party (Norges Kommunistiske Parti; NKP); Socialist Left Party (Sosialistisk Venstreparti; SV); Workers' Communist Party (Marxist-Leninist) (Arbeidernes Kommunistiske Parti [marxist-leninistene]; AKP [m-l]), which commonly participates in elections as Red Electoral Alliance (Rød Valgallianse; RV)
Founded. NKP: 1923; SV: 1975; AKP: 1973
Membership. NKP: 1,500–2,000 (est.); SV: 11,000 dues-paying members (official figure); AKP: 5,000–7,000 (est.)
Chairs. NK: Kåre André Nilsen (journalist); SV: Erik Solheim; AKP: Siri Jensen (bookbinder)
Central Committees. NKP: 8 full members: Kåre André Nilsen, Ingrid Negård (deputy chair), Trygve Horgen (deputy chair), Paul Midtlyng, Grete Trondsen, Åsmund Langsether, Gunnar Wahl, Ørnulf Godager; 2 alternate members: Knut Vidar Paulsen, Knut Jarle Berg; SV: 4 members: Erik Solheim, Kjellbjørg Lunde (deputy chair), Per Eggum Maurseth (deputy chair), Hilde Vogt (party secretary); AKP: 17 full members: Siri Jensen (41 years old), Aksel Nærstad

(deputy chair for political affairs, 37), Arne Lauritzen (deputy chair for organizational affairs, 41), Eli Aaby (leader for women's affairs, 34), Frode Bygdnes (leader for labor affairs, 37), Sigurd Allern (editor in charge, *Klassekampen*, 43), Kjersti Ericsson (45), Pål Steigan (39), Tellef Hansen (41), Vidar Våde (46), Marion Palmer (36), Torild Nustad (36), Torstein Dahle (41), Solveig Aamdal (42), Geir Johnsen (40), Tone Anne Ødegaard (45), Bente Moseng (39)
Status. Legal
Last Congress. NKP: Nineteenth, 23–26 April 1987, in Oslo; SV: April 1989, in Skien; AKP: December 1988, "somewhere in Norway" (*Klassekampen*, 13 December 1988)
Last Election. 1989: Joint lists of NKP and AKP ("County Lists for the Environment and Solidarity"): 22,139 votes (0.84 percent), no representation; SV: 266,782 votes (10.08 percent), 17 representatives. 1985: NKP: 0.16 percent, no representation; SV: 5.46 percent, 6 out of 157 representatives; RV: 0.57 percent, no representation
Auxiliary Organizations. NKP: Norwegian Communist Youth League (NKU); SV: Socialist Youth League, Socialist Information League; AKP: Norwegian Communist Student League (NKS)
Publications. NKP: *Friheten* (Freedom), semiweekly, Arne Jørgensen, editor; SV: *Ny Tid* (New times), weekly; AKP: *Klassekampen* (Class struggle), daily, Sigurd Allern, editor

The Norwegian Labor Party (*Det Norske Arbeiderparti*; DNA)—a moderate, generally pro-Western social-democratic reform movement—controlled the Norwegian government continuously from 1935 to 1963. Through most of this period, the Labor Party could count on parliamentary majorities. However, in 1961 the Labor Party lost its parliamentary majority, which it has never managed to regain. In 1963, the Labor government was defeated by a coalition of nonsocialist parties and the Socialist People's Party, and since then the Norwegian government has alternated between Labor Party minority governments and various coalitions of nonsocialist parties. None of the parties to the left of the Labor Party has ever been in government.

In the 1981 election the Labor Party was ousted from power by a center-right coalition headed by Conservative Party leader Kåre Willoch. Willoch served as prime minister throughout the 1981–1985 parliamentary term, during which Norway experienced strong economic growth. In the general election of 9 September 1985, Willoch's three-party coalition lost its parliamentary majority, and in May 1986 Willoch resigned after losing a vote to increase gasoline taxes in order to cope with the fiscal crisis caused by declining oil revenues.

The leader of the DNA, Gro Harlem Brundtland, became the new prime minister. Brundtland, the first Norwegian woman to hold this office, had previously served as prime minister for eight months in 1981. Her Labor government held only 71 parliamentary seats and faced a nonsocialist majority in the Storting (parliament). However, Brundtland was able to serve out the remainder of the 1985–1989 parliamentary term, thanks to the support of the SV and the unwillingness of the agrarian Center Party to defeat her government. The Brundtland government introduced a variety of austerity measures to reduce inflation, private-sector spending, and the current account deficit. The general election of 11 September 1989 resulted in stunning setbacks for Mrs. Brundtland's Labor Party, as well as for its main adversary, the Conservatives. The Labor Party received only 34.3 percent of the popular vote, its worst result since 1930, whereas the Conservatives declined from 30.4 percent to 22.2 percent. The big winners of the election were the right-wing libertarian Progress Party, which won 22 seats in parliament (in contrast with 2 previously held), and the Socialist Left Party, which increased its representation from 6 seats to 17. Despite the electoral setback of its dominant party, a nonsocialist coalition government headed by Conservative leader Jan P. Syse took office in October 1989. This government has no legislative majority and had to seek the support of the Progress Party for its first budget. Syse promised to give the country a "change of course," with more favorable conditions for private enterprise.

The Norwegian Communist Party. The NKP began as the minority faction of the DNA, when the majority of the latter party decided in 1923 to sever its ties with Moscow. The NKP gained 6.1 percent of the vote and six representatives in the general election of 1924, but later fell into continual decline and could not elect a single member of parliament during the 1930s. During World War II, NKP support for the war effort against Nazi Germany and the Soviet liberation of northern Norway boosted the party's popularity, giving it 11 seats (out of 150) in the first postwar parliament. During these early postwar years, the NKP had as many as 35,000 members, according to official sources. However, the party's fortunes fell quickly with the onset of the

Cold War. Since 1945, the NKP's vote share has declined in every single general election. In 1985 the party received no more than 4,245 votes. Thus the NKP remains one of the weakest communist parties in Western Europe. It has elected no member of parliament since 1973, when it ran as part of the Socialist Electoral Alliance and elected its chairman, Reidar Larsen, to the national assembly. In 1989, the party ran jointly with the AKP and other left-wing groups as "The County Lists for the Environment and Solidarity" ("Fylkeslistene for miljø og solidaritet"). The election results represented a modest gain for these parties collectively, but even jointly their candidates were not in serious contention for representation in any district. Due to its extremism and electoral weakness, the NKP has virtually no influence on Norwegian political debate.

The weakness of the NKP was exacerbated in 1975 when the party split in two over whether to participate in the formation of the Socialist Left Party (SV). Under the leadership of Martin Gunnar Knudsen, the majority faction decided to withdraw from the SV and remain a staunchly pro-Soviet, Stalinist party. However, Chairman Larsen and several other party leaders abandoned the NKP and joined the SV. The gulf between the NKP and the SV has remained wide, although both parties have in recent years called for a broad united front of Norwegian left-wing parties, including the DNA, the SV, and the NKP. Former NKP chairman Hans I. Kleven has supported cooperation both in the union movement and in the form of joint electoral lists. A party congress of the NKP in April 1988 advocated a "red-green" alliance for the general election of September 1989. Such an alliance would consist of "forces in the union movement, the peace movement, the environmental movement, the women's movement, the solidarity movement, and the progressive women's movement" (*Friheten*, 13 April 1988). Such an alliance did materialize in the formation of the County Lists for the Environment and Solidarity.

A national party conference in Oslo on 23 April decided by a sweeping majority to rehabilitate former NKP leader Peder Furubotn and 170 other former members, who had been expelled by the party after its defeat in the election of 1949. Furubotn and the other expelled members were at that time accused of factionalism, Titoism, Trotskyism, and various right-wing deviations. The decision to exonerate Furubotn and his associates was made on the recommendation of a committee consisting of Arne Pettersen, Arne Jørgensen (editor of *Friheten*), and Hans I. Kleven (who himself had been expelled as a Titoist in 1950). The committee, which had been appointed at the party conference in April 1988, concluded that the expulsions had been due to dogmatism, fanaticism, and a failure of democratic communication. (*Aftenposten*, 24 April 1989.)

At its nineteenth congress in 1987, the NKP adopted a new party program ("program of principle"), replacing its previous program, adopted in 1973. In its new program, the NKP reaffirms its commitment to Marxism-Leninism, scientific socialism, and class struggle. However, the new program puts greater emphasis on international peace, "the most important issue of all." The NKP sees the threat of war as a consequence of imperialism and the boundless greed for profit and power in monopoly capitalism. The deterioration of the international situation since the mid-1970s has its primary cause in the United States and its military-industrial complex. In the main resolution adopted at the congress, the NKP advocated forcing the United States to accept a nuclear test–ban treaty, preventing the implementation of the Strategic Defense Initiative, and the creation of a Nordic nuclear weapons–free zone. The Communists also rejected Norwegian membership in the European Community. Domestically, the NKP favors greater restrictions on finance capital and expansion of public credit institutions. The party also supports greater subsidies for moderate-income housing. The 1987 party congress also elected Kåre André Nilsen the new party chair. Nilsen, a veteran journalist for *Friheten* and a former manual worker, has been associated with the Knudsen/Jørgensen faction (and against Kleven) in the recent factional struggle in the NKP. However, Nilsen seems most concerned to unite the party. His main political interests are in international and security affairs.

In an article published in *World Marxist Review* (August), Nilsen called for an international dialog with working-class, progressive, left-wing, and democratic forces. Admitting that communists no longer monopolize the truth, and that the class structure of Norwegian society has changed remarkably, Nilsen advocated systematic participation in new and old social movements, such as the peace movement. The NKP leader also expressed support for *perestroika* in the Soviet Union and acknowledged that the low living standards of socialist states make them unattractive examples for millions of working-class people in the West.

The NKP maintains international contacts primarily with the communist parties of the Soviet Union and Eastern Europe. However, the party also has ties to orthodox communist parties in Western Europe.

The Socialist Left Party. The SV is the strongest party to the left of the Labor Party. Although the party includes Marxist elements, it does not define itself as a communist party, and the current program of principle is more moderate and pragmatic than the previous version. The SV was the result of a merger of the previous Socialist People's Party (Sosialistisk Folkeparti; SF), the Democratic Socialists (Demokratiske Sosialister; DS-AIK), an anti-EC splinter group of former members of the DNA, and segments of the NKP. These three parties had previously run jointly in the 1973 general election. The electoral support of the SV increased steadily in the 1980s. In the general election of September 1989 the party won 10.1 percent of the national vote and became the fourth-largest Norwegian party, trailing Labor, the Conservatives, and the Progress party. The party won seventeen seats in parliament, an increase of eleven since 1985.

In parliament, the SV has tended to support Labor minority governments, such as the one led by Gro Harlem Brundtland (1986–1989). However, the party has never held cabinet office. Although the SV frequently criticized the Brundtland government, it made no attempt to oust the Labor Party, presumably because the only alternative would have been a more conservative government.

A leadership struggle in the SV became apparent when party chairman Erik Solheim challenged parliamentary leader Theo Koritzinsky for the party's safe Oslo seat in the 1989 general election. Solheim was eventually persuaded to withdraw his candidacy and let himself be nominated elsewhere. At the 1989 party congress, Arent M. Henriksen, a member of parliament and a prominent figure in the party's right wing, criticized the election of Kåre Syltebø as leader for labor affairs. According to Henriksen, Syltebø had undesirable ties to the Workers' Communist Party (AKP).

According to party reports, the SV currently has a membership of about 11,000 dues payers, whereas the official rolls stand at approximately 14,000 members. The party has particular strengths among people 35 to 40 years old, women, the well-educated, and urban voters. More than half of all SV supporters work in the public sector; one-third are industrial workers.

The SV platform for the 1989–1993 parliamentary term was adopted at its party congress in Skien in April 1989. The program stresses environmental issues, such as large additional taxes on fossil fuels, restrictions on the use of automobiles in urban areas, and expansion of public transportation. The party wants to combat unemployment through expansion of the public sector (especially in the area of health care and welfare), increased taxation of high incomes and property, and public funds for industrial development. The SV further favors better care for children and the elderly and extension of the national maternity leave. Internationally, the SV anticipates renewed discussion of Norwegian membership in the European Community, which it opposes. The SV is also the only Norwegian parliamentary party opposed to the country's membership in NATO. The party has in the past criticized U.S. naval strategy in the North Atlantic and called for disarmament and the creation of a nuclear weapons–free zone in the Nordic area. The party wants no foreign bases or arms depots on Norwegian soil and favors prohibiting entry into Norwegian ports of any ship not certifiably free of nuclear weapons.

The SV maintains international contacts with a variety of socialist and Marxist parties, but has particularly close ties to such Nordic parties as the Swedish Communists (VPK) and the Danish Socialist People's Party (SF).

The Workers' Communist Party. The AKP was born in the late 1960s as a splinter group from the Socialist People's Party (SF). It comprises parts of the youth movement of the latter party. The founders were generally Maoist and revolutionary in orientation and dissatisfied with the moderate course of the SF. The AKP emerged as a formal organization in 1973, but has generally contested elections as the Red Electoral Alliance (RV) (see below). The RV has not fared well in elections, never reaching one percent of the national vote in general elections or electing a single member of parliament. However, the party has had greater success in local elections in some of the larger cities (particularly Tromsø) and has representation on several city councils.

The AKP has recruited its members mainly among students and other youth and is not a genuine working-class party. However, the party has adopted a policy of proletarianization of its cadres. The party draws a disproportionate share of votes from individuals between the ages of 35 and 45, mainly former student radicals. The party has until

recently been highly secretive and sectarian. While the AKP has maintained an estimated 5,000 to 7,000 members, its support among Norwegian students and intellectuals has declined precipitously since its heyday in the 1970s. The AKP currently stresses its opposition to austerity policies and especially wage controls. The party also opposes Norwegian membership in the European Community and favors an open immigration policy and efforts to improve the conditions of women.

The fifth congress of the AKP took place somewhere in Norway in the first half of December 1988. Contrary to previous practice, the party subsequently held simultaneous press conferences in Oslo, Tromsø, and Bodø, in which the names of all members of the newly elected Central Committee were released. Out of seventeen members, nine are women, eight are workers, and three are from northern Norway. With one exception, all were at that time between the ages of 35 and 45. The congress decided that congresses should henceforth take place every two years, as opposed to every four years, as in the past. During the press conferences, party leaders stressed the economic crisis in northern Norway, a national plan for public-sector employment, higher corporate taxes, women's issues, and support for refugees and immigrants. Party leaders declined to take a more critical position on Stalin than in the past. There was considerable discussion of the proper evaluation of Stalin during the party congress, which narrowly decided to retain him among the "classics of socialism" (*Klassekampen*, 13 December 1988).

The Red Electoral Alliance. The RV is mainly an offshoot of the AKP, but also contains independent Socialists. In the 1989 parliamentary election, the RV joined forces with the NKP and other Socialists in the County Lists for the Environment and Solidarity (see above). For electoral results, see above under AKP.

The decision to participate in joint lists was made at the national congress of the Red Electoral Alliance in Oslo, 8–9 April. The party congress elected Aksel Nærstad (who also holds the office of deputy chair of the AKP) as chair and Taran Sæther and Bente Volder as deputy chairs. The congress witnessed a conflict between the national party organization and the local organization in the city of Tromsø. The conflict revolved in part around the lack of orthodoxy in the Tromsø chapter and its policy of serving alcohol at public meetings (*Aften-posten*, 10 April 1989).

Kaare Strom
University of Minnesota, Minneapolis

Portugal

Population. 10,459,701 (July 1989) (*World Fact Book*, 1989)
Party. Portuguese Communist Party (Partido Comunista Português; PCP)
Founded. 1921
Membership. 199,275 (claimed, November 1988)
General Secretary. Álvaro Cunhal (since 1961)
Secretariat. 7 full members: Álvaro Cunhal (75), Carlos Costa, Domingos Abrantes, Fernando Blanqui Teixeira, Jorge Araújo, Luísa Araújo, Octávio Pato; 3 alternate members: Albano Nunes, Artur Vidal Pinto, Francisco Lopes
Political Secretariat. 8 members: Álvaro Cunhal, Agostinho Lopes, Ângelo Veloso, Carlos Brito, Domingos Abrantes, José Casanova, José Soeiro, Luís Sá
Political Commission. 12 full members: Álvaro Cunhal, Ângelo Veloso, António Gervásio, António Lopes, Carlos Brito, Domingos Abrantes, Edgar Maciel Correia, Jorge Araújo, José Casanova, José Soeiro, Luís Sá, Raimundo Cabral; 10 alternate members: Agostinho Ferreira Lopes, António Orcinha, António Casmarrinha, Bernardina Sebastião, Carlos Carvalhas, Carlos Fraião, Carlos Luís Figueira, Decq Mota, Manuel Sobral, Sérgio Teixeira
Central Committee. 175 members
Status. Legal
Last Congress. Twelfth, 1–4 December 1988, in Oporto
Last Election. 1987, United Democratic Coalition (CDU, communist coalition), 11 percent, 30 of 250 seats
Auxiliary Organization. General Confederation of Portuguese Workers (Confederação Geral de Trabalhadores Portugueses–Intersindical Nacional; CGTP), which, with 1.6 million members (*WMR*, April 1988), represents more than half of Portugal's 2.5 million-member unionized labor force out of a work force of 4.58 million (*World Fact Book*, 1989)
Publications. *Avante!* weekly newspaper, António Dias Lorenço, editor; *O Militante*, theoretical journal; and *O Diário*, semiofficial daily newspaper (all published in Lisbon)

The Portuguese communist movement and most of the unionized labor force are controlled by the PCP, now the most Stalinist party in Western Europe. Though it expresses support for current Soviet policy, it resists internal Soviet-style reforms demanded by "renewalist" party rebels. The PCP's political influence has declined since it won 19 percent of the national vote in 1979, though it claims to be the leading municipal force in 30 percent of the country (*WMR*, January). Communist strength is limited to the industrial belt, Lisbon, and the southern Alentejo region. Other far-leftist groups, such as the Popular Forces of April 25 and the Reconstructed Communist Party of Portugal, now appear to be relatively inactive.

Organization and Leadership. Aging Álvaro Cunhal's two-month stay in Moscow for surgery and rest early in 1989 fed speculation about his health and his successor (Lisbon International Service, 3 February; *Expresso*, 18 March; *FBIS*, 3 February, 11 May). The most likely official candidate to succeed him was thought by some to be Domingos Abrantes, a hard-liner who was the only leader elected at the last congress, along with Cunhal, to all three executive bodies (*Expresso*, 11 March; *FBIS*, 4 April). Cunhal denied that there was any political significance to this and, in fact, indicated at one point that he would prefer to be succeeded by a team; there are periods, he said, when "no one man has all the suitable qualities to be general secretary" (*Expresso*, 10 December 1988; *FBIS*, 14 February). In August, Cunhal proposed to the Political Commission that a debate on his eventual replacement be given urgent priority. It was reported that there were growing differences of opinion between the Secretariat and the Political Commission. (Radio Renascença, Lisbon, 13 August; *FBIS*, 19 August.)

Concern over the succession revived jockeying between the PCP's hard-line conservatives and "renewalist" challengers. Considering inevitable the general secretary's replacement before long, the rebels were said early in the year to be preparing strategy for the next party congress (Lisbon,

Tempo, 12 January; *FBIS*, 21 March). They were still chafing after their direct challenge to orthodoxy at the December 1988 congress had been repulsed (see *YICA*, 1989).

The greatest degree of agreement among the "renewalists" concerning a candidate to be fielded for new party head was reportedly generated by the name of José Luís Judas, a charismatic and influential CGTP leader. Judas appeared to be more moderate and less acerbic in his opposition to the party's Stalinist line than other critics. Even so, the Central Committee, presumably considering him a threat, voted in August to exclude him from its meetings. He had previously been invited to attend even though he was not an elected member. Party leaders explained that this invitation was no longer necessary since a considerable number of trade-union representatives had been elected to the committee at the last congress. (Ibid.; Lisbon, *O Independente*, 1 September; Lisbon, *Diário de Notícias*, 2 September; *FBIS*, 14 September, 20 October.) Judas himself explained that his exclusion was the logical result of the decision that the Central Committee "should be a cohesive team, on the basis of tendentiously monolithic principles" (*Expresso*, 9 September; *FBIS*, 20 October). The snubbing was vigorously denounced by party renewalists in statements to the press (*Diário de Notícias*, 2 September; *FBIS*, 14 September).

Another critic, António da Silva Graça, resigned in August from the PCP, convinced that it would not budge from its rigid positions. He was a member of the "Group of Six" that had rocked the party in 1987 with a proposal for renewal (see *YICA*, 1989). His decision to leave was precipitated, he said, by Cunhal's criticism of changes taking place in Eastern Europe and by the party's failure to denounce repression in China (*O Jornal*, 8 September; *FBIS*, 20 October). A document published in *O Militante* made it clear that members who condemn the PCP's course publicly were of no interest to the party. All such troublemakers were urged to leave, though Cunhal himself later denied calling for anyone's departure. (*Expresso*, 9 September; *Diário de Notícias*, 19 September; *FBIS*, 2, 23 October.) One PCP member was expelled in June after he had made some public pronouncements that were contrary to party positions (*Diário de Notícias*, 24 June; *FBIS*, 9 August).

Domestic Affairs. After years of categorically rejecting PCP proposals for an electoral alliance, the Socialist Party (Partido Socialista; PS) agreed in 1989 to form a "popular front" with the communists for municipal elections in Lisbon. Heading the slate, as candidate for mayor, was newly elected PS head Jorge Sampaio. He was said to regard this agreement as a trial run for the 1991 legislative elections, in which he felt his party alone had very slim chances of defeating the incumbent Social Democratic Party (Partido Social Democrático; PSD). In joining with the communists, Sampaio rejected a PSD proposal for coalitions in 21 municipal councils. According to one critic, he thereby delivered many chambers south of the Tagus River to the communists "on a platter." (*O Diabo*, 8 August; *FBIS*, 20 September.)

Both communists and socialists undertook discussions with some trepidation. The PCP "old guard" was said to fear that its party, as a mere "appendage" to PS slates, would risk being "smothered." Many socialists feared a coalition with the PCP might breathe new life into a party that was "isolated and afflicted with hardening of the arteries," thereby hurting the PS in the long run. (*Tempo*, 23 February; *Expresso*, 15 July; *FBIS*, 14 April, 10 August.) One critic spoke of a "suicidal love affair which the PS knows it should not have but which it cannot resist" (*Semanário*, 1 July).

In December elections, the coalition won in Lisbon, and at the national level the socialists secured the most votes and control of the most city councils. The PCP slightly improved its showing in its traditional areas of strength in southern Portugal. (Lisbon Domestic Service, 17 December; *FBIS*, 18 December.)

A package of reforms that removed traces of Marxism from the 1976 constitution went into effect in August (*Keesing's Record of World Events*, August). The PCP assailed the PS for its collaboration with the "forces of reaction" in passing the amendments in parliament (Sofia, *Rabotnichesko Delo*, 7 August; *FBIS*, 10 August).

Polls in July and August found Cunhal among Portugal's least-liked political figures, with 42 percent of voters unsympathetic to him. Only 5 percent could even imagine him as prime minister. (*O Independente*, 14 July, 25 August; *FBIS*, 13 September, 1 November.)

International Views and Activities. Cunhal was said to be bitterly perturbed over the instability in Eastern Europe. He visited East Germany, Poland, Czechoslovakia, Bulgaria, and Yugoslavia in July and August. State and party practices had often departed from ideals of socialism and communism, he said, but the communist movement was certainly "not on the way out." He insisted that communists held the solution to human problems that capitalism could not solve. (Prague, *Rudé právo*, 30 June; *Expresso*, 15 July; Lisbon Domestic Service, 15 November, 20 December.) Cunhal was reportedly especially disturbed over the fall of East German general secretary Erich Honecker, whose party he had cited as a model of true socialism. That party had taken over a previous Soviet role of subsidizing some PCP activities. (*O Independente*, 2 October; *FBIS*, 8 December.)

In Moscow, Cunhal was awarded the Order of Lenin, but not by Mikhail Gorbachev himself. Some observers noted that the Portuguese leader was treated with a "certain coolness" by Soviet authorities. (*Pravda*, 16 March; *Expresso*, 18 March; *FBIS*, 17 March, 11 May.) A direct criticism of a major PCP position even appeared for the first time in the Soviet press. An article in *Novoye Vremya* concluded that the first years of Portuguese membership in the European Community "clearly show" that predictions of catastrophe for the country were "unjustified." (*Expresso*, 18 March; *FBIS*, 11 May.) Portuguese communists continued to insist that the country's participation in the EC directly subordinates Portugal's development and national sovereignty to the interests "of big capital, the multinational corporations and foreign states." Incidentally, four communists were elected in Portugal, with 14.4 percent of the vote, to be members of the European Parliament. (Sofia, *Rabotnichesko Delo*, 7 August; *FBIS*, 10 August.)

The Chinese government's violent suppression of student rebellion in June provoked two opposite reactions within the PCP. A score of members signed a document criticizing their party's "exoneration" of those responsible for the massacres "under the pretext of a lack of information." The Central Committee deplored this "divisive interference" by its own members. It did urge clemency toward those sentenced to capital punishment, but also denounced the "lack of objectivity" of many reports in the "international campaign" against the Chinese communist government. (*Expresso*, 9, 10 June; *Avante!*, 29 June; *FBIS*, 19 June, 7 July, 3 October.) This view contrasted sharply with the PCP's hostile attitude toward China prior to 1987, when relations began to be normalized. Chinese delegations visited the PCP in March and April (*FBIS*, 28 March, 3 May).

Other Left-Wing Groups. The Supreme Court in May freed Lt. Col. Otelo Saraiva de Carvalho and 28 others from prison pending a new hearing. Members of the Popular Forces of April 25 movement, they had been convicted in 1987 on charges of terrorism, but there were alleged to have been irregularities during the trial. (*NYT*, 18 May.)

A Central Committee member of the Reconstructed Communist Party of Portugal visited Albania in October (Tiranë Domestic Service, 14 October; *FBIS*, 25 October). This far-left party, one of many that appeared in Portugal after the revolution of April 1974, was thought to be inactive in recent years.

H. Leslie Robinson, Professor Emeritus
University of the Pacific

San Marino

Population. 22,980 (0.6 percent birthrate; *World Fact Book*, 1989, p. 366)
Party. Communist Party of San Marino (PCS)
Founded. 1921
Membership. 1,200 claimed (*WMR*, July 1987; also *Europa World Yearbook 1989*, p. 2205; 300 est., *World Fact Book*, 1989)
General Secretary. Gilberto Ghiotti
Honorary Chairman. Gildo Gasperoni
Last Congress. Eleventh, 27 January 1986 (twelfth scheduled for 1990); general conference, 3–4 March
Last Election. 29 May 1988, 28.71 percent of vote, 18 of 60 seats
Publication. *La Scintilla* (The spark), published monthly, but not regularly (for example this year's issues were for January, February, May, and October); editor, Giuseppe Morganti

The first part of the year found the small republic busily tending to relations with important erstwhile communist hard-liners and reformers (the German Democratic Republic and China), as well as the chief proponent of *perestroika*, the USSR.

San Marino's new consul general to the GDR, Giuseppi Renzi, voiced his appreciation to Foreign

Minister Oskar Fischer for GDR's efforts on behalf of peace, and reduction of arms and chances for confrontation in Europe. Both expressed a desire for meaningful dialog and bilateral relations. (*ND*, 31 January.) In turn, the GDR offered congratulations to the newly elected captains regent (*ND*, 1–2 April), and on the occasion of San Marino's national holiday (*ND*, 2–3 September).

After attending the Italian Communist Party's eighth congress, the Chinese Communist Party (CCP) delegation, headed by CCP Politburo member Song Ping, visited state and political leaders of San Marino. Captains regent Luciano Cardelli and Reves Salvatore (a CPS member) expressed hope for further cooperation between their two countries, as did Christian Democratic Party (PDCS) leader Pier-Marino Menicucci at this very first contact between the CCP and PDCS (*FBIS-China*, 27 March; Xinhua, 24 March).

The chairman of the Friendship Association of China and San Marino, Gian-Franco Terenzi, used the occasion of the CCP delegation's stay in San Marino to have a "friendly visit" with Song Ping (*FBIS-China*, 27 March; Xinhua, 24 March).

Secretary General Ghiotti visited the USSR and attended the session of the Supreme Soviet on 24 November. During a brief discussion with Mikhail Gorbachev, he recounted the novel experience of its party's coalition government with the PDSC, and commented on the activity of the new Soviet parliament (*FBIS-SOV*, 5 December; Moscow Domestic Service, 24 November). Whether or not he told Mr. Gorbachev of the various disagreements with the PCS's coalition partner on government problems (*La Scintilla*, October) is not known.

As San Marino is now a member of the Council of Europe (since November 1988), the minister of culture and education, PCS member, and frequent contributor to *La Scintilla*, Fausta Morganti feels that the university, with its new research capabilities, has a role to play in the political development of the republic (*La Scintilla*, January); and in turn, it is the duty of San Marino to participate responsibly in the unifying cultural, political, and economic life and values of Europe (*La Scintilla*, May).

This new consciousness of being part of a larger community was also evident from an eight-page leaflet inserted in the February issue of *La Scintilla*. It detailed the agenda for discussion at the general party conference on 3 and 4 March. This agenda consisted mainly of topics pertaining to matters international, such as support for the Council of Europe in view of San Marino's joining the Common Market in 1992; enhancement of relations between Italy and San Marino; contribution of the CPS to new ideas of the European left and progressive forces; and active participation in work for self-determination of peoples. To be sure, this agenda also reflects the soul-searchings of the PCS's parent, the Italian Communist Party, as well as the general ferment in communist thinking in Eastern and Western Europe.

In domestic affairs, local elections for the nine castles (municipalities) took place on 4 June, with no notable ripple except the publication in *La Scintilla* (May) of the slate (not wholly communist) recommended by the PCS. Election results have not been available.

The regularly scheduled changes (1 April and 1 October) of captains regent, who jointly act as head of state, and who are selected from among the 60-member Great and General Council, included two CPS members: from 1 October 1988 to end of March 1989, Reves Salvatore; from 1 April to end of September, Mauro Fiorini, who also writes on administrative matters for the party newspaper (*La Scintilla*, January). The ten members of Congress of State, of whom four are PCS members (see *YICA*, 1988), remain in place for the five-year term of the Great and General Council.

The Information Commission of the PCS held a convention on 4 February in cooperation with print and TV journalists; the topic was the dissemination of accurate and significant information at conventions and congresses (*La Scintilla*, February). The general conference in March was held in preparation for the twelfth congress scheduled for 1990 (*La Scintilla*, February; *Pravda*, 16 July). In view of the events in Eastern Europe of the last quarter of 1989, this congress may herald changes in the attitudes and programs of the PCS.

Margit N. Grigory
Hoover Institution

Spain

Population. 39,417,220 (July 1989) (*World Fact Book*, 1989)
Parties.

• Spanish Communist Party (Partido Comunista de España; PCE)
Founded. 1920
Membership. Over 83,000 (claimed) (Sofia, *Rabotnichesko Delo*, 13 August; *FBIS*, 17 August)
General Secretary. Julio Anguita González (48)
Secretariat. 9 members: Julio Anguita González, Juan José Azcona, Juan Berga, José María Coronas, Francisco Frutos, Lucía García, Salvador Jové, Josep Palau, Francisco Palero
Political Commission. 28 members
Central Committee. 101 members
Status. Legal
Last Congress. Twelfth, 19–21 February 1988, in Madrid
Last Election. 1989, United Left (PCE electoral front), 9.05 percent, 18 of 350 seats
Auxiliary Organizations. Workers' Commissions (Comisiones Obreras; CC OO), claimed membership of about 1 million, almost a third of Spain's approximately 3.4 million unionized workers, Antonio Gutiérrez, chairman. (The CC OO are considered an auxiliary organization of the PCE, but all three Spanish communist parties have direct influence in it; 90 to 95 percent of the CC OO officials are claimed to be PCE members—*Pravda*, 3 June; *FBIS*, 8 June.)
Publications. *Mundo Obrero* (Labor world), weekly, Juan B. Berga, editor; *Nuestra Bandera* (Our flag), bimonthly ideological journal, Pedro Marset, editor (both published in Madrid)

• Communist Party of the Peoples of Spain (Partido Comunista de los Pueblos de España; PCPE)
Founded. 1984
Membership. 16,000–17,000 (claimed)
General Secretary. Juan Ramos Camarero
Secretariat. 9 members: Juan Ramos Camarero, Leopoldo Alcaraz Redondo, Jaime Ballesteros Pulido, Quim Boix Lluch, Josep Cónsola, José Antonio García Rubio, Carmen Morente, Mariá

Pere Lizandara, Margarita Sanz Alonso (*Nuevo Rumbo*, 20 March)
Executive Committee. 22 members: Juan Ramos Camarero, Leopoldo Alcaraz Redondo, Jaime Ballesteros Pulido, Quim Boix Lluch, Estéban Cerdán Francés, José Miguel Céspedes, Josep Cónsola, Leopoldo del Prado, Juan Luis García Córdoba, José Antonio García Rubio, Guillermo Gil Vázquez, Manuel Guerra Lobo, Carlos Gutiérrez García-Alix, M. Angels Martínez Castells, Carmen Morente, Juan Muñiz Acedo, Vicente Peragón Herranz, Mariá Pere Lizandara, Miguel Roselló del Rosal, Nicasio Sancho González, Margarita Sanz Alonso, Francisco Trives Mesequer (ibid.)
Central Committee. 72 full members, 23 alternate members
Status. Legal
Last Congress. Third (Extraordinary), March 1989
Last Election. 1989
Publications. *Nuevo Rumbo* (New direction), biweekly, José Antonio García Rubio, editor; *Revista Teórica* (Theoretic journal), Carmen Morente, editor

• Spanish Workers' Party–Communist Unity (Partido de los Trabajadores de España–Unidad Comunista; PTE-UC)
Founded. 1987
Membership. 14,000
General Secretary. Adolfo Pinedo
Chairman. Santiago Carrillo (74)
Status. Legal
Last Congress. First, 8 February 1987
Last Election. 1989, no seats
Publication. *Ahora* (Now), weekly, Santiago Carrillo, editor

A fractured communist movement in Spain has been gradually reuniting in recent years under the aegis of the mainstream PCE. The latter lost 63 percent of its members after 1977, but now claims it has in its ranks 78 percent of all Spanish communists (*Pravda*, 3 June; *FBIS*, 8 June). The PCPE was formed by dissidents who protested the PCE's Eurocommunism; the PTE-UC was founded by former General Secretary Santiago Carrillo, who left the PCE in 1986 in disrepute for having presided over the party's decline.

A Marxist guerrilla group called Basque Homeland and Liberty (Euzkadi ta Askatasuna; ETA) carries out occasional terrorist acts in an attempt to extort Spanish recognition of Basque independence. Since it began its armed insurgency in 1968, over 600 victims have died (*NYT*, 21 September). ETA has lost its pivotal role of earlier years, but its political arm, Herri Batasuna, appears to be increasingly influential among Basque voters (*NYT*, 1 April).

Little is known about a less active terrorist ring, the October First Antifascist Resistance Group (Grupo de Resistencia Antifascista Primero de Octubre; GRAPO). Its name commemorates the killing of four policemen in Madrid on 1 October 1975. During 1988, there was no reported activity by Iraultza (Revolution), created in 1981 to support the Basque labor movement, or by the Catalan separatist groups called Free Land (Terra Lliure) and the Catalan Red Army of Liberation.

Organization and Leadership. At a January unification congress, PCPE chairman Ignacio Gallego led a sizable contingent of his renegade group back into the PCE (TASS, 14 January; *Pravda*, 15 February; *FBIS*, 18 January, 17 February). In August, PCE general secretary Julio Anguita said 80 percent of the PCPE members had rallied to the PCE, and that numerous followers of Santiago Carrillo were also ready to return (Sofia, *Rabotnichesko Delo*, 13 August; *FBIS*, 17 August). Enrique Líster, a former dissenter who rejoined in 1986, declared that communist parties had lost prestige "due to their own mistakes." He said Carrillo had led the PCE to catastrophe using Stalinist methods "in the worst sense." (*NYT*, 23 January.)

Anguita announced in November that the PCE was considering lowering its profile in the United Left coalition (Izquierda Unida; IU) that it headed. He said that if the party rank and file approved, much decisionmaking and activity would be ceded to the IU. (Madrid Domestic Service, 11 November; *FBIS*, 15 November; *NYT*, 17 November.)

PCE president Dolores Ibarruri, known during the Spanish Civil War as "La Pasionaria" (Passion Flower), died in November at the age of 93 (*NYT*, 13 November).

Domestic Affairs. Communists made a dramatic political recovery in two Spanish elections during 1989. In June, the IU picked up 6.1 percent of the vote and four of Spain's 60 seats in the European Parliament (*CSM*, 22 June). In October elections for the Spanish parliament, it won 9.05 percent of the vote and 18 seats, up from 4.6 percent and 7 seats in 1986. Anguita exulted that this com-

munist gain, which barely dislodged the socialists from their majority status, made the IU the nation's third political force in votes and seats. (*NYT*, 12 November.) He taunted Prime Minister Felipe González that now he would have to govern in a different way—with dialogue and negotiation (ibid., 30 October).

Communists were able to pick up support by appealing to socialists disenchanted with a "pro-business, antilabor" government. Also, candidate Anguita reportedly projected an image of a reasoned, statesmanlike leader rather than that of a revolutionary, communist firebrand. A poll revealed in July that he had moved into second place in the public ranking of political leaders. In his campaign, Anguita emphasized that Spain had the highest rate of unemployment among the Common-Market countries; this was caused, he said, by foreign investment in technological equipment that had "shaken Spain's fragile economy without replacing it." (*Diario 16*, 2 July; Sofia, BTA, 12 August; *FBIS*, 18 July, 14 August; *CSM*, 23 October; *NYT*, 12 November.)

Anguita also warned workers not to be deceived by new promises by socialists, who would "make the people pay dearly" with belt-tightening measures after the election (*NYT*, 29 October). He deplored the "shelving" of an investigation of "more or less acknowledged" government spying on political parties; "apparently that doesn't constitute a crime—just a scandal" (*Ya*, 1 August; *FBIS*, 22 August).

Worried by pre-election surveys that anticipated significant communist advances, socialists concentrated their attacks on the IU during the campaign. Spaniards were reminded that the group was "merely a front for the PCE, though they don't dare say so because communism has failed throughout the world." (*Diario 16*, 13 September; *FBIS*, 15 October.) Prime Minister Felipe González said that despite the Soviet Union's revolution 70 years ago, "today there is no bread and no flour" in that country. He also asked communists whether they would rather, by dividing the left-wing vote, permit the right to rule again. (*NYT*, 29 October.)

In a bid for the youth vote, many Spanish political parties favored the reduction or replacement of required military service. The IU called for a national referendum on the issue. (*CSM*, 1 November.)

Auxiliary Organization. The communist and socialist trade unions continued jointly to press the government for hefty wage increases. Unbudging officials replied that wealth had to be redistributed through taxes rather than wages so as to minimize unemployment and inflationary pressures. CC OO leader Antonio Gutiérrez blamed the prime minister for "charging the batteries" of social tensions and demanded his resignation. A cabinet minister accused the head of the socialist union confederation of having become an ally of the "most reactionary" communist party in Europe. (*NYT*, 22 January, 10 and 13 February; *Cambio 16*, 27 February; *FBIS*, 29 March.)

A few days before the general elections in October, a fire at Spain's oldest nuclear reactor near Tarragona ignited CC OO charges that fire-extinguishing equipment and training procedures were inadequate. It was said that local firefighters "had not the slightest idea" of how to respond to such an incident. (*NYT*, 26 October.)

International Views and Activities. The PCE enthusiastically endorsed Eastern Europe's political changes in late 1989 "because they derive from the will of the people." Anguita declared that he could make no excuses for such outmoded systems as were being displaced but added that neither was capitalism compatible with a decent human existence. He also criticized NATO for "not supporting Warsaw Pact efforts at disarmament." (*Mundo Obrero*, 18 October; *CSM*, 23 October; Madrid Domestic Service, 11 November; *FBIS*, 15 November.) In a visit to Bulgaria prior to the upheaval in that country, Anguita hailed the PCE's longstanding good relations with Bulgarian communists, whom he praised for their helpful and "correct" approach to the party split in Spain (*Rabotnichesko Delo*, 13 August; *FBIS*, 17 August).

Enrique Líster said he had great confidence in what Chairman Gorbachev was doing in the Soviet Union, which had yet to achieve a truly communist society. Líster said Stalin was a great revolutionary, but his crimes had greatly harmed socialist development. (*NYT*, 23 January.) A Soviet Foreign Ministry spokesman participated in Spain in extensive seminar discussions of labor and ethnic tensions in his country (Madrid Domestic Service, 24 July; *FBIS*, 25 July).

Spain's four IU members of the European Parliament joined with some Italian, Danish, and Greek communist MPs to form a caucus called "For a United European Left." It seeks legislative powers for the parliament through which left-wing goals could be achieved. A separate and pre-existing caucus of French, Portuguese, and Greek communists holds to an old-style orthodox resistance to the EC. (ANSA, Rome, 20, 21 July; *FBIS*, 21 July.)

Anguita said he was tired of hearing the left talk about "resistance"; he urged instead an "offensive" to try to bring economic planning into the EC so as to equalize the development of various regions of Western Europe (*Granma*, Havana, 9 April; *WMR*, May). He also said it was important for the parliament to disband military blocs (*Rabotnichesko Delo*, 13 August; *FBIS*, 15 and 17 August). During the Spanish election campaign, Anguita was applauded when he spoke of "helping both NATO and the Warsaw Pact die peacefully" (*CSM*, 23 October).

The PCE expressed its outrage at the Chinese authorities' "brutal" repression of student protest and rejected the "fantastic" explanations offered for this "intolerable behavior" (*Mundo Obrero*, 28 June–4 July, 12 July; *FBIS*, 10, 21 July).

The PCE reaffirmed its support for an independent Palestinian state and demanded that the Israeli occupation army withdraw from the Golan Heights. Anguita cabled the Arab Socialist Ba'th Party the PCE's desire to consolidate relations with that party. (Damascus, SANAS, 26 February; *FBIS*, 27 February.) In May a PCE group visited the Yemeni Council for Peace, Solidarity, and Friendship with Nations (*FBIS*, 5 May). A PCE delegation in Tripoli expressed its support for the Libyan Arab people's struggle against "imperialist forces" (Tripoli, JANA, 21 November; *FBIS*, 22 November).

Rival Communist Parties. Juan Ramos, who headed a PCPE group that refused to participate in the communist unification congress in January, was re-elected general secretary of his party in March at its Third Congress. The delegates decided to support their own—rather than the IU—candidate to the European Parliament in June elections. (*Pravda*, 12 March; *FBIS*, 13 March.) The PCPE reported that the PCE had resolved in February that henceforth there should be only one communist party in the IU (*Nuevo Rumbo*, 25 January–10 February).

Ramos contradicted Anguita's claim that most PCPE members had rejoined the PCE; he said only about 400 of the group's 16,000–17,000 members had defected. Actually, it would seem that a much larger number must have deserted it in view of the PCPE's 1988 claim of a membership of 25,000–26,000. Ramos explained that his faction had rejected reunification because the PCE, having renounced Leninism, was trying to build the party along the lines of the Italian Communist Party. He qualified the January congress as an "attack on our own party" and asserted that it had provided no opportunity to discuss basic problems. (*Pravda*, 3 June; *FBIS*, 8 June.)

Left-Wing Terrorist Groups. The arrest of a top ETA leader in France in January encouraged Spanish authorities to believe that the organization had been severely crippled. About 500 militants were already in high-security prisons. In the face of increasingly effective Spanish-French antiterrorist cooperation, the beleaguered guerrilla group declared a truce in January in exchange for what it claimed was a government promise of "political conversations." (*NYT*, 13 January; *CSM*, 31 January; *Ya*, 15 March; *FBIS*, 27 April.)

The truce and tentative talks in Algiers were ended by ETA in late March when the latter bridled at a government communiqué that only aimed for an "agreed and final solution" rather than a "negotiated, political" settlement (Madrid Domestic Service, 29 March; *FBIS*, 29 March). Spanish officials insisted that from the beginning they had made clear there could be no negotiation of the Basque region's political status. They said an end to terrorism and amnesty for those not guilty of violent crimes was all Madrid was prepared to discuss. (*NYT*, 26 April.)

The ETA action was explained by some as the result of squabbling within the organization, with the hard-line sector finally imposing its views on those favoring dialogue (*Ya*, 30 March; *FBIS*, 4 May). All national and Basque parties, except for the ETA-supported Herri Batasuna, backed the government's policy and blamed ETA alone for the collapse of peace talks. A PCE spokesman called ETA's decision a "tragic and stupid error." (ABC, 30 March; *NYT*, 5 April; *FBIS*, 4 May.)

A rash of fresh terrorist murders and bombings followed, but ETA was further disabled in September when police killed two guerrillas and captured 34 others. Algeria acceded to Spanish requests that it arrest and deport a number of ETA leaders. (*NYT*, 26 April, 21 September.)

In October legislative elections, Herri Batasuna won four seats in parliament with 1.06 percent of the votes (ibid., 30 October). Opinion polls suggest the party may now have the support of a quarter of the Basque population (*NYT*, 1 April).

A GRAPO terrorist band, inactive since 1983, renewed its violence in December, shooting and

wounding an army officer in Valencia (Madrid Domestic Service, 20 December; *FBIS*, 24 December).

H. Leslie Robinson, Professor Emeritus
University of the Pacific

Sweden

Population. 8,401,098 (July 1989), growth rate 0.1 percent (1989)
Party. Left Party Communists (Vänsterpartiet Kommunisterna; VPK)
Founded. 1921 (VPK, 1967)
Membership. Ca. 17,800, principally in the far north, Stockholm, and Göteborg
Chairman. Lars Werner
Executive Committee. 9 members: Lars Werner, Lennart Beijer, Bertil Mabrink (vice-chairman), Gudrun Schyman (vice-chairman), Kenneth Kvist (chairman), Bo Leinderdahl, Bitte Engsell, Birgit Hansson, Gerd Mabrink
Party Board. 35 members
Status. Legal
Last Congress. Twenty-eighth, 23–25 May 1987
Last Election. September 1988, 314,031 votes, 5.8 percent, 21 out of 349 seats
Auxiliary Organizations. Communist Youth (KU)
Publications. *Ny Dag* (New day), semiweekly; *Volkvillan* (People's will), weekly; *Socialistick Debatt* (Socialist debate), monthly theoretical journal

The ancestor of the VPK, Sweden's Communist Party (Sveriges Kommunistiska Partiet), was established in 1921. Its greatest moment came right after World War II, when it obtained 11.2 percent of the vote in local elections, largely due to the popularity of the Soviet Union at the end of the war. Since that time the communist party (later the VPK) has usually won between 4 to 6 percent of the vote. The party, which has never made a truly major contribution to communist history, has had marginal influence in Swedish politics. Its most important role has been to allow the Social Democrats to govern during much of Sweden's recent history. During the last half-century, the Swedish Social Democrats have been Europe's most dominant social democratic party, and during many of their years in power, they have relied on a combined majority with the Communists in the Riksdag (parliament). The Communists, however, have never been a part of the government. In Sweden, a party has to clear 4 percent in order to be represented in the Riksdag, and after the bitter reaction to the Soviet invasion of Czechoslovakia in 1968, the VPK fell beneath 4 percent and was not represented. In the 1970 and 1976 elections, it received 4.8 percent; and in 1979 and 1982, 5.6 percent of the vote. The VPK dropped to 5.4 percent of the vote in 1985 and went up to 5.8 percent in 1988.

The Communists changed both the name and the direction of the party during the party congress in 1967. Blue-collar workers had constituted the majority of the communist electorate in previous years, but during the 1970 elections the VPK increasingly attracted white-collar and younger voters. In the 1979 elections, 56 percent of the voters were under the age of 30, and 36 percent of the voters were in the white-collar class. In the 1982 elections, those under 30 years of age slipped to 45 percent, but those from the white-collar class rose from 36 to 41 percent. Over the years, the VPK has projected a Marxist image, even though it has been regarded as one of the more moderate West European communist parties.

The history of the VPK has been characterized by stormy internal fighting, and the internecine battling in 1987 was worse than usual. The arguments focused on policy and personnel decisions that were made by the Twenty-Eighth Party Congress in May of that year. Much of the dispute centered around the chairman, Lars Werner, who by 1987 had served twelve years as party leader, longer than any other leader in the history of the VPK. (His predecessor, C. H. Hermansson, served eleven years.) Werner came under increasing criticism from members of the party's inner circle, because they felt he should take a tougher line against the Social Democrats in the parliament. Some wanted to oust Werner at the Twenty-Eighth Party Congress, but it voted to retain him and to remove three of Werner's opponents from the Executive Committee. Another major opponent of Werner resigned as vice-chairman of the Executive Committee in 1988. Even though some of Werner's opponents remained on the Executive Committee, he seemed to be in a stronger position in relation to his

VPK opponents at the end of 1988 than he had been two years previously.

The dominant political event in Sweden in 1988 was the September election. Based on polls taken early in 1988, there were predictions that the Communists might not surmount the barrier of 4 percent and so not be represented in the Riksdag. A poll by SIFO in February 1988 showed the VPK getting only 2.8 percent of the vote. It therefore surprised many observers when the VPK received 5.8 percent in the election. It was widely speculated that part of the VPK vote came from Social Democrats who wanted to see the Communists reach the 4 percent threshold so that they would be represented in parliament, thereby helping the Social Democrats form the government. Much of Swedish voters' attention in 1988 was focused on environmental issues, and, indeed, the Green Party won 5.5 percent of the vote, and was, for the first time, represented in the parliament.

Eastern European Developments. Much of the world's attention focused in the autumn of 1989 on Eastern Europe. The VPK also concentrated on the seismic events in Eastern Europe. Werner acknowledged in a wide-ranging interview published in *Svenska Dagbladet* in late November that the VPK was rethinking its policies and even considering changing its name by removing the word *Communists*. He seemed to imply that events in Eastern Europe had led to soul-searching in the VPK. When asked by the interviewer whether the party would remove the "k" from VPK, Werner said: "I have not said that I want to remove it. I want primarily to discuss what the party's nature should be—whether we should be a broad-based left-wing party, a socialist alternative where people who are communists, socialists or left-wing socialists would be welcome. If the name were an obstacle, I think that a change of name should be discussed . . . The question is whether developments in East Europe and the process of democratization do not occasion a change of program." (*Svenska Dagbladet*, 23 November.)

In the interview Werner went on to say that he gave President Gorbachev great credit for unleashing the pent-up feelings in East Germany and Czechoslovakia. In all of his statements, Werner made it clear that he identified himself with the progressive changes in Eastern Europe, and that he had long-standing good relations with the current leadership in Hungary and the GDR. Werner said, "I froze when I read that Honecker had intended to order the military onto the streets of Leipzig before he was removed." (*Svenska Dagbladet*, 23 November.)

Werner's comments were made in connection with the awarding of this year's Olof Palme Prize to President Vaclav Havel of Czechoslovakia for his "consistent and courageous work for truth and democracy." The Olof Palme Prize was awarded by Foreign Minister Sten Andersson in the Swedish embassy in Prague. (*Svenska Dagbladet*, 25 November.)

Prior to the dramatic autumn events in Eastern Europe, the VPK had issued a sharp protest against the massacre in Tiananmen Square. The party statement "demanded" that the Chinese government revoke the death sentences, and that democracy not be silenced (*Dagens Nyheter*, 23 June).

Party Internal Affairs. Chairman Werner, who in recent years had fought off several vigorous attempts to unseat him, seemed to be sailing in relatively tranquil political waters in 1989. As the year came to an end, he seemed unchallenged for the leadership. He stated his intention of running for another three-year term as the party's chairman at the party congress in 1990. Werner has even said that he doesn't plan to retire until the year 2000. (*Dagens Nyheter*, 11 March.)

One of the major reasons for Werner's high standing in the party ranks is that, according to the SIFO public-opinion poll, the VPK in general and Werner in particular seemed to have gained in popularity. According to a SIFO poll reported in June, the VPK figure of 7.7 percent was the highest recorded so far, except for the period immediately after World War II. Perhaps even more remarkable was the finding that Werner, for the first time ever, headed SIFO's "top party leader list." The sample surveyed ranked Werner 4 percentage points ahead of Prime Minister Ingvar Carlsson as the leader most trusted. (*Dagens Nyheter*, 12 June.) According to the poll, many members of the public seem to view the VPK program as being the following: "Cheaper milk for children, higher wages for the workers, more places at the day-care centers and hospitals, fewer billions for the military" (*Dagens Nyheter*, 13 June).

The major controversy surrounding Werner related to allegations that Jorn Svensson, then-chairman of the Executive Committee and Werner's archfoe, made about the drinking habits of Werner. First, Svensson wrote an article for *Dagens Nyheter* in which he complained about the effects that drink-

ing had on some leading members of the Riksdag. This led to a storm of media criticism that Svensson was being deceitful, that people knew that his remarks were really aimed at Werner. (*Dagens Nyheter*, August 18.) Later, Svensson directly stated that Werner's political policies and performance were being affected by his drinking. He also accused him of dictatorial behavior. This direct confrontation led to Svensson's resignation as chairman of the Executive Committee. Kenneth Kvist replaced him, and Lennart Beijer from Hultsfred was appointed to the Executive Committee to replace the departing Svensson. (*Dagens Nyheter* 11 September.)

Virtually nothing was written in 1989 about international party contacts or about rival communist groups. The Communist Workers' party (APK), founded in 1977, has continued to play a minuscule role in Swedish politics. Rolf Hagel, who was reelected secretary of that party in May of 1989, reaffirmed the role of his hard-line party: "The historical role of the working class is to vanquish capitalism" (*Norrskensflamman*, 5 May). The Swedish TT news agency reported that *Norrskensflamman*, the organ of the APK, which was founded in 1904, was very near closure because its circulation was down to 4,000 and because of heavy financial losses (AFP, 6 August).

Peter Grothe
Monterey Institute of International Studies

Switzerland

Population. 6,611,019 (July 1989)
Party. Swiss Labor Party (Partei der Arbeit der Schweiz/Parti suisse du travail/Partito Svizzero del Lavoro; PdAS)
Founded. 1921; outlawed 1940; re-established 15 October 1944
Membership. 4,500 (estimated)
General Secretary. Jean Spielmann
Honorary President. Jean Vincent (deceased March 1989)
Politburo. 14 members
Secretariat. 5 members

Central Committee. 50 members
Status. Legal
Last Congress. Thirteenth, 27 February–1 March 1987
Last Election. 18 October 1987 (app. 0.8 percent); one seat in the National Council, the lower chamber of the national parliament; 8.72 percent of the vote in canton of Geneva, and in addition represented in the parliaments of the Vaud, Neuchatel, and Jura cantons
Auxiliary Organizations. Communist Youth League of Switzerland (KVJS), Marxist Student League, Swiss Women's Organization for Peace and Progress, Swiss Peace Movement, Swiss-Soviet Union Society, Swiss-Cuban Society, Central Sanitaire Swiss
Publications. *Voix Ouvrière* (Geneva), weekly, circulation ca. 8,000 copies; *Vorwärts* (Basel), weekly, circulation ca. 6,000 copies; *Il Lavatore*, Italian-language newspaper; *Zunder*, KVJS organ

Despite the dramatic death of Marxism and socialism of all stripes throughout Eastern Europe, Switzerland's leftist organizations—though not addressing the apparent collapse of their dream ideology—gained some influence.

Switzerland has three organizations of some significance that can be labeled communist parties. The largest and oldest of these three groups is the Partei der Arbeit der Schweiz (Swiss Party of Labor; PdAS), which is the only communist organization officially recognized by other communist fraternal parties. The two others are the Sozialistische Arbeiterpartei (Socialist Workers' Party; SAP), of which Werner Carrobio is secretary, and the Progressive Organizations of Switzerland (POCH), which is led by Georg Degen. Forced by the rapid change in the Eastern bloc, almost all of these organizations apparently ceased emphasizing their old ideological positions and shifted their political efforts more toward human-rights issues, environmental problems, the excessive size of Swiss military forces, and to the Third World.

The SAP was founded in 1969 by a group of young Trotskyists who left the PdAS. It was renamed in 1980, and operates mainly in larger cities. Because it is organized as a cadre party, its membership seems to remain constant at about 2,000, but these are supported by at least 3,000 sympathizers nationwide. The leading theoretician still is Fritz Osterwalder. In recent years, a few SAP members have attained some important positions, especially in the educational system and the trade

unions. The party exercises, therefore, a far greater influence than its small membership would indicate. The SAP somewhat sticks to revolutionary class struggle in the Swiss centers of production (*WMR*, January). The obsolete ideas of central economic planning and the nationalization of the means of production play a major role in its program. In 1989 under the name Revolutionary Socialist Youth (RSJ), it became active especially among students and supported the antinuclear-power movement. Its main weekly publication appears in four languages: *Bresche, La Breche, Rosso,* and *Roia*.

The small but influential POCH was founded in 1972 in Basel by students disappointed with the sterile politics of the PdAS. Under Georg Degen, the now-Zürich-based organization replaced old-fashioned, doctrinaire Marxism with the more attractive ideological concepts of the Greens movement and presents itself as the "voice of conscience" (*WMR*, June). A POCH subsidiary, the Organization for Women's Affairs, is the most important women's group in Switzerland, and is quite active among students. POCH publishes the weekly *POCH-Zeitung*, with an estimated circulation of 6,000 copies. The membership is reported to be somewhat lower, with 65 percent women. This organization was more active than the other.

There are several other leftist organizations which, with some support by the above-mentioned groups, gained some influence during 1989. It is important to note that left-extremist SPS members gained strength within this party's leadership. The Social Democratic Party of Switzerland (SPS), which has some radical wings, won more than 18 percent of the votes in the last election two years ago; it was the only major party not to oppose the call for the abolition of the army. The SPS enjoyed the help of the SAP-connected Gruppe Schweiz ohne Armee (Group for a Switzerland Without Military; GSoA). This active group collected the signatures leading to the "antimilitary" referendum of 26 November, which was supported by 35.6 percent of the votes (*NYT*, 6 December).

In addition, there are several other radical socialist splinter organizations. Due to the fact that the Swiss proletariat is made up more and more of foreign workers, mainly from southern European countries, the Autonomous Socialist Party (PSA), under the leadership of Werner Carrobbio, operates exclusively in the Italian part of Switzerland. The estimated membership is about 1,000. This fairly agile party is the result of a split within the SPS in 1960. Again in 1989 there were some indications of a forthcoming merger with the SPS. The Communist Party of Switzerland/Marxist-Leninist (KPS/ML) must also be mentioned. The two major Swiss peace groups—the Schweizerische Friedensbewegung (Swiss Section of the World Peace Council; SFB) and the International Women's League for Peace and Freedom (IFFF)—are controlled by the PdAS. There are some indications that all of the leftist organizations have somewhat contributed to the success of the antiarmy referendum. The Political Bureau of the PdAS again proposed to POCH, SAP, and the Green alliance that a single left opposition in parliament be formed. According to Erica Deuber-Pauli, deputy to the Greater Council of Geneva and member of the PdAS, the Swiss Party of Labor "is open now to all social movements" (*WMR*, June).

In addition there are two Green parties in Switzerland: the first group, the Swiss Ecologist Party is known as a "cucumber" because it is (supposedly) all-Green; the second organization, the Green Socialist Alternative is called a "watermelon," because its green peel covers a red, or Marxist, core (*NYT*, 18 October 1987). POCH's new policies along the latter party's lines proved quite successful in the November election, in which the "watermelons" gained nine seats.

Leadership and Organization. While the center of Swiss political and economic power lies in the German-speaking part of the country, the PdAS's strongholds are located in the French-speaking areas. Since Jean-Philippe Becker organized the first international socialist congress in 1866, Geneva has developed a long tradition as an open and "progressive" city. The fact that almost half of its population are foreigners certainly plays a role. It is therefore not surprising that the old socialist ideas are more attractive in the country's western part and in Basel, whereas the more modern, environmentally oriented approaches have more followers among intellectuals in the other German-speaking urban areas. Probably due to a lack of active support of the Basel section of the party, though, in 1989 the Central Committee of the PdAS made the decision to dissolve that section (*WMR*, December 1988).

Despite all its efforts, the party has no cantonal groups in small rural and conservative cantons. Its organization is a territorial one and follows the historically developed regions.

The main organizational change and one of the most notable aspects of recent years continues to be the strong effort to rejuvenate the party's leading bodies. The age factor in 1987 was reflected in the replacement of eleven members of the Central Committee with younger delegates. By now 39 percent of the delegates are under 40, and 26 percent are aged between 40 and 50 (*IB*, June 1987). Although the *World Marxist Review* claims that "the age problem is no longer a headache for the party organization" (June 1988), the PdAS apparently struggles with its establishment and its members' old-fashioned class-conscious ideology, vocabulary, and slogans. The bitter defeat in the last federal election reflects the party's failure to adjust quickly to sociological changes.

Domestic Affairs. The death in March of Jean Vincent, honorary president of the PdSA and perhaps the only figure with at least some international stature, represented a great loss for the PdAS. Even the CPSU published a touching condolence message (*Pravda*, 19 March; *FBIS-SOV*, 29 March).

In order to gain new appeal, the PdSA continued to emphasize radical options, such as completely banning arms exports, which would hurt the Swiss economy badly, the reduction of military spending, the lifting of banking secrecy, and even calling for a workweek of 35 hours with full pay. According to ADN, the PdSA organized a national party conference in Bern and issued a document underlining the party's continuing efforts to fight for concrete disarmament, solidarity with Nicaragua, and Radio Freedom, a radio station of the African National Congress (*ND*, 6 March). These hollow slogans surprisingly proved to be somewhat successful with a few students, but failed to attract the disoriented working-class movement. Nevertheless, since 1987 the PdAS has 10 members sitting on Geneva's municipal council.

In January, *Vorwärts*, the party's German-language newspaper held its traditional annual press festival in Zürich. The festival serves as an important fund-raiser. Several antiwar organizations and delegations from fraternal parties attended and celebrated their solidarity with the "just cause" of the PLO. How this poorly funded small party can finance its multilanguage publications and its various other activities remains somewhat mysterious. The old rumor persists that the PdAS is aided financially by some Kremlin sources.

International Affairs. One of the most important events of 1989 was the visit of Jozef Lenart, a member of the Presidium and secretary of the

CPCZ (Czechoslovak Communist Party). It is almost pathetic that as late as 3 November, shortly before the overdue downfall of the hard-line communist regime in Czechoslovakia, Jozef Lenart and Jean Spielmann signed their first protocol on cooperation between the CPCZ and the PdAS for 1990. (One wonders whether there will be something left which can be called the CPCZ by 1990.) The most intense relationship with a foreign party was that maintained with what was the hard-line establishment in East Germany. The party's main international resolution of its 1987 congress upgraded the party's policies as outlined in the 1971 theses, the 1979 Regensdorf program, and the 1982 decisions, and promoted the idea of a "peace-advancing economy." This approach aims at five areas: the repudiation of the arms race; orienting and controlling the economy to solve important problems; balancing scientific and technological progress and protection of the environment; massive support of the Third World and of radical changes in Switzerland's political ties with lesser-developed countries; and peaceful coexistence.

In contrast to 1988 the party's general secretary did not travel a great deal. During his stay in Bulgaria in 1988 Spielmann on several occasions emphasized the importance of *perestroika* and *glasnost'* for the international communist movement (*FBIS*, 26 August 1988).

General Activities. Jean Spielmann seems to understand that the Swiss left nowadays is more focused on problems of disarmament, environmental protection, or the Third World, than old-fashioned, class-struggle slogans. Swiss society traditionally is not too tolerant of radical politics. During 1989 there was some cooperation between more or less autonomous leftist groups on the referendum and occasionally on environmental issues. Following international patterns, several anti-apartheid actions and organized divestment demonstrations took place in the major urban centers and universities. Among the politically most active universities in Switzerland now are those of Zürich, Basel, and Geneva, the last having a tradition of student political activity. But besides the well organized actions which helped to gather the signatures needed for the antiarmy referendum, and which were organized mainly by POCH and SAP-connected groups, and a few helpless solidarity appeals, there were no signs of significant political activity.

Kurt R. Leube
California State University at Hayward

Turkey

Population. 55,355,831
Parties. United Communist Party of Turkey (UCPT), established through merger of the Communist Party of Turkey (TCP) and the Workers' Party of Turkey (WPT)
Date Founded. TCP: 1920; WPT: 1961; UCPT: 1988
Membership. Negligible
General Secretary. UCPT/TCP: Nabi Yağci (aka Haydar Kutlu); other officers of UCPT: Nihat Sargin, chairman; Mehmet Karaca, deputy general secretary; Osman Sakalsiz, deputy chairman
Leading Bodies. No data
Status. Illegal
Last Congress. UCPT: October 1988; TCP: November 1983
Last Election. N/a
Auxiliary Organizations. N/a
Publications. The following publications were listed in the indictment of the UCPT/TCP general secretary and attributed to Kutlu's own testimony in the periodical *Atilim* (Progress)—domestic: *Alinteri* (Toil); *Görüş* (Viewpoint); foreign: *Atilim*; *Sol Birlik* (Left union); *Türkiye Postasi* (Mail of Turkey); *Yol ve Amaç* (Means and goals); *Yeni Çağ* (New age); *Gerçeğin Sesi* (The voice of truth); *Proleter Istanbul* (Proletarian Istanbul); *Ileri* (Forward)

While 1989 was not very eventful for the UCPT, significant extreme-leftist activities dominated the political scene. The Central Committee of the UCPT announced in its New Year message that the party would struggle to protect the interests of the workers, to gain legality, to support every step toward democratization, and to resist those circles that insisted on maintaining the conditions of the period beginning with 12 September 1980. The UCPT also declared that it would make every effort to develop the dialogue and cooperation between the democratic and leftist forces (Our Radio [clandestine radio of UCPT], 1 January; *FBIS*, 3 January). Furthermore, the UCPT/TCP attended an international symposium in the Ruhr, West Germany, on "New Aspects of Communists' Activities in the

Community and at the Workplace in European Capitalist Countries." During this symposium, the TCP emphasized that they had easier access to large numbers of workers in Turkey because these individuals lived in socially homogeneous population centers and neighborhoods. The declaration of the symposium stated that since Turkey lacked an effective Green Party, the TCP should take advantage of recent citizens' concerns, such as pollution and environment, and establish contact with the masses. (*WMR*, January.)

Despite this optimism, the events of 1989 did not favor the UCPT. Ten leaders of the UCPT, who had lived in self-imposed exile in West Germany and Greece since the 1980 coup, returned to Turkey on 23 September and were immediately arrested by the security forces (*FBIS*, 25 September). These leaders were Şeref Yildiz, Mehmet Bozok, Erdal Talu, Ahmet Kardan, Talat Ulusoy, Fikret Temir, Fahrettin Filiz, Aynur Ilkay, Alaaddin Taş, and Ihsan Baştan. Of these individuals, Baştan was later released. This development is similar to the case of Haydar Kutlu and Nihat Sargin who returned to Turkey on 16 November 1987, ostensibly to formally establish the new UCPT, and were arrested by security officials upon their arrival at the airport. According to Önder Sezgin, who is a member of the UCPT's Central Committee, the return of the party leaders to Turkey was a conscious decision of the Central Committee aimed securing legality for the party and contributing to the democratization process in Turkey (*Pravda*, 24 September).

Meanwhile, the State Security Court twice rejected Kutlu's and Sargin's requests for release (*FBIS*, 25 May, 20 November). The two men cited the statements of President Kenan Evren, Prime Minister Turgut Özal, Parliament Speaker Yildirim Akbulut, main opposition leader Erdal Inönü, business tycoons, and university professors that a communist party could be permitted in Turkey. Kutlu and Sargin argued that these statements made their continued detention on the grounds of "committing a crime damaging the prestige of the state" irrational. The court rejected their argument and denied the requests.

In other extreme-leftist activities, the First State Security Court in Istanbul sentenced two of the twelve defendants accused of being members of the Turkish Communist Party-Unity Group to eight years and four months imprisonment each (*Cumhuriyet*, 7 November). The trial in Ankara of 723 people accused of belonging to the Revolutionary Path Organization, which began in 1982, also

ended. The Military Court handed down various sentences to 392 suspects. Of these, 7 were sentenced to death, 39 to life imprisonment, and one to 21 years in prison. Another 345 suspects received prison terms ranging from 2 to 20 years. (Ankara Domestic Service, 19 July; *FBIS*, 20 July.)

In addition, Turkish security forces continued to carry out operations against illegal leftist groups. They arrested a total of 189 members of the extreme leftist DEV-SOL (Revolutionary Left) and other organizations (*FBIS*, various issues through 25 November). In another development, the names of seven of the police chiefs who have hindered the illegal Marxist-Leninist Turkish Workers-Peasants Liberation Army (TWPLA), which is affiliated with the TCP, have been included in the death list of the TWPLA. The bulletin drawn up by leading TWPLA members in foreign countries and sent to the militants in Turkey instructed them to shoot and kill on sight the police chiefs whose names were included in the bulletin (*FBIS*, 13 June). Furthermore, thirteen members of an illegal leftist organization were apprehended in Istanbul in July. According to the Istanbul Security Directorate, Ali Gülmez, who escaped from the Mescit Military Prison in 1988, was in this group (*FBIS*, 6 July).

On other leftist fronts, the activities of the separatist Marxist-Leninist Kurdish Workers Party (PKK) intensified in 1989. Some illegal extreme-leftist organizations, which are active outside Turkey, formed a union with the PKK in order to wage a joint struggle against the government. These organizations are the Socialist Motherland Party, the Turkish Communist Party-Unity, the Turkish People's Liberation Party Front-Emergency Group, and the Socialist Newspaper (*Milliyet*, 31 January; *FBIS*, 2 February). In a joint statement, the group claimed that there was a fascist dictatorship in Turkey, and that the struggle against that regime, which had previously been waged separately, would be united in a single front. The declaration also accused the UCPT of trying to gain the sympathy of the ruling classes in Turkey (*FBIS*, 2 February).

In a related development, Yilmaz Çelik, PKK supervisor for Central Europe and all its training camps abroad and the person in charge of Diyarbakir and Bingöl provinces, revealed that the organization's leader, Abdullah Öcalan (aka Apo), planned to increase his combatant forces to 2,000. But Turkish forces captured Çelik while he was trying to contact organization members in Diyarbakir. The State Security Court's Prosecutor's Office asked for the death sentence against him (*FBIS*,

9 February). The Turkish forces also captured a suspected PKK leader, Ismail Yeşilmen (aka Zana), who was carrying important documents revealing the rules and regulations of the PKK's United Kurdistan People's Revolutionary Army (UKPRA). The documents' eight sections contained thirty points which stated the organization's ideology as being Marxism-Leninism with an operational sphere spanning Turkey, Iran, Iraq, and Syria (*Hürriyet*, 11 February).

Turkish intelligence units also established that agents of the Syrian Secret Service are among the members of the PKK's brain trust. Turkish security forces acquired a photograph of one of the Syrian agents, who is known by his code name Ömer the Syrian. He is known to have personally planned operations and participated in a number of them. In his photograph, Ömer carries a rosette depicting Mahsun Korkmaz, who was the right-hand man of PKK leader Abdullah Öcalan until he was killed in a clash in Şirnak some time ago. The documents captured by Turkish forces revealed that Ömer personally led the operations in the Nusaybin, Cizre, Idil, and Midyat regions (*FBIS*, 20 March).

Related to this issue, Fatih Tan, a PKK militant who surrendered to security forces in Şemdilli, disclosed at his court hearings that Kurdish fighters also receive training in camps inside Iran. According to Tan, Osman Öcalan (alias Ferhat), who is the brother of Apo, is in charge of the training centers (Ahmet Kesip and the Örencik Martyrs Resistance camps) in Iran (*Tercüman*, 6 July; *FBIS*, 11 July). Soon after this disclosure, the Turkish security forces declared that some 132 PKK centers have been ascertained in the territories of Iraq, Iran, Syria, and Lebanon. They further disclosed that 69 PKK centers are in Iraqi territory controlled by the Democratic Party of Kurdistan (DPK), led by Barzani, and by the Patriotic Union of Kurdistan (PUK), led by Talabani. Some 27 centers existed in Iranian territory controlled by the Kurdish Democratic Party of Iran (KDPI), led by Qassemlou; 25 centers were in Syria; and 11 centers were located in the al-Biqa' Valley of Lebanon. (*Tercüman*, 29 September.) According to reports, Turkish workers in Europe who joined the PKK as a result of propaganda, and people kidnapped in eastern and southeastern Anatolia, are taken to the PKK centers in these countries where they undergo political and armed training. The PKK calls some of these centers schools and conducts political indoctrination in them. In the military camps jointly used by the PKK and the DPK, PUK, and KDPI, Iranian officers and training experts called *paskars* train alongside Syrian officers. These military camps teach the use of light long-barreled weapons, as well as of heavy weapons such as missiles, automatic rifles, mortars, and so on. The militants are also trained in guerrilla warfare and tactics. (Ibid.) Ismail Sezgin, a former PKK militant, disclosed the PKK militants are trained in a refugee camp on Lavrion island in Greece and in camps in southern Cyprus as well. In these camps, Greek and Greek Cypriot officers provide the training. (*FBIS*, 16 November.)

These developments in southeastern Anatolia present a serious challenge to central authorities. According to State of Emergency Governor Hayri Kozakcioğlu, there are 2,500 PKK militants and 40,000 Turkish troops in southeastern Turkey. He also revealed that 15,000 village guards have been hired to assist the security forces in the region. (*Cumhuriyet*, 25 October.) The results of the various guerrilla activities and operations by the security forces have been costly to both sides. Between January and November the total casualties were: PKK: 47 dead and 86 captured; security forces: 17 dead; village guards: 3 dead; and civilians: 56 dead and 107 kidnapped (*FBIS*, tabulated from various issues; *Hürriyet*, 28 November).

The PKK was also involved in the local elections in March. Apparently, 55 candidate mayors in southeast Turkey were supported by the PKK. A high-ranking official said that the Marxist-Leninist Turkish Communist Party-Partisan Organization and the Turkish Workers-Peasants Liberation Army also backed the PKK decision (*Günaydin*, 13 March).

In domestic politics, 1989 has been an eventful year for the Turkish political scene. In the local elections in March, voters turned massively against Prime Minister Özal. The Social Democratic Populist Party (SDPP) received 28.71 percent of the votes. The True Path Party (TPP) of Süleyman Demirel was second with 25.15 percent of the votes, and the Motherland Party (MP) of Özal was third with 21.75 percent of the votes. (Ankara Domestic Service, 31 March.) The results were a serious blow to Özal's popularity. The MP showed a decrease from the 36 percent it had won in the last legislative elections in 1987 and from the 41 percent it had won in the last local elections, held five years ago (*WP*, 28 March).

Following local elections, the opposition demanded Özal's resignation. However, Özal brushed aside these demands, reshuffled his cabinet, and in October announced his candidacy for the presidency. This announcement was not unexpected. Throughout the period following the local elections, Özal maintained that the next president of Turkey would most certainly come from the ranks of the MP, since this party held the majority of seats in the Grand National Assembly. On 31 October, the Grand National Assembly elected Özal as the eighth president of the republic. The main opposition SDPP and the right wing TPP, with 155 votes between them, both boycotted the voting as a protest against Özal's candidacy (*Anatolia*, 31 October; *FBIS*, 1 November). In a statement after the presidential election results were announced, SDPP leader Erdal İnönü declared that a period of a presidency without public support has begun in Turkey (Ankara, TRT, 31 October). Süleyman Demirel, leader of the TPP, also argued that the country would suffer because the MP, which is the third most popular party in Turkey, acted alone in electing the president (*Anatolia*, 31 October).

Upon taking an oath as president of Turkey on 9 November, Turgut Özal appointed Yildirim Akbulut, speaker of the parliament, as the next prime minster. Following the appointment of Akbulut as prime minister, the Grand National Assembly moved to elect Kaya Erdem as the new speaker of the parliament on 22 November. This was an important development because Erdem's election was against the advice of the president. Apparently, President Özal favored another candidate, Metin Emiroğlu, to replace Akbulut. However, some members of the MP who were upset at Özal's choice for prime minister joined ranks with the opposition parties to elect Erdem, an opponent of Özal, as the next speaker of the parliament. (*Hürriyet*, 23 November.)

Regarding her communist neighbors, Turkey improved its economic ties with the Soviet Union in 1989 by signing several trade agreements. However, relations with Bulgaria deteriorated to reach a new low. Turkey and Bulgaria have been at odds for over four years, following Sofia's campaign, launched at the end of 1984, to redesignate Bulgaria's ethnic Turks as "Muslim Bulgarians." In fact, the Bulgarian authorities consistently denied that these Turks, who account for about 11 percent of the country's nine million inhabitants, are anything other than Slavs forcibly converted to Islam during the five centuries of Ottoman rule. Turkey and other Western countries called on the Bulgarian authorities to stop their campaign of eradicating Turkish names, the use of the Turkish language, and many Muslim practices. The Bulgarian officials responded by increasing their attempts to assimilate the Turkish minority by forcibly changing their names. (BBC Current Affairs Unit, 9 August.) According to Turkish sources, the Bulgarians often punished those who refused to accept Slavic names, and in many instances ethnic Turks were killed. These developments provoked a serious critique of the Özal government for lack of action from opposition parties in Turkey (Ankara Domestic Service, 28 May; *FBIS*, 1 June).

Following a series of demonstrations by ethnic Turks in May, and a demand from Prime Minister Özal to Bulgaria to let them go, Bulgaria opened up its border to Turkey. In the three following months more than 300,000 Bulgarian Turks fled to Turkey. This uncontrolled influx, the largest population movement in Europe since the aftermath of WW II, found the Özal government totally unprepared. The prime minister, who was under attack from the opposition for being ineffective and hesitant in pursuing the dispute with Bulgaria, also faced criticism for failing to provide suitable assistance to the refugees. Given these problems, the Özal government announced that it would require visas for all Bulgarian Turks who wished to emigrate to Turkey (*Anatolia*, 22 August). Following this decision, the number of Turks crossing the border from Bulgaria declined significantly to an average of 234 per week (*Anatolia*, 29 August; *FBIS*, 30 August). In an attempt to influence the Bulgarian officials, Turkey appealed for international public support through efforts at the EC, the UN, the Islamic Conference Organization (ICO), the Council of Europe, and even the Kremlin. However, because the refugees had not received proper support from Turkish officials in resettling, more than 50,000 Bulgarian Turks had returned to Bulgaria by the end of October (*Miiliyet*, 24 October).

Birol Yeşilada
University of Missouri at Columbia

Select Bibliography, 1988–1989

GENERAL

Becker, Jörg and Tamás Szecskö, eds. *Europe Speaks to Europe: International Information Flows between Eastern and Western Europe.* New York: Pergamon Press, 1989. 445 pp.

Clesse, Armand, and Thomas C. Schelling, eds. *The Western Community and the Gorbachev Challenge.* Baden-Baden: Nomos Verlag, 1989. 408 pp.

Coffey, Peter, ed. *Main Economic Policy of the EEC– towards 1992.* Dordrecht: Kluwer Academic Publishers, 1988. 166 pp.

Crenshaw, Martha. *Terrorism and International Cooperation.* New York: Institute for East-West Security Studies, 1989. 91 pp.

European Strategy Group. *Gorbachev Challenge and European Security.* Baden-Baden: Nomos Verlagsgesellschaft, 1988. 137 pp.

Federal Republic of Germany. *Der Besuch von Generalsekretär Honecker in der Bundesrepublik Deutschland.* Bonn: Bundesministerium für Innerdeutsche Beziehungen, 1988. 168 pp.

Felkay, Andrew. *Hungary and the USSR, 1956–1988: Kádár's Political Leadership.* Westport, Conn.: Greenwood Press, 1989. 334 pp.

Gabrisch, Hubert, ed. *Economic Reforms in Eastern Europe and the Soviet Union.* Boulder, Colo.: Westview Press, 1989. 214 pp.

Goldfarb, Jeffrey C. *Beyond Glasnost: The Post-Totalitarian Mind.* Chicago: University of Chicago Press, 1989. 248 pp.

Goldman, Kjell. *Strategies for Peace: The Political Parties, Churches and Activists in West Germany, Great Britain and Sweden.* Stockholm: University of Stockholm Press, 1988. 102 pp.

Hardt, John P., and Carl H. McMillan, eds. *Planned Economies: Confronting the Challenges of the 1980's.* New York: Cambridge University Press, 1988. 191 pp.

Höffkes, Karl. *Deutsch-sowjetische Geheimverbindungen.* Tübingen: Gräbert Verlag, 1989. 301 pp.

Kim, Dalchoong, Werner Gumpel, and Gottfried-Karl Kindermann, eds. *New Dynamics in East-West Relations.* Seoul: Yonsei University, Institute of East and West Studies, 1989. 200 pp.

Lee, Vl. F. *Eastern Societies: Revolution, Power, Progress.* Moscow: Nauka, 1989. 236 pp.

Link, Werner. *Der Ost-West Konflikt: Die Organisation der internationalen Beziehungen im 20. Jahrhundert.* 2nd rev. ed. Stuttgart: Kohlhammer, 1988. 257 pp.

Maresceau, Marc, ed. *The Political and Legal Framework of Trade Relations between the European Community and Eastern Europe.* Dordrecht: Martinus Nijhoff Publishers, 1989. 349 pp.

Mouritzen, Hans. *Finlandization: Towards a General Theory of Adaptive Politics.* Aldershot: Avebury Publishers, 1988. 463 pp.

Nee, Victor, and David Stark, eds. *Remaking the Economic Institutions of Socialism: China and Eastern Europe.* Stanford, Calif.: Stanford University Press. 1989. 405 pp.

Pijpers, A. *European Political Cooperation in the 1980's.* Dordrecht: Kluwer Academic Publishers, 1988. 398 pp.

Pilevsky, Philip. *Captive Continent: The Stockholm Syndrome in European-Soviet Relations.* Westport, Conn.: Praeger, 1989. 144 pp.

Rimbert, Pierre. *Du Capital de Marx au socialisme.* Paris, Editions de L'OURS, 1988. 522 pp.

Schultz, Brigitte H., and William W. Hansen, eds. *The Soviet Bloc and the Third World.* Boulder, Colo.: Westview Press, 1989. 246 pp.

Staar, Richard F., ed. *1989 Yearbook on International Communist Affairs.* Stanford, Calif.: Hoover Institution Press, 1989. 676 pp.

Stariz, Dietrich and Hermann Weber, eds. *Einheitsfront–Einheitspartei.* Cologne: Verlag Wissenschaft und Politik, 1989. 467 pp.

Taras, Raymond C., ed. *Leadership Change in Communist States.* Winchester, Mass.: Unwin Hyman Inc., 1989. 210 pp.

Weber, Hermann. *Kommunistische Bewegung und realsozialistischer Staat; Beiträge zum deutschen und internationalen Kommunismus.* Cologne: Bund-Verlag, 1989. 354 pp.

AFRICA

Angola Watch. *Angola: Violations of the Laws of War by Both Sides.* London: Human Rights Watch, 1989. 149 pp.

Alekseev, Valerii. *Gdrani Almaza: Povest' o Patrise Emeri Lumumbe.* Moscow: Politizdat, 1988. 332 pp.

Allen, Chris, and Michael Radu. *Benin and the Congo.* Philadelphia: Foreign Policy Research Institute, 1989. 220 pp.

———, et al. *Benin, The Congo, Burkina Faso: Economics, Politics and Society.* London: Pinter Publishers, 1989. 300 pp.

Aye, Edward Jide. *Development Planning in Nigeria.* Nigeria: University Press, 1988. 199 pp.

Bardis, Panos. *South Africa and the Marxist Movement.* Lewiston, Wales: The Edwin Mellen Press, 1989. 270 pp.

Becker, Joachim. *Angola, Mosambik und Zimbabwe: Im Visier Südafrikas.* Cologne: Pahl-Rugenstein Verlag, 1988. 329 pp.

Bennuzzi, Nadia. *Le Donne nei processi di sviluppo dell'Africa Subsahariana: Materiali esistenti nelle Biblioteche del Centro Amilcar Cabral e del Centro di Documentazine delle Donne.* Bologna: Centro Amilcar Cabral, 1989. 186 pp.

Bienen, Henry. *Armed Forces, Conflict, and Change in Africa.* Boulder, Colo.: Westview Press, 1989. 211 pp.

Brittain, Victoria. *Hidden Lives, Hidden Deaths: South Africa's Crippling of a Continent.* London: Faber, 1988. 189 pp.

Braginskii, M. I., and V. M. Kirko, eds. *Afrika: Problemy zaniatosti: sbornik statei.* Moscow: "Nauka," 1988. 219 pp.

Bulcha, Mekuria. *Flight and Integration: Causes of Mass Exodus from Ethiopia and Problems of Integration in the Sudan.* Uppsala: Scandinavian Institute of African Studies, 1988. 256 pp.

Callinicos, Alex. *South Africa between Reform and Revolution.* London: Bookmarks, 1988. 231 pp.

Chatenet, Pierre. *Décolonisation: Souvenirs et réflexions.* Paris: Buchet/Chastel, 1988. 245 pp.

Chazan, Naomi. *Politics and Society in Contemporary Africa.* Hampshire: Macmillan, 1988. 459 pp.

Cliffe, Lionel, and Basil Davidson, eds. *The Long Struggle of Eritrea.* Trenton, N.J.: The Red Sea Press, 1988. 215 pp.

Cobbett, William, ed. *Popular Struggles in South Africa.* Trenton, N.J.: Africa World Press, 1988. 234 pp.

Dawit, Wolde Giorgis. *Red Tears: War, Famine, and Revolution in Ethiopia.* Trenton, N.J.: The Red Sea Press, 1989. 375 pp.

Diamond, Larry, ed. *Democracy in Developing Countries: Africa.* Boulder, Colo.: L. Rienner Publishers, 1988. 309 pp.

Downs, R. E., and S. P. Reyna, eds. *Land and Society in Contemporary Africa.* Hanover: University Press of New England, 1988. 383 pp.

Dreijmanis, John. *The Role of the South African Government in Tertiary Education.* Braamfontein: South African Institute of Race Relations, 1988. 156 pp.

Emergency Situation in Mozambique: Priority Requirements for the Period 1989–1990. New York: United Nations, Office for Emergencies in Africa, 1989. 290 pp.

Friedman, Steven. *A New Mood in Moscow: Soviet Attitudes to South Africa.* Braamfontein: South African Institute of Race Relations, 1989. 27 pp.

Gebre-Medhin, Jordan. *Peasants and Nationalism in Eritrea: A Critique of Ethiopian Studies.* Trenton, N.J.: Red Sea Press, 1989. 220 pp.

Gritzner, Jeffrey A. *The West African Sahel: Human Agency and Environmental Change.* Chicago: University of Chicago, Committee on Geographical Studies, 1988. 170 pp.

Hargreaves, John D. *Decolonization in Africa.* London: Longman, 1988. 263 pp.

Hermele, Kenneth. *Country Report, Mozambique: War & Stabilization.* Stockholm: Swedish International Development Authority, 1988. 53 pp.

Hirschmann, David. *Changing Attitudes of Black South Africans Toward the United States of America.* Grahamstown: Rhodes University, 1988. 70 pp.

Hodges, Tony, and Malyn Newitt. *São Tome and Príncipe; from Plantation Colony to Microstate.* Boulder, Colo.; Westview Press, 1988. 173 pp.

Houser, George M. *No One Can Stop the Rain: Glimpses of Africa's Liberation Struggle.* New York: Pilgrim Press, 1988. 388 pp.

Ihonvbere, Julius Omozuanvbo. *Towards a Political Economy of Nigeria: Petroleum and Politics at the (Semi)-Periphery.* Aldershot: Avebury Publishers, 1988. 213 pp.

Jackson, J. C. *Incomes, Poverty and Food Security in the Communal Lands of Zimbabwe.* Harare: University of Zimbabwe, 1988. 45 pp.

Johnson, Phyllis, and David Martin, eds. *Frontline Southern Africa: Destructive Engagement.* New York: Four Walls Eight Windows, 1988. 530 pp.

Kempton, Daniel R. *Soviet Strategy Toward Southern Africa: The National Liberation Movement Connection.* New York: Praeger, 1989. 261 pp.

Kgosana, Philip Ata. *Lest We Forget: An Autobiography.* Johannesburg: Skotaville, 1988. 108 pp.

Lazic, Branko M., with Pierre Rigoulot. *Angola, 1974–1988: Un Échec du communisme en Afrique.* Paris: Est & Ouest, 1988. 109 pp.

Mahmud, Abdulmalik Bappa. *A Brief History of Shari'ah in the Defunct Northern Nigeria.* Jos, Nigeria: Jos University Press, 1988. 61 pp.

Meli, Francis. *South Africa Belongs to Us: A History of the ANC.* Harare: Zimbabwe Publishing House, 1988. 258 pp.

Moore, Susanna. *The Whiteness of Bones.* New York: Doubleday, 1989. 277 pp.

Mungazi, Dickson A. *The Struggle for Social Change in Southern Africa: Visions of Liberty.* New York: Crane, Russak, 1989. 145 pp.

Namibia: The Facts. London: IDAF Publications, 1989. 112 pp.

Norval, Morgan. *Red Star over Southern Africa.* Washington, D.C.: Selous Foundation Press, 1988. 217 pp.

Obasanjo, Olusegun. *Africa Embattled: Selected Essays on Contemporary African Development.* Ibadan: Fountain Publications, 1988. 118 pp.

Oyugi, Walter O., ed. *Democratic Theory and Practice in Africa.* Portsmouth, N.H.: Heinemann, 1988. 237 pp.

Parpart, Jane L., ed. *Women and the State in Africa.* Boulder, Colo.: L. Rienner Publishers, 1989. 229 pp.

Radu, Michael. *Final Report: Soviet Activities in Sub-Saharan Africa.* Philadelphia, Pa.: Foreign Policy Research Institute, 1988. 132 pp.

Roux, Helene, ed. *How Revolutionaries Use Children.* Johannesburg: Lone Tree Publications, 1988. 62 pp.

Samatar, Ahmed I. *Socialist Somalia: Rhetoric and Reality.* London: Zed Books, Ltd., 1988. 186 pp.

Selassie, Bereket H. *Eritrea and the United Nations and Other Essays.* Trenton, N.J.: Red Sea Press, 1989. 174 pp.

Slovo, Joe. *The South African Working Class and the National Democratic Revolution.* (No place given): South African Communist Party, 1988. 36 pp.

Sudan. New York: United Nations, 1988. 164 pp.

Stoneman, Colin. *Zimbabwe: Politics, Economics, and Society.* London: Pinter Publishers, 1989. 210 pp.

Torp, Jens Erik. *Mozambique.* New York: Columbia University Press, 1989. 257 pp.

Urdang, Stephanie. *And Still They Dance: Women, War and the Struggle for Change in Mozambique.* New York: Monthly Review Press, 1989, 256 pp.

Van der Merwe, Hendrik W. *Pursuing Justice and Peace in South Africa.* New York: Routledge, 1989. 127 pp.

Venter, Al J., ed. *Challenge: Southern Africa Within the African Revolutionary Context: An Overview.* Johannesburg: Ashanti Publishing, 1989. 526 pp.

Voice of the South African People: A Survey of South Africans on the Subject of Sanctions and Foreign Corporate Divestment: A Gallup Survey. Princeton, N.J.: Gallup Organization, 1989. 54 pp.

Whitaker, Jennifer Seymour. *How Can Africa Survive?* New York: Harper & Row, 1988. 264 pp.

Wuyts, Marc. *Money and Planning for Socialist Transition: The Mozambican Experience.* Aldershot: Gower, 1989. 167 pp.

AMERICAS

Aguila, Juan M. del. *Cuba: Dilemmas of a Revolution.* Boulder, Colo.: Westview Press, 1988. 228 pp.

Ai Camp, Roderic. *Who's Who in Mexico Today.* Boulder, Colo.: Westview Press, 1988. 193 pp.

Bacha, Edmar L., and Herbert S. Klein, ed. *Social Change in Brazil, 1934–1985: The Incomplete Transition.* Albuquerque: University of New Mexico Press, 1989. 346 pp.

Bellegarde-Smith, Patrick. *Haiti: The Beached Citadel.* Boulder, Colo.: Westview Press, 1989. 217 pp.

Blandon, Chuno. *Cuartel General.* Managua: La Ocarina, 1988. 272 pp.

Booth, John A., and Mitchell A. Seligson. *Elections and Democracy in Central America.* Chapel Hill: University of North Carolina Press, 1989. 214 pp.

Clerc, Jean-Pierre. *Fidel de Cuba.* Paris: Editions Ramsey, 1988. 492 pp.

Davis, Charles L. *Working-Class Mobilization and Political Control: Venezuela and Mexico.* Lexington: University Press of Kentucky, 1989. 211 pp.

Dominguez, Jorge I. *To Make the World Safe for Revo-*

lution: Cuba's Foreign Policy. Cambridge: Harvard University Press, 1989. 365 pp.

Dupuy, Alex. *Haiti in the World Economy: Class, Race and Underdevelopment since 1700*. Boulder, Colo.: Westview Press, 1989. 245 pp.

Eckstein, Susan, ed. *Power and Popular Protest: Latin American Social Movements*. Berkeley: University of California Press, 1989. 342 pp.

Faúndez, Julio. *Marxism and Democracy in Chile: From 1932 to the Fall of Allende*. New Haven, Conn.: Yale University Press, 1988. 305 pp.

Fernández, Damián J. *Cuba's Foreign Policy in the Middle East*. Boulder, Colo.: Westview Press, 1988. 160 pp.

Fontaine, Roger W. *Terrorism: The Cuban Connection*. New York: Crane, Russak, 1988. 197 pp.

Foroohar, Manzar. *The Catholic Church and Social Change in Nicaragua*. Albany: State University of New York Press, 1989. 262 pp.

Hellinger, Daniel Charles. *Venezuela*. 1989. Boulder, Colo.: Westview Press, 1989. 200 pp.

Horowitz, Irving L., ed. *Cuban Communism*. 7th ed. New Brunswick, N.J.: Transaction Publishers, 1989. 854 pp.

Isaula, Roger. *Honduras: Crisis e Incertidumbre Nacional: Hacia una Analisis de Coyuntura, 1986–1987*. Tegucigalpa: Editores Unidos, 1988. 194 pp.

Israel Zipper, Ricardo. *Politics and Ideology in Allende's Chile*. Tempe: Arizona State University Center for Latin American Studies, 1989. 306 pp.

Julio, Agosto. *Brecha: Informe sobre la situacion Centroamerica*. San José, Costa Rica: La Comision, 1988.

Kirk, John M., and George W. Schuyler, eds. *Central America: Democracy, Development and Change*. New York: Praeger Publishers, 1988. 224 pp.

Klehr, Harvey. *Far Left of Center: The American Radical Left Today*. New Brunswick, N.J.: Transaction Books, 1988. 310 pp.

Lamperti, John. *What Are We Afraid of?* Boston, Mass.: South End Press, 1988. 109 pp.

Larkin, Bruce D. *Vital Interest: The Soviet Issue In U.S. Central American Policy*. Boulder, Colo.: L. Rienner Publishers, 1988. 500 pp.

Lievens, Karin. *El Quinto piso de la Alegria: Tres años con la guerrilla: El Salvador*. Managua: Ediciones Sistema Radio Venceremos, 1988. 189 pp.

Manwaring, Max G., and Court Prisk, eds. *El Salvador at War: An Oral History*. Washington, D.C.: National Defense University Press, 1988. 500 pp.

Martz, John D., ed. *United States Policy in Latin America: A Quarter Century of Crisis and Challenge, 1961–1986*. Lincoln: University of Nebraska Press, 1988. 336 pp.

Matias, Andreo. *CIA, Sendero Luminoso: Guerra Politica*. Lima: El Universo Gráfico, 1988. 240 pp.

Mayorga, Juan Manual Ulloa, et al. *Apuntes de Historia de Nicaragua*. Nicaragua: Editorial Universitaria, 1988. 234 pp.

McDonald, Ronald H., and J. Mark Ruhl. *Party Politics and Elections in Latin America*. Boulder, Colo.: Westview Press, 1989. 358 pp.

Medal, José Luis. *Nicaragua: Politica económica, crisis y cambio social*. Managua: CINASE, 1988. 135 pp.

Meditz, Sandra W., and Dennis M. Hanratty, eds. *Islands of the Commonwealth Caribbean: A Regional Study*. Washington, D.C.: Department of the Army, 1989. 771 pp.

Mercado, Rogger. *La Realidad Politica del Peru*. Peru: Ediciones Latinoamericanas, 1988. 64 pp.

Mora, Arnoldo, ed. *Los Origenes del pensamiento socialista en Costa Rica*. San José, Costa Rica: Departamento Ecumenico De Investigaciones, 1988. 47 pp.

Morse, Richard M., ed. *Haiti's Future: Views of Twelve Haitian Leaders*. Washington, D.C.: Wilson Center Press, 1988. 129 pp.

Movimiento Civilista: Junio 1987–Junio 1988: Fases y cronologia de Panameño por su democratizacion: Partido Democrata Cristiano. Panama City: Instituto Panameño de Estudios Comunitarios, 1988?. 144 pp.

Nuñez Soto, Orlando. *La Insurreccion de la Conciencia*. Managua: Editorial Escuela de Sociologia de la Universidad Centroamericana (ESUCA), 1988. 209 pp.

Ortega, Daniel. *Combatiendo por la paz*. Havana: Editora Politica, 1988. 283 pp.

Palmer, Bryan D. *A Communist Life: Jack Scott and the Canadian Labour Movement, 1927–1985*. St. John's: Commission on Canadian Labour History, 1989. 276 pp.

Rius. *El Hermano Sandino*. Mexico City: Grijalbo, 1988. 181 pp.

Serrano Caldera, Alejandro. *Entre la nacion y el imperio*. Managua: Vanguardia, 1988. 300 pp.

Sheehan, Edward R. F. *Agony in the Garden: A Stranger in Central America*. Boston: Houghton Mifflin, 1989. 362 pp.

Singh, Chaitram. *Guyana: Politics in a Plantation Society*. New York: Praeger, 1988. 156 pp.

Smith, Wayne S., ed. *Subject to Solution: Problems in Cuban-U.S. Relations.* Boulder, Colo.: L. Rienner Publishers, 1988. 158 pp.

Torres-Rivas, Edelberto. *Repression and Resistance: The Struggle for Democracy in Central America.* Boulder, Colo.: Westview Press, 1989. 165 pp.

Weinstein, Martin. *Uruguay: Democracy at the Crossroads.* Boulder, Colo.: Westview Press, 1988. 160 pp.

Wiarda, Howard J., and Harvey F. Kline, eds. *Latin American Politics and Development.* 3rd ed. Boulder, Colo.: Westview Press, 1989. 670 pp.

Zimbalist, Andrew, ed. *Cuban Political Economy: Controversies in Cubanology.* Boulder, Colo.: Westview Press, 1988. 240 pp.

ASIA AND THE PACIFIC

Beset, Jean-Pierre. *Le Dossier Calédonien.* Paris: La Découverte, 1988. 175 pp.

Bonavia, David. *Deng.* Hong Kong: Longman, 1988. 217 pp.

Bouton, Marshall M., and Philip Oldenburg, eds. *India Briefing, 1989.* Boulder, Colo.: Westview Press, 1989. pp. 198.

Burns, John P., ed. *The Chinese Communist Party's Nomenklatura System.* Armonk, N.Y.: M. E. Sharpe, 1989. 214 pp.

Chang, David Wen-wei. *China Under Deng Xiaoping.* New York: St. Martin's Press, 1988. 304 pp.

Chen, David, ed. *A Day in the Life of China.* San Francisco: Collins Publishers, 1989. 224 pp.

Chen, Philip M., ed. *South Pacific Island States: "Seminar on South Pacific."* Taipei: Asia and World Institute, 1988. 146 pp.

Cima, Ronald J., ed. *Vietnam: A Country Study.* Washington, D.C.: Department of the Army, 1989. 386 pp.

Couper, A.D., ed. *Development and Social Change in the Pacific Islands.* London and New York: Routledge, 1989. 203 pp.

Davis, Leonard. *Revolutionary Struggle in the Philippines.* New York: St. Martin's Press, 1989. 188 pp.

Del Vecchio, John M. *For the Sake of All Living Things.* New York: Bantam Books, 1989. 790 pp.

Duncan, Emma. *Breaking The Curfew: A Political Journey Through Pakistan.* London: Michael Joseph, 1989. 313 pp.

Evans, Grant. *Agrarian Change in Communist Laos.* Singapore: Institute of Southeast Asian Studies, 1988. 88 pp.

The Far East and Australia 1989, 20th ed. London: Europa Publications, 1989. 1,048 pp.

Fathers, Michael, and Andrew Higgins. *Tiananmen: The Rape of Peking.* London: The Independent, 1989. vol. 1.

Flynn, Robert. *A Personnel War in Vietnam.* College Station: Texas A & M University, 1989. 139 pp.

Franz, Uli. *Deng Xiaoping.* San Diego, Calif.: Harcourt Brace Jovanovich, 1988. 340 pp.

Gregor, James. *In the Shadow of Giants: The Major Powers and the Security of Southeast Asia.* Stanford, Calif.: Hoover Institution Press, 1989. 118 pp.

Guzman, Raul P. de, and Mila A. Reforma, eds. *Government and Politics of the Philippines.* Oxford: Oxford University Press, 1988. 304 pp.

Hamilton, John Maxwell. *Edgar Snow: A Biography.* Bloomington: Indiana University Press, 1988. 343 pp.

Hamrin, Carol Lee. *China and the Challenge of the Future.* Boulder, Colo.: Westview Press, 1989. 257 pp.

Hartford, Kathleen, and Steven M. Goldstein, eds. *Single Sparks: China's Rural Revolutions.* Armonk, N.Y.: M. E. Sharpe, 1989. 270 pp.

Heitzman, James, and Robert L. Worden. *Bangladesh: A Country Study.* Washington, D.C.: Department of the Army, 1989. 306 pp.

Jackson, Karl D., ed. *Cambodia 1975–1978: Rendezvous with Death.* Princeton, N.J.: Princeton University Press, 1989. 334 pp.

Jane's Information Group, comp. *China in Crisis.* London: Jane's Information Group, 1989. 119 pp.

Jones, Gregg R. *Red Revolution: Inside the Philippine Guerrilla Movement.* Boulder, Colo.: Westview Press, 1989. 360 pp.

Kallgren, Joyce, Noordin Sopiee, and Soedjati Djiwandono, eds. *ASEAN and China: an Evolving Relationship.* Berkeley: University of California, Institute of East Asian Studies, 1988. 368 pp.

Kane, Anthony J., ed. *China Briefing, 1989.* Boulder, Colo.: Westview Press, 1989. 159 pp.

Kim, Samuel S. *China and the World: New Directions in Chinese Foreign Relations.* Boulder, Colo.: Westview Press, 1989. 339 pp.

Lal, Brij V. *Power and Prejudice: The Making of the Fiji Crisis.* Wellington: New Zealand Institute of International Affairs, 1988. 257 pp.

Lam, Willy Wo-Lap. *The Era of Zhao Ziyang: Power*

Struggle in China, 1986–88. Hong Kong: A.B. Books and Stationery International, 1989. 281 pp.

Lee, Suck-Ho. *Party-Military Relations in North Korea: A Comparative Analysis.* Seoul: Research Center for Peace and Unification of Korea, 1989. 278 pp.

Leng Shao-chuan. *Changes in China: Party, State and Society.* Lanham, Md.: University Press of America, 1989, 368 pp.

LePoer, Barbara Leitch, ed. *Thailand: A Country Study.* Washington, D.C.: Department of the Army, 1989. 365 pp.

Lieberthal, Kenneth J., and Michael Oksenberg. *Policy Making in China: Leaders, Structures and Processes.* Princeton, N.J.: Princeton University Press, 1988. 445 pp.

Lintner, Bertil. *Outrage: Burma's Struggle for Democracy.* Hong Kong: Review Publishing Company, 1989. 267 pp.

Longman, David. *Deng.* San Diego: Harcourt Brace Jovanovich, 1988. 340 pp.

Marr, David G., and Christine P. White, eds. *Postwar Vietnam: Dilemmas in Socialist Development.* Ithaca, N.Y.: Southeast Asia Program, Cornell University, 1988. 248 pp.

Minford, John, and Geremie Barme, eds. *Seeds of Fire: Chinese Voices of Conscience.* New York: Hill and Wang, 1988. 491 pp.

Okonogi, Masao, ed. *North Korea at the Crossroads.* Tokyo: Japan Institute of International Affairs, 1988. 196 pp.

Oliver, Douglas L. *The Pacific Islands.* 3rd ed. Honolulu: University of Hawaii Press, 1989. 304 pp.

Parker, F. Charles, IV. *Vietnam, Strategy for a Stalemate.* New York: Paragon House, 1989. 257 pp.

Plenel, Edwy. *Mourir à Ouvéa.* Paris: Ed. La Découverte, 1988. 276 pp.

Ramanathan, Sankaran, and Mohd. Hamdan Adnan. *Malaysia's 1986 General Election: The Urban-Rural Dichotomy.* Singapore: Institute of Southeast Asian Studies, 1988. 88 pp.

Salisbury, Harrison E. *Tiananmen Square: Thirteen Days in June.* Boston: Little Brown, 1989. 176 pp.

Scalapino, Robert A., and Dalchoong Kim, eds. *Asian Communism: Continuity and Transition.* Berkeley: University of California, Institute of East Asian Studies, 1989. 365 pp.

——and Masataka Kosaka, eds. *Peace, Politics, and Economics in Asia.* Washington, D.C.: Pergamon-Brassey's, 1988. 209 pp.

Selden, Mark. *The Political Economy of Chinese So-cialism.* Armonk, N.Y.: M. E. Sharpe, 1989. 241 pp.

de Silva, K. M., and Howard Wriggins. *J. R. Jayewardene: A Political Biography. Vol. 1: The First Fifty Years.* Honolulu: University of Hawaii Press, 1989. 336 pp.

Sison, Jose Maria, with Rainer Werning. *The Philippine Revolution: The Leader's View.* New York: Crane, Russak, 1989. 241 pp.

Spencer, Michael, ed. *New Caledonia: Essays in Nationalism and Dependency.* New York: University of Queensland Press, 1988. 253 pp.

TIME Magazine. *Massacre in Beijing: China's Struggle for Democracy.* New York: Warner Books, 1989. 280 pp.

Walsh, J. Richard. *Change, Continuity and Commitment: China's Adaptive Foreign Policy.* Lanham, Md.: University Press of America, 1988. 174 pp.

White, Lynn T., III. *Policies of Chaos: The Organizational Causes of Violence in China's Cultural Revolution.* Princeton, N.J.: Princeton University Press, 1989. 367 pp.

Woetzel, Jonathan R. *China's Economic Opening to the Outside World: The Politics of Empowerment.* New York: Praeger, 1989. 208 pp.

Woodruff, John. *China in Search of Its Future; Years of Great Reform, 1982–87.* Seattle: University of Washington Press, 1989. 218 pp.

Wurfel, David. *Filipino Politics: Development and Decay.* Ithaca, N.Y.: Cornell University Press. 1988. 361 pp.

Yang, Richard H., editor-in-chief. *SCPS Yearbook on PLA Affairs.* Taipei: Sun Yat-sen University, Center for Policy Studies, 1989. 196 pp.

Yang Zhongmei. *Hu Yaobang: A Chinese Biography.* Armonk, N.Y.: M.E. Sharpe, 1988. 208 pp.

Zweig, David. *Agrarian Radicalism in China, 1968–81.* Cambridge, Mass.: Harvard University Press, 1989. 270 pp.

EASTERN EUROPE

Alia, Ramiz. *Our Enver.* Tirana: "8 Nëntori," 1988. 481 pp.

Allen, Bruce. *Germany East: Dissent and Opposition.* Montreal: Black Rose Books, 1989. 171 pp.

Banac, Ivo. *With Stalin against Tito: Cominformist Splits in Yugoslav Communism.* Ithaca, N.Y.: Cornell University Press, 1988. 295 pp.

Blumenwitz, Dieter, and Gottfried Ziezel. *Deutsche*

Frage im Spiegel der Parteien. Cologne: Verlag Wissenschaft und Politik, 1989. 191 pp.

Borsányi, György. *The History of the Working Class Movement in Hungary.* Budapest: Corvina, 1988. 225 pp.

Boyadjieff, Christo. *Saving the Bulgarian Jews in World War II.* Ottawa: Free Bulgarian Center, 1989. 167 pp.

Bozyk, Pawel, ed. *Global Challenges and East European Responses.* Warsaw: PWN Scientific Publishers, 1988. 367 pp.

Brada, Joseph C., and István Dobozi, eds. *The Hungarian Economy in the 1980s: Reforming the System and Adjusting to External Shocks.* Greenwich, Conn.: Jai Press, 1988. 277 pp.

Broun, Janice, and Grazyna Sikorska. *Conscience and Captivity: Religion in Eastern Europe.* Washington, D.C.: Ethics and Public Policy Center, 1988. 376 pp.

Brown, J. F. *Eastern Europe and Communist Rule.* Durham: Duke University Press, 1988. 562 pp.

Bugajski, Janusz, and Maxine Pollack. *East European Fault Lines: Dissent, Opposition and Social Activism.* Boulder, Colo.: Westview Press, 1989. 332 pp.

Burant, Stephen R., ed. *East Germany: A Country Study.* Washington, D.C.: Department of the Army, 1988. 433 pp.

Childs, David, Thomas A. Baylis, and Marilyn Rueschmeyer, eds. *East Germany in Comparative Perspective.* London: Routledge, 1989. 238 pp.

Carnovale, Marco, and William C. Potter. *Continuity and Change in Soviet-East European Relations: Implications for the West.* Boulder, Colo.: Westview Press, 1989. 413 pp.

Coutouvidis, John, and Jaime Reynolds. *Poland: 1939–1947.* New York: Holmes and Meier, 1988. 393 pp.

DDR Forschung in der BRD. *Veränderungen in Gesellschaft und im Politischen System der DDR.* Cologne: Verlag Wissenschaft und Politik, 1988. 176 pp.

Fischer, Alexander, and Nikolaus Katzer, eds. *Die Deutsche Demokratische Republik: Daten, Fakten, Analysen.* Würzburg: Verlag Ploetz, 1988. 254 pp.

Fischer, Mary Ellen. *Nicolae Ceausescu: A Study in Political Leadership.* Boulder, Colo.: L. Rienner Publishers, 1989. 324 pp.

Forschungsstelle für gesamtdeutsche wirtschaftliche und soziale Fragen. *Glasnost und Perestrojka auch in der DDR?* West Berlin: Verlag Arno Spitz, 1988. 335 pp.

Freedom House. *Romania: A Case of "Dynastic" Communism.* Lanham, Md.: University Press of America, 1989. 130 pp.

Friedrich, Wolfgang-Uwe. *DDR: Deutschland zwischen Elbe und Oder.* 2nd ed. Stuttgart: Verlag W. Kohlhammer, 1989. 272 pp.

Gabrisch, Hubert, ed. *Economic Reforms in Eastern Europe and the Soviet Union.* Boulder, Colo.: Westview Press, 1988. 214 pp.

Gatzka, Rajmund A. *Das Recht der wissenschaftlich-technischen Zusammenarbeit und die DDR.* Cologne: Verlag Wissenschaft und Politik, 1988. 144 pp.

German Democratic Republic. *Die DDR stellt sich vor: 1940–1989.* East Berlin: Panorama Verlag, 1989, 192 pp.

Glaessner, Gert-Joachim, ed. *Die DDR in der Ära Honecker: Politik-Kultur-Gesellschaft.* Opladen: Westdeutscher Verlag, 1988. 689 pp.

Griffith, William E., ed. *Central and Eastern Europe: The Opening Curtain?* Boulder, Colo.: Westview Press, 1989. 458 pp.

Gubcsi, Lajos, ed. *After the Bargain: The Hungarian Reform.* Budapest: Progresprint, 1988. 170 pp.

Gyurkó, László. *János Kádár: Porträtskizze auf historischem Hintergrund.* Kronberg/Budapest: Pergamon Press/Akadémiai Kiadó, 1988. 232 pp.

Hahn, Hans Henning, and Michael G. Müller, eds. *Gesellschaft und Staat in Polen.* West Berlin: Verlag Arno Spitz, 1988. 222 pp.

Hofmann, Jürgen. *Ein neues Deutschland soll es sein.* East Berlin: Dietz Verlag, 1989. 168 pp.

Honecker, Erich. *Reden und Aufsätze.* Vol. 12. East Berlin: Dietz Verlag, 1988. 697 pp.

Jones, Anthony, and William Moskoff, eds. *Perestroika and the Economy.* Armonk, N.Y.: M. E. Sharpe, 1989. 304 pp.

Joó, Rudolf, ed. *Report on the Situation of the Hungarian Minority in Rumania.* Budapest: Hungarian Democratic Forum, 1988. 206 pp.

Kaufman, Michael T. *Mad Dreams, Saving Graces: Poland, A Nation in Conspiracy.* New York: Random House, 1989. 288 pp.

Kostov, Vladimir. *The Bulgarian Umbrella: The Soviet Direction and Operations of the Bulgarian Secret Service in Europe.* New York: St. Martin's Press, 1988. 204 pp.

Kurz, Thomas. *"Blutmai". Sozialdemokraten und*

Kommunisten im Brennpunkt der Berliner Ereignisse von 1929. East Berlin: Dietz, 1988. 179 pp.

Lewis, Paul G. *Political Authority and Party Secretaries in Poland, 1975–1986.* Cambridge: Cambridge University Press, 1989. 344 pp.

Lydall, Harold. *Yugoslavia in Crisis.* New York: Oxford University Press, 1989. 255 pp.

Nelson, Daniel M. *Romanian Politics in the Ceauşescu Era.* New York: Gordon & Breach, 1988. 324 pp.

Nolte, Hans Heinrich, ed. *Patronage und Klientel: Ergebnisse einer polnish-deutschen Konferenz.* Cologne: Böhlau Verlag, 1989. 181 pp.

Pano, Nicholas C. *Albania.* New York: Columbia University Press, 1989. 220 pp.

Pavliwitch, Stevan K. *The Improbable Survivor: Yugoslavia and its Problems, 1918–1988.* London: C. Hurst & Co., 1988. 167 pp.

Poland: Stagnation, Collapse or Growth? London: Centre for Research into Communist Economies, 1988. 100 pp.

Rácz, Barnabás. *The Hungarian Parliament in Transition: Procedure and Politics.* Pittsburgh: University of Pittsburgh Center for Russian and East European Studies, 1989. 38 pp.

Reiquam, Steve W., ed. *Solidarity and Poland: Impacts East and West.* Washington, D.C.: Wilson Center Press, 1988. 60 pp.

Rensenbrink, John. *Poland Challenges a Divided World.* Baton Rouge: Louisiana State University Press, 1988. 246 pp.

Révész, Gábor. *Perestroika in Eastern Europe: Hungary's Economic Transformation.* Boulder, Colo.: Westview Press, 1989. 182 pp.

Royen, Christoph. *Osteuropa: Reformen und Wandel: Erfahrungen und Aussichten vor dem Hintergrund der sowjetischen Perestrojka.* Baden-Baden: Nomos, 1988. 166 pp.

Rudakov, E. V. *Sel'skoe khoziaistvo Bolgarii: Poiski rezervov razvitiia.* Moscow: Nauka, 1988. 122 pp.

Rueschmeyer, Marilyn, and Christiane Lemke, eds. *Quality of Life in the GDR: Change and Development in a State Socialist Society.* New York: M. E. Sharpe, 1989. 256 pp.

Rühmland, Ullrich, comp. *The Warsaw Pact Dictionary.* Bonn: Bonner Druck- und Verlagsgesellschaft, 1988. 288 pp.

Rusinov, Dennison, ed. *Yugoslavia: A Fractured Federalism.* Washington: Wilson Center Press, 1988. 200 pp.

Staar, Richard F., ed. *United States–East European Relations in the 1990s.* New York: Crane, Russak, 1989. 327 pp.

Thomaneck, J. K. A., and James Mellis, eds. *Politics, Society and Government in the German Democratic Republic: Basic Documents.* Oxford: Berg Press, 1989. 357 pp.

Turnock, David. *Eastern Europe: An Historical Geography, 1815–1945.* New York: Routledge, 1989. 357 pp.

United States. Central Intelligence Agency. *Directory of Polish Officials.* Washington, D.C.: CIA, Directorate of Intelligence, 1989. 171 pp.

Weichhardt, Reiner, ed. *The Economies of Eastern Europe under Gorbachev's Influence.* Brussels: NATO, 1988. 345 pp.

Wiatr, Jerzy J. *The Soldier and the Nation: The Role of the Military in Polish Politics, 1918–1985.* Boulder, Colo.: Westview Press, 1988. 204 pp.

Wolchik, Sharon L. *Czechoslovakia.* New York: Columbia University Press, 1989. 220 pp.

World Economic Environment and the Hungarian Economy. Budapest: Akadémiai Kiadó, 1988. 196 pp.

Zieger, Gottfried. *Die Haltung von SED und DDR zur Einheit Deutschlands, 1949–1987.* Cologne: Verlag Wissenschaft und Politik, 1988. 252 pp.

Zwass, Adam. *The Council for Mutual Economic Assistance: The Thorny Path from Political to Economic Integration.* Armonk, N.Y.: M. E. Sharpe, 1989. 269 pp.

USSR

Adams, Jan. *Economic Reforms in the Soviet Union and Eastern Europe since the 1960's.* New York and Oxford: Blackwell, 1988. 264 pp.

Aganbegyan, Abel, ed. *Perestroika 1989.* New York: Charles Scribner's and Sons, 1989. 346 pp.

Allison, Roy. *The Soviet Propaganda Network: A Directory of Organisations Serving Soviet Foreign Policy.* New York: St. Martin's Press, 1989. 313 pp.

———. *The Soviet Union and the Strategy of Nonalignment in the Third World.* Cambridge: Cambridge University Press, 1988. 298 pp.

Antonenko, V. G., et al. *Kommunisticheskii Manifest i sovremennost.* Kiev: Politizdat, 1988. 278 pp.

Åslund, Anders. *Gorbachev's Struggle for Economic Reform.* London: Pinter, 1989. 219 pp.

Bagramov, Edward A. *The CPSU's Nationalities Pol-*

icy: Truth and Lies. Moscow: Progress, 1988. 136 pp.

Barry, Françoise, and Thomas Schreiber, eds. *L'URSS et L'Europe de l'Est.* Paris: Documentation Française, 1988. 284 pp.

Bezuglov, Anatolii Alekseevich. *Glasnost' raboty sovetov.* Moscow: Iurizdat, 1988. 141 pp.

Black, J. L., ed. *1987: The Gorbachev Reforms.* Gulf Breeze, Fla.: Academic International Press, 1988. 398 pp.

Boltenkova, Liubov Fedorovna. *Internatsionalizm v deistvii.* Moscow: Mysl, 1988. 221 pp.

Braun, Aurel, ed. *The Soviet-East European Relationship in the Gorbachev Era.* Boulder, Colo.: Westview Press, 1989. 200 pp.

Brook-Shepherd, Gordon. *The Storm Birds: Soviet Postwar Defectors.* New York: Weidenfeld and Nicolson, 1989. 386 pp.

Brossat, Alain. *Agents de Moscou: Le Stalinisme et son ombre.* Paris: Gallimard, 1988. 310 pp.

Burlatskii, Fedor Mikhailovich. *Novoe myshlenie: Dialogi i suzhdeniia o tekhnologicheskoi revoliutsii i nashikh reformakh.* Moscow: Politizdat, 1988. 332 pp.

Campeanu, Pavel. *The Genesis of the Stalinist Social Order.* Armonk, N.Y.: M. E. Sharpe, 1988. 215 pp.

Clark, Susan L., ed. *Gorbachev's Agenda: Changes in Soviet Domestic and Foreign Policy.* Boulder, Colo.: Westview Press, 1989. 422 pp.

Communist Party of the Soviet Union. Moscow: Politizdat, 1988. 512 pp.

Conquest, Robert. *Stalin and the Kirov Murder.* New York: Oxford University Press, 1989. 164 pp.

D'Agostino, Anthony. *Soviet Succession Struggles.* Boston: Allen & Unwin, 1988. 274 pp.

Dobrokhotov, Leonid N. *Ideologicheskoe protivoborstvo.* Moscow: Sovetskaia Rossiia, 1988. 219 pp.

Duncan, Peter J. S. *The Soviet Union and India.* New York: Routledge, 1989. 150 pp.

Elebaeva, Ainura B. *Osnovnye urovni i mekhanizmy razvitiia sotsialisticheskikh natsional'nykh kul'tur v sovetskom obshchestve.* Frunze: Ilim, 1988. 176 pp.

Ellison, Herbert J. *The Soviet Union and Northeast Asia.* New Lanham, Md.: University Press of America, 1989. 64 pp.

Elmi, Yusuf, ed. *Afghanistan: A Decade of Sovietisation.* Peshawar City: Afghan Jehad Works Translation Centre. 1988. 371 pp.

Gerner, Christian, and Stefan Hedlund. *Ideology and Rationality in the Soviet Model.* London: Routledge, 1989. 455 pp.

Gill, Graeme, ed. *The Rules of the Communist Party of the Soviet Union.* 1988. 280 pp.

Glynn, Patrick, ed. *Unrest in the Soviet Union.* Lanham, Md.: University Press of America, 1989. 60 pp.

Goland, V. Ia., comp. *Ofitsery granitsy.* Moscow: Sov. Rossiia, 1988. 287 pp.

Goldberg, Paul. *The Final Act: The Dramatic Revealing Story of the Moscow Helsinki Watch Group.* New York: William Morrow, 1988. 320 pp.

Gorbachev, Mikhail S. *At the Summit: Speeches and Interviews, February 1987–July 1988.* New York: Richardson, Steirman & Black, 1988. 298 pp.

Gordienko, N. S. *Osnovy nauchnogo ateizma.* Moscow: Prosveshchenie, 1988. 178 pp.

Goriunov, D. P., and L. Iu. Zubkova, comps. *TASS soobshchaet.* Moscow: Politizdat, 1988. 285 pp.

Gorshkov, M. K. *Obshchestvennoe mnenie: istoriia i sovremennost.* Moscow: Politizdat, 1988. 382 pp.

Green, Willam C., and Theodore Karasik, eds. *Gorbachev and His Generals.* Boulder, Colo.: Westview Press, 1989. 200 pp.

Hajda, Lubomyr, and Mark Beissinger, eds. *The Nationalities Factor in Soviet Politics.* Boulder, Colo.: Westview Press, 1989. 160 pp.

Hauner, Milan, and Robert L. Canfield, eds. *Afghanistan and the Soviet Union: Collusion and Transformation.* Boulder, Colo.: Westview Press, 1989. 219 pp.

Hill, Kent R. *The Puzzle of the Soviet Church.* Portland, Ore.: Multnomah Press, 1989. 417 pp.

Horowitz, Tamar. *The Soviet Man in an Open Society.* Lanham, Md.: University Press of America, 1989. 380 pp.

Hough, Jerry F. *Opening up the Soviet Economy.* Washington, D.C.: The Brookings Institution, 100 pp.

Iakovlev, Aleksandr Maksimovich. *Sotsiologiia ekonomicheskoi prestupnosti.* Moscow: Nauka, 1988. 251 pp.

Ioffe, Iakov Abramovich, ed. *My i planeta: tsifry i fakty.* 7th edition. Moskva: Politizdat, 1988. 255 pp.

Judy, Richard W., and Virginia L., *The Information Age and Soviet Society.* Indianapolis: Hudson Institute, 1989. 99 pp.

Karasik, Theodore William. *Directory of Full and Candidate Members of the Soviet Central Commit-*

tee. Sherman Oaks, Calif.: (no publisher given), 1988. 86 pp.

Karsh, Efraim. *The Soviet Union and Syria: The Asad Years.* New York: Routledge. 1988. 125 pp.

Keller, Edmond Joseph. *Revolutionary Ethiopia from Empire to People's Republic.* Bloomington: Indiana University Press, 1988. 307 pp.

Kempton, Daniel R. *Soviet Strategy toward Southern Africa: The National Liberation Movement Connection.* New York: Praeger Publishers, 1989. 261 pp.

Kerblay, Basile. *Gorbachev's Russia.* New York: Pantheon, 1989. 175 pp.

Khalipov, V. F. *Voennaia politika KPSS.* Moscow: Voenizdat, 1988. 271 pp.

Kittrie, Nicholas N., and Iván Völgyes, eds. *The Uncertain Future: Gorbachev's Eastern Bloc.* New York: Paragon Press, 1988. 281 pp.

Kolodziej, Edward, and Roger E. Kanet, eds. *The Limits of Soviet Power in the Developing World.* Baltimore: Johns Hopkins University Press, 1989. 531 pp.

Kubálkova, Vendulka, and Albert A. Cruickshank. *Thinking New about Soviet "New Thinking."* Berkeley: University of California, Institute of International Studies, 1989. 143 pp.

Kuibyshev, Valerian Vladimirovich. *Izabrannye proizvedeniia.* Moscow: Politizdat, 1988. 2 vols.

Kuromiya, Hiroaki. *Stalin's Industrial Revolution: Politics and Workers, 1928–1932.* Cambridge, England: Cambridge University Press, 1988. 369 pp.

Kushnirsky, Fyodor I. *Growth and Inflation in the Soviet Economy.* Boulder, Colo.: Westview Press, 1989. 319 pp.

Lane, David, ed. *Elites and Political Power in the USSR.* Aldershot: Edward Elgar, 1989. 299 pp.

Laqueur, Walter. *The Long Road To Freedom: Russia and Glasnost.* New York: Charles Scribner's and Sons, 1989. 325 pp.

Lavrichev, V. M., and IU. K. Malov, eds. *KPSS o perestroike: Sbornik Dokumentov.* Moscow: Politizdat, 1988. 479 pp.

Lazarev, Boris Mikhailovich. *Gosudarstvennoe upravlenie na etape perestroiki.* Moscow: Iurizdat, 1988. 318 pp.

Lefever, Ernest W., and Robert D. Vander Lugt, eds. *Perestroika: How New is Gorbachev's New Way of Thinking?* Lanham, Md.: University Press of America, 1989. 245 pp.

Lerner, Lawrence W., and Donald W. Treadgold, eds.

Gorbachev and the Soviet Future. Boulder, Colo.: Westview Press, 1989. 284 pp.

Leonhard, Susanne. *Gestohlenes Leben: als Sozialistin in Stalins Gulag.* Frankfurt/Main: Athenäum, 1988. 546 pp.

Levermann, Wolfgang. *Kommunismus und Kapital.* Melsungen: Kasseler Forschungen zur Zeitgeschichte, 1989. 441 pp.

Lieven, Dominic. *Gorbachev and the Nationalities.* London: The Centre for Security and Conflict Studies, 1988. 33 pp.

Linz, Susan J., and William Moskoff, eds. *Reorganization and Reform in the Soviet Economy.* Armonk, N.Y.: M. E. Sharpe, 1988. 147 pp.

Luk'ianenko, Valentina Ivanovna. *Organizatsionno-partiinaia rabota: opyt, problemy.* Moscow: Mysl, 1988. 234 pp.

Marchenko, Mikhail Nikolaevich, and I.N. Rozhko. *Demokratiia v SSSR: Fakty i domysly.* Moscow: Mysl, 1988. 282 pp.

Marples, David R. *The Social Impact of the Chernobyl Disaster.* New York: St. Martin's Press, 1988. 316 pp.

Maslov, N.N., ed. *Istoriia KPSS: Kurs lektsii,* 1988. Moscow: Mysl, vol. 1.

Mastro, Joseph P. *USSR: Calendar of Events, 1987.* Gulf Breeze, Fla.: Academic International Press, 1988. 297 pp.

Matthews, Mervyn, ed. *Party, State, and Citizen in the Soviet Union.* Armonk, N.Y.: M. E. Sharpe, 1989. 385 pp.

McNeal, Robert H. *Stalin: Man and Ruler.* New York: New York University Press, 1988. 389 pp.

Medvedev, Roy. *Let History Judge: The Origins and Consequences of Stalinism.* New York: Columbia University Press, 1989. 903 pp.

Menon, Rajon, and Daniel N. Nelson, eds. *Limits to Soviet Power.* Lexington, Mass.: D. C. Heath, 1989. 230 pp.

Mickiewicz, Ellen. *Split Signals: Television and Politics in The Soviet Union.* New York: Oxford University Press, 1988. 286 pp.

Mikoian, A. I. *Memoirs of Anastas Mikoyan.* Madison, Conn.: Sphinx Press, 1988. 583 pp.

Nove, Alec. *Glasnost' in Action.* Boston: Unwin Hyman, 1989. 251 pp.

Petroff, Serge. *The Red Eminence: A Biography of Mikhail A. Suslov.* Clifton, N.J.: Kingston Press, 1988. 273 pp.

Pinkus, Benjamin. *The Jews of the Soviet Union: The*

History of a National Minority. Cambridge, England: Cambridge University Press, 1988. 397 pp.

Radio Free Europe/Radio Liberty. *Glasnost' and Empire: National Aspirations in the USSR.* Lanham, Md.: University Press of America, 1989. 60 pp.

Rahr, Alexander G., comp. *A Biographic Directory of 100 Leading Soviet Officials.* 4th ed. Munich: Radio Free Europe/Radio Liberty, 1988. 241 pp.

Romerstein, Herbert, and Stanislav Levchenko. *The KGB against the "Main Enemy."* Lexington, Mass.: D. C. Heath, 1989. 369 pp.

Rose, Clive. *The Soviet Propaganda Network.* London: Pinter, 1988. 313 pp.

Rubinstein, Alvin Z. *Moscow's Third World Strategy.* Princeton, N.J.: Princeton University Press, 1989. 311 pp.

————. *Soviet Foreign Policy Since World War II: Imperial and Global.* Boston: Scott, Foresman, 1989. 381 pp.

Rumer, Boris Z. *Soviet Central Asia: A Tragic Experiment.* Boston: Unwin Hyman, Inc., 1989. 204 pp.

————. *Soviet Steel: The Challenge of Industrial Modernization in the USSR.* Ithaca, N.Y.: Cornell University Press, 1989. 251 pp.

Rywkin, Michael. *Soviet Society Today.* Armonk, N.Y.: M. E. Sharpe, 1989. 242 pp.

Saikal, Amin, and William Malley, eds. *The Soviet Withdrawal from Afghanistan.* New York: Cambridge University Press, 1989. 177 pp.

Saivetz, Carol R. *The Soviet Union and the Gulf in the 1980s.* Boulder, Colo.: Westview Press, 1989. 139 pp.

————, ed. *The Soviet Union in the Third World.* Boulder, Colo.: Westview Press, 1989. 230 pp.

Scott, Harriet Fast, and William F. Scott. *Soviet Military Doctrine: Continuity, Formulation, and Dissemination.* Boulder, Colo.: Westview Press, 1988. 315 pp.

S'ezd VLKSM. Moscow: Molodaia Gvardiia, 1988. 191 pp.

Shipley, Peter. *Hostile Action: The KGB and the Secret Soviet Operations in Britain.* London: Pinter, 1989. 280 pp.

Shlapentokh, Vladimir. *Public and Private Life of the Soviet People: Changing Values in Post-Stalin Russia.* New York: Oxford, 1989. 281 pp.

Sicker, Martin. *The Bear and the Lion: Soviet Imperialism and Iran.* New York: Praeger, 1988. 168 pp.

Sinowjew, Alexander. *Katastroika: Gorbatschow's Potemkinsche Dörfer.* West Berlin: Ullstein, 1988. 208 pp.

Steeves, Paul D., ed. *The Modern Encyclopedia of Religions in Russia and the Soviet Union.* Vol. 1. Gulf Breeze, Fla.: Academic International Press, 1988.

Stojanović, Svetozar. *Perestroika: From Marxism and Bolshevism to Gorbachev.* Buffalo, N.Y.: Prometheus Books, 1988. 167 pp.

Subtelny, Orest. *Ukraine: A History.* Toronto: University of Toronto Press, 1988. 666 pp.

Syzrantsev, V. T. et al. *Kratkii slovar'-spravochnik agitatora i politinformatora.* Moscow: Politizdat, 1988. 318 pp.

Taubman, William, and Jane Taubman. *Moscow Spring.* New York: Summit Books, 1989. 296 pp.

Thorniley, Daniel. *The Rise and Fall of the Soviet Rural Communist Party, 1927–1939.* Hampshire: Macmillan Press, 1988. 246 pp.

Toscano, Roberta. *Soviet Human Rights Policy and Perestroika.* Lanham, Md.: University Press of America, 1989. 48 pp.

Tsvietkov, H. M. *SSSR i SShA: Otnosheniia.* Kiev: Vyshcha Shkola, 1988. 269 pp.

Urban, G. R., ed. *Can the Soviet System Survive Reform?* London: Pinter, 1989. 420 pp.

Urban, Mark. *War in Afghanistan.* Basingstoke: Macmillan, 1988. 38 pp.

Valerian Vladimirovich Kuibyshev. Moscow: Politizdat, 1988. 381 pp.

Villemarest, Pierre F. de. *GRU, le Plus Secret des Services Sovietiques, 1918–1988.* Paris: Stock, 1988. 335 pp.

Volkogonov, D. A., chief ed. *Kontrpropaganda: Teoriia i praktika.* Moscow: Voenizdat, 1988. 238 pp.

Weeks, Albert L., ed. *Soviet Nomenklatura.* Washington, D.C.: Washington Institute Press, 1989. 125 pp.

Wettig, Gerhard. *High Road, Low Road: Diplomacy and Public Action in Soviet Foreign Policy.* Washington: Pergamon-Brassey, 1989. 165 pp.

————, et al. *The Soviet Union 1986/1987: Events, Problems, Perspectives.* Boulder, Colo.: Westview Press, 1989. 373 pp.

Woodby, Sylvia. *Gorbachev and the Decline of Ideology in Soviet Foreign Policy.* Boulder, Colo.: Westview Press, 1989. 130 pp.

Zagladin, V. V. *Vneshnepoliticheskaia strategiia KPSS i novoe politicheskoe myshlenie v iadernyi vek.* Moscow: Politizdat, 1988. 367 pp.

Zaslavskaia, Tat'iana I. *A Voice of Reform: Essays by*

Tat'iana Zaslavskaia. Armonk, N.Y.: M. E. Sharpe, 1989. 191 pp.

Zemtsov, Ilya, and John Farrar. *Gorbachev: The Man and the System*. New Brunswick, N.J.: Transaction Publishers, 1989. 462 pp.

Zhukov, Iu. A. *SSSR-SShA—Doroga dlinnoiu v sem'desiat let*. Moscow: Politizdat, 1988. 318 pp.

MIDDLE EAST

Bennoune, Mahfoud. *The Making of Contemporary Algeria, 1830–1987*. New York: Cambridge University Press, 1988. 323 pp.

Buton, Philippe, and Laurent Gervereau. *Le Couteau entre les dents*. Paris: Ed. Du Chene, 1989. 159 pp.

Collelo, Thomas, ed. *Lebanon: A Country Study*. 3d ed. Washington, D.C.: Department of the Army, 1989. 282 pp.

Communist Party of the Soviet Union. Moscow: Novosti, 1988. 159 pp.

Delafon, Gilles. *Beyrouth: Les soldats de l'Islam*. Paris: Stock, 1989. 254 pp.

Friedman, Thomas L. *From Beirut to Jerusalem*. New York: Farrar Strauss Giroux, 1989. 509 pp.

Garbdzhanian, G. B., chief ed. *Voprosy ideologicheskoi bor'by na sovremennom etape*. Erevan: Izd-vo AN Armianskoi SSR, 1988. 147 pp.

Hamizrachi, Beate. *The Emergence of the South Lebanon Security Belt*. New York: Praeger, 1988. 211 pp.

Handourtzel, Remy. *La Collaboration...à gauche aussi*. Paris: Ed. Librairie Académique Perrin, 1989. 276 pp.

Hauner, Milan, and Robert L. Canfield, eds. *Afghanistan and the Soviet Union: Collision and Transformation*. Boulder, Colo.: Westview Press, 1989. 219 pp.

Hinnebush, Raymond A. *Peasant and Bureaucracy in Ba'thist Syria*. Boulder, Colo.: Westview Press, 1989. 325 pp.

Irani, George Emile. *The Papacy and the Middle East*. Notre Dame, Indiana: University of Notre Dame Press, 1989. 218 pp.

al-Khalil, Samir. *Republic of Fear: The Politics of Modern Iraq*. Berkeley: University of California Press, 1989. 327 pp.

Kostiner, Joseph. *South Yemen's Revolutionary Strategy, 1970–1985*. Boulder, Colo.: Westview Press, 1989. 110 pp.

Krogh, Peter E., and Mary C. McDavid. *Palestinians under Occupation: Prospects for the Future*. Washington: Georgetown University Center for Contemporary Arab Studies, 1989. 121 pp.

Laber, Jeri, and Barnett R. Rubin. *A Nation is Dying: Afghanistan under the Soviets, 1979–87*. Evanston, Ill.: Northwestern University Press, 1988. 179 pp.

Lawson, Fred H. *Bahrain: The Modernization of Autocracy*. Boulder, Colo.: Westview Press, 1989. 146 pp.

Mansour, Camille. *Les Palestiniens de l'Intérieur*. Washington: Revue d'Études Palestiniennes, 1989. 291 pp.

Ma'oz, Moshe. *Asad: The Sphinx of Damascus*. New York: Weidenfeld and Nicolson, 1988. 221 pp.

Metz, Helen Chapin, ed. *Iran: A Country Study*. 4th ed. Washington, D.C.: Department of the Army, 1989. 344 pp.

———, ed. *Libya: A Country Study*. Washington, D.C.: U.S. Government, Department of the Army, 1989. 351 pp.

Norton, Augustus R., and Martin H. Greenberg, eds. *The International Relations of the Palestine Liberation Organization*. Carbondale: Southern Illinois University Press, 1989. 233 pp.

Picard, Elizabeth. *Liban: État de discorde*. Paris: Flammarion, 1988. 263 pp.

Picq, Laurence. *Beyond the Horizon*. New York: St. Martin's Press, 1989. 218 pp.

Saiah, Ysabel. *Pieds Noirs et Fiers de l'Être*. Paris: Edition Treize, 1987. 273 pp.

Saikal, Amin, and William Maley, ed. *The Soviet Withdrawal from Afghanistan*. Cambridge, England: Cambridge University Press, 1989. 177 pp.

Seale, Patrick. *Asad: The Struggle for the Middle East*. Berkeley: University of California Press, 1988. 552 pp.

Shafir, Gerson. *Land, Labor and the Origins of the Israeli-Palestinian Conflict, 1882–1924*. Cambridge, England: Cambridge University Press, 1989. 287 pp.

Springborg, Robert. *Mubarak's Egypt: Fragmentation of the Political Order*. Boulder, Colo.: Westview Press, 1989. 307 pp.

Wright, Martin, ed. *Iran: The Khomeini Revolution*. Harlow, England: Longman Group, 1989. 128 pp.

Wright, Robin. *In The Name of God: The Khomeini Decade*. New York: Simon and Schuster, 1989. 284 pp.

WESTERN EUROPE

Balibar, Etienne. *Race, nation, classe: Les identités ambigués*. Paris: La Découverte, 1988. 308 pp.

Barbares, Les. *Les Immigrés et le racisme dans la politique belge*. Brussels: Editions EPO, 1988. 189 pp.

Baring, Arnulf. *Unser Neuer Grössenwahn: Deutschland zwischen Ost und West*. Stuttgart: Deutsche Verlagsanstalt, 1989. 339 pp.

Bon, Frederic. *La France qui vote*. Paris: Pluriel-Hachette, 1988. 464 pp.

Bourderon, Roger, and Ivan Avakoumovitch. *Détruire le PCF: Archives de l'état français et de l'occupant hitlérien, 1940–1944*. Paris: Messidor, 1988. 276 pp.

Buesch, Otto. *Beiträge zur Geschichte der Berliner Demokratie, 1919–1933/45–1985*. West Berlin: Colloquium Verlag, 1988. 405 pp.

Carraud, Michel. *Que faire des jeunes?* Paris: Publisud, 1989. 213 pp.

De Grand, Alexander. *The Italian Left: A History of the Socialist and Communist Parties*. Bloomington: Indiana University Press, 1989. 182 pp.

Demay, Henri. *La Déchirure: Marcel Rigout, les renovateurs limousins et le Parti Communiste Français*. Limoges: L. Souny, 1988. 83 pp.

Di Giacomo, Enzo. *Il Marxismo Italiano: Analisi e critica con particolare riferimento ai problemi dell'organizzazione e della strategia ai fini dela transformazione in Gramsci, Togliatti e Berlinguer*. Naples: Edizioni Scientifiche Italiane, 1988. 430 pp.

Di Loreto, Pietro. *Alle origini della crisi del PCI: Togliatti e il legame di Ferro*. Rome: Euroma-La Goliardica, 1988. 174 pp.

Dumont, René. *Un Monde intolérable: Le libéralisme en Question*. Paris: Editions du Seuil, 1988. 215 pp.

Durupty, Michel. *Les Privatisations en France*. Paris: La Documentation Française, 1988. 144 pp.

Fiori, Giuseppe. *Vita di Enrico Berlinguer*. Rome: Laterza, 1989. 532 pp.

Friend, Julius W. *Seven Years in France: François Mitterrand and the Unintended Revolution, 1981–1988*. Boulder, Colo.: Westview Press, 1989. 249 pp.

Gaffney, John. *The French Left and the Fifth Republic*. Houndmills, Basingstoke: Macmillan, 1989. 299 pp.

Galante, Severino. *Il Partito Comunista Italiano e l'integrazione Europea: il decennio del rifiuto: 1947–1957*. Padua: Liviana, 1988. 159 pp.

Gerome, Noëlle. *La Fête de "L'Humanité": culture communiste, culture populaire*. Paris: Messidor, 1988. 340 pp.

Giraud, Henri-Christian. *De Gaulle et les communistes: L'Alliance juin 1941–mai 1943*. Paris: Albin Michel, 1988. 537 pp.

Guillon, Claude. *De la Révolution 1989: L'inventaire des rêves et des armes*. Paris: A. Moreau, 1989. 270 pp.

Hellman, Stephen. *Italian Communism in Transition*. New York: Oxford University Press, 1988. 274 pp.

Hobsbawm, Eric. *Politics for a Rational Left: Political Writings 1977–88*. London: Verso, 1989. 250 pp.

Italy, Marxist-Leninist Party. *Documenti del Partito Marxista-Leninista Italiano: aprile 1977–aprile 1987*. Florence: PMLI Press, 1988. 613 pp.

Jakobson, Max. *Finland: Myth and Reality*. Oslo: Otava, 1988. 394 pp.

Judice, José Miguel. *PCP: Um Iceberg em Movimento*. Lisboa: Asociação Para a Cooperação e Desenvolvimento Social, 1988. 197 pp.

Lelli, Marcello. *L'Opposizione di stato; Il Partito Comunista e le instituzioni*. Rome: Edizioni Lavoro, 1989. 178 pp.

Macaluso, Emanuele. *Togliatti e i suoi eredi*. Soveria Mannelli: Rubbettino Editore, 1988. 137 pp.

Mazzatosta, Teresa Maria. *I Communisti si raccontano: 1946–1956*. Rome: Armando, 1988. 311 pp.

Moeller, Wulf-Heinrich. *Die Bundesrepublik aus DDR-Perspektive*. Frankfurt a.M.: P. Lang, 1988. 424 pp.

Mueller-Rommel, Ferdinand, ed. *New Politics in Western Europe: The Rise and Success of Green Parties and Alternative Lists*. Boulder, Colo.: Westview Press, 1989. 230 pp.

Paasivirta, Juhani. *Finland and Europe. The Early Years of Independence 1917–1939*. Helsinki: Suomen Historiallinen Seura, 1988. 555 pp.

Partido Comunista Portugues. Lisboa: Ediçoës Avante, 1988. 190 pp.

Partito Comunista Italiano. Roma: Edizioni Associate, 1988. 283 pp.

Pelinka, Anton, and Fritz Plasser, eds. *The Austrian Party System*. Boulder, Colo.: Westview Press, 1989. 458 pp.

Penniman, Howard, ed. *France at the Polls, 1981 and 1986: Three National Elections*. Washington, D.C.: American Enterprise Institute, 1988. 296 pp.

Pitman, Paul M. III, ed. *Turkey: A Country Study.* Washington: Department of the Army, 1988. 463 pp.

Pohl, Manfred. *Geschäft und Politik.* Mainz: Hase und Koehler, 1988. 238 pp.

Schafranek, Hans. *Das Kurze Leben des Kurt Landau: Ein oesterreichischer Kommunist als Opfer der stalinistischen Geheimpolizei.* Vienna: Verlag für Geschichte und Kritik, 1988. 609 pp.

Schoenhals, Kai P. *The Free Germany Movement: A Case of Patriotism or Treason?* Westport, Conn.: Greenwood Press, 1989. 176 pp.

Singer, Daniel. *Is Socialism Doomed? The Meaning of Mitterrand.* New York: Oxford University Press, 1988. 324 pp.

Sundelius, Bengt. *The Committed Neutral: Sweden's Foreign Policy.* Boulder, Colo.: Westview Press, 1989. 214 pp.

Townshend, Charles, ed. *Consensus in Ireland: Approaches and Recessions.* Oxford: Clarendon Press, 1988. 214 pp.

Weber, Hermann. *Kommunistischer Widerstand gegen die Hitler Diktatur, 1933–1939.* West Berlin: Gedenkstätte Deutscher Widerstand, 1988. 24 pp.

Wiarda, Howard J. *The Transition to Democracy in Spain and Portugal.* Washington, D.C.: AEI for Public Policy Research, 1989. 416 pp.

Cumulative Index of Biographies

Index of Names

Thong Khon, 170
Thongsavat Khaikhamphithoun, 235, 237
Thongsing Thammavong, 232, 233
Thongvin Phomvihane, 232
Thorez, Pierre, 625
Thurmer, Gyula, 345, 351
Tiainen, Pekka, 615
Tiamzon, Benito, 257, 259, 265
Tian Jiyun, 183, 185
Tichanov, B., 686
Tie Banh, 168, 171
Tietmeyer, Hans, 651
Tijerino, Santos, 114
Tikhomirov, Sergei, 224
Timakata, Fred, 273
Timoshenko, Anatoly, 47
Tin Yee, 161, 162, 163
Tinoco, Pedro, 150
Tinoco, Victor, 88
Tint Hlaing, 161
Tirado López, Victor, 107, 108, 110, 117
Tisch, Harry, 336
Tito, Josip Broz, 297, 454
Tjibaou, Jean-Marie, 268, 275
Tloome, Dan, 2, 26, 27
Tódero, Domingos, 54
Todorov, Stanko, 313, 316
Todorov-Gorunia, Ivan, 317
Toepfer, Klaus, 341
Togliatti, Palmiro, 670
Tökes, Laszlo, 392, 400, 406
Toledo, Albio, 116
Toledo, Juan Angel, 145
Toledo, Pedro, 145
Tölgyessy, Péter, 352, 353
Toma, Ioan, 385
Tomášek, František Cardinal, 327
Tonner, Joe, 250
Topacio, Eugenia Magpantay, 257, 259
Toriani, Andrés, 145
Torralba González, Diocles, 71, 72
Torres, Carlos Alberto, 54
Torrez, Hugo, 111
Torrijos, Omar, 521
Tortorella, Aldo, 677, 678
Tóth, Károly, 501
Totu, Ion, 385
Touminen, Hannu, 615
Toundas, Giannis, 661
Tozaj, Neshat, 299
Tran Bach Dang, 287
Tran Hoan, 234
Tran Kien, 284
Tran Quang Co, 178
Tran Quoc Hoang, 284

Tran Quyet, 284
Tran Thanh, 46
Tran Van Tra, 287
Tran Xuan Bach, 284
Traustadottir, Stephania, 664
Trentin, Bruno, 674
Tretiyak, I. M., 224
Tret'yak, Ivan, 575
Trifunović, Bogdan, 449
Triki, Abdelmajid, 576
Tripathi, Jagdish, 202
Trives Mesequer, Francisco, 700
Trmala, Josef, 319
Trofimenko, Genrikh, 520
Trondsen, Grete, 692
Trotter, Ron, 251
Troya, Marco, 83
Trûnski, Slavcho, 314
Tsakh, Nikolay, 564, 565
Tsanov, Vasil, 313
Tsedenbal, 243, 245
Tseren, G. Lubsan, 501
Tsfasman, Robert, 519
Tsolakis, Kostas, 659
Tubi, George, 552
Tubi, Tawfiq, 552, 553, 555
Tucker, Marilyn, 248, 249, 250
Tuhanuku, Joses, 274
Tujan, Antonio, 257
Tumaru, Oscar, 276
Tun Lwin, 161
Tupurkovski, Vasil, 449, 451, 453
Turco, Livia, 670, 674, 675, 677
Turf, Jef, 601
Turk, Riyad al-, 573
Twining, Charles, 237
Tyner, Jarvis, 141, 143
Tzanetakis, Tzanis, 659

U Chit Hlaing, 166
'Ubayd, Salih Ahmad, 582
'Ubayd, Sheikh 'Abd-al-Karim, 568
Ueda, Koichiro, 210
Ugarov, Sergei, 487
Uhlig, Mark A., 117
Ukeiwe, Dick, 275
Ulčak, Dusan, 501
Ulloa B., Rodolfo, 69
Ulusoy, Talat, 709
Um Chhunlim, 170
Um Sarit, 169
'Umar, Jarallah, 580
Ung Phan, 169
Ung Sami, 169
Ungo, Guillermo, 42, 85, 86
Unida, Izquierda, 130
Uno, Sosuke, 212, 230, 246, 439
Uotila, Kari, 617

Urbánek, Karel, 319, 322
Urbánek, Zdeněk, 326
Urbany, Dominique, 683
Urbany, Jaqueline, 683
Urbany, René, 591, 592, 682, 683, 684
Urbany, Serge, 682, 683
Urcuyo Castrillo, Daniel, 109
Uregei, Louis Kotra, 275
Uregei, Yann, 275–76
Urnov, A. Yu, 106
Ursu, Ion, 385
Ushwokunze, Herbert, 35
Usmanov, Gumer I., 407, 414, 417
Uthman, al-Gazuli Said, 32
Uutila, Kari, 621
Uzelac, Ugljesa, 449
Uzunov, Dimo, 308, 315

Vaca Narvaja, Fernando, 47
Vaclavik, Milan, 226
Våde, Vidar, 692
Valchev, Vesselin, 508
Valdivieso Alvarenga, Ricardo, 86
Válek, Miroslav, 319
Valenti, Esteban, 145
Valentin, Amaro, 54
Vallejo, Andrés, 83
Vallentine, Jo, 268
Valverde Ruíz, Alberto, 115
Vanderborght, Michel, 601
Van-Dunem, Afonso ("Mbinda"), 4
Van-Dunem, Pedro de Castro ("Loy"), 4, 9
Vang Pao, 236
Van Geyt, Louis, 601, 605, 606
Van Hoek, Ton, 688
Van Houten, Gerry, 57
Varela, Silvio, 149
Varennikov, V. I., 444
Vargas, Mauricio Ernesto, 86
Vargas, Ramón, 80
Vargas, Tancredo, 80
Vargas Carbonell, Humberto, 69, 70
Vargas Llosa, Mario, 74, 130–34 passim
Vargas Pazzos, Frank, 81
Varone, Guillermo, 43
Varošlija, Ljubomir, 449
Vasić, Andejelko, 467
Vásquez, Alvaro, 62, 64
Vásquez, Tabaré, 147
Vass, Csaba, 351
Vassal, Lucien, 629
Vassallo, Anthony, 589, 684
Vassiliev, Aleksey, 25
Vassiliou, George, 607, 608, 609
Vastagh, Pál, 351

Index of Subjects